Industry Analysis	Functional Strategy	Business Level Strategy	Global Strategy (... Strategy)	Corporate...	Limit...	Social Responsibility
X		X				
X		X				
X	X	X				
X	X	X				
		X				
X	X	X	X			
	X	X	X			
X	X	X				
X		X				
X	X	X				
X	X	X				
X	X	X				
X	X	X				
X	X	X	X			
X	X	X				
	X	X	X			
	X	X	X			
X	X	X	X			
X	X	X			X	
X		X			X	
	X	X			X	
	X	X	X		X	
					X	
		X			X	
			X		X	
			X			X
		X				X

5 REASONS
to buy your textbooks and course materials at

CENGAGE**brain**.com

1 **SAVINGS:**
Prices up to 65% off, daily coupons, and free shipping on orders over $25

2 **CHOICE:**
Multiple format options including textbook, eBook and eChapter rentals

3 **CONVENIENCE:**
Anytime, anywhere access of eBooks or eChapters via mobile devices

4 **SERVICE:**
Free eBook access while your text ships, and instant access to online homework products

5 **STUDY TOOLS:**
Free study tools* for your text, plus writing, research, career and job search resources
*availability varies

11TH EDITION

STRATEGIC MANAGEMENT

AN INTEGRATED APPROACH

11TH EDITION

STRATEGIC MANAGEMENT

AN INTEGRATED APPROACH

CHARLES W. L. HILL

University of Washington – Foster School of Business

GARETH R. JONES

MELISSA A. SCHILLING

New York University – Stern School of Business

Australia • Brazil • Japan • Korea • Mexico • Singapore • Spain • United Kingdom • United States

CENGAGE
Learning·

Strategic Management: An Integrated Approach, 11e

Charles W. L. Hill
Gareth R. Jones
Melissa A. Schilling

Product Director: Joe Sabatino

Sr. Product Manager: Scott Person

Sr. Content Developer: Mike Guendelsberger

Product Assistant: Tamara Grega

Sr. Content Project Manager: Cliff Kallemeyn

Media Developer: Courtney J. Bavaro

Sr. Media Developer: Sally Nieman

Sr. Art Director: Stacy Jenkins Shirley

Manufacturing Planner: Ron Montgomery

Sr. Rights Acquisitions Specialist: Amber Hosea

Production Service: MPS Limited

Internal/ Cover Designer: Mike Stratton

Cover Image: © iStockphoto.com/saintho

For product information and technology assistance, contact us at
Cengage Learning Customer & Sales Support, 1-800-354-9706

For permission to use material from this text or product,
submit all requests online at **www.cengage.com/permissions.**
Further permissions questions can be emailed to
permissionrequest@cengage.com.

Library of Congress Control Number: 2013941272

Student Edition:

ISBN-13: 978-1-285-18448-7

ISBN-10: 1-285-18448-3

Cengage Learning
200 First Stamford Place, 4th Floor
Stamford, CT
USA 06902

Cengage Learning is a leading provider of customized learning solutions with office locations around the globe, including Singapore, the United Kingdom, Australia, Mexico, Brazil, and Japan. Locate your local office at: **www.cengage.com/global**

Cengage Learning products are represented in Canada by Nelson Education, Ltd.

To learn more about Cengage Learning Solutions, visit
www.cengage.com

Purchase any of our products at your local college store or at our preferred online store **www.cengagebrain.com**

Printed in Canada
1 2 3 4 5 6 7 17 16 15 14 13

Brief Contents

Contents

PART ONE   INTRODUCTION TO STRATEGIC MANAGEMENT

PART TWO   THE NATURE OF COMPETITIVE ADVANTAGE

PART FOUR   IMPLEMENTING STRATEGY

PART FIVE　CASES IN STRATEGIC MANAGEMENT

Cases

Preface

Consistent with our mission to provide students with the most current and up-to-date account of the changes taking place in the world of strategy and management, there have been some significant changes in the 11th edition of *Strategic Management: An Integrated Approach*.

First, we have a new co-author, Melissa Shilling. Melissa is a Professor of Management and Organization at the Leonard Stern School of Business at New York University, where she teaches courses on strategic management, corporate strategy, and technology and innovation management. She has published extensively in top-tier academic journals and is recognized as one of the leading experts on innovation and strategy in high-technology industries. We are very pleased to have Melissa on the book team. Melissa made substantial contributions to this edition, including revising several chapters and writing seven high-caliber case studies. We believe her input has significantly strengthened the book.

Second, several chapters have been extensively revised. Chapter 5: Business-Level Strategy has been rewritten from scratch. In addition to the standard material on Porter's generic strategies, this chapter now includes discussion of *value innovation* and *blue ocean strategy* following the work of W. C. Kim and R. Mauborgne. Chapter 6: Business-Level Strategy and the Industry Environment has also been extensively rewritten and updated to clarify concepts and bring it into the 21st century. Despite the addition of new materials, both chapters are shorter than in prior editions. Substantial changes have been made to many other chapters, and extraneous material has been cut. For example, in Chapter 13 the section on implementing strategy across countries has been entirely rewritten and updated. This chapter has also been substantially shortened.

Third, the examples and cases contained in each chapter have been revised. We have a new *Running Case* for this edition, Wal-Mart. Every chapter has a new *Opening Case* and a new *Closing Case*. There are also many new *Strategy in Action* features. In addition, there has been significant change in the examples used in the text to illustrate content. In making these changes, our goal has been to make the book relevant for students reading it in the second decade of the 21st century.

Fourth, we have a substantially revised selection of cases for this edition. All of the cases are either new to this edition or are updates of cases that adopters have indicated they like to see in the book. Out of 28 cases, 16 were written either by Charles Hill or Melissa Shilling. This represents a level of commitment to the case collection from the primary authors that you do not see in most strategy textbooks. Many of the cases are current as of 2013. We have made an effort to include cases that have high name recognition with students, and that they will enjoy reading and working on. These include cases on Toyota, Tesla, Apple, Ikea, Starbucks, Intel, Harley-Davidson and Skull Candy.

Practicing Strategic Management: An Interactive Approach

We have received a lot of positive feedback about the usefulness of the end-of-chapter exercises and assignments in the Practicing Strategic Management sections of our book. They offer a wide range of hands-on and digital learning experiences for students. Following the Chapter Summary and Discussion Questions, each chapter contains the following exercises and assignments:

- **Ethical Dilemma**. This feature has been developed to highlight the importance of ethical decision making in today's business environment. With today's current examples of questionable decision making (as seen in companies like Countrywide Financial during the 2007–2009 global financial crisis), we hope to equip students with the tools they need to be strong ethical leaders.
- **Small-Group Exercise.** This short (20-minute) experiential exercise asks students to divide into groups and discuss a scenario concerning some aspect of strategic management. For example, the scenario in Chapter 11 asks students to identify the stakeholders of their educational institution and evaluate how stakeholders' claims are being and should be met.
- The **Strategy Sign-On** section presents an opportunity for students to explore the latest data through digital research activities.

  - First, the Article File requires students to search business articles to identify a company that is facing a particular strategic management problem. For instance, students are asked to locate and research a company pursuing a low-cost or a differentiation strategy, and to describe this company's strategy, its advantages and disadvantages, and the core competencies required to pursue it. Students' presentations of their findings lead to lively class discussions.
  - Then, the **Strategic Management Project: Developing Your Portfolio** asks students to choose a company to study through the duration of the semester. At the end of every chapter, students analyze the company using the series of questions provided at the end of each chapter. For example, students might select Ford Motor Co. and, using the series of chapter questions, collect information on Ford's top managers, mission, ethical position, domestic and global strategy and structure, and so on. Students write a case study of their company and present it to the class at the end of the semester. In the past, we also had students present one or more of the cases in the book early in the semester, but now in our classes, we treat the students' own projects as the major class assignment and their case presentations as the climax of the semester's learning experience.

- **Closing Case.** A short closing case provides an opportunity for a short class discussion of a chapter-related theme.

In creating these exercises, it is not our intention to suggest that they should *all* be used for *every* chapter. For example, over a semester, an instructor might combine a group of Strategic Management Projects with 5 to 6 Article File assignments while incorporating 8 to 10 Small-Group Exercises in class.

We have found that our interactive approach to teaching strategic management appeals to students. It also greatly improves the quality of their learning experience. Our approach is more fully discussed in the *Instructor's Resource Manual*.

Strategic Management Cases

The 28 cases that we have selected for this edition will appeal, we are certain, to students and professors alike, both because these cases are intrinsically interesting and because of the number of strategic management issues they illuminate. The organizations discussed in the cases range from large, well-known companies, for which students can do research to update the information, to small, entrepreneurial businesses that illustrate the uncertainty and challenge of the strategic management process. In addition, the selections include many international cases, and most of the other cases contain some element of global strategy. Refer to the Contents for a complete listing of the cases with brief descriptions.

To help students learn how to effectively analyze and write a case study, we continue to include a special section on this subject. It has a checklist and an explanation of areas to consider, suggested research tools, and tips on financial analysis.

We feel that our entire selection of cases is unrivaled in breadth and depth, and we are grateful to the other case authors who have contributed to this edition.

Teaching and Learning Aids

Taken together, the teaching and learning features of *Strategic Management* provide a package that is unsurpassed in its coverage and that supports the integrated approach that we have taken throughout the book.

For the Instructor

- The **Instructor's Resource Manual: Theory.** For each chapter, we provide a clearly focused synopsis, a list of teaching objectives, a comprehensive lecture outline, teaching notes for the Ethical Dilemma feature, suggested answers to discussion questions, and comments on the end-of-chapter activities. Each Opening Case, Strategy in Action boxed feature, and Closing Case has a synopsis and a corresponding teaching note to help guide class discussion.
- **Case Teaching Notes** include a complete list of case discussion questions as well as a comprehensive teaching notes for each case, which gives a complete analysis of case issues.
- **Cognero Test Bank:** A completely online test bank allows the instructor the ability to create comprehensive, true/false, multiple-choice and essay questions for each chapter in the book. The mix of questions has been adjusted to provide fewer fact-based or simple memorization items and to provide more items that rely on synthesis or application.
- **PowerPoint Presentation Slides:** Each chapter comes complete with a robust Power-Point presentation to aid with class lectures. These slides can be downloaded from the text website.
- **CengageNow.** This robust online course management system gives you more control in less time and delivers better student outcomes—NOW. CengageNow™ includes teaching and learning resources organized around lecturing, creating assignments, casework, quizzing, and gradework to track student progress and performance. Multiple types of quizzes, including video quizzes are assignable and gradable. Flexible assignments, automatic grading, and a gradebook option provide more control while saving you valuable time. CengageNow empowers students to master concepts, prepare for exams, and become more involved in class.

- **Cengage Learning Write Experience 2.0.** This new technology is the first in higher education to offer students the opportunity to improve their writing and analytical skills without adding to your workload. Offered through an exclusive agreement with Vantage Learning, creator of the software used for GMAT essay grading, Write Experience evaluates students' answers to a select set of writing assignments for voice, style, format, and originality.

For the Student

- **CengageNow** includes learning resources organized around assignments, casework, and quizzing, and allows you to track your progress and performance. A Personalized Study diagnostic tool empowers students to master concepts, prepare for exams, and become more involved in class.

Acknowledgments

This book is the product of far more than two authors. We are grateful to our Senior Product Managers, Michele Rhoades and Scott Person; our Senior Content Developer, Mike Guendelsberger; our Content Project Manager, Cliff Kallemeyn; and our Marketing Manager, Emily Horowitz, for their help in developing and promoting the book and for providing us with timely feedback and information from professors and reviewers, which allowed us to shape the book to meet the needs of its intended market. We are also grateful to the case authors for allowing us to use their materials. We also want to thank the departments of management at the University of Washington and New York University for providing the setting and atmosphere in which the book could be written, and the students of these universities who react to and provide input for many of our ideas. In addition, the following reviewers of this and earlier editions gave us valuable suggestions for improving the manuscript from its original version to its current form:

Andac Arikan, *Florida Atlantic University*

Ken Armstrong, *Anderson University*

Richard Babcock, *University of San Francisco*

Kunal Banerji, *West Virginia University*

Kevin Banning, *Auburn University- Montgomery*

Glenn Bassett, *University of Bridgeport*

Thomas H. Berliner, *The University of Texas at Dallas*

Bonnie Bollinger, *Ivy Technical Community College*

Richard G. Brandenburg, *University of Vermont*

Steven Braund, *University of Hull*

Philip Bromiley, *University of Minnesota*

Geoffrey Brooks, *Western Oregon State College*

Jill Brown, *Lehigh University*

Amanda Budde, *University of Hawaii*

Lowell Busenitz, *University of Houston*

Sam Cappel, *Southeastern Louisiana University*

Charles J. Capps III, *Sam Houston State University*

Don Caruth, *Texas A&M Commerce*

Gene R. Conaster, *Golden State University*

Steven W. Congden, *University of Hartford*

Catherine M. Daily, *Ohio State University*

Robert DeFillippi, *Suffolk University Sawyer School of Management*

Helen Deresky, *SUNY—Plattsburgh*

Fred J. Dorn, *University of Mississippi*

Gerald E. Evans, *The University of Montana*

John Fahy, *Trinity College, Dublin*

Patricia Feltes, *Southwest Missouri State University*

Bruce Fern, *New York University*

Mark Fiegener, *Oregon State University*

Chuck Foley, *Columbus State Community College*

Isaac Fox, *Washington State University*

Craig Galbraith, *University of North Carolina at Wilmington*

Scott R. Gallagher, *Rutgers University*

Eliezer Geisler, *Northeastern Illinois University*

Gretchen Gemeinhardt, *University of Houston*

Lynn Godkin, *Lamar University*

Sanjay Goel, *University of Minnesota—Duluth*

Robert L. Goldberg, *Northeastern University*

James Grinnell, *Merrimack College*

Russ Hagberg, *Northern Illinois University*

Allen Harmon, *University of Minnesota—Duluth*

Ramon Henson, *Rutgers University*

David Hoopes, *California State University—Dominguez Hills*

Todd Hostager, *University of Wisconsin—Eau Claire*

David Hover, *San Jose State University*

Graham L. Hubbard, *University of Minnesota*

Tammy G. Hunt, *University of North Carolina at Wilmington*

James Gaius Ibe, *Morris College*

W. Grahm Irwin, *Miami University*

Homer Johnson, *Loyola University—Chicago*

Jonathan L. Johnson, *University of Arkansas Walton College of Business Administration*

Marios Katsioloudes, *St. Joseph's University*

Robert Keating, *University of North Carolina at Wilmington*

Geoffrey King, *California State University—Fullerton*

Rico Lam, *University of Oregon*

Robert J. Litschert, *Virginia Polytechnic Institute and State University*

Franz T. Lohrke, *Louisiana State University*

Paul Mallette, *Colorado State University*

Daniel Marrone, *SUNY Farmingdale*

Lance A. Masters, *California State University—San Bernardino*

Robert N. McGrath, *Embry-Riddle Aeronautical University*

Charles Mercer, *Drury College*

Van Miller, *University of Dayton*

Tom Morris, *University of San Diego*

Joanna Mulholland, *West Chester University of Pennsylvania*

James Muraski, *Marquette University*

John Nebeck, *Viterbo University*

Jeryl L. Nelson, *Wayne State College*

Louise Nemanich, *Arizona State University*

Francine Newth, *Providence College*

Don Okhomina, *Fayetteville State University*

Phaedon P. Papadopoulos, *Houston Baptist University*

John Pappalardo, *Keen State College*

Paul R. Reed, *Sam Houston State University*

Rhonda K. Reger, *Arizona State University*

Malika Richards, *Indiana University*

Simon Rodan, *San Jose State*

Stuart Rosenberg, *Dowling College*

Douglas Ross, *Towson University*

Ronald Sanchez, *University of Illinois*

Joseph A. Schenk, *University of Dayton*

Brian Shaffer, *University of Kentucky*

Leonard Sholtis, *Eastern Michigan University*

Pradip K. Shukla, *Chapman University*

Mel Sillmon, *University of Michigan—Dearborn*

Dennis L. Smart, *University of Nebraska at Omaha*

Barbara Spencer, *Clemson University*

Lawrence Steenberg, *University of Evansville*

Kim A. Stewart, *University of Denver*

Ted Takamura, *Warner Pacific College*

Scott Taylor, *Florida Metropolitan University*

Thuhang Tran, *Middle Tennessee University*

Bobby Vaught, *Southwest Missouri State*

Robert P. Vichas, *Florida Atlantic University*

John Vitton, *University of North Dakota*

Edward Ward, *St. Cloud State University*

Kenneth Wendeln, *Indiana University*

Daniel L. White, *Drexel University*

Edgar L. Williams, Jr., *Norfolk State University*

Jun Zhao, *Governors State University*

Charles W. L. Hill
Gareth R. Jones
Melissa A. Schilling

Dedication

To my children, Elizabeth, Charlotte, and Michelle

– Charles W. L. Hill

For Nicholas and Julia and Morgan and Nia

– Gareth R. Jones

For my children, Julia and Conor

– Melissa A. Schilling

Strategic Leadership: Managing the Strategy-Making Process for Competitive Advantage

OPENING CASE

Wal-Mart's Competitive Advantage

Wal-Mart is one of the most extraordinary success stories in business history. Started in 1962 by Sam Walton, Wal-Mart has grown to become the world's largest corporation. In 2012, the discount retailer—whose mantra is "everyday low prices"—had sales of $440 billion, close to 10,000 stores in 27 countries, and 2.2 million employees. Some 8% of all retail sales in the United States are made at a Wal-Mart store. Wal-Mart is not only large; it is also very profitable. Between 2003 and 2012 the company's average return on invested capital was 12.96%, better than its well-managed rivals Costco and Target, which earned 10.74% and 9.6%, respectively (see Figure 1.1).

Wal-Mart's persistently superior profitability reflects a competitive advantage that is based upon a number of strategies. Back in 1962, Wal-Mart was one of the first companies to apply the self-service supermarket business model developed by grocery chains to general merchandise. Unlike its rivals such as K-Mart and Target that focused on urban and suburban locations, Sam Walton's Wal-Mart concentrated on small southern towns that were ignored by its rivals. Wal-Mart grew quickly by pricing its products lower than those of local retailers, often putting them out of business. By the time its rivals realized that small towns could support a large discount general merchandise store, Wal-Mart had already pre-empted them. These

LEARNING OBJECTIVES

After reading this chapter you should be able to:

1-1 Explain what is meant by "competitive advantage"

1-2 Discuss the strategic role of managers at different levels within an organization

1-3 Identify the primary steps in a strategic planning process

1-4 Discuss the common pitfalls of planning, and how those pitfalls can be avoided

1-5 Outline the cognitive biases that might lead to poor strategic decisions, and explain how these biases can be overcome

1-6 Discuss the role strategic leaders play in the strategy-making process

towns, which were large enough to support one discount retailer but not two, provided a secure profit base for Wal-Mart.

The company was also an innovator in information systems, logistics, and human resource practices. These strategies resulted in higher productivity and lower costs as compared to rivals, which enabled the company to earn a high profit while charging low prices. Wal-Mart led the way among U.S. retailers in developing and implementing sophisticated product tracking systems using bar-code technology and checkout scanners. This information technology enabled Wal-Mart to track what was selling and adjust its inventory accordingly so that the products found in each store matched local demand. By avoiding overstocking, Wal-Mart did not have to hold periodic sales to shift unsold inventory. Over time, Wal-Mart linked this information system to a nationwide network of distribution centers in which inventory was stored and then shipped to stores within a 400-mile radius on a daily basis. The combination of distribution centers and information centers

enabled Wal-Mart to reduce the amount of inventory it held in stores, thereby devoting more of that valuable space to selling and reducing the amount of capital it had tied up in inventory.

With regard to human resources, Sam Walton set the tone. He held a strong belief that employees should be respected and rewarded for helping to improve the profitability of the company. Underpinning this belief, Walton referred to employees as "associates." He established a profit-sharing scheme for all employees, and after the company went public in 1970, a program that allowed employees to purchase Wal-Mart stock at a discount to its market value. Wal-Mart was rewarded for this approach by high employee productivity, which translated into lower operating costs and higher profitability.

As Wal-Mart grew larger, the sheer size and purchasing power of the company enabled it to drive down the prices that it paid suppliers, passing on those saving to customers in the form of lower prices, which enabled Wal-Mart to gain more market share and hence lower prices even further. To take the

Figure 1.1	Profitability of Wal-Mart and Competitors, 2003–2012

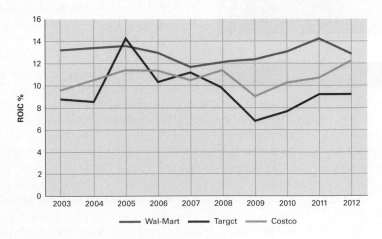

Source: Calculated by the author from Morningstar data.

sting out of the persistent demands for lower prices, Wal-Mart shared its sales information with suppliers on a daily basis, enabling them to gain efficiencies by configuring their own production schedules for sales at Wal-Mart.

By the time the 1990s came along, Wal-Mart was already the largest seller of general merchandise in the United States. To keep its growth going, Wal-Mart started to diversify into the grocery business, opening 200,000-square-foot supercenter stores that sold groceries and general merchandise under the same roof. Wal-Mart also diversified into the warehouse club business with the establishment of Sam's Club. The company began expanding internationally in 1991 with its entry into Mexico.

For all its success, however, Wal-Mart is now encountering very real limits to profitable growth. The U.S. market is saturated, and growth overseas has proved more difficult than the company hoped. The company was forced to exit Germany and South Korea after losing money there, and it has faced difficulties in several other developed nations. Moreover, rivals Target and Costco have continued to improve their performance, and Costco in particular is now snapping at Wal-Mart's heals.

Sources: "How Big Can It Grow?" *The Economist* (April 17, 2004): 74–78; "Trial by Checkout," *The Economist* (June 26, 2004): 74–76; Wal-Mart 10-K, 200, information at Wal-Mart's website, www.walmartstores.com; Robert Slater, *The Wal-Mart Triumph* (New York: Portfolio Trade Books, 2004); and "The Bulldozer from Bentonville Slows; Wal-Mart," *The Economist* (February 17, 2007): 70.

OVERVIEW

Why do some companies succeed, whereas others fail? Why has Wal-Mart been able to persistently outperform its well-managed rivals? In the airline industry, how has Southwest Airlines managed to keep increasing its revenues and profits through both good times and bad, whereas rivals such as United Airlines have had to seek bankruptcy protection? What explains the persistent growth and profitability of Nucor Steel, now the largest steelmaker in the United States, during a period when many of its once-larger rivals disappeared into bankruptcy?

In this book, we argue that the strategies that a company's managers pursue have a major impact on the company's performance relative to that of its competitors. A **strategy** is a set of related actions that managers take to increase their company's performance. For most, if not all, companies, achieving superior performance relative to rivals is the ultimate challenge. If a company's strategies result in superior performance, it is said to have a competitive advantage. Wal-Mart's strategies produced superior performance from 2003 to 2012; as a result, Wal-Mart has enjoyed competitive advantage over its rivals. How did Wal-Mart achieve this competitive advantage? As explained in the opening case, it was due to the successful pursuit of a number of strategies by Wal-Mart's managers, including, most notably, the company's founder, Sam Walton. These strategies enabled the company to lower its cost structure, charge low prices, gain market share, and become more profitable than its rivals. (We will return to the example of Wal-Mart several times throughout this book in the *Running Case* feature that examines various aspects of Wal-Mart's strategy and performance.)

This book identifies and describes the strategies that managers can pursue to achieve superior performance and provide their companies with a competitive advantage. One of its

strategy
A set of related actions that managers take to increase their company's performance.

central aims is to give you a thorough understanding of the analytical techniques and skills necessary to identify and implement strategies successfully. The first step toward achieving this objective is to describe in more detail what superior performance and competitive advantage mean and to explain the pivotal role that managers play in leading the strategy-making process.

strategic leadership
Creating competitive advantage through effective management of the strategy-making process.

Strategic leadership is about how to most effectively manage a company's strategy-making process to create competitive advantage. The strategy-making process is the process by which managers select and then implement a set of strategies that aim to achieve a competitive advantage. **Strategy formulation** is the task of selecting strategies, whereas **strategy implementation** is the task of putting strategies into action, which includes designing, delivering, and supporting products; improving the efficiency and effectiveness of operations; and designing a company's organizational structure, control systems, and culture.

strategy formulation
Selecting strategies based on analysis of an organization's external and internal environment.

strategy implementation
Putting strategies into action.

By the end of this chapter, you will understand how strategic leaders can manage the strategy-making process by formulating and implementing strategies that enable a company to achieve a competitive advantage and superior performance. Moreover, you will learn how the strategy-making process can go wrong, and what managers can do to make this process more effective.

STRATEGIC LEADERSHIP, COMPETITIVE ADVANTAGE, AND SUPERIOR PERFORMANCE

Strategic leadership is concerned with managing the strategy-making process to increase the performance of a company, thereby increasing the value of the enterprise to its owners, its shareholders. As shown in Figure 1.2, to increase shareholder value, managers must pursue strategies that increase the profitability of the company and ensure that profits grow (for more details, see the Appendix to this chapter). To do this, a company must be able to outperform its rivals; it must have a competitive advantage.

| Figure 1.2 | Determinants of Shareholder Value |

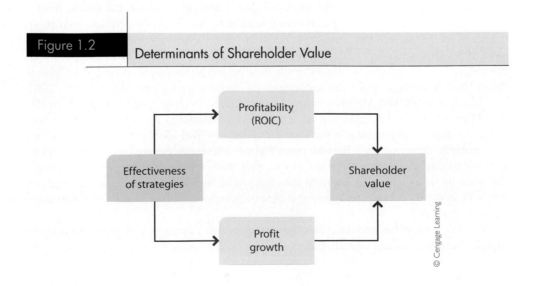

Superior Performance

Maximizing shareholder value is the ultimate goal of profit-making companies, for two reasons. First, shareholders provide a company with the risk capital that enables managers to buy the resources needed to produce and sell goods and services. **Risk capital** is capital that cannot be recovered if a company fails and goes bankrupt. In the case of Wal-Mart, for example, shareholders provided Sam Walton's company with the capital it used to build stores and distribution centers, invest in information systems, purchase inventory to sell to customers, and so on. Had Wal-Mart failed, its shareholders would have lost their money—their shares would have been worthless Thus, shareholders will not provide risk capital unless they believe that managers are committed to pursuing strategies that provide a good return on their capital investment. Second, shareholders are the legal owners of a corporation, and their shares therefore represent a claim on the profits generated by a company. Thus, managers have an obligation to invest those profits in ways that maximize shareholder value. Of course, as explained later in this book, managers must behave in a legal, ethical, and socially responsible manner while working to maximize shareholder value.

By **shareholder value**, we mean the returns that shareholders earn from purchasing shares in a company. These returns come from two sources: (a) capital appreciation in the value of a company's shares and (b) dividend payments.

For example, between January 2 and December 31, 2012, the value of one share in Wal-Mart increased from $60.33 to $68.90, which represents a capital appreciation of $8.57. In addition, Wal-Mart paid out a dividend of $1.59 per share during 2012. Thus, if an investor had bought one share of Wal-Mart on January 2 and held on to it for the entire year, the return would have been $10.16 ($8.57 + $1.59), a solid 16.8% return on the investment. One reason Wal-Mart's shareholders did well during 2012 was that investors believed that managers were pursuing strategies that would both increase the long-term profitability of the company and significantly grow its profits in the future.

One way of measuring the **profitability** of a company is by the return that it makes on the capital invested in the enterprise.[1] The return on invested capital (ROIC) that a company earns is defined as its net profit over the capital invested in the firm (profit/capital invested). By net profit, we mean net income after tax. By capital, we mean the sum of money invested in the company: that is, stockholders' equity plus debt owed to creditors. So defined, *profitability is the result of how efficiently and effectively managers use the capital at their disposal to produce goods and services that satisfy customer needs*. A company that uses its capital efficiently and effectively makes a positive return on invested capital.

The **profit growth** of a company can be measured by the increase in net profit over time. A company can grow its profits if it sells products in markets that are growing rapidly, gains market share from rivals, increases the amount it sells to existing customers, expands overseas, or diversifies profitably into new lines of business. For example, between 1994 and 2012, Wal-Mart increased its net profit from $2.68 billion to $15.7 billion. It was able to do this because the company (a) took market share from rivals, (b) established stores in 27 foreign nations that collectively generated $125 billion in sales by 2012, and (c) entered the grocery business. Due to the increase in net profit, Wal-Mart's earnings per share increased from $0.59 to $4.52, making each share more valuable, and leading in turn to appreciation in the value of Wal-Mart's shares.

Together, profitability and profit growth are the principal drivers of shareholder value (see the Appendix to this chapter for details). *To both boost profitability and grow profits over time, managers must formulate and implement strategies that give their company a competitive advantage over rivals*. Wal-Mart's strategies have enabled the company to maintain a high level

risk capital
Equity capital for which there is no guarantee that stockholders will ever recoup their investment or earn a decent return.

shareholder value
Returns that shareholders earn from purchasing shares in a company.

profitability
The return a company makes on the capital invested in the enterprise.

profit growth
The increase in net profit over time.

of profitability, and to simultaneously grow its profits over time. As a result, investors who purchased Wal-Mart's stock in January 1994, when the shares were trading at $11, would have made a return of more than 620% if they had held onto them through until December 2012. By pursuing strategies that lead to high and sustained profitability, and profit growth, Wal-Mart's managers have thus rewarded shareholders for their decisions to invest in the company.

One of the key challenges managers face is how best to simultaneously generate high profitability and increase the profits of the company. Companies that have high profitability but profits that are not growing will not be as highly valued by shareholders as companies that have both high profitability and rapid profit growth (see the Appendix for details). This was the situation that Dell faced in the later part of the 2000s. At the same time, managers need to be aware that if they grow profits but profitability declines, that too will not be as highly valued by shareholders. What shareholders want to see, and what managers must try to deliver through strategic leadership, is *profitable growth*: that is, high profitability and sustainable profit growth. This is not easy, but some of the most successful enterprises of our era have achieved it—companies such as Apple, Google, and Wal-Mart.

Competitive Advantage and a Company's Business Model

competitive advantage

The achieved advantage over rivals when a company's profitability is greater than the average profitability of firms in its industry.

sustained competitive advantage

A company's strategies enable it to maintain above-average profitability for a number of years.

business model

The conception of how strategies should work together as a whole to enable the company to achieve competitive advantage.

Managers do not make strategic decisions in a competitive vacuum. Their company is competing against other companies for customers. Competition is a rough-and-tumble process in which only the most efficient and effective companies win out. It is a race without end. To maximize shareholder value, managers must formulate and implement strategies that enable their company to outperform rivals—that give it a competitive advantage. A company is said to have a **competitive advantage** over its rivals when its profitability is greater than the average profitability and profit growth of other companies competing for the same set of customers. The higher its profitability relative to rivals, the greater its competitive advantage will be. A company has a **sustained competitive advantage** when its strategies enable it to maintain above-average profitability for a number of years. As discussed in the opening case, Wal-Mart had a significant and sustained competitive advantage over rivals such as Target, Costco, and K-Mart for most of the last two decades.

The key to understanding competitive advantage is appreciating how the different strategies managers pursue over time can create activities that fit together to make a company unique or different from its rivals and able to consistently outperform them. A **business model** is managers' conception of how the set of strategies their company pursues should work together as a congruent whole, enabling the company to gain a competitive advantage and achieve superior profitability and profit growth. In essence, a business model is a kind of mental model, or gestalt, of how the various strategies and capital investments a company makes should fit together to generate above-average profitability and profit growth. A business model encompasses the totality of how a company will:

- Select its customers.
- Define and differentiate its product offerings.
- Create value for its customers.
- Acquire and keep customers.
- Produce goods or services.
- Lower costs.
- Deliver goods and services to the market.
- Organize activities within the company.

- Configure its resources.
- Achieve and sustain a high level of profitability.
- Grow the business over time.

The business model at discount stores such as Wal-Mart, for example, is based on the idea that costs can be lowered by replacing a full-service retail format for with a self-service format and a wider selection of products sold in a large-footprint store that contains minimal fixtures and fittings. These savings are passed on to consumers in the form of lower prices, which in turn grow revenues and help the company to achieve further cost reductions from economies of scale. Over time, this business model has proved superior to the business models adopted by smaller full-service mom-and-pop stores, and by traditional high-service department stores such as Sears. The business model—known as the self-service supermarket business model—was first developed by grocery retailers in the 1950s and later refined and improved on by general merchandisers such as Wal-Mart. More recently, the same basic business model has been applied to toys (Toys "R" Us), office supplies (Staples, Office Depot), and home-improvement supplies (Home Depot and Lowes).

Wal-Mart outperformed close rivals that adopted the same basic business model, such as K-Mart, because of key differences in strategies, and because Wal-Mart implemented the business model more effectively. As a result, over time, Wal-Mart created unique activities that have become the foundation of its competitive advantage. For example, Wal-Mart was one of the first retailers to make strategic investments in distribution centers and information systems, which lowered the costs of managing inventory (see the opening case). This gave Wal-Mart a competitive advantage over rivals such as K-Mart, which suffered from poor inventory controls and thus higher costs. So although Wal-Mart and K-Mart pursued a similar business model, they were not identical. Key differences in the choice of strategies and the effectiveness of implementation created two unique organizations—one that attained a competitive advantage, and one that ended up with a competitive disadvantage.

Industry Differences in Performance

It is important to recognize that in addition to its business model and associated strategies, a company's performance is also determined by the characteristics of the industry in which it competes. Different industries are characterized by different competitive conditions. In some industries, demand is growing rapidly, and in others it is contracting. Some industries might be beset by excess capacity and persistent price wars, others by strong demand and rising prices. In some, technological change might be revolutionizing competition; others may be characterized by stable technology. In some industries, high profitability among incumbent companies might induce new companies to enter the industry, and these new entrants might subsequently depress prices and profits in the industry. In other industries, new entry might be difficult, and periods of high profitability might persist for a considerable time. Thus, the different competitive conditions prevailing in different industries may lead to differences in profitability and profit growth. For example, average profitability might be higher in some industries and lower in other industries because competitive conditions vary from industry to industry.

Figure 1.3 shows the average profitability, measured by ROIC, among companies in several different industries between 2002 and 2011. The computer software industry had a favorable competitive environment: demand for software was high and competition was generally not based on price. Just the opposite was the case in the air transport industry, which was extremely price competitive. Exactly how industries differ is discussed in detail

Figure 1.3   Return on Invested Capital (ROIC) in Selected Industries, 2002–2011

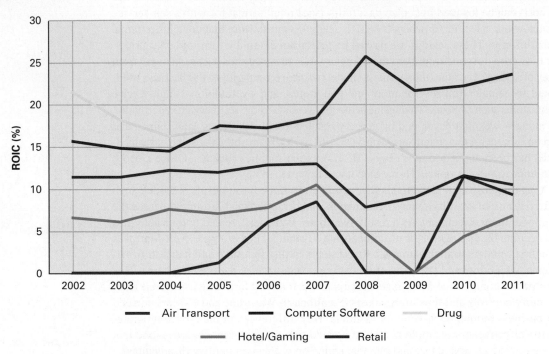

Source: Value Line Investment Survey.

in Chapter 2. For now, it is important to remember that the profitability and profit growth of a company are determined by two main factors: its relative success in its industry and the overall performance of its industry relative to other industries.[2]

Performance in Nonprofit Enterprises

A final point concerns the concept of superior performance in the nonprofit sector. By definition, nonprofit enterprises such as government agencies, universities, and charities are not in "business" to make profits. Nevertheless, they are expected to use their resources efficiently and operate effectively, and their managers set goals to measure their performance. The performance goal for a business school might be to get its programs ranked among the best in the nation. The performance goal for a charity might be to prevent childhood illnesses in poor countries. The performance goal for a government agency might be to improve its services while not exceeding its budget. The managers of nonprofits need to map out strategies to attain these goals. They also need to understand that nonprofits compete with each other for scarce resources, just as businesses do. For example, charities compete for scarce donations, and their managers must plan and develop strategies that lead to high performance and demonstrate a track record of meeting performance goals. A successful strategy gives potential donors a compelling message about why they should contribute additional donations. Thus, planning and thinking strategically are as important for managers in the nonprofit sector as they are for managers in profit-seeking firms.

STRATEGIC MANAGERS

Managers are the linchpin in the strategy-making process. It is individual managers who must take responsibility for formulating strategies to attain a competitive advantage and for putting those strategies into effect. They must lead the strategy-making process. The strategies that made Wal-Mart so successful were not chosen by some abstract entity known as "the company"; they were chosen by the company's founder, Sam Walton, and the managers he hired. Wal-Mart's success was largely based on how well the company's managers performed their strategic roles. In this section, we look at the strategic roles of different managers. Later in the chapter, we discuss strategic leadership, which is how managers can effectively lead the strategy-making process.

In most companies, there are two primary types of managers: **general managers**, who bear responsibility for the overall performance of the company or for one of its major self-contained subunits or divisions, and **functional managers**, who are responsible for supervising a particular function, that is, a task, activity, or operation, such as accounting, marketing, research and development (R&D), information technology, or logistics. Put differently, general managers have profit-and-loss responsibility for a product, a business, or the company as a whole.

A company is a collection of functions or departments that work together to bring a particular good or service to the market. If a company provides several different kinds of goods or services, it often duplicates these functions and creates a series of self-contained divisions (each of which contains its own set of functions) to manage each different good or service. The general managers of these divisions then become responsible for their particular product line. The overriding concern of general managers is the success of the whole company or the divisions under their direction; they are responsible for deciding how to create a competitive advantage and achieve high profitability with the resources and capital they have at their disposal. Figure 1.4 shows the organization of a **multidivisional company**,

general managers
Managers who bear responsibility for the overall performance of the company or for one of its major self-contained subunits or divisions.

functional managers
Managers responsible for supervising a particular function, that is, a task, activity, or operation, such as accounting, marketing, research and development (R&D), information technology, or logistics.

multidivisional company
A company that competes in several different businesses and has created a separate self-contained division to manage each.

| Figure 1.4 | Levels of Strategic Management |

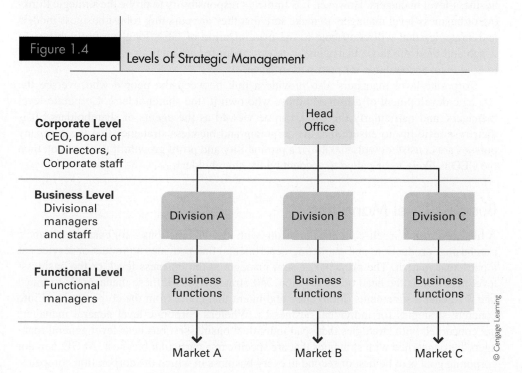

© Cengage Learning

that is, a company that competes in several different businesses and has created a separate self-contained division to manage each. As you can see, there are three main levels of management: corporate, business, and functional. General managers are found at the first two of these levels, but their strategic roles differ depending on their sphere of responsibility.

Corporate-Level Managers

The corporate level of management consists of the chief executive officer (CEO), other senior executives, and corporate staff. These individuals occupy the apex of decision making within the organization. The CEO is the principal general manager. In consultation with other senior executives, the role of corporate-level managers is to oversee the development of strategies for the whole organization. This role includes defining the goals of the organization, determining what businesses it should be in, allocating resources among the different businesses, formulating and implementing strategies that span individual businesses, and providing leadership for the entire organization.

Consider General Electric (GE) as an example. GE is active in a wide range of businesses, including lighting equipment, major appliances, motor and transportation equipment, turbine generators, construction and engineering services, industrial electronics, medical systems, aerospace, aircraft engines, and financial services. The main strategic responsibilities of its CEO, Jeffrey Immelt, are setting overall strategic goals, allocating resources among the different business areas, deciding whether the firm should divest itself of any of its businesses, and determining whether it should acquire any new ones. In other words, it is up to Immelt to develop strategies that span individual businesses; his concern is with building and managing the corporate portfolio of businesses to maximize corporate profitability.

It is the CEO's specific responsibility (in this example, Immelt) to develop strategies for competing in the individual business areas, such as financial services. The development of such strategies is the responsibility of the general managers in these different businesses, or business-level managers. However, it is Immelt's responsibility to probe the strategic thinking of business-level managers to make sure that they are pursuing robust business models and strategies that will contribute to the maximization of GE's long-run profitability, to coach and motivate those managers, to reward them for attaining or exceeding goals, and to hold them accountable for poor performance.

Corporate-level managers also provide a link between the people who oversee the strategic development of a firm and those who own it (the shareholders). Corporate-level managers, and particularly the CEO, can be viewed as the agents of shareholders.[3] It is their responsibility to ensure that the corporate and business strategies that the company pursues are consistent with maximizing profitability and profit growth. If they are not, then the CEO is likely to be called to account by the shareholders.

Business-Level Managers

business unit

A self-contained division that provides a product or service for a particular market.

A **business unit** is a self-contained division (with its own functions—for example, finance, purchasing, production, and marketing departments) that provides a product or service for a particular market. The principal general manager at the business level, or the business-level manager, is the head of the division. The strategic role of these managers is to translate the general statements of direction and intent that come from the corporate level into concrete strategies for individual businesses. Whereas corporate-level general managers are concerned with strategies that span individual businesses, business-level general managers are concerned with strategies that are specific to a particular business. At GE, a major corporate goal is to be first or second in every business in which the corporation competes.

Then, the general managers in each division work out for their business the details of a business model that is consistent with this objective.

Functional-Level Managers

Functional-level managers are responsible for the specific business functions or operations (human resources, purchasing, product development, customer service, etc.) that constitute a company or one of its divisions. Thus, a functional manager's sphere of responsibility is generally confined to one organizational activity, whereas general managers oversee the operation of an entire company or division. Although they are not responsible for the overall performance of the organization, functional managers nevertheless have a major strategic role: to develop functional strategies in their areas that help fulfill the strategic objectives set by business- and corporate-level general managers.

In GE's aerospace business, for instance, manufacturing managers are responsible for developing manufacturing strategies consistent with corporate objectives. Moreover, functional managers provide most of the information that makes it possible for business- and corporate-level general managers to formulate realistic and attainable strategies. Indeed, because they are closer to the customer than is the typical general manager, functional managers themselves may generate important ideas that subsequently become major strategies for the company. Thus, it is important for general managers to listen closely to the ideas of their functional managers. An equally great responsibility for managers at the operational level is strategy implementation: the execution of corporate- and business-level plans.

THE STRATEGY-MAKING PROCESS

We can now turn our attention to the process by which managers formulate and implement strategies. Many writers have emphasized that strategy is the outcome of a formal planning process and that top management plays the most important role in this process.[4] Although this view has some basis in reality, it is not the whole story. As we shall see later in the chapter, valuable strategies often emerge from deep within the organization without prior planning. Nevertheless, a consideration of formal, rational planning is a useful starting point for our journey into the world of strategy. Accordingly, we consider what might be described as a typical formal strategic planning model for making strategy.

A Model of the Strategic Planning Process

The formal strategic planning process has five main steps:

1. Select the corporate mission and major corporate goals.
2. Analyze the organization's external competitive environment to identify opportunities and threats.
3. Analyze the organization's internal operating environment to identify the organization's strengths and weaknesses.
4. Select strategies that build on the organization's strengths and correct its weaknesses in order to take advantage of external opportunities and counter external threats. These strategies should be consistent with the mission and major goals of the organization. They should be congruent and constitute a viable business model.
5. Implement the strategies.

The task of analyzing the organization's external and internal environments and then selecting appropriate strategies constitutes strategy formulation. In contrast, as noted earlier, strategy implementation involves putting the strategies (or plan) into action. This includes taking actions consistent with the selected strategies of the company at the corporate, business, and functional levels; allocating roles and responsibilities among managers (typically through the design of organization structure); allocating resources (including capital and money); setting short-term objectives; and designing the organization's control and reward systems. These steps are illustrated in Figure 1.5 (which can also be viewed as a plan for the rest of this book).

Each step in Figure 1.5 constitutes a sequential step in the strategic planning process. At step 1, each round, or cycle, of the planning process begins with a statement of the corporate mission and major corporate goals. The mission statement, then, is followed by the foundation of strategic thinking: external analysis, internal analysis, and strategic choice. The strategy-making process ends with the design of the organizational structure and the culture and control systems necessary to implement the organization's chosen strategy. This chapter discusses how to select a corporate mission and choose major goals. Other parts of strategic planning are reserved for later chapters, as indicated in Figure 1.5.

Some organizations go through a new cycle of the strategic planning process every year. This does not necessarily mean that managers choose a new strategy each year. In many instances, the result is simply to modify and reaffirm a strategy and structure already in place. The strategic plans generated by the planning process generally project over a period of 1 to 5 years, and the plan is updated, or rolled forward, every year. In most organizations, the results of the annual strategic planning process are used as input into the budgetary process for the coming year so that strategic planning is used to shape resource allocation within the organization.

Mission Statement

The first component of the strategic management process is crafting the organization's mission statement, which provides the framework—or context—within which strategies are formulated. A mission statement has four main components: a statement of the raison d'être of a company or organization—its reason for existence—which is normally referred to as the mission; a statement of some desired future state, usually referred to as the vision; a statement of the key values that the organization is committed to; and a statement of major goals.

mission

The purpose of the company, or a statement of what the company strives to do.

The Mission   A company's **mission** describes what the company does. For example, the mission of Google is *to organize the world's information and make it universally accessible and useful*.[5] Google's search engine is the method that is employed to "organize the world's information and make it accessible and useful." In the view of Google's founders, Larry Page and Sergey Brin, information includes not just text on websites, but also images, video, maps, products, news, books, blogs, and much more. You can search through all of these information sources using Google's search engine.

According to the late Peter Drucker, an important first step in the process of formulating a mission is to come up with a definition of the organization's business. Essentially, the definition answers these questions: "What is our business? What will it be? What should it be?"[6] The responses to these questions guide the formulation of the mission. To answer the question, "What is our business?" a company should define its business in terms of three dimensions: who is being satisfied (what customer groups), what is being satisfied

Figure 1.5	Main Components of the Strategic Planning Process

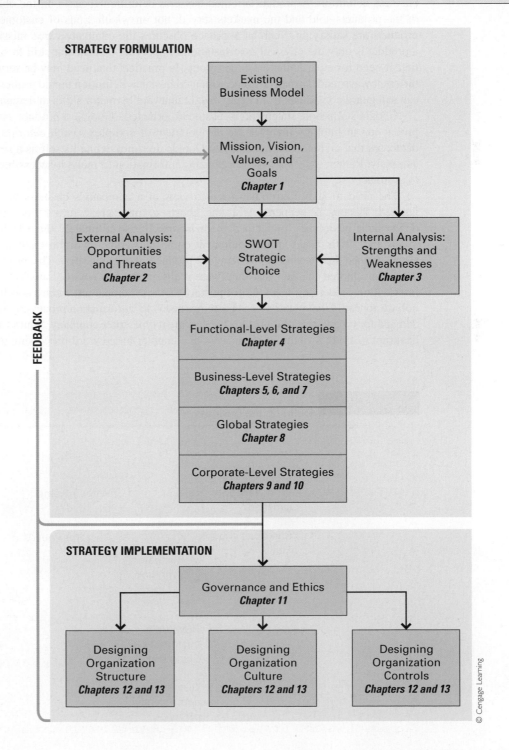

STRATEGY FORMULATION

Existing Business Model

Mission, Vision, Values, and Goals
Chapter 1

External Analysis: Opportunities and Threats
Chapter 2

SWOT Strategic Choice

Internal Analysis: Strengths and Weaknesses
Chapter 3

Functional-Level Strategies
Chapter 4

Business-Level Strategies
Chapters 5, 6, and 7

Global Strategies
Chapter 8

Corporate-Level Strategies
Chapters 9 and 10

FEEDBACK

STRATEGY IMPLEMENTATION

Governance and Ethics
Chapter 11

Designing Organization Structure
Chapters 12 and 13

Designing Organization Culture
Chapters 12 and 13

Designing Organization Controls
Chapters 12 and 13

© Cengage Learning

(what customer needs), and how customers' needs are being satisfied (by what skills, knowledge, or distinctive competencies).[7] Figure 1.6 illustrates these dimensions.

This approach stresses the need for a *customer-oriented* rather than a *product-oriented* business definition. A product-oriented business definition focuses on the characteristics of the products sold and the markets served, not on which kinds of customer needs the products are satisfying. Such an approach obscures the company's true mission because a product is only the physical manifestation of applying a particular skill to satisfy a particular need for a particular customer group. In practice, that need may be served in many different ways, and a broad customer-oriented business definition that identifies these ways can safeguard companies from being caught unaware by major shifts in demand.

Google's mission statement is customer oriented. Google's product is search. Its production technology involves the development of complex search algorithms and vast databases that archive information. But Google does not define its self as a search engine company. Rather, it sees itself as organizing information to make it accessible and useful *to customers*.

The need to take a customer-oriented view of a company's business has often been ignored. History is peppered with the ghosts of once-great corporations that did not define their businesses, or defined them incorrectly, so ultimately they declined. In the 1950s and 1960s, many office equipment companies, such as Smith Corona and Underwood, defined their businesses as being the production of typewriters. This product-oriented definition ignored the fact that they were really in the business of satisfying customers' information-processing needs. Unfortunately for those companies, when a new form of technology appeared that better served customer needs for information processing (computers), demand for typewriters plummeted. The last great typewriter company, Smith Corona, went bankrupt in 1996, a victim of the success of computer-based word-processing technology.

Figure 1.6   Defining the Business

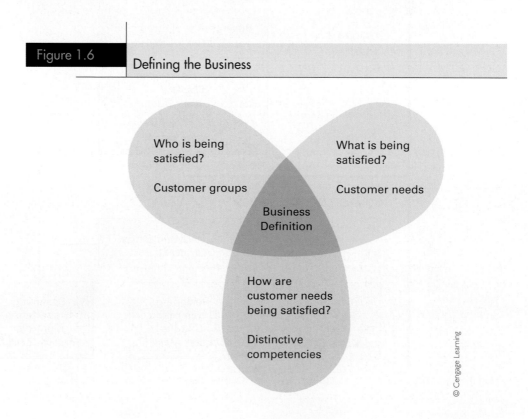

© Cengage Learning

In contrast, IBM correctly foresaw what its business would be. In the 1950s, IBM was a leader in the manufacture of typewriters and mechanical tabulating equipment using punch-card technology. However, unlike many of its competitors, IBM defined its business as providing a means for *information processing and storage*, rather than only supplying mechanical tabulating equipment and typewriters.[8] Given this definition, the company's subsequent moves into computers, software systems, office systems, and printers seem logical.

Vision The **vision** of a company defines a desired future state; it articulates, often in bold terms, what the company would like to achieve. In its early days, Microsoft operated with a very powerful vision of a computer on every desk and in every home. To turn this vision into a reality, Microsoft focused on producing computer software that was cheap and useful to business and consumers. In turn, the availability of powerful and inexpensive software such as Windows and Office helped to drive the penetration of personal computers into homes and offices.

> **vision**
> The articulation of a company's desired achievements or future state.

Values The **values** of a company state how managers and employees should conduct themselves, how they should do business, and what kind of organization they should build to help a company achieve its mission. Insofar as they help drive and shape behavior within a company, values are commonly seen as the bedrock of a company's organizational culture: the set of values, norms, and standards that control how employees work to achieve an organization's mission and goals. An organization's culture is commonly seen as an important source of its competitive advantage.[9] (We discuss the issue of organization culture in depth in Chapter 12.) For example, Nucor Steel is one of the most productive and profitable steel firms in the world. Its competitive advantage is based, in part, on the extremely high productivity of its workforce, which the company maintains is a direct result of its cultural values, which in turn determine how it treats its employees. These values are as follows:

> **values**
> A statement of how employees should conduct themselves and their business to help achieve the company mission.

- "Management is obligated to manage Nucor in such a way that employees will have the opportunity to earn according to their productivity."
- "Employees should be able to feel confident that if they do their jobs properly, they will have a job tomorrow."
- "Employees have the right to be treated fairly and must believe that they will be."
- "Employees must have an avenue of appeal when they believe they are being treated unfairly."[10]

At Nucor, values emphasizing pay for performance, job security, and fair treatment for employees help to create an atmosphere within the company that leads to high employee productivity. In turn, this has helped to give Nucor one of the lowest cost structures in its industry, and helps to explain the company's profitability in a very price-competitive business.

In one study of organizational values, researchers identified a set of values associated with high-performing organizations that help companies achieve superior financial performance through their impact on employee behavior.[11] These values included respect for the interests of key organizational stakeholders: individuals or groups that have an interest, claim, or stake in the company, in what it does, and in how well it performs.[12] They include stockholders, bondholders, employees, customers, the communities in which the company does business, and the general public. The study found that deep respect for the interests of customers, employees, suppliers, and shareholders was associated with high performance. The study also noted that the encouragement of leadership and entrepreneurial behavior by mid- and lower-level managers and a willingness to support change efforts within the organization contributed to high performance. Companies that emphasize such values consistently throughout their organizations include Hewlett-Packard, Wal-Mart, and PepsiCo. The same study identified the values of poorly performing companies—values that, as might be expected, are not articulated in company mission statements: (1) arrogance, particularly to ideas from outside the company; (2) a lack of respect for key stakeholders; and (3) a history of resisting change efforts and "punishing" mid- and lower-level managers who showed "too much leadership." General Motors was held up as an example of one such organization.

MAJOR GOALS

Having stated the mission, vision, and key values, strategic managers can take the next step in the formulation of a mission statement: establishing major goals. A goal is a precise and measurable desired future state that a company attempts to realize. In this context, the purpose of goals is to specify with precision what must be done if the company is to attain its mission or vision.

Well-constructed goals have four main characteristics[13]:

- They are precise and measurable. Measurable goals give managers a yardstick or standard against which they can judge their performance.
- They address crucial issues. To maintain focus, managers should select a limited number of major goals to assess the performance of the company. The goals that are selected should be crucial or important ones.
- They are challenging but realistic. They give all employees an incentive to look for ways of improving the operations of an organization. If a goal is unrealistic in the challenges it poses, employees may give up; a goal that is too easy may fail to motivate managers and other employees.[14]
- They specify a time period in which the goals should be achieved, when that is appropriate. Time constraints tell employees that success requires a goal to be attained by a given date, not after that date. Deadlines can inject a sense of urgency into goal attainment and act as a motivator. However, not all goals require time constraints.

Well-constructed goals also provide a means by which the performance of managers can be evaluated.

As noted earlier, although most companies operate with a variety of goals, the primary goal of most corporations is to maximize shareholder returns, and doing this requires both high profitability and sustained profit growth. Thus, most companies operate with goals for profitability and profit growth. However, it is important that top managers do not make the mistake of overemphasizing current profitability to the detriment of long-term profitability and profit growth.[15] The overzealous pursuit of current profitability to maximize short-term ROIC can encourage such misguided managerial actions as cutting expenditures judged to be nonessential in the short run—for instance, expenditures for research and development, marketing, and new capital investments. Although cutting current expenditures increases current profitability, the resulting underinvestment, lack of innovation, and diminished marketing can jeopardize long-run profitability and profit growth.

To guard against short-run decision making, managers need to ensure that they adopt goals whose attainment will increase the long-run performance and competitiveness of their enterprise. Long-term goals are related to such issues as product development, customer satisfaction, and efficiency, and they emphasize specific objectives or targets concerning such details as employee and capital productivity, product quality, innovation, customer satisfaction, and customer service.

External Analysis

The second component of the strategic management process is an analysis of the organization's external operating environment. The essential purpose of the external analysis is to identify strategic opportunities and threats within the organization's operating environment that will affect how it pursues its mission. Strategy in Action 1.1 describes how an analysis of opportunities and threats in the external environment led to a strategic shift at Time Inc.

Three interrelated environments should be examined when undertaking an external analysis: the industry environment in which the company operates, the country or national environment, and the wider socioeconomic or macroenvironment. Analyzing the industry environment requires an assessment of the competitive structure of the company's industry, including the competitive position of the company and its major rivals. It also requires analysis of the nature, stage, dynamics, and history of the industry. Because many markets are now global markets, analyzing the industry environment also means assessing the impact of globalization on competition within an industry. Such an analysis may reveal that a company should move some production facilities to another nation, that it should aggressively expand in emerging markets such as China, or that it should beware of new competition from emerging nations. Analyzing the macroenvironment consists of examining macroeconomic, social, governmental, legal, international, and technological factors that may affect the company and its industry. We look at external analysis in Chapter 2.

Internal Analysis

Internal analysis, the third component of the strategic planning process, focuses on reviewing the resources, capabilities, and competencies of a company. The goal is to identify the strengths and weaknesses of the company. For example, as described in Strategy in Action 1.1, an internal analysis at Time Inc. revealed that although the company had strong well-known brands such as *Fortune*, *Money*, *Sports Illustrated*, and *People* (a strength), and strong reporting capabilities (another strength), it suffered from a lack of editorial commitment to online publishing (a weakness). We consider internal analysis in Chapter 3.

SWOT Analysis and the Business Model

The next component of strategic thinking requires the generation of a series of strategic alternatives, or choices of future strategies to pursue, given the company's internal strengths and weaknesses and its external opportunities and threats. The comparison of strengths, weaknesses, opportunities, and threats is normally referred to as a **SWOT analysis**.[16] The central purpose is to identify the strategies to exploit external opportunities, counter threats, build on and protect company strengths, and eradicate weaknesses.

SWOT analysis
The comparison of strengths, weaknesses, opportunities, and threats.

At Time Inc., managers saw the move of readership to the Web as both an *opportunity* that they must exploit and a *threat* to Time's established print magazines. Managers recognized that Time's well-known brands and strong reporting capabilities were *strengths* that would serve it well online, but that an editorial culture that marginalized online publishing was a *weakness* that had to be fixed. The *strategies* that managers at Time Inc. came up with included merging the print and online newsrooms to remove distinctions between them; investing significant financial resources in online sites; and entering into a partnership with CNN, which already had a strong online presence.

1.1 STRATEGY IN ACTION

Strategic Analysis at Time Inc.

© iStockPhoto.com/Tom Nulens

Time Inc., the magazine publishing division of media conglomerate Time Warner, has a venerable history. Its magazine titles include *Time*, *Fortune*, *Sports Illustrated*, and *People*, all long-time leaders in their respective categories. By the mid-2000s, however, Time Inc. was confronted with declining subscription rates.

An external analysis revealed what was happening. The readership of Time's magazines was aging. Increasingly, younger readers were getting what they wanted from the Web. This was both a *threat* for Time Inc., as its Web offerings were not strong, and an *opportunity*, because with the right offerings, Time Inc. could capture this audience. Time also realized that advertising dollars were migrating rapidly to the Web, and if the company was going to maintain its share, its Web offerings had to be every bit as good as its print offerings.

An internal analysis revealed why, despite multiple attempts, Time had failed to capitalize on the opportunities offered by the emergence of the Web. Although Time had tremendous *strengths*, including powerful brands and strong reporting, development of its Web offerings had been hindered by a serious *weakness*—an editorial culture that regarded Web publishing as a backwater. At *People*, for example, the online operation used to be "like a distant moon," according to managing editor Martha Nelson. Managers at Time Inc. had also been worried that Web offerings would cannibalize print offerings and help to accelerate the decline in the circulation of magazines, with dire financial consequences for the company. As a result of this culture, efforts to move publications onto the Web were underfunded or were stymied entirely by a lack of management attention and commitment.

It was Martha Nelson at *People* who first showed the way forward for the company. Her *strategy* for overcoming the *weakness* at Time Inc., and better exploiting *opportunities* on the Web, started in 2003 with merging the print and online newsrooms at *People*, removing the distinction between them. Then, she relaunched the magazine's online site, made major editorial commitments to Web publishing, stated that original content should appear on the Web, and emphasized the importance of driving traffic to the site and earning advertising revenues. Over the next 2 years, page views at People.com increased fivefold.

Ann Moore, then the CEO at Time Inc., formalized this strategy in 2005, mandating that all print offerings should follow the lead of People.com, integrating print and online newsrooms and investing significantly more resources in Web publishing. To drive this home, Time hired several well-known bloggers to write for its online publications. The goal of Moore's strategy was to neutralize the cultural *weakness* that had hindered online efforts in the past at Time Inc., and to redirect resources to Web publishing.

In 2006, Time made another strategic move designed to exploit the opportunities associated with the Web when it started a partnership with the 24-hour news channel CNN, putting all of its financial magazines onto a site that is jointly owned, CNNMoney.com. The site, which offers free access to *Fortune*, *Money*, and *Business 2.0*, quickly took the third spot in online financial websites, behind Yahoo! finance and MSN. This was followed with a redesigned website for *Sports Illustrated* that has rolled out video downloads for iPods and mobile phones.

To drive home the shift to Web-centric publishing, in 2007 Time announced another change in strategy—it would sell off 18 magazine titles that, although good performers, did not appear to have much traction on the Web.

In 2007, Ann Moore stated that going forward, Time would be focusing its energy, resources, and investments on the company's largest and most profitable brands: brands that have demonstrated an ability to draw large audiences in digital form. Since then, the big push at Time has been to develop magazine apps for tablet computers, most notably Apple's iPad and tablets that use the Android operating system. By early 2012, Time had its entire magazine catalog on every major tablet platform.

Sources: A. Van Duyn, "Time Inc. Revamp to Include Sale of 18 Titles," *Financial Times* (September 13, 2006): 24; M. Karnitsching, "Time Inc. Makes New Bid to Be Big Web Player," *Wall Street Journal* (March 29, 2006): B1; M. Flamm, "Time Tries the Web Again," *Crain's New York Business* (January 16, 2006): 3; and Tim Carmody, "Time Warner Bringing Digital Magazines, HBO to More Platforms," *Wired* (July 3, 2011).

More generally, the goal of a SWOT analysis is to create, affirm, or fine-tune a company-specific business model that will best align, fit, or match a company's resources and capabilities to the demands of the environment in which it operates. Managers compare and contrast the various alternative possible strategies against each other and then identify the set of strategies that will create and sustain a competitive advantage. These strategies can be divided into four main categories:

- *Functional-level strategies*, directed at improving the effectiveness of operations within a company, such as manufacturing, marketing, materials management, product development, and customer service. We review functional-level strategies in Chapter 4.
- *Business-level strategies*, which encompass the business's overall competitive theme, the way it positions itself in the marketplace to gain a competitive advantage, and the different positioning strategies that can be used in different industry settings—for example, cost leadership, differentiation, focusing on a particular niche or segment of the industry, or some combination of these. We review business-level strategies in Chapters 5, 6, and 7.
- *Global strategies*, which address how to expand operations outside the home country to grow and prosper in a world where competitive advantage is determined at a global level. We review global strategies in Chapter 8.
- *Corporate-level strategies*, which answer the primary questions: What business or businesses should we be in to maximize the long-run profitability and profit growth of the organization, and how should we enter and increase our presence in these businesses to gain a competitive advantage? We review corporate-level strategies in Chapters 9 and 10.

The strategies identified through a SWOT analysis should be congruent with each other. Thus, functional-level strategies should be consistent with, or support, the company's business-level strategies and global strategies. Moreover, as we explain later in this book, corporate-level strategies should support business-level strategies. When combined, the various strategies pursued by a company should constitute a complete, viable business model. In essence, a SWOT analysis is a methodology for choosing between competing business models, and for fine-tuning the business model that managers choose. For example, when Microsoft entered the videogame market with its Xbox offering, it had to settle on the best business model for competing in this market. Microsoft used a SWOT type of analysis to compare alternatives and settled on a business model referred to as "razor and razor blades," in which the Xbox console is priced at cost to build sales (the "razor"), while profits are made from royalties on the sale of games for the Xbox (the "blades").

Strategy Implementation

Once managers have chosen a set of congruent strategies to achieve a competitive advantage and increase performance, managers must put those strategies into action: strategy has to be implemented. Strategy implementation involves taking actions at the functional, business, and corporate levels to execute a strategic plan. Implementation can include, for example, putting quality improvement programs into place, changing the way a product is designed, positioning the product differently in the marketplace, segmenting the marketing and offering different versions of the product to different consumer groups, implementing price increases or decreases, expanding through mergers and acquisitions, or downsizing the company by closing down or selling off parts of the company. These and other topics are discussed in detail in Chapters 4 through 10.

Strategy implementation also entails designing the best organization structure and the best culture and control systems to put a chosen strategy into action. In addition, senior managers need to put a governance system in place to make sure that all within the organization act in a manner that is not only consistent with maximizing profitability and profit growth, but also legal and ethical. In this book, we look at the topic of governance and ethics in Chapter 11; we discuss the organization structure, culture, and controls required to implement business-level strategies in Chapter 12; and we discuss the structure, culture, and controls required to implement corporate-level strategies in Chapter 13.

The Feedback Loop

The feedback loop in Figure 1.5 indicates that strategic planning is ongoing: it never ends. Once a strategy has been implemented, its execution must be monitored to determine the extent to which strategic goals and objectives are actually being achieved, and to what degree competitive advantage is being created and sustained. This information and knowledge is returned to the corporate level through feedback loops, and becomes the input for the next round of strategy formulation and implementation. Top managers can then decide whether to reaffirm the existing business model and the existing strategies and goals, or suggest changes for the future. For example, if a strategic goal proves too optimistic, the next time, a more conservative goal is set. Or, feedback may reveal that the business model is not working, so managers may seek ways to change it. In essence, this is what happened at Time Inc. (see Strategy in Action 1.1).

STRATEGY AS AN EMERGENT PROCESS

The planning model suggests that a company's strategies are the result of a plan, that the strategic planning process is rational and highly structured, and that top management orchestrates the process. Several scholars have criticized the formal planning model for three main reasons: the unpredictability of the real world, the role that lower-level managers can play in the strategic management process, and the fact that many successful strategies are often the result of serendipity, not rational strategizing. These scholars have advocated an alternative view of strategy making.[44, 17]

Strategy Making in an Unpredictable World

Critics of formal planning systems argue that we live in a world in which uncertainty, complexity, and ambiguity dominate, and in which small chance events can have a large and unpredictable impact on outcomes.[18] In such circumstances, they claim, even the most carefully thought-out strategic plans are prone to being rendered useless by rapid and unforeseen change. In an unpredictable world, being able to respond quickly to changing circumstances, and to alter the strategies of the organization accordingly, is paramount. The dramatic rise of Google, for example, with its business model based on revenues earned from advertising links associated with search results (the so-called "pay-per-click" business model), disrupted the business models of companies that made money from online advertising. Nobody could foresee this development or plan for it, but companies had to respond to it, and rapidly. Companies with a strong online advertising presence, including Yahoo.com and Microsoft's MSN network, rapidly changed their strategies to adapt to the threat Google posed. Specifically, both companies developed their own search engines and copied Google's pay-per-click business model. According to critics of formal systems, such a flexible approach to strategy making is not possible within the framework of a traditional strategic planning process, with its implicit assumption that an organization's strategies only need to be reviewed during the annual strategic planning exercise.

Autonomous Action: Strategy Making by Lower-Level Managers

Another criticism leveled at the rational planning model of strategy is that too much importance is attached to the role of top management, particularly the CEO.[19] An alternative view is that individual managers deep within an organization can—and often do—exert a profound influence over the strategic direction of the firm.[20] Writing with Robert Burgelman of Stanford University, Andy Grove, the former CEO of Intel, noted that many important strategic decisions at Intel were initiated not by top managers but by the autonomous action of lower-level managers deep within Intel who, on their own initiative, formulated new strategies and worked to persuade top-level managers to alter the strategic priorities of the firm.[21] These strategic decisions included the decision to exit an important market (the DRAM memory chip market) and to develop a certain class of microprocessors (RISC-based microprocessors) in direct contrast to the stated strategy of Intel's top managers. Another example of autonomous action, this one at Starbucks, is given in Strategy in Action 1.2.

1.2 STRATEGY IN ACTION

Starbucks' Music Business

© iStockPhoto.com/Tom Nulens

Anyone who has walked into a Starbucks cannot help but notice that in addition to various coffee beverages and food, the company also sells music CDs. Most Starbucks stores now have racks displaying anywhere between 5 and 20 CDs right by the cash register. You can also purchase Starbucks music CDs on the company's website, and music published by the company's Hear Music label is available for download via iTunes. The interesting thing about Starbucks' entry into music retailing and publishing is that it was not the result of a formal planning process. The company's journey into music started in the late 1980s when Tim Jones, then the manager of a Starbucks in Seattle's University Village, started to bring his own tapes of music compilations into the store to play. Soon Jones was getting requests for copies from customers. Jones told this to Starbucks' CEO, Howard Schultz, and suggested that Starbucks start to sell music compilations. At first, Schultz was skeptical, but after repeated lobbying efforts by Jones, he eventually took up the suggestion. In the late 1990s, Starbucks purchased Hear Music, a small publishing company, so that it could sell and distribute its own music compilations. Today Starbucks' music business represents a small but healthy part of its overall product portfolio. For some artists, sales through Starbucks can represent an important revenue stream. Although it shifts titles regularly, sales of a CD over, say, 6 weeks, typically accounts for 5 to 10% of the album's overall sales.

Sources: S. Gray and E. Smith, "Coffee and Music Create a Potent Mix at Starbucks," *Wall Street Journal* (July 19, 2005): A1; and J. Leeds, "Starbucks Stumbles into Music," *New York Times* (March 17, 2008).

Autonomous action may be particularly important in helping established companies deal with the uncertainty created by the arrival of a radical new technology that changes the dominant paradigm in an industry.[22] Top managers usually rise to preeminence by successfully executing the established strategy of the firm. Therefore, they may have an emotional commitment to the status quo and are often unable to see things from a different perspective. In this sense, they can be a conservative force that promotes inertia. Lower-level managers, however, are less likely to have the same commitment to the status quo and have more to gain from promoting new technologies and strategies. They may be the first ones to recognize new strategic opportunities and lobby for strategic change. As described in Strategy in Action 1.3, this seems to have been the case at discount stockbroker Charles Schwab, which had to adjust to the arrival of the Web in the 1990s.

Serendipity and Strategy

Business history is replete with examples of accidental events that help to push companies in new and profitable directions. What these examples suggest is that many successful strategies are not the result of well-thought-out plans, but of serendipity—stumbling across good things unexpectedly. One such example occurred at 3M during the 1960s. At that time, 3M was producing fluorocarbons for sale as coolant liquid in air-conditioning equipment. One day, a researcher working with fluorocarbons in a 3M lab spilled some of the liquid on her shoes. Later that day when she spilled coffee over her shoes, she watched with interest as the coffee formed into little beads of liquid and then ran off her shoes without leaving a stain. Reflecting on this phenomenon, she realized that a fluorocarbon-based liquid might turn out to be useful for protecting fabrics from liquid stains, and so the idea for Scotchgard was born. Subsequently, Scotchgard became one of 3M's most profitable products, and took the company into the fabric protection business, an area within which it had never planned to participate.[23]

Serendipitous discoveries and events can open all sorts of profitable avenues for a company. But some companies have missed profitable opportunities because serendipitous discoveries or events were inconsistent with their prior (planned) conception of what their strategy should be. In one of the classic examples of such myopia, a century ago, the telegraph company Western Union turned down an opportunity to purchase the rights to an invention made by Alexander Graham Bell. The invention was the telephone, a technology that subsequently made the telegraph obsolete.

Intended and Emergent Strategies

Henry Mintzberg's model of strategy development provides a more encompassing view of what strategy actually is. According to this model, illustrated in Figure 1.7, a company's realized strategy is the product of whatever planned strategies are actually put into action (the company's deliberate strategies) and any unplanned, or emergent, strategies. In Mintzberg's view, many planned strategies are not implemented because of unpredicted changes in the environment (they are unrealized). Emergent strategies are the unplanned responses to unforeseen circumstances. They arise from autonomous action by individual managers deep within the organization, from serendipitous discoveries or events, or from an unplanned strategic shift by top-level managers in response to changed circumstances. They are not the product of formal top-down planning mechanisms.

Mintzberg maintains that emergent strategies are often successful and may be more appropriate than intended strategies. In the classic description of this process, Richard Pascale described how this was the case for the entry of Honda Motor Co. into the U.S. motorcycle

1.3 STRATEGY IN ACTION

A Strategic Shift at Charles Schwab

© iStockPhoto.com/Tom Nulens

In the mid-1990s, Charles Schwab was the most successful discount stockbroker in the world. Over 20 years, it had gained share from full-service brokers like Merrill Lynch by offering deep discounts on the commissions charged for stock trades. Although Schwab had a nationwide network of branches, most customers executed their trades through a telephone system called TeleBroker. Others used online proprietary software, Street Smart, which had to be purchased from Schwab. It was a business model that worked well—then along came E*Trade.

Bill Porter, a physicist and inventor, started the discount brokerage firm E*Trade in 1994 to take advantage of the opportunity created by the rapid emergence of the World Wide Web. E*Trade launched the first dedicated website for online trading: E*Trade had no branches, no brokers, and no telephone system for taking orders, and thus it had a very-low-cost structure. Customers traded stocks over the company's website. Due to its low-cost structure, E*Trade was able to announce a flat $14.95 commission on stock trades, a figure significantly below Schwab's average commission, which at the time was $65. It was clear from the outset that E*Trade and other online brokers, such as Ameritrade, which soon followed, offered a direct threat to Schwab. Not only were their cost structures and commission rates considerably lower than Schwab's, but the ease, speed, and flexibility of trading stocks over the Web suddenly made Schwab's Street Smart trading software seem limited and its telephone system antiquated.

Deep within Schwab, William Pearson, a young software specialist who had worked on the development of Street Smart, immediately saw the transformational power of the Web. Pearson believed that Schwab needed to develop its own Web-based software, and quickly. Try as he might, though, Pearson could not get the attention of his supervisor. He tried a number of other executives but found little support. Eventually he approached Anne Hennegar, a former Schwab manager who now worked as a consultant to the company. Hennegar suggested that Pearson meet with Tom Seip, an executive vice president at Schwab who was known for his ability to think outside the box. Hennegar approached Seip on Pearson's behalf, and Seip responded positively, asking her to set up a meeting. Hennegar and Pearson arrived, expecting to meet only Seip, but to their surprise, in walked Charles Schwab, his chief operating officer, David Pottruck, and the vice presidents in charge of strategic planning and electronic brokerage.

As the group watched Pearson's demo, which detailed how a Web-based system would look and work, they became increasingly excited. It was clear to those in the room that a Web-based system using real-time information, personalization, customization, and interactivity all advanced Schwab's commitment to empowering customers. By the end of the meeting, Pearson had received a green light to start work on the project. A year later, Schwab launched its own Web-based offering, eSchwab, which enabled Schwab clients to execute stock trades for a low flat-rate commission. eSchwab went on to become the core of the company's offering, enabling it to stave off competition from deep discount brokers like E*Trade.

Sources: John Kador, *Charles Schwab: How One Company Beat Wall Street and Reinvented the Brokerage Industry* (New York: John Wiley & Sons, 2002); and Erick Schonfeld, "Schwab Puts It All Online," *Fortune* (December 7, 1998): 94–99.

market.[24] When a number of Honda executives arrived in Los Angeles from Japan in 1959 to establish a U.S. operation, their original aim (intended strategy) was to focus on selling 250-cc and 350-cc machines to confirmed motorcycle enthusiasts rather than 50-cc Honda Cubs, which were a big hit in Japan. Their instinct told them that the Honda 50s were not suitable for the U.S. market, where everything was bigger and more luxurious than in Japan.

However, sales of the 250-cc and 350-cc bikes were sluggish, and the bikes themselves were plagued by mechanical failure. It looked as if Honda's strategy was going to fail. At the same time, the Japanese executives who were using the Honda 50s to run errands

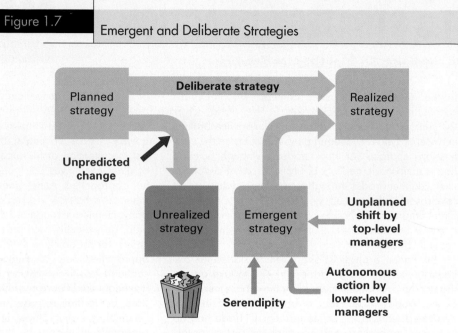

Figure 1.7 Emergent and Deliberate Strategies

Source: Adapted from H. Mintzberg and A. McGugh, *Administrative Science Quarterly* 30:2 (June 1985).

around Los Angeles were attracting a lot of attention. One day, they got a call from a Sears, Roebuck and Co. buyer who wanted to sell the 50-cc bikes to a broad market of Americans who were not necessarily motorcycle enthusiasts. The Honda executives were hesitant to sell the small bikes for fear of alienating serious bikers, who might then associate Honda with "wimpy" machines. In the end, however, they were pushed into doing so by the failure of the 250-cc and 350-cc models.

Honda had stumbled onto a previously untouched market segment that would prove huge: the average American who had never owned a motorbike. Honda had also found an untried channel of distribution: general retailers rather than specialty motorbike stores. By 1964, nearly one out of every two motorcycles sold in the United States was a Honda.

The conventional explanation for Honda's success is that the company redefined the U.S. motorcycle industry with a brilliantly conceived intended strategy. The fact was that Honda's intended strategy was a near-disaster. The strategy that emerged did so not through planning but through unplanned action in response to unforeseen circumstances. Nevertheless, credit should be given to the Japanese management for recognizing the strength of the emergent strategy and for pursuing it with vigor.

The critical point demonstrated by the Honda example is that successful strategies can often emerge within an organization without prior planning, and in response to unforeseen circumstances. As Mintzberg has noted, strategies can take root wherever people have the capacity to learn and the resources to support that capacity.

In practice, the strategies of most organizations are likely a combination of the intended and the emergent. The message for management is that it needs to recognize the process of emergence and to intervene when appropriate, relinquishing bad emergent strategies and nurturing potentially good ones.[25] To make such decisions, managers must be able to judge the worth of emergent strategies. They must be able to think strategically.

Although emergent strategies arise from within the organization without prior planning—that is, without completing the steps illustrated in Figure 1.5 in a sequential fashion—top management must still evaluate emergent strategies. Such evaluation involves comparing each emergent strategy with the organization's goals, external environmental opportunities and threats, and internal strengths and weaknesses. The objective is to assess whether the emergent strategy fits the company's needs and capabilities. In addition, Mintzberg stresses that an organization's capability to produce emergent strategies is a function of the kind of corporate culture that the organization's structure and control systems foster. In other words, the different components of the strategic management process are just as important from the perspective of emergent strategies as they are from the perspective of intended strategies.

STRATEGIC PLANNING IN PRACTICE

Despite criticisms, research suggests that formal planning systems do help managers make better strategic decisions. A study that analyzed the results of 26 previously published studies came to the conclusion that, on average, strategic planning has a positive impact on company performance.[26] Another study of strategic planning in 656 firms found that formal planning methodologies and emergent strategies both form part of a good strategy-formulation process, particularly in an unstable environment.[27] For strategic planning to work, it is important that top-level managers plan not only within the context of the current competitive environment but also within the context of the future competitive environment. To try to forecast what that future will look like, managers can use scenario-planning techniques to project different possible futures. They can also involve operating managers in the planning process and seek to shape the future competitive environment by emphasizing strategic intent.

Scenario Planning

One reason that strategic planning may fail over longer time periods is that strategic managers, in their initial enthusiasm for planning techniques, may forget that the future is entirely unpredictable. Even the best-laid plans can fall apart if unforeseen contingencies occur, and that happens all the time. The recognition that uncertainty makes it difficult to forecast the future accurately led planners at Royal Dutch Shell to pioneer the scenario approach to planning.[28] **Scenario planning** involves formulating plans that are based upon "what-if" scenarios about the future. In the typical scenario-planning exercise, some scenarios are optimistic and some are pessimistic. Teams of managers are asked to develop specific strategies to cope with each scenario. A set of indicators is chosen as signposts to track trends and identify the probability that any particular scenario is coming to pass. The idea is to allow managers to understand the dynamic and complex nature of their environment, to think through problems in a strategic fashion, and to generate a range of strategic options that might be pursued under different circumstances.[29] The scenario approach to planning has spread rapidly among large companies. One survey found that over 50% of the *Fortune* 500 companies use some form of scenario-planning methods.[30]

The oil company Royal Dutch Shell has, perhaps, done more than most to pioneer the concept of scenario planning, and its experience demonstrates the power of the approach.[31] Shell has been using scenario planning since the 1980s. Today, it uses two primary scenarios to anticipate future demand for oil and refine its strategic planning. The first scenario, called "Dynamics as Usual," sees a gradual shift from carbon fuels (such as oil)

scenario planning
Formulating plans that are based upon "what-if" scenarios about the future.

to natural gas, and, eventually, to renewable energy. The second scenario, "The Spirit of the Coming Age," looks at the possibility that a technological revolution will lead to a rapid shift to new energy sources.[32] Shell is making investments that will ensure profitability for the company, regardless of which scenario comes to pass, and it is carefully tracking technological and market trends for signs of which scenario is becoming more likely over time.

The great virtue of the scenario approach to planning is that it can push managers to think outside the box, to anticipate what they might need to do in different situations. It can remind managers that the world is complex and unpredictable, and to place a premium on flexibility, rather than on inflexible plans based on assumptions about the future (which may or may not be correct). As a result of scenario planning, organizations might pursue one dominant strategy related to the scenario that is judged to be most likely, but they make some investments that will pay off if other scenarios come to the fore (see Figure 1.8). Thus, the current strategy of Shell is based on the assumption that the world will only gradually shift away from carbon-based fuels (its "Dynamics as Usual" scenario), but the company is also hedging its bets by investing in new energy technologies and mapping out a strategy to pursue should the second scenario come to pass.

Decentralized Planning

A mistake that some companies have made in constructing their strategic planning process has been to treat planning exclusively as a top-management responsibility. This "ivory tower" approach can result in strategic plans formulated in a vacuum by top managers who have little understanding or appreciation of current operating realities. Consequently, top managers may formulate strategies that do more harm than good. For example, when demographic data indicated that houses and families were shrinking, planners at GE's appliance group concluded that smaller appliances were the wave of the future. Because

| Figure 1.8 | Scenario Planning |

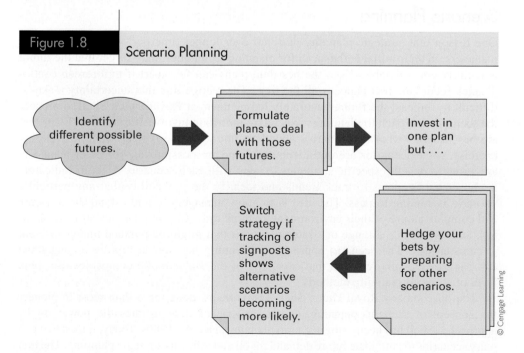

they had little contact with homebuilders and retailers, they did not realize that kitchens and bathrooms were the two rooms that were not shrinking. Nor did they appreciate that families with couples who both worked wanted big refrigerators to cut down on trips to the supermarket. GE ended up wasting a lot of time designing small appliances, for which there was limited demand.

The ivory tower concept of planning can also lead to tensions between corporate-, business-, and functional-level managers. The experience of GE's appliance group is again illuminating. Many of the corporate managers in the planning group were recruited from consulting firms or top-flight business schools. Many of the functional managers took this pattern of recruitment to mean that corporate managers did not believe they were smart enough to think through strategic problems for themselves. They felt shut out of the decision-making process, which they believed to be unfairly constituted. Out of this perceived lack of procedural justice grew an us-versus-them mindset that quickly escalated into hostility. As a result, even when the planners were correct, operating managers would not listen to them. For example, the planners correctly recognized the importance of the globalization of the appliance market and the emerging Japanese threat. However, operating managers, who then saw Sears, Roebuck and Co. as the competition, paid them little heed. Finally, ivory tower planning ignores the important strategic role of autonomous action by lower-level managers and the role of serendipity.

Correcting the ivory tower approach to planning requires recognizing that successful strategic planning encompasses managers at all levels of the corporation. Much of the best planning can and should be done by business and functional managers who are closest to the facts; in other words, planning should be decentralized. Corporate-level planners should take on roles as facilitators who help business and functional managers do the planning by setting the broad strategic goals of the organization and providing the resources necessary to identify the strategies that might be required to attain those goals.

STRATEGIC DECISION MAKING

Even the best-designed strategic planning systems will fail to produce the desired results if managers do not effectively use the information at their disposal. Consequently, it is important that strategic managers learn to make better use of the information they have, and understand why they sometimes make poor decisions. One important way in which managers can make better use of their knowledge and information is to understand how common cognitive biases can result in poor decision making.[33]

Cognitive Biases and Strategic Decision Making

The rationality of decision making is bound by one's cognitive capabilities.[34] Humans are not supercomputers, and it is difficult for us to absorb and process large amounts of information effectively. As a result, when we make decisions, we tend to fall back on certain rules of thumb, or heuristics, that help us to make sense out of a complex and uncertain world. However, sometimes these rules lead to severe and systematic errors in the decision-making process.[35] Systematic errors are those that appear time and time again. They seem to arise from a series of **cognitive biases** in the way that humans process information and reach decisions. Because of cognitive biases, many managers may make poor strategic decisions.

cognitive biases
Systematic errors in human decision making that arise from the way people process information.

prior hypothesis bias

A cognitive bias that occurs when decision makers who have strong prior beliefs tend to make decisions on the basis of these beliefs, even when presented with evidence that their beliefs are wrong.

escalating commitment

A cognitive bias that occurs when decision makers, having already committed significant resources to a project, commit even more resources after receiving feedback that the project is failing.

reasoning by analogy

Use of simple analogies to make sense out of complex problems.

representativeness

A bias rooted in the tendency to generalize from a small sample or even a single vivid anecdote.

illusion of control

A cognitive bias rooted in the tendency to overestimate one's ability to control events.

availability error

A bias that arises from our predisposition to estimate the probability of an outcome based on how easy the outcome is to imagine.

Numerous cognitive biases have been verified repeatedly in laboratory settings, so we can be reasonably sure that these biases exist and that all people are prone to them.[36] The **prior hypothesis bias** refers to the fact that decision makers who have strong prior beliefs about the relationship between two variables tend to make decisions on the basis of these beliefs, even when presented with evidence that their beliefs are incorrect. Moreover, they tend to seek and use information that is consistent with their prior beliefs while ignoring information that contradicts these beliefs. To place this bias in a strategic context, it suggests that a CEO who has a strong prior belief that a certain strategy makes sense might continue to pursue that strategy despite evidence that it is inappropriate or failing.

Another well-known cognitive bias, **escalating commitment**, occurs when decision makers, having already committed significant resources to a project, commit even more resources even if they receive feedback that the project is failing.[37] This may be an irrational response; a more logical response would be to abandon the project and move on (that is, to cut your losses and exit), rather than escalate commitment. Feelings of personal responsibility for a project seemingly induce decision makers to stick with a project despite evidence that it is failing.

A third bias, **reasoning by analogy**, involves the use of simple analogies to make sense out of complex problems. The problem with this heuristic is that the analogy may not be valid. A fourth bias, **representativeness**, is rooted in the tendency to generalize from a small sample or even a single vivid anecdote. This bias violates the statistical law of large numbers, which says that it is inappropriate to generalize from a small sample, let alone from a single case. In many respects, the dot-com boom of the late 1990s was based on reasoning by analogy and representativeness. Prospective entrepreneurs saw some of the early dot-com companies such as Amazon and Yahoo! achieve rapid success, at least as judged by some metrics. Reasoning by analogy from a very small sample, they assumed that any dot-com could achieve similar success. Many investors reached similar conclusions. The result was a massive wave of start-ups that jumped into the Internet space in an attempt to capitalize on the perceived opportunities. The vast majority of these companies subsequently went bankrupt, proving that the analogy was wrong and that the success of the small sample of early entrants was no guarantee that all dot-coms would succeed.

A fifth cognitive bias is referred to as **the illusion of control**, or the tendency to overestimate one's ability to control events. General or top managers seem to be particularly prone to this bias: having risen to the top of an organization, they tend to be overconfident about their ability to succeed. According to Richard Roll, such overconfidence leads to what he has termed the *hubris hypothesis of takeovers*.[38] Roll argues that top managers are typically overconfident about their ability to create value by acquiring another company. Hence, they end up making poor acquisition decisions, often paying far too much for the companies they acquire. Subsequently, servicing the debt taken on to finance such an acquisition makes it all but impossible to make money from the acquisition.

The **availability error** is yet another common bias. The availability error arises from our predisposition to estimate the probability of an outcome based on how easy the outcome is to imagine. For example, more people seem to fear a plane crash than a car accident, and yet statistically one is far more likely to be killed in a car on the way to the airport than in a plane crash. People overweigh the probability of a plane crash because the outcome is easier to imagine, and because plane crashes are more vivid events than car crashes, which affect only small numbers of people at one time. As a result of the availability error, managers might allocate resources to a project with an outcome that is easier to imagine, rather than to one that might have the highest return.

Techniques for Improving Decision Making

The existence of cognitive biases raises a question: How can critical information affect the decision-making mechanism so that a company's strategic decisions are realistic and based on thorough evaluation? Two techniques known to enhance strategic thinking and counteract cognitive biases are devil's advocacy and dialectic inquiry.[39]

Devil's advocacy requires the generation of a plan, and a critical analysis of that plan. One member of the decision-making group acts as the devil's advocate, emphasizing all the reasons that might make the proposal unacceptable. In this way, decision makers can become aware of the possible perils of recommended courses of action.

Dialectic inquiry is more complex because it requires the generation of a plan (a thesis) and a counter-plan (an antithesis) that reflect plausible but conflicting courses of action.[40] Strategic managers listen to a debate between advocates of the plan and counter-plan and then decide which plan will lead to higher performance. The purpose of the debate is to reveal the problems with the definitions, recommended courses of action, and assumptions of both plans. As a result of this exercise, strategic managers are able to form a new and more encompassing conceptualization of the problem, which then becomes the final plan (a synthesis). Dialectic inquiry can promote strategic thinking.

Another technique for countering cognitive biases is the outside view, which has been championed by Nobel Prize winner Daniel Kahneman and his associates.[41] The **outside view** requires planners to identify a reference class of analogous past strategic initiatives, determine whether those initiatives succeeded or failed, and evaluate the project at hand against those prior initiatives. According to Kahneman, this technique is particularly useful for countering biases such as the illusion of control (hubris), reasoning by analogy, and representativeness. For example, when considering a potential acquisition, planners should look at the track record of acquisitions made by other enterprises (the reference class), determine if they succeeded or failed, and objectively evaluate the potential acquisition against that reference class. Kahneman argues that such a reality check against a large sample of prior events tends to constrain the inherent optimism of planners and produce more realistic assessments and plans.

devil's advocacy
A technique in which one member of a decisionmaking team identifies all the considerations that might make a proposal unacceptable.

dialectic inquiry
The generation of a plan (a thesis) and a counterplan (an antithesis) that reflect plausible but conflicting courses of action.

outside view
Identification of past successful or failed strategic initiatives to determine whether those initiatives will work for project at hand.

STRATEGIC LEADERSHIP

One of the key strategic roles of both general and functional managers is to use all their knowledge, energy, and enthusiasm to provide strategic leadership for their subordinates and develop a high-performing organization. Several authors have identified a few key characteristics of good strategic leaders that do lead to high performance: (1) vision, eloquence, and consistency; (2) articulation of a business model; (3) commitment; (4) being well informed; (5) willingness to delegate and empower; (6) astute use of power; and (7) emotional intelligence.[42]

Vision, Eloquence, and Consistency

One of the key tasks of leadership is to give an organization a sense of direction. Strong leaders seem to have a clear and compelling vision of where the organization should go, are eloquent enough to communicate this vision to others within the organization in terms that energize people, and consistently articulate their vision until it becomes part of the organization's culture.[43]

In the political arena, John F. Kennedy, Winston Churchill, Martin Luther King, Jr., and Margaret Thatcher have all been regarded as examples of visionary leaders. Think of the impact of Kennedy's sentence, "Ask not what your country can do for you, ask what you can do for your country," of King's "I have a dream" speech, and of Churchill's "we will never surrender." Kennedy and Thatcher were able to use their political office to push for governmental actions that were consistent with their visions. Churchill's speech galvanized a nation to defend itself against an aggressor, and King was able to pressure the government from outside to make changes within society.

Examples of strong business leaders include Microsoft's Bill Gates; Jack Welch, the former CEO of General Electric; and Sam Walton, Wal-Mart's founder. For years, Bill Gates's vision of a world in which there would be a Windows-based personal computer on every desk was a driving force at Microsoft. More recently, that vision has evolved into one of a world in which Windows-based software can be found on any computing device, from PCs and servers to videogame consoles (Xbox), cell phones, and handheld computers. At GE, Jack Welch was responsible for articulating the simple but powerful vision that GE should be first or second in every business in which it competed, or it should exit from that business. Similarly, it was Wal-Mart founder Sam Walton who established and articulated the vision that has been central to Wal-Mart's success: passing on cost savings from suppliers and operating efficiencies to customers in the form of everyday low prices.

Articulation of the Business Model

Another key characteristic of good strategic leaders is their ability to identify and articulate the business model the company will use to attain its vision. A business model is managers' conception of how the various strategies that the company pursues fit together into a congruent whole. At Dell, for example, it was Michael Dell who identified and articulated the basic business model of the company: the direct sales business model. The various strategies that Dell has pursued over the years have refined this basic model, creating one that is very robust in terms of its efficiency and effectiveness. Although individual strategies can take root in many different places in an organization, and although their identification is not the exclusive preserve of top management, only strategic leaders have the perspective required to make sure that the various strategies fit together into a congruent whole and form a valid and compelling business model. If strategic leaders lack a clear conception of the company's business model (or what it should be), it is likely that the strategies the firm pursues will not fit together, and the result will be lack of focus and poor performance.

Commitment

Strong leaders demonstrate their commitment to their visions and business models by actions and words, and they often lead by example. Consider Nucor's former CEO,

Ken Iverson. Nucor is a very efficient steelmaker with perhaps the lowest cost structure in the steel industry. It has achieved 30 years of profitable performance in an industry where most other companies have lost money due to a relentless focus on cost minimization. In his tenure as CEO, Iverson set the example: he answered his own phone, employed only one secretary, drove an old car, flew coach class, and was proud of the fact that his base salary was the lowest of the *Fortune* 500 CEOs (Iverson made most of his money from performance-based pay bonuses). This commitment was a powerful signal to employees that Iverson was serious about doing everything possible to minimize costs. It earned him the respect of Nucor employees and made them more willing to work hard. Although Iverson has retired, his legacy lives on in the cost-conscious organizational culture that has been built at Nucor, and like all other great leaders, his impact will last beyond his tenure.

Being Well Informed

Effective strategic leaders develop a network of formal and informal sources who keep them well informed about what is going on within the company. At Starbucks, for example, the first thing that former CEO Jim Donald did every morning was call 5 to 10 stores, talk to the managers and other employees there, and get a sense for how their stores were performing. Donald also stopped at a local Starbucks every morning on the way to work to buy his morning coffee. This allowed him to get to know individual employees there very well. Donald found these informal contacts to be a very useful source of information about how the company was performing.[44]

Similarly, Herb Kelleher, the founder of Southwest Airlines, was able to gauge the health of his company by dropping in unannounced on aircraft maintenance facilities and helping workers perform their tasks. Herb Kelleher would also often help airline attendants on Southwest flights, distributing refreshments and talking to customers. One frequent flyer on Southwest Airlines reported sitting next to Kelleher three times in 10 years. Each time, Kelleher asked him (and others sitting nearby) how Southwest Airlines was doing in a number of areas, in order to spot trends and inconsistencies.[45]

Using informal and unconventional ways to gather information is wise because formal channels can be captured by special interests within the organization or by gatekeepers—managers who may misrepresent the true state of affairs to the leader. People like Donald and Kelleher who constantly interact with employees at all levels are better able to build informal information networks than leaders who closet themselves and never interact with lower-level employees.

Willingness to Delegate and Empower

High-performance leaders are skilled at delegation. They recognize that unless they learn how to delegate effectively, they can quickly become overloaded with responsibilities. They also recognize that empowering subordinates to make decisions is a good motivational tool and often results in decisions being made by those who must implement them. At the same time, astute leaders recognize that they need to maintain control over certain key decisions. Thus, although they will delegate many important decisions to lower-level employees, they will not delegate those that they judge to be of critical importance to the future success of the organization, such as articulating the company's vision and business model.

The Astute Use of Power

In a now-classic article on leadership, Edward Wrapp noted that effective leaders tend to be very astute in their use of power.[46] He argued that strategic leaders must often play the power game with skill and attempt to build consensus for their ideas rather than use their authority to force ideas through; they must act as members of a coalition or its democratic leaders rather than as dictators. Jeffery Pfeffer has articulated a similar vision of the politically astute manager who gets things done in organizations through the intelligent use of power.[47] In Pfeffer's view, power comes from control over resources that are important to the organization: budgets, capital, positions, information, and knowledge. Politically astute managers use these resources to acquire another critical resource: critically placed allies who can help them attain their strategic objectives. Pfeffer stresses that one does not need to be a CEO to assemble power in an organization. Sometimes junior functional managers can build a surprisingly effective power base and use it to influence organizational outcomes.

Emotional Intelligence

Emotional intelligence is a term that Daniel Goleman coined to describe a bundle of psychological attributes that many strong and effective leaders exhibit[48]:

- Self-awareness—the ability to understand one's own moods, emotions, and drives, as well as their effect on others.
- Self-regulation—the ability to control or redirect disruptive impulses or moods, that is, to think before acting.
- Motivation—a passion for work that goes beyond money or status and a propensity to pursue goals with energy and persistence.
- Empathy—the ability to understand the feelings and viewpoints of subordinates and to take those into account when making decisions.
- Social skills—friendliness with a purpose.

According to Goleman, leaders who possess these attributes—who exhibit a high degree of emotional intelligence—tend to be more effective than those who lack these attributes. Their self-awareness and self-regulation help to elicit the trust and confidence of subordinates. In Goleman's view, people respect leaders who, because they are self-aware, recognize their own limitations and, because they are self-regulating, consider decisions carefully. Goleman also argues that self-aware and self-regulating individuals tend to be more self-confident and therefore better able to cope with ambiguity and more open to change. A strong motivation exhibited in a passion for work can also be infectious, helping to persuade others to join together in pursuit of a common goal or organizational mission. Finally, strong empathy and social skills can help leaders earn the loyalty of subordinates. Empathetic and socially adept individuals tend to be skilled at remedying disputes between managers, better able to find common ground and purpose among diverse constituencies, and better able to move people in a desired direction compared to leaders who lack these skills. In short, Goleman argues that the psychological makeup of a leader matters.

SUMMARY OF CHAPTER

1. A strategy is a set of related actions that managers take to increase their company's performance goals.
2. The major goal of companies is to maximize the returns that shareholders receive from holding shares in the company. To maximize shareholder value, managers must pursue strategies that result in high and sustained profitability and also in profit growth.
3. The profitability of a company can be measured by the return that it makes on the capital invested in the enterprise. The profit growth of a company can be measured by the growth in earnings per share. Profitability and profit growth are determined by the strategies managers adopt.
4. A company has a competitive advantage over its rivals when it is more profitable than the average for all firms in its industry. It has a sustained competitive advantage when it is able to maintain above-average profitability over a number of years. In general, a company with a competitive advantage will grow its profits more rapidly than its rivals.
5. General managers are responsible for the overall performance of the organization, or for one of its major self-contained divisions. Their overriding strategic concern is for the health of the total organization under their direction.
6. Functional managers are responsible for a particular business function or operation. Although they lack general management responsibilities, they play a very important strategic role.
7. Formal strategic planning models stress that an organization's strategy is the outcome of a rational planning process.
8. The major components of the strategic management process are defining the mission, vision, and major goals of the organization; analyzing the external and internal environments of the organization; choosing a business model and strategies that align an organization's strengths and weaknesses with external environmental opportunities and threats; and adopting organizational structures and control systems to implement the organization's chosen strategies.
9. Strategy can emerge from deep within an organization in the absence of formal plans as lower-level managers respond to unpredicted situations.
10. Strategic planning often fails because executives do not plan for uncertainty and because ivory tower planners lose touch with operating realities.
11. In spite of systematic planning, companies may adopt poor strategies if cognitive biases are allowed to intrude into the decision-making process.
12. Devil's advocacy, dialectic inquiry, and the outside view are techniques for enhancing the effectiveness of strategic decision making.
13. Good leaders of the strategy-making process have a number of key attributes: vision, eloquence, and consistency; ability to craft a business model; commitment; being well informed; a willingness to delegate and empower; political astuteness; and emotional intelligence.

DISCUSSION QUESTIONS

1. What do we mean by strategy? How is a business model different from a strategy?
2. What do you think are the sources of sustained superior profitability?
3. What are the strengths of formal strategic planning? What are its weaknesses?
4. To what extent do you think that cognitive biases may have contributed to the global financial crisis that gripped financial markets in 2008–2009? Explain your answer.
5. Discuss the accuracy of the following statement: Formal strategic planning systems are irrelevant for firms competing in high-technology industries where the pace of change is so rapid that plans are routinely made obsolete by unforeseen events.
6. Pick the current or a past president of the United States and evaluate his performance against the leadership characteristics discussed in the text. On the basis of this comparison, do you think that the president was/is a good strategic leader? Why or why not?

PRACTICING STRATEGIC MANAGEMENT

© iStockPhoto.com/Urilux

Small-Group Exercise: Designing a Planning System

Break up into groups of three to five students and discuss the following scenario. Appoint one group member as a spokesperson who will communicate the group's findings to the class when called on to do so by the instructor.

You are a group of senior managers working for a fast-growing computer software company. Your product allows users to play interactive role-playing games over the Internet. In the past 3 years, your company has gone from being a start-up enterprise with 10 employees and no revenues to a company with 250 employees and revenues of $60 million. It has been growing so rapidly that you have not had time to create a strategic plan, but now members of the board of directors are telling you that they want to see a plan, and they want the plan to drive decision making and resource allocation at the company. They want you to design a planning process that will have the following attributes:

1. It will be democratic, involving as many key employees as possible in the process.
2. It will help to build a sense of shared vision within the company about how to continue to grow rapidly.
3. It will lead to the generation of three to five key strategies for the company.
4. It will drive the formulation of detailed action plans, and these plans will be subsequently linked to the company's annual operating budget.

Design a planning process to present to your board of directors. Think carefully about who should be included in this process. Be sure to outline the strengths and weaknesses of the approach you choose, and be prepared to justify why your approach might be superior to alternative approaches.

STRATEGY SIGN ON

© iStockPhoto.com/Ninoslav Dotlic

Article File 1

At the end of every chapter in this book is an article file task. The task requires you to search newspapers or magazines in the library for an example of a real company that satisfies the task's question or issue.

Your first article file task is to find an example of a company that has recently changed its strategy. Identify whether this change was the outcome of a formal planning process or whether it was an emergent response to unforeseen events occurring in the company's environment.

(continues)

STRATEGY SIGN ON

(continued)

© iStockPhoto.com/Ninoslav Dotlic

Strategic Management Project Module 1

To give you practical insight into the strategic management process, we provide a series of strategic modules; one is at the end of every chapter in this book. Each module asks you to collect and analyze information relating to the material discussed in that chapter. By completing these strategic modules, you will gain a clearer idea of the overall strategic management process.

The first step in this project is to pick a company to study. We recommend that you focus on the same company throughout the book. Remember also that we will be asking you for information about the corporate and international strategies of your company as well as its structure. We strongly recommend that you pick a company for which such information is likely to be available.

There are two approaches that can be used to select a company to study, and your instructor will tell you which one to follow. The first approach is to pick a well-known company that has a lot of information written about it. For example, large publicly held companies such as IBM, Microsoft, and Southwest Airlines are routinely covered in the business and financial press. By going to the library at your university, you should be able to track down a great deal of information on such companies. Many libraries now have comprehensive Web-based electronic data search facilities such as ABI/Inform, the Wall Street Journal Index, Predicasts F&S Index, and the LexisNexis databases. These enable you to identify any article that has been written in the business press on the company of your choice within the past few years. A number of non-electronic data sources are also available and useful. For example, Predicasts F&S publishes an annual list of articles relating to major companies that appeared in the national and international business press. S&P Industry Surveys is also a great source for basic industry data, and Value Line Ratings and Reports contain good summaries of a firm's financial position and future prospects. Collect full financial information on the company that you pick. This information can be accessed from Web-based electronic databases such as the EDGAR database, which archives all forms that publicly quoted companies have to file with the Securities and Exchange Commission (SEC); for example, 10-K filings can be accessed from the SEC's EDGAR database. Most SEC forms for public companies can now be accessed from Internet-based financial sites, such as Yahoo!'s finance site (www.finance.yahoo.com).

A second approach is to choose a smaller company in your city or town to study. Although small companies are not routinely covered in the national business press, they may be covered in the local press. More important, this approach can work well if the management of the company will agree to talk to you at length about the strategy and structure of the company. If you happen to know somebody in such a company or if you have worked there at some point, this approach can be very worthwhile. However, we do not recommend this approach unless you can get a substantial amount of guaranteed access to the company of your choice. If in doubt, ask your instructor before making a decision. The primary goal is to make sure that you have access to enough interesting information to complete a detailed and comprehensive analysis.

Your assignment for Module 1 is to choose a company to study and to obtain enough information about it to carry out the following instructions and answer the questions:

1. Give a short account of the history of the company, and trace the evolution of its strategy. Try to determine whether the strategic evolution of your company is the product of intended strategies, emergent strategies, or some combination of the two.
2. Identify the mission and major goals of the company.
3. Do a preliminary analysis of the internal strengths and weaknesses of the company and the opportunities and threats that it faces in its environment. On the basis of this analysis, identify the strategies that you think the company should pursue. (You will need to perform a much more detailed analysis later in the book.)
4. Who is the CEO of the company? Evaluate the CEO's leadership capabilities.

ETHICAL DILEMMA

© iStockPhoto.com/P_Wei

You are the general manager of a home-mortgage-lending business within a large diversified financial services firm. In the firm's mission statement, there is a value that emphasizes the importance of acting with integrity at all times. When you asked the CEO what this means, she told you that you should "do the right thing, and not try to do all things right." This same CEO has also set your challenging profitability and growth goals for the coming year. The CEO has told you that the goals are "non-negotiable." If you satisfy those goals,

you will earn a large bonus and may get promoted. If you fail to meet the goals, it may negatively affect your career at the company. You know, however, that satisfying the goals will require you to lower lending standards, and it is possible that your unit will lend money to some people whose ability to meet their mortgage payments is questionable. If people do default on their loans, however, your company will be able to seize their homes and resell them, which mitigates the risk. What should you do?

CLOSING CASE

General Electric's Ecomagination Strategy

Back in 2004, GE's top-management team was going through its annual strategic planning review when the management team came to a sudden realization: six of the company's core businesses were deeply involved in environmental and energy-related projects. The appliance business was exploring energy conservation. The plastics business was working on the replacement of PCBs, once widely used in industrial compounds, which had been found to have negative consequences for human health and the environment. The energy business was looking into alternatives to fossil fuels, including wind, solar, and nuclear power. Other businesses were looking at ways to reduce emissions and use energy more efficiently. What was particularly striking was that GE had initiated almost all of these projects in response to requests from its customers.

When these common issues surfaced across different lines of business, the group members realized that something deeper was going on that they needed to understand. They initiated a data-gathering effort. They made an effort to educate themselves on the science behind energy and environmental issues, including greenhouse gas emissions. As CEO Jeff Immelt

later explained, "We went through a process of really understanding and coming to our own points of view on the science." Immelt himself became convinced that climate change was a technical fact. GE executives engaged in "dreaming sessions" with customers in energy and heavy-industry companies to try to understand their concerns and desires. What emerged was a wish list from customers that included cleaner ways to burn coal, more efficient wastewater treatment plants, better hydrogen fuel cells, and so on. At the same time, GE talked to government officials and regulators to try and get a sense for where public policy might be going.

This external review led to the conclusion that energy prices would likely increase going forward, driven by rising energy consumption in developing nations and creating demand for energy-efficient products. The team also saw tighter environmental controls, including caps on greenhouse gas emissions, as all but inevitable. At the same time, team members looked inside GE. Although the company had already been working on numerous energy-efficiency and environmental projects, the team realized there were some gaps in technological capabilities, and there was a lack of overarching strategy.

What emerged from these efforts was a realization that GE could build strong businesses by helping its customers to improve their energy efficiency and environmental performance. As Immelt soon became fond of saying, "green is green." Thus was born GE's ecomagination strategy.

First rolled out in 2005, the ecomagination strategy cut across businesses. Immelt tapped one of the company's promising young leaders to head the program. GE established targets for doubling investments in clean technology to $1.5 billion per year by 2010 and growing annual revenues from eco-products to $20 billion from $10 billion in 2004, twice the growth rate of its overall revenues. In its own operations, GE set out to cut greenhouse gas emissions per unit of output by 30% by 2008, and to cut absolute emissions by 1% by 2010 (as opposed to a forecasted increase of 40% due to the growth of the business). These corporate goals were broken into subgoals and handed down to the relevant businesses. Performance against goals was reviewed on a regular basis, and the compensation of executives was tied to their ability to meet these goals.

The effort soon started to bear fruit. These included a new generation of energy-efficient appliances, more-efficient fluorescent and LED lights, a new jet engine that burned 10% less fuel, a hybrid locomotive that burned 3% less fuel and put out 40% lower emissions than its immediate predecessor, lightweight plastics to replace the steel in cars, and technologies for turning coal into gas in order to drive electric turbines, while stripping most of the carbon dioxide (CO_2) from the turbine exhaust.

By the end of its first 5-year plan, GE had met or exceeded most of its original goals, despite the global financial crisis that hit in 2008. Not only did GE sell more than $20 billion worth of eco-products in 2010, according to management, these products were also among the most profitable in GE's portfolio. In total, GE reported that its ecomagination portfolio included over 140 products and solutions that had generated $105 billion in revenues by 2011. One of the great growth stories in the company has been its wind turbine business, which it bought from Enron in 2002. In that year, it sold $200 million worth of wind turbines. By 2008, this was a $6 billion business that had installed 10,000 turbines. By 2012, GE had installed over 20,000 turbines worldwide and was predicting a surge in orders from developing nations. Sales from Brazil alone were forecasted to be in the range of $1 billion a year for the next decade. Looking forward, GE plans to double clean-tech R&D to $10 billion by 2015, to grow ecomagination revenues at twice the rate of overall revenues, to reduce its own energy intensity by 50% and its greenhouse gas emissions by 25%, and to reduce its water used by 25%.

Sources: D. Fisher, "GE Turns Green," *Forbes* (August 8, 2005): 80–85; R. Kauffeld, A. Malhotra, and S. Higgins, "Green Is a Strategy," *Strategy + Business* (December 21, 2009); J. L. Bower, H. B. Leonard, and L. S. Paine, "Jeffrey Immelt and the Reinvention of GE," *Reuters* (October 14, 2011); and General Electric, "Progress: Ecomagination Report 2011," http://files.gecompany.com/ecomagination/progress/GE_ecomagination_2011AnnualReport.pdf.

CASE DISCUSSION QUESTIONS

1. Where did the original impetus for GE's ecomagination strategy come from? What does this tell you about strategy making?
2. To what extent did GE follow a classic SWOT model when formulating its ecomagination strategy?
3. GE's CEO Jeff Immelt often states that "green is green." What does he mean by this? Is the ecomagination strategy in the best interests of GE's stockholders?
4. By most reports, GE's ecomagination strategy has been successfully implemented. Why do you think this is the case? What did GE do correctly? What are the key lessons here?
5. If GE had not pursued an ecomagination strategy, where do you think it would be today? Where might it be 10 years from now?

KEY TERMS

APPENDIX TO CHAPTER 1: Enterprise Valuation, ROIC, and Growth

The ultimate goal of strategy is to maximize the value of a company to its shareholders (subject to the important constraints that this is done in a legal, ethical, and socially responsible manner). The two main drivers of enterprise valuation are return on invested capital (ROIC) and the growth rate of profits, g.[49]

ROIC is defined as net operating profits less adjusted taxes (NOPLAT) over the invested capital of the enterprise (IC), where IC is the sum of the company's equity and debt (the method for calculating adjusted taxes need not concern us here). That is:

$$ROIC = NOPLAT/IC$$

where:

$$NOPLAT = \text{revenues} - \text{cost of goods sold} -$$
$$\text{operating expenses} - \text{depreciation}$$
$$\text{charges} - \text{adjusted taxes}$$
$$IC = \text{value of shareholders' equity} + \text{value of debt}$$

The growth rate of profits, g, can be defined as the percentage increase in net operating profits (NOPLAT) over a given time period. More precisely:

$$g = [(NOPLAT_{t+1} - NOPLAT_t)/NOPLAT_t] \times 100$$

Note that if NOPLAT is increasing over time, earnings per share will also increase so long as (a) the number of shares stays constant or (b) the number of shares outstanding increases more slowly than NOPLAT.

The valuation of a company can be calculated using discounted cash flow analysis and applying it to future expected free cash flows (free cash flow in a period is defined as NOPLAT − net investments). It can be shown that the valuation of a company so calculated is related to the company's weighted average cost of capital (WACC), which is the cost of the equity and debt that the firm uses to finance its business, and the company's ROIC. Specifically:

- If ROIC > WACC, the company is earning more than its cost of capital and it is creating value.
- If ROIC = WACC, the company is earning its cost of capital and its valuation will be stable.
- If ROIC < WACC, the company is earning less than its cost of capital and it is therefore destroying value.

A company that earns more than its cost of capital is even more valuable if it can grow its net operating profits less adjusted taxes (NOPLAT) over time. Conversely, a firm that is not earning its cost of capital destroys value if it grows its NOPLAT. This critical relationship between ROIC, *g*, and value is shown in Table A1.

In Table A1, the figures in the cells of the matrix represent the discounted present values of future free cash flows for a company that has a starting NOPLAT of $100, invested capital of $1,000, a cost of capital of 10%, and a 25-year time horizon after which ROIC = cost of capital.

Table A1 ROIC, Growth, and Valuation

NOPLAT Growth, *g*	ROIC 7.5%	ROIC 10.0%	ROIC 12.5%	ROIC 15.0%	ROIC 20
3%	887	1000	1058	1113	1170
6%	708	1000	1117	1295	1442
9%	410	1000	1354	1591	1886

The important points revealed by this exercise are as follows:

1. A company with an already high ROIC can create more value by increasing its profit growth rate rather than pushing for an even higher ROIC. Thus, a company with an ROIC of 15% and a 3% growth rate can create more value by increasing its profit growth rate from 3% to 9% than it can by increasing ROIC to 20%.

2. A company with a low ROIC destroys value if it grows. Thus, if ROIC = 7.5%, a 9% growth rate for 25 years will produce less value than a 3% growth rate. This is because unprofitable growth requires capital investments, the cost of which cannot be covered. Unprofitable growth destroys value.

3. The best of both worlds is high ROIC and high growth.

Very few companies are able to maintain an ROIC > WACC and grow NOPLAT over time, but there are some notable examples, including Dell, Microsoft, and Wal-Mart. Because these companies have generally been able to fund their capital investment needs from internally generated cash flows, they have not had to issue more shares to raise capital. Thus, growth in NOPLAT has translated directly into higher earnings per share for these companies, making their shares more attractive to investors and leading to substantial share-price appreciation. By successfully pursuing strategies that result in a high ROIC and growing NOPLAT, these firms have maximized shareholder value.

NOTES

[1]There are several different ratios for measuring profitability, such as return on invested capital, return on assets, and return on equity. Although these different measures are highly correlated with each other, finance theorists argue that the return on invested capital is the most accurate measure of profitability. See Tom Copeland, Tim Koller, and Jack Murrin, *Valuation: Measuring and Managing the Value of Companies* (New York: Wiley, 1996).

[2]Trying to estimate the relative importance of industry effects and firm strategy on firm profitability has been one of the most important areas of research in the strategy literature during the past decade. See Y. E. Spanos and S. Lioukas, "An Examination of the Causal Logic of Rent Generation," *Strategic Management* 22:10 (October 2001): 907–934; and R. P. Rumelt, "How Much Does Industry Matter?" *Strategic Management* 12 (1991): 167–185. See also A. J. Mauri and M. P. Michaels, "Firm and Industry Effects Within Strategic Management: An Empirical Examination," *Strategic Management* 19 (1998): 211–219.

[3]This view is known as "agency theory." See M. C. Jensen and W. H. Meckling, "Theory of the Firm: Managerial Behavior, Agency Costs and Ownership Structure," *Journal of Financial Economics* 3 (1976): 305–360; and E. F. Fama, "Agency Problems and the Theory of the Firm," *Journal of Political Economy* 88 (1980): 375–390.

[4]K. R. Andrews, *The Concept of Corporate Strategy* (Homewood, Ill.: Dow Jones Irwin, 1971); H. I. Ansoff, *Corporate Strategy* (New York: McGraw-Hill, 1965); and C. W. Hofer and D. Schendel, *Strategy Formulation: Analytical Concepts* (St. Paul, Minn.: West, 1978). See also P. J. Brews and M. R. Hunt, "Learning to Plan and Planning to Learn," *Strategic Management* 20 (1999): 889–913; and R. W. Grant, "Planning in a Turbulent Environment," *Strategic Management* 24 (2003): 491–517.

[5]From Google's website, www.google.com/about/company/.

[6]P. F. Drucker, *Management—Tasks, Responsibilities, Practices* (New York: Harper & Row, 1974), pp. 74–94.

[7]Derek F. Abell, *Defining the Business: The Starting Point of Strategic Planning* (Englewood Cliffs, N.J.: Prentice-Hall, 1980).

[8]P. A. Kidwell and P. E. Ceruzzi, *Landmarks in Digital Computing* (Washington, D.C.: Smithsonian Institute, 1994).

[9]J. C. Collins and J. I. Porras, "Building Your Company's Vision," *Harvard Business Review* (September–October 1996): 65–77.

[10]From www.nucor.com.

[11]See J. P. Kotter and J. L. Heskett, *Corporate Culture and Performance* (New York: Free Press, 1992). For similar work, see Collins and Porras, "Building Your Company's Vision."

[12]E. Freeman, *Strategic Management: A Stakeholder Approach* (Boston: Pitman Press, 1984).

[13]M. D. Richards, *Setting Strategic Goals and Objectives* (St. Paul, Minn.: West, 1986).

[14]E. A. Locke, G. P. Latham, and M. Erez, "The Determinants of Goal Commitment," *Academy of Management Review* 13 (1988): 23–39.

[15]R. E. Hoskisson, M. A. Hitt, and C. W. L. Hill, "Managerial Incentives and Investment in R&D in Large Multiproduct Firms," *Organization Science* 3 (1993): 325–341.

[16]Andrews, *Concept of Corporate Strategy;* Ansoff, *Corporate Strategy;* and Hofer and Schendel, *Strategy Formulation.*

[17]For details, see R. A. Burgelman, "Intraorganizational Ecology of Strategy Making and Organizational Adaptation: Theory and Field Research," *Organization Science* 2 (1991): 239–262; H. Mintzberg, "Patterns in Strategy Formulation," *Management Science* 24 (1978): 934–948; S. L. Hart, "An Integrative Framework for Strategy Making Processes," *Academy of Management Review* 17 (1992): 327–351; G. Hamel, "Strategy as Revolution," *Harvard Business Review* 74 (July–August 1996): 69–83; and R. W. Grant, "Planning in a Turbulent Environment," *Strategic Management Journal* 24 (2003): 491–517. See also G. Gavetti, D. Levinthal, and J. W. Rivkin, "Strategy Making in Novel and Complex Worlds: The Power of Analogy," *Strategic Management Journal* 26 (2005): 691–712.

[18]This is the premise of those who advocate that complexity and chaos theory should be applied to strategic management. See S. Brown and K. M. Eisenhardt, "The Art of Continuous Change: Linking Complexity Theory and Time Based Evolution in Relentlessly Shifting Organizations," *Administrative Science Quarterly* 29 (1997): 1–34; and R. Stacey and D. Parker, *Chaos, Management*

and Economics (London: Institute for Economic Affairs, 1994). See also H. Courtney, J. Kirkland, and P. Viguerie, "Strategy Under Uncertainty," *Harvard Business Review* 75 (November–December 1997): 66–79.

[19]Hart, "Integrative Framework"; and Hamel, "Strategy as Revolution."

[20]See Burgelman, "Intraorganizational Ecology"; and Mintzberg, "Patterns in Strategy Formulation."

[21]R. A. Burgelman and A. S. Grove, "Strategic Dissonance," *California Management Review* (Winter 1996): 8–28.

[22]C. W. L. Hill and F. T. Rothaermel, "The Performance of Incumbent Firms in the Face of Radical Technological Innovation," *Academy of Management Review* 28 (2003): 257–274.

[23]This story was related to the author by George Rathmann, who at one time was head of 3M's research activities.

[24]Richard T. Pascale, "Perspectives on Strategy: The Real Story Behind Honda's Success," *California Management Review* 26 (1984): 47–72.

[25]This viewpoint is strongly emphasized by Burgelman and Grove, "Strategic Dissonance."

[26]C. C. Miller and L. B. Cardinal, "Strategic Planning and Firm Performance: A Synthesis of More Than Two Decades of Research," *Academy of Management Journal* 37 (1994): 1649–1665. Also see P. R. Rogers, A. Miller, and W. Q. Judge, "Using Information Processing Theory to Understand Planning/Performance Relationships in the Context of Strategy," *Strategic Management* 20 (1999): 567–577.

[27]P. J. Brews and M. R. Hunt, "Learning to Plan and Planning to Learn," *Strategic Management Journal* 20 (1999): 889–913.

[28]P. Cornelius, A. Van de Putte, and M. Romani, "Three Decades of Scenario Planning at Shell," *California Management Review* 48 (2005): 92–110.

[29]H. Courtney, J. Kirkland, and P. Viguerie, "Strategy Under Uncertainty," *Harvard Business Review*, 75, (November–December 1997): 66–79.

[30]P. J. H. Schoemaker, "Multiple Scenario Development: Its Conceptual and Behavioral Foundation," *Strategic Management Journal* 14 (1993): 193–213.

[31]P. Schoemaker, P. J. H. van der Heijden, and A. J. M. Cornelius, "Integrating Scenarios into Strategic Planning at Royal Dutch Shell," *Planning Review* 20:3 (1992): 41–47; and I. Wylie, "There Is No Alternative to … " *Fast Company* (July 2002): 106–111.

[32]"The Next Big Surprise: Scenario Planning," *The Economist* (October 13, 2001): 71.

[33]See C. R. Schwenk, "Cognitive Simplification Processes in Strategic Decision Making," *Strategic Management* 5 (1984): 111–128; and K. M. Eisenhardt and M. Zbaracki, "Strategic Decision Making," *Strategic Management* 13 (Special Issue, 1992): 17–37.

[34]H. Simon, *Administrative Behavior* (New York: McGraw-Hill, 1957).

[35]The original statement of this phenomenon was made by A. Tversky and D. Kahneman, "Judgment Under Uncertainty: Heuristics and Biases," *Science* 185 (1974): 1124–1131. See also D. Lovallo and D. Kahneman, "Delusions of Success: How Optimism Undermines Executives' Decisions," *Harvard Business Review* 81 (July 2003): 56–67; and J. S. Hammond, R. L. Keeny, and H. Raiffa, "The

Hidden Traps in Decision Making," *Harvard Business Review* 76 (September–October 1998): 25–34.

[36]Schwenk, "Cognitive Simplification Processes," pp. 111–128.

[37]B. M. Staw, "The Escalation of Commitment to a Course of Action," *Academy of Management Review* 6 (1981): 577–587.

[38]R. Roll, "The Hubris Hypotheses of Corporate Takeovers," *Journal of Business* 59 (1986): 197–216.

[39]See R. O. Mason, "A Dialectic Approach to Strategic Planning," *Management Science* 13 (1969): 403–414; R. A. Cosier and J. C. Aplin, "A Critical View of Dialectic Inquiry in Strategic Planning," *Strategic Management* 1 (1980): 343–356; and I. I. Mintroff and R. O. Mason, "Structuring III—Structured Policy Issues: Further Explorations in a Methodology for Messy Problems," *Strategic Management* 1 (1980): 331–342.

[40]Mason, "A Dialectic Approach," pp. 403–414.

[41]Lovallo and Kahneman, "Delusions of Success."

[42]For a summary of research on strategic leadership, see D. C. Hambrick, "Putting Top Managers Back into the Picture," *Strategic Management* 10 (Special Issue, 1989): 5–15. See also D. Goldman, "What Makes a Leader?" *Harvard Business Review* (November–December 1998): 92–105; H. Mintzberg, "Covert Leadership," *Harvard Business Review* (November–December 1998): 140–148; and R. S. Tedlow, "What Titans Can Teach Us," *Harvard Business Review* (December 2001): 70–79.

[43]N. M. Tichy and D. O. Ulrich, "The Leadership Challenge: A Call for the Transformational Leader," *Sloan Management Review* (Fall 1984): 59–68; and F. Westley and

H. Mintzberg, "Visionary Leadership and Strategic Management," *Strategic Management* 10 (Special Issue, 1989): 17–32.

[44]Comments were made by Jim Donald at a presentation to University of Washington MBA students.

[45]B. McConnell and J. Huba. *Creating Customer Evangelists* (Chicago: Dearborn Trade Publishing, 2003).

[46]E. Wrapp, "Good Managers Don't Make Policy Decisions," *Harvard Business Review* (September–October 1967): 91–99.

[47]J. Pfeffer, *Managing with Power* (Boston: Harvard Business School Press, 1992).

[48]D. Goleman, "What Makes a Leader?" *Harvard Business Review* (November–December 1998): 92–105.

[49]Sources: C. Y. Baldwin, *Fundamental Enterprise Valuation: Return on Invested Capital*, Harvard Business School Note 9-801-125, July 3, 2004; T. Copeland et al., *Valuation: Measuring and Managing the Value of Companies* (New York: Wiley, 2000).

External Analysis: The Identification of Opportunities and Threats

OPENING CASE

The Market for Large Commercial Jet Aircraft

Just two companies, Boeing and Airbus, have long dominated the market for large commercial jet aircraft. In early 2012, Boeing planes accounted for 50% of the world's fleet of commercial jet aircraft, and Airbus planes accounted for 31%. The reminder of the global market was split between several smaller players, including Embraer of Brazil and Bombardier of Canada, both of which had a 7% share. Embraer and Bombardier, however, have to date focused primarily on the regional jet market, building planes of less than 100 seats. The market for aircraft with more than 100 seats has been totally dominated by Boeing and Airbus.

The overall market is large and growing. In 2011, Boeing delivered 477 aircraft valued at $33 billion, and Airbus delivered 534 aircraft valued at $32 billion. Demand for new aircraft is driven primarily by demand for air travel, which has grown at 5% per annum compounded since 1980. Looking forward, Boeing predicts that between 2011 and 2031 the world economy will grow at 3.2% per annum, and airline traffic will continue to grow at 5% per annum as more and more people from the world's emerging economies take to the air for business and pleasure trips. Given the anticipated growth in demand, Boeing believes the world's airlines will need 34,000 new aircraft between 2012 and 2031 with a market value of $4.5 trillion dollars in today's prices.

Clearly, the scale of future demand creates an enormous profit opportunity for the two main incumbents, Boeing and Airbus. Given this, many observers wonder if the industry will see new entries. Historically, it has been assumed that the high development cost associated with bringing new commercial jet aircraft to market, and the need to realize substantial economies of scale to cover those costs, has worked as a very effective deterrent to new entries. For example, estimates suggest that it cost Boeing some $18 to $20 billion to develop its latest aircraft, the Boeing 787, and that the company will have to sell 1,100 787s to break even, which will take 10 years. Given the costs, risks, and long time horizon here, it has been argued that only Boeing and Airbus can afford to develop new large commercial jet aircraft.

However, in the last few years, three new entrants have appeared. All three are building narrow-bodied jets with a seat capacity between 100 and 190. Boeing's 737 and the Airbus A320 currently dominate the narrow-bodied segment. The Commercial Aircraft Corporation of China (Comac) is building a 170- to 190-seat narrow-bodied jet, scheduled for introduction in 2016. To date, Comac has 380 firm orders for the aircraft, mostly from Chinese domestic airlines. Bombardier is developing a 100- to 150-seat plane that will bring it into direct competition with Boeing and Airbus for the first time. Scheduled for introduction in late 2014, Bombardier has 352 orders and commitments for these aircraft. Embraer too, is developing a 108- to 125-seat plane to compete in the narrow-bodied segment. The new entry is occurring because all three producers believe that the market for narrow-bodied aircraft is now large enough to support more than Boeing and Airbus. Bombardier and Embraer can leverage the knowhow they developed manufacturing regional jets to help them move upmarket. For its part, Comac can count on orders from Chinese airlines and the tacit support of the Chinese government to help it get off the ground.

In response to these competitive threats, Boeing and Airbus are developing new, more fuel-efficient versions of their own narrow-bodied planes, the 737 and A320. Although they hope their new offerings will keep entrants in check, one thing seems clear: with five producers rather than two in the market, it seems likely that competition will become more intense in the narrow-bodied segment of the industry, which could well drive prices and profits down for the big two incumbent producers.

Sources: R. Marowits, "Bombardier's CSeries Drought Ends," *The Montreal Gazette*, December 20, 2012; D. Gates, "Boeing Projects Break-Even on 787 Manufacturing in 10 Years," *Seattle Times*, October 26, 2011; and Boeing Corporation, "Current Market Outlook 2012–2031," www.boeing.com/commercial/cmo/.

OVERVIEW

opportunities

Elements and conditions in a company's environment that allow it to formulate and implement strategies that enable it to become more profitable.

Strategy formulation begins with an analysis of the forces that shape competition within the industry in which a company is based. The goal is to understand the opportunities and threats confronting the firm, and to use this understanding to identify strategies that will enable the company to outperform its rivals. **Opportunities** arise when a company can take advantage of conditions in its industry environment to formulate and implement strategies that enable it to become more profitable. For example, as discussed in the Opening Case, the growth of demand for airline travel is creating an enormous profit opportunity for Boeing and Airbus. In particular, both companies have developed new wide-bodied aircraft, the Boeing 787 and the Airbus A350, to satisfy growing demand for long-haul aircraft in the 250- to 350-seat range. **Threats** arise when conditions in the external environment endanger the integrity and profitability of the company's business. The biggest threat confronting Boeing and Airbus right now is new entry into the narrow-bodied segment of the large commercial jet aircraft business from Comac, a Chinese company, and two successful manufacturers of regional jets, Bombardier and Embraer. In response to this threat, both Boeing and Airbus are developing next generation versions of their narrow-bodied offerings, the Boeing 737 and the Airbus A320 (see the Opening Case). Their hope is that these next generation aircraft, which make extensive use of composites and new more fuel-efficient jet engines, will keep the new entrants in check. In other words, the product development strategy of Boeing and Airbus is being driven by their assessment of opportunities and threats in the external industry environment.

> **threats**
> Elements in the external environment that could endanger the integrity and profitability of the company's business.

This chapter begins with an analysis of the external industry environment. First, it examines concepts and tools for analyzing the competitive structure of an industry and identifying industry opportunities and threats. Second, it analyzes the competitive implications that arise when groups of companies within an industry pursue similar or different kinds of competitive strategies. Third, it explores the way an industry evolves over time, and the changes present in competitive conditions. Fourth, it looks at the way in which forces in the macroenvironment affect industry structure and influence opportunities and threats. By the end of the chapter, you will understand that a company must either fit its strategy to the external environment in which it operates or be able to reshape the environment to its advantage through its chosen strategy in order to succeed.

DEFINING AN INDUSTRY

An **industry** can be defined as a group of companies offering products or services that are close substitutes for each other—that is, products or services that satisfy the same basic customer needs. A company's closest competitors—its rivals—are those that serve the same basic customer needs. For example, carbonated drinks, fruit punches, and bottled water can be viewed as close substitutes for each other because they serve the same basic customer needs for refreshing, cold, nonalcoholic beverages. Thus, we can talk about the soft drink industry, whose major players are Coca-Cola, PepsiCo, and Cadbury Schweppes. Similarly, desktop computers and notebook computers satisfy the same basic need that customers have for computer hardware on which to run personal productivity software, browse the Internet, send e-mail, play games, and store, display, or manipulate digital images. Thus, we can talk about the personal computer industry, whose major players are Dell, Hewlett-Packard, Lenovo (the Chinese company that purchased IBM's personal computer business), and Apple.

> **industry**
> A group of companies offering products or services that are close substitutes for each other.

External analysis begins by identifying the industry within which a company competes. To do this, managers must start by looking at the basic customer needs their company is serving—that is, they must take a customer-oriented view of their business rather than a product-oriented view (see Chapter 1). An industry is the supply side of a market, and companies within the industry are the suppliers. Customers are the demand side of a market, and are the buyers of the industry's products. The basic customer needs that are served by a market define an industry's boundaries. It is very important for managers to realize this, for if they define industry boundaries incorrectly, they may be caught off-guard by the rise of competitors that serve the same basic customer needs but with different product offerings. For example, Coca-Cola long saw itself as part of the soda industry—meaning carbonated soft drinks—whereas it actually was part of the soft drink industry, which includes noncarbonated soft drinks. In the mid-1990s, the rise of customer demand for bottled water and fruit drinks began to cut into the demand for sodas, which caught Coca-Cola by surprise. Coca-Cola moved quickly to respond to these threats, introducing its own brand of water, Dasani, and acquiring several other beverage companies, including Minute Maid and Glaceau (the owner of the Vitamin Water brand). By defining its industry boundaries too narrowly, Coke almost missed the rapid rise of noncarbonated soft drinks within the soft drinks market.

Industry and Sector

sector

A group of closely related industries.

A distinction can be made between an industry and a sector. A **sector** is a group of closely related industries. For example, as illustrated in Figure 2.1, the computer sector comprises several related industries: the computer component industries (for example, the disk drive industry, the semiconductor industry, and the computer display industry), the computer hardware industries (for example, the personal computer [PC] industry; the handheld computer industry, which includes smartphones such as the Apple iPhone and slates such as Apple's iPad; and the mainframe computer industry), and the computer software industry. Industries within a sector may be involved with one another in many different ways. Companies in the computer component industries are the suppliers of firms in the computer hardware industries. Companies in the computer software industry provide important complements to computer hardware: the software programs that customers purchase to run on their hardware. Companies in the personal, handheld, and mainframe industries indirectly compete with each other because all provide products that are, to one degree or another, substitutes for each other. Thus, in 2012, sales of PCs declined primarily because of booming demand for tablet computers, a substitute product.

Figure 2.1	The Computer Sector: Industries and Segments

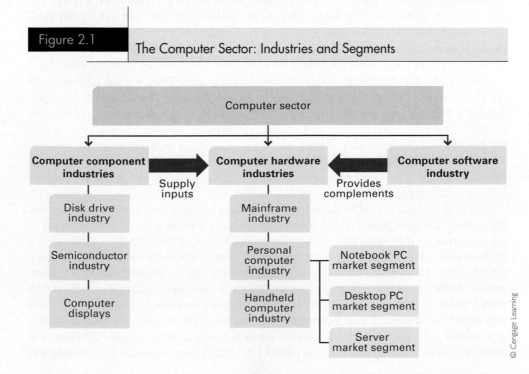

© Cengage Learning

Industry and Market Segments

It is also important to recognize the difference between an industry and the market segments within that industry. Market segments are distinct groups of customers within a market that can be differentiated from each other on the basis of their individual attributes and specific demands. In the beer industry, for example, there are three primary segments: consumers who drink long-established mass-market brands (e.g., Budweiser); weight-conscious consumers who drink less-filling, low-calorie, mass-market brands (e.g., Coors Light); and consumers who prefer premium-priced "craft beer" offered by microbreweries and many importers. Similarly, in the PC industry, there are different market segments in which customers desire desktop machines, lightweight portable machines, or servers that sit at the center of a network of personal computers (see Figure 2.1). Personal computer makers recognize the existence of these different segments by producing a range of product offerings that appeal to customers in the different segments. Customers in all of these market segments, however, share a common need for devices on which to run personal software applications.

Changing Industry Boundaries

Industry boundaries may change over time as customer needs evolve, or as emerging new technologies enable companies in unrelated industries to satisfy established customer needs in new ways. We have noted that during the 1990s, as consumers of soft drinks began to develop a taste for bottled water and noncarbonated fruit-based drinks, Coca-Cola found itself in direct competition with the manufacturers of bottled water and fruit-based soft drinks: all were in the same industry.

For an example of how technological change can alter industry boundaries, consider the convergence that is currently taking place between the computer and telecommunications industries. Historically, the telecommunications equipment industry has been considered an entity distinct from the computer hardware industry. However, as telecommunications equipment has moved from analog technology to digital technology, this equipment increasingly resembles computers. The result is that the boundaries between these different industries are now blurring. A digital wireless smartphone such as Apple's iPhone, for example, is nothing more than a small handheld computer with a wireless connection and telephone capabilities. Thus, Samsung and Nokia, which manufacture wireless phones, are now finding themselves competing directly with traditional computer companies such as Apple.

Industry competitive analysis begins by focusing upon the overall industry in which a firm competes before market segments or sector-level issues are considered. Tools that managers can use to perform industry analysis are discussed in the following sections: the competitive forces model, strategic group analysis, and industry life-cycle analysis.

COMPETITIVE FORCES MODEL

Once the boundaries of an industry have been identified, managers face the task of analyzing competitive forces within the industry environment in order to identify opportunities and threats. Michael E. Porter's well-known framework, the Five Forces model, helps managers with this analysis.[1] An extension of his model, shown in Figure 2.2, focuses on *six* forces that shape competition within an industry: (1) the risk of entry by potential competitors, (2) the intensity of rivalry among established companies within an industry, (3) the bargaining power of buyers, (4) the bargaining power of suppliers, (5) the closeness

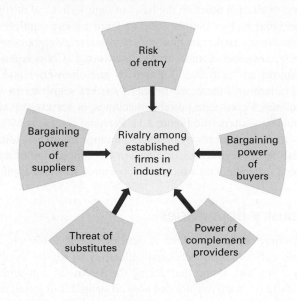

Figure 2.2   Competitive Forces

Source: Based on How Competitive Forces Shape Strategy, by Michael E. Porter, Harvard Business Review, March/April 1979.

of substitutes to an industry's products, and (6) the power of complement providers (Porter did not recognize this sixth force).

As each of these forces grows stronger, it limits the ability of established companies to raise prices and earn greater profits. Within this framework, a strong competitive force can be regarded as a threat because it depresses profits. A weak competitive force can be viewed as an opportunity because it allows a company to earn greater profits. The strength of the six forces may change over time as industry conditions change. Managers face the task of recognizing how changes in the five forces give rise to new opportunities and threats, and formulating appropriate strategic responses. In addition, it is possible for a company, through its choice of strategy, to alter the strength of one or more of the five forces to its advantage. This is discussed in the following chapters.

Risk of Entry by Potential Competitors

potential competitors
Companies that are currently not competing in the industry but have the potential to do so.

Potential competitors are companies that are not currently competing in an industry, but have the capability to do so if they choose. For example, in the last decade, cable television companies have recently emerged as potential competitors to traditional phone companies. New digital technologies have allowed cable companies to offer telephone and Internet service over the same cables that transmit television shows.

Established companies already operating in an industry often attempt to discourage potential competitors from entering the industry because as more companies enter, it becomes more difficult for established companies to protect their share of the market and generate profits. A high risk of entry by potential competitors represents a threat to the profitability of established companies. As discussed in the Opening Case, there is now a high risk of new entry into the market for large commercial jet aircraft. If this entry occurs, it seems probable that one result will be to drive down prices and profits in the industry. If the risk of new entry is low, established companies can take advantage of this opportunity, raise prices, and earn greater returns.

The risk of entry by potential competitors is a function of the height of the barriers to entry, that is, factors that make it costly for companies to enter an industry. The greater the costs potential competitors must bear to enter an industry, the greater the barriers to entry, and the weaker this competitive force. High entry barriers may keep potential competitors out of an industry even when industry profits are high. Important barriers to entry include economies of scale, brand loyalty, absolute cost advantages, customer switching costs, and government regulation.[2] An important strategy is building barriers to entry (in the case of incumbent firms) or finding ways to circumvent those barriers (in the case of new entrants). We shall discuss this topic in more detail in subsequent chapters.

Economies of Scale

Economies of scale arise when unit costs fall as a firm expands its output. Sources of scale economies include: (1) cost reductions gained through mass-producing a standardized output; (2) discounts on bulk purchases of raw material inputs and component parts; (3) the advantages gained by spreading fixed production costs over a large production volume; and (4) the cost savings associated with distributing, marketing, and advertising costs over a large volume of output. If the cost advantages from economies of scale are significant, a new company that enters the industry and produces on a small scale suffers a significant cost disadvantage relative to established companies. If the new company decides to enter on a large scale in an attempt to obtain these economies of scale, it must raise the capital required to build large-scale production facilities and bear the high risks associated with such an investment. In addition, an increased supply of products will depress prices and result in vigorous retaliation by established companies, which constitutes a further risk of large-scale entry. For these reasons, the threat of entry is reduced when established companies have economies of scale.

economies of scale
Reductions in unit costs attributed to a larger output.

Brand Loyalty

Brand loyalty exists when consumers have a preference for the products of established companies. A company can create brand loyalty by continuously advertising its brand-name products and company name, patent protection of its products, product innovation achieved through company research and development (R&D) programs, an emphasis on high-quality products, and exceptional after-sales service. Significant brand loyalty makes it difficult for new entrants to take market share away from established companies. Thus, it reduces the threat of entry by potential competitors; they may see the task of breaking down well-established customer preferences as too costly. In the smartphone business, for example, Apple has generated such strong brand loyalty with its iPhone offering and related products that Microsoft is finding it very difficult to attract customers away from Apple and build demand for its new Windows 8 phone, introduced in late 2011. Despite its financial might, a year after launching the Windows 8 phone, Microsoft's U.S. market share remained mired at around 2.7%, whereas Apple led the market with a 53% share.[3]

brand loyalty
Preference of consumers for the products of established companies.

Absolute Cost Advantages

Sometimes established companies have an **absolute cost advantage** relative to potential entrants, meaning that entrants cannot expect to match the established companies' lower cost structure. Absolute cost advantages arise from three main sources: (1) superior production operations and processes due to accumulated experience, patents, or trade secrets; (2) control of particular inputs required for production, such as labor, materials, equipment, or management skills, that are limited in their supply; and

absolute cost advantage
A cost advantage that is enjoyed by incumbents in an industry and that new entrants cannot expect to match.

(3) access to cheaper funds because existing companies represent lower risks than new entrants. If established companies have an absolute cost advantage, the threat of entry as a competitive force is weaker.

Customer Switching Costs   Switching costs arise when a customer invests time, energy, and money switching from the products offered by one established company to the products offered by a new entrant. When switching costs are high, customers can be locked in to the product offerings of established companies, even if new entrants offer better products.[4] A familiar example of switching costs concerns the costs associated with switching from one computer operating system to another. If a person currently uses Microsoft's Windows operating system and has a library of related software applications and document files, it is expensive for that person to switch to another computer operating system. To effect the change, this person would need to purchase a new set of software applications and convert all existing document files to the new system's format. Faced with such an expense of money and time, most people are unwilling to make the switch unless the competing operating system offers a substantial leap forward in performance. Thus, the higher the switching costs, the higher the barrier to entry for a company attempting to promote a new computer operating system.

switching costs

Costs that consumers must bear to switch from the products offered by one established company to the products offered by a new entrant.

Government Regulations   Historically, government regulation has constituted a major entry barrier for many industries. For example, until the mid-1990s, U.S. government regulation prohibited providers of long-distance telephone service from competing for local telephone service, and vice versa. Other potential providers of telephone service, including cable television service companies such as Time Warner and Comcast (which could have used their cables to carry telephone traffic as well as TV signals), were prohibited from entering the market altogether. These regulatory barriers to entry significantly reduced the level of competition in both the local and long-distance telephone markets, enabling telephone companies to earn higher profits than they might have otherwise. All this changed in 1996 when the government significantly deregulated the industry. In the months that followed this repeal of policy, local, long-distance, and cable TV companies all announced their intention to enter each other's markets, and a host of new players entered the market. The competitive forces model predicts that falling entry barriers due to government deregulation will result in significant new entry, an increase in the intensity of industry competition, and lower industry profit rates, and that is what occurred here.

In summary, if established companies have built brand loyalty for their products, have an absolute cost advantage over potential competitors, have significant scale economies, are the beneficiaries of high switching costs, or enjoy regulatory protection, the risk of entry by potential competitors is greatly diminished; it is a weak competitive force. Consequently, established companies can charge higher prices, and industry profits are therefore higher. Evidence from academic research suggests that the height of barriers to entry is one of the most important determinants of profit rates within an industry.[5] Clearly, it is in the interest of established companies to pursue strategies consistent with raising entry barriers to secure these profits. Additionally, potential new entrants must find strategies that allow them to circumvent barriers to entry.

Rivalry Among Established Companies

The second competitive force is the intensity of rivalry among established companies within an industry. Rivalry refers to the competitive struggle between companies within

2.1 STRATEGY IN ACTION

Circumventing Entry Barriers into the Soft Drink Industry

© iStockPhoto.com/Tom Nulens

Two companies have long dominated the carbonated soft drink industry: Coca-Cola and PepsiCo. By spending large sums of money on advertising and promotion, these two giants have created significant brand loyalty and made it very difficult for new competitors to enter the industry and take market share away. When new competitors have tried to enter, both companies have responded by cutting prices, forcing the new entrants to curtail expansion plans.

However, in the early 1990s, the Cott Corporation, then a small Canadian bottling company, worked out a strategy for entering the carbonated soft drink market. Cott's strategy was deceptively simple. The company initially focused on the cola segment of the market. Cott entered a deal with Royal Crown Cola for exclusive global rights to its cola concentrate. RC Cola was a small player in the U.S. cola market. Its products were recognized as high quality, but RC Cola had never been able to effectively challenge Coke or Pepsi. Next, Cott entered an agreement with a Canadian grocery retailer, Loblaw, to provide the retailer with its own private-label brand of cola. The Loblaw private-label brand, known as "President's Choice," was priced low, became very successful, and took shares from both Coke and Pepsi.

Emboldened by this success, Cott decided to try to convince other retailers to carry private-label cola. To retailers, the value proposition was simple because, unlike its major rivals, Cott spent almost nothing on advertising and promotion. This constituted a major source of cost savings, which Cott passed on to retailers in the form of lower prices. Retailers found that they could

significantly undercut the price of Coke and Pepsi colas and still make better profit margins on private-label brands than on branded colas.

Despite this compelling value proposition, few retailers were willing to sell private-label colas for fear of alienating Coca-Cola and Pepsi, whose products were a major draw for grocery store traffic. Cott's breakthrough came in the 1990s when it signed a deal with Wal-Mart to supply the retailing giant with a private-label cola called "Sam's Choice" (named after Wal-Mart founder Sam Walton). Wal-Mart proved to be the perfect distribution channel for Cott. The retailer was just beginning to appear in the grocery business, and consumers went to Wal-Mart not to buy branded merchandise, but to get low prices. As Wal-Mart's grocery business grew, so did Cott's sales. Cott soon added other flavors to its offering, such as lemon-lime soda, which would compete with 7-Up and Sprite. Moreover, by the late 1990s, other U.S. grocers pressured by Wal-Mart had also started to introduce private-label sodas, and often turned to Cott to supply their needs.

By 2011, Cott's private-label customers included Wal-Mart, Kroger, Costco, and Safeway.

Cott had revenues of $2.33 billion and accounted for 60% of all private-label sales of carbonated beverages in the United States, and 6 to 7% of overall sales of carbonated beverages in grocery stores, its core channel. Although Coca-Cola and PepsiCo remain dominant, they have lost incremental market share to Cott and other companies that have followed Cott's strategy.

Sources: A. Kaplan, "Cott Corporation," *Beverage World*, June 15, 2004, p. 32; J. Popp, "2004 Soft Drink Report," *Beverage Industry*, March 2004, pp. 13–18; L. Sparks, "From Coca-Colonization to Copy Catting: The Cott Corporation and Retailers Brand Soft Drinks in the UK and US," *Agribusiness* 13:2 (March 1997): 153–167; E. Cherney, "After Flat Sales, Cott Challenges Pepsi, Coca-Cola," *Wall Street Journal*, January 8, 2003, pp. B1, B8; "Cott Corporation: Company Profile," *Just Drinks*, August 2006, pp. 19–22; and Cott Corp. 2011 Annual Report, www.cott.com.

an industry to gain market share from each other. The competitive struggle can be fought using price, product design, advertising and promotional spending, direct-selling efforts, and after-sales service and support. Intense rivalry implies lower prices or more spending on non-price-competitive strategies, or both. Because intense rivalry lowers prices and raises costs, it squeezes profits out of an industry. Thus, intense rivalry among established companies constitutes a strong threat to profitability. Alternatively, if rivalry is less intense, companies may have the opportunity to raise prices or reduce spending on non-price-competitive strategies, leading to a higher level of industry profits. Four factors have a major impact on the intensity of rivalry among established companies within an industry: (1) industry competitive structure, (2) demand conditions, (3) cost conditions, and (4) the height of exit barriers in the industry.

Industry Competitive Structure   The competitive structure of an industry refers to the number and size distribution of companies in it, something that strategic managers determine at the beginning of an industry analysis. Industry structures vary, and different structures have different implications for the intensity of rivalry. A fragmented industry consists of a large number of small or medium-sized companies, none of which is in a position to determine industry price. A consolidated industry is dominated by a small number of large companies (an oligopoly) or, in extreme cases, by just one company (a monopoly), and companies often are in a position to determine industry prices. Examples of fragmented industries are agriculture, dry cleaning, health clubs, real estate brokerage, and sun-tanning parlors. Consolidated industries include the aerospace, soft drink, wireless service, and small package express delivery industries. In the small package express delivery industry, for example, two firms, UPS and FedEx, account for over 80% of industry revenues in the United States.

Low-entry barriers and commodity-type products that are difficult to differentiate characterize many fragmented industries. This combination tends to result in boom-and-bust cycles as industry profits rapidly rise and fall. Low-entry barriers imply that new entrants will flood the market, hoping to profit from the boom that occurs when demand is strong and profits are high. The explosive number of video stores, health clubs, and sun-tanning parlors that arrived on the market during the 1980s and 1990s exemplifies this situation.

Often the flood of new entrants into a booming, fragmented industry creates excess capacity, and companies start to cut prices in order to use their spare capacity. The difficulty companies face when trying to differentiate their products from those of competitors can exacerbate this tendency. The result is a price war, which depresses industry profits, forces some companies out of business, and deters potential new entrants. For example, after a decade of expansion and booming profits, many health clubs are now finding that they have to offer large discounts in order to maintain their memberships. In general, the more commodity-like an industry's product, the more vicious the price war will be. The bust part of this cycle continues until overall industry capacity is brought into line with demand (through bankruptcies), at which point prices may stabilize again.

A fragmented industry structure, then, constitutes a threat rather than an opportunity. Economic boom times in fragmented industries are often relatively short-lived because the ease of new entry can soon result in excess capacity, which in turn leads to intense price competition and the failure of less efficient enterprises. Because it is often difficult to differentiate products in these industries, trying to minimize costs is the best strategy for a company so it will be profitable in a boom and survive any subsequent bust. Alternatively, companies might try to adopt strategies that change the underlying structure of fragmented industries and lead to a consolidated industry structure in which the level of industry profitability is increased. (Exactly how companies can do this is something we shall consider in later chapters.)

In consolidated industries, companies are interdependent because one company's competitive actions (changes in price, quality, etc.) directly affect the market share of its rivals, and thus their profitability. When one company makes a move, this generally "forces" a response from its rivals, and the consequence of such competitive interdependence can be a dangerous

2.2 STRATEGY IN ACTION

Price Wars in the Breakfast Cereal Industry

© iStockPhoto.com/Tom Nulens

For decades, the breakfast cereal industry was one of the most profitable in the United States. The industry has a consolidated structure dominated by Kellogg's, General Mills, and Kraft Foods with its Post brand. Strong brand loyalty, coupled with control over the allocation of supermarket shelf space, helped to limit the potential for new entry. Meanwhile, steady demand growth of about 3% per annum kept industry revenues expanding. Kellogg's, which accounted for over 40% of the market share, acted as the price leader in the industry. Every year Kellogg's increased cereal prices, its rivals followed, and industry profits remained high.

This favorable industry structure began to change in the 1990s when growth in demand slowed—and then stagnated—as a latte and bagel or muffin replaced cereal as the American morning fare. Then came the rise of powerful discounters such as Wal-Mart (which entered the grocery industry in 1994) that began to aggressively promote their own cereal brands, and priced their products significantly below the brand-name cereals. As the decade progressed, other grocery chains such as Kroger's started to follow suit, and brand loyalty in the industry began to decline as customers realized that a $2.50 bag of wheat flakes from Wal-Mart tasted about the same as a $3.50 box of Cornflakes from Kellogg's. As sales of cheaper store-brand cereals began to take off, supermarkets, no longer as dependent on brand names to bring traffic into their stores, began to demand lower prices from the branded cereal manufacturers.

For several years, manufacturers of brand-name cereals tried to hold out against these adverse trends, but in the mid-1990s, the dam broke. In 1996, Kraft (then owned by Philip Morris) aggressively cut prices by 20% for its Post brand in an attempt to gain market share. Kellogg's soon followed with a 19% price cut on two-thirds of its brands, and General Mills quickly did the same. The decades of tacit price collusion were officially over.

If breakfast cereal companies were hoping that price cuts would stimulate demand, they were wrong.

Instead, demand remained flat while revenues and margins followed price decreases, and operating margins at Kellogg's dropped from 18% in 1995 to 10.2% in 1996, a trend also experienced by the other brand-name cereal manufacturers.

By 2000, conditions had only worsened. Private-label sales continued to make inroads, gaining over 10% of the market. Moreover, sales of breakfast cereals started to contract at 1% per annum. To cap it off, an aggressive General Mills continued to launch expensive price-and-promotion campaigns in an attempt to take share away from the market leader. Kellogg's saw its market share slip to just over 30% in 2001, behind the 31% now held by General Mills. For the first time since 1906, Kellogg's no longer led the market. Moreover, profits at all three major producers remained weak in the face of continued price discounting.

In mid-2001, General Mills finally blinked and raised prices a modest 2% in response to its own rising costs. Competitors followed, signaling—perhaps—that after a decade of costly price warfare, pricing discipline might once more emerge in the industry. Both Kellogg's and General Mills tried to move further away from price competition by focusing on brand extensions, such as Special K containing berries and new varieties of Cheerios. Efforts with Special K helped Kellogg's recapture market leadership from General Mills, and, more important, the renewed emphasis on non-price competition halted years of damaging price warfare.

However, after a decade of relative peace, price wars broke out in 2010 once more in this industry. The trigger, yet again, appears to have been falling demand for breakfast cereals due to the consumption of substitutes, such as a quick trip to the local coffee shop. In the third quarter of 2010, prices fell by 3.6%, and unit volumes by 3.4%, leading to falling profit rates at Kellogg's. Both General Mills and Kellogg's announced plans to introduce new products in 2011 in an attempt to boost demand and raise prices.

Sources: G. Morgenson, "Denial in Battle Creek," *Forbes*, October 7, 1996, p. 44; J. Muller, "Thinking out of the Cereal Box," *Business Week*, January 15, 2001, p. 54; A. Merrill, "General Mills Increases Prices," *Star Tribune*, June 5, 2001, p. 1D; S. Reyes, "Big G, Kellogg's Attempt to Berry Each Other," *Brandweek*, October 7, 2002, p. 8; and M. Andrejczak, "Kellogg's Profit Hurt by Cereal Price War," *Market Watch*, November 2, 2010.

competitive spiral. Rivalry increases as companies attempt to undercut each other's prices, or offer customers more value in their products, pushing industry profits down in the process.

Companies in consolidated industries sometimes seek to reduce this threat by following the prices set by the dominant company in the industry.[6] However, companies must be careful, for explicit face-to-face price-fixing agreements are illegal. (Tacit, indirect agreements, arrived at without direct or intentional communication, are legal.) Instead, companies set prices by watching, interpreting, anticipating, and responding to one another's strategies. However, tacit price-leadership agreements often break down under adverse economic conditions, as has occurred in the breakfast cereal industry, profiled in Strategy in Action 2.2.

Industry Demand   The level of industry demand is another determinant of the intensity of rivalry among established companies. Growing demand from new customers or additional purchases by existing customers tend to moderate competition by providing greater scope for companies to compete for customers. Growing demand tends to reduce rivalry because all companies can sell more without taking market share away from other companies. High industry profits are often the result. Conversely, declining demand results in increased rivalry as companies fight to maintain market share and revenues (as in the breakfast cereal industry example). Demand declines when customers exit the marketplace, or when each customer purchases less. When this is the case, a company can only grow by taking market share away from other companies. Thus, declining demand constitutes a major threat, for it increases the extent of rivalry between established companies.

Cost Conditions   The cost structure of firms in an industry is a third determinant of rivalry. In industries where fixed costs are high, profitability tends to be highly leveraged to sales volume, and the desire to grow volume can spark intense rivalry. Fixed costs are the costs that must be paid before the firm makes a single sale. For example, before they can offer service, cable TV companies must lay cable in the ground; the cost of doing so is a fixed cost. Similarly, to offer express courier service, a company such as FedEx must first invest in planes, package-sorting facilities, and delivery trucks—all fixed costs that require significant capital investments. In industries where the fixed costs of production are high, firms cannot cover their fixed costs and will not be profitable if sales volume is low. Thus they have an incentive to cut their prices and/or increase promotional spending to drive up sales volume in order to cover fixed costs. In situations where demand is not growing fast enough and too many companies are simultaneously engaged in the same actions, the result can be intense rivalry and lower profits. Research suggests that the weakest firms in an industry often initiate such actions, precisely because they are struggling to cover their fixed costs.[7]

Exit Barriers   Exit barriers are economic, strategic, and emotional factors that prevent companies from leaving an industry.[8] If exit barriers are high, companies become locked into an unprofitable industry where overall demand is static or declining. The result is often excess productive capacity, leading to even more intense rivalry and price competition as companies cut prices, attempting to obtain the customer orders needed to use their idle capacity and cover their fixed costs.[9] Common exit barriers include the following:

- Investments in assets such as specific machines, equipment, or operating facilities that are of little or no value in alternative uses, or cannot be later sold. If the company wishes to leave the industry, it must write off the book value of these assets.
- High fixed costs of exit, such as severance pay, health benefits, or pensions that must be paid to workers who are being made laid off when a company ceases to operate.

- Emotional attachments to an industry, such as when a company's owners or employees are unwilling to exit from an industry for sentimental reasons or because of pride.
- Economic dependence on the industry because a company relies on a single industry for its entire revenue and all profits.
- The need to maintain an expensive collection of assets at or above a minimum level in order to participate effectively in the industry.
- Bankruptcy regulations, particularly in the United States, where Chapter 11 bankruptcy provisions allow insolvent enterprises to continue operating and to reorganize under this protection. These regulations can keep unprofitable assets in the industry, result in persistent excess capacity, and lengthen the time required to bring industry supply in line with demand.

As an example of exit barriers and effects in practice, consider the small package express mail and parcel delivery industry. Key players in this industry, such as FedEx and UPS, rely entirely upon the delivery business for their revenues and profits. They must be able to guarantee their customers that they will deliver packages to all major localities in the United States, and much of their investment is specific to this purpose. To meet this guarantee, they need a nationwide network of air routes and ground routes, an asset that is required in order to participate in the industry. If excess capacity develops in this industry, as it does from time to time, FedEx cannot incrementally reduce or minimize its excess capacity by deciding not to fly to and deliver packages in Miami, for example, because that portion of its network is underused. If it did, it would no longer be able to guarantee to its customers that packages could be delivered to all major locations in the United States, and its customers would switch to another carrier. Thus, the need to maintain a nationwide network is an exit barrier that can result in persistent excess capacity in the air express industry during periods of weak demand.

The Bargaining Power of Buyers

The third competitive force is the bargaining power of buyers. An industry's buyers may be the individual customers who consume its products (end-users) or the companies that distribute an industry's products to end-users, such as retailers and wholesalers. For example, although soap powder made by Procter & Gamble (P&G) and Unilever is consumed by end-users, the principal buyers of soap powder are supermarket chains and discount stores, which resell the product to end-users. The bargaining power of buyers refers to the ability of buyers to bargain down prices charged by companies in the industry, or to raise the costs of companies in the industry by demanding better product quality and service. By lowering prices and raising costs, powerful buyers can squeeze profits out of an industry. Powerful buyers, therefore, should be viewed as a threat. Alternatively, when buyers are in a weak bargaining position, companies in an industry can raise prices and perhaps reduce their costs by lowering product quality and service, thus increasing the level of industry profits. Buyers are most powerful in the following circumstances:

- When the buyers have choice of who to buy from. If the industry is a monopoly, buyers obviously lack choice. If there are two or more companies in the industry, the buyers clearly have choice.
- When the buyers purchase in large quantities. In such circumstances, buyers can use their purchasing power as leverage to bargain for price reductions.
- When the supply industry depends upon buyers for a large percentage of its total orders.
- When switching costs are low and buyers can pit the supplying companies against each other to force down prices.

- When it is economically feasible for buyers to purchase an input from several companies at once so that buyers can pit one company in the industry against another.
- When buyers can threaten to enter the industry and independently produce the product, thus supplying their own needs, also a tactic for forcing down industry prices.

The automobile component supply industry, whose buyers are large manufacturers such as GM, Ford, and Toyota, is a good example of an industry in which buyers have strong bargaining power, and thus a strong competitive threat. Why? The suppliers of auto components are numerous and typically smaller in scale; their buyers, the auto manufacturers, are large in size and few in number. Additionally, to keep component prices down, historically both Ford and GM have used the threat of manufacturing a component themselves rather than buying it from auto component suppliers. The automakers use their powerful position to pit suppliers against one another, forcing down the prices for component parts and demanding better quality. If a component supplier objects, the automaker can use the threat of switching to another supplier as a bargaining tool.

The Bargaining Power of Suppliers

The fourth competitive force is the bargaining power of suppliers—the organizations that provide inputs into the industry, such as materials, services, and labor (which may be individuals, organizations such as labor unions, or companies that supply contract labor). The bargaining power of suppliers refers to the ability of suppliers to raise input prices, or to raise the costs of the industry in other ways—for example, by providing poor-quality inputs or poor service. Powerful suppliers squeeze profits out of an industry by raising the costs of companies in the industry. Thus, powerful suppliers are a threat. Conversely, if suppliers are weak, companies in the industry have the opportunity to force down input prices and demand higher-quality inputs (such as more productive labor). As with buyers, the ability of suppliers to make demands on a company depends on their power relative to that of the company. Suppliers are most powerful in these situations:

- The product that suppliers sell has few substitutes and is vital to the companies in an industry.
- The profitability of suppliers is not significantly affected by the purchases of companies in a particular industry, in other words, when the industry is not an important customer to the suppliers.
- Companies in an industry would experience significant switching costs if they moved to the product of a different supplier because a particular supplier's products are unique or different. In such cases, the company depends upon a particular supplier and cannot pit suppliers against each other to reduce prices.
- Suppliers can threaten to enter their customers' industry and use their inputs to produce products that would compete directly with those of companies already in the industry.
- Companies in the industry cannot threaten to enter their suppliers' industry and make their own inputs as a tactic for lowering the price of inputs.

An example of an industry in which companies are dependent upon a powerful supplier is the PC industry. Personal computer firms are heavily dependent on Intel, the world's largest supplier of microprocessors for PCs. Intel's microprocessor chips are the industry standard for personal computers. Intel's competitors, such as Advanced Micro Devices (AMD), must develop and supply chips that are compatible with Intel's standard. Although AMD has developed competing chips, Intel still supplies approximately 85% of the chips used in PCs primarily because only Intel has the manufacturing capacity required to serve a large share of the market. It is beyond the financial resources of Intel's competitors, such as AMD, to match the scale and efficiency of Intel's manufacturing systems. This means that although PC manufacturers can purchase some microprocessors from Intel's rivals, most notably AMD, they still must turn to Intel for the bulk of their supply. Because Intel is in a powerful bargaining position, it can charge higher prices for its microprocessors than if its competitors were stronger and more numerous (that is, if the microprocessor industry were fragmented).

FOCUS ON: Wal-Mart

Wal-Mart'S Bargaining Power Over Suppliers

© iStockPhoto.com/caracterdesign

When Wal-Mart and other discount retailers began in the 1960s, they were small operations with little purchasing power. To generate store traffic, they depended in large part on stocking nationally branded merchandise from well-known companies such as P&G and Rubbermaid. Because the discounters did not have high sales volume, the nationally branded companies set the price. This meant that the discounters had to look for other ways to cut costs, which they typically did by emphasizing self-service in stripped-down stores located in the suburbs where land was cheaper (in the 1960s, the main competitors for discounters were full-service department stores such as Sears that were often located in downtown shopping areas).

Discounters such as K-Mart purchased their merchandise through wholesalers, which in turned bought from manufacturers. The wholesaler would come into a store and write an order, and when the merchandise arrived, the wholesaler would come in and stock the shelves, saving the retailer labor costs. However, Wal-Mart was located in Arkansas and placed its stores in small towns. Wholesalers were not particularly interested in serving a company that built its stores in such out-of-the-way places. They would do it only if Wal-Mart paid higher prices.

Wal-Mart's Sam Walton refused to pay higher prices. Instead he took his fledgling company public and used the capital raised to build a distribution center to stock merchandise. The distribution center would serve all stores within a 300-mile radius, with trucks leaving the distribution center daily to restock the stores. Because the distribution center was serving a collection of stores and thus buying in larger volumes, Walton found that he was able to cut the wholesalers out of the equation and order directly from manufacturers. The cost savings generated by not having to pay profits to wholesalers were then passed on to consumers in the form of lower prices, which helped Wal-Mart continue growing. This growth increased its buying power and thus its ability to demand deeper discounts from manufacturers.

Today, Wal-Mart has turned its buying process into an art form. Because 8% of all retail sales in the United States are made in a Wal-Mart store, the company has enormous bargaining power over its suppliers. Suppliers of nationally branded products, such as P&G, are no longer in a position to demand high prices. Instead, Wal-Mart is now so important to P&G that it is able to demand deep discounts from P&G. Moreover, Wal-Mart has itself become a brand that is more powerful than the brands of manufacturers. People don't go to Wal-Mart to buy branded goods; they go to Wal-Mart for the low prices. This simple fact has enabled Wal-Mart to bargain down the prices it pays, always passing on cost savings to consumers in the form of lower prices.

Since the early 1990s, Wal-Mart has provided suppliers with real-time information on store sales through the use of individual stock-keeping units (SKUs). These have allowed suppliers to optimize their own production processes, matching output to Wal-Mart's demands and avoiding under- or overproduction and the need to store inventory. The efficiencies that manufacturers gain from such information are passed on to Wal-Mart in the form of lower prices, which then passes on those cost savings to consumers.

Sources: "How Big Can It Grow?—Wal-Mart," *Economist*, April 17, 2004, pp. 74–76; H. Gilman, "The Most Underrated CEO Ever," *Fortune*, April 5, 2004, pp. 242–247; and K. Schaffner, "Psst! Want to Sell to Wal-Mart?," *Apparel Industry Magazine*, August 1996, pp. 18–20.

Substitute Products

The final force in Porter's model is the threat of substitute products: the products of different businesses or industries that can satisfy similar customer needs. For example, companies in the coffee industry compete indirectly with those in the tea and soft drink industries because all three serve customer needs for nonalcoholic drinks. The existence of close substitutes is a strong competitive threat because this limits the price that companies in one industry can charge for their product, which also limits industry profitability. If the price of coffee rises too much relative to that of tea or soft drinks, coffee drinkers may switch to those substitutes.

If an industry's products have few close substitutes (making substitutes a weak competitive force), then companies in the industry have the opportunity to raise prices and earn additional profits. There is no close substitute for microprocessors, which thus gives companies like Intel and AMD the ability to charge higher prices than if there were available substitutes.

Complementors

Andrew Grove, the former CEO of Intel, has argued that Porter's original formulation of competitive forces ignored a sixth force: the power, vigor, and competence of complementors.[10] Complementors are companies that sell products that add value to (complement) the products of companies in an industry because, when used together, the use of the combined products better satisfies customer demands. For example, the complementors to the PC industry are the companies that make software applications to run on the computers. The greater the supply of high-quality software applications running on these machines, the greater the value of PCs to customers, the greater the demand for PCs, and the greater the profitability of the PC industry.

Grove's argument has a strong foundation in economic theory, which has long argued that both substitutes and complements influence demand in an industry.[11] Research has emphasized the importance of complementary products in determining demand and profitability in many high-technology industries, such as the computer industry in which Grove made his mark.[12] When complements are an important determinant of demand for an industry's products, industry profits critically depend upon an adequate supply of complementary products. When the number of complementors is increasing and producing attractive complementary products, demand increases and profits in the industry can broaden opportunities for creating value. Conversely, if complementors are weak, and are not producing attractive complementary products, they can become a threat, slowing industry growth and limiting profitability.

It's also possible for complementors to gain so much power that they are able to extract profit out of the industry they are providing complements to. Complementors this strong can be a competitive threat. For example, in the videogame industry, the companies that produce the consoles—Nintendo, Microsoft (with Xbox), and Sony (with the PlayStation)—have historically made most of the money in the industry. They have done this by charging game-development companies (the complement providers) a royalty fee for every game sold that runs on their consoles. For example, Nintendo used to charge third-party game developers a 20% royalty fee for every game they sold that was written to run on a Nintendo console. However, two things have changed over the last decade. First, game developers have choices. They can, for example, decide to write for

Microsoft Xbox first, and Sony PlayStation a year later. Second, some game franchises are now so popular that consumers will purchase whichever platform runs the most recent version of the game. For example, Madden NFL, which is produced by Electronic Arts, has an estimated 5 to 7 million dedicated fans who will purchase each new release. The game is in such demand that Electronic Arts can bargain for lower royalty rates from Microsoft and Sony in return for writing it to run on their gaming platforms. Put differently, Electronic Arts has gained bargaining power over the console producers, and it uses this to extract profit from the console industry in the form of lower royalty rates paid to console manufacturers. The console manufacturers have responded by trying to develop their own powerful franchises that are exclusive to their platforms. Nintendo has been successful here with its long-running Super Mario series, and Microsoft has had a major franchise hit with its Halo series, which is now in its fourth version.

Summary: Why Industry Analysis Matters

The analysis of forces in the industry environment using the competitive forces framework is a powerful tool that helps managers to think strategically. It is important to recognize that one competitive force often affects others, and all forces need to be considered when performing industry analysis. For example, if new entry occurs due to low entry barriers, this will increase competition in the industry and drive down prices and profit rates, other things being equal. If buyers are powerful, they may take advantage of the increased choice resulting from new entry to further bargain down prices, increasing the intensity of competition and making it more difficult to make a decent profit in the industry. Thus, it is important to understand how one force might impact upon another.

Industry analysis inevitably leads managers to think systematically about strategic choices. For example, if entry barriers are low, managers might ask themselves, "how can we raise entry barriers into this industry, thereby reducing the threat of new competition?" The answer often involves trying to achieve economies of scale, build brand loyalty, create switching costs, and so on, so that new entrants are at a disadvantage and find it difficult to gain traction in the industry. Or they could ask, "How can we modify the intensity of competition in our industry?". They might do this by emphasizing brand loyalty in an attempt to differentiate their products, or by creating switching costs that reduce buyer power in the industry. Wireless service providers, for example, require their customers to sign a new 2-year contract with early termination fees that may run into hundreds of dollars whenever they upgrade their phone equipment. This action effectively increases the costs of switching to a different wireless provider, thus making it more difficult for new entrants to gain traction in the industry. The increase in switching costs also moderates the intensity of rivalry in the industry by making it less likely that consumers will switch from one provider to another in an attempt to lower the price they pay for their service.

When Coca-Cola looked at its industry environment in the early 2000s, it noticed a disturbing trend—per capita consumption of carbonated beverages had started to decline as people switched to noncarbonated soft drinks. In other words, substitute products were becoming a threat. This realization led to a change in the strategy at Coca-Cola. The company started to develop and offer its own noncarbonated beverages, effectively turning the threat into a strategic opportunity. Similarly, in the 2000s, demand for traditional newspapers began to decline as people increasingly started to consume news content on the Web. In other words, the threat from a substitute product was increasing. Several traditional newspapers responded by rapidly developing their own Web-based content.

In all of these examples, an analysis of industry opportunities and threats led directly to a change in strategy by companies within the industry. This, of course, is the crucial point—analyzing the industry environment in order to identify opportunities and threats leads logically to a discussion of what strategies should be adopted to exploit opportunities and counter threats. We will return to this issue again in Chapters 5, 6, and 7 when we look at the different business-level strategies firms can pursue, and how they can match strategy to the conditions prevailing in their industry environment.

STRATEGIC GROUPS WITHIN INDUSTRIES

Companies in an industry often differ significantly from one another with regard to the way they strategically position their products in the market. Factors such as the distribution channels they use, the market segments they serve, the quality of their products, technological leadership, customer service, pricing policy, advertising policy, and promotions affect product position. As a result of these differences, within most industries, it is possible to observe groups of companies in which each company follows a strategy that is similar to that pursued by other companies in the group, but different from the strategy pursued by companies in other groups. These different groups of companies are known as strategic groups.[13]

For example, as noted in the Opening Case, in the commercial aerospace industry there has traditionally been two main strategic groups: the manufacturers of regional jets and the manufacturers of large commercial jets (see Figure 2.3). Bombardier and Embraer are the standouts in the regional jet industry, whereas Boeing and Airbus have lone dominated

| Figure 2.3 | Strategic Groups in the Commercial Aerospace Industry |

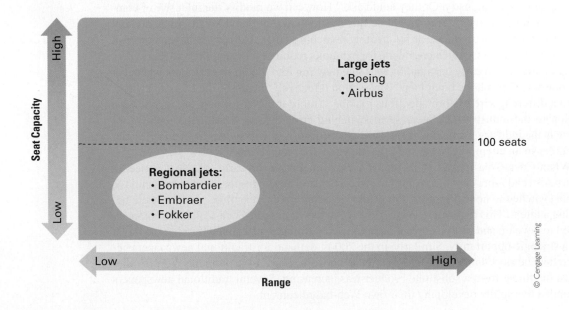

© Cengage Learning

the market for large commercial jets. Regional jets have less than 100 seats and limited range. Large jets have anywhere from 100 to 550 seats, and some models are able to fly across the Pacific Ocean. Large jets are sold to major airlines, and regional jets to small regional carriers. Historically, the companies in the regional jet group have competed against each other, but not against Boeing and Airbus (the converse is also true).

Normally, the basic differences between the strategies that companies in different strategic groups use can be captured by a relatively small number of factors. In the case of commercial aerospace, the differences are primarily in terms of product attributes (seat capacity and range), and customer set (large airlines versus smaller regional airlines). For another example, consider the pharmaceutical industry. Here two primary strategic groups stand out.[14] One group, which includes such companies as Merck, Eli Lilly, and Pfizer, is characterized by a business model based on heavy R&D spending and a focus on developing new, proprietary, blockbuster drugs. The companies in this proprietary strategic group are pursuing a high-risk, high-return strategy because basic drug research is difficult and expensive. Bringing a new drug to market can cost up to $800 million in R&D money and a decade of research and clinical trials. The risks are high because the failure rate in new drug development is very high: only one out of every five drugs entering clinical trials is eventually approved by the U.S. Food and Drug Administration. However, this strategy has potential for a high return because a single successful drug can be patented, giving the innovator a monopoly on the production and sale of the drug for the life of the patent (patents are issued for 20 years). This allows proprietary companies to charge a high price for the drug, earning them millions, if not billions, of dollars over the lifetime of the patent.

The second strategic group might be characterized as the generic-drug strategic group. This group of companies, which includes Forest Labs, Mylan, and Watson Pharmaceuticals, focuses on the manufacture of generic drugs: low-cost copies of drugs that were developed by companies in the proprietary group, which now have expired patents. Low R&D spending, production efficiency, and an emphasis on low prices characterize the business models of companies in this strategic group. They are pursuing a low-risk, low-return strategy. It is low risk because these companies are not investing millions of dollars in R&D, and low return because they cannot charge high prices for their products.

Implications of Strategic Groups

The concept of strategic groups has a number of implications for the identification of opportunities and threats within an industry. First, because all companies in a strategic group are pursuing a similar strategy, customers tend to view the products of such enterprises as direct substitutes for each other. Thus, a company's closest competitors are those in its strategic group, not those in other strategic groups in the industry. The most immediate threat to a company's profitability comes from rivals within its own strategic group. For example, in the retail industry, there is a group of companies that might be characterized as discounters. Included in this group are Wal-Mart, K-mart, Target, and Fred Meyer. These companies compete vigorously with each other, rather than with other retailers in different groups, such as Nordstrom or The Gap. K-Mart, for example, was driven into bankruptcy in the early 2000s, not because Nordstrom or The Gap took its business, but because Wal-Mart and Target gained share in the discounting group by virtue of their superior strategic execution of the discounting business model.

A second competitive implication is that different strategic groups can have different relationships to each of the competitive forces; thus, each strategic group may face a different set of opportunities and threats. Each of the following can be a relatively strong or weak competitive force depending on the competitive positioning approach adopted by each strategic group in the industry: the risk of new entry by potential competitors; the degree of rivalry among companies within a group; the bargaining power of buyers; the bargaining power of suppliers; and the competitive force of substitute and complementary products. For example, in the pharmaceutical industry, companies in the proprietary group historically have been in a very powerful position in relation to buyers because their products are patented and there are no substitutes. Also, rivalry based on price competition within this group has been low because competition in the industry depends upon which company is first to patent a new drug ("patent races"), not on drug prices. Thus, companies in this group have been able to charge high prices and earn high profits. In contrast, companies in the generic group have been in a much weaker position because many companies are able to produce different versions of the same generic drug after patents expire. Thus, in this strategic group, products are close substitutes, rivalry has been high, and price competition has led to lower profits than for the companies in the proprietary group.

The Role of Mobility Barriers

It follows from these two issues that some strategic groups are more desirable than others because competitive forces open up greater opportunities and present fewer threats for those groups. Managers, after analyzing their industry, might identify a strategic group where competitive forces are weaker and higher profits can be made. Sensing an opportunity, they might contemplate changing their strategy and move to compete in that strategic group. However, taking advantage of this opportunity may be difficult because of mobility barriers between strategic groups.

Mobility barriers are within-industry factors that inhibit the movement of companies between strategic groups. They include the barriers to entry into a group and the barriers to exit from a company's existing group. For example, attracted by the promise of higher returns, Forest Labs might want to enter the proprietary strategic group in the pharmaceutical industry, but it might find doing so difficult because it lacks the requisite R&D skills, and building these skills would be an expensive proposition. Over time, companies in different groups develop different cost structures, skills, and competencies that allow them different pricing options and choices. A company contemplating entry into another strategic group must evaluate whether it has the ability to imitate, and outperform, its potential competitors in that strategic group. Managers must determine if it is cost-effective to overcome mobility barriers before deciding whether the move is worthwhile.

At the same time, managers should be aware that companies based in another strategic group within their industry might ultimately become their direct competitors if they can overcome mobility barriers. This now seems to be occurring in the commercial aerospace industry, where two of the regional jet manufacturers, Bombardier and Embraer, have started to move into the large commercial jet business with the development of narrow-bodied aircraft in the 100- to 150-seat range (see the Opening Case). This implies that Boeing and Airbus will be seeing more competition in the years ahead, and their managers need to prepare for this.

INDUSTRY LIFE-CYCLE ANALYSIS

Changes that take place in an industry over time are an important determinant of the strength of the competitive forces in the industry (and of the nature of opportunities and threats). The similarities and differences between companies in an industry often become more pronounced over time, and its strategic group structure frequently changes. The strength and nature of each of the competitive forces also change as an industry evolves, particularly the two forces of risk of entry by potential competitors and rivalry among existing firms.[15]

A useful tool for analyzing the effects that industry evolution has on competitive forces is the industry life-cycle model. This model identifies five sequential stages in the evolution of an industry that lead to five distinct kinds of industry environment: embryonic, growth, shakeout, mature, and decline (see Figure 2.4). The task managers face is to anticipate how the strength of competitive forces will change as the industry environment evolves, and to formulate strategies that take advantage of opportunities as they arise and that counter emerging threats.

Embryonic Industries

An embryonic industry refers to an industry just beginning to develop (for example, personal computers and biotechnology in the 1970s, wireless communications in the 1980s, Internet retailing in the 1990s, and nanotechnology today). Growth at this stage is slow because of factors such as buyers' unfamiliarity with the industry's product, high prices due to the inability of companies to reap any significant scale economies, and poorly developed distribution channels. Barriers to entry tend to be based on access to

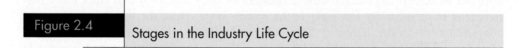

Figure 2.4   Stages in the Industry Life Cycle

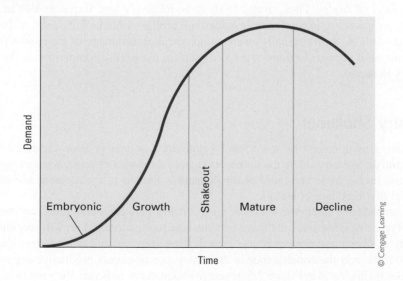

© Cengage Learning

key technological knowhow rather than cost economies or brand loyalty. If the core know how required to compete in the industry is complex and difficult to grasp, barriers to entry can be quite high, and established companies will be protected from potential competitors. Rivalry in embryonic industries is based not so much on price as on educating customers, opening up distribution channels, and perfecting the design of the product. Such rivalry can be intense, and the company that is the first to solve design problems often has the opportunity to develop a significant market position. An embryonic industry may also be the creation of one company's innovative efforts, as happened with microprocessors (Intel), vacuum cleaners (Hoover), photocopiers (Xerox), small package express delivery (FedEx), and Internet search engines (Google). In such circumstances, the developing company has a major opportunity to capitalize on the lack of rivalry and build a strong hold on the market.

Growth Industries

Once demand for the industry's product begins to increase, the industry develops the characteristics of a growth industry. In a growth industry, first-time demand is expanding rapidly as many new customers enter the market. Typically, an industry grows when customers become familiar with the product, prices fall because scale economies have been attained, and distribution channels develop. The U.S. wireless telephone industry remained in the growth stage for most of the 1990s. In 1990, there were only 5 million cellular subscribers in the nation. In 1997, there were 50 million. By 2012, this figure had increased to about 320 million, or roughly one account per person, implying that the market is now saturated and the industry is mature.

Normally, the importance of control over technological knowledge as a barrier to entry has diminished by the time an industry enters its growth stage. Because few companies have yet to achieve significant scale economies or built brand loyalty, other entry barriers tend to be relatively low early in the growth stage. Thus, the threat from potential competitors is typically highest at this point. Paradoxically, however, high growth usually means that new entrants can be absorbed into an industry without a marked increase in the intensity of rivalry. Thus, rivalry tends to be relatively low. Rapid growth in demand enables companies to expand their revenues and profits without taking market share away from competitors. A strategically aware company takes advantage of the relatively benign environment of the growth stage to prepare itself for the intense competition of the coming industry shakeout.

Industry Shakeout

Explosive growth cannot be maintained indefinitely. Sooner or later, the rate of growth slows, and the industry enters the shakeout stage. In the shakeout stage, demand approaches saturation levels: more and more of the demand is limited to replacement because fewer potential first-time buyers remain.

As an industry enters the shakeout stage, rivalry between companies can become intense. Typically, companies that have become accustomed to rapid growth continue to add capacity at rates consistent with past growth. However, demand is no longer growing at historic rates, and the consequence is the emergence of excess productive capacity. This condition is illustrated in Figure 2.5, where the solid curve indicates the growth in demand over time and the broken curve indicates the growth in productive capacity over time.

| Figure 2.5 | Growth in Demand and Capacity |

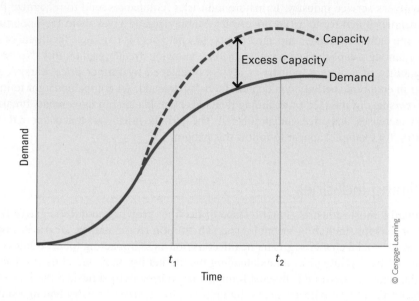

As you can see, past time t_1, demand growth becomes slower as the industry becomes mature. However, capacity continues to grow until time t_2. The gap between the solid and broken lines signifies excess capacity. In an attempt to use this capacity, companies often cut prices. The result can be a price war, which drives the more inefficient companies into bankruptcy and deters new entry.

Mature Industries

The shakeout stage ends when the industry enters its mature stage: the market is totally saturated, demand is limited to replacement demand, and growth is low or zero. Typically, the growth that remains comes from population expansion, bringing new customers into the market, or increasing replacement demand.

As an industry enters maturity, barriers to entry increase, and the threat of entry from potential competitors decreases. As growth slows during the shakeout, companies can no longer maintain historic growth rates merely by holding on to their market share. Competition for market share develops, driving down prices and often producing a price war, as has happened in the airline and PC industries. To survive the shakeout, companies begin to focus on minimizing costs and building brand loyalty. The airlines, for example, tried to cut operating costs by hiring nonunion labor, and build brand loyalty by introducing frequent-flyer programs. Personal computer companies have sought to build brand loyalty by providing excellent after-sales service and working to lower their cost structures. By the time an industry matures, the surviving companies are those that have brand loyalty and efficient low-cost operations. Because both these factors constitute a significant barrier to entry, the threat of entry by potential competitors is often greatly diminished. High entry barriers in mature industries can give companies the opportunity to increase prices and profits—although this does not always occur.

As a result of the shakeout, most industries in the maturity stage have consolidated and become oligopolies. Examples include the beer industry, breakfast cereal industry, and wireless service industry. In mature industries, companies tend to recognize their interdependence and try to avoid price wars. Stable demand gives them the opportunity to enter into tacit price-leadership agreements. The net effect is to reduce the threat of intense rivalry among established companies, thereby allowing greater profitability. Nevertheless, the stability of a mature industry is always threatened by further price wars. A general slump in economic activity can depress industry demand. As companies fight to maintain their revenues in the face of declining demand, price-leadership agreements break down, rivalry increases, and prices and profits fall. The periodic price wars that occur in the airline industry, for example, appear to follow this pattern.

Declining Industries

Eventually, most industries enter a stage of decline: growth becomes negative for a variety of reasons, including technological substitution (for example, air travel instead of rail travel), social changes (greater health consciousness impacting tobacco sales), demographics (the declining birthrate damaging the market for baby and child products), and international competition (low-cost foreign competition helped pushed the U.S. steel industry into decline). Within a declining industry, the degree of rivalry among established companies usually increases. Depending on the speed of the decline and the height of exit barriers, competitive pressures can become as fierce as in the shakeout stage.[16] The largest problem in a declining industry is that falling demand leads to the emergence of excess capacity. In trying to use this capacity, companies begin to cut prices, thus sparking a price war. The U.S. steel industry experienced these problems during the 1980s and 1990s because steel companies tried to use their excess capacity despite falling demand. The same problem occurred in the airline industry in the 1990–1992 period, in 2001–2005, and again in 2008–2009 as companies cut prices to ensure that they would not be flying with half-empty planes (that is, they would not be operating with substantial excess capacity). Exit barriers play a part in adjusting excess capacity. The greater the exit barriers, the harder it is for companies to reduce capacity, and the greater the threat of severe price competition.

Summary

In summary, a third task of industry analysis is to identify the opportunities and threats that are characteristic of different kinds of industry environments in order to develop effective strategies. Managers have to tailor their strategies to changing industry conditions. They must also learn to recognize the crucial points in an industry's development, so they can forecast when the shakeout stage of an industry might begin, or when an industry might be moving into decline. This is also true at the level of strategic groups, for new embryonic groups may emerge because of shifts in customer needs and tastes, or because some groups may grow rapidly due to changes in technology, whereas others will decline as their customers defect.

LIMITATIONS OF MODELS FOR INDUSTRY ANALYSIS

The competitive forces, strategic groups, and life-cycle models provide useful ways of thinking about and analyzing the nature of competition within an industry to identify opportunities and threats. However, each has its limitations, and managers must be aware of their shortcomings.

Life-Cycle Issues

It is important to remember that the industry life-cycle model is a generalization. In practice, industry life-cycles do not always follow the pattern illustrated in Figure 2.4. In some cases, growth is so rapid that the embryonic stage is skipped altogether. In others, industries fail to get past the embryonic stage. Industry growth can be revitalized after long periods of decline through innovation or social change. For example, the health boom brought the bicycle industry back to life after a long period of decline. The revenues of wireless service providers are also now growing at a healthy clip despite a nominally mature market due to the introduction of enhanced products—smartphones—that has resulted in a rapid increase in revenues from data services. Between 2007 and 2012, wireless data revenues in the U.S. increased from $19 billion to $68 billion, which represented essentially all of the growth in industry revenues over this time period (i.e., there was zero growth in revenues from simple wireless voice service).[17]

The time span of these stages can also vary significantly from industry to industry. Some industries can stay in maturity almost indefinitely if their products are viewed as basic necessities, as is the case for the car industry. Other industries skip the mature stage and go straight into decline, as in the case of the vacuum tube industry. Transistors replaced vacuum tubes as a major component in electronic products despite that the vacuum tube industry was still in its growth stage. Still other industries may go through several shakeouts before they enter full maturity, as appears to currently be happening in the telecommunications industry.

Innovation and Change

Over any reasonable length of time, in many industries competition can be viewed as a process driven by innovation.[18] Innovation is frequently the major factor in industry evolution and causes a company's movement through the industry life cycle. Innovation is attractive because companies that pioneer new products, processes, or strategies can often earn enormous profits. Consider the explosive growth of Toys"R"Us, Dell, and Wal-Mart. In a variety of different ways, all of these companies were innovators. Toys"R"Us pioneered a new way of selling toys (through large discount warehouse-type stores), Dell pioneered an entirely new way of selling personal computers (directly via telephone and then the Web), and Wal-Mart pioneered the low-price discount superstore concept.

Successful innovation can transform the nature of industry competition. In recent decades, one frequent consequence of innovation has been to lower the fixed costs of production, thereby reducing barriers to entry and allowing new, and smaller, enterprises to compete with large established organizations. For example, two decades ago, large integrated steel companies such as U.S. Steel, LTV, and Bethlehem Steel dominated the steel industry. The industry was a typical oligopoly, dominated by a small number of large producers, in which tacit price collusion was practiced. Then along came a series of efficient mini-mill producers such as Nucor and Chaparral Steel, which used a new technology: electric arc furnaces. Over the past 20 years, they have revolutionized the structure of the industry. What was once a consolidated industry is now much more fragmented and price competitive. U.S. Steel now has only a 12% market share, down from 55% in the mid-1960s. In contrast, the mini-mills as a group now hold over 40% of the market, up from 5% 20 years ago.[19] Thus, the mini-mill innovation has reshaped the nature of competition in the steel industry.[20] A competitive forces model applied to the industry in 1970 would look very different from a competitive forces model applied in 2012.

Michael Porter talks of innovations as "unfreezing" and "reshaping" industry structure. He argues that after a period of turbulence triggered by innovation, the structure of an industry once more settles down into a fairly stable pattern, and the five forces and strategic group concepts can once more be applied.[21] This view of the evolution of industry structure is often referred to as "punctuated equilibrium."[22] The punctuated equilibrium view holds that long periods of equilibrium (refreezing), when an industry's structure is stable, are punctuated by periods of rapid change (unfreezing), when industry structure is revolutionized by innovation.

Figure 2.6 shows what punctuated equilibrium might look like for one key dimension of industry structure: competitive structure. From time t_0 to t_1, the competitive structure of the industry is a stable oligopoly, and few companies share the market. At time t_1, a major new innovation is pioneered either by an existing company or a new entrant. The result is a period of turbulence between t_1 and t_2. Afterward, the industry settles into a new state of equilibrium, but now the competitive structure is far more fragmented. Note that the opposite could have happened: the industry could have become more consolidated, although this seems to be less common. In general, innovations seem to lower barriers to entry, allow more companies into the industry, and as a result lead to fragmentation rather than consolidation.

During a period of rapid change when industry structure is being revolutionized by innovation, value typically migrates to business models based on new positioning strategies.[23] In the stockbrokerage industry, value migrated from the full-service broker model

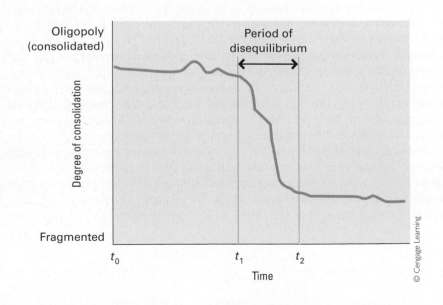

Figure 2.6   Punctuated Equilibrium and Competitive Structure

© Cengage Learning

to the online trading model. In the steel industry, the introduction of electric arc technology led to a migration of value away from large, integrated enterprises and toward small mini-mills. In the book-selling industry, value has migrated first away from small boutique "bricks-and-mortar" booksellers toward large bookstore chains like Barnes & Noble, and more recently toward online bookstores such as Amazon.com. Because the competitive forces and strategic group models are static, they cannot adequately capture what occurs during periods of rapid change in the industry environment when value is migrating.

Company Differences

Another criticism of industry models is that they overemphasize the importance of industry structure as a determinant of company performance, and underemphasize the importance of variations or differences among companies within an industry or a strategic group.[24] As we discuss in the next chapter, there can be enormous variance in the profit rates of individual companies within an industry. Research by Richard Rumelt and his associates, for example, suggests that industry structure explains only about 10% of the variance in profit rates across companies.[25] This implies that individual company differences explain much of the remainder. Other studies have estimated the explained variance at about 20%, which is still not a large figure.[26] Similarly, growing numbers of studies have found only weak evidence linking strategic group membership and company profit rates, despite that the strategic group model predicts a strong link.[27] Collectively, these studies suggest that a company's individual resources and capabilities may be more important determinants of its profitability than the industry or strategic group of which the company is a member. In other words, there are strong companies in tough industries where average profitability is low (e.g., Nucor in the steel industry), and weak companies in industries where average profitability is high.

Although these findings do not invalidate the competitive forces and strategic group models, they do imply that the models are imperfect predictors of enterprise profitability. A company will not be profitable just because it is based in an attractive industry or strategic group. As we will discuss in subsequent chapters, much more is required.

THE MACROENVIRONMENT

Just as the decisions and actions of strategic managers can often change an industry's competitive structure, so too can changing conditions or forces in the wider macroenvironment, that is, the broader economic, global, technological, demographic, social, and political context in which companies and industries are embedded (see Figure 2.7). Changes in the forces within the macroenvironment can have a direct impact on any or all of the forces in Porter's model, thereby altering the relative strength of these forces as well as the attractiveness of an industry.

Macroeconomic Forces

Macroeconomic forces affect the general health and well-being of a nation or the regional economy of an organization, which in turn affect companies' and industries' ability to earn an adequate rate of return. The four most important macroeconomic forces are the growth rate of the economy, interest rates, currency exchange rates, and inflation (or deflation) rates. Economic growth, because it leads to an expansion in customer expenditures, tends to ease competitive pressures within an industry. This gives companies the opportunity to

| Figure 2.7 | The Role of the Macroenvironment |

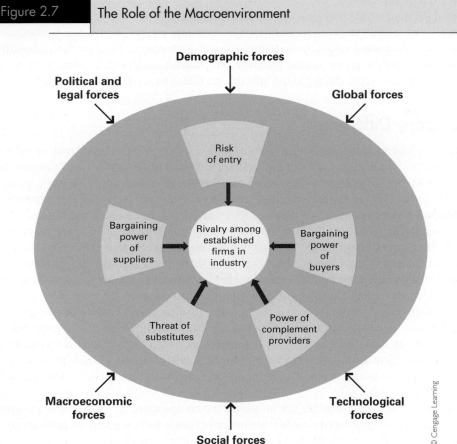

expand their operations and earn higher profits. Because economic decline (a recession) leads to a reduction in customer expenditures, it increases competitive pressures. Economic decline frequently causes price wars in mature industries.

Interest rates can determine the demand for a company's products. Interest rates are important whenever customers routinely borrow money to finance their purchase of these products. The most obvious example is the housing market, where mortgage rates directly affect demand. Interest rates also have an impact on the sale of autos, appliances, and capital equipment, to give just a few examples. For companies in such industries, rising interest rates are a threat, and falling rates an opportunity. Interest rates are also important because they influence a company's cost of capital, and therefore its ability to raise funds and invest in new assets. The lower that interest rates are, the lower the cost of capital for companies, and the more investment there can be.

Currency exchange rates define the comparative value of different national currencies. Movement in currency exchange rates has a direct impact on the competitiveness of a company's products in the global marketplace. For example, when the value of the dollar is low compared to the value of other currencies, products made in the United States are relatively inexpensive and products made overseas are relatively expensive. A low or declining dollar reduces the threat from foreign competitors while creating opportunities for increased sales overseas. The fall in the value of the dollar against several major currencies during 2004–2008 helped to make the U.S. steel industry more competitive.

Price inflation can destabilize the economy, producing slower economic growth, higher interest rates, and volatile currency movements. If inflation continues to increase, investment planning will become hazardous. The key characteristic of inflation is that it makes the future less predictable. In an inflationary environment, it may be impossible to predict with any accuracy the real value of returns that can be earned from a project 5 years later. Such uncertainty makes companies less willing to invest, which in turn depresses economic activity and ultimately pushes the economy into a recession. Thus, high inflation is a threat to companies.

Price deflation also has a destabilizing effect on economic activity. If prices fall, the real price of fixed payments goes up. This is damaging for companies and individuals with a high level of debt who must make regular fixed payments on that debt. In a deflationary environment, the increase in the real value of debt consumes more household and corporate cash flows, leaving less for other purchases and depressing the overall level of economic activity. Although significant deflation has not been seen since the 1930s, in the 1990s it started to take hold in Japan, and in 2008–2009 there were concerns that it might re-emerge in the United States as the country plunged into a deep recession.

Global Forces

Over the last half-century there have been enormous changes in the world's economic system. We review these changes in some detail in Chapter 8 when we discuss global strategy. For now, the important points to note are that barriers to international trade and investment have tumbled, and more and more countries have enjoyed sustained economic growth. Economic growth in places like Brazil, China, and India has created large new markets for companies' goods and services and is giving companies an opportunity to grow their profits faster by entering these nations. Falling barriers to international trade and investment have made it much easier to enter foreign nations. For example, 20 years ago, it was almost impossible for a Western company to set up operations in China. Today, Western and Japanese companies are investing around $100 billion a year in China. By the same token, however, falling barriers to international trade and investment have made it easier for foreign enterprises to enter the domestic markets of many companies (by lowering barriers to entry), thereby increasing the intensity of competition and lowering profitability. Because of these changes, many formerly isolated domestic markets have now become part of a much larger, more competitive global marketplace, creating both threats and opportunities for companies.

Technological Forces

Over the last few decades the pace of technological change has accelerated.[28] This has unleashed a process that has been called a "perennial gale of creative destruction."[29] Technological change can make established products obsolete overnight and simultaneously create a host of new product possibilities. Thus, technological change is both creative and destructive—both an opportunity and a threat.

Most important, the impacts of technological change can affect the height of barriers to entry and therefore radically reshape industry structure. For example, the Internet lowered barriers to entry into the news industry. Providers of financial news must now compete for advertising dollars and customer attention with new Internet-based media organizations that developed during the 1990s and 2000s, such as TheStreet.com, The Motley Fool, Yahoo!'s financial section, and most recently, Google news. Advertisers now have more choices due to the resulting increase in rivalry, enabling them to bargain down the prices that they must pay to media companies.

Demographic Forces

Demographic forces are outcomes of changes in the characteristics of a population, such as age, gender, ethnic origin, race, sexual orientation, and social class. Like the other forces in the general environment, demographic forces present managers with opportunities and threats and can have major implications for organizations. Changes in the age distribution of a population are an example of a demographic force that affects managers and organizations. Currently, most industrialized nations are experiencing the aging of their populations as a consequence of falling birth and death rates and the aging of the baby-boom generation. As the population ages, opportunities for organizations that cater to older people are increasing; the home-health-care and recreation industries, for example, are seeing an upswing in demand for their services. As the baby-boom generation from the late 1950s to the early 1960s has aged, it has created a host of opportunities and threats. During the 1980s, many baby boomers were getting married and creating an upsurge in demand for the customer appliances normally purchased by couples marrying for the first time. Companies such as Whirlpool Corporation and GE capitalized on the resulting upsurge in demand for washing machines, dishwashers, dryers, and the like. In the 1990s, many of these same baby boomers were beginning to save for retirement, creating an inflow of money into mutual funds, and creating a boom in the mutual fund industry. In the next 20 years, many of these same baby boomers will retire, creating a boom in retirement communities.

Social Forces

Social forces refer to the way in which changing social mores and values affect an industry. Like the other macroenvironmental forces discussed here, social change creates opportunities and threats. One of the major social movements of recent decades has been the trend toward greater health consciousness. Its impact has been immense, and companies that recognized the opportunities early have often reaped significant gains. Philip Morris, for example, capitalized on the growing health consciousness trend when it acquired Miller Brewing Company, and then redefined competition in the beer industry with its introduction of low-calorie beer (Miller Lite). Similarly, PepsiCo was able to gain market share from its rival, Coca-Cola, by being the first to introduce diet colas and fruit-based soft drinks. At the same time, the health trend has created a threat for many industries. The tobacco industry, for example, is in decline as a direct result of greater customer awareness of the health implications of smoking.

Political and Legal Forces

Political and legal forces are outcomes of changes in laws and regulations, and significantly affect managers and companies. Political processes shape a society's laws, which constrain the operations of organizations and managers and thus create both opportunities and threats.[30] For example, throughout much of the industrialized world, there has been a strong trend toward deregulation of industries previously controlled by the state, and privatization of organizations once owned by the state. In the United States, deregulation of the airline industry in 1979 allowed 29 new airline companies to enter the industry between 1979 and 1993.

The increase in passenger-carrying capacity after deregulation led to excess capacity on many routes, intense competition, and fare wars. To respond to this more competitive task environment, airlines needed to look for ways to reduce operating costs. The development of hub-and-spoke systems, the rise of nonunion airlines, and the introduction of no-frills discount service are all responses to increased competition in the airlines' task environment. Despite these innovations, the airline industry still experiences intense fare wars, which have lowered profits and caused numerous airline-company bankruptcies. The global telecommunications service industry is now experiencing the same kind of turmoil following the deregulation of that industry in the United States and elsewhere.

SUMMARY OF CHAPTER

1. An industry can be defined as a group of companies offering products or services that are close substitutes for each other. Close substitutes are products or services that satisfy the same basic customer needs.

2. The main technique used to analyze competition in the industry environment is the competitive forces model. The six forces are: (1) the risk of new entry by potential competitors, (2) the extent of rivalry among established firms, (3) the bargaining power of buyers, (4) the bargaining power of suppliers, (5) the threat of substitute products, and (6) the power of complement providers. The stronger each force is, the more competitive the industry and the lower the rate of return that can be earned.

3. The risk of entry by potential competitors is a function of the height of barriers to entry. The higher the barriers to entry are, the lower is the risk of entry and the greater are the profits that can be earned in the industry.

4. The extent of rivalry among established companies is a function of an industry's competitive structure, demand conditions, cost conditions, and barriers to exit. Strong demand conditions moderate the competition among established companies and create opportunities for expansion. When demand is weak, intensive competition can develop, particularly in consolidated industries with high exit barriers.

5. Buyers are most powerful when a company depends on them for business, but they are not dependent on the company. In such circumstances, buyers are a threat.

6. Suppliers are most powerful when a company depends on them for business but they are not dependent on the company. In such circumstances, suppliers are a threat.

7. Substitute products are the products of companies serving customer needs similar to the needs served by the industry being analyzed. When substitute products are very similar to one another, companies can charge a lower price without losing customers to the substitutes.

8. The power, vigor, and competence of complementors represents a sixth competitive force. Powerful and vigorous complementors may have a strong positive impact on demand in an industry.

9. Most industries are composed of strategic groups: groups of companies pursuing the same or a similar strategy. Companies in different strategic groups pursue different strategies.

10. The members of a company's strategic group constitute its immediate competitors. Because different strategic groups are characterized by different opportunities and threats, a company may improve its performance by switching strategic groups. The feasibility of doing so is a function of the height of mobility barriers.

11. Industries go through a well-defined life cycle: from an embryonic stage, through growth, shakeout, and maturity, and eventually decline. Each stage has different implications for the competitive

structure of the industry, and each gives rise to its own set of opportunities and threats.

12. The competitive forces, strategic group, and industry life-cycles models all have limitations. The competitive forces and strategic group models present a static picture of competition that deemphasizes the role of innovation. Yet innovation can revolutionize industry structure and completely change the strength of different competitive forces. The competitive forces and strategic group models have been criticized for deemphasizing the importance of individual company differences. A company will not be profitable just because it is part of an attractive industry or strategic group; much more is required. The industry life-cycle model is a generalization that is not always followed, particularly when innovations revolutionize an industry.

13. The macroenvironment affects the intensity of rivalry within an industry. Included in the macroenvironment are the macroeconomic environment, the global environment, the technological environment, the demographic and social environment, and the political and legal environment.

DISCUSSION QUESTIONS

1. Under what environmental conditions are price wars most likely to occur in an industry? What are the implications of price wars for a company? How should a company try to deal with the threat of a price war?

2. Discuss the competitive forces model with reference to what you know about the global market for commercial jet aircraft (see the Opening Case). What does the model tell you about the level of competition in this industry?

3. Identify a growth industry, a mature industry, and a declining industry. For each industry, identify the following: (a) the number and size distribution of companies, (b) the nature of barriers to entry, (c) the height of barriers to entry, and (d) the extent of product differentiation. What do these factors tell you about the nature of competition in each industry? What are the implications for the company in terms of opportunities and threats?

4. Assess the impact of macroenvironmental factors on the likely level of enrollment at your university over the next decade. What are the implications of these factors for the job security and salary level of your professors?

PRACTICING STRATEGIC MANAGEMENT

© iStockPhoto.com/Urilux

Small-Group Exercise: Competing with Microsoft

Break into groups of three to five people, and discuss the following scenario. Appoint one group member as a spokesperson who will communicate your findings to the class.

You are a group of managers and software engineers at a small start-up. You have developed a revolutionary new operating system for personal computers that offers distinct advantages over Microsoft's Windows operating system: it takes up less memory space on the hard drive of a personal computer; it takes full advantage of the power of the personal computer's microprocessor, and in theory can run software applications much faster than Windows; it is much easier to install and use than Windows; and it responds to voice instructions with an accuracy of 99.9%, in addition to input from a keyboard or mouse. The operating system is the only product offering that your company has produced.

(continues)

PRACTICING STRATEGIC MANAGEMENT

© iStockPhoto.com/Urilux

(continued)

Complete the following exercises:

1. Analyze the competitive structure of the market for personal computer operating systems. On the basis of this analysis, identify what factors might inhibit adoption of your operating system by customers.
2. Can you think of a strategy that your company might pursue, either alone or in conjunction with other enterprises, in order to "beat Microsoft"? What will it take to execute that strategy successfully?

STRATEGY SIGN ON

© iStockPhoto.com/Ninoslav Dotlic

Article File 2

Find an example of an industry that has become more competitive in recent years. Identify the reasons for the increase in competitive pressure.

Strategic Management Project: Module 2

This module requires you to analyze the industry environment in which your company is based using the information you have already gathered:

1. Apply the competitive forces model to the industry in which your company is based. What does this model tell you about the nature of competition in the industry?
2. Are any changes taking place in the macroenvironment that might have an impact, positive or negative, on the industry in which your company is based? If so, what are these changes, and how might they affect the industry?
3. Identify any strategic groups that might exist in the industry. How does the intensity of competition differ across these strategic groups?
4. How dynamic is the industry in which your company is based? Is there any evidence that innovation is reshaping competition or has done so in the recent past?
5. In what stage of its life cycle is the industry in which your company is based? What are the implications of this for the intensity of competition now? In the future?
6. Is your company part of an industry that is becoming more global? If so, what are the implications of this change for competitive intensity?
7. Analyze the impact of the national context as it pertains to the industry in which your company is based. Does the national context help or hinder your company in achieving a competitive advantage in the global marketplace?

ETHICAL DILEMMA

© iStockPhoto.com/P_Wei

You are a strategic analyst at a successful hotel enterprise that has been generating substantial excess cash flow. Your CEO instructed you to analyze the competitive structure of closely related industries to find one that the company could enter, using its cash reserve to build up a sustainable position. Your analysis, using the competitive forces model, suggests that the highest profit opportunities are to be found in the gambling industry. You realize that it might be possible to add casinos to several of your existing hotels, lowering entry costs into this industry. However, you personally have strong moral objections to gambling. Should your own personal beliefs influence your recommendations to the CEO?

CLOSING CASE

The U.S. Airline Industry

The U.S. airline industry has long struggled to make a profit. In the 1990s, investor Warren Buffet famously quipped that investors in the airline industry would have been more fortunate if the Wright Brothers had crashed at Kitty Hawk. Buffet's point was that the airline industry had cumulatively lost more money than it had made—it has always been an economically losing proposition. Buffet once made the mistake of investing in the industry when he took a stake in US Airways. A few years later, he was forced to write off 75% of the value of that investment. He told his shareholders that if he ever invested in another airline, they should shoot him.

The 2000s have not been kinder to the industry. The airline industry lost $35 billion between 2001 and 2006. It managed to earn meager profits in 2006 and 2007, but lost $24 billion in 2008 as oil and jet fuel prices surged throughout the year. In 2009, the industry lost $4.7 billion as a sharp drop in business travelers—a consequence of the deep recession that followed the global financial crisis—more than offset the beneficial effects of falling oil prices. The industry returned to profitability in 2010–2012, and in 2012 actually managed to make $13 billion in net profit on revenues of $140.5 billion.

Analysts point to a number of factors that have made the industry a difficult place in which to do business. Over the years, larger carriers such as United, Delta, and American have been hurt by low-cost budget carriers entering the industry, including Southwest Airlines, Jet Blue, AirTran Airways, and Virgin America. These new entrants have used nonunion labor, often fly just one type of aircraft (which reduces maintenance costs), have focused on the most lucrative routes, typically fly point-to-point (unlike the incumbents, which have historically routed passengers through hubs), and compete by offering very low fares. New entrants have helped to create a situation of excess capacity in the industry, and have taken share from the incumbent airlines, which often have a much higher cost structure (primarily due to higher labor costs).

The incumbents have had little choice but to respond to fare cuts, and the result has been a protracted industry price war. To complicate matters, the rise of Internet travel sites such as Expedia, Travelocity, and Orbitz has made it much easier for consumers to comparison shop, and has helped to keep fares low.

Beginning in 2001, higher oil prices also complicated matters. Fuel costs accounted for 32% of total revenues in 2011 (labor costs accounted for 26%;

together they are the two biggest variable expense items). From 1985 to 2001, oil prices traded in a range between $15 and $25 a barrel. Then, prices began to rise due to strong demand from developing nations such as China and India, hitting a high of $147 a barrel in mid-2008. The price for jet fuel, which stood at $0.57 a gallon in December 2001, hit a high of $3.70 a gallon in July 2008, plunging the industry deep into the red. Although oil prices and fuel prices subsequently fell, they remain far above historic levels. In late 2012, jet fuel was hovering around $3.00 a gallon.

Many airlines went bankrupt in the 2000s, including Delta, Northwest, United, and US Airways. The larger airlines continued to fly, however, as they reorganized under Chapter 11 bankruptcy laws, and excess capacity persisted in the industry. These companies thereafter came out of bankruptcy protection with lower labor costs, but generating revenue still remained challenging for them.

The late 2000s and early 2010s were characterized by a wave of mergers in the industry. In 2008, Delta and Northwest merged. In 2010, United and Continental merged, and Southwest Airlines announced plans to acquire AirTran. In late 2012, American Airlines put itself under Chapter 11 bankruptcy protection. US Airways subsequently pushed for a merger agreement with American Airlines, which was under negotiation in early 2013. The driving forces behind these mergers include the desire to reduce excess capacity and lower costs by eliminating duplication. To the extent that they are successful, they could lead to a more stable pricing environment in the industry, and higher profit rates. That, however, remains to be seen.

Sources: J. Corridore, "Standard & Poors Industry Surveys: Airlines," June 28, 2012; B. Kowitt, "High Anxiety," *Fortune*, April 27, 2009, p. 14; and "Shredding Money," *The Economist*, September 20, 2008.

CASE DISCUSSION QUESTIONS

1. Conduct a competitive forces analysis of the U.S. airline industry. What does this analysis tell you about the causes of low profitability in this industry?

2. Do you think there are any strategic groups in the U.S. airline industry? If so, what might they be? How might the nature of competition vary from group to group?

3. The economic performance of the airline industry seems to be very cyclical. Why do you think this is the case?

4. Given your analysis, what strategies do you think an airline should adopt in order to improve its chances of being persistently profitable?

KEY TERMS

Opportunities 44
Threats 45
Industry 45

Sector 46
Potential competitors 48
Economies of scale 49

Brand loyalty 49
Absolute cost
  advantage 49

Switching costs 50

NOTES

[1]M. E. Porter, *Competitive Strategy* (New York: Free Press, 1980).

[2]J. E. Bain, *Barriers to New Competition* (Cambridge, Mass.: Harvard University Press, 1956). For a review of the modern literature on barriers to entry, see R. J. Gilbert, "Mobility Barriers and the Value of Incumbency," in R. Schmalensee and R. D. Willig (eds.), *Handbook of Industrial Organization,* vol. 1 (Amsterdam: North-Holland, 1989). See also R. P. McAfee, H. M. Mialon, and M. A. Williams, "What Is a Barrier to Entry?" *American Economic Review* 94 (May 2004): 461–468.

[3]J. Koetsier, "Old Phones and New Users Are Key Reasons Apple Topped 53% of U.S. Smart Phone Market Share," *Venture Beat*, January 4, 2013.

[4]A detailed discussion of switching costs can be found in C. Shapiro and H. R. Varian, *Information Rules: A Strategic Guide to the Network Economy* (Boston: Harvard Business School Press, 1999).

[5]Most of this information on barriers to entry can be found in the industrial organization economics literature. See especially the following works: Bain, *Barriers to New Competition;* M. Mann, "Seller Concentration, Barriers to Entry and Rates of Return in 30 Industries," *Review of Economics and Statistics* 48 (1966): 296–307; W. S. Comanor and T. A. Wilson, "Advertising, Market Structure and Performance," *Review of Economics and Statistics* 49 (1967): 423–440; Gilbert, "Mobility Barriers"; and K. Cool, L.-H. Roller, and B. Leleux, "The Relative Impact of Actual and Potential Rivalry on Firm Profitability in the Pharmaceutical Industry," *Strategic Management Journal* 20 (1999): 1–14.

[6]For a discussion of tacit agreements, see T. C. Schelling, *The Strategy of Conflict* (Cambridge, Mass.: Harvard University Press, 1960).

[7]M. Busse, "Firm Financial Condition and Airline Price Wars," *Rand Journal of Economics* 33 (2002): 298–318.

[8]For a review, see F. Karakaya, "Market Exit and Barriers to Exit: Theory and Practice," *Psychology and Marketing* 17 (2000): 651–668.

[9]P. Ghemawat, *Commitment: The Dynamics of Strategy* (Boston: Harvard Business School Press, 1991).

[10]A. S. Grove, *Only the Paranoid Survive* (New York: Doubleday, 1996).

[11]In standard microeconomic theory, the concept used for assessing the strength of substitutes and complements is the cross elasticity of demand.

[12]For details and further references, see Charles W. L. Hill, "Establishing a Standard: Competitive Strategy and Technology Standards in Winner Take All Industries," *Academy of Management Executive* 11 (1997): 7–25; and Shapiro and Varian, *Information Rules.*

[13]The development of strategic group theory has been a strong theme in the strategy literature. Important contributions include the following: R. E. Caves and Michael E. Porter, "From Entry Barriers to Mobility Barriers," *Quarterly Journal of Economics* (May 1977): 241–262; K. R. Harrigan, "An Application of Clustering for Strategic Group Analysis," *Strategic Management Journal* 6 (1985): 55–73; K. J. Hatten and D. E. Schendel, "Heterogeneity Within an Industry: Firm Conduct in the U.S. Brewing Industry, 1952–71," *Journal of Industrial Economics* 26 (1977): 97–113; Michael E. Porter, "The Structure Within Industries and Companies' Performance," *Review of Economics and Statistics* 61 (1979): 214–227. See also K. Cool and D. Schendel, "Performance Differences Among Strategic Group Members," *Strategic Management Journal* 9 (1988): 207–233; A. Nair and S. Kotha, "Does Group Membership Matter? Evidence from the Japanese Steel Industry," *Strategic Management Journal* 20 (2001): 221–235; and G. McNamara, D. L. Deephouse, and R. A. Luce, "Competitive Positioning Within and Across a Strategic Group Structure,"*Strategic Management Journal* 24 (2003): 161–180.

[14]For details on the strategic group structure in the pharmaceutical industry, see K. Cool and I. Dierickx, "Rivalry, Strategic Groups, and Firm Profitability," *Strategic Management Journal* 14 (1993): 47–59.

[15]Charles W. Hofer argued that life-cycle considerations may be the most important contingency when formulating business strategy. See Hofer, "Towards a Contingency Theory of Business Strategy," *Academy of Management Journal* 18 (1975): 784–810. There is empirical evidence to support this view. See C. R. Anderson and C. P. Zeithaml, "Stages of the Product Life Cycle, Business Strategy, and Business Performance," *Academy of Management Journal* 27 (1984): 5–24; and D. C. Hambrick and D. Lei, "Towards an Empirical Prioritization

of Contingency Variables for Business Strategy," *Academy of Management Journal* 28 (1985): 763–788. See also G. Miles, C. C. Snow, and M. P. Sharfman, "Industry Variety and Performance," *Strategic Management Journal* 14 (1993): 163–177; G. K. Deans, F. Kroeger, and S. Zeisel, "The Consolidation Curve," *Harvard Business Review* 80 (December 2002): 2–3.

[16]The characteristics of declining industries have been summarized by K. R. Harrigan, "Strategy Formulation in Declining Industries," *Academy of Management Review* 5 (1980): 599–604. See also J. Anand and H. Singh, "Asset Redeployment, Acquisitions and Corporate Strategy in Declining Industries," *Strategic Management Journal* 18 (1997): 99–118.

[17]Data from CTIA, a wireless industry association, www.ctia.org/advocacy/research/index.cfm/aid/10323.

[18]This perspective is associated with the Austrian school of economics, which goes back to Schumpeter. For a summary of this school and its implications for strategy, see R. Jacobson, "The Austrian School of Strategy," *Academy of Management Review* 17 (1992): 782–807; and C. W. L. Hill and D. Deeds, "The Importance of Industry Structure for the Determination of Industry Profitability: A Neo-Austrian Approach," *Journal of Management Studies* 33 (1996): 429–451.

[19]"A Tricky Business," *Economist,* June 30, 2001, pp. 55–56.

[20]D. F. Barnett and R. W. Crandall, *Up from the Ashes* (Washington, D.C.: Brookings Institution, 1986).

[21]M. E. Porter, *The Competitive Advantage of Nations* (New York: Free Press, 1990).

[22]The term *punctuated equilibrium* is borrowed from evolutionary biology. For a detailed explanation of the concept, see M. L. Tushman, W. H. Newman, and E. Romanelli, "Convergence and Upheaval: Managing the Unsteady Pace of Organizational Evolution," *California Management Review* 29:1 (1985): 29–44; C. J. G. Gersick, "Revolutionary Change Theories: A Multilevel Exploration of the Punctuated Equilibrium Paradigm," *Academy of Management Review* 16 (1991): 10–36; and R. Adner and D. A. Levinthal, "The Emergence of Emerging Technologies,"*California Management Review* 45 (Fall 2002): 50–65.

[23]A. J. Slywotzky, *Value Migration: How to Think Several Moves Ahead of the Competition* (Boston: Harvard Business School Press, 1996).

[24]Hill and Deeds, "Importance of Industry Structure."

[25]R. P. Rumelt, "How Much Does Industry Matter?" *Strategic Management Journal* 12 (1991): 167–185. See also A. J. Mauri and M. P. Michaels, "Firm and Industry Effects Within Strategic Management: An Empirical Examination," *Strategic Management Journal* 19 (1998): 211–219.

[26]See R. Schmalensee, "Inter-Industry Studies of Structure and Performance," in Schmalensee and Willig (eds.), *Handbook of Industrial Organization*. Similar results were found by A. N. McGahan and M. E. Porter, "How Much Does Industry Matter, Really?" *Strategic Management Journal* 18 (1997): 15–30.

[27]For example, see K. Cool and D. Schendel, "Strategic Group Formation and Performance: The Case of the U.S. Pharmaceutical Industry, 1932–1992," *Management Science* (September 1987): 1102–1124.

[28]See M. Gort and J. Klepper, "Time Paths in the Diffusion of Product Innovations," *Economic Journal* (September 1982): 630–653. Looking at the history of 46 products, Gort and Klepper found that the length of time before other companies entered the markets created by a few inventive companies declined from an average of 14.4 years for products introduced before 1930 to 4.9 years for those introduced after 1949.

[29]The phrase was originally coined by J. Schumpeter, *Capitalism, Socialism and Democracy* (London: Macmillan, 1950), p. 68.

[30]For a detailed discussion of the importance of the structure of law as a factor explaining economic change and growth, see D. C. North, *Institutions, Institutional Change, and Economic Performance* (Cambridge: Cambridge University Press, 1990).

3

Internal Analysis: Distinctive Competencies, Competitive Advantage, and Profitability

OPENING CASE

After reading this chapter you should be able to:

3-1 Discuss the source of competitive advantage

3-2 Identify and explore the role of efficiency, quality, innovation, and customer responsiveness in building and maintaining a competitive advantage

3-3 Explain the concept of the value chain

3-4 Understand the link between competitive advantage and profitability

3-5 Explain what impacts the durability of a company's competitive advantage

Verizon Wireless

Spencer Platt/Getty Images

Established in 2000 as a joint venture between Verizon Communications and Britain's Vodafone, over the last 12 years Verizon Wireless has emerged as the largest and consistently most profitable enterprise in the fiercely competitive U.S. wireless service market. Today the company has almost 100 million subscribers and a 35% market share.

One of the most significant facts about Verizon is that it has the lowest churn rate in the industry. Customer churn refers to the number of subscribers who leave a service within a given time period. Churn is important because it costs between $400 and $600 to acquire a customer (with phone subsidies accounting for a large chunk of that). It can take months just to recoup the fixed costs of a customer acquisition. If churn rates are high, profitability is eaten up by the costs of acquiring customers who do not stay long enough to provide a profit to the service provider.

The risk of churn increased significantly in the United States after November 2003, when the Federal Communications Commission (FCC) allowed wireless subscribers to take their numbers with them when they switched to a new service provider. Over the next few years Verizon Wireless emerged as a clear winner in the battle to limit customer defections. By mid-2006, Verizon's churn rate was 0.87% a month, implying that 10.4% of the company's customers were leaving the service each year. This was lower than the churn rate at its competitors. Verizon retained its churn advantage through 2012. In that year, its monthly churn rate was 0.84%, compared to a 0.97% churn rate for AT&T, 1.69% for Sprint, and 2.10% for T-Mobile. Verizon's low churn rate has enabled the company to grow its subscriber base faster than rivals, which allows the company to better achieve economies of scale by spreading the fixed costs of building a wireless network over a larger customer base.

The low customer churn at Verizon is due to a number of factors. First, it has the most extensive network in the United States, blanketing 95% of the nation. This means fewer dropped calls and dead zones as compared to its rivals. For years Verizon communicated its coverage and quality advantage to customers with its "Test Man" advertisements. In these ads, a Verizon Test Man wearing horn-rimmed glasses and a Verizon uniform wanders around remote spots in the nation asking on his Verizon cell phone, "Can you hear me now?" Verizon says that the Test Man was actually the personification of a crew of 50 Verizon employees who each drive some 100,000 miles annually in specially outfitted vehicles to test the reliability of Verizon's network.

Second, the company has invested aggressively in high-speed wireless networks, including 3G and now 4G LTE, enabling fast download rates on smartphones. Complementing this, Verizon has a high-speed fiber-optic backbone for transporting data between cell towers. In total, Verizon has invested some

$70 billion in its wireless and fiber optic network since 2000. For customers, this means a high-quality user experience when accessing data, such as streaming video, on their smartphones. To drive this advantage home, in 2011 Verizon started offering Apple's market-leading iPhone in addition to the full range of Android smartphones it was already offering (the iPhone was originally exclusive to AT&T).

To further reduce customer churn, Verizon has invested heavily in its customer care function. Verizon's automated software programs analyze the call habits of individual customers. Using that information, Verizon representatives will contact customers and suggest alternative plans that might better suit their needs. For example, Verizon might contact a customer and say, "We see that because of your heavy use of data, an alternative plan might make more sense for you and help reduce your monthly bills." The goal is to anticipate customer needs and proactively satisfy them, rather than have the customer take the initiative and possibly switch to another service provider.

Surveys by J.D. Power have repeatedly confirmed Verizon's advantages. An August 2012 J.D. Power study ranked Verizon best in the industry in terms of overall network performance. The ranking was based on a number of factors which included dropped calls, late text message notifications, Web connection errors, and slow download rates. Another J.D. Power study looked at customer care in three customer contact channels—telephone, walk-in (retail store), and online. Again, Verizon had the best score in the industry, reflecting faster service and greater satisfaction with the efficiency with which costumer service reps resolved problems.

Sources: R. Blackden, "Telecom's Giant Verizon Is Conquering America," *The Telegraph*, January 6, 2013; S. Woolley, "Do You Fear Me Now?", *Forbes*, November 10, 2003, pp. 78–80; A. Z. Cuneo, "Call Verizon Victorious," *Advertising Age*, March 24, 2004, pp. 3–5; M. Alleven, "Wheels of Churn," *Wireless Week*, September 1, 2006; J.D. Power, "2012 U.S. Wireless Customer Care Full-Service Performance Study," July 7, 2012; and J.D. Power, "2012 U.S. Wireless Network Quality Performance Study," August 23, 2012.

OVERVIEW

Why, within a particular industry or market, do some companies outperform others? What is the basis of their (sustained) competitive advantage? The Opening Case provides some clues.

Verizon has placed a lot of emphasis on building the highest-*quality* service in the business as measured by network coverage and download speeds. It has also been an *innovator*, rolling out the most technologically advanced 4G LTE network ahead of rivals. In addition, Verizon has successfully emphasized *customer responsiveness*. According to surveys by J.D. Power, the company has the best customer care function in the industry. The high quality of its service, coupled with excellent customer responsiveness, has enabled Verizon to drive down its churn rate, which in turn has lowered the company's costs, making it more *efficient*. As you will see in this chapter, efficiency, customer responsiveness, quality, and innovation are the building blocks of competitive advantage.

This chapter focuses on internal analysis, which is concerned with identifying the strengths and weaknesses of the company. Internal analysis, coupled with an analysis of the company's external environment, gives managers the information they need to choose the strategy and business model that will enable their company to attain a sustained competitive advantage. Internal analysis is a three-step process. First, managers must understand the process by which companies create value for customers and profit for the company. Managers must also understand the role of resources, capabilities, and distinctive competencies in this process. Second, they need to understand the importance of superior efficiency, innovation, quality, and customer responsiveness when creating value and generating high profitability. Third, they must be able to analyze the sources of their company's competitive advantage to identify what drives the profitability of their enterprise, and where opportunities for improvement might lie. In other words, they must be able to identify how the strengths of the enterprise boost its profitability and how any weaknesses result in lower profitability.

Three more critical issues in internal analysis are addressed in this chapter. First: What factors influence the durability of competitive advantage? Second: Why do successful companies sometimes lose their competitive advantage? Third: How can companies avoid competitive failure and sustain their competitive advantage over time?

After reading this chapter, you will understand the nature of competitive advantage and why managers need to perform internal analysis (just as they must conduct industry analysis) to achieve superior performance and profitability.

THE ROOTS OF COMPETITIVE ADVANTAGE

A company has a *competitive advantage* over its rivals when its profitability is greater than the average profitability of all companies in its industry. It has a *sustained competitive advantage* when it is able to maintain above-average profitability over a number of years (as Wal-Mart has done in the retail industry and Verizon has done in wireless service). The primary objective of strategy is to achieve a sustained competitive advantage, which in turn will result in superior profitability and profit growth. What are the sources of competitive advantage, and what is the link between strategy, competitive advantage, and profitability?

Distinctive Competencies

Competitive advantage is based upon distinctive competencies. **Distinctive competencies** are firm-specific strengths that allow a company to differentiate its products from those offered by rivals, and/or achieve substantially lower costs than its rivals. Verizon, for example, has a distinctive competence in customer care, which creates value for customers, helps to lower churn rates, and ultimately translates into higher costs (see the Opening case). Similarly, it can be argued that Toyota, which historically has been the stand-out performer in the automobile industry, has distinctive competencies in the development and operation of manufacturing processes (although the company has struggled somewhat since 2008). Toyota pioneered an entire range of manufacturing techniques, such as just-in-time inventory systems, self-managing teams, and reduced setup times for complex equipment. These competencies, collectively known as the "Toyota lean production system," helped the company attain superior efficiency and product quality as the basis of its competitive advantage in the global automobile industry.[1] Distinctive competencies arise from two complementary sources: resources and capabilities.[2]

Resources   **Resources** refer to the assets of a company. A company's resources can be divided into two types: tangible and intangible resources. **Tangible resources** are physical entities, such as land, buildings, manufacturing plants, equipment, inventory, and money. In the case of Verizon, its ubiquitous high-speed wireless network is a tangible resource. **Intangible resources** are nonphysical entities that are created by managers and other employees, such as brand names, the reputation of the company, the knowledge that employees have gained through experience, and the intellectual property of the company, including patents, copyrights, and trademarks.

Resources are particularly *valuable* when they enable a company to create strong demand for its products, and/or to lower its costs. Toyota's valuable *tangible resources* include the equipment associated with its lean production system, much of which has been engineered specifically by Toyota for exclusive use in its factories. These valuable tangible resources allow Toyota to lower its costs, relative to competitors. Similarly, Microsoft has a number of valuable *intangible resources*, including its brand name and the software code that comprises its Windows operating system. These valuable resources have historically allowed Microsoft to sell more of its products, relative to competitors.

Valuable resources are more likely to lead to a sustainable competitive advantage if they are *rare*, in the sense that competitors do not possess them, and difficult for rivals to imitate; that is, if there are *barriers to imitation* (we will discuss the source of barriers to imitation in more detail later in this chapter). For example, the software code underlying Windows is *rare* because only Microsoft has full access to it. The code is also difficult to imitate. A rival cannot simply copy the software code underlying Windows and sell a repackaged version of Windows because copyright law protects the code, and reproducing it is illegal.

Capabilities   **Capabilities** refer to a company's resource-coordinating skills and productive use. These skills reside in an organization's rules, routines, and procedures, that is, the style or manner through which it makes decisions and manages its internal processes to achieve organizational objectives.[3] More generally, a company's capabilities are the product of its organizational structure, processes, control systems, and hiring strategy. They specify how and where decisions are made within a company, the kind of behaviors the company rewards, and the company's cultural norms and values. (We will discuss how organizational

distinctive competencies
Firm-specific strengths that allow a company to differentiate its products and/or achieve substantially lower costs to achieve a competitive advantage.

resources
Assets of a company.

tangible resources
Physical entities, such as land, buildings, equipment, inventory, and money.

intangible resources
Nonphysical entities such as brand names, company reputation, experiential knowledge, and intellectual property, including patents, copyrights, and trademarks.

capabilities
A company's skills at coordinating its resources and putting them to productive use.

structure and control systems help a company obtain capabilities in Chapters 12 and 13.) Capabilities are intangible. They reside not in individuals, but in the way individuals interact, cooperate, and make decisions within the context of an organization.[4]

Like resources, capabilities are particularly valuable if they enable a company to create strong demand for its products, and/or to lower its costs. The competitive advantage of Southwest Airlines is based largely upon its capability to select, motivate, and manage its workforce in such a way that leads to high employee productivity and lower costs. As with resources, valuable capabilities are also more likely to lead to a sustainable competitive advantage if they are both *rare* and protected from copying by *barriers to imitation.*

Resources, Capabilities, and Competencies   The distinction between resources and capabilities is critical to understanding what generates a distinctive competency. A company may have firm-specific and valuable resources, but unless it also has the capability to use those resources effectively, it may not be able to create a distinctive competency. Additionally, it is important to recognize that a company may not need firm-specific and valuable resources to establish a distinctive competency so long as it has capabilities that no other competitor possesses. For example, the steel mini-mill operator Nucor is widely acknowledged to be the most cost-efficient steel maker in the United States. Its distinctive competency in low-cost steel making does not come from any firm-specific and valuable resources. Nucor has the same resources (plant, equipment, skilled employees, knowhow) as many other mini-mill operators. What distinguishes Nucor is its unique capability to manage its resources in a highly productive way. Specifically, Nucor's structure, control systems, and culture promote efficiency at all levels within the company.

In sum, for a company to possess a distinctive competency, it must—at a minimum— have either (1) a firm-specific and valuable resource, and the capabilities (skills) necessary to take advantage of that resource, or (2) a firm-specific capability to manage resources (as exemplified by Nucor). A company's distinctive competency is strongest when it possesses both firm-specific and valuable resources and firm-specific capabilities to manage those resources.

The Role of Strategy   Figure 3.1 illustrates the relationship of a company's strategies, distinctive competencies, and competitive advantage. Distinctive competencies shape the strategies that the company pursues, which lead to competitive advantage and superior profitability. However, it is also very important to realize that the strategies a company adopts can build new resources and capabilities or strengthen the existing resources and capabilities of the company, thereby enhancing the distinctive competencies of the enterprise. Thus, the relationship between distinctive competencies and strategies is not a linear one; rather, it is a reciprocal one in which distinctive competencies shape strategies, and strategies help to build and create distinctive competencies.[5]

The history of the Walt Disney Company illustrates the way this process works. In the early 1980s, Disney suffered a string of poor financial years that culminated in a 1984 management shakeup when Michael Eisner was appointed CEO. Four years later, Disney's sales had increased from $1.66 billion to $3.75 billion, its net profits from $98 million to $570 million, and its stock market valuation from $1.8 billion to $10.3 billion. What brought about this transformation was the company's deliberate attempt to use its resources and capabilities more aggressively: Disney's enormous film library, its brand name, and its filmmaking skills, particularly in animation. Under Eisner, many old Disney classics were re-released, first in movie theaters and then on video, earning the company millions in the process. Then Eisner reintroduced the product that had originally made Disney famous:

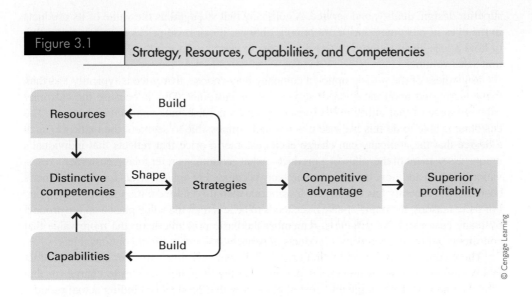

Figure 3.1   Strategy, Resources, Capabilities, and Competencies

© Cengage Learning

the full-length animated feature. Putting together its brand name and in-house animation capabilities, Disney produced a stream of major box office hits, including *The Little Mermaid, Beauty and the Beast, Aladdin, Pocahontas,* and *The Lion King.* Disney also started a cable television channel, the Disney Channel, to use this library and capitalize on the company's brand name. In other words, Disney's existing resources and capabilities shaped its strategies.

Through his choice of strategies, Eisner also developed new competencies in different parts of the business. In the filmmaking arm of Disney, for example, Eisner created a new low-cost film division under the Touchstone label, and the company had a string of low-budget box-office hits. It entered into a long-term agreement with the computer animation company Pixar to develop a competency in computer-generated animated films. This strategic collaboration produced several hits, including *Toy Story* and *Monsters, Inc.* (in 2004 Disney acquired Pixar). In sum, Disney's transformation was based not only on strategies that took advantage of the company's existing resources and capabilities, but also on strategies that built new resources and capabilities, such as those that underlie the company's competency in computer-generated animated films.

Competitive Advantage, Value Creation, and Profitability

Competitive advantage leads to superior profitability. At the most basic level, a company's profitability depends on three factors: (1) the value customers place on the company's products, (2) the price that a company charges for its products, and (3) the costs of creating those products. The value customers place on a product reflects the *utility* they get from a product, or the happiness or satisfaction gained from consuming or owning the product. Value must be distinguished from price. Value is something that customers receive from a product. It is a function of the attributes of the product, such as its performance, design, quality, and point-of-sale and after-sale service. For example, most customers would place a much higher value on a top-end Lexus car from Toyota than on a low-end basic economy car from Kia, precisely because they perceive Lexus to have better performance and superior design, quality, and service. A company that strengthens the value of its products in the eyes of customers has more pricing options: it can raise prices to reflect that value or hold prices lower to induce more customers to purchase its products, thereby expanding unit sales volume.

Regardless of the pricing option a company may choose, that price is typically less than the value placed upon the good or service by the customer. This is because the customer captures some of that utility in the form of what economists call a *consumer surplus*.[6] The customer is able to do this because it is normally impossible to segment the market to such a degree that the company can charge each customer a price that reflects that individual's unique assessment of the value of a product—what economists refer to as a customer's reservation price. In addition, because the company is competing against rivals for the customer's business, it frequently has to charge a lower price than it could were it a monopoly supplier. For these reasons, the point-of-sale price tends to be less than the value placed on the product by many customers. Nevertheless, remember the basic principle here: the more value that consumers get from a company's products or services, the more pricing options it has.

These concepts are illustrated in Figure 3.2: V is the *average* value per unit of a product to a customer, P is the average price per unit that the company decides to charge for that product, and C is the average unit cost of producing that product (including actual production costs and the cost of capital investments in production systems). The company's average profit per unit is equal to $P - C$, and the consumer surplus is equal to $V - P$. In other words, $V - P$ is a measure of the value the consumer captures, and $P - C$ is a measure of the value the company captures. The company makes a profit so long as P is more than C, and its profitability will be greater the lower C is relative to P. Bear in mind that the difference between V and P is in part determined by the intensity of competitive pressure in the marketplace; the lower the competitive pressure's intensity, the higher the price that can be charged relative to V, but the difference between V and P is also determined by the company's pricing choice.[7] As we shall see, a company may choose to keep prices low relative to volume because lower prices enable the company to sell more products, attain scale economies, and boost its profit margin by lowering C relative to P.

Also, note that the value created by a company is measured by the difference between the value or utility a consumer gets from the product (V) and the costs of production (C),

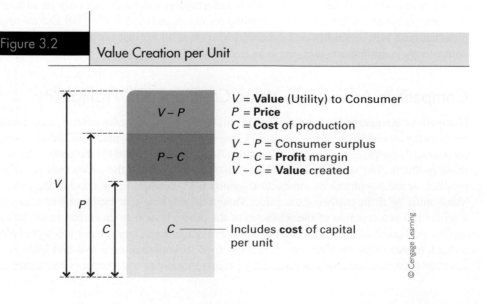

| Figure 3.2 | Value Creation per Unit |

V = **Value** (Utility) to Consumer
P = **Price**
C = **Cost** of production

$V - P$ = Consumer surplus
$P - C$ = **Profit** margin
$V - C$ = **Value** created

C —— Includes **cost** of capital per unit

© Cengage Learning

that is, $V - C$. A company creates value by converting factors of production that cost C into a product from which customers receive a value of V. A company can create more value for its customers by lowering C or making the product more attractive through superior design, performance, quality, service, and other factors. When customers assign a greater value to the product (V increases), they are willing to pay a higher price (P increases). This discussion suggests that a company has a competitive advantage and high profitability when it creates more value for its customers than rivals.[8]

The company's pricing options are captured in Figure 3.3. Suppose a company's current pricing option is the one pictured in the middle column of Figure 3.3. Imagine that the company decides to pursue strategies to increase the utility of its product offering from V to V^* in order to boost its profitability. Increasing value initially raises production costs because the company must spend money in order to increase product performance, quality, service, and other factors. Now there are two different pricing options that the company can pursue. Option 1 is to raise prices to reflect the higher value: the company raises prices more than its costs increase, and profit per unit $(P - C)$ increases. Option 2 involves a very different set of choices: the company lowers prices in order to expand unit volume. Generally, customers recognize that they are getting a great bargain because the price is now much lower than the value (the consumer surplus has increased), so they rush out to buy more (demand has increased). As unit volume expands due to increased demand, the company is able to realize scale economies and reduce its average unit costs. Although creating the extra value initially costs more, and although margins are initially compressed by aggressive pricing, ultimately profit margins widen because the average per-unit cost of production falls as volume increases and scale economies are attained.

Managers must understand the dynamic relationships among value, pricing, demand, and costs in order to make decisions that will maximize competitive advantage and profitability. Option 2 in Figure 3.3, for example, may not be a viable strategy if demand did

---

Figure 3.3   **Value Creation and Pricing Options**

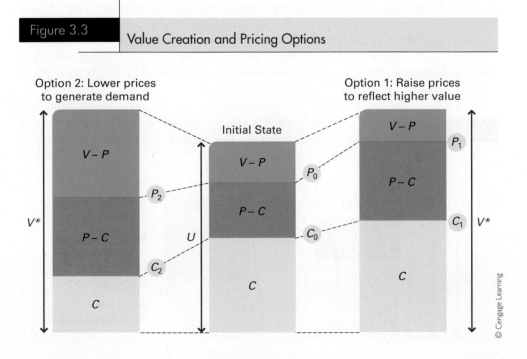

© Cengage Learning

not increase rapidly with lower prices, or if few economies of scale will result by increasing volume. Managers must understand how value creation and pricing decisions affect demand, as well as how unit costs change with increases in volume. In other words, they must have a good grasp of the demand for the company's product and its cost structure at different levels of output if they are to make decisions that maximize profitability.

Consider the automobile industry. According to a 2008 study by Oliver Wyman, Toyota made $922 in profit on every vehicle it manufactured in North America in 2007. General Motors (GM), in contrast, lost $729 on every vehicle it made.[9] What accounted for the difference? First, Toyota had the best reputation for quality in the industry. According to annual surveys issued by J.D. Power and Associates, Toyota consistently topped the list in terms of quality, whereas GM cars were—at best—in the middle of the pack. Higher quality equaled a higher value and allowed Toyota to charge 5 to 10% higher prices than General Motors for equivalent cars. Second, Toyota had a lower cost per vehicle than General Motors, in part because of its superior labor productivity. For example, in Toyota's North American plants, it took an average of 30.37 employee hours to build one car, compared to 32.29 at GM plants in North America. The 1.94-hour productivity advantage meant lower total labor costs for Toyota, and hence a lower overall cost structure. Therefore, as summarized in Figure 3.4, Toyota's advantage over GM came from greater value (V), which allowed the company to charge a higher price (P) for its cars, and from a lower cost structure (C), which taken together implies greater profitability per vehicle ($P - C$).

Toyota's pricing decisions are guided by its managers' understanding of the relationships between utility, prices, demand, and costs. Given its ability to build more utility into its products, Toyota could have charged even higher prices than those illustrated in Figure 3.4, but that might have led to lower sales volume, fewer scale economies, higher unit costs, and lower profit margins. Toyota's managers sought to find the pricing option that enabled the company to maximize its profits given their assessment of demand for its products and its cost function. Thus, to create superior value, a company does not need to tout the lowest cost structure in an industry, nor create the product with the highest value in the eyes of customers. All that is necessary is that the gap between perceived value (V) and costs of production (C) is greater than the gap attained by competitors.

Note that Toyota has differentiated itself from General Motors by its superior quality, which allows it to charge higher prices, and its superior productivity translates into a lower cost structure. Thus, its competitive advantage over General Motors is the result of

| Figure 3.4 | Comparing Toyota and General Motors |

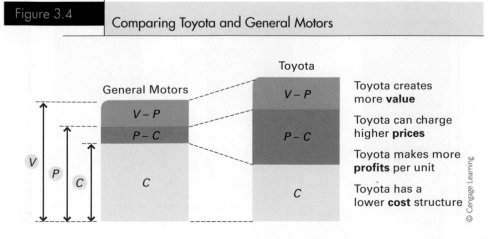

strategies that have led to distinctive competencies, resulting in greater differentiation and a lower cost structure.

Indeed, at the heart of any company's business model is the combination of congruent strategies aimed at creating distinctive competencies that (1) differentiate its products in some way so that its consumers derive more value from them, which gives the company more pricing options, and (2) result in a lower cost structure, which also gives it a broader range of pricing choices.[10] Achieving superior profitability and a sustained competitive advantage requires the right choices regarding utility through differentiation and pricing (given the demand conditions in the company's market), and the company's cost structure at different levels of output. This issue is addressed in detail in the following chapters.

THE VALUE CHAIN

All of the functions of a company—such as production, marketing, product development, service, information systems, materials management, and human resources—have a role in lowering the cost structure and increasing the perceived value of products through differentiation. As the first step in examining this concept, consider the value chain, which is illustrated in Figure 3.5.[11] The term **value chain** refers to the idea that a company is a chain of activities that transforms inputs into outputs that customers value. The transformation process involves both primary activities and support activities that add value to the product.

value chain
The idea that a company is a chain of activities that transforms inputs into outputs that customers value.

Primary Activities

Primary activities include the design, creation, and delivery of the product, the product's marketing, and its support and after-sales service. In the value chain illustrated in Figure 3.5, the primary activities are broken down into four functions: research and development, production, marketing and sales, and customer service.

primary activities
Activities related to the design, creation, and delivery of the product, its marketing, and its support and after-sales service.

Figure 3.5	The Value Chain

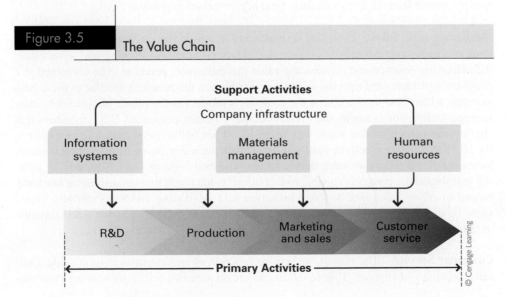

Support Activities

Company infrastructure

Information systems

Materials management

Human resources

R&D

Production

Marketing and sales

Customer service

Primary Activities

© Cengage Learning

Research and Development   Research and development (R&D) refers to the design of products and production processes. Although we think of R&D as being associated with the design of physical products and production processes in manufacturing enterprises, many service companies also undertake R&D. For example, banks compete with each other by developing new financial products and new ways of delivering those products to customers. Online banking and smart debit cards are two examples of the fruits of new-product development in the banking industry. Earlier examples of innovation in the banking industry included ATM machines, credit cards, and debit cards.

By creating superior product design, R&D can increase the functionality of products, making them more attractive to customers, and thereby adding value. Alternatively, the work of R&D may result in more efficient production processes, thereby lowering production costs. Either way, the R&D function can help to lower costs or raise the utility of a product and permit a company to charge higher prices. At Intel, for example, R&D creates value by developing ever more powerful microprocessors and helping to pioneer ever-more-efficient manufacturing processes (in conjunction with equipment suppliers).

It is important to emphasize that R&D is not just about enhancing the features and functions of a product, it is also about the elegance of a product's design, which can create an impression of superior value in the minds of consumers. For example, part of Apple's success with the iPhone has been based upon the elegance and appeal of the iPhone design, which has turned a piece of electronic equipment into a fashion accessory. For another example of how design elegance can create value, see Strategy in Action 3.1, which discusses value creation at the fashion house Burberry.

Production   Production refers to the creation process of a good or service. For physical products, this generally means manufacturing. For services such as banking or retail operations, "production" typically takes place while the service is delivered to the customer, as when a bank makes a loan to a customer. By performing its activities efficiently, the production function of a company helps to lower its cost structure. For example, the efficient production operations of Honda and Toyota help those automobile companies achieve higher profitability relative to competitors such as General Motors. The production function can also perform its activities in a way that is consistent with high product quality, which leads to differentiation (and higher value) and lower costs.

Marketing and Sales   There are several ways in which the marketing and sales functions of a company can help to create value. Through brand positioning and advertising, the marketing function can increase the value that customers perceive to be contained in a company's product (and thus the utility they attribute to the product). Insofar as these help to create a favorable impression of the company's product in the minds of customers, they increase utility. For example, the French company Perrier persuaded U.S. customers that slightly carbonated bottled water was worth $1.50 per bottle rather than a price closer to the $0.50 that it cost to collect, bottle, and distribute the water. Perrier's marketing function increased the perception of value that customers ascribed to the product. Similarly, by helping to re-brand the company and its product offering, the marketing department at Burberry helped to create value (see Strategy in Action 3.1). Marketing and sales can also create value by discovering customer needs and communicating them back to the R&D function of the company, which can then design products that better match those needs.

Customer Service   The role of the service function of an enterprise is to provide after-sales service and support. This function can create superior utility by solving customer

3.1 STRATEGY IN ACTION

Value Creation at Burberry

© iStockPhoto.com/Tom Nulens

When Rose Marie Bravo, the highly regarded president of Saks Fifth Avenue, announced in 1997 that she was leaving to become CEO of ailing British fashion house Burberry, people thought she was crazy. Burberry, best known as a designer of raincoats with a trademark tartan linings, had been described as an outdated, stuffy business with a fashion cachet of almost zero. When Bravo stepped down in 2006, she was heralded in Britain and the United States as one of the world's best managers. In her tenure at Burberry, she had engineered a remarkable turnaround, leading a transformation of Burberry into what one commentator called an "achingly hip" high-end fashion brand whose famous tartan bedecks everything from raincoats and bikinis to handbags and luggage in a riot of color from pink to blue to purple. In less than a decade, Burberry had become one of the most valuable luxury fashion brands in the world.

When asked how she achieved the transformation, Bravo explains that there was hidden value in the brand, which was unleashed by constant creativity and innovation. Bravo hired world-class designers to redesign Burberry's tired fashion line and bought in

Christopher Bailey, one of the very best, to lead the design team. The marketing department worked closely with advertisers to develop hip ads that would appeal to a younger, well-heeled audience. The ads featured supermodel Kate Moss promoting the line, and Burberry hired a top fashion photographer to shoot Moss in Burberry. Burberry exercised tight control over distribution, pulling its products from stores whose image was not consistent with the Burberry brand, and expanding its own chain of Burberry stores.

Bravo also noted that "creativity doesn't just come from designers......ideas can come from the sales floor, the marketing department, even from accountants, believe it or not. People at whatever level they are working have a point of view and have something to say that is worth listening to." Bravo emphasized the importance of teamwork: "One of the things I think people overlook is the quality of the team. It isn't one person, and it isn't two people. It is a whole group of people—a team that works cohesively toward a goal—that makes something happen or not." She notes that her job is to build the team and then motivate the team, "keeping them on track, making sure that they are following the vision."

Sources: Quotes from S. Beatty, "Bass Talk: Plotting Plaid's Future," *Wall Street Journal*, September 9, 2004, p. B1. Also see C. M. Moore and G. Birtwistle, "The Burberry Business Model," *International Journal of Retail and Distribution Management* 32 (2004): 412–422; and M. Dickson, "Bravo's Legacy in Transforming Burberry," *Financial Times*, October 6, 2005, p. 22.

problems and supporting customers after they have purchased the product. For example, Caterpillar, the U.S.-based manufacturer of heavy-earthmoving equipment, can ship spare parts to any location in the world within 24 hours, thereby minimizing the amount of downtime its customers have to face if their Caterpillar equipment malfunctions. This is an extremely valuable support capability in an industry where downtime is very expensive. The extent of customer support has helped to increase the utility that customers associate with Caterpillar products, and therefore the price that Caterpillar can charge for its products.

Support Activities

The **support activities** of the value chain provide inputs that allow the primary activities to take place. These activities are broken down into four functions: materials management (or logistics), human resources, information systems, and company infrastructure (see Figure 3.5).

support activities
Activities of the value chain that provide inputs that allow the primary activities to take place.

Materials Management (Logistics)   The materials-management (or logistics) function controls the transmission of physical materials through the value chain, from procurement through production and into distribution. The efficiency with which this is carried out can significantly lower cost, thereby creating more profit. Dell Inc. has a very efficient materials-management process. By tightly controlling the flow of component parts from its suppliers to its assembly plants, and into the hands of consumers, Dell has dramatically reduced its inventory holding costs. Lower inventories equate to lower costs, and hence greater profitability. Another company that has benefited from very efficient materials management, the Spanish fashion company Zara, is discussed in Strategy in Action 3.2.

Human Resources   There are numerous ways in which the human resource function can help an enterprise to create more value. This function ensures that the company

3.2 STRATEGY IN ACTION

© iStockPhoto.com/Tom Nulens

Competitive Advantage at Zara

The fashion retailer Zara is one of Spain's fastest-growing and most successful companies, with sales of some $10 billion and a network of 2,800 stores in 64 countries. Zara's competitive advantage centers around one thing: speed. Whereas it takes most fashion houses 6 to 9 months to go from design to having merchandise delivered to a store, Zara can complete the entire process in just 5 weeks. This rapid response time enables Zara to quickly respond to changing fashion trends.

Zara achieves this by breaking many of the rules of operation in the fashion business. Whereas most fashion houses outsource production, Zara has its own factories and keeps approximately half of its production in-house. Zara also has its own designers and own stores. Its designers are in constant contact with the stores, to track what is selling on a real-time basis through information systems, and talk to store managers once a week to get their subjective impressions of what is "hot." This information supplements data gathered from other sources, such as fashion shows.

Drawing on this information, Zara's designers create approximately 40,000 new designs a year from which 10,000 are selected for production. Zara then purchases basic textiles from global suppliers, but performs capital-intensive production activities in its own factories. These factories use computer-controlled machinery to cut pieces for garments. Zara does not produce in large volumes to attain economies of scale; instead it produces in small lots. Labor-intensive activities, such as sewing, are performed by subcontractors located close to Zara's factories. Zara makes a practice of retaining more production capacity than necessary, so that if a new fashion trend emerges, it can quickly respond by designing garments and ramping-up production.

Once a garment has been made, it is delivered to one of Zara's own warehouses, and then shipped to its own stores once a week. Zara deliberately underproduces products, supplying small batches of products in hot demand before quickly shifting to the next fashion trend. Often its merchandise sells out quickly. The empty shelves in Zara stores create a scarcity value—which helps to generate demand. Customers quickly snap up products they like because they know these styles may soon be out of stock, and never produced again.

As a result of this strategy, which is supported by competencies in design, information systems, and logistics management, Zara carries fewer inventories than competitors (Zara's inventory equals about 10% of sales, compared to 15% at rival stores such as The Gap and Benetton). This means fewer price reductions to move products that haven't sold, and higher profit margins.

Sources: "Shining Examples," *The Economist: A Survey of Logistics*, June 17, 2006, pp. 4–6; K. Capell et al., "Fashion Conquistador," *Business Week*, September 4, 2006, pp. 38–39; and K. Ferdows et al., "Rapid Fire Fulfillment," *Harvard Business Review* 82 (November 2004): 101–107.

has the right combination of skilled people to perform its value creation activities effectively. It is also the job of the human resource function to ensure that people are adequately trained, motivated, and compensated to perform their value creation tasks. If the human resources are functioning well, employee productivity rises (which lowers costs) and customer service improves (which raises utility), thereby enabling the company to create more value.

Information Systems   Information systems are, primarily, the electronic systems for managing inventory, tracking sales, pricing products, selling products, dealing with customer service inquiries, and so on. Information systems, when coupled with the communications features of the Internet, are holding out the promise of being able to improve the efficiency and effectiveness with which a company manages its other value creation activities. Again, Dell uses Web-based information systems to efficiently manage its global logistics network and increase inventory turnover. World-class information systems are also an aspect of Zara's competitive advantage (see Strategy in Action 3.2).

Company Infrastructure   Company infrastructure is the companywide context within which all the other value creation activities take place: the organizational structure, control systems, and company culture. Because top management can exert considerable influence upon shaping these aspects of a company, top management should also be viewed as part of the infrastructure of a company. Indeed, through strong leadership, top management can shape the infrastructure of a company and, through that, the performance of all other value creation activities that take place within it. A good example of this process is given in Strategy in Action 3.1, which looks at how Rose Marie Bravo helped to engineer a turnaround at Burberry.

THE BUILDING BLOCKS OF COMPETITIVE ADVANTAGE

Four factors help a company to build and sustain competitive advantage: superior efficiency, quality, innovation, and customer responsiveness. Each of these factors is the product of a company's distinctive competencies. Indeed, in a very real sense they are "generic" distinctive competencies. These generic competencies allow a company to (1) differentiate its product offering, and hence offer more value to its customers, and (2) lower its cost structure (see Figure 3.6). These factors can be considered generic distinctive competencies because any company, regardless of its industry or the products or services it produces, can pursue these competencies. Although each one is discussed sequentially in the following discussion, all are highly interrelated, and the important ways these competencies affect each other should be noted. For example, superior quality can lead to superior efficiency, and innovation can enhance efficiency, quality, and responsiveness to customers.

Efficiency

In one sense, a business is simply a device for transforming inputs into outputs. Inputs are basic factors of production such as labor, land, capital, management, and technological knowhow. Outputs are the goods and services that the business produces. The simplest

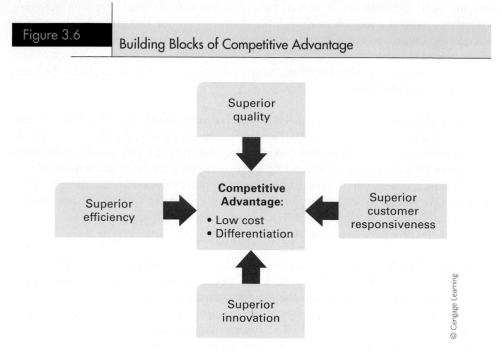

Figure 3.6   Building Blocks of Competitive Advantage

Superior quality

Superior efficiency

Competitive Advantage:
- Low cost
- Differentiation

Superior customer responsiveness

Superior innovation

© Cengage Learning

measure of efficiency is the quantity of inputs that it takes to produce a given output, that is, efficiency = outputs/inputs. The more efficient a company is, the fewer inputs required to produce a particular output, and the lower its costs will be.

One common measure of efficiency is employee productivity. **Employee productivity** refers to the output produced per employee. For example, if it takes General Motors 30 hours of employee time to assemble a car, and it takes Ford 25 hours, we can say that Ford has higher employee productivity than GM, and is more efficient. As long as other factors are equal, such as wage rates, we can assume from this information that Ford will have a lower cost structure than GM. Thus, employee productivity helps a company attain a competitive advantage through a lower cost structure.

employee productivity

The output produced per employee.

Quality as Excellence and Reliability

A product can be thought of as a bundle of attributes.[12] The attributes of many physical products include their form, features, performance, durability, reliability, style, and design.[13] A product is said to have *superior quality* when customers perceive that its attributes provide them with higher utility than the attributes of products sold by rivals. For example, a Rolex watch has attributes—such as design, styling, performance, and reliability—that customers perceive as being superior to the same attributes in many other watches. Thus, we can refer to a Rolex as a high-quality product: Rolex has differentiated its watches by these attributes.

When customers evaluate the quality of a product, they commonly measure it against two kinds of attributes: those related to *quality as excellence* and those related to *quality as reliability*. From a quality-as-excellence perspective, the important attributes are things such as a product's design and styling, its aesthetic appeal, its features and functions, the level of service associated with the delivery of the product, and so on. For example,

---

Figure 3.7 | A Quality Map for Wireless Service

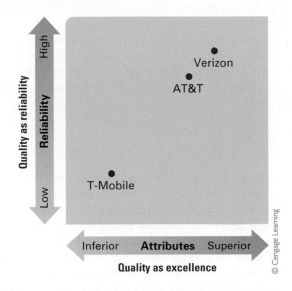

© Cengage Learning

customers can purchase a pair of imitation leather boots for $20 from Wal-Mart, or they can buy a handmade pair of butter-soft leather boots from Nordstrom for $500. The boots from Nordstrom will have far superior styling, feel more comfortable, and look much better than those from Wal-Mart. The value consumers will get from the Nordstrom boots will in all probability be much greater than the value derived from the Wal-Mart boots, but of course, they will have to pay far more for them. That is the point: when excellence is built into a product offering, consumers must pay more to own or consume it.

With regard to quality as reliability, a product can be said to be reliable when it consistently performs the function it was designed for, performs it well, and rarely, if ever, breaks down. As with excellence, reliability increases the value (utility) a consumer gets from a product, and thus the price the company can charge for that product and/or demand for the product.

The position of a product against two dimensions, reliability and other attributes, can be plotted on a figure similar to Figure 3.7. For example, as we saw in the Opening Case, Verizon has the most reliable network in the wireless service industry as measured by factors such as coverage, number of dropped calls, dead zones, and so on. Verizon also has the best ratings when it comes to excellence, as measured by download speeds, customer care, and the like. According to J.D. Power surveys, T-Mobile has the worst position in the industry as measured by reliability and excellence.

The concept of quality applies whether we are talking about Toyota automobiles, clothes designed and sold by Zara, Verizon's wireless service, the customer service department of Citibank, or the ability of airlines to arrive on time. Quality is just as relevant to services as it is to goods.[14] The impact of high product quality on competitive advantage is twofold.[15] First, providing high-quality products increases the value (utility) those products provide to customers, which gives the company the option of charging a higher price for the products. In the automobile industry, for example, Toyota has historically been able to charge a higher price for its cars because of the higher quality of its products.

Second, greater efficiency and lower unit costs associated with reliable products of high quality impact competitive advantage. When products are reliable, less employee time is wasted making defective products, or providing substandard services, and less time has to be spent fixing mistakes—which means higher employee productivity and lower unit costs. Thus, high product quality not only enables a company to differentiate its product from that of rivals, but, if the product is reliable, it also lowers costs.

The importance of reliability in building competitive advantage has increased dramatically over the past 20 years. The emphasis many companies place on reliability is so crucial to achieving high product reliability that it can no longer be viewed as just one way of gaining a competitive advantage. In many industries, it has become an absolute imperative for a company's survival.

Innovation

product innovation

Development of products that are new to the world or have superior attributes to existing products.

process innovation

Development of a new process for producing products and delivering them to customers.

Innovation refers to the act of creating new products or processes. There are two main types of innovation: product innovation and process innovation. **Product innovation** is the development of products that are new to the world or have superior attributes to existing products. Examples are Intel's invention of the microprocessor in the early 1970s, Cisco's development of the router for routing data over the Internet in the mid-1980s, and Apple's development of the iPod, iPhone, and iPad in the 2000s. **Process innovation** is the development of a new process for producing products and delivering them to customers. Examples include Toyota, which developed a range of new techniques collectively known as the "Toyota lean production system" for making automobiles: just-in-time inventory systems, self-managing teams, and reduced setup times for complex equipment.

Product innovation creates value by creating new products, or enhanced versions of existing products, that customers perceive as having more value, thus increasing the company's pricing options. Process innovation often allows a company to create more value by lowering production costs. Toyota's lean production system, for example, helped to boost employee productivity, thus giving Toyota a cost-based competitive advantage.[16] Similarly, Staples dramatically lowered the cost of selling office supplies by applying the supermarket business model to retail office supplies. Staples passed on some of this cost savings to customers in the form of lower prices, which enabled the company to increase its market share rapidly.

In the long run, innovation of products and processes is perhaps the most important building block of competitive advantage.[17] Competition can be viewed as a process driven by innovations. Although not all innovations succeed, those that do can be a major source of competitive advantage because, by definition, they give a company something unique—something its competitors lack (at least until they imitate the innovation). Uniqueness can allow a company to differentiate itself from its rivals and charge a premium price for its product, or, in the case of many process innovations, reduce its unit costs far below those of competitors.

Customer Responsiveness

To achieve superior responsiveness to customers, a company must be able to do a better job than competitors of identifying and satisfying its customers' needs. Customers will then attribute more value to its products, creating a competitive advantage based on differentiation. Improving the quality of a company's product offering is consistent with achieving responsiveness, as is developing new products with features that existing products lack. In other words, achieving superior quality and innovation is integral to achieving superior responsiveness to customers.

Another factor that stands out in any discussion of responsiveness to customers is the need to customize goods and services to the unique demands of individual customers or customer groups. For example, the proliferation of soft drinks and beers can be viewed partly as a response to this trend.

An aspect of responsiveness to customers that has drawn increasing attention is **customer response time**: the time that it takes for a good to be delivered or a service to be performed.[18] For a manufacturer of machinery, response time is the time it takes to fill customer orders. For a bank, it is the time it takes to process a loan, or that a customer must stand in line to wait for a free teller. For a supermarket, it is the time that customers must stand in checkout lines. For a fashion retailer, it is the time required to take a new product from design inception to placement in a retail store (see Strategy in Action 3.2 for a discussion of how the Spanish fashion retailer Zara minimizes this). Customer survey after customer survey has shown slow response time to be a major source of customer dissatisfaction.[19]

customer response time
Time that it takes for a good to be delivered or a service to be performed.

Other sources of enhanced responsiveness to customers are superior design, superior service, and superior after-sales service and support. All of these factors enhance responsiveness to customers and allow a company to differentiate itself from its less responsive competitors. In turn, differentiation enables a company to build brand loyalty and charge a premium price for its products. Consider how much more people are prepared to pay for next-day delivery of Express Mail, compared to delivery in 3 to 4 days. In 2012, a two-page letter sent by overnight Express Mail within the United States cost about $10, compared to $0.48 for regular mail. Thus, the price premium for express delivery (reduced response time) was $9.52, or a premium of 1983% over the regular price.

BUSINESS MODELS, THE VALUE CHAIN, AND GENERIC DISTINCTIVE COMPETENCIES

As noted in Chapter 1, a business model is a manager's conception, or gestalt, of how the various strategies that a firm pursues fit together into a congruent whole, enabling the firm to achieve a competitive advantage. More precisely, a business model represents the way in which managers configure the value chain of the firm through their choice of strategy. It includes the investments they make to support that configuration, so that they can build the distinctive competencies necessary to attain the efficiency, quality, innovation, and customer responsiveness required to support the firm's low-cost or differentiated position, thereby achieving a competitive advantage and generating superior profitability (see Figure 3.8).

For example, the primary strategic goal of Wal-Mart is to be the lowest-cost operator offering a wide display of general merchandise in the retail industry. Wal-Mart's business model involves offering general merchandise in a self-service supermarket type of setting. Wal-Mart's strategies flesh out this business model and help the company to attain its strategic goal. To reduce costs, Wal-Mart limits investments in the fittings and fixtures of its stores. One of the keys to generating sales and lowering costs in this setting

Figure 3.8   Competitive Advantage and the Value Creation Cycle

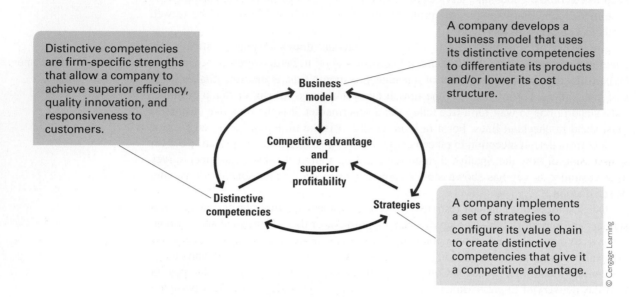

Distinctive competencies are firm-specific strengths that allow a company to achieve superior efficiency, quality innovation, and responsiveness to customers.

A company develops a business model that uses its distinctive competencies to differentiate its products and/or lower its cost structure.

A company implements a set of strategies to configure its value chain to create distinctive competencies that give it a competitive advantage.

© Cengage Learning

is rapid inventory turnover, which is achieved through strategic investments in logistics and information systems. Wal-Mart makes major investments in process innovation to improve the effectiveness of its information and logistics systems, which enables the company to respond to customer demands for low-priced goods, and to do so in a very efficient manner.

Wal-Mart's business model is very different from those of retailers such as Nordstrom. Nordstrom's business model is to offer high quality, and high-priced apparel, in a full-service and sophisticated setting. This implies differences in the way the value chain is configured. Nordstrom devotes far more attention to in-store customer service than Wal-Mart does, which implies significant investments in its salespeople. Moreover, Nordstrom invests far more in the furnishings and fittings for its stores compared to Wal-Mart, whose stores have a basic warehouse feel to them. Nordstrom recaptures the costs of this investment by charging higher prices for higher-quality merchandise. Although Wal-Mart and Nordstrom both sell apparel (Wal-Mart is in fact the biggest seller of apparel in the United States), their business models imply very different positions in the marketplace, and very different configurations of value chain activities and investments.

ANALYZING COMPETITIVE ADVANTAGE AND PROFITABILITY

If a company's managers are to perform a good internal analysis, they must be able to analyze the financial performance of their company, identifying how its strategies contribute (or not) to profitability. To identify strengths and weaknesses effectively, they must be able to compare, or benchmark, the performance of their company against competitors, as well as against the historic performance of the company itself. This will help them determine whether they are more or less profitable than competitors and whether the performance of the company has been improving or deteriorating through time; whether their company strategies are maximizing the value being created; whether their cost structure is out of alignment compared to competitors; and whether they are using the resources of the company to the greatest effect.

As we noted in Chapter 1, the key measure of a company's financial performance is its profitability, which captures the return that a company is generating on its investments. Although several different measures of profitability exist, such as return on assets and return on equity, many authorities on the measurement of profitability argue that return on invested capital (ROIC) is the best measure because "it focuses on the true operating performance of the company."[20] (However, return on assets is very similar in formulation to return on invested capital.)

ROIC is defined as net profit over invested capital, or ROIC = net profit/invested capital. Net profit is calculated by subtracting the total costs of operating the company from its total revenues (total revenues − total costs). *Net profit* is what is left over after the government takes its share in taxes. *Invested capital* is the amount that is invested in the operations of a company: property, plant, equipment, inventories, and other assets. Invested capital comes from two main sources: interest-bearing debt and shareholders' equity. Interest-bearing debt is money the company borrows from banks and those who purchase its bonds. Shareholders' equity is the money raised from selling shares to the public, plus earnings that the company has retained in prior years (and that are available to fund current investments). ROIC measures the effectiveness with which a company is using the capital funds that it has available for investment. As such, it is recognized to be an excellent measure of the value a company is creating.[21]

A company's ROIC can be algebraically divided into two major components: return on sales and capital turnover.[22] Specifically:

$$ROIC = \text{net profits/invested capital}$$
$$= \text{net profits/revenues} \times \text{revenues/invested capital}$$

where net profits/revenues is the return on sales, and revenues/invested capital is capital turnover. Return on sales measures how effectively the company converts revenues into profits. Capital turnover measures how effectively the company employs its invested capital to generate revenues. These two ratios can be further divided into some basic accounting ratios, as shown in Figure 3.9 (these ratios are defined in Table 3.1).[23]

Figure 3.9 notes that a company's managers can increase ROIC by pursuing strategies that increase the company's return on sales. To increase the company's return on sales, they can pursue strategies that reduce the cost of goods sold (COGS) for a given level of sales revenues (COGS/sales); reduce the level of spending on sales-force, marketing, general, and administrative expenses (SG&A) for a given level of sales revenues (SG&A/sales); and reduce R&D spending for a given level of sales revenues (R&D/sales). Alternatively, they can increase return on sales by pursuing strategies that increase sales revenues more than they increase the costs of the business, as measured by COGS, SG&A, and R&D expenses. That is, they can increase the return on sales by pursuing strategies that lower costs or increase value through differentiation, and thus allow the company to increase its prices more than its costs.

Figure 3.9 also tells us that a company's managers can boost the profitability of their company by obtaining greater sales revenues from their invested capital, thereby increasing capital turnover. They do this by pursuing strategies that reduce the amount of working capital, such as the amount of capital invested in inventories, needed to generate a given

Figure 3.9   Drivers of Profitability (ROIC)

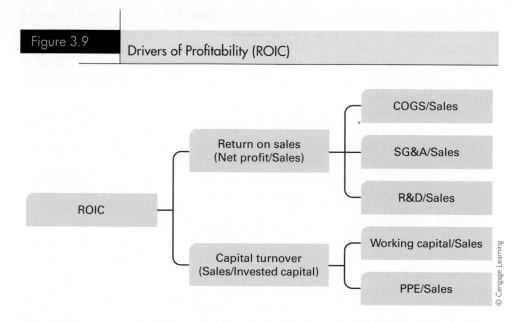

© Cengage Learning

Table 3.1   Definitions of Basic Accounting Terms

Term	Definition	Source
Cost of Goods Sold (COGS)	Total costs of producing products	Income statement
Sales, General, and Administrative Expenses (SG&A)	Costs associated with selling products and administering the company	Income statement
R&D Expenses (R&D)	Research and development expenditure	Income statement
Working Capital	The amount of money the company has to "work" with in the short term: Current assets – current liabilities	Balance sheet
Property, Plant, and Equipment (PPE)	The value of investments in the property, plant, and equipment that the company uses to manufacture and sell its products; also known as *fixed capital*	Balance sheet
Return on Sales (ROS)	Net profit expressed as a percentage of sales; measures how effectively the company converts revenues into profits	Ratio
Capital Turnover	Revenues divided by invested capital; measures how effectively the company uses its capital to generate revenues	Ratio
Return on Invested Capital (ROIC)	Net profit divided by invested capital	Ratio
Net Profit	Total revenues minus total costs before tax	Income statement
Invested Capital	Interest-bearing debt plus shareholders' equity	Balance sheet

level of sales (working capital/sales) and then pursuing strategies that reduce the amount of fixed capital that they have to invest in plant, property, and equipment (PPE) to generate a given level of sales (PPE/sales). That is, they pursue strategies that reduce the amount of capital that they need to generate every dollar of sales, and therefore their cost of capital. Recall that cost of capital is part of the cost structure of a company (see Figure 3.2), so strategies designed to increase capital turnover also lower the cost structure.

To see how these basic drivers of profitability help us to understand what is going on in a company and to identify its strengths and weaknesses, let us compare the financial performance of Wal-Mart against one of its more effective competitors, Target. This is done in the following Running Case.

FOCUS ON: Wal-Mart

Wal-Mart and Target

© iStockPhoto.com/caracterdesign

For the financial year ending January 2012, Wal-Mart earned a ROIC of 13.61%, and Target earned a respectable 10.01%. Wal-Mart's superior profitability can be understood in terms of the impact of its strategies on the various ratios identified in Figure 3.9. These are summarized in Figure 3.10.

Figure 3.10   Comparing Wal-Mart and Target, 2012

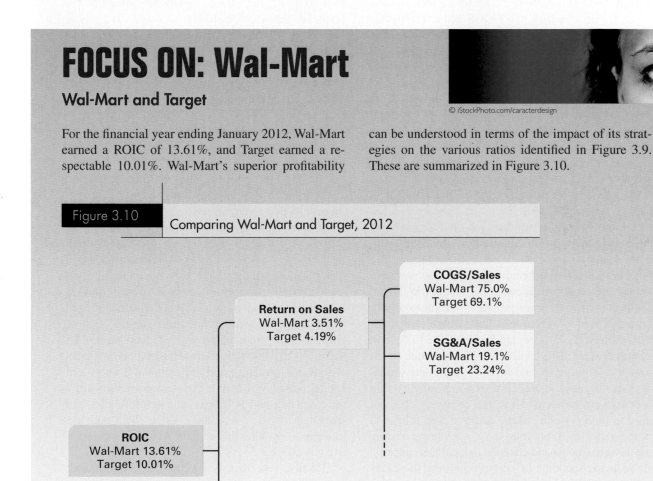

© Cengage Learning

(*continues*)

FOCUS ON: Wal-Mart

(continued)

© iStockPhoto.com/caracterdesign

First, note that Wal-Mart has a *lower* return on sales than Target. The main reason for this is that Wal-Mart's cost of goods sold (COGS) as a percentage of sales is higher than Target's (75% against 69.1%). For a retailer, the COGS reflects the price that Wal-Mart pays to its suppliers for merchandise. The lower COGS/sales ratio implies that Wal-Mart does not mark up prices much as Target—its profit margin on each item sold is lower. Consistent with its long-time strategic goal, Wal-Mart passes on the low prices it gets from suppliers to customers. Wal-Mart's higher COGS/sales ratio reflects its strategy of being the lowest-price retailer.

On the other hand, you will notice that Wal-Mart spends less on sales, general, and administrative (SG&A) expenses as a percentage of sales than Target (19.1% against 22.24%). There are three reasons for this. First, you will recall that Wal-Mart's early strategy was to focus on small towns that could only support one discounter. In small towns, the company does not have to advertise heavily because it is not competing against other discounters. Second, Wal-Mart has become such a powerful brand that the company does not need to advertise as heavily as its competitors, even when its stores are located close to them in suburban areas. Third, because Wal-Mart sticks to its low-price philosophy, and because the company manages its inventory so well, it does not usually have an overstocking problem. Thus, the company does not need to hold periodic sales—and nor does it have to bear the costs of promoting those sales (e.g., sending out advertisements and coupons in local newspapers). By reducing spending of sales promotions, these factors reduce Wal-Mart's SG&A/sales ratio.

In addition, Wal-Mart operates with a flat organization structure that has very few layers of management between the head office and store managers (the company has no regional headquarters). This reduces administrative expenses (which are a component of SG&A) and hence the SG&A/sales ratio. Wal-Mart can operate with such flat structure because its information systems allow the company's top managers to monitor and control individual stores directly, rather than rely upon intervening layers of subordinates to do that for them.

It is when we turn to consider the capital turnover side of the ROIC equation, however, that financial impact of Wal-Mart's competitive advantage in information systems and logistics becomes apparent. Wal-Mart generates $3.87 for every dollar of capital invested in the business, whereas Target generates $2.39 for every dollar of capital invested. Wal-Mart is much more efficient in its use of capital than Target. Why?

One reason is that Wal-Mart has a lower working capital/sales ratio than Target. In fact, Wal-Mart has a *negative* ratio (–1.64%), whereas Target has a positive ratio (3.10%). The negative working capital ratio implies that Wal-Mart does not need any capital to finance its day-to-day operations—in fact, Wal-Mart is using its suppliers' capital to finance its day-to-day operations! This is very unusual, but Wal-Mart is able to do this for two reasons. First, Wal-Mart is so powerful that it can demand and get very favorable payment terms from its suppliers. It does not have to pay for merchandise for 60 days after it is delivered. Second, Wal-Mart turns over its inventory so rapidly—around 8 times a year—that it typically sells merchandise *before* it has to pay its suppliers. Thus, suppliers finance Wal-Mart's inventory and the company's short-term capital needs! Wal-Mart's high inventory turnover is the result of strategic investments in information systems and logistics. It is these value chain activities more than any other that explain Wal-Mart's competitive advantage.

Finally, note that Wal-Mart has a significantly lower PPE/sales ratio than Target: 20.72% versus 41.72%. There are several explanations for this. First, many of Wal-Mart's stores are still located in small towns where land is cheap, whereas most of Target's stores are located in more expensive suburban locations. Thus, on average, Wal-Mart needs to spend less on a store than Target. Again, strategy has a clear impact on financial performance! Second, because Wal-Mart turns its inventory over so rapidly, it does not need to devote as much space in stores to storing

(*continues*)

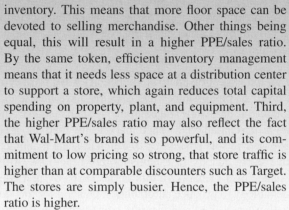

FOCUS ON: Wal-Mart

(continued)

© iStockPhoto.com/caracterdesign

inventory. This means that more floor space can be devoted to selling merchandise. Other things being equal, this will result in a higher PPE/sales ratio. By the same token, efficient inventory management means that it needs less space at a distribution center to support a store, which again reduces total capital spending on property, plant, and equipment. Third, the higher PPE/sales ratio may also reflect the fact that Wal-Mart's brand is so powerful, and its commitment to low pricing so strong, that store traffic is higher than at comparable discounters such as Target. The stores are simply busier. Hence, the PPE/sales ratio is higher.

In sum, Wal-Mart's high profitability is a function of its strategy, and the distinctive competencies that strategic investments have built over the years, particularly in the area of information systems and logistics. As in the Wal-Mart example, the methodology described in this section can be a very useful tool for analyzing why and how well a company is achieving and sustaining a competitive advantage. It highlights a company's strengths and weaknesses, showing where there is room for improvement and where a company is excelling. As such, it can drive strategy formulation. Moreover, the same methodology can be used to analyze the performance of competitors, and gain a greater understanding of their strengths and weakness, which can in turn inform strategy.

Source: Calculated by the author from 2010 company 10K statements.

THE DURABILITY OF COMPETITIVE ADVANTAGE

The next question we must address is how long a competitive advantage will last once it has been created. In other words: What is the durability of competitive advantage given that other companies are also seeking to develop distinctive competencies that will give them a competitive advantage? The answer depends on three factors: barriers to imitation, the capability of competitors, and the general dynamism of the industry environment.

Barriers to Imitation

A company with a competitive advantage will earn higher-than-average profits. These profits send a signal to rivals that the company has valuable, distinctive competencies allowing it to create superior value. Naturally, its competitors will try to identify and imitate that competency, and insofar as they are successful, ultimately their increased success may whittle away the company's superior profits.[24]

How quickly rivals will imitate a company's distinctive competencies is an important issue, because the speed of imitation has a bearing on the durability of a company's competitive advantage. Other factors being equal, the more rapidly competitors imitate a company's distinctive competencies, the less durable its competitive advantage will be, and the more important it is that the company endeavor to improve its competencies to stay one step ahead of imitators. It is important to stress at the outset that a competitor can imitate almost any distinctive competency. The critical issue is time: the longer it takes competitors to imitate a distinctive competency, the greater the opportunity the company has to build a strong market position and reputation with customers—which are then more difficult for competitors to attack. Moreover, the longer it takes to achieve an imitation, the greater the opportunity for the imitated company to improve on its competency or build other competencies, thereby remaining one step ahead of the competition.

Barriers to imitation are a primary determinant of the speed of imitation. Barriers to imitation are factors that make it difficult for a competitor to copy a company's distinctive competencies; the greater the barriers to imitation, the more sustainable a company's competitive advantage.[25] Barriers to imitation differ depending on whether a competitor is trying to imitate resources or capabilities.

Imitating Resources   In general, the easiest distinctive competencies for prospective rivals to imitate tend to be those based on possession of firm-specific and valuable tangible resources, such as buildings, manufacturing plants, and equipment. Such resources are visible to competitors and can often be purchased on the open market. For example, if a company's competitive advantage is based on sole possession of efficient-scale manufacturing facilities, competitors may move fairly quickly to establish similar facilities. Although Ford gained a competitive advantage over General Motors in the 1920s by first adopting assembly-line manufacturing technology to produce automobiles, General Motors quickly imitated that innovation, competing away Ford's distinctive competency in the process. A similar process is occurring in the auto industry today as rival automakers try to imitate Toyota's famous production system.

Intangible resources can be more difficult to imitate. This is particularly true of brand names, which are important because they symbolize a company's reputation. In the heavy-earthmoving equipment industry, for example, the Caterpillar brand name is synonymous with high quality and superior after-sales service and support. Similarly, the St. Michael's brand name used by Marks & Spencer, Britain's largest clothing retailer, symbolizes high-quality but reasonably priced clothing. Customers often display a preference for the products of such companies because the brand name is an important guarantee of high quality. Although competitors might like to imitate well-established brand names, the law prohibits them from doing so.

Marketing and technological knowhow are also important intangible resources and can be relatively easy to imitate. The movement of skilled marketing personnel between companies may facilitate the general dissemination of marketing knowhow. More generally, successful marketing strategies are relatively easy to imitate because they are so visible to competitors. Thus, Coca-Cola quickly imitated PepsiCo's Diet Pepsi brand with the introduction of its own brand, Diet Coke.

With regard to technological knowhow, the patent system in theory should make technological knowhow relatively immune to imitation. Patents give the inventor of a new product a 20-year exclusive production agreement. However, this is not always the case. In electrical and computer engineering, for example, it is often possible to invent and circumnavigate the patent process—that is, produce a product that is functionally equivalent but does not rely on the patented technology. One study found that 60% of patented innovations were successfully invented in around 4 years.[26] This suggests that, in general, distinctive competencies based on technological knowhow can be relatively short-lived.

Imitating Capabilities   Imitating a company's capabilities tends to be more difficult than imitating its tangible and intangible resources, chiefly because capabilities are based on the way in which decisions are made and processes are managed deep within a company. It is hard for outsiders to discern them.

The invisible nature of capabilities would not be enough to halt imitation; competitors could still gain insights into how a company operates by hiring people away from that company. However, a company's capabilities rarely reside in a single individual. Rather, they are the product of how numerous individuals interact within a unique organizational setting.[27] It is possible that no one individual within a company may be familiar with the totality of a company's internal operating routines and procedures. In such cases, hiring people away from a successful company in order to imitate its key capabilities may not be helpful.

Capability of Competitors

According to work by Pankaj Ghemawat, a major determinant of the capability of competitors to rapidly imitate a company's competitive advantage is the nature of the competitors' prior strategic commitments.[28] By *strategic commitment*, Ghemawat means a company's commitment to a particular way of doing business—that is, to developing a particular set of resources and capabilities. Ghemawat states that once a company has made a strategic commitment, it will have difficulty responding to new competition if doing so requires a break with this commitment. Therefore, when competitors have long-established commitments to a particular way of doing business, they may be slow to imitate an innovating company's competitive advantage. The innovator's competitive advantage may be relatively durable as a result.

The U.S. automobile industry again offers an example. From 1945 to 1975, General Motors, Ford, and Chrysler dominated this stable oligopoly, and all three companies directed their operations to the production of large cars, which American customers demanded at the time. When the market shifted from large cars to small, fuel-efficient vehicles during the late 1970s, U.S. companies lacked the resources and capabilities required to produce these cars. Their prior commitments had built the wrong kind of skills for this new environment. As a result, foreign producers, particularly the Japanese, stepped into the market breach by providing compact, fuel-efficient, high-quality low-cost cars. U.S. auto manufacturers failed to react quickly to the distinctive competency of Japanese auto companies, giving them time to build a strong market position and brand loyalty, which subsequently proved difficult to attack.

Another determinant of the ability of competitors to respond to a company's competitive advantage is the absorptive capacity of competitors.[29] **Absorptive capacity** refers to the ability of an enterprise to identify, value, assimilate, and use new knowledge. For example, in the 1960s, 1970s, and 1980s Toyota developed a competitive advantage based on its innovation of lean production systems. Competitors such as General Motors were slow to imitate this innovation, primarily because they lacked the necessary absorptive capacity. In those days General Motors was such a bureaucratic and inward-looking organization that it was very difficult for the company to identify, value, assimilate, and use the knowledge underscoring lean production systems. Long after General Motors had identified and understood the importance of lean production systems, it was still struggling to assimilate and use that new knowledge. Put differently, internal forces of inertia can make it difficult for established competitors to respond to rivals whose competitive advantage is based on new products or internal processes—that is, on innovation.

Together, factors such as existing strategic commitments and low absorptive capacity limit the ability of established competitors to imitate the competitive advantage of a rival, particularly when that competitive advantage is based on innovative products or processes. This is why value often migrates away from established competitors and toward new enterprises that are operating with new business models when innovations reshape the rules of industry competition.

absorptive capacity
The ability of an enterprise to identify, value, assimilate, and use new knowledge.

Industry Dynamism

A dynamic industry environment is one that changes rapidly. We examined some of the factors that determine the dynamism and intensity of competition in an industry in Chapter 2 when we discussed the external environment. The most dynamic industries tend to be those with a very high rate of product innovation—for instance, the customer electronics industry, the computer industry, and the telecommunications industry. In dynamic industries, the rapid rate of innovation means that product life cycles are shortening and that competitive advantage can be fleeting. A company that has a competitive advantage today may find its market position outflanked tomorrow by a rival's innovation.

In the personal computer industry, the rapid increase in computing power during the past three decades has contributed to a high degree of innovation and a turbulent environment. Reflecting the persistence of computer innovation, Apple had an industry-wide competitive advantage due to its innovation in the late 1970s and early 1980s. In 1981, IBM seized the advantage by introducing its first personal computer. By the mid-1980s, IBM had lost its competitive advantage to high-power "clone" manufacturers, such as Compaq, that had beaten IBM in the race to introduce a computer based on Intel's 386 chip. In the 1990s, Compaq subsequently lost its competitive advantage to Dell, which pioneered new low-cost ways of delivering computers to customers using the Internet as a direct-selling device. In recent years, Apple has again seized the initiative with its innovative product designs and successful differentiation strategy.

Summary

The durability of a company's competitive advantage depends upon the height of barriers to imitation, the capability of competitors to imitate its innovation, and the general level of dynamism in the industry environment. When barriers to imitation are low, capable competitors abound, and innovations are rapidly being developed within a dynamic environment, then competitive advantage is likely to be transitory. But even within such industries, companies can build a more enduring competitive advantage—if they are able to make investments that build barriers to imitation.

AVOIDING FAILURE AND SUSTAINING COMPETITIVE ADVANTAGE

How can a company avoid failure and escape the traps that have snared so many once-successful companies? How can managers build a sustainable competitive advantage? Much of the remainder of this book addresses these questions. Here, we outline a number of key points that set the scene for the coming discussion.

Why Companies Fail

When a company loses its competitive advantage, its profitability falls. The company does not necessarily fail; it may just have average or below-average profitability and can remain in this mode for a considerable time, although its resource and capital base is shrinking. Failure implies something more drastic. A failing company is one whose profitability is substantially lower than the average profitability of its competitors; it has lost the ability to attract and generate resources and its profit margins and invested capital are rapidly shrinking.

Why does a company lose its competitive advantage and fail? This question is particularly pertinent because some of the most successful companies of the last half-century have seen their competitive position deteriorate at one time or another. IBM, General Motors, American Express, and Sears (among many others), which all were astute examples of managerial excellence, have gone through periods of poor financial performance, during which any competitive advantage was distinctly lacking. We explore three related reasons for failure: inertia, prior strategic commitments, and the Icarus paradox.

Inertia   The inertia argument states that companies find it difficult to change their strategies and structures in order to adapt to changing competitive conditions.[30] IBM is a classic example of this problem. For 30 years, it was viewed as the world's most successful computer company. Then, in only a few years, its success turned into a disaster: it lost $5 billion in 1992, and laid off more than 100,000 employees. The underlying cause of IBM's troubles was a dramatic decline in the cost of computing power as a result of innovations in microprocessors. With the advent of powerful low-cost microprocessors, the locus of the computer market shifted from mainframes to small, low-priced personal computers, leaving IBM's huge mainframe operations with a diminished market. Although IBM had a significant presence in the personal computer market, it had failed to shift the focus of its efforts away from mainframes and toward personal computers. This failure meant deep trouble for one of the most successful companies of the 20th century. (IBM has now executed a very successful turnaround, repositioning itself as a provider of information technology infrastructure and solutions.)

One reason companies find it so difficult to adapt to new environmental conditions is the role of capabilities in causing inertia. Organizational capabilities—the way a company makes decisions and manages its processes—can be a source of competitive advantage, but they are often difficult to change. IBM always emphasized close coordination among operating units and favored decision-making processes that stressed consensus among interdependent operating units as a prerequisite for decisions to go forward.[31] This capability was a source of advantage for IBM during the 1970s, when coordination among its worldwide operating units was necessary to develop, manufacture, and sell complex mainframes. But the slow-moving bureaucracy that it had spawned was a source of failure in the 1990s, when organizations needed to readily adapt to rapid environmental change.

Capabilities are difficult to change because distribution of power and influence is embedded within the established decision-making and management processes of an organization. Those who play key roles in a decision-making process clearly have more power. It follows that changing the established capabilities of an organization means changing its existing distribution of power and influence. Most often, those whose power and influence would diminish resist such change; proposals for change trigger turf battles. Power struggles and the hierarchical resistance associated with trying to alter the way in which an organization makes decisions and manages its process—that is, trying to change its capabilities—bring on inertia. This is not to say that companies cannot change. However, those who feel threatened by change often resist it; change in most cases is induced by a crisis. By then, the company may already be failing, as exemplified by IBM.

Prior Strategic Commitments   A company's prior strategic commitments not only limit its ability to imitate rivals but may also cause competitive disadvantage.[32] IBM, for instance, had major investments in the mainframe computer business, so when the market shifted, it was stuck with significant resources specialized to that particular business: its manufacturing facilities largely produced mainframes, and its research organization and sales force were similarly specialized. Because these resources were not well suited to the newly emerging personal computer business, IBM's difficulties in the early 1990s were in a sense inevitable. Its prior strategic commitments locked it into a business that was shrinking. Shedding these resources inevitably caused hardship for all organization stakeholders.

The Icarus Paradox   Danny Miller has postulated that the roots of competitive failure can be found in what he termed the "Icarus paradox."[33] Icarus is a figure in Greek mythology who used a pair of wings, made for him by his father, to escape from an island where he was being held prisoner. He flew so well that he climbed higher and higher, ever closer to the sun, until the heat of the sun melted the wax that held his wings together, and he plunged to his death in the Aegean Sea. The paradox is that his greatest asset, his ability to fly, caused his demise. Miller argues that the same paradox applies to many once-successful companies. According to Miller, many companies become so dazzled by their early success that they believe more of the same type of effort is the way to future success. As a result, they can become so specialized and myopic that they lose sight of market realities and the fundamental requirements for achieving a competitive advantage. Sooner or later, this leads to failure. For example, Miller argues that Texas Instruments and Digital Equipment Corporation (DEC) achieved early success through engineering excellence. But thereafter, they became so obsessed with engineering details that they lost sight of market realities. (The story of DEC's demise is summarized in Strategy in Action 3.3.)

Steps to Avoid Failure

Given that so many pitfalls await companies, the question arises as to how strategic managers can use internal analysis to find and escape them. We now look at several steps that managers can take to avoid failure.

Focus on the Building Blocks of Competitive Advantage   Maintaining a competitive advantage requires a company to continue focusing on all four generic building blocks of competitive advantage—efficiency, quality, innovation, and responsiveness to customers—and to develop distinctive competencies that contribute to superior performance in these areas. Miller's Icarus paradox promotes the message that many successful companies become unbalanced in their pursuit of distinctive competencies. DEC, for example, focused on engineering quality at the expense of almost everything else, including, most importantly, responsiveness to customers.

Institute Continuous Improvement and Learning   Change is constant and inevitable. Today's source of competitive advantage may soon be rapidly imitated by capable competitors or made obsolete by the innovations of a rival. In a dynamic, fast-paced environment, the only way that a company can maintain a competitive advantage over time is to continually improve its efficiency, quality, innovation, and responsiveness to customers. The way to do this is to recognize the importance of learning within the organization.[34] The most successful companies are not those that stand still, resting on their laurels. Companies that are always seeking ways to improve their operations and constantly upgrade the value of their distinctive competencies or create new competencies are the most successful. General Electric and Toyota, for example, have reputations as learning organizations; they are continually analyzing the processes that underlie their efficiency, quality, innovation,

3.3 STRATEGY IN ACTION

The Road to Ruin at DEC

© iStockPhoto.com/Tom Nulens

Digital Equipment Corporation (DEC) was one of the premier computer companies of the 1970s and 1980s. DEC's original success was founded on the minicomputer, a cheaper, more flexible version of its mainframe cousins that Ken Olson and his brilliant team of engineers invented in the 1960s. They then improved on their original minicomputers until they could not be beat for quality and reliability. In the 1970s, their VAX series of minicomputers was widely regarded as the most reliable series of computers ever produced, and DEC was rewarded by high profit rates and rapid growth. By 1990, it was number 27 on the *Fortune* 500 list of the largest corporations in America.

Buoyed by its success, DEC turned into an engineering monoculture: its engineers became idols; marketing and accounting staff, however, were barely tolerated. Component specs and design standards were all that senior managers understood. Technological fine-tuning became such an obsession that the customer's needs for smaller, more economical, user-friendly computers were ignored. DEC's personal computers, for example, bombed because they were out of touch with the needs of customers. The company failed to respond to the threat to its core market, presented by the rise of computer workstations and client–server architecture. Ken Olson was known for dismissing such new products. He once said, "We always say that customers are right, but they are not always right." Perhaps. But DEC, blinded by its early success, failed to remain responsive to its customers and to changing market conditions. In another famous statement, when asked about personal computers in the early 1980s, Olson said: "I can see of no reason why anybody would ever want a computer on their desk."

By the early 1990s, DEC was in deep trouble. Olson was forced out in July 1992, and the company lost billions of dollars between 1992 and 1995. It returned to profitability in 1996, primarily because its turnaround strategy, aimed at reorienting the company to serve the areas that Olson had dismissed, was a success. In 1998, Compaq purchased DEC (which Hewlett Packard later purchased) and DEC disappeared from the business landscape as an independent entity.

Sources: D. Miller, *The Icarus Paradox* (New York: HarperBusiness, 1990); P. D. Llosa, "We Must Know What We Are Doing," *Fortune*, November 14, 1994, p. 68.

and responsiveness to customers. Learning from prior mistakes and seeking out ways to improve processes over time is the primary objective. This approach has enabled Toyota, for instance, to continually upgrade its employee productivity and product quality, and stay one step ahead of imitators.

Track Best Industrial Practice and Use Benchmarking   Identifying and adopting best industrial practice is one of the best ways to develop distinctive competencies that contribute to superior efficiency, quality, innovation, and responsiveness to customers. Only in this way will a company be capable of building and maintaining the resources and capabilities that underpin excellence in efficiency, quality, innovation, and responsiveness to customers. (We discuss what constitutes best industrial practice in some depth in Chapter 4.) It requires tracking the practice of other companies, and perhaps the best way to do so is through benchmarking: measuring the company against the products, practices, and services of some of its most efficient global competitors.

Overcome Inertia   Overcoming the internal forces that are a barrier to change within an organization is one of the key requirements for maintaining a competitive advantage.

Identifying barriers to change is an important first step. Once barriers are identified, implementing change to overcome these barriers requires good leadership, the judicious use of power, and appropriate subsequent changes in organizational structure and control systems.

The Role of Luck   Some scholars have argued that luck plays a critical role in determining competitive success and failure.[35] In its most extreme version, the luck argument devalues the importance of strategy altogether. Instead, it states that in the face of uncertainty, some companies just happen to choose the correct strategy.

Although luck may be the reason for a company's success in particular cases, it is an unconvincing explanation for the persistent success of a company. Recall our argument that the generic building blocks of competitive advantage are superior efficiency, quality, innovation, and responsiveness to customers. In addition, keep in mind that competition is a process in which companies are continually trying to outdo each other in their ability to achieve high efficiency, superior quality, outstanding innovation, and rapid responsiveness to customers. It is possible to imagine a company getting lucky and coming into possession of resources that allow it to achieve excellence within one or more of these dimensions. It is difficult, however, to imagine how sustained excellence within any of these four dimensions could be produced by anything other than conscious effort—that is, by strategy. Luck may indeed play a role in success, and managers must always exploit a lucky break. However, to argue that success is entirely a matter of luck is to strain credibility. As the prominent banker of the early 20th century, J. P. Morgan, once said, "The harder I work, the luckier I seem to get." Managers who strive to formulate and implement strategies that lead to a competitive advantage are more likely to be lucky.

SUMMARY OF CHAPTER

1. Distinctive competencies are the firm-specific strengths of a company. Valuable distinctive competencies enable a company to earn a profit rate that is above the industry average.

2. The distinctive competencies of an organization arise from its resources (its financial, physical, human, technological, and organizational assets) and capabilities (its skills at coordinating resources and putting them to productive use).

3. In order to achieve a competitive advantage, a company needs to pursue strategies that build on its existing resources and capabilities and formulate strategies that build additional resources and capabilities (develop new competencies).

4. The source of a competitive advantage is superior value creation.

5. To create superior value (utility) a company must lower its costs or differentiate its product so that it creates more value and can charge a higher price, or do both simultaneously.

6. Managers must understand how value creation and pricing decisions affect demand and how costs change with increases in volume. They must have a good grasp of the demand conditions in the company's market, and the cost structure of the company at different levels of output, if they are to make decisions that maximize the profitability of their enterprise.

7. The four building blocks of competitive advantage are efficiency, quality, innovation, and responsiveness to customers. These are generic distinctive competencies. Superior efficiency enables a company to lower its costs, superior quality allows it to charge a higher price and lower its costs, and superior customer service lets it charge a higher price. Superior innovation can lead to higher prices, particularly in

the case of product innovations, or lower unit costs, as in the case of process innovations.

8. If a company's managers are to perform a good internal analysis, they need to be able to analyze the financial performance of their company, identifying how the strategies of the company relate to its profitability, as measured by the return on invested capital.

9. The durability of a company's competitive advantage depends on the height of barriers to imitation, the capability of competitors, and environmental dynamism.

10. Failing companies typically earn low or negative profits. Three factors seem to contribute to failure: organizational inertia in the face of environmental change, the nature of a company's prior strategic commitments, and the Icarus paradox.

11. Avoiding failure requires a constant focus on the basic building blocks of competitive advantage: continuous improvement, identification and adoption of best industrial practice, and victory over inertia.

DISCUSSION QUESTIONS

1. What are the primary implications of the material discussed in this chapter for strategy formulation?

2. When is a company's competitive advantage most likely to endure over time?

3. It is possible for a company to be the lowest-cost producer in its industry and simultaneously have an output that is the most valued by customers. Discuss this statement.

4. Why is it important to understand the drivers of profitability, as measured by the return on invested capital?

5. Which is more important in explaining the success and failure of companies: strategizing or luck?

PRACTICING STRATEGIC MANAGEMENT

© iStockPhoto.com/Urilux

Small-Group Exercise: Analyzing Competitive Advantage

Break up into groups of three to five people. Drawing on the concepts introduced in this chapter, analyze the competitive position of your business school in the market for business education. Then answer the following questions:

1. Does your business school have a competitive advantage?
2. If so, upon what is this advantage based, and is this advantage sustainable?
3. If your school does not have a competitive advantage in the market for business education, identify the inhibiting factors that are holding it back.
4. How might the Internet change the way in which business education is delivered?
5. Does the Internet pose a threat to the competitive position of your school in the market for business education, or is it an opportunity for your school to enhance its competitive position?

STRATEGY SIGN ON

© iStockPhoto.com/Ninoslav Dotlic

Article File 3

Find a company that has sustained its competitive advantage for more than 10 years. Identify the source or sources of this competitive advantage, and explain why it has lasted so long.

Strategic Management Project: Module 3

This module deals with the competitive position of your company. With the information you have available, perform the following tasks and answer the listed questions:

1. Identify whether your company has a competitive advantage or disadvantage in its primary industry. (Its primary industry is the one in which it has the most sales.)
2. Evaluate your company against the four generic building blocks of competitive advantage: efficiency, quality, innovation, and responsiveness to customers. How does this exercise help you understand the performance of your company relative to its competitors?
3. What are the distinctive competencies of your company?
4. What roles have prior strategies played in shaping the distinctive competencies of your company? What has been the role of luck?
5. Do the strategies your company is currently pursuing build on its distinctive competencies? Are they an attempt to build new competencies?
6. What are the barriers to imitating the distinctive competencies of your company?
7. Is there any evidence that your company finds it difficult to adapt to changing industry conditions? If so, why do you think this is the case?

ETHICAL DILEMMA

© iStockPhoto.com/P_Wei

Your friend manages a retailer that has a history of superior profitability. She believes that one of the principal sources of competitive advantage for her enterprise are low labor costs. The low labor costs are due to her hiring of minimum-wage workers, the decision not to give them any benefits (such as health benefits), and her consistent opposition to unionization at the company (the workforce is not unionized). Although she acknowledges that this approach does lead to high employee turnover, she argues that the jobs are low skilled, and that it is easy to replace someone who leaves. Is your friend's approach to doing business ethical? Are there ways of achieving low labor costs that do not rely upon the hiring of minimum-wage workers? Would you counsel your friend to use an alternative approach?

CLOSING CASE

Competitive Advantage at Starbucks

The growth of Starbucks is the stuff of business legend. In the 1980s, when the company had only a handful of stores, the company's director of marketing, Howard Schultz, returned from a trip to Italy enchanted with the Italian coffeehouse experience. Schultz, who later purchased the company and became CEO, persuaded the owners to experiment with the coffeehouse format, and the Starbucks experience was born. The strategy was to sell the company's own premium roasted coffee and freshly brewed espresso-style coffee beverages, along with a variety of pastries, coffee accessories, and other products, in a tastefully designed coffeehouse setting. The idea was to transform the act of buying and drinking coffee into a social experience. The stores were to be "third places," where people could meet and talk or relax and read. The company focused on providing superior customer service. Reasoning that motivated employees provide the best customer service, Starbucks' executives devoted much attention to employee hiring and training programs, and progressive compensation policies that gave full-time and part-time employees stock-option grants and medical benefits.

This formula was the bedrock of Starbucks' competitive advantage. Starbucks went from obscurity to one of the best-known brands in the United States within a decade. Between 1995 and 2005, Starbucks added U.S. stores at an annual rate of 27%, reaching almost 12,000 total locations. It also expanded aggressively internationally. Schultz himself stepped down from the CEO role in 2000, although he remained chairman.

By 2008, however, the company was hitting serious headwinds. Competitors from small boutique coffee houses to chains like Tully's and Pete's Coffee, and even McDonald's, were beginning to erode Starbucks' competitive advantage. Although the company was still adding stores at a break-neck pace, same-store sales started to fall. Profitability, measured by return on invested capital (ROIC), slumped from around 21% to just 8.6% in 2008. The stock price tumbled.

At this point, Howard Schultz fired the CEO and again reclaimed the position. His strategy was to return Starbucks to its roots. He wanted the company to reemphasize the creation of value through great customer experiences, and he wanted the company to do that as efficiently as possible. He first closed all Starbucks' stores for a day, and retrained baristas in the art of making coffee. A number of other changes followed. The company redesigned many of its stores to give them a contemporary feel. It stopped selling breakfast sandwiches because Schultz thought that the smell detracted from the premium coffeehouse experience. Instead of grinding enough coffee for an entire day, he told employees to grind more coffee each time a new pot was brewed to create the aroma of freshly brewed coffee. He gave store managers more freedom to decide on specific aspects of their stores, such as the type of artwork displayed. Starbucks also dramatically expanded its fair-trade policy, purchasing its coffee beans from growers adhering to environmentally friendly policies, and it promoted this to customers.

To reduce costs, Schultz announced the closure of 600 underperforming U.S. stores. Starbucks used the threat of possible closure to renegotiate many store leases at lower rates. It cut back on the number of suppliers of pastries and negotiated volume discounts. A lean thinking team was created, and it was tasked with the job of improving employee productivity; baristas needed to become more efficient. The team found that by making simple changes, such as placing commonly ordered syrup flavors closer to where drinks are made, they could shave several seconds off the time it took to make a drink, and give employees more time to interact with customers. Faster customer service meant higher customer satisfaction.

The results have been impressive. What was once nearly dismissed as a stale brand has been reinvigorated. Between 2008 and 2012, Starbucks' revenues expanded from $10.4 billion to $13.3 billion against the background of a weak economy, and ROIC surged from 8.6% to an impressive 26.13%.

Sources: J. Jargon, "Latest Starbucks Buzzword: Lean Japanese Techniques," *Wall Street Journal*, August 4, 2009, p. A1; J. Adamy, "Starbucks Moves to Cut Costs, Retain Customers," *Wall Street Journal*, December 5, 2008, p. B3; "Coffee Wars," *The Economist*, December 1, 2008, pp. 57–59; and R. Lowenstein, "What Latte Lost Its Luster," *Wall Street Journal*, March 29, 2011, p. A17.

CASE DISCUSSION QUESTIONS

1. What is the value that Starbucks creates for its customers? How does the company create this value?
2. How important have innovation, efficiency, quality, and customer responsiveness been to Starbucks' competitive position?
3. Does Starbucks have any distinctive competencies? If so, how do they affect the business?
4. Why do you think the performance of Starbucks started to decline after 2005? What was Schultz trying to do with the changes he made after 2008?

KEY TERMS

Distinctive competencies 83
Resources 83
Tangible resources 83
Intangible resources 83

Capabilities 83
Value chain 89
Primary activities 89
Support activities 91
Employee productivity 94

Product innovation 96
Process innovation 96
Customer response time 97
Barriers to imitation 104

Absorptive capacity 105
Total quality management xx

NOTES

[1]M. Cusumano, *The Japanese Automobile Industry* (Cambridge, Mass.: Harvard University Press, 1989); S. Spear and H. K. Bowen, "Decoding the DNA of the Toyota Production System," *Harvard Business Review* (September–October 1999): 96–108.

[2]The material in this section relies on the resource-based view of the company. For summaries of this perspective, see J. B. Barney, "Company Resources and Sustained Competitive Advantage," *Journal of Management* 17 (1991): 99–120; J. T. Mahoney and J. R. Pandian, "The Resource-Based View Within the Conversation of Strategic Management," *Strategic Management Journal* 13 (1992): 63–380; R. Amit and P. J. H. Schoemaker, "Strategic Assets and Organizational Rent," *Strategic Management Journal* 14 (1993): 33–46; M. A. Peteraf, "The Cornerstones of Competitive Advantage: A Resource-Based View," *Strategic Management Journal* 14 (1993): 179–191; B. Wernerfelt, "A Resource Based View of the Company," *Strategic Management Journal* 15 (1994): 171–180; and K. M. Eisenhardt and J. A. Martin, "Dynamic Capabilities: What Are They?" *Strategic Management Journal* 21 (2000): 1105–1121.

[4]For a discussion of organizational capabilities, see R. R. Nelson and S. Winter, *An Evolutionary Theory of Economic Change* (Cambridge, Mass.: Belknap Press, 1982).

[5]W. Chan Kim and R. Mauborgne, "Value Innovation: The Strategic Logic of High Growth," *Harvard Business Review,* January–February 1997, pp. 102–115.

[6]The concept of consumer surplus is an important one in economics. For a more detailed exposition, see D. Besanko, D. Dranove, and M. Shanley, *Economics of Strategy* (New York: Wiley, 1996).

[7]However, $P = U$ only in the special case when the company has a perfect monopoly and it can charge each customer a unique price that reflects the utility of the product to that

customer (i.e., where perfect price discrimination is possible). More generally, except in the limiting case of perfect price discrimination, even a monopolist will see most customers capture some of the utility of a product in the form of a consumer surplus.

[8]This point is central to the work of Michael Porter. See M. E. Porter, *Competitive Advantage* (New York: Free Press, 1985). See also P. Ghemawat, *Commitment: The Dynamic of Strategy* (New York: Free Press, 1991), chap. 4.

[9]Oliver Wyman, "The Harbor Report," 2008, www.oliverwyman.com/ow/automotive.htm.

[10]Porter, *Competitive Advantage.*

[11]Ibid.

[12]This approach goes back to the pioneering work by K. Lancaster: *Consumer Demand, a New Approach* (New York: 1971).

[13]D. Garvin, "Competing on the Eight Dimensions of Quality," *Harvard Business Review,* November–December 1987, pp. 101–119; P. Kotler, *Marketing Management* (Millennium ed.) (Upper Saddle River, N.J.: Prentice Hall, 2000).

[14]C. K. Prahalad and M. S. Krishnan, "The New Meaning of Quality in the Information Age," *Harvard Business Review,* September–October 1999, pp. 109–118.

[15]See D. Garvin, "What Does Product Quality Really Mean,?" *Sloan Management Review* 26 (Fall 1984): 25–44; P. B. Crosby, *Quality Is Free* (New York: Mentor, 1980); and A. Gabor, *The Man Who Discovered Quality* (New York: Times Books, 1990).

[16]M. Cusumano, *The Japanese Automobile Industry* (Cambridge, Mass.: Harvard University Press, 1989); and S. Spear and H. K. Bowen, "Decoding the DNA of the Toyota Production System," *Harvard Business Review,* September–October 1999, pp. 96–108.

[17]Kim and Mauborgne, "Value Innovation."

[18]G. Stalk and T. M. Hout, *Competing Against Time* (New York: Free Press, 1990).

[19]Ibid.

[20]Tom Copeland, Tim Koller, and Jack Murrin, *Valuation: Measuring and Managing the Value of Companies* (New York: Wiley, 1996). See also S. F. Jablonsky and N. P. Barsky, *The Manager's Guide to Financial Statement Analysis* (New York: Wiley, 2001).

[21]Copeland, Koller, and Murrin, *Valuation.*

[22]This is done as follows. Signifying net profit by π, invested capital by K, and revenues by R, then ROIC $= \pi/K$. If we multiply through by revenues, R, this becomes $R \times (K) = (\pi \times R)/(K \times R)$, which can be rearranged as $\pi/R \times R/K$, where π/R is the return on sales and R/K is capital turnover.

[23]Note that Figure 3.9 is a simplification and ignores some other important items that enter the calculation, such as depreciation/sales (a determinant of ROS) and other assets/sales (a determinant of capital turnover).

[24]This is the nature of the competitive process. For more detail, see C. W. L. Hill and D. Deeds, "The Importance of Industry Structure for the Determination of Company Profitability: A Neo-Austrian Perspective," *Journal of Management Studies* 33 (1996): 429–451.

[25]As with resources and capabilities, so the concept of barriers to imitation is also grounded in the resource-based view of the company. For details, see R. Reed and R. J. DeFillippi, "Causal Ambiguity, Barriers to Imitation, and Sustainable Competitive Advantage," *Academy of Management Review* 15 (1990): 88–102.

[26]E. Mansfield, "How Economists See R&D," *Harvard Business Review,* November–December 1981, pp. 98–106.

[27]S. L. Berman, J. Down, and C. W. L. Hill, "Tacit Knowledge as a Source of Competitive Advantage in the National Basketball Association," *Academy of Management Journal* 45:1 (2002): 13–33.

[28]P. Ghemawat, *Commitment: The Dynamic of Strategy* (New York: Free Press, 1991).

[29]W. M. Cohen and D. A. Levinthal, "Absorptive Capacity: A New Perspective on Learning and Innovation," *Administrative Science Quarterly* 35 (1990): 128–152.

[30]M. T. Hannah and J. Freeman, "Structural Inertia and Organizational Change," *American Sociological Review* 49 (1984): 149–164.

[31]See "IBM Corporation," Harvard Business School Case #180-034.

[32]Ghemawat, *Commitment.*

[33]D. Miller, *The Icarus Paradox* (New York: HarperBusiness, 1990).

[34]P. M. Senge, *The Fifth Discipline: The Art and Practice of the Learning Organization* (New York: Doubleday, 1990).

[35]The classic statement of this position was made by A. A. Alchain, "Uncertainty, Evolution, and Economic Theory," *Journal of Political Economy* 84 (1950): 488–500.

Building Competitive Advantage Through Functional-Level Strategies

Amazon.Com

When Jeff Bezos started Amazon.com back in 1995, the online retailer focused just on selling books. Music and videos were soon added to the mix. Today, you can purchase a wide range of media and general-merchandise products from Amazon, which is now the world's largest online retailer, with over $60 billion in annual sales. According to Bezos, Amazon's success is based on three main factors: a relentless focus on delivering value to customers, operating efficiencies, and a willingness to innovate.

Amazon offers customers a much wider selection of merchandise than they can find in a physical store, and does so at a low price. Online shopping and purchasing is made easy with a user-friendly interface, product recommendations, customer wish lists, and a one-click purchasing option for repeat customers. The percentage of traffic that Amazon gets from

search engines such as Google has been falling for several years, whereas other online retailers are becoming more dependent on third-party search engines. This indicates that Amazon is increasingly becoming the starting point for online purchases. As a result, its active customer base in now approaching 200 million.

To deliver products to customers quickly and accurately, Amazon has been investing heavily in a network of distribution centers. In the United States alone there are now over 40 such centers. Sophisticated software analyzes customer purchasing patterns and tells the company what to order, where to store it in the distribution network, what to charge for it, and when to mark it down to shift it. The goal is to reduce inventory holding costs while always having product in stock. The increasingly dense network of distribution centers enables Amazon to reduce the time it takes to deliver products to consumers and to cut down on delivery costs. As Amazon becomes larger, it can support a denser distribution network, which it turn enables it to fulfill customer orders more rapidly, and at a lower cost, thereby solidifying its competitive advantage over smaller rivals.

To make its distribution centers work more efficiently, Amazon is embracing automation. Until recently, most of the picking and packing of products at Amazon distribution centers was done by hand, with employees walking as much as 20 miles a shift to pick merchandise off shelves and bring it to packing stations. Although walking 20 miles a day may be good for the physical health of employees, it represents a lot of wasted time and hurts productivity. In 2012 Amazon purchased Kiva, a leading manufacturer of robots that service warehouses. Kiva has announced that for the next 2 to 3 years, it will not take any external orders, and instead focus on automating Amazon's distribution centers. Kiva's robots pick products from shelves and deliver them to packing stations. This reduces the number of employees needed per distribution center by 30 to 40%, and boosts productivity accordingly.

On the innovation front, Amazon has been a leader in pushing the digitalization of media. Its invention of the Kindle digital reader, and the ability of customers to use that reader either on a dedicated Kindle device or on a general-purpose device such as an iPad, turbo charged the digital distribution of books, a market segment where Amazon is the clear leader. Digitalization of books is disrupting the established book retailing industry and strengthening Amazon's advantage in this segment. To store digital media, from books to films and music, and to enable rapid customer download, Amazon has built huge server farms. Its early investment in "cloud-based" infrastructure has turned Amazon into a leader in this field. It is now leveraging its expertise and infrastructure to build another business. Known as Amazon Web Services (AWS), Amazon will host websites, data, and associated software for other companies. In 2012 this new business generated $2.1 billion in revenues, making Amazon one of the early leaders in the emerging field of cloud computing. By 2015, analysts predict that AWS will be a $15 billion business. Jeff Bezos is on record as stating that he believes AWS will ultimately match Amazon's online retail business in sales volume.

Sources: "Amazon to Add 18 New Distribution Centers," *Supply Chain Digest*, August 7, 2012; Adam Lashinsky, "Jeff Bezos: The Ultimate Disrupter," *Fortune*, December 3, 2012, pp. 34–41; S. Banker, "The New Amazon Distribution Model," *Logistics Viewpoints*, August 6, 2012; and G. A. Fowler, "Holiday Hiring Call: People Vs Robots," *Wall Street Journal*, December 10, 2010, p. B1.

OVERVIEW

In this chapter, we take a close look at **functional-level strategies**: those aimed at improving the effectiveness of a company's operations and its ability to attain superior efficiency, quality, innovation, and customer responsiveness.

It is important to keep in mind the relationships between functional strategies, distinctive competencies, differentiation, low cost, value creation, and profitability (see Figure 4.1). Distinctive competencies shape the functional-level strategies that a company can pursue. Managers, through their choices related to functional-level strategies, can build resources

functional-level strategies
Strategy aimed at improving the effectiveness of a company's operations and its ability to attain superior efficiency, quality, innovation, and customer responsiveness.

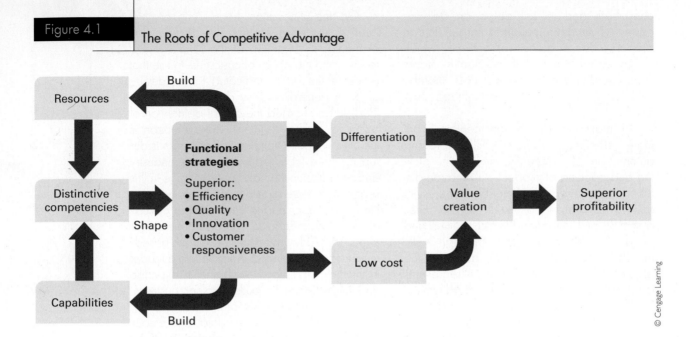

Figure 4.1   The Roots of Competitive Advantage

© Cengage Learning

and capabilities that enhance a company's distinctive competencies. Also, note that a company's ability to attain superior efficiency, quality, innovation, and customer responsiveness will determine if its product offering is differentiated from that of rivals, and if it has a low-cost structure. Recall that companies that increase the value (utility) consumers get from their products through differentiation, while simultaneously lowering their cost structure, create more value than their rivals—and this leads to a competitive advantage, superior profitability, and profit growth.

The Opening Case illustrates some of these relationships. Amazon has always focused on customer responsiveness. Its wide product selection, low prices, rapid order fulfillment, user-friendly interface, product recommendations, customer wish lists, and one-click purchasing option are all aspects of this. Taken together, these factors *differentiate* Amazon from its rivals in online and physical retailing. Over time, Amazon has also become increasingly efficient and effective at managing inventory and running its growing network of distribution centers. By opening more distribution centers and increasing the density of its distribution network, Amazon is able to deliver products to customers more rapidly (boosting customer satisfaction) and to do so at a lower cost. The current strategy of automating much of the work at its distribution centers promises to further boost employee productivity. All of this helps Amazon to achieve a *low-cost* position. The company is also innovative, developing new products (the Kindle reader, digital downloads of books) and services (Amazon Web Services) that are helping it to solidify its competitive advantage.

Much of this chapter is devoted to looking at the basic strategies that can be adopted at the functional level to improve competitive position, as the Amazon.com example illustrates. By the end of this chapter, you will understand how functional-level strategies can be used to build a sustainable competitive advantage.

ACHIEVING SUPERIOR EFFICIENCY

A company is a device for transforming inputs (labor, land, capital, management, and technological knowhow) into outputs (the goods and services produced). The simplest measure of efficiency is the quantity of inputs that it takes to produce a given output; that is, efficiency = outputs/inputs. The more efficient a company, the fewer the inputs required to produce a given output, and therefore the lower its cost structure. Put another way, an efficient company has higher productivity, and therefore lower costs, than its rivals. Here we review the steps that companies can take at the functional level to increase their efficiency and thereby lower cost structure.

Efficiency and Economies of Scale

Economies of scale are unit cost reductions associated with a large scale of output. You will recall from the last chapter that it is very important for managers to understand how the cost structure of their enterprise varies with output because this understanding should help to drive strategy. For example, if unit costs fall significantly as output is expanded—that is, if there are significant economies of scale—a company may benefit by keeping prices down and increasing volume.

economies of scale
Reductions in unit costs attributed to a larger output.

One source of economies of scale is the ability to spread fixed costs over a large production volume. **Fixed costs** are costs that must be incurred to produce a product regardless of the level of output; examples are the costs of purchasing machinery, setting up machinery for individual production runs, building facilities, advertising, and research and development (R&D). For example, Microsoft spent approximately $5 billion to develop the latest version of its Windows operating system, Windows 8. It can realize substantial scale economies by distributing the fixed costs associated with developing the new operating system over the enormous unit sales volume it expects for this system (over 90% of the world's 1.6 billion personal computers [PCs] use the Windows operating system). These scale economies are significant because of the trivial incremental (or marginal) cost of producing additional copies of Windows 8. For example, once the master copy has been produced, original equipment manufacturers (OEMs) can install additional copies of Windows 8 on new PCs for a marginal cost of zero to Microsoft. The key to Microsoft's efficiency and profitability (and that of other companies with high fixed costs and trivial incremental or marginal costs) is to increase sales rapidly enough that fixed costs can be spread out over a large unit volume and substantial scale economies can be realized.

fixed costs
Costs that must be incurred to produce a product regardless of the level of output.

Another source of scale economies is the ability of companies producing in large volumes to achieve a greater division of labor and specialization. Specialization is said to have a favorable impact on productivity, primarily because it enables employees to become very skilled at performing a particular task. The classic example of such economies is Ford's Model T car. The Model T Ford was introduced in 1923, and was the world's first mass-produced car. Until 1923, Ford had made cars using an expensive hand-built craft production method. Introducing mass-production techniques allowed the company to achieve greater division of labor (it split assembly into small, repeatable tasks) and specialization, which boosted employee productivity. Ford was also able to distribute the fixed costs of developing a car and setting up production machinery over a large volume of output. As a result of these economies, the cost of manufacturing a car at Ford fell from $3,000 to less than $900 (in 1958 dollars).

The concept of scale economies is depicted in Figure 4.2, which illustrates that as a company increases its output, unit costs decrease. This process comes to an end at an

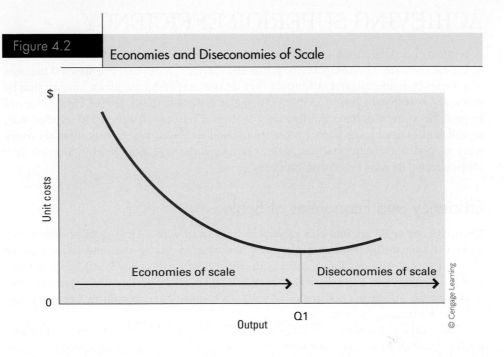

Figure 4.2   Economies and Diseconomies of Scale

© Cengage Learning

diseconomies of scale

Unit cost increases associated with a large scale of output.

output of Q1, where all scale economies are exhausted. Indeed, at outputs of greater than Q1, the company may encounter **diseconomies of scale**, which are the unit cost increases associated with a large scale of output. Diseconomies of scale occur primarily because of the increased bureaucracy associated with large-scale enterprises and the managerial inefficiencies that can result.[1] Larger enterprises have a tendency to develop extensive managerial hierarchies in which dysfunctional political behavior is commonplace. Information about operating matters can accidentally and deliberately be distorted by the number of managerial layers through which the information must travel to reach top decision makers. The result is poor decision making. Therefore, past a specific point—such as Q1 in Figure 4.2—inefficiencies result from such developments, and outweigh any additional gains from economies of scale. As output expands, unit costs begin to rise.

Managers must know the extent of economies of scale, and where diseconomies of scale begin to occur. At Nucor Steel, for example, the realization that diseconomies of scale exist has led to the company's decision to build plants that only employ 300 individuals or less. The belief is that it is more efficient to build two plants, each employing 300 people, than one plant employing 600 people. Although the larger plant may theoretically make it possible to reap greater scale economies, Nucor's management believes that larger plants would suffer from the diseconomies of scale associated with larger organizational units.

Efficiency and Learning Effects

learning effects

Cost savings that come from learning by doing.

Learning effects are cost savings that come from learning by doing. Labor, for example, learns by repetition how to best carry out a task. Therefore, labor productivity increases over time, and unit costs decrease as individuals learn the most efficient way to perform a particular task. Equally important, management in new manufacturing facilities typically learns over time how best to run the new operation. Hence, production costs decline because of increasing labor productivity and management efficiency.

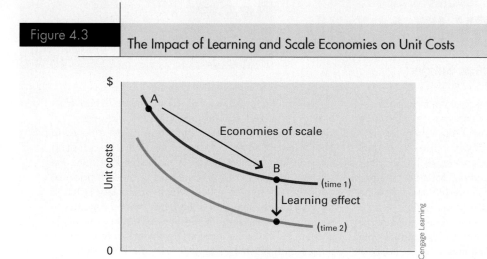

Figure 4.3

The Impact of Learning and Scale Economies on Unit Costs

© Cengage Learning

Japanese companies such as Toyota are noted for making learning a central part of their operating philosophy.

Learning effects tend to be more significant when a technologically complex task is repeated because there is more to learn. Thus, learning effects will be more significant in an assembly process that has 1,000 complex steps than in a process with 100 simple steps. Although learning effects are normally associated with the manufacturing process, there is plenty of evidence that they are just as important in service industries. One famous study of learning in the health-care industry discovered that more experienced medical providers posted significantly lower mortality rates for a number of common surgical procedures, suggesting that learning effects are at work in surgery.[2] The authors of this study used the evidence to argue in favor of establishing regional referral centers for the provision of highly specialized medical care. These centers would perform many specific surgical procedures (such as heart surgery), replacing local facilities with lower volumes and presumably higher mortality rates. Another recent study found strong evidence of learning effects in a financial institution. This study looked at a newly established document-processing unit with 100 staff members and found that, over time, documents were processed much more rapidly as the staff learned the process. Overall, the study concluded that unit costs decreased every time the cumulative number of documents processed doubled.[3] Strategy in Action 4.1 looks at the determinants of differences in learning effects across a sample of hospitals performing cardiac surgery.

In terms of the unit cost curve of a company, economies of scale imply a movement along the curve (say, from A to B in Figure 4.3). The realization of learning effects implies a downward shift of the entire curve (B to C in Figure 4.3) as both labor and management become more efficient over time at performing their tasks at every level of output. In accounting terms, learning effects in a production setting will reduce the cost of goods sold as a percentage of revenues, enabling the company to earn a higher return on sales and return on invested capital.

No matter how complex the task is, however, learning effects typically diminish in importance after a period of time. Indeed, it has been suggested that they are most important during the start-up period of a new process, and become trivial after 2 or 3 years.[4] When changes occur to a company's production system—as a result of the use of new information technology, for example—the learning process must begin again.

4.1 STRATEGY IN ACTION

Learning Effects in Cardiac Surgery

© iStockPhoto.com/Tom Nulens

A study carried out by researchers at the Harvard Business School tried to estimate the importance of learning effects in the case of a specific new technology for minimally invasive heart surgery that was approved by federal regulators. The researchers looked at 16 hospitals and obtained data on the operations for 660 patients. They examined how the time required to undertake the procedure varied with cumulative experience. Across the 16 hospitals, they found that average time decreased from 280 minutes for the first procedure with the new technology to 220 minutes once a hospital had performed 50 procedures (note that not all of the hospitals performed 50 procedures, and the estimates represent an extrapolation based on the data).

Next, the study observed differences across hospitals; here they found evidence of very large differences in learning effects. One hospital, in particular, stood out. This hospital, which they called "Hospital M," reduced its net procedure time from 500 minutes on case 1 to 132 minutes by case 50. Hospital M's 88-minute procedure time advantage over the average hospital at case 50 meant a cost savings of approximately $2,250 per case, which allowed surgeons at the hospital to complete one more revenue-generating procedure per day.

The researchers tried to find out why Hospital M was so superior. They noted that all hospitals had similar state-of-the-art operating rooms, all used the same set of devices approved by the Food and Drug Administration (FDA), all adopting surgeons completed the

same training courses, and all surgeons came from highly respected training hospitals. Follow-up interviews, however, suggested that Hospital M differed in how it implemented the new procedure. The adopting surgeon handpicked the team that would perform the surgery. Members of the team had significant prior experience working together, which was a key criterion for member selection, and the team trained together to perform the new surgery. Before undertaking a single procedure, the entire team met with the operating room nurses and anesthesiologists to discuss the procedure. In addition, the adopting surgeon mandated that the surgical team and surgical procedure was stable in the early cases. The initial team completed 15 procedures before any new members were added or substituted, and completed 20 cases before the procedures were modified. The adopting surgeon also insisted that the team meet prior to each of the first 10 cases and after the first 20 cases to debrief.

The picture that emerges is one of a core team that was selected and managed to maximize the gains from learning. Unlike other hospitals where team members and procedures were less consistent, and where there was not the same attention to briefing, debriefing, and learning, surgeons at Hospital M learned much faster, and ultimately achieved higher productivity than their peers in other institutions. Clearly, differences in the implementation of the new procedure were very significant.

Source: G. P. Pisano, R. M. J. Bohmer, and A. C. Edmondson, "Organizational Differences in Rates of Learning: Evidence from the Adoption of Minimally Invasive Cardiac Surgery," *Management Science* 47 (2001): 752–768.

Efficiency and the Experience Curve

experience curve

The systematic lowering of the cost structure, and consequent unit cost reductions, that have been observed to occur over the life of a product.

The **experience curve** refers to the systematic lowering of the cost structure, and consequent unit cost reductions, that have been observed to occur over the life of a product.[5] According to the experience-curve concept, per-unit production costs for a product typically decline by some characteristic amount each time accumulated output of the product is doubled (accumulated output is the total output of a product since its introduction). This relationship was first observed in the aircraft industry, where it was found that each time the accumulated output of airframes doubled, unit costs declined to 80% of their previous level.[6] As such, the 4th airframe typically cost only 80% of the 2nd airframe to produce, the 8th airframe only 80% of the 4th,

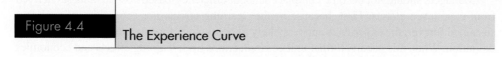

Figure 4.4   The Experience Curve

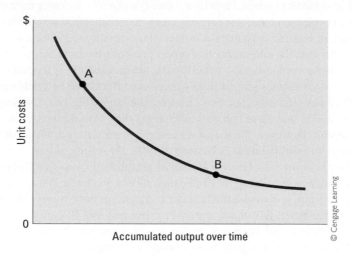

the 16th only 80% of the 8th, and so on. The outcome of this process is a relationship between unit manufacturing costs and accumulated output similar to the illustration in Figure 4.4. Economies of scale and learning effects underlie the experience-curve phenomenon. Put simply, as a company increases the accumulated volume of its output over time, it is able to realize both economies of scale (as volume increases) and learning effects. Consequently, unit costs and cost structure fall with increases in accumulated output.

The strategic significance of the experience curve is clear: increasing a company's product volume and market share will lower its cost structure relative to its rivals. In Figure 4.4, Company B has a cost advantage over Company A because of its lower cost structure, and because it is farther down the experience curve. This concept is very important in industries that mass-produce a standardized output, for example, the manufacture of semiconductor chips. A company that wishes to become more efficient and lower its cost structure must try to move down the experience curve as quickly as possible. This means constructing efficient scale manufacturing facilities (even before it has generated demand for the product), and aggressively pursuing cost reductions from learning effects. It might also need to adopt an aggressive marketing strategy, cutting prices drastically and stressing heavy sales promotions and extensive advertising, in order to build up demand and accumulated volume as quickly as possible. A company is likely to have a significant cost advantage over its competitors because of its superior efficiency once it is down the experience curve. For example, it has been argued that Intel uses such tactics to ride down the experience curve and gain a competitive advantage over its rivals in the market for microprocessors.[7]

It is worth emphasizing that this concept is just as important outside of manufacturing. For example, as it invests in its distribution network, online retailer Amazon is trying to both realize economies of scale (spreading the fixed costs of its distribution centers over a large sales volume) and improve the efficiency of its inventory management and order-fulfillment process at distribution centers (a learning effect). Together these two sources of cost savings should enable Amazon to ride down the experience curve ahead of its rivals, thereby gaining a low-cost position that enables it to make greater profits at lower prices than its rivals (see the Opening Case for details).

Managers should not become complacent about efficiency-based cost advantages derived from experience effects. First, because neither learning effects nor economies of scale are sustained forever, the experience curve is likely to bottom out at some point; it must do so by definition. When this occurs, further unit cost reductions from learning effects and economies of scale will be difficult to attain. Over time, other companies can lower their cost structures and match the cost leader. Once this happens, many low-cost companies can have cost parity with each other. In such circumstances, a sustainable competitive advantage must rely on strategic factors other than the minimization of production costs by using existing technologies—factors such as better responsiveness to customers, product quality, or innovation.

Second, cost advantages gained from experience effects can be made obsolete by the development of new technologies. For example, the large "big box" bookstores Borders and Barnes & Noble may have had cost advantages that were derived from economies of scale and learning. However, these cost advantages were reduced when Amazon utilized Web technology to start its online bookstore in 1994. By selling online, Amazon was able to offer a larger selection at a lower cost than its established rivals that had physical storefronts. When Amazon introduced its Kindle digital book reader in 2007, and started to sell books in digital form, it changed the basis of competition once more, effectively nullifying the experience-based advantage enjoyed by Borders and Barnes & Noble. By 2012, Borders was bankrupt, and Barnes & Noble was in financial trouble and closing stores. Amazon, in the meantime, has gone from strength to strength.

Efficiency, Flexible Production Systems, and Mass Customization

Central to the concept of economies of scale is the idea that a lower cost structure, through the mass production of a standardized output, is the best way to achieve high efficiency. The tradeoff implicit in this idea is between unit costs and product variety. Producing greater product variety from a factory implies shorter production runs, which implies an inability to realize economies of scale, and thus higher costs. That is, a wide product variety makes it difficult for a company to increase its production efficiency and reduce its unit costs. According to this logic, the way to increase efficiency and achieve a lower cost structure is to limit product variety and produce a standardized product in large volumes (see Figure 4.5a).

This view of production efficiency has been challenged by the rise of flexible production technologies. The term **flexible production technology** covers a range of technologies designed to reduce setup times for complex equipment, increase the use of individual machines through better scheduling, and improve quality control at all stages of the manufacturing process.[8] Flexible production technologies allow the company to produce a wider variety of end products at a unit cost that at one time could be achieved only through the mass production of a standardized output (see Figure 4.5b). Research suggests that the adoption of flexible production technologies may increase efficiency and lower unit costs relative to what can be achieved by the mass production of a standardized output, while at the same time enabling the company to customize its product offering to a much greater extent than was once thought possible. The term **mass customization** has been coined to describe the company's ability to use flexible manufacturing technology to reconcile two goals that were once thought to be incompatible: low cost and differentiation through product customization.[9]

Dell Computer is pursuing a mass-customization strategy when it allows its customers to build their own machines online. Dell keeps costs and prices under control by allowing customers to make choices within a limited menu of options (e.g., different amounts of memory, hard drive size, video card, microprocessor, etc). The result is to create more value for customers than is possible for rivals that sell a limited range of PC models through retail

flexible production technology

A range of technologies designed to reduce setup times for complex equipment, increase the use of individual machines through better scheduling, and improve quality control at all stages of the manufacturing process.

mass customization

The use of flexible manufacturing technology to reconcile two goals that were once thought to be incompatible: low cost, and differentiation through product customization.

Figure 4.5   Tradeoff Between Costs and Product Variety

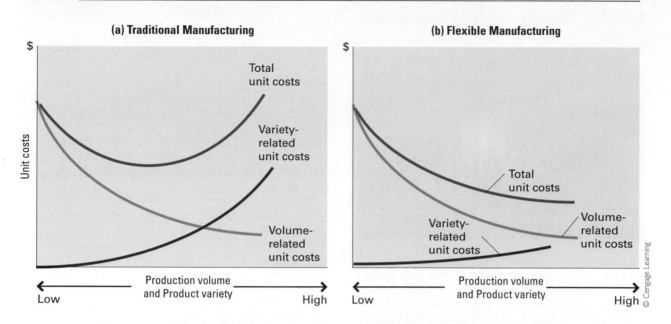

outlets. Similarly, Mars offers a service that enables customers to design their own "personalized" M&Ms over the Web. Called My M&Ms, customers can pick different colors and have messages or pictures printed on their M&Ms. Another example of mass customization is the Internet radio service Pandora, which is discussed in Strategy in Action 4.2.

The effects of installing flexible production technology on a company's cost structure can be dramatic. Over the last decade, the Ford Motor Company has been introducing flexible production technologies into its automotive plants around the world. These technologies have enabled Ford to produce multiple models from the same line and to switch production from one model to another much more quickly than in the past. Ford took $2 billion out of its cost structure between 2006 and 2010 through flexible manufacturing, and is striving to take out more.[10]

Marketing and Efficiency

The marketing strategy that a company adopts can have a major impact on efficiency and cost structure. **Marketing strategy** refers to the position that a company takes with regard to market segmentation, pricing, promotion, advertising, product design, and distribution. Some of the steps leading to greater efficiency are fairly obvious. For example, moving down the experience curve to achieve a lower cost structure can be facilitated by aggressive pricing, promotions, and advertising—all of which are the task of the marketing function. Other aspects of marketing strategy have a less obvious—but no less important impact—on efficiency. One important aspect is the relationship of customer defection rates, cost structure, and unit costs.[11]

Customer defection (or "churn rates") are the percentage of a company's customers who defect every year to competitors. Defection rates are determined by customer loyalty, which in turn is a function of the ability of a company to satisfy its customers. Because

marketing strategy ✂
The position that a company takes with regard to pricing, promotion, advertising, product design, and distribution.

customer defection ✂
Rate percentage of a company's customers who defect every year to competitors.

4.2 STRATEGY IN ACTION

Pandora: Mass Customizing Internet Radio

© iStockPhoto.com/Tom Nulens

M4OS Photos/Alamy

Pandora Media streams music to PCs and mobile devices. Customers start by typing in the kind of music that they want to listen to. With a database of over 100,000 artists, there is a good chance that Pandora has something for you, however obscure your tastes. Customers can then rate the music that Pandora plays for them (thumbs up or down). Pandora takes this feedback and refines the music it streams to a customer. The company also uses sophisticated predictive statistical analysis (what do other customers who also like this song listen to?) and product analysis (what Pandora calls its Music Genome, which analyzes songs and identifies similar songs) to further customize the experience for the individual listener. The Music Genome has the added benefit of introducing listeners to new songs they might like based on an analysis of their listening habits. The result is a radio station that is uniquely tuned into each individual's unique listening preferences. This is mass customization at its most pure.

Started in 2000, by late 2012 Pandora's annualized revenue run rate was close to 500 million. There were 175 million registered users and 63 million active users, giving Pandora a 75% share of the online radio market in the United States. Pandora's revenue comes primarily from advertising, although premium subscribers can pay $36 a year and get commercial-free music.

Despite its rapid growth—a testament to the value of mass customization—Pandora does have its problems. Pandora pays more than half of its revenue in royalties to music publishers. By comparison, satellite radio company Sirius-XM pays out only 7.5% of its revenue in the form of royalties, and cable companies that stream music pay only 15%. The different royalty rates are due to somewhat arcane regulations under which three judges who serve on the Copyright Royalty Board, an arm of the Library of Congress, set royalty fees for radio broadcasters. This method of setting royalty rates has worked against Pandora, although the company is lobbying hard to have the law changed. Pandora is also facing growing competition from Spotify and Rdio, two customizable music-streaming services that have sold equity stakes to recording labels in exchange for access to their music libraries. There are also reports that Apple will soon be offering its own customizable music-streaming service. Whatever happens to Pandora in the long run, however, it would seem that the mass customization of Internet radio is here to stay.

Soures: A. Fixmer, "Pandora Is Boxed in by High Royalty Fees," *Bloomberg Businessweek*, December 24, 2012; E. Smith and J. Letzing, "At Pandora Each Sales Drives up Losses," *Wall Street Journal*, December 6, 2012; and E. Savitz, "Pandora Swoons on Weak Outlook," *Forbes.com*, December 5, 2012.

acquiring a new customer often entails one-time fixed costs, there is a direct relationship between defection rates and costs. For example, when a wireless service company signs up a new subscriber, it has to bear the administrative costs of opening up a new account and the cost of a subsidy that it pays to the manufacturer of the handset the new subscriber decides to use. There are also the costs of advertising and promotions designed to attract new subscribers. The longer a company retains a customer, the greater the volume of customer-generated unit sales that can be set against these fixed costs, and the lower the average unit cost of each sale. Thus, lowering customer defection rates allows a company to achieve a lower cost structure.

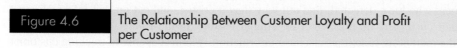

Figure 4.6 | The Relationship Between Customer Loyalty and Profit per Customer

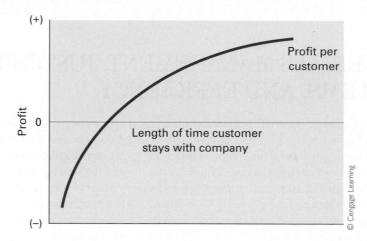

One consequence of the defection–cost relationship depicted is illustrated in Figure 4.6. Because of the relatively high fixed costs of acquiring new customers, serving customers who stay with the company only for a short time before switching to competitors often leads to a loss on the investment made to acquire those customers. The longer a customer stays with the company, the more the fixed costs of acquiring that customer can be distributed over repeat purchases, boosting the profit per customer. Thus, there is a positive relationship between the length of time that a customer stays with a company and profit per customer. If a company can reduce customer defection rates, it can make a much better return on its investment in acquiring customers, and thereby boost its profitability.

For an example, consider the credit card business.[12] Most credit card companies spend an average of $50 per customer for recruitment and new account setup. These costs are derived from the advertising required to attract new customers, the credit checks required for each customer, and the mechanics of setting up an account and issuing a card. These one-time fixed costs can be recouped only if a customer stays with the company for at least 2 years. Moreover, when customers stay a second year, they tend to increase their use of the credit card, which raises the volume of revenues generated by each customer over time. As a result, although the credit card business loses $50 per customer in year 1, it makes a profit of $44 in year 3 and $55 in year 6.

Another economic benefit of long-time customer loyalty is the free advertising that customers provide for a company. Loyal customers can dramatically increase the volume of business through referrals. A striking example is Britain's largest retailer, the clothing and food company Marks & Spencer, whose success is built on a well-earned reputation for providing its customers with high-quality goods at reasonable prices. The company has generated such customer loyalty that it does not need to advertise in Britain, a major source of cost savings.

The key message, then, is that reducing customer defection rates and building customer loyalty can be major sources of a lower cost structure. One study has estimated that a 5% reduction in customer defection rates leads to the following increases in profits per customer over average customer life: 75% in the credit card business, 50% in the insurance brokerage industry, 45% in the industrial laundry business, and 35% in the computer software industry.[13]

A central component of developing a strategy to reduce defection rates is to identify customers who have defected, find out why they defected, and act on that information so that other customers do not defect for similar reasons in the future. To take these measures, the marketing function must have information systems capable of tracking customer defections.

MATERIALS MANAGEMENT, JUST-IN-TIME SYSTEMS, AND EFFICIENCY

The contribution of materials management (logistics) to boosting the efficiency of a company can be just as dramatic as the contribution of production and marketing. Materials management encompasses the activities necessary to get inputs and components to a production facility (including the costs of purchasing inputs), through the production process, and out through a distribution system to the end-user.[14] Because there are so many sources of cost in this process, the potential for reducing costs through more efficient materials-management strategies is enormous. For a typical manufacturing company, materials and transportation costs account for 50 to 70% of its revenues, so even a small reduction in these costs can have a substantial impact on profitability. According to one estimate, for a company with revenues of $1 million, a return on invested capital of 5%, and materials-management costs that amount to 50% of sales revenues (including purchasing costs), increasing total profits by $15,000 would require either a 30% increase in sales revenues or a 3% reduction in materials costs.[15] In a typical competitive market, reducing materials costs by 3% is usually much easier than increasing sales revenues by 30%.

just-in-time (JIT) inventory system

System of economizing on inventory holding costs by scheduling components to arrive just in time to enter the production process or as stock is depleted.

Improving the efficiency of the materials-management function typically requires the adoption of a **just-in-time (JIT) inventory system**, which is designed to economize on inventory holding costs by scheduling components to arrive at a manufacturing plant just in time to enter the production process, or to have goods arrive at a retail store only when stock is almost depleted. The major cost saving comes from increasing inventory turnover, which reduces inventory holding costs, such as warehousing and storage costs, and the company's need for working capital. For example, through efficient logistics, Wal-Mart can replenish the stock in its stores at least twice a week; many stores receive daily deliveries if they are needed. The typical competitor replenishes its stock every 2 weeks, so it must carry a much higher inventory, which requires more working capital per dollar of sales. Compared to its competitors, Wal-Mart can maintain the same service levels with a lower investment in inventory, a major source of its lower cost structure. Thus, faster inventory turnover has helped Wal-Mart achieve an efficiency-based competitive advantage in the retailing industry.[16]

More generally, in terms of the profitability model developed in Chapter 3, JIT inventory systems reduce the need for working capital (because there is less inventory to finance) and the need for fixed capital to finance storage space (because there is less to store), which reduces capital needs, increases capital turnover, and, by extension, boosts the return on invested capital.

The drawback of JIT systems is that they leave a company without a buffer stock of inventory. Although buffer stocks are expensive to store, they can help a company prepare for shortages on inputs brought about by disruption among suppliers (for instance, a labor dispute at a key supplier), and can help a company respond quickly to increases in demand. However, there are ways around these limitations. For example, to reduce the risks linked to dependence on just one supplier for an important input, a company might decide to source inputs from multiple suppliers.

Recently, the efficient management of materials and inventory has been recast in terms of **supply chain management**: the task of managing the flow of inputs and components from suppliers into the company's production processes to minimize inventory holding and maximize inventory turnover. Dell, whose goal is to streamline its supply chain to such an extent that it "replaces inventory with information," is exemplary in terms of supply chain management.

supply chain management
The task of managing the flow of inputs and components from suppliers into the company's production processes to minimize inventory holding and maximize inventory turnover.

Value Chain

R&D Strategy and Efficiency

The role of superior research and development (R&D) in helping a company achieve a greater efficiency and a lower cost structure is twofold. First, the R&D function can boost efficiency by designing products that are easy to manufacture. By cutting down on the number of parts that make up a product, R&D can dramatically decrease the required assembly time, which results in higher employee productivity, lower costs, and higher profitability. For example, after Texas Instruments redesigned an infrared sighting mechanism that it supplies to the Pentagon, it found that it had reduced the number of parts from 47 to 12, the number of assembly steps from 56 to 13, the time spent fabricating metal from 757 minutes per unit to 219 minutes per unit, and unit assembly time from 129 minutes to 20 minutes. The result was a substantial decline in production costs. Design for manufacturing requires close coordination between the production and R&D functions of the company. Cross-functional teams that contain production and R&D personnel who work jointly can best achieve this.

Pioneering process innovations is the second way in which the R&D function can help a company achieve a lower cost structure. A process innovation is a new, unique way that production processes can operate to improve their efficiency. Process innovations have often been a major source of competitive advantage. Toyota's competitive advantage is based partly on the company's invention of new flexible manufacturing processes that dramatically reduce setup times. This process innovation enabled Toyota to obtain efficiency gains associated with flexible manufacturing systems years ahead of its competitors.

Human Resource Strategy and Efficiency

Employee productivity is one of the key determinants of an enterprise's efficiency, cost structure, and profitability.[17] Productive manufacturing employees can lower the cost of goods sold as a percentage of revenues, a productive sales force can increase sales revenues for a given level of expenses, and productive employees in the company's R&D function can boost the percentage of revenues generated from new products for a given level of R&D expenses. Thus, productive employees lower the costs of generating revenues, increase the return on sales, and, by extension, boost the company's return on invested capital. The challenge for a company's human resource function is to devise ways to increase employee productivity. Among its choices are using certain hiring strategies, training employees, organizing the workforce into self-managing teams, and linking pay to performance.

Hiring Strategy Many companies that are well known for their productive employees devote considerable attention to hiring. Southwest Airlines hires people who have a positive attitude and who work well in teams because it believes that people who have a positive attitude will work hard and interact well with customers, therefore helping to create customer loyalty. Nucor hires people who are self-reliant and goal-oriented, because its employees, who work in self-managing teams, require these skills to perform well. As these examples suggest, it is important to be sure that the hiring strategy of the company is consistent with its own internal organization, culture, and strategic priorities. The people a company hires should have attributes that match the strategic objectives of the company.

Employee Training

Employees are a major input into the production process. Those who are highly skilled can perform tasks faster and more accurately, and are more likely to learn the complex tasks associated with many modern production methods than individuals with lesser skills. Training upgrades employee skill levels, bringing the company productivity-related efficiency gains from learning and experimentation.[18]

Self-Managing Teams

self-managing teams
Teams where members coordinate their own activities and make their own hiring, training, work, and reward decisions.

The use of **self-managing teams**, whose members coordinate their own activities and make their own hiring, training, work, and reward decisions, has been spreading rapidly. The typical team comprises 5 to 15 employees who produce an entire product or undertake an entire task. Team members learn all team tasks and rotate from job to job. Because a more flexible workforce is one result, team members can fill in for absent coworkers and take over managerial duties such as scheduling work and vacation, ordering materials, and hiring new members. The greater responsibility thrust on team members and the empowerment it implies are seen as motivators. (*Empowerment* is the process of giving lower-level employees decision-making power.) People often respond well to being given greater autonomy and responsibility. Performance bonuses linked to team production and quality targets work as an additional motivator.

The effect of introducing self-managing teams is reportedly an increase in productivity of 30% or more and a substantial increase in product quality. Further cost savings arise from eliminating supervisors and creating a flatter organizational hierarchy, which also lowers the cost structure of the company. In manufacturing companies, perhaps the most potent way to lower the cost structure is to combine self-managing teams with flexible manufacturing cells. For example, after the introduction of flexible manufacturing technology and work practices based on self-managing teams, a General Electric (GE) plant in Salisbury, North Carolina, increased productivity by 250% compared with GE plants that produced the same products 4 years earlier.[19]

Still, teams are no panacea; in manufacturing companies, self-managing teams may fail to live up to their potential unless they are integrated with flexible manufacturing technology. Also, teams place a lot of management responsibilities upon team members, and helping team members to cope with these responsibilities often requires substantial training—a fact that many companies often forget in their rush to drive down costs. Haste can result in teams that don't work out as well as planned.[20]

Pay for Performance

It is hardly surprising that linking pay to performance can help increase employee productivity, but the issue is not quite so simple as just introducing incentive pay systems. It is also important to define what kind of job performance is to be rewarded and how. Some of the most efficient companies in the world, mindful that cooperation among employees is necessary to realize productivity gains, link pay to group or team (rather than individual) performance. Nucor Steel divides its workforce into teams of about 30, with bonus pay, which can amount to 30% of base pay, linked to the ability of the team to meet productivity and quality goals. This link creates a strong incentive for individuals to cooperate with each other in pursuit of team goals; that is, it facilitates teamwork.

FOCUS ON: Wal-Mart

Human Resource Strategy and Productivity at Wal-Mart

© iStockPhoto.com/caracterdesign

Wal-Mart has one of the most productive workforces of any retailer. The roots of Wal-Mart's high productivity go back to the company's early days and the business philosophy of the company's founder, Sam Walton. Walton started off his career as a management trainee at J.C. Penney. There he noticed that all employees were called associates, and moreover, that treating them with respect seemed to reap dividends in the form of high employee productivity.

When he founded Wal-Mart, Walton decided to call all employees "associates" to symbolize their importance to the company. He reinforced this by emphasizing that at Wal-Mart, "Our people make the difference." Unlike many managers who have stated this mantra, Walton believed it and put it into action. He believed that if you treat people well, they will return the favor by working hard, and that if you empower them, then ordinary people can work together to achieve extraordinary things. These beliefs formed the basis for a decentralized organization that operated with an open-door policy and open books. This allowed associates to see just how their stores and the company were doing.

Consistent with the open-door policy, Walton continually emphasized that management needed to listen to associates and their ideas. As he noted: "The folks on the front lines—the ones who actually talk to the customer—are the only ones who really know what's going on out there. You'd better find out what they know. This really is what total quality is all about. To push responsibility down in your organization, and to force good ideas to bubble up within it, you must listen to what your Associates are trying to tell you."

For all of his belief in empowerment, however, Walton was notoriously tight on pay. Walton opposed unionization, fearing that it would lead to higher pay and restrictive work rules that would sap productivity. The culture of Wal-Mart also encouraged people to work hard. One of Walton's favorite homilies was the "sundown rule," which stated that one should never leave until tomorrow what can be done today. The sundown rule was enforced by senior managers, including Walton, who would drop in unannounced at a store, peppering store managers and employees with questions, but at the same time praising them for a job well done and celebrating the "heroes" who took the sundown rule to heart, and did today what could have been done tomorrow.

The key to getting extraordinary effort out of employees, while paying them meager salaries, was to reward them with profit-sharing plans and stock-ownership schemes. Long before it became fashionable in American business, Walton was placing a chunk of Wal-Mart's profits into a profit-sharing plan for associates, and the company put matching funds into employee stock-ownership programs. The idea was simple: reward associates by giving them a stake in the company, and they will work hard for low pay, because they know they will make it up in profit sharing and stock price appreciation.

For years this formula worked extraordinarily well, but there are now signs that Wal-Mart's very success is creating problems. In 2012 the company had a staggering 2.2 million associates, making it the largest private employer in the world. As the company has grown, it has become increasingly difficult to hire the kinds of people that Wal-Mart has traditionally relied on—those willing to work long hours for low pay based on the promise of advancement and reward through profit sharing and stock ownership. The company has come under attack for paying its associates low wages and pressuring them to work long hours without overtime pay. Labor unions have made a concerted but so far unsuccessful attempt to unionize stores, and the company itself is the target of lawsuits from employees alleging sexual discrimination. Wal-Mart claims that the negative publicity is based on faulty data, and perhaps that is right, but if the company has indeed become too big to put Walton's principles into practice, the glory days may be over.

Sources: Sam Walton, *Made in America* (New York: Bantam, 1992), S. Maich, "Wal-Mart's Mid-Life Crisis," *Maclean's*, August 23, 2004, p. 45; "The People Make It All Happen," *Discount Store News*, October 1999, pp 103–106; and www.walmartstores.com.

Information Systems and Efficiency

With the rapid spread of computer use, the explosive growth of the Internet and corporate intranets (internal corporate computer networks based on Internet standards), and the spread of high-bandwidth fiber-optics and digital wireless technology, the information systems function has moved to center stage in the quest for operating efficiencies and a lower cost structure.[21] The impact of information systems on productivity is wide ranging and potentially affects all other activities of a company. For example, Cisco Systems was able to realize significant cost savings by moving its ordering and customer service functions online. The company found it could operate with just 300 service agents handling all of its customer accounts, compared to the 900 it would need if sales were not handled online. The difference represented an annual savings of $20 million a year. Moreover, without automated customer service functions, Cisco calculated that it would need at least 1,000 additional service engineers, which would cost around $75 million.[22]

Like Cisco, many companies are using Web-based information systems to reduce the costs of coordination between the company and its customers and the company and its suppliers. By using Web-based programs to automate customer and supplier interactions, they can substantially reduce the number of people required to manage these interfaces, thereby reducing costs. This trend extends beyond high-tech companies. Banks and financial service companies are finding that they can substantially reduce costs by moving customer accounts and support functions online. Such a move reduces the need for customer service representatives, bank tellers, stockbrokers, insurance agents, and others. For example, it costs an average of about $1.07 to execute a transaction at a bank, such as shifting money from one account to another; executing the same transaction over the Internet costs $0.01.[23]

Similarly, the theory behind Internet-based retailers such as Amazon.com is that replacing physical stores and their supporting personnel with an online virtual store and automated ordering and checkout processes allows a company to take significant costs out of the retailing system. Cost savings can also be realized by using Web-based information systems to automate many internal company activities, from managing expense reimbursements to benefits planning and hiring processes, thereby reducing the need for internal support personnel.

Infrastructure and Efficiency

A company's infrastructure—that is, its structure, culture, style of strategic leadership, and control system—determines the context within which all other value creation activities take place. It follows that improving infrastructure can help a company increase efficiency and lower its cost structure. Above all, an appropriate infrastructure can help foster a companywide commitment to efficiency, and promote cooperation among different functions in pursuit of efficiency goals. These issues are addressed at length in Chapters 12 and 13.

For now, it is important to note that strategic leadership is especially important in building a companywide commitment to efficiency. The leadership task is to articulate a vision that recognizes the need for all functions of a company to focus on improving efficiency. It is not enough to improve the efficiency of production, or of marketing, or of R&D in a piecemeal fashion. Achieving superior efficiency requires a companywide commitment to this goal that must be articulated by general and functional managers. A further leadership task is to facilitate the cross-functional cooperation needed to achieve superior efficiency.

For example, designing products that are easy to manufacture requires that production and R&D personnel communicate; integrating JIT systems with production scheduling requires close communication between materials management and production; and designing self-managing teams to perform production tasks requires close cooperation between human resources and production.

Summary

Table 4.1 summarizes the primary roles of various functions in achieving superior efficiency. Keep in mind that achieving superior efficiency is not something that can be tackled on a function-by-function basis. It requires an organization-wide commitment and an ability to ensure close cooperation among functions. Top management, by exercising leadership and influencing the infrastructure, plays a significant role in this process.

Table 4.1 — Primary Roles of Value Creation Functions in Achieving Superior Efficiency

Value Creation Function	Primary Roles
Infrastructure (leadership)	1. Provide company-wide commitment to efficiency
	2. Facilitate cooperation among functions
Production	1. Where appropriate, pursue economies of scale and learning economics
	2. Implement flexible manufacturing systems
Marketing	1. Where appropriate, adopt aggressive marketing to ride down the experience curve
	2. Limit customer defection rates by building brand loyalty
Materials management	1. Implement JIT systems
	2. Implement supply-chain coordination
R&D	1. Design products for ease of manufacture
	2. Seek process innovations
Information systems	1. Use information systems to automate processes
	2. Use information systems to reduce costs of coordination
Human resources	1. Institute training programs to build skills
	2. Implement self-managing teams
	3. Implement pay for performance

© Cengage Learning

ACHIEVING SUPERIOR QUALITY

In Chapter 3, we noted that quality can be thought of in terms of two dimensions: *quality as reliability* and *quality as excellence*. High-quality products are reliable, do well the job for which they were designed, and are perceived by consumers to have superior attributes. We also noted that superior quality provides a company with two advantages. First, a strong reputation for quality allows a company to differentiate its products from those offered by rivals, thereby creating more value in the eyes of customers, and giving the company the option of charging a premium price for its products. Second, eliminating defects or errors from the production process reduces waste, increases efficiency, lowers the cost structure of the company, and increases its profitability. For example, reducing the number of defects in a company's manufacturing process will lower the cost of goods sold as a percentage of revenues, thereby raising the company's return on sales and return on invested capital. In this section, we look in more depth at what managers can do to enhance the reliability and other attributes of the company's product offering.

Attaining Superior Reliability

total quality management increasing product reliability so that it consistently performs as it was designed to and rarely breaks down.

The principal tool that most managers now use to increase the reliability of their product offering is the Six Sigma quality improvement methodology. The Six Sigma methodology is a direct descendant of the **total quality management** (TQM) philosophy that was widely adopted, first by Japanese companies and then by American companies, during the 1980s and early 1990s.[24] The TQM concept was developed by a number of American management consultants, including W. Edwards Deming, Joseph Juran, and A. V. Feigenbaum.[25]

Originally, these consultants won few converts in the United States. However, managers in Japan embraced their ideas enthusiastically, and even named their premier annual prize for manufacturing excellence after Deming. The philosophy underlying TQM, as articulated by Deming, is based on the following five-step chain reaction:

1. Improved quality means that costs decrease because of less rework, fewer mistakes, fewer delays, and better use of time and materials.
2. As a result, productivity improves.
3. Better quality leads to higher market share and allows the company to raise prices.
4. Higher prices increase the company's profitability and allow it to stay in business.
5. Thus, the company creates more jobs.[26]

Deming identified a number of steps that should be part of any quality improvement program:

1. Management should embrace the philosophy that mistakes, defects, and poor-quality materials are not acceptable and should be eliminated.
2. Quality of supervision should be improved by allowing more time for supervisors to work with employees, and giving employees appropriate skills for the job.
3. Management should create an environment in which employees will not fear reporting problems or recommending improvements.
4. Work standards should not only be defined as numbers or quotas, but should also include some notion of quality to promote the production of defect-free output.
5. Management is responsible for training employees in new skills to keep pace with changes in the workplace.
6. Achieving better quality requires the commitment of everyone in the company.

Western businesses were blind to the importance of the TQM concept until Japan rose to the top rank of economic powers in the 1980s. Since that time, quality improvement programs have spread rapidly throughout Western industry. Strategy in Action 4.3 describes one of the most successful implementations of a quality improvement process, General Electric's Six Sigma program.

4.3 STRATEGY IN ACTION

General Electric's Six Sigma Quality Improvement Process

© iStockPhoto.com/Tom Nulens

Six Sigma, a quality and efficiency program adopted by many major corporations, including Motorola, General Electric, and AlliedSignal, aims to reduce defects, boost productivity, eliminate waste, and cut costs throughout a company. "Sigma" comes from the Greek letter that statisticians use to represent a standard deviation from a mean: the higher the number of sigmas, the smaller the number of errors. At Six Sigma, a production process would be 99.99966% accurate, creating just 3.4 defects per million units. Although it is almost impossible for a company to achieve such perfection, several companies strive toward that goal.

General Electric (GE) is perhaps the most well-known adopter of the Six Sigma program. Under the direction of long-serving CEO Jack Welch, GE spent nearly $1 billion to convert all of its divisions to the Six Sigma method.

One of the first products designed using Six Sigma processes was a $1.25 million diagnostic computer tomography (CT) scanner, the LightSpeed VCT, which produces rapid three-dimensional images of the human body. The new scanner captured multiple images simultaneously, requiring only 20 seconds to do full-body scans that once took 3 minutes—important because patients must remain perfectly still during the scan. GE spent $50 million to run 250 separate Six Sigma analyses designed to improve the reliability and lower the manufacturing cost of the new scanner. Its efforts were rewarded when LightSpeed VCT's first customers soon noticed that it ran without downtime between patients—a testament to the reliability of the machine.

Achieving that reliability took immense work. GE's engineers deconstructed the scanner into its basic components and tried to improve the reliability of each component through a detailed step-by-step analysis. For example, the most important part of CT scanners is the vacuum tubes that focus x-ray waves. The tubes that GE used in previous scanners, which cost $60,000 each, suffered from low reliability. Hospitals and clinics wanted the tubes to operate for 12 hours a day for at least 6 months, but typically they lasted only half that long. Moreover, GE was scrapping some $20 million in tubes each year because they failed preshipping performance tests, and disturbing numbers of faulty tubes were slipping past inspection, only to be determined as dysfunctional upon arrival.

To try to solve the reliability problem, the Six Sigma team took the tubes apart. They knew that one problem was a petroleum-based oil used in the tubes to prevent short circuits by isolating the anode (which has a positive charge) from the negatively charged cathode. The oil often deteriorated after a few months, leading to short circuits, but the team did not know why. By using statistical "what-if" scenarios on all parts of the tube, the researchers learned that the lead-based paint on the inside of the tube was contaminating the oil. Acting on this information, the team developed a paint that would preserve the tube and protect the oil.

By pursuing this and other improvements, the Six Sigma team was able to extend the average life of a vacuum tube in the CT scanner from 3 months to over 1 year. Although the improvements increased the cost of the tube from $60,000 to $85,000, the increased cost was outweighed by the reduction in replacement costs, making it an attractive proposition for customers.

Sources: C. H. Deutsch, "Six-Sigma Enlightenment," *New York Times*, December 7, 1998, p. 1; J. J. Barshay, "The Six-Sigma Story," *Star Tribune*, June 14, 1999, p. 1; D. D. Bak, "Rethinking Industrial Drives," *Electrical/Electronics Technology*, November 30, 1998, p. 58.

Implementing Reliability Improvement Methodologies

Among companies that have successfully adopted quality improvement methodologies, certain imperatives stand out. These are discussed in the following sections in the order in which they are usually tackled in companies implementing quality improvement programs. What needs to be stressed first, however, is that improvement in product reliability is a cross-functional process. Its implementation requires close cooperation among all functions in the pursuit of the common goal of improving quality; it is a process that works across functions. The roles played by the different functions in implementing reliability improvement methodologies are summarized in Table 4.2.

First, it is important that senior managers agree to a quality improvement program and communicate its importance to the organization. Second, if a quality improvement program is to be successful, individuals must be identified to lead the program. Under the Six Sigma methodology, exceptional employees are identified and put through a "black belt" training course on the Six Sigma methodology. The black belts are taken out of their normal job roles,

Table 4.2	Roles Played by Different Functions in Implementing Reliability Improvement Methodologies
Infrastructure (leadership)	1. Provide leadership and commitment to quality
	2. Find ways to measure quality
	3. Set goals and create incentives
	4. Solicit input from employees
	5. Encourage cooperation among functions
Production	1. Shorten production runs
	2. Trace defects back to the source
Marketing	1. Focus on the customer
	2. Provide customers' feedback on quality
Materials management	1. Rationalize suppliers
	2. Help suppliers implement quality-improvement methodologies
	3. Trace defects back to suppliers
R&D	1. Design products that are easy to manufacture
Information systems	1. Use information systems to monitor defect rates
Human resources	1. Institute quality-improvement training programs
	2. Identify and train "black belts"
	3. Organize employees into quality teams

and assigned to work solely on Six Sigma projects for the next 2 years. In effect, the black belts become internal consultants *and* project leaders. Because they are dedicated to Six Sigma programs, the black belts are not distracted from the task at hand by day-to-day operating responsibilities. To make a black belt assignment attractive, many companies now endorse the program as an advancement in a career path. Successful black belts might not return to their prior job after 2 years, but could instead be promoted and given more responsibility.

Third, quality improvement methodologies preach the need to identify defects that arise from processes, trace them to their source, find out what caused the defects, and make corrections so that they do not recur. Production and materials management are primarily responsible for this task. To uncover defects, quality improvement methodologies rely upon the use of statistical procedures to pinpoint variations in the quality of goods or services. Once variations have been identified, they must be traced to their respective sources and eliminated.

One technique that helps greatly in tracing defects to the source is reducing lot sizes for manufactured products. With short production runs, defects show up immediately. Consequently, they can quickly be sourced, and the problem can be addressed. Reducing lot sizes also means that when defective products are produced, there will not be a large number produced, thus decreasing waste. Flexible manufacturing techniques can be used to reduce lot sizes without raising costs. JIT inventory systems also play a part. Under a JIT system, defective parts enter the manufacturing process immediately; they are not warehoused for several months before use. Hence, defective inputs can be quickly spotted. The problem can then be traced to the supply source and corrected before more defective parts are produced. Under a more traditional system, the practice of warehousing parts for months before they are used may mean that suppliers produce large numbers of defects before entering the production process.

Fourth, another key to any quality improvement program is to create a metric that can be used to measure quality. In manufacturing companies, quality can be measured by criteria such as defects per million parts. In service companies, suitable metrics can be devised with a little creativity. For example, one of the metrics Florida Power & Light uses to measure quality is meter-reading errors per month.

Fifth, once a metric has been devised, the next step is to set a challenging quality goal and create incentives for reaching it. Under Six Sigma programs, the goal is 3.4 defects per million units. One way of creating incentives to attain such a goal is to link rewards, such as bonus pay and promotional opportunities, to the goal.

Sixth, shop-floor employees can be a major source of ideas for improving product quality, so these employees must participate and must be incorporated into a quality improvement program.

Seventh, a major source of poor-quality finished goods is poor-quality component parts. To decrease product defects, a company must work with its suppliers to improve the quality of the parts they supply.

Eighth, the more assembly steps a product requires, the more opportunities there are for mistakes. Thus, designing products with fewer parts is often a major component of any quality improvement program.

Finally, implementing quality improvement methodologies requires organization-wide commitment and substantial cooperation among functions. R&D must cooperate with production to design products that are easy to manufacture; marketing must cooperate with production and R&D so that customer problems identified by marketing can be acted on; and human resource management must cooperate with all the other functions of the company in order to devise suitable quality-training programs.

Improving Quality as Excellence

As we stated in Chapter 3, a product is comprised of different attributes, and reliability is just one attribute, albeit an important one. Products can also be *differentiated* by attributes that collectively define product excellence. These attributes include the form, features, performance, durability, and styling of a product. In addition, a company can create quality as excellence by emphasizing attributes of the service associated with the product, such as ordering ease, prompt delivery, easy installation, the availability of customer training and consulting, and maintenance services. Dell Inc., for example, differentiates itself on ease of ordering (via the Web), prompt delivery, easy installation, and the ready availability of customer support and maintenance services. Differentiation can also be based on the attributes of the people in the company with whom customers interact when making a product purchase, such as their competence, courtesy, credibility, responsiveness, and communication. Singapore Airlines enjoys an excellent reputation for quality service, largely because passengers perceive their flight attendants as competent, courteous, and responsive to their needs. Thus, we can talk about the product attributes, service attributes, and personnel attributes associated with a company's product offering (see Table 4.3).

For a product to be regarded as high in the excellence dimension, a company's product offering must be seen as superior to that of rivals. Achieving a perception of high quality on any of these attributes requires specific actions by managers. First, it is important for managers to collect marketing intelligence indicating which of these attributes are most important to customers. For example, consumers of personal computers (PCs) may place a low weight on durability because they expect their PCs to be made obsolete by technological advances within 3 years, but they may place a high weight on features and performance. Similarly, ease of ordering and timely delivery may be very important attributes for customers of online booksellers (as they indeed are for customers of Amazon.com), whereas customer training and consulting may be very important attributes for customers who purchase complex business-to-business software to manage their relationships with suppliers.

Second, once the company has identified the attributes that are important to customers, it needs to design its products (and the associated services) in such a way that those attributes are embodied in the product. It also needs to make sure that personnel in the company

Table 4.3	Attributes Associated with a Product Offering

Product Attributes	Service Attributes	Associated Personnel Attributes
Form	Ordering ease	Competence
Features	Delivery	Courtesy
Performance	Installation	Credibility
Durability	Customer training	Reliability
Reliability	Customer consulting	Responsiveness
Style	Maintenance and repair	Communication

© Cengage Learning

are appropriately trained so that the correct attributes are emphasized during design creation. This requires close coordination between marketing and product development (the topic of the next section) and the involvement of the human resource management function in employee selection and training.

Third, the company must decide which of the significant attributes to promote and how best to position them in the minds of consumers, that is, how to tailor the marketing message so that it creates a consistent image in the minds of customers.[27] At this point, it is important to recognize that although a product might be differentiated on the basis of six attributes, covering all of those attributes in the company's communication messages may lead to an unfocused message. Many marketing experts advocate promoting only one or two central attributes to customers. For example, Volvo consistently emphasizes the safety and durability of its vehicles in all marketing messages, creating the perception in the minds of consumers (backed by product design) that Volvo cars are safe and durable. Volvo cars are also very reliable and have high performance, but the company does not emphasize these attributes in its marketing messages. In contrast, Porsche emphasizes performance and styling in all of its marketing messages; thus, a Porsche is positioned differently in the minds of consumers than Volvo. Both are regarded as high-quality products because both have superior attributes, but the attributes that each of the two companies have chosen to emphasize are very different; they are differentiated from the average car in different ways.

Finally, it must be recognized that competition is not stationary, but instead continually produces improvement in product attributes, and often the development of new-product attributes. This is obvious in fast-moving high-tech industries where product features that were considered leading edge just a few years ago are now obsolete—but the same process is also at work in more stable industries. For example, the rapid diffusion of microwave ovens during the 1980s required food companies to build new attributes into their frozen food products: they had to maintain their texture and consistency while being cooked in the microwave; a product could not be considered high quality unless it could do that. This speaks to the importance of having a strong R&D function in the company that can work with marketing and manufacturing to continually upgrade the quality of the attributes that are designed into the company's product offerings. Exactly how to achieve this is covered in the next section.

ACHIEVING SUPERIOR INNOVATION

In many ways, innovation is the most important source of competitive advantage. This is because innovation can result in new products that better satisfy customer needs, can improve the quality (attributes) of existing products, or can reduce the costs of making products that customers want. The ability to develop innovative new products or processes gives a company a major competitive advantage that allows it to: (1) *differentiate* its products and charge a premium price, and/or (2) *lower its cost structure* below that of its rivals. Competitors, however, attempt to imitate successful innovations and often succeed. Therefore, maintaining a competitive advantage requires a continuing commitment to innovation.

Successful new-product launches are major drivers of superior profitability. Robert Cooper reviewed more than 200 new-product introductions and found that of those classified as successes, some 50% achieve a return on investment in excess of 33%, half have a payback period of 2 years or less, and half achieve a market share in excess of 35%.[28] Many companies have established a track record for successful innovation. Among them are Apple, whose successes include the iPod, iPhone, and iPad; Pfizer, a drug company that during the 1990s and early 2000s produced eight new blockbuster drugs; 3M, which has applied its core competency in tapes and adhesives to developing a wide range of new products; Intel, which has consistently managed to lead in the development of innovative new microprocessors to run personal computers; and Cisco Systems, whose innovations in communications equipment helped to pave the way for the rapid growth of the Internet.

The High Failure Rate of Innovation

Although promoting innovation can be a source of competitive advantage, the failure rate of innovative new products is high. Research evidence suggests that only 10 to 20% of major R&D projects give rise to commercial products.[29] Well-publicized product failures include Apple's Newton, an early handheld computer that flopped in the market place; Sony's Betamax format in the videocassette recorder segment; Sega's Dreamcast video-game console; and Windows Mobile, an early smartphone operating system created by Microsoft that was made obsolete in the eyes of consumers by the arrival of Apple's iPhone. Although many reasons have been advanced to explain why so many new products fail to generate an economic return, five explanations for failure repeatedly appear.[30]

First, many new products fail because the demand for innovations is inherently uncertain. It is impossible to know prior to market introduction whether the new product has tapped an unmet customer need, and if there sufficient market demand to justify manufacturing the product. Although good market research can reduce the uncertainty about likely future demand for a new technology, that uncertainty cannot be fully eradicated; a certain failure rate is to be expected.

Second, new products often fail because the technology is poorly commercialized. This occurs when there is definite customer demand for a new product, but the product is not well adapted to customer needs because of factors such as poor design and poor quality. For instance, the failure of Microsoft to establish an enduring dominant position in the market for smartphones, despite the fact that phones using the Windows Mobile operating system were introduced in 2003, which was 4 years before Apple's iPhone hit the market, can be traced to its poor design. Windows Mobile phones had a physical keyboard, and a small and cluttered screen that was difficult to navigate, which made them unattractive to many consumers. In contrast, the iPhone's large touchscreen and associated keyboard was very appealing to many consumers, who rushed out to buy it in droves.

positioning strategy
The specific set of options a company adopts for a product based upon four main dimensions of marketing: price, distribution, promotion and advertising, and product features.

Third, new products may fail because of poor positioning strategy. **Positioning strategy** is the specific set of options a company adopts for a product based upon four main dimensions of marketing: price, distribution, promotion and advertising, and product features. Apart from poor design, another reason for the failure of Windows Mobile phones was poor positioning strategy. They were targeted at business users, whereas Apple developed a mass market by targeting the iPhone at retail consumers.

Fourth, many new-product introductions fail because companies often make the mistake of marketing a technology for which there is not enough demand. A company can become blinded by the wizardry of a new technology and fail to determine whether there is sufficient customer demand for the product. A classic example concerns the Segway two-wheeled personal transporter. Despite the fact that its gyroscopic controls were highly sophisticated, and that the product introduction was accompanied by massive media hype, sales fell well below expectations when it transpired that most consumers had no need for such a device.

Finally, companies fail when products are slowly marketed. The more time that elapses between initial development and final marketing—the slower the "cycle time"—the more likely it is that a competitor will beat the company to market and gain a first-mover advantage.[31] In the car industry, General Motors long suffered from being a slow innovator. Its typical product development cycle used to be about 5 years, compared with 2 to 3 years at Honda, Toyota, and Mazda, and 3 to 4 years at Ford. Because GM's offerings were based on 5-year-old technology and design concepts, they are already out of date when they reached the market.

Reducing Innovation Failures

One of the most important things that managers can do to reduce the high failure rate associated with innovation is to make sure that there is tight integration between R&D, production, and marketing.[32] Tight cross-functional integration can help a company ensure that:

1. Product development projects are driven by customer needs.
2. New products are designed for ease of manufacture.
3. Development costs are not allowed to spiral out of control.
4. The time it takes to develop a product and bring it to market is minimized.
5. Close integration between R&D and marketing is achieved to ensure that product development projects are driven by the needs of customers.

A company's customers can be a primary source of new-product ideas. The identification of customer needs, and particularly unmet needs, can set the context within which successful product innovation takes place. As the point of contact with customers, the marketing function can provide valuable information. Moreover, integrating R&D and marketing is crucial if a new product is to be properly commercialized—otherwise, a company runs the risk of developing products for which there is little or no demand.

Integration between R&D and production can help a company to ensure that products are designed with manufacturing requirements in mind. Design for manufacturing lowers manufacturing costs and leaves less room for mistakes; thus it can lower costs and increase product quality. Integrating R&D and production can help lower development costs and speed products to market. If a new product is not designed with manufacturing capabilities in mind, it may prove too difficult to build with existing manufacturing technology. In that case, the product will need to be redesigned, and both overall development costs and time to market may increase significantly. Making design changes during product planning can increase overall development costs by 50% and add 25% to the time it takes to bring the product to market.[33]

One of the best ways to achieve cross-functional integration is to establish cross-functional product development teams composed of representatives from R&D, marketing, and production. The objective of a team should be to oversee a product development project from initial concept development to market introduction. Specific attributes appear to be important in order for a product development team to function effectively and meet all its development milestones.[34]

First, a project manager who has high status within the organization and the power and authority required to secure the financial and human resources that the team needs to succeed should lead the team and be dedicated primarily, if not entirely, to the project. The leader should believe in the project (be a champion for the project) and be skilled at integrating the perspectives of different functions and helping personnel from different functions work together for a common goal. The leader should also be able to act as an advocate of the team to senior management.

Second, the team should be composed of at least one member from each key function or position. Individual team members should have a number of attributes, including an ability to contribute functional expertise, high standing within their function, a willingness to share responsibility for team results, and an ability to put functional advocacy aside. It is generally preferable if core team members are 100% dedicated to the project for its duration. This ensures that their focus is upon the project, not upon their ongoing individual work.

Third, the team members should be physically co-located to create a sense of camaraderie and facilitate communication. Fourth, the team should have a clear plan and clear goals, particularly with regard to critical development milestones and development budgets. The team should have incentives to attain those goals; for example, pay bonuses when major development milestones are attained. Fifth, each team needs to develop its own processes for communication, as well as conflict resolution. For example, one product development team at Quantum Corporation, a California-based manufacturer of disk drives for personal

4.4 STRATEGY IN ACTION

Corning—learning from Innovation Failures

© iStockPhoto.com/Tom Nulens

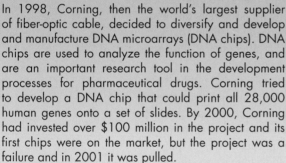

In 1998, Corning, then the world's largest supplier of fiber-optic cable, decided to diversify and develop and manufacture DNA microarrays (DNA chips). DNA chips are used to analyze the function of genes, and are an important research tool in the development processes for pharmaceutical drugs. Corning tried to develop a DNA chip that could print all 28,000 human genes onto a set of slides. By 2000, Corning had invested over $100 million in the project and its first chips were on the market, but the project was a failure and in 2001 it was pulled.

What went wrong? Corning was late to market—a critical mistake. Affymetrix, which had been in the business since the early 1990s, dominated the market. By 2000, Affymetrix's DNA chips were the dominant design—researchers were familiar with them, they performed well, and few people were willing to switch to chips from unproven competitors. Corning was late because it adhered to its long-established innovation processes, which were not entirely appropriate in the biological sciences. In particular, Corning's own in-house experts in the physical sciences insisted on sticking to rigorous quality standards that customers and life scientists felt were higher than necessary. These quality standards proved to be very difficult to achieve, and as a result, the product launch was delayed, giving Affymetrix time to consolidate its hold on the market.

Additionally, Corning failed to allow potential customers to review prototypes of its chips, and consequently, it missed incorporating some crucial features that customers wanted.

After reviewing this failure, Corning decided that in the future, it needed to bring customers into the development process earlier. The company also needed to hire additional outside experts if it planned to diversify into an area where it lacked competencies—and to allow those experts extensive input in the development process.

The project was not a total failure, however, for through it Corning discovered a vibrant and growing market—the market for drug discovery. By combining what it had learned about drug discovery with another failed business, photonics, which manipulates data using light waves, Corning created a new product called "Epic." Epic is a revolutionary technology for drug testing that uses light waves instead of fluorescent dyes (the standard industry practice). Epic promises to accelerate the process of testing potential drugs and save pharmaceutical companies valuable R&D money. Unlike in its DNA microarray project, Corning had 18 pharmaceutical companies test Epic before development was finalized. Corning used this feedback to refine Epic. The product is now an important product offering for the company.

Sources: V. Govindarajan and C. Trimble, "How Forgetting Leads to Innovation," *Chief Executive*, March 2006, pp. 46–50; and J. McGregor, "How Failure Breeds Success," *Business Week*, July 10, 2006, pp. 42–52.

computers, mandated that all major decisions would be made and conflicts resolved during meetings that were held every Monday afternoon. This simple rule helped the team to meet its development goals.[35]

Finally, there is sufficient evidence that developing competencies in innovation requires managers to proactively learn from their experience with product development, and to incorporate the lessons from past successes and failures into future new-product development processes.[36] This is easier said than done. To learn, managers need to undertake an objective assessment process after a product development project has been completed, identifying key success factors and the root causes of failures, and allocating resources toward repairing failures. Leaders also must admit their own failures if they are to encourage other team members to responsibly identify what they did wrong. Strategy in Action 4.4 looks at how Corning learned from a prior mistake to develop a potentially promising new product.

The primary role that the various functions play in achieving superior innovation is summarized in Table 4.4. The table makes two matters clear. First, top management must bear primary responsibility for overseeing the entire development process. This entails both managing the development process and facilitating cooperation among the functions. Second, the effectiveness of R&D in developing new products and processes depends upon its ability to cooperate with marketing and production.

Table 4.4

Functional Roles for Achieving Superior Innovation

Value Creation Function	Primary Roles
Infrastructure (leadership)	1. Manage overall project (i.e., manage the development function)
	2. Facilitate cross-functional cooperation
Production	1. Cooperate with R&D on designing products that are easy to manufacture
	2. Work with R&D to develop process innovations
Marketing	1. Provide market information to R&D
	2. Work with R&D to develop new products
Materials management	No primary responsibility
R&D	1. Develop new products and processes
	2. Cooperate with other functions, particularly marketing and manufacturing, in the development process
Information systems	1. Use information systems to coordinate cross-functional and cross-company product development work
Human resources	1. Hire talented scientists and engineers

ACHIEVING SUPERIOR RESPONSIVENESS TO CUSTOMERS

To achieve superior responsiveness to customers, a company must give customers what they want, when they want it, and at a price they are willing to pay—so long as the company's long-term profitability is not compromised in the process. Customer responsiveness is an important differentiating attribute that can help to build brand loyalty. Strong product differentiation and brand loyalty give a company more pricing options; it can charge a premium price for its products, or keep prices low to sell more goods and services to customers. Whether prices are at a premium or kept low, the company that is the most responsive to its customers' needs will have the competitive advantage.

Achieving superior responsiveness to customers means giving customers value for money, and steps taken to improve the efficiency of a company's production process and the quality of its products should be consistent with this aim. In addition, giving customers what they want may require the development of new products with new features. In other words, achieving superior efficiency, quality, and innovation are all part of achieving superior responsiveness to customers. There are two other prerequisites for attaining this goal. First, a company must develop a competency in listening to its customers, focusing on its customers, and in investigating and identifying their needs. Second, it must constantly seek better ways to satisfy those needs.

Focusing on the Customer

A company cannot be responsive to its customers' needs unless it knows what those needs are. Thus, the first step to building superior responsiveness to customers is to motivate the entire company to focus on the customer. The means to this end are: demonstrating leadership, shaping employee attitudes, and using mechanisms for making sure that the needs of the customer are well known within the company.

Demonstrating Leadership   Customer focus must begin at the top of the organization. A commitment to superior responsiveness to customers brings attitudinal changes throughout a company that can only be built through strong leadership. A mission statement that puts customers first is one way to send a clear message to employees about the desired focus. Another avenue is top management's own actions. For example, Tom Monaghan, the founder of Domino's Pizza, stayed close to the customer by eating Domino's pizza regularly, visiting as many stores as possible every week, running some deliveries himself, and insisting that other top managers do the same.[37]

Shaping Employee Attitudes   Leadership alone is not enough to attain a superior customer focus. All employees must see the customer as the focus of their activity, and be trained to focus on the customer—whether their function is marketing, manufacturing, R&D, or accounting. The objective should be to make employees think of themselves as customers—to put themselves in customers' shoes. From that perspective, employees become better able to identify ways to improve the quality of a customer's experience with the company.

To reinforce this mindset, incentive systems within the company should reward employees for satisfying customers. For example, senior managers at the Four Seasons hotel chain, who pride themselves on customer focus, like to tell the story of Roy Dyment, a doorman in Toronto who neglected to load a departing guest's briefcase into his taxi. The doorman called the guest, a lawyer, in Washington, D.C., and found that he desperately needed the briefcase for a morning meeting. Dyment hopped on a plane to Washington and returned it—without first securing approval from his boss. Far from punishing Dyment for making a mistake and for not checking with management before going to Washington, the Four Seasons responded by naming Dyment Employee of the Year.[38] This action sent a powerful message to Four Seasons employees, stressing the importance of satisfying customer needs.

Knowning Customer Needs "Know thy customer" is one of the keys to achieving superior responsiveness to customers. Knowing the customer not only requires that employees think like customers themselves; it also demands that they listen to what customers have to say. This involves bringing in customers' opinions by soliciting feedback from customers on the company's goods and services, and by building information systems that communicate the feedback to the relevant people.

For an example, consider direct-selling clothing retailer Lands' End. Through its catalog, the Internet, and customer service telephone operators, Lands' End actively solicits comments from its customers about the quality of its clothing and the kind of merchandise they want it to supply. Indeed, it was customers' insistence that initially prompted the company to move into the clothing segment. Lands' End formerly supplied equipment for sailboats through mail-order catalogs. However, it received so many requests from customers to include outdoor clothing in its offering that it responded by expanding the catalog to fill this need. Soon clothing became its main business, and Lands' End ceased selling the sailboat equipment. Today, the company continues to pay close attention to customer requests. Every month, data on customer requests and comments is reported to managers. This feedback helps the company to fine-tune the merchandise it sells; new lines of merchandise are frequently introduced in response to customer requests.

Satisfying Customer Needs

Once customer focus is an integral part of the company, the next requirement is to satisfy the customer needs that have been identified. As already noted, efficiency, quality, and innovation are crucial competencies that help a company satisfy customer needs. Beyond that, companies can provide a higher level of satisfaction if they differentiate their products by (1) customizing them, where possible, to the requirements of individual customers, and (2) reducing the time it takes to respond to or satisfy customer needs.

Customization Customization means varying the features of a good or service to tailor it to the unique needs or tastes of groups of customers, or—in the extreme case—individual customers. Although extensive customization can raise costs, the development of flexible manufacturing technologies has made it possible to customize products to a greater extent than was feasible 10 to 15 years ago, without experiencing a prohibitive rise in cost structure (particularly when flexible manufacturing technologies are linked with Web-based information systems). For example, online retailers such as Amazon.com have used Web-based technologies to develop a homepage customized for each individual user. When a customer accesses Amazon.com, he or she is offered a list of recommended books and music to purchase based on an analysis of prior buying history—a powerful competency that gives Amazon.com a competitive advantage.

The trend toward customization has fragmented many markets, particularly customer markets, into ever-smaller niches. An example of this fragmentation occurred in Japan in the early 1980s when Honda dominated the motorcycle market there. Second-place Yamaha had decided to surpass Honda's lead. It announced the opening of a new factory that, when operating at full capacity, would make Yamaha the world's largest manufacturer of motorcycles. Honda responded by proliferating its product line, and increasing its rate of new-product introduction. At the start of what became known as the "motorcycle wars," Honda had 60 motorcycles in its product line. Over the next 18 months thereafter, it rapidly increased its range to 113 models, customizing them to ever-smaller niches. Honda was able to accomplish this without bearing a prohibitive cost penalty due to its competency in flexible manufacturing. The flood of Honda's customized models pushed Yamaha out of much of the market, effectively stalling its bid to overtake Honda.[39]

Response Time   To gain a competitive advantage, a company must often respond to customer demands very quickly, whether the transaction is a furniture manufacturer's delivery of a product once it has been ordered, a bank's processing of a loan application, an automobile manufacturer's delivery of a spare part for a car that broke down, or the wait in a supermarket checkout line. We live in a fast-paced society, where time is a valuable commodity. Companies that can satisfy customer demands for rapid response build brand loyalty, differentiate their products, and can charge higher prices for products.

Increased speed often lets a company choose a premium pricing option, as the mail delivery industry illustrates. The air express niche of the mail delivery industry is based on the notion that customers are often willing to pay substantially more for overnight express mail than for regular mail. Another example of the value of rapid response is Caterpillar, the manufacturer of heavy-earthmoving equipment, which can deliver a spare part to any location in the world within 24 hours. Downtime for heavy-construction equipment is very costly, so Caterpillar's ability to respond quickly in the event of equipment malfunction is

Table 4.5	Primary Roles of Different Functions in Achieving Superior Responsiveness to Customers

Value Creation Function	Primary Roles
Infrastructure (leadership)	• Through leadership by example, build a company-wide commitment to responsiveness to customers
Production	• Achieve customization through implementation of flexible manufacturing • Achieve rapid response through flexible manufacturing
Marketing	• Know the customer • Communicate customer feedback to appropriate functions
Materials management	• Develop logistics systems capable of responding quickly to unanticipated customer demands (JIT)
R&D	• Bring customers into the product development process
Information systems	• Use Web-based information systems to increase responsiveness to customers
Human resources	• Develop training programs that get employees to think like customers themselves

© Cengage Learning

of prime importance to its customers. As a result, many customers have remained loyal to Caterpillar despite the aggressive low-price competition from Komatsu of Japan.

In general, reducing response time requires: (1) a marketing function that can quickly communicate customer requests to production, (2) production and materials-management functions that can quickly adjust production schedules in response to unanticipated customer demands, and (3) information systems that can help production and marketing in this process.

Table 4.5 summarizes the steps different functions must take if a company is to achieve superior responsiveness to customers. Although marketing plays a critical role in helping a company attain this goal (primarily because it represents the point of contact with the customer), Table 4.5 shows that the other functions also have major roles. Achieving superior responsiveness to customers requires top management to lead in building a customer orientation within the company.

SUMMARY OF CHAPTER

1. A company can increase efficiency through a number of steps: exploiting economies of scale and learning effects; adopting flexible manufacturing technologies; reducing customer defection rates; implementing just-in-time systems; getting the R&D function to design products that are easy to manufacture; upgrading the skills of employees through training; introducing self-managing teams; linking pay to performance; building a companywide commitment to efficiency through strong leadership; and designing structures that facilitate cooperation among different functions in pursuit of efficiency goals.

2. Superior quality can help a company lower its costs, differentiate its product, and charge a premium price.

3. Achieving superior quality demands an organization-wide commitment to quality, and a clear focus on the customer. It also requires metrics to measure quality goals and incentives that emphasize quality; input from employees regarding ways in which quality can be improved; a methodology for tracing defects to their source and correcting the problems that produce them; a rationalization of the company's supply base; cooperation with the suppliers that remain to implement total quality management programs; products that are designed for ease

of manufacturing; and substantial cooperation among functions.

4. The failure rate of new-product introductions is high because of factors such as uncertainty, poor commercialization, poor positioning strategy, slow cycle time, and technological myopia.

5. To achieve superior innovation, a company must build skills in basic and applied research; design good processes for managing development projects; and achieve close integration between the different functions of the company, primarily through the adoption of cross-functional product development teams and partly parallel development processes.

6. To achieve superior responsiveness to customers often requires that the company achieve superior efficiency, quality, and innovation.

7. To achieve superior responsiveness to customers, a company must give customers what they want, when they want it. It must ensure a strong customer focus, which can be attained by emphasizing customer focus through leadership; training employees to think like customers; bringing customers into the company through superior market research; customizing products to the unique needs of individual customers or customer groups; and responding quickly to customer demands.

DISCUSSION QUESTIONS

1. How are the four generic building blocks of competitive advantage related to each other?
2. What role can top management play in helping a company achieve superior efficiency, quality, innovation, and responsiveness to customers?
3. Over time, will the adoption of Six Sigma quality improvement processes give a company a competitive advantage, or will it be required only to achieve parity with competitors?
4. From what perspective might innovation be called "the single most important building block" of competitive advantage?

PRACTICING STRATEGIC MANAGEMENT

© iStockPhoto.com/Urilux

Small-Group Exercise: Identifying Excellence

Break up into groups of three to five people, and appoint one group member as a spokesperson who will communicate your findings to the class.

You are the management team of a start-up company that will produce hard drives for the personal computer (PC) industry. You will sell your product to manufacturers of PCs (original equipment manufacturers [OEMs]). The disk drive market is characterized by rapid technological change, product life cycles of only 6 to 9 months, intense price competition, high fixed costs for manufacturing equipment, and substantial manufacturing economies of scale. Your customers, the OEMs, issue very demanding technological specifications that your product must comply with. They also pressure you to deliver your product on time so that it fits in within their company's product introduction schedule.

1. In this industry, what functional competencies are the most important for you to build?
2. How will you design your internal processes to ensure that those competencies are built within the company?

STRATEGY SIGN ON

© iStockPhoto.com/Ninoslav Dotlic

Article File 4

Choose a company that is widely regarded as excellent. Identify the source of its excellence, and relate it to the material discussed in this chapter. Pay particular attention to the role played by the various functions in building excellence.

(continues)

STRATEGY SIGN ON

(continued)

© iStockPhoto.com/Ninoslav Dotlic

Strategic Management Project: Module 4

This module deals with the ability of your company to achieve superior efficiency, quality, innovation, and responsiveness to customers. With the information you have at your disposal, perform the following tasks and answer the listed questions:

1. Is your company pursuing any of the efficiency-enhancing practices discussed in this chapter?
2. Is your company pursuing any of the quality-enhancing practices discussed in this chapter?
3. Is your company pursuing any of the practices designed to enhance innovation discussed in this chapter?
4. Is your company pursuing any of the practices designed to increase responsiveness to customers discussed in this chapter?
5. Evaluate the competitive position of your company with regard to your answers to questions 1–4. Explain what, if anything, the company must do to improve its competitive position.

ETHICAL DILEMMA

© iStockPhoto.com/P_Wei

Is it ethical for Wal-Mart to pay its employees minimum wage and to oppose unionization, given that the organization also works its people very hard?

Are Wal-Mart's employment and compensation practices for lower-level employees ethical?

CLOSING CASE

Lean Production at Virginia Mason

In the early 2000s, Seattle's Virginia Mason Hospital was not performing as well as it should have been. Financial returns were low, patient satisfaction was subpar, too many errors were occurring during patient treatment, and staff morale was suffering. Gary Kaplan, the CEO, was wondering what to do about this when he experienced a chance encounter with Ian Black, the director of lean thinking at Boeing. Black told Kaplan that Boeing had been implementing aspects of Toyota's famous lean production system in its aircraft assembly operations, and Boeing was seeing positive results. Kaplan soon became convinced that the same system that had helped Toyota build more reliable cars at a lower cost could also be applied to health care to improve patient outcomes at a lower cost.

In 2002, Kaplan and a team of executives began annual trips to Japan to study the Toyota production system. They learned that "lean" meant doing without things that were not needed; it meant removing unnecessary steps in a process so that tasks were performed more efficiently. It meant eliminating waste and elements that didn't add value. Toyota's system applied to health care meant improving patient outcomes through more rapid treatment the elimination of errors in the treatment process.

Kaplan and his team returned from Japan believing in the value of lean production. They quickly set about applying what they had learned to Virginia Mason. Teams were created to look at individual processes in what Virginia Mason called "rapid process improvement workshops." The teams, which included doctors as well as other employees, were freed from their normal duties for 5 days. They learned the methods of lean production, analyzed systems and processes, tested proposed changes, and were empowered to implement the chosen change the following week.

The gains appeared quickly, reflecting the fact that there was a lot of inefficiency in the hospital. One of the first changes involved the delay between a doctor's referral to a specialist and the patient's first consultation with that specialist. By examining the process, it was found that secretaries, whose job it was to arrange these referrals, were not needed. Instead, the doctor would send a text message to the consultant the instant he or she decided that a specialist was required. The specialist then needed to respond within 10 minutes, even if only to confirm the receipt of the message. Delays in referral-to-treatment time dropped by 68% as a consequence of this simple change, which improved patient satisfaction.

On another occasion, a team in the radiation oncology department mapped out the activities that the department performed when processing a patient with the intention of eliminating time wasted in performing those activities. By removing unnecessary workflow activities, patient time spent in the department fell from 45 minutes to just 15 minutes. A similar exercise at Virginia Mason's back clinic cut treatment time from an average of 66 days to just 12.

By 2012, Virginia Mason was claiming that lean production had transformed the hospital into a more efficient, customer-responsive organization where medical errors during treatment had been significantly reduced. Among other gains, lean processes reduced annual inventory costs by more than $1 million, reduced the time it took to report lab tests to a patient by more than 85%, freed up the equivalent of 77 full-time employee positions through more efficient processes, and reduced staff walking distance by 60 miles a day, giving both doctors and nurses more time to spend with patients. These, and many other similar changes, lowered costs, increased the organization's customer responsiveness, improved patient outcomes, and increased the financial performance of the hospital.

Sources: C. Black, "To Build a Better Hospital, Virginia Mason Takes Lessons from Toyota Plants," *Seattle PI*, March 14, 2008; P. Neurath, "Toyota Gives Virginia Mason Docs a Lesson in Lean," *Puget Sound Business Journal*, September 14, 2003; and K. Boyer and R. Verma, *Operations and Supply Chain Management for the 21stCentury* (New York: Cengage, 2009).

CASE DISCUSSION QUESTIONS

1. What do you think were the *underlying* reasons for the performance problems that Virginia Mason Hospital was encountering in the early 2000s?

2. Which of the four building blocks of competitive advantage did lean production techniques help improve at Virginia Mason?

3. What do you think was the key to the apparently successful implementation of lean production techniques at Virginia Mason?

4. Lean production was developed at a manufacturing firm, Toyota, yet it is being applied in this case at a hospital. What does that tell you about the nature of the lean production philosophy for performance improvement?

KEY TERMS

NOTES

[1]G. J. Miller, *Managerial Dilemmas: The Political Economy of Hierarchy* (Cambridge: Cambridge University Press, 1992).

[2]H. Luft, J. Bunker, and A. Enthoven, "Should Operations Be Regionalized?" *New England Journal of Medicine* 301 (1979): 1364–1369.

[3]S. Chambers and R. Johnston, "Experience Curves in Services," *International Journal of Operations and Production Management* 20 (2000): 842–860.

[4]G. Hall and S. Howell, "The Experience Curve from an Economist's Perspective," *Strategic Management Journal* 6 (1985): 197–212; M. Lieberman, "The Learning Curve and Pricing in the Chemical Processing Industries," *RAND Journal of Economics* 15 (1984): 213–228; and R. A. Thornton and P. Thompson, "Learning from Experience and Learning from Others," *American Economic Review* 91 (2001): 1350–1369.

[5]Boston Consulting Group, *Perspectives on Experience* (Boston: Boston Consulting Group, 1972); Hall and Howell, "The Experience Curve," pp. 197–212; and W. B. Hirschmann, "Profit from the Learning Curve," *Harvard Business Review* (January–February 1964): 125–139.

[6]A. A. Alchian, "Reliability of Progress Curves in Airframe Production," *Econometrica* 31 (1963): 679–693.

[7]M. Borrus, L. A. Tyson, and J. Zysman, "Creating Advantage: How Government Policies Create Trade in the Semi-Conductor Industry," in P. R. Krugman (ed.), *Strategic Trade Policy and the New International Economics* (Cambridge, Mass.: MIT Press, 1986); and S. Ghoshal and C. A. Bartlett, "Matsushita Electrical Industrial (MEI) in 1987," Harvard Business School Case #388-144 (1988).

[8]See P. Nemetz and L. Fry, "Flexible Manufacturing Organizations: Implications for Strategy Formulation," *Academy of Management Review* 13 (1988): 627–638; N. Greenwood, *Implementing Flexible Manufacturing Systems* (New York: Halstead Press, 1986); J. P. Womack, D. T. Jones, and D. Roos, *The Machine That Changed the World* (New York: Rawson Associates, 1990); and R. Parthasarthy and S. P. Seith, "The Impact of Flexible Automation on Business Strategy and Organizational Structure," *Academy of Management Review* 17 (1992): 86–111.

[9]B. J. Pine, *Mass Customization: The New Frontier in Business Competition* (Boston: Harvard Business School Press, 1993); S. Kotha, "Mass Customization: Implementing the Emerging Paradigm for Competitive Advantage," *Strategic Management Journal* 16 (1995): 21–42; and J. H. Gilmore and B. J. Pine II, "The Four Faces of Mass Customization," *Harvard Business Review* (January–February 1997): 91–101.

[10]P. Waurzyniak, "Ford's Flexible Push," *Manufacturing Engineering*, September 1, 2003, pp. 47–50.

[11]F. F. Reichheld and W. E. Sasser, "Zero Defections: Quality Comes to Service," *Harvard Business Review*, September–October 1990, pp. 105–111.

[12]The example comes from ibid.

[13]Ibid.

[14]R. Narasimhan and J. R. Carter, "Organization, Communication and Coordination of International Sourcing," *International Marketing Review* 7 (1990): 6–20.

[15]H. F. Busch, "Integrated Materials Management," *IJDP & MM* 18 (1990): 28–39.

[16]G. Stalk and T. M. Hout, *Competing Against Time* (New York: Free Press, 1990).

[17]See Peter Bamberger and Ilan Meshoulam, *Human Resource Strategy: Formulation, Implementation, and Impact* (Thousand Oaks, Calif.: Sage, 2000); and P. M. Wright and S. Snell, "Towards a Unifying Framework for Exploring Fit and Flexibility in Human Resource Management," *Academy of Management Review* 23 (October 1998): 756–772.

[18]A. Sorge and M. Warner, "Manpower Training, Manufacturing Organization, and Work Place Relations in Great Britain and West Germany," *British Journal of Industrial Relations* 18 (1980): 318–333; and R. Jaikumar, "Postindustrial Manufacturing," *Harvard Business Review,* November–December 1986, pp. 72–83.

[19]J. Hoerr, "The Payoff from Teamwork," *Business Week,* July 10, 1989, pp. 56–62.

[20]"The Trouble with Teams," *Economist,* January 14, 1995, p. 61.

[21]T. C. Powell and A. Dent-Micallef, "Information Technology as Competitive Advantage: The Role of Human, Business, and Technology Resource," *Strategic Management Journal* 18 (1997): 375–405; and B. Gates, *Business @ the Speed of Thought* (New York: Warner Books, 1999).

[22]"Cisco@speed," *Economist,* June 26, 1999, p. 12; S. Tully, "How Cisco Mastered the Net," *Fortune,* August 17, 1997, pp. 207–210; and C. Kano, "The Real King of the Internet," *Fortune,* September 7, 1998, pp. 82–93.

[23]Gates, *Business @ the Speed of Thought.*

[24]See the articles published in the special issue of the *Academy of Management Review on Total Quality Management* 19:3 (1994). The following article provides a good overview of many of the issues involved from an academic perspective: J. W. Dean and D. E. Bowen, "Management Theory and Total Quality," *Academy of Management Review* 19 (1994): 392–418. See also T. C. Powell, "Total Quality Management as Competitive Advantage," *Strategic Management Journal* 16 (1995): 15–37.

[25]For general background information, see "How to Build Quality," *Economist,* September 23, 1989, pp. 91–92; A. Gabor, *The Man Who Discovered Quality* (New York: Penguin, 1990); and P. B. Crosby, *Quality Is Free* (New York: Mentor, 1980).

[26]W. E. Deming, "Improvement of Quality and Productivity Through Action by Management," *National Productivity Review* 1 (Winter 1981–1982): 12–22.

[27]A. Ries and J. Trout, *Positioning: The Battle for Your Mind* (New York: Warner Books, 1982).

[28]R. G. Cooper, *Product Leadership* (Reading, Mass.: Perseus Books, 1999).

[29]See Cooper, *Product Leadership*; A. L. Page "PDMA's New Product Development Practices Survey: Performance and Best Practices," presentation at PDMA 15th Annual International Conference, Boston, MA, October 16, 1991; and E. Mansfield, "How Economists See R&D," *Harvard Business Review,* November–December 1981, pp. 98–106.

[30]S. L. Brown and K. M. Eisenhardt, "Product Development: Past Research, Present Findings, and Future Directions," *Academy of Management Review* 20 (1995): 343–378; M. B. Lieberman and D. B. Montgomery, "First Mover Advantages," *Strategic Management Journal* 9 (Special Issue, Summer 1988): 41–58; D. J. Teece, "Profiting from Technological Innovation: Implications for Integration, Collaboration, Licensing and Public Policy," *Research Policy* 15 (1987): 285–305; G. J. Tellis and P. N. Golder, "First to Market, First to Fail?" *Sloan Management Review,* Winter 1996, pp. 65–75; and G. A. Stevens and J. Burley, "Piloting the Rocket of Radical Innovation," *Research Technology Management* 46 (2003): 16–26.

[31]G. Stalk and T. M. Hout, *Competing Against Time* (New York: Free Press, 1990).

[32]K. B. Clark and S. C. Wheelwright, *Managing New Product and Process Development* (New York: Free Press, 1993); and M. A. Schilling and C. W. L. Hill, "Managing the New Product Development Process," *Academy of Management Executive* 12:3 (August 1998): 67–81.

[33]O. Port, "Moving Past the Assembly Line," *Business Week* (Special Issue, Reinventing America, 1992): 177–180.

[34]K. B. Clark and T. Fujimoto, "The Power of Product Integrity," *Harvard Business Review,* November–December 1990, pp. 107–118; Clark and Wheelwright, *Managing New Product and Process Development;* Brown and Eisenhardt, "Product Development"; and Stalk and Hout, *Competing Against Time.*

[35]C. Christensen, "Quantum Corporation—Business and Product Teams," Harvard Business School Case, #9-692-023.

[36]H. Petroski, *Success Through Failure: The Paradox of Design* (Princeton, NJ: Princeton University Press, 2006). See also A. C. Edmondson, "Learning from Mistakes Is Easier Said Than Done," *Journal of Applied Behavioral Science* 40 (2004): 66–91.

[37]S. Caminiti, "A Mail Order Romance: Lands' End Courts Unseen Customers," *Fortune,* March 13, 1989, pp. 43–44.

[38]Sellers, "Getting Customers to Love You."

[39]Stalk and Hout, *Competing Against Time.*

Business-Level Strategy

OPENING CASE

nick barounis/Alamy

Nordstrom

Nordstrom is one of American's most successful fashion retailers. John Nordstrom, a Swedish immigrant, established the company in 1901 with a single shoe store in Seattle. Right from the start, Nordstrom's approach to business was to provide exceptional customer service, selection, quality, and value. This approach is still the hallmark of Nordstrom today.

The modern Nordstrom is a fashion specialty chain with some 240 stores in 31 states. Nordstrom generated almost $12 billion of sales in 2012 and makes consistently higher-than-average returns on invested capital. Its return on invested capital (ROIC) has exceeded 30% since 2006, and was 36% in 2012, a remarkable performance for a retailer. Wal-Mart, in contrast, earns an ROIC in the 12% to 14% range.

Nordstrom is a niche company. It focuses on a relatively affluent customer base that is looking for affordable luxury. The stores themselves are located in upscale areas, and have expensive fittings and fixtures that convey an impression of luxury. The stores are inviting and easy to browse in. Touches such as live music being played on a grand piano help create an appealing atmosphere. The merchandise is high quality and fashionable. What really differentiates the company from many of its rivals, however, is Nordstrom's legendary excellence in customer service.

LEARNING OBJECTIVES

After reading this chapter, you should be able to:

5-1 Explain the difference between low-cost and differentiation strategies.

5-2 Articulate how the attainment of a differentiated or low-cost position can give a company a competitive advantage.

5-3 Explain how a company executes its business-level strategy through function-level strategies and organizational arrangements.

5-4 Describe what is meant by the term "value innovation."

5-5 Discuss the concept of blue ocean strategy, and explain how innovation in business-level strategy can change the competitive game in an industry, giving the innovator a sustained competitive advantage.

153

Nordstrom's salespeople are typically well groomed and dressed, polite and helpful, and known for their attention to detail. They are selected for their ability to interact with customers in a positive way. During the interview process for new employees, one of the most important questions asked of candidates is their definition of good customer service. Thank-you cards, home deliveries, personal appointments, and access to personal shoppers are the norm at Nordstrom. There is a no-questions-asked returns policy, with no receipt required. Nordstrom's philosophy is that the customer is always right. The company's salespeople are also well compensated, with good benefits and commissions on sales that range from 6.75% to 10% depending on the department. Top salespeople at Nordstrom have the ability to earn over $100,000 a year, mostly in commissions.

The customer service ethos is central to the culture and organization of Nordstrom. The organization chart is an inverted pyramid, with salespeople on the top, and the CEO at the bottom. According to the CEO, Blake Nordstrom, this is because "I work for them. My job is to make them as successful as possible." Management constantly tells stories emphasizing the primacy of customer service at Nordstrom in order to reinforce the culture. One story relates that when a customer in Fairbanks, Alaska, wanted to return two tires (which Nordstrom does not sell), bought a while ago from another store on the same site, a sales clerk looked up their price and gave him his money back!

Despite its emphasis on quality and luxury, Nordstrom has not taken its eye off operating efficiency. Sales per square foot are $400 despite the large open-plan nature of the stores, and inventory turns exceed 5 times per year, up from 3.5 times a decade ago. Both of these figures are good for a high-end department store. Management is constantly looking for ways to improve efficiency and customer service. Today it is putting mobile checkout devices into the hands of 5,000 salespeople, eliminating the need to wait in line at a checkout stand.

Sources: A. Martinez, "Tale of Lost Diamond Adds Glitter to Nordstrom's Customer Service," *Seattle Times*, May 11, 2011; C. Conte, "Nordstrom Built on Customer Service," *Jacksonville Business Journal*, September 7, 2012; W. S. Goffe, "How Working as a Stock Girl at Nordstrom Prepared Me for Being a Lawyer," *Forbes*, December 3, 2012; and P. Swinand, "Nordstrom Inc," *Morningstar*, February 22, 2013.

OVERVIEW

business-level strategy

The business's overall competitive theme, the way it positions itself in the marketplace to gain a competitive advantage, and the different positioning strategies that can be used in different industry settings

In this chapter we look at the formulation of **business-level strategy**. As you may recall from Chapter 1, business-level strategy refers to the overarching competitive theme of a company in a given market. At its most basic, business-level strategy is about *who* a company decides to serve (which customer segments), what customer *needs* and *desires* the company is trying to satisfy, and *how* the company decides to satisfy those needs and desires.[1] If this sounds familiar, it is because we have already discussed this in Chapter 1 when we considered how companies construct a mission statement.

The high-end retailer Nordstrom provides us with an illustration of how this works. As discussed in the Opening Case, Nordstrom *focuses* on serving mid- to upper-income consumers who *desire* fashionable high-quality merchandise. Nordstrom attempts to satisfy the desires of this customer segment not only through merchandising, but also through excellence in customer service. To the extent it has been successful, Nordstrom has *differentiated* itself from rivals in that segment of the retail space. In essence, Nordstrom is pursuing a business-level strategy of *focused differentiation* that is built on a *distinctive competence* in customer service. Nordstrom has been so successful at pursuing this strategy that it has been consistently profitable, measured by ROIC, while also continuing to grow both its sales revenues and its net operating profit. In other words, through successful execution of its chosen business-level strategy, Nordstrom has built a sustainable competitive advantage.

In this chapter we will look at how managers decide what business-level strategy to pursue, and how they go about executing that strategy in order to attain a sustainable competitive advantage. We start by looking at two basic ways that companies chose how to compete in a market—by *lowering costs* and by *differentiating* their good or service from that offered by rivals so that they create more value. Next we consider the issue of *customer choice* and *market segmentation*, and discuss the choices that managers must make when it comes to their company's segmentation strategy. Then we then put this together and discuss the various business-level strategies that an enterprise can adopt, and what must be done to successfully implement those strategies. The chapter closes with a discussion of how managers can think about formulating an innovative business-level strategy that gives their company a unique and defendable position in the marketplace.

LOW COST AND DIFFERENTIATION

Strategy is about the search for competitive advantage. As we saw in Chapter 3, at the most fundamental level, a company has a competitive advantage if it can lower costs relative to rivals and/or if it can differentiate its product offering from those of rivals, thereby creating more value. We will look at lowering costs first, and then at differentiation.[2]

Lowering Costs

Imagine that all enterprises in an industry offer products that are very similar in all respects except for price, and that each company is small relative to total market demand so that they are unable to influence the prevailing price. This is the situation that exists in many commodity markets, such as the market for oil, or wheat, or aluminum, or steel. In the world oil market, for example, prices are set by the interaction of supply and demand. Even the world's largest private oil producer, Exxon Mobile, only produces around 3.5% of world output and cannot influence the prevailing price.

In commodity markets, competitive advantage goes to the company that has the lowest costs. Low costs will enable a company to make a profit at price points where its rivals are losing money. Low costs can also allow a company to undercut rivals on price, gain market share, and maintain or even increase profitability. Being the low-cost player in an industry can be a very advantageous position.

Although lowering costs below those of rivals is a particularly powerful strategy in a pure commodity industry, it can also have great utility in other settings. General merchandise retailing, for example, is not a classic commodity business. Nevertheless, Wal-Mart has built a very strong competitive position in United States market by being the low-cost player. Because its costs are so low, Wal-Mart can cut prices, grow its market share, and still make profits at price points where its competitors are losing money. The same is true in the airline industry, where Southwest Airlines has established a low-cost position. Southwest's operating efficiencies have enabled it to make money in an industry that has been hit by repeated bouts of price warfare, and where many of its rivals have been forced into bankruptcy. Strategy in Action 5.1 describes some of actions Southwest has taken to achieve this low-cost position.

5.1 STRATEGY IN ACTION

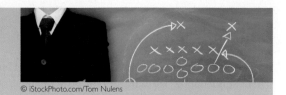

Low Costs at Southwest Airlines

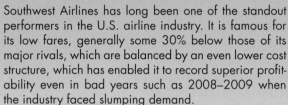

© iStockPhoto.com/Tom Nulens

Southwest Airlines has long been one of the standout performers in the U.S. airline industry. It is famous for its low fares, generally some 30% below those of its major rivals, which are balanced by an even lower cost structure, which has enabled it to record superior profitability even in bad years such as 2008–2009 when the industry faced slumping demand.

A major source of Southwest's low-cost structure seems to be its very high employee productivity. One way airlines measure employee productivity is by the ratio of employees to passengers carried. According to figures from company 10K statements, in 2012 Southwest had an employee-to-passenger ratio of 1 to 1,999, one of the best in the industry. By comparison, the ratio at one of the better major airlines, Delta, was in the range of 1 to 1,500. These figures suggest that holding size constant, Southwest runs its operation with fewer people than competitors. How does it do this?

First, Southwest's managers devote enormous attention to whom they hire. On average, Southwest hires only 3% of those interviewed in a year. When hiring, it places a big emphasis on teamwork and a positive attitude. Southwest's managers rationalize that skills can be taught, but a positive attitude and a willingness to pitch in cannot. Southwest also creates incentives for its employees to work hard. All employees are covered by a profit-sharing plan, and at least 25% of an employee's share of the profit-sharing plan has to be invested in Southwest Airlines stock. This gives rise to a simple

formula: the harder employees work, the more profitable Southwest becomes, and the richer the employees get. The results are clear. At other airlines, one would never see a pilot helping to check passengers onto the plane. At Southwest, pilots and flight attendants have been known to help clean the aircraft and check in passengers at the gate. They do this to turn around an aircraft as quickly as possible and get it into the air again—because they all know that an aircraft doesn't make money when it is sitting on the ground.

Southwest also reduces its costs by striving to keep its operations as simple as possible. By operating only one type of plane, the Boeing 737, it reduces training costs, maintenance costs, and inventory costs while increasing efficiency in crew and flight scheduling. The operation is nearly ticketless, which reduces cost and back-office accounting functions. There is no seat assignment, which again reduces costs. There are no meals or movies in flight, and the airline will not transfer baggage to other airlines, reducing the need for baggage handlers. Another major difference between Southwest and most other airlines is that Southwest flies point to point rather than operating from congested airport hubs. As a result, its costs are lower because there is no need for dozens of gates and thousands of employees needed to handle banks of flights that come in and then disperse within a 2-hour window, leaving the hub empty until the next flights a few hours later.

Sources: M. Brelis, "Simple Strategy Makes Southwest a Model for Success," *Boston Globe*, November 5, 2000, p. F1; M. Trottman, "At Southwest, New CEO Sits in the Hot seat," *Wall Street Journal*, July 19, 2004, p. B1; J. Helyar, "Southwest Finds Trouble in the Air," *Fortune*, August 9, 2004, p. 38; J. Reingold, "Southwest's Herb Kelleher: Still Crazy After All These Years," *Fortune*, January 14, 2013; and Southwest Airlines 10K 2012.

Differentiation   Now let's look at the differentiation side of the equation. Differentiation implies distinguishing yourself from rivals by offering something that they find hard to match. As we saw in the Opening Case, Nordstrom has differentiated itself from its rivals through excellence in customer service. There are many ways that a company can differentiate itself from rivals. A product can be differentiated by superior reliability (it breaks down less often, or not at all), better design, superior functions and features, better point-of-sale service, better after sales service and support, better branding, and so on. A Rolex watch is differentiated from a Timex watch by superior design, materials, and reliability; a Toyota car is differentiated from a General Motors car by superior reliability (historically new Toyota cars have had fewer defects than new GM cars); Apple differentiates its iPhone from rival offerings through superior product design, ease of use, excellent customer service at its Apple stores, and easy synchronization with other Apple products, such as its computers, tablets, iTunes, and iCloud.

Differentiation gives a company two advantages. First, it can allow the company to charge a premium price for its good or service, should it chose to do so. Second, it can help the company to grow overall demand and capture market share from its rivals. In the case of the iPhone, Apple has been able to reap both of these benefits through its successful differentiation strategy. Apple charges more for its iPhone than people pay for rival smartphone offerings, and the differential appeal of Apple products has led to strong demand growth.

It is important to note that differentiation often (but not always) raises the cost structure of the firm. It costs Nordstrom a lot to create a comfortable and luxurious shopping experience. Nordstrom's stores are sited at expensive locations, and use top-of-the-line fittings and fixtures. The goods Nordstrom sells are also expensive, and turn over far less often than the cheap clothes sold at a Wal-Mart store. This too, will drive up Nordstrom's costs. Then there is the expense associated with hiring, training, and compensating the best salespeople in the industry. None of this is cheap, and as a consequence, it is inevitable that Nordstrom will have a much higher costs structure than lower-end retail establishments.

On the other hand, there are situations where successful differentiation, because it increases primary demand so much, can actually lower costs. Apple's iPhone is a case in point. Apple uses very expensive materials in the iPhone—Gorilla glass for the screen, brushed aluminum for the case. It could have used cheap plastic, but then the product would not have looked as good and would have scratched easily. Although these decisions about materials originally raised the unit costs of the iPhone, the fact is that Apple has sold so many iPhones that it now enjoys economies of scale in purchasing and can effectively bargain down the price it pays for expensive materials. The result for Apple—successful differentiation of the iPhone—not only helped the company to charge a premium price, it has also gown demand to the point where it can lower costs through the attainment of scale economies, thereby widening profit margins. This is why Apple captured 75% of all profits in the global smartphone business in 2012.

More generally, the Apple example points to an essential truth here: successful differentiation gives managers options. One option that managers have is to raise the price to reflect the differentiated nature of the product offering and cover any incremental increase in costs (see Figure 5.1). This is an option that many pursue and it can by itself enhance profitability so long as prices increase by more than costs. For example, the Four Seasons chain has very luxurious hotels. It certainly costs a lot to provide that luxury, but Four Seasons also charges very high prices for its rooms, and the firm is profitable as a result. Nordstrom also pursues such a strategy.

However, as the Apple example suggests, increased profitability and profit growth can also come from the increased demand associated with successful differentiation, which enables the firm to use its assets more efficiently and thereby realize *lower costs* from scale economies. This leads to another option: the successful differentiator can also hold prices constant, or only increase prices slightly, sell more, and boost profitability through the attainment of scale economies (see Figure 5.1).[3]

For another example, consider Starbucks. The company has successfully differentiated its product offering from that of rivals such as Tully's by the excellent quality of its coffee-based drinks; by the quick, efficient, and friendly service that its baristas offer customers; by the comfortable atmosphere created by the design of its stores; and by its strong brand image. This differentiation increases the volume of traffic in each Starbucks store, thereby

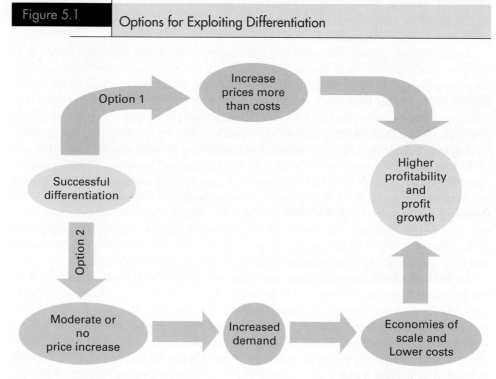

Figure 5.1 Options for Exploiting Differentiation

Option 1 → Increase prices more than costs

Successful differentiation

Option 2 → Moderate or no price increase → Increased demand → Economies of scale and Lower costs → Higher profitability and profit growth

Source: Charles W.L. Hill © Copyright 2013.

increasing the productivity of employees in the store (they are always busy), and the productivity of the capital invested in the store itself. The result: each store realizes scale economies from greater volume, which lowers the average unit costs at each store. Spread that across the 12,000 stores that Starbucks operates, and you have potentially huge cost savings that translate into higher profitability. Add this to the enhanced demand that comes from successful differentiation, which in the case of Starbucks not only enables the firm to sell more from each store, but also to open more stores, and profit growth will also accelerate.

The Differentiation–Low Cost Tradeoff The thrust of our discussion so far is that a low-cost position and a differentiated position are two very different ways of gaining a competitive advantage. The enterprise that is striving for the lowest costs does everything it can to be productive and drive down its cost structure, whereas the enterprise striving for differentiation necessarily has to bear higher costs to achieve that differentiation. Put simply, one cannot be Wal-Mart and Nordstrom, Porsche and Kia, Rolex and Timex. Managers must make a choice between these two basic ways of attaining a competitive advantage.

However, presenting the choice between differentiation and low costs in these terms is something of a simplification. As we have already noted, the successful differentiator might be able to subsequently reduce costs if differentiation leads to significant demand growth and the attainment of scale economies. But in actuality, the relationship between low cost and differentiation is subtler than this. In reality, strategy is not so much about making discrete choices as it is about deciding what the right balance is between differentiation and low costs.

To understand the issues here, look at Figure 5.2. The convex curve in Figure 5.2 illustrates what is known as an *efficiency frontier* (also known in economics as a production possibility frontier).[4] The efficiency frontier shows all of the different positions that a company can adopt with regard to differentiation and low cost, *assuming* that its internal functions and organizational arrangements are configured efficiently to support a particular position (note that the horizontal axis in Figure 5.2 is reverse scaled—moving along the axis to the right implies lower costs). The efficiency frontier has a convex shape because of diminishing returns. Diminishing returns imply that when an enterprise already has significant differentiation built into its product offering, increasing differentiation by a relatively small amount requires significant additional costs. The converse also holds: when a company already has a low-cost structure, it has to give up a lot of differentiation in its product offering to get additional cost reductions.

The efficiency frontier shown in Figure 5.2 is for the U.S. retail apparel business (Wal-Mart sells more than apparel, but that need not concern us here). As you will see, Nordstrom and Wal-Mart are both shown to be on the frontier, implying that both organizations have configured their internal functions and organizations efficiently. However, they have adopted very different positions; Nordstrom has high differentiation and high costs, whereas Wal-Mart has low costs and low differentiation. These are not the only viable positions in the industry, however. We have also shown The Gap to be on the frontier. The Gap offers higher-quality apparel merchandise than Wal-Mart, sold in a more appealing store format, but its offering is nowhere near as differentiated as that of Nordstrom; it is positioned between Wal-Mart and Nordstrom. This mid-level position, offering moderate differentiation at a higher cost than Wal-Mart, makes perfect sense because there are enough consumers demanding this kind of offering. They don't want to look as if they purchased their clothes at Wal-Mart, but they do want fashionable causal clothes that are more affordable than those available at Nordstrom.

Figure 5.2	The Differentiation–Low Cost Tradeoff

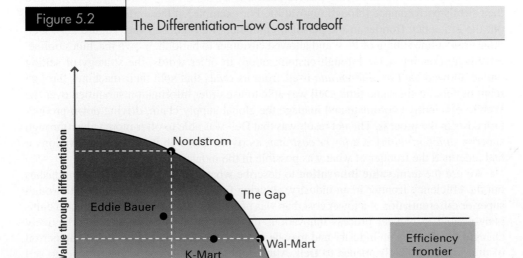

Source: Charles W.L. Hill © Copyright 2013.

The essential point here is that *there are often multiple positions on the differentiation–low cost continuum that are viable in the sense that they have enough demand to support an offering.* The task for managers is to identify a position in the industry that is viable and then configure the functions and organizational arrangements of the enterprise so that they are run as efficiently and effectively as possible, and enable the firm to reach the frontier. Not all companies are able to do this. Only those that can get to the frontier have a competitive advantage. Getting to the frontier requires excellence in strategy implementation. As has been suggested already in this chapter, business-level strategy is implemented through function and organization. Therefore: *to successfully implement a business-level strategy and get to the efficiency frontier, a company must be pursuing the right functional-level strategies, and it must be appropriately organized. Business-level strategy, functional-level strategy, and organizational arrangement must all be aligned with each other.*

It should be noted that not all positions on an industry's efficiency frontier are equally as attractive. For some positions, there may not be sufficient demand to support a product offering. For other positions, there may be too many competitors going after the same basic position—the competitive space might be too crowded—and the resulting competition might drive prices down below levels that are acceptable.

In Figure 5.2, K-Mart is shown to be inside the frontier. K-Mart is trying to position itself in the same basic space as Wal-Mart, but its internal operations are not efficient (the company was operating under bankruptcy protection in the early 2000s, although it is now out of bankruptcy). Also shown in Figure 5.2 is the Seattle-based clothing retailer Eddie Bauer, which is owned by Spiegel. Like K-Mart, Eddie Bauer is not an efficiently run operation relative to its rivals. Its parent company has operated under bankruptcy protection three times in the last 20 years.

Value Innovation: Greater Differentiation at a Lower Cost   The efficiency frontier is not static; it is continually being pushed outwards by the efforts of managers to improve their firm's performance through innovation. For example, in the mid-1990s Dell pushed out the efficiency frontier in the personal computer (PC) industry (see Figure 5.3). Dell pioneered online selling of PCs, and allowed customer to build their own machines online, effectively creating value through customization. In other words, the strategy of selling online allowed Dell to *differentiate* itself from its rivals that sold their machines through retail outlets. At the same time, Dell was able to use order information submitted over the Web to efficiently coordinate and manage the global supply chain, driving down production costs in the process. The net result was that Dell was able to offer more value (through superior *differentiation*) at a *lower cost* than its rivals. Through its process innovations it had redefined the frontier of what was possible in the industry.

value innovation

When innovations push out the efficiency frontier in an industry, allowing for greater value to be offered through superior differentiation at a lower cost than was previously thought possible.

We use the term **value innovation** to describe what happens when innovation pushes out the efficiency frontier in an industry, allowing for greater value to be offered through superior differentiation at a lower cost than was previously thought possible.[5] When a company is able to pioneer process innovations that lead to value innovation, it effectively changes the game in an industry and may be able to outperform its rivals for a long period of time. This is what happened to Dell. After harnessing the power of the Internet to sell PCs online, and coordinate the global supply chain, Dell outperformed its rivals in the industry for over a decade while they scrambled to catch up with the industry leader.

Toyota is another company that benefitted from value innovation. As we have discussed in Chapters 3 and 4, Toyota pioneered lean production systems that improved the quality of automobiles, while simultaneously lowering costs. Toyota *redefined what was possible in the automobile industry*, effectively pushing out the efficiency frontier and enabling the company to better differentiate its product offering at a cost level that its rivals couldn't match. The result was a competitive advantage that persisted for over two decades.

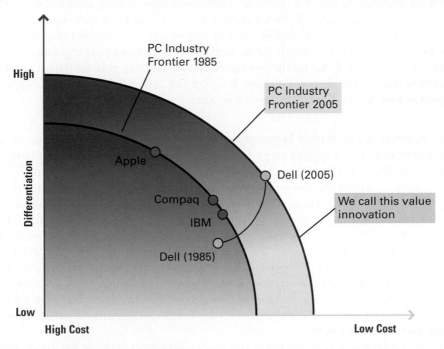

Figure 5.3 Value Innovation in the PC Industry

PC Industry Frontier 1985

PC Industry Frontier 2005

Apple

Dell (2005)

Compaq

IBM

We call this value innovation

Dell (1985)

High / Low (Differentiation)

High Cost / Low Cost

Source: Charles W.L. Hill © Copyright 2013

WHO ARE OUR CUSTOMERS? MARKET SEGMENTATION

As noted in the introduction to this chapter, business-level strategy begins with the customer. It starts with deciding *who* the company is going to serve, what *needs* or *desires* it is trying to satisfy, and *how* it is going to satisfy those needs and desires. Answering these questions is not straightforward, because the customers in a market are not homogenous. They often differ in fundamental ways. Some are wealthy, some are not; some are old, some are young; some are women, some are men; some are influenced by popular culture, some never watch TV; some live in cities, some in the suburbs; some care deeply about status symbols, others do not; some place a high value on luxury, some on value for money; some exercise every day, others have never seen the inside of a gym; some speak English most of the time, for others, Spanish is their first language; and so on.

One of the most fundamental questions that any company faces is whether to recognize such differences in customers, and if it does, how to tailor its approach depending on which customer segment or segments it decides to serve. The first step toward answering these questions is to segment the market according to differences in customer demographics, needs, and desires.

Market segmentation refers to the process of subdividing a market into clearly identifiable groups of customers with similar needs, desires, and demand characteristics.

market segmentation
The way a company decides to group customers based on important differences in their needs to gain a competitive advantage.

Customers within these segments are relatively homogenous, whereas they differ in important ways from customers in other segments of the market. For example, Nike segments the athletic shoe market according to sport (running, basketball, football, soccer, and training) and gender (men's shoes and women's shoes). It does this because it believes that people participating in different sports need different things from an athletic shoe (a shoe designed for running is not suitable for playing basketball) and that men and women also desire different things from a shoe in terms of styling and construction (most men don't want to wear pink shoes). Similarly, in the market for colas, Coca-Cola segments the market by needs—regular Coke for the average consumer, and diet cola for those concerned about their weight. The diet cola segment is further subdivided by gender, with *Diet Coke* targeted at women, and *Coke Zero* targeted at men.

Three Approaches to Market Segmentation   There are three basic approaches to market segmentation that companies adopt. One is to choose not to tailor different offerings to different segments, and instead produce and sell a standardized product that is targeted at the *average* customer in that market. This was the approach adopted by Coca-Cola until the early 1980s before the introduction of Diet Coke and different flavored cola drinks such as Cherry Cola. In those days Coke was *the* drink for everyone. Coke was differentiated from the offerings of rivals, and particularly Pepsi Cola, by lifestyle advertising that positioned Coke as the iconic American drink, the "real thing." Some network broadcast news programs also choose to adopt this approach today. The coverage offered by ABC News, for example, is tailored toward the average American viewer. The giant retailer Wal-Mart also targets the average customer in the market, although unlike Coca-Cola, Wal-Mart's goal is to drive down costs so that it can charge everyday low prices, give its customers value for money, and still make a profit.

A second approach is to recognize differences between segments and create different product offerings for the different segments. This is the approach that Coca-Cola has adopted since the 1980s. In 1982 it introduced Diet Coke, targeting that drink at the weight and health conscious. In 2007 it introduced Coke Zero, also a diet cola, but this time targeted at men. Coca Cola did this because company research found that men tended to associate Diet Coke with women. Since 2007, Diet Coke has been repositioned as more of a women's diet drink. Similarly, in the automobile industry, Toyota has brands that address the entire market—Scion for budget-constrained young entry-level buyers, Toyota for the middle market, and the Lexus for the luxury end of the market. In each of these segments Toyota pursues a differentiation strategy; it tries to differentiate itself from rivals in the segment by the excellent reliability and high quality of its offerings.

A third approach is to target only a limited number of market segments, or just one, and to become the very best at serving that particular segment. In the automobile market, for example, Porsche focuses exclusively on the very top end of the market, targeting wealthy middle-aged male consumers who have a passion for the speed, power, and engineering excellence associated with its range of sports cars. Porsche is clearly pursuing a differentiation strategy with regard to this segment, although it emphasizes a different type of differentiation than Toyota. Alternatively, Kia of South Korea has positioned itself as low-cost player in the industry, selling vehicles that are aimed at value-conscious buyers in the middle- and lower-income brackets. In the network broadcasting news business, Fox News and MSNBC have also adopted a focused approach. Fox tailors its content toward those on the right of the political spectrum, whereas MSNBC is orientated towards the left.

When managers decide to ignore different segments, and produce a standardized product for the average consumer, we say that they are pursuing a **standardization strategy**.

standardization strategy
When a company decides to ignore different segments, and produce a standardized product for the average consumer.

When they decide to serve many segments, or even the entire market, producing different **segmentation strategy**
offerings for different segments, we say that they are pursuing a **segmentation strategy**.
When they decide to serve a limited number of segments, or just one segment, we say that
they are pursuing a **focus strategy**. Today Wal-Mart is pursuing a standardization strategy,
Toyota a segmentation strategy, and Nordstrom a focus strategy.

segmentation strategy
When a company
decides to serve many
segments, or even the
entire market, producing
different offerings for
different segments.

focus strategy
When a company
decides to serve a limited
number of segments, or
just one segment.

Market Segmentation, Costs and Revenues   It is important to understand that these
different approaches to market segmentation have different implications for costs and revenues. Consider first the comparison between a standardization strategy and a segmentation strategy.

A standardization strategy is typically associated with lower costs than a segmentation
strategy. A standardization strategy involves the company producing one basic offering,
and trying to attain economies of scale by achieving a high volume of sales. Wal-Mart, for
example, pursues a standardization strategy and achieves enormous economies of scale in
purchasing, driving down its cost of goods sold.

In contrast, a segmentation strategy requires that the company customize its product offering to different segments, producing multiple offerings, one for each segment. Customization can drive up costs for two reasons; first, the company may sell less of each offering,
making it harder to achieve economies of scale, and second, products targeted at segments
at the higher-income end of the market may require more functions and features, which can
raise the costs of production and delivery.

On the other hand, it is important not to lose sight of the fact that advances in production technology, and particularly lean production techniques, have allowed for *mass
customization*—that is, the production of more product variety without a large cost penalty
(see Chapter 4 for details). In addition, by designing products that share common components, some manufacturing companies are able to achieve substantial economies of scale
in component production, while still producing a variety of end products aimed at different
segments. This is an approach adopted by large automobile companies, which try to utilize
common components and platforms across a wide range of models. To the extent that mass
customization and component sharing is possible, the cost penalty borne by a company
pursuing a segmentation strategy may be limited.

Although a standardization strategy may have lower costs that a segmentation strategy,
a segmentation strategy does have one big advantage: it allows the company to capture
incremental revenues by customizing its offerings to the needs of different groups of consumers, and thus selling more in total. A company pursuing a standardization strategy
where the product is aimed at the average consumer may lose sales from customers who
desire more functions and features, and are prepared to pay more for that. Similarly, it may
lose sales from customers who cannot afford to purchase the average product, but might
enter the market if a more basic offering was available.

This reality was first recognized in the automobile industry back in the 1920s. The early
leader in the automobile industry was Ford with its Model T offering. Henry Ford famously
said that consumers could have it "any color as long as it's black." Ford was in essence
pursuing a standardization strategy. However, in the 1920s Ford rapidly lost market share
to General Motors, a company that pursued a segmentation strategy and offered a range of
products aimed at different customer groups.

As for a focus strategy, here the impact on costs and revenues is subtler. Companies
that focus on the higher-income or higher-value end of the market will tend to have a
higher cost structure for two reasons. First, they will have to add features and functions
to their product to appeal to higher-income consumers, and this will raises costs. For

example, Nordstrom locates its stores in areas where real estate is expensive, its stores have costly fittings and fixtures and a wide open store plan with lots of room to walk around, and the merchandise is expensive and does not turn over as fast as the basic clothes and shoes sold at somewhere like Wal-Mart. Second, the relatively limited nature of demand associated with serving just a segment of the market may make it harder to attain economies of scale. Offsetting this, however, is that the customization and exclusivity associated with a strategy of focusing on the high-income end of the market may enable such a firm to charge significantly higher prices than those enterprises pursuing standardization and segmentation strategies.

For companies focusing on the lower-income end of the market, or a segment that desires value for money, a different calculus comes into play. First, such companies tend to produce a more basic offering that is relatively inexpensive to produce and deliver. This may help them to drive down their cost structures. The retailer Costco, for example, focuses on consumers who are looking for "value for money", and are less concerned about brands than they are about price. Costco sells a limited range of merchandise in large warehouse-type stores. A Costco store has about 3,750 stock-keeping units (SKUs) compared to 142,000 SKUs at the average Wal-Mart superstore. Products are stored on pallets stacked on utilitarian metal shelves. It offers consumers the opportunity to make bulk purchases of basic goods, such as breakfast cereal, dog food, and paper towels, at lower prices than found elsewhere. It turns over its inventory rapidly, typically selling it before it has to pay its suppliers and thereby reducing its working capital needs. Thus, by tailoring its business to the needs of a segment, Costco is able to undercut the cost structure and pricing of a retail gain such as Wal-Mart, even though it lacks Wal-Mart's enormous economies of scale in purchasing. The drawback, of course, is that Costco offers nowhere near the range of goods that you might get at a Wal-Mart superstore, so for customers looking for one stop-shopping at a low price, Wal-Mart is always going to be the store of choice.

BUSINESS-LEVEL STRATEGY CHOICES

We now have enough information to be able to identify the basic business-level strategy choices that companies make. These basic choices are sometimes called **generic business-level strategy**. The various choices are illustrated in Figure 5.4.

Companies that pursue a standardized or segmentation strategy both target a broad market. However, those pursuing a segmentation strategy recognize different segments, and tailor their offering accordingly, whereas those pursuing a standardization strategy just focus on serving the average consumer. Companies that target the broad market can either concentrate on lowering their costs so that they can lower prices and still make a profit, in which case we say they are pursuing a **broad low-cost strategy**, or they can try to differentiate their product in some way, in which case they are pursuing a **broad differentiation strategy**. Companies that decide to recognize different segments, and offer different product to each segment, are by default pursuing a broad differentiation strategy. It is possible, however, to pursue a differentiation strategy while not recognizing different segments, as Coca-Cola did prior to the 1980s. Today, Wal-Mart is pursuing a broad low-cost strategy, whereas Toyota and Coca-Cola are both pursuing a broad differentiation strategy.

Companies that target a few segments, or more typically, just one, are pursuing a focus or niche strategy. These companies can either try to be the low-cost player in that niche,

generic business-level strategy

A strategy that gives a company a specific form of competitive position and advantage vis-à-vis its rivals that results in above-average profitability.

broad low-cost strategy

When a company lowers costs so that it can lower prices and still make a profit.

broad differentiation strategy

When a company differentiates its product in some way, such as by recognizing different segments or offering different products to each segment.

Figure 5.4	Generic Business-Level Strategies

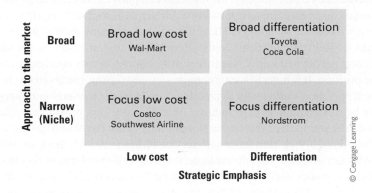

It is important to understand that there is often no one best way of competing in an industry. Different strategies may be equally viable. Wal-Mart, Costco, and Nordstrom are all in the retail industry, all three compete in different ways, and all three have done very well financially. The important thing for managers is to know what their business-level strategy is, to have a clear logic for pursuing that strategy, to have an offering that matches their strategy, and to align the functional activities and organization arrangements of the company with that strategy so that the strategy is well executed.

Michael Porter, who was the originator of the concept of generic business-level strategies, has argued that companies must make a clear choice between the different options outline in Figure 5.4.[6] If they don't, Porter argues, they may become "*stuck in the middle*" and experience poor relative performance. Central to Porter's thesis is the assertion that it is not possible to be both a differentiated company, and a low-cost enterprise. According to Porter, differentiation by its very nature raises costs and makes it impossible to attain the low-cost position in an industry. By the same token, to achieve a low-cost position, companies necessarily have to limit spending on product differentiation.

At the limit, there is certainly considerable value in this perspective. As noted, one cannot be Nordstrom and Wal-Mart, Timex and Rolex, Porsche and Kia. Low cost and differentiation are very different ways of competing—they require different functional strategies and different organizational arrangements, so trying to do both at the same time may not work. On the other hand, there are some important caveats to this argument.

First, as we have already seen in this chapter when we discussed value innovation, through improvements in process and product, a company can push out the efficiency frontier in its industry, redefining what is possible, and deliver more differentiation at a lower cost than its rivals. In such circumstances, a company might find itself in the fortunate position of being both the differentiated player in its industry and having a low-cost position. Ultimately its rivals might catch up, in which case it may well have to make a choice between emphasizing low cost and differentiation, but as we have seen

focus low-cost strategy
When a company targets a certain segment or niche, and tries to be the low-cost player in that niche.

focus differentiation strategy
When a company targets a certain segment or niche, and customizes its offering to the needs of that particular segment through the addition of features and functions.

as Costco has done, in which case we say that they pursuing a **focus low-cost strategy**, or they can try to customizing their offering to the needs of that particular segment through the addition of features and functions, as Nordstrom has done, in which case we say that they are pursuing a **focus differentiation strategy**.

from the case histories of Dell and Toyota, value innovators can gain a sustain competitive advantage that lasts for years, if not decades (another example of value innovation is given in Strategy in Action 5.2, which looks at the history of Microsoft Office).

Second, it is important for the differentiated company to recognize that it cannot take its eye off the efficiency ball. Similarly, the low-cost company cannot ignore product differentiation. The task facing a company pursuing a differentiation strategy is to be as efficient as possible given its choice of strategy. The differentiated company should not cut costs so far that it harms its ability to differentiate its offering from that of rivals. At the same time, it cannot let costs get out of control. Nordstrom, for example, is very efficient given its choice of strategic position. It is not a low-cost company by any means, but given its choice of how to compete it operates as efficiently as possible. Similarly, the low-cost company cannot totally ignore key differentiators in its industry. Wal-Mart does not provide anywhere near the level of customer service that is found at Nordstrom, but nor can Wal-Mart ignore customer service. Even though Wal-Mart has a self-service business model, there are still people in the store who are available to help customers with questions if that is required. The task for low-cost companies such as Wal-Mart is to be "good enough" with regard to key differentiators. For another example of how this plays out, see Strategy in Action 5.2, which looks at how Google and Microsoft compete in the market for office productivity software.

BUSINESS-LEVEL STRATEGY, INDUSTRY AND COMPETITIVE ADVANTAGE

Properly executed, a well-chosen and well-crafted business-level strategy can give a company a competitive advantage over actual and potential rivals. More precisely, it can put the company in an advantageous position relative to each of the competitive forces that we discussed in Chapter 2—specifically, the threat of entrants, the power of buyers and suppliers, the threat posed by substitute goods or services, and the intensity of rivalry between companies in the industry.

Consider first the low-cost company; by definition, the low-cost enterprise can make profits at price points that its rivals cannot profitably match. This makes it very hard for rivals to enter its market. In other words, the low-cost company can build an entry barrier into its market. It can, in effect, erect an economic moat around its business that keeps higher-cost rivals out. This is what Amazon has done in the online retail business. Through economies of scale and other operating efficiencies, Amazon has attained a very-low-cost structure that effectively constitutes a high entry barrier into this business. Rivals with less volume and fewer economies of scale than Amazon cannot match Amazon on price without losing money—not a very appealing proposition.

A low-cost position and the ability to charge low prices and still make profits also give a company protection against substitute goods or services. Low costs can help a company to absorb cost increases that may be passed on downstream by powerful suppliers. Low costs can also enable the company to respond to demands for deep price discounts from powerful buyers and still make money. The low-cost company is often best positioned to survive price rivalry in its industry. Indeed, a low-cost company may deliberately initiate a price war in order to grow volume and drive its weaker rivals out of the industry. This is what Dell did during its glory days in the early 2000s when it repeatedly cut prices for PCs in order to drive up sales volume and force marginal competitors out of the business. Pursuing such a strategy enabled Dell to become the largest computer company in the world by the mid-2000s.

5.2 STRATEGY IN ACTION

Microsoft Office versus Google Apps

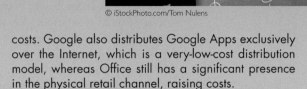

© iStockPhoto.com/Tom Nulens

Microsoft has long been the dominant player in the market for office productivity software with its Office suite of programs that includes a word processor, spreadsheet, presentation software, and e-mail client. Microsoft's rise to dominance in this market was actually the result of an important innovation—in 1989 Microsoft was the first company to bundle word processing, spreadsheet, and presentation programs together into a single offering that was interoperable. At the time, the market leader in word processing software was Word Perfect, in spreadsheet software it was Lotus, and in presentation software it was Harvard Graphics. Microsoft was number 2 in each of these markets. However, by offering a bundle, and pricing the bundle below the price of each program purchased on its own, Microsoft was able to grab share from its competitors, none of which had a full suite of offerings. In effect, Microsoft Office offered consumers more value (interoperability), at a lower price, than could be had from rivals.

As demand for Office expanded, Microsoft was able to spread the fixed costs of product development over a much larger volume than its rivals, and unit costs fell, giving Microsoft the double advantage of a differentiated product offering and a low-cost position. The results included the creation of a monopoly position in office productivity software and two decades of extraordinary high returns for Microsoft in this market.

Things started to shift in 2006 when Google introduced Google Apps, an online suite of office productivity software that was aimed squarely at Microsoft's profitable Office franchise. Unlike Office at the time, Google Apps was an online service. The basic programs reside on the cloud, and documents were saved on the cloud. At first Google lacked a full suite of programs, and traction was slow, but since 2010 adoption of Google Apps has started to accelerate. Today Google Apps has the same basic programs as Office—a word processer, spreadsheet, presentation software, and an e-mail client—but nowhere near the same number of features. Google's approach is not to match Office on features, but to *be good enough* for the majority of users. This helps to reduce development costs. Google also distributes Google Apps exclusively over the Internet, which is a very-low-cost distribution model, whereas Office still has a significant presence in the physical retail channel, raising costs.

In other words, Google is pursuing a low-cost strategy with regard to Google Apps. Consistent with this, Google Apps is also priced significantly below Office. Google charges $50 a year for each person using its product. In contrast, Microsoft Office costs $400 per computer for business users (although significant discounts are often negotiated). Initially Google Apps was targeted at small businesses and start-ups, but more recently, Google seems to be gaining some traction in the enterprise space, which is Microsoft's core market for Office. In 2012, Google scored an impressive string of wins, including the Swiss drug company Hoffman La Roche, where over 80,000 employees use the package, and the U.S. Interior Department, where 90,000 use it. In total, Google Apps earned around $1 billion in revenue in 2012 and estimates suggest that the company has more than 30 million paying subscribers. This still makes it a small offering relative to Microsoft Office, which is installed on over 1 billion computers worldwide. Microsoft Office generated $24 billion in revenue in 2012 and it remains Microsoft's most profitable business. However, Microsoft cannot ignore Google Apps.

Indeed, Microsoft is not standing still. In 2012, Microsoft rolled out its own cloud-based Office offering, Office 365. Office 365 starts at a list price of $72 a year per person, and can cost as much as $240 a person annually in versions that offer many more features and software development capabilities. According to a Microsoft spokesperson, demand for Office 365 has been strong. Microsoft argues that Google cannot match the "quality enterprise experience in areas like privacy, data handling and security" that Microsoft offers. Microsoft's message is clear—it still believes that Office is the superior product offering, differentiated by features, functions, privacy, data handing, and security. Whether Office 365 will keep Google Apps in check, however, remains to be seen.

Sources: Author interviews at Microsoft and Google; Quentin Hardy, "Google Apps Moving onto Microsoft's Business Turf," *New York Times*, December 26, 2012; and A. R. Hickey, "Google Apps: A $1 Billion Business?" *CRN*, February 3, 2012.

Now consider the differentiated company. The successful differentiator is also protected against each of the competitive forces we discussed in Chapter 2. The brand loyalty associated with differentiation can constitute an important entry barrier, protecting the company's market from potential competitors. The brand loyalty enjoyed by Apple in the smartphone business, for example, has set a very high hurdle for any new entrant to match, and effectively acts as a deterrent to entry. Because the successful differentiator sells on non-price factors, such as design or customer service, it is also less exposed to pricing pressure from powerful buyers. Indeed, the converse may be the case—the successful differentiator may be able to implement price increases without encountering much, if any, resistance from buyers. The differentiated company can also fairly easy absorb price increases from powerful suppliers and pass those on downstream in the form of higher prices for its offerings, without suffering much, if any, loss in market share. The brand loyalty enjoyed by the differentiated company also gives it protection from substitute goods and service.

The differentiated company is protected from intense price rivalry within its industry by its brand loyalty, and by the fact that non-price factors are important to its customer set. At the same time, the differentiated company often does have to invest significant effort and resources in non-price rivalry, such as brand building through marketing campaigns or expensive product development efforts, but to the extent that it is successful, it can reap the benefits of these investments in the form of stable or higher prices.

Having said this, it is important to note that focused companies often have an advantage over their broad market rivals in the segment or niche that they compete in. For example, although Wal-Mart and Costco are both low-cost companies, Costco has a cost advantage over Wal-Mart in the segment that it serves. This primarily comes from the fact that Costco carries far fewer SKUs, and those it does are sold in bulk. However, if Costco tried to match Wal-Mart and serve the broader market, the need to carry a wider product selection (Wal-Mart has over 140,000 SKUs) means that its cost advantage would be lost.

The same can be true for a differentiated company. By focusing on a niche, and customizing the offering to that segment, a differentiated company can often outsell differentiated rivals that target a broader market. Thus Porsche can outsell broad market companies like Toyota or General Motors in the high-end sports car niche of the market, in part because the company does not sell outside of its core niche. Thus Porsche creates an image of exclusivity that appeals to its customer base. Were Porsche to start moving down-market, it would lose this exclusive appeal and become just another broad market differentiator.

IMPLEMENTING BUSINESS-LEVEL STRATEGY

As we have already suggested in this chapter, for a company's business-level strategy to translate into a competitive advantage, it must be well implemented. This means that actions taken at the functional level should support the business-level strategy, as should the organizational arrangements of the enterprise. There must, in other words, be *alignment* or *fit* between business-level strategy, functional strategy, and organization (see Figure 5.5). We have already discussed functional strategy in Chapter 4; detailed discussion of organizational arrangements is postponed until Chapter 12. Notwithstanding this, here we do make some basic observations about the functional strategies and organizational arrangements required to implement the business-level strategies of low cost and differentiation.

| Figure 5.5 | Strategy is Implemented through Function and Organization |

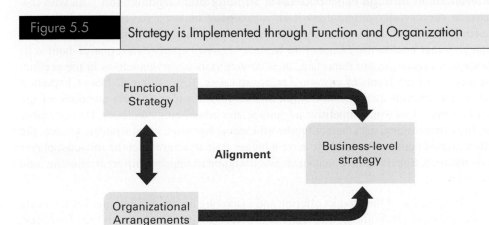

Source: Charles W.L. Hill © Copyright 2013.

Lowering Costs through Functional Strategy and Organization How do companies achieve a low-cost position? They do this primarily through pursuing those functional-level strategies that result in *superior efficiency* and *superior product reliability*, which we discussed in detail in Chapter 4 when we looked at functional-level strategy and the building blocks of competitive advantage. As you will recall from Chapter 4, the following are clearly important:

- Achieving economies of scale and learning effects.
- Adopting lean production and flexible manufacturing technologies.
- Implementing quality improvement methodologies to ensure that the goods or services the company produces are reliable, so that time, materials, and effort are not wasted producing and delivering poor-quality products that have to be scrapped, reworked, or produced again from scratch
- Streamlining processes to take out unnecessary steps
- Using information systems to automate business process
- Implementing just-in-time inventory control systems
- Designing products so that they can be produced and delivered at as low a cost as possible
- Taking steps to increase customer retention and reduce customer churn

In addition, to lower costs the firm must be *organized* in such a way that the structure, control systems, incentive systems, and culture of the company all emphasize and reward employee behaviors and actions that are consistent with, or lead to, higher productivity and greater efficiency. As will be explained in detail in Chapter 12, the kinds of organizational arrangements that are favored in such circumstances include a flat organizational structure with very few levels in the management hierarchy, clear lines of accountability and control, measurement and control systems that focus on productivity and cost containment, incentive systems that encourage employees to work in as productive a manner as possible and empower employees to suggest and pursue initiatives that are consistent with productivity improvements, and a frugal culture that emphasizes the need to control costs. Companies that operate with these kinds of organizational arrangements include Amazon and Wal-Mart.

Differentiation through Functional-Level Strategy and Organization   As with low costs, to successfully differentiate itself a company must pursue the right actions at the functional level, and it must organize itself appropriately. Pursuing functional-level strategies that enable the company to achieve *superior quality* in terms of both reliability and excellence are important, as is an emphasis upon *innovation* in the product offering, and high levels of *customer responsiveness*. You will recall from Chapters 3 and 4 that superior quality, innovation, and customer responsiveness are three of the four building blocks of competitive advantage, the other being *efficiency*. Do remember that the differentiated firm cannot ignore efficiency; by virtue of its strategic choice, the differentiated company is likely to have a higher cost structure than the low-cost player in its industry. Specific functional strategies designed to improve differentiation include the following:

- Customization of the product offering and marketing mix to different market segments
- Designing product offerings that have high perceived quality in terms of their functions, features, and performance, in addition to being reliable
- A well-developed customer care function for quickly handling and responding to customer inquiries and problems
- Marketing efforts focused on brand building and perceived differentiation from rivals
- Hiring and employee development strategies designed to ensure that employees act in a manner that is consistent with the image that the company is trying to project to the world

As we saw in the opening case, Nordstrom's successful differentiation is due to its excellent customer service, which is an element of customer responsiveness. Nordstrom also pays close attention to employee recruitment and training to ensure that salespeople at Nordstrom behave in a manner that is consistent with Nordstrom's customer service values when interacting with customers. Similarly, Apple has an excellent customer care function, as demonstrated by its in-store "genius bars" where well-trained employees are available to help customers with inquiries and problems, and give tutorials to help them get the best value out of their purchases. Apple has also been very successful at building a brand that differentiates it from rivals such as Microsoft (for example, the long-running TV advertisements featuring "Mac," a very hip guy, and "PC," the short, overweight man in a shabby gray suit).

As for organizing, creating the right structure, controls, incentives, and culture can all help a company to differentiate itself from rivals. In a differentiated enterprise, one key issue is to make sure that marketing, product design, customer service, and customer care functions all play a key role. Again consider Apple; following the return of Steve Jobs to the company in 1997, he reorganized to give the industrial design group the lead on all new product development efforts. Under this arrangement, industrial design, headed by Johnny Ive, reported directly to Jobs, and engineering reported to industrial design for purposes of product development. This meant that the designers, rather than engineers, specified the look and feel of a new product, and engineers then had to design according to the parameters imposed by the design group. This is in contrast to almost all other companies in the computer and smartphone business, where engineering typically takes the lead on product development. Jobs felt that this organizational arrangement was necessary to ensure that Apple produced beautiful products that not only worked well, but also looked and felt elegant. Because Apple under Jobs was differentiating by design, design was given a pivotal position in the organization.[7]

Making sure that control systems, incentive systems, and culture are aligned with the strategic thrust is also extremely important for differentiated companies. Thus leaders at

Nordstrom constantly emphasize the importance of customer service in order to build a company-wide culture that internalizes this key value. Actions consistent with this include an inverted organizations chart that shows the CEO working for salespeople, and the salespeople working for customers, as well as the repetition of stories that celebrate employees who have gone beyond the call of duty to serve customers. We will return to and expand upon these themes in Chapter 12.

COMPETING DIFFERENTLY: SEARCHING FOR A BLUE OCEAN

We have already suggested in this chapter that sometimes companies can fundamentally shift the game in their industry by figuring out ways to offer more value through differentiation at a lower cost than their rivals. We referred to this as *value innovation*, a term that was first coined by Chan Kim and Renee Mauborgne.[8] Kim and Mauborgne developed their ideas further in the best-selling book *Blue Ocean Strategy*.[9] Their basic proposition is that many successful companies have built their competitive advantage by redefining their product offering through value innovation and, in essence, creating a new market space. They describe the process of thinking through value innovation as searching for the blue ocean—which they characterize as a wide open market space where a company can chart its own course.

One of their examples of a company that found its own blue ocean is Southwest Airlines (see Strategy in Action 5.1 for more details about Southwest Airlines). From its conception, Southwest competed differently than other companies in the U.S. airline industry. Most important, Southwest saw its main competitors not as other airlines, but people who would typically drive or take a bus to travel. For Southwest, the focus was to reduce travel time for its customer set, and to do so in a way that was cheap, reliable, and convenient, so that they would prefer to fly rather than drive.

The very first route that Southwest operated was between Houston and Dallas. To reduce total travel time, it decided to fly into the small downtown airports in both cities, Hobby in Houston and Love Field in Dallas, rather than the large inter-continental airports outside located an hour drive outside of both cities. The goal was to reduce total travel time by eliminating the need to dive to reach a big airport outside the city before even beginning the journey. Southwest then put as many flights a day on the route as possible to make it convenient, and did everything possible to drive down operating costs so that it could charge low prices and still make a profit.

As the company grew and opened more routes, it followed the same basic strategy. Southwest always flew point to point, never routing passengers through hubs. Changing planes in a hub adds to total travel time and can hurt reliability, measured by on-time departures and arrivals, if connections are slow coming into or leaving a hub due to adverse events, such as bad weather delaying arrivals or departures somewhere in an airline's network. Southwest also cut out in-flight meals, only offers coach-class seating, does not have lounges in airports for business-class passengers, and has standardized on one type of aircraft, the Boeing 737, which helps to raise reliability. As we saw in Strategy in Action 5.1, Southwest has also taken a number of steps to boost employee productivity. The net result is that Southwest delivers more value *to its customer set*, and does so at a lower cost than its rivals, enabling it to price lower than them and still make a profit. Southwest is a value innovator.

Kim and Mauborgne use the concept of a *strategy canvas* to map out how value innovators differ from their rivals. A strategy canvas for Southwest is shown in Figure 5.6. This shows that Southwest charges a low price and does not provide meals or lounges in airports, or business-class seating, or connections through hubs (it flies point to point), but does provide a friendly, quick, convenient, and reliable low-cost service, *which is exactly what its customer set values*.

The whole point of the Southwest example, and other business case histories Kim and Mauborgne review, is to illustrate how many successful enterprises compete differently than their less successful rivals: they carve out a unique market space for themselves through value innovation. When thinking about how a company might redefine its market and craft a new business-level strategy, Kim and Mauborgne suggest that managers ask themselves the following questions:

1. **Eliminate**: Which factors that rivals take for granted in our industry can be eliminated, thereby reducing costs?
2. **Reduce**: Which factors should be reduced well below the standard in our industry, thereby lowering costs?
3. **Raise**: Which factors should be raised above the standard in our industry, thereby increasing value?
4. **Create**: What factors can we create that rivals do not offer, thereby increasing value?

Figure 5.6	A Strategy Canvas for Southwest Airlines

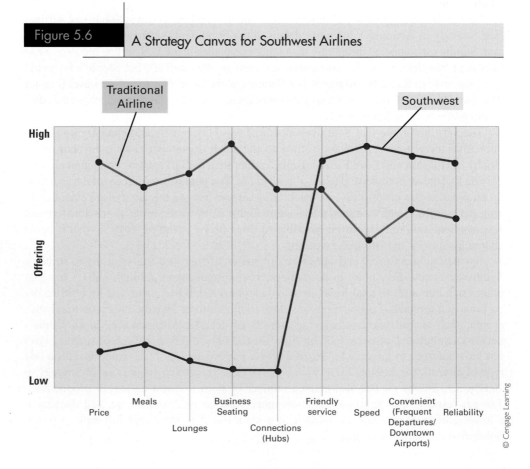

© Cengage Learning

Southwest, for example, *eliminated* lounges, business seating, and meals in flight—it *reduced* in-flight refreshment to way below industry standards; but by flying point to point it *raised* speed (reducing travel time) and convenience and reliability. Southwest also *created* more value by flying between smaller downtown airports whenever possible, something that other airlines did not typically do.

This is a useful framework, and it directs managerial attention to the need to think differently than rivals in order to create an offering and strategic position that are unique. If such efforts are successful, they can help a company to build a sustainable advantage.

One of the great advantages of successful value innovation is that it can catch rivals off guard and make it difficult for them to catch up. For example, when Dell Computer started to sell direct over the Internet, it was very difficult for rivals to respond because they had already invested in a different way of doing business—selling though a physical retail channel. Dell's rivals could not easily adopt the Dell model without alienating their channel, which would have resulted in lost sales. The prior strategic investment of Dell's rivals in distribution channels, which at the time they were made seemed reasonable, became a source of inertia that limited their ability to respond in a timely manner to Dell's innovations. The same has been true in the airline industry, where the prior strategic investments of traditional airlines have made it very difficult for them to respond to the threat posed by Southwest.

In sum, value innovation, because it shifts the basis of competition, can result in a sustained competitive advantage for the innovating company due to the relative inertia of rivals and their inability to respond in a timely manner without breaking prior strategic commitments.

SUMMARY OF CHAPTER

1. Business-level strategy refers to the overarching competitive theme of a company in a given market.
2. At the most basic level, a company has a competitive advantage if it can lower costs relative to rivals and/or differentiate its product offering from those of rivals.
3. A low-cost position enables a company to make money at price points where its rivals are losing money.
4. A differentiated company can charge a higher price for its offering, and/or it can use superior value to generate growth in demand.
5. There are often multiple positions along the differentiation–low cost continuum that are viable in a market.
6. Value innovation occurs when a company develops new products, or processes, or strategies that enable it to offer more value through differentiation at a lower cost than its rivals.
7. Formulating business-level strategy starts with deciding *who* the company is going to serve, what *needs* or *desires* it is trying to satisfy, and *how* it is going to satisfy those needs and desires.
8. Market segmentation is the process of subdividing a market into clearly identifiable groups of customers that have similar needs, desires, and demand characteristics.
9. A company's approach to market segmentation is an important aspect of its business-level strategy.
10. There are four generic business-level strategies: broad low cost, broad differentiation, focus low cost, and focus differentiation.
11. Business-level strategy is executed through actions taken at the functional level, and through organizational arrangements.
12. Many successful companies have built their competitive advantage by redefining their

product offering through value innovation and creating a new market space. The process of thinking through value innovation has been described as searching for a "blue ocean"—a wide open market space where a company can chart its own course.

DISCUSSION QUESTIONS

1. What are the main differences between a low-cost strategy and a differentiation strategy?
2. Why is market segmentation such an important step in the process of formulating a business-level strategy?
3. How can a business-level strategy of (a) low cost and (b) differentiation offer some protection against competitive forces in a company's industry?
4. What is required to transform a business-level strategy from an idea into reality?
5. What do we mean by the term *value innovation*? Can you identify a company not discussed in the text that has established a strong competitive position through value innovation?

KEY TERMS

Business-level
    strategy 154
Value innovation 160
Market
    segmentation 161

Standardization
    strategy 162
Segmentation
    strategy 163
Focus strategy 163

Generic business-level
    strategy 164
Broad low-cost
    strategy 164
Broad differentiation
    strategy 164

Focus low-cost
    strategy 165
Focus differentiation
    strategy 165

PRACTICING STRATEGIC MANAGEMENT

© iStockPhoto.com/Urilux

Small-Group Exercise

Break up into groups of three to five each. Appoint one group member as a spokesperson who will communicate the group's findings to the class when called on to do so by the instructor. Discuss the following scenario: Identify a company that you are familiar with that seems to have gained a competitive advantage by being a value innovator within its industry. Explain how this company has (a) created more value that rivals in its industry, and (b) simultaneously been able to drive down its cost structure. How secure do you think this company's competitive advantage is? Explain your reasoning.

STRATEGY SIGN ON

© iStockPhoto.com/Ninoslav Dotlic

Article File 5

Find examples of companies that are pursuing each of the generic business-level strategies identified in Figure 5.4. How successful has each of these companies been at pursuing its chosen strategy?

Strategic Management Project: Developing Your Portfolio 5

This module deals with the business-level strategy pursued by your company:

1. Which market segments is your company serving?
2. What business-level strategy is your company pursuing?
3. How is your company executing its business-level strategy through actions at the functional level, and through organizational arrangements? How well is it doing? Are there things it could do differently?
4. Take a blue ocean approach to the business of your company, and ask if it could and/or should change its business-level strategy by eliminating, reducing, raising, or creating factors related to its product offering.

ETHICAL DILEMMA

© iStockPhoto.com/P_Wei

Costco is pursuing a low-cost strategy. As result of its pressures on suppliers to reduce prices, many of them have outsourced manufacturing to low-wage countries such as China. This may have contributed to the "hollowing out" of the manufacturing base in the United States. Are Costco's actions ethical?

CLOSING CASE

Lululemon

Back in 1998, self-described snowboarder and surfer dude Chip Wilson took his first commercial yoga class. The Vancouver native loved the exercises, but he hated doing them in the cotton clothing that was standard yoga wear at the time. For Wilson, who had worked in the sportswear business and had a passion for technical athletic fabrics, wearing cotton clothes to do sweaty, stretchy power yoga exercises seemed totally inappropriate. And so the idea for Lululemon was born.

Wilson's vision was to create high-quality and stylishly designed clothing for yoga and related sports activities using the very best technical fabrics. He built up a design team, but outsourced manufacturing to low-cost producers, primarily in South East Asia. Rather than selling clothing through existing retailers, Wilson elected to open his own stores. The idea was to staff the stores with employees who were themselves passionate about exercise, and could act as ambassadors for healthy living through yoga and other sports such as running and cycling.

The first store opened in Vancouver, Canada, in 2000. It quickly became a runaway success, and other stores soon followed. In 2007 the company went public, using the capital raised to accelerate its expansion plans. By 2013, Lululemon had over 210 stores, mostly in North America, sales in excess of $1.4 billion, and a market capitalization of $8 to 9 billion. Sales per square foot were estimated to be around $1,800—more than four times that of luxury department store Nordstrom, making Lululemon one of the top retailers in the world on this metric. Along the way, Chip Wilson stepped up into the chairman role. Wilson hired Christine Day to be the CEO in 2008, while he continued to focus on branding. Day had spent 20 years at Starbucks overseeing retail operations in North America, and then around the world.

As it has evolved, Lululemon's strategy focuses on a number of key issues. Getting the product right is undoubtedly a central part of the company's strategy. The company's yoga-inspired athletic clothes are well designed, stylish, comfortable, and use the very best technical fabrics. An equally important part of the strategy is to only stock a limited supply of an item. New colors and seasonal items, for example, get 3- to 12-week life cycles, which keeps the product offerings feeling fresh. The goal is to sell gear at full price, and to condition customers to buy when they see it, rather than wait, because if they do, it may soon be "out of stock." The company only allows product returns if the clothes have not been worn and still have the price tags attached. "We are not Nordstrom," says Day, referring to that retailer's policy of taking products back, no questions asked.

The scarcity strategy has worked; Lululemon never holds sales, and its clothing sells for a premium price. For example, its yoga pants are priced from $78 to $128 a pair, whereas low-priced competitors like Gap Inc.'s Athleta sell yoga pants on their websites for $25 to $50.

Lululemon continues to hire employees who are passionate about fitness. Part of the hiring process involves taking prospective employees to a yoga or spin class. Some 70% of store managers are internal hires; most started on the sales floor and grew up in the culture. Store managers are given $300 to repaint their stores (any color) twice a year. The look and interior design of each store are completely up to its manager. Each store is also given $2,700 a year for employees to contribute to a charity or local event of their own choosing. One store manager in D.C. used the funds to create, with regional community leaders, a global yoga event in 2010. The result, Salutation Nation, is now an annual event in which over 70 Lululemon stores host a free, all-level yoga practice at the same time.

Employees are trained to eavesdrop on customers, who are called "guests." Clothes-folding tables are placed on the sales floor near the fitting rooms rather than in a back room so that employees can overhear complaints. Nearby, a large chalkboard lets customers write suggestions or complaints that are sent back to headquarters. This feedback is then incorporated into the product design process.

CEO Christine Day is not a fan of using "big data" to analyze customer purchases. She believes that software-generated data can give a company a false sense of security about the customer. Instead, Day personally spends hours each week in Lululemon stores observing how customers shop, listening to their complaints, and then using their feedback to tweak product development efforts. On one visit to a store in Whistler, British Columbia, Day noticed that women trying on a knit sweater found the sleeves too tight. After asking store associates if they had heard similar complaints, she canceled all future orders.

Despite the company's focus on providing quality, it has not all been plain sailing for Lululemon. In 2010, Wilson caused a stir when he had the company's tote bags emblazoned with the phrase "Who is John Galt," the opening line from Ayn Rand's 1957 novel, *Atlas Shrugged*. *Atlas Shrugged* has become a libertarian bible, and the underlying message that

Lululemon supported Rand's brand of unregulated capitalism did not sit too well with many of the stores' customers. After negative feedback, the bags were quickly pulled from stores. Wilson himself stepped down from any day-to-day involvement in the company in January 2012, although he remains chairman.

In early 2013, Lululemon found itself dealing with another controversy when it decided to recall some black yoga pants that were apparently too sheer, and effectively "see through" when stretched due to the lack of "rear-end coverage." In addition to the negative fallout from the product itself, some customers report being mistreated by employees who demanded that customers put the pants on and bend over to determine whether the clothing was see-through enough to warrant a refund! Despite this misstep, however, most observers in the media and financial community believe that the company will deal with this issue, and be able to continue its growth trajectory going forward.

Sources: Dana Mattoili, "Lululemon's Secret Sauce," *Wall Street Journal,* March 22, 2012; C. Leahey, "Lululemon CEO: How to Build Trust Inside Your Company," *CNN Money,* March 16, 2012; Tiffany Hsu "Panysgate to Hurt Lululemon Profit: Customer Told to Bend Over," *latimes.com,* March 21, 2013; and C. O'Commor, "Billionaire Founder Chip Wilson out at Yoga Giant Lululemon," *Forbes,* January 9, 2012.

CASE DISCUSSION QUESTIONS

1. How would you describe Lululemon's market segmentation strategy? Who do you think are Lululemon's typical customers?
2. What generic business-level strategy is Lululemon pursuing? Does this strategy give it an advantage over its rivals in the athletic clothing business? If so, how?
3. In order to successfully implement its business-level strategy, what does Lululemon need to do at the functional level? Has the company done these things?
4. How might the marketing and product missteps cited in the case impact upon Lululemon's ability to successfully execute its business-level strategy? What should Lululemon do to make sure that it does not make similar mistakes going forward?

NOTES

[1] Derek F. Abell, *Defining the Business: The Starting Point of Strategic Planning* (Englewood Cliffs NJ: Prentice-Hall, 1980).

[2] M. E. Porter, *Competitive Advantage* (New York: Free Press, 1985); and M. E. Porter, *Competitive Strategy* (New York, Free Press, 1980)

[3] C. W. L. Hill, "Differentiation Versus Low Cost or Differentiation and Low Cost: A Contingency Framework," *Academy of Management Review* 13 (1988): 401–412.

[4] M. E. Porter, "What Is Strategy?" *Harvard Business Review,* On-point Enhanced Edition Article, February 1, 2000.

[5] W.C. Kim and R. Mauborgne, "Value Innovation: The Strategic Logic of High Growth," *Harvard Business Review,* January–February 1997.

[6] Porter, *Competitive Advantage;* and, *Competitive Strategy.*

[7] The story was told to the author, Charles Hill, by an executive at Apple.

[8] Kim and Mauborgne, "Value Innovation: The Strategic Logic of High Growth."

[9] W.C. Kim and R. Mauborgne, Blue Ocean Strategy (Boston, Mass: Harvard Business School Press, 2005).

6

Business-Level Strategy and the Industry Environment

LEARNING OBJECTIVES

After reading this chapter, you should be able to:

6-1 Identify the strategies managers can develop to increase profitability in fragmented industries

6-2 Discuss the special problems that exist in embryonic and growth industries and how companies can develop strategies to effectively compete

6-3 Understand competitive dynamics in mature industries and discuss the strategies managers can develop to increase profitability even when competition is intense

6-4 Outline the different strategies that companies in declining industries can use to support their business models and profitability

OPENING CASE

How to Make Money in Newspaper Advertising

The U.S. newspaper business is a declining industry. Since 1990 newspaper circulation has been in a steady fall, with the drop accelerating in recent years. According to the Newspaper Association of America, in 1990 62.3 million newspapers were sold every day. By 2011 this figure had dropped to 44.4 million. The fall in advertising revenue has been even steeper, with revenues peaking in 2000 at $48.7 billion, and falling to just $20.7 billion in 2011. The reasons for the declines in circulation and advertising revenue are not hard to find; digitalization has disrupted the industry, news consumption has moved to the Web, and advertising has followed suit.

Declining demand for printed newspapers has left established players in the industry reeling. Gannett Co., which publishes USA Today

and a host of local newspapers, has seen its revenues slip to $5.3 billion in 2012, down from $6.77 billion in 2008. The venerable New York Times has watched revenues fall from $2.9 billion to $1.99 billion over the same period. The industry has responded by downsizing newsrooms, shutting down unprofitable newspaper properties, including numerous local newspapers, and expanding Web-based news properties as rapidly as possible. It has proved to be anything but easy. Whereas consumers were once happy to subscribe to their daily print newspaper, they seem to loathe paying for anything on the Web, particularly given the large amount of "free" content that they can access.

Against this background, one local newspaper company is swimming against the tide, and making money at it. The company, Community Impact Newspaper, produces 13 hyper-local editions that are delivered free each month to 855,000 homes in the Austin, Houston, and Dallas areas. The paper was the brainchild of John Garrett, who used to work as an advertising director for the *Austin Business Journal*. Back in 2005, Garrett noticed that the large-circulation local newspapers in Texas did not cover news that was relevant to smaller neighborhoods— such as the construction of a local toll road, or the impact of a new corporate campus for Exxon Mobil. Nor could news about these projects be gleaned from the Web. Yet Garrett believed that local people were still hungry for news about local projects and events that might impact them. So he started the paper, launching the inaugural issue in September 2005, and financing it with $40,000 borrowed from low-interest credit cards.

Today the paper has a staff of 30 journalists, about 35% of the total workforce.

The reporting is pretty straight stuff—there is no investigative reporting—although Impact will do in-depth stories on controversial local issues, but it is careful not to take sides. "That would just lose us business," says Garrett. About half of each edition is devoted to local advertisements, and this is where Impact makes its money. For their part, the advertisers seem happy with the paper. "We've tried everything, from Google Ads to Groupon, but this is the most effective," says Richard Hunter, who spends a few hundred dollars each month to advertise his Houston restaurant, Catfish Station. Another advertiser, Rob Sides, who owns a toy store, Toy Time, places 80% of his advertising dollars with Impact's local edition in order to reach 90,000 homes in the area.

An analysis by *Forbes* estimated that each 40-page issue of Impact brings in about $2.50 in ad revenue per printed copy. About 50 cents of that goes to mailing and distribution costs, 80 cents to payroll, and another 80 cents to printing and overhead, leaving roughly 40 cents per copy for Garrett and his wife, who own the entire company. If this analysis is right, Impact is making very good money for its owners in an industry where most players are struggling just to survive.

Sources: C. Helman, "Breaking: A Local Newspaper Chain That's Actually Making Good Money," *Forbes*, January 21, 2013; News Paper Association of America, "Trends and Numbers," www.naa.org/Trends-and-Numbers/Research.aspx; and J. Agnese, "Publishing and Advertising," S&P netAdvantage, April 12, 2012, http://eresources.library.nd.edu/databases/netadvantage.

OVERVIEW

In Chapter 2 we saw industries go through a life cycle. Some industries are young and dynamic, with rapidly growing demand. Others are mature and relatively stable, whereas still other industries, like the newspaper industry profiled in the opening case, are in decline.

In this chapter we look at the different strategies that companies can pursue to strengthen their competitive position in each of these different stages of the industry life cycle. What we will see is that each stage in the evolution of its industry raises some interesting challenges for a business. Managers must adopt the appropriate strategies to deal with these challenges.

For example, as explained in the Opening Case, the print newspaper business is a declining industry. Due to digital substitution, print circulation and advertising revenues from print have been falling for years. Most incumbents in the industry have responded by downsizing their print operations, while trying to grow their online presence. However, paradoxically, there is often still good money to be made in a declining industry if managers can figure out the right strategy. A niche strategy of focusing on market segments where demand remains strong is one of the classic ways of making money in a declining industry. This is exactly the strategy pursued by Community Impact Newspaper, the small hyperlocal print newspaper chain profiled in the Opening Case.

Before we look at the different stages of an industry life cycle, however, we first consider strategy in a fragmented industry. We do this because fragmented industries can offer unique opportunities for enterprises to pursue strategies that result in the consolidation of those industries, often creating significant wealth for the consolidating enterprise and its owners.

STRATEGY IN A FRAGMENTED INDUSTRY

fragmented industry
An industry composed of a large number of small- and medium-sized companies.

A **fragmented industry** is one composed of a large number of small- and medium-sized companies. Examples of fragmented industries include the dry-cleaning, hair salon, restaurant, health club, massage, and legal services industries. There are several reasons that an industry may consist of many small companies rather than a few large ones.[1]

Reasons for Fragmentation

First, a lack of scale economies may mean that there are few, if any, cost advantages to large size. There are no obvious scale economies in landscaping and massage services, for example, which helps explain why these industries remain highly fragmented. In some industries customer needs are so specialized that only a small amount of a product is required; hence, there is no scope for a large mass-production operation to satisfy the market. Custom-made jewelry or catering is an example of this. In some industries there may even be diseconomies of scale. In the restaurant business, for example, customers often prefer the unique food and style of a popular local restaurant, rather than the standardized offerings of some national chain. This diseconomy of scale places a limit on the ability of large restaurant chains to dominate the market.

Second, brand loyalty in the industry may primarily be local. It may be difficult to build a brand through differentiation that transcends a particular location or region. Many homebuyers, for example, prefer dealing with local real estate agents, whom they perceive as having better local knowledge than national chains. Similarly, there are no large chains in the massage services industry because differentiation and brand loyalty are primarily driven by differences in the skill sets of individual massage therapists.

Third, the lack of scale economies and national brand loyalty implies low entry barriers. When this is the case, a steady stream of new entrants may keep the industry fragmented. The massage services industry exemplifies this situation. Due to the absence of scale requirements, the costs of opening a massage services business are minor and can be shouldered by a single entrepreneur. The same is true of landscaping services, which helps to keep that industry fragmented.

In industries that have these characteristics, focus strategies tend to work best. Companies may specialize by customer group, customer need, or geographic region. Many small specialty companies may operate in local or regional markets. All kinds of specialized or custom-made products—furniture, clothing, hats, boots, houses, and so forth—fall into this category, as do all small service operations that cater to personalized customer needs, including dry-cleaning services, landscaping services, hair salons, and massage services.

Consolidating a Fragmented Industry Through Value Innovation

Business history is full of examples of entrepreneurial organizations that have pursued strategies to create meaningful scale economies and national brands where none previously existed. In the process they have consolidated industries that were once fragmented, reaping enormous gains for themselves and their shareholders in the process.

For example, until the 1980s the office supplies business was a highly fragmented industry composed of many small "mom-and-pop" enterprises that served local markets. The typical office supplies enterprise in those days had a limited selection of products, low inventory turnover, limited operating hours, and a focus on providing personal service to local businesses. Customer service included having a small sales force, which visited businesses and took orders, along with several trucks that delivered merchandise to larger customers. Then along came Staples, started by executives who had cut their teeth in the grocery business; they opened a big-box store with a wide product selection, long operating hours, and a self-service business model. They implemented computer information systems to track product sales and make sure that inventory was replenished just before it was out of stock, which drove up inventory turnover. Staples focused on selling to small businesses, and offered them something that established enterprises had not—value from a wide product selection that was always in stock, and long operating hours, all at a low price. True, Staples did not initially offer the same level of personal service that established office supplies enterprises did, but the managers of Staples made a bet that small business customers were more interested in a wide product selection, long opening hours, and low prices—and they were right! Put differently, the managers at Staples had a different view of what was important to their customer set than established enterprises. Today Staples, Office Depot, and Office Max dominate the office supplies business, and most of their small rivals have gone out of businesses.

You may recognize in the Staples story a theme that we discussed in the last chapter: Staples is a *value innovator*.[2] The company's founders figured out a way to offer more value to their customer set, and to do so at a lower cost. Nor have they been alone in doing this. In the retail sector, for example, Wal-Mart and Target did a similar thing in general merchandise, Lowes and Home Depot pulled off the same trick in building materials and home improvement, and Barnes and Noble did this in book retailing. In the restaurant sector, MacDonald's, Taco Bell, Kentucky Fried Chicken, and, more recently, Starbucks have all done a similar thing. In each case, these enterprises succeeded in consolidating once-fragmented industries.

The lesson is clear; fragmented industries are wide open market spaces—blue oceans—just waiting for entrepreneurs to transform them through the pursuit of value innovation. A key to understanding this process is to recognize that in each case, the value innovator defines value differently than established companies, and finds a way to offer that value that lowers costs through the creation of scale economies. In fast food, for example, McDonald's offers reliable, quick, and convenient fast food, and does so at a low cost. The low cost comes from two sources—first the standardization of processes within each store, which boosts labor productivity, and second, the attainment of scale economies on the input side due to McDonald's considerable purchasing power (which has gotten bigger and bigger over time as McDonald's grew). McDonald's, then, was also a value innovator in its day, and through its choice of strategy the company helped to drive consolidation in the fast-food segment of the restaurant industry.

Chaining and Franchising

In many fragmented industries that have been consolidated through value innovation, the transforming company often starts with a single location, or just a few locations. This was true for Staples, which started with a single store in Boston, and Starbucks, which had just three stores when Howard Shultz took over and started to transform the business. The key is to get the strategy right at the first few locations, and then expand as rapidly as possible to build a national brand and realize scale economies before rivals move into the market. If this is done right, the value innovator can build formidable barriers to new entry by establishing strong brand loyalty and enjoying the scale economies that come from large size (often, these scale economies are associated with purchasing power).

There are two strategies that enterprises use to *replicate* their offering once they get it right. One is chaining and the other is franchising.[3]

Chaining involves opening additional locations that adhere to the same basic formulae, *and that the company owns*. Thus, Staples pursued a chaining strategy when it quickly opened additional stores after perfecting its formula at its original Boston location. Today Staples has over 2,000 stores worldwide. Starbucks too has pursued a chaining strategy, offering the same basic formula in every store that it opens. Its store count now exceeds 18,000 in some 60 countries. Wal-Mart, Barnes & Noble, and Home depot have also all pursued a chaining strategy.

By expanding through chaining, a value innovator can quickly build a national brand. This may be of significant value in a mobile society, such as the United States, where people move and travel frequently, and when in a new town or city they look for familiar offerings. At the same time, by rapidly opening locations, and by knitting those locations together through good information systems, the value innovator can start to realize many of the cost advantages that come from large size. Wal-Mart, for example, tightly controls the flow of inventory through its stores, which allows for rapid inventory turnover (a major source of cost savings). In addition, as Wal-Mart grew, it was able to exercise more and more buying power, driving down the price for the goods that it then resold in its stores (for more details on the Wal-Mart story, see the Running Case in this chapter).

Franchising is similar in many respects to chaining, except that in the case of franchising the founding company—the franchisor—licenses the right to open and operate a new location to another enterprise—franchisee—in return for a fee. Typically, franchisees must adhere to some strict rules that require them to adopt the same basic business model and operate in a certain way. Thus, a McDonald's franchisee has to have the same basic look, feel, offerings, pricing, and business processes as other restaurants in the system, and has to report standardized financial information to McDonald's on a regular basis.

There are some advantages to using a franchising strategy. First, normally the franchisee puts up some or all of the capital to establish his or her operation. This helps to finance the growth of the system, and can result in more rapid expansion. Second, because franchisees are the owners of their operations, and because they often put up capital, they have a

chaining
A strategy designed to obtain the advantages of cost leadership by establishing a network of linked merchandising outlets interconnected by information technology that functions as one large company.

franchising
A strategy in which the franchisor grants to its franchisees the right to use the franchisor's name, reputation, and business model in return for a franchise fee and often a percentage of the profits.

strong incentive to make sure that their operations are run as efficiently and effectively as possible, which is good for the franchisor.

Third, because the franchisees are themselves entrepreneurs, who own their own businesses, they have an incentive to improve the efficiency and effectiveness of their operations by developing new offerings and/or processes. Typically, the franchisor will give them some latitude to do this, so long as they do not deviate too far from the basic business model. Ideas developed in this way may then be transferred to other locations in the system, improving the performance of the entire system. For example, McDonald's has recently been changing the design and menu of its restaurants in the United States based on ideas first pioneered by a franchisee in France.

The drawbacks of a franchising strategy are threefold. First, there may not be the same tight control that can be achieved through a chaining strategy, as, by definition, with a franchising strategy some authority is being delegated to the franchisee. Howard Shultz of Starbucks, for example, decided to expand via a chaining strategy rather than a franchising strategy because he felt that franchising would not give Starbucks the necessary control over customer service in each store. Second, in a franchising system the franchisee captures some of the economic profit from a successful operation, whereas in a chaining strategy it all goes back to the company. Third, because franchisees are small relative to the founding enterprise, they may face a higher cost of capital, which raises system costs and lowers profitability. Given these various pros and cons, the choice between chaining and franchising depends on managers evaluating which is the best strategy given the circumstances facing the founding enterprise.

Horizontal Mergers

Another way of consolidating a fragmented industry is to merge with or acquire competitors, combining them together into a single larger enterprise that is able to realize scale economies and build a more compelling national brand. For example, in the aerospace and defense contracting business there are many small niche producers that make the components that find their way into large products, such as Boeing jets or military aircraft. Esterline, a company based in Bellevue, Washington, has been pursuing horizontal mergers and acquisitions, trying to consolidate this tier of suppliers. Esterline started off as a small supplier itself. Over the last decade it has acquired another 30 or so niche companies, building a larger enterprise that now has sales of almost $2 billion. Esterline's belief is that as a larger enterprise offering a full portfolio of defense and avionic products, it can gain an edge over smaller rivals when selling to companies like Boeing and Lockheed, while its larger size enables it to realize scale economies and lowers its cost of capital.

We will consider the benefits, costs, and risk associated with a strategy of horizontal mergers and acquisitions in Chapters 9 and 10 when we look at corporate-level strategy. For now, it is worth noting that although mergers and acquisitions can help a company to consolidate a fragmented industry, the road to success when pursuing this strategy is littered with failures. Some acquiring companies pay too much for the companies they purchase. Others find out after the acquisition that they have bought a "lemon" that is nowhere as efficient as they thought prior to the acquisition. Still others discover that the gains envisaged for an acquisition are difficult to realize due to a clash between the culture of the acquiring and acquired enterprises. We discuss all of these issues, and how to guard against them, in Chapters 9 and 10.

FOCUS ON: Wal-Mart

Value Innovation at Wal-Mart: Consolidating a Fragmented Market

© iStockPhoto.com/caracterdesign

When Sam Walton opened the first Wal-Mart store in 1967 there were no large-scale general merchandise retailers. The industry was very fragmented. The general merchandise retailers that did exist in its original target markets—small southern towns—were "mom-and-pop stores." These stores offered a limited selection of merchandise in a full-service setting, with store employees helping customers to find the right products for their needs. Open hours were limited (10 a.m. to 6 p.m. being fairly standard), and the stores were often closed 1 or 2 days a week. The storeowners had to pay high prices for the goods they sold, so prices were high too. Inventory turnover was typically low, and infrequent restocking implied that a desired item could be out of stock for a while before the inventory was replenished. If customers wanted an item that was not typically stocked by the store, they would have to place a special order, and wait days or weeks before the item was delivered, or they would have to drive to the nearest city, which could be a 3-hour trip.

Sam Walton's vision was simple: Provide a wide selection of merchandise, stay open seven days a week, and have long operating hours. Buy in bulk to drive down the costs of goods sold, and then pass those cost savings on to customers in the form of lower prices. Reduce costs further by switching from a full-service format to a self-service format. Use good information systems to track what is sold in a store, and make sure that desired products are never out of stock. Gain further efficiencies by *chaining*, opening additional stores in a cluster around a common distribution center. Buy goods in still larger volumes, negotiating deep volume discounts with suppliers. Ship the goods to distribution centers, and then out from the centers to the stores so that inventory arrives just in time, thereby increasing inventory turnover and reducing working capital needs.

It was a brilliant vision. Execution required the development of processes that did not exist at the time, including state-of-the-art information systems to track store sales and inventory turnover, and a logistics system to optimize the flow of inventory from distribution centers to stores. Over the years, as Wal-Mart grew and built these systems, it was able to offer its customer set *more value* on the attributes that mattered to them—wide product selection, always-in-stock inventory, and the convenience of extended opening hours. At the same time, Wal-Mart dispensed with the value that did not matter to its customer set—full service—replacing that with self-service. Due to its increasingly low cost structure, it was able to offer all this at prices significantly below those of its smaller rivals, effectively driving them out of business. Through such value innovation, Wal-Mart was able to consolidate what was once a fragmented market, building a powerful national brand wrapped around the concept of everyday low prices and wide product selection.

STRATEGIES IN EMBRYONIC AND GROWTH INDUSTRIES

As Chapter 2 discusses, an embryonic industry is one that is just beginning to develop, and a growth industry is one in which first-time demand is rapidly expanding as many new customers enter the market. Choosing the strategies needed to succeed in such industries poses special challenges because new groups of customers with different kinds of needs start to enter the market. Managers must be aware of the way competitive forces in embryonic and growth industries change over time because they frequently need to build and develop new kinds of competencies, and refine their business strategy, in order to effectively compete in the future.

Most embryonic industries emerge when a technological innovation creates a new product opportunity. For example, in 1975, the personal computer (PC) industry was born after Intel developed the microprocessor technology that allowed companies to build the world's first PCs; this spawned the growth of the PC software industry that took off after Microsoft developed an operating system for IBM.[4]

Customer demand for the products of an embryonic industry is initially limited for a variety of reasons. Reasons for slow growth in market demand include: (1) the limited performance and poor quality of the first products; (2) customer unfamiliarity with what the new product can do for them; (3) poorly developed distribution channels to get the product to customers; (4) a lack of complementary products that might increase the value of the product for customers; and (5) high production costs because of small volumes of production.

Customer demand for the first cars, for example, was limited by their poor performance (they were no faster than a horse, far noisier, and frequently broke down), a lack of important complementary products (such as a network of paved roads and gas stations), and high production costs that made these cars an expensive luxury (before Ford invented the assembly line, cars were built by hand in a craft-based production setting). Similarly, demand for the first PCs was limited because buyers had to know how to program computers to use them: There were no software programs to purchase that could run on the original PCs. Because of such problems, early demand for the products of embryonic industries typically comes from a small set of technologically savvy customers willing and able to tolerate, and even enjoy, the imperfections in their new purchase.

An industry moves from the embryonic stage to the growth stage when a mass market starts to develop for its product (a **mass market** is one in which large numbers of customers enter the market). Mass markets start to emerge when three things happen: (1) ongoing technological progress makes a product easier to use, and increases its value for the average customer; (2) complementary products are developed that also increase its value; and (3) companies in the industry work to find ways to reduce the costs of producing the new products so they can lower their prices and stimulate high demand.[5] For example, the mass market for cars emerged and the demand for cars surged when: (1) technological progress increased the performance of cars; (2) a network of paved roads and gas stations was established; and (3) Henry Ford began to mass-produce cars using an assembly-line process, something that dramatically reduced production costs and enabled him to decrease car prices and build consumer demand. Similarly, the mass market for PCs emerged when technological advances made computers easier to use, a supply of complementary software (such as spreadsheets and word processing programs) was developed, and companies in the industry (such as Dell) began to use mass production to build PCs at a low cost.

mass market
One in which large numbers of customers enter the market.

The Changing Nature of Market Demand

Managers who understand how the demand for a product is affected by the changing needs of customers can focus on developing new strategies that will protect and strengthen their competitive position, such as building competencies to lower production costs or speed product development. In most product markets, the changing needs of customers lead to the S-shaped growth curve in Figure 6.1. This illustrates how different groups of customers with different needs enter the market over time. The curve is S-shaped because as the stage of market development moves from embryonic to mature, customer demand first accelerates then decelerates as the market approaches the saturation point—where most customers have already purchased the product for the first time, and demand is increasingly limited to replacement demand. This curve has major implications for a company's differentiation, cost, and pricing decisions.

The first group of customers to enter the market is referred to as *innovators*. Innovators are "technocrats" or "gadget geeks"; people who are delighted to be the first to purchase and

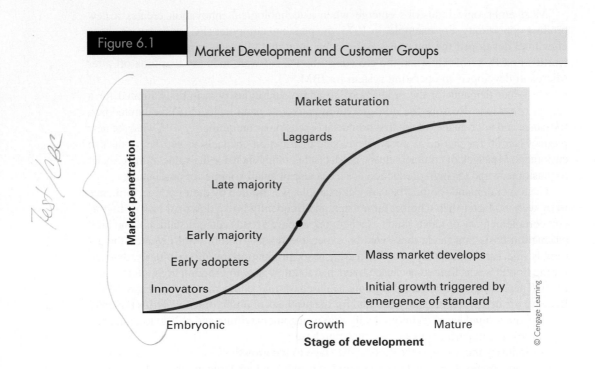

Figure 6.1 | Market Development and Customer Groups

experiment with a product based on a new technology—even if it is imperfect and expensive. Frequently, innovators have technical talents and interests and that makes them want to "own" and develop the technology because it is so new. In the PC market, the first customers were software engineers and computer hobbyists who wanted to write computer code at home.[6]

Early adopters are the second group of customers to enter the market; they understand that the technology may have important future applications and are willing to experiment with it to see if they can pioneer new uses for the technology. Early adopters are often people who envision how the technology may be used in the future, and they try to be the first to profit from its use. Jeff Bezos, the founder of Amazon.com, was an early adopter of Web technology. In 1994, before anyone else, he saw that the Web could be used in innovative ways to sell books.

Both innovators and early adopters enter the market while the industry is in its embryonic stage. The next group of customers, the _early majority_, forms the leading wave or edge of the mass market. Their entry into the market signifies the beginning of the growth stage. Customers in the early majority are practical and generally understand the value of new technology. They weigh the benefits of adopting new products against the costs, and wait to enter the market until they are confident they will benefit. When the early majority decides to enter the market, a large number of new buyers may be expected. This is what happened in the PC market after IBM's introduction of the PC in 1981. For the early majority, IBM's entry into the market signaled that the benefits of adopting the new PC technology would be worth the cost to purchase and time spent to learn how to use a PC. The growth of the PC market was further strengthened by the development of applications that added value to the PC, such as new spreadsheet and word processing programs. These applications transformed the PC from a hobbyist's toy into a business productivity tool. The same process started to unfold in the smartphone market after Apple introduced its iPhone in 2007. The early majority entered the market at that point because these customers saw the value that a smartphone could have, and they were comfortable adopting new technology.

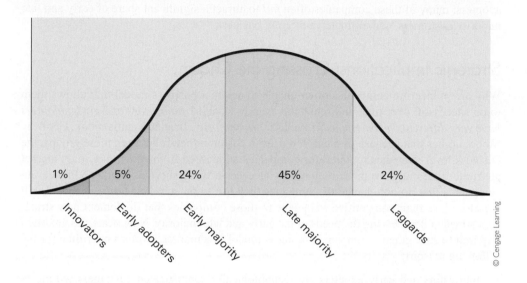

Figure 6.2

Market Share of Different Customer Segments

1% — Innovators
5% — Early adopters
24% — Early majority
45% — Late majority
24% — Laggards

© Cengage Learning

When the mass market reaches a critical mass, with about 30% of the potential market penetrated, the next group of customers enters the market. This group is characterized as the *late majority*, the customers who purchase a new technology or product only when it is obvious the technology has great utility and is here to stay. A typical late majority customer group is a somewhat "older" and more behaviorally conservative set of customers. They are familiar with technology that was around when they were younger, but are often unfamiliar with the advantages of new technology. The late majority can be a bit nervous about buying new technology, but they will do so once they see large numbers of people adopting it and getting value out of it. The late majority did not start to enter the PC market until the mid-1990s. In the smartphone business, the late majority started to enter the market in 2012 when it became clear that smartphones had great utility and would be here to stay. Although members of the late majority are hesitant to adopt new technology, they do so when they see that people around them are doing so in large numbers, and they will be left out if they do not do the same. Many older people, for example, started to purchase PCs for the first time when they saw people around them engaging in email exchanges and browsing the Web, and it became clear that these technologies were here to stay and had value for them.

Laggards, the last group of customers to enter the market, are people who are inherently conservative and unappreciative of the uses of new technology. Laggards frequently refuse to adopt new products even when the benefits are obvious, or unless they are forced to do so by circumstances—for example, due to work-related reasons. People who use typewriters rather than computers to write letters and books are an example of laggards. Given the fast rate of adoption of smartphones in the United States, it will not be long before the only people not in the smartphone market are the laggards. These people with either continue to use basic wireless phones, or may not even have a wireless phone, continuing to rely instead on increasingly outdated traditional wire-line phones.

In Figure 6.2, the bell-shaped curve represents the total market, and the divisions in the curve show the average percentage of buyers who fall into each of these customer groups. Note that early adopters are a very small percentage of the market; hence, the figure illustrates a vital competitive dynamic—the highest market demand and industry profits arise when the early and late majority groups enter the market. Additionally, research has found that although early pioneering companies succeed in attracting innovators and early adopters, many of these companies often *fail* to attract a significant share of early and late majority customers, and ultimately go out of business.[7]

Strategic Implications: Crossing the Chasm

Why are pioneering companies often unable to create a business model that allows them to be successful over time and remain as market leaders? *Innovators and early adopters have very different customer needs from the early majority.* In an influential book, Geoffrey Moore argues that because of the differences in customer needs between these groups, the business-level strategies required for companies to succeed in the emerging mass market are quite different from those required to succeed in the embryonic market.[8] Pioneering companies that do not change the strategies they use to pursue their business model will therefore lose their competitive advantage to those companies that implement new strategies aimed at best serving the needs of the early and late majority. New strategies are often required to strengthen a company's business model as a market develops over time for the following reasons:

- Innovators and early adopters are technologically sophisticated customers willing to tolerate the limitations of the product. The early majority, however, values ease of use and reliability. Companies competing in an embryonic market typically pay more attention to increasing the performance of a product than to its ease of use and reliability. Those competing in a mass market need to make sure that the product is reliable and easy to use. Thus, the product development strategies required for success are different as a market develops over time.
- Innovators and early adopters are typically reached through specialized distribution channels, and products are often sold by word of mouth. Reaching the early majority requires mass-market distribution channels and mass-media advertising campaigns that require a different set of marketing and sales strategies.
- Because innovators and the early majority are relatively few in number and are not particularly price sensitive, companies serving them typically pursue a focus model, produce small quantities of a product, and price high. To serve the rapidly growing mass-market, large-scale mass production may be critical to ensure that a high-quality product can be reliably produced at a low price point.

In sum, the business models and strategies required to compete in an embryonic market populated by early adopters and innovators are very different from those required to compete in a high-growth mass market populated by the early majority. As a consequence, the transition between the embryonic market and the mass market is not a smooth, seamless one. Rather, it represents a *competitive chasm* or gulf that companies must cross. According to Moore, many companies do not or cannot develop the right business model; they fall into the chasm and go out of business. Thus, although embryonic markets are typically populated by a large number of small companies, once the mass market begins to develop, the number of companies sharply decreases.[9] For a detailed example of how this unfolds, see Strategy in Action 6.1, which explains how Microsoft and Research in Motion fell into the chasm in the smartphone market, whereas Apple leaped across it with its iPhone, a product designed for the early majority.

6.1 STRATEGY IN ACTION

© iStockPhoto.com/Tom Nulens

Crossing the Chasm in the Smartphone Market

The first smartphones started to appear in the early 2000s. The early market leaders included Research in Motion (RIM), with its Blackberry line of smartphones, and Microsoft, whose Windows Mobile operating system powered a number of early smartphone offerings made by companies such as Motorola. These phones were sold to business users, and marketed as a business productivity tool. They had small screens, and a physical keyboard that was crammed onto a relatively small form factor. Although they had an ability to send and receive e-mails, browse the Web, and so on, there was no independent applications market, and consequently, the utility of the phones was very limited. Nor were they always easy to use. System administrators were often required to set up basic features such as corporate e-mail access. They were certainly not consumer-friendly devices. The customers at this time were primarily innovators and early adopters.

The market changed dramatically after the introduction of the Apple iPhone in 2007 (see Figure 6.3). First, this phone was aimed not at power business users, but at a broader consumer market. Second, the phone was easy to use, with a large touch-activated screen and a virtual keyboard that vanished when not in use. Third,

the phone was stylishly designed, with an elegance that appealed to many consumers. Fourth, Apple made it very easy for independent developers to write applications that could run on the phone, and they set up an App store that made it easy for developers to market their apps. Very quickly new applications started to appear that added value to the phone. These included mapping applications, news feeds, stock information, and a wide array of games, several of which soon became big hits. Clearly, the iPhone was a device aimed squarely not at business users, but at consumers. The ease of use and utility of the iPhone quickly drew the early majority into the market, and sales surged. Meanwhile, sales of Blackberry devices and Windows Mobile phones started to spiral downward.

Both Microsoft and Blackberry were ultimately forced to abandon their existing phone platforms and strategies, and reorient themselves. Both developed touch-activated screens, similar to those on the iPhone, started app stores, and targeted consumers. However, it may have been too late for them. By early 2013 both former market leaders had market share numbers in the single digits, whereas Apple controlled 45% of the market. Smartphones that used Google's

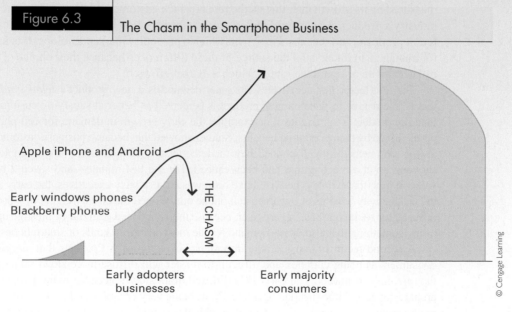

Figure 6.3   The Chasm in the Smartphone Business

© Cengage Learning

(continues)

6.1 STRATEGY IN ACTION

(continued)

Android operating system took up the remaining market share. Introduced some 12 months after the iPhone, Android phones shared many of the same features as the iPhone. Google also supported an app store, and devices makers using the Android operating system, such as Samsung, marketed their phones to consumers who now very clearly constituted the early and late majority of the market.

The implication is clear: to cross the chasm successfully, managers must correctly identify the customer needs of the first wave of early majority users—the leading edge of the mass market. Then they must adjust their business models by developing new strategies to redesign products and create distribution channels and marketing campaigns to satisfy the needs of the early majority. They must have a suitable product available at a reasonable price to sell to the early majority when they begin to enter the market in large numbers. At the same time, the industry pioneers must abandon their outdated, focused business models directed at the needs of innovators and early adopters. Focusing on the outdated model will lead managers to ignore the needs of the early majority—and the need to develop the strategies necessary to pursue a differentiation or cost-leadership business model in order to remain a dominant industry competitor.

Strategic Implications of Differences in Market Growth Rates

Managers must understand a final important issue in embryonic and growth industries: different markets develop at different rates. The speed at which a market develops can be measured by its growth rate, that is, the rate at which customers in that market purchase the industry's product. A number of factors explain the variation in market growth rates for different products, and thus the speed with which a particular market develops. It is important for managers to understand the source of these differences because their choice of strategy can accelerate or retard the rate at which a market grows.[10]

The first factor that accelerates customer demand is a new product's _relative advantage_, that is, the degree to which a new product is perceived as better at satisfying customer needs than the product it supersedes. For example, the early growth in demand for cell phones was partly driven by their economic benefits. Studies showed that because business customers could always be reached by cell phone, they made better use of their time—for example, by not showing up at a meeting that had been cancelled at the last minute—and saved 2 hours per week in time that would otherwise have been wasted. For busy executives, the early adopters, the productivity benefits of owning a cell phone outweighed the costs. Cell phones also rapidly diffused for social reasons, in particular, because they conferred glamour or prestige upon their users (something that also drives demand for the most advanced kinds of smartphones today).

A second factor of considerable importance is _complexity_. Products that are viewed by consumers as being complex and difficult to master will diffuse more slowly than products that are easy to master. The early PCs diffused quite slowly because many people saw the archaic command lines needed operate a PC as being very complex and intimidating. PCs did not become a mass-market device until graphical user interfaces with onscreen icons became widespread, enabling users to open programs and perform functions by pointing and clicking with a mouse. In contrast, the first cell phones were simple to use and quickly adopted.

Another factor driving growth in demand is *compatibility*, the degree to which a new product is perceived as being consistent with the current needs or existing values of potential adopters. Demand for cell phones grew rapidly because their operation was compatible with the prior experience of potential adopters who used traditional landline phones. A fourth factor is *trialability*, the degree to which potential customers can experiment with a new product during a hands-on trial basis. Many people first used cell phones when borrowing them from colleagues to make calls, and positive experiences helped accelerate growth rates. In contrast, early PCs were more difficult to experiment with because they were rare and expensive and because some training was needed in how to use them. These complications led to slower growth rates for PCs. A final factor is *observability*, the degree to which the results of using and enjoying a new product can be seen and appreciated by other people. Originally, the iPhone and Android phones diffused rapidly because it became obvious how their owners could put them to so many different uses.

Thus managers must be sure to devise strategies that help to educate customers about the value of their new products if they are to grow demand over time. In addition, they need to design their products so that they overcome some of the barriers to adoption by making them less complex and intimidating, and easy to use, and by showcasing their relative advantage over prior technology. This is exactly what Apple did with the iPhone, which helps explain the rapid diffusion of smartphones after Apple introduced its first iPhone in 2007.

When a market is rapidly growing, and the popularity of a new product increases or spreads in a way that is analogous to a *viral model of infection*, a related strategic issue arises. Lead adopters (the first customers who buy a product) in a market become "infected" or enthused with the product, as exemplified by iPhone users. Subsequently, lead adopters infect other people by telling others about the advantages of products. After observing the benefits of the product, these people also adopt and use the product. Companies promoting new products can take advantage of viral diffusion by identifying and aggressively courting opinion leaders in a particular market—the customers whose views command respect. For example, when the manufacturers of new high-tech medical equipment, such as magnetic resonance imaging (MRI) scanners, start to sell a new product, they try to get well-known doctors at major research and teaching hospitals to use the product first. Companies may give these opinion leaders (the doctors) free machines for their research purposes, and work closely with the doctors to further develop the technology. Once these opinion leaders commit to the product and give it their stamp of approval, other doctors at additional hospitals often follow.

In sum, understanding competitive dynamics in embryonic and growth industries is an important strategic issue. The ways in which different kinds of customer groups emerge and the ways in which customer needs change are important determinants of the strategies that need to be pursued to make a business model successful over time. Similarly, understanding the factors that affect a market's growth rate allows managers to tailor their business model to a changing industry environment. (More about competition in high-tech industries is discussed in the next chapter.)

STRATEGY IN MATURE INDUSTRIES

A mature industry is commonly dominated by a small number of large companies. Although a mature industry may also contain many medium-sized companies and a host of small, specialized companies, the large companies often determine the nature of competition in the industry because they can influence the six competitive forces. Indeed, these large companies hold their leading positions because they have developed the most successful business models and strategies in an industry.

By the end of the shakeout stage, companies have learned how important it is to analyze each other's business model and strategies. They also know that if they change their strategies, their actions are likely to stimulate a competitive response from industry rivals. For example, a differentiator that starts to lower its prices because it has adopted a more cost-efficient technology not only threatens other differentiators, but may also threaten cost leaders that see their competitive advantage being eroded. Hence, by the mature stage of the life cycle, companies have learned the meaning of competitive interdependence.

As a result, in mature industries, business-level strategy revolves around understanding how established companies *collectively* attempt to moderate the intensity of industry competition in order to preserve both company and industry profitability. Interdependent companies can help protect their competitive advantage and profitability by adopting strategies and tactics, first, to deter entry into an industry, and second, to reduce the level of rivalry within an industry.

Strategies to Deter Entry

In mature industries successful enterprises have normally gained substantial economies of scale and established strong brand loyalty. As we saw in Chapter 2, the economies of scale and brand loyalty enjoyed by incumbents in an industry constitute strong barriers to new entry. However, there may be cases in which scale and brand, although significant, are not sufficient to deter entry. In such circumstances there are other strategies that companies can pursue to make new entry less likely. These strategies include product proliferation, limit pricing, and strategic commitments.[11]

Product Proliferation   One way in which companies try to enter a mature industry is by looking for market segments or niches that are poorly served by incumbent enterprises. The entry strategy involves entering these segments, gaining experience, scale and brand in that segment, and then progressively moving upmarket. This is how Japanese automobile companies first entered the U.S. market in the late 1970s and early 1980s. They targeted segments at the bottom end of the market for small inexpensive cars that were fuel-efficient. These segments were not well served by large American manufacturers such as Ford and GM. Once companies like Toyota and Honda had gained a strong position in these segments, they started to move upmarket with larger offerings, and ultimately entering the pick-up truck and SUV segments, which historically had been the most profitable parts of the automobile industry for American companies.

A **product proliferation strategy** involves incumbent companies attempting to forestall entry by making sure that *every* niche or segment in the marketplace is well served. Had U.S. automobile companies pursued product proliferation in the 1970s and early 1980s, and produced a line of smaller, fuel-efficient cars, it may have been more difficult for Japanese automobile companies to enter the U.S. market. Another example concerns breakfast cereal companies, which are famous for pursuing a product proliferation strategy. Typically they produce many different types of cereal, so that they can cater to all likely consumer needs. The net result is that the three big breakfast cereal companies—General Mills, Post, and Kellogg—have been able to occupy all of the valuable real estate in the industry, which is shelf space in supermarkets, filling it up with a multiplicity of offerings and leaving very little room for new entrants. Moreover, when new entry does occur—as happened when smaller companies entered the market selling granola and organic cereals—the big three

product proliferation strategy

The strategy of "filling the niches," or catering to the needs of customers in all market segments to deter entry by competitors.

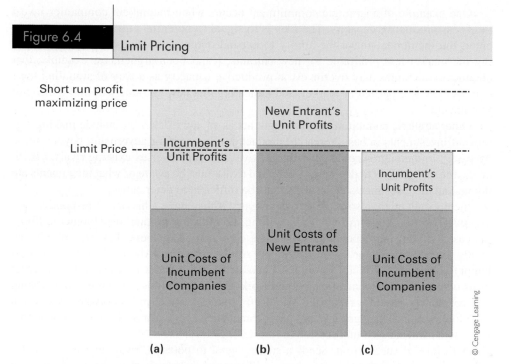

Figure 6.4   Limit Pricing

© Cengage Learning

have moved rapidly to offer their own versions of these products, effectively foreclosing entry. A product proliferation strategy therefore, because it gives new entrants very little opportunity to find an unoccupied niche in an industry, can effectively deter entry.

Limit Price   A limit price strategy may be used to deter entry when incumbent companies in an industry enjoy economies of scale, but the resulting cost advantages are *not* enough to keep potential rivals out of the industry. A **limit price strategy** involves charging a price that is lower than that required to maximize profits in the short run, but is above the cost structure of potential entrants.

For illustration, consider Figure 6.4; this shows that incumbent companies have a unit cost structure that is lower than that of potential entrants. However, if incumbents charge the price that the market will bear (Figure 6.4a), this will be above the unit cost structure of new entrants (Figure 6.4b), allowing them to enter and still make a profit under the pricing umbrella set by incumbents. In this situation, the best option for incumbents might be to charge a price that is still above their own cost structure, but just below the cost structure of any potential new entrants (Figure 6.4c). Now there is no incentive for potential entrants to enter the market, because at the lower "limit" price they cannot make a profit. Thus, because it deters entry, the limit price might be thought of as the long-run profit-maximizing price.

Strategic Commitments   Incumbent companies can deter entry by engaging in strategic commitments that send a signal to any potential new entrants that entry will be difficult. **Strategic commitments** are investments that signal an incumbent's long-term commitment to a market, or a segment of that market.[12] As an entry-deterring strategy, strategic commitments involve raising the perceived costs of entering a market, thereby reducing the likelihood of entry. To the extent that such actions are successful, strategic commitments can help to protect an industry and lead to greater long-run profits for those already in the industry.

limit price strategy
Charging a price that is lower than that required to maximize profits in the short run, but is above the cost structure of potential entrants.

strategic commitments
Investments that signal an incumbent's long-term commitment to a market, or a segment of that market.

One example of a strategic commitment occurs when incumbent companies invest in excess productive capacity. The idea is to signal to potential entrants that if they do enter, the incumbents have the ability to expand output and drive down prices, making the market less profitable for new entrants. It has been argued, for example, that chemical companies may overinvest in productive capacity as a way of signaling their commitment to a particular market, and indicating that new entrants will find it difficult to compete.[13]

Other strategic commitments that might act as an entry deterrent include making significant investments in basic research, product development, or advertising beyond those necessary to maintain a company's competitive advantage over its existing rivals.[14] In all cases, for such actions to deter entry, potential rivals must be aware of what incumbents are doing, and the investments themselves must be sufficient to deter entry.

Incumbents might also be able to deter entry if they have a history of responding aggressively to new entry through price cutting, accelerating product development efforts, increased advertising expenditures, or some combination of these. For example, in the 1990s when a competitor announced a new software product, Microsoft would often attempt to make entry difficult by quickly announcing that it had a similar software product of its own under development that would work well with Windows (the implication being that consumers should wait for the Microsoft product). The term "vaporware" was often used to describe such aggressive product preannouncements. Many observers believe that the practice did succeed on occasion in forestalling entry.[15]

A history of such actions sends a strong signal to potential rivals that market entry will not be easy, and that the incumbents will respond vigorously to any encroachment on their turf. When established companies have succeeded in signaling this to potential rivals through past actions, we say that they have established a *credible commitment* to respond to new entry.

One thing to note here is that when making strategic commitments, a company must be careful not to fall foul of antitrust law. For example, it is illegal to engage in predatory pricing, or pricing a good or service below the cost of production with the expressed intent of driving a rival out of business and monopolizing a market. In the late 1990s Microsoft fell afoul of antitrust laws when it told PC manufacturers that they had to display Internet Explorer on the PC desktop if they wanted to license the company's Windows operating system. Because Windows was the only viable operating system for PCs at the time, this was basically viewed as strong-arming PC makers. The intent was to give Internet Explorer an edge over rival browsers, and particularly one produced by Netscape. The U.S. Justice Department ruled Microsoft's actions as predatory behavior. Microsoft was forced to pay fines and change its practices.

Strategies to Manage Rivalry

Beyond seeking to deter entry, companies also wish to develop strategies to manage their competitive interdependence and decrease price rivalry. Unrestricted competition over prices reduces both company and industry profitability. Several strategies are available to companies to manage industry rivalry. The most important are price signaling, price leadership, non-price competition, and capacity control.

Price Signaling   A company's ability to choose the price option that leads to superior performance is a function of several factors, including the strength of demand for a product and the intensity of competition between rivals. Price signaling is a method by which companies attempt to control rivalry among competitors to allow the *industry* to choose the most favorable pricing option. **price signaling** is the process by which companies increase or decrease product prices to convey their intentions to other companies and influence the way other companies price their products. Companies use price signaling to improve industry profitability.

Companies may use price signaling to announce that they will vigorously respond to hostile competitive moves that threaten them. For example, they may signal that if one company starts to aggressively cut prices, they will respond in kind. A *tit-for-tat strategy* is a well-known price signaling maneuver in which a company does exactly what its rivals do: if its rivals cut prices, the company follows; if its rivals raise prices, the company follows. By consistently pursuing this strategy over time, a company sends a clear signal to its rivals that it will mirror any pricing moves they make; sooner or later, rivals will learn that the company will always pursue a tit-for-tat strategy. Because rivals know that the company will match any price reductions and cutting prices will only reduce profits, price cutting becomes less common in the industry. Moreover, a tit-for-tat strategy also signals to rivals that price increases will be imitated, growing the probability that rivals will initiate price increases to raise profits. Thus, a tit-for-tat strategy can be a useful way of shaping pricing behavior in an industry.[16]

The airline industry is a good example of the power of price signaling when prices typically rise and fall depending upon the current state of customer demand. If one carrier signals the intention to lower prices, a price war frequently ensues as other carriers copy one another's signals. If one carrier feels demand is strong, it tests the waters by signaling an intention to increase prices, and price signaling becomes a strategy to obtain uniform price increases. Nonrefundable tickets or charges for a second bag, another strategy adopted to allow airlines to charge higher prices, also originated as a market signal by one company that was quickly copied by all other companies in the industry (it is estimated that extra bag charges have so far allowed airlines to raise over $1 billion in revenues). Carriers have recognized that they can stabilize their revenues and earn interest on customers' money if they collectively act to force customers to assume the risk of buying airline tickets in advance. In essence, price signaling allows companies to give one another information that enables them to understand each other's competitive product or market strategy and make coordinated, price-competitive moves.

Price Leadership When one company assumes the responsibility for setting the pricing option that maximizes industry profitability, that company assumes the position as price leader—a second tactic used to reduce price rivalry between companies in a mature industry. Formal price leadership, or when companies jointly set prices, is illegal under antitrust laws; therefore, the process of **price leadership** is often very subtle. In the car industry, for example, prices are set by imitation. The price set by the weakest company—that is, the company with the highest cost structure—is often used as the basis for competitors' pricing. Thus, in the past, U.S. carmakers set their prices and Japanese carmakers then set their prices in response to the U.S. prices. The Japanese are happy to do this because they have lower costs than U.S. carmakers, and still make higher profits without having to compete on price. Pricing is determined by market segment. The prices of different auto models in a particular range indicate the customer segments that the companies are targeting, and the price range the companies believe the market segment can tolerate. Each manufacturer prices a model in the segment with reference to the prices charged by its competitors, not by reference to competitors' costs. Price leadership also allows differentiators to charge a premium price.

price signaling
The process by which companies increase or decrease product prices to convey their intentions to other companies and influence the price of an industry's products.

price leadership
When one company assumes the responsibility for determining the pricing strategy that maximizes industry profitability.

Although price leadership can stabilize industry relationships by preventing head-to-head competition and raising the level of profitability within an industry, it has its dangers. It helps companies with high cost structures, allowing them to survive without needing to implement strategies to become more efficient. In the long term, such behavior makes them vulnerable to new entrants that have lower costs because they have developed new low-cost production techniques. This is what happened in the U.S. car industry. After decades of tacit price fixing, and GM as the price leader, U.S. carmakers were subjected to growing low-cost overseas competition that was threatening their survival. In 2009, the U.S. government decided to bail out Chrysler and GM by loaning them billions of dollars after the financial crisis, while forcing them to enter, and then emerge from, bankruptcy. This dramatically lowered the cost structures of these companies, and has made them more competitive today. (This also applies to Ford, which obtained similar benefits while managing to avoid bankruptcy.)

non-price competition
The use of product differentiation strategies to deter potential entrants and manage rivalry within an industry.

Non-price Competition   A third very important aspect of product and market strategy in mature industries is the use of **non-price competition** to manage rivalry within an industry. The use of strategies to try to prevent costly price cutting and price wars does not preclude competition by product differentiation. In many industries, product-differentiation strategies are the principal tools companies use to deter potential entrants and manage rivalry within their industries.

Product differentiation allows industry rivals to compete for market share by offering products with different or superior features, such as smaller, more powerful, or more sophisticated computer chips, as AMD, Intel, and NVIDIA compete to offer, or by applying different marketing techniques, as Procter & Gamble, Colgate, and Unilever do. In Figure 6.5, product and market segment dimensions are used to identify four non-price-competitive strategies based on product differentiation: market penetration, product development, market development, and product proliferation. (Note that this model applies to new market segments, *not* new markets.)

Market Penetration   When a company concentrates on expanding market share in its existing product markets, it is engaging in a strategy of **market penetration**. Market penetration involves heavy advertising to promote and build product differentiation. For example, Intel has actively pursued penetration with its aggressive marketing campaign of "Intel Inside."

Figure 6.5 | Four Nonprice Competitive Strategies

© Cengage Learning

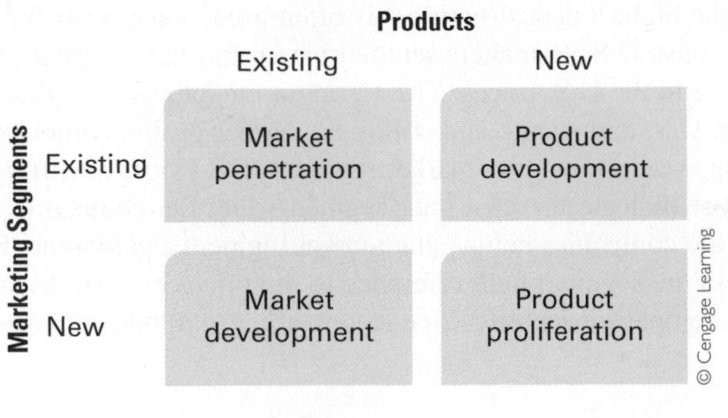

In a mature industry, advertising aims to influence customers' brand choice and create a brand-name reputation for the company and its products. In this way, a company can increase its market share by attracting its rival's customers. Because brand-name products often command premium prices, building market share in this situation is very profitable.

In some mature industries—for example, soap and detergent, disposable diapers, and brewing—a market-penetration strategy becomes a long-term strategy. In these industries, all companies engage in intensive advertising and battle for market share. Each company fears that if it does not advertise, it will lose market share to rivals who do. Consequently, in the soap and detergent industry, Procter & Gamble spends more than 20% of sales revenues on advertising, with the aim of maintaining, and perhaps building, market share. These huge advertising outlays constitute a barrier to entry for prospective competitors.

Product Development   **Product development** is the creation of new or improved products to replace existing ones. The wet-shaving industry depends on product replacement to create successive waves of customer demand, which then create new sources of revenue for companies in the industry. Gillette, for example, periodically unveils a new and improved razor, such as its vibrating razor (that competes with Schick's four-bladed razor), to try to boost its market share. Similarly, in the car industry, each major car company replaces its models every 3 to 5 years to encourage customers to trade in old models and purchase new ones.

Product development is crucial for maintaining product differentiation and building market share. For instance, the laundry detergent Tide has gone through more than 50 changes in formulation during the past 40 years to improve its performance. The product is always advertised as Tide, but it is a different product each year. Refining and improving products is a crucial strategy companies use to fine-tune and improve their business models in a mature industry, but this kind of competition can be as vicious as a price war because it is very expensive and can dramatically increase a company's cost structure. This happened in the computer chip industry, where intense competition to make the fastest or most powerful chip and become the market leader has dramatically increased the cost structure of Intel, AMD, and NVIDIA and sharply reduced their profitability.

Market Development   **Market development** finds new market segments for a company's products. A company pursuing this strategy wants to capitalize on the brand name it has developed in one market segment by locating new market segments in which to compete—just as Mattel and Nike do by entering many different segments of the toy and shoe markets, respectively. In this way, a company can leverage the product differentiation advantages of its brand name. The Japanese auto manufacturers provide an interesting example of the use of market development. When each manufacturer entered the market, it offered a car model aimed at the economy segment of the auto market, such as the Toyota Corolla and the Honda Accord. Then, these companies upgraded each model over time; now each company is directed at a more expensive market segment. The Honda Accord is a leading contender in the mid-sized car segment, and the Toyota Corolla fills the small-car segment. By redefining their product offerings, Japanese manufacturers have profitably developed their market segments and successfully attacked their U.S. rivals, wresting market share from these companies. Although the Japanese used to compete primarily as cost leaders, market development has allowed them to become differentiators as well. In fact, as we noted in the previous chapter, Toyota has used market development to become a broad differentiator. Over time, Toyota has used market development to create a vehicle for almost every segment of the car market, a tactic discussed in Strategy in Action 6.2.

product development
The creation of new or improved products to replace existing products.

market development
When a company searches for new market segments for a company's existing products to increase sales.

6.2 STRATEGY IN ACTION

Toyota Uses Market Development to Become the Global Leader

The car industry has always been one of the most competitive in the world because of the huge revenues and profits that are at stake. Given the difficult economic conditions in the late-2000s, it is hardly surprising that rivalry has increased as global carmakers struggle to develop new car models that better satisfy the needs of particular groups of buyers. One company at the competitive forefront is Toyota.

Toyota produced its first car 40 years ago, the ugly, boxy vehicle that was, however, cheap. As the quality of its car became apparent, sales increased. Toyota, which was then a focused cost leader, reinvested its profits into improving the styling of its vehicles, and into efforts to continually reduce production costs. Over time, Toyota has taken advantage of its low-cost structure to make an ever-increasing range of reasonably priced vehicles tailored to different segments of the car market. The company's ability to begin with the initial design stage and move to the production stage in 2 to 3 years allowed it to make new models available faster than its competitors, and capitalize on the development of new market segments.

Toyota has been a leader in positioning its entire range of vehicles to take advantage of new, emerging market segments. In the SUV segment, for example, its first offering was the expensive Toyota Land Cruiser, even then priced at over $35,000. Realizing the need for SUVs in lower price ranges, it next introduced the 4Runner, priced at $20,000 and designed for the average SUV customer; the RAV4, a small SUV in the low $20,000 range, followed; then came the Sequoia, a bigger, more powerful version of the 4Runner in the upper $20,000 range. Finally, taking the technology from its Lexus division, it introduced the luxury Highlander SUV in the low $30,000 range. Today it offers six SUV models, each offering a particular combination of price, size, performance, styling, and luxury to appeal to a particular customer group within the SUV segment of the car market. In a similar way, Toyota positions its sedans to appeal to the needs of different sets of customers. For example, the Camry is targeted at the middle of the market to customers who can afford to pay about $25,000 and want a balance of luxury, performance, safety, and reliability.

Toyota's broad differentiation business model is geared toward making a range of vehicles that optimizes the amount of value it can create for different groups of customers. At the same time, the number of models it makes is constrained by the need to keep costs under strict control so it can make car-pricing options that will generate maximum revenues and profits. Because competition in each car market segment is now intense, all global carmakers need to balance the advantages of showcasing more cars to attract customers against the increasing costs that result when the number of different car models they make expands to suit the needs of different customers.

Product Proliferation We have already seen how product proliferation can be used to deter entry into an industry. The same strategy can be used to manage rivalry within an industry. As noted earlier, product proliferation generally means that large companies in an industry have a product in each market segment (or niche) If a new niche develops, such as SUVs, designer sunglasses, or shoe-selling websites, the leader gets a first-mover advantage—but soon thereafter, all the other companies catch up. Once again, competition is stabilized, and rivalry within the industry is reduced. Product proliferation thus allows the development of stable industry competition based on product differentiation, not price— that is, non-price competition based on the development of new products. The competitive battle is over a product's perceived uniqueness, quality, features, and performance, not over its price. Strategy in Action 6.3 looks at Nike's history of non-price competition, and how that has helped the company to differentiate itself from rivals.

6.3 STRATEGY IN ACTION

Non-Price Competition at Nike

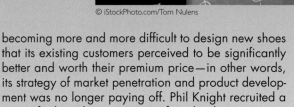

© iStockPhoto.com/Tom Nulens

The way in which Nike has used non-price-competitive strategies to strengthen its differentiation strategy is highly instructive. Bill Bowerman, a former University of Oregon track coach, and Phil Knight, an entrepreneur in search of a profitable business opportunity, founded Nike, now headquartered in Beaverton, Oregon. Bowerman's dream was to create a new type of sneaker tread that would enhance a runner's traction and speed, and after studying the waffle iron in his home, he came up with the idea for Nike's "waffle tread." Bowerman and Knight made this shoe, and began by selling it out of car trunks at track meets. Nike has since grown into a company that sells almost 45% of the shoes sold in the global $50 billion athletic footwear and apparel industries each year, and made more than $2 billion in profit in 2012.

Nike's amazing success came from its business model, which was always based on differentiation; its strategy was to innovate state-of-the-art athletic shoes and then to publicize the qualities of its shoes through dramatic "guerrilla" marketing. Nike's marketing is designed to persuade customers that its shoes are not only superior, but also a high-fashion statement and a necessary part of a lifestyle based on sporting or athletic interests. Nike's strategy to emphasize the uniqueness of its product obviously paid off, as its market share soared. However, the company received a shock in 1998, when its sales suddenly began to fall; it was

becoming more and more difficult to design new shoes that its existing customers perceived to be significantly better and worth their premium price—in other words, its strategy of market penetration and product development was no longer paying off. Phil Knight recruited a team of talented top managers from leading consumer products companies to help him change Nike's strategy in some fundamental ways.

In the past, Nike shunned sports like golf, soccer, rollerblading, and so on, and focused most of its efforts on making shoes for the track and basketball market segments. However, when its sales started to fall, it realized that using marketing to increase sales in a particular market segment (market penetration) could only grow sales and profits so much. Nike decided to take its existing design and marketing competencies and began to craft new lines of shoes for new market segments. In other words, it began to pursue market development and product proliferation as well as the other non-price strategies.

For example, it revamped its aerobics shoes, launched a line of soccer shoes, and perfected the company's design over time; by the mid-2000s, it took over as the market leader from its archrival Adidas. Nike's strategies significantly strengthened its differentiation business model, which is why its market share and profitability have continued to increase, and also why Nike is the envy of competitors.

Capacity Control   Although non-price competition helps mature industries avoid the cutthroat price cutting that reduces company and industry levels of profitability, price competition does periodically occur when excess capacity exists in an industry. Excess capacity arises when companies collectively produce too much output; to dispose of it, they cut prices. When one company cuts prices, other companies quickly do the same because they fear that the price cutter will be able to sell its entire inventory, while they will be left with unwanted goods. The result is a developing price war.

Excess capacity may be caused by a shortfall in demand, as when a recession lowers the demand for cars and causes car companies to give customers price incentives to purchase new cars. In this situation, companies can do nothing but wait for better times. By and large, however, excess capacity results from companies within an industry simultaneously responding to favorable conditions; they all invest in new plants to be able to take advantage of the predicted upsurge in demand. Paradoxically, each individual company's effort to outperform the others means that, collectively, companies create industry overcapacity, which hurts all companies. Although demand is rising, the consequence of each company's decision to increase capacity is a surge in industry capacity, which drives down prices. To prevent the accumulation of costly excess capacity, companies must devise strategies that let them control—or at least benefit from—capacity expansion programs. Before we examine these strategies, however, we need to consider in greater detail the factors that cause excess capacity.[17]

Factors Causing Excess Capacity   The problem of excess capacity often derives from technological developments. Sometimes new low-cost technology can create an issue because all companies invest in it simultaneously to prevent being left behind. Excess capacity occurs because the new technology can produce more than the old. In addition, new technology is often introduced in large increments, which generates overcapacity. For instance, an airline that needs more seats on a route must add another plane, thereby adding hundreds of seats even if only 50 are needed. To take another example, a new chemical process may efficiently operate at the rate of only 1,000 gallons per day, whereas the previous process was efficient at 500 gallons per day. If all companies within an industry change technologies, industry capacity may double, and enormous problems can potentially result.

Overcapacity may also be caused by competitive factors within an industry. Entry into an industry is one such a factor. The recent economic recession caused global overcapacity and the price of steel plunged; with global recovery the price has increased. Sometimes the age of a company's physical assets is the source of the problem. For example, in the hotel industry, given the rapidity with which the quality of hotel room furnishings decline, customers are always attracted to new hotels. When new hotel chains are built alongside the old chains, excess capacity can result. Often, companies are simply making simultaneous competitive moves based on industry trends—but these moves lead to head-to-head competition. Most fast-food chains, for instance, establish new outlets whenever demographic data show population increases. However, companies seem to forget that all other chains use the same data—they are not anticipating their rivals' actions. Thus, a certain locality that has few fast-food outlets may suddenly have several new outlets being built at the same time. Whether all the outlets can survive depends upon the growth rate of customer demand, but most often the least popular outlets close down.

Choosing a Capacity-Control Strategy   Given the various ways in which capacity can expand, companies clearly need to find some means of controlling it. If companies are always plagued by price cutting and price wars, they will be unable to recoup the investments in their generic strategies. Low profitability within an industry caused by overcapacity forces not only the weakest companies but also sometimes the major players to exit the industry. In general, companies have two strategic choices: (1) each company individually must try to preempt its rivals and seize the initiative, or (2) the companies must collectively find indirect means of coordinating with each other so that they are all aware of the mutual effects of their actions.

To *preempt* rivals, a company must forecast a large increase in demand in the product market and then move rapidly to establish large-scale operations that will be able to satisfy the predicted demand. By achieving a first-mover advantage, the company may deter other firms from entering the market because the preemptor will usually be able to move down the experience curve, reduce its costs, and therefore reduce its prices as well—and threaten a price war if necessary.

This strategy, however, is extremely risky, for it involves investing resources before the extent and profitability of the future market are clear. A preemptive strategy is also risky if it does not deter competitors, and they decide to enter the market. If competitors can develop a stronger generic strategy, or have more resources, such as Google or Microsoft, they can make the preemptor suffer. Thus, for the strategy to succeed, the preemptor must generally be a credible company with enough resources to withstand a possible advertising/price war.

To *coordinate* with rivals as a capacity-control strategy, caution must be exercised because collusion on the timing of new investments is illegal under antitrust law. However, tacit coordination is practiced in many industries as companies attempt to understand and forecast one another's competitive moves. Generally, companies use market signaling to secure coordination. They make announcements about their future investment decisions in trade journals and newspapers. In addition, they share information about their production levels and their forecasts of demand within an industry to bring supply and demand into equilibrium. Thus, a coordination strategy reduces the risks associated with investment in the industry. This is very common in the chemical refining and oil businesses, where new capacity investments frequently cost hundreds of millions of dollars.

STRATEGIES IN DECLINING INDUSTRIES

Sooner or later, many industries enter into a decline stage, in which the size of the total market begins to shrink. Examples are the railroad industry, the tobacco industry, the steel industry, and the newspaper business (see the Opening Case). Industries start declining for a number of reasons, including technological change, social trends, and demographic shifts. The railroad and steel industries began to decline when technological changes brought viable substitutes for their products. The advent of the internal combustion engine drove the railroad industry into decline, and the steel industry fell into decline with the rise of plastics and composite materials. Similarly, as noted in the Opening Case, the newspaper industry is in decline because of the rise of news sites on the Web. As for the tobacco industry, changing social attitudes toward smoking, which come from growing concerns about the health effects of smoking, have caused the decline.

The Severity of Decline

When the size of the total market is shrinking, competition tends to intensify in a declining industry, and profit rates tend to fall. The intensity of competition in a declining industry depends on four critical factors, which are indicated in Figure 6.6. First, the intensity of competition is greater in industries in which decline is rapid, as opposed to industries such as tobacco, in which decline is slow and gradual.

Second, the intensity of competition is greater in declining industries in which exit barriers are high. Recall from Chapter 2 that high exit barriers keep companies locked into an industry, even when demand is falling. The result is the emergence of excess productive capacity, and hence an increased probability of fierce price competition.

Third, and related to the previous point, the intensity of competition is greater in declining industries in which fixed costs are high (as in the steel industry). The reason is that the need to cover fixed costs, such as the costs of maintaining productive capacity, can make companies try to use any excess capacity they have by slashing prices, which can trigger a price war.

Finally, the intensity of competition is greater in declining industries in which the product is perceived as a commodity (as it is in the steel industry) in contrast to industries in

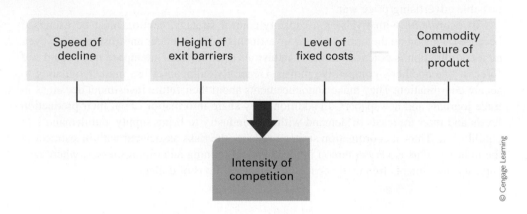

Figure 6.6 Factors that Determine the Intensity of Competition in Declining Industries

© Cengage Learning

leadership strategy
When a company develops strategies to become the dominant player in a declining industry.

niche strategy
When a company focuses on pockets of demand that are declining more slowly than the industry as a whole to maintain profitability.

harvest strategy
When a company reduces to a minimum the assets it employs in a business to reduce its cost structure and extract or "milk" maximum profits from its investment.

divestment strategy
When a company decides to exit an industry by selling off its business assets to another company.

which differentiation gives rise to significant brand loyalty, as was true (until very recently) of the declining tobacco industry.

Not all segments of an industry typically decline at the same rate. In some segments, demand may remain reasonably strong despite decline elsewhere. The steel industry illustrates this situation. Although bulk steel products, such as sheet steel, have suffered a general decline, demand has actually risen for specialty steels, such as those used in high-speed machine tools. Vacuum tubes provide another example. Although demand for the tubes collapsed when transistors replaced them as a key component in many electronics products, vacuum tubes still had some limited applications in radar equipment for years afterward. Consequently, demand in this vacuum tube segment remained strong despite the general decline in the demand for vacuum tubes. The point, then, is that there may be pockets of demand in an industry in which demand is declining more slowly than in the industry as a whole—or where demand is not declining at all. Price competition may be far less intense among the companies serving pockets of demand than within the industry as a whole.

Choosing a Strategy

There are four main strategies that companies can adopt to deal with decline: (1) a **leadership strategy**, by which a company seeks to become the dominant player in a declining industry; (2) a **niche strategy**, which focuses on pockets of demand that are declining more slowly than the industry as a whole; (3) a **harvest strategy**, which optimizes cash flow; and (4) a **divestment strategy**, by which a company sells the business to others.[18] Figure 6.7 provides a simple framework for guiding strategic choice. Note that the intensity of competition in the declining industry is measured on the vertical axis, and a company's strengths relative to remaining pockets of demand are measured on the horizontal axis.

Leadership Strategy   A leadership strategy aims at growing in a declining industry by picking up the market share of companies that are leaving the industry. A leadership

Figure 6.7	Strategy Selection in a Declining Industry

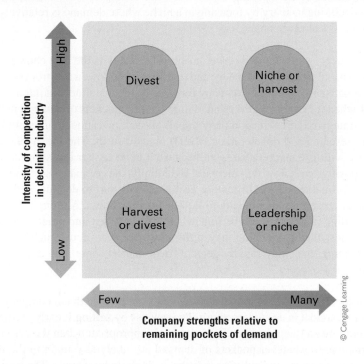

strategy makes most sense when (1) the company has distinctive strengths that allow it to capture market share in a declining industry and (2) the speed of decline and the intensity of competition in the declining industry are moderate. Philip Morris used this strategy in the tobacco industry. Through strong marketing, Philip Morris increased its market share in a declining industry and earned enormous profits in the process.

The tactical steps companies might use to achieve a leadership position include using aggressive pricing and marketing to build market share, acquiring established competitors to consolidate the industry, and raising the stakes for other competitors, for example, by making new investments in productive capacity. Competitive tactics such as these signal to other competitors that the company is willing and able to stay and compete in the declining industry. These signals may persuade other companies to exit the industry, which would further enhance the competitive position of the industry leader.

Niche Strategy   A niche strategy focuses on pockets of demand in the industry in which demand is stable, or declining less rapidly than the industry as a whole. This strategy makes sense when the company has some unique strengths relative to those niches in which demand remains relatively strong. As an example, consider Naval, a company that manufactures whaling harpoons (and small guns to fire them) and makes adequate profits. This might be considered rather odd because the world community has outlawed whaling. However, Naval survived the terminal decline of the harpoon industry by focusing on the one group of people who are still allowed to hunt whales, although only in very limited numbers: North American Inuits. Inuits are permitted to hunt bowhead whales, provided that they do so only for food and not for commercial purposes. Naval is the sole supplier of small harpoon whaling guns to Inuit communities, and its monopoly position allows the company to earn a healthy return in this small market. Community Impact Newspapers, which was profiled in the Opening Case, is another example of a company that has made money in a declining industry by focusing in a niche where demand is relatively strong—in this case hyper-local newspapers.

Harvest Strategy   As we noted earlier, a harvest strategy is the best choice when a company wishes to exit a declining industry and optimize cash flow in the process. This strategy makes the most sense when the company foresees a steep decline and intense future competition, or when it lacks strengths relative to remaining pockets of demand in the industry. A harvest strategy requires the company to halt all new investments in capital equipment, advertising, research and development (R&D), and so forth. The inevitable result is that the company will lose market share, but because it is no longer investing in the business, initially its positive cash flow will increase. Essentially, the company is accepting cash flow in exchange for market share. Ultimately, cash flow will start to decline, and when that occurs, it makes sense for the company to liquidate the business. Although this strategy can be very appealing in theory, it can be somewhat difficult to put into practice. Employee morale in a business that is declining may suffer. Furthermore, if customers realize what the company is doing, they may rapidly defect. Then, market share may decline much faster than the company expects.

Divestment Strategy   A divestment strategy rests on the idea that a company can recover most of its investment in an underperforming business by selling it early, before the industry has entered into a steep decline. This strategy is appropriate when the company has few strengths relative to whatever pockets of demand are likely to remain in the industry and when the competition in the declining industry is likely to be intense. The best option may be to sell to a company that is pursuing a leadership strategy in the industry. The drawback of the divestment strategy is that its success depends upon the ability of the company to spot industry decline before it becomes detrimental, and to sell while the company's assets are still valued by others.

ETHICAL DILEMMA

© iStockPhoto.com/P_Wei

A team of marketing managers for a major differentiated consumer products company has been instructed by top managers to develop new strategies to increase the profitability of the company's products. One idea is to lower the cost of ingredients, which will reduce product quality; another is to reduce the content of the products while maintaining the size of the packaging; a third is to slightly change an existing product and then offer it as a "new" premium brand that can be sold at a higher price.

Do you think it is ethical to pursue these strategies and present them to management? In what ways could these strategies backfire and cause the company harm?

SUMMARY OF CHAPTER

1. In fragmented industries composed of a large number of small- and medium-sized companies, the principal forms of competitive strategy are chaining, franchising, and horizontal merger.

2. In embryonic and growth industries, strategy is partly determined by market demand. Innovators and early adopters have different needs than the early and the late majority, and a company must have the right strategies in place to cross the chasms and survive. Similarly, managers must understand the factors that affect a market's growth rate so that they can tailor their business model to a changing industry environment.

3. Mature industries are composed of a few large companies whose actions are so highly interdependent that the success of one company's strategy depends upon the responses of its rivals.

4. The principal strategies used by companies in mature industries to deter entry are product proliferation, price cutting, and maintaining excess capacity.

5. The principal strategies used by companies in mature industries to manage rivalry are price signaling, price leadership, non-price competition, and capacity control.

6. In declining industries, in which market demand has leveled off or is decreasing, companies must tailor their price and non-price strategies to the new competitive environment. Companies also need to manage industry capacity to prevent the emergence of capacity expansion problems.

7. There are four main strategies a company can pursue when demand is falling: leadership, niche, harvest, and divestment. The strategic choice is determined by the severity of industry decline and the company's strengths relative to the remaining pockets of demand.

DISCUSSION QUESTIONS

1. Why are industries fragmented? What are the primary ways in which companies can turn a fragmented industry into a consolidated industry?

2. What are the key problems in maintaining a competitive advantage in embryonic and growth industry environments? What are the dangers associated with being the leader in an industry?

3. What investment strategies should be made by: (a) differentiators in a strong competitive position, and (b) differentiators in a weak competitive position, while managing a company's growth through the life cycle?

4. Discuss how companies can use: (a) product differentiation, and (b) capacity control to manage rivalry and increase an industry's profitability.

5. What kinds of strategies might: (a) a small pizza place operating in a crowded college market, and (b) a detergent manufacturer seeking to unveil new products in an established market use to strengthen their business models?

PRACTICING STRATEGIC MANAGEMENT

© iStockPhoto.com/Urilux

Small-Group Exercises: Creating a Nationwide Health Club

Break into groups of three to five people and discuss the following scenario. Appoint one group member as a spokesperson who will communicate your findings to the class. You are the founders of a health club. The health club industry is quite fragmented, with many small players, and just a few larger players such as LA Fitness, 24 Hour Fitness, and Gold's Gym. Your backers want you to devise a strategy for growing your business, quickly establishing a nationwide chain of health clubs.

1. Is there scope for value innovation in this industry? What might a value innovation strategy look like?
2. Describe how your chosen strategy would enable you to create a national brand and/or attain scale economies.
3. What would your growth strategy be: chaining or franchising? Be sure to justify your answer.

STRATEGY SIGN ON

© iStockPhoto.com/Ninoslav Dotlic

Article File 6

Choose a company (or group of companies) in a particular industry environment and explain how it has adopted a competitive strategy to protect or enhance its business-level strategy.

Strategic Management Project: Developing Your Portfolio 6

This part of the project considers how conditions in the industry environment affect the success of your company's business model and strategies. With the information you have available, perform the tasks and answer the questions listed:

1. In what kind of industry environment (e.g., embryonic, mature, etc.) does your company operate? Use the information from Strategic Management Project: Module 2 to answer this question.
2. Discuss how your company has attempted to develop strategies to protect and strengthen its business model. For example, if your company is operating in an embryonic industry, how has it attempted to increase its competitive advantage over time? If it operates in a mature industry, discuss how it has tried to manage industry competition.
3. What new strategies would you advise your company to pursue to increase its competitive advantage? For example, how should your company attempt to differentiate its products in the future, or lower its cost structure?
4. On the basis of this analysis, do you think your company will be able to maintain its competitive advantage in the future? Why or why not?

CLOSING CASE

Consolidating Dry Cleaning

No large companies dominate the U.S. dry-cleaning industry. The industry has some 30,000 individual businesses employing around 165,000 people. Most establishments are very small. The top 50 enterprises in the industry are estimated to account for no more than 40% of industry revenues. According to the Dry-cleaning & Laundry Institute, the median annual sales for a commercial dry cleaner are less than $250,000. The industry is a favored starting point for many immigrants, who are attracted by the low capital requirements. More than 80% of industry revenues can be attributed to individual retail customers, with hospitals, hotels, and restaurants accounting for much of the balance. The larger companies in the industry tend to focus on serving larger establishments, such as hospitals and hotels.

Total industry revenues are estimated to be around $9 billion. Between 2007 and 2012 demand shrunk at 2.5% per annum. A weak economy with persistently high unemployment, the rise of "business casual" dress norms in many companies, and the development of new clothing materials that do not need dry cleaning or pressing are all cited as reasons for the weak demand conditions.

Demand for dry-cleaning services is very local. All dry cleaners within a 10-minute drive of each other are often viewed as direct competitors. Convenience seems to be one of the major factors leading a consumer to pick one dry cleaner over another. Dry cleaning has been described as a classic low-interest category—there is very little about dry cleaning that excites consumers.

The industry has defied efforts to consolidate it. The largest national dry-cleaning chain in the United States is Martinizing. Started more than 60 years ago, in 2012 Martinizing had some 160 franchisees that operate more than 456 stores. However, as recently as 2001 its franchisees operated almost 800 stores, so the company seems to have been shrinking steadily over the last decade.

In the late 1990s the founders of Staples, the office supplies superstore, entered the dry-cleaning industry, establishing a Boston-based chain known as Zoots. Backed with up to $40 million in capital, they had visions of transforming the dry-cleaning industry (as they had done with office supplies), consolidating a fragmented industry and creating enormous economic value for themselves in the process. They created of cluster of 7 to 10 stores around a central cleaning hub. Each store had a drive through window, self-service lockers for leaving and picking up clothes, and one or two full-time staff members on hand to help customers. The hub had about 40 employees engaged in cleaning processes. Zoots promised to get dry cleaning done right, reliably, and conveniently, and to do this at a reasonable price. Unfortunately, Zoots found that the service-intensive nature of dry cleaning and the very high variability of clothing made it all but impossible to standardize processes. Costs were significantly higher than anticipated, quality was not as good as management hoped, employee turnover was high, and demand came in below forecasts. Today Zoots has less than 40 stores and remains concentrated in the Boston area. The founders are no longer involved in the business and, clearly, it did not come close to transforming the industry.

Sources: IBIS World, "Dry Cleaners in the US: Market Research Report," October 2012; Myra M. Hart and Sharon Peyus, "Zoots: The Cleaner Cleaner," *Harvard Business School*, September 20, 2000; and Fulcrum Inquiry, "Valuation Guide: Dry Cleaners," www .fulcrum.com/drycleaning_appraisal.htm.

CASE DISCUSSION QUESTIONS

1. Why do you think that the dry-cleaning industry has a fragmented structure?

2. The larger enterprises in the industry seem to serve large customers with standardized

needs, such as hotels and hospitals. Why do you think this is the case?

3. Why do you think that Zoots was unable to consolidate the dry-cleaning industry, despite adequate capital and the managerial talent that created Staples?

4. If you were to try to consolidate the dry-cleaning industry, what strategy would you pursue and why?

KEY TERMS

NOTES

[1] M. E. Porter, *Competitive Strategy: Techniques for Analyzing Industries and Competitors* (New York: Free Press, 1980), pp. 191–200.

[2] W. C. Kim and R. Mauborgne, "Value Innovation: The Strategic Logic of High Growth," *Harvard Business Review*, January–February 1997.

[3] S. A. Shane, "Hybrid Organizational Arrangements and Their Implications for Firm Growth and Survival: A Study of New Franchisors," *Academy of Management Journal* 1 (1996): 216–234.

[4] Microsoft is often accused of not being an innovator, but the fact is that Gates and Allen wrote the first commercial software program for the first commercially available personal computer. Microsoft was the first mover in its industry. See P. Freiberger and M. Swaine, *Fire in the Valley* (New York: McGraw-Hill, 2000).

[5] J. M. Utterback, *Mastering the Dynamics of Innovation* (Boston: Harvard Business School Press, 1994).

[6] See Freiberger and Swaine, *Fire in the Valley*.

[7] Utterback, *Mastering the Dynamics of Innovation*.

[8] G. A. Moore, *Crossing the Chasm* (New York: HarperCollins, 1991).

[9] Utterback, *Mastering the Dynamics of Innovation*.

[10] E. Rogers, *Diffusion of Innovations* (New York: Free Press, 1995).

[11] R. J. Gilbert, "Mobility Barriers and the Value of Incumbency," in R. Schmalensee and R. D. Willig (eds.), *Handbook of Industrial Organization* (Elsevier Science Publishers, 1989).

[12] P. Ghemawat, *Commitment: The Dynamic of Strategy* (Harvard Business School Press, 1991).

[13] M. B. Lieberman, "Excess Capacity as a Barrier to Entry: An Empirical Appraisal," *Journal of Industrial Economics* 35 (1987): 607–627.

[14] R. Lukach, P. M. Kort, and J. Plasmans, "Optimal R&D Investment Strategies Under the Threat of New Technology Entry," *International Journal of Industrial Organization* 25 (February 2007): 103–119.

[15] W. B. Arthur, "Increasing Returns and the New World of Business," *Harvard Business Review*, July 1996.

[16] R. Axelrod, *The Evolution of Cooperation* (New York: Basic Books, 1984).

[17] The next section draws heavily on Marvin B. Lieberman, "Strategies for Capacity Expansion," *Sloan Management Review* 8 (1987): 19–27; Porter, *Competitive Strategy*, 324–338.

[18] K. R. Harrigan, "Strategy Formulation in Declining Industries," *Academy of Management Review* 5 (1980): 599–604.

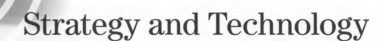

7

Strategy and Technology

LEARNING OBJECTIVES

After reading this chapter you should be able to:

7-1 Understand the tendency toward standardization in many high-technology markets

7-2 Describe the strategies that firms can use to establish their technology as the standard in a market

7-3 Explain the cost structure of many high-technology firms, and articulate the strategic implications of this structure

7-4 Explain the nature of technological paradigm shifts and their implications for enterprise strategy

A Battle Emerging in Mobile Payments

In 2012, 75% of the world population was using mobile phones, and 80% of those mobile users accessed the mobile Web. Mobile payment systems offered the potential of enabling all of these users to perform financial transactions on their phones, similar to how they would perform those transactions using personal computers. However, in 2012, there was no dominant mobile payment system, and a battle among competing mobile payment mechanisms and standards was unfolding.

In the United States, several large players, including Google and a joint venture called ISIS between AT&T, T-Mobile, and Verizon Wireless, were developing systems based on Near Field Communication (NFC) chips that were increasingly being incorporated into smartphones. NFC chips enable communication between a mobile device and a point-of-sale system just by having the devices in close proximity. The systems being developed by Google and ISIS would transfer the customer's information wirelessly, and then use merchant banks and credit card systems such as Visa or MasterCard to complete the transaction. These systems were thus very much like existing ways of using credit cards, but enabled completion of the purchase without contact.

Other competitors, such as Square (with Square Wallet) and PayPal, did not require a smartphone with an NFC chip, but instead used a downloadable application and the Web to transmit a customer's information. Square had gained early fame by offering small, free, credit card readers that could be plugged into the audio jack of a smartphone. These readers enabled vendors that would normally only take cash (street vendors, babysitters, etc.) to accept major credit cards. By mid-2012, merchants were processing over $6 billion a year using Square readers, making the company one of the fastest growing tech start-ups in Silicon Valley. In terms of installed base, however, PayPal had the clear advantage, with over 100 million active registered accounts. With PayPal, customers could complete purchases simply by entering their phone numbers and a pin number, or use a PayPal-issued magnetic stripe cards linked to their PayPal accounts. Users could opt to link their PayPal accounts to their credit cards, or directly to their bank accounts. This meant that of the systems described so far, only the PayPal system offered the possibility of excluding the major credit card companies (and their billions of dollars in transaction fees) from mobile transactions.

In other parts of the world, intriguing alternatives for mobile banking were gaining traction even faster. In India and Africa, for example, there are enormous populations of "unbanked" or "underbanked" people (individuals who do not have bank accounts or make limited use of banking services). In these regions, the proportion of people with mobile phones vastly exceeds the proportion of people with credit cards. The opportunity, then, of giving such people access to fast and inexpensive funds transfer is enormous. The leading system in India is the Inter-bank Mobile Payment Service developed by National Payments Corporation of India (NPCI). NPCI leveraged its ATM network (connecting more than 60 large banks in India) to create a person-to-person mobile banking system that works on mobile phones. The system uses a unique identifier for each individual that links directly to his or her bank account. In parts of Africa, where the proportion of people who are unbanked is even larger, a system called M-Pesa ("M" for *mobile* and "pesa," which is kiswahili for *money*) enables any individual with a passport or national ID card to deposit money into his or her phone account, and transfer money to other users using Short Message Service (SMS). By mid-2012, the M-Pesa system had almost 15 million active users.

By early 2013, it was clear that mobile payments represented a game-changing opportunity that could accelerate e-commerce, smartphone adoption, and the global reach of financial services. However, lack of compatibility between many of the mobile payment systems and uncertainty over what type of mobile payment system would become dominant still posed significant obstacles to consumer and merchant adoption.

Sources: "Mobile Phone Access Reaches Three Quarters of Planet's Population," *The World Bank*, July 17, 2012; J. Kent, "Dominant Mobile Payment Approaches and Leading Mobile Payment Solution Providers: A Review," *Journal of Payments Strategy & Systems* 6:4 (2012): 315–324; V. Govindarajan and M. Balakrishnan, "Developing Countries Are Revolutionizing Mobile Banking," *Harvard Business Review Blog Network*, April 30, 2012; and M. Helft, "The Death of Cash," *Fortune* 166:2 (2012): 118–128.

OVERVIEW

The high-stakes battle that is brewing in mobile payments is typical of the nature of competition in high-technology industries (see the Opening Case). In industries where standards and compatibility are important strategic levers, a technology that gains an initial advantage can sometimes rise to achieve a nearly insurmountable position. Such industries can thus become "winner-take-all" markets. Being successful in such industries can require very different strategies than in more traditional industries. Firms may aggressively subsidize adoption of their preferred technology (including sometimes giving away products for free) in order to win the standards battle.

In this chapter, we will take a close look at the nature of competition and strategy in high-technology industries. Technology refers to the body of scientific knowledge used in the production of goods or services. High-technology (high-tech) industries are those in which the underlying scientific knowledge that companies in the industry use is rapidly advancing, and, by implication, so are the attributes of the products and services that result from its application. The computer industry is often thought of as the quintessential example of a high-technology industry. Other industries often considered high-tech are: telecommunications, where new technologies based on wireless and the Internet have proliferated in recent years; consumer electronics, where the digital technology underlying products from high-definition DVD players to videogame terminals and digital cameras is advancing rapidly; pharmaceuticals, where new technologies based on cell biology, recombinant DNA, and genomics are revolutionizing the process of drug discovery; power generation, where new technologies based on fuel cells and cogeneration may change the economics of the industry; and aerospace, where the combination of new composite materials, electronics, and more efficient jet engines is giving birth to a new era of super-efficient commercial jet aircraft such as Boeing's 787.

This chapter focuses on high-technology industries for a number of reasons. First, technology is accounting for an ever-larger share of economic activity. Estimates suggest that in the last decade, nearly 25% of growth in domestic product was accounted for by information technology industries.[1] This figure actually underestimates the true impact of technology on the economy, because it ignores the other high-technology areas we just mentioned. Moreover, as technology advances, many low-technology industries are becoming more high-tech. For example, the development of biotechnology and genetic engineering transformed the production of seed corn, long considered a low-technology business, into a high-technology business. Retailing was once considered a low technology business, but the shift to online retailing, led by companies like Amazon.com, has changed this. In addition, high-technology products are making their way into a wide range of businesses; today most automobiles contain more computing power than the multimillion-dollar mainframe computers used in the *Apollo* space program, and the competitive advantage of physical stores, such as Wal-Mart, is based on their use of information technology. The circle of high-technology industries is both large and expanding, and technology is revolutionizing aspects of the product or production system even in industries not typically considered high-tech.

Although high-tech industries may produce very different products, when developing a business model and strategies that will lead to a competitive advantage and superior profitability and profit growth, they often face a similar situation. For example, "winner-take-all" format wars are common in many high-technology industries, such as the consumer electronics and computer industries. In mobile payments, for example, it is possible that a new payment system will emerge that could displace Visa, MasterCard, and American Express as the dominant firms for managing payment transactions worldwide—this could result in a tremendous windfall for the firm(s) controlling the new standard (and a tremendous loss for Visa, MasterCard, and American Express). Firms are thus carefully forging alliances and backing standards they believe will best position them to capture the billions of dollars in transactions fees that are at stake (see the Opening Case). This chapter examines the competitive features found in many high-tech industries and the kinds of strategies that companies must adopt to build business models that will allow them to achieve superior profitability and profit growth.

By the time you have completed this chapter, you will have an understanding of the nature of competition in high-tech industries, and the strategies that companies can pursue to succeed in those industries.

TECHNICAL STANDARDS AND FORMAT WARS

Especially in high-tech industries, ownership of **technical standards**—a set of technical specifications that producers adhere to when making the product, or a component of it—can be an important source of competitive advantage.[2] Indeed, in many cases the source of product differentiation is based on the technical standard. Often, only one standard will dominate a market, so many battles in high-tech industries involve companies that are competing to set the standard. For example, for the last three decades, Microsoft has controlled the market as the dominant operating system for personal computers, sometimes exceeding a 90% market share, and with roughly an 85% share by the end of 2012. Notably, however, Microsoft held a very small share (roughly 3% in 2013) of the tablet and smartphone operating system market, suggesting the possibility of turbulent times ahead for the firm (see Strategy in Action 7.1).

technical standards
A set of technical specifications that producers adhere to when making the product, or a component of it.

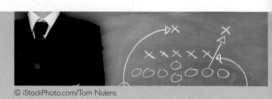

7.1 STRATEGY IN ACTION

"Segment Zero"—A Serious Threat to Microsoft?

© iStockPhoto.com/Tom Nulens

From 1980 to 2012, Microsoft was entrenched as the dominant personal computer operating system, giving it enormous influence over many aspects of the computer hardware and software industries. Although competing operating systems had been introduced during that time (e.g., Unix, Geoworks, NeXTSTEP, Linux, and the Mac OS), Microsoft's share of the personal computer operating system market held stable at roughly 85% throughout most of that period. In 2013, however, Microsoft's dominance in computer operating systems was under greater threat than it had ever been. A high-stakes race for dominance over the next generation of computing was well under way, and Microsoft was not even in the front pack.

"Segment Zero"

As Andy Grove, former CEO of Intel, noted in 1998, in many industries—including microprocessors, software, motorcycles, and electric vehicles—technologies improve faster than customer demands of those technologies increase. Firms often add features (speed,

power, etc.) to products faster than customers' capacity to absorb them. Why would firms provide higher performance than that required by the bulk of their customers? The answer appears to lie in the market segmentation and pricing objectives of a technology's providers. As competition in an industry drives prices and margins lower, firms often try to shift sales into progressively higher tiers of the market. In these tiers, high-performance and feature-rich products can command higher margins. Although customers may also expect to have better-performing products over time, their ability to fully utilize such performance improvements is slowed by the need to learn how to use new features and adapt their work and lifestyles. Thus, both the trajectory of technology improvement and the trajectory of customer demands are upward sloping, but the trajectory for technology improvement is steeper.

In Figure 7.1 the technology trajectory begins at a point where it provides performance close to that demanded by the mass market, but over time it increases faster than the expectations of the mass market

(continues)

7.1 STRATEGY IN ACTION

(continued)

© iStockPhoto.com/Tom Nulens

Figure 7.1	Trajectories of Technology Improvement and Customer Requirements

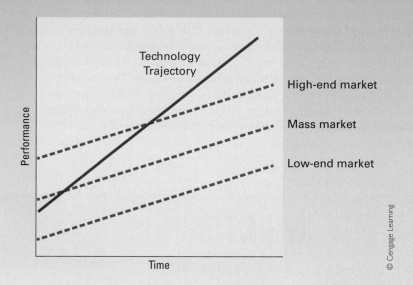

© Cengage Learning

as the firm targets the high-end market. As the price of the technology rises, the mass market may feel it is overpaying for technological features it does not value. In Figure 7.1 the low-end market is not being served; it either pays far more for technology that it does not need, or it goes without. It is this market that Andy Grove, former CEO of Intel, refers to as segment zero.

For Intel, segment zero was the market for low-end personal computers (those less than $1,000). Although segment zero may seem unattractive in terms of margins, if it is neglected, it can become the breeding ground for companies that provide lower-end versions of the technology. As Grove notes, "The overlooked, underserved, and seemingly unprofitable end of the market can provide fertile ground for massive competitive change."

As the firms serving low-end markets with simpler technologies ride up their own trajectories (which are also steeper than the slope of the trajectories of customer expectations), they can eventually reach a performance level that meets the demands of the mass market, while offering a much lower price than the

Gmargittai/Dreamstime.com

premium technology (see Figure 7.2). At this point, the firms offering the premium technology may suddenly find they are losing the bulk of their sales revenue to industry contenders that do not look so low-end anymore. For example, by 1998, the combination of rising microprocessor power and decreasing prices enabled personal computers priced under $1,000 to capture 20% of the market.

7.1 STRATEGY IN ACTION

(continued)

© iStockPhoto.com/Tom Nulens

| Figure 7.2 | Low-End Technology's Trajectory Intersects Mass-Market Trajectory |

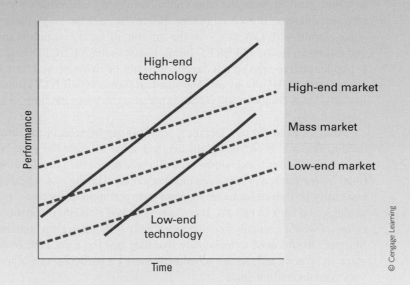

© Cengage Learning

The Threat to Microsoft

So where was the "segment zero" that could threaten Microsoft? Look in your pocket. In 2013, Apple's iPhone operating system (iOS) and Google's Android collectively controlled over 90% of the worldwide market for smartphones, followed by Research in Motion's Blackberry. Gartner estimates put Microsoft's share at 3%. The iOS and Android interfaces offered a double whammy of beautiful aesthetics and remarkable ease of use. The applications business model used for the phones was also extremely attractive to both developers and customers, and quickly resulted in enormous libraries of applications that ranged from the ridiculous to the indispensable.

From a traditional economics perspective, the phone operating system market should not be that attractive to Microsoft—people do not spend as much on the applications, and the carriers have too much bargaining power, among other reasons. However, those smartphone operating systems soon became tablet operating systems, and tablets were rapidly becoming fully functional computers. Suddenly, all of that mindshare that Apple and Google had achieved in smartphone operating systems was transforming into mindshare in personal computer operating systems. Despite years of masterminding the computing industry, Microsoft's dominant position was at risk of evaporating. The outcome was still uncertain—in 2013 Microsoft had an impressive arsenal of capital, talent, and relationships in its armory, but for the first time, it was fighting the battle from a disadvantaged position.

Sources: Adapted from M. A. Schilling, "'Segment Zero': A Serious Threat to Microsoft?", Conceptual note, New York University, 2013; A. S. Grove, "Managing Segment Zero," *Leader to Leader*, 11 (1999); and L. Dignan, "Android, Apple iOS Flip Consumer, Corporate Market Share. *Between the Lines*", February 13 (2013).

✴format wars

Battles to control the source of differentiation, and thus the value that such differentiation can create for the customer.

Battles to set and control technical standards in a market are referred to as **format wars**—essentially, battles to control the source of differentiation, and thus the value that such differentiation can create for the customer. Because differentiated products often command premium prices and are often expensive to develop, the competitive stakes are enormous. The profitability and survival of a company may depend on the outcome of the battle.

Examples of Standards

A familiar example of a standard is the layout of a computer keyboard. No matter what keyboard you purchase, the letters are all arranged in the same pattern.[3] The reason is quite obvious. Imagine if each computer maker changed the ways the keys were laid out—if some started with QWERTY on the top row of letters (which is indeed the format used and is known as the QWERTY format), some with YUHGFD, and some with ACFRDS. If you learned to type on one layout, it would be irritating and time consuming to have to relearn on a YUHGFD layout. The standard format (QWERTY) it makes it easy for people to move from computer to computer because the input medium, the keyboard, is set in a standard way.

Another example of a technical standard can be seen in the dimensions of containers used to ship goods on trucks, railcars, and ships: all have the same basic dimensions—the same height, length, and width—and all make use of the same locking mechanisms to hold them onto a surface or to bolt against each other. Having a standard ensures that containers can easily be moved from one mode of transportation to another—from trucks, to railcars, to ships, and back to railcars. If containers lacked standard dimensions and locking mechanisms, it would suddenly become much more difficult to ship containers around the world. Shippers would need to make sure that they had the right kind of container to go on the ships and trucks and railcars scheduled to carry a particular container around the world—a very complicated process.

Consider, finally, the personal computer (PC). Most share a common set of features: an Intel or Intel-compatible microprocessor, random access memory (RAM), a Microsoft operating system, an internal hard drive, a DVD drive, a keyboard, a monitor, a mouse, a modem, and so on. We call this set of features the dominant design for personal computers (a **dominant design** refers to a common set of features or design characteristics). Embedded in this design are several technical standards (see Figure 7.3). For example, there is the Wintel technical standard based on an Intel microprocessor and a Microsoft operating system. Microsoft and Intel "own" that standard, which is central to the personal computer. Developers of software applications, component parts, and peripherals such as printers adhere to this standard when developing their own products because this guarantees that their products will work well with a personal computer based on the Wintel standard. Another technical standard for connecting peripherals to the PC is the Universal Serial Bus (or USB), established by an industry-standards-setting board. No one owns it; the standard is in the public domain. A third technical standard is for communication between a PC and the Internet via a modem. Known as TCP/IP, this standard was also set by an industry association and is in the public domain. Thus, as with many other products, the PC is actually based on several technical standards. It is also important to note that when a company owns a standard, as Microsoft and Intel do with the Wintel standard, it may be a source of competitive advantage and high profitability.

✴dominant design

Common set of features or design characteristics.

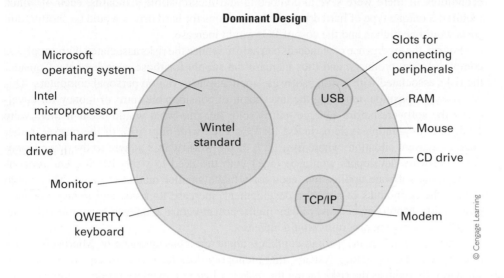

Figure 7.3 Technical Standards for Personal Computers

Benefits of Standards

Standards emerge because there are economic benefits associated with them. First, a technical standard helps to guarantee compatibility between products and their complements. For example, containers are used with railcars, trucks, and ships, and PCs are used with software applications. Compatibility has the tangible economic benefit of reducing the costs associated with making sure that products work well with each other.

Second, having a standard can help to reduce confusion in the minds of consumers. A few years ago, several consumer electronics companies were vying with each other to produce and market the first generation of DVD players, and they were championing different variants of the basic DVD technology—different standards—that were incompatible with each other; a DVD disc designed to run on a DVD player made by Toshiba would not run on a player made by Sony, and vice versa. The companies feared that selling these incompatible versions of the same technology would produce confusion in the minds of consumers, who would not know which version to purchase and might decide to wait and see which technology would dominate the marketplace. With lack of demand, the technology might fail to gain traction in the marketplace and would not be successful. To avoid this possibility, the developers of DVD equipment established a standard-setting body for the industry, the DVD Forum, which established a common technical standard for DVD players and disks that all companies adhered to. The result was that when DVDs were introduced, there was a common standard and no confusion in consumers' minds. This helped to boost demand for DVD players, making this one of the fastest-selling technologies of the late-1990s and early-2000s.

Third, the emergence of a standard can help to reduce production costs. Once a standard emerges, products that are based on the standard design can be mass produced, enabling the manufacturers to realize substantial economies of scale while lowering their cost structures. The fact that there is a central standard for PCs (the Wintel standard) means that the component parts for a PC can be mass produced. A manufacturer of internal hard drives, for example, can mass produce drives for Wintel PCs, and so can realize substantial scale economies. If there were several competing and incompatible standards, each of which required a unique type of hard drive, production runs for hard drives would be shorter, unit costs would be higher, and the cost of PCs would increase.

Fourth, the emergence of standards can help to reduce the risks associated with supplying complementary products, and thus increase the supply for those complements. Consider the risks associated with writing software applications to run on personal computers. This is a risky proposition, requiring the investment of considerable sums of money for developing the software before a single unit is sold. Imagine what would occur if there were 10 different operating systems in use for PCs, each with only 10% of the market, rather than the current situation, where over 90% of the world's PCs adhere to the Wintel standard. Software developers would be faced with the need to write 10 different versions of the same software application, each for a much smaller market segment. This would change the economics of software development, increase its risks, and reduce potential profitability. Moreover, because of their higher cost structure and fewer economies of scale, the price of software programs would increase.

Thus, although many people complain about the consequences of Microsoft's near monopoly of PC operating systems, that monopoly does have at least one good effect: it substantially reduces the risks facing the makers of complementary products and the costs of those products. In fact, standards lead to both low-cost and differentiation advantages for individual companies and can help raise the level of industry profitability.

Establishment of Standards

Standards emerge in an industry in three primary ways. First, when the benefits of establishing a standard are recognized, companies in an industry might lobby the government to mandate an industry standard. In the United States, for example, the Federal Communications Commission (FCC), after detailed discussions with broadcasters and consumer electronics companies, mandated a single technical standard for digital television broadcasts (DTV) and required analog television broadcasts to be terminated in 2009. The FCC took this step because it believed that without government action to set the standard, the DTV rollout would be very slow. With a standard set by the government, consumer electronics companies can have greater confidence that a market will emerge, and this should encourage them to develop DTV products.

Second, technical standards are often set by cooperation among businesses, without government help, and often through the medium of an industry association, as the example of the DVD forum illustrates. Companies cooperate in this way when they decide that competition to create a standard might be harmful because of the uncertainty that it would create in the minds of consumers or the risk it would pose to manufacturers and distributors.

When the government or an industry association sets standards, these standards fall into the **public domain**, meaning that any company can freely incorporate the knowledge and technology upon which the standard is based into its products. For example, no one owns the QWERTY format, and therefore no one company can profit from it directly. Similarly, the language that underlies the presentation of text and graphics on the Web, hypertext markup language (HTML), is in the public domain; it is free for all to use. The same is true for TCP/IP, the communications standard used for transmitting data on the Internet.

public domain
Government- or association-set standards of knowledge or technology that any company can freely incorporate into its product.

Often, however, the industry standard is selected competitively by the purchasing patterns of customers in the marketplace—that is, by market demand. In this case, the strategy and business model a company has developed for promoting its technological standard are of critical importance because ownership of an industry standard that is protected from imitation by patents and copyrights is a valuable asset—a source of sustained competitive advantage and superior profitability. Microsoft and Intel, for example, both owe their competitive advantage to their ownership of a specific technological standard or format. As noted earlier, format wars occur when two or more companies compete against each other to get their designs adopted as the industry standard. Format wars are common in high-tech industries where standards are important. The Wintel standard became the dominant standard for PCs only after Microsoft and Intel won format wars against Apple's proprietary system, and later against IBM's OS/2 operating system. The Opening Case describes how a number of firms are engaged in a format war in mobile payments. There is also an ongoing format war within the smartphone business, as Apple, Google, Research in Motion, and Microsoft all battle to get their respective operating systems and phones adopted as the industry standard, as described in Strategy in Action 7.1.

Network Effects, Positive Feedback, and Lockout

There has been a growing realization that when standards are set by competition between companies promoting different formats, network effects are a primary determinant of how standards are established.[4] **Network effects** arise in industries where the size of the "network" of complementary products is a primary determinant of demand for an industry's product. For example, the demand for automobiles early in the 20th century was an increasing function of the network of paved roads and gas stations. Similarly, the demand for telephones is an increasing function of the multitude of other numbers that can be called with that phone; that is, of the size of the telephone network (the telephone network is the complementary product). When the first telephone service was introduced in New York City, only 100 numbers could be called. The network was very small because of the limited number of wires and telephone switches, which made the telephone a relatively useless piece of equipment. But, as an increasing number of people got telephones, and as the network of wires and switches expanded, the telephone connection gained value. This led to an upsurge in demand for telephone lines, which further increased the value of owning a telephone, setting up a positive feedback loop.

To understand why network effects are important in the establishment of standards, consider the classic example of a format war: the battle between Sony and Matsushita to establish their respective technologies for videocassette recorders (VCRs) as the standard in the marketplace. Sony was first to market with its Betamax technology, followed by JVC with its VHS technology. Both companies sold VCR recorder-players, and movie studios issued films prerecorded on VCR tapes for rental to consumers. Initially, all tapes were issued in Betamax format to play on Sony's machine. Sony did not license its Betamax technology, preferring to make all of the player-recorders itself. Because Japan's Ministry of International Trade and Industry (MITI) appeared poised to select Sony's Betamax as a standard for Japan, JVC decided to liberally license its format, and turned to Matsushita (now called Panasonic) to ask for its support. Matsushita was the largest Japanese electronics manufacturer at that time. JVC and Matushita realized that to make the VHS format players valuable to consumers, they would need to encourage movie studios to issue movies for rental on VHS tapes. The only way to do that, they reasoned, was to increase the installed base of VHS players as rapidly as possible. They believed that the greater the

network effects ✳
The network of complementary products as a primary determinant of the demand for an industry's product.

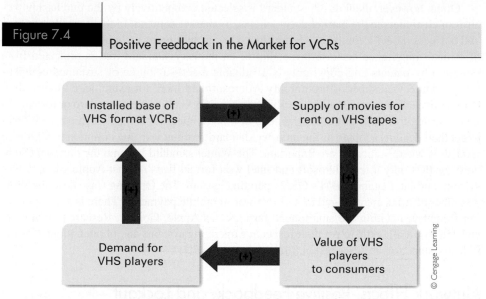

Figure 7.4   Positive Feedback in the Market for VCRs

© Cengage Learning

installed base of VHS players, the greater the incentive for movie studios to issue films on VHS-format tapes for rental. As more prerecorded VHS tapes were made available for rental, the VHS player became more valuable to consumers, and therefore the demand for VHS players increased (see Figure 7.4). JVC and Matsushita wanted to exploit a positive feedback loop.

To do this, JVC and Matsushita chose a licensing strategy under which any consumer electronics company was allowed to manufacture VHS-format players under license. This strategy worked. A large number of companies signed on to manufacture VHS players, and soon far more VHS players were available for purchase in stores than Betamax players. As sales of VHS players started to grow, movie studios issued more films for rental in VHS format, and this stoked demand. Before long, it was clear to anyone who entered a video rental store that there were more VHS tapes available for rent, and fewer Betamax tapes available. This served to reinforce the positive feedback loop, and ultimately Sony's Betamax technology was shut out of the market. The pivotal difference between the two companies was strategy: JVC and Matsushita chose a licensing strategy, and Sony did not. As a result, JVC's VHS technology became the de facto standard for VCRs, whereas Sony's Betamax technology was locked out.

The general principle that emerges from this example is that when two or more companies are competing with each other to get technology adopted as a standard in an industry, and when network effects and positive feedback loops are important, *the company that wins the format war will be the one whose strategy best exploits positive feedback loops*. This is a very important strategic principle in many high-technology industries, particularly computer hardware, software, telecommunications, and consumer electronics. Microsoft is where it is today because it exploited a positive feedback loop. Dolby presents us with another example of a company that exploited a positive feedback loop. When Ray Dolby invented a technology for reducing the background hiss in professional tape recording, he adopted a licensing model that charged a very modest fee. He knew his technology was valuable, but he also understood that charging a high fee would encourage manufacturers to develop their own noise-reduction technology. He also decided to license the technology for use on prerecorded tapes for free, collecting licensing fees on the players only. This set up a powerful positive feedback loop: Growing sales of prerecorded tapes encoded with Dolby technology created a demand for tape players that contained Dolby technology, and as the installed base of tape players with Dolby technology grew, the proportion of prerecorded tapes that were encoded with Dolby technology surged—further boosting demand for players incorporating Dolby technology. By the mid-1970s, virtually all prerecorded tapes were encoded with Dolby noise-reduction technology.

As the market settles on a standard, an important implication of the positive feedback process occurs: companies promoting alternative standards can become locked out of the market when consumers are unwilling to bear the switching costs required to abandon the established standard and adopt the new standard. In this context, switching costs are the costs that consumers must bear to switch from a product based on one technological standard to a product based on another technological standard.

For illustration, imagine that a company developed an operating system for personal computers that was both faster and more stable than the current standard in the marketplace, Microsoft Windows. Would this company be able to gain significant market share from Microsoft? Only with great difficulty. Consumers choose personal computers not for their operating system, but for the applications that run on the operating system. A new operating system would initially have a very small installed base, so few developers would be willing to take the risks in writing word processing programs, spreadsheets, games, and other applications for that operating system. Because there would be very few applications available, consumers who did make the switch would have to bear the switching costs associated with giving up some of their applications—something that they might be unwilling to do. Moreover, even if applications were available for the new operating system, consumers would have to bear the costs of purchasing those applications, another source of switching costs. In addition, they would have to bear the costs associated with learning to use the new operating system, yet another source of switching costs. Thus, many consumers would be unwilling to switch even if the new operating system performed better than Windows, and the company promoting the new operating system would be locked out of the market.

However, consumers will bear switching costs if the benefits of adopting the new technology outweigh the costs of switching. For example, in the late 1980s and early 1990s, millions of people switched from analog record players to digital CD players despite that switching costs were significant: consumers had to purchase the new player technology, and many people purchased duplicate copies of their favorite musical recordings. Nevertheless, people made the switch because, for many, the perceived benefit—the incredibly better sound quality associated with CDs—outweighed the costs of switching.

As this switching process continued, a positive feedback loop started to develop, and the installed base of CD players grew, leading to an increase in the number of musical recordings issued on CDs, as opposed to, or in addition to, vinyl records. The installed base of CD players got so big that mainstream music companies began to issue recordings only in CD format. Once this occurred, even those who did not want to switch to the new technology were required to if they wished to purchase new music recordings. The music industry standard had shifted: new technology had locked in as the standard, and the old technology was locked out.

Extrapolating from this example, it can be argued that despite its dominance, the Wintel standard for personal computers could one day be superseded if a competitor finds a way of providing sufficient benefits that enough consumers are willing to bear the switching costs associated with moving to a new operating system. Indeed, there are signs that Apple is starting to chip away at the dominance of the Wintel standard, primarily by using elegant design and ease of use as tools to get people to bear the costs of switching from Wintel computers to Apple machines.

STRATEGIES FOR WINNING A FORMAT WAR

From the perspective of a company pioneering a new technological standard in a marketplace where network effects and positive feedback loops operate, the key question becomes: "What strategy should we pursue to establish our format as the dominant one?"

The various strategies that companies should adopt in order to win format wars are centered upon *finding ways to make network effects work in their favor and against their competitors.* Winning a format war requires a company to build the installed base for its standard as rapidly as possible, thereby leveraging the positive feedback loop, inducing consumers to bear switching costs, and ultimately locking the market into its technology. It requires the company to jump-start and then accelerate demand for its technological standard or format such that it becomes established as quickly as possible as the industry standard, thereby locking out competing formats. There are a number of key strategies and tactics that can be adopted to try to achieve this.[5]

Ensure a Supply of Complements

It is important for the company to make sure that, in addition to the product itself, there is an adequate supply of complements. For example, no one will purchase the Sony PlayStation 3 unless there is an adequate supply of games to run on that machine. Companies typically take two steps to ensure an adequate supply of complements.

First, they may diversify into the production of complements and seed the market with sufficient supply to help jump-start demand for their format. Before Sony produced the original PlayStation in the early 1990s, for example, it established its own in-house unit to produce videogames for the PlayStation. When it launched the PlayStation, Sony also simultaneously issued 16 games to run on the machine, giving consumers a reason to purchase the format. Second, companies may create incentives or make it easy for independent companies to produce complements. Sony also licensed the right to produce games to a number of independent game developers, charged the developers a lower royalty rate than they had to pay to competitors (such as Nintendo and Sega), and provided them with software tools that made it easier for them to develop the games (note that Apple is now doing the same thing with its smartphones). Thus, the launch of the Sony PlayStation was accompanied by the simultaneous launch of approximately 30 games, which quickly helped to stimulate demand for the machine.

Leverage Killer Applications

killer applications
Applications or uses of a new technology or product that are so compelling that customers adopt them in droves, killing the competing formats.

Killer applications are applications or uses of a new technology or product that are so compelling that they persuade customers to adopt the new format or technology in droves, thereby "killing" demand for competing formats. Killer applications often help to jump-start demand for the new standard. For example, the killer applications that induced consumers to sign up for online services such as AOL in the 1990s were e-mail, chat rooms, and the ability to browse the Web.

Ideally, the company promoting a technological standard will also want to develop its own killer applications—that is, develop the appropriate complementary products. However, it may also be able to leverage the applications that others develop. For example, the early sales of the IBM PC following its 1981 introduction were primarily driven by IBM's decision to license two important software programs for the PC: VisiCalc (a spreadsheet program) and EasyWriter (a word processing program), both developed by independent companies. IBM saw that they were driving rapid adoption of rival personal computers, such as the Apple II, so it quickly licensed software, produced versions that would run on the IBM PC, and sold these programs as complements to the IBM PC, a strategy that was very successful.

Aggressive Pricing and Marketing

A common tactic to jump-start demand is to adopt a **razor and blade strategy**: pricing the product (razor) low in order to stimulate demand and increase the installed base, and then trying to make high profits on the sale of complements (razor blades), which are priced relatively high. This strategy owes its name to Gillette, the company that pioneered this strategy to sell its razors and razor blades. Many other companies have followed this strategy—for example, Hewlett-Packard typically sells its printers at cost but makes significant profits on the subsequent sales of its replacement cartridges. In this case, the printer is the "razor," and it is priced low to stimulate demand and induce consumers to switch from their existing printer, while the cartridges are the "blades," which are priced high to make profits. The inkjet printer represents a proprietary technological format because only HP cartridges can be used with HP printers; cartridges designed for competing inkjet printers, such as those sold by Canon, will not work in HP printers. A similar strategy is used in the videogame industry: manufacturers price videogame consoles at cost to induce consumers to adopt their technology, while they make profits on the royalties received from the sales of games that run on the game system.

Aggressive marketing is also a key factor in jump-starting demand to get an early lead in an installed base. Substantial upfront marketing and point-of-sales promotion techniques are often used to try to attract potential early adopters who will bear the switching costs associated with adopting the format. If these efforts are successful, they can be the start of a positive feedback loop. Again, the Sony PlayStation provides a good example. Sony co-linked the introduction of the PlayStation with nationwide television advertising aimed at its primary demographic (18- to 34-year-olds) and in-store displays that allowed potential buyers to play games on the machine before making a purchase.

razor and blade strategy Pricing the product low in order to stimulate demand, and pricing complements high.

Cooperate with Competitors

Companies have been close to simultaneously introducing competing and incompatible technological standards a number of times. A good example is the compact disc. Initially four companies—Sony, Philips, JVC, and Telefunken—were developing CD players using different variations of the underlying laser technology. If this situation had persisted, they might have introduced incompatible technologies into the marketplace; a CD made for a Philips CD player would not play on a Sony CD player. Understanding that the nearly simultaneous introduction of such incompatible technologies can create significant confusion among consumers, and often lead them to delay their purchases, Sony and Philips decided to join forces and cooperate on developing the technology. Sony contributed its error correction technology, and Philips contributed its laser technology. The result of this cooperation was that momentum among other players in the industry shifted toward the

Sony–Philips alliances; JVC and Telefunken were left with little support. Most important, recording labels announced that they would support the Sony–Philips format but not the Telefunken or JVC format. Telefunken and JVC subsequently decided to abandon their efforts to develop CD technology. The cooperation between Sony and Philips was important because it reduced confusion in the industry and allowed a single format to rise to the fore, which accelerated adoption of the technology. The cooperation was a win-win situation for both Philips and Sony, which eliminated the competitors and enabled them to share in the success of the format.

License the Format

Licensing the format to other enterprises so that those others can produce products based on the format is another strategy often adopted. The company that pioneered the format gains from the licensing fees that return to it, as well as from the enlarged supply of the product, which can stimulate demand and help accelerate market adoption. This was the strategy that JVC and Matsushita adopted with its VHS format for the VCR. As discussed previously, in addition to producing VCRs at Matsushita's factory in Osaka, JVC let a number of other companies produce VHS format players under license, and so VHS players were more widely available. (Sony decided not to license its competing Betamax format and produced all Betamax format players itself.)

The correct strategy to pursue in a particular scenario requires that the company consider all of these different strategies and tactics and pursue those that seem most appropriate given the competitive circumstances prevailing in the industry and the likely strategy of rivals. Although there is no single best combination of strategies and tactics, the company must keep the goal of rapidly increasing the installed base of products based on its standard at the front of its mind. By helping to jump-start demand for its format, a company can induce consumers to bear the switching costs associated with adopting its technology and leverage any positive feedback process that might exist. It is also important not to pursue strategies that have the opposite effect. For example, pricing high to capture profits from early adopters, who tend not to be as price sensitive as later adopters, can have the unfortunate effect of slowing demand growth and allowing a more aggressive competitor to pick up share and establish its format as the industry standard.

COSTS IN HIGH-TECHNOLOGY INDUSTRIES

In many high-tech industries, the fixed costs of developing the product are very high, but the costs of producing one extra unit of the product are very low. This is most obvious in the case of software. For example, it reportedly cost Microsoft $5 billion to develop Windows Vista, but the cost of producing one more copy of Windows Vista is virtually zero. Once the Windows Vista program was complete, Microsoft duplicated its master disks and sent the copies to PC manufacturers, such as Dell Computer, which then installed a copy of Windows Vista onto every PC sold. Microsoft's cost was, effectively, zero, and yet the company receives a significant licensing fee for each copy of Windows Vista installed on a PC.[6] For Microsoft, the marginal cost of making one more copy of Windows Vista is close to zero, although the fixed costs of developing the product were around $5 billion.

Many other high-technology products have similar cost economics: very high fixed costs and very low marginal costs. Most software products share these features, although if the software is sold through stores, the costs of packaging and distribution will raise the marginal costs, and if it is sold by a sales force direct to end-users, this too will raise the marginal costs. Many consumer electronics products have the same basic economics. The fixed costs of developing a DVD player or a videogame console can be very expensive, but the costs of producing an incremental unit are very low. Similarly, the fixed costs of developing a new drug can run to over $800 million, but the marginal cost of producing each additional pill is at most a few cents.

Comparative Cost Economics

To grasp why this cost structure is strategically important, a company must understand that, in many industries, marginal costs rise as a company tries to expand output (economists call this the *law of diminishing returns*). To produce more of a good, a company must hire more labor and invest in more plant and machinery. At the margin, the additional resources used are not as productive, so this leads to increasing marginal costs. However, the law of diminishing returns often does not apply in many high-tech settings, such as the production of software, or sending bits of data through a digital telecommunications network.

Consider two companies, α and β (see Figure 7.5). Company α is a conventional producer and faces diminishing returns, so as it tries to expand output, its marginal

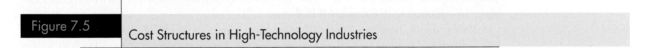

Figure 7.5   Cost Structures in High-Technology Industries

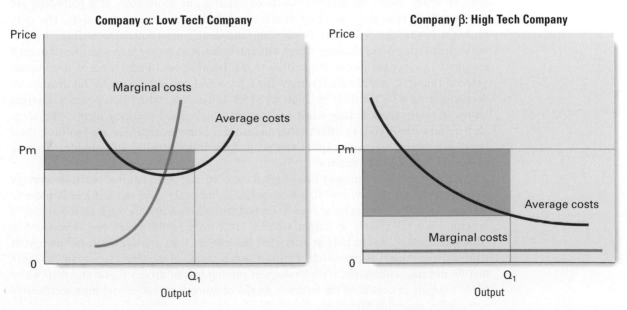

© Cengage Learning

costs rise. Company β is a high-tech producer, and its marginal costs do not rise at all as output is increased. Note that in Figure 7.5, company β's marginal cost curve is drawn as a straight line near to the horizontal axis, implying that marginal costs are close to zero and do not vary with output, whereas company α's marginal costs rise as output is expanded, illustrating diminishing returns. Company β's flat and low marginal cost curve means that its average cost curve will continuously fall over all ranges of output as it spreads its fixed costs out over greater volume. In contrast, the rising marginal costs encountered by company α mean that its average cost curve is the U-shaped curve familiar from basic economics texts. For simplicity, assume that both companies sell their product at the same price, Pm, and both sell exactly the same quantity of output, $0 - Q_1$. You will see from Figure 7.5 that at an output of Q_1, company β has much lower average costs than company α and as a consequence is making far more profit (profit is the shaded area in Figure 7.5).

Strategic Significance

If a company can shift from a cost structure where it encounters increasing marginal costs to one where fixed costs may be high but marginal costs are much lower, its profitability may increase. In the consumer electronics industry, such a shift has been playing out for two decades. Musical recordings were once based on analog technology where marginal costs rose as output expanded due to diminishing returns (as in the case of company α in Figure 7.5). In the 1980s and 1990s, digital systems such as CD players replaced analog systems. Digital systems are software based, and this implies much lower marginal costs of producing one more copy of a recording. As a result, music companies were able to lower prices, expand demand, and see their profitability increase (their production system has more in common with company β in Figure 7.5).

This process, however, was still unfolding. The latest technology for copying musical recordings is based on distribution over the Internet (e.g., by downloading songs onto an iPod). Here, the marginal costs of making one more copy of a recording are lower still. In fact, they are close to zero, and do not increase with output. The only problem is that the low costs of copying and distributing music recordings lead to widespread illegal fire sharing, which ultimately leads to a very large decline in overall revenues in recorded music. According to the International Federation of the Phonographic Industry, worldwide revenues for CDs, vinyl, cassettes and digital downloads dropped from $36.9 billion in 2000 to $15.9 billion in 2010. We discuss copyright issues in more detail shortly when we consider intellectual property rights. The same shift is now beginning to affect other industries. Some companies are building their strategies around trying to exploit and profit from this shift. For an example, Strategy in Action 7.2 looks at SonoSite.

When a high-tech company faces high fixed costs and low marginal costs, its strategy should emphasize the low-cost structure option: deliberately drive down prices in order to increase volume. Look again at Figure 7.5 and you will see that the high-tech company's average costs fall rapidly as output expands. This implies that prices can be reduced to stimulate demand, and so long as prices fall less rapidly than average costs, per unit profit margins will expand as prices fall. This is a consequence of the firm's low marginal costs that do not rise with output. This strategy of pricing low to drive volume and reap wider profit margins is central to the business model of some very successful high-technology companies, including Microsoft.

7.2 STRATEGY IN ACTION

Lowering the Cost of Ultrasound Equipment Through Digitalization

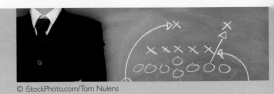
© iStockPhoto.com/Tom Nulens

The ultrasound unit has been an important piece of diagnostic equipment in hospitals for some time. Ultrasound units use the physics of sound to produce images of soft tissues in the human body. Ultrasounds can produce detailed three-dimensional color images of organs and, by using contrast agents, track the flow of fluids through an organ. A cardiologist, for example, can use an ultrasound in combination with contrast agents injected into the bloodstream to track the flow of blood through a beating heart. In addition to the visual diagnosis, ultrasound also produces an array of quantitative diagnostic information of great value to physicians.

Modern ultrasound units are sophisticated instruments that cost about $250,000 to $300,000 each for a top-line model. They are fairly bulky instruments, weighing approximately 300 pounds, and are wheeled around hospitals on carts.

A few years ago, a group of researchers at ATL, one of the leading ultrasound companies, proposed an idea for reducing the size and cost of a basic machine. They theorized that it might be possible to replace up to 80% of the solid circuits in an ultrasound unit with software, and in the process significantly shrink the size and reduce the weight of machines, thereby producing portable ultrasound units. Moreover, by digitalizing much of the ultrasound (replacing hardware with software), they could considerably decrease the marginal costs of making additional units, and would thus be able to make a better profit at much lower price points.

The researchers reasoned that a portable and inexpensive ultrasound unit would find market opportunities in totally new niches. For example, a small, inexpensive ultrasound unit could be placed in an ambulance or carried into battle by an army medic, or purchased by family physicians for use in their offices. Although they realized that it would be some time, perhaps decades, before such small, inexpensive machines could attain the image quality and diagnostic sophistication of top-of-the-line machines, they saw the opportunity in terms of creating market niches that previously could not be served by ultrasound companies because of the high costs and bulk of the product.

The researchers later became part of a project team within ATL, and thereafter became an entirely new company, SonoSite. In late-1999, SonoSite introduced its first portable product, which weighed just 6 pounds and cost about $25,000. SonoSite targeted niches that full-sized ultrasound products could not reach: ambulatory care and foreign markets that could not afford the more expensive equipment. In 2010, the company sold over $275 million of product. In 2011, Fujifilm Holdings bought SonoSite for $995 million to expand its range of medical imaging products and help it overtake the dominant portable ultrasound equipment producer, General Electric.

Source: Interviews by Charles W. L. Hill.

CAPTURING FIRST-MOVER ADVANTAGES

In high-technology industries, companies often compete by striving to be the first to develop revolutionary new products, that is, to be a **first mover**. By definition, the first mover that creates a revolutionary product is in a monopoly position. If the new product satisfies unmet consumer needs and demand is high, the first mover can capture significant revenues and profits. Such revenues and profits signal to potential rivals that imitating the first mover makes money. Figure 7.6 implies that in the absence of strong barriers to imitation, imitators will rush into the market created by the first mover, competing away the first mover's monopoly profits and leaving all participants in the market with a much lower level of returns.

first mover
A firm that pioneers a particular product category or feature by being first to offer it to market.

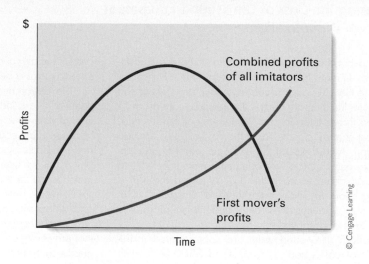

Figure 7.6 The Impact of Imitation on Profits of a First Mover

Despite imitation, some first movers have the ability to capitalize on and reap substantial first-mover advantages—the advantages of pioneering new technologies and products that lead to an enduring competitive advantage. Intel introduced the world's first microprocessor in 1971, and, today, still dominates the microprocessor segment of the semiconductor industry. Xerox introduced the world's first photocopier and for a long time enjoyed a leading position in the industry. Cisco introduced the first Internet protocol network router in 1986, and still leads the market for that equipment today. Microsoft introduced the world's first software application for a personal computer in 1979, Microsoft BASIC, and it remains a dominant force in PC software.

Some first movers can reap substantial advantages from their pioneering activities that lead to an enduring competitive advantage. They can, in other words, limit or slow the rate of imitation.

But there are plenty of counterexamples suggesting that first-mover advantages might not be easy to capture and, in fact, that there might be **first-mover disadvantages—** the competitive disadvantages associated with being first. For example, Apple was the first company to introduce a handheld computer, the Apple Newton, but the product failed; a second mover, Palm, succeeded where Apple had failed (although Apple has recently had major success as a first mover with the first true tablet computer, the iPad). In the market for commercial jet aircraft, DeHavilland was first to market with the Comet, but it was the second mover, Boeing, with its 707 jetliner, that went on to dominate the market.

Clearly, being a first mover does not by itself guarantee success. As we shall see, the difference between innovating companies that capture first-mover advantages and those that fall victim to first-mover disadvantages in part incites the strategy that the first mover pursues. Before considering the strategy issue, however, we need to take a closer look at the nature of first-mover advantages and disadvantages.[7]

first-mover disadvantages
Competitive disadvantages associated with being first.

First-Mover Advantages

There are five primary sources of first-mover advantages.[8] First, the first mover has an opportunity to exploit network effects and positive feedback loops, locking consumers into its technology. In the VCR industry, Sony could have exploited network effects by licensing its technology, but instead the company ceded its first-mover advantage to the second mover, Matsushita.

Second, the first mover may be able to establish significant brand loyalty, which is expensive for later entrants to break down. Indeed, if the company is successful in this endeavor, its name may become closely associated with the entire class of products, including those produced by rivals. People still talk of "Xeroxing" when making a photocopy, or "FedExing" when they will be sending a package by overnight mail.

Third, the first mover may be able to increase sales volume ahead of rivals and thus reap cost advantages associated with the realization of scale economies and learning effects (see Chapter 4). Once the first mover has these cost advantages, it can respond to new entrants by cutting prices in order to retain its market share and still earn significant profits.

Fourth, the first mover may be able to create switching costs for its customers that subsequently make it difficult for rivals to enter the market and take customers away from the first mover. Wireless service providers, for example, will give new customers a "free" wireless phone, but customers must sign a contract agreeing to pay for the phone if they terminate the service contract within a specified time period, such as 1 or 2 years. Because the real cost of a wireless phone may run from $100 to $200, this represents a significant switching cost that later entrants must overcome.

Finally, the first mover may be able to accumulate valuable knowledge related to customer needs, distribution channels, product technology, process technology, and so on. Knowledge so accumulated can give it an advantage that later entrants might find difficult or expensive to match. Sharp, for example, was the first mover in the commercial manufacture of active matrix liquid crystal displays used in laptop computers. The process for manufacturing these displays is very difficult, with a high rejection rate for flawed displays. Sharp has accumulated such an advantage with regard to production processes that it has been very difficult for later entrants to match it on product quality, and therefore on costs.

First-Mover Disadvantages

Balanced against these first-mover advantages are a number of disadvantages.[9] First, the first mover has to bear significant pioneering costs that later entrants do not. The first mover must pioneer the technology, develop distribution channels, and educate customers about the nature of the product. All of this can be expensive and time consuming. Later entrants, by way of contrast, might be able to free-ride on the first mover's investments in pioneering the market and customer education. That is, they do not have to bear the pioneering costs of the first mover.

Related to this, first movers are more prone to make mistakes because there are so many uncertainties in a new market. Later entrants may learn from the mistakes made by first movers, improve on the product or the way in which it is sold, and come to market with a superior offering that captures significant market share from the first mover. For example, one of the reasons that the Apple Newton failed was that the handwriting software in the handheld computer failed to recognize human handwriting. The second mover in this market, Palm, learned from Apple's error. When it introduced the PalmPilot, it used software that recognized letters written in a particular way, Graffiti, and then persuaded customers to learn this method of inputting data into the handheld computer.

Third, first movers run the risk of building the wrong resources and capabilities because they are focusing on a customer set that is not going to be characteristic of the mass market. This is the "crossing the chasm" problem that we discussed in the previous chapter. You will recall that the customers in the early market—those we categorized as innovators and early adopters—have different characteristics from the first wave of the mass market, the early majority. The first mover runs the risk of directing its resources and capabilities to the needs of innovators and early adopters, and not being able to switch when the early majority enters the market. As a result, first movers run a greater risk of plunging into the chasm that separates the early market from the mass market.

Finally, the first mover may invest in inferior or obsolete technology. This can happen when its product innovation is based on underlying technology that is rapidly advancing. By basing its product on an early version of the technology, it may become locked into something that rapidly becomes obsolete. In contrast, later entrants may be able to leap-frog the first mover and introduce products that are based on later versions of the underlying technology. This happened in France during the 1980s when, at the urging of the government, France Telecom introduced the world's first consumer online service, Minitel. France Telecom distributed crude terminals to consumers for free, which connected to the phone line and could be used to browse phone directories. Other simple services were soon added, and before long the French could shop, bank, make travel arrangements, and check weather and news "online"—years before the Web was invented. The problem was that by the standards of the Web, Minitel was very crude and inflexible, and France Telecom, as the first mover, suffered. The French were very slow to adopt personal computers and the Internet primarily because Minitel had such a presence. As late as 1998, only 1/5 of French households had a computer, compared with 2/5 in the United States, and only 2% of households were connected to the Internet, compared to over 30% in the United States. As the result of a government decision, France Telecom, and the entire nation of France, was slow to adopt a revolutionary new online medium—the Web—because they were the first to invest in a more primitive version of the technology.[10]

Strategies for Exploiting First-Mover Advantages

First movers must strategize and determine how to exploit their lead and capitalize on first-mover advantages to build a sustainable long-term competitive advantage while simultaneously reducing the risks associated with first-mover disadvantages. There are three basic strategies available: (1) develop and market the innovation; (2) develop and market the innovation jointly with other companies through a strategic alliance or joint venture; and (3) license the innovation to others and allow them to develop the market.

The optimal choice of strategy depends on the answers to three questions:

1. Does the innovating company have the complementary assets to exploit its innovation and capture first-mover advantages?
2. How difficult is it for imitators to copy the company's innovation? In other words, what is the height of barriers to imitation?
3. Are there capable competitors that could rapidly imitate the innovation?

Complementary Assets   Complementary assets are the assets required to exploit a new innovation and gain a competitive advantage.[11] Among the most important complementary assets are competitive manufacturing facilities capable of handling rapid growth in customer demand while maintaining high product quality. State-of-the-art manufacturing facilities enable the first mover to quickly move down the experience curve without encountering production bottlenecks or problems with the quality of the product. The inability to satisfy demand because of these problems, however, creates the opportunity for imitators to enter the marketplace. For example, in 1998, Immunex was the first company to introduce a revolutionary new biological treatment for rheumatoid arthritis. Sales for this product, Enbrel, very rapidly increased, reaching $750 million in 2001. However, Immunex had not invested in sufficient manufacturing capacity. In mid-2000, it announced that it lacked the capacity to satisfy demand and that bringing additional capacity on line would take at least 2 years. This manufacturing bottleneck gave the second mover in the market, Johnson & Johnson, the opportunity to rapidly expand demand for its product, which by early 2002 was outselling Enbrel. Immunex's first-mover advantage had been partly eroded because it lacked an important complementary asset, the manufacturing capability required to satisfy demand.

Complementary assets also include marketing knowhow, an adequate sales force, access to distribution systems, and an after-sales service and support network. All of these assets can help an innovator build brand loyalty and more rapidly achieve market penetration.[12] In turn, the resulting increases in volume facilitate more rapid movement down the experience curve and the attainment of a sustainable cost-based advantage due to scale economies and learning effects. EMI, the first mover in the market for computerized tomography (CT) scanners, ultimately lost out to established medical equipment companies, such as GE Medical Systems, because it lacked the marketing knowhow, sales force, and distribution systems required to effectively compete in the world's largest market for medical equipment, the United States.

Developing complementary assets can be very expensive, and companies often need large infusions of capital for this purpose. That is why first movers often lose out to late movers that are large, successful companies in other industries with the resources to quickly develop a presence in the new industry. Microsoft and 3M exemplify companies that have moved quickly to capitalize on the opportunities when other companies open up new product markets, such as compact discs or floppy disks. For example, although Netscape pioneered the market for Internet browsers with the Netscape Navigator, Microsoft's Internet Explorer ultimately dominated that market.

Height of Barriers to Imitation   Recall from Chapter 3 that barriers to imitation are factors that prevent rivals from imitating a company's distinctive competencies and innovations. Although any innovation can be copied, the higher the barriers are, the longer it takes for rivals to imitate the innovation, and the more time the first mover has to build an enduring competitive advantage.

Barriers to imitation give an innovator time to establish a competitive advantage and build more enduring barriers to entry in the newly created market. Patents, for example, are among the most widely used barriers to imitation. By protecting its photocopier technology with a thicket of patents, Xerox was able to delay any significant imitation of its product for 17 years. However, patents are often easy to "invent around." For example, one study found that this happened to 60% of patented innovations within 4 years.[13] If patent protection is weak, a company might try to slow imitation by developing new products and processes in secret. The most famous example of this approach is Coca-Cola, which has kept the formula for Coke a secret for generations. But Coca-Cola's success in this regard is an exception. A study of 100 companies has estimated that rivals learn about a company's decision to develop a major new product or process and its related proprietary information within about 12–18 months of the original development decision.[14]

Capable Competitors   Capable competitors are companies that can move quickly to imitate the pioneering company. Competitors' capability to imitate a pioneer's innovation depends primarily on two factors: (1) research and development (R&D) skills; and (2) access to complementary assets. In general, the greater the number of capable competitors with access to the R&D skills and complementary assets needed to imitate an innovation, the more rapid imitation is likely to be.

In this context, R&D skills refer to the ability of rivals to reverse-engineer an innovation in order to find out how it works and quickly develop a comparable product. As an example, consider the CT scanner. GE bought one of the first CT scanners produced by EMI, and its technical experts reverse-engineered the machine. Despite the product's technological complexity, GE developed its own version, which allowed it to quickly imitate EMI and replace EMI as the major supplier of CT scanners.

Complementary assets, or the access that rivals have to marketing, sales knowhow, and manufacturing capabilities, is one of the key determinants of the rate of imitation. If would-be imitators lack critical complementary assets, not only will they have to imitate the innovation, but they may also need to imitate the innovator's complementary assets. This is expensive, as AT&T discovered when it tried to enter the personal computer business in 1984. AT&T lacked the marketing assets (sales force and distribution systems) necessary to support personal computer products. The lack of these assets and the time it takes to build the assets partly explains why: 4 years after it entered the market, AT&T had lost $2.5 billion and still had not emerged as a viable contender. It subsequently exited this business.

Three Innovation Strategies   The way in which these three factors—complementary assets, height of barriers to imitation, and the capability of competitors—influence the choice of innovation strategy is summarized in Table 7.1. The competitive strategy of developing and marketing the innovation alone makes most sense when: (1) the innovator has the complementary assets necessary to develop the innovation, (2) the barriers to imitating a new innovation are high, and (3) the number of capable competitors is limited. Complementary assets allow rapid development and promotion of the innovation. High barriers to imitation give the innovator time to establish a competitive advantage and build enduring barriers to entry through brand loyalty or experience-based cost advantages. The fewer capable competitors there are, the less likely it is that any one of them will succeed in circumventing barriers to imitation and quickly imitating the innovation.

The competitive strategy of developing and marketing the innovation jointly with other companies through a strategic alliance or joint venture makes most sense when:

Table 7.1	Strategies for Profiting from Innovation		
Strategy	**Does the Innovator Have the Required Complementary Assets?**	**Likely Height of Barriers to Imitation**	**Number of Capable Competitors**
Going it alone	Yes	High	Very few
Entering into an alliance	No	High	Moderate number
Licensing the innovation	No	Low	Many

(1) the innovator lacks complementary assets, (2) barriers to imitation are high, and (3) there are several capable competitors. In such circumstances, it makes sense to enter into an alliance with a company that already has the complementary assets—in other words, with a capable competitor. Theoretically, such an alliance should prove to be mutually beneficial, and each partner can share in high profits that neither could earn on its own. Moreover, such a strategy has the benefit of co-opting a potential rival. For example, had EMI teamed with a capable competitor to develop the market for CT scanners, such as GE Medical Systems, instead of going it alone, the company might have been able to build a more enduring competitive advantage, and also have co-opted a potentially powerful rival into its camp.

The third strategy, licensing, makes most sense when: (1) the innovating company lacks the complementary assets, (2) barriers to imitation are low, and (3) there are many capable competitors. The combination of low barriers to imitation and many capable competitors makes rapid imitation almost certain. The innovator's lack of complementary assets further suggests that an imitator will soon capture the innovator's competitive advantage. Given these factors, because rapid diffusion of the innovator's technology through imitation is inevitable, the innovator can at least share in some of the benefits of this diffusion by licensing out its technology.[15] Moreover, by setting a relatively modest licensing fee, the innovator may be able to reduce the incentive that potential rivals have to develop their own competing, and possibly superior, technology. As described previously, this seems to have been the strategy Dolby adopted to get its technology established as the standard for noise reduction in the music and film businesses.

TECHNOLOGICAL PARADIGM SHIFTS

Technological paradigm shifts occur when new technologies revolutionize the structure of the industry, dramatically alter the nature of competition, and require companies to adopt new strategies in order to survive. A good example of a paradigm shift is the evolution of photography from chemical to digital printing processes. For over half a century, the large incumbent enterprises in the photographic industry such as Kodak and Fujifilm have generated most of their revenues from selling and processing film using traditional silver halide technology. The rise of digital photography has been a huge disruptive threat to their business models. Digital cameras do not use film, the mainstay of Kodak's and Fuji's business. In addition, these cameras are more like specialized computers than conventional cameras, and are therefore based on scientific knowledge in which Kodak and Fuji have little expertise. Although both Kodak and Fuji have heavily invested in the development of digital cameras, they are facing intense competition from companies such as Sony, Canon, and Hewlett-Packard, which have developed their own digital cameras; from software developers such as Adobe and Microsoft, which make software for manipulating digital images; and from printer companies such as Hewlett-Packard and Canon, which are making the printers that consumers can use to print high-quality pictures from home. As digital substitution gathers speed in the photography industry, it is not clear that the traditional incumbents will be able to survive this shift; the new competitors might rise to dominance in the new market.

Kodak and Fuji are hardly the first large incumbents to be felled by a technological paradigm shift in their industry. In the early 1980s, the computer industry was revolutionized by the arrival of personal computer technology, which gave rise to client–server networks that replaced traditional mainframe and minicomputers for many business uses. Many incumbent companies in the mainframe era, such as Wang, Control Data, and DEC, ultimately did

technological paradigm shift
Shifts in new technologies that revolutionize the structure of the industry, dramatically alter the nature of competition, and require companies to adopt new strategies in order to survive.

not survive, and even IBM went through a decade of wrenching changes and large losses before it reinvented itself as a provider of e-business solutions. Instead, new entrants such as Microsoft, Intel, Dell, and Compaq rose to dominate this new computer industry.

Today, many believe that the advent of cloud computing is ushering in a paradigm shift in the computer industry. Microsoft, the dominant incumbent in the PC software business, is very vulnerable to this shift. If the center of computing does move to the cloud, with most data and applications stored there, and if all one needs to access data and run applications is a Web browser, then the value of a PC operating system such as Windows is significantly reduced. Microsoft understands this as well as anyone, which is why the company is pushing aggressively into the cloud computing market with Windows Azure.

Examples such as these raise four questions:

1. When do paradigm shifts occur, and how do they unfold?
2. Why do so many incumbents go into decline following a paradigm shift?
3. What strategies can incumbents adopt to increase the probability that they will survive a paradigm shift and emerge on the other side of the market abyss created by the arrival of new technology as a profitable enterprise?
4. What strategies can new entrants into a market adopt to profit from a paradigm shift?

We shall answer each of these questions in the remainder of this chapter.

Paradigm Shifts and the Decline of Established Companies

Paradigm shifts appear to be more likely to occur in an industry when one, or both, of the following conditions are in place.[16] First, the established technology in the industry is mature and approaching or at its "natural limit," and second, a new "disruptive technology" has entered the marketplace and is taking root in niches that are poorly served by incumbent companies using the established technology.

The Natural Limits to Technology Richard Foster has formalized the relationship between the performance of a technology and time in terms of what he calls the technology S-curve (see Figure 7.7).[17] This curve shows the relationship over time of cumulative

Figure 7.7   The Technology S-Curve

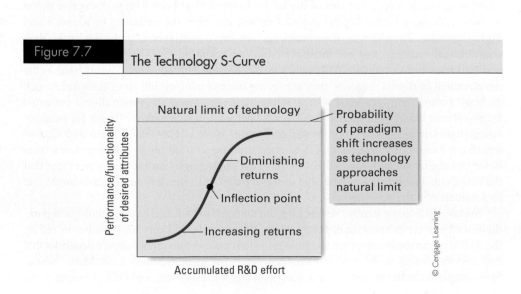

© Cengage Learning

investments in R&D and the performance (or functionality) of a given technology. Early in its evolution, R&D investments in a new technology tend to yield rapid improvements in performance as basic engineering problems are solved. After a time, diminishing returns to cumulative R&D begin to set in, the rate of improvement in performance slows, and the technology starts to approach its natural limit, where further advances are not possible. For example, one can argue that there was more improvement in the first 50 years of the commercial aerospace business following the pioneering flight by the Wright Brothers than there has been in the second 50 years. Indeed, the venerable Boeing 747 is based on a 1960s design. In commercial aerospace, therefore, we are now in the region of diminishing returns and may be approaching the natural limit to improvements in the technology of commercial aerospace.

Similarly, it can be argued that we are approaching the natural limit to technology in the performance of silicon-based semiconductor chips. Over the past two decades, the performance of semiconductor chips has been increased dramatically; companies can now manufacture a larger amount of transistors in one single, small silicon chip. This process has helped to increase the power of computers, lower their cost, and shrink their size. But we are starting to approach limits to the ability to shrink the width of lines on a chip and therefore pack ever more transistors onto a single chip. The limit is imposed by the natural laws of physics. Light waves are used to help etch lines onto a chip, and one cannot etch a line that is smaller than the wavelength of light being used. Semiconductor companies are already using light beams with very small wavelengths, such as extreme ultraviolet, to etch lines onto a chip, but there are limits to how far this technology can be pushed, and many believe that we will reach those limits within the decade. Does this mean that our ability to make smaller, faster, cheaper computers is coming to an end? Probably not. It is more likely that we will find another technology to replace silicon-based computing and enable us to continue building smaller, faster, cheaper computers. In fact, several exotic competing technologies are already being developed that may replace silicon-based computing. These include self-organizing molecular computers, three-dimensional microprocessor technology, quantum computing technology, and using DNA to perform computations.[18]

What does all of this have to do with paradigm shifts? According to Foster, when a technology approaches its natural limit, research attention turns to possible alternative technologies, and sooner or later one of those alternatives might be commercialized and replace the established technology. That is, the probability that a paradigm shift will occur increases. Thus, sometime in the next decade or two, another paradigm shift might shake up the foundations of the computer industry as exotic computing technology replaces silicon-based computing. If history is any guide, if and when this happens, many of the incumbents in today's computer industry will go into decline, and new enterprises will rise to dominance.

Foster pushes this point a little further, noting that, initially, the contenders for the replacement technology are not as effective as the established technology in producing the attributes and features that consumers demand in a product. For example, in the early years of the 20th century, automobiles were just beginning to be produced. They were valued for their ability to move people from place to place, but so was the horse and cart (the established technology). When automobiles originally appeared, the horse and cart was still quite a bit better than the automobile (see Figure 7.8). After all, the first cars were slow, noisy, and prone to breakdown. Moreover, they needed a network of paved roads and gas stations to be really useful, and that network didn't yet exist. For most applications, the horse and cart was still the preferred mode of transportation—including the fact that it was cheaper.

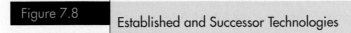

Figure 7.8   Established and Successor Technologies

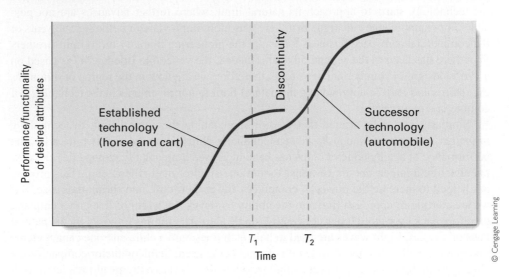

However, this comparison ignored the fact that in the early 20th century, automobile technology was at the very start of its S-curve and was about to experience dramatic improvements in performance as major engineering problems were solved (and those paved roads and gas stations were built). In contrast, after 3,000 years of continuous improvement and refinement, the horse and cart was almost definitely at the end of its technological S-curve. The result was that the rapidly improving automobile soon replaced the horse and cart as the preferred mode of transportation. At time T_1 in Figure 7.8, the horse and cart was still superior to the automobile. By time T_2, the automobile had surpassed the horse and cart.

Foster notes that because the successor technology is initially less efficient than the established technology, established companies and their customers often make the mistake of dismissing it, only to be surprised by its rapid performance improvement. A final point here is that often there is not one potential successor technology but a swarm of potential successor technologies, only one of which might ultimately rise to the fore (see Figure 7.9). When this is the case, established companies are put at a disadvantage. Even if they recognize that a paradigm shift is imminent, companies may not have the resources to invest in all the potential replacement technologies. If they invest in the wrong one, something that is easy to do given the uncertainty that surrounds the entire process, they may be locked out of subsequent development.

Disruptive Technology   Clayton Christensen has built on Foster's insights and his own research to develop a theory of disruptive technology that has become very influential in high-technology circles.[19] Christensen uses the term *disruptive technology* to refer to a new technology that gets its start away from the mainstream of a market and then, as its functionality improves over time, invades the main market. Such technologies are disruptive because they revolutionize industry structure and competition, often causing the decline of established companies. They cause a technological paradigm shift.

Christensen's greatest insight is that established companies are often aware of the new technology but do not invest in it because they listen to their customers, and their customers do not want it. Of course, this arises because the new technology is early in its development,

Swarm of Successor Technologies

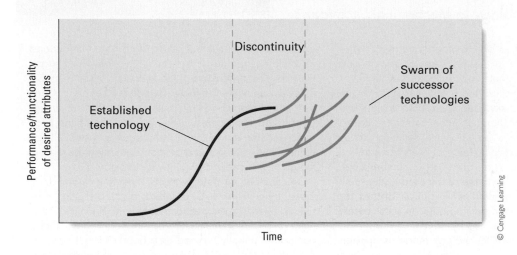

© Cengage Learning

and only at the beginning of the S-curve for that technology. Once the performance of the new technology improves, customers will want it, but by this time it is new entrants (as opposed to established companies), that have accumulated the required knowledge to bring the new technology into the mass market. Christensen supports his view by several detailed historical case studies, one of which is summarized in Strategy in Action 7.3.

In addition to listening too closely to their customers, Christensen also identifies a number of other factors that make it very difficult for established companies to adopt a new disruptive technology. He notes that many established companies decline to invest in new disruptive technologies because initially they serve such small market niches that it seems unlikely there would be an impact on the company's revenues and profits. As the new technology starts to improve in functionality and invade the main market, their investment can often be hindered by the difficult implementation of a new business model required to exploit the new technology.

Both of these points can be illustrated by reference to one more example: the rise of online discount stockbrokers during the 1990s, such as Ameritrade and E*TRADE, which made use of a new technology—the Internet—to allow individual investors to trade stocks for a very low commission fee, whereas full-service stockbrokers, such as Merrill Lynch, which required that orders be placed through a stockbroker who earned a commission for performing the transaction, did not.

Christensen also notes that a new network of suppliers and distributors typically grows alongside the new entrants. Not only do established companies initially ignore disruptive technology, so do their suppliers and distributors. This creates an opportunity for new suppliers and distributors to enter the market to serve the new entrants. As the new entrants grow, so does the associated network. Ultimately, Christensen suggests, the new entrants and their network may replace not only established enterprises, but also the entire network of suppliers and distributors associated with established companies. Taken to its logical extreme, this view suggests that disruptive technologies may result in the demise of the entire network of enterprises associated with established companies in an industry.

The established companies in an industry that is being rocked by a technological paradigm shift often must cope with internal inertia forces that limit their ability to adapt,

7.3 STRATEGY IN ACTION

Disruptive Technology in Mechanical Excavators

© iStockPhoto.com/Tom Nulens

Excavators are used to dig out foundations for large buildings, trenches to lay large pipes for sewers and related components, and foundations and trenches for residential construction and farm work. Prior to the 1940s, the dominant technology used to manipulate the bucket on a mechanical excavator was based on a system of cables and pulleys. Although these mechanical systems could lift large buckets of earth, the excavators themselves were quite large, cumbersome, and expensive. Thus, they were rarely used to dig small trenches for house foundations, irrigation ditches for farmers, and projects of similar scale. In most cases, these small trenches were dug by hand.

In the 1940s, a new technology made its appearance: hydraulics. In theory, hydraulic systems had certain advantages over the established cable and pulley systems. Most important, their energy efficiency was higher: for a given bucket size, a smaller engine would be required using a hydraulic system. However, the initial hydraulic systems also had drawbacks. The seals on hydraulic cylinders were prone to leak under high pressure, effectively limiting the size of bucket that could be lifted. Notwithstanding this drawback, when hydraulics first appeared, many of the incumbent firms in the mechanical excavation industry took the technology seriously enough to ask their primary customers whether they would be interested in hydraulic products. Because the primary customers of incumbents needed

excavators with large buckets to dig out the foundations for buildings and large trenches, their reply was negative. For this customer set, the hydraulic systems of the 1940s were neither reliable nor powerful enough. Consequently, after consulting with their customers, these established companies in the industry made the strategic decision not to invest in hydraulics. Instead, they continued to produce excavation equipment based on the dominant cable and pulley technology.

A number of new entrants, which included J. I. Case, John Deere, J. C. Bamford, and Caterpillar, pioneered hydraulic excavation equipment. Because of the limits on bucket size imposed by the seal problem, these companies initially focused on a poorly served niche in the market that could make use of small buckets: residential contractors and farmers. Over time, these new entrants were able to solve the engineering problems associated with weak hydraulic seals, and as they did this, they manufactured excavators with larger buckets. Ultimately, they invaded the market niches served by the old-line companies: general contractors that dug the foundations for large buildings, sewers, and large-scale projects. At this point, Case, Deere, Caterpillar, and similar companies rose to dominance in the industry, whereas the majority of established companies from the prior era lost share. Of the 30 or so manufacturers of cable-actuated equipment in the United States in the late-1930s, only four survived to the 1950s.

Source: Adapted from Christensen, *The Innovator's Dilemma*

but the new entrants do not, and thereby have an advantage. New entrants do not have to deal with an established, conservative customer set, and an obsolete business model. Instead, they can focus on optimizing the new technology, improving its performance, and riding the wave of disruptive technology into new market segments until they invade the main market and challenge the established companies. By then, they may be well equipped to surpass the established companies.

Strategic Implications for Established Companies

Although Christensen has uncovered an important tendency, it is by no means written in stone that all established companies are doomed to fail when faced with disruptive technologies, as we have seen with IBM and Merrill Lynch. Established companies must meet the challenges created by the emergence of disruptive technologies.[20]

First, having access to the knowledge about how disruptive technologies can revolutionize markets is a valuable strategic asset. Many of the established companies that Christensen examined failed because they took a myopic view of the new technology and asked their customers the wrong question. Instead of asking: "Are you interested in this new technology?" they should have recognized that the new technology was likely to improve rapidly over time and instead have asked: "Would you be interested in this new technology if it improves its functionality over time?" If established enterprises had done this, they may have made very different strategic decisions.

Second, it is clearly important for established enterprises to invest in newly emerging technologies that may ultimately become disruptive technologies. Companies have to hedge their bets about new technology. As we have noted, at any time, there may be a swarm of emerging technologies, any one of which might ultimately become a disruptive technology. Large, established companies that are generating significant cash flows can, and often should, establish and fund central R&D operations to invest in and develop such technologies. In addition, they may wish to acquire newly emerging companies that are pioneering potentially disruptive technologies, or enter into alliances with others to jointly develop the technology. The strategy of acquiring companies that are developing potentially disruptive technology is one that Cisco Systems, a dominant provider of Internet network equipment, is famous for pursuing. At the heart of this strategy must be a recognition on behalf of the incumbent enterprise that it is better for the company to develop disruptive technology and then cannibalize its established sales base than to have the sales base taken away by new entrants.

However, Christensen makes a very important point: even when established companies undertake R&D investments in potentially disruptive technologies, they often fail to commercialize those technologies because of internal forces that suppress change. For example, managers who are currently generating the most cash in one part of the business may claim that they need the greatest R&D investment to maintain their market position, and may lobby top management to delay investment in a new technology. This can be a powerful argument when, early in the S-curve, the long-term prospects of a new technology are very unclear. The consequence, however, may be that the company fails to build competence in the new technology, and will suffer accordingly.

In addition, Christensen argues that the commercialization of new disruptive technology often requires a radically different value chain with a completely different cost structure—a new business model. For example, it may require a different manufacturing system, a different distribution system, and different pricing options, and may involve very different gross margins and operating margins. Christensen argues that it is almost impossible for two distinct business models to coexist within the same organization. When companies try to implement both models, the already established model will almost inevitably suffocate the model associated with the disruptive technology.

The solution to this problem is to separate out the disruptive technology and create an autonomous operating division solely for this new technology. For example, during the early 1980s, HP built a very successful laser jet printer business. Then ink jet technology was invented. Some employees at HP believed that ink jet printers would cannibalize sales of laser jet printers, and consequently argued that HP should not produce ink jet printers. Fortunately for HP, senior management saw ink jet technology for what it was: a potential disruptive technology. Instead of choosing not to invest in ink jet technology, HP allocated significant R&D funds toward its commercialization. Furthermore, when the technology was ready for market introduction, HP established an autonomous ink jet division at a different geographical location, including manufacturing, marketing, and distribution departments. HP senior managers accepted that the ink jet division might take sales away from the laser jet division and decided that it was better for an HP division to cannibalize the sales of another HP division, than allow those sales to be cannibalized by another company. Happily for HP, ink jets cannibalize sales of laser jets only on the margin, and both laser jet and ink jet printers have profitable market niches. This felicitous outcome, however, does not detract from the message of this example: if a company is developing a potentially disruptive technology, the chances for success will be enhanced if it is placed in a stand-alone product division and given its own mandate.

Strategic Implications for New Entrants

Christensen's work also holds implications for new entrants. The new entrants, or attackers, have several advantages over established enterprises. Pressures to continue the existing out-of-date business model do not hamstring new entrants, which do not need to worry about product cannibalization issues. They do not need to worry about their established customer base, or about relationships with established suppliers and distributors. Instead, they can focus all their energies on the opportunities offered by the new disruptive technology, move along the S-curve of technology improvement, and rapidly grow with the market for that technology. This does not mean that the new entrants do not have problems to solve. They may be constrained by a lack of capital or must manage the organizational problems associated with rapid growth; most important, they may need to find a way to take their technology from a small out-of-the-way niche into the mass market.

Perhaps one of the most important issues facing new entrants is choosing whether to partner with an established company, or go it alone in an attempt to develop and profit from a new disruptive technology. Although a new entrant may enjoy all of the advantages of the attacker, it may lack the resources required to fully exploit them. In such a case, the company might want to consider forming a strategic alliance with a larger, established company to gain access to those resources. The main issues here are the same as those discussed earlier when examining the three strategies that a company can pursue to capture first-mover advantages: go it alone, enter into a strategic alliance, or license its technology.

7.1 ETHICAL DILEMMA

© iStockPhoto.com/P_Wei

Your company is in a race with two other enterprises to develop a new technological standard for streaming high-definition video over the Internet. The three technologies are incompatible with each other, and switching costs are presumed to be high. You know that your technology is significantly inferior to the technology being developed by your rivals, but you strongly suspect that you will be the first to the market. Moreover, you know that by bundling your product with one that your company already sells (which is very popular among computer users), you should be able to ensure wide early adoption. You have even considered initially pricing the product at zero in order to ensure rapid take up, thereby shutting out the superior technology that your rivals are developing. You are able to do this because you make so much money from your other products. Once the market has locked into your offering, the strategy will be to raise the price on your technology.

One of your colleagues has suggested that it is not ethical for your company to use its financial muscle and bundling strategies to lock out a superior technology in this manner. Why do you think he makes this argument?

Do you agree with him? Why?

Can you think of a real-world situation that is similar to this case?

SUMMARY OF CHAPTER

1. Technical standards are important in many high-tech industries: they guarantee compatibility, reduce confusion in the minds of customers, allow for mass production and lower costs, and reduce the risks associated with supplying complementary products.
2. Network effects and positive feedback loops often determine which standard will dominate a market.
3. Owning a standard can be a source of sustained competitive advantage.
4. Establishing a proprietary standard as the industry standard may require the company to win a format war against a competing and incompatible standard. Strategies for doing this include producing complementary products, leveraging killer applications, using aggressive pricing and marketing, licensing the technology, and cooperating with competitors.
5. Many high-tech products are characterized by high fixed costs of development but very low or zero marginal costs of producing one extra unit of output. These cost economics create a presumption in favor of strategies that emphasize aggressive pricing to increase volume and drive down average total costs.
6. It is very important for a first mover to develop a strategy to capitalize on first-mover advantages. A company can choose from three strategies: develop and market the technology itself, do so jointly with another company, or license the technology to existing companies. The choice depends on the complementary assets required to capture a first-mover advantage, the height of barriers to imitation, and the capability of competitors.
7. Technological paradigm shifts occur when new technologies come along that revolutionize the structure of the industry, dramatically alter the nature of competition, and require companies to adopt new strategies in order to succeed.
8. Technological paradigm shifts are more likely to occur when progress in improving the established technology is slowing because of diminishing returns and when a new disruptive technology is taking root in a market niche.
9. Established companies can deal with paradigm shifts by investing in technology or setting up a stand-alone division to exploit the technology.

DISCUSSION QUESTIONS

1. What is different about high-tech industries? Were all industries once high tech?
2. Why are standards so important in high-tech industries? What are the competitive implications of this?
3. You work for a small company that has the leading position in an embryonic market. Your boss believes that the company's future is ensured because it has a 60% share of the market, the lowest cost structure in the industry, and the most reliable and highest-valued product. Write a memo to your boss outlining why the assumptions posed might be incorrect.
4. You are working for a small company that has developed an operating system for PCs that is faster and more stable than Microsoft's Windows operating system. What strategies might the company pursue to unseat Windows and establish its own operating system as the dominant technical standard in the industry?
5. You are a manager for a major music record label. Last year, music sales declined by 10%, primarily because of very high piracy rates for CDs. Your boss has asked you to develop a strategy for reducing piracy rates. What would you suggest that the company do?
6. Reread the opening case on the emerging standards battles in mobile payments. Which mobile payment system do you think will become dominant?

PRACTICING STRATEGIC MANAGEMENT

© iStockPhoto.com/Urilux

Small-Group Exercises: Digital Books

Break up into groups of three to five people, and discuss the following scenario. Appoint one group member as a spokesperson who will communicate your findings to the class.

You are a group of managers and software engineers at a small start-up that has developed software that enables customers to easily download and view digital books on a variety of digital devices, including PCs, iPods, and e-book readers. The same software also allows customers to share digital books using peer-to-peer technology (the same technology that allows people to share music files on the Web), and to "burn" digital books onto DVDs.

1. How do you think the market for this software is likely to develop? What factors might inhibit adoption of this software?
2. Can you think of a strategy that your company might pursue in combination with book publishers that will enable your company to increase revenues and the film companies to reduce piracy rates?

STRATEGY SIGN-ON

© iStockPhoto.com/Ninoslav Dotlic

Article File 7

Find an example of an industry that has undergone a technological paradigm shift in recent years. What happened to the established companies as that paradigm shift unfolded?

Strategic Management Project: Developing Your Portfolio 7

This module requires you to analyze the industry environment in which your company is based and determine if it is vulnerable to a technological paradigm shift. With the information you have at your disposal, answer the following questions:

1. What is the dominant product technology used in the industry in which your company is based?
2. Are technical standards important in your industry? If so, what are they?
3. What are the attributes of the majority of customers purchasing the product of your company (e.g., early adopters, early majority, late majority)? What does this tell you about the strategic issues that the company is likely to face in the future?
4. Did the dominant technology in your industry diffuse rapidly or slowly? What drove the speed of diffusion?

STRATEGY SIGN ON (continued)

© iStockPhoto.com/Ninoslav Dotlic

5. Where is the dominant technology in your industry on its S-curve? Are alternative competing technologies being developed that might give rise to a paradigm shift in your industry?
6. Are intellectual property rights important to your company? If so, what strategies is it adopting to protect those rights? Is it doing enough?

CLOSING CASE

The Rise of Cloud Computing

There is a paradigm shift beginning in the world of computing. Over the next decade, increasing numbers of businesses will stop purchasing their own computer servers and mainframes, and instead move their applications and data to "the cloud." The cloud is a metaphor for large data centers or "server farms"—collections of hundreds of thousands of co-located and interlinked computer servers. Corporations will be able to "host" their data and applications on cloud computing providers' servers. To run an application hosted on the cloud, all a person will need is a computing device with a Web browser and an Internet connection.

There are significant cost advantages associated with shifting data and applications to the cloud. Business will no longer need to invest in information technology hardware that rapidly becomes obsolete. Cloud providers will instead be responsible for maintenance costs of servers and hardware. Moreover, businesses will no longer need to purchase many software applications. Instead, businesses will utilize a pay-as-you-go pricing model for any applications that they use, which also holds out the promise of reducing costs. (Some studies have concluded that 70% of software purchased by corporations is either underutilized or not used at all.) The Brookings Institute estimates that companies could reduce their information technology costs by as much as 50% by moving to the cloud.

Early adopters of cloud computing services have included InterContinental Hotel Group (IHG), which has 650,000 rooms in 4,400 hotels around the world. Rather than upgrade its own information technology hardware, IHG has decided to move its central reservation system onto server farms owned by Amazon.com, the online retail store that is also emerging as an early leader in the cloud computing market. Similarly, Netflix has decided to utilize Amazon's cloud services for distributing its movies digitally, rather than investing in its own server farms. Another early user of cloud services is Starbucks, which has moved its entire corporate e-mail system off its servers and onto Microsoft's cloud computing system.

Amazon and Microsoft are two of the early leaders in the embryonic cloud computing market. The other significant player is Google. All three companies had to build large server farms to run parts of their own businesses (online retail in the case of Amazon, and Web-searching capabilities in the case of Google and Microsoft). When these corporations soon realized that they could rent out capacity on these server farms to other businesses, the concept of cloud computing was born. Other companies that have announced their intentions to enter the cloud computing market as providers of hosting services include IBM and Hewlett-Packard.

Right now the cloud is small—IDC indicates that worldwide, cloud services accounted for $40 billion in 2012 (just over 1% of the 3.6 trillion spent worldwide on information technology in 2012), and expects that number to grow to 100 billion by 2016. However, cloud services also threatened to redistribute who earned those revenues in information technology, attracting the attention of companies such as Microsoft and Google.

Microsoft has developed an operating system, known as Windows Azure, which is designed to run software applications very efficiently on server farms, allocating workloads and balancing capacity across hundreds of thousands of servers. Microsoft is rewriting many of its own applications, such as Office and SQL server, to run on Azure. The belief is that this will help the company retain existing clients as they transition their data and applications from their own servers onto the cloud. Microsoft has also developed tools to help clients write their own custom applications for the cloud; it has recognized that the shift to the cloud threatens its existing Windows monopoly, and that its best strategy is to try to become the dominant company on the cloud.

Microsoft's rivals were not idly standing by. Google, for example, has developed a cloud-based operating system, Google App Engine, which allows clients to efficiently run their custom software applications on the cloud, and also offers the Chrome OS for individuals to use on dedicated Chrome tablets. Amazon, too, has its own cloud-based operating system, known as Elastic Compute Cloud, or "EC2." Other companies, including IBM and VM Ware, are developing similar software. Software applications that are written for one cloud-based operating system will not run on another cloud operating system without a complete rewrite— meaning that there will be significant switching costs involved in moving an application from one cloud provider to another. This strongly suggests that we are witnessing the beginnings of a format war in cloud computing, much like the format war during the early 1990s between Microsoft, IBM, and Apple to dominate the desktop computer—a war that Microsoft won with its Windows operating system. If business history is any guide, at most only two or three formats will survive, with most other formats falling by the wayside.

Sources: R. Harms and M. Yamartino, "The Economics of the Cloud," *Microsoft White Paper*, November 2011; A. Vance, "The Cloud: Battle of the Tech Titans," *Bloomberg Businessweek*, March 3, 2011; and K. D. Schwartz, "Cloud Computing Can Generate Massive Savings for Agencies," *Federal Computer Week*, January 2011.

CASE DISCUSSION QUESTIONS

1. What are the advantages and disadvantages of using cloud services for individuals and businesses?

2. How does the adoption of cloud services affect the revenues for computer and software makers? Which companies will "win" and "lose" if individuals and businesses continue to shift to using cloud services?

3. What forces would create pressure for a dominant cloud-based operating system to emerge?

4. What individual advantages do you think Microsoft, Amazon, and Google have in promoting their cloud-based operating systems?

KEY TERMS

Technical standards 215
Format wars 218
Dominant design 218

Public domain 220
Network effects 221
Killer applications 224

Razor and blade
strategy 225
First mover 229

First-mover
disadvantages 230
Technological paradigm
shift 235

NOTES

[1]Data from Bureau of Economic Analysis, 2013, www.bea.gov.

[2]J. M. Utterback, *Mastering the Dynamics of Innovation* (Boston: Harvard Business School Press, 1994); C. Shapiro and H. R. Varian, *Information Rules: A Strategic Guide to the Network Economy* (Boston: Harvard Business School Press, 1999).

[3]The layout is not universal, although it is widespread. The French, for example, use a different layout.

[4]For details, see Charles W. L. Hill, "Establishing a Standard: Competitive Strategy and Technology Standards in Winner Take All Industries," *Academy of Management Executive* 11 (1997): 7–25; Shapiro and Varian, *Information Rules;* B. Arthur, "Increasing Returns and the New World of Business," *Harvard Business Review,* July–August 1996, 100–109; G. Gowrisankaran and J. Stavins, "Network Externalities and Technology Adoption: Lessons from Electronic Payments," *Rand Journal of Economics* 35 (2004): 260–277; V. Shankar and B. L. Bayus, "Network Effects and Competition: An Empirical Analysis of the Home Video Game Industry," *Strategic Management Journal* 24 (2003): 375–394; and R. Casadesus-Masanell and P. Ghemawat, "Dynamic Mixed Duopoly: A Model Motivated by Linux vs Windows," *Management Science,* 52 (2006): 1072–1085.

[5]See Shapiro and Varian, *Information Rules;* Hill, "Establishing a Standard"; and M. A. Schilling, "Technological Lockout: An Integrative Model of the Economic and Strategic Factors Driving Technology Success and Failure," *Academy of Management Review* 23:2 (1998): 267–285.

[6]Microsoft does not disclose the per unit licensing fee that it receives from original equipment manufacturers, although media reports speculate it is around $50 a copy.

[7]Much of this section is based on Charles W. L. Hill, Michael Heeley, and Jane Sakson, "Strategies for Profiting from Innovation," in *Advances in Global High Technology Management* 3 (Greenwich, CT: JAI Press, 1993), pp. 79–95.

[8]M. Lieberman and D. Montgomery, "First Mover Advantages," *Strategic Management Journal* 9 (Special Issue, Summer 1988): 41–58.

[9]W. Boulding and M. Christen, "Sustainable Pioneering Advantage? Profit Implications of Market Entry Order?" *Marketing Science* 22 (2003): 371–386; C. Markides and P. Geroski, "Teaching Elephants to Dance and Other Silly Ideas," *Business Strategy Review* 13 (2003): 49–61.

[10]J. Borzo, "Aging Gracefully," *Wall Street Journal,* October 15, 2001, p. R22.

[11]The importance of complementary assets was first noted by D. J. Teece. See D. J. Teece, "Profiting from Technological Innovation," in D. J. Teece (ed.), *The Competitive Challenge* (New York: Harper & Row, 1986), pp. 26–54.

[12]M. J. Chen and D. C. Hambrick, "Speed, Stealth, and Selective Attack: How Small Firms Differ from Large Firms in Competitive Behavior," *Academy of Management Journal* 38 (1995): 453–482.

[13]E. Mansfield, M. Schwartz, and S. Wagner, "Imitation Costs and Patents: An Empirical Study," *Economic Journal* 91 (1981): 907–918.

[14]E. Mansfield, "How Rapidly Does New Industrial Technology Leak Out?" *Journal of Industrial Economics* 34 (1985): 217–223.

[15]This argument has been made in the game theory literature. See R. Caves, H. Cookell, and P. J. Killing, "The Imperfect Market for Technology Licenses," *Oxford Bulletin of Economics and Statistics* 45 (1983): 249–267; N. T. Gallini, "Deterrence by Market Sharing: A Strategic Incentive for Licensing," *American Economic Review* 74 (1984): 931–941; and C. Shapiro, "Patent Licensing and R&D Rivalry," *American Economic Review* 75 (1985): 25–30.

[16]M. Christensen, *The Innovator's Dilemma* (Boston: Harvard Business School Press, 1997); and R. N. Foster, *Innovation: The Attacker's Advantage* (New York: Summit Books, 1986).

[17]Foster, *Innovation.*

[18]Ray Kurzweil, *The Age of the Spiritual Machines* (New York: Penguin Books, 1999).

[19]See Christensen, *The Innovator's Dilemma;* and C. M. Christensen and M. Overdorf, "Meeting the Challenge of Disruptive Change," *Harvard Business Review,* March–April 2000, pp. 66–77.

[20]Charles W. L. Hill and Frank T. Rothaermel, "The Performance of Incumbent Firms in the Face of Radical Technological Innovation," *Academy of Management Review* 28 (2003): 257–274; and F. T. Rothaermel and Charles W. L. Hill, "Technological Discontinuities and Complementary Assets: A Longitudinal Study of Industry and Firm Performance," *Organization Science* 16:1(2005): 52–70.

8

Strategy in the Global Environment

LEARNING OBJECTIVES

After this chapter, you should be able to:

8-1 Understand the process of globalization and how it impacts a company's strategy

8-2 Discuss the motives for expanding internationally

8-3 Review the different strategies that companies use to compete in the global market place

8-4 Explain the pros and cons of different modes for entering foreign markets

Ford's Global Strategy

When Ford CEO Alan Mulally arrived at the company in 2006 after a long career at Boeing, he was shocked to learn that the company produced one Ford Focus for Europe, and a totally different one for the United States. "Can you imagine having one Boeing 737 for Europe and one 737 for the United States?" he said at the time. Due to this product strategy, Ford was unable to buy common parts for the vehicles, could not share development costs, and couldn't use its European Focus plants to make cars for the United States, or vice versa. In a business where economies of scale are important, the result was high costs. Nor were these problems limited to the Ford Focus—the strategy of designing and building different cars for different regions was the standard approach at Ford.

Ford's long-standing strategy of regional models was based upon the assumption that consumers in different regions had different tastes and preferences, which required considerable local customization. Americans, it was

© iStockPhoto.com/GYI NSEA

argued, loved their trucks and SUVs, whereas Europeans preferred smaller, fuel-efficient cars. Notwithstanding such differences, Mulally still could not understand why small car models like the Focus or the Escape SUV, which were sold in different regions, were not built on the same platform and did not share common parts. In truth, the strategy probably had more to do with the autonomy of different regions within Ford's organization, a fact that was deeply embedded in Ford's history as one of the oldest multinational corporations.

When the global financial crisis rocked the world's automobile industry in 2008–2009, and precipitated the steepest drop in sales since the Great Depression, Mulally decided that Ford had to change its long-standing practices in order to get its costs under control. Moreover, he felt that there was no way that Ford would be able to compete effectively in the large developing markets of China and India unless Ford leveraged its global scale to produce low-cost cars. The result was Mulally's "One Ford" strategy, which aims to create a handful of car platforms that Ford can use everywhere in the world.

Under this strategy, new models—such as the 2013 Fiesta, Focus, and Escape—share a common design, are built on a common platform, use the same parts, and will be built in identical factories around the world. Ultimately, Ford hopes to have only five platforms to deliver sales of more than 6 million vehicles by 2016. In 2006 Ford had 15 platforms that accounted for sales of 6.6 million vehicles. By pursuing this strategy, Ford can share the costs of design and tooling, and it can attain much greater scale economies in the production of component parts. Ford has stated that it will take about one-third out of the $1 billion cost of developing a new car model and should significantly reduce its $50 billion annual budget for component parts. Moreover, because the different factories producing these cars are identical in all respects, useful knowledge acquired through experience in one factory can quickly be transferred to other factories, resulting in system-wide cost savings.

What Ford hopes is that this strategy will bring down costs sufficiently to enable Ford to make greater profit margins in developed markets, and be able to make good margins at lower price points in hypercompetitive developing nations, such as China, now the world's largest car market, where Ford currently trails its global rivals such as General Motors and Volkswagen. Indeed, the strategy is central to Mulally's goal for growing Ford's sales from 5.5 million in 2010 to 8 million by mid-decade.

Sources: M. Ramsey, "Ford SUV Marks New World Car Strategy," *Wall Street Journal*, November 16, 2011; B. Vlasic, "Ford Strategy Will Call for Stepping up Expansion, Especially in Asia," *New York Times*, June 7, 2011; and "Global Manufacturing Strategy Gives Ford Competitive Advantage," Ford Motor Company, http://media.ford.com/article_display.cfm?article_id=13633.

OVERVIEW

This chapter begins with a discussion of ongoing changes in the global competitive environment and discusses models managers can use for analyzing competition in different national markets. Next, the chapter discusses the various ways in which international expansion can increase a company's profitability and profit growth. We then discuss the advantages and disadvantages of the different strategies companies can pursue to gain a competitive advantage in the global marketplace. This is followed by a discussion of two related strategic issues: (1) how managers decide which foreign markets to enter, when to enter them, and on what scale; and (2) what kind of vehicle or method a company should use to expand globally and enter a foreign country.

Ford Motor Company's One Ford strategy, profiled in the Opening Case, gives a preview of some issues explored in this chapter. Historically Ford pursued a *localization* strategy, selling cars in the different regions that were designed and produced locally (i.e., one design for Europe, another for North America). Although this strategy did have the virtue of ensuring that the offering was tailored to the tastes and preferences of consumers in different regions, it also involved considerable duplication and high costs. By the late 2000s, Alan Mulally, Ford's CEO, decided that the company could no longer afford the high costs associated with this approach, and he pushed the company to adopt his One Ford strategy. Under this *global standardization strategy,* Ford aims to design and sell the same models worldwide. The idea is to reap substantial cost reduction from sharing design costs, building on common platforms, sharing component parts across models, and building cars in identical factories around the world to share tooling costs. To the extent that Ford can do this, the company should be able to lower prices and still make good profits, which should help it not only to hold on to share in developed markets, but also to gain share in rapidly growing emerging markets such as India and China. Although there is a risk that the lack of local customization will lead to some loss of sales at the margin, Mulally clearly feels that the benefits in terms of lower costs and more competitive pricing clearly outweigh this risk. Only time will tell if he is correct.

As we shall see later in this chapter, many other companies have made a similar shift in the last two decades, moving from what can be characterized as a *localization strategy*, where local country managers have considerable autonomy over manufacturing and marketing, to a *global strategy*, where the corporate center exercises more control over manufacturing, marketing, and product development decisions. The tendency to make such a shift in many international businesses is a response to the globalization of markets. We shall discuss this process later in the chapter.

By the time you have completed this chapter, you will have a good understanding of the various strategic issues that companies face when they decide to expand their operations abroad to achieve competitive advantage and superior profitability.

THE GLOBAL AND NATIONAL ENVIRONMENTS

Fifty years ago, most national markets were isolated from one another by significant barriers to international trade and investment. In those days, managers could focus on analyzing only those national markets in which their company competed. They did not need to pay much attention to entry by global competitors, for there were few and entry was difficult. Nor did they need to pay much attention to entering foreign markets, because that was often prohibitively expensive. All of this has now changed. Barriers to international trade and investment have tumbled, huge global markets for goods and services have been created, and companies from different nations are entering each other's home markets on an unprecedented scale, increasing the intensity of competition. Rivalry can no longer be understood merely in terms of what happens within the boundaries of a nation; managers now need to consider how globalization is impacting the environment in which their company competes and what strategies their company should adopt to exploit the unfolding opportunities and counter competitive threats. In this section we look at the changes ushered in by falling barriers to international trade and investment, and we discuss a model for analyzing the competitive situation in different nations.

The Globalization of Production and Markets

The past half-century has seen a dramatic lowering of barriers to international trade and investment. For example, the average tariff rate on manufactured goods traded between advanced nations has fallen from around 40% to under 4%. Similarly, in nation after nation, regulations prohibiting foreign companies from entering domestic markets and establishing production facilities, or acquiring domestic companies, have been removed. As a result of these developments, there has been a surge in both the volume of international trade and the value of foreign direct investment. The volume of world merchandise trade has been growing faster than the world economy since the 1950s. Between 1970 and 2011, the volume of world merchandise trade increased 30-fold, compared to a 10-fold increase in the size of the world economy. Even in the economically troubled years of 2005–2011, world merchandise trade grew at 3.7% per annum, versus a 2.3% per annum growth in the size of the world economy.[1] As for foreign direct investment, between 1992 and 2011, the total flow of foreign direct investment from all countries increased over 500%, while world trade by value grew by some 150% and world output by around 40%.[2] These trends have led to the globalization of production and the globalization of markets.[3]

The globalization of production has been increasing as companies take advantage of lower barriers to international trade and investment to disperse important parts of their production processes around the globe. Doing so enables them to take advantage of national differences in the cost and quality of factors of production such as labor, energy, land, and capital, which allows companies to lower their cost structures and boost profits. For example, foreign companies build nearly 65% by value of the Boeing Company's 787 commercial jet aircraft. Three Japanese companies build 35% of the 787, and another 20% is allocated to companies located in Italy, Singapore, and the UK.[4] Part of Boeing's rationale for outsourcing so much production to foreign suppliers is that these suppliers are the best in the world at performing their particular activity. Therefore, the result of having foreign suppliers build specific parts is a better final product and higher profitability for Boeing.

As for the globalization of markets, it has been argued that the world's economic system is moving from one in which national markets are distinct entities, isolated from each other by trade barriers and barriers of distance, time, and culture, toward a system in which national markets are merging into one huge global marketplace. Increasingly, customers around the world demand and use the same basic product offerings. Consequently, in many industries, it is no longer meaningful to talk about the German market, the U.S. market, or the Chinese market; there is only the global market. The global acceptance of Coca-Cola, Citigroup credit cards, Starbucks, McDonald's hamburgers, Samsung and Apple smartphones, IKEA furniture, and Microsoft's Windows operating system are examples of this trend.[5]

The trend toward the globalization of production and markets has several important implications for competition within an industry. First, industry boundaries do not stop at national borders. Because many industries are becoming global in scope, competitors and potential future competitors exist not only in a company's home market, but also in other national markets. Managers who analyze only their home market can be caught unprepared by the entry of efficient foreign competitors. The globalization of markets and production implies that companies around the globe are finding their home markets under attack from foreign competitors. For example, in Japan, American financial institutions such as J.P. Morgan have been making inroads against Japanese financial service institutions. In the United States, South Korea's Samsun has been battling Apple for a share of the smartphone market. In the European Union, the once-dominant Dutch company Philips has seen its market share in the customer electronics industry taken by Japan's Panasonic and Sony, and Samsung of South Korea.

Second, the shift from national to global markets has intensified competitive rivalry in many industries. National markets that once were consolidated oligopolies, dominated by three or four companies and subjected to relatively little foreign competition, have been transformed into segments of fragmented global industries in which a large number of companies battle each other for market share in many countries. This rivalry has threatened to drive down profitability and has made it more critical for companies to maximize their efficiency, quality, customer responsiveness, and innovative ability. The painful restructuring and downsizing that has been occurring at companies such as Kodak is as much a response to the increased intensity of global competition as it is to anything else. However, not all global industries are fragmented. Many remain consolidated oligopolies, except that now they are consolidated global (rather than national) oligopolies. In the videogame industry, for example, three companies are battling for global dominance: Microsoft from the United States and Nintendo and Sony from Japan. In the market for smartphones, Nokia of Finland is in a global battle with Apple of the United States, Samsung and LG from South Korea, and HTC from China.

Finally, although globalization has increased both the threat of entry and the intensity of rivalry within many formerly protected national markets, it has also created enormous opportunities for companies based in those markets. The steady decline in barriers to cross-border trade and investment has opened up many once-protected national markets to companies based outside these nations. Thus, for example, Western European, Japanese, and U.S. companies have accelerated their investments in the nations of Eastern Europe, Latin America, and Southeast Asia as they try to take advantage of growth opportunities in those areas.

National Competitive Advantage

Despite the globalization of production and markets, many of the most successful companies in certain industries are still clustered in a small number of countries. For example, many of the world's most successful biotechnology and computer companies are based in the United States, and many of the most successful consumer electronics companies are based in Japan, Taiwan, and South Korea. Germany is the base for many successful chemical and engineering companies. These facts suggest that the nation-state within which a company is based may have an important bearing on the competitive position of that company in the global marketplace.

In a study of national competitive advantage, Michael Porter identified four attributes of a national or country-specific environment that have an important impact on the global competitiveness of companies located within that nation:[6]

- *Factor endowments*: A nation's position in factors of production such as skilled labor or the infrastructure necessary to compete in a given industry
- *Local demand conditions*: The nature of home demand for the industry's product or service
- *Related and supporting industries*: The presence or absence in a nation of supplier industries and related industries that are internationally competitive
- *Firm strategy, structure, and rivalry*: The conditions in the nation governing how companies are created, organized, and managed, and the nature of domestic rivalry

Porter speaks of these four attributes as constituting the "diamond," arguing that companies from a given nation are most likely to succeed in industries or strategic groups in which the four attributes are favorable (see Figure 8.1). He also argues that the diamond's attributes form a mutually reinforcing system in which the effect of one attribute is dependent on the state of others.

Factor Endowments Factor endowments—the cost and quality of factors of production—are a prime determinant of the competitive advantage that certain countries might have in certain industries. Factors of production include basic factors, such as land, labor, capital, and raw materials, and advanced factors, such as technological knowhow, managerial

Figure 8.1	National Competitive Advantage

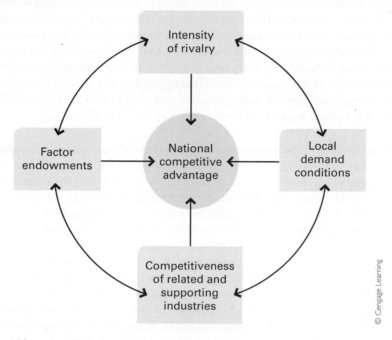

© Cengage Learning

Source: Adapted from M. E. Porter, "The Competitive Advantage of Nations," *Harvard Business Review,* March–April 1990, p. 77.

sophistication, and physical infrastructure (roads, railways, and ports). The competitive advantage that the United States enjoys in biotechnology might be explained by the presence of certain advanced factors of production—for example, technological knowhow—in combination with some basic factors, which might be a pool of relatively low-cost venture capital that can be used to fund risky start-ups in industries such as biotechnology.

Local Demand Conditions   Home demand plays an important role in providing the impetus for "upgrading" competitive advantage. Companies are typically most sensitive to the needs of their closest customers. Thus, the characteristics of home demand are particularly important in shaping the attributes of domestically made products and creating pressures for innovation and quality. A nation's companies gain competitive advantage if their domestic customers are sophisticated and demanding, and pressure local companies to meet high standards of product quality and produce innovative products. Japan's sophisticated and knowledgeable buyers of cameras helped stimulate the Japanese camera industry to improve product quality and introduce innovative models. A similar example can be found in the cellular phone equipment industry, where sophisticated and demanding local customers in Scandinavia helped push Nokia of Finland and Ericsson of Sweden to invest in cellular phone technology long before demand for cellular phones increased in other developed nations. As a result, Nokia and Ericsson, together with Motorola, became significant players in the global cellular telephone equipment industry.

Competitiveness of Related and Supporting Industries   The third broad attribute of national advantage in an industry is the presence of internationally competitive suppliers or related industries. The benefits of investments in advanced factors of production by related and supporting industries can spill over into an industry, thereby helping it achieve a strong competitive position internationally. Swedish strength in fabricated steel products (such as ball bearings and cutting tools) has drawn on strengths in Sweden's specialty steel industry. Switzerland's success in pharmaceuticals is closely related to its previous international success in the technologically related dye industry. One consequence of this process is that successful industries within a country tend to be grouped into clusters of related industries. Indeed, this is one of the most pervasive findings of Porter's study. One such cluster is the German textile and apparel sector, which includes high-quality cotton, wool, synthetic fibers, sewing machine needles, and a wide range of textile machinery.

Intensity of Rivalry   The fourth broad attribute of national competitive advantage in Porter's model is the intensity of rivalry of firms within a nation. Porter makes two important points here. First, different nations are characterized by different management ideologies, which either help them or do not help them to build national competitive advantage. For example, Porter noted the predominance of engineers in top management at German and Japanese firms. He attributed this to these firms' emphasis on improving manufacturing processes and product design. In contrast, Porter noted a predominance of people with finance backgrounds leading many U.S. firms. He linked this to U.S. firms' lack of attention to improving manufacturing processes and product design. He argued that the dominance of finance led to an overemphasis on maximizing short-term financial returns. According to Porter, one consequence of these different management ideologies was a relative loss of U.S. competitiveness in those engineering-based industries where manufacturing processes and product design issues are all-important (such as the automobile industry).

Porter's second point is that there is a strong association between vigorous domestic rivalry and the creation and persistence of competitive advantage in an industry. Rivalry compels companies to look for ways to improve efficiency, which makes them better international competitors. Domestic rivalry creates pressures to innovate, improve quality, reduce costs, and invest in upgrading advanced factors. All this helps to create world-class competitors.

Using the Framework   The framework just described can help managers to identify from where their most significant global competitors are likely to originate. For example, there is a cluster of computer service and software companies in Bangalore, India, that includes two of the fastest-growing information technology companies in the world, Infosys and Wipro. These companies have emerged as aggressive competitors in the global market. Both companies have recently opened up offices in the European Union and United States so they can better compete against Western rivals such as IBM and Hewlett Packard, and both are gaining share in the global marketplace.

The framework can also be used to help managers decide where they might want to locate certain productive activities. Seeking to take advantage of U.S. expertise in biotechnology, many foreign companies have set up research facilities in San Diego, Boston, and Seattle, where U.S. biotechnology companies tend to be clustered. Similarly, in an attempt to take advantage of Japanese success in consumer electronics, many U.S. electronics companies have set up research and production facilities in Japan, often in conjunction with Japanese partners.

Finally, the framework can help a company assess how tough it might be to enter certain national markets. If a nation has a competitive advantage in certain industries, it might be challenging for foreigners to enter those industries. For example, the highly competitive retailing industry in the United States has proved to be a very difficult industry for foreign companies to enter. Successful foreign retailers such as Britain's Tesco and Sweden's IKEA have found it tough going into the United States because the U.S. retailing industry is the most competitive in the world.

INCREASING PROFITABILITY AND PROFIT GROWTH THROUGH GLOBAL EXPANSION

Here we look at a number of ways in which global expansion can enable companies to increase and rapidly grow profitability. At the most basic level, global expansion increases the size of the market in which a company is competing, thereby boosting profit growth. Moreover, as we shall see, global expansion offers opportunities for reducing the cost structure of the enterprise or adding value through differentiation, thereby potentially boosting profitability.

Expanding the Market: Leveraging Products

A company can increase its growth rate by taking goods or services developed at home and selling them internationally; almost all multinationals started out doing this. Procter & Gamble, (P&G) for example, developed most of its best-selling products at home and then sold them around the world. Similarly, from its earliest days, Microsoft has always focused on selling its software around the world. Automobile companies such as Ford, Volkswagen, and Toyota also grew by developing products at home and then selling them in international markets. The returns from such a strategy are likely to be greater if indigenous competitors in the nations a company enters lack comparable products. Thus, Toyota has grown its profits by entering the large automobile markets of North America and Europe and by offering products that are differentiated from those offered by local rivals (Ford and GM) by superior quality and reliability.

It is important to note that the success of many **multinational companies** is based not just on the goods or services that they sell in foreign nations, but also upon the distinctive competencies (unique skills) that underlie the production and marketing of those goods or services. Thus Toyota's success is based on its distinctive competency in manufacturing automobiles. International expansion can be seen as a way for Toyota to generate greater returns from this competency. Similarly, P&G global success was based on more than its portfolio of consumer products; it was also based on the company's skills in mass-marketing consumer goods. P&G grew rapidly in international markets between 1950 and 1990 because it was one of the most skilled mass-marketing enterprises in the world and could "out-market" indigenous competitors in the nations it entered. Global expansion was, therefore, a way of generating higher returns from its competency in marketing.

Furthermore, one could say that because distinctive competencies are the most valuable aspects of a company's business model, the successful global expansion of manufacturing companies such as Toyota and P&G was based on the ability to transfer aspects of the business model and apply it to foreign markets.

The same can be said of companies engaged in the service sectors of an economy, such as financial institutions, retailers, restaurant chains, and hotels. Expanding the market

multinational company
A company that does business in two or more national markets.

for their services often means replicating their business model in foreign nations (albeit with some changes to account for local differences, which we will discuss in more detail shortly). Starbucks, for example, has expanded globally by taking the basic business model it developed in the United States and using that as a blueprint for establishing international operations. As detailed in the Running Case, Wal-Mart has done the same thing, establishing stores in 27 other nations since 1992 following the blueprint it developed in the United States.

FOCUS ON: Wal-Mart

Wal-Mart's Global Expansion

© iStockPhoto.com/caracterdesign

In the early 1990s, managers at Wal-Mart realized that the company's opportunities for growth in the United States were becoming more limited. By 1995 the company would be active in all 50 states. Management calculated that by the early 2000s, domestic growth opportunities would be constrained due to market saturation. So the company decided to expand globally. The critics scoffed. Wal-Mart, they said, was too American a company. Although its business model was well suited to the United States, it would not work in other countries where infrastructure was different, consumer tastes and preferences varied, and where established retailers already dominated.

Unperturbed, in 1991 Wal-Mart started to expand internationally with the opening of its first stores in Mexico. The Mexican operation was established as a joint venture with Cifera, the largest local retailer. Initially, Wal-Mart made a number of missteps that seemed to prove the critics right. Wal-Mart had problems replicating its efficient distribution system in Mexico. Poor infrastructure, crowded roads, and a lack of leverage with local suppliers, many of which could not or would not deliver directly to Wal-Mart's stores or distribution centers, resulted in stocking problems and raised costs and prices. Initially, prices at Wal-Mart in Mexico were some 20% above prices for comparable products in the company's U.S. stores, which limited Wal-Mart's ability to gain market share. There were also problems with merchandise selection. Many of the stores in Mexico carried items that were popular in the United States. These included ice skates, riding lawn mowers, leaf blowers, and fishing tackle. Not surprisingly, these items did not sell well in Mexico, so managers would slash prices to move inventory, only to find that the company's automated information systems would immediately order more inventory to replenish the depleted stock.

By the mid-1990s, however, Wal-Mart had learned from its early mistakes and adapted its operations in

Mexico to match the local environment. A partnership with a Mexican trucking company dramatically improved the distribution system, and more careful stocking practices meant that the Mexican stores sold merchandise that appealed more to local tastes and preferences. As Wal-Mart's presence grew, many of Wal-Mart's suppliers built factories close by its Mexican distribution centers so that they could better serve the company, which helped to further drive down inventory and logistics costs. In 1998, Wal-Mart acquired a controlling interest in Cifera. Today, Mexico is a leading light in Wal-Mart's international operations, where the company is more than twice the size of its nearest rival.

The Mexican experienced proved to Wal-Mart that it could compete outside of the United States. It has subsequently expanded into 27 other countries. In Canada, Britain, Germany, and Japan, Wal-Mart entered by acquiring existing retailers and then transferring its information systems, logistics, and management expertise. In Puerto Rico, Brazil, Argentina, and China, Wal-Mart established its own stores (although it added to its Chinese operations with a major acquisition in 2007). As a result of these moves, by 2013 the company had over 6,000 stores outside the United States, included 800,000 foreign employees on the payroll, and generated international revenues of more than $125 billion.

In addition to greater growth, expanding internationally has bought Wal-Mart two other major benefits. First, Wal-Mart has also been able to reap significant economies of scale from its global buying power. Many of Wal-Mart's key suppliers have long been international companies; for example, GE (appliances), Unilever (food products), and P&G (personal care products) are all major Wal-Mart suppliers that have long had their own global operations. By building international reach, Wal-Mart has been able to use its enhanced size to demand deeper discounts from the local operations

(continues)

FOCUS ON: Wal-Mart

(continued)

© iStockPhoto.com/caracterdesign

of its global suppliers, increasing the company's ability to lower prices to consumers, gain market share, and ultimately earn greater profits. Second, Wal-Mart has found that it is benefiting from the flow of ideas across the countries in which it now competes. For example, Wal-Mart's Argentina team worked with Wal-Mart's Mexican management to replicate a Wal-Mart store format developed first in Mexico, and to adopt the best practices in human resources and real estate that had been developed in Mexico. Other ideas, such as wine departments in its stores in Argentina, have now been integrated into layouts worldwide.

Moreover, Wal-Mart realized that if it didn't expand internationally, other global retailers would beat it to the punch. In fact, Wal-Mart does face significant global competition from Carrefour of France, Ahold of Holland, and Tesco from the United Kingdom. Carrefour, the world's second-largest retailer, is perhaps the most global of the lot. The pioneer of the hypermarket concept now operates in 26 countries and generates more than 50% of its sales outside France. Compared to this, Wal-Mart is a laggard with just 28% of its sales in 2012 generated from international operations. However, there is still room for significant global expansion—the global retailing market remains very fragmented.

For all of its success, Wal-Mart has hit some significant speed bumps in its drive for global expansion. In 2006 the company pulled out of two markets, South Korea—where it failed to decode the shopping habits of local customers—and Germany, where it could not beat incumbent discount stores on price. It is also struggling in Japan, where the company does not seem to have grasped the market's cultural nuances. One example is Wal-Mart's decision to sell lower-priced gift fruits at Japanese holidays, which failed because customers felt spending less would insult the recipient! It is interesting to note that the markets where Wal-Mart has struggled were all developed markets that it entered through acquisitions, where it faced long-established and efficient local competitors, and where shopping habits were very different than in the United States. In contrast, many of those markets where it has done better have been developing nations that lacked strong local competitors, and where Wal-Mart has built operations from the ground up (e.g., Mexico, Brazil, and, increasingly, China).

Source: A. Lillo, "Wal-Mart Says Global Going Good," *Home Textiles Today*, September 15, 2003, pp. 12–13; A. de Rocha and L. A. Dib, "The Entry of Wal-Mart into Brazil," *International Journal of Retail and Distribution Management* 30 (2002): 61–73; "Wal-Mart: Mexico's Biggest Retailer," *Chain Store Age*, June 2001, pp. 52–54; M. Flagg, "In Asia, Going to the Grocery Increasingly Means Heading for a European Retail Chain," *Wall Street Journal*, April 24, 2001, p. A21; "A Long Way from Bentonville," *The Economist*, September 20, 2006, pp. 38–39; "How Wal-Mart Should Right Itself," *Wall Street Journal*, April 20, 2007, pp. C1, C5; and Wal-Mart website, www.walmart.com.

Realizing Cost Economies from Global Volume

In addition to growing profits more rapidly, a company can realize cost savings from economies of scale, thereby boosting profitability, by expanding its sales volume through international expansion. Such scale economies come from several sources. First, by spreading the fixed costs associated with developing a product and setting up production facilities over its global sales volume, a company can lower its average unit cost. Thus, Microsoft can garner significant scale economies by spreading the $5 to $10 billion it cost to develop Windows 8 over global demand.

Second, by serving a global market, a company can potentially utilize its production facilities more intensively, which leads to higher productivity, lower costs, and greater profitability. For example, if Intel sold microprocessors only in the United States, it might only be able to keep its factories open for 1 shift, 5 days a week. But by serving a global market from the same factories, it might be able to utilize those assets for 2 shifts, 7 days a week. In other words, the capital invested in those factories is used more intensively if Intel sells to a global—as opposed to a national—market, which translates into higher capital productivity and a higher return on invested capital.

Third, as global sales increase the size of the enterprise, its bargaining power with suppliers increases, which may allow it to bargain down the cost of key inputs and boost profitability that way. For example, Wal-Mart has been able to use its enormous sales volume as a lever to bargain down the price it pays to suppliers for merchandise sold through its stores (see the Running Case).

In addition to the cost savings that come from economies of scale, companies that sell to a global rather than a local marketplace may be able to realize further cost savings from learning effects. We first discussed learning effects in Chapter 4, where we noted that employee productivity increases with cumulative increases in output over time. (For example, it costs considerably less to build the 100th aircraft from a Boeing assembly line than the 10th because employees learn how to perform their tasks more efficiently over time.) By selling to a global market, a company may be able to increase its sales volume more rapidly, and thus the cumulative output from its plants, which in turn should result in accelerated learning, higher employee productivity, and a cost advantage over competitors that are growing more slowly because they lack international markets.

Realizing Location Economies

Earlier in this chapter we discussed how countries differ from each other along a number of dimensions, including differences in the cost and quality of factors of production. These differences imply that some locations are more suited than others for producing certain goods and services.[7] **Location economies** are the economic benefits that arise from performing a value creation activity in the optimal location for that activity, wherever in the world that might be (transportation costs and trade barriers permitting). Thus, if the best designers for a product live in France, a firm should base its design operations in France. If the most productive labor force for assembly operations is in Mexico, assembly operations should be based in Mexico. If the best marketers are in the United States, the marketing strategy should be formulated in the United States—and so on. Apple, for example, designs the iPhone and develops the associated software in California, but undertakes final assembly in China, precisely because the company believes that these are the best locations in the world for carrying out these different value creation activities (Please see the opening case for Chapter 9).

location economies
The economic benefits that arise from performing a value creation activity in an optimal location.

Locating a value creation activity in the optimal location for that activity can have one of two effects: (1) it can lower the costs of value creation, helping the company achieve a low-cost position; or (2) it can enable a company to differentiate its product offering, which gives it the option of charging a premium price or keeping prices low and using differentiation as a means of increasing sales volume. Thus, efforts to realize location economies are consistent with the business-level strategies of low cost and differentiation.

In theory, a company that realizes location economies by dispersing each of its value creation activities to the optimal location for that activity should have a competitive advantage over a company that bases all of its value creation activities at a single location. It should be able to better differentiate its product offering and lower its cost structure more than its single-location competitor. In a world where competitive pressures are increasing, such a strategy may well become an imperative for survival.

Introducing transportation costs and trade barriers can complicate the process of realizing location economies. New Zealand might have a comparative advantage for low-cost car assembly operations, but high transportation costs make it an uneconomical location from which to serve global markets. Factoring transportation costs and trade barriers into the cost equation helps explain why some U.S. companies have shifted their production from Asia to Mexico. Mexico has three distinct advantages over many Asian countries as a location for value creation activities: low labor costs; Mexico's proximity to the large U.S. market, which reduces transportation costs; and the North American Free Trade Agreement (NAFTA), which has removed many trade barriers between Mexico, the United States, and Canada, increasing Mexico's attractiveness as a production site for the North American market. Thus, although the relative costs of value creation are important, transportation costs and trade barriers also must be considered in location decisions.

Leveraging the Skills of Global Subsidiaries

Initially, many multinational companies develop the valuable competencies and skills that underpin their business model in their home nation and then expand internationally, primarily by selling products and services based on those competencies. However, for more mature multinational enterprises that have already established a network of subsidiary operations in foreign markets, the development of valuable skills can just as well occur in foreign subsidiaries.[8] Skills can be created anywhere within a multinational's global network of operations, wherever people have the opportunity and incentive to try new ways of doing things. The creation of skills that help to lower the costs of production, or to enhance perceived value and support higher product pricing, is not the monopoly of the corporate center.

Leveraging the skills created within subsidiaries and applying them to other operations within the firm's global network may create value. For example, McDonald's is increasingly finding that its foreign franchisees are a source of valuable new ideas. Faced with slow growth in France, its local franchisees have begun to experiment with the menu, as well as the layout and theme of restaurants. Gone are the ubiquitous Golden Arches; gone too are many of the utilitarian chairs and tables and other plastic features of the fast-food giant. Many McDonald's restaurants in France now have hardwood floors, exposed brick walls, and even armchairs. Half of the 930 or so outlets in France have been upgraded to a level that would make them unrecognizable to an American. The menu, too, has been changed to include premier sandwiches, such as chicken on focaccia bread, priced some 30% higher than the average hamburger. In France, this strategy seems to be working. Following these changes, increases in same-store sales rose from 1% annually to 3.4%. Impressed with the impact, McDonald's executives are now considering adopting similar changes at other McDonald's restaurants in markets where same-store sales growth is sluggish, including the United States.[9]

For the managers of a multinational enterprise, this phenomenon creates important new challenges. First, managers must have the humility to recognize that valuable skills can arise anywhere within the firm's global network, not just at the corporate center. Second, they must establish an incentive system that encourages local employees to acquire new competencies. This is not as easy as it sounds. Creating new competencies involves a degree of risk. Not all new skills add value. For every valuable idea created by a McDonald's subsidiary in a foreign country, there may be several failures. The management of the multinational must install incentives that encourage employees to take necessary risks, and the company must reward people for successes and not sanction them unnecessarily for taking risks that did not pan out. Third, managers must have a process for identifying when valuable new skills have been created in a subsidiary, and, finally, they need to act as facilitators, helping to transfer valuable skills within the firm.

COST PRESSURES AND PRESSURES FOR LOCAL RESPONSIVENESS

Companies that compete in the global marketplace typically face two types of competitive pressures: *pressures for cost reductions and pressures to be locally responsive* (see Figure 8.2).[10] These competitive pressures place conflicting demands on a company. Responding to pressures for cost reductions requires that a company attempt to minimize its unit costs. To attain this goal, it may have to base its productive activities at the most favorable low-cost location, wherever in the world that might be. It may also need to offer a standardized product to the global marketplace in order to realize the cost savings that come from economies of scale and learning effects. On the other hand, responding to pressures to be locally responsive requires that a company differentiate its product offering and marketing strategy from country to country in an effort to accommodate the diverse demands arising from national differences in consumer tastes and preferences, business practices, distribution channels, competitive conditions, and government policies. Because differentiation across countries can involve significant duplication and a lack of product standardization, it may raise costs.

Whereas some companies, such as Company A in Figure 8.2, face high pressures for cost reductions and low pressures for local responsiveness, and others, such as Company B, face low pressures for cost reductions and high pressures for local responsiveness, many companies are in the position of Company C. They face high pressures for both cost reductions and local responsiveness. Dealing with these conflicting and contradictory pressures is a difficult strategic challenge, primarily because local responsiveness tends to raise costs.

Figure 8.2	Pressures for Cost Reductions and Local Responsiveness

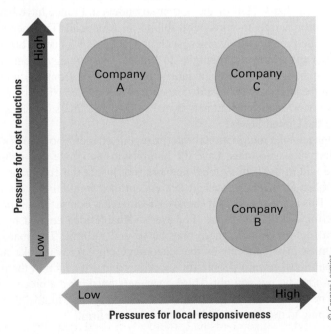

© Cengage Learning

Pressures for Cost Reductions

In competitive global markets, international businesses often face pressures for cost reductions. To respond to these pressures, a firm must try to lower the costs of value creation. A manufacturer, for example, might mass-produce a standardized product at an optimal location in the world to realize economies of scale and location economies. Alternatively, it might outsource certain functions to low-cost foreign suppliers in an attempt to reduce costs. Thus, many computer companies have outsourced their telephone-based customer service functions to India, where qualified technicians who speak English can be hired for a lower wage rate than in the United States. In the same vein, a retailer like Wal-Mart might push its suppliers (which are manufacturers) to also lower their prices. (In fact, the pressure that Wal-Mart has placed on its suppliers to reduce prices has been cited as a major cause of the trend among North American manufacturers to shift production to China.)[11] A service business, such as a bank, might move some back-office functions, such as information processing, to developing nations where wage rates are lower.

Cost reduction pressures can be particularly intense in industries producing commodity-type products where meaningful differentiation on non-price factors is difficult, and price is the main competitive weapon. This tends to be the case for products that serve universal needs. Universal needs exist when the tastes and preferences of consumers in different nations are similar if not identical, such as for bulk chemicals, petroleum, steel, sugar, and similar products. Pressures for cost reductions also exist for many industrial and consumer products—for example, hand-held calculators, semiconductor chips, personal computers, and liquid crystal display screens. Pressures for cost reductions are also intense in industries where major competitors are based in low-cost locations, where there is persistent excess capacity, and where consumers are powerful and face low switching costs. Many commentators have argued that the liberalization of the world trade and investment environment in recent decades, by facilitating greater international competition, has generally increased cost pressures.[12]

Pressures for Local Responsiveness

Pressures for local responsiveness arise from differences in consumer tastes and preferences, infrastructure and traditional practices, distribution channels, and host government demands. Responding to pressures to be locally responsive requires that a company differentiate its products and marketing strategy from country to country to accommodate these factors, all of which tend to raise a company's cost structure.

Differences in Customer Tastes and Preferences   Strong pressures for local responsiveness emerge when customer tastes and preferences differ significantly between countries, as they may for historic or cultural reasons. In such cases, a multinational company's products and marketing message must be customized to appeal to the tastes and preferences of local customers. The company is then typically pressured to delegate production and marketing responsibilities and functions to a company's overseas subsidiaries.

For example, the automobile industry in the 1980s and early 1990s moved toward the creation of "world cars." The idea was that global companies such as General Motors, Ford, and Toyota would be able to sell the same basic vehicle globally, sourcing it from centralized production locations. If successful, the strategy would have enabled automobile companies to reap significant gains from global scale economies. However, this strategy frequently ran aground upon the hard rocks of consumer reality. Consumers in different automobile markets have historically had different tastes and preferences, and these require different types of vehicles. North American consumers show a strong demand for pickup trucks. This is particularly true in the South and West where many families have a pickup truck as a second or third car. But in European countries, pickup trucks are seen purely as utility vehicles and are purchased primarily by firms rather than individuals. As a consequence, the product mix and marketing message need to be tailored to take into account the different nature of demand in North America and Europe.

Some commentators have argued that customer demands for local customization are on the decline worldwide.[13] According to this argument, modern communications and transport technologies have created the conditions for a convergence of the tastes and preferences of customers from different nations. The result is the emergence of enormous global markets for standardized consumer products. The worldwide acceptance of McDonald's hamburgers, Coca-Cola, GAP clothes, the Apple iPhone, and Sony television sets, all of which are sold globally as standardized products, is often cited as evidence of the increasing homogeneity of the global marketplace.

However, this argument may not hold in many consumer goods markets. Significant differences in consumer tastes and preferences still exist across nations and cultures. Managers in international businesses do not yet have the luxury of being able to ignore these differences, and they may not for a long time to come. For an example of a company that has discovered how important pressures for local responsiveness can still be, read the accompanying Strategy in Action 8.1 on MTV Networks.

8.1 STRATEGY IN ACTION

Local Responsiveness at MTV Networks

© iStockPhoto.com/Tom Nulens

MTV Networks has become a symbol of globalization. Established in 1981, the U.S.-based TV network has been expanding outside of its North American base since 1987 when it opened MTV Europe. Today MTV Networks figures that every second of every day over 2 million people are watching MTV around the world, the majority outside the United States. Despite its international success, MTV's global expansion got off to a weak start. In the 1980s, when the main programming fare was still music videos, it piped a single feed across Europe almost entirely composed of American programming with English-speaking veejays. Naively, the network's U.S. managers thought Europeans would flock to the American programming. But although viewers in Europe shared a common interest in a handful of global superstars, their tastes turned out to be surprisingly local. After losing share to local competitors, which focused more on local tastes, MTV changed it strategy in the 1990s. It broke its service into "feeds" aimed at national or regional markets. Although MTV Networks exercises creative control over these different feeds, and although all the channels have the same familiar frenetic look and feel of MTV in the United States, a significant share of the programming and content is now local.

Today an increasing share of programming is local in conception. Although many programming ideas still originate in the United States, with staples such as "The Real World" having equivalents in different countries, an increasing share of programming is local in conception. In Italy, "MTV Kitchen" combines cooking with a music countdown. "Erotica" airs in Brazil and features a panel of youngsters discussing sex. The Indian channel produces 21 homegrown shows hosted by local veejays who speak "Hinglish," a city-bred version of Hindi and English. Many feeds still feature music videos by locally popular performers. This localization push reaped big benefits for MTV, allowing the network to capture viewers back from local imitators.

Sources: M. Gunther, "MTV's Passage to India," *Fortune*, August 9, 2004, pp. 117–122; B. Pulley and A. Tanzer, "Sumner's Gemstone," *Forbes*, February 21, 2000, pp. 107–11; K. Hoffman, "Youth TV's Old Hand Prepares for the Digital Challenge," *Financial Times*, February 18, 2000, p. 8; presentation by Sumner M. Redstone, chairman and CEO, Viacom Inc., delivered to Salomon Smith Barney 11th Annual Global Entertainment Media, Telecommunications Conference, Scottsdale, AZ, January 8, 2001, archived at www.viacom.com; and Viacom 10K Statement, 2005.

Differences in Infrastructure and Traditional Practices   Pressures for local responsiveness also arise from differences in infrastructure or traditional practices among countries, creating a need to customize products accordingly. To meet this need, companies may have to delegate manufacturing and production functions to foreign subsidiaries. For example, in North America, consumer electrical systems are based on 110 volts, whereas in some European countries 240-volt systems are standard. Thus, domestic electrical appliances must be customized to take this difference in infrastructure into account. Traditional social practices also often vary across nations. In Britain, people drive on the left-hand side of the road, creating a demand for right-hand-drive cars, whereas in France and the rest of Europe, people drive on the right-hand side of the road (and therefore want left-hand-drive cars).

Although many of the country differences in infrastructure are rooted in history, some are quite recent. In the wireless telecommunications industry, different technical standards are found in different parts of the world. A technical standard known as GSM is common in Europe, and an alternative standard, CDMA, is more common in the United States and parts of Asia. The significance of these different standards is that equipment designed for GSM will not work on a CDMA network, and vice versa. Thus, companies that manufacture wireless handsets and infrastructure such as switches need to customize their product offerings according to the technical standard prevailing in a given country.

Differences in Distribution Channels   A company's marketing strategies may have to be responsive to differences in distribution channels among countries, which may necessitate delegating marketing functions to national subsidiaries. In the pharmaceutical industry, for example, the British and Japanese distribution system is radically different from the U.S. system. British and Japanese doctors will not accept or respond favorably to a U.S.-style high-pressure sales force. Thus, pharmaceutical companies must adopt different marketing practices in Britain and Japan compared with the United States—soft sell versus hard sell.

Similarly, Poland, Brazil, and Russia all have similar per capita income on the basis of purchasing power parity, but there are big differences in distribution systems across the three countries. In Brazil, supermarkets account for 36% of food retailing, in Poland for 18%, and in Russia for less than 1%.[14] These differences in channels require that companies adapt their own distribution and sales strategies.

Host Government Demands   Finally, economic and political demands imposed by host country governments may require local responsiveness. For example, pharmaceutical companies are subject to local clinical testing, registration procedures, and pricing restrictions, all of which make it necessary that the manufacturing and marketing of a drug should meet local requirements. Moreover, because governments and government agencies control a significant portion of the health-care budget in most countries, they are in a powerful position to demand a high level of local responsiveness. More generally, threats of protectionism, economic nationalism, and local content rules (which require that a certain percentage of a product should be manufactured locally) can dictate that international businesses manufacture locally.

CHOOSING A GLOBAL STRATEGY

Pressures for local responsiveness imply that it may not be possible for a firm to realize the full benefits from economies of scale and location economies. It may not be possible to serve the global marketplace from a single low-cost location, producing a globally standardized product, and marketing it worldwide to achieve economies of scale. In practice, the need to customize the product offering to local conditions may work against the implementation of such a strategy.

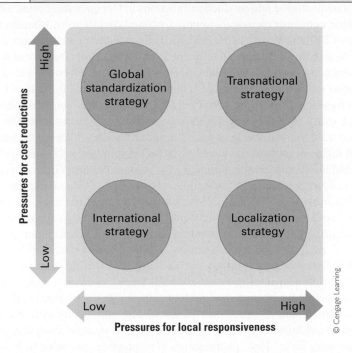

Figure 8.3   Four Basic Strategies

For example, automobile firms have found that Japanese, American, and European consumers demand different kinds of cars, and this necessitates producing products that are customized for local markets. In response, firms such as Honda, Ford, and Toyota are pursuing a strategy of establishing top-to-bottom design and production facilities in each of these regions so that they can better serve local demands. Although such customization brings benefits, it also limits the ability of a firm to realize significant scale economies and location economies.

In addition, pressures for local responsiveness imply that it may not be possible to leverage skills and products associated with a firm's distinctive competencies wholesale from one nation to another. Concessions often have to be made to local conditions. Despite being depicted as "poster child" for the proliferation of standardized global products, even McDonald's has found that it has to customize its product offerings (its menu) in order to account for national differences in tastes and preferences.

Given the need to balance the cost and differentiation (value) sides of a company's business model, how do differences in the strength of pressures for cost reductions versus those for local responsiveness affect the choice of a company's strategy? Companies typically choose among four main strategic postures when competing internationally: a global standardization strategy, a localization strategy, a transnational strategy, and an international strategy.[15] The appropriateness of each strategy varies with the extent of pressures for cost reductions and local responsiveness. Figure 8.3 illustrates the conditions under which each of these strategies is most appropriate.

Global Standardization Strategy

global standardization strategy

A business model based on pursuing a low-cost strategy on a global scale.

Companies that pursue a **global standardization strategy** focus on increasing profitability by reaping the cost reductions that come from economies of scale and location economies; that is, their business model is based on pursuing a low-cost strategy on a global scale. The production, marketing, and research and development (R&D) activities of companies pursuing a global strategy are concentrated in a few favorable locations. These companies try not to customize their product offerings and marketing strategy to local conditions because customization, which involves shorter production runs and the duplication of functions, can raise costs. Instead, they prefer to market a standardized product worldwide so that they can reap the maximum benefits from economies of scale. They also tend to use their cost advantage to support aggressive pricing in world markets. Dell is a good example of a company that pursues such a strategy.

This strategy makes most sense when there are strong pressures for cost reductions and demand for local responsiveness is minimal. Increasingly, these conditions prevail in many industrial goods industries, whose products often serve universal needs. In the semiconductor industry, for example, global standards have emerged, creating enormous demands for standardized global products. Accordingly, companies such as Intel, Texas Instruments, and Motorola all pursue a global strategy.

These conditions are not always found in many consumer goods markets, where demands for local responsiveness remain high. However, even some consumer goods companies are moving toward a global standardization strategy in an attempt to drive down their costs. P&G, which is featured in the Strategy in Action 8.2 feature, is one example of such a company.

Localization Strategy

A **localization strategy** focuses on increasing profitability by customizing the company's goods or services so that the goods provide a favorable match to tastes and preferences in different national markets. Localization is most appropriate when there are substantial differences across nations with regard to consumer tastes and preferences, and where cost pressures are not too intense. By customizing the product offering to local demands, the company increases the value of that product in the local market. On the downside, because it involves some duplication of functions and smaller production runs, customization limits the ability of the company to capture the cost reductions associated with mass-producing a standardized product for global consumption. The strategy may make sense, however, if the added value associated with local customization supports higher pricing, which would enable the company to recoup its higher costs, or if it leads to substantially greater local demand, enabling the company to reduce costs through the attainment of scale economies in the local market.

MTV is a good example of a company that has had to pursue a localization strategy. If MTV localized its programming to match the demands of viewers in different nations, it would have lost market share to local competitors, its advertising revenues would have fallen, and its profitability would have declined. Thus, even though it raised costs, localization became a strategic imperative at MTV.

At the same time, it is important to realize that companies like MTV still have to closely monitor costs. Companies pursuing a localization strategy still need to be efficient and, whenever possible, capture some scale economies from their global reach. As noted earlier, many automobile companies have found that they have to customize some of their product offerings to local market demands—for example, by producing large pickup trucks for U.S. consumers and small fuel-efficient cars for European and Japanese consumers. At the same time, these companies try to get some scale economies from their global volume by using common vehicle platforms and components across many different models and by manufacturing those platforms and components at efficiently scaled factories that are

localization strategy
A strategy focused on increasing profitability by customizing the company's goods or services so that the goods provide a favorable match to tastes and preferences in different national markets.

optimally located. By designing their products in this way, these companies have been able to localize their product offerings, yet simultaneously capture some scale economies.

Transnational Strategy

We have argued that a global standardization strategy makes most sense when cost pressures are intense and demands for local responsiveness limited. Conversely, a localization strategy makes most sense when demands for local responsiveness are high but cost pressures are moderate or low. What happens, however, when the company simultaneously faces both strong cost pressures and strong pressures for local responsiveness? How can managers balance out such competing and inconsistent demands? According to some researchers, pursuing what has been called a transnational strategy is the answer.

Two of these researchers, Christopher Bartlett and Sumantra Ghoshal, argue that in today's global environment, competitive conditions are so intense that, to survive, companies must do all they can to respond to pressures for both cost reductions and local responsiveness. They must try to realize location economies and economies of scale from global volume, transfer distinctive competencies and skills within the company, and simultaneously pay attention to pressures for local responsiveness.[15]

Moreover, Bartlett and Ghoshal note that, in the modern multinational enterprise, distinctive competencies and skills do not reside just in the home country but can develop in any of the company's worldwide operations. Thus, they maintain that the flow of skills and product offerings should not be all one way, from home company to foreign subsidiary. Rather, the flow should also be from foreign subsidiary to home country and from foreign subsidiary to foreign subsidiary. Transnational companies, in other words, must also focus on leveraging subsidiary skills.

transnational strategy
A business model that simultaneously achieves low costs, differentiates the product offering across geographic markets, and fosters a flow of skills between different subsidiaries in the company's global network of operations.

In essence, companies that pursue a **transnational strategy** are trying to develop a business model that simultaneously achieves low costs, differentiates the product offering across geographic markets, and fosters a flow of skills between different subsidiaries in the company's global network of operations. As attractive as this may sound, the strategy is not an easy one to pursue because it places conflicting demands on the company. Differentiating the product to respond to local demands in different geographic markets raises costs, which runs counter to the goal of reducing costs. Companies such as 3M and ABB (a Swiss-based multinational engineering conglomerate) have tried to embrace a transnational strategy and have found it difficult to implement in practice.

Indeed, how best to implement a transnational strategy is one of the most complex questions that large global companies are grappling with today. It may be that few, if any, companies have perfected this strategic posture. But some clues to the right approach can be derived from a number of companies. Consider, for example, the case of Caterpillar. The need to compete with low-cost competitors such as Komatsu of Japan forced Caterpillar to look for greater cost economies. However, variations in construction practices and government regulations across countries meant that Caterpillar also had to be responsive to local demands. Therefore, Caterpillar confronted significant pressures for cost reductions and for local responsiveness.

To deal with cost pressures, Caterpillar redesigned its products to use many identical components and invested in a few large-scale component-manufacturing facilities, sited at favorable locations, to fill global demand and realize scale economies. At the same time, the company augments the centralized manufacturing of components with assembly plants in each of its major global markets. At these plants, Caterpillar adds local product features, tailoring the finished product to local needs. Thus, Caterpillar is able to realize many of the benefits of global manufacturing while reacting to pressures for local responsiveness by differentiating its product among national markets.[16] Caterpillar started to pursue this strategy in the 1980s. By the 2000s it had succeeded in doubling output per employee, significantly reducing its overall cost structure in the process. Meanwhile, Komatsu and Hitachi, which are still wedded to a Japan-centric global strategy, have seen their cost advantages evaporate and have been steadily losing market share to Caterpillar.

However, building an organization capable of supporting a transnational strategy is a complex and challenging task. Indeed, some would say it is too complex, because the strategy implementation problems of creating a viable organizational structure and set of control systems to manage this strategy are immense. We shall return to this issue in Chapter 13.

International Strategy

Sometimes it is possible to identify multinational companies that find themselves in the fortunate position of being confronted with low cost pressures and low pressures for local responsiveness. Typically these enterprises are selling a product that serves universal needs, but because they do not face significant competitors, they are not confronted with pressures to reduce their cost structure. Xerox found itself in this position in the 1960s after its invention and commercialization of the photocopier. Strong patents protected the technology comprising the photocopier, so for several years Xerox did not face competitors—it had a monopoly. Because the product was highly valued in most developed nations, Xerox was able to sell the same basic product all over the world, and charge a relatively high price for it. At the same time, because it did not face direct competitors, the company did not have to deal with strong pressures to minimize its costs.

Historically, companies like Xerox have followed a similar developmental pattern as they build their international operations. They tend to centralize product development functions such as R&D at home. However, companies also tend to establish manufacturing and marketing functions in each major country or geographic region in which they do business. Although they may undertake some local customization of product offering and marketing strategy, this tends to be rather limited in scope. Ultimately, in most international companies, the head office retains tight control over marketing and product strategy.

Other companies that have pursued this strategy include P&G, which had historically always developed innovative new products in Cincinnati and thereafter transferred them wholesale to local markets. Microsoft is another company that has followed a similar strategy. The bulk of Microsoft's product development work takes place in Redmond, Washington, where the company is headquartered. Although some localization work is undertaken elsewhere, this is limited to producing foreign-language versions of popular Microsoft programs such as Office.

Changes in Strategy over Time

The Achilles heel of the international strategy is that, over time, competitors inevitably emerge, and if managers do not take proactive steps to reduce their cost structure, their company may be rapidly outflanked by efficient global competitors. This is exactly what happened to Xerox. Japanese companies such as Canon ultimately invented their way

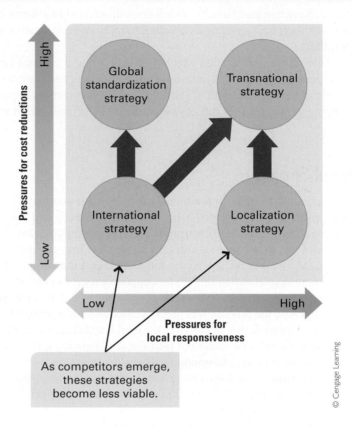

Figure 8.4   Changes over Time

As competitors emerge, these strategies become less viable.

© Cengage Learning

around Xerox's patents, produced their own photocopying equipment in very efficient manufacturing plants, priced the machines below Xerox's products, and rapidly took global market share from Xerox. Xerox's demise was not due to the emergence of competitors, for ultimately that was bound to occur, but rather to its failure to proactively reduce its cost structure in advance of the emergence of efficient global competitors. The message in this story is that an international strategy may not be viable in the long term, and to survive, companies that are able to pursue it need to shift toward a global standardization strategy, or perhaps a transnational strategy, ahead of competitors (see Figure 8.4).

The same can be said about a localization strategy. Localization may give a company a competitive edge, but if it is simultaneously facing aggressive competitors, the company will also need to reduce its cost structure—and the only way to do that may be to adopt a transnational strategy. Thus, as competition intensifies, international and localization strategies tend to become less viable, and managers need to orientate their companies toward either a global standardization strategy or a transnational strategy. Strategy in Action 8.2 describes how this process occurred at Coca-Cola.

8.2 STRATEGY IN ACTION

The Evolving Strategy of Coca-Cola

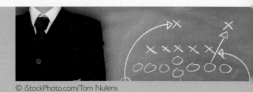
© iStockPhoto.com/Tom Nulens

Coca-Cola, the iconic American soda maker, has long been among the most international of enterprises. The company made its first move outside the United States in 1902, when it entered Cuba. By 1929, Coke was marketed in 76 countries. In World War II, Coke struck a deal to supply the U.S. military with Coca-Cola, wherever soldiers might be stationed. During this era, the company built 63 bottling plants around the world. Its global push continued after the war, fueled in part by the belief that the U.S. market would eventually reach maturity, and by the perception that huge growth opportunities were overseas. By 2012 Coca Cola was operating in more than 200 countries and over 80% of Coke's case volume was in international markets.

Through until the early 1980s, Coke's strategy could best be characterized as one of considerable localization. Local operations were granted a high degree of independence to oversee operations as managers saw fit. This changed in the 1980s and 1990s under the leadership of Roberto Goizueta, a talented Cuban immigrant who became the CEO of Coke in 1981. Goizueta placed renewed emphasis on Coke's flagship brands, which were extended with the introduction of Diet Coke, Cherry Coke, and similar flavors. His prime belief was that the main difference between the United States and international markets was the lower level of penetration overseas, where consumption per capita of colas was only 10 to 15% of the U.S. figure. Goizueta pushed Coke to become a global company, centralizing a great deal of management and marketing activities at the corporate headquarters in Atlanta, focusing on core brands, and taking equity stakes in foreign bottlers so that the company could exert more strategic control over them. This one-size-fits-all strategy was built around standardization and the realization of economies of scale by, for example, using the same advertising message worldwide.

Goizueta's global strategy was adopted by his successor, Douglas Ivester, but by the late 1990s the drive toward a one-size-fits-all strategy was running out of steam, as smaller, more nimble local competitors that were marketing local beverages began to halt the Coke growth engine. When Coke began failing to hit its financial targets for the first time in a generation,

Ivester resigned in 2000 and was replaced by Douglas Daft. Daft instituted a 180-degree shift in strategy. Daft's belief was that Coke needed to put more power back in the hands of local country managers. He thought that strategy, product development, and marketing should be tailored to local needs. He laid off 6,000 employees, many of them in Atlanta, and granted country managers much greater autonomy. Moreover, in a striking move for a marketing company, he announced that the company would stop using global advertisements, and he placed advertising budgets and control over creative content back in the hands of country managers.

Ivester's move was, in part, influenced by the experience of Coke in Japan, the company's second most profitable market, where the best-selling Coca-Cola product is not a carbonated beverage, but a canned cold coffee drink, Georgia Coffee, that is sold in vending machines. The Japanese experience seemed to signal that products should be customized to local tastes and preferences, and that Coke would do well to decentralize more decision-making authority to local managers.

However, the shift toward localization didn't produce the growth that had been expected, and by 2002, the trend was moving back toward more central coordination, with Atlanta exercising *oversight* over marketing and product development in different nations outside the United States. But this time, it was not the one-size-fits-all ethos of the Goizueta era. Under the leadership of Neville Isdell, who became CEO in March 2004, senior managers at the corporate head office now reviewed and helped to guide local marketing and product development. However, Isdell adopted the belief that strategy (including pricing, product offerings, and marketing message) should be varied from market to market to match local conditions. Isdell's position, in other words, represented a midpoint between the strategy of Goizueta and the strategy of Daft. Moreover, Isdell has stressed the importance of leveraging good ideas across nations, for example, such as Georgia Coffee. Having seen the success of this beverage in Japan, in 2007, Coke entered into a strategic alliance with Illycaffè, one of Italy's premier coffee makers, to build a global franchise for canned or bottled cold coffee beverages. Similarly,

(continues)

8.2 STRATEGY IN ACTION

(continued)

© iStockPhoto.com/Tom Nulens

in 2003, the Coke subsidiary in China developed a low-cost non-carbonated orange-based drink that has rapidly become one of the best-selling drinks in that nation. Seeing the potential of the drink, Coke rolled it out in other Asian countries such as Thailand, where it has been a huge hit.

Sources: "Orange Gold," *The Economist*, March 3, 2007, p. 68; P. Bettis, "Coke Aims to Give Pepsi a Routing in Cold Coffee War," *Financial Times*, October 17, 2007, p. 16; P. Ghemawat, *Redefining Global Strategy* (Boston, Mass: Harvard Business School Press, 2007); D. Foust, "Queen of Pop," *Business Week*, August 7, 2006, pp. 44–47; and W. J. Holstein, "How Coca-Cola Manages 90 Emerging Markets," *Strategy+Business*, November 7, 2011, www.strategy-business.com/article/00093?pg=0.

THE CHOICE OF ENTRY MODE

Any firm contemplating entering a different national market must determine the best mode or vehicle for such entry. There are five primary choices of entry mode: exporting, licensing, franchising, entering into a joint venture with a host country company, and setting up a wholly owned subsidiary in the host country. Each mode has its advantages and disadvantages, and managers must weigh these carefully when deciding which mode to use.[17]

Exporting

Most manufacturing companies begin their global expansion as exporters and only later switch to one of the other modes for serving a foreign market. Exporting has two distinct advantages: it avoids the costs of establishing manufacturing operations in the host country, which are often substantial, and it may be consistent with scale economies and location economies. By manufacturing the product in a centralized location and then exporting it to other national markets, the company may be able to realize substantial scale economies from its global sales volume. That is how Sony came to dominate the global television market, how many Japanese auto companies originally made inroads into the U.S. auto market, and how Samsung gained share in the market for computer memory chips.

There are a number of drawbacks to exporting. First, exporting from the company's home base may not be appropriate if there are lower-cost locations for manufacturing the product abroad (that is, if the company can achieve location economies by moving production elsewhere). Thus, particularly in the case of a company pursuing a global standardization or transnational strategy, it may pay to manufacture in a location where conditions are most favorable from a value creation perspective and then export from that location to the rest of the globe. This is not so much an argument against exporting, but rather an argument against exporting from the company's home country. For example, many U.S. electronics companies have moved some of their manufacturing to Asia because low-cost but highly skilled labor is available there. They export from Asia to the rest of the globe, including the United States (this is what Apple does with the iPhone, see the opening case for Chapter 9.

Another drawback is that high transport costs can make exporting uneconomical, particularly in the case of bulk products. One way of alleviating this problem is to manufacture bulk products on a regional basis, thereby realizing some economies from large-scale production while limiting transport costs. Many multinational chemical companies manufacture their products on a regional basis, serving several countries in a region from one facility.

Tariff barriers, too, can make exporting uneconomical, and a government's threat to impose tariff barriers can make the strategy very risky. Indeed, the implicit threat from the U.S. Congress to impose tariffs on Japanese cars imported into the United States led directly to the decision by many Japanese auto companies to set up manufacturing plants in the United States.

Finally, a common practice among companies that are just beginning to export also poses risks. A company may delegate marketing activities in each country in which it does business to a local agent, but there is no guarantee that the agent will act in the company's best interest. Often, foreign agents also carry the products of competing companies and thus have divided loyalties. Consequently, agents may not perform as well as the company would if it managed marketing itself. One way to solve this problem is to set up a wholly owned subsidiary in the host country to handle local marketing. In this way, the company can reap the cost advantages that arise from manufacturing the product in a single location and exercise tight control over marketing strategy in the host country.

Licensing

International licensing is an arrangement whereby a foreign licensee purchases the rights to produce a company's product in the licensee's country for a negotiated fee (normally, royalty payments on the number of units sold). The licensee then provides most of the capital necessary to open the overseas operation.[18] The advantage of licensing is that the company does not have to bear the development costs and risks associated with opening up a foreign market. Licensing therefore can be a very attractive option for companies that lack the capital to develop operations overseas. It can also be an attractive option for companies that are unwilling to commit substantial financial resources to an unfamiliar or politically volatile foreign market where political risks are particularly high.

Licensing has three serious drawbacks, however. First, it does not give a company the tight control over manufacturing, marketing, and strategic functions in foreign countries that it needs to have in order to realize scale economies and location economies—as companies pursuing both global standardization and transnational strategies try to do. Typically, each licensee sets up its manufacturing operations. Hence, the company stands little chance of realizing scale economies and location economies by manufacturing its product in a centralized location. When these economies are likely to be important, licensing may not be the best way of expanding overseas.

Second, competing in a global marketplace may make it necessary for a company to coordinate strategic moves across countries so that the profits earned in one country can be used to support competitive attacks in another. Licensing, by its very nature, severely limits a company's ability to coordinate strategy in this way. A licensee is unlikely to let a multinational company take its profits (beyond those due in the form of royalty payments) and use them to support an entirely different licensee operating in another country.

Third, there is risk associated with licensing technological knowhow to foreign companies. For many multinational companies, technological knowhow forms the basis of their competitive advantage, and they would want to maintain control over how this competitive advantage is put to use. By licensing its technology, a company can quickly lose control over it. RCA, for instance, once licensed its color television technology to a number of Japanese companies. The Japanese companies quickly assimilated RCA's technology and then used it to enter the U.S. market. Now the Japanese have a bigger share of the U.S. market than the RCA brand does.

There are ways of reducing this risk. One way is by entering into a cross-licensing agreement with a foreign firm. Under a cross-licensing agreement, a firm might license some valuable intangible property to a foreign partner and, in addition to a royalty payment, also request that the foreign partner license some of its valuable knowhow to the firm. Such agreements are reckoned to reduce the risks associated with licensing technological knowhow, as the licensee realizes that if it violates the spirit of a licensing contract (by using the knowledge obtained to compete directly with the licensor), the licensor can do the same to it. Put differently, cross-licensing agreements enable firms to hold each other hostage, thereby reducing the probability that they will behave opportunistically toward each other.[19] Such cross-licensing agreements are increasingly common in high-technology industries. For example, the U.S. biotechnology firm Amgen licensed one of its key drugs, Neupogen, to Kirin, the Japanese pharmaceutical company. The license gives Kirin the right to sell Neupogen in Japan. In return, Amgen receives a royalty payment, and through a licensing agreement it gains the right to sell certain Kirin products in the United States.

Franchising

In many respects, franchising is similar to licensing, although franchising tends to involve longer-term commitments than licensing. Franchising is basically a specialized form of licensing in which the franchiser not only sells intangible property to the franchisee (normally a trademark), but also insists that the franchisee agree to abide by strict rules governing how it does business. The franchiser will often assist the franchisee to run the business on an ongoing basis. As with licensing, the franchiser typically receives a royalty payment, which amounts to a percentage of the franchisee revenues.

Whereas licensing is a strategy pursued primarily by manufacturing companies, franchising, which resembles it in some respects, is a strategy employed chiefly by service companies. McDonald's provides a good example of a firm that has grown by using a franchising strategy. McDonald's has set down strict rules as to how franchisees should operate a restaurant. These rules extend to control the menu, cooking methods, staffing policies, and restaurant design and location. McDonald's also organizes the supply chain for its franchisees and provides management training and financial assistance.[20]

The advantages of franchising are similar to those of licensing. Specifically, the franchiser does not need to bear the development costs and risks associated with opening up a foreign market on its own, for the franchisee typically assumes those costs and risks. Thus, using a franchising strategy, a service company can build up a global presence quickly and at a low cost.

The disadvantages of franchising are less pronounced than in licensing. Because service companies often use franchising, there is no reason to consider the need for coordination of manufacturing to achieve experience curve and location economies. But, franchising may inhibit the firm's ability to take profits out of one country to support competitive attacks in another. A more significant disadvantage of franchising is quality control. The foundation of franchising arrangements is that the firm's brand name conveys a message to consumers about the quality of the firm's product. Thus, a business traveler checking in at a Four Seasons hotel in Hong Kong can reasonably expect the same quality of room, food, and service that would be received in New York, Hawaii, or Ontario, Canada. The Four Seasons name is supposed to guarantee consistent product quality. This presents a problem in that foreign franchisees may not be as concerned about quality as they are supposed to be, and the result of poor quality can extend beyond lost sales in a particular foreign market to a decline in the firm's worldwide reputation. For example, if the business traveler has a bad experience at the Four Seasons in Hong Kong, the traveler may never go to another Four Seasons hotel and may urge colleagues to do likewise. The geographical distance of the firm from its foreign franchisees can make poor quality difficult to detect. In addition, the numbers of franchisees—in the case of McDonald's, tens of thousands—can make quality control difficult. Due to these factors, quality problems may persist.

To reduce this problem, a company can set up a subsidiary in each country or region in which it is expanding. The subsidiary, which might be wholly owned by the company or a joint venture with a foreign company, then assumes the rights and obligations to establish franchisees throughout that particular country or region. The combination of proximity and the limited number of independent franchisees that need to be monitored reduces the quality control problem. Besides, because the subsidiary is at least partly owned by the company, the company can place its own managers in the subsidiary to ensure the kind of quality monitoring it wants. This organizational arrangement has proved very popular in practice; it has been used by McDonald's, KFC, and Hilton Worldwide to expand international operations, to name just three examples.

Joint Ventures

Establishing a joint venture with a foreign company has long been a favored mode for entering a new market. One of the most famous long-term joint ventures is the Fuji–Xerox joint venture to produce photocopiers for the Japanese market. The most typical form of joint venture is a 50/50 joint venture, in which each party takes a 50% ownership stake, and a team of managers from both parent companies shares operating control. Some companies have sought joint ventures in which they have a majority shareholding (for example, a 51% to 49% ownership split), which permits tighter control by the dominant partner.[21]

Joint ventures have a number of advantages. First, a company may feel that it can benefit from a local partner's knowledge of a host country's competitive conditions, culture, language, political systems, and business systems. Second, when the development costs and risks of opening up a foreign market are high, a company might gain by sharing these costs and risks with a local partner. Third, in some countries, political considerations make joint ventures the only feasible entry mode. Historically, for example, many U.S. companies found it much easier to obtain permission to set up operations in Japan if they joined with a Japanese partner than if they tried to enter on their own. This is why Xerox originally teamed up with Fuji to sell photocopiers in Japan.

Despite these advantages, there are major disadvantages with joint ventures. First, as with licensing, a firm that enters into a joint venture risks giving control of its technology to its partner. Thus, a proposed joint venture in 2002 between Boeing and Mitsubishi Heavy Industries to build a new wide-body jet (the 787), raised fears that Boeing might unwittingly give away its commercial airline technology to the Japanese. However, joint-venture agreements can be constructed to minimize this risk. One option is to hold majority ownership in the venture. This allows the dominant partner to exercise greater control over its technology—but it can be difficult to find a foreign partner who is willing to settle for minority ownership. Another option is to "wall off" from a partner technology that is central to the core competence of the firm, while sharing other technology.

A second disadvantage is that a joint venture does not give a firm the tight control over subsidiaries that it might need to realize experience curve or location economies. Nor does it give a firm the tight control over a foreign subsidiary that it might need for engaging in coordinated global attacks against its rivals. Consider the entry of Texas Instruments (TI) into the Japanese semiconductor market. When TI established semiconductor facilities in Japan, it did so for the dual purpose of checking Japanese manufacturers' market share and limiting the cash they had available for invading TI's global market. In other words, TI was engaging in global strategic coordination. To implement this strategy, TI's subsidiary in Japan had to be prepared to take instructions from corporate headquarters regarding competitive strategy. The strategy also required the Japanese subsidiary to run at a loss if necessary. Few if any potential joint-venture partners would have been willing to accept such conditions, as it would have necessitated a willingness to accept a negative return on investment. Indeed, many joint ventures establish a degree of autonomy that would make such direct control over strategic decisions all but impossible to establish.[22] Thus, to implement this strategy, TI set up a wholly owned subsidiary in Japan.

Wholly Owned Subsidiaries

A wholly owned subsidiary is one in which the parent company owns 100% of the subsidiary's stock. To establish a wholly owned subsidiary in a foreign market, a company can either set up a completely new operation in that country or acquire an established host country company and use it to promote its products in the host market.

Setting up a wholly owned subsidiary offers three advantages. First, when a company's competitive advantage is based on its control of a technological competency, a wholly owned subsidiary will normally be the preferred entry mode, because it reduces the company's risk of losing this control. Consequently, many high-tech companies prefer wholly owned subsidiaries to joint ventures or licensing arrangements. Wholly owned subsidiaries tend to be the favored entry mode in the semiconductor, computer, electronics, and pharmaceutical industries.

Second, a wholly owned subsidiary gives a company the kind of tight control over operations in different countries that it needs if it is going to engage in global strategic coordination—taking profits from one country to support competitive attacks in another.

Third, a wholly owned subsidiary may be the best choice if a company wants to realize location economies and the scale economies that flow from producing a standardized output from a single or limited number of manufacturing plants. When pressures on costs are intense, it may pay a company to configure its value chain in such a way that value added at each stage is maximized. Thus, a national subsidiary may specialize in manufacturing only part of the product line or certain components of the end product, exchanging parts and products with other subsidiaries in the company's global system. Establishing such a global production system requires a high degree of control over the operations of national affiliates. Different national operations must be prepared to accept centrally determined decisions as to how they should produce, how much they should produce, and how their output should be priced for transfer between operations. A wholly owned subsidiary would have to comply with these mandates, whereas licensees or joint-venture partners would most likely shun such a subservient role.

On the other hand, establishing a wholly owned subsidiary is generally the most costly method of serving a foreign market. The parent company must bear all the costs and risks of setting up overseas operations—in contrast to joint ventures, where the costs and risks are shared, or licensing, where the licensee bears most of the costs and risks. But the risks of learning to do business in a new culture diminish if the company acquires an established host country enterprise. Acquisitions, however, raise a whole set of additional problems, such as trying to marry divergent corporate cultures, and these problems may more than offset the benefits. (The problems associated with acquisitions are discussed in Chapter 10.)

Choosing an Entry Strategy

The advantages and disadvantages of the various entry modes are summarized in Table 8.1. Inevitably, there are tradeoffs in choosing one entry mode over another. For example, when considering entry into an unfamiliar country with a track record of nationalizing foreign-owned enterprises, a company might favor a joint venture with a local enterprise. Its rationale might be that the local partner will help it establish operations in an unfamiliar environment and speak out against nationalization should the possibility arise. But if the company's distinctive competency is based on proprietary technology, entering into a joint venture might mean risking loss of control over that technology to the joint venture partner, which would make this strategy unattractive. Despite such hazards, some generalizations can be offered about the optimal choice of entry mode.

Table 8.1 The Advantages and Disadvantages of Different Entry Modes

Entry Mode	Advantages	Disadvantages
Exporting	• Ability to realize location- and scale-based economies	• High transport costs • Trade barriers • Problems with local marketing agents
Licensing	• Low development costs and risks	• Inability to realize location- and scale-based economies • Inability to engage in global strategic coordination • Lack of control over technology
Franchising	• Low development costs and risks	• Inability to engage in global strategic coordination • Lack of control over quality
Joint Ventures	• Access to local partner's knowledge • Shared development costs and risks • Political dependency	• Inability to engage in global strategic coordination • Inability to realize location- and scale-based economies • Lack of control over technology
Wholly Owned Subsidiaries	• Protection of technology • Ability to engage in global strategic coordination • Ability to realize location- and scale-based economies	• High costs and risks

© Cengage Learning

Distinctive Competencies and Entry Mode   When companies expand internationally to earn greater returns from their differentiated product offerings, entering markets where indigenous competitors lack comparable products, the companies are pursuing an international strategy. The optimal entry mode for such companies depends to some degree upon the nature of their distinctive competency. In particular, we need to distinguish between companies with a distinctive competency in technological knowhow and those with a distinctive competency in management knowhow.

If a company's competitive advantage—its distinctive competency—derives from its control of proprietary technological knowhow, licensing and joint-venture arrangements should be avoided if possible to minimize the risk of losing control of that technology. Thus, if a high-tech company is considering setting up operations in a foreign country in order to profit from a distinctive competency in technological knowhow, it should probably do so through a wholly owned subsidiary.

However, this should not be viewed as a hard-and-fast rule. For instance, a licensing or joint-venture arrangement might be structured in such a way as to reduce the risks that licensees or joint-venture partners will expropriate a company's technological knowhow. (We consider this kind of arrangement in more detail later in the chapter when we discuss the issue of structuring strategic alliances.) Or consider a situation where a company believes its technological advantage will be short lived, and expects rapid imitation of its core technology by competitors. In this situation, the company might want to license its technology as quickly as possible to foreign companies in order to gain global acceptance of its technology before imitation occurs.[23] Such a strategy has some advantages. By licensing its technology to competitors, the company may deter them from developing their own, possibly superior, technology. It also may be able to establish its technology as the dominant design in the industry, ensuring a steady stream of royalty payments. Such situations aside, however, the attractions of licensing are probably outweighed by the risks of losing control of technology, and therefore licensing should be avoided.

The competitive advantage of many service companies, such as McDonald's or Hilton Worldwide, is based on management knowhow. For such companies, the risk of losing control of their management skills to franchisees or joint-venture partners is not that great. The reason is that the valuable asset of such companies is their brand name, and brand names are generally well protected by international laws pertaining to trademarks. Given this fact, many of the issues that arise in the case of technological knowhow do not arise in the case of management knowhow. As a result, many service companies favor a combination of franchising and subsidiaries to control franchisees within a particular country or region. The subsidiary may be wholly owned or a joint venture. In most cases, however, service companies have found that entering into a joint venture with a local partner in order to set up a controlling subsidiary in a country or region works best because a joint venture is often politically more acceptable and brings a degree of local knowledge to the subsidiary.

Pressures for Cost Reduction and Entry Mode   The greater the pressures for cost reductions, the more likely that a company will want to pursue some combination of exporting and wholly owned subsidiaries. By manufacturing in the locations where factor conditions are optimal and then exporting to the rest of the world, a company may be able to realize substantial location economies and substantial scale economies. The company might then want to export the finished product to marketing subsidiaries based in various countries. Typically, these subsidiaries would be wholly owned and have the responsibility for overseeing distribution in a particular country. Setting up wholly owned marketing subsidiaries is preferable to a joint venture arrangement or using a foreign marketing agent because it gives the company the tight control over marketing that might be required to coordinate a globally dispersed value chain. In addition, tight control over a local operation enables the company to use the profits generated in one market to improve its competitive position in another market. Hence companies pursuing global or transnational strategies prefer to establish wholly owned subsidiaries.

GLOBAL STRATEGIC ALLIANCES

Global strategic alliances are cooperative agreements between companies from different countries that are actual or potential competitors. Strategic alliances range from formal joint ventures, in which two or more companies have an equity stake, to short-term contractual agreements, in which two companies may agree to cooperate on a particular problem (such as developing a new product).

global strategic alliances
Cooperative agreements between companies from different countries that are actual or potential competitors.

Advantages of Strategic Alliances

Companies enter into strategic alliances with competitors to achieve a number of strategic objectives.[24] First, strategic alliances may facilitate entry into a foreign market. For example, many firms feel that if they are to successfully enter the Chinese market, they need a local partner who understands business conditions, and who has good connections. Thus, Warner Brothers entered into a joint venture with two Chinese partners to produce and distribute films in China. As a foreign film company, Warner found that if it wanted to produce films on its own for the Chinese market, it had to go through a complex approval process for every film. It also had to farm out distribution to a local company, which made doing business in China very difficult. Due to the participation of Chinese firms, however, the joint-venture films will require a streamlined approval process, and the venture will be able to distribute any films it produces. Moreover, the joint venture will be able to produce films for Chinese TV, something that foreign firms are not allowed to do.[25]

Second, strategic alliances allow firms to share the fixed costs (and associated risks) of developing new products or processes. An alliance between Boeing and a number of Japanese companies to build Boeing's latest commercial jetliner, the 787, was motivated by Boeing's desire to share the estimated $8 billion investment required to develop the aircraft.

Third, an alliance is a way to bring together complementary skills and assets that neither company could easily develop on its own.[26] In 2011, for example, Microsoft and Nokia established an alliance aimed at developing and marketing smartphones that used Microsoft's Windows 8 operating system. Microsoft contributed its software engineering skills, particularly with regard to the development of a version of its Windows operating system for smartphones, and Nokia contributed its design, engineering, and marketing knowhow. The first phones resulting from this collaboration reached the market in late 2012.

Fourth, it can make sense to form an alliance that will help firms establish technological standards for the industry that will benefit the firm. This was also a goal of the alliance between Microsoft and Nokia. The idea is to try to establish Windows 8 as the de facto operating system for smartphones in the face of strong competition from Apple, with its iPhone, and Google, whose Android operating system was the most widely used smartphone operating system in the world in 2012.

Disadvantages of Strategic Alliances

The advantages we have discussed can be very significant. Despite this, some commentators have criticized strategic alliances on the grounds that they give competitors a low-cost route to new technology and markets.[27] For example, a few years ago some commentators argued that many strategic alliances between U.S. and Japanese firms were part of an implicit Japanese strategy to keep high-paying, high-value-added jobs in Japan while gaining the project engineering and production process skills that underlie the competitive success of many U.S. companies.[28] They argued that Japanese success in the machine tool and semiconductor industries was built on U.S. technology acquired through strategic alliances. And they argued that U.S. managers were aiding the Japanese by entering alliances that channel new inventions to Japan and provide a U.S. sales and distribution network for the resulting products. Although such deals may generate short-term profits, so the argument goes, in the long term, the result is to "hollow out" U.S. firms, leaving them with no competitive advantage in the global marketplace.

These critics have a point; alliances have risks. Unless a firm is careful, it can give away more than it receives. But there are so many examples of apparently successful alliances between firms—including alliances between U.S. and Japanese firms—that this position appears extreme. It is difficult to see how the Microsoft–Toshiba alliance, the Boeing–Mitsubishi alliance for the 787, or the Fuji–Xerox alliance fit the critics' thesis. In these cases, both partners seem to have gained from the alliance. Why do some alliances benefit both firms while others benefit one firm and hurt the other? The next section provides an answer to this question.

Making Strategic Alliances Work

The failure rate for international strategic alliances is quite high. For example, one study of 49 international strategic alliances found that two-thirds run into serious managerial and financial troubles within 2 years of their formation, and that although many of these problems are ultimately solved, 33% are rated as failures by the parties involved.[29] The success of an alliance seems to be a function of three main factors: partner selection, alliance structure, and the manner in which the alliance is managed.

Partner Selection   One of the keys to making a strategic alliance work is to select the right kind of partner. A good partner has three principal characteristics. First, a good partner helps the company achieve strategic goals such as achieving market access, sharing the costs and risks of new-product development, or gaining access to critical core competencies. In other words, the partner must have capabilities that the company lacks and that it values. Second, a good partner shares the firm's vision for the purpose of the alliance. If two companies approach an alliance with radically different agendas, the chances are great that the relationship will not be harmonious and the partnership will end.

Third, a good partner is unlikely to try to exploit the alliance opportunistically for its own ends—that is, to expropriate the company's technological knowhow while giving away little in return. In this respect, firms with reputations for fair play probably make the best partners. For example, IBM is involved in so many strategic alliances that it would not pay the company to trample over individual alliance partners.[30] This would tarnish IBM's reputation of being a good ally and would make it more difficult for IBM to attract alliance partners. Because IBM attaches great importance to its alliances, it is unlikely to engage in the kind of opportunistic behavior that critics highlight. Similarly, their reputations make it less likely (but by no means impossible) that such Japanese firms as Sony, Toshiba, and Fuji, which have histories of alliances with non-Japanese firms, would opportunistically exploit an alliance partner.

To select a partner with these three characteristics, a company needs to conduct some comprehensive research on potential alliance candidates. To increase the probability of selecting a good partner, the company should collect as much pertinent, publicly available information about potential allies as possible; collect data from informed third parties, including companies that have had alliances with the potential partners, investment bankers who have had dealings with them, and some of their former employees; and get to know potential partners as well as possible before committing to an alliance. This last step should include face-to-face meetings between senior managers (and perhaps middle-level managers) to ensure that the chemistry is right.

Alliance Structure   Having selected a partner, the alliance should be structured so that the company's risk of giving too much away to the partner is reduced to an acceptable level. First, alliances can be designed to make it difficult (if not impossible) to transfer technology not meant to be transferred. Specifically, the design, development, manufacture, and service of a product manufactured by an alliance can be structured to "wall off" sensitive technologies to prevent their leakage to the other participant. In the alliance between General Electric and Snecma to build commercial aircraft engines, for example, GE reduced the risk of "excess transfer" by walling off certain steps of the production process. The modularization effectively cut off the transfer of what GE regarded as key competitive technology while permitting Snecma access to final assembly. Similarly, in the alliance between Boeing and the Japanese to build the 787, Boeing walled off research, design, and marketing functions considered central to its competitive position, while allowing the Japanese to share in production technology. Boeing also walled off new technologies not required for 787 production.[31]

Second, contractual safeguards can be written into an alliance agreement to guard against the risk of **opportunism** by a partner. For example, TRW has three strategic alliances with large Japanese auto component suppliers to produce seat belts, engine valves, and steering gears for sale to Japanese-owned auto assembly plants in the United States. TRW has clauses in each of its alliance contracts that bar the Japanese firms from competing with TRW to supply U.S.-owned auto companies with component parts. By doing this, TRW protects itself against the possibility that the Japanese companies are entering into the alliances merely as a means of gaining access to the North American market to compete with TRW in its home market.

Third, both parties in an alliance can agree in advance to exchange skills and technologies that the other covets, thereby ensuring a chance for equitable gain. Cross-licensing agreements are one way to achieve this goal.

Fourth, the risk of opportunism by an alliance partner can be reduced if the firm extracts a significant credible commitment from its partner in advance. The long-term alliance between Xerox and Fuji to build photocopiers for the Asian market perhaps best illustrates this. Rather than enter into an informal agreement or a licensing arrangement (which Fujifilm initially wanted), Xerox insisted that Fuji invest in a 50/50 joint venture to serve Japan and East Asia. This venture constituted such a significant investment in people, equipment, and facilities that Fujifilm was committed from the outset to making the alliance work in order to earn a return on its investment. By agreeing to the joint venture, Fuji essentially made a credible commitment to the alliance. Given this, Xerox felt secure in transferring its photocopier technology to Fuji.

opportunism
Seeking one's own self-interest, often through the use of guile.

Managing the Alliance   Once a partner has been selected and an appropriate alliance structure agreed on, the task facing the company is to maximize the benefits from the alliance. One important ingredient of success appears to be sensitivity to cultural differences. Many differences in management style are attributable to cultural differences, and managers need to make allowances for these when dealing with their partners. Beyond this, maximizing the benefits from an alliance seems to involve building trust between partners and learning from partners.[32]

Managing an alliance successfully requires building interpersonal relationships between the firms' managers, or what is sometimes referred to as *relational capital*.[33] This is one lesson that can be drawn from a strategic alliance between Ford and Mazda. Ford and Mazda set up a framework of meetings within which their managers not only discuss matters pertaining to the alliance, but also have time to get to know one another better. The belief is that the resulting friendships help build trust and facilitate harmonious relations between the two firms. Personal relationships also foster an informal management network between the firms. This network can then be used to help solve problems arising in more formal contexts (such as in joint committee meetings between personnel from the two firms).

Academics have argued that a major determinant of how much acquiring knowledge a company gains from an alliance is its ability to learn from its alliance partner.[34] For example, in a study of 15 strategic alliances between major multinationals, Gary Hamel, Yves Doz, and C. K. Prahalad focused on a number of alliances between Japanese companies and Western (European or American) partners.[35] In every case in which a Japanese company emerged from an alliance stronger than its Western partner, the Japanese company had made a greater effort to learn. Few Western companies studied seemed to want to learn from their Japanese partners. They tended to regard the alliance purely as a cost-sharing or risk-sharing device, rather than as an opportunity to learn how a potential competitor does business.

For an example of an alliance in which there was a clear learning asymmetry, consider the agreement between General Motors and Toyota Motor Corp. to build the Chevrolet Nova. This alliance was structured as a formal joint venture, New United Motor Manufacturing, in which both parties had a 50% equity stake. The venture owned an auto plant in Fremont, California. According to one of the Japanese managers, Toyota achieved most of its objectives from the alliance: "We learned about U.S. supply and transportation. And we got the confidence to manage U.S. workers." All that knowledge was then quickly transferred to Georgetown, Kentucky, where Toyota opened a plant of its own. By contrast, although General Motors (GM) got a new product, the Chevrolet Nova, some GM managers complained that their new knowledge was never put to good use inside GM. They say that they should have been kept together as a team to educate GM's engineers and workers about the Japanese system. Instead, they were dispersed to different GM subsidiaries.[36]

When entering an alliance, a company must take some measures to ensure that it learns from its alliance partner and then puts that knowledge to good use within its own organization. One suggested approach is to educate all operating employees about the partner's strengths and weaknesses and make clear to them how acquiring particular skills will bolster their company's competitive position. For such learning to be of value, the knowledge acquired from an alliance must be diffused throughout the organization—which did not happen at GM. To spread this knowledge, the managers involved in an alliance should be used as a resource in familiarizing others within the company about the skills of an alliance partner.

SUMMARY OF CHAPTER

1. For some companies, international expansion represents a way of earning greater returns by transferring the skills and product offerings derived from their distinctive competencies to markets where indigenous competitors lack those skills. As barriers to international trade have fallen, industries have expanded beyond national boundaries and industry competition and opportunities have increased.

2. Because of national differences, it pays for a company to base each value creation activity it performs at the location where factor conditions are most conducive to the performance of that activity. This strategy is known as focusing on the attainment of location economies.

3. By building sales volume more rapidly, international expansion can help a company gain a cost advantage through the realization of scale economies and learning effects.

4. The best strategy for a company to pursue may depend on the kind of pressures it must cope with: pressures for cost reductions or for local responsiveness. Pressures for cost reductions are greatest in industries producing commodity-type products, where price is the main competitive weapon. Pressures for local responsiveness arise from differences in consumer tastes and preferences, as well as from national infrastructure and traditional practices, distribution channels, and host government demands.

5. Companies pursuing an international strategy transfer the skills and products derived from distinctive competencies to foreign markets, while undertaking some limited local customization.

6. Companies pursuing a localization strategy customize their product offerings, marketing strategies, and business strategies to national conditions.

7. Companies pursuing a global standardization strategy focus on reaping the cost reductions that come from scale economies and location economies.

8. Many industries are now so competitive that companies must adopt a transnational strategy. This involves a simultaneous focus upon reducing costs, transferring skills and products, and being locally responsive. Implementing such a strategy may not be easy.

9. There are five different ways of entering a foreign market: exporting, licensing, franchising, entering into a joint venture, and setting up a wholly owned subsidiary. The optimal choice among entry modes depends on the company's strategy.

10. Strategic alliances are cooperative agreements between actual or potential competitors. The advantages of alliances are that they facilitate entry into foreign markets, enable partners to share the fixed costs and risks associated with new products and processes, facilitate the transfer of complementary skills between companies, and help companies establish technical standards.

11. The drawbacks of a strategic alliance are that the company risks giving away technological knowhow and market access to its alliance partner while getting very little in return.

12. The disadvantages associated with alliances can be reduced if the company selects partners carefully, paying close attention to reputation, and structures the alliance in order to avoid unintended transfers of knowhow.

DISCUSSION QUESTIONS

1. Plot the position of the following companies on Figure 8.3: Microsoft, Google, Coca-Cola, Dow Chemicals, Pfizer, and McDonald's. In each case, justify your answer.

2. Are the following global standardization industries, or industries where localization is more important: bulk chemicals, pharmaceuticals, branded food products, moviemaking, television manufacture, personal computers, airline travel, fashion retailing?

3. Discuss how the need for control over foreign operations varies with the strategy and distinctive competencies of a company. What are the implications of this relationship for the choice of entry mode?

4. Licensing proprietary technology to foreign competitors is the best way to give up a company's competitive advantage. Discuss.

5. What kind of companies stand to gain the most from entering into strategic alliances with potential competitors? Why?

PRACTICING STRATEGIC MANAGEMENT

© iStockPhoto.com/Urilux

Small-Group Exercise: Developing a Global Strategy

Break into groups of three to five people, and discuss the following scenario. Appoint one group member as a spokesperson who will communicate your findings to the class. You work for a company in the soft drink industry that has developed a line of carbonated fruit-based drinks. You have already established a significant presence in your home market, and now you are planning the global strategy development of the company in the soft drink industry. You need to decide the following:

1. What overall strategy to pursue: a global standardization strategy, a localization strategy, an international strategy, or a transnational strategy
2. Which markets to enter first
3. What entry strategy to pursue (e.g., franchising, joint venture, wholly owned subsidiary)
4. What information do you need to make this kind of decision? Considering what you do know, what strategy would you recommend?

STRATEGY SIGN-ON

© iStockPhoto.com/Ninoslav Dotlic

Article File 8

Find an example of a multinational company that in recent years has switched its strategy from a localization, international, or global standardization strategy to a transnational strategy. Identify why the company made the switch and any problems that the company may be encountering while it tries to change its strategic orientation.

Strategic Management Project: Module 8

This module requires you to identify how your company might profit from global expansion, the strategy that your company should pursue globally, and the entry mode that it might favor. With the information you have at your disposal, answer the questions regarding the following two situations:

Your company is already doing business in other countries.

1. Is your company creating value or lowering the costs of value creation by realizing location economies, transferring distinctive competencies abroad, or realizing cost economies from the economies of scale? If not, does it have the potential to do so?

(continues)

STRATEGY SIGN ON

© iStockPhoto.com/Ninoslav Dotlic

(continued)

2. How responsive is your company to differences among nations? Does it vary its product and marketing message from country to country? Should it?
3. What are the cost pressures and pressures for local responsiveness in the industry in which your company is based?
4. What strategy is your company pursuing to compete globally? In your opinion, is this the correct strategy, given cost pressures and pressures for local responsiveness?
5. What major foreign market does your company serve, and what mode has it used to enter this market? Why is your company active in these markets and not others? What are the advantages and disadvantages of using this mode? Might another mode be preferable?

Your company is not yet doing business in other countries.

1. What potential does your company have to add value to its products or lower the costs of value creation by expanding internationally?
2. On the international level, what are the cost pressures and pressures for local responsiveness in the industry in which your company is based? What implications do these pressures have for the strategy that your company might pursue if it chose to expand globally?
3. What foreign market might your company enter, and what entry mode should it use to enter this market? Justify your answer.

ETHICAL DILEMMA

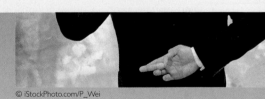

© iStockPhoto.com/P_Wei

Your company has established a manufacturing subsidiary in southern China. Labor costs at this factory are much lower than in your home market. Employees also work 10 hours a day, 6 days a week, with mandatory overtime often pushing that to 12 hours a day. They are paid the local minimum wage. The factory also does not adhere to the same standards for environmental protection and employee safety as those mandated in your home nation. On a visit to the factory you notice these things, and ask the expatriate manager who heads up the operation if he should be doing something to improve working conditions and environmental protection. He replies that his view is that "when in Rome, do as the Romans

do." He argues that the situation at the factory is normal for China, and he is complying at with all local regulations and laws. Moreover, he notes that the company established this subsidiary to have a low-cost manufacturing base. Improving working conditions and environmental standards beyond those mandated by local laws would not be consistent with this goal.

Is the position taken by the expatriate manager the correct one? Is it ethical? What are the potential negative consequences, if any, of continuing to operate in this manner? What benefits might there be to the company of taking steps to raise working conditions and environmental protection beyond those mandated by local regulations?

CLOSING CASE

For six years after Andrea Jung became CEO in 1999 of Avon Products, the beauty products company famous for its direct sales model, revenues grew in excess of 10% a year. Profits tripled, making Jung a Wall Street favorite. Then in 2005, the success story started to turn ugly. Avon, which derives as much as 70% of its revenues from international markets, mostly in developing nations, suddenly began losing sales across the globe. A ban on direct sales had hurt its business in China (the Chinese government had accused companies that used a direct sales model of engaging in pyramid schemes and of creating "cults"). To compound matters, economic weakness in Eastern Europe, Russia, and Mexico, all drivers of Avon's success, stalled growth there. The dramatic turn of events took investors by surprise. In May 2005 Jung had told investors that Avon would exceed Wall Street's targets for the year. By September she was rapidly backpedaling, and the stock fell 45%.

With her job on the line, Jung began to reevaluate Avon's global strategy. Until this point, the company had expanded primarily by replicating its U.S. strategy and organization in other countries. When it entered a nation, it gave country managers considerable autonomy. All used the Avon brand name and adopted the direct sales model that has been the company's hallmark. The result was an army of 5 million Avon representatives around the world, all independent contractors, who sold the company's skin care and makeup products. However, many country managers also set up their own local manufacturing operations and supply chains, were responsible for local marketing, and developed their own new products. In Jung's words, "they were the king or queen of every decision." The result was a lack of consistency in marketing strategy from nation to nation, extensive duplication of manufacturing operations and supply chains, and a profusion of new products, many of which were not profitable. In Mexico, for example, the roster of products for sale had ballooned to 13,000. The company had 15 layers of management, making accountability and communication problematic. There was also a distinct lack of data-driven analysis of new-product opportunities, with country managers often making decisions based on their intuition or gut feeling.

Jung's turnaround strategy involved several elements. To help transform Avon, she hired seasoned managers from well-known global consumer products companies such as P&G and Unilever. She flattened the organization to improve communication, performance visibility, and accountability, reducing the number of management layers to just eight and laying off 30% of managers. Manufacturing was consolidated in a number of regional centers, and supply chains were rationalized, eliminating duplication and reducing costs by more than $1 billion a year. Rigorous return-on-investment criteria were introduced to evaluate product profitability. As a consequence, 25% of Avon's products were discontinued. New-product decisions were centralized at Avon's headquarters. Jung also invested in centralized product development. The goal was to develop and introduce blockbuster new products that could be positioned as global brands. And Jung pushed the company to emphasize its value proposition in every national market, which could be characterized as high quality at a low price.

By 2007 this strategy was starting to yield dividends. The company's performance improved and growth resumed. It didn't hurt that Jung, a Chinese-American who speaks Mandarin, was instrumental in persuading Chinese authorities to rescind the ban on direct sales, allowing Avon to recruit 400,000 new representatives in China. Then in 2008 and 2009, the global financial crisis hit. Jung's reaction: This was an opportunity for Avon to expand its business. In 2009, Avon ran ads around the world aimed at recruiting sales representatives. In the ads, female sales representatives talked about working for Avon. "I can't get laid off, I can't get fired," is what one said. Phones started to ring of the hook, and Avon was quickly able to expand its global sales force. She also instituted an aggressive pricing strategy, and packaging was redesigned for a more elegant look at no additional cost. The idea was to emphasize the "value for money" the Avon products represented. Media stars were used in ads to help market the company's products, and Avon pushed its representatives to use online social networking sites as a medium for representatives to market themselves.

The result of all this was initially good: In the difficult years of 2008 and 2009, Avon gained global market share and its financial performance improved. However, the company started to stumble again in 2010 and 2011. The reasons were complex. In many of Avon's important emerging markets the company found itself increasingly on the defensive against rivals such as P&G that were building a strong retail presence there. Meanwhile, sales in developed markets sputtered

in the face of persistently slow economic growth. To complicate matters, there were reports of numerous operational mistakes—problems with implementing information systems, for example—that were costly for the company. Avon also came under fire for a possible violation of the Foreign Corrupt Practices Act when it was revealed that some executives in China had been paying bribes to local government officials. Under pressure from investors, in December 2011 Andrea Jung relinquished her CEO role, although she will stay on as Chairman until at least 2014.

Sources: A. Chang, "Avon's Ultimate Makeover Artist," *Market-Watch,* December 3, 2009; N. Byrnes, "Avon: More Than Cosmetic Change," *Businessweek,* March 3, 2007, pp. 62–63; J. Hodson, "Avon 4Q Profit Jumps on Higher Overseas Sales," *Wall Street Journal* (online), February 4, 2010; and M. Boyle, "Avon Surges After Saying That Andrea Jung Will Step Down as CEO," Bloomberg Business Week, December 15, 2011.

CASE DISCUSSION QUESTIONS

1. What strategy was Avon pursuing until the mid-2000s? What were the advantages of this strategy? What were the disadvantages?
2. What changes did Andrea Jung make in Avon's strategy after 2005? What were the benefits of these changes? Can you see any drawbacks?
3. In terms of the framework introduced in this chapter, what strategy was Avon pursuing by the late 2000s?
4. Do you think that Avon's problems in 2010 and 2011 were a result of the changes in its strategy, or were there other reasons for this?

KEY TERMS

Multinational company 256
Location economies 259
Global standardization strategy 265
Localization strategy 266
Transnational strategy 267
Global strategic alliances 278
Opportunism 280

NOTES

[1]World Trade Organization (WTO), *International Trade Statistics 2012* (Geneva: WHO, 2012).

[2]Ibid.; and United Nations, *World Investment Report, 2012* (New York and Geneva: United Nations, 2012).

[3]P. Dicken, *Global Shift* (New York: Guilford Press, 1992).

[4]D. Pritchard, "Are Federal Tax Laws and State Subsides for Boeing 7E7 Selling America Short?" *Aviation Week,* April 12, 2004, pp. 74–75.

[5]T. Levitt, "The Globalization of Markets," *Harvard Business Review,* May–June 1983, pp. 92–102.

[6]M. E. Porter, *The Competitive Advantage of Nations* (New York: Free Press, 1990). See also R. Grant, "Porter's Competitive Advantage of Nations: An Assessment," *Strategic Management Journal* 7 (1991): 535–548.

[7]Porter, *Competitive Advantage of Nations.*

[8]See J. Birkinshaw and N. Hood, "Multinational Subsidiary Evolution: Capability and Charter Change in Foreign Owned Subsidiary Companies," *Academy of Management Review* 23 (October 1998), pp. 773–795; A. K. Gupta and V. J. Govindarajan, "Knowledge Flows Within Multinational Corporations," *Strategic Management Journal* 21 (2000), pp. 473–496; V. J. Govindarajan and A. K. Gupta, *The Quest for Global Dominance* (San Francisco: Jossey-Bass, 2001); T. S. Frost, J. M. Birkinshaw, and P. C. Ensign, "Centers of Excellence in Multinational Corporations," *Strategic Management Journal* 23 (2002), pp. 997–1018; and U. Andersson, M. Forsgren, and U. Holm, "The Strategic Impact of External Networks,"

Strategic Management Journal 23 (2002), pp. 979–996.

[9]S. Leung, "Armchairs, TVs and Espresso: Is It McDonald's?" *Wall Street Journal,* August 30, 2002, pp. A1, A6.

[10]C. K. Prahalad and Yves L. Doz, *The Multinational Mission: Balancing Local Demands and Global Vision* (New York: Free Press, 1987). See also J. Birkinshaw, A. Morrison, and J. Hulland, "Structural and Competitive Determinants of a Global Integration Strategy," *Strategic Management Journal* 16 (1995): 637–655.

[11]J. E. Garten, "Walmart Gives Globalization a Bad Name," *Business Week*, March 8, 2004, p. 24.

[12]Prahalad and Doz, *Multinational Mission.* Prahalad andDoz actually talk about local responsivenessrather than local customization.

[13]Levitt, "Globalization of Markets."

[14]W.W. Lewis. *The Power of Productivity* (Chicago, University of Chicago Press, 2004).

[15]Bartlett and Ghoshal, *Managing Across Borders.*

[16]Ibid.

[17]T. Hout, M. E. Porter, and E. Rudden, "How Global Companies Win Out," *Harvard Business Review,* September–October 1982, pp. 98–108.

[18]This section draws on numerous studies, including: C. W. L. Hill, P. Hwang, and W. C. Kim, "An Eclectic Theory of the Choice of International Entry Mode," *Strategic Management Journal* 11 (1990), pp. 117–28; C. W. L. Hill and W. C. Kim, "Searching for a Dynamic Theory of the Multinational Enterprise:

A Transaction Cost Model," *Strategic Management Journal* 9 (Special Issue on Strategy Content, 1988), pp. 93–104; E. Anderson and H. Gatignon, "Modes of Foreign Entry: A Transaction Cost Analysis and Propositions," *Journal of International Business Studies* 17 (1986), pp. 1–26; F. R. Root, *Entry Strategies for International Markets* (Lexington, MA: D. C. Heath, 1980); A. Madhok, "Cost, Value and Foreign Market Entry: The Transaction and the Firm," *Strategic Management Journal* 18 (1997), pp. 39–61; K. D. Brouthers and L. B. Brouthers, "Acquisition or Greenfield Start-Up?" *Strategic Management Journal* 21:1 (2000): 89–97; X. Martin and R. Salmon, "Knowledge Transfer Capacity and Its Implications for the Theory of the Multinational Enterprise," *Journal of International Business Studies,* July 2003, p. 356; and A. Verbeke, "The Evolutionary View of the MNE and the Future of Internalization Theory," *Journal of International Business Studies,* November 2003, pp. 498–515.

[19]F. J. Contractor, "The Role of Licensing in International Strategy," *Columbia Journal of World Business*, Winter 1982, pp. 73–83.

[20]Andrew E. Serwer, "McDonald's Conquers the World," *Fortune,* October 17, 1994, pp. 103–116.

[21]For an excellent review of the basic theoretical literature of joint ventures, see B. Kogut, "Joint Ventures: Theoretical and Empirical Perspectives," *Strategic Management Journal* 9 (1988), pp. 319–32. More recent studies include T. Chi, "Option to Acquire or Divest a Joint Venture," *Strategic Management Journal* 21:6

(2000): 665–688; H. Merchant and D. Schendel, "How Do International Joint Ventures Create Shareholder Value?" *Strategic Management Journal* 21:7 (2000): 723–37; H. K. Steensma and M. A. Lyles, "Explaining IJV Survival in a Transitional Economy Through Social Exchange and Knowledge Based Perspectives," *Strategic Management Journal* 21:8 (2000): 831–851; and J. F. Hennart and M. Zeng, "Cross Cultural Differences and Joint Venture Longevity," *Journal of International Business Studies,* December 2002, pp. 699–717.

22J. A. Robins, S. Tallman, and K. Fladmoe-Lindquist, "Autonomy and Dependence of International Cooperative Ventures," *Strategic Management Journal,* October 2002, pp. 881–902.

23C. W. L. Hill, "Strategies for Exploiting Technological Innovations," *Organization Science* 3 (1992): 428–441.

24See K. Ohmae, "The Global Logic of Strategic Alliances," *Harvard Business Review*, March–April 1989, pp. 143–154; G. Hamel, Y. L. Doz, and C. K. Prahalad, "Collaborate with Your Competitors and Win!" *Harvard Business Review,* January–February 1989, pp. 133–139; W. Burgers, C. W. L. Hill, and W. C. Kim, "Alliances in the Global Auto Industry," *Strategic Management Journal* 14 (1993): 419–432; and P. Kale, H. Singh, and H. Perlmutter, "Learning and Protection of Proprietary Assets in Strategic Alliances: Building Relational Capital," *Strategic Management Journal* 21 (2000): 217–237.

25L. T. Chang, "China Eases Foreign Film Rules," *Wall Street Journal,* October 15, 2004, p. B2.

26B. L. Simonin, "Transfer of Marketing Knowhow in International Strategic Alliances," *Journal of International Business Studies,* 1999, pp. 463–91, and J. W. Spencer, "Firms' Knowledge Sharing Strategies in the Global Innovation System," *Strategic Management Journal* 24 (2003): 217–233.

27Kale et al., "Learning and Protection of Proprietary Assets."

28R. B. Reich and E. D. Mankin, "Joint Ventures with Japan Give Away Our Future," *Harvard Business Review,* March–April 1986, pp. 78–90.

29J. Bleeke and D. Ernst, "The Way to Win in Cross-Border Alliances," *Harvard Business Review,* November–December 1991, pp. 127–135.

30E. Booker and C. Krol, "IBM Finds Strength in Alliances," *B to B,* February 10, 2003, pp. 3, 27.

31W. Roehl and J. F. Truitt, "Stormy Open Marriages Are Better," *Columbia Journal of World Business,* Summer 1987, pp. 87–95.

32See T. Khanna, R. Gulati, and N. Nohria, "The Dynamics of Learning Alliances: Competition, Cooperation, and Relative Scope," *Strategic Management Journal* 19 (1998): 193–210; Kale et al., "Learning and Protection of Proprietary Assets."

33Kale, Singh, and Perlmutter, "Learning and Protection of Proprietary Assets."

34Hamel et al., "Collaborate with Competitors"; Khanna et al., "The Dynamics of Learning Alliances"; and E. W. K. Tang, "Acquiring Knowledge by Foreign Partners from International Joint Ventures in a Transition Economy: Learning by Doing and Learning Myopia," *Strategic Management Journal* 23 (2002): 835–854.

35Hamel et al., "Collaborate with Competitors."

36B. Wysocki, "Cross Border Alliances Become Favorite Way to Crack New Markets," *Wall Street Journal,* March 4, 1990, p. A1.

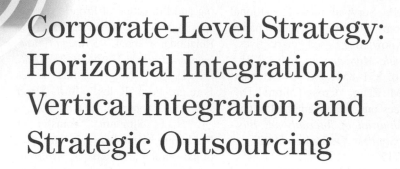

© iStockPhoto.com/Chepko Danil

9

Corporate-Level Strategy: Horizontal Integration, Vertical Integration, and Strategic Outsourcing

LEARNING OBJECTIVES

After reading this chapter, you should be able to:

9-1 Discuss how corporate-level strategy can be used to strengthen a company's business model and business-level strategies

9-2 Define *horizontal integration* and discuss the primary advantages and disadvantages associated with this corporate-level strategy

9-3 Explain the difference between a company's internal value chain and the industry value chain

9-4 Describe why, and under what conditions, cooperative relationships such as strategic alliances and outsourcing may become a substitute for vertical integration

OPENING CASE

Outsourcing and Vertical Integration at Apple

At a dinner for Silicon Valley's luminaries in February of 2011, U.S. President Barack Obama asked Steve Jobs of Apple, "What would it take to make iPhones in the United States?" Steve Jobs replied, "Those jobs aren't coming back." Apple's management had concluded that overseas factories provided superior scale, flexibility, diligence, and access to industrial skills—"Made in the U.S.A." just did not make sense for Apple anymore.

As an example of the superior responsiveness of Chinese factories to Apple's needs, an executive described a recent event when Apple wanted to revamp its iPhone manufacturing just weeks before it was scheduled for delivery to stores. At the last minute, Apple had redesigned the screen, and new screens arrived at the Chinese factory at midnight. Fortunately, the 8,000 workers slept in dormitories at the factory—they

were woken, given a cookie and a cup of tea, and were at work fitting glass screens into their beveled frames within 30 minutes. Soon the plant was producing 10,000 iPhones per day. The executive commented, "The speed and flexibility is breathtaking. . . There's no American plant that can match that."

"Foxconn City," a complex where the iPhone is assembled, has 230,000 employees, many of whom work 6 days a week and up to 12 hours a day. It is owned by Foxconn Technology, which has dozens of factories in Asia, Eastern Europe, Mexico, and Brazil. It is estimated that Foxconn assembles 40% of the world's consumer electronics, and boasts a customer list that includes Amazon, Dell, Hewlett-Packard, Motorola, Nintendo, Nokia, Samsung, and Sony, in addition to Apple. Foxconn can hire thousands of engineers overnight and put them up in dorms—something no American firm could do. Nearly 8,700 industrial engineers were needed to oversee the 200,000 assembly-line workers required to manufacture iPhones. Apple's analysts estimated that it could take 9 months to find that many qualified engineers in the United States. It only took 15 days in China. Moreover, China's advantage was not only in assembly; it offered advantages across the entire supply chain. As noted by an Apple executive, "The entire supply chain is in China now. You need a thousand rubber gaskets? That's the factory next door. You need a million screws? That factory is a block away. You need that screw made a little bit different? It will take three hours." Of Apple's 64,000 employees, nearly one-third are outside of the United States. In response to criticisms about failing to support employment in its home country, Apple executives responded, "We sell iPhones in over a hundred countries. . . . Our only obligation is making the best product possible."

Although Apple epitomizes the opportunities for strategic outsourcing, Apple is also—paradoxically perhaps—more vertically integrated than most computer or smartphone firms. Apple's decision to produce its own hardware and software—and tie them tightly together and sell them its own retail stores—was widely known and hotly debated. However, the vertical integration did not end there. Apple also spends billions of dollars buying production equipment that is used to outfit new and existing Asian factories that will be run by others (an example of *quasi vertical integration*), and then requires those factories to commit to producing for Apple exclusively. By providing the upfront investment, Apple removes most of the risk for its suppliers in investing

in superior technology or scale. For decades, the computer and mobile phone industries have been characterized by commoditization and rapid cost reduction—suppliers had to work hard to reduce costs to win competitive bids, and standardized production facilities trumped specialized facilities as they enabled the suppliers to smooth out the volatility in scale by working with multiple buyers. This meant that most suppliers to the computer and phone industry could produce cost-efficient hardware, but not "insanely great" hardware. Apple's strategy of paying upfront for both the technology and capacity enabled it to induce its suppliers to make specialized investments in technologies that were well beyond the industry standard, and to hold excess capacity that would enable rapid scaling. The net result is that Apple ends up with superior flexibility and technological sophistication that its competitors cannot match.

Seeming to acknowledge the advantages of Apple's strategy of controlling device design and production, Microsoft announced on June 18, 2012, that it too would design and produce its own tablet, the Surface. It also launched its own chain of dedicated Microsoft retail stores that looked remarkably similar to Apple stores. The success of this strategy is far from assured, however. Although Microsoft can imitate some of the individual integration strategies of Apple, it lacks both the tightly woven ecosystem that Apple has developed around those strategies, and its decades of experience in implementing them.

Sources: C. Duhigg and K. Bradsher, "How the U.S. Lost Out on iPhone Work", *New York Times*, January 21, 2012, p. 1; and C. Guglielmo, "Apple's Secret Plan for Its Cash Stash," *Forbes*, May 7, 2012, pp. 116–120.

OVERVIEW

The overriding goal of managers is to maximize the value of a company for its shareholders. The opening case about Apple's outsourcing and vertical integration moves shows how a firm's decisions about what activities to get into—and get out of—influence its profitability. In Apple's case, strategic outsourcing helps it to be more cost efficient, faster to market, and more flexible in scale, and its vertical integration moves give it a technological advantage that is difficult for its competitors to match.

In general, corporate-level strategy involves choices strategic managers must make: (1) deciding in which businesses and industries a company should compete; (2) selecting which value creation activities it should perform in those businesses; and (3) determining how it should enter, consolidate, or exit businesses or industries to maximize long-term profitability. When formulating corporate-level strategy, managers must adopt a long-term perspective and consider how changes taking place in an industry and in its products, technology, customers, and competitors will affect their company's current business model and its future strategies. They then decide how to implement specific corporate-level strategies that redefine their company's business model to allow it to increase its competitive advantage in a changing industry environment by taking advantage of opportunities and countering threats. Thus, the principal goal of corporate-level strategy is to enable a company to sustain or promote its competitive advantage and profitability in its present business—*and in any new businesses or industries that it chooses to enter.*

This chapter is the first of two that describe the role of corporate-level strategy in repositioning and redefining a company's business model. We discuss three corporate-level strategies—horizontal integration, vertical integration, and strategic outsourcing—that are primarily directed toward improving a company's competitive advantage and profitability in its current business or industry. Diversification, which entails entry into new kinds of businesses or industries, is examined in the next chapter, along with guidelines for choosing the most profitable way to enter new businesses or industries, or to exit others. By the end of this chapter and the next, you will understand how the different levels of strategy contribute to the creation of a successful and profitable business or multibusiness model. You will also be able to distinguish between the types of corporate strategies managers use to maximize long-term company profitability.

CORPORATE-LEVEL STRATEGY AND THE MULTIBUSINESS MODEL

The choice of corporate-level strategies is the final part of the strategy-formulation process. Corporate-level strategies drive a company's business model over time and determine which types of business- and functional-level strategies managers will choose to maximize long-term profitability. The relationship between business-level strategy and functional-level strategy was discussed in Chapter 5. Strategic managers develop a business model and strategies that use their company's distinctive competencies to strive for a cost-leadership position and/or to differentiate its products. Chapter 8 described how global strategy is also an extension of these basic principles.

In this chapter and the next, we repeatedly emphasize that to increase profitability, a corporate-level strategy should enable a company or one or more of its business divisions or units *to perform value-chain functional activities (1) at a lower cost and/or (2) in a way that results in increased differentiation.* Only when it selects the appropriate corporate-level strategies can a company choose the pricing option (lowest, average, or premium price) that will allow it to maximize profitability. In addition, corporate-level strategy will increase profitability if it helps a company reduce industry rivalry by reducing the threat of damaging price competition. In sum, a company's corporate-level strategies should be chosen to promote the success of its business-level strategies, which allows it to achieve a sustainable competitive advantage, leading to higher profitability.

Many companies choose to expand their business activities beyond one market or industry and enter others. When a company decides to expand into new industries, it must construct its business model at two levels. First, it must develop a business model and strategies for each business unit or division in every industry in which it competes. Second, it must also develop a higher-level *multibusiness model* that justifies its entry into different businesses and industries. This multibusiness model should explain how and why entering a new industry will allow the company to use its existing functional competencies and business strategies to increase its overall profitability. This model should also explain any other ways in which a company's involvement in more than one business or industry can increase its profitability. IBM, for example, might argue that its entry into online computer consulting, data storage, and cloud computing enables it to offer its customers a lineup of computer services, which allows it to better compete with HP, Oracle, or Amazon.com. Apple might argue that its entry into digital music and entertainment has given it a commanding lead over rivals such as Sony or Microsoft (which ended sales of its Zune music player in October 2011).

This chapter first focuses on the advantages of staying inside one industry by pursuing horizontal integration. It then looks at why companies use vertical integration and expand into new industries. In the next chapter, we examine two principal corporate strategies companies use to enter new industries to increase their profitability, related and unrelated diversification, and several other strategies companies may use to enter and compete in new industries.

HORIZONTAL INTEGRATION: SINGLE-INDUSTRY CORPORATE STRATEGY

Managers use corporate-level strategy to identify which industries their company should compete in to maximize its long-term profitability. For many companies, profitable growth and expansion often entail finding ways to successfully compete within a single market or industry over time. In other words, a company confines its value creation activities to just one business or industry. Examples of such single-business companies include McDonald's, with its focus on the global fast-food business, and Walmart, with its focus on global discount retailing.

Staying within one industry allows a company to focus all of its managerial, financial, technological, and functional resources and capabilities on competing successfully in one area. This is important in fast-growing and changing industries in which demands on a company's resources and capabilities are likely to be substantial, but where the long-term profits from establishing a competitive advantage are also likely to be substantial.

A second advantage of staying within a single industry is that a company "sticks to the knitting," meaning that it stays focused on what it knows and does best. A company does not make the mistake of entering new industries in which its existing resources and capabilities create little value and/or where a whole new set of competitive industry forces—new competitors, suppliers, and customers—present unanticipated threats. Coca-Cola, like many other companies, has committed this strategic error in the past. Coca-Cola once decided to expand into the movie business and acquired Columbia Pictures; it also acquired a large California winemaker. It soon found it lacked the competencies to successfully compete in these new industries and had not foreseen the strong competitive forces that existed in these industries from movie companies such as Paramount and winemakers such as Gallo. Coca-Cola concluded that entry into these new industries had reduced rather than created value and lowered its profitability; it divested or sold off these new businesses at a significant loss.

Even when a company stays in one industry, sustaining a successful business model over time can be difficult because of changing conditions in the environment, such as advances in technology that allow new competitors into the market, or because of changing customer needs. Two decades ago, the strategic issue facing telecommunications providers was how to shape their landline phone services to best meet customer needs in local and long-distance telephone service. When a new kind of product—wireless telephone service—emerged and quickly gained in popularity, landline providers like Verizon and AT&T had to quickly change their business models, lower the price of landline service, merge with wireless companies, and offer broadband services to ensure their survival.

Even within one industry, it is very easy for strategic managers to fail to see the "forest" (changing nature of the industry that results in new product/market opportunities) for the "trees" (focusing only on how to position current products). A focus on corporate-level strategy can help managers anticipate future trends and then change their business models to position their companies to compete successfully in a changing environment. Strategic managers must not become so committed to improving their company's *existing* product lines that they fail to recognize *new* product opportunities and threats. Apple has been so successful because it did recognize the increasing number of product opportunities offered by digital entertainment. The task for corporate-level managers is to analyze how new emerging technologies will impact their business models, how and why these technologies might change customer needs and customer groups in the future, and what kinds of new distinctive competencies will be needed to respond to these changes.

One corporate-level strategy that has been widely used to help managers strengthen their company's business model is horizontal integration, a strategy discussed in the chapter-closing case on the airline industry. **Horizontal integration** is the process of acquiring or merging with industry competitors to achieve the competitive advantages that arise from a large size and scope of operations. An **acquisition** occurs when one company uses its capital resources, such as stock, debt, or cash, to purchase another company, and a **merger** is an agreement between equals to pool their operations and create a new entity.

Mergers and acquisitions are common in most industries. In the aerospace industry, Boeing merged with McDonnell Douglas to create the world's largest aerospace company; in the pharmaceutical industry, Pfizer acquired Warner-Lambert to become the largest pharmaceutical firm; and global airlines are increasingly merging their operations (as the chapter-closing case suggests) in order to rationalize the number of flights offered between destinations and increase their market power. The pace of mergers and acquisitions has been rising as companies try to gain a competitive advantage over their rivals. The reason for this is that horizontal integration often significantly improves the competitive advantage and profitability of companies whose managers choose to stay within one industry and focus on managing its competitive position to keep the company at the value creation frontier.

Benefits of Horizontal Integration

In pursuing horizontal integration, managers decide to invest their company's capital resources to purchase the assets of industry competitors to increase the profitability of its single-business model. Profitability increases when horizontal integration (1) lowers the cost structure, (2) increases product differentiation, (3) leverages a competitive advantage

Horizontal integration
The process of acquiring or merging with industry competitors to achieve the competitive advantages that arise from a large size and scope of operations.

Acquisition
When a company uses its capital resources to purchase another company.

Merger
An agreement between two companies to pool their resources and operations and join together to better compete in a business or industry.

more broadly, (4) reduces rivalry within the industry, and (5) increases bargaining power over suppliers and buyers.

Lower Cost Structure Horizontal integration can lower a company's cost structure because it creates increasing *economies of scale*. Suppose five major competitors exist, each of which operates a manufacturing plant in some region of the United States, but none of the plants operate at full capacity. If one competitor buys another and closes that plant, it can operate its own plant at full capacity and reduce its manufacturing costs. Achieving economies of scale is very important in industries that have a high-fixed-cost structure. In such industries, large-scale production allows companies to spread their fixed costs over a large volume, and in this way drive down average unit costs. In the telecommunications industry, for example, the fixed costs of building advanced 4G and LTE broadband networks that offer tremendous increases in speed are enormous, and to make such an investment profitable, a large volume of customers is required. Thus, companies such as AT&T and Verizon purchased other telecommunications companies to acquire their customers, increase their customer base, increase utilization rates, and reduce the cost of servicing each customer. In 2011, AT&T planned to acquire T-Mobile, but abandoned the deal in response to antitrust concerns raised by the U.S. Department of Justice and the Federal Communications Commission. Similar considerations were involved in the hundreds of acquisitions that have taken place in the pharmaceutical industry in the last decade because of the need to realize scale economies in research and development (R&D) and sales and marketing. The fixed costs of building a nationwide pharmaceutical sales force are enormous, and pharmaceutical companies such as Pfizer and Merck must possess a wide portfolio of drugs to sell to effectively make use of their sales forces.

A company can also lower its cost structure when horizontal integration allows it to *reduce the duplication of resources* between two companies, such as by eliminating the need for two sets of corporate head offices, two separate sales teams, and so forth. Notably, however, these cost savings are often overestimated. If two companies are operating a function such as a call center, for example, and both are above the minimum efficient scale for operating such a center, there may be few economies from consolidating call center operations: if each center was already optimally utilized, the consolidated call center may require just as many service people, computers, phone lines, and real estate as the two call centers previously required. Similarly, when banks were consolidating during the late 1990s, one of the justifications was that the banks could save by consolidating their information technology (IT) resources. Ultimately, however, most of the merged banks realized that their potential savings were meager at best, and the costs of attempting to harmonize their information systems were high, so most of the merged banks continued to run the separate legacy systems the banks had prior to merging.

Increased Product Differentiation Horizontal integration may also increase profitability when it increases product differentiation, for example, by increasing the flow of innovative new products that a company's sales force can sell to customers at premium prices. Desperate for new drugs to fill its pipeline, for example, Eli Lilly paid $6.5 billion to ImClone Systems to acquire its new cancer-preventing drugs in order to outbid rival Bristol-Myers Squibb. Google, anxious to provide its users with online coupons, offered to pay $6 billion for Groupon to fill this niche in its online advertising business in order to increase its differentiation advantage—and reduce industry rivalry.

Horizontal integration may also increase differentiation when it allows a company to combine the product lines of merged companies so that it can offer customers a wider range of products that can be bundled together. **Product bundling** involves offering customers

Product bundling
Offering customers the opportunity to purchase a range of products at a single combined price; this increases the value of a company's product line because customers often obtain a price discount when purchasing a set of products at one time, and customers become used to dealing with only one company and its representatives.

FOCUS ON: WAL-MART

Walmart's Expansion into Other Retail Formats

© iStockPhoto.com/caracterdesign

In 2013, Walmart was the largest firm in the world, with sales of $469.2 billion, more than 10,000 stores worldwide, and employing 2.2 million people. However, as the U.S. discount retail market was mature (where Walmart earned 70% of its revenues), it looked for other opportunities to apply its exceptional retailing power and expertise. In the United States it had expanded into Supercenters (that sold groceries in addition to general merchandise) and even-lower-priced warehouse store formats (Sam's Club), both of which were doing well. These stores could directly leverage Walmart's bargaining power over suppliers (for many producers of general merchandise, Walmart accounted for more than 70% of their sales, giving it unrivaled power to negotiate prices and delivery terms), and benefitted from its exceptionally efficient system for transporting, managing, and tracking inventory. Walmart had invested relatively early in advanced information technology: it adopted radio frequency identification (RFID) tagging well ahead of its competitors, and satellites tracked inventory in real time. Walmart knew where each item of inventory was at all times and when it had sold, enabling it to simultaneously minimize its inventory holding costs while optimizing the inventory mix in each store. As a result, it had higher sales per square foot and inventory turnover than either Target or Kmart. It handled inventory through a massive hub-and-spoke distribution system that included more than 140 distribution centers that each served approximately 150 stores within a 150 miles radius. As Supercenters and Sam's Clubs were also approaching saturation, however, growth had become harder and harder to sustain. Walmart began to pursue other types of expansion opportunities. It expanded into smaller-format neighborhood stores, international stores (many of which were existing chains that were acquired), and was considering getting into organic foods and trendy fashions. While expansion into contiguous geographic regions (e.g., Canada and Mexico) had gone well, its success at overseas expansions was spottier. Walmart's forays into Germany and South Korea, for example, resulted in large losses, and Walmart ultimately exited the markets. Walmart's entry into Japan was also not as successful as hoped, resulting in many years of losses and never gaining a large share of the market. The challenge was that many of these markets already had tough competitors by the time Walmart entered—they weren't the sleepy underserved markets that had initially helped it to grow in the United States. Furthermore, Walmart's IT and logistics advantages could not easily be leveraged into overseas markets—they would require massive upfront investments to replicate, and it would be hard to break even on those investments without having massive scale in those markets. Which of Walmart's advantages could be leveraged overseas and to which markets? Was Walmart better off trying to diversify its product offerings within North America? Or should it perhaps reconsider its growth objectives altogether?

Sources: www.walmart.com.

Cross-selling

When a company takes advantage of or "leverages" its established relationship with customers by way of acquiring additional product lines or categories that it can sell to customers. In this way, a company increases differentiation because it can provide a "total solution" and satisfy all of a customer's specific needs.

the opportunity to purchase a range of products at a single combined price. This increases the value of a company's product line because customers often obtain a price discount when purchasing a set of products at one time, and customers become used to dealing with only one company and its representatives. A company may obtain a competitive advantage from increased product differentiation.

Another way to increase product differentiation is through **cross-selling**, which is when a company takes advantage of or "leverages" its established relationship with customers by way of acquiring additional product lines or categories that it can sell to customers. In this way, a company increases differentiation because it can provide a "total solution" and satisfy all of a customer's specific needs. Cross-selling and becoming a total solution provider is an important rationale for horizontal integration in the computer sector, where IT companies attempt to increase the value of their offerings by satisfying all of the hardware and

9.1 STRATEGY IN ACTION

Larry Ellison Wants Oracle to Become the Biggest and the Best

© iStockPhoto.com/Tom Nulens

Oracle Corporation, based in Redwood Shores, California, is the world's largest maker of database software and the third-largest global software company after Microsoft and IBM. This commanding position is not enough for Oracle, however, which has set its sights on becoming the global leader in the corporate applications software market. In this market, Germany's SAP, with 45% of the market, is the acknowledged leader, and Oracle, with 25%, is a distant second. Corporate applications are a fast-growing and highly profitable market, however, and Oracle has been snapping up leading companies in this segment. Its goal is to quickly build the distinctive competencies it needs to expand the range of products that it can offer to its existing customers and attract new customers to compete with SAP.

Beginning in the mid-2000s Oracle's CEO Larry Ellison has spent over $29 billion to acquire more than 20 leading suppliers of corporate software and hardware, including 2 of the top 5 companies: PeopleSoft, a leading human resource management (HRM) software supplier it bought for $10 billion, and Siebel Systems, a leader in customer relationship management (CRM) software, that it purchased for $5.8 billion.

Oracle expects several competitive advantages to result from its use of acquisitions to pursue the corporate strategy of horizontal integration. First, it is now able to bundle the best software applications of these acquired companies—with Oracle's own first-class set of corporate and database software programs—to create a new integrated software suite that will allow companies to manage all their functional activities, such as accounting, marketing, sales, HRM, CRM, and supply-chain management. Second, through these acquisitions, Oracle obtained access to thousands of new customers—especially the medium and small companies that use the software of the companies it acquired. All of these companies have become potential customers for Oracle's other database and corporate software offerings, and therefore its market share has steadily increased during the 2010s. Third, Oracle's acquisitions have consolidated the corporate software industry. By taking over some of its largest rivals, Oracle has become the second-largest supplier of corporate software and is better positioned to compete with leader SAP. As a result, its stock price has soared in the 2010s—at a much faster rate than that of archrival SAP.

Sources: www.oracle.com and www.sap.com.

---

service needs of corporate customers. Providing a total solution saves customers' time and money because they do not have to work with several suppliers, and a single sales team can ensure that all the components of a customer's IT seamlessly work together. When horizontal integration increases the differentiated appeal and value of the company's products, the total solution provider gains market share. This was the business model Oracle pursued when it acquired many IT software companies, as discussed in Strategy in Action 9.1.

Leveraging a Competitive Advantage More Broadly   For firms that have resources or capabilities that could be valuably deployed across multiple market segments or geographies, horizontal integration may offer opportunities to become more profitable. In the retail industry, for example, Walmart's enormous bargaining power with suppliers and its exceptional efficiency in inventory logistics enabled it to have a competitive advantage in other discount retail store formats, such as its chain of Sam's Clubs (an even-lower-priced warehouse segment). It also expanded the range of products it offers customers when it entered the supermarket business and established a nationwide chain of Walmart supercenters that sell groceries as well as all the clothing, toys, and electronics sold in regular

Walmart stores. It has also replicated its business model globally, although not always with as much success as it had in the United States because many of its efficiencies in logistics (such as its hub-and-spoke distribution system and inventory tracked by satellite) employ fixed assets that are geographically limited (see the Focus on Walmart box for more on this).

Reduced Industry Rivalry   Horizontal integration can help to reduce industry rivalry in two ways. First, acquiring or merging with a competitor helps to *eliminate excess capacity* in an industry, which, as we discuss in Chapter 6, often triggers price wars. By taking excess capacity out of an industry, horizontal integration creates a more benign environment in which prices might stabilize—or even increase.

Second, by reducing the number of competitors in an industry, horizontal integration often makes it easier to implement *tacit price coordination* between rivals, that is, coordination reached without communication. (Explicit communication to fix prices is illegal in most countries.) In general, the larger the number of competitors in an industry, the more difficult it is to establish informal pricing agreements—such as price leadership by the dominant company—which increases the possibility that a price war will erupt. By increasing industry concentration and creating an oligopoly, horizontal integration can make it easier to establish tacit coordination among rivals.

Both of these motives also seem to have been behind Oracle's many software acquisitions. There was significant excess capacity in the corporate software industry, and major competitors were offering customers discounted prices that had led to a price war and falling profit margins. Oracle hoped to be able to eliminate excess industry capacity that would reduce price competition. By 2009, it was clear that the major corporate software competitors were focusing on finding ways to better differentiate their product suites to prevent a price war and continuing to make major acquisitions to help their companies build competitive advantage.

Increased Bargaining Power   Finally, some companies use horizontal integration because it allows them to obtain bargaining power over suppliers or buyers and increase their profitability at the expense of suppliers or buyers. By consolidating the industry through horizontal integration, a company becomes a much larger buyer of suppliers' products and uses this as leverage to bargain down the price it pays for its inputs, thereby lowering its cost structure. Walmart, for example, is well known for pursuing this strategy. Similarly, by acquiring its competitors, a company gains control over a greater percentage of an industry's product or output. Other things being equal, the company then has more power to raise prices and profits because customers have less choice of suppliers and are more dependent on the company for their products—something both Oracle and SAP are striving for to protect their customer base. When a company has greater ability to raise prices to buyers or bargain down the price paid for inputs, it has obtained increased market power.

Problems with Horizontal Integration

Although horizontal integration can strengthen a company's business model in several ways, there are problems, limitations, and dangers associated with pursuing this corporate-level strategy. *Implementing* a horizontal integration strategy is not an easy task for managers. As we discuss in Chapter 10, there are several reasons why mergers and acquisitions may fail to result in higher profitability: problems associated with merging very different company cultures, high management turnover in the acquired company when the acquisition is a hostile one, and a tendency of managers to overestimate the potential benefits from a merger or acquisition and underestimate the problems involved in merging their operations.

When a company uses horizontal integration to become a dominant industry competitor, in an attempt to keep using the strategy to continue to grow business, the company comes into conflict with the Federal Trade Commission (FTC), the government agency responsible for enforcing antitrust laws. Antitrust authorities are concerned about the potential for abuse of market power; more competition is generally better for consumers than less competition. The FTC is concerned when a few companies within one industry try to make acquisitions that will allow them to raise consumer prices above the level that would exist in a more competitive situation, and thus abuse their market power. The FTC also wishes to prevent dominant companies from using their market power to crush potential competitors, for example, by cutting prices when a new competitor enters the industry and forcing the competitor out of business, then raising prices after the threatening company has been eliminated.

JASON REED/Reuters/Corbis

Because of these concerns, any merger or acquisition the FTC perceives as creating too much consolidation, and the *potential* for future abuse of market power, may, for antitrust reasons, be blocked. The proposed merger between the two dominant satellite radio companies Sirius and XM was blocked for months until it became clear that customers had many other ways to obtain high-quality radio programming, for example, through their computers and cell phones, so substantial competition would still exist in the industry. In 2011, AT&T's attempt to acquire T-Mobile faced similar hurdles, although as the chapter-closing case discusses, airlines have been permitted to merge in order to reduce their cost structures.

VERTICAL INTEGRATION: ENTERING NEW INDUSTRIES TO STRENGTHEN THE "CORE" BUSINESS MODEL

Many companies that use horizontal integration to strengthen their business model and improve their competitive position also use the corporate-level strategy of vertical integration for the same purpose. When pursuing vertical integration, however, a company is entering new industries to support the business model of its "core" industry, that is, the industry which is the primary source of its competitive advantage and profitability. At this point, therefore, a company must formulate a multibusiness model that explains how entry into a new industry using vertical integration will enhance its long-term profitability. The model that justifies the pursuit of vertical integration is based on a company entering industries that *add value* to its core products because this increases product differentiation and/or lowers its cost structure, thus increasing its profitability.

A company pursuing a strategy of **vertical integration** expands its operations either backward into an industry that produces inputs for the company's products (*backward*

Vertical integration

When a company expands its operations either backward into an industry that produces inputs for the company's products (*backward vertical integration*) or forward into an industry that uses, distributes, or sells the company's products (forward vertical integration).

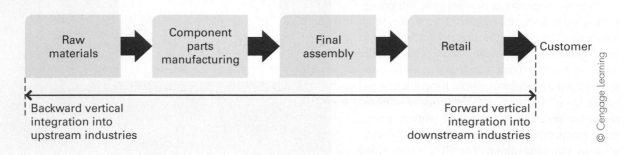

Figure 9.1   Stages in the Raw-Materials-to-Customer Value-Added Chain

© Cengage Learning

vertical integration) or forward into an industry that uses, distributes, or sells the company's products (*forward vertical integration*). To enter an industry, it may establish its own operations and build the value chain needed to compete effectively in that industry, or it may acquire a company that is already in the industry. A steel company that supplies its iron ore needs from company-owned iron ore mines illustrates backward integration. A maker of personal computers (PCs) that sells its laptops through company-owned retail outlets illustrates forward integration. For example, Apple entered the retail industry in 2001 when it decided to establish a chain of Apple stores to sell, promote, and service its products. IBM is a highly vertically integrated company; it integrated backward into the chip and memory disk industry to produce the components that work inside its mainframes and servers, and integrated forward into the computer software and consulting services industries.

Figure 9.1 illustrates four *main* stages in a typical raw-materials-to-customer value-added chain. For a company based in the final assembly stage, backward integration means moving into component parts manufacturing and raw materials production. Forward integration means moving into distribution and sales (retail). At each stage in the chain, *value is added* to the product, meaning that a company at one stage takes the product produced in the previous stage and transforms it in some way so that it is worth more to a company at the next stage in the chain and, ultimately, to the customer. It is important to note that each stage of the value-added chain is a separate industry or industries in which many different companies are competing. Moreover, within each industry, every company has a value chain composed of the value creation activities we discussed in Chapter 3: R&D, production, marketing, customer service, and so on. In other words, we can think of a value chain that runs *across* industries, and embedded within that are the value chains of companies *within* each industry.

As an example of the value-added concept, consider how companies in each industry involved in the production of a PC contribute to the final product (Figure 9.2). The first stage in the chain includes raw materials companies that make specialty ceramics, chemicals, and metal, such as Kyocera of Japan, which manufactures the ceramic substrate for semiconductors. Companies at the first stage in the chain sell their products to the makers of PC component products, such as Intel and AMD, which transform the ceramics, chemicals, and metals they purchase into PC components such as microprocessors, disk drives, and memory chips. In the process, companies *add value* to the raw materials they purchase. At the third stage, the manufactured components are then sold to PC makers such as Apple, Dell, and HP, and these companies decide which of the components to purchase and assemble to *add value* to the final PCs (that they make or outsource to a contract manufacturer). At stage four, the finished PCs are then either sold directly to the final customer over the Internet, or sold to

| Figure 9.2 | The Raw-Materials-to-Customer Value-Added Chain in the PC Industry |

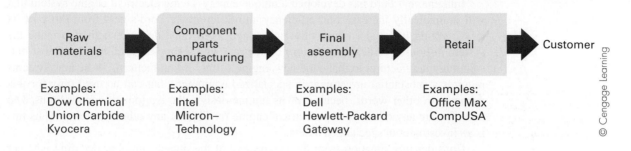

Examples:
Dow Chemical
Union Carbide
Kyocera

Examples:
Intel
Micron–
Technology

Examples:
Dell
Hewlett-Packard
Gateway

Examples:
Office Max
CompUSA

© Cengage Learning

retailers such as Best Buy and Staples, which distribute and sell them to the final customer. Companies that distribute and sell PCs also *add value* to the product because they make the product accessible to customers and provide customer service and support.

Thus, companies in different industries add value at each stage in the raw-materials-to-customer chain. Viewed in this way, vertical integration presents companies with a choice about within which industries in the raw-materials-to-customer chain to operate and compete. This choice is determined by how much establishing operations at a stage in the value chain will increase product differentiation or lower costs—and therefore increase profitability—as we discuss in the following section.

Increasing Profitability Through Vertical Integration

As noted earlier, a company pursues vertical integration to strengthen the business model of its original or core business and to improve its competitive position.[1] Vertical integration increases product differentiation, lowers costs, or reduces industry competition when it (1) facilitates investments in efficiency-enhancing specialized assets, (2) protects product quality, and (3) results in improved scheduling.

Facilitating Investments in Specialized Assets A specialized asset is one that is designed to perform a specific task and whose value is significantly reduced in its next-best use.[2] The asset may be a piece of equipment that has a firm-specific use or the knowhow or skills that a company or employees have acquired through training and experience. Companies invest in specialized assets because these assets allow them to lower their cost structure or to better differentiate their products, which facilitates premium pricing. A company might invest in specialized equipment to lower manufacturing costs, as Toyota does, for example, or it might invest in an advanced technology that allows it to develop better-quality products than its rivals, as Apple does. Thus, specialized assets can help a company achieve a competitive advantage at the business level.

Just as a company invests in specialized assets in its own industry to build competitive advantage, it is often necessary that suppliers invest in specialized assets to produce the inputs that a specific company needs. By investing in these assets, a supplier can make higher-quality inputs that provide its customers with a differentiation advantage, or inputs at a lower cost so it can charge its customers a lower price to keep their business. However, it is often difficult to persuade companies in adjacent stages of the raw-materials-to-customer value-added chain to make investments in specialized assets. Often, to realize the benefits associated with such investments, a company must vertically integrate and enter into adjacent industries and invest its own resources. Why does this happen?

Imagine that Ford has developed a unique energy-saving electrical engine system that will dramatically increase fuel efficiency and differentiate Ford's cars from those of its rivals, giving it a major competitive advantage. Ford must decide whether to make the system in-house (vertical integration) or contract with a supplier such as a specialist outsourcing manufacturer to make the new engine system. Manufacturing these new systems requires a substantial investment in specialized equipment that can be used only for this purpose. In other words, because of its unique design, the equipment cannot be used to manufacture any other type of electrical engine for Ford or any other carmaker. Thus this is an investment in specialized assets.

Consider this situation from the perspective of the outside supplier deciding whether or not to make this investment. The supplier might reason that once it has made the investment, it will become dependent on Ford for business because *Ford is the only possible customer for the electrical engine made by this specialized equipment*. The supplier realizes that this puts Ford in a strong bargaining position and that Ford might use its buying power to demand lower prices for the engines. Given the risks involved, the supplier declines to make the investment in specialized equipment.

Now consider Ford's position. Ford might reason that if it outsources production of these systems to an outside supplier, it might become too dependent on that supplier for a vital input. Because specialized equipment is required to produce the engine systems, Ford cannot switch its order to other suppliers. Ford realizes that this increases the bargaining power of the supplier, which might use its bargaining power to demand higher prices.

The situation of *mutual dependence* that would be created by the investment in specialized assets makes Ford hesitant to allow outside suppliers to make the product and makes suppliers hesitant to undertake such a risky investment. The problem is a lack of trust—neither Ford nor the supplier can trust the other to operate fairly in this situation. The lack of trust arises from the risk of **holdup**—that is, being taken advantage of by a trading partner *after* the investment in specialized assets has been made.[3] Because of this risk, Ford reasons that the only cost-effective way to get the new engine systems is for it to make the investment in specialized assets and manufacture the engine in-house.

To generalize from this example, if achieving a competitive advantage requires one company to make investments in specialized assets so it can trade with another, *the risk of holdup* may serve as a deterrent, and the investment may not take place. Consequently, the potential for higher profitability from specialization will be lost. To prevent such loss, companies vertically integrate into adjacent stages in the value chain. Historically, the problems surrounding specific assets have driven automobile companies to vertically integrate backward into the production of component parts, steel companies to vertically integrate backward into the production of iron, computer companies to vertically integrate backward into chip production, and aluminum companies to vertically integrate backward into bauxite mining. Often such firms practice **tapered integration**, whereby the firm makes some of the input and buys some of the input. Purchasing part or most of its needs for a given input from suppliers enables the firm to tap the advantages of the market (e.g., being able to choose from more suppliers that are competing to improve quality or lower the cost of the product). At the same time, meeting some of its needs for the input through internal production improves the firm's bargaining power by reducing its likelihood of holdup by a supplier. A firm that is engaged in production of an input is also better able to evaluate the cost and quality of

Holdup
When a company is taken advantage of by another company it does business with after it has made an investment in expensive specialized assets to better meet the needs of the other company.

Tapered integration
When a firm uses a mix of vertical integration and market transactions for a given input. For example, a firm might operate limited semiconductor manufacturing itself, while also buying semiconductor chips on the market. Doing so helps to prevent supplier holdup (because the firm can credibly commit to not buying from external suppliers) and increases its ability to judge the quality and cost of purchased supplies.

9.2 STRATEGY IN ACTION

Specialized Assets and Vertical Integration in the Aluminum Industry

© iStockPhoto.com/Tom Nulens

The metal content and chemical composition of bauxite ore, used to produce aluminum, vary from deposit to deposit, so each type of ore requires a specialized refinery—that is, the refinery must be designed for a particular type of ore. Running one type of bauxite through a refinery designed for another type reportedly increases production costs from 20% to 100%. Thus, the value of an investment in a specialized aluminum refinery and the cost of the output produced by that refinery depend on receiving the right kind of bauxite ore.

Imagine that an aluminum company must decide whether to invest in an aluminum refinery designed to refine a certain type of ore. Also assume that the ore is extracted by a company that owns a single bauxite mine. Using a different type of ore would raise production costs by 50%. Therefore, the value of the aluminum company's investment is dependent on the price it must pay the bauxite company for this material. Recognizing this, once the aluminum company has made the investment in a new refinery, what is to stop the bauxite company from raising prices? Nothing. Once it has made

the investment, the aluminum company is locked into its relationship with its bauxite supplier. The bauxite supplier can increase prices because it knows that as long as the increase in the total production costs of the aluminum company is less than 50%, the aluminum company will continue to buy its ore. Thus, once the aluminum company has made the investment, the bauxite supplier can *hold up* the aluminum company.

How can the aluminum company reduce the risk of holdup? The answer is by purchasing the bauxite supplier. If the aluminum company can purchase the bauxite supplier's mine, it no longer needs to fear that bauxite prices will be increased after the investment in an aluminum refinery has been made. In other words, vertical integration eliminates the risk of holdup, making the specialized investment worthwhile. In practice, it has been argued that these kinds of considerations have driven aluminum companies to pursue vertical integration to such a degree that, according to one study, more than 90% of the total volume of bauxite is transferred within vertically integrated aluminum companies.

Sources: J .F. Hennart, "Upstream Vertical Integration in the Aluminum and Tin Industries," *Journal of Economic Behavior and Organization* 9 (1988): 281–299; and www.alcoa.com.

---

external suppliers of that input.[4] The way specific asset issues have led to vertical integration in the global aluminum industry is discussed in Strategy in Action 9.2.

Enhancing Product Quality   By entering industries at other stages of the value-added chain, a company can often enhance the quality of the products in its core business and strengthen its differentiation advantage. For example, the ability to control the reliability and performance of complex components such as engine and transmission systems may increase a company's competitive advantage in the luxury sedan market and enable it to charge a premium price. Conditions in the banana industry also illustrate the importance of vertical integration in maintaining product quality. Historically, a problem facing food companies that import bananas has been the variable quality of delivered bananas, which often arrive on the shelves of U.S. supermarkets too ripe or not ripe enough. To correct this problem, major U.S. food companies such as Del Monte have integrated backward and now own banana plantations, putting them in control over the banana supply. As a result, they can distribute and sell bananas of a standard quality at the optimal time to better satisfy customers. Knowing they can rely on the quality of these brands, customers are also willing to pay more for them. Thus, by vertically integrating backward into plantation ownership, banana companies have built customer confidence, which has, in turn, enabled them to charge a premium price for their product.

The same considerations can promote forward vertical integration. Ownership of retail outlets may be necessary if the required standards of after-sales service for complex products are to be maintained. For example, in the 1920s, Kodak owned the retail outlets that distributed its photographic equipment because the company felt that few existing retail outlets had the skills necessary to sell and service its complex equipment. By the 1930s, new retailers had emerged that could provide satisfactory distribution and service for Kodak products, so it left the retail industry.

McDonald's has also used vertical integration to protect product quality and increase efficiency. By the 1990s, McDonald's faced a problem: after decades of rapid growth, the fast-food market was beginning to show signs of market saturation. McDonald's responded to the slowdown by rapidly expanding abroad. In 1980, 28% of the chain's new restaurant openings were abroad; in 1990 it was 60%, and by 2000, 70%. In 2011, more than 12,000 restaurants in 110 countries existed outside the United States.[5] Replication of its value creation skills was the key to successful global expansion and spurred the growth of McDonald's in the countries and world regions in which it operates. McDonald's U.S. success was built on a formula of close relations with suppliers, nationwide marketing might, and tight control over store-level operating procedures.

The biggest global problem McDonald's has faced is replicating its U.S. supply chain in other countries; its domestic suppliers are fiercely loyal to the company because their fortunes are closely linked to its success. McDonald's maintains very rigorous specifications for all the raw ingredients it uses—the key to its consistency and quality control. Outside of the United States, however, McDonald's has found suppliers far less willing to make the investments required to meet its specifications. In Great Britain, for example, McDonald's had problems getting local bakeries to produce the hamburger bun. After experiencing quality problems with two local bakeries, McDonald's had to vertically integrate backward and build its own bakeries to supply its British stores. When McDonald's decided to operate in Russia, it found that local suppliers lacked the capability to produce ingredients of the quality it demanded. It was then forced to vertically integrate through the local food industry on a heroic scale, importing potato seeds and bull semen and indirectly managing dairy farms, cattle ranches, and vegetable plots. It also needed to construct the world's largest food-processing plant at a huge cost. In South America, McDonald's also purchased huge ranches in Argentina, upon which it could raise its own cattle. In short, vertical integration has allowed McDonald's to protect product quality and reduce its global cost structure.[6]

Improved Scheduling   Sometimes important strategic advantages can be obtained when vertical integration makes it quicker, easier, and more cost-effective to plan, coordinate, and schedule the transfer of a product, such as raw materials or component parts, between adjacent stages of the value-added chain.[7] Such advantages can be crucial when a company wants to realize the benefits of just-in-time (JIT) inventory systems. For example, in the 1920s, Ford profited from the tight coordination and scheduling that backward vertical integration made possible. Ford integrated backward into steel foundries, iron ore shipping, and iron ore production—it owned mines in Upper Michigan! Deliveries at Ford were coordinated to such an extent that iron ore unloaded at Ford's steel foundries on the Great Lakes was turned into engine blocks within 24 hours, which lowered Ford's cost structure.

Problems with Vertical Integration

Vertical integration can often be used to strengthen a company's business model and increase profitability. However, the opposite can occur when vertical integration results in (1) an increasing cost structure, (2) disadvantages that arise when technology is changing fast, and (3) disadvantages that arise when demand is unpredictable. Sometimes these disadvantages are so great that vertical integration, rather than increasing profitability, may actually reduce it—in which case a company engages in **vertical disintegration** and exits industries adjacent to its core industry in the industry value chain. For example, Ford, which was highly vertically integrated, sold all its companies involved in mining iron ore and making steel when more efficient and specialized steel producers emerged that were able to supply lower-priced steel.

Increasing Cost Structure   Although vertical integration is often undertaken to lower a company's cost structure, it can raise costs if, over time, a company makes mistakes, such as continuing to purchase inputs from company-owned suppliers when low-cost independent suppliers that can supply the same inputs exist. For decades, for example, GM's company-owned suppliers made more than 60% of the component parts for its vehicles; this figure was far higher than that for any other major carmaker, which is why GM became such a high-cost carmaker. In the 2000s, it vertically disintegrated by selling off many of its largest component operations, such as Delhi, its electrical components supplier. Thus, vertical integration can be a major disadvantage when company-owned suppliers develop a higher cost structure than those of independent suppliers. Why would a company-owned supplier develop such a high cost structure?

In this example, company-owned or "in-house" suppliers know that they can always sell their components to the car-making divisions of their company—they have a "captive customer." Because company-owned suppliers do not have to compete with independent, outside suppliers for orders, they have much less *incentive* to look for new ways to reduce operating costs or increase component quality. Indeed, in-house suppliers simply pass on cost increases to the car-making divisions in the form of higher **transfer prices**, the prices one division of a company charges other divisions for its products. Unlike independent suppliers, which constantly need to increase their efficiency to protect their competitive advantage, in-house suppliers face no such competition, and the resulting rising cost structure reduces a company's profitability.

The term *bureaucratic costs* refers to the costs of solving the transaction difficulties that arise from managerial inefficiencies and the need to manage the handoffs or exchanges between business units to promote increased differentiation, or to lower a company's cost structure. Bureaucratic costs become a significant component of a company's cost structure because considerable managerial time and effort must be spent to reduce or eliminate managerial inefficiencies, such as those that result when company-owned suppliers lose their incentive to increase efficiency or innovation.

Technological Change   When technology is changing fast, vertical integration may lock a company into an old, inefficient technology and prevent it from changing to a new one that would strengthen its business model.[8] Consider Sony, which had integrated backward to become the leading manufacturer of the now outdated cathode ray tubes (CRTs) used in TVs and computer monitors. Because Sony was locked into the outdated CRT technology, it was slow to recognize that the future was flatscreen liquid crystal display (LCD) screens and did not exit the CRT business. Sony's resistance to change in technology forced it to

Vertical disintegration
When a company decides to exit industries either forward or backward in the industry value chain to its core industry to increase profitability.

Transfer pricing
The price that one division of a company charges another division for its products, which are the inputs the other division requires to manufacture its own products.

enter into a strategic alliance with Samsung to supply the LCD screens that are used in its BRAVIA TVs. As a result, Sony lost its competitive advantage and experienced a major loss in TV market share. Thus, vertical integration can pose a serious disadvantage when it prevents a company from adopting new technology, or changing its suppliers or distribution systems to match the requirements of changing technology.

Demand Unpredictability   Suppose the demand for a company's core product, such as cars or washing machines, is predictable, and a company knows how many units it needs to make each month or year. Under these conditions, vertical integration allows a company to schedule and coordinate efficiently the flow of products along the industry value-added chain and may result in major cost savings. However, suppose the demand for cars or washing machines wildly fluctuates and is unpredictable. If demand for cars suddenly plummets, the carmaker may find itself burdened with warehouses full of component parts it no longer needs, which is a major drain on profitability—something that has hurt major carmakers during the recent recession. Thus, vertical integration can be risky when demand is unpredictable because it is hard to manage the volume or flow of products along the value-added chain.

For example, a PC maker might vertically integrate backward to acquire a supplier of memory chips so that it can make exactly the number of chips it needs each month. However, if demand for PCs falls because of the popularity of mobile computing devices, the PC maker finds itself locked into a business that is now inefficient because it is not producing at full capacity, and therefore its cost structure starts to rise. In general, high-speed environmental change (e.g., technological change, changing customer demands, and major shifts in institutional norms or competitive dynamics) provides a disincentive for integration, as the firm's asset investments are at greater risk of rapid obsolescence.[9] It is clear that strategic managers must carefully assess the advantages and disadvantages of expanding the boundaries of their company by entering adjacent industries, either backward (upstream) or forward (downstream), in the industry value-added chain. Moreover, although the decision to enter a new industry to make crucial component parts may have been profitable in the past, it may make no economic sense today because so many low-cost global component parts suppliers exist that compete for the company's business. The risks and returns on investing in vertical integration must be continually evaluated, and companies should be as willing to vertically disintegrate, as vertically integrate, to strengthen their core business model.

ALTERNATIVES TO VERTICAL INTEGRATION: COOPERATIVE RELATIONSHIPS

Is it possible to obtain the differentiation and cost-savings advantages associated with vertical integration without having to bear the problems and costs associated with this strategy? In other words, is there another corporate-level strategy that managers can use to obtain the advantages of vertical integration while allowing other companies to perform upstream and downstream activities? Today, companies have found that they can realize many of the benefits associated with vertical integration by entering into *long-term cooperative relationships* with companies in industries along the value-added chain, also known as

quasi integration. Such moves could include, for example, sharing the expenses of investment in production assets or inventory, or making long-term supply or purchase guarantees. Apple's decision to invest in production equipment for its suppliers (in the opening case) is a prime example.

Short-Term Contracts and Competitive Bidding

Many companies use short-term contracts that last for a year or less to establish the price and conditions under which they will purchase raw materials or components from suppliers or sell their final products to distributors or retailers. A classic example is the carmaker that uses a *competitive bidding strategy,* in which independent component suppliers compete to be chosen to supply a particular component, such as brakes, made to agreed-upon specifications, at the lowest price. For example, GM typically solicits bids from global suppliers to produce a particular component and awards a 1-year contract to the supplier that submits the lowest bid. At the end of the year, the contract is once again put out for competitive bid, and once again the lowest-cost supplier is most likely to win the bid.

The advantage of this strategy for GM is that suppliers are forced to compete over price, which drives down the cost of its car components. However, GM has no long-term commitment to outside suppliers—and it drives a hard bargain. For this reason, suppliers are unwilling to make the expensive long-term investments in specialized assets that are required to produce higher-quality or better-designed component parts over time. In addition, suppliers will be reluctant to agree upon the tight scheduling that makes it possible to use a JIT inventory system because this may help GM lower its costs but will increase a supplier's costs and reduce its profitability.

As a result, short-term contracting does not result in the specialized investments that are required to realize differentiation and cost advantages *because it signals a company's lack of long-term commitment to its suppliers.* Of course, this is not a problem when there is minimal need for cooperation, and specialized assets are not required to improve scheduling, enhance product quality, or reduce costs. In this case, competitive bidding may be optimal. However, when there is a need for cooperation, something that is becoming increasingly significant today, the use of short-term contracts and competitive bidding can be a serious drawback.

Strategic Alliances and Long-Term Contracting

Unlike short-term contracts, **strategic alliances** between buyers and suppliers are long-term, cooperative relationships; both companies agree to make specialized investments and work jointly to find ways to lower costs or increase product quality so that they both gain from their relationship. A strategic alliance becomes a *substitute* for vertical integration because it creates a relatively stable long-term partnership that allows both companies to obtain the same kinds of benefits that result from vertical integration. However, it also avoids the problems (bureaucratic costs) that arise from managerial inefficiencies that result when a company owns its own suppliers, such as those that arise because of a lack of incentives, or when a company becomes locked into an old technology even when technology is rapidly changing.

Consider the cooperative relationships that often were established decades ago, which many Japanese carmakers have with their component suppliers (the *keiretsu* system). Japanese carmakers and suppliers cooperate to find ways to maximize the "value added" they

Quasi integration
The use of long-term relationships, or investment into *some* of the activities normally performed by suppliers or buyers, in place of full ownership of operations that are backward or forward in the supply chain.

Strategic alliances
Long-term agreements between two or more companies to jointly develop new products or processes that benefit all companies that are a part of the agreement.

can obtain from being a part of adjacent stages of the value chain. For example, they do this by jointly implementing JIT inventory systems, or sharing future component-parts designs to improve quality and lower assembly costs. As part of this process, suppliers make substantial investments in specialized assets to better serve the needs of a particular carmaker, and the cost savings that result are shared. Thus, Japanese carmakers have been able to capture many of the benefits of vertical integration without having to enter the component industry.

Similarly, component suppliers also benefit because their business and profitability grow as the companies they supply grow, and they can invest their profits in investing in ever more specialized assets.[10] An interesting example of this is the computer chip outsourcing giant Taiwan Semiconductor Manufacturing Company (TSMC) that makes the chips for many companies, such as NVIDIA, Acer, and AMD. The cost of investing in the machinery necessary to build a state-of-the-art chip factory can exceed $10 billion. TSMC is able to make this huge (risky) investment because it has developed cooperative long-term relationships with its computer chip partners. All parties recognize that they will benefit from this outsourcing arrangement, which does not preclude some hard bargaining between TSMC and the chip companies, because all parties want to maximize their profits and reduce their risks. An interesting example of how strategic alliances can go wrong and lead to major problems occurred in 2011, as discussed in Strategy in Action 9.3.

9.3 STRATEGY IN ACTION

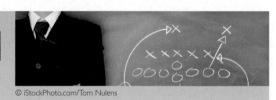

© iStockPhoto.com/Tom Nulens

Apple, Samsung, and Nokia Battle in the Smartphone Market

For several years, Apple had formed a strategic alliance with Samsung to make the proprietary chips it uses in its iPhones and iPads, which are based on the designs of British chip company ARM Holdings, the company that dominates the smartphone chip industry. Samsung used its low-cost skills in chip-making to make Apple's new chips—despite that Samsung was one of Apple's competitors, as it also makes its own smartphones. In 2010, Samsung introduced its new generation of Galaxy smartphones and tablet computers that do not use the same chip as Apple's, but perform similar functions, look similar to Apple's products, and have proven to be very popular with customers globally.

In 2011, Apple decided that its alliance with Samsung had allowed that company to imitate the designs of its smartphones and tablet computers and it sued Samsung, arguing that it had infringed on Apple's patents and specialized knowledge. The alliance between the two companies quickly dissolved as

Samsung countersued Apple, arguing that Apple had infringed upon Samsung's own patented designs, and analysts expect Apple to turn to another company to make its chips in the future. At the same time, Nokia, which has spent $60 billion on R&D to develop new smartphone technology in the last decade, was suing Apple! Nokia claimed that Apple had violated its patents and this had allowed it to innovate the iPhone so quickly. Apple countersued Nokia, arguing that Nokia had violated its patents, in particular the touchscreen technology for which it is now so well known. In June 2011, however, Apple agreed to settle with Nokia and to pay Nokia billions of dollars for the right to license its patents and use its technology. Then, also in June 2011, Apple was awarded a patent that protected its touchscreen technology, and it looked like a new round of lawsuits would begin between these smartphone companies to dominate this highly profitable and growing market.

Sources: www.samsung.com, www.nokia.com, and www.apple.com.

Building Long-Term Cooperative Relationships

How does a company create a long-term strategic alliance with another company when the fear of holdup exists, and the possibility of being cheated arises if one company makes a specialized investment with another company? How do companies such as GM or Nissan manage to develop such profitable, enduring relationships with their suppliers?

There are several strategies companies can adopt to promote the success of a long-term cooperative relationship and lessen the chance that one company will renege on its agreement and cheat the other. One strategy is for the company that makes the specialized investment to demand a *hostage* from its partner. Another is to establish a *credible commitment* from both companies that will result in a trusting, long-term relationship.[11]

Hostage Taking   **Hostage taking** is essentially a means of guaranteeing that each partner will keep its side of the bargain. The cooperative relationship between Boeing and Northrop Grumman illustrates this type of situation. Northrop is a major subcontractor for Boeing's commercial airline division, providing many components for its aircraft. To serve Boeing's special needs, Northrop has had to make substantial investments in specialized assets, and, in theory, because of this investment, Northrop has become dependent on Boeing—which can threaten to change orders to other suppliers as a way of driving down Northrop's prices. In practice, Boeing is highly unlikely to make a change of suppliers because it is, in turn, a major supplier to Northrop's defense division and provides many parts for its Stealth aircraft; it also has made major investments in specialized assets to serve Northrop's needs. Thus, the companies are *mutually dependent*; each company holds a hostage—the specialized investment the other has made. Thus, Boeing is unlikely to renege on any pricing agreements with Northrop because it knows that Northrop would respond the same way.

Credible Commitments   A **credible commitment** is a believable promise or pledge to support the development of a long-term relationship between companies. Consider the way GE and IBM developed such a commitment. GE is one of the major suppliers of advanced semiconductor chips to IBM, and many of the chips are customized to IBM's requirements. To meet IBM's specific needs, GE has had to make substantial investments in specialized assets that have little other value. As a consequence, GE is dependent on IBM and faces a risk that IBM will take advantage of this dependence to demand lower prices. In theory, IBM could back up its demand by threatening to switch its business to another supplier. However, GE reduced this risk by having IBM enter into a contractual agreement that committed IBM to purchase chips from GE for a 10-year period. In addition, IBM agreed to share the costs of the specialized assets needed to develop the customized chips, thereby reducing the risks associated with GE's investment. Thus, by publicly committing itself to a long-term contract and putting some money into the chip development process, IBM made a *credible commitment* that it would continue to purchase chips from GE. When a company violates a credible commitment with its partners, the results can be dramatic, as discussed in Strategy in Action 9.4.

Maintaining Market Discipline   Just as a company pursuing vertical integration faces the problem that its company-owned suppliers might become inefficient, a company that forms a strategic alliance with an independent component supplier runs the risk that its alliance partner might become inefficient over time, resulting in higher component costs or lower quality. This also happens because the outside supplier knows it does not need to compete

Hostage taking

A means of exchanging valuable resources to guarantee that each partner to an agreement will keep its side of the bargain.

Credible commitment

A believable promise or pledge to support the development of a long-term relationship between companies.

9.4 STRATEGY IN ACTION

Ebay's Changing Commitment to Its Sellers

© iStockPhoto.com/Tom Nulens

Since its founding in 1995, eBay has always cultivated good relationships with the millions of sellers that advertise their goods for sale on its website. Over time, however, to increase its revenues and profits, eBay has steadily increased the fees it charges sellers to list their products on its sites, to insert photographs, to use its PayPal online payment service, and for other additional services. Although this has caused some grumbling among sellers because it reduced their profit margins, eBay increasingly engages in extensive advertising to attract millions more buyers to its website, so sellers can receive better prices and also increase their total profits. As a result, they remained largely satisfied with eBay's fee structure.

These policies changed when a new CEO, John Donohue, took the place of eBay's long-time CEO, Meg Whitman, who had built the company into a dot.com giant. By 2008, eBay's profits had not increased rapidly enough to keep its investors happy, and its stock price plunged. To increase performance, one of Donohue's first moves was to announce a major overhaul of eBay's fee structure and feedback policy. The new fee structure would reduce upfront seller listing costs, but increase back-end commissions on completed sales and payments. For smaller sellers that already had thin profit margins, these fee hikes were painful. In addition, in the future, eBay announced it would block sellers from leaving negative feedback about buyers—feedback such as buyers didn't pay for the goods they purchased, or buyers took too long to pay for goods. The feedback system that eBay had originally developed had been a major source of its success; it allowed buyers to be certain they were dealing with reputable sellers—and vice versa. All sellers and buyers have feedback scores that provide them with a reputation as good—or bad—individuals to do business with, and these scores helped reduce the risks involved in online transactions. Donohue claimed this change was implemented in order to improve the buyer's experience because many buyers

had complained that if they left negative feedback for a seller, the seller would then leave negative feedback for the buyer!

Together, however, throughout 2009, these changes resulted in conflict between eBay and its millions of sellers, who perceived they were being harmed by these changes. Their bad feelings resulted in a revolt. Blogs and forums all over the Internet were filled with messages claiming that eBay had abandoned its smaller sellers, and was pushing them out of business in favor of high-volume "powersellers" who contributed more to eBay's profits. Donohue and eBay received millions of hostile e-mails, and sellers threatened they would do business elsewhere, such as on Amazon.com and Yahoo!, two companies that were both trying to break into eBay's market. Sellers also organized a 1-week boycott of eBay during which they would list no items with the company to express their dismay and hostility! Many sellers did shut down their eBay online storefronts and moved to Amazon.com, which claimed in 2011 that its network of sites had overtaken eBay in monthly unique viewers or "hits" for the first time. The bottom line was that the level of commitment between eBay and its sellers had fallen dramatically; the bitter feelings produced by the changes eBay had made were likely to result in increasing problems that would hurt its future performance.

Realizing that his changes had backfired, Donohue reversed course and eliminated several of eBay's fee increases and revamped its feedback system; sellers and buyers can now respond to one another's comments in a fairer way. These changes did improve hostility and smooth over the bad feelings between sellers and eBay, but the old "community relationship" it had enjoyed with sellers in its early years largely disappeared. As this example suggests, finding ways to maintain cooperative relationships—such as by testing the waters in advance and asking sellers for their reactions to fee and feedback changes—could have avoided many of the problems that arose.

Source: www.ebay.com.

with other suppliers for the company's business. Consequently, a company seeking to form a mutually beneficial, long-term strategic alliance needs to possess some kind of power that it can use to discipline its partner—should the need arise.

A company holds two strong cards over its supplier partner. First, all contracts, including long-term contracts, are periodically renegotiated, usually every 3 to 5 years, so the supplier knows that if it fails to live up to its commitments, its partner may refuse to renew the contract. Second, many companies that form long-term relationships with suppliers use **parallel sourcing policies**—that is, they enter into long-term contracts with at least *two* suppliers for the *same* component (this is Toyota's policy, for example).[12] This arrangement protects a company against a supplier that adopts an uncooperative attitude because the supplier knows that if it fails to comply with the agreement, the company can switch *all* its business to its other supplier partner. When both the company and its suppliers recognize that the parallel sourcing policy allows a supplier to be replaced at short notice, most suppliers behave because the policy brings market discipline into their relationship.

The growing importance of JIT inventory systems as a way to reduce costs and enhance quality and differentiation is increasing the pressure on companies to form strategic alliances in a wide range of industries. The number of strategic alliances formed each year, especially global strategic alliances, is increasing, and the popularity of vertical integration is falling because so many low-cost global suppliers exist in countries like Malaysia, Korea, and China.

STRATEGIC OUTSOURCING

Vertical integration and strategic alliances are alternative ways of managing the value chain *across industries* to strengthen a company's core business model. However, just as low-cost suppliers of component parts exist, so today many *specialized companies* exist that can perform one of a company's *own value-chain activities* in a way that contributes to a company's differentiation advantage or that lowers its cost structure. For example, as noted in the opening case, Apple found that using Foxconn factories in China to assemble its iPhones enabled it to not only benefit by lower costs, but to also much more rapidly incorporate design changes and scale up production.

Strategic outsourcing is the decision to allow one or more of a company's value-chain activities or functions to be performed by independent specialist companies that focus all their skills and knowledge on just one kind of activity. The activity to be outsourced may encompass an entire function, such as the manufacturing function, or it may be just one kind of activity that a function performs. For example, many companies outsource the management of their pension systems while keeping other human resource management (HRM) activities within the company. When a company chooses to outsource a value-chain activity, it is choosing to focus on a *fewer* number of value creation activities to strengthen its business model.

There has been a clear move among many companies to outsource activities that managers regard as being "noncore" or "nonstrategic," meaning they are not a source of a company's distinctive competencies and competitive advantage.[13] The vast majority of companies outsource manufacturing or some other value-chain activity to domestic or overseas companies today; some estimates are that over 60% of all global product manufacturing is outsourced to manufacturing specialists because of pressures to reduce costs. Some well-known companies that outsource include Nike, which does not make its athletic shoes; Gap Inc., which does not make its jeans and clothing; and Microsoft, which does not

Parallel sourcing policy
A policy in which a company enters into long-term contracts with at least two suppliers for the same component to prevent any problems of opportunism.

Strategic outsourcing
The decision to allow one or more of a company's value-chain activities to be performed by independent, specialist companies that focus all their skills and knowledge on just one kind of activity to increase performance.

9.5 STRATEGY IN ACTION

Apple Tries to Protect Its New Products and the Workers Who Make Them

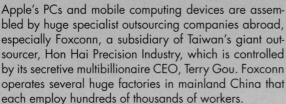

© iStockPhoto.com/Tom Nulens

Apple's PCs and mobile computing devices are assembled by huge specialist outsourcing companies abroad, especially Foxconn, a subsidiary of Taiwan's giant outsourcer, Hon Hai Precision Industry, which is controlled by its secretive multibillionaire CEO, Terry Gou. Foxconn operates several huge factories in mainland China that each employ hundreds of thousands of workers.

Apple has long been known for its concern for secrecy; it strives to keep the details of its new or improved products, such as its updated iPhone 4S launched in October 2011, hidden while under development. Steve Jobs, who also passed away in October 2011, was always concerned with protecting Apple's secrets. His concern for security led Apple to sue a college student who published a website featuring details of Apple's future products; it has also brought legal action against many bloggers who reveal details about its new products. Even in its own U.S. product engineering units Apple has strict rules that prevent engineers from discussing the projects they are working on with engineers from other units to prevent information flows between engineering units and so protect product secrecy.

Apple has also developed uncompromising rules that govern how its outsourcers should protect product secrecy. To keep Apple's business, outsourcers like Foxconn go to extreme lengths to follow Apple's rules and follow stringent security guidelines in their manufacturing plants to keep the details of Apple's new products secret. For example, Apple dictates that the final product should not be assembled until as late as possible to meet its launch date; so, while workers learn how to assemble components, they have no idea what collection of components will go into the final product. Also, Foxconn strictly controls its factories to make it easier to enforce such rules. For example, Foxconn's massive plant in Longhua, China, employs over 350,000 workers who are discouraged from leaving the factory; it offers them a full array of low-cost services such as canteens, dormitories, and recreational facilities. If employees leave the plant, they are searched; metal detectors are used to ensure they do not take components with them, and they are also scanned when they return. Truck drivers who deliver components to the factory are also scanned, as well as anyone else who enters the factory. Apple's contracts include a confidentiality clause with stiff penalties in the event of a security breach, and

Apple's inspectors perform surprise factory visits to ensure outsourcers follow its rules.

Although Apple insists its outsourcers create elaborate "secrecy" walls around their assembly plants, these same walls make it much more difficult to enforce the extensive and well-publicized rules Apple has developed regarding the fair and equitable treatment of employees who work in these gigantic "sweatshops." For example, in 2006, after reports claimed Foxconn was not following Apple's rules regarding employee treatment, Apple audited its factories and found many violations that were never publicly disclosed. Apple has been criticized for allowing its products to be made at plants with poor employment practices—despite the fact that it claims to enforce many rules governing how employees should be treated. In 2010, Apple announced that new audits had revealed that child labor had been used in Foxconn's and other Chinese factories that made its iPods and other electronic devices: "In each of the three facilities, we required a review of all employment records for the year as well as a complete analysis of the hiring process to clarify how under-age people had been able to gain employment." Also, Apple admitted that sweatshop-like conditions existed inside these factories and at least 55 of the 102 factories had ignored rules that employees should work no more than 60 hours per week. Apple said another of its outsourcers had repeatedly falsified its records to conceal child labor practices and long employee hours; it terminated all contracts with that company: "When we investigated, we uncovered records and conducted worker interviews that revealed excessive working hours and 7 days of continuous work."

Apple's ethical position came under increased scrutiny in 2010 when it was widely publicized that at Foxconn's biggest factory in Shenzhen, which assembles Apple's iPhone, 11 workers had committed suicide by jumping off buildings within a period of 12 months. Once again Apple sent inspectors, including its chief operating officer (COO), to investigate, and within months Foxconn's Terry Gou announced that it would almost double workers' wages and improve working conditions to improve employee morale. These circumstances beg the questions: Which rules does Apple spend the most time and effort to develop and enforce? Which rules does it regard as being most important—the rules that protect the secrecy of its products, or the rules that protect the rights of the workers who make those products?

Source: www.apple.com.

make its Xbox consoles. These products are made under contract at low-cost, global locations by contract manufacturers that specialize in low-cost assembly—and many problems can arise as a result, as Strategy in Action 9.5 discusses.

Although manufacturing is the most common form of strategic outsourcing, as we noted earlier, many other kinds of noncore activities are also outsourced. Microsoft has long outsourced its entire customer technical support operation to an independent company, as does Dell. Both companies have extensive customer support operations in India staffed by skilled operatives who are paid a fraction of what their U.S. counterparts earn. BP outsourced almost all of its human resource function to Exult, a San Antonio company, in a 5-year deal worth $600 million; a few years later Exult won a 10-year, $1.1 billion contract to handle HRM activities for all Bank of America's 150,000 employees. Similarly, American Express outsourced its entire IT function to IBM in a 7-year deal worth $4 billion. In 2006, IBM announced it was outsourcing its purchasing function to an Indian company to save $2 billion a year, and it has steadily increased its use of outsourcing ever since. For example, in 2009, IBM announced it would lay off 5,000 IT employees in the United States and move their jobs to India.[14]

Companies engage in strategic outsourcing to strengthen their business models and increase their profitability. The process of strategic outsourcing typically begins with strategic managers identifying the value-chain activities that form the basis of a company's competitive advantage; these are obviously kept within the company to protect them from competitors. Managers then systematically review the noncore functions to assess whether independent companies that specialize in those activities can perform them more effectively and efficiently. Because these companies specialize in particular activities, they can perform them in ways that lower costs or improve differentiation. If managers decide there are differentiation or cost advantages, these activities are outsourced to those specialists.

This is illustrated in Figure 9.3, which shows the primary value-chain activities and boundaries of a company before and after it has pursued strategic outsourcing. In this

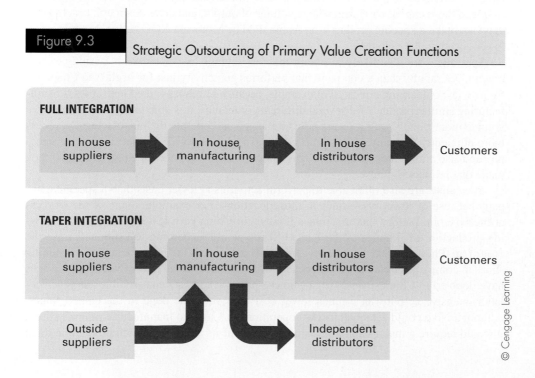

Figure 9.3 **Strategic Outsourcing of Primary Value Creation Functions**

© Cengage Learning

example, the company decided to outsource its production and customer service functions to specialist companies, leaving only R&D and marketing and sales within the company. Once outsourcing has been executed, the relationships between the company and its specialists are then often structured as long-term contractual relationships, with rich information sharing between the company and the specialist organization to which it has contracted the activity. The term **virtual corporation** has been coined to describe companies that have pursued extensive strategic outsourcing.[15]

Virtual corporation

When companies pursued extensive strategic outsourcing to the extent that they only perform the central value creation functions that lead to competitive advantage.

Benefits of Outsourcing

Strategic outsourcing has several advantages. It can help a company to (1) lower its cost structure, (2) increase product differentiation,[16] and (3) focus on the distinctive competencies that are vital to its long-term competitive advantage and profitability.

Lower Cost Structure   Outsourcing will reduce costs when the price that must be paid to a specialist company to perform a particular value-chain activity is less than what it would cost the company to internally perform that activity in-house. Specialists are often able to perform an activity at a lower cost than the company, because they are able to realize scale economies or other efficiencies not available to the company. For example, performing HRM activities, such as managing benefit and pay systems, requires a significant investment in sophisticated HRM IT; purchasing these IT systems represents a considerable fixed cost for one company. But, by aggregating the HRM IT needs of many individual companies, companies that specialize in HRM, such as Exult and Paychex, can obtain huge economies of scale in IT that any single company could not hope to achieve. Some of these cost savings are then passed to the client companies in the form of lower prices, which reduces their cost structure. A similar dynamic is at work in the contract manufacturing business. Once again, manufacturing specialists like Foxconn, Flextronics, and Jabil Circuit make large capital investments to build efficient-scale manufacturing facilities, but then are able to spread those capital costs over a huge volume of output, and drive down unit costs so that they can make a specific product—an Apple iPod or Motorola XOOM, for example—at a lower cost than the company.

Specialists are also likely to obtain the cost savings associated with learning effects much more rapidly than a company that performs an activity just for itself (see Chapter 4 for a review of learning effects). For example, because a company like Flextronics is manufacturing similar products for several different companies, it is able to build up *cumulative* volume more rapidly, and it learns how to manage and operate the manufacturing process more efficiently than any of its clients could. This drives down the specialists' cost structure and also allows them to charge client companies a lower price for a product than if they made that product in-house.

Specialists are also often able to perform activities at lower costs than a specific company because of lower wage rates in those locations. For example, many of the workers at the Foxconn factory that assembles iPhones in China earn less than $17 a day; moving production of iPhones to the United States would, according to estimates, raise the cost of an iPhone by $65.[17] Similarly, Nike also outsources the manufacture of its running shoes to companies based in China because of much lower wage rates. Even though wages have doubled in China since 2010, a Chinese-based specialist can assemble shoes (a very labor-intensive activity) at a much lower cost than could be done in the United States. Although Nike could establish its own operations in China to manufacture running shoes, it would require a major capital investment and limit its ability to switch production to an even lower-cost location later, for example, Vietnam—and many companies are moving to Vietnam because wage rates are lower there. So, for Nike and most other consumer goods companies, outsourcing manufacturing activities lowers costs and gives the companies the flexibility to switch to a more favorable location if labor costs change is the most efficient way to handle production.

Enhanced Differentiation   A company may also be able to differentiate its final products better by outsourcing certain noncore activities to specialists. For this to occur, the *quality* of the activity performed by specialists must be greater than if that same activity was performed by the company. On the reliability dimension of quality, for example, a specialist may be able to achieve a lower error rate in performing an activity, precisely because it focuses solely on that activity and has developed a strong distinctive competency in it. Again, this is one advantage claimed for contract manufacturers. Companies like Flextronics have adopted Six Sigma methodologies (see Chapter 4) and driven down the defect rate associated with manufacturing a product. This means they can provide more reliable products to their clients, which can now differentiate their products on the basis of their superior quality.

A company can also improve product differentiation by outsourcing to specialists when they stand out on the excellence dimension of quality. For example, the excellence of Dell's U.S. customer service is a differentiating factor, and Dell outsources its PC repair and maintenance function to specialist companies. A customer who has a problem with a product purchased from Dell can get excellent help over the phone, and if there is a defective part in the computer, a maintenance person will be dispatched to replace the part within a few days. The excellence of this service differentiates Dell and helps to guarantee repeat purchases, which is why HP has worked hard to match Dell's level of service quality. In a similar way, carmakers often outsource specific kinds of vehicle component design activities, such as microchips or headlights, to specialists that have earned a reputation for design excellence in this particular activity.

Focus on the Core Business   A final advantage of strategic outsourcing is that it allows managers to focus their energies and their company's resources on performing those core activities that have the most potential to create value and competitive advantage. In other words, companies can enhance their core competencies and are able to push out the value frontier and create more value for their customers. For example, Cisco Systems remains the dominant competitor in the Internet router industry because it has focused on building its competencies in product design, marketing and sales, and supply-chain management. Companies that focus on the core activities essential for competitive advantage in their industry are better able to drive down the costs of performing those activities, and better differentiate their final products.

Risks of Outsourcing

Although outsourcing noncore activities has many benefits, there are also risks associated with it, risks such as holdup and the possible loss of important information when an activity is outsourced. Managers must assess these risks before they decide to outsource a particular activity, although, as we discuss the following section, these risks can be reduced when the appropriate steps are taken.

Holdup   In the context of outsourcing, holdup refers to the risk that a company will become too dependent upon the specialist provider of an outsourced activity and that the specialist will use this fact to raise prices beyond some previously agreed-upon rate. As with strategic alliances, the risk of holdup can be reduced by outsourcing to several suppliers and pursuing a parallel sourcing policy, as Toyota and Cisco do. Moreover, when an activity can be performed well by any one of several different providers, the threat that a contract will not be renewed in the future is normally sufficient to keep the chosen provider from exercising bargaining power over the company. For example, although IBM enters into long-term contracts to provide IT services to a wide range of companies, it would be unadvisable to attempt to raise prices after the contract has been signed because it knows full well that such an action would reduce its chance of getting the contract renewed in the future. Moreover, because IBM has many strong competitors in the IT services business, such as Accenture, Capgemini, and HP, it has a very strong incentive to deliver significant value to its clients.

Increased Competition   As firms employ contract manufacturers for production, they help to build an industry-wide resource that lowers the barriers to entry in that industry. In industries that have efficient and high-quality contract manufacturers, large firms may find that their size no longer affords them protection against competitive pressure; their high investments in fixed assets can become a constraint rather than a source of advantage.[18] Furthermore, firms that use contract manufacturing pay, in essence, for the contract manufacturer to progress down its own learning curve. Over time, the contract manufacturer's capabilities improve, putting it at an even greater manufacturing advantage over the firm. Contract manufacturers in many industries increase the scope of their activities over time, adding a wider range of services (e.g., component purchasing, redesign-for-manufacturability, testing, packaging, and after-sales service) and may eventually produce their own end products in competition with their customers. Contracts to manufacture goods for U.S. and European electronics manufacturers, for example, helped to build the electronics manufacturing giants that exist today in Japan and Korea.

Loss of Information and Forfeited Learning Opportunities   A company that is not careful can lose important competitive information when it outsources an activity. For example, many computer hardware and software companies have outsourced their customer technical support function to specialists. Although this makes good sense from a cost and differentiation perspective, it may also mean that a critical point of contact with the customer, and a source of important feedback, is lost. Customer complaints can be useful pieces of information and valuable inputs into future product design, but if those complaints are not clearly communicated to the company by the specialists performing the technical support activity, the company can lose the information. Similarly, a firm that manufactures its own products also gains knowledge about how to improve their design in order to lower the costs of manufacturing or produce more reliable products. Thus, a firm that forfeits the development of manufacturing knowledge could unintentionally forfeit opportunities for improving its capabilities in product design. The firm risks becoming "hollow."[19] These are not arguments against outsourcing. Rather, they are arguments for ensuring that there is appropriate communication between the outsourcing specialist and the company. At Dell, for example, a great deal of attention is paid to making sure that the specialist responsible for providing technical support and onsite maintenance collects and communicates all relevant data regarding product failures and other problems to Dell, so that Dell can design better products.

Ethical Dilemma

© iStockPhoto.com/P_Wei

Google pursued a strategy of horizontal integration and has bought hundreds of small software companies to become the dominant online advertising company and a major software provider for PCs and mobile computing devices. Google has been accused of using its monopoly power to overcome or undermine its rivals, such as Yahoo! and perhaps Groupon, and in 2011, it was under investigation by the FTC. Google's managers have responded that online advertising costs have actually fallen because its search engine technology allows it to better target customers. in addition, it has given many products away for free such as its Chrome Web browser and Android software, and dramatically improved other online offerings.

If you were on a committee charged with deciding whether Google has behaved in an unethical manner, what kind of criteria would you use to determine the outcome?

SUMMARY OF CHAPTER

1. A corporate strategy should enable a company, or one or more of its business units, to perform one or more of the value creation functions at a lower cost or in a way that allows for differentiation and a premium price.

2. The corporate-level strategy of horizontal integration is pursued to increase the profitability of a company's business model by (a) reducing costs, (b) increasing the value of the company's products through differentiation, (c) replicating the business model, (d) managing rivalry within the industry to reduce the risk of price warfare, and (e) increasing bargaining power over suppliers and buyers.

3. There are two drawbacks associated with horizontal integration: (a) the numerous pitfalls associated with making mergers and acquisitions and (b) the fact that the strategy can bring a company into direct conflict with antitrust authorities.

4. The corporate-level strategy of vertical integration is pursued to increase the profitability of a company's "core" business model in its original industry. Vertical integration can enable a company to achieve a competitive advantage by helping build barriers to entry, facilitating investments in specialized assets, protecting product quality, and helping to improve scheduling between adjacent stages in the value chain.

5. The disadvantages of vertical integration include (i) increasing bureaucratic costs if a company-owned or in-house supplier becomes lazy or inefficient, (ii) potential loss of focus on those resources and capabilities that create the most value for the firm, and (iii), reduced flexibility to adapt to a fast-changing environment. Entering into a long-term contract can enable a company to realize many of the benefits associated with vertical integration without having to bear the same level of bureaucratic costs. However, to avoid the risks associated with becoming too dependent upon its partner, it needs to seek a credible commitment from its partner or establish a mutual hostage-taking situation.

6. The strategic outsourcing of noncore value creation activities may allow a company to lower its costs, better differentiate its products, and make better use of scarce resources, while also enabling it to respond rapidly to changing market conditions. However, strategic outsourcing may have a detrimental effect if the company outsources important value creation activities or becomes too dependent upon the key suppliers of those activities.

DISCUSSION QUESTIONS

1. Under what conditions might horizontal integration be inconsistent with the goal of maximizing profitability?
2. What is the difference between a company's internal value chain and the industry value chain? What is the relationship between vertical integration and the industry value chain?
3. Why was it profitable for GM and Ford to integrate backward into component-parts manufacturing in the past, and why are both companies now buying more of their parts from outside suppliers?
4. What value creation activities should a company outsource to independent suppliers? What are the risks involved in outsourcing these activities?
5. What steps would you recommend that a company take to build mutually beneficial long-term cooperative relationships with its suppliers?

PRACTICING STRATEGIC MANAGEMENT

© iStockPhoto.com/Urilux

Small-Group Exercise: Comparing Vertical Integration Strategies

Break up into small groups of three to five people, and discuss the following scenario. Appoint one group member as a spokesperson who will communicate your findings to the class. Read the following description of the activities of Seagate Technologies and Quantum Corporation, both of which manufacture computer disk drives. On the basis of this description, outline the pros and cons of a vertical integration strategy. Which strategy do you think makes most sense in the context of the computer disk drive industry?

Quantum Corporation and Seagate Technologies are major producers of disk drives for PCs and workstations. The disk drive industry is characterized by sharp fluctuations in the level of demand, intense price competition, rapid technological change, and product life cycles of only 12 to 18 months. Quantum and Seagate have pursued very different vertical integration strategies to meet this challenge.

Seagate is a vertically integrated manufacturer of disk drives, both designing and manufacturing the bulk of its own disk drives. On the other hand, Quantum specializes in design; it outsources most of its manufacturing to a number of independent suppliers, including, most important, Matsushita Kotobuki Electronics (MKE) of Japan. Quantum makes only its newest and most expensive products in-house. Once a new drive is perfected and ready for large-scale manufacturing, Quantum turns over manufacturing to MKE. MKE and Quantum have cemented their partnership over 8 years. At each stage in designing a new product, Quantum's engineers send the newest drawings to a production team at MKE. MKE examines the drawings and proposes changes that make new disk drives easier to manufacture. When the product is ready for manufacture, 8 to 10 Quantum engineers travel to MKE's plant in Japan for at least 1 month to work on production ramp-up.

STRATEGY SIGN-ON

© iStockPhoto.com/Ninoslav Dotlic

Article File 9

Find an example of a company whose horizontal or vertical integration strategy appears to have dissipated rather than created value. Identify why this has been the case and what the company should do to rectify the situation.

Strategic Management Project: Module 9

This module requires you to assess the horizontal and vertical integration strategy being pursued by your company. With the information you have at your disposal, answer the questions and perform the tasks listed:

1. Has your company ever pursued a horizontal integration strategy? What was the strategic reason for pursuing this strategy?
2. How vertically integrated is your company? In what stages of the industry value chain does it operate?
3. Assess the potential for your company to increase profitability through vertical integration. In reaching your assessment, also consider the bureaucratic costs of managing vertical integration.
4. On the basis of your assessment in question 3, do you think your company should (a) outsource some operations that are currently performed in-house or (b) bring some operations in-house that are currently outsourced? Justify your recommendations.
5. Is your company involved in any long-term cooperative relationships with suppliers or buyers? If so, how are these relationships structured? Do you think that these relationships add value to the company? Why or why not?
6. Is there any potential for your company to enter into (additional) long-term cooperative relationships with suppliers or buyers? If so, how might these relationships be structured?

CLOSING CASE

The Rapid Consolidation of the U.S. Airline Industry

In July 2008, American Airlines (AA) was the largest air carrier in the world, and it competed against five other established U.S. airlines as well as newer airlines such as Southwest and JetBlue. Then, oil prices, which are approximately 35% of an airline's total operating costs, were rising, and the recent financial recession occurred that led to a significant decrease in the number of business travelers (who are the most lucrative source of revenue for an airline). These circumstances led to billions of dollars in losses for most major U.S.

airlines, including American and JetBlue. Southwest, however, was the exception because it has always pursued a cost-leadership strategy and so had been able to withstand falling ticket prices and rising costs better than the older, more established airlines.

With many major airlines facing bankruptcy, the Justice Department began to look more favorably upon requests by airlines to merge their operations, expand their route structures, and reduce their cost structures. The downside for passengers of merger and horizontal integration, of course, is that if there are fewer airlines, the remaining carriers are able to reduce the number of flights they offer and services they provide—and the result is that ticket prices increase. For example, industry consolidation makes it easier for carriers to announce changes such as charging for a second checked bag or the right to be seated first, all of which provide airlines with additional sources of revenue.

Nevertheless, in 2009 the Justice Department allowed Delta and Northwest Airlines to merge, resulting in the new Delta becoming the largest U.S. airline. Then in 2010, the merger between United and Continental Airlines was also approved, and by 2011, the newly merged United-Continental Airlines was competing with Delta to become the largest U.S. carrier. American Airlines, by that time, was now number three after its proposal to merge with British Airways (and become the largest global airline) was not approved for antitrust reasons—despite that the global airline industry was also rapidly consolidating.

By 2011, the largest U.S. airlines had achieved most of their goals of reducing costs; they had slashed the number of flights they offered, mothballed hundreds of older planes, laid off thousands of employees, and instituted new surcharges for fuel, baggage, and even for carrying pets onboard. In 2012, Delta and US Airways posted modest profits (Delta earned a net profit margin of 2.4% and a return on assets of 2%; US Airways earned a net profit margin of 4.6% and a return on assets of 6.8%). United-Continental and American Airlines, however, were still posting losses.

While its rivals had lost many billions over the decade beginning in 2000, Southwest celebrated an unbroken string of consecutive annual profits. By 2011, Southwest served most major U.S. cities, and its managers also saw an opportunity to expand market share and simultaneously keep its cost structure low by acquiring one of its low-cost rivals, Air Tran Holdings, owner of AirTran Airways. AirTran offered low-cost passenger transportation to almost 70 cities, mainly in the United States and the Caribbean. Like Southwest Airlines, it operated an all-Boeing fleet, facilitating its integration with Southwest's operations (Southwest's use of only Boeing 737s was said to be a major source of efficiencies, for example, by reducing parts inventory requirements and increasing pilot flexibility). The revenues of the combined companies reached $17.1 billion in 2012, roughly half the size of the world's largest airlines.

Many analysts, watching Southwest's ever-changing online fares, noted that it, too, was raising fares in response to the moves of other airlines. Although it had staunchly refused to impose baggage fees (in order to not erode its low-cost image), it began to create fees for such services as bringing pets into the cabin and for the travel of unaccompanied minors.

Sources: Hoovers.com; "Southwest Airlines – Details and Fleet History – Planespotters.net Just Aviation," Planespotters.net; and "AirTran Airways – Details and Fleet History – Planespotters.net Just Aviation," Planespotters.net.

CASE DISCUSSION QUESTIONS

1. How does consolidation improve airlines' revenues? How might it improve their costs?
2. Are there any disadvantages to the airlines of consolidating?
3. Why do you think Southwest Airlines is (on average) the most profitable of the U.S. airlines? Should it attempt to integrate with other airlines? Why or why not?

KEY TERMS

NOTES

[1]This is the essence of Chandler's argument. See A. D. Chandler, *Strategy and Structure* (Cambridge: MIT Press, 1962). The same argument is also made by J. Pfeffer and G. R. Salancik, *The External Control of Organizations* (New York: Harper & Row, 1978). See also K. R. Harrigan, *Strategic Flexibility* (Lexington: Lexington Books, 1985); K. R. Harrigan, "Vertical Integration and Corporate Strategy," *Academy of Management Journal* 28 (1985): 397–425; and F. M. Scherer, *Industrial Market Structure and Economic Performance* (Chicago: Rand McNally, 1981).

[2]O. E. Williamson, *The Economic Institutions of Capitalism* (New York: Free Press, 1985). For a more recent empirical work that uses this framework, see L. Poppo and T. Zenger, "Testing Alternative Theories of the Firm: Transaction Cost, Knowledge Based, and Measurement Explanations for Make or Buy Decisions in Information Services," *Strategic Management Journal* 19 (1998): 853–878.

[3]Williamson, *Economic Institutions of Capitalism*.

[4]J. M. deFigueiredo and B. S. Silverman, "Firm Survival and Industry Evolution in Vertically Related Populations," *Management Science* 58 (2012):1632–1650.

[5]www.mcdonalds.com.

[6]Ibid.

[7]A. D. Chandler, *The Visible Hand* (Cambridge: Harvard University Press, 1977).

[8]Harrigan, *Strategic Flexibility*, pp. 67–87. See also A. Afuah, "Dynamic Boundaries of the Firm: Are Firms Better Off Being Vertically Integrated in the Face of a Technological Change?" *Academy of Management Journal* 44 (2001): 1121–1228.

[9]K. M. Gilley, J. E. McGee, and A. A. Rasheed, "Perceived Environmental Dynamism and Managerial Risk Aversion as Antecedents of Manufacturing Outsourcing: The Moderating Effects of Firm Maturity," *Journal of Small Business Management*, 42 (2004): 117–134; and M. A. Schilling and H. K. Steensma, "The Use of Modular Organizational Forms: An Industry-Level Analysis," *Academy of Management Journal*, 44(2001): 1149–1169.

[10]X. Martin, W. Mitchell, and A. Swaminathan, "Recreating and Extending Japanese Automobile Buyer-Supplier Links in North America," *Strategic Management Journal* 16 (1995): 589–619; and C. W. L. Hill, "National Institutional Structures, Transaction Cost Economizing, and Competitive Advantage," *Organization Science* 6 (1995): 119–131.

[11]Williamson, *Economic Institutions of Capitalism*. See also J. H. Dyer, "Effective Inter-Firm Collaboration: How Firms Minimize Transaction Costs and Maximize Transaction Value," *Strategic Management Journal* 18 (1997): 535–556.

[12]Richardson, "Parallel Sourcing."

[13]W. H. Davidow and M. S. Malone, *The Virtual Corporation* (New York: Harper & Row, 1992).

[14]J. Krane, "American Express Hires IBM for $4 Billion," *Columbian*, February 26, 2002, p. E2; www.ibm.com.

[15]Davidow and Malone, *The Virtual Corporation*.

[16]Ibid.; H. W. Chesbrough and D. J. Teece, "When Is Virtual Virtuous? Organizing for Innovation," *Harvard Business Review*, January–February 1996, pp. 65–74; J. B. Quinn, "Strategic Outsourcing: Leveraging Knowledge Capabilities," *Sloan Management Review*, Summer 1999, pp. 9–21.

[17]C. Duhigg and K. Bradsher, "How the U.S. Lost Out on iPhone Work," *New York Times*, January 21, 2012, p. 1.

[18]Schilling and Steensma, "The Use of Modular Organizational Forms."

[19]R. Venkatesan, "Strategic Sourcing: To Make or Not to Make. *Harvard Business Review*, November–December 1992, pp. 98–107.

10

Corporate-Level Strategy: Related and Unrelated Diversification

© iStockPhoto.com/Chepko Danil

LEARNING OBJECTIVES

After reading this chapter, you should be able to:

10-1 Differentiate between multibusiness models based on related and unrelated diversification

10-2 Explain the five primary ways in which diversification can increase company profitability

10-3 Discuss the conditions that lead managers to pursue related diversification versus unrelated diversification and explain why some companies pursue both strategies

10-4 Describe the three methods companies use to enter new industries—internal new venturing, acquisitions, and joint ventures—and discuss the advantages and disadvantages associated with each of these methods

OPENING CASE

Citigroup: The Opportunities and Risks of Diversification

Helen Sessions/Alamy

In 2013, Citigroup was a $90.1 billion diversified financial services firm known around the world. However, its history had not always been smooth. From the late 1990s through 2010, the company's diversification moves, and its role in the mortgage crisis, combined to bring the company to its knees, making many fear that the venerable bank—one of the oldest and largest in the United States—would not survive.

Citigroup traces its history all the way back to 1812, when it was formed by a group of merchants in response to the abolishment of the First Bank of the United States (the First Bank's charter had been permitted to lapse due to Thomas Jefferson's arguments about the dangers of centralized control of the economy). The merchants, led by Alexander Hamilton, created the City Bank of New York in 1812, which they hoped would be large enough to replicate the scale advantages that had been offered by the First Bank. The bank played some key roles in the rise of the United States as a global power, including lending money to support the purchasing of armaments for the War of 1812, financing the Union war effort in the mid-1800s, and later pioneering foreign-exchange trading, which helped to bring the United States to the world stage in the early 1900s. By 1929, it was the largest commercial bank in the world.

The bank's capital resources and its trusted brand name enabled it to successfully diversify into a range of consumer banking services. The highly innovative company was, for example, the first to introduce savings accounts with compound interest, unsecured personal loans, checking accounts, and 24-hour ATMs, among other things. However, its business remained almost entirely within traditional retail banking services. That would soon change with the rise of a new concept: the "financial supermarket."

During the 1990s, there was much buzz in the financial industry about the value of having a wider range of financial services within the same bank. Why have your savings account in New Jersey, your stock broker in California, and your insurance agent in Maryland, when you could have everything under one roof? Merging such services under one roof would enable numerous "cross-selling" opportunities: Each company's customer bases could be more fully leveraged by promoting other financial products to them. Furthermore, cost savings might be realized by consolidating operations such as information technology, customer service and billing, and so forth. In 1998, Sanford "Sandy" Weill, who had already begun creating his own financial supermarket that included Travelers insurance, Aetna, Primerica, Salomon Brothers, and Smith Barney Holdings, convinced Citicorp chairman and CEO John Reed that the two companies should merge. Travelers Group purchased all of Citicorp's shares for $70 billion, and issued 2.5 new Citigroup shares for each Citicorp Share. Existing shareholders of each company thus owned approximately half of the new firm. The merger created a $140 billion firm with assets of $700 billion. Renamed Citigroup, it was now the largest financial services organization in the world.

Unfortunately, at almost exactly the same time, the Internet rendered the bricks-and-mortar financial supermarket obsolete: the best deals were to be found at the financial supermarket on the Web. To make matters worse, rather than cross-selling, the different divisions of Citi and Travelers began battling each other to protect their turf. Savings in consolidating back-office operations also turned out to be meager and costly to realize. Harmonizing each company's information technology systems, for example, was going to be so expensive that ultimately the legacy systems were just left intact. Additionally,

though the merged company shed more than 10,000 employees, it was harder to part with other executive—instead, the company kept so many pairs of executives with "co" titles (including co-CEOs Weill and Reed) that some people compared Citi to Noah's Ark. According to Meredith Whitney, a banking analyst who was an early critic of Citi's megabank model, Citi had become "a gobbledygook of companies that were never integrated. . . The businesses didn't communicate with each other. There were dozens of technology systems and dozens of financial ledgers."

To boost earnings, Citi began investing in subprime loans, whose risk was camouflaged by bundling them into mortgage-backed securities known as collateralized debt obligations (CDOs). Trouble began brewing before even Citi knew the scale of risk it had undertaken. Loose lending policies had resulted in a large number of poor-quality mortgages, the vast majority of which had adjustable-rate mortgages (i.e., the initial rate was very low, but would increase over time). This combined with a steep decline in housing prices that made it next to impossible for homebuyers to refinance their mortgages as their interest rates climbed—their homes were now worth less than what they owed. Delinquencies and foreclosures soared, meaning that banks holding those mortgages had assets whose value was rapidly declining. A lawsuit by Citi's shareholders in 2006 accused the company of using a "CDO-related quasi-Ponzi scheme" to falsely give the appearance that it had a healthy asset base and conceal the true risks the company was facing, but even Citi's CEO at the time, Charles O. Prince III, did not know how much the company had invested in mortgage-related assets. Prince found out at a September 2007 meeting that the company had $43 billion in mortgage-related assets, but was assured by Thomas Maheras (who oversaw trading at the bank) that everything was fine. Soon the company was posting billions in losses and its stock price fell to the lowest it had been in a decade (see the accompanying graphs). To Lynn Turner, a former chief accountant with the Securities and Exchange Commission, Citi's crisis was no surprise. He pointed out that Citi was too large, did not have the right controls, and lacked sufficient accountability for individuals undertaking risks on the company's behalf, making such problems inevitable. The amalgamation of businesses had created conflicts of interest, and Citi's managers lacked the ability to accurately gauge the risk of the exotic financial instruments that were proliferating. As the true scope of the problem was revealed, Citi found itself in very dire circumstances. The losses from writing down its mortgage assets threatened to destroy the entire company, bringing down even its profitable lines of business.

While the U.S. government kept the bank from failing with a $45 billion bailout (for fear that Citi's failure would cause an even greater economic collapse—giving rise to the phrase "too big to fail"), Citigroup began reducing its workforce, and selling off everything it could, dismantling its financial supermarket. Over the next 2 years it slashed over 80,000 jobs and sold Smith Barney, Phibro (its commodities-trading unit), Diner's Club (a credit card), its Japanese brokerage operations, Primerica, and more. Furthermore, to raise capital it sold 5% of its equity to the Abu Dhabi Investment

authority for $7.5 billion, and then raised another $12 billion by selling shares to a group of investors that included Prince Alwaleed Bin Talal of Saudi Arabia in 2008. It also restructured itself into two operating units: Citicorp for retail and institutional client business, and Citi Holdings for its brokerage and asset management. This reorganization would help to isolate Citi's banking operations from the riskier assets it wished to sell.

In 2010, Citigroup finally returned to profitability. It repaid its U.S. government loans, and its managers and the investment community breathed a sigh of relief, optimistic that the worst was over. In 2012, Citi posted $71 billion in revenues and $7.5 billion in net income (Citi's consumer and institutional businesses earned $14.1 billion in profits, but were offset by $6.6 billion in losses from Citi Holdings). Today, roughly 50% of its revenues come from its consumer businesses (retail banking, credit cards, mortgages, and commercial banking for small-to-medium businesses), 50% comes from its Institutional Clients group (which provides investment and banking services for corporations, governments, institutions and ultra-high-net-worth individuals), and Citi Holdings posts zero to negative revenues.

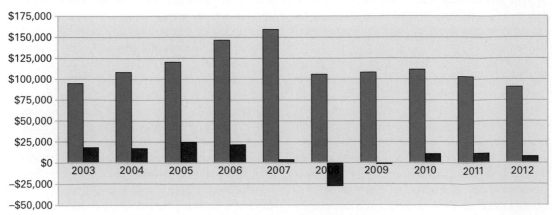

Citigroup's Revenues and Net Income (in $US millions), 2003–2012

Source: Hoovers.com

The saga of Citi seriously undermined the investment community's faith in the financial supermarket model, although in the wake of the mortgage crisis it was difficult to assess how much had been gained and lost through the diversification of the firm. One thing that was clear, however, was that having a very large and complex organization had made it more difficult to provide sufficient, and effective, oversight within the firm. This, in turn, allowed problems to grow very large before being detected. Citi's managers knew they would have to think much more carefully about their business choices in the future, and about how to manage the interdependencies between those businesses.

Sources: R. Wile, "Dramatic Highlights from Citi's 200-Year History," *Business Insider,* April 4, 2012, www.businessinsider.com/presenting-a-history-of-citi-2012-4?op=1); "About Citi—Citibank, N.A.," www.citigroup.com; M. Martin, "Citicorp and Travelers Plan to Merge in Record $70 Billion Deal," *New York Times,* April 7, 1998, p. 1; A. Kessler, "The End of Citi's Financial Supermarket," *Wall Street Journal,* January 16, 2009, p. A11; "Fall Guy," *The Economist,* November 5, 1998; E. Dash and J. Creswell, "Citigroup Saw No Red Flags Even as It Made Bolder Bets," *New York Times,* November 22, 2008, p. 14; P. Hurtado and D. Griffin, "Citigroup Settles Investors' CDO Suit for $590 Million," Bloomberg.com, August 29, 2012; and D. Ellis, "Citi Plunges 26%—Lowest in 15 Years," CNNMoney.com, November 20, 2008.

Citigroup's Stock Price, 2004–2013

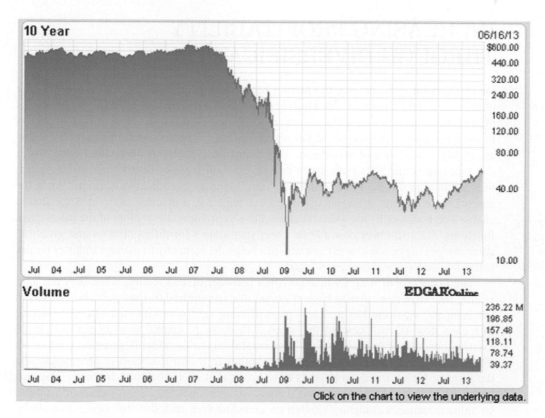

Source: NASDAQ.com

OVERVIEW

The chapter-opening case illustrates how diversification can create, and destroy, value. Citibank's reputation, brand name, expertise, and capital had enabled it to profitably expand both its product and geographic scope. However, overestimates of synergies led the firm to diversify into activities that strayed from its key strengths in consumer retail banking. Furthermore, as it became increasingly diversified, it became difficult for managers to provide adequate oversight within the organization. Problems, including conflicts of interest and underestimates of the risk of its assets, grew without being detected. By the time management knew there was trouble within the firm, the company was in desperate circumstances, and may not have survived had it not been bailed out by the U.S. government.

In this chapter, we continue to discuss both the challenges and opportunities created by corporate-level strategies of related and unrelated diversification. A diversification strategy is based upon a company's decision to enter one or more new industries to take advantage of its existing distinctive competencies and business model. We examine the different kinds of multibusiness models upon which related and unrelated diversification are based. Then, we discuss three different ways companies can implement a diversification strategy: internal new ventures, acquisitions, and joint ventures. By the end of this chapter, you will understand the advantages and disadvantages associated with strategic managers' decisions to diversify and enter new markets and industries.

INCREASING PROFITABILITY THROUGH DIVERSIFICATION

diversification

The process of entering new industries, distinct from a company's core or original industry, to make new kinds of products for customers in new markets.

diversified company

A company that makes and sells products in two or more different or distinct industries.

Diversification is the process of entering new industries, distinct from a company's core or original industry, to make new kinds of products that can be sold profitably to customers in these new industries. A multibusiness model based on diversification aims to find ways to use a company's existing strategies and distinctive competencies to make products that are highly valued by customers in the new industries it enters. A **diversified company** is one that makes and sells products in two or more different or distinct industries (industries *not* in adjacent stages of an industry value chain as in vertical integration). As in the case of the corporate strategies discussed in Chapter 9, a diversification strategy should enable a company or its individual business units to perform one or more of the value-chain functions: (1) at a lower cost, (2) in a way that allows for differentiation and gives the company pricing options, or (3) in a way that helps the company to manage industry rivalry better—*in order to increase profitability*.

The managers of most companies often consider diversification when they are generating *free cash flow*. that is, cash in excess of that required to fund new investments in the company's current business and meet existing debt commitments.[1] In other words, free cash flow is cash beyond that needed to make profitable new investments in its existing business. When a company's successful business model is generating free cash flow and profits, managers must decide whether to return that cash to shareholders in the form of higher dividend payouts or to invest it in diversification. In theory, any free cash flow belongs to the company's owners—its shareholders. So, for diversification to be value creating, a company's return on investing free cash flow to pursue diversification opportunities, that is, its future ROIC, *must* exceed the value shareholders would reap by returning the cash to them. When a firm does not pay out its free cash flow to its shareholders, the shareholders bear an opportunity cost equal to their next best use of those funds (i.e., another investment that pays a similar return at a similar risk, an investment that pays a higher return at a higher risk, or an investment that pays a lower return but at a lower risk). Thus, a diversification strategy must pass the "better off" test: the firm must be more valuable than it was before the diversification, and that value must not be fully capitalized by the cost of the diversification move (i.e., the cost of entry into the new industry must be taken into account when assessing the value created by the diversification move). Thus managers might defer paying dividends now to invest in diversification, but they should do so only when this is expected to create even greater cash flow (and thus higher dividends) in the future.

There are five primary ways in which pursuing a multibusiness model based on diversification can increase company profitability. Diversification can increase profitability when strategic managers (1) transfer competencies between business units in different industries, (2) leverage competencies to create business units in new industries, (3) share resources between business units to realize synergies or economies of scope, (4) use product bundling, and (5) utilize *general* organizational competencies that increase the performance of *all* a company's business units.

Transferring Competencies Across Businesses

Transferring competencies involves taking a distinctive competency developed by a business unit in one industry and implanting it in a business unit operating in another industry. The second business unit is often one a company has acquired. Companies that base their diversification strategy on transferring competencies aim to use one or more of their existing distinctive competencies in a value-chain activity—for example, in manufacturing, marketing, materials management, or research and development (R&D)—to significantly strengthen the business model of the acquired business unit or company. For example, over time, Philip Morris developed distinctive competencies in product development, consumer marketing, and brand positioning that had made it a leader in the tobacco industry. Sensing a profitable opportunity, it acquired Miller Brewing, which at the time was a relatively small player in the brewing industry. Then, to create valuable new products in the brewing industry, Philip Morris transferred some of its best marketing experts to Miller, where they applied the skills acquired at Philip Morris to turn around Miller's lackluster brewing business (see Figure 10.1). The result was the creation of Miller Light, the first "light" beer, and a marketing campaign that helped to push Miller from number 6 to number 2 in market share in the brewing industry.

Companies that base their diversification strategy on transferring competencies tend to acquire new businesses *related* to their existing business activities because of commonalities between one or more of their value-chain functions. A **commonality** is some kind of skill or attribute that, when it is shared or used by two or more business units, allows both businesses to operate more effectively and efficiently and create more value for customers.

For example, Miller Brewing was related to Philip Morris's tobacco business because it was possible to create important marketing commonalities; both beer and tobacco are mass-market consumer goods in which brand positioning, advertising, and product development skills are crucial to create successful new products. In general, such competency transfers increase profitability when they either (1) lower the cost structure of one or more of a diversified company's business units or (2) enable one or more of its business units to better differentiate their products, both of which give business unit pricing options to lower a product's price to increase market share or to charge a premium price.

transferring competencies

The process of taking a distinctive competency developed by a business unit in one industry and implanting it in a business unit operating in another industry.

commonality

Some kind of skill or competency that when shared by two or more business units allows them to operate more effectively and create more value for customers.

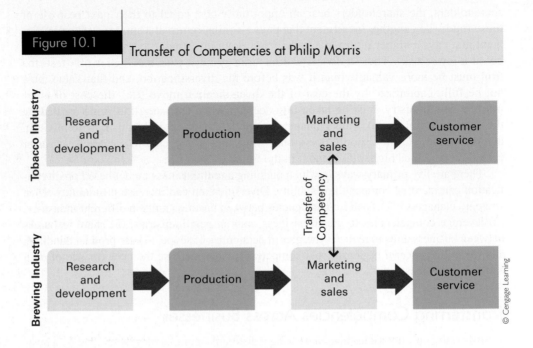

Figure 10.1   Transfer of Competencies at Philip Morris

© Cengage Learning

For competency transfers to increase profitability, the competencies transferred must involve value-chain activities that become an important source of a specific business unit's competitive advantage in the future. In other words, the distinctive competency being transferred must have real strategic value. However, all too often companies assume that *any* commonality between their value chains is sufficient for creating value. When they attempt to transfer competencies, they find the anticipated benefits are not forthcoming because the different business units did not share some important attribute in common. For example, Coca-Cola acquired Minute Maid, the fruit juice maker, to take advantage of commonalities in global distribution and marketing, and this acquisition has proved to be highly successful. On the other hand, Coca-Cola once acquired the movie studio Columbia Pictures because it believed it could use its marketing prowess to produce blockbuster movies. This acquisition was a disaster that cost Coca-Cola billions in losses, and Columbia was eventually sold to Sony, which was then able to base many of its successful PlayStation games on the hit movies the studio produced.

Leveraging Competencies to Create a New Business

leveraging competencies

The process of taking a distinctive competency developed by a business unit in one industry and using it to create a new business unit in a different industry.

Firms can also **leverage their competencies** by using them to develop a new business in a different industry. For example, Apple leveraged its competencies in personal computer (PC) hardware and software to enter the smartphone industry. Once again, the multibusiness model is based on the premise that the set of distinctive competencies that are the source of a company's competitive advantage in one industry might be applied to create a differentiation or cost-based competitive advantage for a new business unit or division in a different industry. For example, Canon used its distinctive competencies in precision mechanics, fine optics, and electronic imaging to produce laser jet printers, which, for Canon, was a new business in a new industry. Its competencies enabled it to produce high-quality (differentiated) laser printers that could be manufactured at a low cost, which created its competitive advantage, and made Canon a leader in the printer industry.

Many companies have based their diversification strategy on leveraging their competencies to create new business units in different industries. Microsoft leveraged its longtime experience and relationships in the computer industry, skills in software development, and its expertise in managing industries characterized by network externalities to create new business units in industries such as videogames (with its Xbox videogame consoles and game), online portals and search engines (e.g., MSN and Bing), and tablet computers (with the introduction of the Surface).

Sharing Resources and Capabilities

A third way in which two or more business units that operate in different industries can increase a diversified company's profitability is when the shared resources and capabilities results in economies of scope, or synergies.[2] **Economies of scope** arise when one or more of a diversified company's business units are able to realize cost-saving or differentiation synergies because they can more effectively pool, share, and utilize expensive resources or capabilities, such as skilled people, equipment, manufacturing facilities, distribution channels, advertising campaigns, and R&D laboratories. If business units in different industries can share a common resource or function, they can collectively lower their cost structure; the idea behind synergies is that $2 + 2 = 5$, not 4, in terms of value created.[3] For example, the costs of GE's consumer products advertising, sales, and service activities reduce costs *across* product lines because they are spread over a wide range of products such as light bulbs, appliances, air conditioners, and furnaces. There are two major sources of these cost reductions.

First, when companies can share resources or capabilities across business units, it lowers their cost structure compared to a company that operates in only one industry and bears the full costs of developing resources and capabilities. For example, P&G makes disposable diapers, toilet paper, and paper towels, which are all paper-based products that customers value for their ability to absorb fluids without disintegrating. Because these products need the same attribute—absorbency—P&G can share the R&D costs associated with developing and making even more advanced absorbent paper-based products across the three distinct businesses (only two are shown in Figure 10.2). Similarly, because all of these products are sold to retailers, P&G can use the same sales force to sell all its products (see Figure 10.2). In contrast, P&G competitors that make only one or two of these products cannot share these costs across industries, so their cost structures are higher. As a result, P&G has lower costs; it can use its marketing function to better differentiate its products, and it achieves a higher ROIC than companies that operate only in one or a few industries—which are unable to obtain economies of scope from the ability to share resources and obtain synergies across business units.

Similarly, Nike, which began strictly as a maker of running shoes, realized that its brand image, and its relationships with athletes and sports events, could be profitably leveraged into other types of athletic footwear, athletic apparel, and accessories such as sunglasses and headphones. Those products were more differentiated because of the Nike brand name and had better exposure because Nike was able to place them in suitable endorsement spots via its relationships with athletes and events, and Nike is able to amortize the cost of its brand-building activities across a wider range of products, thus achieving economies of scope.

Once again, diversification to obtain economies of scope is possible only when there are *significant* commonalities between one or more of the value-chain functions in a company's different business units or divisions that result in synergies that increase profitability.

economies of scope
The synergies that arise when one or more of a diversified company's business units are able to lower costs or increase differentiation because they can more effectively pool, share, and utilize expensive resources or capabilities.

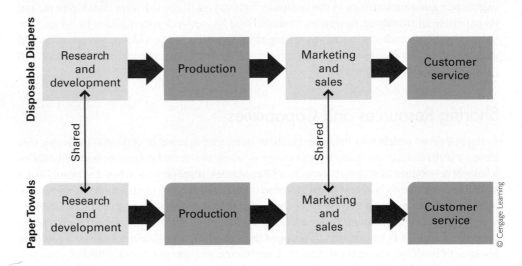

Figure 10.2   Sharing Resources at Proctor & Gamble

In addition, managers must be aware that the costs of coordination necessary to achieve synergies or economies of scope within a company may sometimes be *higher* than the value that can be created by such a strategy.[4] As noted in the opening case, although Citibank had anticipated major cost savings from consolidating operations across its acquisitions, and revenue-increasing opportunities from cross-selling, some of those synergies turned out to be smaller or more difficult to reap than anticipated. In retrospect, the coordination costs that Citi bore (in the form of massive losses due to inadequate oversight over its investment activities) probably vastly exceeded the synergies it gained. Consequently, diversification based on obtaining economies of scope should be pursued only when the sharing of competencies will result in *significant* synergies that will achieve a competitive advantage for one or more of a company's new or existing business units.

Using Product Bundling

In the search for new ways to differentiate products, more and more companies are entering into industries that provide customers with new products that are connected or related to their existing products. This allows a company to expand the range of products it produces in order to be able to satisfy customers' needs for a complete package of related products. This is currently happening in telecommunications, in which customers are increasingly seeking package prices for wired phone service, wireless phone service, high-speed access to the Internet, voice over Internet protocol (VOIP) phone service, television programming, online gaming, video-on-demand, or any combination of these services. To meet this need, large phone companies such as AT&T and Verizon have been acquiring other companies that provide one or more of these services, and cable companies such as Comcast have acquired or formed strategic alliances with companies that can offer their customers a package of these services. In 2010, for example, Comcast acquired GE's NBC division to gain control of its library of content programming. The goal, once again, is to bundle products to offer customers lower prices and/or a superior set of services.

Just as manufacturing companies strive to reduce the number of their component suppliers to reduce costs and increase quality, final customers want to obtain the convenience and reduced price of a bundle of related products—such as from Google or Microsoft's cloud-based commercial, business-oriented online applications. Another example of product bundling comes from the medical equipment industry in which companies that, in the past, made one kind of product, such as operating theater equipment, ultrasound devices, magnetic imaging or X-ray equipment, have now merged with or been acquired by other companies to allow a larger diversified company to provide hospitals with a complete range of medical equipment. This industry consolidation has also been driven by hospitals and health maintenance organizations (HMOs) that wish to obtain the convenience and lower prices that often follow from forming a long-term contract with a single supplier.

It is important to note here that product bundling often does not require joint ownership. In many instances, bundling can be achieved through market contracts. For example, McDonald's does not need to manufacture toys in order to bundle them into Happy Meals—it can buy them through a supply contract. Disney does need to own airline services to offer a package deal on a vacation—an alliance contract will serve just as well. For product bundling to serve as a justification for diversification, there must be a strong need for coordination between the producers of the different products that cannot be overcome through market contracts.

Utilizing General Organizational Competencies

General organizational competencies transcend individual functions or business units and are found at the top or corporate level of a multibusiness company. Typically, **general organizational competencies** are the result of the skills of a company's top managers and functional experts. When these general competencies are present—and many times they are not—they help each business unit within a company perform at a higher level than it could if it operated as a separate or independent company—this increases the profitability of the *entire* corporation.[5] Three kinds of general organizational competencies help a company increase its performance and profitability: (1) entrepreneurial capabilities, (2) organizational design capabilities, and (3) strategic capabilities.

Entrepreneurial Capabilities A company that generates significant excess cash flow can take advantage of it only if its managers are able to identify new opportunities and act on them to create a stream of new and improved products, in its current industry and in new industries. Some companies seem to have a greater capability to stimulate their managers to act in entrepreneurial ways than others, for example, Apple, 3M, Google, and Samsung.[6]

These companies are able to promote entrepreneurship because they have an organizational culture that stimulates managers to act entrepreneurially. As a result, they are able to create profitable new business units more quickly than other companies; this allows them to take advantage of profitable opportunities for diversification. We discuss one of the strategies required to generate profitable new businesses later in this chapter: internal new venturing. For now, it is important to note that to promote entrepreneurship, a company must (1) encourage managers to take risks, (2) give managers the time and resources to pursue novel ideas, (3) not punish managers when a new idea fails, and (4) make sure that the company's free cash flow is not wasted in pursuing too many risky new ventures that have a low probability of generating a profitable return on investment. Strategic managers

general organizational competencies
Competencies that result from the skills of a company's top managers that help every business unit within a company perform at a higher level than it could if it operated as a separate or independent company.

face a significant challenge in achieving all four of these objectives. On the one hand, a company must encourage risk taking, and on the other hand, it must limit the number of risky ventures in which it engages.

Companies that possess strong entrepreneurial capabilities achieve this balancing act. For example, 3M's goal of generating 40% of its revenues from products introduced within the past 4 years focuses managers' attention on the need to develop new products and enter new businesses. 3M's long-standing commitment to help its customers solve problems also ensures that ideas for new businesses are customer focused. The company's celebration of employees who have created successful new businesses helps to reinforce the norm of entrepreneurship and risk taking. Similarly, there is a norm that failure should not be punished but viewed as a learning experience.

organizational design skills

The ability of the managers of a company to create a structure, culture, and control systems that motivate and coordinate employees to perform at a high level.

Capabilities in Organizational Design   **Organizational design skills** are a result of managers' ability to create a structure, culture, and control systems that motivate and coordinate employees to perform at a high level. Organizational design is a major factor that influences a company's entrepreneurial capabilities; it is also an important determinant of a company's ability to create the functional competencies that give it a competitive advantage. The way strategic managers make organizational design decisions, such as how much autonomy to give to managers lower in the hierarchy, what kinds of norms and values should be developed to create an entrepreneurial culture, and even how to design its headquarters buildings to encourage the free flow of ideas, is an important determinant of a diversified company's ability to profit from its multibusiness model. Effective organizational structure and controls create incentives that encourage business-unit (divisional) managers to maximize the efficiency and effectiveness of their units. Moreover, good organizational design helps prevent strategic managers from missing out on profitable new opportunities, as happens when employees become so concerned with protecting their company's competitive position in *existing* industries that they lose sight of new or improved ways to do business and gain profitable opportunities to enter new industries.

The last two chapters of this book look at organizational design in depth. To profit from pursuing the corporate-level strategy of diversification, a company must be able to continuously manage and change its structure and culture to motivate and coordinate its employees to work at a high level and develop the resources and capabilities upon which its competitive advantage depends. The ever-present need to align a company's structure with its strategy is a complex, never-ending task, and only top managers with superior organizational design skills can do it.

Superior Strategic Management Capabilities   For diversification to increase profitability, a company's top managers must have superior capabilities in strategic management. They must possess the intangible, hard-to-define governance skills that are required to manage different business units in a way that enables these units to perform better than they would if they were independent companies.[7] These governance skills are a rare and valuable capability. However, certain CEOs and top managers seem to have them; they have developed the aptitude of managing multiple businesses simultaneously and encouraging the top managers of those business units to devise strategies and achieve superior performance. Examples of CEOs famous for their superior strategic management capabilities include Jeffrey Immelt at GE, Steve Jobs at Apple, and Larry Ellison at Oracle.

An especially important governance skill in a diversified company is the ability to diagnose the underlying source of the problems of a poorly performing business unit, and then to understand how to proceed to solve those problems. This might involve recommending new strategies to the existing top managers of the unit or knowing when to replace them with a new management team that is better able to fix the problems. Top managers who have such governance skills tend to be very good at probing business unit managers for information and helping them to think through strategic problems, as the example of United Technologies Corporation (UTC) discussed in Strategy in Action 10.1 suggests.

Related to strategic management skills is the ability of the top managers of a diversified company to identify inefficient and poorly managed companies in other industries and then to acquire and restructure them to improve their performance—and thus the profitability of

10.1 STRATEGY IN ACTION

United Technologies Has an "ACE" in Its Pocket

© iStockPhoto.com/Tom Nulens

United Technologies Corporation (UTC), based in Hartford, Connecticut, is a *conglomerate*, a company that owns a wide variety of other companies that operate separately in many different businesses and industries. UTC has businesses in two main groups, aerospace and building systems. Its aerospace group includes Sikorsky aircraft, Pratt & Whitney Engines, and UTC Aerospace systems, which was formed through the merger of Hamilton Sundstrand and Goodrich. Its building systems group includes Otis elevators and escalators; Carrier and Noresco heating and air-conditioning solutions; building automation businesses that include AutomatedLogic, Onity, Lenel, and UTEC; and fire detection and security businesses that include Chubb, Kidde, Edwards, Fenwal, Marioff, Supra, and Interlogix. Today, investors frown upon companies like UTC that own and operate companies in widely different industries. There is a growing perception that managers can better manage a company's business model when the company operates as an independent or stand-alone entity. How can UTC justify holding all these companies together in a conglomerate? Why would this lead to a greater increase in total profitability than if they operated as independent companies? In the last decade, the boards of directors and CEOs of many conglomerates, such as Tyco and Textron, have realized that by holding diverse companies together they were reducing, not increasing, the profitability of their companies. As a result, many conglomerates have been broken up and their individual companies spun off to allow them to operate as separate, independent entities.

UTC's CEO George David claims that he has created a unique and sophisticated multibusiness model that adds value across UTC's diverse businesses. David joined Otis Elevator as an assistant to its CEO in 1975, but within 1 year, UTC acquired Otis. The 1970s was a decade when a "bigger is better" mindset ruled corporate America, and mergers and acquisitions of all kinds were seen as the best way to grow profits. UTC sent David to manage its South American operations and later gave him responsibility for its Japanese operations. Otis had formed an alliance with Matsushita to develop an elevator for the Japanese market, and the resulting "Elevonic 401," after being installed widely in Japanese buildings, proved to be a disaster. It broke down much more often than elevators made by other Japanese companies, and customers were concerned about the reliability and safety of this model.

Matsushita was extremely embarrassed about the elevator's failure and assigned one of its leading total quality management (TQM) experts, Yuzuru Ito, to head a team of Otis engineers to find out why it performed so poorly. Under Ito's direction, all the employees—managers, designers, and production workers—who had produced the elevator analyzed why the elevators were malfunctioning. This intensive study led to a total redesign of the elevator, and when the new and improved elevator was launched worldwide, it met with great success. Otis's share of the global elevator market dramatically increased, and David was named president of UTC in 1992. He was given the responsibility to cut costs across the entire corporation, including its

10.1 STRATEGY IN ACTION

(continued)

© iStockPhoto.com/Tom Nulens

important Pratt & Whitney division, and his success in reducing UTC's cost structure and increasing its ROIC led to his appointment as CEO in 1994.

Now responsible for all of UTC's diverse companies, David decided that the best way to increase UTC's profitability, which had been declining, was to find ways to improve efficiency and quality in *all* its constituent companies. He convinced Ito to move to Hartford and take responsibility for championing the kinds of improvements that had by now transformed the Otis division. Ito began to develop UTC's TQM system, also known as "Achieving Competitive Excellence," or ACE.

ACE is a set of tasks and procedures that are used by employees from the shop floor to top managers to analyze all aspects of the way a product is made. The goal is to find ways to improve *quality and reliability*, to *lower the costs* of making a product, and, especially, to find ways to make the next generation of a particular product perform better—in other words, to encourage *technological innovation*. David makes every employee in every function and at every level personally responsible for achieving the incremental, step-by-step gains that result in state-of-the-art innovative and efficient products that allow a company to dominate its industry.

David calls these techniques "process disciplines," and he has used them to increase the performance of all UTC companies. Through these techniques, he has created the extra value for UTC that justifies it owning and operating such a diverse set of businesses. David's success can be seen in the performance that his company has achieved in the decade since he took control: he has quadrupled UTC's earnings per share, and its sales and profits have soared. UTC has been in the top three performers of the companies that make up the Dow Jones industrial average for most of the 2000s, and the company has consistently outperformed GE, another huge conglomerate, in its return to investors.

David and his managers believe that the gains that can be achieved from UTC's process disciplines are never-ending because its own R&D—in which it invests more than $2.5 billion a year—is constantly producing product innovations that can help all its businesses. Recognizing that its skills in creating process improvements are specific to manufacturing companies, UTC's strategy is to only acquire companies that make products that can benefit from the use of its ACE program—hence its Chubb acquisition. At the same time, David invests only in companies that have the potential to remain leading companies in their industries and can therefore charge above-average prices. His acquisitions strengthen the competencies of UTC's existing businesses. For example, he acquired a company called Sundstrand, a leading aerospace and industrial systems company, and combined it with UTC's Hamilton Aerospace Division to create Hamilton Sundstrand, which is now a major supplier to Boeing and makes products that command premium prices. In October 2011, UTC acquired Goodrich, a major supplier of airline components, for over $22 billion to strengthen its aircraft division.

Source: http://utc.com.

turnaround strategy

When managers of a diversified company identify inefficient and poorly managed companies in other industries and then acquire and restructure them to improve their performance—and thus the profitability of the total corporation.

the total corporation. This is known as a **turnaround strategy**.[8] There are several ways to improve the performance of the acquired company. First, the top managers of the acquired company are replaced with a more aggressive top-management team. Second, the new top-management team sells off expensive assets, such as underperforming divisions, executive jets, and elaborate corporate headquarters; it also terminates managers and employees to reduce the cost structure. Third, the new management team works to devise new strategies to improve the performance of the operations of the acquired business and improve its efficiency, quality, innovativeness, and customer responsiveness.

Fourth, to motivate the new top-management team and the other employees of the acquired company to work toward such goals, a company-wide pay-for-performance bonus system linked to profitability is introduced to reward employees at all levels for their hard work. Fifth, the acquiring company often establishes "stretch" goals for employees at all levels; these are challenging, hard-to-obtain goals that force employees at all levels to work to increase the company's efficiency and effectiveness. Finally, the members of the new top-management team clearly understand that if they fail to increase their division's performance and meet these stretch goals within some agreed-upon amount of time, they will be replaced. In sum, the system of rewards and sanctions that corporate managers of the acquiring company establish provide the new top managers of the acquired unit with strong incentive to develop strategies to improve their unit's operating performance.

TWO TYPES OF DIVERSIFICATION

The last section discussed five principal ways in which companies can use diversification to transfer and implant their business models and strategies into other industries and so increase their long-term profitability. The two corporate strategies of *related diversification* and *unrelated diversification* can be distinguished by how they attempt to realize these five profit-enhancing benefits of diversification.[9]

Related Diversification

Related diversification is a corporate-level strategy that is based on the goal of establishing a business unit (division) in a new industry that is *related* to a company's existing business units by some form of commonality or linkage between the value-chain functions of the existing and new business units. As you might expect, the goal of this strategy is to obtain the benefits from transferring competencies, leveraging competencies, sharing resources, and bundling products, as just discussed.

The multibusiness model of related diversification is based on taking advantage of strong technological, manufacturing, marketing, and sales commonalities between new and existing business units that can be successfully "tweaked" or modified to increase the competitive advantage of one or more business units. Figure 10.3 illustrates the commonalities or linkages possible among the different functions of three different business units or divisions. The greater the number of linkages that can be formed among business units, the greater the potential to realize the profit-enhancing benefits of the five reasons to diversify discussed previously.

One more advantage of related diversification is that it can also allow a company to use any general organizational competency it possesses to increase the overall performance of *all* its different industry divisions. For example, strategic managers may strive to create a structure and culture that encourages entrepreneurship across divisions, as Google, Apple, and 3M have done; beyond these general competences, these companies all have a set of distinctive competences that can be shared among their different business units and that they continuously strive to improve.

Unrelated Diversification

Unrelated diversification is a corporate-level strategy whereby firms own unrelated businesses and attempt to increase their value through an internal capital market, the use of general organizational competencies, or both. Companies pursuing this strategy are

related diversification
A corporate-level strategy that is based on the goal of establishing a business unit in a new industry that is related to a company's existing business units by some form of commonality or linkage between their value-chain functions.

unrelated diversification
A corporate-level strategy based on a multibusiness model that uses general organizational competencies to increase the performance of all the company's business units.

Figure 10.3

Commonalities Between the Value Chains of Three Business Units

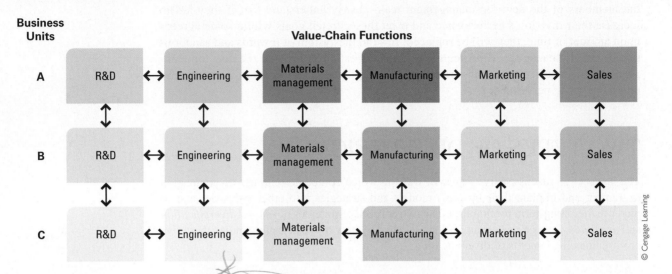

Business Units — **Value-Chain Functions**

A: R&D ↔ Engineering ↔ Materials management ↔ Manufacturing ↔ Marketing ↔ Sales

B: R&D ↔ Engineering ↔ Materials management ↔ Manufacturing ↔ Marketing ↔ Sales

C: R&D ↔ Engineering ↔ Materials management ↔ Manufacturing ↔ Marketing ↔ Sales

internal capital market

A corporate-level strategy whereby the firm's headquarters assesses the performance of business units and allocates money across them. Cash generated by units that are profitable but have poor investment opportunities within their business is used to cross-subsidize businesses that need cash and have strong promise for long-run profitability.

often called *conglomerates*, business organizations that operate in many diverse industries. An **internal capital market** refers to a situation whereby a corporate headquarters assesses the performance of business units and allocates money across them. Cash generated by units that are profitable but have poor investment opportunities within their business is used to cross-subsidize businesses that need cash and have strong promise for long-run profitability. A large and diverse firm may both have free cash generated from its internal businesses and/or have access to cheaper cash on the external capital market than an individual business unit might have. For example, GE's large capital reserves and excellent credit rating enable it to provide funding to advanced technology businesses within its corporate umbrella (e.g., solar power stations, subsea oil production equipment, avionics, photonics) that would otherwise pay a high price (either in interest payments or equity shares) for funding due to their inherent uncertainty.

The benefits of an internal capital market are limited, however, by the efficiency of the external capital market (banks, stockholders, venture capitalists, angel investors, etc.). If the external capital market were perfectly efficient, managers could not create additional value by cross-subsidizing businesses with internal cash. An internal capital market is, in essence, an arbitrage strategy where managers make money by making better investment decisions within the firm than the external capital market would. Often this is because managers have superior information than the external capital market. The amount of value that can be created through an internal capital market is thus directly proportional to the inefficiency of the external capital market. In the United States, where capital markets have become fairly efficient due to (i) reporting requirements mandated by the Securities and Exchange Commission (SEC), (ii) large numbers of research analysts, (iii) an extremely large and active investment community, (iv) strong communication systems, and (v) strong contract law, it is not common to see firms create significant value through an internal capital market. As a result, few large conglomerates have survived, and many of those that do survive trade at a discount (i.e., their stock is worth less than the stock of more specialized firms operating in the same industries). On the other hand, in a market with a less efficient capital market, conglomerates may create significant value. Tata Group, for example, is an extremely large and diverse business holding group in India. It was founded during the 1800s and took on many projects that its founders felt were crucial to India's development (developing rail system, hotels, power production, etc.) The lack of a well-developed investment community and poor contract law to protect investors and bankers meant that funds were often not available to entrepreneurs in India, or were available only at a very high cost. Tata Group was thus able to use cross-subsidization to fund projects much more cheaply than independent businesses could. Furthermore, the reputation of the company served as a strong guarantee that the company would fulfill its promises (which was particularly important in the absence of strong contract law), and its long and deep relationships with the government gave it an advantage in securing licenses and permits.

Companies pursuing a strategy of unrelated diversification have *no* intention of transferring or leveraging competencies between business units or sharing resources other than cash and general organizational competencies. If the strategic managers of conglomerates have the special skills needed to manage many companies in diverse industries, the strategy can result in superior performance and profitability; often they do not have these skills, as is discussed later in the chapter. Some companies, such as UTC, discussed in Strategy in Action 10.1, have top managers who do possess these special skills.

THE LIMITS AND DISADVANTAGES OF DIVERSIFICATION

Many companies, such as 3M, Samsung, UTC, and Cisco, have achieved the benefits of pursuing either or both of the two diversification strategies just discussed, and they have managed to sustain their profitability over time. On the other hand, companies such as GM, Tyco, Textron, and Philips that pursued diversification failed miserably and became unprofitable. There are three principal reasons why a business model based on diversification may lead to a loss of competitive advantage: (1) changes in the industry or inside a company that occur over time, (2) diversification pursued for the wrong reasons, and (3) excessive diversification that results in increasing bureaucratic costs.

Changes in the Industry or Company

Diversification is a complex strategy. To pursue diversification, top managers must have the ability to recognize profitable opportunities to enter new industries and to implement the strategies necessary to make diversification profitable. Over time, a company's top-management team often changes; sometimes its most able executives join other companies and become their CEOs, and sometimes successful CEOs decide to retire or step down. When the managers who possess the hard-to-define skills leave, they often take their visions with them. A company's new leaders may lack the competency or commitment necessary to pursue diversification successfully over time; thus, the cost structure of the diversified company increases and eliminates any gains the strategy may have produced.

In addition, the environment often changes rapidly and unpredictably over time. When new technology blurs industry boundaries, it can destroy the source of a company's competitive advantage; for example, by 2011, it was clear that Apple's iPhone and iPad had become a direct competitor with Nintendo's and Sony's mobile gaming consoles. When such a major technological change occurs in a company's core business, the benefits it has previously achieved from transferring or leveraging distinctive competencies disappear. The company is then saddled with a collection of businesses that have all become poor performers in their respective industries because they are not based on the new technology—something that has happened to Sony. Thus, a major problem with diversification is that the future success of a business is hard to predict when this strategy is used. For a company to profit from it over time, managers must be as willing to divest business units as they are to acquire them. Research suggests managers do not behave in this way, however.

Diversification for the Wrong Reasons

As we have discussed, when managers decide to pursue diversification, they must have a clear vision of how their entry into new industries will allow them to create new products that provide more value for customers and increase their company's profitability. Over time, however, a diversification strategy may result in falling profitability for reasons noted earlier, but managers often refuse to recognize that their strategy is failing. Although they know they should divest unprofitable businesses, managers "make up" reasons why they should keep their collection of businesses together.

In the past, for example, one widely used (and false) justification for diversification was that the strategy would allow a company to obtain the benefits of risk pooling. The idea behind risk pooling is that a company can reduce the risk of its revenues and profits rising and falling sharply (something that sharply lowers its stock price) if it acquires and operates companies in several industries that have different business cycles. The business cycle is the tendency for the revenues and profits of companies in an industry to rise and fall over time because of "predictable" changes in customer demand. For example, even in a recession, people still need to eat—the profits earned by supermarket chains will be relatively stable; sales at Safeway, Kroger, and also at "dollar stores" actually rise as shoppers attempt to get more value for their dollars. At the same time, a recession can cause the demand for cars and luxury goods to plunge. Many CEOs argue that diversifying into industries that have different business cycles would allow the sales and revenues of some of their divisions to rise, while sales and revenues in other divisions would fall. A more stable stream of revenue and profits is the net result over time. An example of risk pooling occurred when U.S. Steel diversified into the oil and gas industry in an attempt to offset the adverse effects of cyclical downturns in the steel industry.

This argument ignores two important facts. First, stockholders can eliminate the risk inherent in holding an individual stock by diversifying their *own* portfolios, and they can do so at a much lower cost than a company can. Thus, attempts to pool risks through diversification represent an unproductive use of resources; instead, profits should be returned to shareholders in the form of increased dividends. Second, research suggests that corporate diversification is not an effective way to pool risks because the business cycles of different industries are *inherently difficult to predict,* so it is likely that a diversified company will find that an economic downturn affects *all* its industries simultaneously. If this happens, the company's profitability plunges.[10]

When a company's core business is in trouble, another mistaken justification for diversification is that entry into new industries will rescue the core business and lead to long-term growth and profitability. An example of a company that made this mistake is Kodak. In the 1980s, increased competition from low-cost Japanese competitors, such as Fuji, combined with the beginnings of the digital revolution, soon led its revenues and profits to plateau and then fall. Its managers should have done all they could to reduce its cost structure; instead they took its huge free cash flow and spent tens of billions of dollars to enter new industries, such as health care, biotechnology, and computer hardware, in a desperate and mistaken attempt to find ways to increase profitability.

This was a disaster because every industry Kodak entered was populated by strong companies such as 3M, Canon, and Xerox. Also, Kodak's corporate managers lacked any general competencies to give their new business units a competitive advantage. Moreover, the more industries Kodak entered, the greater the range of threats the company encountered, and the more time managers had to spend dealing with these threats. As a result, they could spend much less time improving the performance of their core film business that continued to decline.

In reality, Kodak's diversification was just for growth itself, but *growth does not create value for stockholders*; growth is just the by-product, not the objective, of a diversification strategy. However, in desperation, companies diversify for reasons of growth alone rather than to gain any well-thought-out strategic advantage.[11] In fact, many studies suggest that too much diversification may reduce rather than improve company profitability.[12] That is, the diversification strategies many companies pursue may *reduce* value instead of creating it.[13]

The Bureaucratic Costs of Diversification

A major reason why diversification often fails to boost profitability is that very often the *bureaucratic costs* of diversification exceed the benefits created by the strategy (that is, the increased profit that results when a company makes and sells a wider range of differentiated products and/or lowers its cost structure). As we mention in the previous chapter, **bureaucratic costs** are the costs associated with solving the transaction difficulties that arise between a company's business units and between business units and corporate headquarters, as the company attempts to obtain the benefits from transferring, sharing, and leveraging competencies. They also include the costs associated with using general organizational competencies to solve managerial and functional inefficiencies. The level of bureaucratic costs in a diversified organization is a function of two factors: (1) the number of business units in a company's portfolio and (2) the degree to which coordination is required between these different business units to realize the advantages of diversification.

bureaucratic costs
The costs associated with solving the transaction difficulties between business units and corporate headquarters as a company obtains the benefits from transferring, sharing, and leveraging competencies.

Number of Businesses   The greater the number of business units in a company's portfolio, the more difficult it is for corporate managers to remain informed about the complexities of each business. Managers simply do not have the time to assess the business model of each unit. This problem occurred at GE in the 1970s when its growth-hungry CEO Reg Jones acquired many new businesses, as he commented:

> I tried to review each plan [of each business unit] in great detail. This effort took untold hours and placed a tremendous burden on the corporate executive office. After a while I began to realize that no matter how hard we would work, we could not achieve the necessary in-depth understanding of the 40-odd business unit plans.[14]

The inability of top managers in extensively diversified companies to maintain control over their multibusiness model over time often leads managers to base important resource allocation decisions only on the most superficial analysis of each business unit's competitive position. For example, a promising business unit may be starved of investment funds, while other business units receive far more cash than they can profitably reinvest in their operations. Furthermore, because they are distant from the day-to-day operations of the business units, corporate managers may find that business unit managers try to hide information on poor performance to save their own jobs. For example, business unit managers might blame poor performance on difficult competitive conditions, even when it is the result of their inability to craft a successful business model. As such organizational problems increase, top managers must spend an enormous amount of time and effort to solve these problems. This increases bureaucratic costs and cancels out the profit-enhancing advantages of pursuing diversification, such as those obtained from sharing or leveraging competencies.

Coordination Among Businesses   The amount of coordination required to realize value from a diversification strategy based on transferring, sharing, or leveraging competencies is a major source of bureaucratic costs. The bureaucratic mechanisms needed to oversee and manage the coordination and handoffs between units, such as cross-business-unit teams and management committees, are a major source of these costs. A second source of bureaucratic costs arises because of the enormous amount of managerial time and effort required to accurately measure the performance and unique profit contribution of a business unit that is transferring or sharing resources with another. Consider a company that has two business units, one making household products (such as liquid soap and laundry detergent) and another making packaged food products. The products of both units are sold through supermarkets. To lower the cost structure, the parent company decides to pool the marketing and sales functions of each business unit, using an organizational structure similar to that illustrated in Figure 10.4. The company is organized into three divisions: a household products division, a food products division, and a marketing division.

Although such an arrangement may significantly lower operating costs, it can also give rise to substantial control problems, and hence bureaucratic costs. For example, if the performance of the household products business begins to slip, identifying who is to be held accountable—managers in the household products division or managers in the marketing division—may prove difficult. Indeed, each may blame the other for poor performance. Although these kinds of problems can be resolved if corporate management performs an in-depth audit of both divisions, the bureaucratic costs (managers' time and effort) involved in doing so may once again cancel out any value achieved from diversification. The need to reduce bureaucratic costs is evident from the experience of Pfizer discussed in Strategy in Action 10.2.

Figure 10.4	Coordination Among Related Business Units

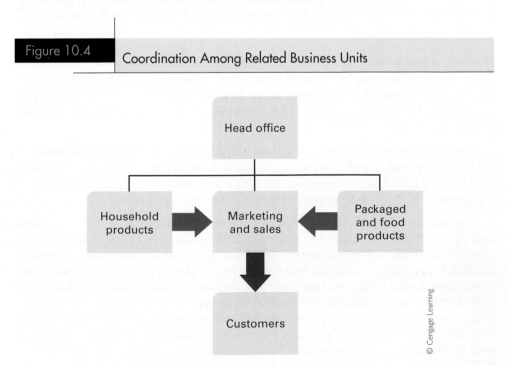

© Cengage Learning

10.2 STRATEGY IN ACTION

How Bureaucratic Costs Rose Then Fell at Pfizer

© iStockPhoto.com/Tom Nulens

Pfizer is the largest global pharmaceuticals company, with sales of almost $50 billion in 2011. Its research scientists have innovated some of the most successful and profitable drugs in the world, such as the first cholesterol reducer, Lipitor. In the 2000s, however, Pfizer encountered major problems in its attempt to innovate new blockbuster drugs while its current blockbuster drugs, such as Lipitor, lost their patent protection. Whereas Lipitor once earned a $13 billion in profits per year, its sales were now fast declining. Pfizer desperately needed to find ways to make its product development pipeline work—and one manager, Martin Mackay, believed he knew how to do it.

When Pfizer's R&D chief retired, Mackay, his deputy, made it clear to CEO Jeffrey Kindler that he wanted the job. Kindler made it equally clear he thought the company could use some new talent and fresh ideas to solve its problems. Mackay realized he had to quickly devise a convincing plan to change the way Pfizer's scientists worked to develop new drugs, gain Kindler's support, and get the top job. Mackay created a detailed plan for changing the way Pfizer's thousands of researchers made decisions, ensuring that the company's resources and its talent and funds would be best put to use. After Kindler reviewed the plan, he was so impressed he promoted Mackay to the top R&D position. What was Mackay's plan?

As Pfizer had grown over time as a result of mergers with two other large pharmaceutical companies, Warner Lambert and Pharmacia, Mackay noted how decision-making problems and conflict between the managers of Pfizer's different drug divisions had increased. As it grew, Pfizer's organizational structure had become taller and taller, and the size of its headquarters staff grew. With more managers and levels in the company's hierarchy there was a greater need for committees to integrate across activities.

However, in these meetings, different groups of managers fought to promote the development of the drugs they had the most interest in, and managers increasingly came into conflict with one another in order to ensure they got the resources needed to develop these drugs. In short, Mackay felt that too many managers and committees resulted in too much conflict between those who

were actively lobbying the managers and the CEO to promote the interests of their own product groups—and the company's performance was suffering as a result. In addition, although Pfizer's success depended upon innovation, this growing conflict had resulted in a bureaucratic culture that reduced the quality of decision making, creating more difficulty when identifying promising new drugs—and increasing bureaucratic costs.

Mackay's bold plan to reduce conflict and bureaucratic costs involved slashing the number of management layers between top managers and scientists from 14 to 7, which resulted in the layoff of thousands of Pfizer's managers. He also abolished the product development committees whose wrangling he believed was slowing down the process of transforming innovative ideas into blockbuster drugs. After streamlining the hierarchy, he focused on reducing the number of bureaucratic rules scientists had to follow, many of which were unnecessary and had promoted conflict. He and his team eliminated every kind of written report that was slowing the innovation process. For example, scientists had been in the habit of submitting quarterly and monthly reports to top managers explaining each drug's progress; Mackay told them to choose which report they wanted to keep, and the other would be eliminated.

As you can imagine, Mackay's efforts caused enormous upheaval in the company as managers fought to keep their positions, and scientists fought to protect the drugs they had in development. However, Mackay was resolute and pushed his agenda through with the support of the CEO, who defended his efforts to create a new R&D product development process that empowered Pfizer's scientists and promoted innovation and entrepreneurship. Pfizer's scientists reported that they felt "liberated" by the new work flow; the level of conflict decreased, and new drugs were manufactured more quickly. By 2011, Pfizer had secured the approval of the Food and Drug Administration (FDA) for a major new antibacterial drug, and Mackay announced that several potential new blockbuster drugs under development were on track. Finding ways to control and reduce bureaucratic costs is a vital element of managing corporate-level strategy.

Source: www.pfizer.com.

In sum, although diversification can be a highly profitable strategy to pursue, it is also the most complex and difficult strategy to manage because it is based on a complex multi-business model. Even when a company has pursued this strategy successfully in the past, changing conditions both in the industry environment and inside a company may quickly reduce the profit-creating advantages of pursuing this strategy. For example, such changes may result in one or more business units losing their competitive advantage, as happened to Sony. Or, changes may cause the bureaucratic costs associated with pursuing diversification to rise sharply and cancel out its advantages. Thus, the existence of bureaucratic costs places a limit on the amount of diversification that a company can profitably pursue. It makes sense for a company to diversify only when the profit-enhancing advantages of this strategy *exceed* the bureaucratic costs of managing the increasing number of business units required when a company expands and enters new industries.

CHOOSING A STRATEGY

Related Versus Unrelated Diversification

Because related diversification involves more sharing of competencies, one might think it can boost profitability in more ways than unrelated diversification, and is therefore the better diversification strategy. However, some companies can create as much or more value from pursuing unrelated diversification, so this strategy must also have some substantial benefits. An unrelated company does *not* need to achieve coordination between business units; it has to cope only with the bureaucratic costs that arise from the number of businesses in its portfolio. In contrast, a related company must achieve coordination *among* business units if it is to realize the gains that come from utilizing its distinctive competencies. Consequently, it has to cope with the bureaucratic costs that arise *both* from the number of business units in its portfolio *and* from coordination among business units. Although it is true that related diversified companies can create value and profit in more ways than unrelated companies, they also have to bear higher bureaucratic costs to do so. These higher costs may cancel out the higher benefits, making the strategy no more profitable than one of unrelated diversification.

How, then, does a company choose between these strategies? The choice depends upon a comparison of the benefits of each strategy against the bureaucratic costs of pursuing it. It pays a company to pursue related diversification when (1) the company's competencies can be applied across a greater number of industries and (2) the company has superior strategic capabilities that allow it to keep bureaucratic costs under close control—perhaps by encouraging entrepreneurship or by developing a value-creating organizational culture.

Using the same logic, it pays a company to pursue unrelated diversification when (1) each business unit's functional competencies have few useful applications across industries, but the company's top managers are skilled at raising the profitability of poorly run businesses and (2) the company's managers use their superior strategic management competencies to improve the competitive advantage of their business units and keep bureaucratic costs under control. Some well-managed companies, such as UTC, discussed in Strategy in Action 10.1, have managers who can successfully pursue unrelated diversification and reap its rewards.

The Web of Corporate-Level Strategy

Finally, it is important to note that although some companies may choose to pursue a strategy of related or unrelated diversification, there is nothing that stops them from pursuing both strategies at the same time. The purpose of corporate-level strategy is to increase long-term profitability. A company should pursue any and all strategies as long as strategic managers have weighed the advantages and disadvantages of those strategies and arrived at a multibusiness model that justifies them. Figure 10.5 illustrates how Sony developed a web of corporate strategies to compete in many industries—a program that proved a mistake and actually *reduced* its differentiation advantage and increased its cost structure in the 2000s.

First, Sony's core business is its electronic consumer products business, and in the past, it has been well known for its innovative products that have made it a leading global brand. To protect the quality of its electronic products, Sony decided to manufacture a high percentage of the component parts for its televisions, DVD players, and other units and pursued a strategy of backward vertical integration. Sony also engaged in forward vertical integration: for example, it acquired Columbia Pictures and MGM to enter the movie or "entertainment software" industry, and it opened a chain of Sony stores in shopping malls (to compete with Apple). Sony also shared and leveraged its distinctive competencies by developing its own business units to operate in the computer and smartphone industries, a strategy of related diversification. Finally, when it decided to enter the home videogame industry and develop its PlayStation to compete with Nintendo, it was pursuing a strategy of unrelated diversification. In the 2000s, this division contributed more to Sony's profits than its core electronics business, but the company has not been doing well, as Strategy in Action 10.3 suggests.

| Figure 10.5 | Sony's Web of Corporate-Level Strategy |

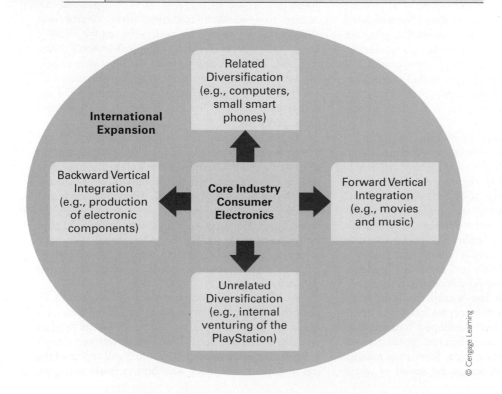

© Cengage Learning

As this discussion suggests, Sony's profitability has fallen dramatically because its multibusiness model led the company to diversify into too many industries, in each of which the focus was upon innovating high-quality products—as a result, its cost structure increased so much it swallowed up all the profits its businesses were generating. Sony's strategy of individual-business-unit autonomy also resulted in each unit pursuing its own goals at the expense of the company's multibusiness model—which escalated bureaucratic costs and drained its profitability. In particular, because its different divisions did not share their knowledge and expertise, this incongruence allowed competitors such as Samsung to supersede Sony, especially with smartphones and flatscreen LCD TV products.

10.3 STRATEGY IN ACTION

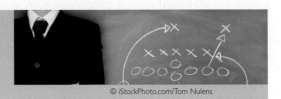

© iStockPhoto.com/Tom Nulens

Sony's "Gaijin" CEO Is Changing the Company's Strategies

Sony was renowned in the 1990s for using its engineering prowess to develop blockbuster new products such as the Walkman, Trinitron TV, and PlayStation. Its engineers churned out an average of four new product ideas every day, something attributed to its culture, called the "Sony Way," which emphasized communication, cooperation, and harmony among its company-wide product engineering teams. Sony's engineers were empowered to pursue their own ideas, and the leaders of its different divisions and hundreds of product teams were allowed to pursue their own innovations—no matter what the cost. Although this approach to leadership worked so long as Sony could churn out blockbuster products, it did not work in the 2000s as agile global competitors from Taiwan, Korea, and the United States innovated new technologies and products that began to beat Sony at its own game.

Companies such as LG, Samsung, and Apple innovated new technologies—including advanced liquid crystal display (LCD) flatscreens, flash memory, touchscreen commands, mobile digital music and video, global positioning system (GPS) devices, and 3D displays—that made many of Sony's technologies (such as its Trinitron TV and Walkman) obsolete. For example, products such as Apple's iPod and iPhone and Nintendo's Wii game console better met customer needs than Sony's out-of-date and expensive products. Why did Sony lose its leading competitive position?

One reason was that Sony's corporate-level strategies no longer worked in its favor; the leaders of its different product divisions had developed business-level strategies to pursue their own divisions' goals and not those of the whole company. Also, Sony's top managers had been slow to recognize the speed at which

technology was changing, and as each division's performance fell, competition between corporate and divisional managers increased. The result was slower decision making and increased operating costs as each division competed to obtain the funding necessary to develop successful new products.

By 2005, Sony was in big trouble, and at this crucial point in their company's history, Sony's top managers turned to a *gaijin*, or non-Japanese, executive to lead their company. Their choice was Welshman Sir Howard Stringer, who, as the head of Sony's U.S. operations, had been instrumental in cutting costs and increasing profits. Stringer was closely involved in all U.S. top-management decisions, but, nevertheless, he still gave his top executives the authority to develop successful strategies to implement these decisions.

When he became Sony's CEO in 2005, Stringer faced the immediate problem of reducing operating costs that were *double* those of its competitors because divisional managers had seized control of Sony's top-level decision-making authority. Stringer recognized how the extensive power struggles among Sony's different product-division managers were hurting the company. So, he made it clear they needed to work quickly to reduce costs and cooperate, sharing resources and competencies to speed product development across divisions.

By 2008, it was clear that many of Sony's most important divisional leaders were still pursuing their own goals, so Stringer replaced all the divisional leaders who resisted his orders. Then, he downsized Sony's bloated corporate headquarters staff and replaced the top functional managers who had pursued strategies

10.3 STRATEGY IN ACTION

(continued)

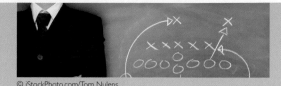

© iStockPhoto.com/Tom Nulens

favoring their interests. He promoted younger managers to develop new strategies for its divisions and functions—managers who would obey his orders and focus on creating commonalities between the company's different businesses.

But, Sony's performance continued to decline, and in 2009, Stringer announced that he would assume more control over the divisions' business-level strategies, taking charge of the core electronics division, and continuing to reorganize and streamline Sony's divisions to increase differentiation and reduce costs. He also told managers to prioritize new products and invest only in those with the greatest chance of success in order to reduce out-of-control R&D costs. By 2010, Sony's financial results suggested that Stringer's initiatives were finally paying off; his strategies to reduce costs had stemmed Sony's huge losses and its new digital products were selling better.

In January 2011, Stringer announced that Sony's performance had increased so much that it would be profitable in the second half of 2011. Then, within months, hackers invaded Sony's PlayStation website and stole the private information of millions of its users. Sony was forced to shut down the website for

weeks and compensate users, which eventually cost it hundreds of millions of dollars. In addition, it also became clear that customers were not buying Sony's expensive new 3D flatscreen TVs and that its revenues from other consumer products would be lower than expected because of intense competition from companies like Samsung. Stringer reported that he expected Sony to make a record loss in 2011, and that his turnaround efforts had been foiled, as the company desperately strived to meet challenges from Apple and Samsung. In 2012, Sony replaced Stringer with Kazuo Hirai, who had been head of Sony Computer Entertainment. Hirai implemented a company-wide initiative named "One Sony," and a focus on three core areas: digital imaging, games, and mobile. Hirai implemented a cost-cutting program that targeted the cost of components, logistics, and operations. He shifted many of the engineering resources out of Japan and into Malaysia, which further cut costs. He sold Sony's chemical business, and he also dissolved Sony's joint venture with Samsung so that the company could purchase LCD panels on the open market to get better pricing. At the end of 2012, Sony finally posted a profit, after 4 straight years of losses.

Sources: B. Gruley, "Kazuo Hirai on Where He's Taking Sony," *Bloomberg Businessweek*, August 9, 2012, www.businessweek.com/printer/articles/66252-kazuo-hirai-on-where-hes-taking-sony); and www.sony.com, 2011 press releases.

ENTERING NEW INDUSTRIES: INTERNAL NEW VENTURES

We have discussed the sources of value managers seek through corporate-level strategies of related and unrelated diversification (and the challenges and risks these strategies also impose). Now we turn to the three main methods managers employ to enter new industries: internal new ventures, acquisitions, and joint ventures. In this section, we consider the pros and cons of using internal new ventures. In the following sections, we look at acquisitions and joint ventures.

The Attractions of Internal New Venturing

Internal new venturing is typically used to implement corporate-level strategies when a company possesses one or more distinctive competencies in its core business model that

internal new venturing

The process of transferring resources to and creating a new business unit or division in a new industry to innovate new kinds of products.

can be leveraged or recombined to enter a new industry. **Internal new venturing** is the process of transferring resources to and creating a new business unit or division in a new industry. Internal venturing is used most by companies that have a business model based upon using their technology or design skills to innovate new kinds of products and enter related markets or industries. Thus, technology-based companies that pursue related diversification, like DuPont, which has created new markets with products such as cellophane, nylon, Freon, and Teflon, are most likely to use internal new venturing. 3M has a near-legendary knack for creating new or improved products from internally generated ideas, and then establishing new business units to create the business model that enables it to dominate a new market. Similarly, HP entered into the computer and printer industries by using internal new venturing.

A company may also use internal venturing to enter a newly emerging or embryonic industry—one in which no company has yet developed the competencies or business model to give it a dominant position in that industry. This was Monsanto's situation in 1979 when it contemplated entering the biotechnology field to produce herbicides and pest-resistant crop seeds. The biotechnology field was young at that time, and there were no incumbent companies focused on applying biotechnology to agricultural products. Accordingly, Monsanto internally ventured a new division to develop the required competencies necessary to enter and establish a strong competitive position in this newly emerging industry.

Pitfalls of New Ventures

Despite the popularity of internal new venturing, there is a high risk of failure. Research suggests that somewhere between 33% and 60% of all new products that reach the marketplace do not generate an adequate economic return[15] and that most of these products were the result of internal new ventures. Three reasons are often put forward to explain the relatively high failure rate of internal new ventures: (1) market entry on too small a scale, (2) poor commercialization of the new-venture product, and (3) poor corporate management of the new-venture division.[16]

Scale of Entry   Research suggests that large-scale entry into a new industry is often a critical precondition for the success of a new venture. In the short run, this means that a substantial capital investment must be made to support large-scale entry; thus, there is a risk of major losses if the new venture fails. But, in the long run, which can be as long as 5 to 12 years (depending on the industry), such a large investment results in far greater returns than if a company chooses to enter on a small scale to limit its investment and reduce potential losses.[17] Large-scale entrants can more rapidly realize scale economies, build brand loyalty, and gain access to distribution channels in the new industry, all of which increase the probability of a new venture's success. In contrast, small-scale entrants may find themselves handicapped by high costs due to a lack of scale economies, and a lack of market presence limits the entrant's ability to build brand loyalty and gain access to distribution channels. These scale effects are particularly significant when a company is entering an *established* industry in which incumbent companies possess scale economies, brand loyalty, and access to distribution channels. In that case, the new entrant must make a major investment to succeed.

Figure 10.6 plots the relationship between scale of entry and profitability over time for successful small-scale and large-scale ventures. The figure shows that successful small-scale entry is associated with lower initial losses, but in the long term, large-scale entry generates greater returns. However, because of the high costs and risks associated with large-scale entry, many companies make the mistake of choosing a small-scale entry strategy, which often means they fail to build the market share necessary for long-term success.

Figure 10.6	Scale of Entry and Profitability

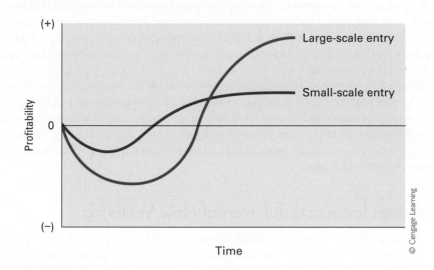

Commercialization   Many internal new ventures are driven by the opportunity to use a new or advanced technology to make better products for customers and outperform competitors. But, to be commercially successful, the products under development must be tailored to meet the needs of customers. Many internal new ventures fail when a company ignores the needs of customers in a market. Its managers become so focused on the technological possibilities of a new product that customer requirements are forgotten.[18] Thus, a new venture may fail because it is marketing a product based on a technology for which there is no demand, or the company fails to correctly position or differentiate the product in the market at attract customers.

For example, consider the desktop PC marketed by NeXT, the company that was started by the founder of Apple, Steve Jobs. The NeXT system failed to gain market share because the PC incorporated an array of expensive technologies that consumers simply did not want, such as optical disk drives and hi-fidelity sound. The optical disk drives, in particular, turned off customers because it was difficult to move work from PCs with floppy drives to NeXT machines with optical drives. In other words, NeXT failed because its founder was so dazzled by leading-edge technology that he ignored customer needs. However, Jobs redeemed himself and was named "CEO of the Decade" by *Fortune* magazine in 2010, after he successfully commercialized Apple's iPod, which dominates the MP3 player market. Also, the iPhone set the standard in the smartphone market, and the iPad quickly dominated the tablet computer market following its introduction in 2010.

Poor Implementation   Managing the new-venture process, and controlling the new-venture division, creates many difficult managerial and organizational problems.[19] For example, one common mistake some companies make to try to increase their chances of introducing successful products is to establish *too many* different internal new-venture divisions at the same time. Managers attempt to spread the risks of failure by having many divisions, but this places enormous demands upon a company's cash flow. Sometimes, companies are forced to reduce the funding each division receives to keep the entire company profitable, and this can result in the most promising ventures being starved of the cash they need to succeed.[20] Another common mistake is when corporate managers fail to do the extensive advanced planning necessary to ensure that the new venture's business model is sound and contains all the elements that will be needed later if it is to succeed. Sometimes corporate managers leave this process to the scientists and engineers championing the new technology. Focused on the new technology, managers may innovate new products that have little strategic or commercial value. Corporate managers and scientists must work together to clarify how and why a new venture will lead to a product that has a competitive advantage and jointly establish strategic objectives and a timetable to manage the venture until the product reaches the market.

The failure to anticipate the time and costs involved in the new-venture process constitutes a further mistake. Many companies have unrealistic expectations regarding the time frame and expect profits to flow in quickly. Research suggests that some companies operate with a philosophy of killing new businesses if they do not turn a profit by the end of the third year, which is unrealistic given that it can take 5 years or more before a new venture generates substantial profits.

Guidelines for Successful Internal New Venturing

To avoid these pitfalls, a company should adopt a well-thought-out, structured approach to manage internal new venturing. New venturing is based on R&D. It begins with the *exploratory research* necessary to advance basic science and technology (the "R" in R&D) and *development research* to identify, develop, and perfect the commercial applications of a new technology (the "D" in R&D). Companies with strong track records of success at internal new venturing excel at both kinds of R&D; they help to advance basic science and discover important commercial applications for it.[21] To advance basic science, it is important for companies to have strong links with universities, where much of the scientific knowledge that underlies new technologies is discovered. It is also important to make sure that research funds are being controlled by scientists who understand the importance of both "R" and "D" research. If the "D" is lacking, a company will probably generate few successful commercial ventures no matter how well it does basic research. Companies can take a number of steps to ensure that good science ends up with good, commercially viable products.

First, many companies must place the funding for research into the hands of business unit managers who have the skill or knowhow to narrow down and then select the best set of research projects—those that have the best chance of a significant commercial payoff. Second, to make effective use of its R&D competency, a company's top managers must work with its R&D scientists to continually develop and improve the business model and strategies that guide their efforts and make sure *all* its scientists and engineers understand what they have to do to make it succeed.[22]

Third, a company must also foster close links between R&D and marketing to increase the probability that a new product will be a commercial success in the future. When marketing works to identify the most important customer requirements for a new product and then communicates these requirements to scientists, it ensures that research projects meet the needs of their intended customers. Fourth, a company should also foster close links between R&D and manufacturing to ensure that it has the ability to make a proposed new product in a cost-effective way. Many companies successfully integrate the activities of the different functions by creating cross-functional project teams to oversee the development of new products from their inception to market introduction. This approach can significantly reduce the time it takes to bring a new product to market. For example, while R&D

is working on design, manufacturing is setting up facilities, and marketing is developing a campaign to show customers how much the new product will benefit them.

Finally, because large-scale entry often leads to greater long-term profits, a company can promote the success of internal new venturing by "thinking big." A company should construct efficient-scale manufacturing facilities and give marketing a large budget to develop a future product campaign that will build market presence and brand loyalty quickly, and well in advance of that product's introduction. And, corporate managers should not panic when customers are slow to adopt the new product; they need to accept the fact there will be initial losses and recognize that as long as market share is expanding, the product will eventually succeed.

ENTERING NEW INDUSTRIES: ACQUISITIONS

In Chapter 9, we explained that *acquisitions* are the main vehicle that companies use to implement a horizontal integration strategy. Acquisitions are also a principal way companies enter new industries to pursue vertical integration and diversification, so it is necessary to understand both the benefits and risks associated with using acquisitions to implement a corporate-level strategy.

The Attraction of Acquisitions

In general, acquisitions are used to pursue vertical integration or diversification when a company lacks the distinctive competencies necessary to compete in a new industry, so it uses its financial resources to purchase an established company that has those competencies. A company is particularly likely to use acquisitions when it needs to move fast to establish a presence in an industry, commonly an embryonic or growth industry. Entering a new industry through internal venturing is a relatively slow process; acquisition is a much quicker way for a company to establish a significant market presence. A company can purchase a leading company with a strong competitive position in months, rather than waiting years to build a market leadership position by engaging in internal venturing. Thus, when speed is particularly important, acquisition is the favored entry mode. Intel, for example, used acquisitions to build its communications chip business because it sensed that the market was developing very quickly, and that it would take too long to develop the required competencies.

In addition, acquisitions are often perceived as being less risky than internal new ventures because they involve less commercial uncertainty. Because of the risks of failure associated with internal new venturing, it is difficult to predict its future success and profitability. By contrast, when a company makes an acquisition, it acquires a company with an already established reputation, and it knows the magnitude of the company's market share and profitability.

Finally, acquisitions are an attractive way to enter an industry that is protected by high barriers to entry. Recall from Chapter 2 that barriers to entry arise from factors such as product differentiation, which leads to brand loyalty and high market share that leads to economies of scale. When entry barriers are high, it may be very difficult for a company to enter an industry through internal new venturing because it will have to construct large-scale manufacturing facilities and invest in a massive advertising campaign to establish brand loyalty—difficult goals that require huge capital expenditures. In contrast, if a company acquires another company already established in the industry, possibly the market leader, it can circumvent most entry barriers because that company has already achieved economies of scale and obtained brand loyalty. In general, the higher the barriers to entry, the more likely it is that acquisitions will be the method used to enter the industry.

Acquisition Pitfalls

For these reasons, acquisitions have long been the most common method that companies use to pursue diversification. However, as we mentioned earlier, research suggests that many acquisitions fail to increase the profitability of the acquiring company and may result in losses. For example, a study of 700 large acquisitions found that although 30% of these resulted in higher profits, 31% led to losses and the remainder had little impact.[23] Research suggests that many acquisitions fail to realize their anticipated benefits.[24] One study of the post-acquisition performance of acquired companies found that the profitability and market share of an acquired company often declines afterward, suggesting that many acquisitions destroy rather than create value.[25]

Acquisitions may fail to raise the performance of the acquiring companies for four reasons: (1) companies frequently experience management problems when they attempt to integrate a different company's organizational structure and culture into their own; (2) companies often overestimate the potential economic benefits from an acquisition; (3) acquisitions tend to be so expensive that they do not increase future profitability; and (4) companies are often negligent in screening their acquisition targets and fail to recognize important problems with their business models.

Integrating the Acquired Company   Once an acquisition has been made, the acquiring company has to integrate the acquired company and combine it with its own organizational structure and culture. Integration involves the adoption of common management and financial control systems, the joining together of operations from the acquired and the acquiring company, the establishment of bureaucratic mechanisms to share information and personnel, and the need to create a common culture. Experience has shown that many problems can occur as companies attempt to integrate their activities.

After an acquisition, many acquired companies experience high management turnover because their employees do not like the acquiring company's way of operating—its structure and culture.[26] Research suggests that the loss of management talent and expertise, and the damage from constant tension between the businesses, can materially harm the performance of the acquired unit.[27] Moreover, companies often must take on an enormous amount of debt to fund an acquisition, and they are frequently unable to pay it once these management problems (and sometimes the weaknesses) of the acquired company's business model become clear.

Overestimating Economic Benefits   Even when companies find it easy to integrate their activities, they often overestimate by how much combining the different businesses can increase future profitability. Managers often overestimate the competitive advantages that will derive from the acquisition and so pay more for the acquired company than it is worth. One reason is that top managers typically overestimate their own personal general competencies to create valuable new products from an acquisition. Why? The very fact that they have risen to the top of a company gives managers an exaggerated sense of their own capabilities, and a self-importance that distorts their strategic decision making.[28] Coca-Cola's acquisition of a number of medium-sized winemaking companies illustrates this. Reasoning that a beverage is a beverage, Coca-Cola's then-CEO decided he would be able to mobilize his company's talented marketing managers to develop the strategies needed to dominate the U.S. wine industry. After purchasing three wine companies and enduring 7 years of marginal profits because of failed marketing campaigns, he subsequently decided that wine and soft drinks are very different products; in particular, they have different kinds of appeal, pricing systems, and distribution networks. Coca-Cola eventually sold the wine operations to Joseph E. Seagram and took a substantial loss.[29]

The Expense of Acquisitions   Perhaps the most important reason for the failure of acquisitions is that acquiring a company with stock that is publicly traded tends to be very expensive—and the expense of the acquisition can more than wipe out the value of the stream of future profits that are expected from the acquisition. One reason is that the top managers of a company that is "targeted" for acquisition are likely to resist any takeover attempt unless the acquiring company agrees to pay a substantial premium above its current market value. These premiums are often 30 to 50% above the usual value of a company's stock. Similarly, the stockholders of the target company are unlikely to sell their stock unless they are paid major premiums over market value prior to a takeover bid. To pay such high premiums, the acquiring company must be certain it can use its acquisition to generate the stream of future profits that justifies the high price of the target company. This is frequently a difficult thing to do given how fast the industry environment can change and the other problems discussed earlier, such as integrating the acquired company. This is a major reason why acquisitions are frequently unprofitable for the acquiring company.

The reason why the acquiring company must pay such a high premium is that the stock price of the acquisition target increases enormously during the acquisition process as investors speculate on the final price the acquiring company will pay to capture it. In the case of a contested bidding contest, where two or more companies simultaneously bid to acquire the target company, its stock price may surge. Also, when many acquisitions are occurring in one particular industry, investors speculate that the value of the remaining industry companies that have *not* been acquired has increased, and that a bid for these companies will be made at some future point. This also drives up their stock price and increases the cost of making acquisitions. This happened in the telecommunications sector when, to make sure they could meet the needs of customers who were demanding leading-edge equipment, many large companies went on acquisition "binges." Nortel and Alcatel-Lucent engaged in a race to purchase smaller, innovative companies that were developing new telecommunications equipment. The result was that the stock prices for these companies were bid up by investors, and they were purchased at a hugely inflated price. When the telecommunications boom turned to bust, the acquiring companies found that they had vastly overpaid for their acquisitions and had to take enormous accounting write-downs; Nortel was forced to declare bankruptcy and sold off all its assets, and the value of Alcatel-Lucent's stock plunged almost 90%, although by 2011, there were signs of possible recovery.

Inadequate Pre-acquisition Screening   As the problems of these companies suggest, top managers often do a poor job of pre-acquisition screening, that is, evaluating how much a potential acquisition may increase future profitability. Researchers have discovered that one important reason for the failure of an acquisition is that managers make the decision to acquire other companies without thoroughly analyzing potential benefits and costs.[30] In many cases, after an acquisition has been completed, many acquiring companies discover that instead of buying a well-managed business with a strong business model, they have purchased a troubled organization. Obviously, the managers of the target company may manipulate company information or the balance sheet to make their financial condition look much better than it is. The acquiring company must remain aware and complete extensive research. In 2009, IBM was in negotiations to purchase chip-maker Sun Microsystems. After spending one week examining its books, IBM reduced its offer price by 10% when its negotiators found its customer base was not as solid as they had expected. Sun Microsystems was eventually sold to Oracle in 2010, and so far the acquisition has not proven a success, as Sun Microsystems's server sales fell in both 2011 and 2012.[31]

Guidelines for Successful Acquisition

To avoid these pitfalls and make successful acquisitions, companies need to follow an approach to targeting and evaluating potential acquisitions that is based on four main steps: (1) target identification and pre-acquisition screening, (2) bidding strategy, (3) integration, and (4) learning from experience.[32]

Identification and Screening　Thorough pre-acquisition screening increases a company's knowledge about a potential takeover target and lessens the risk of purchasing a problem company—one with a weak business model. It also leads to a more realistic assessment of the problems involved in executing a particular acquisition so that a company can plan how to integrate the new business and blend organizational structures and cultures. The screening process should begin with a detailed assessment of the strategic rationale for making the acquisition, an identification of the kind of company that would make an ideal acquisition candidate, and an extensive analysis of the strengths and weaknesses of the prospective company's business model compared to other possible acquisition targets.

Indeed, an acquiring company should select a set of top potential acquisition targets and evaluate each company using a set of criteria that focus on revealing (1) its financial position, (2) its distinctive competencies and competitive advantage, (3) changing industry boundaries, (4) its management capabilities, and (5) its corporate culture. Such an evaluation helps the acquiring company perform a detailed strength, weakness, opportunities, and threats (SWOT) analysis that identifies the best target, for example, by measuring the potential economies of scale and scope that can be achieved between the acquiring company and each target company. This analysis also helps reveal the potential integration problems that might exist when it is necessary to integrate the corporate cultures of the acquiring and acquired companies. For example, managers at Microsoft and SAP, the world's leading provider of enterprise resource planning (ERP) software, met to discuss a possible acquisition by Microsoft. Both companies decided that despite the strong strategic rationale for a merger—together they could dominate the software computing market, satisfying the need of large global companies—they would have challenges to overcome. The difficulties of creating an organizational structure that could successfully integrate their hundreds of thousands of employees throughout the world, and blend two very different cultures, were insurmountable.

Once a company has reduced the list of potential acquisition candidates to the most favored one or two, it needs to contact expert third parties, such as investment bankers like Goldman Sachs and Merrill Lynch. These companies' business models are based on providing valuable insights about the attractiveness of a potential acquisition, and assessing current industry competitive conditions, and handling the many other issues surrounding an acquisition, such as how to select the optimal bidding strategy for acquiring the target company's stock and keep the purchase price as low as possible.

Bidding Strategy   The objective of the bidding strategy is to reduce the price that a company must pay for the target company. The most effective way a company can acquire another is to make a friendly takeover bid, which means the two companies decide upon an amicable way to merge the two companies, satisfying the needs of each company's stockholders and top managers. A friendly takeover prevents speculators from bidding up stock prices. By contrast, in a hostile bidding environment, such as between Oracle and PeopleSoft, and Microsoft and Yahoo!, the price of the target company often gets bid up by speculators who expect that the offer price will be raised by the acquirer or by another company that might have a higher counteroffer.

Another essential element of a good bidding strategy is timing. For example, Hanson PLC, one of the most successful companies to pursue unrelated diversification, searched for sound companies suffering from short-term problems because of the business cycle or because performance was being seriously impacted by one underperforming division. Such companies are often undervalued by the stock market, so they can be acquired without paying a high stock premium. With good timing, a company can make a bargain purchase.

Integration   Despite good screening and bidding, an acquisition will fail unless the acquiring company possesses the essential organizational design skills needed to integrate the acquired company into its operations, and quickly develop a viable multibusiness model. Integration should center upon the source of the potential strategic advantages of the acquisition, for instance, opportunities to share marketing, manufacturing, R&D, financial, or management resources. Integration should also involve steps to eliminate any duplication of facilities or functions. In addition, any unwanted business units of the acquired company should be divested.

Learning from Experience   Research suggests companies that acquire many companies over time become expert in this process, and can generate significant value from their experience of the acquisition process.[33] Their past experience enables them to develop a "playbook," a clever plan that they can follow to execute an acquisition most efficiently and effectively. One successful company, Tyco International, never made hostile acquisitions; it audited the accounts of the target companies in detail, acquired companies to help it achieve a critical mass in an industry, moved quickly to realize cost savings after an acquisition, promoted managers one or two layers down to lead the newly acquired entity, and introduced profit-based incentive pay systems in the acquired unit.[34] Over time, however, Tyco tended to become too large and diversified, leading both investors and management to suspect Tyco was not generating as much value as it could. In 2007, Tyco's health-care and electronics divisions were spun off. Then in 2012, plans Tyco was split again into three parts that would each have their own stock: Tyco Fire and Security, ADT (which provided residential and small business security installation), and Flow Control (which sold water and fluid valves and controls).[35]

ENTERING NEW INDUSTRIES: JOINT VENTURES

Joint ventures, where two or more companies agree to pool their resources to create new business, are most commonly used to enter an embryonic or growth industry. Suppose a company is contemplating creating a new-venture division in an embryonic industry; such a move involves substantial risks and costs because the company must make the huge investment necessary to develop the set of value-chain activities required to make and sell products in the new industry. On the other hand, an acquisition can be a dangerous proposition because there is rarely an established leading company in an emerging industry; even if there is it will be extremely expensive to purchase.

In this situation, a joint venture frequently becomes the most appropriate method to enter a new industry because it allows a company to share the risks and costs associated with establishing a business unit in the new industry with another company. This is especially true when the companies share *complementary* skills or distinctive competencies because this increases the probability of a joint venture's success. Consider the 50/50 equity joint venture formed between UTC and Dow Chemical to build plastic-based composite parts for the aerospace industry. UTC was already involved in the aerospace industry (it builds Sikorsky helicopters), and Dow Chemical had skills in the development and manufacture of plastic-based composites. The alliance called for UTC to contribute its advanced aerospace skills and Dow to contribute its skills in developing and manufacturing plastic-based composites. Through the joint venture, both companies became involved in new product markets. They were able to realize the benefits associated with related diversification without having to merge their activities into one company or bear the costs and risks of developing new products on their own. Thus, both companies enjoyed the profit-enhancing advantages of entering new markets without having to bear the increased bureaucratic costs.

Although joint ventures usually benefit both partner companies, under some conditions they may result in problems. First, although a joint venture allows companies to share the risks and costs of developing a new business, it also requires that they share in the profits if it succeeds. So, if one partner's skills are more important than the other partner's skills, the partner with more valuable skills will have to "give away" profits to the other party because of the 50/50 agreement. This can create conflict and sour the working relationship as time passes. Second, the joint-venture partners may have different business models or time horizons, and problems can arise if they start to come into conflict about how to run the joint venture; these kinds of problems can disintegrate a business and result in failure. Third, a company that enters into a joint venture runs the risk of giving away important company-specific knowledge to its partner, which might then use the new knowledge to compete with its other partner in the future. For example, having gained access to Dow's expertise in plastic-based composites, UTC might have dissolved the alliance and produced these materials on its own. As the previous chapter discussed, this risk can be minimized if Dow gets a *credible commitment* from UTC, which is what Dow did. UTC had to make an expensive asset-specific investment to make the products the joint venture was formed to create.

Restructuring

restructuring
The process of reorganizing and divesting business units and exiting industries to refocus upon a company's core business and rebuild its distinctive competencies

Many companies expand into new industries to increase profitability. Sometimes, however, companies need to exit industries to increase their profitability and split their existing businesses into separate, independent companies. **Restructuring** is the process of reorganizing and divesting business units and exiting industries to refocus upon a company's core business and rebuild its distinctive competencies.[36] Why are so many companies restructuring and how do they do it?

Why Restructure?

One main reason that diversified companies have restructured in recent years is that the stock market has valued their stock at a *diversification discount*, meaning that the stock of highly diversified companies is valued lower, relative to their earnings, than the stock of less-diversified companies.[37] Investors see highly diversified companies as less attractive investments for four reasons. First, as we discussed earlier, investors often feel these companies no longer have multibusiness models that justify their participation in many different industries. Second, the complexity of the financial statements of highly diversified enterprises disguises the performance of individual business units; thus, investors cannot identify if their multibusiness models are succeeding. The result is that investors perceive the company as being riskier than companies that operate in one industry, whose competitive advantage and financial statements are more easily understood. Given this situation, restructuring can be seen as an attempt to boost the returns to shareholders by splitting up a multibusiness company into separate and independent parts.

The third reason for the diversification discount is that many investors have learned from experience that managers often have a tendency to pursue too much diversification or do it for the wrong reasons: their attempts to diversify *reduce* profitability.[38] For example, some CEOs pursue growth for its own sake; they are empire builders who expand the scope of their companies to the point where fast-increasing bureaucratic costs become greater than the additional value that their diversification strategy creates. Restructuring thus becomes a response to declining financial performance brought about by over-diversification.

A final factor leading to restructuring is that innovations in strategic management have diminished the advantages of vertical integration or diversification. For example, a few decades ago, there was little understanding of how long-term cooperative relationships or strategic alliances between a company and its suppliers could be a viable alternative to vertical integration. Most companies considered only two alternatives for managing the supply chain: vertical integration or competitive bidding. As we discuss in Chapter 9, in many situations, long-term cooperative relationships can create the most value, especially because they avoid the need to incur bureaucratic costs or dispense with market discipline. As this strategic innovation has spread throughout global business, the relative advantages of vertical integration have declined.

ETHICAL DILEMMA

© iStockPhoto.com/P_Wei

Recently, many top managers have been convicted of illegally altering their company's financial statements or providing false information to hide the poor performance of their company from stockholders—or simply for personal gain. You have been charged with the task of creating a control system for your company to ensure managers behave ethically and legally when reporting the performance of their business. To help develop the control system, you identify the five main ways managers use diversification to increase profitability—transferring and leveraging competences, sharing resources, product bundling, and the use of general managerial competencies.

How might these five methods be associated with unethical behavior? Can you determine rules or procedures that could prevent managers from behaving in an unethical way?

SUMMARY OF CHAPTER

1. Strategic managers often pursue diversification when their companies are generating free cash flow, that is, financial resources they do not need to maintain a competitive advantage in the company's core industry that can be used to fund profitable new business ventures.

2. A diversified company can create value by (a) transferring competencies among existing businesses, (b) leveraging competencies to create new businesses, (c) sharing resources to realize economies of scope, (d) using product bundling, (e) taking advantage of general organizational competencies that enhance the performance of all business units within a diversified company, and (f) operating an internal capital market. The bureaucratic costs of diversification rise as a function of the number of independent business units within a company and the extent to which managers must coordinate the transfer of resources between those business units.

3. Diversification motivated by a desire to pool risks or achieve greater growth often results in falling profitability.

4. There are three methods companies use to enter new industries: internal new venturing, acquisition, and joint ventures.

5. Internal new venturing is used to enter a new industry when a company has a set of valuable competencies in its existing businesses that can be leveraged or recombined to enter a new business or industry.

6. Many internal ventures fail because of entry on too small a scale, poor commercialization, and poor corporate management of the internal venture process. Guarding against failure involves a carefully planned approach toward project selection and management, integration of R&D and marketing to improve the chance new products will be commercially successful, and entry on a scale large enough to result in competitive advantage.

7. Acquisitions are often the best way to enter a new industry when a company lacks the competencies required to compete in a new industry, and it can purchase a company that does have those competencies at a reasonable price. Acquisitions are also the method chosen to enter new industries when there are high barriers to entry and a company is unwilling to accept the time frame, development costs, and risks associated with pursuing internal new venturing.

8. Acquisitions are unprofitable when strategic managers (a) underestimate the problems associated with integrating an acquired company, (b) overestimate the profit that can be created from an acquisition, (c) pay too much for the acquired company, and (d) perform inadequate pre-acquisition screening to ensure the acquired company will increase the profitability of the whole company. Guarding against acquisition failure requires careful pre-acquisition screening, a carefully selected bidding strategy, effective organizational design to successfully integrate the operations of the acquired company into the whole company, and managers who develop a general managerial competency by learning from their experience of past acquisitions.

9. Joint ventures are used to enter a new industry when (a) the risks and costs associated with setting up a new business unit are more than a company is willing to assume on its own and (b) a company can increase the probability that its entry into a new industry will result in a successful new business by teaming up with another company that has skills and assets that complement its own.

10. Restructuring is often required to correct the problems that result from (a) a business model that no longer creates competitive advantage, (b) the inability of investors to assess the competitive advantage of a highly diversified company from its financial statements, (c) excessive diversification because top managers desire to pursue empire building that results in growth without profitability, and (d) innovations in strategic management such as strategic alliances and outsourcing that reduce the advantages of vertical integration and diversification.

DISCUSSION QUESTIONS

1. When is a company likely to choose (a) related diversification and (b) unrelated diversification?
2. What factors make it most likely that (a) acquisitions or (b) internal new venturing will be the preferred method to enter a new industry?
3. Imagine that IBM has decided to diversify into the telecommunications business to provide online cloud computing data services and broadband access for businesses and individuals. What method would you recommend that IBM pursue to enter this industry? Why?
4. Under which conditions are joint ventures a useful way to enter new industries?
5. Identify Honeywell's (www.honeywell.com) portfolio of businesses that can be found by exploring its website. In how many different industries is Honeywell involved? Would you describe Honeywell as a related or an unrelated diversification company? Has Honeywell's diversification strategy increased profitability over time?

KEY TERMS

Diversification 322
Diversified company 322
Transferring competencies 323
Commonality 323

Leveraging competencies 324
Economies of scope 325
General organizational competencies 327
Organizational design skills 329

Turnaround strategy 330
Related diversification 331
Unrelated diversification 331

Internal capital market 332
Bureaucratic costs 335
Internal new venturing 342
Restructuring 350

PRACTICING STRATEGIC MANAGEMENT

© iStockPhoto.com/Urilux

Small-Group Exercises

Small-Group Exercise: Visiting General Electric

Break up into groups of three to five students, and explore GE's website (www.ge.com) to answer the following questions. Then appoint one member of the group as spokesperson who will communicate the group's findings to the class.

1. Review GE's portfolio of major businesses. Upon what multibusiness model is this portfolio of businesses based? How profitable has that model been in past?
2. Has GE's multibusiness model been changing? Has its CEO, Jeffrey Immelt, announced any new strategic initiatives?
3. What kinds of changes would you make to its multibusiness model to boost its profitability?

STRATEGY SIGN ON

© iStockPhoto.com/Ninoslav Dotlic

Article File 10

Find an example of a diversified company that made an acquisition that apparently failed to create any value. Identify and critically evaluate the rationale that top management used to justify the acquisition when it was made. Explain why the acquisition subsequently failed.

Strategic Management Project: Module 10

This module requires you to assess your company's use of acquisitions, internal new ventures, and joint ventures as ways to enter a new business or restructure its portfolio of businesses.

A. Your Company Has Entered a New Industry During the Past Decade

1. Pick one new industry that your company has entered during the past 10 years.
2. Identify the rationale for entering this industry.
3. Identify the strategy used to enter this industry.
4. Evaluate the rationale for using this particular entry strategy. Do you think that this was the best entry strategy to use? Why or why not?
5. Do you think that the addition of this business unit to the company increased or reduced profitability? Why?

B. Your Company Has Restructured Its Corporate Portfolio During the Past Decade

1. Identify the rationale for pursuing a restructuring strategy.
2. Pick one industry from which your company has exited during the past 10 years.
3. Identify the strategy used to exit from this particular industry. Do you think that this was the best exit strategy to use? Why or why not?
4. In general, do you think that exiting from this industry has been in the company's best interest?

CLOSING CASE

VF Corp. Acquires Timberland to Realize the Benefits from Related Diversification

In June 2011, U.S.-based VF Corp., the global apparel and clothing maker, announced that it would acquire Timberland, the U.S.-based global footwear maker, for $2 billion, which was a 40% premium on Timberland's stock price. VF is the maker of such established clothing brands as Lee and Wrangler Jeans, Nautica, lucy, 7 For All Mankind, Vans, Kipling, and outdoor apparel brands such as The North Face, JanSport, and Eagle Creek.

Timberland is well known for its tough waterproof leather footwear, such as its best-selling hiking boots and its classic boat shoes; it also licenses the right to make clothing and accessories under its brand name. Obviously, Timberland's stockholders were thrilled that they had made a 40% profit overnight on their investment; but why would a clothing maker purchase a footwear company that primarily competes in a different industry?

The reason, according to VF's CEO Eric Wiseman, is that the Timberland deal would be a "transformative" acquisition that would add footwear to VF's fastest-growing division, the outdoor and action sports business, which had achieved a 14% gain in revenues in 2010 and contributed $3.2 billion of VF's total revenues of $7.7 billion. By combining the products of the clothing and footwear division, Wiseman claimed that VF could almost double Timberland's profitability by increasing its global sales by at least 15%. At the same time, the addition of the Timberland brand would increase the sales of VF's outdoor brands such as The North Face by 10%. The result would be a major increase in VF's revenues and profitability—an argument its investors agreed with because whereas the stock price of a company that acquires another company normally declines after the announcement, VF's stock price soared by 10%!

Why would this merger of two very different companies result in so much more value being created? The first reason is that it would allow the company to offer an extended range of outdoor products—clothing, shoes, backpacks, and accessories—which could all be packaged together, distributed to retailers, and marketed and sold to customers. The result would be substantial cost savings because purchasing, distribution, and marketing costs would now be shared between the different brands or product lines in VF's expanded portfolio. In addition, VF would be able to increasingly differentiate its outdoor products by, for example, linking its brand The North Face with the Timberland brand, so customers purchasing outdoor clothing would be more likely to purchase Timberland hiking boots and related accessories such as backpacks offered by VF's other outdoor brands.

In addition, although Timberland is a well-known popular brand in the United States, it generates more than 50% of its revenues from global sales (especially in high-growth markets such as China), and it has a niche presence in many countries such as the United Kingdom and Japan. In 2011 VF was only generating 30% of its revenues from global sales; by taking advantage of the commonalities between its outdoor brands, VF argued that purchasing Timberland would increase its sales in overseas markets and also increase the brand recognition and sales of its other primary brands such as Wrangler Jeans and Nautica. For example, hikers could wear VF's Wrangler or Lee Jeans, as well as The North Face clothing, at the same time they put on their Timberland hiking boots. In short, Timberland's global brand cachet and the synergies between the two companies' outdoor lifestyle products would result in major new value creation. Thus, the acquisition would allow VF to increase the global differentiated appeal of all its brands, resulting in lower costs. VF would be able to negotiate better deals with specialist outsourcing companies abroad, and economies of scale would result from reduced global shipping and distribution costs.

In a conference call to analysts, Wiseman said that: "Timberland has been our Number 1 acquisition priority. It knits together two powerful companies into a new global player in the outdoor and action sports space."

After the acquisition, the combined companies had more than 1,225 VF-operated retail stores, of which most were single-brand shops. VF also operated 80 U.S. outlet stores that sold a wide range of excess VF products. VF also sold to specialty stores, department stores, national chains, and mass merchants such as Walmart (Walmart accounted for 8% of VF's total sales in 2012—primarily due to its purchases of jeanswear). The Timberland acquisition increased the range of products VF could distribute and sell through its many distribution channels, resulting in synergies and cost savings. VF's organizational structure leveraged the advantage of centralized purchasing, distribution, and IT to reduce costs across the organization.

Timberland's 2010 sales (prior to the acquisition) had been $1.4 billion, and its net income had been $96 million—a net profit margin of just under 7%. VF's sales in 2010 had been $7.7 billion with net income of $571 million, for a net profit margin of 7.4%. After the acquisition, VF Corporation posted revenues of $9.4 billion and $10.9 billion while also showing an increase in net profit margin to 9.4% and 10.0% in 2011 and 2012, respectively. Although it is difficult to know how much of these gains could be directly attributable to the Timberland acquisition, VF's strategy of related diversification appeared to be paying off!

Sources: www.vfc.com and www.timberland.com.

CASE DISCUSSION QUESTIONS

1. What kinds of resources can likely be shared across different brands between an apparel maker and a footwear maker? What kinds of resources are unlikely to be shared?
2. How much does being a larger, more diversified apparel and footwear company increase VF's market power over its suppliers or customers? How could we assess how much this is worth?
3. If VF had increased its sales only by the amount of Timberland's sales and had not reaped an increase in profitability, would you consider the acquisition successful?
4. How might you compare VF's increase in profits to the premium it paid for Timberland?

NOTES

[1]This resource-based view of diversification can be traced to Edith Penrose's seminal book *The Theory of the Growth of the Firm* (Oxford: Oxford University Press, 1959).

[2]D. J. Teece, "Economies of Scope and the Scope of the Enterprise," *Journal of Economic Behavior and Organization* 3 (1980): 223–247. For more recent empirical work on this topic, see C. H. St. John and J. S. Harrison, "Manufacturing Based Relatedness, Synergy and Coordination," *Strategic Management Journal* 20 (1999): 129–145.

[3]Teece, "Economies of Scope." For more recent empirical work on this topic, see St. John and Harrison, "Manufacturing Based Relatedness, Synergy and Coordination."

[4]For a detailed discussion, see C. W. L. Hill and R. E. Hoskisson, "Strategy and Structure in the Multiproduct Firm," *Academy of Management Review* 12 (1987): 331–341.

[5]See, for example, G. R. Jones and C. W. L. Hill, "A Transaction Cost Analysis of Strategy Structure Choice," *Strategic Management Journal* 2 (1988): 159–172; and O. E. Williamson, *Markets and Hierarchies, Analysis and Antitrust Implications* (New York: Free Press, 1975), pp. 132–175.

[6]R. Buderi, *Engines of Tomorrow* (New York: Simon & Schuster, 2000).

[7]See, for example, Jones and Hill, "A Transaction Cost Analysis"; and Williamson, *Markets and Hierarchies.*

[8]C. A. Trahms, H. A. Ndofor, and D. G. Sirmon, "Organizational Decline and Turnaround: A Review and Agenda for Future Research," *Journal of Management,* 39 (2013): 1277–1307.

[9]The distinction goes back to R. P. Rumelt, *Strategy, Structure and Economic Performance* (Cambridge: Harvard Business School Press, 1974).

[10]For evidence, see C. W. L. Hill, "Conglomerate Performance over the Economic Cycle," *Journal of Industrial Economics* 32 (1983): 197–212; and D. T. C. Mueller, "The Effects of Conglomerate Mergers," *Journal of Banking and Finance* 1 (1977): 315–347.

[11]For reviews of the evidence, see V. Ramanujam and P. Varadarajan, "Research on Corporate Diversification: A Synthesis," *Strategic Management Journal* 10 (1989): 523–551; G. Dess, J. F. Hennart, C. W. L. Hill, and A. Gupta, "Research Issues in Strategic Management," *Journal of Management* 21 (1995): 357–392; and D. C. Hyland and J. D. Diltz, "Why Companies Diversify: An Empirical Examination," *Financial Management* 31 (Spring 2002): 51–81.

[12]M. E. Porter, "From Competitive Advantage to Corporate Strategy," *Harvard Business Review,* May–June 1987, pp. 43–59.

[13]For reviews of the evidence, see Ramanujam and Varadarajan, "Research on Corporate Diversification"; Dess et al., "Research Issues in Strategic Management"; and Hyland and Diltz, "Why Companies Diversify."

[14]C. R. Christensen et al., *Business Policy Text and Cases* (Homewood: Irwin, 1987), p. 778.

[15]See Booz, Allen, and Hamilton, *New Products Management for the 1980s* (New York: Booz, Allen and Hamilton, 1982); A. L. Page, "PDMA's New Product Development Practices Survey: Performance and Best Practices" (presented at the PDMA 15th Annual International Conference, Boston, October 16, 1991); and E. Mansfield, "How Economists See R&D," *Harvard Business Review*, November–December 1981, pp. 98–106.

[16]See R. Biggadike, "The Risky Business of Diversification," *Harvard Business Review*, May–June 1979, pp. 103–111; R. A. Burgelman, "A Process Model of Internal Corporate Venturing in the Diversified Major Firm," *Administrative Science Quarterly* 28 (1983): 223–244; and Z. Block and I. C. MacMillan, *Corporate Venturing* (Boston: Harvard Business School Press, 1993).

[17]Biggadike, "The Risky Business of Diversification"; Block and Macmillan, *Corporate Venturing*.

[18]Buderi, *Engines of Tomorrow*.

[19]I. C. MacMillan and R. George, "Corporate Venturing: Challenges for Senior Managers," *Journal of Business Strategy* 5 (1985): 34–43.

[20]See R. A. Burgelman, M. M. Maidique, and S. C. Wheelwright, *Strategic Management of Technology and Innovation* (Chicago: Irwin, 1996), 493–507. See also Buderi, *Engines of Tomorrow*.

[21]Buderi, *Engines of Tomorrow*.

[22]See Block and Macmillan, *Corporate Venturing*; Burgelman et al., *Strategic Management of Technology and Innovation*; and Buderi, *Engines of Tomorrow*.

[23]For evidence on acquisitions and performance, see R. E. Caves, "Mergers, Takeovers, and Economic Efficiency," *International Journal of Industrial Organization* 7 (1989): 151–174; M. C. Jensen and R. S. Ruback, "The Market for Corporate Control: The Scientific Evidence," *Journal of Financial Economics* 11 (1983): 5–50; R. Roll, "Empirical Evidence on Takeover Activity and Shareholder Wealth," in J. C. Coffee, L. Lowenstein, and S. Rose (eds.), *Knights, Raiders and Targets* (Oxford: Oxford University Press, 1989), pp. 112–127; A. Schleifer and R. W. Vishny, "Takeovers in the 60s and 80s: Evidence and Implications," *Strategic Management Journal* 12 (Special Issue, Winter 1991), pp. 51–60; T. H. Brush, "Predicted Changes in Operational Synergy and Post Acquisition Performance of Acquired Businesses," *Strategic Management Journal* 17 (1996): 1–24; and T. Loughran and A. M. Vijh, "Do Long Term Shareholders Benefit from Corporate Acquisitions?" *Journal of Finance* 5 (1997): 1765–1787.

[24]Ibid.

[25]D. J. Ravenscraft and F. M. Scherer, *Mergers, Sell-offs, and Economic Efficiency* (Washington: Brookings Institution, 1987).

[26]See J. P. Walsh, "Top Management Turnover Following Mergers and Acquisitions," *Strategic Management Journal* 9 (1988): 173–183.

[27]See A. A. Cannella and D. C. Hambrick, "Executive Departure and Acquisition Performance," *Strategic Management Journal* 14 (1993): 137–152.

[28]R. Roll, "The Hubris Hypothesis of Corporate Takeovers," *Journal of Business* 59 (1986): 197–216.

[29]"Coca-Cola: A Sobering Lesson from Its Journey into Wine," *Business Week*, June 3, 1985, pp. 96–98.

[30]P. Haspeslagh and D. Jemison, *Managing Acquisitions* (New York: Free Press, 1991).

[31]A. Ricadela, "Oracle Unveils Faster Servers to Combat Hardware Slump," Bloomberg.com, March 27, 2013.

[32]For views on this issue, see L. L. Fray, D. H. Gaylin, and J. W. Down, "Successful Acquisition Planning," *Journal of Business Strategy* 5 (1984): 46–55; C. W. L. Hill, "Profile of a Conglomerate Takeover: BTR and Thomas Tilling," *Journal of General Management* 10 (1984): 34–50; D. R. Willensky, "Making It Happen: How to Execute an Acquisition," *Business Horizons*, March–April 1985, pp. 38–45; Haspeslagh and Jemison, *Managing Acquisitions*; and P. L. Anslinger and T. E. Copeland, "Growth Through Acquisition: A Fresh Look," *Harvard Business Review*, January–February 1996, pp. 126–135.

[33]M. L. A. Hayward, "When Do Firms Learn from Their Acquisition Experience? Evidence from 1990–1995," *Strategic Management Journal* 23 (2002): 21–39; K. G. Ahuja, "Technological Acquisitions and the Innovation Performance of Acquiring Firms: A Longitudinal Study," *Strategic Management Journal* 23 (2001): 197–220; and H. G. Barkema and F. Vermeulen, "International Expansion Through Startup or Acquisition," *Academy of Management Journal* 41 (1998): 7–26.

[34]Hayward, "When Do Firms Learn from Their Acquisition Experience?"

[35]N. Zieminski, "Tyco Shareholders Approve Three-Way Break-Up," Reuters, September 17, 2012.

[36]For a review of the evidence and some contrary empirical evidence, see D. E. Hatfield, J. P. Liebskind, and T. C. Opler, "The Effects of Corporate Restructuring on Aggregate Industry Specialization," *Strategic Management Journal* 17 (1996): 55–72.

[37]A. Lamont and C. Polk, "The Diversification Discount: Cash Flows Versus Returns," *Journal of Finance* 56 (October 2001): 1693–1721; and R. Raju, H. Servaes, and L. Zingales, "The Cost of Diversity: The Diversification Discount and Inefficient Investment," *Journal of Finance* 55 (2000): 35–80.

[38]For example, see Schleifer and Vishny, "Takeovers in the '60s and '80s."

Corporate Performance, Governance, and Business Ethics

LEARNING OBJECTIVES

After reading this chapter you should be able to:

11-1 Understand the relationship between stakeholder management and corporate performance

11-2 Explain why maximizing returns to stockholders is often viewed as the preeminent goal in many corporations

11-3 Describe the various governance mechanisms that are used to align the interests of stockholders and managers

11-4 Explain why these governance mechanisms do not always work as intended

11-5 Identify the main ethical issues that arise in business and the causes of unethical behavior

11-6 Identify what managers can do to improve the ethical climate of their organization, and to make sure that business decisions do not violate good ethical principles

OPENING CASE

Imaginechina/Corbis

HP's Disastrous Acquisition of Autonomy

In 2011, HP was churning on many fronts simultaneously. It had decided to abandon its tablet computer, and was struggling with a decision about whether to exit its $40 billion-a-year personal computer (PC) business altogether. It also had a new CEO, Leo Apotheker (formerly the head of German software company SAP AG) who was intent on making a high-impact acquisition that would transform the firm from being primarily a hardware manufacturer into a fast-growing software firm. The firm also had a new chairman of the board, Ray Lane, who was also a software specialist as well as former president of Oracle.

Leo Apotheker had proposed buying two mid-sized software companies, but both deals fell through—the first was nixed by the board's finance committee, and the second fell apart during negotiations over price. In frustration, Apotheker told Lane, "I'm running out of software companies."

Then in the summer of 2011, Apotheker proposed looking at Autonomy, a British firm that makes software that enables firms to search for relevant information in text files, video files, and other corporate

359

documents. Lane was enthusiastic about the idea. When Apotheker brought the proposal to the board members in July of 2011, half of them were already busy analyzing the decision to jettison the PC business, so only half of the board evaluated the acquisition proposal. The board ended up approving a price for Autonomy that was about a 50% premium over its market value, and its market value was already high at about 15 times its operating profit. HP announced the acquisition on August 18, 2011, on the same day that it announced it would abandon its tablet computer and was considering exiting the PC industry. The price of the acquisition was $11.1 billion—12.6 times Autonomy's 2010 revenue. Notably, Oracle had already considered acquiring Autonomy and decided that even if the numbers Autonomy was presenting were taken at face value, it was not worth buying even at a $6 billion price tag. HP's stock fell by 20% the next day.

In the days following the announcement, HP's stock continued to tumble, and backlash from shareholders and others in the investment community was scathing. Ray Lane asked HP's advisers if the company could back out of the deal and was told that, according to U.K. takeover rules, backing out was only possible if HP could show that Autonomy engaged in financial impropriety. HP began frantically examining the financials of Autonomy, hoping for a way to get out of the deal. In the midst of harsh disapproval from HP's largest stockholders and other senior executives within the firm, HP fired Leo Apotheker on September 22, 2012, less than a month after the acquisition's announcement, and only 11 months into his job as CEO.

By May of 2012 it was clear that Autonomy was not going to hit its revenue targets, and Michael Lynch, Autonomy's founder (who had been asked to stay on and run the company) was fired. In late November 2012, HP wrote down 8.8 billion of the acquisition, essentially admitting that the company was worth 79% less than it had paid for it. Then the finger pointing began in earnest. HP attributed more than $5 billion of the write-down to a "willful

effort on behalf of certain former Autonomy employees to inflate the underlying financial metrics of the company in order to mislead investors and potential buyers. . . .These misrepresentations and lack of disclosure severely impacted management's ability to fairly value Autonomy at the time of the deal."

Michael Lynch denied the charges, insisting he knew of no wrongdoing at Autonomy, arguing that auditors from Deloitte had approved its financial statements, and pointing out that the firm followed British accounting guidelines, which differ in some ways from American rules. Lynch also accused HP of mismanaging the acquisition, saying "Can HP really state that no part of the $5 billion write-down was, or should be, attributed to HP's operational and financial mismanagement of Autonomy since acquisition?... Why did HP senior management apparently wait six months to inform its shareholders of the possibility of a material event related to Autonomy?"

Many shareholders and analysts also pointed their fingers at HP by saying that the deal was shockingly overpriced. Bernstein analyst Toni Sacconaghi wrote, "We see the decision to purchase Autonomy as value-destroying," and Richard Kugele, an analyst at Needham & Company, wrote, "HP may have eroded what remained of Wall Street's confidence in the company" with the "seemingly overly expensive acquisition of Autonomy for over $10B." Apotheker responded by saying, "We have a pretty rigorous process inside HP that we follow for all our acquisitions, which is a D.C.F.-based model.... Just take it from us. We did that analysis at great length, in great detail, and we feel that we paid a very fair price for Autonomy." However, when Ray Lane was questioned, he seemed unfamiliar with any cash flow analysis done for the acquisition. He noted instead that he believed the price was fair because Autonomy was unique and critical to HP's strategic vision.

According to an article in *Fortune*, Catherine A. Lesjak, the chief financial officer at HP, had spoken out against the deal before it transpired, arguing that it was not in the best interests of the shareholders and that HP could not afford it. Furthermore, outside auditors for Autonomy apparently informed HP (during a call in the days leading up to the announcement) that an executive at Autonomy had raised allegations of improper accounting at the firm, but a review had deemed the allegations baseless and they were never passed on to HP's board or CEO.

In the third quarter of 2012, HP lost $6.9 billion, largely because of the Autonomy mess. Its stock was trading at $13—almost 60% less than it had been worth when the Autonomy deal was announced. By April 4, 2013, Ray Lane stepped down as chairman of the board (although he continued on as a board member).

Did Autonomy intentionally inflate its financial metrics? Did Apotheker and Lane's eagerness for a "transformative acquisition" cause them to be sloppy in their valuation of Autonomy? Or was the value of Autonomy lost due to the more mundane cause of integration failure? Financial forensic investigators are still at work trying to answer these questions, but irrespective of the underlying causes, Toni Sacconaghi notes that Autonomy "will arguably go down as the worst, most value-destroying deal in the history of corporate America."

Sources: J. Bandler, "HP Should Have Listened to Its CFO," *Fortune*, November 20, 2012; J. B. Stewart, "From HP, a Blunder That Seems to Beat All," *New York Times*, November 30, 2012; M. G. De La Merced, "Autonomy's Ex-Chief Calls on HP to Defend Its Claims," *New York Times Dealbook*, November 27, 2012; and B. Worthen and J. Scheck, "Inside H-P's Missed Chance to Avoid a Disastrous Deal," *Wall Street Journal*, January 21, 2013, pp. A1–A16.

OVERVIEW

The story of HP's acquisition of Autonomy told in the Opening Case highlights some of the issues that we will discuss in this chapter. HP entered into an acquisition that seems to have been driven more by enthusiasm than by diligence or concern for its shareholders. Many shareholders and analysts appear to believe that HP recklessly overpaid for the firm, resulting in many billions of dollars being lost. HP, in turn, blamed Autonomy, stating that the company had not fairly represented its financials and had willfully misled HP. Autonomy's founder denied HP's charges, and blamed HP for mismanaging the acquisition. The acquisition appears to have come at a time when the company was at risk of making a poor decision: it had a new CEO who was looking to make an impression with a large, transformative acquisition; it had a new chairman of the board who understood software more than hardware; and it was in the middle of decisions to drastically reduce its hardware lines, including its tablet computer and potentially the rest of its PC business. Although it is likely that no one will be found legally to blame for the debacle, it seems apparent that at least one party to the transaction (and maybe all of the parties) may have behaved unethically.

We open this chapter with a close look at the governance mechanisms that shareholders implement to ensure that managers are acting in the company's interest and are pursuing strategies that maximize shareholder value. We also discuss how managers need to pay attention to other stakeholders as well, such as employees, suppliers, and customers. Balancing the needs of different stakeholder groups is in the long-term interests of the company's owners, its shareholders. Good governance mechanisms recognize this truth. In addition, we will spend some time reviewing the ethical implications of strategic decisions, and we will discuss how managers can make sure that their strategic decisions are founded upon strong ethical principles.

STAKEHOLDERS AND CORPORATE PERFORMANCE

stakeholders

Individuals or groups with an interest, claim, or stake in the company—in what it does and in how well it performs.

internal stakeholders

Stockholders and employees, including executive officers, other managers, and board members.

external stakeholders

All other individuals and groups that have some claim on the company.

A company's **stakeholders** are individuals or groups with an interest, claim, or stake in the company, in what it does, and in how well it performs.[1] They include stockholders, creditors, employees, customers, the communities in which the company does business, and the general public. Stakeholders can be divided into two groups: internal stakeholders and external stakeholders (see Figure 11.1). **Internal stakeholders** are stockholders and employees, including executive officers, other managers, and board members. **External stakeholders** are all other individuals and groups that have some claim on the company. Typically, this group comprises customers, suppliers, creditors (including banks and bondholders), governments, unions, local communities, and the general public.

All stakeholders are in an exchange relationship with their company. Each of the stakeholder groups listed in Figure 11.1 supplies the organization with important resources (or contributions), and in exchange, each expects its interests to be satisfied (by inducements).[2] Stockholders provide the enterprise with risk capital and in exchange expect management to attempt to maximize the return on their investment. Creditors, and particularly bondholders, also provide the company with capital in the form of debt, and they expect to be repaid on time, with interest. Employees provide labor and skills and in exchange expect commensurate income, job satisfaction, job security, and good working conditions. Customers provide a company with its revenues, and in exchange want high-quality, reliable products that represent value for money. Suppliers provide a company with inputs and in exchange seek revenues and dependable buyers. Governments provide a company with rules and regulations that govern business practice and maintain fair competition. In exchange they want companies that adhere to these rules. Unions help to provide a company with productive employees, and in exchange they want benefits for their members in proportion to their contributions to the company. Local communities provide companies with local infrastructure, and in exchange want companies that are responsible citizens. The general public provides companies with national infrastructure, and in exchange seeks some assurance that the quality of life will be improved as a result of the company's existence.

A company must take these claims into account when formulating its strategies, or else stakeholders may withdraw their support. For example, stockholders may sell their shares, bondholders may demand higher interest payments on new bonds, employees may leave

---

Figure 11.1   Stakeholders and the Enterprise

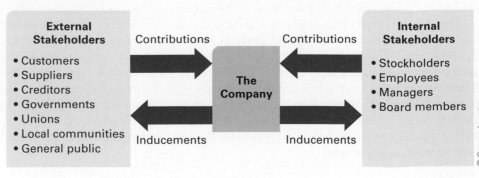

their jobs, and customers may buy elsewhere. Suppliers may seek more dependable buyers, and unions may engage in disruptive labor disputes. Government may take civil or criminal action against the company and its top officers, imposing fines and, in some cases, jail terms. Communities may oppose the company's attempts to locate its facilities in their area, and the general public may form pressure groups, demanding action against companies that impair the quality of life. Any of these reactions can have a damaging impact on an enterprise.

Stakeholder Impact Analysis

A company cannot always satisfy the claims of all stakeholders. The goals of different groups may conflict, and, in practice, few organizations have the resources to manage all stakehold-ers.[3] For example, union claims for higher wages can conflict with consumer demands for reasonable prices and stockholder demands for acceptable returns. Often the company must make choices. To do so, it must identify the most important stakeholders and give highest priority to pursuing strategies that satisfy their needs. Stakeholder impact analysis can provide such identification. Typically, stakeholder impact analysis follows these steps:

1. Identify stakeholders.
2. Identify stakeholders' interests and concerns.
3. As a result, identify what claims stakeholders are likely to make on the organization.
4. Identify the stakeholders who are most important from the organization's perspective.
5. Identify the resulting strategic challenges.[4]

Such an analysis enables a company to identify the stakeholders most critical to its survival and to make sure that the satisfaction of their needs is paramount. Most companies that have gone through this process quickly come to the conclusion that three stakeholder groups must be satisfied above all others if a company is to survive and prosper: customers, employees, and stockholders.

The Unique Role of Stockholders

A company's stockholders are usually put in a different class from other stakeholder groups, and for good reason. Stockholders are the legal owners and the providers of **risk capital**, a major source of the capital resources that allow a company to operate its business. The capital that stockholders provide to a company is seen as risk capital because there is no guarantee that stockholders will ever recoup their investments and/or earn a decent return.

Recent history demonstrates all too clearly the nature of risk capital. For example, many investors who bought shares in Washington Mutual, the large Seattle-based bank and home loan lender, believed that they were making a low-risk investment. The company had been around for decades and paid a solid dividend, which it increased every year. It had a large branch network and billions in deposits. However, during the 2000s, Washington Mutual was also making increasingly risky mortgage loans, reportedly giving mortgages to people without ever properly verifying if they had the funds to pay back those loans on time. By 2008, many of the borrowers were beginning to default on their loans, and Washington Mutual had to take multibillion-dollar write-downs on the value of its loan portfolio, effectively destroying its once-strong balance sheet. The losses were so large that people with deposits at the bank started to worry about its stability, and they withdrew nearly $16 billion in November 2008 from accounts at Washington Mutual. The stock price collapsed from around $40 at the start of 2008 to under $2 a share, and with the bank teetering on the brink of collapse, the federal government intervened, seized the bank's

risk capital
Capital that cannot be recovered if a company fails and goes bankrupt.

assets, and engineered a sale to JP Morgan. What did Washington Mutual's shareholders get? Absolutely nothing! They were wiped out.

Over the past decade, maximizing returns to stockholders has taken on significant importance as an increasing number of employees have become stockholders in the companies for which they work through employee stock ownership plans (ESOPs). At Walmart, for example, all employees who have served for more than 1 year are eligible for the company's ESOP. Under an ESOP, employees are given the opportunity to purchase stock in the company, sometimes at a discount or less than the market value of the stock. The company may also contribute a certain portion of the purchase price to the ESOP. By making employees stockholders, ESOPs tend to increase the already strong emphasis on maximizing returns to stockholders, for they now help to satisfy two key stakeholder groups: stockholders and employees.

Profitability, Profit Growth, and Stakeholder Claims

Because of the unique position assigned to stockholders, managers normally seek to pursue strategies that maximize the returns that stockholders receive from holding shares in the company. As we noted in Chapter 1, stockholders receive a return on their investment in a company's stock in two ways: from dividend payments and from capital appreciation in the market value of a share (that is, by increases in stock market prices). The best way for managers to generate the funds for future dividend payments and keep the stock price appreciating is to pursue strategies that maximize the company's long-term profitability (as measured by the return on invested capital or ROIC) and grow the profits of the company over time.[5]

As we saw in Chapter 3, ROIC is an excellent measure of the profitability of a company. It tells managers how efficiently they are using the capital resources of the company (including the risk capital provided by stockholders) to generate profits. A company that is generating a positive ROIC is covering all of its ongoing expenses and has money left over, which is then added to shareholders' equity, thereby increasing the value of a company and thus the value of a share of stock in the company. The value of each share will increase further if a company can grow its profits over time, because then the profit that is attributable to every share (that is, the company's earnings per share) will also grow. As we have seen in this book, to grow profits, companies must be doing one or more of the following: (a) participating in a market that is growing, (b) taking market share from competitors, (c) consolidating the industry through horizontal integration, and (d) developing new markets through international expansion, vertical integration, or diversification.

Although managers should strive for profit growth if they are trying to maximize shareholder value, the relationship between profitability and profit growth is a complex one because attaining future profit growth may require investments that reduce the current rate of profitability. The task of managers is to find the right balance between profitability and profit growth.[6] Too much emphasis on current profitability at the expense of future profitability and profit growth can make an enterprise less attractive to shareholders. Too much emphasis on profit growth can reduce the profitability of the enterprise and have the same effect. In an uncertain world where the future is unknowable, finding the right balance between profitability and profit growth is as much art as it is science, but it is something that managers must try to do.

In addition to maximizing returns to stockholders, boosting a company's profitability and profit growth rate is also consistent with satisfying the claims of several other key stakeholder groups. When a company is profitable and its profits are continuing to grow, it can pay higher salaries to productive employees and can also afford benefits such as health insurance coverage, all of which help to satisfy employees. In addition, companies with a high level of profitability and profit growth have no problem meeting their debt commitments, which provides creditors, including bondholders, with a measure of security. More profitable companies are also better able to undertake philanthropic investments, which can help to satisfy some of the claims that local communities and the general public place on a company. Pursuing strategies that maximize the long-term profitability and profit growth of the company is therefore generally consistent with satisfying the claims of various stakeholder groups.

Stakeholder management requires consideration of how the firm's practices affect the cooperation of stakeholders in the short-term, the benefits of building trust and a knowledge-sharing culture with stakeholders in the long run, and the firm's profitability and growth that will enable it to serve stakeholder interests in the future.[7] The company that overpays its employees in the current period, for example, may have very happy employees for a short while, but such action will raise the company's cost structure and limit its ability to attain a competitive advantage in the marketplace, thereby depressing its long-term profitability and hurting its ability to award future pay increases. As far as employees are concerned, the way many companies deal with this situation is to make future pay raises contingent upon improvements in labor productivity. If labor productivity increases, labor costs as a percentage of revenues will fall, profitability will rise, and the company can afford to pay its employees more and offer greater benefits.

Of course, not all stakeholder groups want the company to maximize its long-run profitability and profit growth. Suppliers are more comfortable about selling goods and services to profitable companies because they can be assured that the company will have the funds to pay for those products. Similarly, customers may be more willing to purchase from profitable companies because they can be assured that those companies will be around in the long term to provide after-sales services and support. But neither suppliers nor customers want the company to maximize its profitability at their expense. Rather, they would like to capture some of these profits from the company in the form of higher prices for their goods and services (in the case of suppliers), or lower prices for the products they purchase from the company (in the case of customers). Thus, the company is in a bargaining relationship with some of its stakeholders, a phenomenon we discussed in Chapter 2.

Moreover, despite the argument that maximizing long-term profitability and profit growth is the best way to satisfy the claims of several key stakeholder groups, it should be noted that a company must do so within the limits set by the law and in a manner consistent with societal expectations. The unfettered pursuit of profit can lead to behaviors that are outlawed by government regulations, opposed by important public constituencies, or simply unethical. Governments have enacted a wide range of regulations to govern business behavior, including antitrust laws, environmental laws, and laws pertaining to health and safety in the workplace. It is incumbent on managers to make sure that the company is in compliance with these laws when pursuing strategies.

Unfortunately, there is plenty of evidence that managers can be tempted to cross the line between the legal and illegal in their pursuit of greater profitability and profit growth. For example, in mid-2003 the U.S. Air Force stripped Boeing of $1 billion in contracts to launch satellites when it was discovered that Boeing had obtained thousands of pages of proprietary information from rival Lockheed Martin. Boeing had used that information to prepare its winning bid for the satellite contract. This was followed by the revelation that Boeing's CFO, Mike Sears, had offered a government official, Darleen Druyun, a lucrative job at Boeing while Druyun was still involved in evaluating whether Boeing should be awarded a $17 billion contract to build tankers for the Air Force. Boeing won the contract against strong competition from Airbus, and Boeing hired Druyun. It was clear that the job offer may have had an impact on the Air Force decision. Boeing fired Druyun and the CFO, and shortly thereafter, Boeing CEO Phil Condit resigned in a tacit acknowledgment that he bore responsibility for the ethics violations that had occurred at Boeing during his tenure as leader.[8] In another case, the chief executive of Archer Daniels Midland, one of the world's largest producers of agricultural products, was sent to jail after the Federal Bureau of Investigation (FBI) determined that the company had systematically tried to fix the price for lysine by colluding with other manufacturers in the global marketplace. In another example of price fixing, the 76-year-old chairman of Sotheby's auction house was sentenced to a jail term and the former CEO to house arrest for fixing prices with rival auction house Christie's over a 6-year period (see Strategy in Action 11.1).

Examples such as these beg the question of why managers would engage in such risky behavior. A body of academic work collectively known as agency theory provides an explanation for why managers might engage in behavior that is either illegal or, at the very least, not in the interest of the company's shareholders.

11.1 STRATEGY IN ACTION

Price Fixing at Sotheby's and Christie's

© iStockPhoto.com/Tom Nulens

Sotheby's and Christie's are the two largest fine-art auction houses in the world. In the mid-1990s, the two companies controlled 90% of the fine-art auction market, which at the time was worth approximately $4 billion per year. Traditionally, auction houses make their profit by the commission they charge on auction sales. In good times, these commissions can be as high as 10% on some items, but in the early 1990s, the auction business was in a slump, with the supply of art for auction shriveling. With Sotheby's and Christie's desperate for works of art, sellers played the two houses against each other, driving commissions down to 2%, or sometimes lower.

To try to control this situation, Sotheby's CEO, Dede Brooks, met with Christie's CEO Christopher Davidge in a series of clandestine meetings held in car parking lots that began in 1993. Brooks claimed that she was acting on behalf of her boss, Alfred Taubman, the chairman and controlling shareholder of Sotheby's. According to Brooks, Taubman had agreed with the chairman of Christie's, Anthony Tennant, to work together in the weak auction market and limit price competition. In their meetings, Brooks and Davidge agreed to a fixed and nonnegotiable commission structure. Based on a sliding scale, the commission structure would range from 10% on a $100,000 item to 2% on a $5 million item. In effect, Brooks and Davidge were agreeing to eliminate price competition between them, thereby guaranteeing both auction houses higher profits. The price-fixing agreement started in 1993 and continued unabated for 6 years until federal investigators uncovered the arrangement and brought charges against Sotheby's and Christie's.

With the deal out in the open, lawyers filed several class-action lawsuits on behalf of the sellers that Sotheby's and Christie's had defrauded. Ultimately, at least 100,000 sellers signed on to the class-action lawsuits, which the auction houses settled with a $512 million payment. The auction houses also pleaded guilty to price fixing and paid $45 million in fines to U.S. antitrust authorities. As for the key players, the chairman of Christie's, as a British subject, was able to avoid prosecution in the United States (price fixing is not an offense for which someone can be extradited). Christie's CEO, Davidge, struck a deal with prosecutors, and in return for amnesty turned incriminating documents in to the authorities. Brooks also cooperated with federal prosecutors and avoided jail (in April 2002 she was sentenced to 3 years of probation, 6 months of home detention, 1,000 hours of community service, and a $350,000 fine). Taubman, ultimately isolated by all his former coconspirators, was sentenced to 1 year in jail and fined $7.5 million.

Sources: S. Tully, "A House Divided," *Fortune*, December 18, 2000, pp. 264–275; J. Chaffin, "Sotheby's Ex CEO Spared Jail Sentence," *Financial Times*, April 30, 2002, p. 10; and T. Thorncroft, "A Courtroom Battle of the Vanities," *Financial Times*, November 3, 2001, p. 3.

AGENCY THEORY

Agency theory looks at the problems that can arise in a business relationship when one person delegates decision-making authority to another. It offers a way of understanding why managers do not always act in the best interests of stakeholders and why they might sometimes behave unethically, and, perhaps, also illegally.[9] Although agency theory was originally formulated to capture the relationship between management and stockholders, the basic principles have also been extended to cover the relationship with other key stakeholders, such as employees, as well as relationships between different layers of management within a corporation.[10] Although the focus of attention in this section is on the relationship between senior management and stockholders, some of the same language can be applied to the relationship between other stakeholders and top managers and between top management and lower levels of management.

Principal–Agent Relationships

The basic propositions of agency theory are relatively straightforward. First, an agency relationship is held to arise whenever one party delegates decision-making authority or control over resources to another. The principal is the person delegating authority, and the agent is the person to whom authority is delegated. The relationship between stockholders and senior managers is the classic example of an agency relationship. Stockholders, who are the principals, provide the company with risk capital but delegate control over that capital to senior managers, and particularly to the CEO, who, as their agent, is expected to use that capital in a manner that is consistent with the best interests of stockholders. As we have seen, this means using that capital to maximize the company's long-term profitability and profit growth rate.

The agency relationship continues down the hierarchy within the company. For example, in the large, complex, multibusiness company, top managers cannot possibly make all the important decisions; therefore, they delegate some decision-making authority and control over capital resources to business unit (divisional) managers. Thus, just as senior managers—such as the CEO—are the agents of stockholders, business unit managers are the agents of the CEO (and in this context, the CEO is the principal). The CEO entrusts business unit managers to use the resources over which they have control in the most effective manner in order to maximize the performance of their units. This helps the CEO ensure that he or she maximizes the performance of the entire company, thereby discharging agency obligation to stockholders. More generally, whenever managers delegate authority to managers below them in the hierarchy and give them the right to control resources, an agency relation is established.

The Agency Problem

Although agency relationships often work well, problems may arise if agents and principals have different goals and if agents take actions that are not in the best interests of their principals. Agents may be able to do this because there is an **information asymmetry** between the principal and the agent: agents almost always have more information about the resources they are managing than the principal does. Unscrupulous agents can take advantage of any information asymmetry to mislead principals and maximize their own interests at the expense of principals.

information asymmetry

A situation where an agent has more information about resources he or she is managing than the principal has.

In the case of stockholders, the information asymmetry arises because they delegate decision-making authority to the CEO, their agent, who, by virtue of his or her position inside the company, is likely to know far more than stockholders do about the company's operations. Indeed, there may be certain information about the company that the CEO is unwilling to share with stockholders because that information would also help competitors. In such a case, withholding some information from stockholders may be in the best interest of all. More generally, the CEO, involved in the day-to-day running of the company, is bound to have an information advantage over stockholders, just as the CEO's subordinates may have an information advantage over the CEO with regard to the resources under their control.

The information asymmetry between principals and agents is not necessarily a bad thing, but it can make it difficult for principals to measure how well an agent is performing and thus hold the agent accountable for how well he or she is using the entrusted resources. There is a certain amount of performance ambiguity inherent in the relationship between a principal and agent: principals cannot know for sure if the agent is acting in his or her best interests. They cannot know for sure if the agent is using the resources to which he or she has been entrusted as effectively and efficiently as possible. This ambiguity is amplified by the fact that agents must engage in behavior that has outcomes for different time horizons. For example, investing in research and development may lower profits today but help to ensure the firm is profitable in the future. Principals who reward only immediate performance outcomes could induce myopic ("short-sighted") behavior on the part of the agent. To an extent, principals must trust the agent to do the right thing.

Of course, this trust is not blind: principals do put mechanisms in place with the purpose of monitoring agents, evaluating their performance, and, if necessary, taking corrective action. As we shall see shortly, the board of directors is one such mechanism, for, in part, the board exists to monitor and evaluate senior managers on behalf of stockholders. In Germany, the codetermination law (*Mitbestimmungsgesetz*) requires that firms with over 2,000 employees have boards of directors that represent the interests of employees—just under half of a firm's supervisory board members must represent workers. Other mechanisms serve a similar purpose. In the United States, publicly owned companies must regularly file detailed financial statements with the Securities and Exchange Commission (SEC) that are in accordance with generally agreed-upon accounting principles (GAAP). This requirement exists to give stockholders consistent and detailed information about how well management is using the capital with which it has been entrusted. Similarly, internal control systems within a company are there to help the CEO ensure that subordinates are using the resources with which they have been entrusted as efficiently and effectively as possible.

Despite the existence of governance mechanisms and comprehensive measurement and control systems, a degree of information asymmetry will always remain between principals and agents, and there is always an element of trust involved in the relationship. Unfortunately, not all agents are worthy of this trust. A minority will deliberately mislead principals for personal gain, sometimes behaving unethically or breaking laws in the process. The interests of principals and agents are not always the same; they diverge, and some agents may take advantage of information asymmetries to maximize their own interests at the expense of principals and to engage in behaviors that the principals would never condone.

For example, some authors have argued that, like many other people, senior managers are motivated by desires for status, power, job security, and income.[11] By virtue of their position within the company, certain managers, such as the CEO, can use their authority and control over corporate funds to satisfy these desires at the cost of returns to stockholders. CEOs might use their positions to invest corporate funds in various perks that enhance their status—executive jets, lavish offices, and expense-paid trips to exotic locations—rather than investing those funds in ways that increase stockholder returns. Economists have termed such behavior **on-the-job consumption**.[12]

Aside from engaging in on-the-job consumption, CEOs, along with other senior managers, might satisfy their desires for greater income by using their influence or control over the board of directors to persuade the compensation committee of the board to grant pay increases. Critics of U.S. industry claim that extraordinary pay has now become an endemic problem and that senior managers are enriching themselves at the expense of stockholders and other employees. They point out that CEO pay has been increasing far more rapidly than the pay of average workers, primarily because of very liberal stock option grants that enable a CEO to earn huge pay bonuses in a rising stock market, even if the company underperforms the market and competitors.[13] In 1980, the average CEO in *Business Week's* survey of CEOs of the largest 500 American companies earned 42 times what the average blue-collar worker earned. By 1990, this figure had increased to 85 times. In 2012, the AFL-CIO's Executive PayWatch database reported that American CEOs made 354 times the pay of average workers.[14]

What rankles critics is the size of some CEO pay packages and their apparent lack of relationship to company performance.[15] In 2010, a study by Graef Crystal evaluated the relationship between CEO pay and performance and concluded that there virtually is none. For example, if CEOs were paid according to shareholder return, the CEO of CBS Corporation, Leslie Moonves, who earned an impressive $43.2 million in 2009, should have gotten a $28 million paycut, according to Crystal.[16] Critics feel that the size of pay awards to many CEOs is disproportionate to their achievement, representing a clear example of the agency problem. However, in response to shareholder pressure, in recent years more companies have begun adopting compensation practices that more closely tie CEO pay to performance. For example, at Air Products & Chemicals, when the earnings per share fell short of its 9% growth target in 2012, its CEO John McGlade paid the price in the form of a 65% cut in his annual bonus. His stock grants and stock options decreased as well, reducing his total direct compensation 19%, to 9.1 million.[17] A further concern is that in trying to satisfy a desire for status, security, power, and income, a CEO might engage in empire building—buying many new businesses in an attempt to increase the size of the company through diversification.[18] Although such growth may depress the company's long-term profitability and thus stockholder returns, it increases the size of the empire under the CEO's control and, by extension, the CEO's status, power, security, and income (there is a strong relationship between company size and CEO pay). Instead of trying to maximize stockholder returns by seeking the right balance between profitability and profit growth, some senior managers may trade long-term profitability for greater company growth via new business purchases. For example, in the mid-1970s, Compagnie Générale des Eaux was primarily a water utility and waste-management company, operating "near monopolies" in local municipalities in France and generating strong (and stable) cash flows for its shareholders. However, a series of audacious debt-funded acquisitions in the 1980s and 1990s, first by CEO Guy DeJouany and later by his successor Jean-Marie Messier, rapidly transformed the company into one of the world's largest media and telecom empires, renamed "Vivendi." Then in the 2000s, as the tech, media, and telecom bubble began to burst, the Vivendi empire came crashing down under the weight of its debt burden. Jean-Marie Messier was investigated by both French and U.S. courts, and was accused of misleading shareholders, misappropriating funds, and worsening the company's precarious position. He was fined, and forced to resign.[19]

Figure 11.2 graphs long-term profitability against the rate of growth in company revenues. A company that does not grow is likely missing out on some profitable opportunities.[20]

on-the-job consumption

A term used by economists to describe the behavior of senior management's use of company funds to acquire perks (such as lavish offices, jets, etc.) that will enhance their status, instead of investing it to increase stockholder returns.

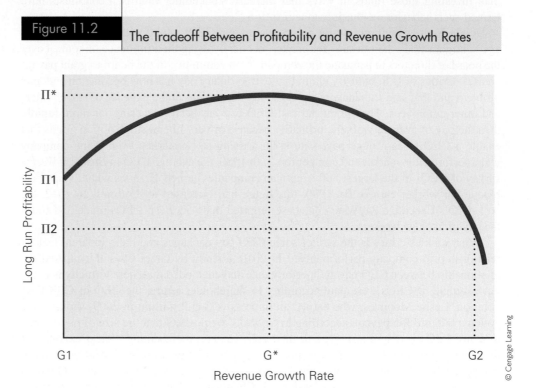

Figure 11.2   The Tradeoff Between Profitability and Revenue Growth Rates

© Cengage Learning

A moderate revenue growth rate of *G** allows a company to maximize long-term profit-ability, generating a return of π^*. Thus, a growth rate of *G1* in Figure 11.2 is not consistent with maximizing profitability ($\pi1 < \pi^*$). By the same token, however, attaining growth in excess of *G2* requires diversification into areas that the company knows little about. Conse-quently, it can be achieved only by sacrificing profitability; that is, past *G**, the investment required to finance further growth does not produce an adequate return, and the company's profitability declines. Yet *G2* may be the growth rate favored by an empire-building CEO, for it will increase his or her power, status, and income. At this growth rate, profitability is equal only to $\pi2$. Because $\pi^* > \pi2$, a company growing at this rate is clearly not maximiz-ing its long-run profitability or the wealth of its stockholders.

The magnitude of agency problems was emphasized in the early 2000s when a series of scandals swept through the corporate world, many of which could be attributed to self-interest-seeking senior executives and a failure of corporate governance mechanisms to hold the largess of those executives in check. In 2003, an investigation revealed that the CEO of Hollinger, Conrad Black, had used "tunneling" to divert over $400 million in company funds to his family and friends (see the Strategy in Action 11.2 for more details on Hollinger and Black). Between 2001 and 2004, accounting scandals also unfolded at a number of major corporations, including Enron, WorldCom, Tyco, Computer Associ-ates, HealthSouth, Adelphia Communications, Dynegy, Royal Dutch Shell, and Parmalat, a major Italian food company. At Enron, $27 billion in debt was hidden from sharehold-ers, employees, and regulators in special partnerships that were removed from the balance sheet. At Parmalat, managers apparently "invented" $8 to $12 billion in assets to shore up the company's balance sheet—assets that never existed. In the case of Royal Dutch Shell,

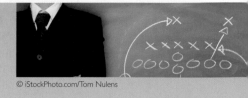

11.2 STRATEGY IN ACTION

Self-Dealing at Hollinger International Inc.

© iStockPhoto.com/Tom Nulens

From 1999 to 2003, Conrad Black, CEO, and F. David Radler, chief operating officer (COO), of Hollinger International Inc. illegally diverted cash and assets to themselves, family members, and other corporate insiders. Hollinger International was a global publishing empire that owned newspapers around the world, such as the *Chicago Sun-Times*, the *Daily Telegraph* (in London), the *National Post* (in Toronto), and the *Jerusalem Post* (in Israel), among others. According to Stephen Cutler, the director of the SEC's Division of Enforcement, "Black and Radler abused their control of a public company and treated it as their personal piggy bank. Instead of carrying out their responsibilities to protect the interest of public shareholders, the defendants cheated and defrauded these shareholders through a series of deceptive schemes and misstatements." In a practice known as "tunneling," Black and Radler engaged in a series of self-dealing transactions, such as selling some of Hollinger's newspapers at below-market prices to companies privately held by Black and Radler themselves—sometimes for a price as low as one dollar! They also directly channeled money out of the firm under the guise of "non-competition payments." The managers also fraudulently used corporate perks, such as using a company jet to fly to the South Pacific for a vacation, and using corporate funds to live in a swanky New York apartment on Park Avenue and throw a lavish $62,000 birthday party for Black's wife. Black's ill-gotten gains are thought to total more than $400 million, and fallout from the scandal resulted in a loss of $2 billion in shareholder value. Although Black was originally sentenced to 6½ years in jail, he ultimately only served 42 months.

Sources: S. Taub, "SEC Charges Hollinger, Two Executives," *CFO*, November 16, 2004; U.S. Department of Justice, "Former Hollinger Chairman Conrad Black and Three Other Executives Indicted in U.S.–Canada Corporate Fraud Schemes," indictment released November 17, 2005; "Ex-Media Mogul Black Convicted of Fraud," *Associated Press*, July 13, 2007; and A. Stern, "Ex-Media Mogul Conrad Black Sent Back to Prison," *Reuters*, June 24, 2011.

senior managers knowingly inflated the value of the company's oil reserves by 1/5, which amounted to 4 billion barrels of oil that never existed, making the company appear much more valuable than it actually was. At the other companies, earnings were systematically overstated, often by hundreds of millions of dollars, or even billions of dollars in the case of Tyco and WorldCom, which understated its expenses by $3 billion in 2001. In all of these cases, the prime motivation seems to have been an effort to present a more favorable view of corporate affairs to shareholders than was actually the case, thereby securing senior executives significantly higher pay packets.[21]

It is important to remember that the agency problem is not confined to the relationship between senior managers and stockholders. It can also bedevil the relationship between the CEO and subordinates and between them and their subordinates. Subordinates might use control over information to distort the true performance of their unit in order to enhance their pay, increase their job security, or make sure their unit gets more than its fair share of company resources.

Confronted with agency problems, the challenge for principals is to (1) shape the behavior of agents so that they act in accordance with the goals set by principals, (2) reduce the information asymmetry between agents and principals, and (3) develop mechanisms for removing agents who do not act in accordance with the goals of principals and mislead them. Principals try to deal with these challenges through a series of governance mechanisms.

GOVERNANCE MECHANISMS

Governance mechanisms are mechanisms that principals put in place to align incentives between principals and agents and to monitor and control agents. The purpose of governance mechanisms is to reduce the scope and frequency of the agency problem: to help ensure that agents act in a manner that is consistent with the best interests of their principals. In this section, the primary focus is on the governance mechanisms that exist to align the interests of senior managers (as agents) with their principals, stockholders. It should not be forgotten, however, that governance mechanisms also exist to align the interests of business-unit managers with those of their superiors, and likewise down the hierarchy within the organization.

Here we look at four main types of governance mechanisms for aligning stockholder and management interests: the board of directors, stock-based compensation, financial statements, and the takeover constraint. The section closes with a discussion of governance mechanisms within a company to align the interest of senior and lower-level managers.

The Board of Directors

The board of directors is the centerpiece of the corporate governance system. Board members are directly elected by stockholders, and under corporate law, they represent the stockholders' interests in the company. Hence, the board can be held legally accountable for the company's actions. Its position at the apex of decision making within the company allows it to monitor corporate strategy decisions and ensure that they are consistent with stockholder interests. If the board believes that corporate strategies are not in the best interest of stockholders, it can apply sanctions, such as voting against management nominations to the board of directors or submitting its own nominees. In addition, the board has the legal authority to hire, fire, and compensate corporate employees, including, most important, the CEO.[22] The board is also responsible for making sure that audited financial statements of the company present a true picture of its financial situation. Thus, the board exists to reduce the information asymmetry between stockholders and managers and to monitor and control management actions on behalf of stockholders.

The typical board of directors is composed of a mix of inside and outside directors. **Inside directors** are senior employees of the company, such as the CEO. They are required on the board because they have valuable information about the company's activities. Without such information, the board cannot adequately perform its monitoring function. But because insiders are full-time employees of the company, their interests tend to be aligned with those of management. Hence, outside directors are needed to bring objectivity to the monitoring and evaluation processes. **Outside directors** are not full-time employees of the company. Many of them are full-time professional directors who hold positions on the boards of several companies. The need to maintain a reputation as competent outside directors gives them an incentive to perform their tasks as objectively and effectively as possible.[23]

There is little doubt that many boards perform their assigned functions admirably. For example, when the board of Sotheby's discovered that the company had been engaged in price fixing with Christie's, board members moved quickly to oust both the CEO and the chairman of the company (see Strategy in Action 11.1). But not all boards perform as well as they should. The board of now-bankrupt energy company Enron approved the company's audited financial statements, which were later discovered to be grossly misleading.

Critics of the existing governance system charge that inside directors often dominate the outsiders on the board. Insiders can use their position within the management hierarchy to exercise control over what kind of company-specific information the board receives. Consequently, they

inside directors

Senior employees of the company, such as the CEO.

outside directors

Directors who are not full-time employees of the company, needed to provide objectivity to the monitoring and evaluation of processes.

can present information in a way that puts them in a favorable light. In addition, because insiders have intimate knowledge of the company's operations and because superior knowledge and control over information are sources of power, they may be better positioned than outsiders to influence boardroom decision making. The board may become the captive of insiders and merely rubber-stamp management decisions instead of guarding stockholder interests.

Some observers contend that many boards are dominated by the company CEO, particularly when the CEO is also the chairman of the board.[24] To support this view, they point out that both inside and outside directors are often the personal nominees of the CEO. The typical inside director is subordinate to the CEO in the company's hierarchy and therefore unlikely to criticize the boss. Because outside directors are frequently the CEO's nominees as well, they can hardly be expected to evaluate the CEO objectively. Thus, the loyalty of the board may be biased toward the CEO, not the stockholders. Moreover, a CEO who is also chairman of the board may be able to control the agenda of board discussions in such a manner as to deflect any criticisms of his or her leadership. Notably, although shareholders ostensibly vote on board members, board members are not legally required to resign if they do not receive a majority of the vote. The Council of Institutional Investors (which represents pension funds, endowments, and other large investors) published a list of "zombie directors" in 2012—directors who were retained on boards despite being rejected by shareholders. The list includes a wide range of companies, from Boston Beer Company to Loral Space and Communications to Cablevision. In fact, Cablevision was listed as having three directors who lost their shareholder votes twice between 2010 and 2012 yet remained on the board.[25]

In the aftermath of a wave of corporate scandals that hit the corporate world in the early 2000s, there are clear signs that many corporate boards are moving away from merely rubber-stamping top-management decisions and are beginning to play a much more active role in corporate governance. In part, they have been prompted by new legislation, such as the 2002 Sarbanes-Oxley Act in the United States, which tightened rules regulating corporate reporting and corporate governance. A growing trend on the part of the courts to hold directors liable for corporate misstatements has also been important. Powerful institutional investors such as pension funds have also been more aggressive in exerting their power, often pushing for more outside representation on the board of directors and for a separation between the roles of chairman and CEO—with the chairman role going to an outsider. Partly as a result, 43% of firms on the Standard & Poor's 500 index split the chairman and CEO jobs as of November 2012—up from 25% 10 years earlier.[26] Separating the role of chairman and CEO limits the ability of corporate insiders, and particularly of the CEO, to exercise control over the board. Regardless, it must be recognized that boards of directors do not work as well as they should in theory, and other mechanisms are needed to align the interests of stockholders and managers.

Stock-Based Compensation

According to agency theory, one of the best ways to reduce the scope of the agency problem is for principals to establish incentives for agents to behave in the company's best interest through pay-for-performance systems. In the case of stockholders and top managers, stockholders can encourage top managers to pursue strategies that maximize a company's long-term profitability and profit growth, and thus the gains from holding its stock, by linking the pay of those managers to the performance of the stock price.

Giving managers **stock options**— the right to purchase the company's shares at a predetermined (strike) price at some point in the future, usually within 10 years of the grant date—has been the most common pay-for-performance system. Typically, the strike price is the price at which the stock was trading when the option was originally granted. Ideally, stock options will

stock options
The right to purchase company stock at a predetermined price at some point in the future, usually within 10 years of the grant date.

motivate managers to adopt strategies that increase the share price of the company, for in doing so managers will also increase the value of their own stock options. Granting managers stock if they attain predetermined performance targets is another stock-based pay-for-performance system.

Several academic studies suggest that stock-based compensation schemes for executives, such as stock options and stock grants, can align management and stockholder interests. For instance, one study found that managers were more likely to consider the effects of their acquisition decisions on stockholder returns if they were significant shareholders.[27] According to another study, managers who were significant stockholders were less likely to pursue strategies that would maximize the size of the company rather than its profitability.[28] More generally, it is difficult to argue with the proposition that the chance to get rich from exercising stock options is the primary reason for the 14-hour days and 6-day workweeks that many employees of fast-growing companies experience.

However, the practice of granting stock options has become increasingly controversial. Many top managers often earn huge bonuses from exercising stock options that were granted several years prior. Critics claim that these options are often too generous, but do not deny that they motivate managers to improve company performance. A particular cause for concern is that stock options are often granted at such low strike prices that the CEO can hardly fail to make a significant amount of money by exercising them, even if the company underperforms in the stock market by a significant margin. A serious example of the agency problem emerged in 2005 and 2006 when the SEC started to investigate a number of companies that had granted stock options to senior executives and apparently "backdated" the stock to a time when the price was lower, enabling executives to earn more money than if those options had simply been dated on the day they were granted.[29] By late 2006, the SEC was investigating nearly 130 companies for possible fraud related to stock-option dating. Major corporations such as Apple, Jabil Circuit, United Healthcare, and Home Depot were included in the list.[30]

Other critics of stock options, including the famous investor Warren Buffett, complain that huge stock-option grants increase the outstanding number of shares in a company and therefore dilute the equity of stockholders; accordingly, they should be shown in company accounts as an expense against profits. Under accounting regulations that were enforced until 2005, stock options, unlike wages and salaries, were not expensed. However, this has since changed, and as a result, many companies are beginning to reduce their use of options. Microsoft, for example, which had long given generous stock-option grants to high-performing employees, replaced stock options with stock grants in 2005. Requiring senior management to hold large numbers of shares in the company is also not without its downside: Managers holding a large portion of their personal wealth in the company they are managing are likely to be underdiversified. This can lead to excessively risk-averse behavior, or overdiversification of the firm.

Financial Statements and Auditors

Publicly traded companies in the United States are required to file quarterly and annual reports with the SEC that are prepared according to GAAP. The purpose of this requirement is to give consistent, detailed, and accurate information about how efficiently and effectively the agents of stockholders—the managers—are running the company. To make sure that managers do not misrepresent this financial information, the SEC also requires that the accounts be audited by an independent and accredited accounting firm. Similar regulations exist in most other developed nations. If the system works as intended, stockholders can have a lot of faith that the information contained in financial statements accurately reflects the state of affairs at a company. Among other things, such information can enable a stockholder to calculate the profitability (ROIC) of a company in which he or she invests and to compare its ROIC against that of competitors.

Unfortunately, this system has not always worked as intended in the United States. Despite that the vast majority of companies do file accurate information in their financial statements, and although most auditors review that information accurately, there is substantial evidence that a minority of companies have abused the system, aided in part by the compliance of auditors. This was clearly an issue at bankrupt energy trader Enron, where the CFO and others misrepresented the true financial state of the company to investors by creating off-balance-sheet partnerships that hid the true state of Enron's indebtedness from public view. Enron's auditor, Arthur Andersen, was complicit with this deception and in direct violation of its fiduciary duty. Arthur Anderson also had lucrative consulting contracts with Enron that it did not want to jeopardize by questioning the accuracy of the company's financial statements. The losers in this mutual deception were shareholders, who relied only upon inaccurate information to make their investment decisions.

There have been numerous examples in recent years of managers' gaming of financial statements to present a distorted picture of their company's finances to investors (see the accusations made by HP about Autonomy in the chapter-opening case, for example). The typical motive has been to inflate the earnings or revenues of a company, thereby generating investor enthusiasm and propelling the stock price higher, which gives managers an opportunity to cash in stock-option grants for huge personal gain, obviously at the expense of stockholders, who have been mislead by the reports.

The gaming of financial statements by companies such as Enron raises serious questions about the accuracy of the information contained in audited financial statements. In response, the United States passed the Sarbanes-Oxley Act in 2002, representing the biggest overhaul of accounting rules and corporate governance procedures since the 1930s. Among other things, Sarbanes-Oxley set up a new oversight board for accounting firms, required CEOs and CFOs to endorse their company's financial statements, and barred companies from hiring the same accounting firm for auditing and consulting services.

The Takeover Constraint

Given the imperfections in corporate governance mechanisms, it is clear that the agency problem may still exist at some companies. However, stockholders still have some residual power—they can always sell their shares. If stockholders sell in large numbers, the price of the company's shares will decline. If the share price falls far enough, the company might be worth less on the stock market than the actual value of its assets. At this point, the company may become an attractive acquisition target and runs the risk of being purchased by another enterprise, against the wishes of the target company's management.

The risk of being acquired by another company is known as the **takeover constraint**—it limits the extent to which managers can pursue strategies and take actions that put their own interests above those of stockholders. If they ignore stockholder interests and the company is acquired, senior managers typically lose their independence, and likely their jobs as well. Therefore, the threat of takeover can constrain management action and limit the worst excesses of the agency problem.

takeover constraint The risk of being acquired by another company.

During the 1980s and early 1990s, the threat of takeover was often enforced by corporate raiders: individuals or corporations that purchase large blocks of shares in companies that appear to be pursuing strategies inconsistent with maximizing stockholder wealth. Corporate raiders argue that if these underperforming companies pursued different strategies, they could create more wealth for stockholders. Raiders purchase stock in a company either to take over the business and run it more efficiently or to precipitate a change in the top management, replacing the existing team with one more likely to maximize stockholder returns. Raiders are motivated not by altruism but by gain. If they succeed in their takeover bid, they can institute strategies that create value for stockholders, including themselves. Even if a takeover bid fails, raiders can still earn millions, for their stockholdings will typically be bought out by the defending company for a hefty premium. Called **greenmail**, this source of gain has stirred much controversy and debate about its benefits. Whereas some claim that the threat posed by raiders has had a salutary effect on enterprise performance by pushing corporate management to run their companies better, others claim there is little evidence of this.[31]

Although the incidence of hostile takeover bids has fallen off significantly since the early 1990s, this should not imply that the takeover constraint has ceased to operate. Unique circumstances existed in the early 2000s that made it more difficult to execute hostile takeovers. The boom years of the 1990s left many corporations with excessive debt (corporate America entered the new century with record levels of debt on its balance sheets), limiting the ability to finance acquisitions, particularly hostile acquisitions, which are often particularly expensive. In addition, the market valuations of many companies became maligned with underlying fundamentals during the stock market bubble of the 1990s, and after a substantial fall in certain segments of the stock market, such as the technology sector, present valuations are still high relative to historic norms—making the hostile acquisition of even poorly run and unprofitable companies expensive. However, takeovers tend to occur in cycles, and it seems likely that once excesses are worked out of the stock market and off corporate balance sheets, the takeover constraint will begin to reassert itself again. It should be remembered that the takeover constraint is the governance mechanism of last resort and is often invoked only when other governance mechanisms have failed.

Governance Mechanisms Inside a Company

Thus far, this chapter has focused on the governance mechanisms designed to reduce the agency problem that potentially exists between stockholders and managers. Agency relationships also exist within a company, and the agency problem can arise between levels of management. In this section, we explore how the agency problem can be reduced within a company by using two complementary governance mechanisms to align the incentives and behavior of employees with those of upper-level management: strategic control systems and incentive systems.

Strategic Control Systems   Strategic control systems are the primary governance mechanisms established within a company to reduce the scope of the agency problem between levels of management. These systems are the formal target-setting, measurement, and feedback systems that allow managers to evaluate whether a company is executing the strategies necessary to maximize its long-term profitability and, in particular, whether the company is achieving superior efficiency, quality, innovation, and customer responsiveness. They are discussed in more detail in subsequent chapters.

The purpose of strategic control systems is to (1) establish standards and targets against which performance can be measured, (2) create systems for measuring and monitoring performance on a regular basis, (3) compare actual performance against the established targets, and (4) evaluate results and take corrective action if necessary. In governance terms, their purpose is to ensure that lower-level managers, as the agents of top managers, are acting in a way that is consistent with top managers' goals, which should be to maximize the wealth of stockholders, subject to legal and ethical constraints.

One increasingly influential model that guides managers through the process of creating the right kind of strategic control systems to enhance organizational performance is the balanced scorecard model.[32] According to the balanced scorecard model, managers

greenmail

A source of gaining wealth by corporate raiders who benefit by pushing companies to either change their corporate strategy to one that will benefit stockholders, or by charging a premium for these stocks when the company wants to buy them back.

have traditionally emphasized financial measures of performance such as ROIC to gauge and evaluate organizational performance. Financial information is extremely important, but it is not enough alone. If managers are to obtain a true picture of organizational performance, financial information must be supplemented with performance measures that indicate how well an organization has been achieving the four building blocks of competitive advantage: efficiency, quality, innovation, and responsiveness to customers. This is because financial results simply inform strategic managers about the results of decisions they have already taken; the other measures balance this picture of performance by informing managers about how accurately the organization has in place the building blocks that drive future performance.[33]

One version of the way the balanced scorecard operates is presented in Figure 11.3. Based on an organization's mission and goals, strategic managers develop a set of criteria for assessing performance according to multiple perspectives, such as:

- *The financial perspective:* for example, the return on capital, cash flow, and revenue growth
- *The customer perspective:* for example, satisfaction, product reliability, on-time delivery, and level of service

Figure 11.3   A Balanced Scorecard Approach

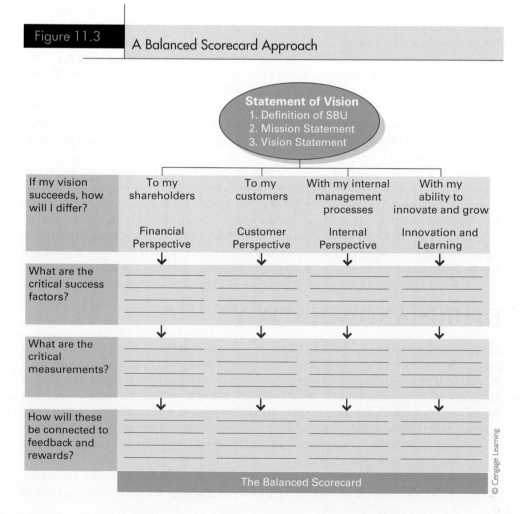

© Cengage Learning

- *The internal perspective:* for example, efficiency, timeliness, and employee satisfaction
- *Innovation and learning:* for example, the number of new products introduced, the percentage of revenues generated from new products in a defined period, the time taken to develop the next generation of new products versus the competition, and the productivity of research and development (R&D)—how much R&D spending is required to produce a successful product

As Kaplan and Norton, the developers of this approach, suggest, "Think of the balanced scorecard as the dials and indicators in an airplane cockpit. For the complex task of navigating and flying an airplane, pilots need detailed information about many aspects of the flight. They need information on fuel, air speed, altitude, learning, destination, and other indicators that summarize the current and predicted environment. Reliance on one instrument can be fatal. Similarly, the complexity of managing an organization today requires that managers be able to view performance in several areas simultaneously."[34]

Based on an evaluation of the complete set of measures in the balanced scorecard, strategic managers are in a good position to reevaluate the company's mission and goals and take corrective action to rectify problems, limit the agency problem, or exploit new opportunities by changing the organization's strategy and structure—which is the purpose of strategic control.

Employee Incentives   Control systems alone may not be sufficient to align incentives between stockholders, senior management, and the rest of the organization. To help do this, positive incentive systems are often put into place to motivate employees to work toward goals that are central to maximizing long-term profitability. As already noted, ESOPs are one form of positive incentive, as are stock-option grants. In the 1990s, ESOPs and stock-ownership grants were pushed down deep within many organizations, meaning that employees at many levels of the firm were eligible for the plans. The logic behind such systems is straightforward: recognizing that the stock price, and therefore their own wealth, is dependent upon the profitability of the company, employees will work toward maximizing profitability.

In addition to stock-based compensation systems, employee compensation can also be tied to goals that are linked to the attainment of superior efficiency, quality, innovation, and customer responsiveness. For example, the bonus pay of a manufacturing employee might depend upon attaining quality and productivity targets, which, if reached, will lower the costs of the company, increase customer satisfaction, and boost profitability. Similarly, a salesperson's bonus pay might be dependent upon surpassing sales targets, and an R&D employee's bonus pay may be contingent upon the success of the new products he or she had worked on developing.

ETHICS AND STRATEGY

The term **ethics** refers to accepted principles of right or wrong that govern the conduct of a person, the members of a profession, or the actions of an organization. **Business ethics** are the accepted principles of right or wrong governing the conduct of businesspeople. Ethical decisions are in accordance with those accepted principles, whereas unethical decisions violate accepted principles. This is not as straightforward as it sounds. Managers may be confronted with **ethical dilemmas**, which are situations where there is no agreement over exactly what the accepted principles of right and wrong are, or where none of the available alternatives seems ethically acceptable.

In our society, many accepted principles of right and wrong are not only universally recognized but also codified into law. In the business arena, there are laws governing product

ethics
Accepted principles of right or wrong that govern the conduct of a person, the members of a profession, or the actions of an organization.

business ethics
Accepted principles of right or wrong governing the conduct of businesspeople.

ethical dilemmas
Situations where there is no agreement over exactly what the accepted principles of right and wrong are, or where none of the available alternatives seems ethically acceptable.

liability (tort laws), contracts and breaches of contract (contract law), the protection of intellectual property (intellectual property law), competitive behavior (antitrust law), and the selling of securities (securities law). Not only is it unethical to break these laws, it is illegal.

In this book we argue that the preeminent goal of managers in a business should be to pursue strategies that maximize the long-term profitability and profit growth of the enterprise, thereby boosting returns to stockholders. Strategies, of course, must be consistent with the laws that govern business behavior: managers must act legally while seeking to maximize the long-term profitability of the enterprise. Unfortunately, as we have already seen in this chapter, managers do break laws. Moreover, managers may take advantage of ambiguities and gray areas in the law, of which there are many in our common law system, to pursue actions that are at best legally suspect and, in any event, clearly unethical. It is important to realize, however, that behaving ethically surpasses staying within the bounds of the law. In the chapter-closing case, we discuss how Goldman Sachs sold bonds to investors that were deliberately structured to increase the risk of failure, and did so without informing clients. Although the legality of this action is unclear (Goldman did pay a fine, but it admitted to no wrongdoing), it pushes the boundaries of ethical behavior.

For another example, see Strategy in Action 11.3, which discusses Nike's use of "sweatshop labor" in developing nations to make sneakers for consumers in the developed world. Although Nike was not breaking any laws by using poorly paid laborers who worked long hours for low wages in poor working conditions, and neither were its subcontractors, many considered it unethical to use subcontractors that by Western standards clearly exploited their workforce. In this section, we take a closer look at the ethical issues that managers may confront when developing strategy, and at the steps managers can take to ensure that strategic decisions are not only legal, but also ethical.

11.3 STRATEGY IN ACTION

Nike–the Sweatshop Debate

© iStockPhoto.com/Tom Nulens

Nike is in many ways the quintessential global corporation. Established in 1972 by former University of Oregon track star Phil Knight, Nike is today one of the leading marketers of athletic shoes and apparel in the world, with sales in 140 countries. Nike does not do any manufacturing; rather, it designs and markets its products and contracts for their manufacture from a global network of 600 factories owned by subcontractors scattered around the globe, which together employ nearly 550,000 people. This huge corporation has made founder Phil Knight one of the richest people in the United States. Nike's marketing phrase "Just Do It!" has become as recognizable in popular culture as its "swoosh" logo, or the faces of its celebrity sponsors, such as Tiger Woods.

For years the company was dogged by repeated and persistent accusations that its products are made in "sweatshops" where workers, many of them children,

slave away in hazardous conditions for wages below subsistence level. Nike's wealth, its detractors claim, has been built upon the backs of the world's poor. Many critics paint the Nike symbol as a sign of the evils of globalization: a rich Western corporation exploiting the world's poor to provide expensive shoes and apparel to the pampered consumers of the developed world. Nike's "Niketown" stores have become standard targets for anti-globalization protestors. Several nongovernmental organizations, such as San Francisco–based Global Exchange, a human rights organization dedicated to promoting environmental, political, and social justice around the world, targeted Nike for repeated criticism and protests. News organizations such as CBS's *48 Hours*, hosted by Dan Rather, ran exposés on working conditions in foreign factories that supply Nike. Students on the campuses of several

(continues)

11.3 STRATEGY IN ACTION

(continued)

© iStockPhoto.com/Tom Nulens

major U.S. universities, with which Nike entertains lucrative sponsorship deals, have protested against those deals, citing Nike's use of sweatshop labor.

Typical of the allegations were those detailed in the CBS news program *48 Hours* in 1996. The report painted a picture of young women at a Vietnamese subcontractor who worked 6 days per week, in poor working conditions with toxic materials, for only $0.20 per hour. The report also stated that a living wage in Vietnam was at least $3 per day, an income that could not be achieved without working substantial overtime. Nike was not breaking any laws, and nor were its subcontractors, but this report and others like it raised questions about the ethics of using "sweatshop labor" to make what were essentially fashion accessories. These actions may have been legal and may have helped the company to increase its profitability, but was it ethical to use subcontractors that, by Western standards, clearly exploited their workforce? Nike's critics thought not, and the company found itself at the focus of a wave of demonstrations and consumer boycotts.

Adding fuel to the fire, in November 1997, Global Exchange obtained and leaked a confidential report by Ernst & Young of an audit that Nike had commissioned of a Vietnam factory owned by a Nike subcontractor. The factory had 9,200 workers and made 400,000 pairs of shoes per month. The Ernst & Young report painted a dismal picture of thousands of young women, most under age 25, laboring 10½ hours per day, 6 days a week, in excessive heat and noise and foul air, for slightly more than $10 a week. The report also found that workers with skin or breathing problems had not been transferred to departments free of chemicals. More than half the workers who dealt with dangerous chemicals did not wear protective masks or gloves. The report stated that, in parts of the plant, workers were exposed to carcinogens that exceeded local legal standards by 177 times and that 77% of the employees suffered from respiratory problems.

These exposés surrounding Nike's use of subcontractors forced the company to reexamine its policies. Realizing that its subcontracting policies were perceived as unethical, Nike's managers took a number of steps. They established a code of conduct for Nike subcontractors and set up a system whereby independent auditors would annually monitor all subcontractors. Nike's code of conduct required that all employees at footwear factories be at least 18 years old and that exposure to potentially toxic materials would not exceed the permissible exposure limits established by the U.S. Occupational Safety and Health Administration for workers in the United States. In short, Nike concluded that behaving ethically required going beyond the requirements of the law. It required the establishment and enforcement of rules that adhere to accepted moral principles of right and wrong.

Sources: "Boycott Nike," CBS News *48 Hours*, October 17, 1996; D. Jones, "Critics Tie Sweatshop Sneakers to 'Air Jordan,'" *USA Today*, June 6, 1996, p. 1B; "Global Exchange Special Report: Nike Just Don't Do It," www.globalexchange.org/education/publications/newsltr6.97p2.html#nike; S. Greenhouse, "Nike Shoeplant in Vietnam Is Called Unsafe for Workers," *New York Times*, November 8, 1997; and V. Dobnik, "Chinese Workers Abused Making Nikes, Reeboks," *Seattle Times*, September 21, 1997, p. A4.

Ethical Issues in Strategy

The ethical issues that strategic managers confront cover many topics, but most are due to a potential conflict between the goals of the enterprise, or the goals of individual managers, and the fundamental rights of important stakeholders, including stockholders, customers, employees, suppliers, competitors, communities, and the general public. Stakeholders have basic rights that should be respected, and it is unethical to violate those rights.

Stockholders have the right to timely and accurate information about their investments (in accounting statements), and it is unethical to violate that right. Customers have the right to be fully informed about the products and services they purchase, including the right to information about how those products might cause them harm, and it is unethical to restrict their access to such information. Employees have the right to safe working conditions, fair compensation for the work they perform, and just treatment by managers. Suppliers have the right to expect contracts to be respected, and the company should not take advantage of a power disparity between it and a supplier to opportunistically rewrite a contract. Competitors have the right to expect that the firm will abide by the rules of competition and not violate the basic principles of antitrust laws. Communities and the general public, including their political representatives in government, have the right to expect that a firm will not violate the basic expectations that society places on enterprises—for example, by dumping toxic pollutants into the environment, or overcharging for work performed on government contracts.

Those who take the stakeholder view of business ethics often argue that it is in the enlightened self-interest of managers to behave in an ethical manner that recognizes and respects the fundamental rights of stakeholders, because doing so will ensure the support of stakeholders and, ultimately, benefit the firm and its managers. Others go beyond this instrumental approach to ethics and argue that, in many cases, acting ethically is simply the right thing to do. They argue that businesses need to recognize their *noblesse oblige*, a French term that refers to honorable and benevolent behavior that is considered the responsibility of people of high (noble) birth, and give something back to the society that made their success possible. In a business setting, it is understood that benevolent behavior is the moral responsibility of successful enterprises.

Unethical behavior often arises in a corporate setting when managers decide to put the attainment of their own personal goals, or the goals of the enterprise, above the fundamental rights of one or more stakeholder groups (in other words, unethical behavior may arise from agency problems). The most common examples of such behavior involve self-dealing, information manipulation, anticompetitive behavior, opportunistic exploitation of other players in the value chain in which the firm is embedded (including suppliers, complement providers, and distributors), the maintenance of substandard working conditions, environmental degradation, and corruption.

Self-dealing occurs when managers find a way to feather their own nests with corporate monies, as we have already discussed in several examples in this chapter (such as Conrad Black at Hollinger). **Information manipulation** occurs when managers use their control over corporate data to distort or hide information in order to enhance their own financial situation or the competitive position of the firm, such as HP accused Autonomy of in the chapter-opening case. As we have seen, many accounting scandals have involved the deliberate manipulation of financial information. Information manipulation can also occur with nonfinancial data. An example of this is when managers at the tobacco companies suppressed internal research that linked smoking to health problems, violating the rights of consumers to accurate information about the dangers of smoking. When this evidence came to light, lawyers filed class-action suits against the tobacco companies, claiming that they had intentionally caused harm to smokers: they had broken tort law by promoting a product that they knew was seriously harmful to consumers. In 1999, the tobacco companies settled a lawsuit brought by the states that sought to recover health-care costs associated with tobacco-related illnesses; the total payout to the states was $260 billion.

Anticompetitive behavior covers a range of actions aimed at harming actual or potential competitors, most often by using monopoly power, and thereby enhancing the long-run prospects of the firm. For example, in the 1990s, the Justice Department claimed that Microsoft used its monopoly in operating systems to force PC makers to bundle Microsoft's Web browser, Internet Explorer, with the Windows operating system, and to display the Internet Explorer logo prominently on the computer desktop. Microsoft

self-dealing
Managers using company funds for their own personal consumption, as done by Enron, for example, in previous years.

information manipulation
When managers use their control over corporate data to distort or hide information in order to enhance their own financial situation or the competitive position of the firm.

anticompetitive behavior
A range of actions aimed at harming actual or potential competitors, most often by using monopoly power, and thereby enhancing the long-run prospects of the firm.

reportedly told PC makers that it would not supply them with Windows unless they did this. Because the PC makers needed Windows to sell their machines, this was a powerful threat. The alleged aim of the action, which exemplifies "tie-in sales"—which are illegal under antitrust laws—was to drive a competing browser maker, Netscape, out of business. The courts ruled that Microsoft was indeed abusing its monopoly power in this case, and under a 2001 consent decree, the company was forced to cease this practice.

Legality aside, the actions Microsoft managers allegedly engaged in are unethical on at least three counts; first, by violating the rights of end-users by unfairly limiting their choice; second, by violating the rights of downstream participants in the industry value chain, in this case PC makers, by forcing them to incorporate a particular product in their design; and third, by violating the rights of competitors to free and fair competition.

opportunistic exploitation

Unethical behavior sometimes used by managers to unilaterally rewrite the terms of a contract with suppliers, buyers, or complement providers in a way that is more favorable to the firm.

Opportunistic exploitation of other players in the value chain in which the firm is embedded is another example of unethical behavior. Exploitation of this kind typically occurs when the managers of a firm seek to unilaterally rewrite the terms of a contract with suppliers, buyers, or complement providers in a way that is more favorable to the firm, often using their power to force a revision to the contract. For example, in the late 1990s, Boeing entered into a $2 billion contract with Titanium Metals Corporation to purchase certain amounts of titanium annually for 10 years. In 2000, after Titanium Metals had already spent $100 million to expand its production capacity to fulfill the contract, Boeing demanded that the contract be renegotiated, asking for lower prices and an end to minimum purchase agreements. As a major purchaser of titanium, managers at Boeing probably thought they had the power to push this contract revision through, and Titanium's investment meant that it would be unlikely that the company walk away from the deal. Titanium promptly sued Boeing for breach of contract. The dispute was settled out of court, and under a revised agreement, Boeing agreed to pay monetary damages to Titanium Metals (reported to be in the $60 million range) and entered into an amended contract to purchase titanium.[35] This action was arguably unethical because it violated the supplier's rights to have buyers do business in a fair and open way, regardless of any legality.

substandard working conditions

Arise when managers underinvest in working conditions, or pay employees below-market rates, in order to reduce their production costs.

Substandard working conditions arise when managers underinvest in working conditions, or pay employees below-market rates, in order to reduce their production costs. The most extreme examples of such behavior occur when a firm establishes operations in countries that lack the workplace regulations found in developed nations such as the United States. The example of Nike, mentioned earlier, falls into this category. In another example, The Ohio Art Company ran into an ethical storm when newspaper reports alleged that it had moved production of its popular Etch A Sketch toy from Ohio to a supplier in Shenzhen Province where employees—mostly teenagers—work long hours for $0.24 per hour, below the legal minimum wage of $0.33 per hour. Moreover, production reportedly started at 7:30 a.m. and continued until 10 p.m., with breaks only for lunch and dinner; Saturdays and Sundays were treated as normal workdays, meaning that employees worked 12 hours per day, 7 days per week, or 84 hours per week—well above the standard 40-hour week authorities set in Shenzhen. Working conditions such as these clearly violate employees' rights in China, as specified by local regulations (which are poorly enforced). Is it ethical for the The Ohio Art Company to use such a supplier? Many would say it is not.[36]

environmental degradation

Occurs when a company's actions directly or indirectly result in pollution or other forms of environmental harm.

Environmental degradation occurs when a company's actions directly or indirectly result in pollution or other forms of environmental harm. Environmental degradation can violate the rights of local communities and the general public for things such as clean air and water, land that is free from pollution by toxic chemicals, and properly managed forests.

Finally, **corruption** can arise in a business context when managers pay bribes to gain access to lucrative business contracts. For example, it was alleged that Halliburton was part of a consortium that paid nearly $180 million in bribes to win a lucrative contract to build a natural gas plant in Nigeria.[37] Similarly, between 2006 and 2009, Siemens was found guilty of paying hundreds of millions of dollars in bribes to secure sales contracts; the company was ultimately forced to pay hefty fines, and one of the Chinese executives who accepted $5.1 million in bribes was sentenced to death by Chinese courts.[38] Corruption is clearly unethical because it violates many rights, including the right of competitors to a level playing field when bidding for contracts, and, when government officials are involved, the right of citizens to expect that government officials will act in the best interest of the local community (or nation) and not in response to corrupt payments.

corruption
Can arise in a business context when managers pay bribes to gain access to lucrative business contracts.

The Roots of Unethical Behavior

Why do some managers behave unethically? What motivates managers to engage in actions that violate accepted principals of right and wrong, trample on the rights of one or more stakeholder groups, or simply break the law? Although there is no simple answer to this question, a few generalizations can be made.[39] First, it is important to recognize that business ethics are not divorced from **personal ethics**, which are the generally accepted principles of right and wrong governing the conduct of individuals. As individuals we are taught that it is wrong to lie and cheat and that it is right to behave with integrity and honor and to stand up for what we believe to be right and true. The personal ethical code that guides behavior comes from a number of sources, including parents, schools, religion, and the media. A personal ethical code will exert a profound influence on the way individuals behave as businesspeople. An individual with a strong sense of personal ethics is less likely to behave in an unethical manner in a business setting; in particular, he or she is less likely to engage in self-dealing and more likely to behave with integrity.

personal ethics
Generally accepted principles of right and wrong governing the conduct of individuals.

Second, many studies of unethical behavior in a business setting have come to the conclusion that businesspeople sometimes do not realize that they are behaving unethically, primarily because they simply fail to ask the relevant question: Is this decision or action ethical? Instead, they apply straightforward business calculus to what they perceive to be a business decision, forgetting that the decision may also have an important ethical dimension.[40] The fault here is within the processes that do not incorporate ethical considerations into business decision making. This may have been the case at Nike when managers originally made subcontracting decisions (see the Strategy in Action 11.3). Those decisions were probably made on the basis of good economic logic. Subcontractors were probably chosen on the basis of business variables such as cost, delivery, and product quality, and key managers simply failed to ask: "How does this subcontractor treat its workforce?" If managers pondered this question at all, they probably reasoned that it was the subcontractor's concern, not the company's.

Unfortunately, the climate in some businesses does not encourage people to think through the ethical consequences of business decisions. This brings us to the third cause of unethical behavior in businesses: an organizational culture that de-emphasizes business ethics and considers all decisions to be purely economic ones. Individuals may believe their decisions within the workplace are not subject to the same ethical principles that govern their personal lives, or that their decisions within the firm do not really "belong" to them, but rather that they are merely acting as agents of the firm. A related fourth cause of unethical behavior may be pressure from top management to meet performance goals that are unrealistic and can only be attained by cutting corners or acting in an unethical manner. Thus the pressure to perform induces individuals to behave in ways they otherwise would not.

An organizational culture can "legitimize" behavior that society would judge as unethical, particularly when this is mixed with a focus upon unrealistic performance goals, such as maximizing short-term economic performance regardless of the costs. In such circumstances, there is a greater-than-average probability that managers will violate their own personal ethics and engage in behavior that is unethical. By the same token, an organization's culture can do just the opposite and reinforce the need for ethical behavior. Recreational Equipment Inc. (REI), for example, has a strong culture around valuing environmental sustainability, respect for individuals, and trustworthiness. The firm backs up this belief system with such policies as producing an annual environmental stewardship report and providing health-care benefits for all workers (including part-time employees), a retirement plan that does not require individual contributions, and grants for employees to contribute to their communities or to buy gear to pursue personal outdoor challenges. The company ranked 17th on *Fortune*'s 2013 100 "Best Companies to Work For" and has been on that list every year since 1998.

This brings us to a fifth root cause of unethical behavior: *unethical leadership*. Leaders help to establish the culture of an organization, and they set the example that others follow. Other employees in a business often take their cues from business leaders, and if those leaders do not behave in an ethical manner, employees may not either. It is not what leaders say that matters, but what they do. A good example is Ken Lay, the former CEO of the failed energy company Enron. While constantly referring to Enron's code of ethics in public statements, Lay simultaneously engaged in behavior that was ethically suspect. Among other things, he failed to discipline subordinates who had inflated earnings by engaging in corrupt energy trading schemes. Such behavior sent a very clear message to Enron's employees—unethical behavior would be tolerated if it could boost earnings.

Behaving Ethically

What is the best way for managers to ensure that ethical considerations are taken into account? In many cases, there is no easy answer to this question, for many of the most vexing ethical problems involve very real dilemmas and suggest no obvious right course of action. Nevertheless, managers can and should do at least seven things to ensure that basic ethical principles are adhered to and that ethical issues are routinely considered when making business decisions. They can (1) favor hiring and promoting people with a well-grounded sense of personal ethics, (2) build an organizational culture that places a high value on ethical behavior, (3) make sure that leaders within the business not only articulate the rhetoric of ethical behavior but also act in a manner that is consistent with that rhetoric, (4) put decision-making processes in place that require people to consider the ethical dimension of business decisions, (5) use ethics officers, (6) put strong governance processes in place, and (7) act with moral courage.

Hiring and Promotion It seems obvious that businesses should strive to hire people who have a strong sense of personal ethics and would not engage in unethical or illegal behavior. Similarly, you would rightly expect a business to not promote people, and perhaps fire people, whose behavior does not match generally accepted ethical standards. But doing this is actually very difficult. How do you know if someone has a poor sense of personal ethics? In this society, if someone lacks personal ethics, he or she may hide this fact to retain people's trust.

Is there anything that businesses can do to ensure they do not hire people who have poor personal ethics, particularly given that people have an incentive to hide this from public view (indeed, unethical people may well lie about their nature)? Businesses can give potential employees psychological tests to try to discern their ethical predisposition, and they can check with prior employees regarding someone's reputation, such as by asking for letters of reference and talking to people who have worked with the prospective employee. The latter approach is certainly not uncommon and does influence the hiring process. Promoting people who have displayed poor ethics should not occur in a company where the organization's culture values ethical behavior and where leaders act accordingly.

Organization Culture and Leadership To foster ethical behavior, businesses must build an organization culture that places a high value on ethical behavior. Three actions are particularly important. First, businesses must explicitly articulate values that place a strong emphasis on ethical behavior. Many companies now do this by drafting a **code of ethics**, a formal statement of the ethical priorities to which a business adheres—in fact, both the New York Stock Exchange and Nasdaq listing services require listed companies to have a code of ethics that identifies areas of ethical risk, provides guidance for recognizing and dealing with ethical issues, provides mechanisms for reporting unethical conduct, and notes procedures to ensure prompt action against violations.[41] Firms also sometimes incorporate ethical statements into documents that articulate the values or mission of the business. For example, the food and consumer products giant Unilever's code of ethics includes the following points: "We will not use any form of forced, compulsory or child labor" and "No employee may offer, give or receive any gift or payment which is, or may be construed as being, a bribe. Any demand for, or offer of, a bribe must be rejected immediately and reported to management."[42] Unilever's principles send a very clear message to managers and employees within the organization. Data from the National Business Ethics Survey, administered by the Ethics Resource Center, a U.S. nonprofit, has found that firms with strong and well-implemented ethics programs have significantly fewer cases of ethical misconduct.[42]

> **code of ethics**
> Formal statement of the ethical priorities to which a business adheres.

Having articulated values in a code of ethics or some other document, it is important that leaders in the business give life and meaning to those words by repeatedly emphasizing their importance and then acting on them. This means using every relevant opportunity to stress the importance of business ethics and making sure that key business decisions not only make good economic sense but also are ethical. Many companies have gone a step further and hired independent firms to audit them and make sure that they are behaving in a manner consistent with their ethical codes. Nike, for example, has in recent years hired independent auditors to make sure that its subcontractors are adhering to Nike's code of conduct.

Finally, building an organization culture that places a high value on ethical behavior requires incentive and reward systems, including promotional systems that reward people who engage in ethical behavior and sanction those who do not.

Decision-Making Processes In addition to establishing the right kind of ethical culture in an organization, businesspeople must be able to think through the ethical implications of decisions in a systematic way. To do this, they need a moral compass, and beliefs about what determines individual rights and justice. Some experts on ethics have proposed a straightforward practical guide, or ethical algorithm, to determine whether a decision is ethical. A decision is acceptable on ethical grounds if a businessperson can answer "yes" to each of these questions:

1. Does my decision fall within the accepted values or standards that typically apply in the organizational environment (as articulated in a code of ethics or some other corporate statement)?
2. Am I willing to see the decision communicated to all stakeholders affected by it—for example, by having it reported in newspapers or on television?
3. Would the people with whom I have a significant personal relationship, such as family members, friends, or even managers in other businesses, approve of the decision?

FOCUS ON: Wal-Mart

Walmart's Statement of Ethics

© iStockPhoto.com/caracterdesign

Walmart has a 35-page "Statement of Ethics" (available in 14 languages) that covers a wide range of issues spanning from harassment and nondiscrimination to fair competition, insider trading, corruption, and money laundering. The statement is organized around the following guiding principles:

- Always act with integrity.
- Lead with integrity, and expect others to work with integrity.
- Follow the law at all times.
- Be honest and fair.
- Reveal and report all information truthfully, without manipulation or misrepresentation.
- Work, actions, and relationships outside of your position with the company should be free of any conflicts of interest.
- Respect and encourage diversity, and never discriminate against anyone.
- Ask your manager or the Global Ethics Office for help if you have questions about this Statement of Ethics, or if you face an ethical problem.
- Promptly report suspected violations of the Statement of Ethics.
- Cooperate with and maintain the private nature of any investigation of a possible ethics violation.

- When involved in an ethics investigation, you should reveal and report all information truthfully. You should present all the facts you are aware of without personal opinion, bias, or judgment.

The statement details what Walmart employees cannot do, and provides helpful examples with Q&A sections such as "Q: A supplier I work with has offered me two tickets to the World Cup if I pay face value for them. Can I buy the tickets?

A: You should decline the offer. Although you may be paying face value for the tickets, it may not necessarily reflect the market value of the item. Some areas allow you to resell tickets, and you might be able to make a profit if you sold them. Also, there could be a gift of prestige in receiving the ability to attend a coveted event, such as the World Cup."

Walmart has a Global Ethics Office that is responsible for developing Walmart's ethics policies, promoting an ethical culture, and providing an anonymous reporting system for misconduct. Walmart also has ethics committees organized by region that employees can contact, and global ethics helplines that employees can call when they have questions.

Source: Data retrieved from http://ethics.walmartstores.com/statementofethics on April 26, 2013.

Ethics Officers   To make sure that a business behaves in an ethical manner, a number of firms now have ethics officers. These individuals are responsible for making sure that all employees are trained to be ethically aware, that ethical considerations enter the business decision-making process, and that employees adhere to the company's code of ethics. Ethics officers may also be responsible for auditing decisions to ensure that they are consistent with this code. In many businesses, ethics officers act as an internal ombudsperson with responsibility for handling confidential inquiries from employees, investigating complaints from employees or others, reporting findings, and making recommendations for change.

United Technologies, a large aerospace company with worldwide revenues of about $60 billion, has had a formal code of ethics since 1990. There are now some 450 "business practice officers" (this is the company's name for ethics officers) within United Technologies who are responsible for making sure that employees adhere to the code. United Technologies also established an ombudsperson program in 1986 that allows employees to inquire anonymously about ethics issues.[43]

Strong Corporate Governance   Strong corporate governance procedures are needed to ensure that managers adhere to ethical norms, in particular, that senior managers do not engage in self-dealing or information manipulation. Strong corporate governance procedures require an independent board of directors that is willing to hold top managers accountable for self-dealing and is capable of verifying the information managers provide. If companies like Tyco, WorldCom, and Enron had had strong boards of directors, it is unlikely that these companies would have experienced accounting scandals, or that top managers would have been able to access the funds of these corporations as personal treasuries.

There are five cornerstones of strong governance. The first is a board of directors that is composed of a majority of outside directors who have no management responsibilities in the firm, who are willing and able to hold top managers accountable, and who do not have business ties with important insiders. Outside directors should be individuals of high integrity whose reputation is based on their ability to act independently. The second cornerstone is a board where the positions of CEO and chairman are held by separate individuals and the chairman is an outside director. When the CEO is also chairman of the board of directors, he or she can control the agenda, thereby furthering his or her own personal agenda (which may include self-dealing) or limiting criticism against current corporate policies. The third cornerstone is a compensation committee formed by the board that is composed entirely of outside directors. It is the compensation committee that sets the level of pay for top managers, including stock-option grants and additional benefits. The scope of self-dealing is reduced by making sure that the compensation committee is independent of managers. Fourth, the audit committee of the board, which reviews the financial statements of the firm, should also be composed of outsiders, thereby encouraging vigorous independent questioning of the firm's financial statements. Finally, the board should use outside auditors that are truly independent and do not have a conflict of interest. This was not the case in many recent accounting scandals, where outside auditors were also consultants to the corporation and therefore less likely to ask management hard questions for fear that doing so would jeopardize lucrative consulting contracts.

Moral Courage   It is important to recognize that sometimes managers and others need significant moral courage. It is moral courage that enables managers to walk away from a decision that is profitable but unethical, that gives employees the strength to say no to superiors who instruct them to behave unethically, and that gives employees the integrity to go to the media and blow the whistle on persistent unethical behavior in a company. Moral courage does not come easily; there are well-known cases where individuals have lost their jobs because they blew the whistle on unethical corporate behaviors.

Companies can strengthen the moral courage of employees by making a commitment to refuse to seek retribution against employees who exercise moral courage, say no to superiors, or otherwise complain about unethical actions. For example, Unilever's code of ethics includes the following:

> *Any breaches of the Code must be reported in accordance with the procedures specified by the Joint Secretaries. The Board of Unilever will not criticize management for any loss of business resulting from adherence to these principles and other mandatory policies and instructions. The Board of Unilever expects employees to bring to their attention, or to that of senior management, any breach or suspected breach of these principles. Provision has been made for employees to be able to report in confidence and no employee will suffer as a consequence of doing so.*

This statement gives "permission" to employees to exercise moral courage. Companies can also set up ethics hotlines that allow employees to anonymously register a complaint with a corporate ethics officer.

Final Words   The steps discussed here can help to ensure that when managers make business decisions, they are fully cognizant of the ethical implications and do not violate basic ethical prescripts. At the same time, not all ethical dilemmas have a clean and obvious solution—that is why they are dilemmas. At the end of the day, there are things that a business should not do, and there are things that a business should do, but there are also actions that present managers with true dilemmas. In these cases a premium is placed upon the ability of managers to make sense out of complex, messy situations and to make balanced decisions that are as just as possible.

11.1 ETHICAL DILEMMA

© iStockPhoto.com/P_Wei

You work for a U.S.-based textile company that is having trouble competing with overseas competitors that have access to low-cost labor. Although you pay your factory workers $14 an hour plus benefits, you know that a similar textile mill in Vietnam is paying its employees around $0.50 an hour, and the mill does not have to comply with the same costly safety and environmental regulations that your company does. After transportation costs have been taken into account, the Vietnamese factory still has a clear cost advantage. Your CEO says that it is time to shut down the mill, lay off employees, and move production to a country in Central America or Southeast Asia where labor and compliance costs are much, much lower. The U.S. mill is the only large employer in this small community. Many of the employees have been working at the mill their entire working lives. The mill is marginally profitable.

What appears to be the right action to take for stockholders? What is the most ethical course of action? Is there a conflict in this situation?

SUMMARY OF CHAPTER

1. Stakeholders are individuals or groups that have an interest, claim, or stake in the company—in what it does and in how well it performs.
2. Stakeholders are in an exchange relationship with the company. They supply the organization with important resources (or contributions) and in exchange expect their interests to be satisfied (by inducements).
3. A company cannot always satisfy the claims of all stakeholders. The goals of different groups may conflict. The company must identify the most important stakeholders and give highest priority to pursuing strategies that satisfy their needs.
4. A company's stockholders are its legal owners and the providers of risk capital, a major source of the capital resources that allow a company

to operate its business. As such, they have a unique role among stakeholder groups.

5. Maximizing long-term profitability and profit growth is the route to maximizing returns to stockholders, and it is also consistent with satisfying the claims of several other key stakeholder groups.

6. When pursuing strategies that maximize profitability, a company has the obligation to do so within the limits set by the law and in a manner consistent with societal expectations.

7. An agency relationship is held to arise whenever one party delegates decision-making authority or control over resources to another.

8. The essence of the agency problem is that the interests of principals and agents are not always the same, and some agents may take advantage of information asymmetries to maximize their own interests at the expense of principals.

9. Numerous governance mechanisms serve to limit the agency problem between stockholders and managers. These include the board of directors, stock-based compensation schemes, financial statements and auditors, and the threat of a takeover.

10. The term *ethics* refers to accepted principles of right or wrong that govern the conduct of a person, the members of a profession, or the actions of an organization. Business ethics are the accepted principles of right or wrong governing the conduct of businesspeople, and an ethical strategy is one that does not violate these accepted principles.

11. Unethical behavior is rooted in poor personal ethics; the inability to recognize that ethical issues are at stake; failure to incorporate ethical issues into strategic and operational decision making; a dysfunctional culture; and failure of leaders to act in an ethical manner.

12. To make sure that ethical issues are considered in business decisions, managers should (a) favor hiring and promoting people with a well-grounded sense of personal ethics, (b) build an organizational culture that places a high value on ethical behavior, (c) ensure that leaders within the business not only articulate the rhetoric of ethical behavior but also act in a manner that is consistent with that rhetoric, (d) put decision-making processes in place that require people to consider the ethical dimension of business decisions, (e) use ethics officers, (f) have strong corporate governance procedures, and (g) be morally courageous and encourage others to be the same.

DISCUSSION QUESTIONS

1. How prevalent has the agency problem been in corporate America during the last decade? During the late 1990s there was a boom in initial public offerings of Internet companies (dot.com companies). The boom was supported by sky-high valuations often assigned to Internet start-ups that had no revenues or earnings. The boom came to an abrupt end in 2001, when the Nasdaq stock market collapsed, losing almost 80% of its value. Who do you think benefited most from this boom: investors (stockholders) in those companies, managers, or investment bankers?

2. Why is maximizing ROIC consistent with maximizing returns to stockholders?

3. How might a company configure its strategy-making processes to reduce the probability that managers will pursue their own self-interest at the expense of stockholders?

4. In a public corporation, should the CEO of the company also be allowed to be the chairman of the board (as allowed for by the current law)? What problems might this give rise to?

5. Under what conditions is it ethically defensible to outsource production to producers in the developing world who have much lower labor costs when such actions involve laying off long-term employees in the firm's home country?

6. Is it ethical for a firm faced with a shortage of labor to employ illegal immigrants to meet its needs?

KEY TERMS

Stakeholders   362
Internal stakeholders   362
External
    stakeholders   362
Risk capital   363
Information
    asymmetry   367
On-the-job
    consumption   369

Inside directors   372
Outside directors   372
Stock options   374
Takeover constraint   375
Greenmail   376
Ethics   378
Business ethics   378
Ethical dilemmas   378
Self-dealing   381

Information
    manipulation   381
Anticompetitive
    behavior   381
Opportunistic
    exploitation   382
Substandard working
    conditions   382

Environmental
    degradation   385
Corruption   386
Personal ethics   386
Code of ethics   388

PRACTICING STRATEGIC MANAGEMENT

© Yuri_aRCuRS/iStock Photo

Small Group Exercises

Small-Group Exercise: Evaluating Stakeholder Claims

Break up into groups of three to five people, and appoint one group member as a spokesperson who will communicate your findings to the class when called on by the instructor. Discuss the following:

1. Identify the key stakeholders of your educational institution. What claims do they place on the institution?
2. Strategically, how is the institution responding to those claims? Do you think the institution is pursuing the correct strategies in view of those claims? What might it do differently, if anything?
3. Prioritize the stakeholders in order of their importance for the survival and health of the institution. Do the claims of different stakeholder groups conflict with each other? If the claims do conflict, whose claim should be tackled first?

STRATEGY SIGN ON

© iStockPhoto.com/Ninoslav Dotlic

Article File 11

Find an example of a company that ran into trouble because it failed to take into account the rights of one of its stakeholder groups when making an important strategic decision.

STRATEGY SIGN ON

(continued)

© iStockPhoto.com/Ninoslav Dotlic

Strategic Management Project: Module 11

This module deals with the relationships your company has with its major stakeholder groups. With the information you have at your disposal, perform the tasks and answer the questions that follow:

1. Identify the main stakeholder groups in your company. What claims do they place on the company? How is the company trying to satisfy those claims?
2. Evaluate the performance of the CEO of your company from the perspective of (a) stockholders, (b) employees, (c) customers, and (d) suppliers. What does this evaluation tell you about the ability of the CEO and the priorities that he or she is committed to?
3. Try to establish whether the governance mechanisms that operate in your company do a good job of aligning the interests of top managers with those of stockholders.
4. Pick a major strategic decision made by your company in recent years, and try to think through the ethical implications of that decision. In the light of your review, do you think that the company acted correctly?

CLOSING CASE

Did Goldman Sachs Commit Fraud?

In the mid-2000s, when housing prices in the United States were surging, hedge fund manager John Paulson approached Goldman Sachs. Paulson believed that housing prices had risen too much. There was, he felt, a speculative bubble in housing. In his view, the bubble had been fueled by cheap money from banks. The banks were enticing people to purchase homes with adjustable-rate mortgages with very low interest rates for the first 1 to 3 years. Many of the borrowers, however, could probably not afford their monthly payments once higher rates would later begin. Paulson thought that homeowners would start to default on their mortgage payments in large numbers. When that happened, the housing market would be flooded with distressed sales and house prices would collapse. Paulson wanted to find a way to make money from this situation.

Goldman Sachs devised an investment vehicle that would allow Paulson to do just this. During the early 2000s, mortgage originators had started to pool thousands of individual mortgages together into bonds known as collateralized debt obligations, or CDOs. They then sold the bonds to institutional investors. The underlying idea was simple: the pool of mortgage payments generated income for the bondholders. As long as people continued to make their mortgage payments, the CDOs would generate good income and their price would be stable. Many of these bonds were given favorable ratings from the two main rating agencies, Moody's and Standard & Poor's, suggesting that they were safe investments. At the time, institutional investors were snapping up CDOs. Paulson, however, took a very different view. He believed that the rating agencies were wrong and

(continued)

that many CDOs were far more risky than investors thought. He believed that when people started to default on their mortgage payments, the price of these CDOs would collapse.

Goldman Sachs decided to offer bonds for sale to institutional investors that were a collection of 90 or so CDOs. These bonds were referred to as *synthetic CDOs*. They asked Paulson to identify the CDOs that he thought were very risky and grouped them together into *synthetic CDOs*. Goldman then sold these very same bonds to institutional investors—many were long-time Goldman Sachs clients. Goldman did not tell investors that Paulson had helped to pick the CDOs that were pooled into the bonds, nor did the company tell investors that the underlying CDOs might be a lot more risky than the rating agencies thought. Paulson then took a short position in these synthetic CDOs. Short selling is a technique whereby the investor will make money if the price of the asset goes down over time. Paulson was effectively betting against the synthetic CDOs, a fact that Goldman knew, while he was actively marketing these bonds to institutions.

Shortly thereafter, Paulson was proved correct. People did start to default on their housing payments, the price of houses did fall, and the value of CDOs and the synthetic CDOs that Goldman had created plunged. Paulson made an estimated $3.7 billion in 2007 alone from this event. Goldman Sachs, too, made over $1 billion by betting against the very same bonds that it had been selling.

The SEC soon started to investigate the transactions. Some at the SEC believed that Goldman had knowingly committed fraud by failing to inform buyers that Paulson had selected the CDOs. The SEC's case was strengthened by internal Goldman e-mails. In one, a senior executive described the synthetic CDOs it was selling as "one shitty deal." In another, a colleague applauded the deal for making "lemonade from some big old lemons."

In April 2010, the SEC formally charged Goldman Sachs with civil fraud, arguing that the company had knowingly mislead investors about the risk and value of the synthetic CDOs, and failed to inform them of John Paulson's involvement in selecting the underlying CDOs. Goldman provided a vigorous defense; it argued that a market maker like Goldman Sachs owes no fiduciary duty to clients and offers no warranties—it is up to clients to make their own assessment of the value of a security. However, faced with a barrage of negative publicity, Goldman opted to settle the case out of court and pay a $550 million fine. In doing so, Goldman admitted no legal wrongdoing, but did say that the company had made a "mistake" in not disclosing Paulson's role, and vowed to raise its standards for the future.

Sources: L. Story and G. Morgenson, "SEC Accuses Goldman of Fraud in Housing Deal," *New York Times*, April 16, 2010; J. Stempel and S. Eder, "Goldman Sachs Charged with Fraud by SEC," *Reuters*, April 16, 2010; and "Sachs and the Shitty," *The Economist*, May 1, 2010.

CASE DISCUSSION QUESTIONS

1. Did Goldman Sachs break the law by not telling investors that Paulson had created the synthetic CDOs and was betting against them? Was it unethical for Goldman Sachs to market the CDOs?

2. Would your answer to the question above change if Goldman had not made billions from selling the CDOs? Would your answer to the question above change if Paulson had been wrong, and the CDOs had increased in value?

3. If opinions vary about the quality or riskiness of an investment, does a firm like Goldman Sachs owe a fiduciary duty to its clients to try to represent all of those opinions?

4. Is it unethical for a company like Goldman to permit its managers to trade on the company's account (i.e., invest on the company's behalf rather than an external client's behalf)? If not, how should compensation policies be designed to prevent conflicts of interest from arising between trades on behalf of the firm and trades on behalf of clients?

NOTES

[1] E. Freeman, *Strategic Management: A Stakeholder Approach* (Boston: Pitman Press, 1984).

[2] C. W. L. Hill and T. M. Jones, "Stakeholder-Agency Theory," *Journal of Management Studies* 29 (1992): 131–154; and J. G. March and H. A. Simon, *Organizations* (New York: Wiley, 1958).

[3] Hill and Jones, "Stakeholder-Agency Theory"; and C. Eesley and M. J. Lenox, "Firm Responses to Secondary Stakeholder Action," *Strategic Management Journal* 27 (2006): 13–24.

[4] I. C. Macmillan and P. E. Jones, *Strategy Formulation: Power and Politics* (St. Paul: West, 1986).

[5] Tom Copeland, Tim Koller, and Jack Murrin, *Valuation: Measuring and Managing the Value of Companies* (New York: Wiley, 1996).

[6] R. S. Kaplan and D. P. Norton, *Strategy Maps* (Boston: Harvard Business School Press, 2004).

[7] J. S. Harrison, D. A. Bosse, and R. A. Phillips, "Managing for Stakeholders, Stakeholder Utility Functions, and Competitive Advantage," *Strategic Management Journal* 31 (2010): 58–74.

[8] A. L. Velocci, D. A. Fulghum, and R. Wall, "Damage Control," *Aviation Week*, December 1, 2003, pp. 26–27.

[9] M. C. Jensen and W. H. Meckling, "Theory of the Firm: Managerial Behavior, Agency Costs and Ownership Structure," *Journal of Financial Economics* 3 (1976): 305–360; and E. F. Fama, "Agency Problems and the Theory of the Firm," *Journal of Political Economy* 88 (1980): 375–390.

[10] Hill and Jones, "Stakeholder-Agency Theory."

[11] For example, see R. Marris, *The Economic Theory of Managerial Capitalism* (London: Macmillan, 1964); and J. K. Galbraith, *The New Industrial State* (Boston: Houghton Mifflin, 1970).

[12] Fama, "Agency Problems and the Theory of the Firm."

[13] A. Rappaport, "New Thinking on How to Link Executive Pay with Performance," *Harvard Business Review,* March–April 1999, pp. 91–105.

[14] AFL-CIO's Executive PayWatch Database, www.aflcio.org/CorporateWatch/CEO-Pay-and-You.

[15] For academic studies that look at the determinants of CEO pay, see M. C. Jensen and K. J. Murphy, "Performance Pay and Top Management Incentives," *Journal of Political Economy* 98 (1990): 225–264; Charles W. L. Hill and Phillip Phan, "CEO Tenure as a Determinant of CEO Pay," *Academy of Management Journal* 34 (1991): 707–717; H. L. Tosi and L. R. Gomez-Mejia, "CEO Compensation Monitoring and Firm Performance," *Academy of Management Journal* 37 (1994): 1002–1016; and Joseph F. Porac, James B. Wade, and Timothy G. Pollock, "Industry Categories and the Politics of the Comparable Firm in CEO Compensation," *Administrative Science Quarterly* 44 (1999): 112–144.

[16] J. Silver-Greenberg and A. Leondis, "CBS Overpaid Moonvest $28 Million, Says Study of CEO Pay," *Bloomberg News*, May 6, 2010.

[17] "'Pay for Performance' No Longer a Punchline," *Wall Street Journal*, March 20, 2013.

[18] For research on this issue, see Peter J. Lane, A. A. Cannella, and M. H. Lubatkin, "Agency Problems as Antecedents to Unrelated Mergers and Diversification: Amihud and Lev Reconsidered," *Strategic Management Journal* 19 (1998): 555–578.

[19] M. Saltmarsh and E. Pfanner, "French Court Convicts Executives in Vivendi Case," *New York Times*, January 21, 2011.

[20] E. T. Penrose, *The Theory of the Growth of the Firm* (London: Macmillan, 1958).

[21] G. Edmondson and L. Cohn, "How Parmalat Went Sour," *Business Week*, January 12, 2004, pp. 46–50; and "Another Enron? Royal Dutch Shell," *Economist,* March 13, 2004, p. 71.

[22] O. E. Williamson, *The Economic Institutions of Capitalism* (New York: Free Press, 1985).

[23] Fama, "Agency Problems and the Theory of the Firm."

[24] S. Finkelstein and R. D'Aveni, "CEO Duality as a Double Edged Sword," *Academy of Management Journal* 37 (1994): 1079–1108; B. Ram Baliga and R. C. Moyer, "CEO Duality and Firm Performance," *Strategic Management Journal* 17 (1996): 41–53; M. L. Mace, *Directors: Myth and Reality* (Cambridge: Harvard University Press, 1971); and S. C. Vance, *Corporate Leadership: Boards of Directors and Strategy* (New York: McGraw-Hill, 1983).

[25] J. B. Stewart, "When Shareholder Democracy Is a Sham," *New York Times*, April 12, 2013.

[26] "Goldman Union Deal Lets Blankfein Keep Dual Roles," *Reuters*, April 11, 2013.

[27]W. G. Lewellen, C. Eoderer, and A. Rosenfeld, "Merger Decisions and Executive Stock Ownership in Acquiring Firms," *Journal of Accounting and Economics* 7 (1985): 209–231.

[28]C. W. L. Hill and S. A. Snell, "External Control, Corporate Strategy, and Firm Performance," *Strategic Management Journal* 9 (1988): 577–590.

[29]The phenomenon of back dating stock options was uncovered by academic research, and then picked up by the SEC. See Erik Lie, "On the Timing of CEO Stock Option Awards," *Management Science* 51 (2005): 802–812.

[30]G. Colvin, "A Study in CEO Greed," *Fortune*, June 12, 2006, pp. 53–55.

[31]J. P. Walsh and R. D. Kosnik, "Corporate Raiders and Their Disciplinary Role in the Market for Corporate Control," *Academy of Management Journal* 36 (1993): 671–700.

[32]R. S. Kaplan and D. P. Norton, "The Balanced Scorecard—Measures That Drive Performance," *Harvard Business Review,* January–February 1992, pp. 71–79; and Kaplan and Norton, *Strategy Maps* (Boston: Harvard Business School Press, 2004).

[33]R. S. Kaplan and D. P. Norton, "Using the Balanced Scorecard as a Strategic Management System," *Harvard Business Review,* January–February 1996, pp. 75–85; and Kaplan and Norton, *Strategy Maps.*

[34]Kaplan and Norton, "The Balanced Scorecard," p. 72.

[35]"Timet, Boeing Settle Lawsuit," *Metal Center News* 41 (June 2001): 38–39.

[36]Joseph Kahn, "Ruse in Toyland: Chinese Workers Hidden Woe," *New York Times,* December 7, 2003, pp. A1, A8.

[37]N. King, "Halliburton Tells the Pentagon Workers Took Iraq Deal Kickbacks," *Wall Street Journal,* 2004, p. A1; "Whistleblowers Say Company Routinely Overcharged," *Reuters,* February 12, 2004; and R. Gold and J. R. Wilke, "Data Sought in Halliburton Inquiry," *Wall Street Journal,* 2004, p. A6.

[38]L. Jieqi and Z. Hejuan, "Siemens Bribery Scandal Ends in Death Sentence," *Caixin Online*, June 30, 2011.

[39]Saul W. Gellerman, "Why Good Managers Make Bad Ethical Choices," *Ethics in Practice: Managing the Moral Corporation*, ed. Kenneth R. Andrews (Harvard Business School Press, 1989).

[40]Ibid.

[41]S. Hopkins, "How Effective Are Ethics Codes and Programs?" *Financial Executive*, March 2013.

[42]Can be found on Unilever's website, www.unilever.com/company/ourprinciples/.

[43]www.utc.com/governance/ethics.

Implementing Strategy in Companies That Compete in a Single Industry

12

OPENING CASE

Organization at Apple

Apple has a legendary ability to produce a steady stream of innovative new products and product improvements that are differentiated by design elegance and ease of use. Product innovation is in many ways the essence of what the company has always done, and what it strives to continue doing. Innovation at Apple began with the Apple II in 1979. The original Macintosh computer, the first personal computer (PC) to use a graphical user interface, a mouse, and onscreen icons, followed in 1984. After founder and former CEO the late Steve Jobs returned to the company in 1997, the list of notable innovations expanded to include the iPod and iTunes, the Mac Airbook, the iPhone, the Apple App store, and the iPad. Apple's ability to continue to innovate, and to improve its existing product offerings, is in large part a result of its organizational structure, controls, and culture.

Unlike most companies of its size, Apple has a functional structure. The people reporting directly to current CEO Tim Cook include the senior vice presidents of operations, Internet software and services, industrial design, software engineering, hardware engineering, and worldwide marketing, along with the CFO and company general council. This group meets every Monday morning to review the strategy of the company, its operations, and ongoing product development efforts.

The industrial design group takes the lead on new-product development efforts, dictating the look and feel of a new product, and the materials that must be used. The centrality of industrial design is unusual—in most companies engineers first develop products, with industrial design coming into the picture quite late in the process. The key role played by industrial design at Apple, however, is consistent with the company's mission of designing beautiful products that change the world. The industrial design group works closely with hardware and software engineering to develop features and functions for each new product, with operations to ensure that manufacturing can be rapidly scaled up following a product launch, and with worldwide marketing to plan the product launch strategy.

Thus, product development at Apple is a cross-functional effort that requires intense coordination. This coordination is achieved through a centralized command and control structure, with the top-management group driving collaboration and the industrial design group setting key parameters. During his long tenure as CEO, Steve Jobs was well known for clearly articulating who was responsible for what in the product development process, and for holding people accountable if they failed to meet his high standards. His management style could be unforgiving and harsh—there are numerous stories of people

being fired on the spot for failing to meet his standards—but it did get the job done.

Even though Jobs passed away in 2011, the focus on accountability persists at Apple. Each task is given a "directly responsible individual," or DRI in "Apple-speak." Typically, the DRI's name will appear on an agenda for a meeting, so everyone knows who is responsible. Meetings at Apple have an action list, and next to each action item will be a DRI. By such clear control processes, Apple pushes accountability down deep within the ranks.

A key feature of the culture of Apple is the secrecy surrounding much of what the company does. Not only is information that reaches the outside world tightly controlled, so is the flow of information within the company. Many employees are kept in the dark about new-product development efforts and frequently do not know what people in other parts of the company are working on. Access to buildings where teams are developing new products or features is tightly controlled, with only team members allowed in. Cameras monitor sensitive workspaces to make sure that this is not violated. Disclosing what the company is doing to an outside source, or an unauthorized inside source, is grounds for termination—something that all employees are told when they join the company. The idea is to keep new products under very tight wraps until launch day. Apple wants to control the message surrounding new products. It does not want to give the competition time to respond, or media critics time to bash ideas under development, rather than actual products.

Sources: J. Tyrangiel, "Tim Cook's Freshman Year: The Apple CEO Speaks," *Bloomberg Businessweek*, December 6, 2012; A. Lashinsky, "The Secrets Apple Keeps," *CNNMoney*, January 10, 2012; and B. Stone, "Apple's Obsession with Secrecy Grows Stronger," *New York Times*, June 23, 2009.

OVERVIEW

As the story of Apple suggests, organizational structure and culture can have a direct effect on a company's profits. Apple's functional organization, the tight coordination between functions, the strong power vested in the industrial design function, the tradition of responsibility and accountability at the level of individual tasks, and a culture that keeps new product ideas under wraps until they hit the market all come together to support the company's goal of producing revolutionary new products that surprise and change the world. In other words, Apple's organizational structure and culture supports the company's strategy of differentiation through product innovation.

This chapter examines how managers can best implement their strategies through their organization's structure and culture to achieve a competitive advantage and superior performance. A well-thought-out strategy becomes profitable only if it can be implemented successfully. In practice, however, implementing strategy through structure and culture is a difficult, challenging, and never-ending task. Managers cannot create an organizing framework for a company's value-chain activities and assume it will keep working efficiently and effectively over time—just as they cannot select strategies and assume that these strategies will still be effective in the future—in a changing competitive environment.

We begin by discussing the primary elements of organizational design and the way these elements work together to create an organizing framework that allows a company to implement its chosen strategy. We also discuss how strategic managers can use structure, control, and culture to pursue functional-level strategies that create and build distinctive competencies. We will also discuss the implementation issues facing managers in a single industry at the industry level. The next chapter examines strategy implementation across industries and countries—that is—corporate and global strategy. By the end of this chapter and the next, you will understand why the fortunes of a company often rest on its managers' ability to design and manage its structure, control systems, and culture to best implement its business model.

IMPLEMENTING STRATEGY THROUGH ORGANIZATIONAL DESIGN

Strategy implementation involves the use of **organizational design**, the process of deciding how a company should create, use, and combine organizational structure, control systems, and culture to pursue a business model successfully. **Organizational structure** assigns employees to specific value creation tasks and roles and specifies how these tasks and roles are to work together in a way that increases efficiency, quality, innovation, and responsiveness to customers—the distinctive competencies that build competitive advantage. The purpose of organizational structure is to *coordinate and integrate* the efforts of employees at all levels—corporate, business, and functional—and across a company's functions and business units so that all levels work together in a way that will allow the company to achieve the specific set of strategies in its business model.

Organizational structure does not, by itself, provide the set of incentives through which people can be *motivated* to make the company work. Hence, there is a need for control systems. The purpose of a **control system** is to provide managers with (1) a set of incentives to motivate employees to work toward increasing efficiency, quality, innovation, and responsiveness to customers and (2) specific feedback on how well an organization and its members are performing and building competitive advantage so that managers can continuously take action to strengthen a company's business model. Structure provides an organization with a skeleton; control gives it the muscles, sinews, nerves, and sensations that allow managers to regulate and govern its activities.

Organizational culture, the third element of organizational design, is the specific collection of values, norms, beliefs, and attitudes that are shared by people and groups in an organization and that control the way they interact with each other and with stakeholders outside

organizational design
The process of deciding how a company should create, use, and combine organizational structure, control systems, and culture to pursue a business model successfully.

organizational structure
The means through which a company assigns employees to specific tasks and roles and specifies how these tasks and roles are to be linked together to increase efficiency, quality, innovation, and responsiveness to customers.

control system
Provides managers with incentives for employees as well as feedback on how the company performs.

organizational culture
The specific collection of values, norms, beliefs, and attitudes that are shared by people and groups in an organization and that control the way they interact with each other and with stakeholders outside the organization.

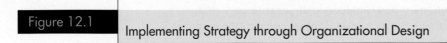
Figure 12.1   Implementing Strategy through Organizational Design

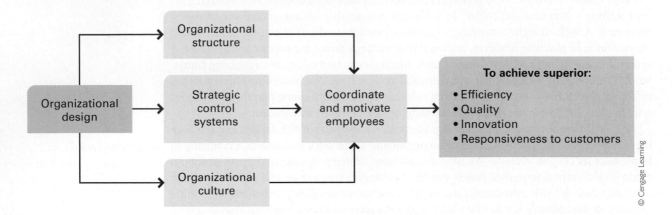

© Cengage Learning

the organization.[1] Organizational culture is a company's way of doing something: it describes the characteristic ways—"this is the way we do it around here"—in which members of an organization get the job done. Top managers, because they can influence which kinds of beliefs and values develop in an organization, are an important determinant of how organizational members will work toward achieving organizational goals, as we discuss later.[2]

Figure 12.1 sums up what has been discussed in this chapter. Organizational structure, control, and culture are the means by which an organization motivates and coordinates its members to work toward achieving the building blocks of competitive advantage.

Top managers who wish to find out why it takes a long time for people to make decisions in a company, why there is a lack of cooperation between sales and manufacturing, or why product innovations are few and far between, need to understand how the design of a company's structure and control system, and the values and norms in its culture, affect employee motivation and behavior. *Organizational structure, control, and culture shape people's behaviors, values, and attitudes and determine how they will implement an organization's business model and strategies.*[3] On the basis of such an analysis, top managers can devise a plan to reorganize or change their company's structure, control systems, and culture to improve coordination and motivation. Effective organizational design allows a company to obtain a competitive advantage and achieve above-average profitability.

BUILDING BLOCKS OF ORGANIZATIONAL STRUCTURE

After formulating a company's business model and strategies, managers must make designing an organizational structure their next priority. The value creation activities of organizational members are meaningless unless some type of structure is used to assign people to tasks and connect the activities of different people and functions.[4] Managers must make three basic choices:

1. How best to group tasks into functions and to group functions into business units or divisions to create distinctive competencies and pursue a particular strategy.

2. How to allocate authority and responsibility to these functions and divisions.
3. How to increase the level of coordination or integration between functions and divisions as a structure evolves and becomes more complex.

We first discuss basic issues and then revisit them when considering appropriate choices of structure at different levels of strategy.

Grouping Tasks, Functions, and Divisions

Because an organization's tasks are, to a large degree, a function of its strategy, the dominant view is that companies choose a form of structure to match their organizational strategy. Perhaps the first person to address this issue formally was Harvard business historian Alfred D. Chandler.[5] After studying the organizational problems experienced in large U.S. corporations such as DuPont and GM as they grew in the early decades of the 20th century, Chandler reached two conclusions: (1) in principle, organizational structure follows the range and variety of tasks that the organization chooses to pursue and (2) the structures of U.S. companies' change as their strategies change in a predictable way over time.[6] In general, this means that most companies first group people and tasks into functions and then functions into divisions.[7]

As we discussed earlier, a *function* is a collection of people who work together and perform the same types of tasks or hold similar positions in an organization.[8] For example, the salespeople in a car dealership belong to the sales function. Together, car sales, car repair, car parts, and accounting are the set of functions that allow a car dealership to sell and maintain cars.

As organizations grow and produce a wider range of products, the amount and complexity of the *handoffs*—that is, the work exchanges or transfers among people, functions, and subunits—increase. The communications and measurement problems and the managerial inefficiencies surrounding these transfers or handoffs are a major source of *bureaucratic costs*, which we discussed in Chapter 10. Recall that these are the costs associated with monitoring and managing the functional exchanges necessary to add value to a product as it flows along a company's value chain to the final customer.[9] We discuss why bureaucratic costs increase as companies pursue more complex strategies later in the chapter.

For now, it is important to note that managers first group tasks into functions, and second, group functions into a business unit or division, to reduce bureaucratic costs. A *division* is a way of grouping functions to allow an organization to better produce and transfer its goods and services to customers. In developing an organizational structure, managers must decide how to group an organization's activities by function and division in a way that achieves organizational goals effectively.[10]

Top managers can choose from the many kinds of structures to group their activities. The choice is made on the basis of the structure's ability to successfully implement the company's business models and strategies.

Allocating Authority and Responsibility

As organizations grow and produce a wider range of goods and services, the size and number of their functions and divisions increase. The number of handoffs, or transfers, between employees also increases. To economize on bureaucratic costs and effectively coordinate the activities of people, functions, and divisions, managers must develop a clear and unambiguous **hierarchy of authority**, or chain of command, that defines each manager's

hierarchy of authority
The clear and unambiguous chain of command that defines each manager's relative authority from the CEO down through top, middle, to first-line managers.

span of control

The number of subordinates reporting directly to a particular manager.

relative authority beginning with the CEO, continuing through middle managers and first-line managers, and then to the employees who directly make goods or provide services.[11] Every manager, at every level of the hierarchy, supervises one or more subordinates. The term **span of control** refers to the number of subordinates who report directly to a manager. When managers know exactly what their authority and responsibilities are, information distortion problems that promote managerial inefficiencies are kept to a minimum, and handoffs or transfers can be negotiated and monitored to economize on bureaucratic costs. For example, managers are less likely to risk invading another manager's turf and can avoid the costly conflicts that inevitably result from such encroachments.

Tall and Flat Organizations   Companies choose the number of hierarchical levels they need on the basis of their strategies and the functional tasks necessary to create distinctive competencies.[12] As an organization grows in size or complexity (measured by the number of its employees, functions, and divisions), its hierarchy of authority typically lengthens, making the organizational structure "taller." A *tall structure* has many levels of authority relative to company size; a *flat structure* has fewer levels relative to company size (see Figure 12.2). As the hierarchy becomes taller, problems that make the organization's structure less flexible and slow managers' response to changes in the competitive environment may result. It is vital that managers understand how these problems arise so they know how to change a company's structure to respond accordingly.

First, communication problems may arise. When an organization has many levels in the hierarchy, it can take a long time for the decisions and orders of top managers to reach other managers in the hierarchy, and it can take a long time for top managers to learn how well

| Figure 12.2 | Tall and Flat Structures |

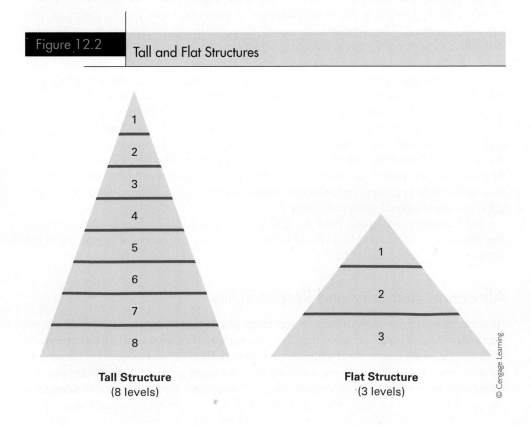

Tall Structure
(8 levels)

Flat Structure
(3 levels)

© Cengage Learning

the actions based upon their decisions work. Feeling out of touch, top managers may want to verify that lower-level managers are following orders and may require written confirmation from them. Lower-level managers, who know they will be held strictly accountable for their actions, start devoting more time to the process of making decisions to improve their chances of being right. They might even try to avoid responsibility by making top managers decide what actions to take.

A second communication problem that can result is the distortion of commands and orders as they are transmitted up and down the hierarchy, which causes managers at different levels to interpret what is happening in their own unique way. Accidental distortion of orders and messages occurs when different managers interpret messages from their own narrow functional perspectives. Intentional distortion can occur when managers lower in the hierarchy decide to interpret information in a way that increases their own personal advantage.

Tall hierarchies usually indicate that an organization is employing too many expensive managers, creating a third problem. Managerial salaries, benefits, offices, and secretaries are a huge expense for organizations. Large companies such as IBM, Ford, and Google pay their managers billions of dollars per year. In the recent recession, millions of middle and lower managers were laid off as companies strived to survive by reorganizing and simplifying their structures, and downsizing their workforce to reduce their cost structure.

The Minimum Chain of Command   To avoid the problems that result when an organization becomes too tall and employs too many managers, top managers need to ascertain whether they are employing the right number of top, middle, and first-line managers, and see whether they can redesign their hierarchies to reduce the number of managers. Top managers might follow a basic organizing principle: the **principle of the minimum chain of command**, which states that a company should choose the hierarchy with the *fewest* levels of authority necessary to use organizational resources efficiently and effectively.

Effective managers constantly scrutinize their hierarchies to see whether the number of levels can be reduced—for example, by eliminating one level and giving the responsibilities of managers at that level to managers above, while empowering employees below. This practice has become increasingly common as companies battle with low-cost overseas competitors and search for ways to reduce costs. Many well-known managers such as Alan Mulally continually strive to empower employees and keep the hierarchy as flat as possible; their message is that employees should feel free to go above and beyond their prescribed roles to find ways to better perform their job tasks.

When companies become too tall, and the chain of command too long, strategic managers tend to lose control over the hierarchy, which means they lose control over their strategies. Disaster often follows because a tall organizational structure decreases, rather than promotes, motivation and coordination between employees and functions, and bureaucratic costs escalate as a result. Strategy in Action 12.1 discusses how this happened at Walt Disney.

Centralization or Decentralization?   One important way to reduce the problems associated with too-tall hierarchies and reduce bureaucratic costs is to *decentralize authority*—that is, vest authority in managers at lower levels in the hierarchy as well as at the top. Authority is *centralized* when managers at the upper levels of a company's hierarchy retain the authority to make the most important decisions. When authority is decentralized, it is delegated to divisions, functions, and employees at lower levels in the company. Delegating authority in this fashion reduces bureaucratic costs because it avoids the communication and coordination problems that arise when information is sent up the hierarchy, sometimes to the top of

principle of the minimum chain of command

The principle that a company should design its hierarchy with the fewest levels of authority necessary to use organizational resources effectively.

12.1 STRATEGY IN ACTION

Bob Iger Flattens Walt Disney

© iStockPhoto.com/Tom Nulens

When Bob Iger, who had been COO of Disney under its then-CEO Michael Eisner, took control of the troubled Walt Disney company, he decided to immediately act upon a problem he had observed with the way the company was operating. For several years, Disney had been plagued by slow decision making, and analysts claimed it had made many mistakes in putting its new strategies into action. Disney stores were losing money, its Internet properties were not getting many "hits," and even its theme parks seemed to have lost their luster as few new rides or attractions had been introduced.

Iger believed that one of the main reasons for Disney's declining performance was that it had become too tall and bureaucratic, and its top managers were following financial rules that did not lead to innovative strategies. To turn around the performance of the poorly performing company, one of Iger's first decisions was to dismantle Disney's central strategic planning office.

In this office, several levels of managers were responsible for sifting through all the new ideas and innovations suggested by Disney's different business divisions (such as theme parks, movies, gaming) and then deciding which ideas to present to the CEO. Iger saw the strategic planning office as a bureaucratic bottleneck that actually reduced the number of ideas coming from below. He dissolved the office and reassigned its managers to Disney's different business units.

More new ideas are being generated by the different business units as a result of eliminating this unnecessary layer in Disney's hierarchy. The level of innovation has also increased because managers are more willing to speak out and champion ideas when they know they are working directly with the CEO and a top-management team searching for innovative new ways to improve performance rather than a layer of strategic planning "bureaucrats" only concerned for the bottom line.

Source: www.waltdisney.com.

the organization, and then back down again in order for decisions to be made. There are three advantages to decentralization, as discussed next.

First, when top managers delegate operational decision-making responsibility to middle- and first-level managers, they reduce information overload and are able to spend more time on competitively positioning the company and strengthening its business model. Second, when managers in the bottom layers of the company become responsible for implementing strategies to suit local conditions, their motivation and accountability increase. The result is that decentralization promotes flexibility and reduces bureaucratic costs because lower-level managers are authorized to make on-the-spot decisions; handoffs are not needed. The third advantage is that when lower-level employees are given the right to make important decisions, fewer managers are needed to oversee their activities and tell them what to do—a company can flatten its hierarchy.

If decentralization is so effective, why don't all companies decentralize decision making and avoid the problems of tall hierarchies? The answer is that centralization has its advantages, too. Centralized decision making allows for easier coordination of the organizational activities needed to pursue a company's strategy. Thus, we saw in Opening Case that Apple centralizes its product development efforts to ensure tight coordination between industrial design, hardware and software engineering, operations, and marketing. If managers at all levels can make their own decisions, overall planning becomes extremely difficult, and the company may lose control of its decision making.

Centralization also means that decisions fit an organization's broad objectives. When its branch operations managers were getting out of control, for example, Merrill Lynch increased centralization by installing more information systems to give corporate managers greater control over branch activities. Similarly, the centralization of product development at Apple makes for a very clearly directed strategy. Furthermore, in times of crisis, centralization of authority permits strong leadership because authority is focused upon one person or group. This focus allows for speedy decision making and a concerted response by the whole organization. When Steve Jobs came back to Apple in 1997, for example, he had to quickly execute a turnaround strategy. The centralization of power and authority under Jobs allowed him to make some very quick decisions and effectively save Apple from bankruptcy.

How to choose the right level of centralization for a particular strategy is discussed later. Strategy in Action 12.2 discusses one company that benefits from centralizing authority and one company that benefits from decentralizing authority.

Integration and Integrating Mechanisms

Much coordination takes place among people, functions, and divisions through the hierarchy of authority. Often, however, as a structure becomes complex, this is not enough, and top managers need to use various **integrating mechanisms** to increase communication and coordination among functions and divisions. The greater the complexity of an organization's structure, the greater is the need for coordination among people, functions, and divisions to make the organizational structure work efficiently.[13] We discuss three kinds of integrating mechanisms that illustrate the kinds of issues involved.[14] Once again, these mechanisms are employed to economize on the information distortion problems that commonly arise when managing the handoffs or transfers among the ideas and activities of different people, functions, and divisions.

integrating mechanisms Ways to increase communication and coordination among functions and divisions.

Direct Contact   Direct contact among managers creates a context within which managers from different functions or divisions can work together to solve mutual problems. However, several issues are associated with establishing this contact. Managers from different functions may have different views about what must be done to achieve organizational goals. But if the managers have equal authority (as functional managers typically do), the only manager who can tell them what to do is the CEO. If functional managers cannot reach agreement, no mechanism exists to resolve the conflict apart from the authority of the boss. In fact, one sign of a poorly performing organizational structure is the number of problems sent up the hierarchy for top managers to solve. The need to solve everyday conflicts and hand off or transfer problems raises bureaucratic costs. To reduce such conflicts and solve transfer problems, top managers use more complex integrating mechanisms to increase coordination among functions and divisions.

Liaison Roles   Managers can increase coordination among functions and divisions by establishing liaison roles. When the volume of contacts between two functions increases, one way to improve coordination is to give one manager in each function or division the responsibility for coordinating with the other. These managers may meet daily, weekly, monthly, or as needed to solve handoff issues and transfer problems. The responsibility for coordination is part of the liaison's full-time job, and usually an informal relationship forms between the people involved, greatly easing strains between functions. Furthermore, liaison roles provide a way of transmitting information across an organization, which is important in large organizations where employees may know no one outside their immediate function or division.

12.2 STRATEGY IN ACTION

Centralization and Decentralization at Union Pacific and Yahoo!

© iStockPhoto.com/Tom Nulens

Union Pacific (UP), one of the biggest railroad freight carriers in the United States, faced a crisis when an economic boom in the early 2000s led to a record increase in the amount of freight the railroad had to transport. At the same time, the railroad was experiencing record delays in moving this freight. UP's customers complained bitterly about the problem, and the delivery delays cost the company tens of millions of dollars in penalty payments. Why the problem? UP's top managers decided to centralize authority high in the organization and to standardize operations to reduce operating costs. All scheduling and route planning were handled centrally at headquarters to increase efficiency. The job of regional managers was largely to ensure the smooth flow of freight through their regions.

Recognizing that efficiency had to be balanced by the need to be responsive to customers, UP announced a sweeping reorganization. Regional managers would have the authority to make everyday operational decisions; they could alter scheduling and routing to accommodate customer requests even if it raised costs. UP's goal was to "return to excellent performance by simplifying our processes and becoming easier to deal with." In deciding to decentralize authority, UP was following the lead of its competitors that had already decentralized their operations. Its managers would continue to "decentralize decision making into the field, while fostering improved customer responsiveness, operational excellence, and personal accountability." The result has been continued success for the company; in fact, in 2011 several large companies recognized UP as the top railroad in on-time service performance and customer service.

Yahoo! has been forced by circumstances to pursue a different approach to decentralization. In 2009, after Microsoft failed to take over Yahoo! because of the resistance of Jerry Wang, a company founder, the company's stock price plunged. Wang, who had come under intense criticism for preventing the merger, resigned as CEO and was replaced by Carol Bartz, a manager with a long history of success in managing online companies. Bartz moved quickly to find ways to reduce Yahoo!'s cost structure and simplify its operations to maintain its strong online brand identity. Intense competition from the growing popularity of online companies such as Google, Facebook, and Twitter also threatened its popularity.

Bartz decided the best way to restructure Yahoo! was to recentralize authority. To gain more control over its different business units and reduce operating costs, she decided to centralize functions that had previously been performed by Yahoo!'s different business units, such as product development and marketing activities. For example, all the company's publishing and advertising functions were centralized and placed under the control of a single executive. Yahoo!'s European, Asian, and emerging markets divisions were centralized, and another top executive took control. Bartz's goal was to find out how she could make the company's resources perform better. While she was centralizing authority, she was also holding many "town hall" meetings to ask Yahoo! employees from all functions, "What would you do if you were me?" Even as she centralized authority to help Yahoo! recover its dominant industry position, she was looking for the input of employees at every level in the hierarchy.

Nevertheless, in 2011, Yahoo! was still in a precarious position. It had signed a search agreement with Microsoft to use the latter's search technology, Bing; Bartz had focused on selling off Yahoo!'s noncore business assets to reduce costs and gain the money for strategic acquisitions. But the company was still in an intense battle with other dot-coms that had more resources, such as Google and Facebook, and in September 2011 Bartz was fired by Yahoo!'s board of directors. In October 2011, both Microsoft and Google were reportedly planning to acquire the troubled company for around $20 billion—obviously Yahoo! is still for sale—at the right price.

Source: www.up.com and www.yahoo.com 2011.

Teams   When more than two functions or divisions share many common problems, direct contact and liaison roles may not provide sufficient coordination. In these cases, a more complex integrating mechanism, the **team**, may be appropriate. One manager from each relevant function or division is assigned to a team that meets to solve a specific mutual problem; team members are responsible for reporting back to their subunits on the issues addressed and the solutions recommended. Teams are increasingly being used at all organizational levels.

team

Formation of a group that represents each division or department facing a common problem, with the goal of finding a solution to the problem.

STRATEGIC CONTROL SYSTEMS

Managers choose the organizational strategies and structure they hope will allow the organization to use its resources most effectively to pursue its business model and create value and profit. Then they create **strategic control systems**, tools that allow them to monitor and evaluate whether, in fact, their strategies and structure are working as intended, how they could be improved, and how they should be changed if they are not working.

Strategic control is not only about monitoring how well an organization and its members are currently performing, or about how well the firm is using its existing resources. It is also about how to create the incentives to keep employees motivated and focused on the important problems that may confront an organization in the future so that the employees work together and find solutions that can help an organization perform better over time.[15] To understand the vital importance of strategic control, consider how it helps managers obtain superior efficiency, quality, innovation, and responsiveness to customers—the four basic building blocks of competitive advantage:

strategic control systems

The mechanism that allows managers to monitor and evaluate whether their business model is working as intended and how it could be improved.

1. *Control and efficiency.* To determine how *efficiently* they are using organizational resources, managers must be able to accurately measure how many units of inputs (raw materials, human resources, and so on) are being used to produce a unit of output. They must also be able to measure the number of units of outputs (goods and services) they produce. A control system contains the measures or yardsticks that allow managers to assess how efficiently they are producing goods and services. Moreover, if managers experiment to find a more efficient way to produce goods and services, these measures tell managers how successful they have been. Without a control system in place, managers have no idea how well their organizations are performing nor how to perform better in the future—something that is becoming increasingly important in today's highly competitive environment.[16]

2. *Control and quality.* Today, competition often revolves around increasing the *quality* of goods and services. In the car industry, for example, within each price range, cars compete against one another over features, design, and reliability. Whether a customer buys a Ford 500, a GM Impala, a Chrysler 300, a Toyota Camry, or a Honda Accord depends significantly upon the quality of each company's product. Strategic control is important in determining the quality of goods and services because it gives managers feedback on product quality. If managers consistently measure the number of customers' complaints and the number of new cars returned for repairs, they have a good indication of how much quality they have built into their product.

3. *Control and innovation.* Strategic control can help to raise the level of *innovation* in an organization. Successful innovation takes place when managers create an organizational setting in which employees feel empowered to be creative and in which

authority is decentralized to employees so that they feel free to experiment and take risks, such as at 3M and Google. Deciding upon the appropriate control systems to encourage risk taking is an important management challenge. As discussed later in the chapter, an organization's culture becomes important in this regard.

4. *Control and responsiveness to customers.* Finally, strategic managers can help make their organizations more *responsive to customers* if they develop a control system that allows them to evaluate how well employees with customer contact are performing their jobs. Monitoring employees' behavior can help managers find ways to help increase employees' performance level, perhaps by revealing areas in which skills training can help employees, or by finding new procedures that allow employees to perform their jobs more efficiently. When employees know their behaviors are being monitored, they may have more incentive to be helpful and consistent in the way they act toward customers.

Strategic control systems are the formal target-setting, measurement, and feedback systems that allow strategic managers to evaluate whether a company is achieving superior efficiency, quality, innovation, and customer responsiveness and implementing its strategy successfully. An effective control system should have three characteristics. It should be *flexible* enough to allow managers to respond as necessary to unexpected events; it should provide *accurate information*, thus giving a true picture of organizational performance; and it should supply managers with the information in a *timely manner* because making decisions on the basis of outdated information is a recipe for failure.[17] As Figure 12.3 shows, designing an effective strategic control system requires four steps: establishing standards and targets, creating measuring and monitoring systems, comparing performance against targets, and evaluating results.

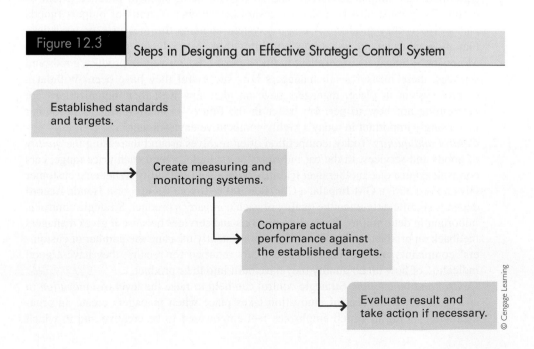

| Figure 12.3 | Steps in Designing an Effective Strategic Control System |

Established standards and targets.

Create measuring and monitoring systems.

Compare actual performance against the established targets.

Evaluate result and take action if necessary.

© Cengage Learning

Levels of Strategic Control

Strategic control systems are developed to measure performance at four levels in a company: corporate, divisional, functional, and individual. Managers at all levels must develop the most appropriate set of measures to evaluate corporate-, business-, and functional-level performance. As the balanced scorecard approach discussed in Chapter 11 suggests, these measures should be tied as closely as possibly to the goals of developing distinctive competencies in efficiency, quality, innovativeness, and responsiveness to customers. Care must be taken, however, to ensure that the standards used at each level do not cause problems at the other levels—for example, that a division's attempts to improve its performance do not conflict with corporate performance. Furthermore, controls at each level should provide the basis upon which managers at lower levels design their control systems. Figure 12.4 illustrates these relationships.

Types of Strategic Control Systems

In Chapter 11, the balanced scorecard approach was discussed as a way to ensure that managers complement the use of return on invested capital (ROIC) with other kinds of strategic controls to ensure they are pursuing strategies that maximize long-run profitability. In this chapter, we consider three more types of control systems: *personal control, output control*, and *behavior control*.

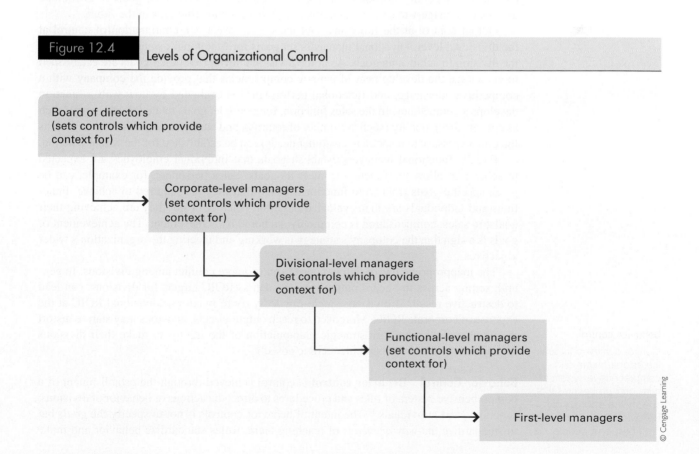

| Figure 12.4 | Levels of Organizational Control |

Board of directors
(sets controls which provide context for)

Corporate-level managers
(set controls which provide context for)

Divisional-level managers
(set controls which provide context for)

Functional-level managers
(set controls which provide context for)

First-level managers

© Cengage Learning

personal control

The way one manager shapes and influences the behavior of another in a face-to-face interaction in the pursuit of a company's goals.

Personal Control   **Personal control** is the desire to shape and influence the behavior of a person in a *face-to-face interaction* in the pursuit of a company's goals. The most obvious kind of personal control is direct supervision from a manager farther up in the hierarchy. The personal approach is useful because managers can question subordinates about problems or new issues they are facing to get a better understanding of the situation and to ensure that subordinates are performing their work effectively and that they are not hiding any information that could cause additional problems later. Personal control also can come from a group of peers, such as when people work in teams. Once again, personal control at the group level means that there is more possibility for learning to occur and competencies to develop, as well as greater opportunities to prevent free-riding or shirking.

output control

The control system managers use to establish appropriate performance goals for each division, department, and employee and then measure actual performance relative to these goals.

Output Control   **Output control** is a system in which strategic managers estimate or forecast appropriate performance goals for each division, department, and employee, and then measure actual performance relative to these goals. Often a company's reward system is linked to performance on these goals, so output control also provides an incentive structure for motivating employees at all levels in the organization. Goals keep managers informed about how well their strategies are creating a competitive advantage and building the distinctive competencies that lead to future success. Goals exist at all levels in an organization.

Divisional goals state corporate managers' expectations for each division concerning performance on dimensions such as efficiency, quality, innovation, and responsiveness to customers. Generally, corporate managers set challenging divisional goals to encourage divisional managers to create more effective strategies and structures in the future.

Output control at the functional and individual levels is a continuation of control at the divisional level. Divisional managers set goals for functional managers that will allow the division to achieve its goals. As at the divisional level, functional goals are established to encourage the development of generic competencies that provide the company with a competitive advantage, and functional performance is evaluated by how well a function develops a competency. In the sales function, for example, goals related to efficiency (such as cost of sales), quality (such as number of returns), and customer responsiveness (such as the time necessary to respond to customer needs) can be established for the whole function.

Finally, functional managers establish goals that individual employees are expected to achieve to allow the function to meet its goals. Sales personnel, for example, can be given specific goals (related to functional goals) that they are required to achieve. Functions and individuals are then evaluated based on whether or not they are achieving their goals; in sales, compensation is commonly anchored by achievement. The achievement of goals is a sign that the company's strategy is working and meeting the organization's wider objectives.

The inappropriate use of output control can promote conflict among divisions. In general, setting across-the-board output targets, such as ROIC targets for divisions, can lead to destructive results if divisions single-mindedly try to maximize divisional ROIC at the expense of corporate ROIC. Moreover, to reach output targets, divisions may start to distort the numbers and engage in strategic manipulation of the figures to make their divisions look good—which increases bureaucratic costs.[18]

behavior control

Control achieved through the establishment of a comprehensive system of rules and procedures that specify the appropriate behavior of divisions, functions, and people.

Behavior Control   **Behavior control** is control achieved through the establishment of a comprehensive system of rules and procedures to direct the actions or behavior of divisions, functions, and individuals.[19] The intent of behavior controls is not to specify the *goals* but to standardize the *way or means* of reaching them. Rules standardize behavior and make outcomes predictable. If employees follow the rules, then actions are performed and decisions are handled the same way time and time again. The result is predictability and accuracy, the aim of all control systems. The primary kinds of behavior controls are operating budgets, standardization, and rules and procedures.

Once managers at each level have been given a goal to achieve, they establish operating budgets that regulate how managers and workers are to attain those goals. An **operating budget** is a blueprint that outlines how managers intend to use organizational resources to most efficiently achieve organizational goals. Most commonly, managers at one level allocate to managers at a lower level a specific amount of resources to use in the production of goods and services. Once a budget is determined, lower-level managers must decide how they will allocate finances for different organizational activities. Managers are then evaluated on the basis of their ability to stay within the budget and make the best use of it. For example, managers at GE's washing machine division might have a budget of $50 million to develop and sell a new line of washing machines; they must decide how much money to allocate to research and development (R&D), engineering, sales, and so on, to ensure that the division generates the most revenue possible, and hence makes the biggest profit. Most commonly, large companies treat each division as a stand-alone profit center, and corporate managers evaluate each division's performance by its relative contribution to corporate profitability, something discussed in detail in the next chapter.

Standardization refers to the degree to which a company specifies how decisions are to be made so that employees' behavior becomes predictable.[20] In practice, there are three things an organization can standardize: *inputs, conversion activities*, and *outputs*.

When managers standardize, they screen *inputs* according to preestablished criteria, or standards that determine which inputs to allow into the organization. If employees are the input, for example, then one way of standardizing them is to specify which qualities and skills they must possess, and only selecting applicants who possess those qualities. If the inputs are raw materials or component parts, the same considerations apply. The Japanese are renowned for the high quality and precise tolerances they demand from component parts to minimize problems with the product at the manufacturing stage. Just-in-time (JIT) inventory systems also help standardize the flow of inputs.

The aim of standardizing *conversion activities* is to program work activities so that they can be done the same way time and time again; the goal is predictability. Behavior controls, such as rules and procedures, are among the chief means by which companies can standardize throughputs. Fast-food restaurants such as McDonald's and Burger King standardize all aspects of their restaurant operations; the result is consistent fast food.

The goal of standardizing *outputs* is to specify what the performance characteristics of the final product or service should be—the dimensions or tolerances the product should conform to, for example. To ensure that their products are standardized, companies apply quality control and use various criteria to measure this standardization. One criterion might be the number of goods returned from customers, or the number of customer complaints. On production lines, periodic sampling of products can indicate whether they are meeting performance characteristics.

As with other kinds of controls, the use of behavior control is accompanied by potential pitfalls that must be managed if the organization is to avoid strategic problems. Top management must be careful to monitor and evaluate the usefulness of behavior controls over time. Rules constrain people and lead to standardized, predictable behavior. However, rules are always easier to establish than to get rid of, and over time the number of rules an organization uses tends to increase. As new developments lead to additional rules, often the old rules are not discarded, and the company becomes overly bureaucratized. Consequently, the

operating budget
A blueprint that states how managers intend to use organizational resources to most efficiently achieve organizational goals.

standardization
The degree to which a company specifies how decisions are to be made so that employees' behavior becomes measurable and predictable.

organization and the people within it become inflexible and are slow to react to changing or unusual circumstances. Such inflexibility can reduce a company's competitive advantage by lowering the pace of innovation and reducing its responsiveness to customers.

Strategic Reward Systems

Organizations strive to control employees' behavior by linking reward systems to their control systems.[21] Based on a company's strategy (cost leadership or differentiation, for example), strategic managers must decide which behaviors to reward. They then create a control system to measure these behaviors and link the reward structure to them. Determining how to relate rewards to performance is a crucial strategic decision because it determines the incentive structure that affects the way managers and employees behave at all levels in the organization. As Chapter 11 pointed out, top managers can be encouraged to work on behalf of shareholders' interests when rewarded with stock options linked to a company's long-term performance. Companies such as GM require managers to purchase company stock. When managers become shareholders, they are more motivated to pursue long-term rather than short-term goals. Similarly, in designing a pay system for salespeople, the choice is whether to motivate them through salary alone, or salary plus a bonus based on how much they sell. Neiman Marcus, the luxury retailer, pays employees only salary because it wants to encourage high-quality service and discourage a hard-sell approach. Thus, there are no incentives based on quantities sold. On the other hand, the pay system for rewarding car salespeople encourages high-pressure selling; it typically contains a large bonus based on the number and price of cars sold.

ORGANIZATIONAL CULTURE

The third element of successful strategy implementation is managing *organizational culture*, the specific collection of values and norms shared by people and groups in an organization.[22] Organizational values are beliefs and ideas about what kinds of goals the members of an organization should pursue and about the appropriate kinds or standards of behavior organizational members should use to achieve these goals. Microsoft founder Bill Gates is famous for the set of organizational values that he created for Microsoft: entrepreneurship, ownership, creativity, honesty, frankness, and open communication. By stressing entrepreneurship and ownership, he strives to get his employees to feel that Microsoft is not one big bureaucracy but a collection of smaller companies run by the members. Gates emphasizes that lower-level managers should be given autonomy and encouraged to take risks—to act like entrepreneurs, not corporate bureaucrats.[23]

From organizational values develop organizational norms, guidelines, or expectations that prescribe appropriate kinds of behavior by employees in particular situations and control the behavior of organizational members toward one another. Behavioral norms for software programmers at Microsoft include working long hours to ship products, wearing whatever clothing is comfortable (but never a suit and tie), consuming junk food, and communicating with other employees using the company's state-of-the-art communications products such as SharePoint.

Organizational culture functions as a kind of control because strategic managers can influence the kind of values and norms that develop in an organization—values and norms that specify appropriate and inappropriate behaviors, and that shape and influence the way its members behave.[24] Strategic managers such as Gates deliberately cultivate values that tell their subordinates how they should perform their roles; at 3M and Google innovation and creativity are stressed. These companies establish and support norms that tell employees they should be innovative and entrepreneurial and should experiment even if there is a significant chance of failure.

Other managers might cultivate values that tell employees they should always be conservative and cautious in their dealings with others, consult with their superiors before they make important decisions, and record their actions in writing so they can be held accountable for what happens. Managers of organizations such as chemical and oil companies, financial institutions, and insurance companies—any organization in which great caution is needed—may encourage a conservative, vigilant approach to decision making.[25] In a bank or mutual fund, for example, the risk of losing investors' money makes a cautious approach to investing highly appropriate. Thus, we might expect that managers of different kinds of organizations will deliberately attempt to cultivate and develop the organizational values and norms that are best suited to their strategy and structure.

Organizational socialization is the term used to describe how people learn organizational culture. Through socialization, people internalize and learn the norms and values of the culture so that they become organizational members.[26] Control through culture is so powerful that once these values have been internalized, they become part of the individual's values, and the individual follows organizational values without thinking about them.[27] Often the values and norms of an organization's culture are transmitted to its members through the stories, myths, and language that people in the organization use, as well as by other means.

Culture and Strategic Leadership

Strategic leadership is also provided by an organization's founder and top managers, who help create its organizational culture. The organization's founder is particularly important in determining culture because the founder imprints his or her values and management style on the organization. Walt Disney's conservative influence on the company he established continued well after his death. In the past, managers were afraid to experiment with new forms of entertainment because they were afraid "Walt Disney wouldn't like it." It wasn't until the installation of a new management team under Michael Eisner that the company turned around its fortunes, which allowed it to deal with the realities of the new entertainment industry.

The founder's established leadership style is transmitted to the company's managers; as the company grows, it typically attracts new managers and employees who share the same values. Moreover, members of the organization typically recruit and select only those who share their values. Thus, a company's culture becomes more distinct as its members become more similar. The virtue of these shared values and common culture is that they *increase integration and improve coordination among organizational members*. For example, the common language that typically emerges in an organization when people share the same beliefs and values facilitates cooperation among managers. Similarly, rules and procedures and direct supervision are less important when shared norms and values control behavior and motivate employees. When organizational members buy into cultural norms and values, they feel a bond with the organization and are more committed to finding new ways to help it succeed. The Running Case profiles the way in which Walmart's founder Sam Walton built a strong culture.

FOCUS ON: Wal-Mart

How Sam Walton Shaped Wal-Mart's Culture

© iStockPhoto.com/caracterdesign

Walmart, headquartered in Bentonville, Arkansas, is the largest retailer in the world. In 2012, it sold more than $440 billion worth of products. A large part of Walmart's success is due to the nature of the culture that its founder, the late Sam Walton, established for the company. Walton wanted all his managers and workers to take a hands-on approach to their jobs and be committed to Walmart's primary goal, which he defined as total customer satisfaction. To motivate his employees, Walton created a culture that gave all employees, called "associates," continuous feedback about their performance and the company's performance.

To involve his associates in the business and encourage them to develop work behaviors focused on providing quality customer service, Walton established strong cultural values and norms for his company. One of the norms associates are expected to follow is the "10-foot attitude." This norm encourages associates, in Walton's words, to "promise that whenever you come within 10 feet of a customer, you will look him in the eye, greet him, and ask him if you can help him." The "sundown rule" states that employees should strive to answer customer requests by sundown of the day they are made. The Walmart cheer ("Give me a W, give me an A," and so on) is used in all its stores.

The strong customer-oriented values that Walton has created are exemplified in the stories Walmart members tell one another about associates' concern for customers. They include stories such as the one about Sheila, who risked her own safety when she jumped in front of a car to prevent a little boy from being struck; about Phyllis, who administered cardiopulmonary resuscitation (CPR) to a customer who had suffered a heart attack in her store; and about Annette, who gave up the Power Ranger she had on layaway for her own son to fulfill the birthday wish of a customer's son. The strong Walmart culture helps to control and motivate employees to achieve the stringent output and financial targets the company sets.

A notable way Walmart builds its culture is through its annual stockholders' meeting, its extravagant ceremony celebrating the company's success. Every year, Walmart flies thousands of its highest-performing associates to an annual meeting at its corporate headquarters in Arkansas for entertainment featuring famous singers, rock bands, and comedians. Walmart feels that expensive entertainment is a reward its employees deserve and that the event reinforces the company's high-performance values and culture. The proceedings are also broadcast live to all Walmart stores so that all employees can celebrate the company's achievements together.

Since Sam Walton's death, the public attention's to Walmart, which has more than 2 million employees, has revealed the "hidden side" of its culture. Critics claim that few Walmart employees receive reasonably priced health care or other benefits, and that the company pays employees at little above the minimum wage. They also contend that employees do not question these policies because managers have convinced them into believing that this has to be the case—that the only way Walmart can keep its prices low is by keeping their pay and benefits low. Walmart has been forced to respond to these issues and to public pressure as well as lawsuits. Not only has it paid billions of dollars of fines to satisfy the claims of employees who have been discriminated against, it has also been forced to offer many of its employees increased health benefits—although it is constantly searching for ways to reduce these benefits and make its employees pay a higher share of their costs.

Source: www.walmart.com.

Strategic leadership also affects organizational culture through the way managers design organizational structure—that is, the way they delegate authority and divide task relationships. Thus, the way an organization designs its structure affects the cultural norms and values that develop within the organization. Managers need to be aware of this fact when implementing their strategies. Michael Dell, for example, has always kept his company's structure as flat as possible. He has decentralized authority to lower-level managers and employees to make them responsible for getting as close to the customer as possible. As a result, he has created a cost-conscious customer service culture at Dell, and employees strive to provide high-quality customer service.

Traits of Strong and Adaptive Corporate Cultures

Few environments are stable for a prolonged period of time. If an organization is to survive, managers must take actions that enable it to adapt to environmental changes. If they do not take such action, they may find themselves faced with declining demand for their products.

Managers can try to create an **adaptive culture**, one that is innovative and that encourages and rewards middle- and lower-level managers for taking initiative.[28] Managers in organizations with adaptive cultures are able to introduce changes in the way the organization operates, including changes in its strategy and structure that allow it to adapt to changes in the external environment. Organizations with adaptive cultures are more likely to survive in a changing environment and should have higher performance than organizations with inert cultures.

Several scholars have tried to uncover the common traits that strong, adaptive corporate cultures share, to find out whether there is a particular set of values that dominates adaptive cultures not present in weak or inert ones. An early but still influential attempt is T. J. Peters and R. H. Waterman's account of the values and norms characteristic of successful organizations and their cultures.[29] They argue that adaptive organizations show three common value sets. First, successful companies have values promoting a *bias for action*. The emphasis is on autonomy and entrepreneurship, and employees are encouraged to take risks—for example, to create new products—despite that there is no assurance that these products will be popular. Managers are closely involved in the day-to-day operations of the company and do not simply make strategic decisions isolated in some ivory tower. Employees have a hands-on, value-driven approach.

The second set of values stems from the *nature of the organization's mission*. The company must continue to do what it does best and develop a business model focused on its mission. A company can easily divert and pursue activities outside its area of expertise because other options seem to promise a quick return. Management should cultivate values so that a company "sticks to its knitting," which means strengthening its business model. A company must also establish close relationships with customers as a way of improving its competitive position. After all, who knows more about a company's performance than those who use its products or services? By emphasizing customer-oriented values, organizations are able to identify customer needs and improve their ability to develop products and services that customers desire. All of these management values are strongly represented in companies such as McDonald's, Walmart, and Toyota, each of which is sure of its mission and continually take steps to maintain it.

The third set of values determines *how to operate the organization*. A company should attempt to establish an organizational design that will motivate employees to perform best. Inherent in this set of values is the belief that productivity is obtained through people and that respect for the individual is the primary means by which a company can create the right atmosphere for productive behavior. An emphasis on entrepreneurship and respect for the employee leads to the establishment of a structure that gives employees the latitude to make decisions and motivates them to succeed. Because a simple structure and a lean staff best fit this situation, the organization should be designed with only the number of managers and hierarchical levels necessary to get the job done. The organization should

adaptive culture
A culture that is innovative and encourages and rewards middle- and lower-level managers for taking the initiative to achieve organizational goals.

also be sufficiently decentralized to permit employees' participation but centralized enough for management to ensure that the company pursues its strategic mission and that cultural values are followed.

In summary, these three primary sets of values are at the center of an organization's culture, and management transmits and maintains these values through strategic leadership. Strategy implementation continues as managers build strategic control systems that help perpetuate a strong adaptive culture, further the development of distinctive competencies, and provide employees with the incentive to build a company's competitive advantage. Finally, organizational structure contributes to the implementation process by providing the framework of tasks and roles that reduces transaction difficulties and allows employees to think and behave in ways that enable a company to achieve superior performance.

BUILDING DISTINCTIVE COMPETENCIES AT THE FUNCTIONAL LEVEL

In this section, we discuss the issue of creating specific kinds of structures, control systems, and cultures to implement a company's business model. The first level of strategy to examine is the functional level because, as Chapters 3 and 4 discussed, a company's business model is implemented through the functional strategies managers adopt to develop the distinctive competencies that allow a company to pursue a particular business model.[30] What is the best kind of structure to use to group people and tasks to build competencies? The answer for most companies is to group them by function and create a functional structure.

Functional Structure: Grouping by Function

In the quest to deliver a final product to the customer, two related value-chain-management problems increase. First, the range of value-chain activities that must be performed expands, and it quickly becomes clear that a company lacks the expertise needed to perform these activities effectively. For example, in a new company, the expertise necessary to effectively perform activities is lacking. It becomes apparent, perhaps, that the services of a professional accountant, a production manager, or a marketing expert are needed to take control of specialized tasks as sales increase. Second, it also becomes clear that a single person cannot successfully perform more than one value-chain activity without becoming overloaded. The new company's founder, for instance, who may have been performing many value-chain activities simultaneously, realizes that he or she can no longer make and sell the product. As most entrepreneurs discover, they must decide how to group new employees to perform the various value-chain activities most efficiently. Most choose the functional structure.

functional structure
Grouping of employees on the basis of their common expertise and experience or because they use the same resources.

Functional structures group people on the basis of their common expertise and experience or because they use the same resources.[31] For example, engineers are grouped in a function because they perform the same tasks and use the same skills or equipment. Figure 12.5 shows a typical functional structure. Each of the rectangles represents a different functional specialization—R&D, sales and marketing, manufacturing, and so on—and each function concentrates upon its own specialized task.[32]

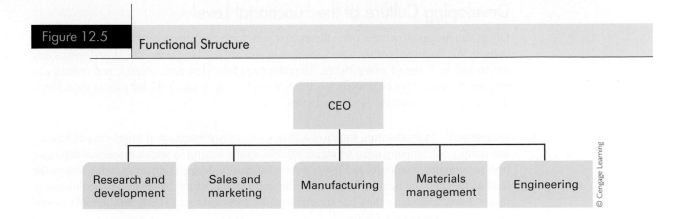

Figure 12.5 Functional Structure

Functional structures have several advantages. First, if people who perform similar tasks are grouped together, they can learn from one another and become more specialized and productive at what they do. This can create capabilities and competencies in each function. Second, they can monitor each other to make sure that all are performing their tasks effectively and not shirking their responsibilities. As a result, the work process becomes more efficient by reducing manufacturing costs and increasing operational flexibility. A third important advantage of functional structures is that they give managers greater control of organizational activities. As already noted, many difficulties arise when the number of levels in the hierarchy increases. If people are grouped into different functions, each with their own managers, then *several different hierarchies are created*, and the company can avoid becoming too tall. There will be one hierarchy in manufacturing, for example, and another in accounting and finance. Managing a business is much easier when different groups specialize in different organizational tasks and are managed separately.

The Role of Strategic Control

An important element of strategic control is to design a system that sets ambitious goals and targets for all managers and employees and then develops performance measures that *stretch and encourage managers and employees* to excel in their quest to raise performance. A functional structure promotes this goal because it increases the ability of managers and employees to monitor and make constant improvements to operating procedures. The structure also encourages organizational learning because managers working closely with subordinates can mentor them and help develop their technical skills.

Grouping by function also makes it easier to apply output control. Measurement criteria can be developed to suit the needs of each function to encourage members to stretch themselves. Each function knows how well it is contributing to overall performance and the part it plays in reducing the cost of goods sold or the gross margin. Managers can look closely to see if they are following the principle of the minimum chain of command and whether or not they need several levels of middle managers. Perhaps, instead of using middle managers, they could practice **management by objectives**, a system in which employees are encouraged to help set their own goals so that managers *manage by exception*, intervening only when they sense something is not going right. Given this increase in control, a functional structure also makes it possible to institute an effective strategic reward system in which pay can be closely linked to performance, and managers can accurately assess the value of each person's contributions.

management by objectives

A system in which employees are encouraged to help set their own goals so that managers *manage by exception*, intervening only when they sense something is not going right.

Developing Culture at the Functional Level

Often, functional structures offer the easiest way for managers to build a strong, cohesive culture. We discussed earlier how Sam Walton worked hard to create values and norms that are shared by Walmart's employees. To understand how structure, control, and culture can help create distinctive competencies, think about how they affect the way these three functions operate: production, R&D, and sales.

Production   In production, functional strategy usually centers upon improving efficiency and quality. A company must create an organizational setting in which managers can learn how to economize on costs and lower the cost structure. Many companies today follow the lead of Japanese companies such as Toyota and Honda, which have strong capabilities in manufacturing because they pursue total quality management (TQM) and flexible manufacturing systems (see Chapter 4).

When pursuing TQM, the inputs and involvement of all employees in the decision-making process are necessary to improve production efficiency and quality. Thus, it becomes necessary to decentralize authority to motivate employees to improve the production process. In TQM, work teams are created, and workers are given the responsibility and authority to discover and implement improved work procedures. Managers assume the role of coach and facilitator, and team members jointly take on the supervisory burdens. Work teams are often given the responsibility to control and discipline their own members and also decide who should work in their teams. Frequently, work teams develop strong norms and values, and work-group culture becomes an important means of control; this type of control matches the new decentralized team approach. Quality control circles are created to exchange information and suggestions about problems and work procedures. A bonus system or employee stock-ownership plan is frequently established to motivate workers and to allow them to share in the increased value that TQM often produces.

Nevertheless, to move down the experience curve quickly, most companies still exercise tight control over work activities and create behavior and output controls that standardize the manufacturing process. For example, human inputs are standardized through the recruitment and training of skilled personnel; the work process is programmed, often by computers; and quality control is used to make sure that outputs are being produced correctly. In addition, managers use output controls such as operating budgets to continuously monitor costs and quality. The extensive use of output controls and the continuous measurement of efficiency and quality ensure that the work team's activities meet the goals set for the function by management. Efficiency and quality increase as new and improved work rules and procedures are developed to raise the level of standardization. The aim is to find the match between structure and control and a TQM approach so that manufacturing develops the distinctive competency that leads to superior efficiency and quality.

R&D   The functional strategy for an R&D department is to develop distinctive competencies in innovation, quality, and excellence that result in products that fit customers' needs. Consequently, the R&D department's structure, control, and culture should provide the coordination necessary for scientists and engineers to bring high-quality products quickly to market. Moreover, these systems should motivate R&D scientists to develop innovative products.

In practice, R&D departments typically have a flat, decentralized structure that gives their members the freedom and autonomy to experiment and be innovative. Scientists and engineers are also grouped into teams because their performance can typically be judged only over the long term (it may take several years for a project to be completed). Consequently, extensive supervision by managers and the use of behavior control are a waste of managerial time and effort.[33] Managers avoid the information distortion problems that cause bureaucratic costs by letting teams manage their own transfer and handoff issues rather than using managers and the hierarchy of authority to coordinate work activities. Strategic managers take advantage of scientists' ability to work jointly to solve problems and enhance each other's performance. In small teams, too, the professional values and norms that highly trained employees bring to the situation promote coordination. A culture for innovation frequently emerges to control employees' behavior, as it did at Nokia, Intel, and Microsoft, where the race to be first energizes the R&D teams. To create an innovative culture and speed product development, Intel uses a team structure in its R&D function. Intel has many work teams that operate side by side to develop the next generation of chips. When the company makes mistakes, as it has recently, it can act quickly to join each team's innovations together to make a state-of-the-art chip that meets customer needs, such as multimedia chips. At the same time, to sustain its leading-edge technology, the company creates healthy competition between teams to encourage its scientists and engineers to champion new-product innovations that will allow Intel to control the technology of tomorrow.[34]

To spur teams to work effectively, the reward system should be linked to the performance of the team and company. If scientists, individually or in a team, do not share in the profits a company obtains from its new products, they may have little motivation to contribute wholeheartedly to the team. To prevent the departure of their key employees and encourage high motivation, companies such as Merck, Intel, and Microsoft give their researchers stock options, stock, and other rewards that are tied to their individual performance, their team's performance, and the company's performance.

Sales   Salespeople work directly with customers, and when they are dispersed in the field, these employees are especially difficult to monitor. The cost-effective way to monitor their behavior and encourage high responsiveness to customers is usually to develop sophisticated output and behavior controls. Output controls, such as specific sales goals or goals for increasing responsiveness to customers, can be easily established and monitored by sales managers. These controls can then be linked to a bonus reward system to motivate salespeople. Behavioral controls, such as detailed reports that salespeople file describing their interactions with customers, can also be used to standardize behavior and make it easier for supervisors to review performance.[35]

Usually, few managers are needed to monitor salespeople's activities, and a sales director and regional sales managers can oversee large sales forces because outputs and behavior controls are employed. Frequently, however, and especially when salespeople deal with complex products, such as pharmaceutical drugs or even luxury clothing, it becomes important to develop shared employee values and norms about the importance of patient safety or high-quality customer service; managers spend considerable time training and educating employees to create such norms.

Similar considerations apply to the other functions, such as accounting, finance, engineering, and human resource management. Managers must implement functional strategy through the combination of structure, control, and culture to allow each function to create the competencies that lead to superior efficiency, quality, innovation, and responsiveness to customers. Strategic managers must also develop the incentive systems that motivate and align employees' interests with those of their companies.

Functional Structure and Bureaucratic Costs

No matter how complex their strategies become, most companies retain a functional orientation because of its many advantages. Whenever different functions work together, however, bureaucratic costs inevitably arise because of information distortions that lead to the communications and measurement problems discussed in Chapter 10. These problems often arise from the transfers or handoffs across different functions that are necessary to deliver the final product to the customer.[36] The need to economize on the bureaucratic costs of solving such problems leads managers to adopt new organizational arrangements that reduce the scope of information distortions. Usually, companies divide their activities according to more complex plans to match their business models and strategies in discriminating ways. These more complex structures are discussed later in the chapter. First, we review five areas in which information distortions can arise: communications, measurement, customers, location, and strategy.

Communication Problems   As separate functional hierarchies evolve, functions can grow more remote from one another, and it becomes increasingly difficult to communicate across functions and coordinate their activities. This communication problem stems from *differences in goal orientations*—the various functions develop distinct outlooks or understandings of the strategic issues facing a company.[37] For example, the pursuit of different competencies can often lead to different time or goal orientations. Some functions, such as manufacturing, have a short time frame and concentrate on achieving short-term goals, such as reducing manufacturing costs. Others, such as R&D, have a long-term point of view; their product development goals may have a time horizon of several years. These factors may cause each function to develop a different view of the strategic issues facing the company. Manufacturing, for example, may see the strategic issue as the need to reduce costs, sales may see it as the need to increase customer responsiveness, and R&D may see it as the need to create new products. These communication and coordination problems among functions increase bureaucratic costs.

Measurement Problems   Often a company's product range widens as it develops new competencies and enters new market segments. When this happens, a company may find it difficult to gauge or measure the contribution of a product or a group of products to its overall profitability. Consequently, the company may turn out some unprofitable products without realizing it and may also make poor decisions about resource allocation. This means that the company's measurement systems are not complex enough to serve its needs.

Customer Problems   As the range and quality of an organization's goods and services increase, often more and different kinds of customers are attracted to its products. Servicing the needs of more customer groups and tailoring products to suit new kinds of customers will result in increasing the handoff problems among functions. It becomes increasingly difficult to coordinate the activities of value-chain functions across the growing product range. Also, functions such as production, marketing, and sales have little opportunity to differentiate products and increase value for customers by specializing in the needs of particular customer groups. Instead, they are responsible for servicing the complete product range. Thus, the ability to identify and satisfy customer needs may fall short in a functional structure.

Location Problems   Being in a particular location or geographical region may also hamper coordination and control. Suppose a growing company in the Northeast begins to expand and sell its products in many different regional areas. A functional structure will not be able to provide the flexibility needed for managers to respond to the different customer needs or preferences in the various regions.

Strategic Problems   The combined effect of all these factors results in long-term strategic considerations that are frequently ignored because managers are preoccupied with solving communication and coordination problems. The result is that a company may lose direction and fail to take advantage of new strategic opportunities—thus bureaucratic costs escalate.

Experiencing one or more of these problems is a sign that bureaucratic costs are increasing. If this is the case, managers must change and adapt their organization's structure, control systems, and culture to economize on bureaucratic costs, build new distinctive competencies, and strengthen the company's business model. These problems indicate that the company has outgrown its structure and that managers need to develop a more complex structure that can meet the needs of their competitive strategy. An alternative, however, is to reduce these problems by adopting the outsourcing option.

The Outsourcing Option

Rather than move to a more complex, expensive structure, companies are increasingly turning to the outsourcing option (discussed in Chapter 9) and solving the organizational design problem by contracting with other companies to perform specific functional tasks. Obviously, it does not make sense to outsource activities in which a company has a distinctive competency, because this would lessen its competitive advantage; but it does make sense to outsource and contract with companies to perform particular value-chain activities in which they specialize and therefore have a competitive advantage.

Thus, one way of avoiding the kinds of communication and measurement problems that arise when a company's product line becomes complex is to reduce the number of functional value-chain activities it performs. This allows a company to focus on those competencies that are at the heart of its competitive advantage and to economize on bureaucratic costs. Today, responsibility for activities such as a company's marketing, pension and health benefits, materials management, and information systems is being increasingly outsourced to companies that specialize in the needs of a company in a particular industry. More outsourcing options, such as using a global network structure, are considered in Chapter 13.

IMPLEMENTING STRATEGY IN A SINGLE INDUSTRY

Building capabilities in organizational design that allow a company to develop a competitive advantage begins at the functional level. However, to pursue its business model successfully, managers must find the right combination of structure, control, and culture that *links and combines* the competencies in a company's value-chain functions so that it enhances its ability to differentiate products or lower the cost structure. Therefore, it is important to coordinate and integrate across functions and business units or divisions. In organizational design, managers must consider two important issues: one concerns the revenue portion of the profit equation and the other concerns the cost portion, as Figure 12.6 illustrates.

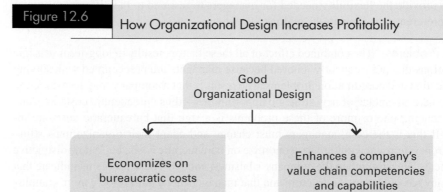

Figure 12.6   How Organizational Design Increases Profitability

Good Organizational Design

Economizes on bureaucratic costs

Enhances a company's value chain competencies and capabilities

Leading to a low-cost structure and the ability to choose a low price option

Leading to differentiation advantages and option of charging a premium price

That leads to competitive advantage, profitability, and superior return on investment

© Cengage Learning

First, effective organizational design improves the way in which people and groups choose the business-level strategies that lead to increasing differentiation, more value for customers, and the opportunity to charge a premium price. For example, capabilities in managing its structure and culture allow a company to more rapidly and effectively combine its distinctive competencies or transfer or leverage competencies across business units to create new and improved, differentiated products.

Second, effective organizational design reduces the bureaucratic costs associated with solving the measurement and communications problems that derive from factors such as transferring a product in progress between functions or a lack of cooperation between marketing and manufacturing or between business units. A poorly designed or inappropriate choice of structure or control system or a slow-moving bureaucratic culture (e.g., a structure that is too centralized, an incentive system that causes functions to compete instead of cooperate, or a culture in which value and norms have little impact on employees) can cause the motivation, communication, measurement, and coordination problems that lead to high bureaucratic costs.

Effective organizational design often means moving to a more complex structure that economizes on bureaucratic costs. A more complex structure will cost more to operate because additional, experienced, and more highly paid managers will be needed; a more expensive information technology (IT) system will be required; there may be a need for extra offices and buildings; and so on. However, these are simply costs of doing business, and a company will happily bear this extra expense provided its new structure leads to increased revenues from product differentiation and/or new ways to lower its *overall* cost structure by obtaining economies of scale or scope from its expanded operations.

In the following sections, we first examine the implementation and organizational design issues involved in pursuing a cost-leadership or differentiation business model. Then we describe different kinds of organizational structures that allow companies to pursue business models oriented at (1) managing a wide range of products; (2) being responsive to customers; (3) expanding nationally; (4) competing in a fast-changing, high-tech environment; and (5) focusing on a narrow product line.

Implementing Cost Leadership

The aim of a company pursuing cost leadership is to become the lowest-cost producer in the industry, and this involves reducing costs across *all* functions in the organization, including R&D and sales and marketing.[38] If a company is pursuing a cost-leadership strategy, its R&D efforts probably focus on product and process development rather than on the more expensive product innovation, which carries no guarantee of success. In other words, the company stresses competencies that improve product characteristics or lower the cost of making existing products. Similarly, a company tries to decrease the cost of sales and marketing by offering a standard product to a mass market rather than different products aimed at different market segments, which is also more expensive.[39]

To implement cost leadership, a company chooses a combination of structure, control, and culture compatible with lowering its cost structure while preserving its ability to attract customers. In practice, the functional structure is the most suitable provided that care is taken to select integrating mechanisms that will reduce communication and measurement problems. For example, a TQM program can be effectively implemented when a functional structure is overlaid with cross-functional teams because team members can now search for ways to improve operating rules and procedures that lower the cost structure or standardize and raise product quality.[40]

Cost leadership also requires that managers continuously monitor their structures and control systems to find ways to restructure or streamline them so that they operate more effectively. For example, managers need to be alert to ways of using IT to standardize operations and lower costs. To reduce costs further, cost leaders use the cheapest and easiest forms of control available: output controls. For each function, a cost leader adopts output controls that allow it to closely monitor and evaluate functional performance. In the manufacturing function, for example, the company imposes tight controls and stresses meeting budgets based on production, cost, or quality targets.[41] In R&D, the emphasis also falls on the bottom line; to demonstrate their contribution to cost savings, R&D teams focus on improving process technology. Cost leaders are likely to reward employees through generous incentive and bonus plans to encourage high performance. Their culture is often based on values that emphasize the bottom line, such as those of Walmart, McDonald's, and Dell.

Implementing Differentiation

Effective strategy implementation can improve a company's ability to add value and to differentiate its products. To make its product unique in the eyes of the customer, for example, a differentiated company must design its structure, control, and culture around the *particular source* of its competitive advantage.[42] Specifically, differentiators need to design their structures around the source of their distinctive competencies, the differentiated qualities of their products, and the customer groups they serve. Commonly, in pursuing differentiation, a company starts to produce a wider range of products to serve more market segments, which means it must customize its products for different groups of customers. These factors make it more difficult to standardize activities and usually increase the bureaucratic costs associated with managing the handoffs or transfers between functions. Integration becomes much more of a problem; communications, measurement, location, and strategic problems increasingly arise; and the demands upon functional managers increase.

To respond to these problems, managers develop more sophisticated control systems, increasingly make use of IT, focus on developing cultural norms and values that overcome problems associated with differences in functional orientations, and focus on cross-functional objectives. The control systems used to match the structure should be aligned to a company's distinctive competencies. For successful differentiation, it is important that the various functions do not pull in different directions; indeed, cooperation among the functions is vital for cross-functional integration. However, when functions work together, output controls become much harder to use. In general, it is much more difficult to measure the performance of people in different functions when they are engaged in cooperative efforts. Consequently, a differentiator must rely more upon behavior controls and shared norms and values.

This explains why companies pursuing differentiation often have a markedly different kind of culture from those pursuing cost leadership. Because human resources—scientists, designers, or marketing employees—are often the source of differentiation, these organizations have a culture based on professionalism or collegiality that emphasizes the distinctiveness of the human resources rather than the high pressure of the bottom line.[43] HP, Motorola, and Coca-Cola, all of which emphasize some kind of distinctive competency, exemplify companies with professional cultures.

In practice, the implementation decisions that confront managers who must simultaneously strive for differentiation and a low-cost structure are dealt with together as strategic managers move to implement new, more complex kinds of organizational structure. As a company's business model and strategies evolve, strategic managers usually start to *superimpose* a more complex divisional grouping of activities on its functional structure to better coordinate value-chain activities. This is especially true of companies seeking to become *broad differentiators*—companies that have the ability to simultaneously increase differentiation and lower their cost structures. These companies are the most profitable in their industries, and they have to be especially adept at organizational design—a major source of a differentiation and cost advantage (see Figure 12.6). No matter what the business model, however, more complex structures cost more to operate than a simple functional structure. Managers are willing to bear this extra cost, however, as long as the new structure makes better use of functional competencies, increases revenues, and lowers the overall cost structure.

Product Structure: Implementing a Wide Product Line

The structure that organizations most commonly adopt to solve the control problems that result from producing many different kinds of products for many different market segments is the *product structure*. The intent is to break up a company's growing product line into a number of smaller, more manageable subunits to reduce bureaucratic costs due to communication, measurement, and other problems.

Figure 12.7   Nokia's Product Structure

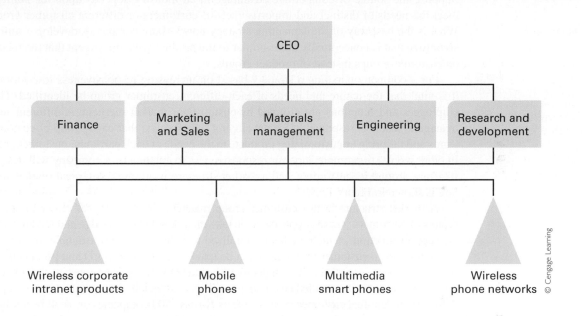

An organization that chooses a **product structure** first divides its overall product line into product groups or categories (see Figure 12.7, which uses Nokia as an example). Each product group focuses on satisfying the needs of a particular customer group and is managed by its own team of managers. Second, to keep costs as low as possible, value-chain support functions such as basic R&D, marketing, materials, and finance are centralized at the top of the organization, and the different product groups share their services. Each support function, in turn, is divided into product-oriented teams of functional specialists who focus on the needs of one particular product group. This arrangement allows each team to specialize and become expert in managing the needs of its product group. Because all of the R&D teams belong to the same centralized function, however, they can share knowledge and information with each other and build their competence over time.

Strategic control systems can now be developed to measure the performance of each product group separately from the others. Thus, the performance of each product group is easy to monitor and evaluate, and corporate managers at the center can move more quickly to intervene if necessary. Also, the strategic reward system can be linked more closely to the performance of each product group, although top managers can still decide to make rewards based on corporate performance an important part of the incentive system. Doing so will encourage the different product groups to share ideas and knowledge and promote the development of a corporate culture, as well as the product group culture that naturally develops inside each product group. A product structure is commonly used by food processors, furniture makers, personal and health products companies, and large electronics companies such as Nokia.

product structure

A way of grouping employees into separate product groups or units so that each product group can focus on the best ways to increase the effectiveness of the product.

Market Structure: Increasing Responsiveness to Customer Groups

market structure

A way of grouping employees into separate customer groups so that each group can focus on satisfying the needs of a particular customer group in the most effective way.

Suppose the source of competitive advantage in an industry depends upon the ability to meet the needs of distinct and important sets of customers or different customer groups. What is the best way of implementing strategy now? Many companies develop a **market structure** that is conceptually quite similar to the product structure except that the focus is on customer groups instead of product groups.

For a company pursuing a strategy based on increasing responsiveness to customers, it is vital that the nature and needs of each different customer group be identified. Then, employees and functions are grouped by customer or market segment. A different set of managers becomes responsible for developing the products that each group of customers wants and tailoring or customizing products to the needs of each particular customer group. In other words, to promote superior responsiveness to customers, a company will design a structure around its customers, and a market structure is adopted. A typical market structure is shown in Figure 12.8.

A market structure brings customer group managers and employees closer to specific groups of customers. These people can then take their detailed knowledge and feed it back to the support functions, which are kept centralized to reduce costs. For example, information about changes in customer preferences can be quickly fed back to R&D and product design so that a company can protect its competitive advantage by supplying a constant stream of improved products for its installed customer base. This is especially important when a company serves well-identified customer groups such as *Fortune* 500 companies or small businesses.

Geographic Structure: Expanding by Location

geographic structure

A way of grouping employees into different geographic regions to best satisfy the needs of customers within different regions of a state or country.

Suppose a company begins to expand locally, regionally, or nationally through internal expansion or by engaging in horizontal integration and merging with other companies to expand its geographical reach. A company pursuing this competitive approach frequently moves to a **geographic structure** in which geographic regions become the basis for the

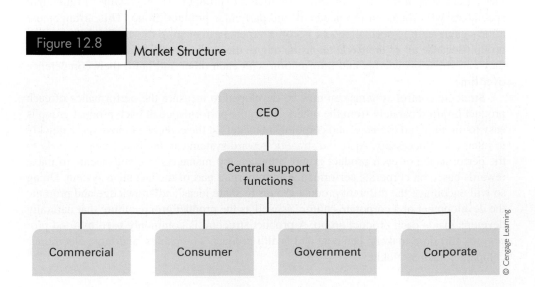

| Figure 12.8 | Market Structure |

© Cengage Learning

Figure 12.9   Geographic Structure

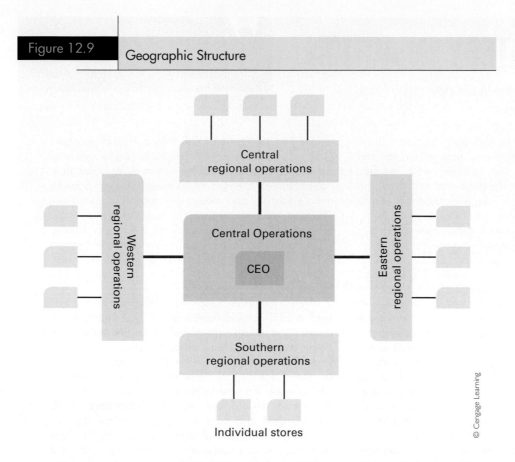

Central regional operations

Western regional operations

Central Operations

CEO

Eastern regional operations

Southern regional operations

Individual stores

© Cengage Learning

grouping of organizational activities (see Figure 12.9). A company may divide its manufacturing operations and establish manufacturing plants in different regions of the country, for example. This allows the company to be responsive to the needs of regional customers and reduces transportation costs. Similarly, as a service organization such as a store chain or bank expands beyond one geographic area, it may begin to organize sales and marketing activities on a regional level to better serve the needs of customers in different regions.

A geographic structure provides more coordination and control than a functional structure does because several regional hierarchies are created to take over the work, as in a product structure, where several product group hierarchies are created. A company such as FedEx clearly needs to operate a geographic structure to fulfill its corporate goal: next-day delivery. Large merchandising organizations, such as Neiman Marcus, Dillard's Department Stores, and Walmart, also moved to a geographic structure as they started building stores across the country. With this type of structure, different regional clothing needs (e.g., sunwear in the South, down coats in the Midwest) can be handled as required. At the same time, because the information systems, purchasing, distribution, and marketing functions remain centralized, companies can leverage their skills across all the regions. When using a geographic structure, a company can achieve economies of scale in buying, distributing, and selling and lower its cost structure, while simultaneously being more responsive (differentiated) to customer needs. One organization that moved from a geographic to a market structure to provide better-quality service and reduce costs is discussed in Strategy in Action 12.3.

12.3 STRATEGY IN ACTION

The HISD Moves from a Geographic to a Market Structure

© iStockPhoto.com/Tom Nulens

Like all organizations, state and city government agencies such as school districts may become too tall and bureaucratic over time and, as they grow, develop ineffective and inefficient organizational structures. This happened to the Houston Independent School District (HISD) when the explosive growth of the city during the last decades added over 1 million new students to its schools. As Houston expanded many miles in every direction to become the fourth-largest U.S. city, successive HISD superintendents adopted a geographic structure to coordinate and control all of the teaching functions involved in creating high-performing elementary, middle, and high schools. The HISD eventually created five different geographic regions or regional school districts. And over time, each regional district sought to control more of its own functional activities and became increasingly critical of HISD's central administration. The result was a slowdown in decision making, infighting between districts, an increasingly ineffectual team of district administrators, and falling student academic test scores across the city.

In 2010, a new HISD superintendent was appointed, who, working on the suggestions of HISD's top managers,

decided to reorganize HISD into a market structure. HISD's new organizational structure is now grouped by the needs of its customers—its students—and three "chief officers" oversee all of Houston's high schools, middle schools, and elementary schools, respectively. The focus will now be upon the needs of its three types of students, not on the needs of the former five regional managers. Over 270 positions were eliminated in this restructuring, saving over $8 million per year, and many observers hope to see more cost savings ahead.

Many important support functions were recentralized to HISD's headquarters office to eliminate redundancies and reduce costs, including teacher professional development. Also, a new support function called school improvement was formed, with managers charged to share ideas and information between schools and oversee their performance on many dimensions to improve service and student performance. HISD administrators also hope that eliminating the regional geographic structure will encourage schools to share best practices and cooperate so student education and test scores will improve over time.

Source: By 2011, major cost savings had been achieved, but a huge budget deficit forced the HISD to close 12 middle and elementary schools and relocate students to new facilities in which class sizes would be higher. The result is a streamlined, integrated divisional structure that HISD hopes will increase performance—student scores—in the years ahead, but at a lower cost.

Neiman Marcus developed a geographic structure similar to the one shown in Figure 12.9 to manage its nationwide chain of stores. In each region, it established a team of regional buyers to respond to the needs of customers in each geographic area, for example, the western, central, eastern, and southern regions. The regional buyers then fed their information to the central buyers at corporate headquarters, who coordinated their demands to obtain purchasing economies and ensure that Neiman Marcus's high-quality standards, upon which its differentiation advantage depends, were maintained nationally.

Matrix and Product-Team Structures: Competing in High-Tech Environments

The communication and measurement problems that lead to bureaucratic costs escalate quickly when technology is rapidly changing and industry boundaries are blurring.

Frequently, competitive success depends upon rapid mobilization of a company's skills and resources, and managers face complex strategy implementation issues. A new grouping of people and resources becomes necessary, often one that is based on fostering a company's distinctive competencies in R&D. Managers need to make structure, control, and culture choices around the R&D function. At the same time, they need to ensure that implementation will result in new products that cost-effectively meet customer needs and will not result in products so expensive that customers will not wish to buy them.

matrix structure
A way of grouping employees in two ways simultaneously—by function and by product or project—to maximize the rate at which different kinds of products can be developed.

Matrix Structure   To address these problems, many companies choose a matrix structure.[44]
In a **matrix structure**, value-chain activities are grouped in two ways (see Figure 12.10). First, activities are grouped vertically by *function* so that there is a familiar differentiation of tasks into functions such as engineering, sales and marketing, and R&D. In addition, superimposed upon this vertical pattern is a horizontal pattern based on grouping by *product*

Figure 12.10	Matrix Structure

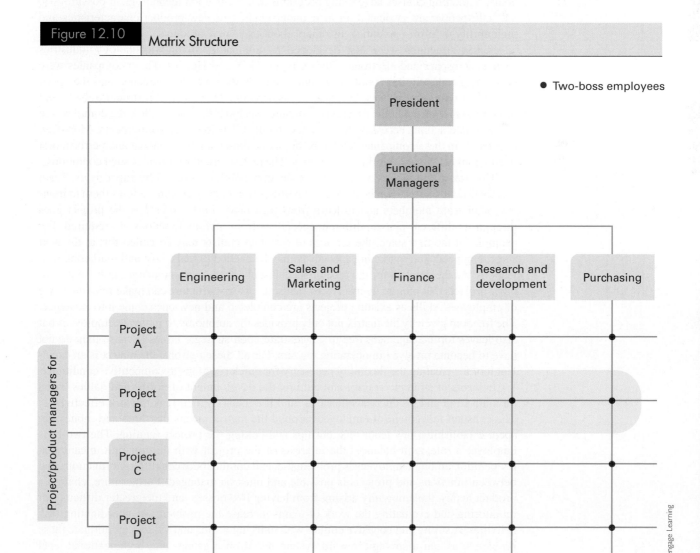

• Two-boss employees

© Cengage Learning

or project, in which people and resources are grouped to meet ongoing product development needs. The resulting network of reporting relationships among projects and functions is designed to make R&D the focus of attention.

Matrix structures are flat and decentralized, and employees inside a matrix have two bosses: a *functional boss*, who is the head of a function, and a *product or project boss*, who is responsible for managing the individual projects. Employees work on a project team with specialists from other functions and report to the project boss on project matters and the functional boss on matters relating to functional issues. All employees who work on a project team are called **two-boss employees** and are responsible for managing coordination and communication among the functions and projects.

Implementing a matrix structure can promote innovation and speeds product development because this type of structure permits intensive cross-functional integration. Integrating mechanisms such as teams help transfer knowledge among functions and are designed around the R&D function. Sales, marketing, and production targets are geared to R&D goals, marketing devises advertising programs that focus upon technological possibilities, and salespeople are evaluated on their understanding of new-product characteristics and their ability to inform potential customers about these new products.

Matrix structures were first developed by companies in high-technology industries such as aerospace and electronics, for example, TRW and Hughes. These companies were developing radically new products in uncertain, competitive environments, and the speed of product development was the crucial consideration. They needed a structure that could respond to this need, but the functional structure was too inflexible to allow the complex role and task interactions necessary to meet new-product development requirements. Moreover, employees in these companies tend to be highly qualified and professional and perform best in autonomous, flexible working conditions. The matrix structure provides such conditions.

This structure requires a minimum of direct hierarchical control by supervisors. Team members control their own behavior, and participation in project teams allows them to monitor other team members and to learn from each other. Furthermore, as the project goes through its different phases, different specialists from various functions are required. For example, at the first stage, the services of R&D specialists may be called for; at the next stage, engineers and marketing specialists may be needed to make cost and marketing projections. As the demand for the type of specialist changes, team members can be moved to other projects that require their services. Thus, the matrix structure can make maximum use of employees' skills as existing projects are completed and new ones come into existence. The freedom given by the matrix not only provides the autonomy to motivate employees but also leaves top management free to concentrate upon strategic issues because they do not have to become involved in operating matters. For all these reasons, the matrix is an excellent tool for creating the flexibility necessary for quick reactions to competitive conditions.

In terms of strategic control and culture, the development of norms and values based on innovation and product excellence is vital if a matrix structure is to work effectively.[45] The constant movement of employees around the matrix means that time and money are spent establishing new team relationships and getting the project running. The two-boss employee's role, as it balances the interests of the project with the function, means that cooperation among employees is problematic, and conflict between different functions and between functions and projects is possible and must be managed. Furthermore, changing product teams, the ambiguity arising from having two bosses, and the greater difficulty of monitoring and evaluating the work of teams increase the problems of coordinating task activities. A strong and cohesive culture with unifying norms and values can mitigate these problems, as can a strategic reward system based on a group- and organizational-level reward system.

two-boss employees

Employees who report both to a project boss and a functional boss.

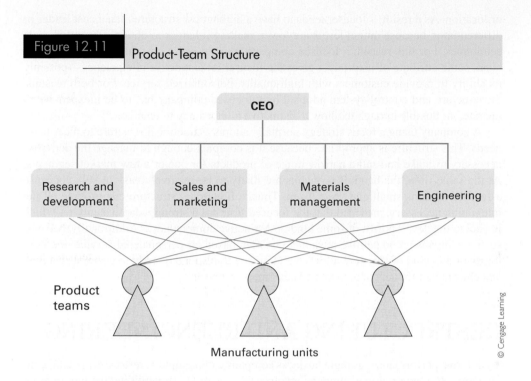

Figure 12.11   Product-Team Structure

Product-Team Structure   A major structural innovation in recent years is the *product-team structure*. Its advantages are similar to those of a matrix structure, but it is much easier and far less costly to operate because of the way people are organized into permanent cross-functional teams, as Figure 12.11 illustrates. In the **product-team structure**, as in the matrix structure, tasks are divided along product or project lines. However, instead of being assigned only *temporarily* to different projects, as in the matrix structure, functional specialists become part of a *permanent* cross-functional team that focuses on the development of one particular range of products, such as luxury cars or computer workstations. As a result, the problems associated with coordinating cross-functional transfers or hand-offs are much lower than in a matrix structure, in which tasks and reporting relationships change rapidly. Moreover, cross-functional teams are formed at the beginning of the product development process so that any difficulties that arise can be ironed out early, before they lead to major redesign problems. When all functions have direct input from the beginning, design costs and subsequent manufacturing costs can be kept low. Moreover, the use of cross-functional teams speeds innovation and customer responsiveness because, when authority is decentralized, team decisions can be made more quickly.

product-team structure
A way of grouping employees by product or project line but employees focus on the development of only one particular type of product.

A product-team structure groups tasks by product, and each product group is managed by a cross-functional product team that has all the support services necessary to bring the product to market. This is why it is different from the product structure, in which support functions remain centralized. The role of the product team is to protect and enhance a company's differentiation advantage and at the same time coordinate with manufacturing to lower costs.

Focusing on a Narrow Product Line

As Chapter 5 discussed, a focused company concentrates on developing a narrow range of products aimed at one or two market segments, which may be defined by type of customer or location. As a result, a focuser tends to have a higher cost structure than a cost leader or differentiator, because output levels are lower, making it harder to obtain substantial scale economies. For this reason, a focused company must exercise cost control. On the other hand, some attribute of its product gives the focuser its distinctive competency—possibly its ability to provide customers with high-quality, personalized service. For both reasons, the structure and control system adopted by a focused company has to be inexpensive to operate but flexible enough to allow a distinctive competency to emerge.

A company using a focus strategy normally adopts a functional structure to meet these needs. This structure is appropriate because it is complex enough to manage the activities necessary to make and sell a narrow range of products for one or a few market segments. At the same time, the handoff problems are likely to be relatively easy to solve because a focuser remains small and specialized. Thus, a functional structure can provide all the integration necessary, provided that the focused firm has a strong, adaptive culture, which is vital to the development of some kind of distinctive competency.[46] Additionally, because such a company's competitive advantage is often based on personalized service, the flexibility of this kind of structure allows the company to respond quickly to customers' needs and change its products in response to customers' requests.

RESTRUCTURING AND REENGINEERING

restructuring

The process by which a company streamlines its hierarchy of authority and reduces the number of levels in its hierarchy to a minimum to lower operating costs.

To improve performance, a single business company often employs restructuring and reengineering. **Restructuring** a company involves two steps: (1) streamlining the hierarchy of authority and reducing the number of levels in the hierarchy to a minimum and (2) reducing the number of employees to lower operating costs. Restructuring and downsizing become necessary for many reasons.[47] Sometimes a change in the business environment occurs that could not have been foreseen; perhaps a shift in technology made the company's products obsolete. Sometimes an organization has excess capacity because customers no longer want the goods and services it provides; perhaps the goods and services are outdated or offer poor value for the money. Sometimes organizations downsize because they have grown too tall and inflexible and bureaucratic costs have become much too high. Sometimes they restructure even when they are in a strong position simply to build and improve their competitive advantage and stay ahead of competitors.

All too often, however, companies are forced to downsize and lay off employees because they fail to monitor and control their basic business operations and have not made the incremental changes to their strategies and structures over time that allow them to adjust to changing conditions. Advances in management, such as the development of new models for organizing work activities, or IT advances, offer strategic managers the opportunity to implement their strategies in more effective ways.

reengineering

The process of redesigning business processes to achieve dramatic improvements in performance, such as cost, quality, service, and speed.

A company may operate more effectively using **reengineering**, which involves the "fundamental rethinking and radical redesign of business processes to achieve dramatic improvements in critical, contemporary measures of performance, such as cost, quality, service, and speed."[48] As this definition suggests, strategic managers who use reengineering must completely rethink how they organize their value-chain activities. Instead of focusing on how a company's *functions* operate, strategic managers make business *processes* the focus of attention.

A *business process* is any activity that is vital to delivering goods and services to customers quickly or that promotes high quality or low costs (such as IT, materials management, or product development). It is not the responsibility of any one function but *cuts across functions*. Because reengineering focuses on business processes, not on functions, a company that reengineers always has to adopt a different approach to organizing its activities. Companies that take up reengineering deliberately ignore the existing arrangement of tasks, roles, and work activities. They start the reengineering process with the customer (not the product or service) and ask: "How can we reorganize the way we do our work—our business processes—to provide the best quality and the lowest-cost goods and services to the customer?"

Frequently, when managers ask this question, they realize that there are more effective ways to organize their value-chain activities. For example, a business process that encompasses members of 10 different functions working sequentially to provide goods and services might be performed by one person or a few people at a fraction of the cost. Often individual jobs become increasingly complex, and people are grouped into cross-functional teams as business processes are reengineered to reduce costs and increase quality.

Hallmark Cards, for example, reengineered its card design process with great success. Before the reengineering effort, artists, writers, and editors worked separately in different functions to produce all kinds of cards. After reengineering, these same artists, writers, and editors were put on cross-functional teams, each of which now works on a specific type of card, such as birthday, Christmas, or Mother's Day. The result is that the production time to bring a new card to market decreased from years to months, and Hallmark's performance increased dramatically.

Reengineering and TQM, discussed in Chapter 4, are highly interrelated and complementary. After reengineering has taken place and value-chain activities have been altered to speed the product to the final customer, TQM takes over, with its focus on how to continue to improve and refine the new process and find better ways of managing task and role relationships. Successful organizations examine both issues simultaneously and continuously attempt to identify new and better processes for meeting the goals of increased efficiency, quality, and customer responsiveness. Thus, companies are always seeking to improve their visions of their desired future.

Another example of reengineering is the change program that took place at IBM Credit, a wholly owned division of IBM that manages the financing and leasing of IBM computers—particularly mainframes—to IBM's customers. Before reengineering took place, a financing request arrived at the division's headquarters in Old Greenwich, Connecticut, and completed a five-step approval process that involved the activities of five different functions. First, the IBM salesperson called the credit department, which logged the request and recorded details about the potential customer. Second, this information was taken to the credit-checking department, where a credit check on the potential customer was done. Third, when the credit check was complete, the request was taken to the contracts department, which wrote the contract. Fourth, from the contracts department, it went to the pricing department, which determined the actual financial details of the loan, such as the interest rate and the term of the loan. Finally, the whole package of information was assembled by the dispatching department and delivered to the sales representative, who presented it to the customer.

This series of cross-functional activities took an average of 7 days to complete, and sales representatives constantly complained that the delay resulted in a low level of customer responsiveness that reduced customer satisfaction. Also, potential customers were tempted to shop around for financing and look at competitors' machines in the process. The delay in closing the deal caused uncertainty for all involved.

The change process began when two senior IBM credit managers reviewed the finance approval process. They found that the time different specialists spent on the different functions processing a loan application was only 90 minutes. The 7-day approval process was caused by the delay in transmitting information and requests between departments. Managers also learned that the activities taking place in each department were not complex; each department had its own computer system containing its own work procedures, but the work done in each department was routine.

Armed with this information, IBM managers realized that the approval process could be reengineered into one overarching process handled by one person with a computer system containing all the necessary information and work procedures to perform the five loan-processing activities. If the application happened to be complex, a team of experts stood ready to help process it, but IBM found that, after the reengineering effort, a typical application could be done in 4 hours rather than the previous 7 days. A sales representative could speak with the customer the same day to close the deal, and all the uncertainty surrounding the transaction was removed.

As reengineering consultants Hammer and Champy note, this dramatic performance increase was instigated by a radical change to the whole process. Change through reengineering requires managers to assess the most basic level and look at each step in the work process to identify a better way to coordinate and integrate the activities necessary to provide customers with goods and services. As this example makes clear, the introduction of new IT is an integral aspect of reengineering. IT also allows a company to restructure its hierarchy because it provides more and better-quality information. IT today is an integral part of the strategy implementation process.

ETHICAL DILEMMA

© iStockPhoto.com/P_Wei

Suppose a poorly performing organization has decided to terminate hundreds of middle managers. Top managers making the termination decisions might choose to keep subordinates whom they like rather than the best performers, or terminate the most highly paid subordinates even if they are top performers. Remembering that organizational structure and culture affect all company stakeholders, which ethical principles about equality, fairness, and justice would you use to redesign the organizational hierarchy? Keep in mind that some employees may feel they have as strong a claim on the organization as some of its stockholders, even claiming to "own" their jobs from contributions to past successes.

Do you think this is an ethical claim? How would it factor into your design?

SUMMARY OF CHAPTER

1. The successful implementation of a company's business model and strategies depends upon organizational design—the process of selecting the right combination of organizational structure, control systems, and culture. Companies must monitor and oversee the organizational design process to achieve superior profitability.

2. Effective organizational design can increase profitability in two ways. First, it economizes on bureaucratic costs and helps a company lower its cost structure. Second, it enhances the ability of a company's value creation functions to achieve superior efficiency, quality, innovativeness, and customer responsiveness and obtain the advantages of differentiation.

3. The main issues in designing organizational structure are how to group tasks, functions, and divisions; how to allocate authority and responsibility (whether to have a tall or flat organization and whether to have a centralized or decentralized

structure); and how to use integrating mechanisms to improve coordination between functions (such as direct contacts, liaison roles, and teams).

4. Strategic control provides the monitoring and incentive systems necessary to make an organizational structure work as intended and extends corporate governance down to all levels inside the company. The main kinds of strategic control systems are personal control, output control, and behavior control. IT is an aid to output and behavior control, and reward systems are linked to every control system.

5. Organizational culture is the set of values, norms, beliefs, and attitudes that help to energize and motivate employees and control their behavior. Culture is a way of doing something, and a company's founder and top managers help determine which kinds of values emerge in an organization.

6. At the functional level, each function requires a different combination of structure and control system to achieve its functional objectives.

7. To successfully implement a company's business model, structure, control, and culture must be combined in ways that increase the relationships among all functions to build distinctive competencies.

8. Cost leadership and differentiation each require a structure and control system that strengthens the business model that is the source of their competitive advantage. Managers must use organizational design in a way that balances pressures to increase differentiation against pressures to lower the cost structure.

9. Other specialized kinds of structures include the product, market, geographic, matrix, and product-team structures. Each has a specialized use and is implemented as a company's strategy warrants.

10. Restructuring and reengineering are two ways of implementing a company's business model more effectively.

DISCUSSION QUESTIONS

1. What is the relationship among organizational structure, control, and culture? Give some examples of when and under what conditions a mismatch among these components might arise.

2. What kind of structure best describes the way your (a) business school and (b) university operate? Why is the structure appropriate? Would another structure fit better?

3. When would a company choose a matrix structure? What are the problems associated with managing this type of structure, and in what circumstances might a product-team structure be preferable?

4. For each of the structures discussed in the chapter, outline the most suitable control systems.

5. What kind of structure, controls, and culture would you be likely to find in (a) a small manufacturing company, (b) a chain store, (c) a high-tech company, and (d) a Big Four accounting firm?

KEY TERMS

Organizational design 397
Organizational structure 397
Control system 397
Organizational culture 397
Hierarchy of authority 399
Span of control 400

Principle of the minimum chain of command 401
Integrating mechanisms 403
Team 405
Strategic control systems 405
Personal control 408
Output control 408

Behavior control 408
Operating budget 409
Standardization 409
Adaptive culture 413
Functional structure 414
Management by objectives 415
Product structure 423
Market structure 424

Geographic structure 424
Matrix structure 427
Two-boss employees 428
Product-team structure 429
Restructuring 430
Reengineering 430

PRACTICING STRATEGIC MANAGEMENT

© iStockPhoto.com/Urilux

Small-Group Exercises

Small-Group Exercise: Deciding on an Organizational Structure

Break up into groups of three to five people and discuss the following scenario. You are a group of managers of a major soft drink company that is going head-to-head with Coca-Cola to increase market share. Your business model is based on increasing your product range to offer a soft drink in every segment of the market to attract customers. Currently you have a functional structure. What you are trying to work out now is how best to implement your business model to launch your new products. Should you move to a more complex kind of product structure, and if so which one? Alternatively, should you establish new-venture divisions and spin off each kind of new soft drink into its own company so that it can focus its resources on its market niche? Thinking strategically, debate the pros and cons of the possible organizational structures and decide which structure you will implement.

STRATEGY SIGN ON

© iStockPhoto.com/Ninoslav Dotlic

Article File 12

Find an example of a company that competes in one industry and has recently changed the way it implements its business model and strategies. What changes did it make? Why did it make these changes? What effect did these changes have on the behavior of people and functions?

Strategic Management Project: Module 12

This module asks you to identify how your company implements its business model and strategy. For this part of your project, you need to obtain information about your company's structure, control systems, and culture. This information may be hard to obtain unless you can interview managers directly. But you can make many inferences about the company's structure from the nature of its activities, and if you write to the company, it may provide you with an organizational chart and other information. Also, published information, such as compensation for top management, is available in the company's annual reports or 10-K reports. If your company is well known, magazines such as *Fortune* and *Businessweek* frequently report on corporate culture or control issues. Nevertheless, you may be forced to make some bold assumptions to complete this part of the project.

1. How large is the company as measured by the number of its employees? How many levels in the hierarchy does it have from the top to the bottom? Based on these two measures and any other information you may have, would you say your company operates with a relatively tall or flat structure? Does your company have a centralized or decentralized approach to decision making?

(continues)

...

STRATEGY SIGN ON

(continued)

© iStockPhoto.com/Ninoslav Dotlic

2. What changes (if any) would you make to the way the company allocates authority and responsibility?

3. Draw an organizational chart showing the primary way in which your company groups its activities. Based on this chart, decide what kind of structure (functional, product, or divisional) your company is using.

4. Why did your company choose this structure? In what ways is it appropriate for its business model? In what ways is it inappropriate?

5. What kind of integration or integration mechanisms does your company use?

6. What are the primary kinds of control systems your company is using? What kinds of behaviors is the organization trying to (a) shape and (b) motivate through the use of these control systems?

7. What role does the top-management team play in creating the culture of your organization? Can you identify the characteristic norms and values that describe the way people behave in your organization? How does the design of the organization's structure affect its culture?

8. What are the sources of your company's distinctive competencies? Which functions are most important to it? How does your company design its structure, control, and culture to enhance its (a) efficiency, (b) quality, (c) innovativeness, and (d) responsiveness to customers?

9. How does it design its structure and control systems to strengthen its business model? For example, what steps does it take to further cross-functional integration? Does it have a functional, product, or matrix structure?

10. How does your company's culture support its business model? Can you determine any ways in which its top-management team influences its culture?

11. Based on this analysis, would you say your company is coordinating and motivating its people and subunits effectively? Why or why not? What changes (if any) would you make to the way your company's structure operates? What use could it make of restructuring or reengineering?

CLOSING CASE

Alan Mulally Transforms Ford's Structure and Culture

After a loss of more than $13 billion in 2006, William Ford III, who had been Ford Motor's CEO for 5 years, decided he was not the right person to turn around the company's performance. In fact, it became apparent that he was a part of Ford's management problems because he and other top managers at Ford tried to build and protect their own corporate empires, and none would ever admit that mistakes had occurred over the

years. As a result, the entire company's performance had suffered; its future was in doubt. Deciding they needed an outsider to change the way the company operated, Ford recruited Alan Mulally from Boeing to become the new CEO.

After arriving at Ford, Mulally attended hundreds of executive meetings with his new managers. At one meeting, he became confused about why one top-division manager, who obviously did not know the answer to one of Mulally's questions concerning the performance of his car division, rambled on for several minutes trying to disguise his ignorance. Mulally turned to his second-in-command Mark Fields and asked him why the manager had done that. Fields explained that "at Ford you never admit when you don't know something." He also told Mulally that when he arrived as a middle manager at Ford and wanted to ask his boss to lunch to gain information about divisional operations, he was told: "What rank are you at Ford? Don't you know that a subordinate never asks a superior to lunch?"

Mulally discovered that over the years Ford had developed a tall hierarchy composed of managers whose primary goal was to protect their turf and avoid any direct blame for its plunging car sales. When asked why car sales were falling, they did not admit to bad design and poor-quality issues in their divisions; instead they hid in the details. Managers brought thick notebooks and binders to meetings, using the high prices of components and labor costs to explain why their own particular car models were not selling well—or why they had to be sold at a loss. Why, Mulally wondered, did Ford's top executives have this inward-looking, destructive mind-set? How could he change Ford's organizational structure and culture to reduce costs and speed product development to build the kinds of vehicles customers wanted?

First, Mulally decided he needed to change Ford's structure, and that a major reorganization of the company's hierarchy was necessary. He decided to flatten Ford's structure and recentralize control at the top so that all top divisional managers reported to him. But, at the same time, he emphasized teamwork and the development of a cross-divisional approach to manage the enormous value-chain challenges that confronted Ford in its search for ways to reduce its cost structure. He eliminated two levels in the top-management hierarchy and clearly defined each top manager's role in the turnaround process so the company could begin to act as a whole instead of as separate divisions in which managers pursued their own interests.

Mulally also realized, however, that simply changing Ford's structure was not enough to change the way it operated; its other major organizational problem was that the values and norms in Ford's culture that had developed over time hindered cooperation and teamwork. These values and norms promoted secrecy and ambiguity; they emphasized status and rank so managers could protect their information—the best way managers of its different divisions and functions believed to maintain jobs and status was to hoard, rather than share, information. The reason only the boss could ask a subordinate to lunch was to allow superiors to protect their information and positions!

What could Mulally do? He issued a direct order that the managers of every division share with every other Ford division a detailed statement of the costs they incurred to build each of its vehicles. He insisted that each of Ford's divisional presidents should attend a weekly (rather than a monthly) meeting to openly share and discuss the problems all the company's divisions faced. He also told managers they should bring a different subordinate with them to each meeting so every manager in the hierarchy would learn of the problems that had been kept hidden.

Essentially, Mulally's goal was to demolish the dysfunctional values and norms of Ford's culture that focused managers' attention on their own empires at the expense of the entire company. Mulally's goal was to create new values and norms that encouraged employees to admit mistakes, share information about all aspects of model design and costs, and, of course, find ways to speed development and reduce costs. He also wanted to change Ford's culture to allow norms of cooperation to develop both within and across divisions to allow its new structure to work effectively and improve company performance.

By 2011, it was clear that Mulally's attempts to change Ford's structure and culture had succeeded. The company reported a profit in the spring of 2010, for which Mulally received over $17 million in salary and other bonuses, and by 2011 it was reporting record profits as the sales of its vehicles soared. In 2011, Mulally had reached 65, the normal retirement age for Ford's top managers, but in a press conference announcing Ford's record results, William Ford joked that he hoped Mulally would still be in charge of the transformed company in 2025.

Sources: www.ford.com; D. Kiley, "The New Heat on Ford," June 4, 2007, www.businessweek.com; and B. Koenig, "Ford Reorganizes Executives Under New Chief Mulally," December 14, 2006, www.bloomberg.com.

CASE DISCUSSION QUESTIONS

1. How did organizational structure and culture contribute to the poor performance of Ford prior to the arrival of Alan Mulally?

2. One of the first things Mulally did was to flatten the organizational structure at Ford and clearly articulate lines of responsibility. How do you think this contributed to improving Ford's performance?

3. Why was changing the organizational structure not enough to improve Ford's performance?

4. How did Mulally go about changing the culture of Ford? How did this cultural change impact the company's performance?

NOTES

[1] L. Smircich, "Concepts of Culture and Organizational Analysis," *Administrative Science Quarterly* 28 (1983): 339–358.

[2] G. R. Jones and J. M. George, "The Experience and Evolution of Trust: Implications for Cooperation and Teamwork," *Academy of Management Review* 3 (1998): 531–546.

[3] Ibid.

[4] J. R. Galbraith, *Designing Complex Organizations* (Reading: Addison-Wesley, 1973).

[5] A. D. Chandler, *Strategy and Structure* (Cambridge: MIT Press, 1962).

[6] The discussion draws heavily on Chandler, *Strategy and Structure*, and B. R. Scott, *Stages of Corporate Development* (Cambridge: Intercollegiate Clearing House, Harvard Business School, 1971).

[7] R. L. Daft, *Organizational Theory and Design*, 3rd ed. (St. Paul: West, 1986), p. 215.

[8] J. Child, *Organization 9: A Guide for Managers and Administrators* (New York: Harper & Row, 1977), pp. 52–70.

[9] G. R. Jones and J. Butler, "Costs, Revenues, and Business Level Strategy," *Academy of Management Review* 13 (1988): 202–213; and G. R. Jones and C. W. L. Hill, "Transaction Cost Analysis of Strategy-Structure Choice," *Strategic Management Journal* 9 (1988): 159–172.

[10] G. R. Jones, *Organizational Theory, Design, and Change: Text and Cases* (Englewood Cliffs: Pearson, 2011).

[11] Blau, P. M., "A Formal Theory of Differentiation in Organizations," *American Sociological Review* 35 (1970): 684–695.

[12] G. R. Jones, "Organization-Client Transactions and Organizational Governance Structures," *Academy of Management Journal* 30 (1987): 197–218.

[13] P. R. Lawrence and J. Lorsch, *Organization and Environment* (Boston: Division of Research, Harvard Business School, 1967), pp. 50–55.

[14] Galbraith, *Designing Complex Organizations*, Chapter 1; and J. R. Galbraith and R. K. Kazanjian, *Strategy Implementation: Structure System and Process*, 2nd ed. (St. Paul: West, 1986), Chapter 7.

[15] R. Simmons, "Strategic Orientation and Top Management Attention to Control Systems," *Strategic Management Journal* 12 (1991): 49–62.

[16] R. Simmons, "How New Top Managers Use Control Systems as Levers of Strategic Renewal," *Strategic Management Journal* 15 (1994): 169–189.

[17] W. G. Ouchi, "The Transmission of Control Through Organizational Hierarchy," *Academy of Management Journal* 21 (1978):

173–192; and W. H. Newman, *Constructive Control* (Englewood Cliffs: Prentice-Hall, 1975).

[18]E. Flamholtz, "Organizational Control Systems as a Managerial Tool," *California Management Review,* Winter 1979, pp. 50–58.

[19]O. E. Williamson, *Markets and Hierarchies: Analysis and Antitrust Implications* (New York: Free Press, 1975); and W. G. Ouchi, "Markets, Bureaucracies, and Clans," *Administrative Science Quarterly* 25 (1980): 129–141.

[20]H. Mintzberg, *The Structuring of Organizations* (Englewood Cliffs: Prentice-Hall, 1979), pp. 5–9.

[21]E. E. Lawler III, *Motivation in Work Organizations* (Monterey: Brooks/Cole, 1973); and Galbraith and Kazanjian, *Strategy Implementation*, Chapter 6.

[22]Smircich, "Concepts of Culture and Organizational Analysis."

[23]www.microsoft.com, 2011.

[24]Ouchi, "Markets, Bureaucracies, and Clans," 130.

[25]Jones, *Organizational Theory, Design, and Change.*

[26]J. Van Maanen and E. H. Schein, "Towards a Theory of Organizational Socialization," in B. M. Staw (ed.), *Research in Organizational Behavior 1* (Greenwich: JAI Press, 1979), pp. 209–264.

[27]G. R. Jones, "Socialization Tactics, Self-Efficacy, and Newcomers' Adjustments to Organizations," *Academy of Management Journal* 29 (1986): 262–279.

[28]J. P. Kotter and J. L. Heskett, "Corporate Culture and Performance," *Sloan Management Review* 33:3 (1992): 91–92.

[29]T. J. Peters and R. H. Waterman, *In Search of Excellence: Lessons from America's Best-Run Companies* (New York: Harper & Row, 1982).

[30]G. Hamel and C. K. Prahalad, "Strategic Intent," *Harvard Business Review,* May–June 1989, p. 64.

[31]Galbraith and Kazanjian, *Strategy Implementation*; Child, *Organization*; and R. Duncan, "What Is the Right Organization Structure?" *Organizational Dynamics*, Winter 1979, pp. 59–80.

[32]J. Pettet, "Walmart Yesterday and Today," *Discount Merchandiser*, December 1995, pp. 66–67; M. Reid, "Stores of Value," *Economist*, March 4, 1995, ss5–ss7; M. Troy, "The Culture Remains the Constant," *Discount Store News*, June 8, 1998, pp. 95–98; and www.walmart.com.

[33]W. G. Ouchi, "The Relationship Between Organizational Structure and Organizational Control," *Administrative Science Quarterly* 22 (1977): 95–113.

[34]R. Bunderi, "Intel Researchers Aim to Think Big While Staying Close to Development," *Research-Technology Management*, March–April 1998, pp. 3–4.

[35]K. M. Eisenhardt, "Control: Organizational and Economic Approaches," *Management Science* 16 (1985): 134–148.

[36]Williamson, *Markets and Hierarchies.*

[37]P. R. Lawrence and J. W. Lorsch, *Organization and Environment* (Boston: Graduate School of Business Administration, Harvard University, 1967).

[38]M. E. Porter, *Competitive Strategy: Techniques for Analyzing Industries and Competitors* (New York: Free Press, 1980); and D. Miller, "Configurations of Strategy and Structure," *Strategic Management Journal* 7 (1986): 233–249.

[39]D. Miller and P. H. Freisen, *Organizations: A Quantum View* (Englewood Cliffs: Prentice-Hall, 1984).

[40]J. Woodward, *Industrial Organization: Theory and Practice* (London: Oxford University Press, 1965); and Lawrence and Lorsch, *Organization and Environment.*

[41]R. E. White, "Generic Business Strategies, Organizational Context and Performance: An Empirical Investigation," *Strategic Management Journal* 7 (1986): 217–231.

[42]G. Rivlin, "He Naps. He Sings. And He Isn't Michael Dell," *New York Times,* September 11, 2005, p. 31.

[43]Porter, *Competitive Strategy;* and Miller, "Configurations of Strategy and Structure."

[44]S. M. Davis and R. R. Lawrence, *Matrix* (Reading: Addison-Wesley, 1977); and J. R. Galbraith, "Matrix Organization Designs: How to Combine Functional and Project Forms," *Business Horizons* 14 (1971): 29–40.

[45]Duncan, "What Is the Right Organizational Structure?"; and Davis and Lawrence, *Matrix.*

[46]D. Miller, "Configurations of Strategy and Structure," in R. E. Miles and C. C. Snow (eds.), *Organizational Strategy, Structure, and Process* (New York: McGraw-Hill, 1978).

[47]G. D. Bruton, J. K. Keels, and C. L. Shook, "Downsizing the Firm: Answering the Strategic Questions," *Academy of Management Executive*, May 1996, pp. 38–45.

[48]M. Hammer and J. Champy, *Reengineering the Corporation* (New York: HarperCollins, 1993).

13

Implementing Strategy in Companies That Compete Across Industries and Countries

OPENING CASE

Justin Sullivan/Getty Images

Google Reorganizes

In April of 2011, Larry Page, one of Google's two founders, became CEO of the company. Page had been CEO of Google from its establishment in 1998 through 2001, when Eric Schmidt became the CEO. After 10 years, Schmidt decided to step down and handed the reins back to Page. One of Page's first actions was to reorganize the company into business units.

Under Schmidt, Google was organized into two main entities—an engineering function and a product management group under the leadership of Jonathan Rosenberg. The engineering group was responsible for creating, building, and maintaining Google's products, and the product management group focused on selling Google's offerings, particularly its advertising services. There were, however, two main exceptions to this structure, YouTube and the Android group, both of which were the result of acquisitions, and both of which were left to run their own operations in a largely autonomous manner. Notably, both had been more successful than many of Google's own internally generated new-product ideas.

The great virtue claimed for Google's old organization structure was that it was a flat structure, based around teams, where innovation was encouraged. Indeed, numerous articles were written about the bottom-up new product-development process at Google. Engineers were encouraged to spend 20% of their own time on

LEARNING OBJECTIVES

After reading this chapter, you should be able to:

13-1 Discuss the reasons why companies pursuing different corporate strategies need to implement these strategies using different combinations of organizational structure, control, and culture

13-2 Describe the advantages and disadvantages of a multidivisional structure

13-3 Explain why companies that pursue different kinds of global expansion strategies choose different kinds of global structures and control systems to implement these strategies

13-4 Discuss the strategy-implementation problems associated with the three primary methods used to enter new industries: internal new venturing, joint ventures, and mergers

projects of their own choosing. They were empowered to form teams to flesh out product ideas, and could get funding to take those products to market by going through a formal process that ended with a presentation in front of Page and Google cofounder Sergey Brin. The products that came out of this process included Google News, Google Earth, and Google Apps.

However, by 2011 it was becoming increasingly clear that there were limitations to this structure. There was a lack of accountability for products once they had been developed. The core engineers might move on to other projects. Projects could stay in the beta stage for years, essentially unfinished offerings. No one was really responsible for taking products and making them into stand-alone businesses. Many engineers complained that the process for approving new products had become mired in red tape. It was too slow. A structure that had worked well when Google was still a small start-up was no longer scaling. Furthermore, the structure did not reflect the fact that Google was essentially becoming a multibusiness enterprise, albeit one in which search-based advertising income was still the main driver of the company's revenues. Indeed, that in itself was viewed as an issue, for despite creating many new-product offerings, Google was still dependent upon search-based advertising for the bulk of its income.

Page's solution to this problem was to reorganize Google into seven core product areas or business units: Search, Advertising, YouTube, Mobile (Android), Chrome, Social (Google + and Blogger), and Commerce (Google Apps). A senior vice president who reports directly to Page heads each unit. The heads of each unit have full responsibility (and accountability) for their fates. Getting a new product started no longer requires convincing executives from across the company to get on board. And once a product ships, engineers and managers can't jump to the next thing and leave important products like Gmail in unfinished beta for years. "Now you are accountable not only for delivering something, but for revising and fixing it," said one Google spokesperson.

Sources: Miguel Helft, "The Future According to Google's Larry Page," *CNNMoney*, January 3, 2013; Liz Gannes, "GoogQuake: The Larry Page Reorg Promotes Top Lieutenants to SVP," *All Things Digital*, April 7, 2011; Jessica Guynn, "Google CEO Larry Page Completes Major Reorganization of Internet Search Giant," *Los Angeles Times*, April 7, 2011.

OVERVIEW

As explained in the Opening Case, in 2011 Google reorganized itself to try to improve its performance. Although Google has had stellar financial performance over the years, many of its new business ideas have failed to become big revenue generators. In attempt to solve this problem, CEO Larry Page has essentially created a *multidivisional structure* at Google, with each "division" been given full responsibility to run its own operations, and being held accountable for its own performance. Google is not the first company to wrestle with the problem of how best to manage a company as it grows and starts to generate new-product offerings; there is in fact a long history of companies moving from a functional toward a multidivisional structure as they grow and start to diversify. The organizational structures that are optimal for managing a single business turn out to be inappropriate for managing a more diversified multibusiness enterprise, which Google is in the process of becoming. Indeed, by reorganizing itself, Google may promote more profitable business diversification.

This chapter begins where the last one ends; it examines how to implement strategy when a company decides to enter and compete in new business areas, new industries, or in new countries when it expands globally. The strategy-implementation issue remains the same; however, deciding how to use organizational design and combine organizational structure, control, and culture to strengthen a company's strategy and increase its profitability.

Once a company decides to compete across businesses, industries, and countries, it confronts a new set of problems; some of them are continuations of the organizational problems we discussed in Chapter 12, and some of them are a direct consequence of the decision to enter and compete in overseas markets and new industries. As a result, managers must make a new series of organizational design decisions to successfully implement their company's corporate strategy. By the end of the chapter, you will appreciate the many complex issues that confront global multibusiness companies and understand why effective strategy implementation is an integral part of achieving competitive advantage and superior performance.

CORPORATE STRATEGY AND THE MULTIDIVISIONAL STRUCTURE

As Chapters 10 and 11 discuss, there are many ways in which corporate-level strategies such as vertical integration or diversification can be used to strengthen a company's performance and improve its competitive position. However, important implementation problems also arise when a company enters new industries, often due to the increasing bureaucratic costs associated with managing a collection of business units that operate in different industries. Bureaucratic costs are especially high when a company seeks to gain the differentiation and low-cost advantages of transferring, sharing, or leveraging its distinctive competencies across its business units in different industries. Companies that pursue a strategy of related diversification, for example, face many problems and costs in managing the handoffs or transfers between the value-chain functions of their business units in different industries or around the world to boost profitability. The need to economize on these costs propels managers to search for improved ways to implement corporate-level strategies.

As a company begins to enter new industries and produce different kinds of products, the structures described in Chapter 12, such as the functional and product structures, are not up to the task. These structures cannot provide the level of coordination between managers, functions, and business units necessary to effectively implement corporate-level strategy. As a result, the control problems that give rise to bureaucratic costs, such as those related to measurement, customers, location, or strategy, escalate.

Experiencing these problems is a sign that a company has once again outgrown its structure. Managers need to invest additional resources to develop a different structure—one that allows the company to implement its corporate strategies successfully. The answer for most large, complex companies is to move to a multidivisional structure, design a cross-industry control system, and fashion a global corporate culture to reduce these problems and economize on bureaucratic costs.

A **multidivisional structure** has two organizational design advantages over a functional or product structure that allow a company to grow and diversify while also reducing the coordination and control problems that inevitably arise as it enters and competes in new industries. First, in each industry in which a company operates, managers group all its different business operations in that industry into one division or subunit. Each industry division contains all the value-chain functions it needs to pursue its industry business model

multidivisional structure
A complex organizational design that allows a company to grow and diversify while also reducing coordination and control problems because it uses self-contained divisions and has a separate corporate headquarters staff.

self-contained division

An independent business unit or division that contains all the value-chain functions it needs to pursue its business model successfully.

corporate headquarters staff

The team of top executives, as well as their support staff, who are responsible for overseeing a company's long-term multibusiness model and providing guidance to increase the value created by the company's self-contained divisions.

and is thus called a **self-contained division**. For example, GE competes in eight different industries—and each of its eight main business divisions is self-contained and performs all the value creation functions necessary to give it a competitive advantage.

Second, the office of *corporate headquarters staff* is created to monitor divisional activities and exercise financial control over each division.[1] This office contains the corporate-level managers who oversee the activities of divisional managers. Hence, the organizational hierarchy is taller in a multidivisional structure than in a product or functional structure. An important function of the new level of corporate management is to develop strategic control systems that lower a company's overall cost structure, including finding ways to economize on the costs of controlling the handoffs and transfers between divisions. The extra cost of these corporate managers is more than justified if their actions lower the cost structure of the operating divisions or increase their ability to differentiate their products—both of which boost total company profitability.

In the multidivisional structure, the day-to-day operations of each division are the responsibility of divisional management; that is, divisional managers have *operating responsibility*. The **corporate headquarters staff**, which includes top executives as well as their support staff, is responsible for overseeing the company's long-term growth strategy and providing guidance for increasing the value created by interdivisional projects. These executives have *strategic responsibility*. Such an organizational grouping of self-contained divisions with centralized corporate management results in an organizational structure that provides the extra coordination and control necessary to compete in new industries or world regions successfully.

Figure 13.1 illustrates a typical multidivisional structure found in a large chemical company such as DuPont. Although this company has at least 20 different divisions, only

| Figure 13.1 | Multidivisional Structure |

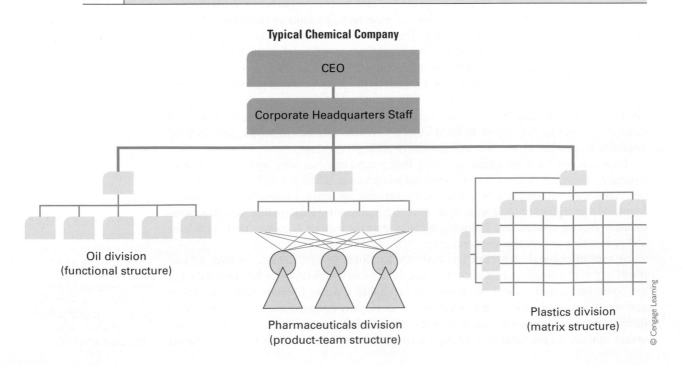

Typical Chemical Company

Oil division
(functional structure)

Pharmaceuticals division
(product-team structure)

Plastics division
(matrix structure)

© Cengage Learning

three—the oil, pharmaceuticals, and plastics divisions—are represented in this figure. Each division possesses the value-chain functions it needs to pursue its own strategy. Each division is treated by corporate managers as an independent profit center, and measures of profitability such as return on invested capital (ROIC) are used to monitor and evaluate each division's individual performance.[2] The use of this kind of output control makes it easier for corporate managers to identify high-performing and underperforming divisions and to take corrective action as necessary.

Because each division operates independently, the divisional managers in charge of each individual division can choose which organizational structure (e.g., a product, matrix, or market structure), control systems, and culture to adopt to implement its business model and strategies most effectively. Figure 13.1 illustrates how this process works. It shows that managers of the oil division have chosen a functional structure (the one that is the least costly to operate) to pursue a cost-leadership strategy. The pharmaceuticals division has adopted a product-team structure that allows each separate product development team to focus its efforts on the speedy development of new drugs. And, managers of the plastics division have chosen to implement a matrix structure that promotes cooperation between teams and functions and allows for the continuous innovation of improved plastic products that suit the changing needs of customers. These two divisions are pursuing differentiation based on a distinctive competence in innovation.

The CEO famous for employing the multidivisional structure to great advantage was Alfred Sloan, GM's first CEO, who implemented a multidivisional structure in 1921, noting that GM "needs to find a principle for coordination without losing the advantages of decentralization." Sloan placed each of GM's different car brands in a self-contained division so it possessed its own functions—sales, production, engineering, and finance. Each division was treated as a profit center and evaluated on its return on investment. Sloan was clear about the main advantage of decentralization: it made it much easier to evaluate the performance of each division. And, Sloan observed, it: (1) "increases the morale of the organization by placing each operation on its own foundation . . . assuming its own responsibility and contributing its share to the final result"; (2) "develops statistics correctly reflecting . . . the true measure of efficiency"; and (3) "enables the corporation to direct the placing of additional capital where it will result in the greatest benefit to the corporation as a whole."[3]

Sloan recommended that exchanges or handoffs between divisions be set by a *transfer-pricing system* based on the cost of making a product plus some agreed-upon rate of return. He recognized the risks that internal suppliers might become inefficient and raise the cost structure, and he recommended that GM should benchmark competitors to determine the fair price for a component. He established a centralized headquarters management staff to perform these calculations. Corporate management's primary role was to audit divisional performance and plan strategy for the entire organization. Divisional managers were to be responsible for all competitive product-related decisions.

Advantages of a Multidivisional Structure

When managed effectively at both the corporate and the divisional levels, a multidivisional structure offers several strategic advantages. Together, they can raise corporate profitability to a new peak because they allow a company to more effectively implement its corporate-level strategies.

Enhanced Corporate Financial Control   The profitability of different business divisions is clearly visible in the multidivisional structure.[4] Because each division is its own **profit center**, financial controls can be applied to each business on the basis of profitability criteria such as ROIC. Corporate managers establish performance goals for each

profit center
When each self-contained division is treated as a separate financial unit and financial controls are used to establish performance goals for each division and measure profitability.

division, monitor their performance on a regular basis, and intervene selectively if a division starts to underperform. They can then use this information to identify the divisions in which investment of the company's financial resources will yield the greatest long-term ROIC. As a result, they can allocate the company's funds among competing divisions in an optimal way—that is, a way that will maximize the profitability of the *whole* company. Essentially, managers at corporate headquarters act as "internal investors" who channel funds to high-performing divisions in which they will produce the most profits.

Enhanced Strategic Control The multidivisional structure makes divisional managers responsible for developing each division's business model and strategies; this allows corporate managers to focus on developing corporate strategy, which is their main responsibility. The structure gives corporate managers the time they need to contemplate wider long-term strategic issues and develop a coordinated response to competitive changes, such as quickly changing industry boundaries. Teams of managers at corporate headquarters can also be created to collect and process crucial information that leads to improved functional performance at the divisional level. These managers also perform long-term strategic and scenario planning to find new ways to increase the performance of the entire company, such as evaluating which of the industries they compete in will likely be the most profitable in the future. Then managers can decide which industries they should expand into and which they should exit.

Profitable Long-Term Growth   The division of responsibilities between corporate and divisional managers in the multidivisional structure allows a company to overcome organizational problems, such as communication problems and information overload. Divisional managers work to enhance their divisions' profitability; teams of managers at corporate headquarters devote their time to finding opportunities to expand or diversify existing businesses so that the entire company enjoys profitable growth. Communication problems are also reduced because corporate managers use the same set of standardized accounting and financial output controls to evaluate all divisions. Also, from a behavior control perspective, corporate managers can implement a policy of management by exception, which means that they intervene only when problems arise.

Stronger Pursuit of Internal Efficiency   As a single-business company grows, it often becomes difficult for top managers to accurately assess the profit contribution of each functional activity because their activities are so interdependent. This means that it is often difficult for top managers to evaluate how well their company is performing relative to others in its industry—and to identify or pinpoint the specific source of the problem. As a result, inside one company, considerable degrees of **organizational slack**—that is, the unproductive use of functional resources—can go undetected. For example, the head of the finance function might employ a larger staff than is required for efficiency to reduce work pressures inside the department and to bring the manager higher status. In a multidivisional structure, however, corporate managers can compare the performance of one division's cost structure, sales, and the profit it generates against another. The corporate office is therefore in a better position to identify the managerial inefficiencies that result in bureaucratic costs; divisional managers have no excuses for poor performance.

organizational slack
The unproductive use of functional resources by divisional managers that can go undetected unless corporate managers monitor their activities.

Problems in Implementing a Multidivisional Structure

Although research suggests large companies that adopt multidivisional structures outperform those that retain functional structures, multidivisional structures have their disadvantages as well.[5] Good management can eliminate some of these disadvantages, but some problems are inherent in the structure. Corporate managers must continually pay attention to the way they operate and detect problems.

Establishing the Divisional–Corporate Authority Relationship

The authority relationship between corporate headquarters and the subordinate divisions must be correctly established. The multidivisional structure introduces a new level in the management hierarchy: the corporate level. Corporate managers face the problem of deciding how much authority and control to delegate to divisional managers, and how much authority to retain at corporate headquarters to increase long-term profitability. Sloan encountered this problem when he implemented GM's multidivisional structure.[6] He found that when corporate managers retained too much power and authority, the managers of its business divisions lacked the autonomy required to change its business model to meet rapidly changing competitive conditions; the need to gain approval from corporate managers slowed down decision making. On the other hand, when too much authority is delegated to divisions, managers may start to pursue strategies that benefit their own divisions, but add little to the whole company's profitability. Strategy in Action 13.1 describes the problems CEO Andrea Jung experienced as Avon recentralized control over its functional operations to U.S. corporate managers from overseas divisional managers when under order to overcome this problem.

As this example suggests, the most important issue in managing a multidivisional structure is how much authority should be *centralized* at corporate headquarters and how much should be *decentralized* to the divisions—in different industries or countries. Corporate managers must consider how their company's corporate strategies will be affected by the way they make this decision now and in the future. There is no easy answer because every company is different. In addition, as the environment changes or a company alters its corporate strategy, the optimal balance between centralization and decentralization of authority will also change.

Restrictive Financial Controls Lead to Short-Run Focus Suppose corporate managers place too much emphasis on each division's *individual* profitability, for example, by establishing very high and stringent ROIC targets for each division. Divisional managers may engage in **information distortion**—that is, they may manipulate the facts they supply to corporate managers to hide declining divisional performance, or start to pursue strategies that increase short-term profitability but reduce future profitability. For example, divisional managers may attempt to make the ROIC of their division look better by cutting investments in R&D, product development, or marketing—all of which increase ROIC in the short run. In the long term, however, cutting back on the investments and expenditures necessary to maintain the division's performance, particularly the crucial R&D investments that lead a stream of innovative products, will reduce its long-term profitability. Hence, corporate managers must carefully control their interactions with divisional managers to ensure that both the short- and long-term goals of the business are being met. In sum, a problem can stem from the use of financial controls that are too restrictive; Chapter 11 discusses the "balanced scorecard" approach that helps solve it.

information distortion
The manipulation of facts supplied to corporate managers to hide declining divisional performance.

Competition for Resources The third problem of managing a multidivisional structure is that when the divisions compete among themselves for scarce resources, this rivalry can make it difficult—or sometimes impossible—to obtain the gains from transferring, sharing, or leveraging distinctive competencies across business units. For example, every year the funds available to corporate managers to allocate or distribute to their divisions is fixed, and, usually, the divisions that have obtained the highest ROIC proportionally

13.1 STRATEGY IN ACTION

Organizational Change at Avon

© iStockPhoto.com/Tom Nulens

After a decade of profitable growth, Avon began to experience falling sales in the mid-2000s, both at home and in developing markets abroad. After spending several months visiting the managers of its worldwide divisions, Andrea Jung, Avon's CEO, decided that Avon had lost the balance between centralization and decentralization of authority. Managers abroad had gained so much authority to control operations in their respective countries and world regions that they had made decisions to benefit their own divisions, and these decisions had hurt the performance of the whole company. Specifically, Avon's operating costs were out of control, and it was losing both low-cost and differentiation advantages. Avon's country-level managers from Poland to Mexico ran their own factories, made their own product development decisions, and spearheaded their own advertising campaigns. These decisions were often based on poor marketing knowledge and with little concern for operating costs because the goal was to increase sales as rapidly as possible.

When too much authority is decentralized to managers lower in an organization's hierarchy, these managers often recruit more and more managers to help them build their country "empires." At Avon, the result was an expansion of the global hierarchy—it had risen from 7 levels to 15 levels of managers in a decade as tens of thousands of additional managers were hired around the globe! Because Avon's profits were rising fast, Jung and her top-management team had not paid enough attention to the way Avon's organizational structure was becoming taller and taller—and how this was taking away its competitive advantage.

Once Jung recognized this problem she had to confront the need to lay off thousands of managers and restructure the hierarchy. She embarked on a program to take away the authority of Avon's country-level managers and to transfer authority to regional and corporate headquarters managers to streamline decision making and reduce costs. She cut out seven levels of management and laid off 25% of Avon's global managers in its 114 worldwide markets. Then, using teams of expert managers from corporate headquarters, she embarked on a detailed examination of all Avon's functional activities, country by country, to find out why its costs had risen so quickly, and what could be done to bring them under control. The duplication of marketing efforts in countries around the world was one source of these high costs. In Mexico, one team found that country managers' desire to expand their empires led to the development of a staggering 13,000 different products! Not only had this caused product development costs to soar, it had led to major marketing problems, for how could Avon's Mexican sales reps learn about the differences between 13,000 products—and then find an easy way to tell customers about them?

In Avon's new structure the focus is now upon centralizing all new major product development; Avon develops over 1,000 new products per year, but in the future, the input from different country managers will be used to customize products to country needs, including fragrance, packaging, and so on, and research and development (R&D) will be performed in the United States. Similarly, the future goal is to develop marketing campaigns targeted at the average "global" customer, but that can also be easily customized to any country. Using the appropriate language or changing the nationality of the models used to market the products, for example, could adapt these campaigns. Other initiatives have been to increase the money spent on global marketing and a major push to increase the number of Avon representatives in developing nations in order to attract more customers. By 2011, Avon recruited another 400,000 reps in China alone!

Country-level managers now are responsible for managing this army of Avon reps and for ensuring that marketing dollars are being directed to the right channels for maximum impact. However, they no longer have any authority to engage in major product development or build new manufacturing capacity—or to hire new managers without the agreement of regional- or corporate-level managers. The balance of control has changed at Avon, and Jung and all of her managers are now firmly focused on making operational decisions that lower its costs or increase its differentiation advantage in ways that serve the best interests of the whole company—not just one of the countries in which its cosmetics are sold.

Source: www.avon.com.

receive more of these funds. In turn, because managers have more money to invest in their business, this usually will raise the company's performance the next year, so that strong divisions grow ever stronger. This is what leads to competition for resources and reduces interdivisional coordination; there are many recorded instances in which one divisional manager tells another: "You want our new technology? Well you have to pay us $2 billion to get it." When divisions battle over transfer prices, the potential gains from pursuing a corporate strategy are lost.

Transfer Pricing   As just noted, competition among divisions may lead to battles over **transfer pricing**, that is, conflicts over establishing the fair or "competitive" price of a resource or skill developed in one division that is to be transferred and sold to other divisions that require it. As Chapter 9 discusses, a major source of bureaucratic costs is the problems that arise from handoffs or transfers between divisions to obtain the benefits of corporate strategy when pursuing a vertical integration or related diversification strategy. Setting prices for resource transfers between divisions is a major source of these problems, because every supplying division has the incentive to set the highest possible transfer price for its products or resources to maximize its *own* profitability. The "purchasing" divisions realize the supplying divisions' attempts to charge high prices will reduce their profitability; the result is competition between divisions that undermines cooperation and coordination. Such competition can completely destroy the corporate culture and turn a company into a battleground; if unresolved, the benefits of the strategy will not be achieved. Hence, corporate managers must be sensitive to this problem and work hard with the divisions to design incentive and control systems to make the multidivisional structure work. Indeed, managing transfer pricing is one of corporate managers' most important tasks.

transfer pricing
The problem of establishing the fair or "competitive" price of a resource or skill developed in one division that is to be transferred and sold to another division.

Duplication of Functional Resources   Because each division has its own set of value-chain functions, functional resources are duplicated across divisions; thus, multidivisional structures are expensive to operate. R&D and marketing are especially costly functional activities; to reduce their cost structure, some companies centralize most of the activities of these two functions at the corporate level, in which they service the needs of all divisions. The expense involved in duplicating functional resources does not result in major problems if the differentiation advantages that result from the use of separate sets of specialist functions are substantial. Corporate managers must decide whether the duplication of functions is financially justified. In addition, they should always be on the lookout for ways to centralize or outsource functional activities to reduce a company's cost structure and increase long-run profitability.

In sum, the advantages of divisional structures must be balanced against the problems of implementing them, but an observant, professional set of corporate (and divisional) managers who are sensitive to the complexities involved can respond to and manage these problems. Indeed, advances in information technology (IT) have made strategy implementation easier, as we will discuss later in this chapter.

Structure, Control, Culture, and Corporate-Level Strategy

Once corporate managers select a multidivisional structure, they must then make choices about what kind of integrating mechanisms and control systems are necessary to make the structure work efficiently. Such choices depend on whether a company chooses to pursue a strategy of unrelated diversification, vertical integration, or related diversification.

As Chapter 9 discusses, many possible differentiation and cost advantages derive from vertical integration. A company can coordinate resource transfers between divisions operating in adjacent industries to reduce manufacturing costs and improve quality, for example.[7] This might mean locating a rolling mill next to a steel furnace to save on costs to reheat steel ingots, making it easier to control the quality of the final steel product.

The principal benefits from related diversification also derive from transferring, sharing, or leveraging functional competencies across divisions, such as sharing distribution and sales networks to increase differentiation, or lowering the overall cost structure. With both strategies, the benefits to the company result from some *exchange* of distinctive competencies among divisions. To secure these benefits, managers must coordinate the activities of the various divisions, so an organization's structure and control systems must be designed to manage the handoffs or transfers among divisions.

In the case of unrelated diversification, the strategy is based on using general strategic management capabilities, for example, in corporate finance or organizational design. Corporate managers' ability to create a culture that supports entrepreneurial behavior that leads to rapid product development, or to restructure an underperforming company and establish an effective set of financial controls, can result in substantial increases in profitability. With this strategy, however, there are *no* exchanges among divisions; each division operates separately and independently. The only exchanges that need to be coordinated are those between the divisions and corporate headquarters. Structure and control must therefore be designed to allow each division to operate independently, while making it easy for corporate managers to monitor divisional performance and intervene if necessary.

The choice of structure and control mechanisms depends upon the degree to which a company using a multidivisional structure needs to control the handoffs and interactions among divisions. The more *interdependent divisions are*—that is, the more they depend on each other for skills, resources, and competencies—the greater the bureaucratic costs associated with obtaining the potential benefits from a particular corporate-level strategy.[8] Table 13.1 illustrates what forms of structure and control companies should adopt to economize on the bureaucratic costs associated with the three corporate strategies of unrelated diversification, vertical integration, and related diversification.[9] We examine these strategies in detail in the next sections.

Table 13.1 Corporate Strategy, Structure, and Control

Corporate Strategy	Appropriate Structure	Need for Integration	Type of Control		
			Financial Control	Behavior Control	Organizational Culture
Unrelated Diversification	Multidivisional	Low (no exchanges between divisions)	Great use (e.g., ROIC)	Some use (e.g., budgets)	Little use
Vertical Integration	Multidivisional	Medium (scheduling resource transfers)	Great use (e.g., ROIC, transfer pricing)	Great use (e.g., standardization, budgets)	Some use (e.g., shared norms and values)
Related Diversification	Multidivisional	High (achieving synergies between divisions by integrating roles)	Little use	Great use (e.g., rules, budgets)	Great use (e.g., norms, values, common language)

Unrelated Diversification   Because there are *no exchanges or linkages* among divisions, unrelated diversification is the easiest and cheapest strategy to manage; it is associated with the lowest level of bureaucratic costs. The primary advantage of the structure and control system is that it allows corporate managers to evaluate divisional performance accurately. Thus, companies use multidivisional structures, and each division is evaluated by output controls such as ROIC. A company also uses an IT-based system of financial controls to allow corporate managers to obtain information quickly from the divisions and compare their performance on many dimensions. UTC, Tyco, and Textron are companies well known for their use of sophisticated financial controls to manage their structures and track divisional performance on a daily basis.

Divisions usually have considerable autonomy *unless* they fail to reach their ROIC goals, in which case corporate managers will intervene in the operations of a division to help solve problems. As problems arise, corporate managers step in and take corrective action, such as replacing managers or providing additional funding, depending on the reason for the problem. If they see no possibility of a turnaround, they may decide to divest the division. The multidivisional structure allows the unrelated company to operate its businesses as a portfolio of investments that can be bought and sold as business conditions change. Typically, managers in the various divisions do not know one another; they may not even know what other companies are represented in the corporate portfolio. Hence, the idea of a corporate-wide culture is meaningless.

The use of financial controls to manage a company means that no integration among divisions is necessary. This is why the bureaucratic costs of managing an unrelated company are low. The biggest problem facing corporate managers is to make capital allocations decisions between divisions to maximize the overall profitability of the portfolio and monitor divisional performance to ensure they are meeting ROIC targets.

Alco Standard, once one of the largest U.S. office supply companies, provides an example of how to operate a successful strategy of unrelated diversification. Alco's corporate management believed that authority and control should be completely decentralized to the managers of each of the company's 50 divisions. Each division was then left to make its own manufacturing or purchasing decisions, despite that the potential benefits to be obtained from corporate-wide purchasing or marketing were lost. Corporate managers pursued this nonintervention policy because they judged that the gains from allowing divisional managers to act in an entrepreneurial way exceeded potential cost savings that might result from attempts to coordinate interdivisional activities. Alco believed that a decentralized operating system would allow a big company to act as a small company and avoid the problems that arise when companies become bureaucratic and difficult to change.

Vertical Integration   Vertical integration is a more expensive strategy to manage than unrelated diversification because *sequential resource flows* from one division to the next must be coordinated. Once again, the multidivisional structure economizes on the bureaucratic costs associated with achieving such coordination because it provides the centralized control necessary for a vertically integrated company to benefit from resource transfers. Corporate managers are responsible for devising financial output and behavior controls that solve the problems of transferring resources from one division to the next; for example, they solve transfer pricing problems. Also, rules and procedures are created that specify how resource exchanges are made to solve potential handoff problems; complex resource exchanges may lead to conflict among divisions, and corporate managers must try to prevent this.

The way to distribute authority between corporate and divisional managers must be considered carefully in vertically integrated companies. The involvement of corporate managers in operating issues at the divisional level risks that divisional managers feel they have no autonomy, so their performance suffers. These companies must strike the appropriate balance of centralized control at corporate headquarters and decentralized control at the divisional level if they are to implement this strategy successfully.

Because the interests of their divisions are at stake, divisional managers need to be involved in decisions concerning scheduling and resource transfers. For example, the plastics division in a chemical company has a vital interest in the activities of the oil division because the quality of the products it receives from the oil division determines the quality of its products. Integrating mechanisms must be created between divisions that encourage their managers to freely exchange or transfer information and skills.[10] To facilitate communication among divisions, corporate managers create teams composed of both corporate and divisional managers, called **integrating roles**, whereby an experienced corporate manager assumes the responsibility for managing complex transfers between two or more divisions. The use of integrating roles to coordinate divisions is common in high-tech and chemical companies, for example.

Thus, a strategy of vertical integration is managed through a combination of corporate and divisional controls. As a result, the organizational structure and control systems used to economize upon the bureaucratic costs of managing this strategy are more complex and difficult to implement than those used for unrelated diversification. However, as long as the benefits that derive from vertical integration are realized, the extra expense in implementing this strategy can be justified.

Related Diversification In the case of related diversification, the gains from pursuing this strategy derive from the transfer, sharing, and leveraging of R&D knowledge, industry information, customer bases, and so on, across divisions. Within such companies, the high level of divisional resource sharing and the exchange of functional competencies make it difficult for corporate managers to evaluate the performance of each individual division.[11] Thus, bureaucratic costs are substantial. The multidivisional structure helps to economize on these costs because it provides some of the extra coordination and control that is required. However, if a related company is to obtain the potential benefits from using its competencies efficiently and effectively, it has to adopt more complicated forms of integration and control at the divisional level to make the structure work.

First, output control is difficult to use because divisions share resources, so it is not easy to measure the performance of an individual division. Therefore, a company needs to develop a corporate culture that stresses cooperation among divisions and the corporate team rather than focusing purely on divisional goals. Second, corporate managers must establish sophisticated integrating devices to ensure coordination among divisions. Integrating roles and integrating teams of corporate and divisional managers are essential because these teams provide the forum in which managers can meet, exchange information, and develop a common vision of corporate goals. An organization with a multidivisional structure must have the right mix of incentives and rewards for cooperation if it is to achieve gains from sharing skills and resources among divisions.[12]

With unrelated diversification, divisions operate autonomously, and the company can easily reward managers based upon their division's individual performance. With related diversification, however, rewarding divisions is more difficult because the divisions are engaged in so many shared activities; corporate managers must be alert to the need to achieve equity in the rewards the different divisions receive. The goal is always to design a company's structure and control systems to maximize the benefits from pursuing a particular strategy while economizing on the bureaucratic costs of implementing it.

integrating roles
Managers who work in full-time positions established specifically to improve communication between divisions.

IMPLEMENTING STRATEGY ACROSS COUNTRIES

As companies expand into foreign markets and become multinationals, they face the challenge of how best to organize their activities across different nations and regions. Here we will look at some of the main ways in which multinational companies organize themselves in order to implement their global strategy. Before we review the different organizational types that are used, it is important to remind ourselves of the four different strategies that companies use as they begin to market their products and establish production facilities abroad:

1. A *localization strategy* is oriented toward local responsiveness, and a company decentralizes control to subsidiaries and divisions in each country in which it operates to produce and customize products to local markets.
2. In an *international strategy*, product development is centralized at home and other value creation functions are decentralized to national units.
3. A *global standardization strategy* is oriented toward cost reduction, with all the principal value creation functions centralized at the optimal global location.
4. A *transnational strategy* is focused so that it can achieve local responsiveness and cost reduction. Some functions are centralized; others are decentralized at the global location best suited to achieving these objectives.

international division
A division created by companies that expand abroad and group all of their international activities into one division; often characterizes single businesses and diversified companies that use the multidivisional organizational form.

The International Division

When companies initially expand abroad, they often group all of their international activities into an **international division**. This has tended to be the case for single businesses, and for diversified companies that use the multidivisional organizational form. Regardless of the firm's domestic structure, its international division tends to be organized geographically. Figure 13.2 illustrates this for a firm with a domestic organization based on product divisions.

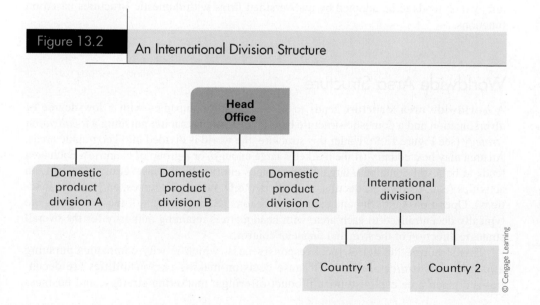

| Figure 13.2 | An International Division Structure |

© Cengage Learning

Many manufacturing enterprises expanded internationally by exporting the product manufactured at home to foreign subsidiaries to sell. Thus, in the firm illustrated in Figure 13.2, the subsidiaries in countries 1 and 2 would sell the products manufactured by divisions A, B, and C. In time, however, it might prove viable to manufacture the product in each country, and so production facilities would be added on a country-by-country basis. For firms with a functional structure at home, this might mean replicating the functional structure in every country in which the firm does business. For firms with a divisional structure, this might mean replicating the divisional structure in every country in which the firm does business.

This structure has been widely used; according to one study, 60% of all firms that have expanded internationally have initially adopted it. A good example of a company that uses this structure is Walmart, which created an international division in 1993 to manage its global expansion (Walmart's international division is profiled in the Running Case). Despite its popularity, an international division structure can give rise to problems. The dual structure it creates contains inherent potential for conflict and coordination problems between domestic and foreign operations. One problem with the structure is that the heads of foreign subsidiaries are not given as much voice in the organization as the heads of domestic functions (in the case of functional firms) or divisions (in the case of divisional firms). Rather, the head of the international division is presumed to be able to represent the interests of all countries to headquarters. This effectively relegates each country's manager to the second tier of the firm's hierarchy, which is inconsistent with a strategy of trying to expand internationally and build a true multinational organization.

Another problem is the implied lack of coordination between domestic operations and foreign operations, which are isolated from each other in separate parts of the structural hierarchy. This can inhibit the worldwide introduction of new products, the transfer of core competencies between domestic and foreign operations, and the consolidation of global production at key locations so as to realize production efficiencies.

As a result of such problems, many companies that continue to expand internationally abandon this structure and adopt one of the worldwide structures discussed next. The two initial choices are a worldwide product divisional structure, which tends to be adopted by diversified firms that have domestic product divisions, and a worldwide area structure, which tends to be adopted by undiversified firms with domestic structures based on functions.

Worldwide Area Structure

worldwide area structure
A structure in which the world is divided into geographic areas; an area may be a country or a group of countries, and each area operates as a self-contained and largely autonomous entity with its own set of value creation activities, with headquarters retaining authority for the overall strategic direction of the firm and financial control; favored by companies with a low degree of diversification and a domestic structure based on functions that are pursuing a localization strategy.

A **worldwide area structure** tends to be favored by companies with a low degree of diversification and a domestic structure based on functions that are pursuing a *localization strategy* (see Figure 13.3). Under this structure, the world is divided into geographic areas. An area may be a country (if the market is large enough) or a group of countries. Each area tends to be a self-contained, largely autonomous entity with its own set of value creation activities (e.g., its own production, marketing, R&D, human resources, and finance functions). Operations authority and strategic decisions relating to each of these activities are typically decentralized to each area, with headquarters retaining authority for the overall strategic direction of the firm and financial control.

This structure facilitates local responsiveness, which is why companies pursuing a *localization strategy* favor it. Because decision-making responsibilities are decentralized, each area can customize product offerings, marketing strategy, and business

FOCUS ON: Wal-Mart

Wal-Mart's International Division

© iStockPhoto.com/caracterdesign

When Walmart started to expand internationally in the early 1990s, it decided to set up an international division to oversee the process. The international division was based in Bentonville, Arkansas, at the company headquarters. Today the division oversees operations in 27 countries that collectively generate more than $109 billion in sales. In terms of reporting structure, the division is divided into three regions—Europe, Asia, and the Americas—with the CEO of each region reporting to the CEO of the international division, who in turn reports to the CEO of Walmart.

Initially, the senior management of the international division exerted tight centralized control over merchandising strategy and operations in different countries. The reasoning was straightforward; Walmart's managers wanted to make sure that international stores copied the format for stores, merchandising, and operations that had served the company so well in the United States. They believed, naively perhaps, that centralized control over merchandising strategy and operations was the way to make sure this was the case.

By the late 1990s, with the international division approaching $20 billion in sales, Walmart's managers concluded this centralized approach was not serving them well. Country managers had to get permission from their superiors in Bentonville before changing strategy and operations, and this was slowing decision making. Centralization also produced information overload at the headquarters, and led to some poor decisions. Walmart found that managers in Bentonville were not necessarily the best ones to decide on store layout in Mexico, merchandising strategy in Argentina, or compensation policy in the United Kingdom. The need to adapt merchandising strategy and operations to local conditions argued strongly for greater decentralization.

The pivotal event that led to a change in policy at Walmart was the company's 1999 acquisition of Britain's ASDA supermarket chain. The ASDA acquisition added a mature and successful $14 billion operation to Walmart's international division. The company realized that it was not appropriate for managers in Bentonville to be making all-important decisions for ASDA. Accordingly, over the next few months, John Menzer, CEO of the international division, reduced the number of staff located in Bentonville who were devoted to international operations by 50%. Country leaders were given greater responsibility, especially in the area of merchandising and operations. In Menzer's own words, "We were at the point where it was time to break away a little bit.... You can't run the world from one place. The countries have to drive the business.... The change has sent a strong message [to country managers] that they no longer have to wait for approval from Bentonville."

Although Walmart has now decentralized decisions within the international division, it is still struggling to find the right formula for managing global procurement. Ideally, the company would like to centralize procurement in Bentonville so that it could use its enormous purchasing power to bargain down the prices it pays suppliers. As a practical matter, however, this has not been easy to attain given that the product mix in Walmart stores has to be tailored to conditions prevailing in the local market. Currently, significant responsibility for procurement remains at the country and regional level. However, Walmart would like to have a global procurement strategy such that it can negotiate on a global basis with key suppliers and can simultaneously introduce new merchandise into its stores around the world.

As merchandising and operating decisions have been decentralized, the international division has increasingly taken on a new role—that of identifying best practices and transferring them between countries. For example, the division has developed a knowledge management system whereby stores in one country, let's say Argentina, can quickly communicate pictures of items, sales data, and ideas on how to market and promote products to stores in another country, such as Japan. The division is also starting to move personnel between stores in different countries as a way of facilitating the flow of best practices across national borders. Finally, the division is at the cutting edge of moving Walmart away from its U.S.-centric mentality and showing the organization that ideas implemented in foreign operations might also be used to improve the efficiency and effectiveness of Walmart's operations at home.

Sources: M. Troy, "Wal-Mart Braces for International Growth with Personnel Moves," *DSN Retailing Today,* February 9, 2004, pp. 5–7; "Division Heads Let Numbers Do the Talking," *DSN Retailing Today,* June 21, 2004, pp. 26–28; and "The Division That Defines the Future," *DSN Retailing Today,* June 2001, pp. 4–7.

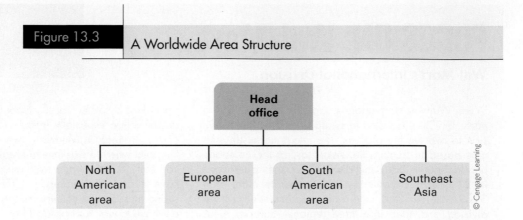

Figure 13.3   A Worldwide Area Structure

strategy to the local conditions. However, this structure encourages fragmentation of the organization into highly autonomous entities. This can make it difficult to transfer distinctive competencies and skills between areas and to realize operating efficiencies. In other words, the structure is consistent with a *localization strategy*, but may make it difficult to realize gains associated with *global standardization*. Companies structured on this basis may encounter significant problems if local responsiveness is less critical than reducing costs or transferring distinctive competencies for establishing a competitive advantage.

Worldwide Product Divisional Structure

worldwide product divisional structure

A structure in which each division is a self-contained, largely autonomous entity with full responsibility for its own value creation activities, with headquarters retaining responsibility for the overall strategic development and financial control of the firm; adopted by firms that are reasonably diversified and originally had domestic structures based on product divisions.

A **worldwide product divisional structure** tends to be adopted by firms that are reasonably diversified and, accordingly, originally had domestic structures based on product divisions. As with the domestic product divisional structure, each division is a self-contained, largely autonomous entity with full responsibility for its own value creation activities. The headquarters retains responsibility for the overall strategic development and financial control of the firm (see Figure 13.4).

Underpinning this organizational form is a belief that the value creation activities of each product division should be coordinated by that division's management, who should be given the responsibility for deciding the geographic location of different activities. Thus, the worldwide product divisional structure is designed to help overcome the coordination problems that arise with the international division and worldwide area structures. This structure provides an organizational context that enhances the consolidation of value creation activities at key locations necessary for realizing location economies and attaining scale economies at the global level (see Chapter 8 for details). It also facilitates the transfer of competencies within a division's worldwide operations and the simultaneous worldwide introduction of new products. As such, the structure is consistent with the implementation of a *global standardization strategy* and an *international strategy*. The main problem with the structure is the limited voice it gives to area or country managers, as they are seen as subservient to product-division managers. The result can be a lack of local responsiveness, which can lead to performance problems.

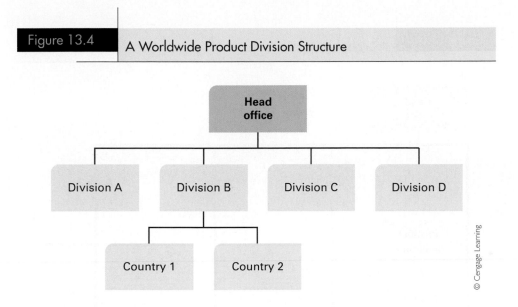

Figure 13.4 A Worldwide Product Division Structure

© Cengage Learning

Global Matrix Structure

Both the worldwide area structure and the worldwide product divisional structure have strengths and weaknesses. The worldwide area structure facilitates *local responsiveness*, but it can inhibit the realization of location and scale economies and the transfer of core competencies between areas. The worldwide product division structure provides a better framework for pursuing location and scale economies and for transferring skills and competencies within product divisions, but it is weak in local responsiveness. Other things being equal, this suggests that a worldwide area structure is more appropriate if the firm is pursuing a *localization strategy*, whereas a worldwide product divisional structure is more appropriate for firms pursuing *global standardization or international strategies*. However, as we saw in Chapter 8, other things are not equal. As Bartlett and Ghoshal have argued, to survive in some industries, companies must adopt a *transnational strategy*. That is, they must focus simultaneously on realizing location and scale economies, on local responsiveness, and on the internal transfer of competencies and skills across national boundaries (worldwide learning).

Some companies have attempted to cope with the conflicting demands of a transnational strategy by using a matrix structure. In the classic **global matrix structure**, horizontal differentiation proceeds along two dimensions: product division and geographic area (see Figure 13.5). The philosophy is that responsibility for operating decisions pertaining to a particular product should be shared by the product division and the various areas of the firm. Thus, the nature of the product offering, the marketing strategy, and the business strategy to be pursued in area 1 for the products produced by division A are determined by conciliation between division A and area 1 management. It is believed that this dual decision-making responsibility should enable the multinational company to simultaneously achieve its particular objectives. In a classic matrix structure, giving product divisions and geographical areas equal status within the organization reinforces the idea of dual responsibility. Individual managers thus belong to two hierarchies (a divisional hierarchy and an area hierarchy) and have two bosses (a divisional boss and an area boss).

global matrix structure
A structure in which horizontal differentiation proceeds along two dimensions: product division and geographic area.

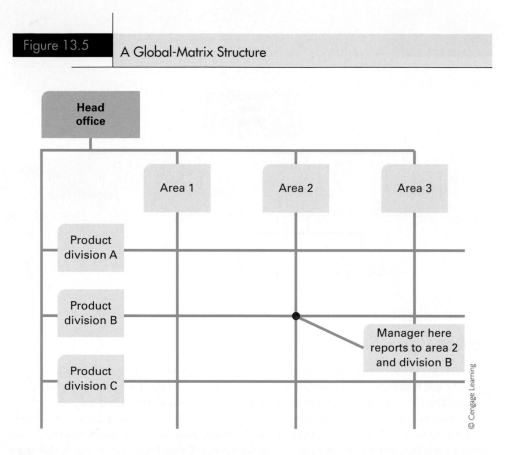

Figure 13.5   A Global-Matrix Structure

The reality of the global matrix structure is that it often does not work as well as the theory predicts. In practice, the matrix often is clumsy and bureaucratic. It can require so many meetings that it is difficult to get any work done. The need to get an area and a product division to reach a decision can slow decision making and produce an inflexible organization unable to respond quickly to market shifts or to innovate. The dual-hierarchy structure can lead to conflict and perpetual power struggles between the areas and the product divisions, catching many managers in the middle. To make matters worse, it can prove difficult to ascertain accountability in this structure. When all critical decisions are the product of negotiation between divisions and areas, one side can always blame the other when things go wrong. As a manager in one global matrix structure, reflecting on a failed product launch, said to the author, "Had we been able to do things our way, instead of having to accommodate those guys from the product division, this would never have happened." (A manager in the product division expressed similar sentiments.) The result of such finger-pointing can be that accountability is compromised, conflict is enhanced, and headquarters loses control over the organization. (See the accompanying Strategy in Action 13.2 for an example of the problems associated with a matrix structure.)

In light of these problems, many companies that pursue a transnational strategy have tried to build "flexible" matrix structures based more on enterprise-wide management knowledge networks, and a shared culture and vision, than on a rigid hierarchical arrangement. Within such companies the informal structure plays a greater role than the formal structure.

13.2 STRATEGY IN ACTION

© iStockPhoto.com/Tom Nulens

Dow Chemical's Matrix Structure

A handful of major players compete head-to-head around the world in the chemical industry. The barriers to the free flow of chemical products between nations largely disappeared in the 1980s. This, along with the commodity nature of most bulk chemicals, has ushered in a prolonged period of intense price competition. In such an environment, the company that wins the competitive race is the one with the lowest costs. Dow Chemical was long among the cost leaders.

For years, Dow's managers insisted that part of the credit should be placed at the feet of its "matrix" organization. Dow's organizational matrix had three interacting elements: functions (e.g., R&D, manufacturing, marketing), businesses (e.g., ethylene, plastics, pharmaceuticals), and geography (e.g., Spain, Germany, Brazil). Managers' job titles incorporated all three elements—for example, plastics marketing manager for Spain—and most managers reported to at least two bosses. The plastics marketing manager in Spain might report to both the head of the worldwide plastics business and the head of the Spanish operations. The intent of the matrix was to make Dow operations responsive to both local market needs and corporate objectives. Thus, the plastics business might be charged with minimizing Dow's global plastics production costs, and the Spanish operation might be charged with determining how best to sell plastics in the Spanish market.

When Dow introduced this structure, the results were less than promising; multiple reporting channels led to confusion and conflict. The large number of bosses made for an unwieldy bureaucracy. The overlapping responsibilities resulted in turf battles and a lack of accountability. Area managers disagreed with managers overseeing business sectors about which plants should be built and where. In short, the structure didn't work. Instead of abandoning the structure, however, Dow decided to see if it could be made more flexible.

Dow's decision to keep its matrix structure was prompted by its move into the pharmaceuticals industry. The company realized that the pharmaceutical business is very different from the bulk chemicals business. In bulk chemicals, the big returns come from achieving economies of scale in production. This dictates establishing large plants in key locations from which regional or global markets can be served. But in pharmaceuticals, regulatory and marketing requirements for drugs vary so much from country to country that local needs are far more important than reducing manufacturing costs through scale economies. A high degree of local responsiveness is essential. Dow realized its pharmaceutical business would never thrive if it were managed by the same priorities as its mainstream chemical operations.

Accordingly, instead of abandoning its matrix, Dow decided to make it more flexible so it could better accommodate the different businesses, each with its own priorities, within a single management system. A small team of senior executives at headquarters helped set the priorities for each type of business. After priorities were identified for each business sector, one of the three elements of the matrix—function, business, or geographic area—was given primary authority in decision making. Which element took the lead varied according to the type of decision and the market or location in which the company was competing. Such flexibility required that all employees understand what was occurring in the rest of the matrix. Although this may seem confusing, for years Dow claimed this flexible system worked well and credited much of its success to the quality of the decisions it facilitated.

By the mid-1990s, however, Dow had refocused its business on the chemicals industry, divesting itself of its pharmaceutical activities, where the company's performance had been unsatisfactory. Reflecting the change in corporate strategy, in 1995 Dow decided to abandon its matrix structure in favor of a more streamlined structure based on global business divisions. The change was also driven by the realization that the matrix structure was just too complex and costly to manage in the intense competitive environment of the 1990s, particularly given the company's renewed focus on its commodity chemicals, where competitive advantage often went to the low-cost producer. As Dow's then CEO put it in a 1999 interview, "We were an organization that was matrixed and depended on teamwork, but there was no one in charge. When things went well, we didn't know whom to reward; and when things went poorly, we didn't know whom to blame. So we created a global divisional structure, and cut out layers of management. There used to be 11 layers of management between me and the lowest-level employees, now there are five." In short, Dow ultimately found that a matrix structure was unsuited to a company that was competing in very cost-competitive global industries, and it had to abandon its matrix to drive down operating costs.

Sources: "Dow Draws Its Matrix Again, and Again, and Again," *The Economist,* August 5, 1989, pp. 55–56; "Dow Goes for Global Structure," *Chemical Marketing Reporter,* December 11, 1995, pp. 4–5; and R. M. Hodgetts, "Dow Chemical CEO William Stavropoulos on Structure and Decision Making," *Academy of Management Executive,* November 1999, pp. 29–35.

ENTRY MODE AND IMPLEMENTATION

As we discuss in Chapter 10, many organizations today are altering their business models and strategies and entering or leaving industries to find better ways to use their resources and capabilities to create value. This section focuses on the implementation issues that arise when companies use internal new venturing, joint ventures, and/or acquisitions to enter new industries.

Internal New Venturing

Chapter 10 discusses how companies enter new industries by using internal new venturing to transfer and leverage their existing competencies to create the set of value-chain activities necessary to compete effectively in a new industry. How can managers create a setting in which employees are encouraged to think about how to apply their functional competencies in new industries? In particular, how can structure, control, and culture be used to increase the success of the new-venturing process?

intrapreneurs
Managers who pioneer and lead new-venture projects or divisions and act as inside or internal entrepreneurs.

Corporate managers must treat the internal new-venturing process as a form of entrepreneurship and the managers who are to pioneer new ventures as **intrapreneurs**, that is, as inside or internal entrepreneurs. This means that organizational structure, control, and culture must be designed to encourage creativity and give new-venture managers real autonomy to develop and champion new products. At the same time, corporate managers want to make sure that their investment in a new market or industry will be profitable because commonalities exist between the new industry and its core industry, so that the potential benefits of transferring or leveraging competencies will be obtained.[13]

3M is an example of a company that carefully selects the right mix of structure, control, and culture to create a work context that facilitates the new-venturing process and promotes product innovation. 3M's goal is that at least 30% of its growth in sales each year should come from new products developed within the past 5 years. To meet this challenging goal, 3M designed a sophisticated control and incentive system that provides its employees with the freedom and motivation to experiment and take risks.

Another approach to internal new venturing is championed by managers who believe that the best way to encourage new-product development is to separate the new-venture unit from the rest of the organization. To provide the new-venture's managers with the autonomy to experiment and take risks, a company establishes a **new-venture division**, that is, a separate and independent division to develop a new product. If a new-venture's managers work within a company's existing structure under the scrutiny of its corporate managers, they will not have the autonomy they need to pursue exciting new-product ideas. In a separate unit in a new location, however, new-venture managers will be able to act as external entrepreneurs as they work to create a new product and develop a business model to bring it to market successfully.

new-venture division
A separate and independent division established to give its managers the autonomy to develop a new product.

The new-venture unit or division uses controls that reinforce its entrepreneurial spirit. Strict output controls are inappropriate because they may promote short-term thinking and inhibit risk taking. Instead, stock options are often used to create a culture for entrepreneurship. Another issue is how to deal with corporate managers. The upfront R&D costs of new venturing are high, and its success is uncertain. After spending millions of dollars, corporate managers often become concerned about how successful the new-venture division will be. As a result, they might attempt to introduce strict output controls, including restrictive budgets, to make the managers of the new venture more accountable—but which at the same time harm its entrepreneurial culture.[14] Corporate managers may believe it is important to use output and behavior controls to limit the autonomy of new-venture managers; otherwise, they might make costly mistakes and waste resources on frivolous ideas.

Recently, there have been some indications that 3M's internal approach may be superior to the use of external new-venture divisions. It appears that many new-venture divisions have failed to bring successful new products to market. And even if they do, the new-venture division eventually begins to operate like other divisions and the entire company's cost structure increases because of the duplication of value-chain activities. Another issue is that scientists lack the formal training necessary to develop successful business models. Just as many medical doctors are earning MBAs today to understand the many strategic issues they must confront when they decide to become hospital managers, so scientists need to be able to think strategically. If strategic thinking is lacking in a new-venture division, the result is failure.

Joint Ventures

Joint ventures are a second method used by large, established companies to maintain momentum and grow their profits by entering new markets and industries.[15] A joint venture occurs when two companies agree to pool resources and capabilities and establish a new business unit to develop a new product and a business model that will allow it bring the new product to market successfully. These companies believe that through collaboration—by sharing their technology or marketing skills to develop an improved product, for example—they will be able to create more value and profit in the new industry than if they decide to "go it alone." Both companies transfer competent managers, who have a proven track record of success, to manage the new subunit that they both own. Sometimes they take an equal "50/50" ownership stake, but sometimes one company insists on having a 51% share or more, giving it the ability to buy out the other party at some point in the future should problems emerge. The way a joint venture is organized and controlled becomes an important issue in this context.

Allocating authority and responsibility is the first major implementation issue upon which companies must decide. Both companies need to be able to monitor the progress of the joint venture so that they can learn from its activities and benefit from their investment in it. Some companies insist on 51% ownership stakes because only then do they have the authority and control over the new ventures. Future problems could arise, such as what to do if the new venture performs poorly, or how to proceed if conflict develops between the parent companies over time—because one partner feels "cheated." For example, what will happen in the future is unknown, and frequently one parent company benefits much more from the product innovations the new company develops; if the other company demands "compensation," the companies come into conflict.[16] As was discussed in Chapter 8, a company also risks losing control of its core technology or competence when it enters into a strategic alliance. One parent company might believe this is taking place and feel threatened by the other. A joint venture can also be dangerous not only because one partner might decide to take the new technology and then "go it alone" in the development process, but also because a company's partner might be acquired by a competitor. For example, Compaq shared its proprietary server technology with a company in the computer storage industry to promote joint product development. Then, it watched helplessly as that company was acquired by Sun Microsystems, which consequently obtained Compaq's technology.

The implementation issues are strongly dependent upon whether the purpose of the joint venture is to share and develop technology, jointly distribute and market products and brands, or share access to customers. Sometimes companies can simply realize the joint benefits from collaboration without having to form a new company. For example, Nestlé and Coca-Cola announced a 10-year joint venture called Beverage Partners Worldwide through which Coca-Cola will distribute and sell Nestlé's Nestea iced tea, Nescafé, and other brands throughout the globe.[17] Similarly, Starbucks' Frappuccino is distributed by Pepsi. In these kinds of joint ventures, both companies can gain from sharing and pooling different competencies so that both realize value that would not otherwise be possible. Issues of ownership and control in these examples are less important.

Once the ownership issue has been settled, one company appoints the CEO, who then becomes responsible for creating a cohesive top-management team out of the managers transferred from the parent companies. The job of the top-management team is to develop a successful business model. These managers then need to choose an organizational structure, such as the functional or product-team structure, that will make the best use of the resources and skills they receive from the parent companies. The need to create an effective organizational design that integrates people and functions is of paramount importance to ensure that the best use is made of limited resources. The need to build a new culture that unites managers who used to work in companies with different cultures is equally as important.

Managing these implementation issues is difficult, expensive, and time consuming, so it is not surprising that when a lot is at stake and the future is uncertain, many companies decide that it would be better to acquire another company and integrate it into their operations. If the risks are lower, however, and it is easier to forecast the future, as in the venture between Coca-Cola and Nestlé, then to reduce bureaucratic costs, a strategic alliance (which does not require the creation of a new subunit) may be capable of managing the transfers of complementary resources and skills between companies.

Mergers and Acquisitions

Mergers and acquisitions are the third method companies use to enter new industries or countries.[18] How to implement structure, control systems, and culture to manage a new acquisition is important because many acquisitions are unsuccessful. One of the primary reasons acquisitions perform poorly is that many companies do not anticipate the difficulties associated with merging or integrating new companies into their existing operations.[19]

At the level of organizational structure, managers of both the acquiring and acquired companies must confront the problem of how to establish new lines of authority and responsibility that will allow them to make the best use of both companies' competencies. The massive merger between HP and Compaq illustrates these issues. Before the merger, the top-management teams of both companies spent thousands of hours analyzing the range of both companies' activities and performing a value-chain analysis to determine how cost and differentiation advantages might be achieved. Based on this analysis, they merged all of the divisions of both companies into four main product groups.

Imagine the problems deciding who would control which group and which operating division, and to whom these divisions would report! To counter fears that infighting would prevent the benefits of the merger from being realized, the CEOs of HP and Compaq were careful to announce in press releases that the process of merging divisions was going smoothly and that battles over responsibilities and control of resources would be resolved. One problem with a mishandled merger is that skilled managers who feel they have been demoted will leave the company, and if many leave, the loss of their skills may prevent the benefits of the merger from being realized. This is why Google, for example, is committed to giving the software experts in the companies it acquires a major role in its current product development efforts, and why it encourages the development of strong cooperative values while working to maintain its innovative organizational culture.

Once managers have established clear lines of authority, they must decide how to coordinate and streamline the operations of both merged companies to reduce costs and leverage and share competencies. For large companies like HP, the answer is to choose the multidivisional structure, but important control issues still must be resolved. In general, the more similar or related are the acquired companies' products and markets, the easier it is to integrate their operations. If the acquiring company has an efficient control system, for example, it can be adapted to the new company to standardize the way its activities are monitored and measured. Alternatively, managers can work hard to combine the best elements of each company's control systems and cultures or introduce a new IT system to integrate their operations.

If managers make unrelated acquisitions, however, and then attempt to interfere with a company's strategy in an industry they know little about, or apply inappropriate structure and controls to manage the new business, then major strategy-implementation problems can arise. For example, if managers try to integrate unrelated companies with related companies, apply the wrong kinds of controls at the divisional level, or interfere in business-level strategy in the search for some elusive benefits, corporate performance can suffer as bureaucratic costs skyrocket. These mistakes explain why related acquisitions are sometimes more successful than unrelated ones.[20]

Even with examples of related diversification, the business processes of each company are frequently different, and their computer systems may be incompatible. The merged company faces the issue of how to use output and behavior controls to standardize business processes and reduce the cost of handing off and transferring resources. After Nestlé installed SAP's enterprise resource planning (ERP) software, for example, managers discovered that each of Nestlé's 150 different U.S. divisions was buying its own supply of vanilla from the same set of suppliers. However, the divisions were not sharing information about these purchases, and vanilla suppliers, dealing with each Nestlé division separately, tried to charge each division as much as they could![21] Each division paid a different price for the same input, and each division used a different code for its independent purchase. Managers at U.S. headquarters did not have the means to discover this discrepancy until SAP's software provided the information.

Finally, even when acquiring a company in a closely related industry, managers must realize that each company has unique norms, values, and culture. Such idiosyncrasies must be understood to effectively integrate the operations of the merged company. Indeed, such idiosyncrasies are likely to be especially important when companies from different countries merge. Over time, top managers can change the culture and alter the internal workings of the company, but this is a difficult implementation task.

In sum, corporate managers' capabilities in organizational design are vital in ensuring the success of a merger or acquisition. Their ability to integrate and connect divisions to leverage competencies ultimately determines how well the newly merged company will perform.[22] The path to merger and acquisition is fraught with danger, which is why some companies claim that internal new venturing is the safest path and that it is best to grow organically from within. Yet with industry boundaries blurring and new global competitors emerging, companies often do not have the time or resources to go it alone. Choosing how to enter a new industry or country is a complex implementation issue that requires thorough strategic analysis.

ETHICAL DILEMMA

© iStockPhoto.com/P_Wei

Unethical and illegal behavior is prevalent in global business. For example, although bribery is considered "acceptable" in some countries, multinational companies are often found guilty of allowing overseas executives to bribe government officials. Many countries, like the United States, have laws and severe penalties to discourage payouts on bribes. In addition to bribery, many U.S. companies have been accused of perpetuating unethical "sweatshop" conditions abroad and turning a blind eye on contract manufacturers' abusive behavior toward workers.

As a manager, if asked to improve your company's structure to prevent unethical and illegal behavior, what kind of control system could you use? In what ways could you develop a global organizational culture that reduces the likelihood of such behavior? What is the best way to decide upon the balance between centralization and decentralization to reduce these problems?

SUMMARY OF CHAPTER

1. A company uses organizational design to combine structure, control systems, and culture in ways that allow it to successfully implement its corporate strategy.

2. As a company grows and diversifies, it adopts a multidivisional structure. Although this structure costs more to operate than a functional or product structure, it economizes on the bureaucratic costs associated with operating through a functional structure and enables a company to handle its value creation activities more effectively.

3. As companies change their corporate strategies over time, they must change their structures because different strategies are managed in different ways. In particular, the move from unrelated diversification to vertical integration to related diversification increases the bureaucratic costs associated with managing a multibusiness strategy. Each requires a different combination of structure, control, and culture to economize on those costs.

4. Companies that start to expand internationally typically do so through an international division.

More mature multinationals can chose between three main structural forms: a worldwide area structure, a worldwide product division structure, and a global matrix structure. Companies pursuing a localization strategy tend to favor a worldwide area structure, whereas those pursuing other strategies favor a worldwide product division structure. Some companies have experimented with global matrix structures, but with mixed results.

5. To encourage internal new venturing, companies must design internal venturing processes that give new-venture managers the autonomy they need to develop new products. Similarly, when establishing a joint venture with another company, managers need to carefully design the new unit's structure and control systems to maximize its chance of success.

6. The profitability of mergers and acquisitions depends on the structure and control systems that companies adopt to manage them and the way a company integrates them into its existing operating structure.

DISCUSSION QUESTIONS

1. When would a company decide to change from a functional to a multidivisional structure?
2. If a related company begins to purchase unrelated businesses, in what ways should it change its structure or control mechanisms to manage the acquisitions?
3. What prompts a company to change from a global standardization strategy to a transnational strategy, and what new implementation problems arise as it does so?
4. How would you design a structure and control system to encourage entrepreneurship in a large, established corporation?
5. What are the problems associated with implementing a strategy of related diversification through acquisitions?

KEY TERMS

Multidivisional structure 441
Self-contained division 442
Corporate headquarters staff 442
Profit center 443
Organizational slack 444
Information distortion 445
Transfer pricing 447
Integrating roles 450
International division 451
Worldwide area structure 452
Worldwide product divisional structure 454
Global matrix structure 455
Intrapreneurs 458
New-venture division 458

PRACTICING STRATEGIC MANAGEMENT

© iStockPhoto.com/Urilux

Small-Group Exercises

Small-Group Exercise: Deciding on an Organizational Structure

This small-group exercise is a continuation of the small-group exercise in Chapter 12. Break into the same groups that you used in Chapter 12, reread the scenario in that chapter, and recall your group's debate about the appropriate organizational structure for your soft drink company. Because it is your intention to compete with Coca-Cola for market share worldwide, your strategy should also have a global dimension, and you must consider the best structure globally as well as domestically. Debate the pros and cons of the types of global structures and decide which is most appropriate and which will best fit your domestic structure.

STRATEGY SIGN ON

© iStockPhoto.com/Ninoslav Dotlic

Article File 13

Find an example of a company pursuing a diversification strategy that has changed its structure and control systems for better management of its strategy. What were the problems with the way it formerly implemented its strategy? What changes did it make to its structure and control systems? What effects does it expect these changes will have on performance?

Strategic Management Project: Module 13

Take the information that you collected in the strategic management project from Chapter 12 on strategy implementation and link it to the multibusiness model. You should collect information to determine if your company competes across industries or countries. If your company *does* operate across countries or industries, answer the following questions:

1. Does your company use a multidivisional structure? Why or why not? What crucial implementation problems must your company tackle to implement its strategy effectively? For example, what kind of integration mechanisms does it employ?
2. What are your company's corporate-level strategies? How do they affect the way it uses organizational structure, control, and culture?
3. What kind of international strategy does your company pursue? How does it control its global activities? What kind of structure does it use? Why?
4. Can you suggest ways of altering the company's structure or control systems to strengthen its business model? Would these changes increase or decrease bureaucratic costs?
5. Does your company have a particular entry mode that it has used to implement its strategy?
6. In what ways does your company use IT to coordinate its value-chain activities?
7. Assess how well your company has implemented its multibusiness (or business) model.

CLOSING CASE

Organizational Change at Unilever

Unilever is one of the world's oldest multinational corporations, with extensive product offerings in the food, detergent, and personal care businesses. It generates annual revenues in excess of $50 billion and sells a wide range of branded products in virtually every country. Detergents, which account for about 25% of corporate revenues, include well-known names such as Omo, which is sold in more than 50 countries. Personal care products, which account for about 15% of sales, include Calvin Klein Cosmetics, Pepsodent toothpaste brands, Faberge hair care products, and Vaseline skin lotions. Food products account for the remaining 60% of sales and include strong offerings in margarine (where Unilever's market share in most countries exceeds 70%), tea, ice cream, frozen foods, and bakery products.

Historically, Unilever was organized on a decentralized basis. Subsidiary companies in each major national market were responsible for the production, marketing, sales, and distribution of products in that market. In Western Europe, for example, the company had 17 subsidiaries in the early 1990s, each focused on a different national market. Each was a profit center and each was held accountable for its own performance. This decentralization was viewed as a source of strength. The structure allowed local managers to match product offerings and marketing strategy to local tastes and preferences and to alter sales and distribution strategies to fit the prevailing retail systems. To drive the localization, Unilever recruited local managers to run local organizations; the U.S. subsidiary (Lever Brothers) was run by Americans, the Indian subsidiary by Indians, and so on.

By the mid-1990s, this decentralized structure was increasingly out of step with a rapidly changing competitive environment. Unilever's global competitors, which include the Swiss firm Nestlé and Procter & Gamble from the United States, had been more successful than Unilever on several fronts—building global brands, reducing cost structure by consolidating manufacturing operations at a few choice locations, and executing simultaneous product launches in several national markets. Unilever's decentralized structure worked against efforts to build global or regional brands. It also meant lots of duplication, particularly in manufacturing; a lack of scale economies; and a high-cost structure. Unilever also found that it was falling behind rivals in the race to bring new products to market. In Europe, for example, while Nestlé and Procter & Gamble moved toward pan-European product launches, it could take Unilever 4 to 5 years to "persuade" its 17 European operations to adopt a new product.

Unilever began to change all this in the late 1990s. It introduced a new structure based on regional business groups. Within each business group were a number of divisions, each focusing on a specific category of products. Thus, in the European Business Group, a division focused on detergents, another on ice cream and frozen foods, and so on. These groups and divisions coordinated the activities of national subsidiaries within their regions to drive down operating costs and speed up the process of developing and introducing new products.

For example, Lever Europe was established to consolidate the company's detergent operations. The 17 European companies reported directly to Lever Europe. Using its newfound organizational clout, Lever Europe consolidated the production of detergents in Europe in a few key locations to reduce costs and speed up new-product introduction. Implicit in this new approach was a bargain: the 17 companies relinquished autonomy in their traditional markets in exchange for opportunities to help develop and execute a unified pan-European strategy. The number of European plants manufacturing soap was cut from 10 to 2, and some new products were manufactured at only one site. Product sizing and packaging were harmonized to cut purchasing costs and to accommodate unified pan-European advertising. By taking these steps, Unilever estimated it saved as much as $400 million a year in its European detergent operations.

By the early 2000, however, Unilever found that it was still lagging its competitors, so the company embarked upon another reorganization. This time the goal was to cut the number of brands that Unilever sold from 1,600 to just 400 that could be marketed on a regional or global scale. To support this new focus, the company reduced the number of manufacturing plants from 380 to about 280. The company also established a new organization based on just two global product divisions—a food division and a home and personal care division. Within each division are a number of regional business groups that focus on developing, manufacturing, and marketing either food or personal care products within a given region. For example, Unilever Bestfoods Europe, which is headquartered in Rotterdam, focuses on selling food brands across Western and Eastern Europe, while Unilever Home and Personal Care Europe does the same for home and personal care products. A similar structure can be found in North America, Latin America, and Asia. Thus, Bestfoods North America, headquartered in New Jersey, has a similar charter to Bestfoods Europe, but in keeping with differences in local history, many of the food brands marketed by Unilever in North America are different from those marketed in Europe.

Sources: H. Connon, "Unilever's Got the Nineties Licked," *The Guardian,* May 24, 1998, p. 5; "Unilever: A Networked Organization," *Harvard Business Review,* November–December 1996, p. 138; C. Christensen and J. Zobel, "Unilever's Butter Beater: Innovation for Global Diversity," Harvard Business School Case No. 9-698-017, March 1998; M. Mayer, A. Smith, and R. Whittington, "Restructuring Roulette," *Financial Times,* November 8, 2002, p. 8; and www.unilever.com.

CASE DISCUSSION QUESTIONS

1. Why did Unilever's decentralized structure make sense in the 1960s and 1970s? Why did this structure start to create problems for the company in the 1980s?
2. What was Unilever trying to do when it introduced a new structure based on business groups in the mid-1990s? Why do you think that this structure failed to cure Unilever's ills?
3. In the 2000s, Unilever switched to a structure based on global product divisions. What do you think is the underlying logic for this shift? Does the structure make sense given the nature of competition in the detergents and food business?

NOTES

[1] A. D. Chandler, *Strategy and Structure* (Cambridge: MIT Press, 1962); O. E. Williamson, *Markets and Hierarchies* (New York: Free Press, 1975); and L. Wrigley, "Divisional Autonomy and Diversification" (Ph.D. Diss., Harvard Business School, 1970).

[2] R. P. Rumelt, *Strategy, Structure, and Economic Performance* (Boston: Division of Research, Harvard Business School, 1974); B. R. Scott, *Stages of Corporate Development* (Cambridge: Intercollegiate Clearing House, Harvard Business School, 1971); and Williamson, *Markets and Hierarchies*.

[3] A. P. Sloan, *My Years at General Motors* (Garden City: Doubleday, 1946); A. Taylor III, "Can GM Remodel Itself?" *Fortune*, January 13, 1992, pp. 26–34; W. Hampton and J. Norman, "General Motors: What Went Wrong?" *Business Week*, March 16, 1987, pp. 102–110; and www.gm.com (2002). The quotations are on pages 46 and 50 in Sloan, *My Years at General Motors*.

[4] The discussion draws on each of the sources cited in endnotes 18–25 and on G. R. Jones and C. W. L. Hill, "Transaction Cost Analysis of Strategy-Structure Choice," *Strategic Management Journal* 9 (1988): 159–172.

[5] H. O. Armour and D. J. Teece, "Organizational Structure and Economic Performance: A Test of the Multidivisional Hypothesis," *Bell Journal of Economics* 9 (1978): 106–122.

[6] Sloan, *My Years at General Motors*.

[7] Jones and Hill, "Transaction Cost Analysis of Strategy-Structure Choice."

[8] Ibid.

[9] R. A. D'Aveni and D. J. Ravenscraft, "Economies of Integration Versus Bureaucracy Costs: Does Vertical Integration Improve Performance?" *Academy of Management Journal* 5 (1994): 1167–1206.

[10] P. R. Lawrence and J. Lorsch, *Organization and Environment* (Boston: Division of Research, Harvard Business School, 1967); J. R. Galbraith, *Designing Complex Organizations* (Reading: Addison-Wesley, 1973); and M. Porter, *Competitive Advantage: Creating and Sustaining Superior Performance* (New York: Free Press, 1985).

[11] P. R. Nayyar, "Performance Effects of Information Asymmetry and Economies of Scope in Diversified Service Firm," *Academy of Management Journal* 36 (1993): 28–57.

[12] L. R. Gomez-Mejia, "Structure and Process of Diversification, Compensation Strategy, and Performance," *Strategic Management Journal* 13 (1992): 381–397.

[13] R. A. Burgelman, "Managing the New Venture Division: Research Findings and the Implications for Strategic Management," *Strategic Management Journal* 6 (1985): 39–54.

[14]Burgelman, "Managing the New Venture Division."

[15]R. A. Burgelman, "Corporate Entrepreneurship and Strategic Management: Insights from a Process Study," *Management Science* 29 (1983): 1349–1364.

[16]G. R. Jones, "Towards a Positive Interpretation of Transaction Cost Theory: The Central Role of Entrepreneurship and Trust," in M. Hitt, R. E. Freeman, and J. S. Harrison (eds.), *Handbook of Strategic Management* (London: Blackwell, 2001), pp. 208–228.

[17]www.nestle.com and www.cocacola.com.

[18]M. S. Salter and W. A. Weinhold, *Diversification Through Acquisition* (New York: Free Press, 1979).

[19]F. T. Paine and D. J. Power, "Merger Strategy: An Examination of Drucker's Five Rules for Successful Acquisitions," *Strategic Management Journal* 5 (1984): 99–110.

[20]H. Singh and C. A. Montgomery, "Corporate Acquisitions and Economic Performance" (unpublished manuscript, 1984).

[21]B. Worthen, "Nestlé's ERP Odyssey," *CIO*, 2002, 1–5.

[22]G. D. Bruton, B. M. Oviatt, and M. A. White, "Performance of Acquisitions of Distressed Firms," *Academy of Management Journal* 4 (1994): 972–989.

Cases

Introduction

Analyzing a Case Study and Writing a Case Study Analysis

WHAT IS CASE STUDY ANALYSIS?

Case study analysis is an integral part of a course in strategic management. The purpose of a case study is to provide students with experience of the strategic management problems that actual organizations face. A case study presents an account of what happened to a business or industry over a number of years. It chronicles the events that managers had to deal with, such as changes in the competitive environment, and charts the managers' response, which usually involved changing the business- or corporate-level strategy. The cases in this book cover a wide range of issues and problems that managers have had to confront. Some cases are about finding the right business-level strategy to compete in changing conditions. Some are about companies that grew by acquisition, with little concern for the rationale behind their growth, and how growth by acquisition affected their future profitability. Each case is different because each organization is different. The underlying thread in all cases, however, is the use of strategic management techniques to solve business problems.

Cases prove valuable in a strategic management course for several reasons. First, cases provide you, the student, with experience of organizational problems that you probably have not had the opportunity to experience firsthand. In a relatively short period of time, you will have the chance to appreciate and analyze the problems faced by many different companies and to understand how managers tried to deal with them.

Second, cases illustrate the theory and content of strategic management. The meaning and implications of this information are made clearer when they are applied to case studies. The theory and concepts help reveal what is going on in the companies studied and allow you to evaluate the solutions that specific companies adopted to deal with their problems. Consequently, when you analyze cases, you will be like a detective who, with a set of conceptual tools, probes what happened and what or who was responsible and then marshals the evidence that provides the solution. Top managers enjoy the thrill of testing their problem-solving abilities in the real world. It is important to remember that no one knows what the right answer is. All that managers can do is to make the best guess. In fact, managers say repeatedly that they are happy if they are right only half the time in solving strategic problems. Strategic management is an uncertain game, and using cases to see how theory can be put into practice is one way of improving your skills of diagnostic investigation.

Third, case studies provide you with the opportunity to participate in class and to gain experience in presenting your ideas to others. Instructors may sometimes call on students as a group to identify what is going on in a case, and through classroom discussion the issues in and solutions to the case problem will reveal themselves. In such a situation, you will have to organize your views and conclusions so that you can present them to the class. Your classmates may have analyzed the issues differently from you, and they will want you to argue your points before they will accept your conclusions, so be prepared for debate. This mode of discussion is an example of the dialectical approach to decision making. This is how decisions are made in the actual business world.

Instructors also may assign an individual, but more commonly a group, to analyze the case before the whole class. The individual or group probably will be responsible for a 30 to 40 minute presentation of the case to the class. That presentation must cover the issues posed, the problems facing the company, and a series of recommendations for resolving the problems. The discussion then will be thrown open to the class, and you will have to defend your ideas. Through such discussions and presentations, you will experience how to convey your ideas effectively to others. Remember that a great deal of managers' time is spent in these kinds of situations: presenting their ideas and engaging in discussion with other managers who have their own views about what is going on. Thus, you will experience in the classroom the actual process of strategic management, and this will serve you well in your future career.

If you work in groups to analyze case studies, you also will learn about the group process involved in working as a team. When people work in groups, it is often difficult to schedule time and allocate responsibility for the case analysis. There are always group members who shirk their responsibilities and group members who are so sure of their own ideas that they try to dominate the group's analysis. Most of the strategic management takes place in groups, however, and it is best if you learn about these problems now.

ANALYZING A CASE STUDY

The purpose of the case study is to let you apply the concepts of strategic management when you analyze the issues facing a specific company. To analyze a case study, therefore, you must examine closely the issues confronting the company. Most often you will need to read the case several times—once to grasp the overall picture of what is happening to the company and then several times more to discover and grasp the specific problems.

Generally, detailed analysis of a case study should include eight areas:

1. The history, development, and growth of the company over time
2. The identification of the company's internal strengths and weaknesses
3. The nature of the external environment surrounding the company
4. A SWOT analysis
5. The kind of corporate-level strategy that the company is pursuing
6. The nature of the company's business-level strategy
7. The company's structure and control systems and how they match its strategy
8. Recommendations

To analyze a case, you need to apply the concepts taught in this course to each of these areas. To help you further, we next offer a summary of the steps you can take to analyze the case material for each of the eight points we just noted:

1. *Analyze the company's history, development, and growth.* A convenient way to investigate how a company's past strategy and structure affect it in the present is to chart the critical incidents in its history—that is, the events that were the most unusual or the most essential for its development into the company it is today. Some

of the events have to do with its founding, its initial products, how it makes new-product market decisions, and how it developed and chose functional competencies to pursue. Its entry into new businesses and shifts in its main lines of business are also important milestones to consider.

2. *Identify the company's internal strengths and weaknesses.* Once the historical profile is completed, you can begin the SWOT analysis. Use all the incidents you have charted to develop an account of the company's strengths and weaknesses as they have emerged historically. Examine each of the value creation functions of the company, and identify the functions in which the company is currently strong and currently weak. Some companies might be weak in marketing; some might be strong in research and development. Make lists of these strengths and weaknesses. The SWOT Checklist (Table 1) gives examples of what might go in these lists.

Table 1   A SWOT Checklist

Potential Internal Strengths	Potential Internal Weaknesses
Many product lines?	Obsolete, narrow product lines?
Broad market coverage?	Rising manufacturing costs?
Manufacturing competence?	Decline in R&D innovations?
Good marketing skills?	Poor marketing plan?
Good materials management systems?	Poor material management systems?
R&D skills and leadership?	Loss of customer good will?
Information system competencies?	Inadequate human resources?
Human resource competencies?	Inadequate information systems?
Brand name reputation?	Loss of brand name capital?
Portfolio management skills?	Growth without direction?
Cost of differentiation advantage?	Bad portfolio management?
New-venture management expertise?	Loss of corporate direction?
Appropriate management style?	Infighting among divisions?
Appropriate organizational structure?	Loss of corporate control?
Appropriate control systems?	Inappropriate organizational
Ability to manage strategic change?	structure and control systems?
Well-developed corporate strategy?	High conflict and politics?
Good financial management?	Poor financial management?
Others?	Others?

Table 1 [*continued*]

Potential Environmental Opportunities	Potential Environment Threats
Expand core business(es)?	Attacks on core business(es)?
Exploit new market segments?	Increases in domestic competition?
Widen product range?	Increase in foreign competition?
Extend cost or differentiation advantage?	Change in consumer tastes?
Diversify into new growth businesses?	Fall in barriers to entry?
Expand into foreign markets?	Rise in new or substitute products?
Apply R&D skills in new areas?	Increase in industry rivalry?
Enter new related businesses?	New forms of industry competition?
Vertically integrate forward?	Potential for takeover?
Vertically integrate backward?	Existence of corporate raiders?
Enlarge corporate portfolio?	Increase in regional competition?
Overcome barriers to entry?	Changes in demographic factors?
Reduce rivalry among competitors?	Changes in economic factors?
Make profitable new acquisitions?	Downturn in economy?
Apply brand name capital in new areas?	Rising labor costs?
Seek fast market growth?	Slower market growth?
Others?	Others?

© Cengage Learning 2013

3. *Analyze the external environment.* To identify environmental opportunities and threats, apply all the concepts on industry and macroenvironments to analyze the environment the company is confronting. Of particular importance at the industry level are the Competitive Forces Model, adapted from Porter's Five Forces Model and the stage of the life-cycle model. Which factors in the macroenvironment will appear salient depends on the specific company being analyzed. Use each factor in turn (for instance, demographic factors) to see whether it is relevant for the company in question.

   Having done this analysis, you will have generated both an analysis of the company's environment and a list of opportunities and threats. The SWOT Checklist table also lists some common environmental opportunities and threats that you may look for, but the list you generate will be specific to your company.

4. *Evaluate the SWOT analysis.* Having identified the company's external opportunities and threats as well as its internal strengths and weaknesses, consider what your findings mean. You need to balance strengths and weaknesses against opportunities and threats. Is the company in an overall strong competitive position? Can it continue to pursue its current business- or corporate-level strategy profitably? What can the company do to turn weaknesses into strengths and threats into opportunities? Can it develop new functional, business, or corporate strategies to accomplish this change? *Never merely generate the SWOT analysis and then put it aside.* Because it provides

a succinct summary of the company's condition, a good SWOT analysis is the key to all the analyses that follow.

5. *Analyze corporate-level strategy.* To analyze corporate-level strategy, you first need to define the company's mission and goals. Sometimes the mission and goals are stated explicitly in the case; at other times, you will have to infer them from available information. The information you need to collect to find out the company's corporate strategy includes such factors as its lines of business and the nature of its subsidiaries and acquisitions. It is important to analyze the relationship among the company's businesses. Do they trade or exchange resources? Are there gains to be achieved from synergy? Alternatively, is the company just running a portfolio of investments? This analysis should enable you to define the corporate strategy that the company is pursuing (for example, related or unrelated diversification, or a combination of both) and to conclude whether the company operates in just one core business. Then, using your SWOT analysis, debate the merits of this strategy. Is it appropriate given the environment the company is in? Could a change in corporate strategy provide the company with new opportunities or transform a weakness into a strength? For example, should the company diversify from its core business into new businesses?

    Other issues should be considered as well. How and why has the company's strategy changed over time? What is the claimed rationale for any changes? Often, it is a good idea to analyze the company's businesses or products to assess its situation and identify which divisions contribute the most to or detract from its competitive advantage. It is also useful to explore how the company has built its portfolio over time. Did it acquire new businesses, or did it internally venture its own? All of these factors provide clues about the company and indicate ways of improving its future performance.

6. *Analyze business-level strategy.* Once you know the company's corporate-level strategy and have done the SWOT analysis, the next step is to identify the company's business-level strategy. If the company is a single-business company, its business-level strategy is identical to its corporate-level strategy. If the company is in many businesses, each business will have its own business-level strategy. You will need to identify the company's generic competitive strategy—differentiation, low-cost, or focus—and its investment strategy, given its relative competitive position and the stage of the life cycle. The company also may market different products using different business-level strategies. For example, it may offer a low-cost product range and a line of differentiated products. Be sure to give a full account of a company's business-level strategy to show how it competes.

    Identifying the functional strategies that a company pursues to build competitive advantage through superior efficiency, quality, innovation, and customer responsiveness and to achieve its business-level strategy is very important. The SWOT analysis will have provided you with information on the company's functional competencies. You should investigate its production, marketing, or research and development strategy further to gain a picture of where the company is going. For example, pursuing a low-cost or a differentiation strategy successfully requires very different sets of competencies. Has the company developed the right ones? If it has, how can it exploit them further? Can it pursue both a low-cost and a differentiation strategy simultaneously?

    The SWOT analysis is especially important at this point if the industry analysis, particularly Porter's model, has revealed threats to the company from the environment. Can the company deal with these threats? How should it change its business-level strategy to counter them? To evaluate the potential of a company's business-level strategy, you must first perform a thorough SWOT analysis that captures the essence of its problems.

Once you complete this analysis, you will have a full picture of the way the company is operating and be in a position to evaluate the potential of its strategy. Thus, you will be able to make recommendations concerning the pattern of its future actions. However, first you need to consider strategy implementation, or the way the company tries to achieve its strategy.

7. *Analyze structure and control systems.* The aim of this analysis is to identify what structure and control systems the company is using to implement its strategy and to evaluate whether that structure is the appropriate one for the company. Different corporate and business strategies require different structures. You need to determine the *degree of fit between the company's strategy and structure.* For example, does the company have the right level of vertical differentiation (e.g., does it have the appropriate number of levels in the hierarchy or decentralized control?) or horizontal differentiation (does it use a functional structure when it should be using a product structure?)? Similarly, is the company using the right integration or control systems to manage its operations? Are managers being appropriately rewarded? Are the right rewards in place for encouraging cooperation among divisions? These are all issues to consider.

In some cases, there will be little information on these issues, whereas in others there will be a lot. In analyzing each case, you should gear the analysis toward its most salient issues. For example, organizational conflict, power, and politics will be important issues for some companies. Try to analyze why problems in these areas are occurring. Do they occur because of bad strategy formulation or because of bad strategy implementation?

Organizational change is an issue in many cases because the companies are attempting to alter their strategies or structures to solve strategic problems. Thus, as part of the analysis, you might suggest an action plan that the company in question could use to achieve its goals. For example, you might list in a logical sequence the steps the company would need to follow to alter its business-level strategy from differentiation to focus.

8. *Make recommendations.* The quality of your recommendations is a direct result of the thoroughness with which you prepared the case analysis. Recommendations are directed at solving whatever strategic problem the company is facing and increasing its future profitability. Your recommendations should be in line with your analysis; that is, they should follow logically from the previous discussion. For example, your recommendation generally will center on the specific ways of changing functional, business, and corporate strategies and organizational structure and control to improve business performance. The set of recommendations will be specific to each case, and so it is difficult to discuss these recommendations here. Such recommendations might include an increase in spending on specific research and development projects, the divesting of certain businesses, a change from a strategy of unrelated to related diversification, an increase in the level of integration among divisions by using task forces and teams, or a move to a different kind of structure to implement a new business-level strategy. Make sure your recommendations are mutually consistent and written in the form of an action plan. The plan might contain a timetable that sequences the actions for changing the company's strategy and a description of how changes at the corporate level will necessitate changes at the business level and subsequently at the functional level.

After following all these stages, you will have performed a thorough analysis of the case and will be in a position to join in class discussion or present your ideas to the class, depending on the format used by your professor. Remember that you must tailor your analysis to suit the specific issue discussed in your case. In some cases, you might completely omit one of the steps in the analysis because it is not relevant to the situation you are considering. You must be sensitive to the needs of the case and not apply the framework we have discussed in this section blindly. The framework is meant only as a guide, not as an outline.

WRITING A CASE STUDY ANALYSIS

Often, as part of your course requirements, you will need to present a written case analysis. This may be an individual or a group report. Whatever the situation, there are certain guidelines to follow in writing a case analysis that will improve the evaluation your work will receive from your instructor. Before we discuss these guidelines and before you use them, make sure that they do not conflict with any directions your instructor has given you.

The structure of your written report is critical. Generally, if you follow the steps for analysis discussed in the previous section, *you already will have a good structure for your written discussion*. All reports begin with an *introduction* to the case. In it, outline briefly what the company does, how it developed historically, what problems it is experiencing, and how you are going to approach the issues in the case write-up. Do this sequentially by writing, for example, "First, we discuss the environment of Company. . . . Third, we discuss Company X's business-level strategy. . . . Last, we provide recommendations for turning around Company X's business."

In the second part of the case write-up, the *strategic analysis* section, do the SWOT analysis, analyze and discuss the nature and problems of the company's business-level and corporate strategies, and then analyze its structure and control systems. Make sure you use plenty of headings and subheadings to structure your analysis. For example, have separate sections on any important conceptual tool you use. Thus, you might have a section on the Competitive Forces Model as part of your analysis of the environment. You might offer a separate section on portfolio techniques when analyzing a company's corporate strategy. Tailor the sections and subsections to the specific issues of importance in the case.

In the third part of the case write-up, present your *solutions and recommendations*. Be comprehensive, and make sure they are in line with the previous analysis so that the recommendations fit together and move logically from one to the next. The recommendations section is very revealing because your instructor will have a good idea of how much work you put into the case from the quality of your recommendations.

Following this framework will provide a good structure for most written reports, though it must be shaped to fit the individual case being considered. Some cases are about excellent companies experiencing no problems. In such instances, it is hard to write recommendations. Instead, you can focus on analyzing why the company is doing so well, using that analysis to structure the discussion. Following are some minor suggestions that can help make a good analysis even better:

1. Do not repeat in summary form large pieces of factual information from the case. The instructor has read the case and knows what is going on. Rather, use the information in the case to illustrate your statements, defend your arguments, or make salient points. Beyond the brief introduction to the company, you must avoid being *descriptive*; instead, you must be *analytical*.

2. Make sure the sections and subsections of your discussion flow logically and smoothly from one to the next. That is, try to build on what has gone before so that the analysis of the case study moves toward a climax. This is particularly important for group analysis, because there is a tendency for people in a group to split up the work and say, "I'll do the beginning, you take the middle, and I'll do the end." The result is a choppy, stilted analysis; the parts do not flow from one to the next, and it is obvious to the instructor that no real group work has been done.

3. Avoid grammatical and spelling errors. They make your work look sloppy.

4. In some instances, cases dealing with well-known companies end in 1998 or 1999 because no later information was available when the case was written. If possible, do a search for more information on what has happened to the company in subsequent years.

   Many libraries now have comprehensive web-based electronic data search facilities that offer such sources as *ABI/Inform, The Wall Street Journal Index,* the *F&S Index,* and the *Nexis-Lexis* databases. These enable you to identify any article that has been written in the business press on the company of your choice within the past few years. A number of nonelectronic data sources are also useful. For example, *F&S Predicasts* publishes an annual list of articles relating to major companies that appeared in the national and international business press. *S&P Industry Surveys* is a great source for basic industry data, and *Value Line Ratings and Reports* can contain good summaries of a firm's financial position and future prospects. You will also want to collect full financial information on the company. Again, this can be accessed from Web-based electronic databases such as the *Edgar* database, which archives all forms that publicly quoted companies have to file with the Securities and Exchange Commission (SEC; e.g., 10-K filings can be accessed from the SEC's *Edgar* database). Most SEC forms for public companies can now be accessed from Internet-based financial sites, such as Yahoo's finance site (http://finance.yahoo.com/).

5. Sometimes instructors hand out questions for each case to help you in your analysis. Use these as a guide for writing the case analysis. They often illuminate the important issues that have to be covered in the discussion.

If you follow the guidelines in this section, you should be able to write a thorough and effective evaluation.

THE ROLE OF FINANCIAL ANALYSIS IN CASE STUDY ANALYSIS

An important aspect of analyzing a case study and writing a case study analysis is the role and use of financial information. A careful analysis of the company's financial condition immensely improves a case write-up. After all, financial data represent the concrete results of the company's strategy and structure. Although analyzing financial statements can be quite complex, a general idea of a company's financial position can be determined through the use of ratio analysis. Financial performance ratios can be calculated from the balance sheet and income statement. These ratios can be classified into five subgroups: profit ratios, liquidity ratios, activity ratios, leverage ratios, and shareholder-return ratios. These ratios should be compared with the industry average or the company's prior years of performance. It should be noted, however, that deviation from the average is not necessarily bad; it simply warrants further investigation. For example, young companies will have purchased assets at a different price and will likely have a different capital structure than older companies do. In addition to ratio analysis, a company's cash flow position is of critical importance and should be assessed. Cash flow shows how much actual cash a company possesses.

Profit Ratios

Profit ratios measure the efficiency with which the company uses its resources. The more efficient the company, the greater is its profitability. It is useful to compare a company's profitability against that of its major competitors in its industry to determine whether the company is operating more or less efficiently than its rivals. In addition, the change in a company's profit ratios over time tells whether its performance is improving or declining.

A number of different profit ratios can be used, and each of them measures a different aspect of a company's performance. Here, we look at the most commonly used profit ratios.

Return on Invested Capital (ROIC).   This ratio measures the profit earned on the capital invested in the company. It is defined as follows:

$$\text{Return on invested capital (ROIC)} = \frac{\text{Net profit}}{\text{Invested capital}}$$

Net profit is calculated by subtracting the total costs of operating the company away from its total revenues (total revenues − total costs). Total costs are the (1) costs of goods sold, (2) sales, general, and administrative expenses, (3) R&D expenses, and (4) other expenses. Net profit can be calculated before or after taxes, although many financial analysts prefer the before-tax figure. Invested capital is the amount that is invested in the operations of a company—that is, in property, plant, equipment, inventories, and other assets. Invested capital comes from two main sources: interest-bearing debt and shareholders' equity. Interest-bearing debt is money the company borrows from banks and from those who purchase its bonds. Shareholders' equity is the money raised from selling shares to the public, *plus* earnings that have been retained by the company in prior years and are available to fund current investments. ROIC measures the effectiveness with which a company is using the capital funds that it has available for investment. As such, it is recognized to be an excellent measure of the value a company is creating.1 Remember that a company's ROIC can be decomposed into its constituent parts.

Return on Total Assets (ROA).   This ratio measures the profit earned on the employment of assets. It is defined as follows:

$$\text{Return on total assests} = \frac{\text{Net profit}}{\text{Total assets}}$$

Return on Stockholders' Equity (ROE).   This ratio measures the percentage of profit earned on common stockholders' investment in the company. It is defined as follows:

$$\text{Return on stockholders equity} = \frac{\text{Net profit}}{\text{Stockholders equity}}$$

If a company has no debt, this will be the same as ROIC.

Liquidity Ratios

A company's liquidity is a measure of its ability to meet short-term obligations. An asset is deemed liquid if it can be readily converted into cash. Liquid assets are current assets such as cash, marketable securities, accounts receivable, and so on. Two liquidity ratios are commonly used.

Current Ratio. The current ratio measures the extent to which the claims of short-term creditors are covered by assets that can be quickly converted into cash. Most companies should have a ratio of at least 1, because failure to meet these commitments can lead to bankruptcy. The ratio is defined as follows:

$$\text{Current ratio} = \frac{\text{Current assets}}{\text{Current liabilities}}$$

Quick Ratio. The quick ratio measures a company's ability to pay off the claims of short-term creditors without relying on selling its inventories. This is a valuable measure since in practice the sale of inventories is often difficult. It is defined as follows:

$$\text{Quick ratio} = \frac{\text{Current assets} - \text{inventory}}{\text{Current liabilities}}$$

Activity Ratios

Activity ratios indicate how effectively a company is managing its assets. Two ratios are particularly useful.

Inventory Turnover. This measures the number of times inventory is turned over. It is useful in determining whether a firm is carrying excess stock in inventory. It is defined as follows:

$$\text{Inventory turnover} = \frac{\text{Cost of goods sold}}{\text{Inventory}}$$

Cost of goods sold is a better measure of turnover than sales because it is the cost of the inventory items. Inventory is taken at the balance sheet date. Some companies choose to compute an average inventory, beginning inventory, and ending inventory, but for simplicity, use the inventory at the balance sheet date.

Days Sales Outstanding (DSO) or Average Collection Period. This ratio is the average time a company has to wait to receive its cash after making a sale. It measures how effective the company's credit, billing, and collection procedures are. It is defined as follows:

$$\text{DSO} = \frac{\text{Accounts receivable}}{\text{Total sales} / 360}$$

Accounts receivable is divided by average daily sales. The use of 360 is the standard number of days for most financial analysis.

Leverage Ratios

A company is said to be highly leveraged if it uses more debt than equity, including stock and retained earnings. The balance between debt and equity is called the *capital structure*. The optimal capital structure is determined by the individual company. Debt has a lower cost because creditors take less risk; they know they will get their interest and principal. However, debt can be risky to the firm because if enough profit is not made to cover the interest and principal payments, bankruptcy can result. Three leverage ratios are commonly used.

Debt-to-Assets Ratio.   The debt-to-assets ratio is the most direct measure of the extent to which borrowed funds have been used to finance a company's investments. It is defined as follows:

$$\text{Debt-to-assets ratio} = \frac{\text{Total debt}}{\text{Total assets}}$$

Total debt is the sum of a company's current liabilities and its long-term debt, and total assets are the sum of fixed assets and current assets.

Debt-to-Equity Ratio.   The debt-to-equity ratio indicates the balance between debt and equity in a company's capital structure. This is perhaps the most widely used measure of a company's leverage. It is defined as follows:

$$\text{Debt-to-equity ratio} = \frac{\text{Total debt}}{\text{Total equity}}$$

Times-Covered Ratio.   The times-covered ratio measures the extent to which a company's gross profit covers its annual interest payments. If this ratio declines to less than 1, the company is unable to meet its interest costs and is technically insolvent. The ratio is defined as follows:

$$\text{Times-covered ratio} = \frac{\text{Profit before interest and tax}}{\text{Total interest charges}}$$

Shareholder-Return Ratios

Shareholder-return ratios measure the return that shareholders earn from holding stock in the company. Given the goal of maximizing stockholders' wealth, providing shareholders with an adequate rate of return is a primary objective of most companies. As with profit ratios, it can be helpful to compare a company's shareholder returns against those of similar companies as a yardstick for determining how well the company is satisfying the demands of this particularly important group of organizational constituents. Four ratios are commonly used.

Total Shareholder Returns.   Total shareholder returns measure the returns earned by time $t + 1$ on an investment in a company's stock made at time t. (Time t is the time at which the initial investment is made.) Total shareholder returns include both dividend payments and appreciation in the value of the stock (adjusted for stock splits) and are defined as follows:

$$\text{Total shareholder returns} = \frac{\text{Stock price } (t+1) - \text{stock price } (t) + \text{sum of annual dividends per share}}{\text{Stock price } (t)}$$

If a shareholder invests $2 at time t and at time $t + 1$ the share is worth $3, while the sum of annual dividends for the period t to $t + 1$ has amounted to $0.20, total shareholder returns are equal to $(3 - 2 + 0.2)/2 = 0.6$, which is a 60% return on an initial investment of $2 made at time t.

Price-Earnings Ratio. The price-earnings ratio measures the amount investors are willing to pay per dollar of profit. It is defined as follows:

$$\text{Price-earnings ratio} = \frac{\text{Market price per share}}{\text{Earnings per share}}$$

Market-to-Book Value. Market-to-book value measures a company's expected future growth prospects. It is defined as follows:

$$\text{Market-to-book value} = \frac{\text{Market price per share}}{\text{Earnings per share}}$$

Dividend Yield. The dividend yield measures the return to shareholders received in the form of dividends. It is defined as follows:

$$\text{Dividend} = \frac{\text{Dividend per share}}{\text{Market price per share}}$$

Market price per share can be calculated for the first of the year, in which case the dividend yield refers to the return on an investment made at the beginning of the year. Alternatively, the average share price over the year may be used. A company must decide how much of its profits to pay to stockholders and how much to reinvest in the company. Companies with strong growth prospects should have a lower dividend payout ratio than mature companies. The rationale is that shareholders can invest the money elsewhere if the company is not growing. The optimal ratio depends on the individual firm, but the key decider is whether the company can produce better returns than the investor can earn elsewhere.

Cash Flow

Cash flow position is cash received minus cash distributed. The net cash flow can be taken from a company's statement of cash flows. Cash flow is important for what it reveals about a company's financing needs. A strong positive cash flow enables a company to fund future investments without having to borrow money from bankers or investors. This is desirable because the company avoids paying out interest or dividends. A weak or negative cash flow means that a company has to turn to external sources to fund future investments. Generally, companies in strong-growth industries often find themselves in a poor cash flow position (because their investment needs are substantial), whereas successful companies based in mature industries generally find themselves in a strong cash flow position.

A company's internally generated cash flow is calculated by adding back its depreciation provision to profits after interest, taxes, and dividend payments. If this figure is insufficient to cover proposed new investments, the company has little choice but to borrow funds to make up the shortfall or to curtail investments. If this figure exceeds proposed new investments, the company can use the excess to build up its liquidity (that is, through investments in financial assets) or repay existing loans ahead of schedule.

CONCLUSION

When evaluating a case, it is important to be *systematic*. Analyze the case in a logical fashion, beginning with the identification of operating and financial strengths and weaknesses and environmental opportunities and threats. Move on to assess the value of a company's current strategies only when you are fully conversant with the SWOT analysis of the company. Ask yourself whether the company's current strategies make sense given its SWOT analysis. If they do not, what changes need to be made? What are your recommendations? Above all, link any strategic recommendations you may make to the SWOT analysis. State explicitly how the strategies you identify take advantage of the company's strengths to exploit environmental opportunities, how they rectify the company's weaknesses, and how they counter environmental threats. Also, do not forget to outline what needs to be done to implement your recommendations.

ENDNOTE

1. Tom Copeland, Tim Koller, and Jack Murrin, *Valuation: Measuring and Managing the Value of Companies* (New York: Wiley, 1996).

Case 1

The Cherry Lady

Alicia Gans, The Cherry Lady

J. Michael Geringer, California Polytechnic State University

In early July 2007, Alicia Gans leaned back against the food mixer in her hot, cramped, rented kitchen after putting another batch of Tart Cherry Caramel chocolates onto racks to cool. As she wiped the perspiration from her brow, she contemplated the challenges that confronted her and her young company. Alicia had founded The Cherry Lady (TCL) in October 2004 to comercially produce her distinctive chocolates. Within three Christmas seasons, TCL's sales had increased tenfold and the customer base had grown to nearly 100. Earlier in the day, Alicia received a voicemail message from a major mail order catalog company, Epicurean Selections, indicating that TCL had received approval to become a preferred vendor. Now Alicia had three weeks to accept their offer, two months until the first trial shipment would be sent, and three months before the peak Christmas season would begin. While this approval was certainly exciting, it intensified the issue of what direction the business should follow. During the past two years, TCL had been a cottage operation, specializing in producing premium quality, hand-made chocolate confections. Alicia had recently explored new market opportunities, and several looked promising for the coming year, but having Epicurean Selections as a customer would drastically alter the scale of her business. Until now, TCL's largest customer had ordered in increments of 100 pounds and orders required a week to process. Epicurean Selections would receive chocolate orders shipped in 5,000 to 10,000-pound lots. The product would be shipped on pallets and transported by a large freight carrier. Since this new catalog customer would initiate a major growth phase for The Cherry Lady, Alicia asked herself, "What kind of company should The Cherry Lady become, and will I be able to successfully build and manage this new business?"

THE CHOCOLATE INDUSTRY

Market Size

Valued at $74.1 billion in 2006, more chocolate was consumed worldwide than any other manufactured food product. The U.S. was the world's top producer of chocolate, with 3.5 billion pounds in 2006, and the production of chocolate and confectionery products was linked directly to approximately 65,000 jobs in the U.S.[1] At the retail level, the chocolate market, with $16 billion in 2006 sales, was the largest segment of the $28 billion U.S. market for retail confectionery. The latter also included sugar candy, licorice, gum, and a variety of other non-chocolate "sweets." Sales of chocolate and chocolate-type confectionery in the U.S. had increased by 26% between 1996 and 2006. An additional growth of 10% was projected by 2012.

Inputs and Traits
of Chocolate Products

Chocolate is derived from processing mature beans from the cacao tree. As a food product, chocolate provides most of the substances required for human nutrition, with roasted beans containing approximately 15 to 20% proteins, 20 to 25% carbohydrates, and 50% fat, as well as a variety of minerals. Fat is a key factor in achieving high quality taste in most confectionery goods, and fat generally constitutes the highest component of ingredient cost, particularly for the premium quality chocolate segment. This high fat content is derived from cocoa butter, which is also responsible for many of chocolate's distinctive characteristics, including its brittle, non-greasy texture at or below room temperatures; excellent keeping qualities, which reduces the risk of spoilage; and rapid melting at close to body temperature.

Many of the ingredients for chocolate confections, such as sugar, are commodities. There are important quality differences, however, among other ingredients, such as chocolate, special flavorings, nuts, and fruits. The quality of chocolate varies and is largely determined by the quality of cacao beans used. In the chocolate-making process, raw beans are selected; roasted; shelled; ground; and made into a thick, plastic-like chocolate liquor that solidifies as it cools, forming unsweetened (bitter) chocolate. The basic ingredient of all chocolate products, chocolate liquor, can be processed further to create products such as cocoa, chocolate syrup, solid chocolate chips, or baking bars, or sold to other manufacturers to be combined with additional ingredients to produce confections, bakery items, and dairy products. Sweet and semi-sweet chocolate are created when the liquor is combined with sugar, cocoa butter, and vanilla. The addition of milk solids creates milk chocolate. While most chocolate products are made from blends of fine and ordinary grades of chocolate, premium products have a higher proportion of finest-grade chocolate and cocoa butter and sometimes use beans from a single nation or region.

Chocolate requires careful tempering to ensure a good set, gloss, and finished shine—qualities that optimize shelf life and appearance. Chocolate also exhibits great sensitivity to temperature fluctuations, requiring careful environmental controls in production, distribution, and storage systems in order to maintain the appearance and integrity of finished products. Chocolate's broad appeal and its versatility as an ingredient results in the potential for many unique products. As a result, a large and growing number of small specialty chocolate and confection companies compete in the North American marketplace, primarily in the premium segment.[2] However, due to the capital and labor-intensive nature of the production of the chocolate itself—as opposed to the production of confections using chocolate as an input—most companies do not produce chocolate in-house. Instead, they outsource their chocolate production to experienced chocolate suppliers such as Guittard, Blommer, or Barry Callebaut, and it is considered to be relatively easy and straightforward for confectioners to gain access to (and switch among) these suppliers.

Competition

While customers often like to see new products, traditional favorites remain dominant among chocolate confections, especially within the mass-market segment. Due to industry consolidation, by 2006 most prominent mass-market brands were owned by large corporations, such as Mars, Nestlé, or Hershey. In contrast, premium chocolate brands included Godiva, Neuhaus, Joseph Schmidt, Lindt, and hundreds of smaller domestic and European specialty companies.

The large chocolate manufacturers have focused extensively on developing bigger, better, and more visible seasonal displays to capture consumers' attention, particularly in key retailer outlets. Holiday periods receive the most advertising and promotional support from manufacturers and the most display and feature treatment from retailers. However, limited space available in candy aisles, especially for seasonal products, have resulted in vigorous competition among manufacturers for shelf space. Many smaller competitors have been forced out of the large food, drug, convenience, and discount stores that constituted the primary channels for most popularly branded, mass-market confections. Smaller specialty stores, mail order and catalog firms, high-end department stores, gift shops, and boutiques—many of which conducted their sales exclusively or partially via the Internet—represented important distribution channels for the premium chocolate segment.

Demand

Chocolate consumption is distributed broadly, spanning gender, age, and socioeconomic differences. A recent poll revealed that 57% of American women and 46%

of men considered chocolate to be their favorite flavor for desserts and sweet snacks. Survey data suggested that more than 39% of adults, and 46% of all women, reported that they wished they could eat something with chocolate every day.[3]

When a consumer reaches for a chocolate product, that decision is the result of a complex interplay of factors, including immediate moods, psychological and emotional needs, nutrition, and personal tastes and values. In the U.S., it was estimated that more than 80% of all candy was bought on impulse. Although recent trends for consumers to decrease dietary consumption of fat suggested cause for concern for the chocolate industry, research suggested that over 70% of consumers still indulged in some form of chocolate at least once a month and 33% ate chocolate at least once a week. Many self-described "chocoholics" regularly enjoy eating chocolate in one of its various forms in order to satisfy their cravings. The consumption of chocolate can produce a euphoria that has been scientifically compared to the effects of marijuana use. One study sponsored by Cadbury suggested that over half of women preferred to have chocolate than sex.[4] As with coffee and tea, the serving of chocolate has traditionally been a symbol of welcome and sociability and it is significant in the customs of many cultures. Whether consumed personally, shared, or used as a gift, chocolate represents one of life's last important, small indulgences for many consumers.

Chocolate consumption tends to be seasonal, with sales in North America increasing sharply during the first and fourth quarters of the year, in conjunction with major holidays. Weather also affects chocolate sales. Consumers generally do not purchase as much chocolate during warm spring and summer months, when higher temperatures could cause melting and harm product quality and appearance. Seasonal candy often served as inexpensive gifts and many customers used seasonal or holiday-themed confections as an integral part of their holiday decorating. With 2006 holiday sales of $1.6 billion, Halloween was the biggest candy holiday, followed by Christmas with $1.4 billion, Easter with $1.3 billion, and Valentine's Day with $1.2 billion. Many of the most familiar confections, such as M&Ms® and Snickers®, are repackaged in appropriate colors, shapes, and packaging for different holidays. For boxed chocolates, winter holidays are the biggest selling season, and 70% of adults report that they gave and/or received a box of chocolate during this time of the year. Valentines Day is also a popular holiday for boxed chocolates. The mass-market manufacturers have traditionally stayed away from the gift box and seasonal chocolate markets. However, maturing markets in the late 1990s and early 2000s enticed these giants to pursue the holiday candy market as well as introduce boxed chocolate products, particularly since customers did not tend to comparison shop as much for these items.

The market for chocolate can be divided into two general segments: (1) mass-market products, such as "candy bars" and coatings for ice cream, which represent approximately 87% of overall chocolate confection sales; and (2) high quality, premium chocolate confections, such as die products offered by The Cherry Lady.

The Premium Chocolate Segment

An interesting contrast to the lower-fat consciousness sweeping North America is the growth in the market for premium chocolate. The proportion of high-fat cocoa typically ranges from 55 to 70% in premium chocolate, versus 35 to 40% for mass-market candy. Many consumers are becoming more sophisticated in their taste for chocolate, preferring the richer "mouth feel" of premium chocolate as they become more experienced. Seeking the pleasure of a little bit of "decadence" or pampering, consumers are increasingly deciding to consume a smaller quantity of premium chocolate, rather than a higher volume of lower quality mass market confectionery that lacked the exquisite taste of a high quality confection.

One result of this trend, combined with an aging American population with significant discretionary spending potential, is the raising sales level of high quality, premium priced chocolates, individually and in gift boxes or other forms. Between 2001 and 2006, sales of non premium chocolate in the U.S. were relatively flat, but sales of premium chocolates increased by 129% to $2.05 billion, or 13% of the over all chocolate market. Sales of premium chocolates were expected to sustain their rapid trajectory, reaching 25% of the industry's total sales 2011.[5] Tinka Gordon, from chocolatier Ghirardelli, stated, as people age, their taste buds mature. Premium chocolate fits perfectly with the increased sophistication and higher income of baby boomers."[6]

Some industry observers mused that chocolate is undergoing a similar process to what coffee and olive oil had done before—a renaissance from a commoditized good into one differentiated on flavor, taste, and geographic origin. Many consumers are becoming sophisticated about the taste of their chocolate and are willing to spend more money for premium quality product. This trend is evidenced by increasing sales of various premium chocolates, including dark, organic, and those with specialty ingredients, such as spices, fruits, berries, and nuts.

Market analyses revealed that the typical customer for premium chocolates is white, married, urban, female, professional, a university graduate, between the ages of 25 and 54, with children, and with an annual income of $40,000 or more.[7] However, chocolate consumption is also prevalent among men. Respondents to a survey on chocolate consumption revealed that 82% of those who ate premium chocolate products in the past three months had purchased it for themselves, 42% purchased for a partner or spouse, 33% for a non family member, and 20% for their children. Further, regarding the preferred type of premium chocolate, 43% of respondents preferred dark chocolate, while 42% preferred milk chocolate. Able to recognize quality in chocolate confections, these consumers are not necessarily price sensitive. Presentation is a key factor for sales success in the premium segment and products with upscale packaging have experienced a tremendous overall level of sales success. Not only is the perceived value higher for products with an upscale presentation, but many buyers are seeking a ready-made gift. Encouraged by tradition, many people regard an elegant box of gourmet chocolates as the ultimate expression of romance, affection, or holiday cheer.

Although the production process is more demanding and expensive for premium chocolates, a growing segment of people seems to be willing to pay for the extra quality. To address this trend, an increasing number of specialty chocolate businesses have emerged throughout North America, primarily small companies that focus on the manufacture or sale of premium quality confections. Many retail stores have expanded their gourmet sections, and premium chocolate often has a prominent place in displays. Recognizing the transformation in consumer behavior, mass-market producers, such as Hershey, Nestlé, and Mars, have been active in adding premium chocolate products to their lines, including through the acquisition of smaller premium chocolate manufacturers. These efforts could impact the ability of new or small premium chocolate companies to enter the market and gain shelf space. However, as Christine Thoreson of chocolatier Lindt and Sprangl said, "Its harder for a company like Hershey and others that are mainstream to try to be premium. We're all about quality and craftsmanship . . . . Ultimately, for the consumer, what is 'premium' will come down to taste."[8]

The chocolate industry is experiencing a recent upward spike in the cost of raw materials, such as cocoa, sweeteners, milk, and other key ingredients, as well as energy, distribution, and packaging costs. Many observers predict that these costs would continue rising during 2007 and beyond. Fortunately for the premium chocolate segment, raw materials account for a relatively minor portion of overall costs, particularly relative to the expense of packaging, marketing, and advertising.

ALICIA'S BACKGROUND

Alicia Gans, a native of California, grew up with an affinity for baking, tasting, and eating anything made from chocolate. Her grandmother had taught her to bake, and Alicia's specialty was chocolate chip and butter cookies.

> My grandmother was a great source of inspiration for me. An excellent baker, Grandma grew up where old-fashioned fun meant whipping up a batch of chocolaty fudge or decorating butter cookies. A perfectionist, Grandma's kitchen was filled with melt-in-the- mouth tasty goodness. Her treasured recipes would win a prize at any state fair. She taught me perfection and the importance of paying attention to detail. She use to say, "Dear Heart, remember always, bake with love and use the freshest ingredients."

While baking was a wonderful hobby, Alicia grew up in the technology-oriented Silicon Valley, and as a youth she had never considered a career in the food industry. After earning her bachelor's degree, and uncertain about a career path to pursue, she began working for an insurance broker. A year later, she moved to Japan to teach English. Two years later, frustrated but determined to find a position she enjoyed, Alicia researched employment in an industry she loved: confectionery. Her candy career began at See's Candies, a well-known chain of retail stores selling premium chocolate candy. While managing one of See's stores, Alicia began to observe and monitor customers' purchasing patterns, including which varieties of candies were the most popular and how extensively the industry relied upon traditional American holidays for sales.

Two years later, Alicia's position had reached a plateau at See's, and she was ready for a change. She accepted a job as a sales and marketing representative for a well-known, family-owned candy manufacturer that specialized in gummy and jelly products.

At [this company], I learned about the non chocolate side of the industry, including what retailers were buying for their stores and which products were the strongest sellers. At See's, I had simply ordered the candy and it was delivered to the retail store. In contrast, the candy company manufactured its products on site, allowing me to experience directly the daily challenges faced by a manufacturer. If a sugar shipment was delayed or if not enough flavor was added to a product, I witnessed how these problems affected production and sales. While I rapidly developed my sales skills, the candy company was experiencing constraints in production capacity. At times, I felt caught in the middle between the respect I should give to my employer and the excellent rapport I had established with my customers. Sometimes I made a sale or acquired a new customer, only to discover that the order could not be filled due to lack of inventory. Integrity was a critical issue for me and I felt that this value was being compromised. It was time for another change.

Alicia had always planned to return to school to pursue an advanced degree and it seemed that the right time had arrived. Feeling that her overall business knowledge was incomplete, she investigated MBA programs. Because of her interest in the food industry, she sought a school with an agribusiness and food science program so that she could customize her degree to include this coursework. Alicia subsequently enrolled in the MBA program at California Polytechnic State University in San Luis Obispo and received her degree in 2003.

The Origin of Tart Cherry Caramels

While completing her MBA studies, Alicia entered and won a product development contest sponsored by the Cherry Marketing Institute (CMI) in Lansing, Michigan. CMI was a grower-supported organization that promoted the use of tart (Montmorency) cherries. The purpose of the contest was to design any product using tart cherries. Commenting on her decision to enter the contest, Alicia said,

My background lent itself to creating a high quality cherry confection and my experience at See's convinced me that a cherry caramel-filled, chocolate covered confection had tremendous potential for success. I was enthusiastic about the challenge of trying to create something new and unique, and the creative, culinary aspect of the contest was a welcome contrast to my MBA studies.

Developing the tart cherry caramel filling took six months. I began by researching confection formulas and observing how each ingredient interacted with and affected the others. I examined how cooking time and temperature influenced the flavor and consistency of a caramel. Reflecting my food science training and baking experience, I maintained a detailed log, documenting how changes in a variable resulted in different product traits. After four months and fifty sample batches, I had developed two prototypes of the filling: a soft, somewhat sticky caramel and a firmer, chewier caramel. The resulting tart cherry caramel filling combined two popular flavors—cherry and caramel—surrounded by chocolate. I began preference testing the new confection, using local chocolate consumers. I sampled 200 people, receiving favorable feedback about the tart cherry caramel. People enjoyed the candy's real fruit filling and tangy flavor. My late night hours of measuring and mixing had resulted in a unique, appealing confection. I was ecstatic when the CMI notified me that I had won the contest, feeling that all of my hard work had really paid off and I had created something new and exciting.

Even though Alicia's primary purpose for developing the tart cherry caramel was in response to the CMI contest, months later Alicia contemplated whether her confection could be a viable business. She started by speaking with entrepreneurial friends, former employers, and colleagues in the industry. Alicia took advantage of Small Business Administration–affiliated SCORE workshops and their individual counseling. She attended several Small Business Administration seminars, participated in various other entrepreneurial conferences, and prepared a rough business plan. From her preliminary research, Alicia believed she had a good understanding of what was necessary to start and operate her own business.

Finally, after spending a year pondering whether or not this was something she should pursue, Alicia thought to herself, "The only way I will know is if I try. If the business is not successful, at least I will know that I gave it a fair chance and will not wonder, 'what if?' "

THE CHERRY LADY

In October 2004, Alicia combined her six years of industry experience with her educational background and started The Cherry Lady as a limited liability company (LLC).

I was living in Santa Clara and while the Bay Area is an expensive location for the company, there was a long history of chocolate manufacturing in the region and I was in close proximity to a variety of suppliers. This gave me quick and convenient access to raw materials. I also had many nearby family members and friends who were able to provide help at a moment's notice. Professionally, I was working in the quality control department of a tomato cannery. October was the start of the off-season and work was slow. These circumstances permitted me the opportunity to start my business. A few weeks before Thanksgiving, I began selling to one customer, a well-established local gourmet cherry stand. In early December, I was temporarily laid off from my job at the cannery, which gave me the entire month to focus on my business and customer. I returned to work in January, only to be laid off permanently in March as the cannery was downsizing and would close the following year. I felt that I was in a unique and ideal situation. I had just experienced a great Christmas selling season, had savings in the bank, and due to the layoff, the opportunity to focus my energy completely on the confectionery business.

When Alicia began selling to the gourmet cherry stand in 2004, the product line consisted, of individually foil-wrapped 1.25 ounce milk, dark, and white chocolate medal lions, as well as a gift box of fifteen smaller pieces packed in a bright red box tied with ribbon. This packaging was simple and gave the product a fresh, hand made appearance. The red box worked well for the cherry stand, as the stand's owners could easily customize it with their store seal. Business for this first Christmas holiday season was outstanding, considering she had only a single retail customer. During the three weeks before Thanksgiving, orders averaged nearly $450 per week, and in the four weeks prior to Christmas nearly $1,000 per week. For the combined seven-week selling season, Alicia sold twelve boxes of seventy-five-count foil medallions and 300 fifteen-piece gift boxes. Alicia participated in the store's holiday open houses by offering tasting samples and explaining the history of the product to the customers. Feedback was extremely positive. What seemed to be an extraordinary success was enough to convince Alicia to invest the necessary time and effort into expanding her business, both locally and nationally.

During this first season, I was handling all aspects of the business: manufacturing, packaging, and delivering the candy, in addition to sales and marketing, finance, and administration. I was working twelve to fourteen hours a day, seven days a week. At this time, the business was small enough that these tasks were manageable. When times were especially busy, I received help from family and friends. I initially produced the product in a rented candy kitchen at one of my former candy company customers. I felt extremely comfortable in this kitchen. It was well equipped, including two 100-pound capacity chocolate-tempering machines that allowed me to manufacture milk or dark chocolate product. My former customer was experienced in chocolate making and was readily available if I had a problem or question.

While renting space helped to control costs, the kitchen was an hour's drive away from my home. The rental site also did not have any storage space, because the kitchen's busy season coincided with TCL's. Production proved to be very demanding in terms of both time and labor requirements. At the start of a production day, I had to load my car with raw materials, drive an hour to the kitchen, unload the car, produce the candy, clean up, load the car, drive home, and unload the car. After a month, this practice was becoming increasingly inconvenient and tedious. Consequently, in early December, I purchased a small capacity chocolate-tempering machine that tempered one flavor of chocolate at a time. I also rented a small local kitchen. Even though the more compact facility was not a candy kitchen and the capacity of my equipment was much smaller than the prior facility, I was able to store ingredients and inventory and I had great flexibility for scheduling production hours. For the remainder of the 2004 Christmas season, I transformed this little kitchen into my own personalized confectionery workshop.

With the success of the first Christmas holiday season behind her, Alicia began to pursue expansion opportunities for TCL beyond the initial single cherry stand customer. From her sales experience at the candy company, she had gained expertise in prospecting for new business. She targeted the northern part of Michigan's lower peninsula, the tart cherry capital of the nation, with the idea that the product would sell well as a souvenir for the many tourists visiting the region. In response to Alicia's request, the CMI provided a list of retail shops in Michigan that might want to sell her chocolates. Alicia mailed sample boxes to these potential customers. At the same time, she personally approached gourmet gift stores in the San Francisco Bay Area. Customers in both Michigan and California responded favorably to the tart cherry caramels and Alicia made a few sales, but the customers were not as enthusiastic about the packaging. Alicia realized that, in order to increase TCL's credibility and perceived commitment to the business, it was necessary to have a more professional package. Moreover, a few prospective customers gave standing orders contingent upon a new, professional package.

I was committed to having TCL be known as a company that produced premium quality chocolate confections. In that respect, I knew from my own experience that the superior quality associated with the premium segment of the market was linked to five main dimensions:

1. The origins and processing of the cocoa beans.
2. The practices associated with production of the chocolate.
3. The quality of the non chocolate ingredients.
4. The technical expertise of the chef making the product.
5. The artistry and presentation associated with the finished product.

For at least the next few years, I knew that TCL would be too small to economically source its own beans and produce its own chocolate, but I committed myself to sourcing TCL's chocolate from the best suppliers that I could afford and then focus my energy on managing the third,

fourth, and fifth dimensions. I recognized that while I had focused on the quality of the product and my own production skills, I had neglected to give enough attention to the presentation of the final product. Yet, creating a new package was a daunting challenge for me.

The first decision was determining the shape of the box, next the artwork, and finally the printing of the box. Upon researching design firms, I learned that the cost to create just the artwork was in the range of $5,000 to $25,000. Although I knew that packaging was extremely important, I also recognized that TCL was very new, with limited resources, and I needed to find a more affordable option. After considering different options, I approached a class of college design students. My reasoning was that tart cherry caramels were the result of a student-developed entry for a contest, so it seemed only natural to continue the contest theme when designing the box. The costs were also substantially more affordable. In March of 2005, work began on designing a new image for TCL.

Three months later, the new box was completed. It was square in shape, red and gray in color. The top of the box had a windowed sleeve, and the top fit snugly over a base that held a fifteen-piece gold candy tray. The outside graphics depicted a 1940s theme and pictured a modest, red-dressed Cherry Lady and her curious Dalmatian. A rectangular window on the right side of the sleeve displayed a row of the tart cherry caramels. Response to the new box was favorable. The box received the first place award for my category from *Fancy Food* magazine's Packaging Award competition. Retailers liked the fun and whimsical design. The square shape also made the package easy to ship, stock, and display. I loved it!

Alicia believed that this new box, made TCL appear to be more of a player in the market, rather than the small cottage business it was. The new Cherry Lady design also served as an image and color theme for TCL. These design elements carried over to a brochure and other promotional material. By creating a company theme and maintaining design consistency with other marketing pieces, Alicia felt that TCL successfully demonstrated its professionalism and commitment to the business. Alicia recognized that creating this image was not only an important element for marketing and advertising the chocolate, but was essential to her long-term goal of growing the business.

Product Line

Tart cherry caramels were manufactured using dark, milk, and white chocolate. Dark chocolate was the most popular flavor, followed by milk and white. Candy was sold in bulk or gift boxed, as shown in Table 1. When sold in bulk, 6.25 pounds (200 half-ounce pieces) of the candy were packed into each stock box, which sold wholesale at $9.91 per pound, or $61.95 per stock box. Bulk candy represented 16% of total sales, although about one-third of this volume was to one customer, a prestigious department store chain that ordered in 100-pound increments and received a 10% quantity discount. Gift boxes were available in two sizes: a four piece box (2.0 ounces) packed assorted or all dark and sold wholesale at $2.75, and a fifteen piece box (7.5 ounces) packed assorted and sold wholesale at $7.35. The four-piece box provided 36% of total sales and the fifteen-piece 45%. Most retailers would double the wholesale price, while a few gourmet supermarkets operated on a 35 to 40% markup. An additional product, a 1.25 ounce foil-wrapped medallion, was a custom item manufactured exclusively for the cherry stand. Packed seventy-five pieces per box, the medallions sold at a wholesale price of $99.95 ($1.33 a piece), with a suggested retail price of $2.49. While the medallion was a great impulse item, the foil wrapping was done by hand and consequently was a labor-intensive activity.

Minimum order requirements were low and TCL did not allow returns. Bulk candy was sold in increments of one 6.25-pound bulk stock box. Both gift boxes were packed twenty-four to a case, although Alicia accommodated new and smaller customers' requests if they wanted to order half a case. Alicia believed that maintaining a low minimum order quantity allowed a retailer to try tart cherry caramels at a minimal investment and risk. Alicia believed that by providing samples, offering low order minimums, and suggesting merchandising ideas, new customers had an attractive prospect for selling the tart cherry caramels.

Markets

As shown in Table 2, the four categories of retailers TCL sold to and their percentage of the business were: specialty food and gift stores (63%), individually-owned candy shops (12%), upscale department stores (5%), and gift basket retailers (20%). Department, specialty food, and gift basket stores generally purchased both sized boxes and arranged them in an attractive display. Overall, the smaller boxes accounted for 44% of the total volume of gift box sales, and larger boxes comprised 56%. While the two boxes complemented each other, Alicia felt that it would have been advantageous to have a third item to supplement the line. It was challenging to create a strong retail presence with only two packaged units. Gift basket companies almost always purchased the four-piece box since its price point and size worked best with basket themes. Many of these gift basket retailers did tremendous volume, which generated a consistent level of sales. Individual candy stores typically purchased in bulk, either to re package or combine with their existing chocolate line. Tart cherry caramels worked well for chocolate storeowners who wanted a unique and high quality confection but did not have the time or ability to make the products themselves.

Almost all of the retailers that TCL sold to were small- and medium-sized businesses. The buyers for

Table 1   The Cherry Lady Product line, July 2007

Item	Percentage of Total Sales	Volume of Candy	Price per Pound	Price per Box
Bulk Wholesale	16	6.25 pounds (200 0.5-ounce pieces)	$9.91	$61.95
Gift Box				
Small	36	2 ounces (4 0.5-ounce pieces)	$22.00	$2.75
Large	45	7.5 ounces (15 0.5-ounce pieces)	$15.68	$7.35
Medallions	3	5.86 pounds (75 1.25-ounce pieces)	$17.06	$99.95

Table 2	Composition of The Cherry Lady's Customer Base, July 2007

Customer Type	Percentage of Total Sales
Specialty Food and Gift Stores	63
Individually-Owned Candy Shops	12
Upscale Department Stores	5
Gift Basket Retailers	20

these stores traditionally started their holiday buying over the summer, placing orders in August and September for shipment in late October and early November. After Thanksgiving, inventory was re evaluated and re orders were usually placed during the first two weeks of December. In contrast, many large chain stores and catalog companies completed their seasonal buying twelve to eighteen months in advance of the holiday, although delivery of the product would be scheduled for later.

TCL strove to provide outstanding customer service. Because the business was small, it was easy for Alicia to maintain a friendly rapport with her customers. She explained the history of the candy, described the unique flavor profile, and gave retailers suggestions on how to market the product in their stores. Pre orders were shipped as scheduled and telephone orders went out the same or following business day. A pound of tasting samples was included with all new orders. When an outside buyer placed an order, Alicia sent a detailed product information sheet with the order to assist in educating the salespeople. Alicia developed this sheet after she had visited several large retailers and recognized that the salespeople were seldom knowledgeable about the products sold in their stores. For local customers, Alicia delivered orders personally and arranged in-store demonstrations. Her commitment and service orientation had helped the business to expand, including through word-of-mouth referrals.

Tart cherry caramels were priced competitively with other premium quality boxed chocolates. Retailers familiar with high-end products were not that price sensitive, as their customers looked for quality and cost was not the primary factor in the purchase decision. Because tart cherry caramels were an unusual confection, the candy sold best in an environment where the retailer strove to carry unique products and enjoyed sharing the background of the product with the customers. Frequently, these were upscale boutiques. While Alicia used ingredients of equal or higher caliber than those of the competition, TCL had the enormous disadvantage of an unknown name in the marketplace. Alicia said,

The best known premium chocolate companies generally have developed national reputations and have existed for twenty or more years. That provides an indication of the time required in the marketplace to build name recognition, which is an important factor driving the boxed chocolate market. Overcoming this obstacle requires regular advertising as well as time in order to establish brand name recognition. TCL has generally been quick on its feet and adaptable, but I have to keep educating the marketplace about our excellent products.

Alicia had developed and placed a wide range of press releases, yet these were onetime-only arrangements. Well-established companies advertised monthly in at least one trade journal. When TCL introduced the four-piece box, Alicia prepared a promotional postcard mailing to existing and prospective customers. TCL sent out 700 cards, of which 85% went to specialty food and gift basket retailers, and the remainder went to a mixture of floral, coffee, and hospitality businesses. Geographically, these businesses were dispersed throughout the United States and approximately 5% consisted of international inquiries. This mailing generated more than a 3% increase in business and the postcard served as an excellent promotional piece. Yet, similar to advertising, Alicia felt that promotional mailings would be most effective when sent monthly. She was considering integration of e-mail and Web-based promotions into her company's efforts, but commented, "The world of marketing is changing so quickly these days, and a challenge for a company of our size is how to take advantage of new technologies without spending a fortune."

TCL's current distribution approach was direct to retailers. While tart cherry caramels were sold nationwide, the largest concentration of sales was in California (split evenly between northern and southern), Michigan, and Florida. Significant interest from the Midwest and New York was demonstrated from the reader response inquiries of various trade journals. Even though strong growth potential existed for these regions, expensive freight charges and the lengthy and somewhat uncertain shipping time resulted in some hesitation to buy. Regardless of the location, some retailers adjusted their prices to include freight whereas others desired a unique product and were willing to accept less of a mark-up in order to carry tart cherry caramels.

TCL was predominately a fourth quarter business, with approximately 70% of sales occurring during the Christmas holiday season, less than 5% for Valentine's, and roughly 25% for the rest of the year. Holidays such as Valentine's Day and Easter were not popular for TCL, as customers desired holiday-specific gifts (i.e., heart-shaped products and boxes for Valentine's Day and chocolate rabbits or decorated eggs for Easter). TCL might have been able to expand business for Valentine's Day, Easter, and Mother's Day through holiday packaging or other special promotional activities, but Alicia was concerned that the incremental volume would not be sufficient to justify the additional expense. Instead, Alicia felt that it would be most effective to concentrate sales on Christmas or on non holiday purchases.

Production

Alicia manufactured the tart cherry caramels by hand. Production included making the tart cherry caramel center and separately preparing the chocolate. The tart cherry caramel filling was a soft butter caramel, flavored with natural cherry and small pieces of dried tart cherries. These bits of cherries added texture and made the product unique, but they also complicated the production process. The dried cherries had to be added at just the right cooking temperature. Otherwise the fruit clumped together, giving the caramel an inconsistent texture and making it difficult to deposit into the chocolate. Three flavors of chocolate surrounded the caramel center: dark, milk, or white. Alicia carefully selected each chocolate flavor so that it complemented the cherry caramel flavor without dominating it.

Alicia purchased raw materials from a variety of sources. She bought sugar, corn syrup, and butter from a local food broker or warehouse club, whichever was the least expensive. Alicia also took advantage of grocery store holiday discounts on butter and sugar. Frequently, these sale prices were lower than the broker or warehouse club prices. After sampling offerings from a variety of suppliers, Alicia selected chocolate from Guittard, a local, high quality chocolate manufacturing company. Guittard's technical support was strong and, when a problem arose, Alicia could get assistance or a replacement quickly and easily. To conserve resources and reduce costs, Alicia picked up raw materials herself when possible, thus eliminating freight charges and providing her a pick-up allowance. She purchased the cherry ingredients from Michigan and they took an average of a week to arrive. Alicia explored West Coast cherry suppliers, but there were only a few and she considered that the flavor of their fruit was not as good as the Michigan cherries. To ensure freshness and achieve the highest product quality, Alicia made the caramel in small batches, without preservatives or additives. Raw material inventory was kept at a minimum to control costs and ensure that the product remained as fresh as possible. Purchasing problems were never really a concern to Alicia, since most ingredients were readily available. Alicia also knew many industry professionals who could rapidly provide ingredients, should she ever encounter a serious shortage. The cost of the raw materials was essentially the same across each of the three types of chocolate, representing approximately 25% of overall sales.

During her first selling season, Alicia manufactured the cherry caramel center in ten-pound batches. She mixed the center by hand, using equipment from a standard kitchen. Small batch production allowed for great flavor and complete quality control, but it was extremely tedious and inefficient. The second season, Alicia found a copacker to produce the center in 100-pound batches. The copacker prepared the caramel in an industrial candy kitchen in an open copper kettle, simultaneously mixing the caramel with a large electric mixer. Still, while the large scale production of the caramel center was certainly timesaving, the cherry pieces were often unevenly mixed, yielding inconsistent batches. The third season, Alicia manufactured the center in thirty-three-pound batches at a research and development lab using a steam-jacketed mixing unit. Although this production method was physically demanding, the result was a more consistent caramel center. Because of the high sugar and fruit acid content, the cherry caramel filling was very stable, with a shelf life of four to six months. No refrigeration or special storage conditions were required and the risk of microbial contamination was extremely low.

Similar to caramel preparation, chocolate production is extremely labor-intensive. The chocolate requires tempering, a process of heating and cooling chocolate in order to stabilize the fat structure of the cocoa butter. I purchased a small, used machine that was in very good condition, and used this to temper chocolate in five-pound batches. When the chocolate reaches the appropriate temperature, I shell-mold the candy. Shell molding is the casting of liquid chocolate into molds, followed by cooling and de-molding. For this technique, chocolate molds are first flooded with liquid chocolate, the air bubbles are removed, and the liquid chocolate is emptied, leaving a shell lining of chocolate to coat the inner surface of the mold. The mold is then cooled in order to set the shell. Second, the hollow chocolate shell is filled by hand with the cherry caramel center, followed by adding more liquid chocolate to cover the filling and create a bottom. Finally, the candy is cooled and the tart cherry caramels are removed from the mold by gently reversing and tapping. The resulting tart cherry caramel is oval in shape, with a raised cherry design on top. Producing these chocolates requires skill, attention to detail, and quite a bit of patience!

On a good day, production yielded fifteen to eighteen pounds, which was approximately 500 to 600 pieces. Problems with production could result from a poor batch of chocolate or humid weather conditions. Alicia said,

> Whenever you are producing a food product like this, there is always an automatic scrap percentage. In fact, even on my best days scrap generally falls around 10%. On TCL's worst days, scrap was 75%. When I had an unusually high quantity of scrap, I either donated the product to homeless shelters or food banks, or gave it to friends.

During the holiday season, September through December, TCL was at peak production. Alicia manufactured for eight to ten hours a day, with three additional hours required for set-up and cleanup. Alicia attempted to schedule her production days for individual chocolate flavors. Occasionally, she was able to build inventory and draw from it as needed. Yet, some of TCL's regular customers were accustomed to rapid turnaround and seldom ordered in advance. Instead, they ordered when they were out of product and expected immediate delivery. Alicia valued these customers and worked to accommodate them, even if it meant sacrificing her scheduled production. Consequently, the business operated mainly on a day-to-day basis, rather than following a strict production schedule.

Completed candy was temporarily put on trays, individually screened for quality, and hand-packed into stock or gift boxes. During the busy holiday season, Alicia's mother and friends performed these jobs, although Alicia recognized that there were limits to how much volunteer labor she could depend on in order to run her company and she had given some thought to hiring a part-time helper for the busy season. During slower time periods, Alicia combined these three tasks and completed them herself while waiting for the chocolate to heat and cool. Once packed, the boxes were cased and generally shipped immediately to the customer.

After the second, hectic holiday season, Alicia began searching for a company to manufacture the tart cherry caramels. Alicia was tired and knew it was neither effective nor realistic to continue manufacturing confections by hand. Not only was Alicia's current method of manufacturing very physically demanding, it also did not allow sufficient time for Alicia to concentrate on the growth of the business. The rate at which TCL could grow was limited by how much Alicia could personally produce. If the business was to grow, TCL needed a stable production department that could turn out a consistent product.

Alicia had three principal options for altering her production processes. First, as a temporary solution, she could purchase two additional chocolate tempering machines, allowing her one tempering machine for each chocolate flavor. This would increase production to perhaps twenty-five to thirty pounds daily, and would allow easier changing between flavors. But three machines also meant additional clean up. Second, she could purchase a larger-capacity tempering machine or a European molding machine designed especially for the chocolate molding. Both of these machines would be expensive, costing $7,000 to $15,000 each, and they were large. If Alicia purchased either one of these machines, she would not only need to rent a much larger kitchen, but she would also need to purchase additional equipment, such as candy molds, cooling racks, and so forth. Depending on the site, rent and utilities for the new kitchen could cost $1,300 to $3,000 per month. The estimated expense for additional molds, racks, and miscellaneous supplies was $1,300. Daily volume could increase to sixty to eighty pounds per day, but Alicia would still be producing the candy by hand. While this was an acceptable short-term solution, she was concerned that it might not be a good investment. The third and seemingly most effective solution appeared to be contracting out production to a copacker, a company that would mass-produce and package the tart cherry caramels for TCL

Mass-producing a shell-molded confection required a sophisticated piece of equipment that would mechanically manufacture the candy either in three steps or in a one deposit sequence. A three-step machine would essentially duplicate Alicia's hand method through automated equipment. The one-deposit machine would deposit the caramel center directly into the liquid chocolate. Of the two machines, the three-step was more sophisticated and could be significantly more expensive Depending upon size and features, the three-step machine would range in price from $250,000 to $1,000,000, whereas the one deposit machine would cost between $300,000 and $500,000. Capacity varied with machine size and type, ranging from 80–250 pounds per hour. Both machines were large and required a sizable production area. While these machines were common in Europe or with national chocolate companies such as Godiva, it would require research to locate chocolate companies that owned a machine and had surplus production capacity.

Coincidentally, the copacker Alicia had used originally to manufacture the tart cherry filling had purchased a one-deposit machine in late 2005. The company had extra machine time available and could be a potential copacker. Alicia started running test batches.

On my first sample run, the original caramel was too thick and could not be pumped through the equipment. During the next six months, I manipulated the original cherry caramel formula, adjusting variables just as I had done when initially developing the caramel. Although this company has successfully used their machine for over a year, they principally manufacture cream centers and solid pieces of chocolate. Creams are softer and less sticky than caramels, making them relatively easy to produce. Solid pieces of chocolate are even easier, as they contained no filling. While this company effectively ran a very thick caramel on their machine, they did not have experience manufacturing a caramel with the same properties as TCL's. The addition of dried cherry pieces further complicated the process. I sought out technical assistance on resolving this problem, making use of former professors and contacts in the confectionery manufacturing facilities, and they contributed many valuable ideas. However, although it appears that I am getting closer to an acceptable prototype, there always seems to be some additional factor preventing the process from making a satisfactory piece of candy.

After spending almost a year experimenting, it became evident to Alicia that she could not rely upon this copacker to produce her product. Alicia commented,

I'm committed to quality. I use high quality ingredients and will only ship the very best product possible. If candy has too many air bubbles or the filling leaks, I will not sell this candy. Maintaining high standards is what is necessary to compete in the premium chocolate market. If you don't have a quality product, consumers are not going to let you stay around too long. There's so much good competition out there, so you absolutely must have high quality. I'm not about to let the company's reputation be blemished by bringing something to the market that is not up to our standards.

Alicia was extremely frustrated by the initial copacking experience and felt that she may have wasted her time and money. But she realized that the process of scaling up any product from small batch production to mass production required fierce trial-and-error and considerable patience, and she refused to give up. After the frustrating experience with the copacker, Alicia felt that because of the consistency of the tart cherry caramel, it was imperative for the candy to be manufactured using a three-step machine.

When initially researching copackers, Alicia located a company in Georgia that had a three-step machine. It successfully ran a very small sample batch of the tart cherry caramels, but the cross-country freight charges compromised Alicia's ability to price the candy competitively. If TCL was only shipping product directly to a single site, such as the Wisconsin town where Epicurean Selections was based, Alicia could potentially use the Georgia copacker. TCL, however, also required product for its other customers. While Alicia was confident that the tart cherry caramel would sell well through Epicurean Selections, the initial vendor approval would only be for a one-year contract. Alicia would need to be prepared in the event that Epicurean Selections did not renew its contract with TCL. Geographically, Alicia felt more comfortable working with a West Coast copacker, located at most a two-hour plane ride away, in case of any production problems. She was also hesitant about relocating her business from California in order to be closer to a copacker. Alicia had recently identified leads for two companies that had a three-step machine, one in Washington and one in Arizona, but she had not yet researched or contacted either firm.

TCL's Financial Resources and Performance

To launch The Cherry Lady, Alicia initially set aside $60,000 of her total savings, an amount that covered TCL's start-up and Alicia's modest living expenses. She received severance compensation from her layoff for several months and felt that she was in a good position financially. Alicia also maintained an extremely frugal lifestyle.

> I spent very little money on myself and tried to economize whenever I could. For business supplies, I only bought what was necessary or obtained a sample of items from suppliers. Through friends, I had access to copier and fax machines and I borrowed other supplies as needed. Professionally, I had a good network of contacts that could offer free advice or services. Finally, when I did spend money, I made certain that I did my homework to guarantee the best value. I also found that if I was flexible on such variables as the delivery date of an item or if I was able to do some of the preparation on a project myself, often I could obtain a better price.

Alicia carefully managed receivables and used a cash accounting system. TCL maintained a strict credit policy; credit was not extended automatically, only after a thorough check of history. Discount terms for early payment were never issued. While some customers and a few potential customers complained about the rigid credit terms, the policy resulted in no bad debt expense.

TCL's first financial statements, for 2004, were relatively simple (see Exhibit 1). The largest expenses were candy molds, a chocolate machine, and mileage from the frequent trips to the rental kitchen to manufacture the candy. All sales were from one customer during the seven-week Christmas sales season. Cherry ingredients during this initial season were donated from the Cherry Marketing Institute and some of the other raw materials were samples from various suppliers. Although the expenses generated a net operating loss, the gross margin was high and Alicia received enough positive feedback and saw sufficient potential to develop the business.

In the income statement for 2005, there was a significant increase in expenses as Alicia undertook efforts to expand the business. The principal new expenses were associated with costs to create and print the new box, product promotion, and participation in a Philadelphia confectionery trade show. The remaining expenses were lower than the net sales. This suggested to Alicia that TCL was still in a favorable position. With the dramatic jump in sales from the first year of business, Alicia was convinced her business was doing well, particularly for such a young company.

In 2006, TCL's sales more than doubled from the prior year and its customer base experienced similar growth. Just as in 2005, a large portion of the expenses was devoted to growing the business. Of the total expenses, a major portion was attributable to the costs of developing a new smaller box and a color postcard for use in a broad mailing to inform customers of this new box. Alicia felt that, except for the "growing the business expenses," TCL was operating above the break-even point, which she believed was a suitable position for a company at TCL's stage of development. Once again, Alicia was convinced the business was progressing well and she was pleased with the progress. She said, "You know what the odds are of a new company succeeding? I think I've heard that around 85% of all new businesses fail within the first year or two. I'm trying to beat the odds, and so far it looks like I'm succeeding."

Alicia was excited about 2007. The new four-piece box had sold well and she expected to generate new business from the non seasonal markets she had been exploring. There was a sufficient inventory of boxes, so she would not incur the cost of creating and printing additional boxes. Based upon her past three years of business, Alicia conservatively estimated her 2007 sales would reach $100,000 and her goal was to increase her customer base to 150 clients. Particularly with several growth initiatives currently underway, Alicia was optimistic that TCL's break-even point would be exceeded on an overall basis and she would begin to receive a well-deserved salary for her efforts in establishing the company.

Despite her optimism, Alicia knew that this would be an important year for the company and she felt some pressure in terms of financial resources that TCL might need in order to achieve the company's potential. Most of Alicia's savings had been exhausted, either invested into the company or for her own modest living

Exhibit 1	The Cherry Lady Balance Sheets and Income Statements for 2004, 2005 and 2006 (December 31 Year End)

	Balance Sheet		
	2004	**2005**	**2006**
Assets			
Current Assets			
Cash	$4,000	$4,360	$6,888
Accounts Receivable	450	5,830	11,224
Merchandise and Packaging Inventory	100	7,220	7,334
Office Supplies	220	294	426
Prepaid Insurance	150	178	234
Total Current Assets	4,920	17,882	26,106
Plant Assets			
Equipment	6,600	7,854	8,680
Less Accumulated Depreciation	(2,004)	(3,670)	(5,194)
Office Equipment	450	450	824
Less Accumulated Depreciation	(90)	(180)	(366)
Total Plant Assets	4,956	4,454	3,944
Total Assets	9,876	22,336	30,050
Liabilities			
Current Liabilities			
Accounts Payable	0	1,074	2,944
Total Current Liabilities	0	1,074	2,944
Total Liabilities	0	1,074	2,944
Owner Equality[9]			
Invested Capital	10,922	30,220	37,373
Retained Earnings	(1,046)	(8,958)	(10,267)
Total owner's Equity	9,876	21,262	27,106
Total Liabilities and Owner's Equity	9,876	22,336	30,050
Income			
Net Sales (After Taxes)	5,522	29,705	63,452
Interested on bank Account	94	374	430
Total Income	5,616	30,079	63,882
Expenses	Income Statement		
Raw Materials for Candy	1,126	7,481	15,842
Packaging	346	4,260	9,080
Postage and Shipping	60	1,838	3,696
Advertising and Promotion	814	3,580	7,698
Depreciation and Amortization	2,092	1,756	1,660
Kitchen Rental and Utilities	800	8,634	10,763
Education and Seminars	190	208	1,004
Telephone	112	1,176	1,560
Business Fees	118	594	648
Insurance	75	610	1,673
Medical/Dental	0	0	1,196
Mileage/Automobile Expense	623	2,144	2,350
Parking and Tolls	0	192	264
Travel and Meals	88	1,034	1,254
Gifts	0	94	129
Trade Shows	0	1,276	1,440
Office Expenses and Supplies	218	728	1,150
Repairs and Maintenance	0	396	274
Graphic Design Services	0	1,990	3,510
Total Expenses	6,662	37,901	65,191
Net Operating Income (Loss)	$(1,046)	$(7,912)	$(1,309)

expenses. She felt that she could access some money from her family members, perhaps as much as $50,000 in loans or investments. Her family had been strongly supportive of Alicia's decision to form and grow TCL, but Alicia was hesitant to ask too much of them and wanted to avoid seeking money from her family unless she felt that there would be little or no risk of losing those funds. Alternatively, Alicia felt confident that she might qualify for a loan under one of the programs coordinated by the U.S. Small Business Administration, particularly if the funds were invested in machinery, inventory, or other assets that would serve as collateral. Further, she thought that she might be able to leverage her network of friends and professional acquaintances to find potential "angel" investors, but she knew that she would need a solid business plan in order to convince them to invest in her company. Outside investors would also want a significant portion of the company's equity in return for their investment. Alicia felt that the company was poised for profitable growth, though, and she was concerned about selling a stake in her company at a price that did not fully reflect her hard work and TCL's growth potential.

GROWTH OPPORTUNITIES

Alicia wondered whether she had effectively pursued TCL's growth during the past three years. During this time, TCL had grown steadily. Retailers in fourteen states and one Canadian province were selling her tart cherry caramels. Up until now, TCL had primarily generated new business from three main sources: targeted mailings to prospective customers, reader response inquiries from trade publications, and periodically from attendees of the two trade shows in which TCL participated. While new customers were obtained from each of these three methods, the overall approach had been somewhat ad hoc. Alicia had not developed and followed a specified expansion plan and she thought that it might be more productive if she concentrated TCL's growth within a specific geographic region. Because of the close proximity to TCL's operations, it seemed to make sense to focus first on pursuing sales along the West Coast. Seattle, Portland, and San Diego were cities where TCL did not have a significant customer base, and the demographics of these three cities matched those of the typical consumer of premium chocolate confections. Alicia

had started to target specific customers in these areas and also began looking for a specialty food broker to represent her product. Typically representing a number of different manufacturers, a specialty food broker would essentially function as an independent salesperson with responsibility for selling TCL's products and transferring orders from customers to TCL. Although a broker could broaden TCL's coverage of the market and help ramp up sales, some control of the business would be relinquished to the broker, such as the close relationships that Alicia had established with her customers. Alicia's inquiries with other small companies in the premium food sector revealed that sometimes these "partnerships" with brokers could be less than satisfying, and it would be important to select the right broker and carefully manage the relationship.

In an effort to expand TCL's business, Alicia had considered broadening her product line. When she developed the tart cherry caramel, she had also formulated a tart cherry jelly and experimented with other caramel flavors. Informal product testing had been positive and Alicia thought that perhaps she could add these confections to increase the product line. Yet, any product change or new offering would require new packaging. Since Alicia already had so much capital invested in packaging, it did not seem feasible to devote any more of her limited funds to packaging for new products. To alter the existing box to accommodate new confections and then have the new packaging manufactured would also be expensive, even if she relied on university students or other low cost sources for the redesign process itself. For the time being, Alicia believed it might be best to concentrate her time and money exclusively on selling the tart cherry caramels.

In an attempt to increase sales during the slower months of the year, Alicia researched non seasonal markets. She tried to concentrate on industries where chocolate might complement the primary business. She narrowed this focus to three sectors: coffee, floral, and hospitality. Each of these three industries tended to augment their core business with outside goods. Coffee shops frequently sold a piece of chocolate to accompany a coffee drink or a box of chocolate to complete a store gift pack. Florists sometimes used a box of chocolate as an add-on item to a floral arrangement. The hospitality industry often used chocolates for turndown service and as a thank-you for returning guests. Alicia pursued these opportunities locally and placed press releases in the corresponding trade magazines. At the same time, Alicia explored the prospect of selling to the United States government, the world's largest retailer. A federal law required government agencies and government contractors to utilize the services, to the maximum extent possible, of small, women and minority-owned businesses. Many of these government agencies and contractors purchased from outside vendors for employee awards, incentives, and commissary products. Alicia worked with a volunteer government consultant on the protocol for selling candy to these agencies. She attended government networking meetings and generated a list of prospective customers. While selling to the government required a great deal of time and patience, Alicia was optimistic she could obtain at least one customer over the next year if she devoted her efforts to this.

In early 2007, a large mail order catalog company, Epicurean Selections, contacted Alicia, expressing its interest in TCL's confections. Upon receiving the request for samples, Alicia was very excited and extremely flattered. After all, Epicurean Selections was a huge customer that had initiated the contact. With headquarters in Wisconsin, Epicurean Selections had been in the business of selling food and confectionery products for seventy-five years. They circulated more than 1.5 million catalogs annually for the Christmas selling season, maintained an extensive website-based retail operation, and serviced customers throughout the United States and Canada. Epicurean Selections' purchasing manager said that they planned to feature the tart cherry caramels as one of their new specialty confections and possibly use the chocolates in one of their gift basket assortments.

If Alicia accepted Epicurean Selections as a customer, they would receive the candy in bulk and repackage them under their own name. When Epicurean Selections first requested samples, they asked Alicia to quote prices in 5,000, 10,000, and 15,000-pound quantities. Alicia had quoted a delivered price of $9.00 per pound, with a 10% discount for 5,000-pound shipments and 15% for individual shipments of 10,000 pounds or more. The company's subsequent proposal to Alicia was for an initial shipment of 1,000 pounds to be delivered on September 17, followed by two 5,000 pound orders, one delivered on October 8 and the other on October 22. TCL's costs to complete this order would include raw materials, co packing fees, labor, and general expenses. Alicia estimated these costs at $5.70 per pound, plus $0.70 per pound for freight, leaving a contribution of $2.60 per pound when priced at $9.00. But again, just as in starting the business, these costs were estimates and they might in actuality be higher.

Alicia needed to respond to Epicurean Selections' inquiry within three weeks. Although it was tempting to accept the offer instantly, Alicia knew that it was crucial for her to carefully evaluate the feasibility of this option. Assuming that either the Washington or the Arizona companies could function as a responsible copacker, was this opportunity a reasonable growth alternative for TCL? She could possibly have the copacker produce in large batches, shipping most of the product directly to Epicurean Selections and any excess to TCL for separate packaging and distribution. Obtaining Epicurean Selections as a customer represented a phenomenal growth opportunity for TCL and Alicia was concerned that declining the proposal might limit TCL's options to serve as a vendor in the future. But as she pondered her decision, Alicia wondered if accepting their business would be the best alternative for growing her business.

Alicia reflected on the growth of her business during the last three Christmas seasons. She felt good about TCL's progress, but recognized that the company was at a turning point. TCL needed to grow, and seemed to have several options available. Alicia sighed deeply and said to herself, "I have invested so much of my time and soul into this company, doing everything I can to make it a success. But what kind of company should The Cherry Lady become, and will I be able to successfully build and manage this new business?" As she pondered those questions, Alicia closed her eyes and inhaled the delicious aroma of the freshly made chocolate treats that infused her small kitchen, bringing a smile of contentment to her face. Then she turned to the sink of hot, sudsy water, pulled on rubber gloves, and began washing the dirty pots and utensils from her last batch of tart cherry caramels.

NOTES

1. Industry data were obtained from:
   Mintel International, *Seasonal Chocolate Confectionery—U.S.* (Chicago: Mintel International, August 2006), http://reports.mintel.com.
   Mintel International, *Sugar Confectionery—U.S.* (Chicago: Mintel International, May 2006), http://reports.mintel.com "The U.S. Market for Chocolate," *Packaged Facts* September 2007: 3.
2. Premium chocolate was generally defined as product with a retail price of more than $8/pound. Some divided the premium chocolate into three segments: everyday gourmet ($8–15.99 per pound), upscale premium

($16–23.99 per pound), and super premium ($24 or more per pound). Most producers of premium chocolates were privately owned companies, making it difficult to obtain reliable, detailed data for this segment of the chocolate industry. Industry participants relied upon estimates, which often evidenced substantial variation.

3. Mintel International, *U.S. Chocolate and Seasonal Chocolate Confectionery* (Chicago, Mintel International, July 2007).

4. "Women Prefer Chocolate to Sex—Survey," *Birmingham Post* June 4, 2007, http://www.birminghampost.net/news/west-midlands-news/tm_headline=women-prefer-chocolate-to-sex—survey&method=full&objectid=19245471&sideid=50002-name_page.html. Accessed August 10, 2010.

5. Allison Linn, "Chocolatiers Jump Onto Gourmet Bandwagon," *MSNBC.com* March 28, 2007, http://www.msnbc.com/id/17646523/.Accessed August 9, 2010. Mintel International, *U.S. Chocolate and Seasonal Chocolate Confectionery* (Chicago, Mintel International, July 2007).

6. Gabriel Pacyniak, "Dark and Decadent Hits the Big Time," *Candy Industry* 170 (7, July 2005): 35.

7. Mintel International, *U.S. Chocolate and Seasonal Chocolate Confectionery* (Chicago, Mintel International, July 2007).

8. Mike Beime, "Industry Nuts for Cacao After Healthy Sales Spike," *Brandweek* 47(24, June 12, 2006): 9.

9. Owner's equity reflects continued investment of owner's funds during 2005 and 2006.

Case 2

Century 21 Sussex and Reilly Residential

Martha A. Martinez, DePaul University

The executive management team of Chicago's Century 21 Sussex and Reilly real estate firm met several times between April and July 2007 to discuss how to achieve their short-term goal of increasing their market share to 5% by 2008 and their long-term goal of 15% by 2013. Sean Conlon, founder and partner, Liz Scheffler, majority partner, and Glen Tomlinson, director manager, were concerned that a new breed of Internet-based real estate firms was bringing new competitive pressures to the industry. While Sussex and Reilly believed in taking advantage of the latest technology to disseminate information and attract clients, the firm's business model remained agent centered, with personal, top-notch, full service as its main marketing incentive. Meanwhile, other companies, some of them national in scope, were developing Web-based applications designed to connect buyers and sellers directly, eliminating part or all of the agent's traditional intermediary role in real estate transactions. At the same time, the real estate market was slowing down; in Chicago, the number of transactions had declined by 33% between 2005 and 2007. When Sussex and Reilly's Mid-Year Report arrived in July 2007, Conlon discovered that the total value of the transactions between July 2006 and July 2007 equaled $1 billion, which was lower than he expected. Conlon wondered whether the company needed to change its strategy in order to accomplish its goals.

Founded in 2000, Sussex and Reilly was a dynamic, young firm, providing services to developers and commercial and residential clients in Chicago. In 2006, Sussex and Reilly's residential division employed 250 agents and had four offices in some of Chicago's most affluent neighborhoods. Gross sales for the period July 2005–July 2006 were slightly over $1 billion. In early 2007, the company set the strategic goal of increasing its market share in the Chicago area from 3% to 5% over the next two years with the aim of becoming the dominant firm in the high-end city market. Sussex and Reilly regarded its main competitor, @ Properties, as a benchmark. Founded at the same time as Sussex and Reilly, @ Properties targeted the same market of affluent young professionals moving to the city, but by the end of 2006, @ Properties had more than 600 agents, five offices, and $1.75 billion in property sales.

How serious a problem was Sussex and Reilly's recent lack of growth? In a contracting market, how should a traditional, full-service firm in an industry that relies heavily on social networking respond to the challenge of new technology (the Internet) that affords potential clients the opportunity to bypass some of an agent's functions or even dispense with agents altogether?

STRUCTURE OF THE REAL ESTATE INDUSTRY

In the United States, real estate business activities were regulated and licensed by state governments, which meant that each of the fifty states had different regulations. In order to obtain a license, individuals were required to pass one or more tests and fulfill certain educational requirements. Licensed real estate practitioners, known in the industry as brokers or agent-brokers, were

Copyright © 2010 by the *Case Research Journal* and Martha A. Martinez. The author thanks Susanne Cannon and DePaul University Real Estate Center for their support in the development of this case.

Exhibit 1	Median House Price in Chicago and National Commission Levels 1991–2007

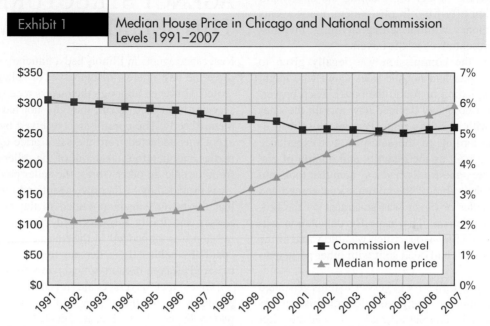

Sources: Median Home Prices provided by Susanne Cannon, Real Estate Center, DePaul University. Figures were calculated using MLS data for the 77 neighborhoods of Chicago. National Commission Levels from 1991 to 2005 obtained from "Competition in the Real Estate Brokerage Industry," a report by the Federal Trade Commission, April 2007, obtained online at http://www.ftc.gov/reports/realestate/V050015.pdf. National Commission Levels for 2006 to 2007 obtained online from the Department of Justice at http://www.usdoj.gov/atr/public/real_estate/faqs.htm.

legally allowed to act as intermediaries between sellers and buyers in a real estate transaction. Brokers hired sales persons, normally known as agents, to help market properties and provide services to buyers, but an unlicensed agent had to act through a licensed broker in order to conclude a purchase or a sale.

Brokers and agents supervised by brokers did not traditionally earn a salary or charge a fee for their services; instead they charged a commission for a successful real estate transaction, which was usually a percentage of the overall value of the property sold or bought. Companies in the real estate industry, as in most other industries in the United States, were forbidden by law to enter into any agreement that would create a particular commission price. Despite this formal prohibition, agents and brokers usually operated according to the "industry standard," a locally established informal consensus on the fair commission percentage. For example, in 2006 commissions in the city of Chicago tended to be close to 5%, while in the Chicago suburbs commissions of 6 to 7% were normal.[1] Agents informally enforced the standard by simply refusing to

accept clients who wanted lower commissions. The local industry standard in the city of Chicago had been 7% during the 1980s, but heightened competition decreased the commissions to 5–6% during the late 1990s and early twenty-first century (Exhibit 1). By 2007, many companies had decided to abandon the informal commission rules, so the market experienced more variation in fees.

The most common and widely used contract between agents and their clients was the Exclusive Right to Sell, which obligated sellers to pay the commission to the agent in the event of a sale, regardless of whether the sale resulted from the agent's efforts or not. Under this type of contract the commission for the agent was protected, so there was a strong incentive to find a buyer as quickly as possible, even if it meant cooperating with other agents. Usually, more than one agent was involved in the transaction, in which case the commission was split among the participating agents. This meant that the commission was divided up between the broker/agent listing the property and the broker/agent who found the buyer. Unless otherwise negotiated, the broker with the listing and the broker representing the buyer split the commission fifty-fifty. In this system, many agents could make money without selling anything; they just served as representatives of the buyers.

In Illinois, the commission was legally given to the licensed broker and not the sales agent who might have made the listing or found the buyer. Each broker/agent or broker company decided how to split the sales commission with its sales agents. Percentage splits usually varied according to the salesperson's experience and success as well as the quantity and quality of his/her work. Sussex and Reilly had a system that took into account both the value of the commissions earned and whether the seller or buyer was generated by the broker or the salesperson. The basis for calculation was the gross sales commission, which was the value of the commission after it had been split with other participating brokers.

In Sussex and Reilly, for buyers or listings generated by the broker company, the gross sales commission was split fifty-fifty. When the salesperson generated the seller or the buyer, he/she was entitled to a compensation that ranged from 70 to 80% of the gross sales commission. Sellers or buyers obtained through Sussex and Reilly's Web site were considered to be generated by the broker and therefore carried a commission split of 50% for the salesperson.

The tool that facilitated cooperation among agents was the Multiple Listing Service (MLS), which allowed brokers in the same local market to share listings with each other. Broker members had to share all of their listings with the MLS and also had access to the listings of all other members. Before the Internet, sales agents could access the information only through their brokers. In order to enter their properties in the MLS, sellers needed to sign an exclusive agreement with an agent and pay the commission asked. In order to get information about houses, potential buyers had to contact an agent and rely on his/her expertise and goodwill to show them the right properties.

In this situation of power, the agents were able to control the time and place of their interactions with the clients. Many agents held part-time and even full-time jobs in addition to their real estate work, because they did not have to provide high-quality services or be flexible to accommodate the needs of their clients. This situation changed in the mid-1990s with the proliferation of new technologies, particularly the Internet.

AGENCY STRUCTURE AND THE SELLERS' DILEMMA

Real estate agents in Illinois had a fiduciary obligation to serve the best interest of the buyer or seller they represented. However, although the buyers received exclusive services from their agent, they did not have to pay for them directly. The commission received by the buyer's agent was deducted from the sales price agreed by the parties and therefore taken out of the seller's final profit from the sale. In other words, the seller paid for the services provided by his/her own agent and for the services that the buyer's agent provided to the buyer. Though Sussex and Reilly formally told clients that the commission was embedded in the transaction and therefore "paid" by neither the seller nor the buyer, most sellers believed the commission came directly from their pocket.

Given that buyers could receive services without paying a fee for them, they had no incentive to completely bypass the real estate agent. However, if sellers could bypass the agent, they would save a considerable amount of money. The MLS structure described above traditionally made it nonetheless appealing for the seller to hire an agent; through the agent, sellers would have access to the buyers represented by any other agent in the MLS region. Before the Internet started making MLS information available, no other mechanism provided exposure and direct contact with other individuals interested in buying and selling a property. Thus, hiring an agent could increase the speed of a sale and the number of potential offers received by a seller.

THE INTERNET AND ITS IMPACT ON THE REAL ESTATE INDUSTRY

One of the first changes to the real estate industry brought about by computer and telecommunication technologies was that the MLS was published online. The computer version of the MLS made accessing the information and searching for properties with specific parameters much easier. Newly listed properties could also be accessed faster. Once the information was available in electronic form, some agents and brokers started making parts of or even the whole MLS listings available online through their Web sites. The purpose of these Web sites was both to increase the visibility of properties and to find new clients.

Information availability through the Internet created a more sophisticated and educated client. Technologically savvy individuals were able to review information about hundreds of properties being sold in particular neighborhoods, compare prices with similar properties and compare different mortgage services. Clients could explore their options without making a definite commitment to an agent. By the time a buyer or a seller contacted an agent, if they ever did, they may have already known how much properties were worth and what they wanted. As a more educated clientele facilitated the work of real estate agents, the difference in knowledge between realtors and clients diminished. With less "leg work" to do for sellers and buyers, clients felt that the work of the agent did not justify the commissions.

The Internet improved the position of real estate buyers, allowing them to compare agents and use some leverage when negotiating their services. New technologies supported the creation and expansion of business models that deviated from the traditional role of the real estate agent and addressed sellers' concerns about commissions. In contrast to Sussex and Reilly, in some of the new breed of firms the agent was no longer a freelancer, paid on commission, but a salaried clerk who merely dealt with paperwork. Among these new actors were the Internet-based ventures, organizations that were usually founded by technology entrepreneurs looking to create new applications that could improve the real estate industry. Table 1 provides information on different Internet companies and their business models.

Another type of real estate firm that benefited from the Internet was discount brokers, defined as anyone charging less than the standard commission. In this

Table 1		Main Estate Internet Ventures				
Company	Founded	Source of Revenue	Main Client	Goal	Role of Agent	Market Covers
Zillow	Feb 2006	Advertising space	Mortgage and real estate brokers, agents, and other service providers.	Make market more efficient by providing free, accurate, and complete information on transactions.	Traditional. Zillow provides marketing opportunities for agents.	National
RedFin	Oct 2004	Real Estate Commissions (discounted)	Buyers, although commission is taken from seller.	Provide high quality service for a fraction of a traditional agent commission.	Salaried employee providing service to smooth transaction.	Boston, Chicago, Los Angeles, Orange County, San Diego, San Francisco Bay, Seattle, and Washington, D.C.
Zip Realty	Aug 1999	Real Estate Commissions (discounted)	Buyers and sellers.	Use the efficiencies of the Internet to streamline process and pass savings to clients.	Independent contractors, similar to agents affiliated with local real estate firms.	Main metropolitan areas in 21 states. Includes Chicago.
Trulia	Sept 2005	Advertising space	Mortgage and real estate brokers, agents, and other service providers.	Provide real estate information at the local level to aid in decision process.	Traditional. Trulia provides marketing opportunities for agents.	National

sense, Internet ventures like ZipRealty and RedFin could be considered discount brokers. Discount brokers predated the Internet by many years, but they proliferated with the introduction of the Internet. The National Association of Realtors classified most discount brokerages according to the services they offered, dividing them into limited- and minimum-service brokers.

Full-service real estate included the following activities: market analysis, setting asking price, marketing (inclusion in MLS, media ads, signs, flyers, and open houses), showings, and transaction management (inspectors, approvals, contracts, etc). Discount brokers "unbundled" the traditional role of the real estate agent and created packages for fixed prices providing certain services and not others. Agents offering less than "full service" but still taking care of most aspects in the real estate transaction were considered limited-service brokers. Minimum-service firms were licensed real estate brokers that, for a flat fee of around $300 to $600, offered a few services for the seller, the most important one being the inclusion of the property on the regional MLS. Sellers hiring a minimum-service broker typically organized their own showings and open houses, negotiated directly with the buyer and/or the buyer's agent, hired a lawyer and took care of closing. In some cases, clients of a discount broker formally committed themselves to paying a 2–3% real estate commission to the buyer's agent. In other cases, the buyer's agent had to negotiate a commission with the seller. Minimum-service brokers could include small entrepreneurs looking to make a living for themselves or more established firms trying to offer a wider array of service options.

The Internet also provided new spaces and services allowing sellers to advertise their properties outside of the MLS. These Web sites did not require the participation of agents, and in some cases were offered for free. Individuals selling or buying real estate without the help of an agent were labeled For Sale by Owner (FSBO). FSBO sellers determined the price of the properties, planned their own marketing strategy, negotiated with buyers and/or their agents, and took care of all the details regarding closing.

Before the popularization of the Internet, the FSBO model usually only included cases where the seller and buyer knew each other (relatives, friends, and acquaintances) and the transaction was private. The Internet provided new ways for sellers to find nonrelated buyers. For example, houses for sale were advertised in places like craigslist.com, and individuals could sell or buy properties directly using ebay.com. Search engines like Yahoo, Google, and MSN started to compile real estate information and offer it to consumers, including lists of inspectors, lawyers, title companies, and other professionals.

INSTITUTIONAL RESPONSES TO DISCOUNT BROKERS

By 2006, Internet ventures and discount brokers were gaining momentum. In that year, the National Association of Realtors (NAR) calculated that of sellers using some kind of agent, 83% used traditional real estate agents, while 9% used limited-service agents, and 8% used minimum-service agents. Only three years earlier, NAR put the market share for both limited- and minimum-service brokers at only 2%. According to NAR, levels of FSBO transactions varied every year without a clear trend, with 12% of all real estate transactions in the country falling under this category in 2006.

Traditional real estate companies, represented by their local MLS associations, tried to oppose these new business models through several strategies. One was to support new state legislation. By 2007, six states, including Illinois, had passed Minimum Service Laws forbidding discount brokers from offering MLS listing services only. Since 2004, Illinois required all brokers entering into an exclusive agreement to assist the client in developing, negotiating, accepting, and delivering offers, as well as to answer any questions related to this process.

Many regional MLS associations set rules regarding access to listings; for example, some associations divided the MLS in sections, one more prominent than another. In order to enter a property with a prominent status, sellers were required to have signs with the name and contact information of the discount broker instead of using the generic For Sale by Owner sign. Other MLS associations restricted the information that could be included online alongside MLS listings. This restriction applied both to non- MLS properties and to other kinds of information like comparative values and neighborhood statistics, directly affecting Internet-only real estate companies, which relied on superior information to attract sellers and buyers.

Although traditional full-service real estate agents saw minimum-service laws and other rules as upholding the standards of the industry, many discount brokers and other consumer advocates interpreted them as strategies to reduce competition and keep the commission system intact. The Department of Justice decided that such laws were unconstitutional and started to challenge them in federal courts. No agreement or judgment had been reached by mid-2007.

THE HISTORY OF SUSSEX AND REILLY

Sussex and Reilly was a result of the combined expertise and experiences of its three major partners: Sean Conlon, Liz Scheffler, and Glen Tomlinson. Conlon arrived in the United States in 1991 looking to achieve the American Dream and become rich. He began working as a janitor while taking night classes in real estate. In 1993, he quit his job as a janitor and began working for a small Chicago firm. As a "rookie" realtor he noticed a new trend: wealthy professionals were coming back from the suburbs to the formerly abandoned inner city. Previously, new construction in the inner city had been considered a difficult or nonexistent market, but this returning population with high spending capacity and expensive tastes created a market for new and more luxurious construction.

While marketing new construction to a young, highly educated, and relatively wealthy group, Conlon broke the city of Chicago sales record with $55 million in 1997 while he was still in his twenties. The average agent at the time sold only $5 million a year. Conlon provided an example of how he created new strategies to take advantage of the new demand for property:

> I don't want to say that I invented the condo, but here in Chicago people would build small, three-flat buildings in places like Lincoln Park and do rental apartments. My first three-flat building I sold as a broker, I basically took the plans and made up prices for each condo because we had no precedent. And I sold a lot of them after that.

Conlon wanted to create a small boutique firm providing full service to a new kind of client: the highly educated, technologically savvy, young professional interested in enjoying city living. He wanted a company that mimicked his target market, with young professional, entrepreneurial, full-time agents at the center of the real estate transaction. He also wanted to use technology to create a relationship between agents and their clients. Conlon sought and found an entrepreneur who already owned a specialized buyer agency; together, they founded Sussex and Reilly in January of 2000. (The name of the company was created using the maiden names of the partners' mothers.)

During Sussex and Reilly's first year of operations, Conlon found organizing and managing a real estate firm more difficult than he expected. About a year after he opened Sussex and Reilly, he contacted Glen Tomlinson, then director of mergers and acquisitions for Cendant Corporation. (The real estate division of Cendant offered franchises under the brands of Century21, Coldwell Banker, and Sotheby's International Realty.) Tomlinson explained:

> Sean asked me to find him some help. He wanted to grow his real estate company, but he didn't know what was needed to do that. He needed help finding the right person. It was very clear to me that Sean was a rain maker, someone who finds and makes amazing deals, but want to be bothered with the day-to-day operations of a business.

Tomlinson believed that for many years the real estate industry had been reactive; agents relied on their monopoly of information to make money. Many agents just waited in their offices for buyers and sellers to reach them. Conlon's idea of professional agents and new technologies could create a real competitive advantage, but he needed someone whose managerial and organizational abilities complemented his entrepreneurial approach.

The best person Tomlinson knew in the greater Chicago marketplace was Liz Scheffler. Scheffler had spent fifteen years managing her own medical billing company in Lake County, suburban Chicago, and started her career as a real estate agent in 1986 at the firm Maki and Associates in Waukegan, Illinois. She became broker-owner in 1993 and since then she had expanded her business in Lake and DuPont Counties, part of the Chicago suburbs, by acquiring several local firms. For Scheffler, the most interesting part of the real estate business was building an organization that efficiently helped real estate agents to succeed. Tomlinson commented:

> Any agent that reaches a certain amount of success needs to delegate the most time-consuming work. What Liz brings to the table at Sussex and

Reilly are the abilities and skills to organize daily work and let the agents concentrate on what they do best: selling.

So Tomlinson contacted Scheffler and arranged a meeting with Conlon. A few months later, in January 2002, they became partners, and Sussex and Reilly joined the Century21 franchise. Both Conlon and Scheffler were so impressed by Tomlinson's mediating skills that, as a requirement for closing their deal, they invited him to come on board as general manager.

The new partnership of Scheffler, Tomlinson, and Conlon ushered in an era of expansion for Sussex and Reilly. The company grew in size, from forty-five agents and two offices when Scheffler and Tomlinson joined, to 250 agents, four offices, and $1 billion in sales in 2006.

SUSSEX AND REILLY'S TARGET MARKET

Sussex and Reilly defined its market first in terms of geographic location and then by demographic characteristics. When the company managers referred to "The City" as their market, they were referring to downtown and nearby neighborhoods mainly in the northeast part of Chicago. These neighborhoods were in a process of gentrification, the displacement of traditional lower-income dwellers by individuals with higher incomes and more expensive tastes. The company expanded its geographical influence as new neighborhoods went through gentrification.

Determining the potential market for Sussex and Reilly depended both on the actual availability of properties to be bought and sold and on the behavior of individuals moving in, out, or within the target area. The area of Chicago covered by Sussex and Reilly had more than 320,000 housing units, but less than one-third of them were owner occupied while the rest were rented or vacant. Of the owner-occupied properties, 75% were condominiums or townhouses. Overall in the city of Chicago approximately 10% of properties were on the market at any particular point in time.[2] Because the area of Chicago covered by Sussex and Reilly has around 96,000 owner-occupied properties, one can infer that around 9,600 were on sale at any particular point in time.

Gentrified neighborhoods were characterized by considerable variation in terms of property characteristics and prices. It was possible to find, within a few feet of each other, a one-bedroom/one-bath "garden"[3] condominium priced at $200,000, a $4 million house with six bedrooms and six bathrooms, and any possible variation in between. However, all these properties were part of the "luxury" market, as they were located in an expensive area in comparison with other neighborhoods in Chicago. What made even the least desirable properties part of the "luxury" or "high-end" market was that potential owners were willing to sacrifice space (and/or amenities) for the benefit of the location.

Variation in properties also meant some variation in terms of the demographic characteristics of potential buyers and sellers. According to the Census Bureau,[4] the people who lived in these neighborhoods were relatively young, with a median age hovering at around thirty. Most of them were single and white, although there were sizable numbers of African Americans, Asians, and Latinos. Married couples tended to be young and have at most one child. The population in the area was also highly educated. Median incomes in Sussex and Reilly's target area varied widely, ranging from $50,000 to $140,000.

Managers at Sussex and Reilly believed that these numbers also reflected the demographic characteristics of individuals wanting to move into the area. There had been some speculation in real estate publications that Baby Boomers, as they reached retirement age, would feel inclined to sell their big houses in the suburbs and move to condos and townhouses in the city. Although Sussex and Reilly's agents had seen some examples of older people moving back to the city after retirement, their numbers were not large enough to be considered a trend.

There was no available information specific to the city of Chicago or to the demographic group targeted by Sussex and Reilly regarding the agent selection process. However, national and Midwest data from the National Association of Realtors (NAR) provided some insights into agent selection preferences. About 77% of buyers and 81% of sellers hired an agent during 2006. In the same year, 80% of Midwest buyers used the Internet[5] as a source of information, but only 24% of overall buyers found the house they bought on the Internet. At the national level, the most common method of finding an agent was through referrals by friends and family, with 49% of first-time buyers, 35% of repeat buyers, and 44% of sellers finding their agent that way. Also at the national level, around 65% of buyers and 69% of sellers contacted only one agent for the transaction. Finally, 82% of sellers and buyers would recommend their agents to family and friends.

The managers at Sussex and Reilly were very aware of the central role of relationships in the real estate industry; they subscribed to the "High Tech, High Touch" principle developed by Conlon. Their business model was agent centric, with technology playing a secondary role to facilitate and improve agent/client relationships. Tomlinson explained:

> They [our customers] are successful in their work life and they spend a lot of time on their jobs. Although they are very technologically savvy, they do not have time to take care of all the little details of the real estate transaction. They do not have time to fax things or bring papers back and forth. We make the transaction as simple and transparent as possible for them. Only a full-time agent could provide the availability and service that young professionals need.

With this in mind, the company hired and developed only agents who would dedicate 100% of their time to real estate, in contrast to the part-time model prevalent in the rest of the industry. Many firms hired housewives looking for half-time employment or older individuals looking for a second career, but the managers at Sussex and Reilly believed that consideration of the target market should determine their choice of agents. The director of training explained:

> With our agents, we try to mimic the demographic and to some extent personal characteristics of our customers, both clients and sellers. For that reason, we hire young, ambitious individuals with a drive to succeed and great technological skills. The average age of our agents is 35, while the industry average is closer to 51. We also try to have agents from different ethnicities be part of our organization.

THE AGENT AT SUSSEX AND REILLY

Sussex and Reilly's agent-centric model followed the traditional view of agents as entrepreneurs. Agents were "hired" as individual contractors and were assumed to be working for themselves and not the company; although the company offered them certain benefits, they did not receive any salary. The agents were required to provide full service to their clients. For sellers, full service meant the use of marketing techniques to increase the number of people exposed to the property (which usually increased sales prices) and generally facilitating the deal. Agents created promotional materials including pamphlets and virtual tours of the property, helped set an optimal price, contacted other agents with potential buyers, took care of the negotiation process, dealt with the paperwork, and

made sure that the transaction complied with state laws and regulations, among other services. Buyers also received full-service attention: agents helped them define their needs, evaluated properties, negotiated price and terms, recommended other professionals like lawyers, inspectors, title companies, and mortgage lenders, and supervised the whole transaction.

Sussex and Reilly had eight managers and thirty employees that monitored and supported the agents. Although each agent was an independent contractor, the company gave them quotas designed to help them grow their business. Tomlinson explained the company's standards:

> For someone just starting their careers, we ask them to perform at least three transactions in the first six months and six transactions during the first year. Those six transactions need to add up to around $2 million in sales for the first year. After that, we work with the agent to create business plans and set up new higher goals. During 2006, our most successful agent engaged in transactions worth $100 million and earned $2 million in net commissions.

SUSSEX AND REILLY'S APPROACH TO INTERNET TECHNOLOGY

Because Sussex and Reilly was formed in 2000 as a direct response to the changing conditions of the real estate industry, Conlon saw his company as a high-technology endeavor. In particular, Sussex and Reilly used technology to increase contact between agents and consumers, and agents and managers. Sussex and Reilly adopted the BlackBerry (a handheld device that sent and received e-mails, served as a mobile phone, and allowed text messaging, Internet faxing, Web browsing, and other wireless information services), which helped connect managers, administrative workers, and agents regardless of time and place.

Sussex and Reilly also applied the combination of technology and a personal touch to the generation of leads, particularly for buyers. Using the computer system Lead Router, the company ran an automated lead generation system that took advantage of company Web sites and other online real estate advertising sites. The company Web site provided potential buyers with access to the company listings, which included photographs and virtual tours of the properties. In addition, Sussex and Reilly fed listings to more than 100 Web sites.

Lead Router matched the lead information with the listing agent and the sales team. The system then converted the data to voice and instantly informed sales associates of the new lead via BlackBerry or phone. Potential clients were called by or received an email from an agent within 20 minutes after visiting the Web site. This system was very important because 70–75% of Sussex and Reilly's residential clients in 2006 initially contacted the company through the Internet. Although the company Web site and the immediate response system generated leads, they did not necessarily make the job of the real estate agent any easier. As one agent explained:

> The Internet . . . means a lot of work. The leads that you receive, you don't know what stage in the process they are or even if they really want to buy. And even with a BlackBerry, it is difficult to send them the information they want right away if you are in a showing and the information is in the office. You need to work a lot to be on top of those leads, but in my experience only 1 in 100 pans out.

COMMISSIONS, TECHNOLOGY, AND MARKET FORCES

Real estate was subject to the normal fluctuations of supply and demand and was affected by other factors such as the interest rates set by the Federal Reserve, the rates of foreclosure, and the levels of new construction. The real estate industry moves in cycles of expansion and contraction. During the 1990s and early 2000s, certain real estate markets, among them the city of Chicago, experienced a long phase of expansion. In Chicago, the movement of people from the suburbs back to the city further increased demand during those years. Historically low interest rates created incentives for potential buyers to become homeowners (Exhibit 2).

High demand translated into incentives for new construction and high appreciation for real estate properties. Individuals who bought homes during a phase

| Exhibit 2 | Number of Sales Chicago and National Mortgage Interest Rate Half Year Data* 2000–2007 |

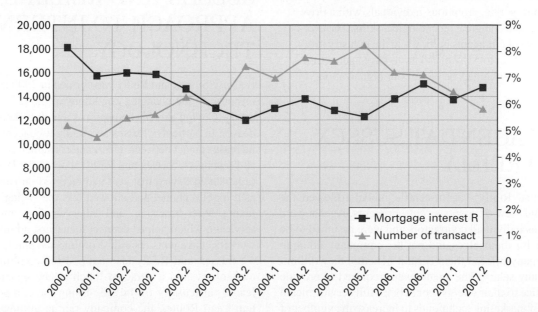

*The Number of Sales data are for six-month periods, the first measured at the end of June and the second at the end of December. Mortgage rates are measured in the first week of July and the first week of January.

**The left axis represents the scale for Number of Sales, and the right axis shows the Mortgage Interest Rate.

Sources: Number of Sales in the Chicago market provided by Susanne Cannon, Real Estate Center, DePaul University. Figures were calculated using MLS data for the 77 neighborhoods of Chicago. Mortgage Interest Rates were obtained from Mortgage-X at the zweb site http://mortgage-x.com/general/ historical_rates.asp. Data represent the National Mortgage 30-Year Fixed-Interest Rates for the first week of January and the first week of July.

of expansion saw the value of their properties increase every year. A homeowner wanting to move to a new place had at his/her disposal the resources created by the appreciation of his/her house over the previous years of ownership. These resources could be used to pay for the real estate commission. By the same token, a booming real estate business attracted many individuals to become agents and brokers. In 2007, the Chicago Association of Realtors (CAR) had around 17,000 members from 3,200 real estate firms. Around 95% of CAR members were dedicated to the residential real estate market. Five years before that, in 2002, CAR had only had 10,000 members.[6]

During boom periods, it was easier to pay for an agent's commission, but it was also very easy to sell a house. Both high demand and the availability of new technologies decreased the difficulty in selling a house; therefore consumers were willing to pay less for the agent's services. Average commissions steadily declined during this period of real estate prosperity, going from above 6% to little more than 5% (Exhibit 1).

"Boom" conditions did not last forever. The Federal Reserve increased federal funds annual interest rates from 1.35% in 2004 to 3.22% in 2005.[7] By the end of 2005, higher federal interest rates translated into higher interests for mortgages. By the beginning of 2006 the real estate market had significantly slowed down; the number of transactions in Chicago for the first six months of 2005 was around 18,000 while the same period of 2007 only registered 12,000 transactions, a 33% reduction (Exhibit 2). The Chicago inventory of houses (residential properties on sale at any given point in time) increased dramatically; it went from 30,000 at the beginning of 2005 to 42,000 at the beginning of 2007. As a consequence of both higher inventories and fewer transactions, the median number of days on the market[8] for a property increased from forty-five in 2005 to sixty-five in 2007. The slowdown of the market was aggravated by an increase in foreclosure levels because of lax underwriting in the subprime market. Appreciation slowed down from 10% annually to 0%. As the crisis continued, property values decreased in some markets. The real estate crisis did not reduce the number of CAR members but created a "revolving door" with some agents leaving the organization while new individuals joined.

Unlike prices in other big cities in the United States, median property prices in Chicago remained relatively stable and, according to some sources, they even increased slightly. However, the price of properties in the 75th percentile of the Chicago market declined from $430,000 to $399,000 between 2005 and early 2007 (Exhibit 3).

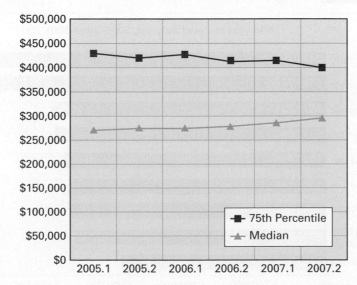

Exhibit 3 Chicago Housing Prices 2005–2007

Source: Information obtained from HousingTracker.net at http://www.housingtracker.net/askingprices/Illinois/Chicago-Naperville-Joliet/Chicago-Naperville-Joliet. Information includes the cities of Aurora, Carol Stream, Chicago, Des Plaines, Evanston, Joliet, McHenry, Naperville, Palatine, Schaumburg, and many others.

SUSSEX AND REILLY'S RESPONSE TO THE NEW COMPETITION

When Sean Conlon received the results of the Mid-Year Review, he was disappointed. He had expected his company's growth to accelerate, but the results were similar to those of the year before. Conlon held a series of conversations to determine if the company needed some corrective actions. Looking at the same results (see Exhibit 4 and Exhibit 5), Tomlinson had a different perspective:

> [Despite the lack of growth] we have the highest levels of annual commission by agent in the Chicago area; on average, our agents earned $10,000 more than agents at @ Properties, our closest competitor. Our agents also had the biggest transaction values and the highest average price per property sold. Our agents are performing well and we have a very successful environment to attract more star agents. But attracting agents is a difficult and time-consuming process.

The training director agreed with Tomlinson that building "star agents" from scratch was a process that took time and effort. However, he thought that there might be something that the company could do to support the agents in the tougher market, so he consulted some of them about their opinions. One agent explained:

> The new competitors, Internet and discount brokers, are affecting the whole market, not just the lower end of it. For example, this gentleman had a $2.2 million property that at the time he was trying to sell by himself. He was already listed in the MLS, so I assumed he hired a discount broker. He told me that he knew the buyer's agent needed to get 2.5% but that I should do the job for only 1%. When I said no, he asked for 1.5%. About 25 to 35% of my potential sellers want to negotiate commissions down.

Scheffler believed that the proliferation of discount brokers was a new and permanent competitive situation. No wishful thinking or legislation would take them out of the market. The director of Sussex and Reilly's Lincoln Park office agreed with Scheffler, but he believed that there had to be a limit to the growth of minimum-service brokers. He explained his view of the transformation of the real estate market:

> Companies will choose to compete in different areas. I've heard the founder of Help-U-Sell

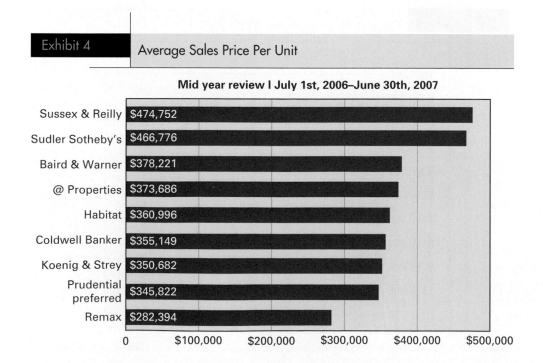

Exhibit 4   Average Sales Price Per Unit

Mid year review I July 1st, 2006–June 30th, 2007

Company	Average Sales Price
Sussex & Reilly	$474,752
Sudler Sotheby's	$466,776
Baird & Warner	$378,221
@ Properties	$373,686
Habitat	$360,996
Coldwell Banker	$355,149
Koenig & Strey	$350,682
Prudential preferred	$345,822
Remax	$282,394

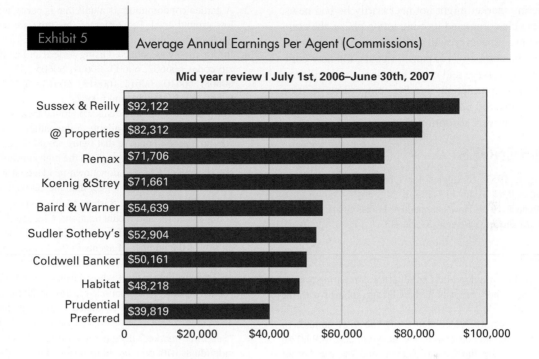

Exhibit 5 | Average Annual Earnings Per Agent (Commissions)

Mid year review I July 1st, 2006–June 30th, 2007

Sussex & Reilly	$92,122
@ Properties	$82,312
Remax	$71,706
Koenig &Strey	$71,661
Baird & Warner	$54,639
Sudler Sotheby's	$52,904
Coldwell Banker	$50,161
Habitat	$48,218
Prudential Preferred	$39,819

speak, and their business model is not to focus on quality but on value. There are different products for different people also in real estate. There are sellers who are not looking for the best, they just want the cheapest, and they will be serviced by flat fee. We should be able to maintain our model and meet our growth objectives.

Conlon was not willing to consider changing the company's business model, and most of his managers agreed with him. The only change that they would seriously consider was a review of the commission level. When Conlon started Sussex and Reilly, commissions in Chicago were about 5.5%, and he entered the market with a lower commission of 5%. Eventually, competitors did catch up, and in 2006, 5% was the industry standard. The lower commission helped the company establish itself during its infancy, but Tomlinson did not agree that a commission reduction would help them grow at this stage:

A year ago the whole industry was moving to commission levels lower than 5% and we were willing to go down. But now, average commissions have increased slightly, we should draw a line in the sand, stay firm and keep our commissions at current levels. In fact, we could increase our commission to 6%. Given the current market, selling houses is a tougher job, so sellers are willing

to pay more for results. That way we could attract agents with higher returns for their work.

Tomlinson was worried that reduced income would make the company less attractive to "star agents" who might otherwise consider transferring to Sussex and Reilly. The training director agreed with him that reducing the commission level was not a good idea, since agents would have to work more for less money. He believed that the company and the agents needed a pricing strategy where superior service was accompanied by reasonably high prices. However, he was not sure that a policy forcing all agents to have higher commission levels would work. His rationale was the following:

Without more information about the behaviors of our target market, we don't know if our clients would be willing to pay the higher commission. Besides, agents do not like change, particularly this kind of risky change. If the higher commission decreased their number of closed transactions, then their total earnings would also be reduced.

Scheffler agreed that a commission change was not practical at the time. She was not sure that the situation required any particular strategic change, since part of the reason the company had not grown was that the market was in a period of contraction. Lack of sales growth in a contracting market might not necessarily be bad news. Once the cycle completed its contraction phase, the company might resume its growth with their present strategies.

Given the company's expansion goals, the new competitive models in the real estate industry, the conditions of a market in contraction, and the competitive position of the company, did Sussex and Reilly need to change its strategy? What were its options?

REFERENCES

Ansoff, Igor. 1957. Strategies for Diversification. *Harvard Business Review*, 35: 113–124.

Porter, Michael. 1979. How Competitive Forces Shape Strategy. *Harvard Business Review,* 57: 86–93.

NOTES

1. Information provided by Liz Scheffler comparing the experience of her company in the Chicago suburbs with the city market.

2. This number was calculated using the total number of owner-occupied households in Chicago in 2007 (499,000) as reported by the Census Bureau and the number of houses on real estate listings (or inventory) reported by Housing Tracker at http://www.housingtracker.net/asking-prices/chicago-illinois for 2006.

3. A garden condominium is a unit that is partly located below ground level. Properties of this type are considered the least desirable.

4. Information was collected using American FactFinder for zip codes 606602, 60603, 60604, 60605, 60606, 60607, 60608, 60610, 60611, 60613, 60614, 60622, 60625, 60640, 60657, 60659, and 60661.

5. The percentage of individuals who found their houses using the Internet was only available at the national level. There was no reason to believe that figure would be too different for the Midwest. However, given the high educational level and income of Chicago downtown residents, it is possible that the local figure was bigger than the national one.

6. Information provided by Barbara Matthopoulos, director of communications and media relations, Chicago Association of Realtors (CAR). CAR membership is only a rough indicator of the number of agents in the Chicago area, since membership in the organization, first, is voluntary and, second, may include realtors whose business is outside the city.

7. Annual federal funds continued to rise in 2006 with a rate of 4.87%. Information obtained online at http://www.federalreserve.gov/releases/h15/data/Annual/H15_FF_O.txt.

8. "Subprime market" designates mortgage loans aimed at individuals with poor credit histories. Because these loans are more risky, investors charge at least 3% more than for the "prime" mortgages granted to individuals with good credit.

Case 3

Estonian Air's Big Buy

Karen Popovich, Saint Michael's College
Diane Lander, Saint Michael's College
Robert Letovsky, Saint Michael's College

It was mid-March 2007, and Rait Kalda, vice president of AS Estonian Air Operations, was in his office looking out at the recently reconstructed Tallinn Airport runway. He checked the departure time table as he watched one of Estonian Air's Boeing 737-300s take off. The plane was bound for Dublin with 93 passengers aboard. He was pleased to note that the flight departed precisely on time.

Kalda's sense of satisfaction quickly faded, however, as he resumed working on the problem at hand. Jet fuel prices had increased, on average, about 32% over the last three years (Exhibit 1). Glancing at the latest industry report, he noted that fuel costs accounted for almost 26% of operating costs, representing an 18% increase from 2005 (Exhibit 2). On the bright side, internal market forecasts predicted a 10–15% increase in the demand for intra-European

Year	Cents/gal.	% Change*
1997	61.30	—
1998	45.00	−26.60
1999	53.30	16.60
2000	88.00	69.00
2001	76.30	−13.80
2002	71.60	−7.50
2003	87.10	22.10
2004	120.80	38.20
2005	172.30	43.90
2006	196.10	14.40

Source: http://www.eia.doe.gov/pub/oil_gas/petroleum/data_publications/petroleum_marketing_monthly/historical/2009/2009_03/pdf/pmmall.pdf.

The case writers prepared this case as the basis for class discussion rather than to illustrate either the effective or ineffective handling of a managerial situation. The case is based on real persons, events, and organizations, though the dialogue and and commentary have been constructed by the authors to provide additional context for analysis. The authors appreciate the efforts of Tupper Cawsey, editor of the *Case Research Journal* and the anonymous reviewers that have helped to make this a more effective case.

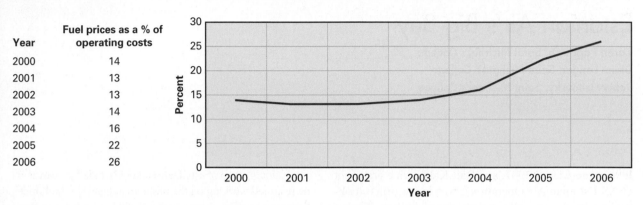

Exhibit 2 | **Jet Fuel Prices as a Percent of Operating Costs: Worldwide Airline Industry**

Year	Fuel prices as a % of operating costs
2000	14
2001	13
2002	13
2003	14
2004	16
2005	22
2006	26

Source: IATA Financial Forecast September 2007. Available at http://www.iata.org/whatwedo/economics/ffarchives.htm.

regional flights. He raised his eyebrows in thought. How would their competition react to these forecasted increases in demand? Should Estonian Air expand its fleet of planes? If they were to expand, an obvious decision was the Boeing 737. Estonian Air currently leased and operated four Boeing 737s. However, considering expected increases in fuel prices, Kalda wondered if it was time to look at the smaller but more fuel efficient turboprops, such as the Bombardier Q400.

The major benefit of using turboprops for short-leg flights, besides greater fuel efficiency, was increased seat utilization (about 90% for the Q400 versus 62% for 737s). Noting that at least 90% of Estonian Air's existing routes could be serviced by Q400 turboprops, Kalda also had to consider operational impacts of smaller planes.

Expanding, whether with jets or turboprops, implied significant new lease payments for Estonian Air.[1] A much less costly alternative would be to accommodate anticipated future growth by leasing used aircraft in the secondary market. All of these choices, however, were predicated on the assumption of continued economic prosperity in Estonia and across Europe.

The next executive team meeting was scheduled for Friday afternoon, and the team expected a recommendation on how Kalda planned to address the expected increase in intra-European regional flight demand in light of both high fuel prices and last year's net loss (about $5 million in U.S. Dollars).[2] The executive team, reporting to the president, consisted of the vice presidents of

operations, finance, and commercial. The vice presidents' responsibilities were as follows:

- Operations included flights, maintenance, quality, security, and crew handling.
- Finance included accounting, risk management, IT, purchasing, and control.
- Commercial covered sales, revenue management, marketing, and in-flight services.

Kalda knew that he would have to calculate and compare fuel efficiency and fuel costs for each alternative plane. He would also need an operational analysis that would evaluate utilization rates under maximum and current operating capacities.[3]

Exhibit 3 | **Coversion Factors**

1 U.S. Gallon = 3.785 Liters	1 Liter = 0.264 U.S. Gallons
1 Foot = 0.304 Meters	1 Meter = 3.281 Feet
1 Mile = 1.609 Kilometers	1 Kilometer = 0.621 Miles
1 Mile = 0.869 Nautical Miles	1 Nautical Mile = 1.151 Miles

EEK to USD Currency Conversion Rates (Interbank rate)

The agerage daily EEK-USD currency conversion rate for
January 1, 2007: $0.0843
March 1, 2007: $0.0844

Source: http://www.oanda.com/convert/. Accessed July 1, 2009.

Rait Kalda had worked for Estonian Air since 1994. A transport engineer by training, he had also studied business administration. Kalda had been around airplanes all of his adult life, having previously worked as an airplane mechanic and then manager at an aviation club. One of his first postings at Estonian Air had been as Operations Manager of the Air Maintenance group. Kalda rose rapidly at Estonian Air, completing a rotation in accounting, then serving as head of the Technical Maintenance Resources group, director of aviation engineering, and ultimately becoming vice president. Not surprisingly, Kalda proudly listed aviation as one of his many hobbies.

Kalda turned to his computer and reviewed his full inbox. He had recently received several e-mails from Andrus Aljas, Estonian Air's new vice president of finance and administration and a member of the airline's board. In his e-mails to Kalda, Aljas outlined a number of additional financial parameters that he was planning to address at the executive meeting. In fact, Aljas had requested a brief meeting with Kalda to discuss the presentation and the entire acquisition question before Friday's executive team meeting.

THE AIRLINE INDUSTRY

The worldwide airline industry in 2007 was composed of three distinct competitive groups: legacy carriers, low cost carriers, and regional carriers. Legacy carriers represented the largest group in terms of passenger revenue, route coverage, and fleet size. These were generally the largest airlines, offering flights within their respective home countries, and between their home countries and overseas destinations. In the United States, this category included Delta, United, American, Continental, and US Airways. In Europe, legacy carriers included British Airways (UK), Lufthansa (Germany), Air France/KLM (France, Netherlands), SAS (Sweden), Iberia (Spain), Finnair (Finland), and Aer Lingus (Ireland). Most European legacy carriers had partial or full government ownership through most of their existence. Since the 1980s, most European governments gradually divested their interests in their "flag carriers," which became private corporations, with ownership spread among a wide range of investing institutions and individuals.

Legacy carriers in both the U.S. and Europe operated large fleets which included planes ranging from 100+ seats (e.g., Boeing 737, Airbus A19/320) to 500+ seats (e.g., Boeing 747, Airbus A380). Legacy carriers typically operated extensive networks of routes, organized around hub-and-spoke systems. Under hub-and-spoke, a carrier would concentrate its operations in a major hub (e.g., London Heathrow), with major international routes flying out of that hub on the carrier's largest planes. In this way, passengers in smaller markets could book a ticket to an international destination served by the carrier while still staying on that carrier's planes for the entire trip, generally flying one of the carrier's smaller planes to arrive at the hub.

Beginning in the late 1960s, a new type of competitor emerged in the U.S. The first and still dominant example of a low cost carrier (LCC) was Southwest Airlines. Southwest's strategy, subsequently emulated by start-ups around the world, was based on several specific decisions. These included:

- Offering direct, point-to-point service instead of routing passengers to a hub;
- Focusing on shorter (i.e., under 800 km) routes;
- Operating a fleet based on only one type of airplane to minimize training and maintenance costs;
- Providing only one class of seating while not offering many of the services typically offered by legacy carriers (e.g., meals) to maximize seating capacity;
- Employing a non union work force to maximize employee flexibility, lowering labor costs;
- Shortening flight turnaround times to ensure maximum output per plane per day.

The real impetus to U.S. airline competition came in the late 1970s, with deregulation of domestic air routes. Over the next thirty years, a number of LCCs started but then disappeared. By 2007, the leading American LCCs were Southwest, AirTran, and Jet Blue Airlines.

The LCC business model arrived relatively later in Europe, taking root in the late 1980s with the launch of Ryanair. The Irish airline grew to become the leading LCC carrier on the continent under the leadership of its charismatic and often controversial CEO, Michael O'Leary.

The LCC model in Europe was given a tremendous boost by the signing of the Maastricht agreement in 1992 and the passage of the Single European Act, creating the structure for the European Union. This reduced trade barriers between member European countries and had a dramatic impact on airlines on the continent.

The process of European economic integration opened new strategic possibilities for legacy carriers, but it also facilitated a number of European airline start-ups directly based on the Southwest LCC model. By 2007, in addition to Ryanair, the continent's LCC carriers included EasyJet (based in the UK), AirBerlin and Germanwings (both based in Germany), and Sky-Europe (based in Slovakia). LCCs generally operated jet fleets based either on small single aisle jets from the large plane manufacturers (i.e., either the Boeing 737 or the Airbus A320) or regional jets (seating 90 or less) offered by firms such as Bombardier, Embraer, BAE, or Fokker.

The third strategic group was regional carriers. These were airlines which specialized in short-haul flights to limited geographic areas, but not at the ultra-low fares offered by LCCs. Regional carriers usually served small cities, connecting them with national or regional capitals. They relied on fleets composed of a mix of small regional jets and turboprop planes.

In the U.S., leading regional carriers included firms such as Midwest Airlines, Skywest Airlines, and Frontier. It was common for many of the short-haul regional routes to be served by legacy carriers, who contracted the business to independent firms such as Republic and Colgan Air, flying planes under the legacy carrier's insignia.

In Europe, there were a larger number of regional carriers. Typical of this type of airline were firms such as Air Nostrum, connecting cities in Spain; SATA Air Açores, connecting the Azores and Canary Islands with mainland Portugal; Luxair, flying between Luxembourg and destinations in Germany, France, and Belgium; and Aero Airlines, connecting Tallinn, Estonia, with cities in Finland. Increasingly, LCCs were making inroads into the regional carriers' market space, offering passengers a combination of lower prices and connections to other destinations in the LCC network. One senior executive of a leading regional aircraft manufacturer went so far as to say that European regional carriers had no choice but " . . . to drive down costs or die."[4]

Regional Aircraft

Regional aircraft, also known as "short-haul aircraft," are built for flights that are typically 800 kilometers or less one way. Starting in the late 1990s, airlines shifted their demand for regional aircraft from turboprops to jets which seated 90 or fewer passengers. Within the last few years, increasing fuel prices and the general decrease in aircraft demand following the 9/11 attacks on the U.S. lead to a switch back to turboprops. Innovations in

turboprop technology included increased fuel capacity and improved fuel efficiency, burning 30 to 40% less fuel than a regional jet. New model turboprops also offered in-flight comfort comparable to jets. They had advanced noise and vibration suppression systems and flew at higher cruising altitudes than their forerunners. By 2006, airlines ranging from legacy carriers, such as Continental, to leading regional carriers, like Horizon Air, were actively considering using new turboprops for regional flights and abandoning the "jets-first" strategy adopted in the late 1990s.[5]

In 2005, orders for turboprops from aircraft manufacturers such as Bombardier and Avions de Transport Régional (ATR) grew more than 240% to 151 aircraft, while similar sized regional jets built by Bombardier and Embraer slumped to just 25 orders. Analysts forecasted that between 2007 and 2016, nearly 1,500 new regional aircraft would be needed in order to keep up with projected demand.[6]

Globalization also has had a tremendous impact on the demand for regional aircraft. Aircraft manufacturers have been supplying more regional aircraft to buyers outside of the U.S. Since 2000, Bombardier has predicted that countries such as China and India would become significant purchasers of both new and used turboprops. Indian carriers Air Deccan and Kingfisher already had ordered increasing numbers of turboprops from both Bombardier and ATR. These developments could mean longer order backlogs for Bombardier and correspondingly, higher list prices for buyers such as Estonian Air.

One key operating cost of all airlines was fuel, which was a function of oil prices on world markets, changes to jet and aircraft fuel prices (which depended on refining capacity and decisions made by refiners), the type of fleet an airline operated (older planes were generally less fuel efficient than newer models), and the nature of an airline's route structure (generally shorter, more frequent routes involving frequent takeoffs and landings consumed more fuel than longer routes involving fewer takeoffs and landings). Given their relatively high number of shorter flights and more frequent takeoffs and landings, fuel efficiency was often a greater priority for regional carriers than for legacy airlines. In 2003, fuel prices rose sharply both in absolute terms (Exhibit 1) and as a percentage of total worldwide airline costs (Exhibit 2). The industry consensus in 2007 was that fuel prices would continue to rise by at least 5% per year for the foreseeable future.

THE ECONOMY OF ESTONIA

The Republic of Estonia, population 1.3 million, is a small country, about twice the size of New Hampshire, located in the Baltic region of Northern Europe (Exhibit 4). Tallinn, Estonia's capital, is the country's most populated city. With the collapse of the Soviet Union in the early 1990s, the Estonian economy grew rapidly as the country adopted a free-market model aimed at attracting foreign investment.

Estonia revamped and simplified its tax structure, with the corporate tax rate on distributed profits lowered until it reached 25%.[7] In 2004, Estonia entered both the European Union and NATO. This made the country eligible for billions of dollars worth of "cohesion funds" (i.e., economic development subsidies) from the European Union. The country's economic growth was also bolstered by a rise in the information technology sector and a boom in real estate. By 2007, annual GDP was approximately equivalent to $14 billion. However, there were potential storm clouds

emerging on the economic horizon. The country's red-hot real estate market seemed to be dependent on access to relatively cheap credit, mainly from European banks.

The country's national currency was the Estonian Kroon (sign: KR, code: EEK). The average daily USD-EEK currency conversion rate as of March 1, 2007 was $1 U.S. = 11.8449 EEK (or 1 EEK = $0.0844 U.S.) (Exhibit 3). Estonia was a heavy importer and any decline in the value of the Kroon could have a serious impact on the prices paid for imported goods.

Estonian Air

The Estonian government, SAS Group (formerly Scandinavian Airlines System), and Cresco, an Estonian investment bank, founded Estonian Air, the national air carrier of Estonia, in 1991. Estonian Air's hub was Tallinn Airport, the largest in Estonia, located approximately four kilometers from the capital city's downtown. By 2005, Tallinn Airport had surpassed the "million passengers" per year mark.

Exhibit 4	The Country of Estonia

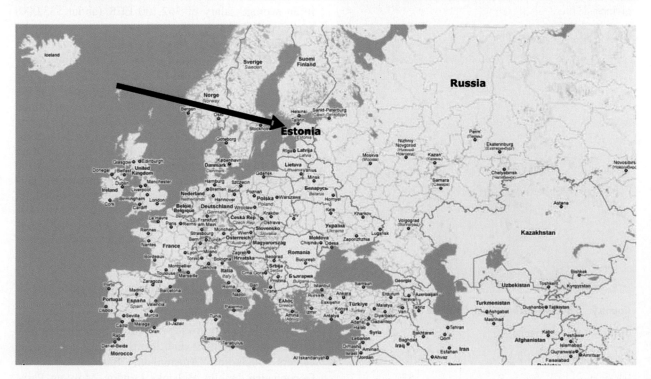

Estonian Air's key strategic goal, as stated in the firm's annual report,[8] was to ensure sustainable and profitable growth through target markets, customer satisfaction, fleet renewal, and employee development. At the end of 2006, Estonian Air provided regularly scheduled regional and long-haul passenger flights to sixteen destinations in Europe (Exhibit 5), as well as charter flights and cargo transport. Its fleet consisted of four leased jets: one Boeing 737-300 and three Boeing 737-500s.[9]

In 2006, Estonian Air carried 689,747 passengers over 9,070 flights, resulting in a load factor (LF)[10] of about 62%. The company saw its available seat per kilometer (ASK)[11] increase by slightly over 11% over the previous year. For 2007, the company expected to see a 1% increase in the total flights, about an 8% increase in total passengers (of which 86% were regular passengers and 14% charter passengers), and a 5% increase in ASK. Average flight length and average aircraft block hours per day[12] were not expected to change. Estonian Air met industry standards for short-range carriers and could operate up to eight flights per day on each of its planes; although operationally, they had been averaging about seven flights per day.[13]

Estonian Air had an enviable on-time record, as measured by its percentage of ontime flights and fifteen-minute punctuality. In 2006, 99.1% of Estonian Air's flights were rated as "regular" and the carrier's fifteen-minute punctuality rating was 84.5%; both measures were slightly down from 2005. Exhibit 6 compares the 2004, 2005, 2006, and expected 2007 key operations indicators.

Even though Estonian Air was not known as a low-wage employer, it could not and did not try to match the salary scales of the large international carriers. Average crew member salaries, based on the last few years' financial statements, increased about 2% each year, resulting in an average salary of 362,100 EEK (about $33,000) expected for 2008.

Selected company financial data are presented in Exhibit 7. The net loss for 2006 was troubling. There were several contributing factors including escalating fuel prices. The most notable factor, however, was the extraordinary costs (73.4m EEK) due to unplanned technical problems leading to unscheduled downtime. The company responded to this by relying on temporary and very high cost capacity leased from other carriers. Even if Estonian Air's technical issues were resolved, planes required extensive maintenance. This was especially true for planes operated by short-haul carriers, with multiple takeoffs and landings each day. Estonian Air estimated that under optimal conditions it could only count on a typical plane operating for 325 days per year.

Exhibit 5	Estonian Air Destinations: Current and Planned

Country	Existing Destinations	Distance from Tallinn (km)
Belgium	Brussels	1,600
Croatia	Dubrovnik	1,900
Denmark	Copenhagen	830
France	Paris	1,900
Germany	Berlin	1,000
	Frankfurt	1,000
	Hamburg	1,100
Ireland	Dublin	2,000
Italy	Milan	1,900
Norway	Oslo	790
Russia	Moscow	900
Spain	Barcelona	2,500
Sweden	Stockholm	375
UK	London	1,800
Ukraine	Kiev	1,100
	Simferopol	1,700
Average Distance (km)		**1,400**

Country	Planned Destinations	Distance from Tallinn (km)
Austria	Vienna	1,350
Finland	Helsinki	85
Lithuania	Vilnius	530

AS Estonian Air's Competitors

In early 2007, commercial passengers could fly into or out of Tallinn on routes within Estonia; to regional capitals in the Baltics; and directly to major European centers, including Amsterdam, Barcelona, Berlin, Copenhagen, Dublin, Helsinki, London, Moscow, Paris,

Exhibit 6   Estonian Air Key Operations Indicators

Key Operations Indicators	E[2007](a)	2006(b)	2005(b)	2007(c)
Flights operated	9,161	9,070	9,051	8,285
Number of seats produced (capacity)*	1,190,232	1,112,366	1,053,395	935,500
Total passengers	744,927	689,747	642,821	546,600
Load factor (passengers/seats)*	62%	62%	61%	58%
Available seat kilometers (ASK)*	1,498,393,000	1,427,041,000	1,284,472,000	1,020,000,000
Average flight distance, km	1,400	1,400	1,220	1,091
Average aircraft block hours per day, hrs*	10.5	10.5	10.2	9.12
Average flight length, hrs	1.5	1.5	1.5	1.5
Operations Quality Measurements:				
Percent on time flights	N/A	99.1%	99.5%	N/A
Fifteen-minute punctuality	N/A	84.5%	87.4%	N/A
Expected Increases:				
Fuel price increase	5%			
Ticket price increase	5%			
Passengers	8%			
Crew salaries	2%			

(a) Case page 8.
(b) 2006 Annual Report, pages 5 and 7.
(c) 2005 Annual Report, page 4.

*See glossary for airline specific terms, Exhibit 9.

Rome, and Vienna.[14] Estonian Air's major competitors into and out of Tallinn included A/S Air Baltic, EasyJet, and Aero Airlines.

A/S Air Baltic Corporation, the national airline of Latvia, a joint venture between the government of Latvia and the Scandinavian airline group SAS, specialized in serving cities within the Baltic region with some flights to major European centers. It had a mixed jet/turboprop fleet composed of fourteen aircraft (Boeing 737 jets and Fokker 50 turboprops).

The second main competitor of Estonian Air, British discount carrier EasyJet, had grown from a small carrier operating two leased jets for flights within the UK in 1995, to one of Europe's largest discount short-haul carriers with over 180 planes and almost 400 routes across the continent. EasyJet scrupulously followed the business model set by other successful LCCs: point-to-point service, internet ticket booking, and a single model fleet (the single-aisle Airbus A320, a direct competitor to the Boeing 737). Though EasyJet only offered five flights per week out of Tallinn, all to the carrier's hub near London, it was a formidable competitor given its reputation for affordable air travel and its extensive European connections.

Aero Airlines, the third competitor, was first established in Helsinki, Finland, in 1923, and for the next seventeen years specialized in flying freight and passengers throughout the Baltics and Scandinavia. With the annexation of the Baltic States by the Soviet Union in 1940, Aero ceased to exist. However, Finnair retained the Aero brand and restarted the airline as a joint venture with another firm in 2000. The then newly incarnated Aero specialized in connecting Tallinn with three cities in Finland, using two ATR 72-200 turboprops leased from Finnair.

Exhibit 7	Selected Estonian Air Financial Data

	2006 (a) EEK '000	2005(a) EEK '000	2004 (b) EEK '000
Assets			
Non-current assets			
Property, plant, and equipment	72,691	78,200	86,010
Intangible assets	2,019	745	492
Investments in joint ventures	14,826	12,698	10,434
Other financial assets	25,401	25,694	22,394
Total non-current assets	*114,937*	*117,337*	*119,330*
Current assets			
Derivative financial assets	–	–	947
Inventories	4,033	4,213	4,363
Trade receivables and prepayments made	166,029	140,124	116,771
Securities	–	–	117
Cash and bank balances	161,990	242,180	208,051
Total current assets	*332,052*	*386,517*	*330,249*
Total assets	**446,989**	**503,854**	**449,579**
Equity and liabilities			
Equity			
Share capital (nominal value)	49,503	49,503	49,503
Share premium	149,997	149,997	149,997
Statutory legal reserves	4,950	4,950	4,950
Retained earnings/(accumulated loss)	46,299	(19,583)	(46,880)
Net profit/(loss) for financial year	(58,937)	65,882	27,297
Total equity	*191,812*	*250,749*	*184,867*
Provisions			
Provisions	24,921	51,518	62,462
Total provisions	*24,921*	*51,518*	*62,462*
Non-current liabilities			
Borrowings	18,034	22,075	29,643
Total non-current liabilities	*18,034*	*22,075*	*29,643*
Current liabilities			
Trade payables and prepayments collected	204,034	165,330	165,044
Borrowings	8,188	7,567	7,563
Derivative financial instruments	–	6,615	–
Total current liabilities	*212,222*	*179,512*	*172,607*
Total liabilities	*255,177*	*253,105*	*264,712*
Total equity and liabilities	**446,989**	**503,854**	**449,579**

continues

	2006 (a) EEK '000	2005(a) EEK '000	2004 (b) EEK '000
Revenue			
Passenger revenue	962,758	867,085	805,631
Charter	214,740	141,207	73,768
Mail and freight	20,725	23,580	20,774
Other traffic revenue	49,683	73,943	18,369
Other operating revenue			
Ground handling	16,644	16,178	10,942
Other services	26,866	29,685	20,392
Total revenue	**1,291,416**	**1,151,678**	**949,876**
Total cost of sales	**1,190,320**	**961,081**	**820,569**
Gross Profit	**101,096**	**190,597**	**129,307**
Other operating income	2,791	20,036	63,049
Marketing expenses	(88,268)	(82,527)	(80,158)
Administrative expenses	(74,946)	(65,880)	(60,313)
Other operating expenses	(12,189)	(4,510)	(26,670)
Operating profit/(loss)	**(71,516)**	**57,716**	**25,215**
Share of profits of joint ventures	5,035	4,670	2,790
Interest income	4,305	6,058	3,423
Interest expense	(1,479)	(1,534)	(1,909)
Net foreign exchange gains/(losses)	(1,753)	6,661	(3,391)
Other financial gains/(losses)	6,471	(7,689)	1,169
Net financial income	**12,579**	**8,166**	**2,082**
Profit/(loss) for the year	**(58,937)**	**65,882**	**27,297**

(a) 2006 Annual Report, page 14
(b) 2005 Annual Report, page 7

Source: Estonian Air Annual Reports, www.estonian-air.ee/estonian_air_annual_reports.

AS Estonian Air's Growth Strategy

Estonian Air's internal analysis assumed that the air transport market in Estonia would continue to grow at a healthy 10 to 15% per year over the next several years. These growth expectations were based on a positive economic outlook for the Estonian economy, market forecasts for intra-European regional flights, and the increasing popularity of Estonia as a tourist destination. Unfortunately, the trend of competing carriers entering the Estonian air transport market was expected to continue.

The growing market on the one hand and the toughening competition on the other hand raised challenges for

Estonian Air. Key success factors for Estonian Air's future included increasing efficiency, ensuring high productivity of flight operations, and maintaining a competitive cost base. In its 2006 Annual Report, Estonian Air clearly expressed its readiness for "implementing a growth strategy and for investing in the development of its fleet." Management projected that, if it increased the fleet, it could:

- increase the frequency of flights to existing destinations and add new routes (Exhibit 5),
- increase general reliability as well as limit the carrier's vulnerability to unplanned technical problems.

A preliminary review of the available aircraft options had shown the Boeing 737 jet (either the 300 or 500 model) and the Bombardier Q400 turboprop to be the most attractive for Estonian Air's purposes. Additionally, within the secondary market, Estonian Air considered one or more Saab 340A turboprops to be on the short list. The turboprops were smaller than the 737 in terms of seating capacity. The Q400, despite smaller capacity, did not necessarily limit Estonian Air's reach, as it could reach about 90% of Estonian Air's current destinations. Due to its smaller size, the Saab would be considered for about 50% of Estonian Air's current destinations (Exhibit 5). Airplanes were generally considered to have a twenty-five year useful life. Though many airlines pushed their planes beyond this point, the consensus in the industry was that added maintenance costs made this increasingly uneconomic, especially for short-haul carriers. Kalda observed that the used Saab had ten years remaining in its useful life.

All of these factors would be discussed and evaluated at Friday's team meeting. Kalda knew that some of the decision factors—such as the extent to which traffic would actually grow and the issues involved in scheduling if smaller planes with shorter ranges were added to the fleet—might not lend themselves easily to a quantitative analysis. Other factors—notably plane-specific performance and productivity data—would be more amenable to a quantitative analysis that could be quickly reviewed at the meeting before arriving at a final decision.

ESTONIAN AIR'S AIRCRAFT OPTIONS

The Boeing 737 Jet

In the late 1960s, in the face of a severe downturn in the airline industry, Boeing launched the 737, a 110 seat, twin engine short range carrier. The 737 became the best selling model in the history of commercial aviation, with over 5,000 planes delivered by 2007. The 737 series, which began with the 737-100 in 1968, included multiple variants up to the newest, the 737-900, and reflected Boeing's design philosophy, introduced by then CEO, T. A. Wilson. Wilson insisted that each Boeing model be designed to generate new versions of itself as airline customers' needs evolved. Though some felt this philosophy added cost to the design process, Wilson claimed that his "family" strategy was a recipe for long-term competitive success: "A new version of an old product line is hard to beat with an entirely new aircraft. You have to have a 20% improvement [in the new model]. The cost of engineering and tooling is more on the new plane, and meanwhile the old version is being improved too."[15] In 2007, the list price for a 737-300 was approximately $40 million, while the larger 737-500 listed for approximately $50 million.

The 737 series offered airlines an increased range of capacities (from 108 passenger seats to 215 passenger seats) and ranges (from 4,204 km to 10,200 km), and had proven to be the workhorse of the global discount and short-range airline industry. Its popularity with such well-known discount carriers as Southwest and Ryanair was due to two key attributes: low cost of operation and flexibility.

Boeing's Web site claimed that the newest model 737s ". . . have the lowest operating costs in their class. In fact, on a typical route the 737s cash operating costs are nearly 4% less than its closest competitor, the Airbus A320 series, in part due to its superior structural efficiency."[16] According to Boeing, the 737s lower weight than its direct competitor, the Airbus A320, not only meant less fuel expense but also lower engine maintenance costs, navigation and landing fees for airlines. In order to reduce maintenance costs even further, the 737 was designed with a low stance, meaning that most equipment could be serviced from the ground without costly lifts. The fact that baggage could also be loaded from the ground made the plane even more appealing to discount and short-range operators, as they could make last-minute baggage additions quickly, reducing costly turnaround time between flights. The plane was redesigned over the years with the aim of reducing the number of parts, further cutting maintenance costs.

As noted, at the end of 2006 Estonian Air's fleet consisted exclusively of Boeing 737s: one Boeing 737-300 and three Boeing 737-500s. Performance data for the Boeing 737-300 and the Boeing 737-500 are given in Exhibit 8.

Bombardier Q400 Turboprop

Bombardier, based in Montreal, Canada, was a leader in both the turboprop and regional jet markets. Its Q400, launched in 1995, had many advantages for regional carriers, such as greater fuel efficiency compared to similar sized jets, decreased cabin noise (the "Q" stands for "quiet"), increased cabin space, and the ability to travel

Exhibit 8	Aircraft Specifications

Specification	Boeing 737-300	Boeing 737-500	Q400 Turboprop	Saab 340A
Cockpit crew	2	2	2	2
Flight attendants	3	3	2 or 3	1
Seating capacity	128–149	108–149	68–78	30–36
Max fuel (gallons)	6,130	6,296	1,724	849
Max fuel (liters)	23,204	23,832	6,526	3,214
Range (km)	4,204	4,444	2,522	1,505
Range (miles)	2,612	2,761	1,567	935
Max altitude (feet)	37,000	37,000	25,000	25,000
Max altitude (meters)	11,278	11,278	7,620	7,600
List price (millions)	$40	$50	$28–30	$1.5–2.5
Average load factor	62%	62%	90%	95%
Landing weight (lbs.)	115,500	115,500	64,500	29,000
Landing fees ($ per 10,000 lbs.)	$2	$2	$2	$2
Estonian Air Operations				
Actual flights per day	7	7	7	5
Maximum flights per day	8	8	8	5
Operating days per year	325	325	325	325
Useful life	25	25	25	10

almost as fast as regional jets over short-haul distances.[17] The Q400s ability to burn 30–40% less fuel than a comparably priced regional jet appealed to airlines, especially as fuel prices increased. The plane also offered environmental benefits, as it emitted only half of the carbon dioxide of a seventy-seater jet. The Q400 had the ability to use shorter runways and fly at lower altitudes, helping to reduce air traffic congestion and alleviate runway delays.[18] Performance data for the Q400 are given in Exhibit 8. As of 2007, the Q400 list price was between $28 and $30 million.

Saab 340A—Secondary Market

Estonian Air could also consider leasing smaller used aircraft. The used market consisted of several internationally-recognized brokers, who had extensive Web sites where potential buyers could search for models that met their needs and desired price points. Aircraft leasing companies were regular re sellers of aircraft that had been returned after the expiration of their lease contracts, as well.

Though there were a number of possible planes Estonian Air could consider in the used market, Kalda felt that the best candidate for acquisition was the Saab 340A, a 30 to 36 seat twin-engine turboprop. It was introduced in 1983 by a joint venture between Saab of Sweden and Fairchild Aircraft of the U.S. After a couple of years, Fairchild withdrew from the project, and Saab took over exclusive responsibility for the plane. Saab sold almost 160 of the initial "A" version. Then, in 1989, the company introduced a second generation version, the 340B, with enhanced power and more sophisticated noise controls. The final version, the 340B Plus, was launched in 1994. Saab had some success with these two versions, selling 200 340Bs, and 100 340B Plus models to commuter airlines around the world. The plane never met Saab's expectations, and the company decided to discontinue the entire line in 1998. Among the 340s' users were commuter airlines from countries around Estonia, including Finland, Germany, Lithuania, and Poland.

Used models of the Saab 340 were available through various brokers for prices ranging from $1.5 to $2.5 million. While leasing one or more used Saab 340s would considerably reduce Estonian Air's up-front investment, it raised other issues for Kalda. Most notably, the 340 was a small plane, having half the capacity and range of the Q400 turboprop and about one-fifth to one-third of the capacity and range of the Boeing 737. This would necessitate an entirely different type of scheduling for Estonian Air, as it probably would have to assign a greater number of flights to any given route to serve a given demand level. The Saab was expected to be operational for 325 days per year. However, the expected number of flights per day for the Saab would be five, versus the seven which Estonian Air typically achieved with jets (and could achieve with the Q400), due to its lower range and corresponding need for refueling stops. Another potential operational concern for Kalda was the availability of spare parts. Since the Saab would have been out of production for almost ten years by the time it was acquired by Estonian Air, Kalda would have to be assured that spare parts could be acquired quickly and affordably, something that might be increasingly problematic in the years going forward.

THE MEETING WITH THE VICE PRESIDENT OF FINANCE

For several weeks, Andrus Aljas had been e-mailing Kalda, outlining various issues he wanted to review for Friday's executive team meeting. In his latest e-mail, he requested a short meeting to discuss some of his concerns. Aljas, new to Estonian Air, joined the airline in 2006 as deputy vice president for finance and member of the board. A graduate of Tallinn University of Technology in production management and the Estonain Business School EMBA program, Aljas had been a financial specialist at Viisnurk, a large wood-processing firm. Kalda felt that it was important to meet with Aljas as soon as possible to gain additional insights into potential questions the board might ultimately raise.

The meeting was held in Aljas's rather sparse office at Estonian Air's headquarters. He began the meeting by thanking Kalda for taking the time to meet with him. Then he surprised Kalda by saying that he had just returned from a one-week trip in Western Europe, where he had had the chance to fly on EasyJet.

"I must say," Aljas quipped, "it wasn't too bad … we arrived on time, and for the money it was a good deal. I could see why people like them."

Aljas added a cautionary note: "Listen, Rait, it's easy for people to laugh at Michael O'Leary, half of what he says is for show. But the other half isn't. These LCCs are going to be very aggressive over the next few years, and I don't think there's a destination in Europe they won't look to expand into if they can."

Then Aljas unveiled the gist for the meeting. "I must confess I am getting a bit anxious about this. How confident are we about the growth projections? What if they are too conservative? Could we end up outgrowing a smaller plane quite quickly?"

Before Kalda could even respond, Aljas continued. "On the other hand, what if we're being too optimistic in the growth projections?"

Passenger volume forecasts were not the only thing Aljas was nervous about. "I know I'm throwing a lot at you, but since we're talking along these lines, there's another thing some board members have been talking about—exchange rates."

Kalda sensed unease, but probed him anyway: "In what sense?" he asked. "Does the board know something I don't? I thought the EEK was doing quite well over the past few years. I've used twelve EEK to the U.S. dollar as a conservative estimate."

"It has," replied Aljas, "but don't forget, this is a large deal for us, in U.S. dollars no less. What happens if, for whatever reason, the Kroon dropped significantly from its present level? Even a one Kroon drop against the dollar would have an impact on our bottom line; wouldn't that affect whatever choice we were looking at?"

As if to reassure Kalda, Aljas added "I recognize we've been doing well. Look, our borrowing costs have come down in the past couple of years—I think the financial institutions are more comfortable with us. We've been using a 11.5% hurdle rate for acquisitions and investments, and that's down even from when I started here."

Kalda sensed that Aljas was speaking for other board members, so he immediately asked him, "How conservatively is the board looking to our future growth? I've assumed that our ticket prices would increase in line with

Exhibit 9	Glossary

Available Seat Kilometers (ASK)—Measures an airline flight's passenger carrying capacity. It is equal to the number of seats onboard an aircraft multiplied by the distance flown. ASK is a standard industry metric.

Block Hour—The time from the moment the aircraft door closes at departure until the moment the aircraft door opens at the arrival gate following its landing. Block hours are a standard industry metric.

Capacity—Number of available seats on each aircraft multiplied by the number of flights.

Flights per Day Average—(Total flights/Working days/Fleet size).

Load Factor—The proportion of sold seats to available seats.

fuel prices. But our future purchasing power depends on the marketplace."

Aljas paused for a moment and, in a very guarded tone, slowly answered Kalda's question. "I think the board is somewhat split. Some of us are optimistic, and think our load factors are bound to go up. In fact some board members want to consider adding new, longer routes. After all, the Estonian economy has been doing well, and we hear of more and more Estonians wanting to travel to new places. And, why not? They can afford it now!" Kalda interjected with a quick "Yes, times have been good over the past few years."

Aljas picked up on that and added, "Just look at how well we've been doing on charters over the past few years. Who can blame someone from the Baltics wanting to get a few days of sunshine in Spain or North Africa, for example?"

Then Aljas countered himself, saying "However, I have to tell you, some board members are very edgy. It's not just the competition. It's the unknown. After all, this run of prosperity we've had is unheard of for us. What happens if the party ends? Maybe we should sit on our money and see how things play out."

Kalda tried to answer, saying "But if we wait, don't we run the risk that the competition will pick up traffic we could have captured?" Aljas chimed in, "Look, I'm not saying the sky is falling, I'm just saying we have to consider all the angles here. We have to think broadly."

"Anyway," Aljas sighed, "I just don't want the board to feel hemmed in on any particular decision. A spreadsheet model will help us look at the bottom line impact on each of the different aircraft options as well as all of these different scenarios. I know that this is the first time that we have analyzed the total cost of ownership from this perspective. At the meeting we will be able to plug in different values and see how the options play out."

Kalda left the meeting feeling he had a lot of work to do, but he was also excited about this new direction of Estonian Air's strategic planning. He was confident his operational analysis would tie in well with Aljas's financial model.

NOTES

1. Estonian Air's lease rate was 4.40%. Estonian Air operated leases on a period of six years.
2. Currency with a $ refers to U.S. Dollars. Estonia currency is referred to as EEK, explained later in the case.
3. Exhibit 3 contains conversion factors (e.g., gallons to liters) and EEK-USD currency conversion rates that may be useful when preparing this case.
4. "Budget Carriers New Driving Force in Regional Business," *Flight Global* June 13, 2005. http://www.flightglobal.com/articles/2005/06/13/199133/budget-carriersnew-driving-force-in-regional-business.html.
5. C. Masters, "Giving Props to the New Turbos," *Time* August 23, 2007. Accessed April 17, 2008. http://www.time.com/time/printout/0,8816,1655707,00.html.
6. M. Kingsley-Jones, "Turboprops Bounce Back," *Flight International* February 3, 2006. Accessed October 4, 2008. http://www.flightglobal.com/articles/2006/02/03/204430/turboprops-bounce-back.html.
7. Corporate taxes in Estonia are on distributed profits only. For planning purposes, assume zero profit distributions (i.e., no taxes).
8. AS Estonian Air 2006 Annual Report. Accessed July 1, 2009. http://www.estonian-air.ee/public/Annual_Report_2006_English_final.pdf.
9. AS Estonian Air 2006 Annual Report, page 4.
10. See glossary for airline specific terms, Exhibit 9.
11. See glossary for airline specific terms, Exhibit 9.

12. See glossary for airline specific terms, Exhibit 9.
13. See glossary for airline specific terms, Exhibit 9.
14. http://www.wego.com/airports/estonia/tallinn/tallinn-tll.
15. W. Guzzardi, "The U.S. Business Hall of Fame," *Fortune* 119(6): 130. Accessed June 11, 2009, from Academic OneFile: http://find.galegroup.com.library. smcvt.edu/itx/start.do?prodId=AONE.
16. "The Secret Behind High Profits at Low-Fare Airlines," *Boeing* June 14, 2002. Accessed June 10, 2009. http://www.boeing.com/commercial/news/feature/profit. html.
17. Q400 Media Guide. http://www.q400.com/q400/pdf/q400_MediaGuide_2008.pdf
18. C. Kjelgaard, "Continental Expects New Q400s to Reduce Newark Flight Delays," *Aviation* February 1, 2008. Accessed April 17, 2008. http://www.aviation. com/travel/080201-continental-connection-q400s-colgan.html.
19. See glossary for airline specific terms, Exhibit 9.
20. See glossary for airline specific terms, Exhibit 9.
21. See glossary for airline specific terms, Exhibit 9.
22. See glossary for airline specific terms, Exhibit 9.

Case 4

Homegrocer.com: Anatomy of a Failure

Terry Drayton, the co-founder and original CEO of the now defunct HomeGrocer.com, left the meeting with his original management team and co-founders feeling charged and hopeful. They had met to discuss the possibility of reviving the online grocery business. Although the company had been the victim of the dot.com bust, and an unsuccessful merger with Webvan, it was attracting interest from investors looking to fund an online grocery venture.

Drayton and his Seattle-based team had started Home-Grocer back in 1997. They raised over $440 million in venture capital, opened eight distribution centers, and in a relatively short time had established operations in six locations along the West Coast. They made plans for more locations and were in midst of a fast rollout at the time of HomeGrocer's IPO on March 9, 2000. One month later, the NASDAQ dropped 35% from its high of 5,132, and the opportunity for a secondary round of funding disappeared. Lacking cash to deliver on the growth plans laid out in their IPO prospectus, HomeGrocer tried to weather the financial crisis by merging with Webvan, a California-based online grocer that was launched in 1999.

Webvan, with its larger capital base (at its 1999 peak it had a market capitalization of $8.8 billion compared with HomeGrocer $725.5 million at IPO), took control of the merged entity. To the chagrin of HomeGrocer executives, Webvan's managers transitioned all of the distribution centers to Webvan technology and created a single Webvan brand. However, despite all their efforts, they burned through cash quickly and their share price plummeted, from $26 in December 1999 to $4 at the time of the merger (August 2000). By January 2001 the price of shares was a mere 5 cents. In June 2001, less than a year after the merger was announced, Webvan filed for bankruptcy.

Drayton had learned a great deal from his experience at HomeGrocer. He strongly believed that he and his team had done many things right, and come close to cracking the online grocery model. As he drove home from meeting with his former partners, he wondered what he might do differently if given the chance. Reflecting on his experience in founding HomeGrocer, Drayton tried to isolate what critical mistakes he and his team would avoid the second time around. This time he was confident that he could pull it off.

THE COMPANY BACKGROUND

Terry Drayton and Mike MacDonald founded HomeGrocer, an Internet-based grocer, in 1994. Drayton had just sold Crystal Springs Water Company, which delivered bottled water to businesses in and around Vancouver, B.C., and was looking for something new. One cold winter day, Drayton's wife remarked that he ought to deliver groceries instead of water; that way busy moms wouldn't have to brave a snowstorm just to go to the store. The idea stuck and Drayton found himself discussing it with his friend MacDonald, president of the largest food broker in the Canadian province of British Columbia. MacDonald was intrigued and agreed to put up some initial capital while

Research Associate Greg Fisher and Professor Suresh Kotha, Olesen/Battelle Chaired Professor, the University of Washington's Foster School of Business prepared this case. The case was developed solely as a basis for class discussion. Cases are not intended as endorsements, sources of primary data, or illustrations of effective or ineffective management.

Drayton wrote the business plan. MacDonald's friend, Ken Deering, with computer and technology expertise soon joined them as vice president of systems. The new venture would be called HomeGrocer.com.

Initial Funding.   By April 1997, Drayton had raised $350,000 in seed capital funding, primarily from friends and family. In search of money, he targeted venture capital (VC) firms in Vancouver, even as the team moved its operations to Seattle, deemed a more "techno-friendly" city. This came at a time when respected Wall Street analysts and investment bankers were touting the Internet's potential to fundamentally "disintermediate" incumbents in a number of industry supply chains. To many, this meant cutting the need for a middleman in the supply chain. Mary Meeker, the Morgan Stanley stock analyst, notes:

> [I]t is important to understand the drivers of supply and demand, and therefore how Internet based distribution may affect this chain and whether there will be disintermediation . . . . For example, Amazon.com would be classified as a disintermediary, as it removes the inventory chain to the bookstore (e.g., brick-and-mortar Barnes & Noble stores) and potentially creates better unit pricing (than the traditional stores), better service, and so forth, while reducing the capital tied up in inventory. [It is] pretty simple—less overhead, more efficiency, better prices for consumers.[1]

Such comments excited investors, fueling the funding of many online ventures by a buoyant venture capital industry. In May 1998, Drayton raised $4 million in Series A (first round) funding. Tom Alberg of Seattle's Madrona Ventures, an early VC investor in HomeGrocer, remembers:

> We had already invested in Amazon.com so we were beginning to see that online commerce could work. This [venture] was much different [in] everything from the delivery to the inventory to a whole lot of issues . . . nonetheless, lots of people are frustrated with the regular grocery stores and the lack of inventory sometimes and having to carry [grocery] bags out, and parking and everything else. So we thought there was an opportunity and that it could be a really big business. Unlike Amazon.com, though, you can't serve the whole country from one warehouse initially. You've got to start by building out in cities. So we really realized it was going to take a lot

more capital. But we were attracted by Terry's idea of doing it in a relatively low-capital way.

Four months later, the HomeGrocer team raised another $6 million in Series B funding, with the legendary Silicon Valley VC firm of Kleiner Perkins Caufield & Byers as lead investor. This was followed by a series C funding round. By this time the market was abuzz with hopes for the Internet grocery business, and HomeGrocer had attracted the attention of some heavy hitters: Amazon.com; Jim Barksdale, an early executive with Netscape and former senior executive with Federal Express; and John Malone, the legendary cable TV operator and Liberty Media Investor. Notes Drayton:

> [W]e actually went out to raise $20 million, but everybody wanted to own more of the company, so the round kept going up. And it was just the math. Amazon.com insisted on owning 35% and so we had a valuation in mind and so we just had to raise way more money—actually $52.5 million—than we ever intended.

A Series D financing round followed in April 1999 with HomeGrocer raising another $110 million. The primary investors during this round of financing were CBS, Inc., the Knight-Ridder Company, Softbank Co. of Japan, Benchmark Capital, Sequoia Capital, and others.

With the frenzy over Internet-based ventures in full swing, Drayton raised a considerable amount from U.S. investors, $172 million, even though his original business plan had only called for $15 million in funding from venture capitalists, followed by an IPO to secure another $50 million in capital. Terry had also assembled an impressive board of advisors that included Jeff Bezos, the founder of Amazon.com, the legendary John Doerr of Kleiner Perkins Caufield & Byers, Jim Barksdale, Martha Stewart, and others.

Going Live in Seattle and Expanding.   According to the business plan, the company would spend the first 12–15 months establishing a distribution center in Seattle, and then roll out new facilities every three months. The idea was to learn as much as possible from the launch and management of the first distribution center so they could perfect the model before replicating it in other regions. In May 1998, its website went "live," and commercial operations were officially underway with a staff of 60. During its first month HomeGrocer attracted 300 customers; they found that on average, each customer ordered three times a month with an order value of $75 per order. According to Drayton's plan, the Seattle facility should break even at 1,100 orders per day (See Exhibit 1 and 2).

A year later, in May 1999, HomeGrocer entered the Portland, Oregon market with a distribution site similar to Seattle's. By September 1999, it had build a distribution center in Orange County, California, where the company employed a more automated system. Items were picked in zones and batches, and conveyors were used instead of having people walk around to do the picking. Instead of its usual 50,000-square feet facility, its Orange County center was double that size. Also multiplying was the number of employees, which doubled every five or six months. By November 1999, payroll had reached over 1,000 employees.

In the next few months, the company opened new distribution centers: a second facility in Orange County, a

second one in Seattle, two in Los Angeles, and one in San Diego. In fact, the company opened eight new distribution centers, at a rate much faster than the original business plan had called for. Drayton himself pointed out:

The biggest consequence of raising a lot of venture capital was [that] with all this money, everyone expects you to grow that much faster. That's very difficult to do in a logistics intensive business like HomeGrocer, especialiy when your business is not yet fully baked. If you're the entrepreneur, what you'd love to do is stuff [the money] in the bank and take your time, knowing that you don't actually have to go spend more time raising money. You can instead focus on the perfecting the venture. Venture capitalists don't

Exhibit 1 — Financial Projections for Homegrocer.com from the Business Plan ($ 000s)

Corporate Financial Performance ($ Thousands)

Year	1998	1999	2000	2001	2002	2003
Number of Centers	1	3	7	15	31	31
Revenue	11,199	49,960	125,718	291,816	634,333	1,125,123
Gross Margin (%)	19.4	16.7	15.3	15.0	14.7	12.0
Net Income Before Tax	(1,349)	(2,901)	(2,821)	(1,065)	2,685	12,467
Net Income (%)	(12.0)	(6.2)	(2.2)	0.4	0.4	1.1
Members	7,700	27,600	69,700	157,000	336,400	547,200
Working Capital	9,622	4,606	44,377	34,289	18,980	25,415
Total Assets	12,149	10,557	57,506	62,185	76,672	92,810
Employees	95	323	800	1,771	3,753	5,684

Prototype Center Financial Performance ($ Thousands)

Year	1	2	3	4	5
Revenue	12,960	30,948	47,108	60,309	72,152
Gross Margin (%)	18.5	13.4	13.0	12.8	12.7
Net Income Before Tax	(629)	618	1,962	2,931	3,903
Net Income (%)	(4.9)	2.0	4.2	4.9	5.4
Members	8,400	15,600	21,600	26,400	31,200
Employees	91	313	784	1,753	3,733
Working Capital	532	918	2,666	5,616	9,656
Total Assets	2,122	3,215	5,572	8,819	13,038

Source: Extracted directly from the HomeGrocer.com Business Plan dated December 31, 1997.

Exhibit 2

Break-Even Analysis for Homegrocer.com from the Business Plan Analysis Per Center

The financial assumes an average order size of $100 with members shopping twice per month. Only 15% of orders are assumed to be less than $75 requiring a $9.95 delivery fee. A membership of $35 is collected from 90% of members. Hence an average member purchases $2467 per year in products from HomeGrocer.com as shown below:

	Amount	% of average grocery sales
Average Sale	$2400.00	100.0%
Average Delivery Fee	35.82	1.5%
Average Membership Fee	31.50	1.3%
	2467.32	102.8%
Average Cost of Sales		
Groceries/shrinkage	1735.20	72.3%
Delivery	223.20	9.3%
Picking	208.80	8.7%
Transaction	19.20	0.8%
Subtotal	2186.40	91.0%
Annual Gross Margin per member	**$280.92**	**11.8%**

The above analysis uses costs at the end of one year and excludes all revenues forecast from manufacturer programs. Revenues from these activities are forecast at $1,740,000 in the first year and $600,000 thereafter.
Fixed costs to operate a HomeGrocer.com site are approximately $3 million annually, which are determined as follows:

Annual Fixed Costs to Operate a HomeGrocer.com Center

Cost	Amount
Warehouse Rental	$243,000
Triple Net and Utilities	102,000
Warehouse Equipment Maintenance	48,000
Insurance	24,000
Office Equipment Maintenance	12,000
Supplies	60,000
Legal and Accounting	60,000
Communications	90,000
Administration	784,700
Member Services	176,229
Sales & Marketing	1,236,000
Depreciation	137,550
Miscellaneous	60,000
Total	**$3,033,875**

As operating efficiencies improve over the year and some expenses are front-end loaded, actual monthly break-even is forecast to occur in month 14. So each site is forecast to achieve a break-even level of operation in just over one year.
Source: Extracted directly from the HomeGrocer.com Business Plan dated December 31, 1997.

like that. They want you to go full speed all the time with the gas pedal pegged to the floor.

Competitors. A number of other companies in the United States were also attempting the online grocery retail model, including Peapod, which delivered products from existing retail stores; Netgrocer.com, which delivered nonperishable packaged items using courier services like FedEx and UPS; and Webvan, the grand project of Louis Borders, co-founder of Borders Books and Music. Webvan attracted large amounts of capital from high profile VCs with its promise to revolutionize retail by creating a web-based storefront that sold "everything from groceries to Palm Pilots." With its massive Bay Area warehouse, fleet of trucks, and highly sophisticated automated picking system, Webvan was considered HomeGrocer's fiercest rival. Both companies were striving to be "first to market" in establishing a web-based retailing presence in the biggest cities in the United States.

Going Public Early. Meanwhile, the investment climate for Internet IPOs seemed strong, and the company prepared to go public. HomeGrocer's financials revealed that it had lost $7.9 million on $1.1 million in revenue in 1998 and $84 million on $21.6 million in revenue in 1999. Prior to its public offering, the board decided to bring in an "experienced CEO" to replace Terry Drayton, along with a new CFO. While Drayton was not overly pleased, he remained supportive of the plan. Board members Doer, Barksdale, and Drayton reviewed candidates with the relevant logistics, financing, and management experience. For CEO, Barksdale recommended Mary Alice Taylor, former CIO at Citigroup and a senior executive of operations at Federal Express. For CFO they hired Dan Lee, former CEO of Mirage Resorts for the preceding ten years (See Exhibit 3). According to company executives, this was common practice for Wall Street bankers at that time: Internet companies would recruit executives from "old-line" businesses who would take

Exhibit 3	Executive Officers and Directors[2]
Mary Alice Taylor (49)	Chief Executive Officer and Chairman of the Board
J. Terrence Drayton (39)*	President and Director
Daniel R. Lee (43)	Senior Vice President and Chief Financial Officer
Mary B. Anderson (44)	Vice President of Finance
Rex L. Carter (47)	Senior Vice President of Systems Development & Technology
Ken Deering (40)*	Vice President of Storefront
Robert G. Duffy (39)	Chief Information Officer
Corwin J. Karaffa (45)	Senior Vice President of Operations
Jonathan W. Landers (47)	Senior Vice President of Marketing and Sales
Daniel J. Murphy (53)	Vice President of Merchandising
David A. Pace (40)	Senior Vice President of People Capability
Kristin H. Stred (40)	Senior Vice President, General Counsel and Secretary
Tom A. Alberg (59)	Director
Charles K. Barbo (58)	Director
James L. Barksdale (56)	Director
Mark P. Gorenberg (44)	Director
Jonathan D. Lazarus (48)	Director
Douglas Mackenzie (40)	Director
David Risher (34)	Director
Philip S. Schlein (65)	Director

*Co-founder of HomeGrocer.com. The third co-founder, Mike Macdonald, was no longer involved in the business at the time of the IPO.

Mary Alice Taylor has served as chairman and chief executive officer of HomeGrocer.com since September 1999. Prior to joining HomeGrocer.com, Ms. Taylor served as corporate executive vice president of Global Operations and Technology for Citigroup, a financial services organization, from January 1997 to September 1999 where she was responsible for standardizing and centralizing worldwide operations and leading quality and cost-effectiveness efforts. From June 1980 until January 1997, Ms. Taylor held various positions with Federal Express, an overnight courier service, serving most recently as senior vice president of Ground Operations where she was responsible for all aspects of pickup and delivery operations in North America. Prior to her positions at Citigroup and Federal Express, from 1977 to 1980 she was the financial planning manager of U.S. Operations with Northern Telecom, Inc., a telecommunications company, From 1973 to 1977 Ms. Taylor was the controller at Cook Investment Properties, a division of Cook Industries and from 1971 to 1973, Ms. Taylor served as senior accountant, oil and gas explorations with Shell Oil. Ms. Taylor also serves as a director on the boards of Autodesk, a supplier of PC design software, and Dell Computer. Previously she served on the boards of The Perrigo Company, a manufacturer of store brand items, and Allstate Insurance Company. Ms. Taylor holds a B.A. in finance from Mississippi State University and is a Certified Public Accountant.

J. Terrence Drayton co-founded HomeGrocer.com and has served as its president since the incorporation of its predecessor in January 1997. Mr. Drayton also served as chief executive officer of HomeGrocer.com from January 1997 until September 1999. From February 1996 through January 1997, Mr. Drayton was the President of Terran Ventures, Inc., a venture capital and consulting company, where he focused on activities leading to the formation of HomeGrocer.com's predecessor company. Prior to co-founding HomeGrocer.com, Mr. Drayton was involved for more than ten years as co-founder and senior manager of two of the leading bottled water companies in Canada. From November 1991 to January 1996, Mr. Drayton was the president of the home and office division of Aquaterra, a Canadian bottled water company producing the brand names Crystal Springs and Labrador. From September 1989 through September 1991 Mr. Drayton served as chairman and chief executive officer of Telepost Communications, a publicly traded Canadian film and video post-production company. From March 1986 to May 1989 Mr. Drayton was the co-founder, executive vice president and co-chief executive officer for Laurentian Spring Valley Water. He holds a B.Comm. from the University of Calgary and an M.B.A. from York University.

Daniel R. Lee joined HomeGrocer.com as chief financial officer in November 1999 and was also appointed senior vice president in December 1999. From February 1992 to September 1999, Mr. Lee served as chief financial officer, treasurer and senior vice president of finance and development for Mirage Resorts, a publicly traded company (NYSE:MIR) that develops and operates large scale resort hotels. From February 1990 to February 1992, he was a director of equity research for CS First Boston, an investment bank. From July 1980 to February 1990, he held various positions with the investment bank Drexel Burnham Lambert, most recently as a managing director. Mr. Lee holds a B.S. and an M.B.A., both from Cornell University, and he is a Chartered Financial Analyst.

Ken Deering co-founded HomeGrocer.com. Since inception, he has held several positions with HomeGrocer.com and its predecessor, including marketing manager from August 1996 to October 1997, vice president of business development from October 1997 to May 1999 and vice president of storefront from May 1999 to the present. Prior to his involvement with HomeGrocer.com, Mr. Deering was an independent management consultant through his firm, Heldeer Ventures, from August 1994 to August 1996. From January 1992 to July 1994, Mr. Deering held the positions of general manager and then vice president of sales and marketing for Offshore Systems, a developer of electronic marine positioning systems. Over the prior 12 years, Mr. Deering held various marketing and operations positions, including six years at Glenayre Technologies, a developer of software for wireless personal communication systems. Mr. Deering has a sales and marketing management diploma from the University of British Columbia.

"new-line" businesses public, and in the process garner a few hundred million in increased market capitalization, just like that.

HomeGrocer went public on March 10, 2000. The stock opened at $12.88, reached a high of $16.25 on day one, but closed at $14.12. While HomeGrocer's top-management team had hoped to raise between $500 and $600 million in capital, they ended the day with $268 million.

The Stock Market Collapses. In April 2000, the NASDAQ index tanked as the Internet "bubble" calamitously burst.[3] Overnight Wall Street's Internet mantra changed from "Get Big Fast" to "Find a Path to

Profitability." HomeGrocer had spent 18 months gearing up for a rapid rollout, but slowing it down would take time and effort. Further, the company lacked the capital needed to achieve positive operating cash flows on its eight distribution centers. In order to remain a viable operation, it needed between $300–500 million in additional capital and when, or if, the financing window would reopen was unclear. Given such uncertainty, growth plans were put on hold. At the same time, rival companies began to compete head-to-head in the new markets.[4] Without additional capital, it was unlikely HomeGrocer could support its large workforce or fund the expansion plans described in its prospectus. Both management and the board were concerned about lawsuits from investors if expansion plans were not carried out.

These were difficult times for HomeGrocer. The company had only $257 million on hand, and financial losses were mounting. By this time, HomeGrocer had over 2,300 employees, and the company's stock was trading at $5, representing a one-month 64% drop in value. By this time Drayton had left the company due to differences with Taylor, the new CEO. Under these trying conditions she began exploring ways to move forward.

THE U.S. GROCERY INDUSTRY IN THE LATE 1990S

The United States grocery industry is mature, and extremely competitive. Exhibit 4 provides an overview of the grocery industry, and Exhibit 5 compares grocery store sales between 1988 and 1998. In 1998, retail supermarket sales were approximately $449 billion. Grocery retailing had experienced growth in real sales during only four of the last ten years, and net profit margins remained thin, at 1% of sales. The industry was (and continues to be)

Exhibit 4	Grocery Industry Overview, 1999
Number of employees	3.5 million
Number of grocery stores	126,000
Total grocery store sales	$449 billion
Total supermarket sales	$346.1 billion
Number of supermarkets ($2 million or more in annual sales)	30,700
Net profit after taxes, 4/98-3/99	1.03%
Typical supermarket size	40,483 sq. ft.
Number of items in a supermarket	40,333
Labor as a % of operating expense	57.5%
Average effective income tax rate (fed, state, local) 4/96-3/97	39%
Percentage of disposable income spend on food	
• food-at-home	6.6%
• food away-from-home	4.2%
Weekly sales per supermarket	$331,411
Weekly sales per square foot of selling area	$9.45
Sales per customer transaction	$10.16
Sales per labor hour	$113.21
Average # of trips per week consumers make to the supermarket, 1/98	2.2
Food basket costs, % of weekly income spent on food	
• Unites States	8.8%
• Canada	10.3%
• Japan	17.6%

Sources: U.S. Department of Labor, U.S. Department of Agriculture, Progressive Grocer magazine, and U.S. Census Bureau

Exhibit 5	Grocery Store Sales 1988 and 1999

	1988				1998			
	$ Sales Billion	%	Number of Stores	%	$ Sales Billion	%	Number of Stores	%
All Stores	329.0	100.0	148,000	100.0	449.0	100.0	126,000	100.0
Supermarkets ($2,000,000 +)	240.4	73.0	30,400	20.5	346.1	77.0	30,700	24.4
Chain Supermarkets	164.3	49.9	16,850	11.4	274.5	61.1	19,530	15.5
Independent Supermarkets	76.1	23.1	13,550	9.1	71.6	15.9	11,170	8.9
Other Stores (Under $2,000,000)	63.1	19.2	62,600	42.3	53.4	11.9	37,550	29.8
Convenience Stores	25.5*	7.8	55,000	37.2	28.0**	6.3	57,000	45.2
Wholesale Club Stores	n/a	n/a	n/a	n/a	21.5**	4.8	750	0.6

Grocery Store — Any retail store selling a line of dry grocery, canned goods or nonfood items plus some perishable items.
Supermarket — Any full-line, self-service grocery store with an annual sales of $2 million or more.
Convenience Store — Compact, drive-to store offering a limited line of high-convenience items. Over half sell gasoline and some sort of fast food. Long hours and easy access.
Independent Supermarkets — An operator of up to 10 retail stores.
Chain Supermarkets — An operator of 11 or more retail stores.

Source: Key Industry Facts — Prepared by FMI Information Service, April 1999.

Notes:
* Excludes sales of gasoline
** Supermarket items only

highly fragmented. In 1997, wholesale industry revenues stood at $315 billion; its largest wholesaler, SuperValu, captured a little over half of one percent while servicing 4,800 stores. Beginning in 1992, the wholesale industry witnessed an average of 20 acquisitions a year. In 1997 alone, 40 mergers and acquisitions occurred. Following the trend set by wholesalers, retailers also engaged in mergers and acquisitions.

According to 1998 reports, the United States population was expected to decline with an average birthrate of 1.3 for every two people. The survival and growth of the grocery industry would have to come from cost-containment efforts, increases in economies of scale and scope, a greater penetration of existing markets, and greater than average consumer expenditure. To increase revenues, grocers had to increase the breadth and depth of fresh produce, meat offerings, organically grown products, while relying on private-label products with higher margins.

To reduce costs, retailers looked to their supply chains. They stepped up the pressure on wholesalers to reduce costs and pass some of those savings on to them. Wholesalers responded by implementing efficiency-driven tactics such as bar coding and scanning, onboard computer systems for delivery trucks, and new delivery trucks with multiple compartments and climate controlled trailers. They adopted just-in-time concepts that minimized non-value-added inventory costs such as product shortages, obsolescence, and spoilage. The grocery wholesale and retail businesses had become deeply interwoven and interdependent. Despite streamlining activities, wholesalers and retailers still had to contend with slim operating margins.

The Market for Online Groceries

According to a 1998 report by IDC, a market research firm, the number of individuals using the Internet in the United States was forecast to grow at a compound annual growth rate (CAGR) of over 23% until 2003, and it was predicted that the number of individuals making purchases online would increase at a CAGR of approximately 28%, from 21.1 million in 1998 to 72.1 million in 2003. Forrester Research, a Cambridge, Massachusetts research firm, forecast the total United States Internet-retail commerce would grow from approximately $20.3 billion in 1999 to approximately $184.5 billion in 2004, representing a CAGR of over 55%. It estimated that online grocery spending would grow at a CAGR of over 100% over the next five years, from $513 million in 1999 to $10.8 billion by 2003. Despite its size in absolute terms, this spending was expected to represent less than 2% of the total United States market for grocery products in 2003.

Forrester categorized the online grocery industry into two segments: full-service retailers and speciality stores. Full-service retailers are those selling a complete range of grocery products, including perishables. They provide home, office, or pickup and delivery options. Speciality stores, in contrast, offer a limited selection of gifts, hard-to-find items, or bulk replenishment products via the PC, and ship directly to consumers. Exhibit 6 provides a detailed breakdown of total electronic grocery spending in the U.S. from 1999–2003. It also highlights the total number of households buying groceries electronically. At the time Forrester Research estimated that by 2003, households buying groceries would reach over 16 million households.

Despite these bold projections, some were skeptical about whether the online grocery industry would achieve these levels. Traditional brick-and-mortar retailers were slow to embrace the Internet as a medium for selling groceries. Albertson's and Hannaford Bros were among the few traditional grocers that experimented with an online model. A major uncertainty was if or when other major chains might enter the online space. Given their ability to source products at a lower cost, compared to new entrants, traditional retailers had significant buying power. In theory this could offer them significant advantages if they chose to compete online. For example, in the mid-1990s Wal-Mart, the world's largest retailer, moved into the grocery business; thanks to its purchasing power, it soon captured a significant share of the market. Many wondered if

Exhibit 6	The Emerging Online Grocer Industry Forecasts				
	1999	**2000**	**2001**	**2002**	**2003**
Online Grocery Sales					
Speciality	$248	$659	$1,548	$3,058	$6,291
Full Service	$265	$473	$911	$1,951	$4,545
Total Revenues	$513	$1,132	$2,459	$5,009	$10,836
Percentage of Industry Total	0.11%	0.23%	0.49%	0.98%	2.05%
Total Number of Households Buying Groceries Electronically (000s)					
Speciality PC-Based	920	1,839	3,678	6,252	10,628
Other Net Devices	35	106	318	1,114	4,454
Total Speciality	**955**	**1,945**	**3,996**	**7,366**	**15,082**
Full-Service PC-Based	187	327	621	1,242	2,546
Other Net Devices	6	12	35	124	495
Phone/Fax	42	42	38	34	31
Total Total Full Service	**235**	**381**	**694**	**1,400**	**3,072**
Household doing both	59	115	243	630	1,536
Total participating household	**1,131**	**2,211**	**4,447**	**8,136**	**16,618**

Source: Forrester Research, Inc

Wal-Mart would enter the online grocery retail business, given their expertise in IT and procurement systems.

While some detractors of online grocery retailing cited a declining population growth rate as a deterrent to the business, others focused on the fact that the demand for online groceries was unclear at best. Notes Tom Alberg:

> I think there's always been people who have said, "It [online markets] will never work for groceries. Margins are too low, how can you purchase at the same competitive prices?" A lot of which is true, but there's also online advantages obviously. You don't have to have the expensive space, parking lots, and as many employees. [These] are huge advantages.

In the meantime, online grocers were not exactly responding to pent-up demand. It first had to be created. Because this kind of service was so novel, potential customers had to be educated about its existence and availability, then build enough trust to place their first order. Many questions about the transaction process had to be answered. Despite such concerns, a number of online grocers began to sell over the Internet and deliver to customers' homes. At that point, however, there was little head-to-head competition among new entrants, since each focused on a specific geographic region.

HOMEGROCER'S ONLINE APPROACH

HomeGrocer was established as a full-service online grocer offering perishable and nonperishable items. The company enabled customers living within a designated region to buy groceries via its website and then have the purchases delivered to their homes. The company invested heavily in creating a website that replicated many aspects of the shopping experience for customers used to buying goods in a traditional grocery store. The website was user-friendly and time-efficient and allowed access to 9,000–12,000 items with an intuitively organized list (a traditional store carried over 100,000 items or SKUs). The customer could either "browse the shelves" or use the "search" function to locate items.

Customers would go online, order groceries, and select a 90-minute window of time, between 1 p.m. and 9 p.m. the following day to have the items delivered. Orders over $75 had no delivery charge, while orders under $75 accrued a $10 delivery charge.

The "Online" Value Proposition

The key advantages to the consumer were convenience, quality, and service. HomeGrocer customers could shop 24/7 without leaving home. Goods were delivered directly to customers' homes, and they no longer needed to carry heavy grocery bags to and from their cars. Because the perishable items sold online hadn't been put out for display or handled by other shoppers, fresh items were higher quality and lasted longer than items purchased in a traditional grocery store. John Landers, vice president of marketing, noted:

> Clearly, our produce was fresher than those bought at a traditional grocery store. We operated on a just-in-time inventory basis and did not require surplus merchandise for display. Theoretically [in a traditional grocery store] customers could select produce to their liking from the available produce by touching and scrutinizing. However, customers damage a good deal of produce by this inspection and are limited to selecting from a picked-over assortment. HomeGrocer.com pickers were able to select fruit to the customer's specifications without damaging the rest of the produce.

HomeGrocer focused on quality customer service. This entailed responding to customer requests, following up after a delivery was completed, and training drivers to be sensitive to customer needs. The driver was seen as a company representative since he was the only employee the customer ever saw. Delivery personnel were instructed to carry groceries into the kitchen or pantry, after asking the customer whether they could enter the house. Wearing surgical booties over their shoes was mandatory in order to leave no impact on the customer's home. Such attentiveness made a big impression on HomeGrocer's customers. Ken Deering observed:

> This is a "loyalty point" that our customers appreciated. About 97 or 98% of all deliveries were taken to the kitchen counter. . . . The drivers were told if you're going through the laundry room, put the soap there, and if you've got the big 20-pound dog food, ask if it goes in the garage and then just put it in the garage. And again, we'd get comments from people calling and saying, "I can't even get my husband to haul the dog food in." Then they'd say, "The best thing about your business is I never have to pick up another 20-pound bag of dog food in the store, and the

driver puts it in garage. He knows that's where we keep it." Or, "I can't believe he took the time to put the soap on top of my washing machine on the way out the door."

In addition, each first-time customer received a phone call from a customer-service representative to make sure he or she was completely satisfied with the order.

Marketing the Service

The company focused on families with incomes over $75,000. It targeted busy middle- to upper-class families with school age children and both parents in professional occupations. Such families were typically short on time, spent enough on groceries to make buying online attractive, and had access to the Internet at home. According to the company's market research, in these homes women made the buying decisions. As a result, the website was designed to appeal to them. Notes Ken Deering:

> The venture chose to build a standalone brand and took on traditional supermarkets as its competitors by providing customers with an alternative to buying groceries from a store. HomeGrocer's pricing and positioning was similar to QFC, better and more expensive than Albertsons, but not as expensive as Larry's, which was the local (Seattle) Whole Foods equivalent at the time HomeGrocer.com was launched.

Initially HomeGrocer's advertising and promotion focused on the convenience of buying online. After Jon Landers joined as VP of marketing in November 2008, the company began promoting the freshness and quality of the products. Landers decided to stress this advantage by sending free sample produce bags with each order. Notes Deering: "This was great consumer marketing and played to the idea that if customers trusted a grocer's produce, they would be happy to order prepackaged food from the company."

Customer Acquisition

The HomeGrocer team put a great deal of effort into customer acquisition. In addition to distributing free fresh produce bags in targeted neighborhoods, they gave away coupons to encourage customers to buy, and eliminated delivery charges for first-time buyers. This was, however, a costly exercise. The company was spending about $300 per customer in acquisition costs but struggling to retain them as customers. Many would stop buying after three or four purchases. Picking up on this, Landers implemented a psychographic profiling process, using GIS (Geographic Information Systems) mapping to ensure that the team was targeting areas with customers who had the appropriate psychographic profile. The move helped bring down acquisition costs and improved customer retention rates, but did not completely solve the problem.

Although all sales were done via the Internet, boosting web traffic was not critical to generating sales. This was at a time before email or Search Engine Marketing. To drive traffic to the company website, HomeGrocer used traditional media including direct mail pamphlets, newspapers, and TV ads. It also used unconventional marketing in the form of Peach Parties (a type of Tupperware party for early Internet users) and extensive sponsorships of local community organizations (such as donating apples and bottled water to school PTA members, who handed them out with direct mail pamphlets which would earn $25 for the organization if people tried HomeGrocer). They also entered into partnerships with AOL and Amazon.com.[5] Of these Drayton remarked:

> These were basically the big players in the Internet and especially for customer acquisitions. We had Amazon.com as a shareholder [and so] we had to deal with them. We signed a big AOL deal because at that stage AOL was so dominant, they were about 40% of the overall market, but for us they were all our target customers, and so it was probably a disproportionate share. Most people who used AOL thought that it was the Internet at the time.

Even though they were able to create customer interest and get people to explore the company's website, there were barriers to getting people to order online the first time and then repeating the process again and again. For many people, buying groceries at a store was such a natural way of doing things that they struggled to move away from the practice. One of the board members called this the "gallon of milk problem":

> Your significant other is on his way home and you call up and say, "We're out of milk. Could you please stop and pick some milk on your way back?" And then he stops to buy a gallon of milk. While he is buying a gallon of milk, he does

some more shopping. If he goes in to buy the gallon of milk he ends up buying more. Because of this, this family ends up not shopping as it should online that week.

As HomeGrocer began planning its expansion beyond the West Coast, they conducted market research focus groups in Atlanta, Georgia, where they discovered that some women were concerned about what people might think if they bought groceries online and had them delivered to their homes. They were concerned their neighbors might think they had gotten "so lazy" that they would shop online. In other words, HomeGrocer's management discovered many behavioral and social concerns that were limiting their ability to acquire and retain customers.

Operations and Delivery

HomeGrocer opted to build its own distribution centers and purchase refrigerated delivery trucks. The distribution centers were built close to the neighborhoods the company planned to serve. Because of the high upfront investment in infrastructure and systems, each facility needed at least 1,100 orders per day, with an average order value of $100, in order to break even and become profitable. The first 55,000 square feet facility was rented just outside Seattle, in Bellevue, Washington.

Since a small operation didn't enjoy the strong wholesaler relationships that brick-and-mortar stores did, it generally paid more since order quantities were smaller. In spite of the increased cost of goods sold,

| Exhibit 7 | HomeGrocer.com and Webvan – A Summary of Revenues and Profits (*thousands* $) |

	HomeGrocer			Webvan		
	1998	1999	2000*	1998	1999	2000**
Net Sales	1,094	21,648	21,215	–	13,305	16,269
Cost of merchandise sold	1,018	19,515	17,515	–	11,289	12,138
Gross Profit	76	2,133	3,700	–	2,016	4,131
Sales, general and marketing expenses	7,455	59,208	13,899	8,825	104,152	47,352
Technology expenses			6,466	3,010	15,237	5,523
Stock based compensation expense	412	28,158	8,143	1,060	36,520	17,720
Customer fulfilment center expenses	–	–	17,644	–	–	–
Pre-opening expenses	–	–	2,015	–	–	–
Loss from operations	–7,791	–85,233	–44,467	–12,895	–153,893	–66,464
Interest Expense	–172	–384	–663	–32	–2,156	–150
Interest Income	54	2,232	1,688	923	11,480	8,799
Other income/(expense)		–608	–23	–	–	–
Net Loss	–7,909	–83,993	–43,465	–12,004	–144,569	–57,815
Unrealized Gain (Loss) on Marketable Securities				4	–729	990
Comprehensive Loss	–7,909	–83,993	–43,465	–12,000	–145,298	–56,825

*13 weeks ended April 1,
** 13 weeks ended March 31,
Source: Hoovers.com

relative to larger retailers, HomeGrocer's original business plan projected net profit margins of 7% over the long term (compared with 1 to 2% for traditional grocery chains). These higher projections were primarily based on its lower location costs and not needing to build retail displays or hire checkout clerks.

Logistically, the business concept presented the company with significant challenges. HomeGrocer's top management agreed the most complicated parts of the business were the supply chain and employees' ability to correctly deliver online orders. To meet the challenge, they built dedicated facilities, invested in high-end distribution equipment, and ordered specially modified delivery vehicles.

When an order came in, a picker would start at one end of the facility and work his way to the other, selecting all items. If items weren't in stock, to complete an order an employees would have to rush out and buy it. While its competitors would simply ship an incomplete order if they did not have an item in stock, HomeGrocer's zeal for customer service insured that customers receive exactly what they ordered. It was a policy that had significant cost and time implications (i.e., pickers would sometimes spend up to 50% of their time filling a few items on an order).

The company's trucks had compartments with three different temperature settings: one for frozen food, a cooler for produce, and room temperature for dry goods. Each truck could deliver 30–40 orders within a narrow geographical area. In this respect the online grocery business departed from other Internet retailers like Amazon.com, which focused on a wide geographical area. HomeGrocer boasted an impressive 98% accurate delivery record. HomeGrocer also used a sophisticated third-party program similar to that used by UPS to route deliveries efficiently. According to Drayton, the company was a pioneer in its technology. At the same time, software development had led to significant cost overruns; website development alone reportedly cost $750,000.

POST-INTERNET BUBBLE OPTIONS FACING HOMEGROCER

The stock market meltdown that occurred days after HomeGrocer's March IPO meant it had no ability to raise capital. Its top management team, under Taylor, faced limited options. One was to scale back expansion plans and focus on reaching profitability by improving its existing operations. Drayton recalled

The biggest thing was we'd just gone public and when you go public you issue a prospectus in which you make all sorts of commitments. Ours was primarily the markets and distribution facilities we committed to opening. And so one of the biggest questions and hardest discussions we ever had with the investment bankers was if and when the market would "reopen." We needed more capital to do that, so if it was going to bounce back we would be fine as long as it didn't take too long. But we had to do our financing probably within five or six months. And so there's that whole thing of "Is the market going to reopen in time?" Or, as we used to say, "Or is it ever going to reopen?" In April 2000, the bankers said, "Oh, it may be a blip, maybe by the summer or perhaps next month." And then by about June 2001, it was "it's all over, who knows when it will reopen?" That's why they supported the Webvan deal: There was nowhere else to get the money needed to open all the facilities [we had committed to opening].

At one point company executives had entertained the idea of restructuring the company under Chapter 11. With contracts to open 15 or more distribution centers over the next year, significantly more capital was needed. However, since the company had just gone public, declaring Chapter 11 would almost guarantee shareholder lawsuits. The company's board was sure to oppose that route.

Another option was merging with a wealthier competitor like Webvan (see Exhibit 8). Louis Borders, the founder of Borders Books and Music, started Webvan with the bold vision of "selling and delivering anything and everything." For him, delivering groceries was just the beginning, a way of getting into the consumers' homes. His plans for Webvan were audacious, as he "sought to outsmart the biggest players around, from Amazon.com and Wal-Mart to UPS and the U.S. Postal Service."[6] Within months of launching Webvan, he was able to raise over a billion dollars from private investors including such marquee VC firms as Benchmark and Sequoia Capital.

Exhibit 8   Map of HomeGrocer.com and Webvan Distribution Centers (2000)

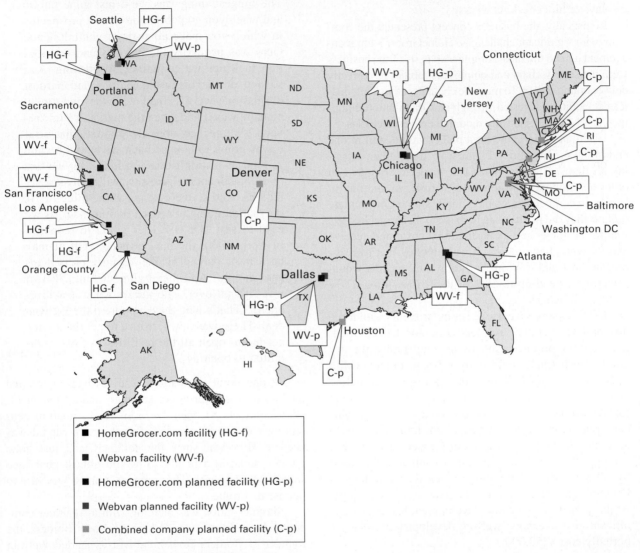

■ HomeGrocer.com facility (HG-f)

■ Webvan facility (WV-f)

■ HomeGrocer.com planned facility (HG-p)

■ Webvan planned facility (WV-p)

■ Combined company planned facility (C-p)

One HomeGrocer executive who wished to remain anonymous recalled,

> [Webvan] had done a secondary offering. They had tons of money and the combined business had tons of cash in it. . . . We had eight operating centers, they had one and they were trying to get organized to do the second one. And so, if we merged things together [we would be] able to get out from most of the commitments we had made. And so we could say, "Oh, well now that we've merged the companies, everything's changed and we've got to cut back this and we'll only open their facilities and away we go." And so we thought, "Here's our green."

If HomeGrocer merged with Webvan, the combined company would have $650 million in cash[7]—enough to weather the storm and move the combined entity toward profitability. But the two companies had very different cost structures. Notes Drayton:

> At that stage one of the key metrics was average order size. You need at least a $100 order to generate $30 in gross margins to pay for the picking, to pay for the shipping and all that. [Webvan] was only running in sort of the $78 or $80 range, and then their picking costs were high because they had these really automated facilities that maybe if you are moving staggering numbers of orders you would get there. But it's kind of like it cost you $100,000 a day whether you pick anything or not, so divide it by 500 orders and all of a sudden it's really expensive to pick your orders. Whereas if we had about 500 orders a day we were doing fine; at a 1,000 we'd break even. I think they needed 3,500 orders a day to break even. And no facility ever in any of the markets we were operating, got close to 3,500. We did about 2,100 in Seattle once, which was a record for one day.

For two years Webvan and HomeGrocer had been fierce competitors. "Merging with the enemy" seemed like a bitter pill to swallow for certain members of the HomeGrocer management team. In the end, HomeGrocer announced a merger with Webvan in an all-stock deal involving 138 million Webvan shares valued at $1 billion on June 26, 2000. Webvan was to exchange 1.076 shares for each share of HomeGrocer.[8] For Webvan, the deal eliminated a tough competitor and gave it an immediate presence in six new markets. The combined company would save an annual $20–30 million in redundant overhead costs.

The acquisition was completed in September. By then, Webvan's stock price stood at $3.88. Its purchase of Home-Grocer was now valued at $535 million, substantially less than its initial offer of $1.2 billion. George Shaheen, CEO of Webvan, remained the president and CEO of the merged entity. At year's end the company operated in 13 markets and was set to open two distribution centers in 2001. Its new goal was to operate 25 facilities by the end of 2002, depending on whether more funding could be raised. At the time of the merger, Webvan had about $650 million in cash, and HomeGrocer about $150 million.

The Death Spiral.   Once Webvan became the controlling entity, its executives began calling the shots on how to proceed as a merged company and things started to quickly unravel.

Webvan switched from HomeGrocer's platform technology to its own. Immediately following the change customer orders in San Diego dropped from 1,000 to 500 a day, and within a week to 300 per day. The decline soon repeated itself seven more times. As Terry Drayton pointed out,

> This was one of the stupidest things Webvan ever did. Webvan's technology did not work with AOL. The 'Buy' buttons and the checkout on the website did not work, so clients could not make purchases even if they wanted to. Plus it was brutally slow since they only tested it on T1 and T3 lines used by their developers. They did not test it under the conditions in which a normal AOL soccer mom user would experience using a dial-up modem. We [HomeGrocer] had an in-house lab that we always tested the releases with representative users. I could forgive them for inadequate testing on the first conversion but not for repeating the mistake seven more times over the following months. Unfortunately, Webvan management repeated this mistake with every facility with the same result, and the end result was a 50% immediate drop in sales, and down to 33% drop within a week. How stupid can you be?

In a related blunder, Webvan had kept on most of HomeGrocer's employees at a 50% premium of their original salaries, but then gave them nothing to do. Notes *The Industry Standard*:

> It [Webvan] kept employees with identical jobs on both sides, paying scores of workers retention bonuses and time-and-a-half on their already high salaries—even as many of them had little to do. "The last month I sat in my office answering maybe one question a day," says Mike Smith director of distribution HomeGrocer. Shortly after the merger, Smith had gone to Foster City, Calif., to meet with his counterparts. At the meeting, five Webvan employees introduced themselves and described their responsibilities. When his turn came, Smith said: "I am director of distribution, and I do all of your jobs." It was all part of a culture where money was no object.[9]

Notes Tom Alberg: "They were spending too much money, and they weren't changing. I mean, there was a lot of talk about it. Well okay, that's not working, obviously. Well, aren't they going to change? No, they're not going to do it. [Webvan's CEO basically said something like] well, you [HomeGrocer] guys failed. There's always a winner in every space and I'm the winner."

By December, the media had begun reporting more cuts were expected at HomeGrocer as Webvan worked to establish a single brand and integrate the two technology platforms. HomeGrocer had six locations; Webvan had one. In the meantime, the HomeGrocer brand had started to gain customer recognition for the Peach logo on its website and delivery trucks. Notes the *Industry Standard*:

> Blinded by their grand vision, Webvan's execs made a string of bad decisions. Even as it was running out of money, the company spent millions on a rebranding campaign to avoid being pegged as a mere grocer: The marketing push promoted Webvan's sterile new blue-and-green "W" logo. Gone were Webvan's earthy grocery bag and HomeGrocer's fuzzy peach.[10]

This move left many customers in Seattle, Portland, and California unsure about the change might mean.

As cash continued to run out, management initiated cutbacks that only made matters worse. For example, during the last quarter of 2000 they decided to cut marketing expenses by 28%; as a result, total orders fell 8% and orders from new customers slid 48%.

By January 2001, in order to conserve cash Webvan postpone planned openings in Washington D.C., Baltimore, and New Jersey. There was some good news: in March, the company's Orange County facility #2 turned a profit, the first and only standalone Internet grocer to do so. Ignoring this achievement, the company released a dismal annual report in April. It included a warning from its auditor that expressed "substantial doubt" the company could survive the year. The report stated that Webvan would probably need to raise an additional $5–15 million by the fourth quarter. By this time investors had soured on Internet-based ventures, and the company could not raise the money. As *The Seattle Times* pointed out, "The gloomy outlook is reflected in Webvan's stock, which closed this week at 12 cents, a far cry from its all-time high of $34. The company has warned that its shares are in danger of being delisted from the NASDAQ if the stock doesn't start trading above $1."[11]

On April 13, 2001, CEO George Shaheen resigned and the company laid-off 1,150 employees. Its new CEO, Robert Swan, was unable to stop the bleeding or turn the company around. In May Drayton made a presentation to the CEO, suggesting ways to rescue the company, including rebranding operations under the HomeGrocer name and rehiring former executives. He even offered to buy back the company's facilities in Seattle and the HomeGrocer name. However, nothing came of the meeting.

On July 9, 2001, Webvan filed for bankruptcy and ceased all operations. Over 2,500 employees lost their jobs, while 400,000 customers in Seattle, Portland, San Francisco, Chicago, Dallas, Atlanta, and Southern California lost their home grocery service. Drayton recalls, "By the time we merged, I think we had about $600 million combined in the bank, and they [Webvan] managed to go through all that money from when the merger closed in September 2000 to July 1st, 2001." A former senior technical manager at Webvan was quoted in *The Industry Standard* as saying, "We bought them out, we killed their stock, we killed their company, and then we killed ourselves."[12]

Alberg, the VC investor from Madrona, reflected on the merger and everything that followed:

> We [HomeGrocer] overextended ourselves by trying to open too many markets too quickly. Then we kind of got in this panic situation like, "Oh, we're going to run out of capital." We'd gone public by then. "We're going to run out of capital, we've got to do this merger." Management just became quite fixated that we had to do the merger as opposed to really trying to find other solutions of really slashing expenses, cutting back our expansion, and just letting Webvan fail. If we hadn't done the merger, Webvan would have failed anyway. It wasn't that clear, but if we were getting nervous about how we were going to keep this going, they would have too. . . . And probably could have gotten some more capital if you'd cut back and so forth. . . . But really, you had both the CEO and the CFO absolutely convinced this was essential or the company would fail. Well, we did the merger and it failed. I think once the merger happened, there was no chance of success. I mean it was just preordained. . . . We invest in a lot of companies that succeed and a lot of them fail and sometimes it's just totally the wrong idea. I don't think web-grocery sales is the wrong idea, it's just hard to execute it. How do you figure out how to do it, and how do you do it without spending too much capital to get there?

Another early investor in HomeGrocer had a different take on what transpired:

It was the concept that you could capture a significant number of customers at a reasonable price and retain those customers and that would make this an interesting business. Those were both inaccuracies, but it took us a long time [and a billion dollars] to find that out. . . . There were two . . . concerns, one is the "critical mass" issue and the other is the profitability per order issue. . . . We discovered them along the way and what we hoped, aggressively, as we went along, was that volume would solve some of these problems. But we never got a single warehouse to profitability; we were unable to raise the volume in warehouses. But now, there's also a whole issue of route management, where you have to do cluster marketing in order to make the truck route sufficient. So you're actually—you're managing your marketing to be able to work in route clusters and that is really, really hard to do. It's so, so easy to look back and see all the problems. I'll tell you the cost of acquisition per order was never really understood until it was too late. That was the core problem. Every other problem is easier if you can solve *that* problem.

HomeGrocer Resurrection?

Soon after Webvan filed for bankruptcy there was talk about HomeGrocer employees reviving the original company. Many showed support for the original founder, Terry Drayton, and his team. Former customers sent emails to the *Seattle Post-Intelligencer* with subject lines like "Bring back the Peach" and "HomeGrocer.com resurrection." John Cook, a reporter and columnist at the newspaper, noted:

To call the two-dozen e-mails I received passionate would be an understatement. These online grocery shoppers clearly want to see the well-polished, peach-colored HomeGrocer.com delivery trucks rumbling down their streets again. . . . [Also] some of the venture capitalists and angel investors I spoke to this week—including a few who invested in HomeGrocer.com in the early venture rounds—didn't rule out the possibility of making another go of it.

Noted David Billstrom, a managing partner at FBR CoMotion Venture Capital firm in Seattle:

[I would] definitely take the meeting if Terry knocked on my door. But he would have to look methodically at the failure points of Webvan/HomeGrocer.com and then he would have to show how he would overcome those failure points in the new incarnation. And then, most importantly, he would have to get a track record showing that the new and improved version did not have the problems of the old.[13]

While in the past selling groceries online had proved to be tough, other aspects of the market and technology landscape were changing. Consumers had become more comfortable with buying products online. Internet broadband connectivity was widely available, the technology related to processing online transactions had improved considerably, and online tools for managing inventory in real time had advanced and were available. As years passed since the failure of Webvan and HomeGrocer, Drayton and the original HomeGrocer team were meeting to figure out whether they should do it all over again. Had they learned enough from the demise of HomeGrocer to make it work the second time around? What should they include in a presentation to investors to convince them that this time they could crack this difficult market? They had lived through a nerve-wracking experience; it was time to relive it and try to make sense of what had gone so very wrong.

NOTES

1. M Meeker & S Pearson, *The Internet Retailing Report*. Morgan Stanley US Investment Research. May 28, 1997.
2. Peapod, an early entrant into the online grocery business, was an early victim when its CEO, Bill Malloy (former COO of AT&T Wireless), resigned. As the news spread, the company's share price dropped from $12 to $4. Internet grocers around the U.S. like Webvan, Streamline, and GroceryWorks.com also felt the impact. Safeway, one of the nation's largest grocery chains, acquired GroceryWorks.com, and Royal Ahold acquired a controlling interest in Peapod. Webvan, Peapod, and Streamline saw their stocks drop below their IPO prices. Webvan shares had come down to around $12, a 20% drop from its $15 IPO price.
3. HomeGrocer had planned to open a center in Dallas in May, where they would compete with GroceryWorks and Peapod, and to move operations into Atlanta during the Fall 2000, where Webvan already operated. There were plans to enter Chicago, Peapod's "stomping ground." Webvan too announced plans to enter Chicago and, more importantly, arrive in the Seattle market, HomeGrocer's home turf, in October.

4. HomeGrocer.com also entered into negotiations with Safeway, a deal that would have given the startup venture leverage in procuring groceries from wholesalers thanks to Safeway's buying power. The catch was that Safeway didn't want HomeGrocer.com to file a public offering, while HomeGrocer was getting ready to do just that. By November, HomeGrocer began working with Morgan Stanley to go public. As a result, its deal with Safeway never materialized.

5. M. Helft. "The End of the Road." *The Industry Standard*, July 23, 2001.

6. K. Hobson. "Out to Lunch? Webvan/HomeGrocer Deal Doesn't Deliver All the Answers." *TheStreet.com*, June 26, 2000. http://www.thestreet.com/tech/internet/977452.html

7. As the deal was announced, Webvan's stock fell 16% to $7.31, while HomeGrocer's declined 15% to close at $6.88.

8. Quoted in M. Helft. "The End of the Road." *The Industry Standard*, July 23, 2001.

9. *The Industry Standard*, July 23, 2001.

10. *The Seattle Times*, April 14, 2001,

11. Quoted in Helft, "The End of the Road."

12. http://seattlepi.nwsource.com/venture/31128_vc13.shtml

13. Taken from HOMEGROCER.COM INC 424B4 filed on 03/10/2000 accessed via Hoovers.com

Case 5

Tenfold™ Organic Textiles

"We believe that organic cotton should be dyed without chemicals."

Inspired to promote change in the world of textiles, Leah Weinstein founded Tenfold Organic Textiles in January 2006. Paul Weinstein, her brother, joined her as president that December. Tenfold designs, manufactures, and markets naturally dyed, branded, organic apparel called "Truly Organic." It markets its product line to specialty boutiques and department stores across the U.S. and Canada. It operates an online store and has plans to open retail outlets to sell its Truly Organic apparel line. It also provides private-label services to help apparel retailers create products using naturally dyed, organic cotton.

With his newly assembled management team, Paul has been pitching the company's business plan to investor groups in Seattle, including the Zino Society, the Alliance of Angels, and the Keiretsu Group. He also entered both the University of Washington's business plan competition and the Executive MBA business plan competition.

Tenfold is seeking $500,000 in investment capital to build the company's brand, Truly Organic, and for working capital. However, investors have been skeptical about the company's retail strategy of developing and branding its own apparel line. They reasoned that building the Truly Organic brand would require significant financial capital and could be overly expensive. Instead, they suggested that Paul focus on the private-label manufacturing and help others create organic apparel using natural dyes and fibers.

The Alliance of Angels seemed genuinely interested in Tenfold, and invited Paul and his team to make another presentation in January, 2009. Because Paul and his management team had presented to this group before, they decided to rethink their strategy this time around.

BACKGROUND

The idea for starting a venture focused on organic apparel came to Leah Weinstein on one of her trips abroad. Between going to art school and working as tree planter, Leah had spent time traveling throughout Africa and South-East Asia. During one trip in 2002, she became fascinated with the beauty of handcrafted textiles and with organic cotton. After graduating from art school, she founded Leah Weinstein Designs, a business venture focused on making quilts using organic cotton. For Leah, the process of designing and making quilts fulfilled a desire to make beautiful functional objects while addressing issues of environmental sustainability. Not satisfied with just using organic cotton, she began to explore sources for natural dyes, and traveled to India in search of fairly traded, naturally dyed, organic cotton supplies. On her return, Leah started the new venture with seed money from her brother Paul and a loan from their family. The company would focus on organic apparel using naturally dyed fibers. Paul describes how his sister came up with the name Tenfold Organic Textiles:

> When Leah was coming up with the name for her new venture, she had a very strong belief in the mantra [that if] you give somebody something good, you get it back tenfold. And because at the time she was dealing in folded fabrics and

Professor Suresh Kotha, Olesen/Battelle Chaired Professor, and Professor Debra Glassman, both from the University of Washington's Foster School of Business, prepared this case. The case was developed solely as the basis for class discussion. This case is not intended to serve as endorsements, sources of primary data, or illustrations of effective or ineffective management. All rights reserved. Copyright © Kotha & Glassman, 2009.

quilting and those kinds of things, the name "Tenfold" kind of stuck. It was later expanded to Tenfold Organic Textiles, because of emphasis on organically dyed fibers.

To date, the Weinsteins have invested $200,000 in the venture. As Paul notes, their goal was simple, yet substantial:

We want to show the world that fashion need not pollute the environment with chemical processing and synthetic dyes. Leah and I believe that style need not be compromised for eco-friendliness and ethical choices. People are paid fair wages, and everything we use is made as eco-friendly as possible, right down to the packaging: tags made from recycled paper and bags made from bio-compostable potato.

Leah and Paul see Tenfold as a way to bring naturally dyed, organic fabric to U.S. and Canadian markets by venturing into a newly emerging category in the garment industry – sustainable apparel.

Market For Sustainable Apparel

There is no universally accepted definition for the term "sustainable apparel." As an emerging market category, the companies and new businesses that sold "sustainable" products were ahead of the regulatory authorities responsible for certifying such products. A report by Packaged Facts, a U.S.-based consumer market research firm explains:

There is no one overarching set of standards for sustainable apparel, but there are many sets of standards that apply to one or more of the dimensions of sustainability that we've identified—materials, processing, or labor. There are some certifications, such as the McDonough Braungart cradle-to-cradle model, that attempt to cover all aspects of sustainability. In terms of a single stamp or benchmark that will support consumer confidence and protection from fraud in clothing marketed as sustainable, nothing now exists that is widely used.[1]

The standards system was somewhat more advanced for textiles, meaning that organically grown fibers like cotton fell under a defined regulatory framework.[2]

As an agricultural product, cotton sold as organic in the United States must meet all of the legal standards mandated by the Organic Foods Production Act of 1990. These standards were finalized in 2001 and implemented in 2002. The National Organic Program (NOP) of the United States Department of Agriculture (USDA) is the oversight body . . . . USDA's National Organic Program standards are quite comprehensive. In broad strokes, they prohibit the use of toxic or synthetic pesticides, herbicides and fertilizers; prohibit genetically modified organisms, irradiation, or sewage sludge used as a farm input . . . and require a comprehensive farm plan and independent third-party certification by an accredited USDA certifier. All agricultural products sold in the United States as organic must comply with this law.[3]

Meeting the organic cotton standard is costly to farmers, as cotton grown without herbicides, pesticides, and synthetic fertilizers typically has a lower yield. Organic cotton is sold for a higher price, but under U.S. standards the cotton must be grown organically for three years before it can be sold as organic.

Such standards applied to the product itself—in this case, cotton—but not to how the fiber was processed. For example, organic cotton fabric could be bleached with chlorine or dyed with a toxic synthetic dye and still be labeled organic. Other aspects of "sustainability" range from the labor practices in manufacturing, to the carbon footprint of the supply chain, to the eco-friendliness of the packaging. Formed in 2002, the Global Organic Textile Standard (GOTS) has been developed to address all of these aspects of sustainability. As described on its website (www.global-standard.org):

The International Working Group on Global Organic Textile Standard was formed as an initiative of leading standard organizations in 2002 with the goal to unify the various existing standards and draft standards which caused confusion with market participants and consumers and were an obstacle to free international trade with organic textiles . . . . The aim of the standard is to define requirements to ensure organic status of textiles, from harvesting of the raw materials, through environmentally and socially responsible manufacturing up to labelling in order to provide a credible assurance to the end consumer.

The process of GOTS certification is quite rigorous; six years of combined effort finally led to its adoption as the leading organic textile-processing standard. In September 2008, a logo indicating certification became available.

Market Projections and Distribution

Retail sales estimates for the emerging category of "sustainable apparel" are neither readily available nor universally accepted. Organic Exchange, an advocacy and education group in California, estimates the global retail sales for organic cotton products, which include apparel, home textiles, and personal care was around $250 million in 2001.[4] In 2006 they estimated global retail sales reached $1.1 billion and $2 billion in 2007 (Packaged Facts estimated the 2007 market at the slightly higher $2.1 billion). Of the Organic Exchange totals, apparel accounted for 85% of the total market in 2006 and 2007, with home textiles accounting for approximately 12%, and personal care products about 3%. Organic Exchange forecast global retail sales of organic cotton apparel would reach $3.5 billion in 2008, $5 billion by 2009, and $6.8 billion by the end of 2010. This represents a CAGR rate of 32% during this period (see Exhibit 1). A 2008 report from Packaged Facts projects the future:

> [G]rowth will be strong for years to come as designers and marketers adapt to the new demands of sustainable business. Growth is predicted to stay in the double-digits through 2012 . . . . With a global apparel market reaching US$450 billion, it's obvious that the sustainable apparel market, even at strong double-digit growth rates, as expected, is still a very small fraction of the total market . . . . Though this sounds insignificant, it parallels the percentage that organic foods have occupied for some time in the total food industry. That small percentage, however, has had a tremendous impact on the food industry and purchasing habits of shoppers, and the industry has set what it believes to be an attainable goal of reaching 10% of food industry sales. Sustainable apparel can make the same kind of impact through strong growth and developing a strong infrastructure at this time.[5]

According to NPD Group, a respected provider of consumer retail information, U.S. apparel sales in 2007 were $195.6 billion, a figure that represented a 3% growth over 2006. Exhibit 2 presents retail apparel information for the U.S. and provides a breakdown of the three primary categories in 2007, women's apparel accounted for 53% of retail sales, men's 29%, and children's 18%. All three categories showed modest growth over the previous year. In 2007 U.S. apparel sales accounted for 43.5% of all global apparel sales.

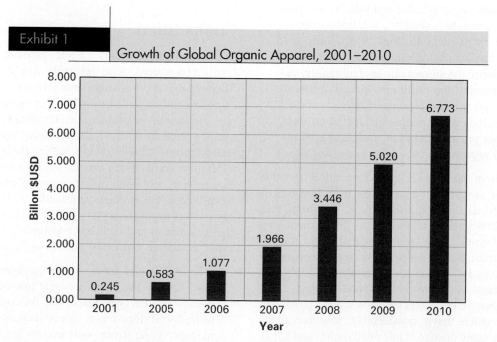

Exhibit 1

Growth of Global Organic Apparel, 2001–2010

Source: Organic Exchange, Market Report, 2007; figures for 2008–2010 are forecasts.

Exhibit 2	U.S. Apparel Market and Categories			
U.S. Apparel (mil)	2006	2007	'07 vs. '06	% of total
Total Apparel	$190,127,200	$195,601,300	+3%	100%
Women's Apparel	$101,976,200	$103,095,100	+1%	53%
Men' Apparel	$54,819,040	$57,212,450	+4%	29%
Children's Apparel	$33,331,990	$35,293,760	+6%	18%

Source: NPD Group, Business Wire.

Applying this figure to Packaged Facts' $450 billion estimate for the global market, the projected U.S. market for organic cotton apparel would be $870 million in 2007 (43.5% of $2 billion) with women's apparel accounting for $461 million (53% of that estimate), men's $252 million (29%) and children's $157 million (18%).[6]

Despite such growth projections, the choices of sustainable apparel products remain limited. According to Packaged Facts:

> The range and variety of sizes and styles available in the conventional clothing industry is not yet available in sustainable equivalents. It is possible, however, to assemble a wardrobe from intimate wear to socks to jeans, shirts, suits, and cocktail dresses made from the fibers and fabrics that comprise the sustainable apparel family, and many garments that fulfill many or all of the additional dimensions of sustainability [such as] low-impact dyes and treatments, socially responsible labor practices and fair trade, and environmentally appropriate packaging and distribution.

The current breakdown of U.S. retail distribution channels for sustainable apparel are as follows: 30% sold through mass merchandisers (e.g., Wal-Mart, J.C. Penney's), 22% through online stores, 18% through outdoor apparel stores, about 16% through department stores (e.g., Nordstrom, Barneys New York), with specialty and boutique stores accounting for the remaining 14%.[7] The mass merchants, department stores, and national chains have strong bargaining power based on scale of purchases. Boutique retailers have considerably less bargaining power, since many operate single retail outlets and buy in smaller quantities relative to the national chains.

For the sustainable apparel market, the recession that began in the U.S. in December 2007 poses both a challenge and a potential opportunity. Generally, apparel sales fall during a recession because apparel is semi-durable and thus purchase that is easily postponed (more so for adult than children's apparel). Currently, consumers are not purchasing not only due to economic uncertainty, but also because they sense it's not the right thing to do. Some observers suggest that consumers are seeking a reason for resuming consumption. They may be enticed to buy if there is a good cause associated with a purchase such as sustainability.

Competition

The sustainable segment of the garment industry is highly fragmented, with relatively low entry barriers. Many small companies outsource primary functions such as design and manufacturing to other specialist companies. Hence, they do not require significant capital to enter or participate in the industry. Some apparel brands start as private-label providers, selling their best designs to retailers and booking production based on the orders they receive, without a major commitment of capital to such fixed assets as plants and facilities. However, new competitors appear every day, styles and consumer tastes change quickly, and rack space is limited to those who garner consumer support. Again, from Packaged Facts:

> [The Industry's] marketers range from private label lines of the world's largest low-cost mass-market retailer, Wal-Mart, and its competitors, to high-end department stores such as Barneys in New York; from well-known international athletic wear brands like Nike and Patagonia to

hundreds of small designer-entrepreneurs; from top-end famous catwalk designers like Stella McCartney and Giorgio Armani to emerging and independent names like Linda Loudermilk; from household names like Levi Straus to newcomers like SeaSalt Organic. Retail outlets include the aforementioned big-box and department stores but also small brick-and-mortar and online eco-boutiques specializing in this category.

Large multinational brands such as Nike, Target, and Wal-Mart are rapidly adding organic apparel to their product lines. Wal-Mart, for example, is now the world's largest user of organic-cotton apparel. Within the last five to ten years, smaller brands have started up, with "sustainability" as their core mission. Examples include Indigenous Designs, Nau, and Historic Futures. They almost exclusively use organic cotton, natural or recycled fibers to create their products. Finally, even some large private-label manufacturers are adopting organic cotton and low-impact processes, offering organic products at relatively low cost. Even so, virtually all of these companies employ "synthetic" chemicals in their dyeing process.

Synthetic versus Natural Dyes

Tenfold Organic Textiles is committed to using natural, herbal dyes. Natural dyes can come from plant, animal, or mineral sources.[8] Herbal dyes are a subset of natural dyes using medicinal herbs such as *tulsi*, *neem*, and *turmeric*. The use of natural dyes in textiles goes back thousands of years. Indigo, a dark blue dye from over thirty different plant species, including the indigo shrub native to India, appeared in Chinese and Indian textiles starting in 2000 BCE (and was used even earlier by the ancient Egyptians).

Both dyes and pigments can be used to color a material, but a dye is a soluble substance while a pigment is insoluble. Generally a dye is dissolved in water, and a fabric is then immersed in the solution. The fabric soaks up the dye and retains the color when dried, because the dye forms a chemical bond with the material. A pigment is generally ground into a powder, mixed with a dispersing agent, and then spread onto a material.

Certain disadvantages are associated with natural dyes. For one thing, the range of colors is limited, and colors are not very bright. For another, it is difficult to produce naturally dyed fabric on a large scale or to

standardize natural dyes; as a result, there may be substantial color variation across different dye lots. Finally, natural dyes are not particularly color- or light-fast and as such tend to fade.

Synthetic dyes, invented in the 1850s, quickly became popular in the textile industry. They were cheaper, more colorfast, and could produce more and brighter colors.[9] Unfortunately, most synthetic dyes also have negative environmental and health impact including toxic exposures for dye workers and the discharge of contaminated water after fabrics are dyed (large quantities of water are needed to rinse dyed fabric).

Whether they're synthetic or natural, not all dyes will form a chemical bond with material. They sometimes require another chemical, called a mordant, to create an insoluble bond. First the mordant is applied to the fabric, the dye is then added, which sticks to the mordant. Thus, the mordant contributes to color-fastness (resistance to color change resulting from light or washing). Mordants range from salt and alum to natural compounds like pomegranate and even toxic heavy metals such as chromium. On average, it takes 80 to 100 liters of water dye one kilogram of finished fabric. Since only 80% of direct dye is retained in the fabric, the rest is emitted as effluent. It is estimated the global textile industry discharges 40,000 to 50,000 tons of dye each year into rivers and streams; in Europe alone, over 200,000 tons of salt used to even out color is discharged each year.

Some mordants also have environmental effects; when metal salts are used, for example, excess metal ions end up in effluent streams. Other mordants like natural pomegranate compounds do not have these effects.

DEVELOPING THE VENTURE

Positioning and Value Proposition

Paul's goal is to position Tenfold as the most "sustainable" brand in the organics category. He believes that being the first to deliver color without synthetic chemicals will allow his venture to differentiate its brand. More important, Tenfold will gain attention from the trade and consumers for its environmentally responsible offerings. Another aspect of Tenfold's differentiation is its emphasis on fashion at an accessible price. Notes Paul:

Our goal is therefore to first win customers as an apparel brand based on fashion, as well as a provider of an environmentally responsible and healthier solution. When you go to a trade show like Magic, the largest apparel selling trade show, which happens twice a year in Las Vegas, you see what is happening. They [the organizers] are beginning to set aside a whole section for what they call the E-Collection for sustainable apparel. So you are seeing "a show within a show" concept where they are setting organics apart because buyers are actively looking for it and they are looking for a destination, somewhere they can find all sorts of organics apparel. When you go into these sections, a lot of what you see is tee-shirts. It is just organic tee-shirts, casual wear, athletic wear, and those kinds of things. Yoga-inspired tee-shirts, hoodies; there is some bamboo, but not a lot. But you don't see a lot of fashion and the fashion you do see is on the very high end—not accessible, very expensive designer couture. So when we looked at how we wanted to design products, we wanted to create something that was definitely fashionable, but also accessible in terms of price.

Paul intends to build relevant brand associations with his customers. These include the innovation of producing organic apparel, greater corporate transparency regarding use and impact of organics, and producing an apparel line that serves the greater good (see Exhibit 3). As Paul explains his company approach,

One of the things that we've taken a look at is all parts of the life cycle of a garment. So much of the sustainable apparel market right now is being built on the concept of using organic cotton, and the fact that it eliminates the use of pesticides and insecticides, a crop that is very hard on the environment. For us, we take our story to the next step of that and say, okay, great, everyone is using organic cotton, but you are all chemically dying and processing it. Over 47% toxicity of an organic tee-shirt is in the wet processing. We're using 100% natural plants and minerals to dye and process our fabrics.

So we're building in the story that our product is organic from farm to garment, all the way, we're looking at all the steps. And in the process of looking at all steps of the life cycle of a garment, we're also looking past ourselves to the consumer and realizing more than 30% of the toxicity of a garment happens after you take it home—it happens in the life and the care of the garment after the initial purchase. So what we're doing is taking a look at that and saying what can we do? We can promote and help consumers reduce their own impact by providing them with Soap Nuts. Soap Nuts is earth's natural laundry soap, it grows on trees, it is a berry and if you use that you are eliminating the toxic

---

Exhibit 3   Tenfold Organic Textiles' Vision and Mission Statement.

Mission Statement: To facilitate the reduction in the use of all chemicals in textile manufacturing by creating powerful brands and products made through the responsible use of natural fibers, dyes, and other resources.

Business Philosophy: To provide people with eco-friendly products, to lessen the use and exposure of harmful chemicals in the world; to be an environmentally responsible company, inspiring others to leave "the lightest footprint possible"™; to profit, but profit from work that lessens our impact on the earth; to operate with honesty, transparency and integrity; to maintain excellence in reputation and craft.

Core Competency: Our major competitive strength is that we can naturally dye textiles on a commercial scale. Most organic textiles today are dyed using low-impact or eco-friendly dyes, which use most of the same chemicals that conventional dyes use. The process used to finish Tenfold Organic's textiles is completely chemical free, which we believe to be an important benefit to our product. Our ability to create high quality, fashionable products from this material will also be a major determining factor in our success.

detergents that are being used. You use cold water and hang to dry and then you've got consumers who are then reducing their own impact on the plant. By addressing the entire life cycle of that tee-shirt, we're actually proving to the consumer that, hey, this is not just a marketing ploy for us; this is something we are taking a serious look from end-to-end of the entire life cycle and trying to make an impact, and help you make that impact with us.

Although some new, smaller brands such as Peligrosa use natural dyes to produce and market a small portion of their apparel line, they lack the technical ability to produce organically dyed fabrics in large volumes. Paul summarizes: "Although there are a lot of players in this industry, none of them offer 100% organic textiles or apparel made without the use of chemicals on a commercial scale." Tenfold found a way to do that which others have not, at least not yet.

Access to Unique Dyeing Technology

During one of her trips to India, Leah discovered a company that could dye organic cotton and fabrics in large volumes without a loss in quality. Located in Ahmedabad, India, Aura Herbal Wear has developed and patented a process to naturally dye fabric in commercial quantities using modern conventional dyeing machinery. Using Aura's herbal dye process, over a thousand meters of cloth can be dyed evenly in the same color; innovative controlled machines replace the need for sun and running water. The company's process is versatile, with the ability to dye yarns, towels, weaves, and knits. It can dye high-fashion fabrics like voile and silk as well as home furnishing fabrics like jute.

Aura's herbal dyes are made from such substances as haritaki, turmeric, indigo, madder, pomegranate, cutch (catechu), and onion. Aura uses only natural mordants, such as myrballams, rubhabs leaves, and alum; they do not use the metal mordants like chrome or copper in their processes. The company even claims the resulting dye effluent can be used to irrigate agriculture, including crops for human consumption. The company holds an Indian patent (and now a U.S. patent) for its dyeing process. Aura has received the GOTS certification.

In March 2007, Tenfold and Aura signed a two-year agreement giving Tenfold exclusive rights to naturally dyed fabric produced by Aura and sold in the U.S. and Canada. In July 2008 Tenfold and Aura agreed in principle to extend the exclusivity of their agreement to July 2013. Under this agreement, Aura is responsible for procuring organic yarn and finished fabric, and then naturally dyeing the fabric or garments to Tenfold's specifications. Paul explains:

Because of our relationship with Aura, we have the ability to create organic textile products that deliver on key environmental benefits few brands have the ability to match. Our advantage is the exclusive access to the Aura's natural dye process, which eliminates the need for chemicals in textile processing, while being flexible, consistent, and scalable.

Using Aura's patented process, Tenfold's strategy is to compete in two distinct but related categories: the branded-apparel market, and private-label manufacturing.

Branded Apparel Market Strategy

Tenfold's apparel line begins with women's lifestyle sportswear and casual clothing, and is targeted at 25- to 40-year-olds. The brand targets "core" female sustainability consumers as defined by the Hartman Group, Inc.[10] This "core" segment is most likely to consider sustainability in their purchasing decisions and are early adopters of sustainable products. According to Paul:

These consumers think beyond themselves and their households when considering the impact of purchasing decisions. They believe, the decisions "I" make and the things that "I" do impact more than just myself. The core sustainability consumers believe in corporate transparency and authenticity. To these folks, company values, policies and practices are an important part of the offering. They want companies and products to be "real" and "values" based.

Amy Thompson, Tenfold's Director of Marketing, adds:

Fundamentally we are talking about a values-based consumer. I think that women have been quicker, perhaps because of their nurturing mother instinct, to think beyond themselves. We're looking at people who are not just thinking about themselves but are starting to think about the community and the impact that their buying decisions has on the larger world around them.

Marketing and Distribution. Tenfold prices its apparel to support its premium organic positioning while remaining accessible for customers. Products are priced at the entry point (low end) of the "better sportswear" market, reflecting the balance between premium positioning and accessibility. Amy claims that this market pricing approach enables them to achieve an average gross margin of 50%, the level required to fund marketing efforts to establish the "Truly Organic" brand.

Tenfold distributes its product line through specialty boutiques and select department stores. Notes Amy, "We've selected these channels because of their ability to communicate the unique benefits of the brand directly to consumers." This was especially true with specialty boutiques. She adds:

> The specialty boutique channel is a good one for us first of all because there are lots of them; they focus less on price, and are relatively easy to reach through trade shows. They are independent, typically owned by one person who has one shop. The owner of the boutique knows almost all of their customers and for sure knows every piece of clothing on their floor, because they bought it.

So what you have is this opportunity for us to have our story told by the retailer, and that can only happen in the boutique setting. We can give them tools like the soap nuts that they can use to spark a conversation about what is organic, and why that is important, and why natural dyes, and the whole farm-to-garment idea.

Thus, the company targets apparel retailers committed to lowering their impact on the environment by offering sustainable products to customers and stakeholders.

In November 2007, Paul hired Wally Barger as the company's in-house national sales manager. Wally directs the sales efforts and makes all major sales calls; to expand the company's reach, he will be supported by a network of multi-line sales representatives in key markets like Los Angeles and New York. In February 2008, Paul hired Carol Morris as Vice President of Merchandising. Carol is responsible for designing the company's product line, sampling, and managing the production processes used by the company. (See Exhibit 4 for details about the current management team.)

Paul estimates that in 2007 the U.S. organic apparel market over $900 million, and that sales through select

---

Exhibit 4   Tenfold Organic's Management Team as of November 2008

Wally Barger, National Sales Manager

Wally Barger joined the company fulltime in November 2007 as National Sales Manager. Wally is an experienced apparel sales executive with over 25 years of branded apparel sales, including ownership and management of boutique retail clothing store earlier in his career. Wally has spent many years selling premium apparel brands.

Carolyn Morris, VP Merchandise

Carolyn Morris spent most of her career on the merchandising and design teams of national retailers and regional department stores. Her last apparel position was Vice President, Merchandise Manager for TJX, a $7 billion retailer based in Framingham, Massachusetts. Carolyn is responsible for merchandising and designing the line, and for designing and managing the design, sampling, and production processes of the company.

Amy Thompson, Director of Marketing

Amy Thompson brings eight years of international marketing experience to Tenfold. In her last position, Amy was responsible for developing and implementing new market entry strategies for U.S.-based industries and businesses. Amy holds an the Executive MBA from the Foster School of Business, University of Washington.

Paul Weinstein, President/General Manager

Paul, formerly a Jones Soda executive, held senior management roles in both Operations and Sales. He was instrumental in the development of the company and in executing its operations strategies from concept in 1995 through its transition to be a national brand name. Paul spent 11.5 years at Jones Soda as the company grew from a concept to a market valuation of over $500 million. Paul completed the Executive MBA program at UW in 2008.

department stores and boutiques should be around $144 million (see Exhibit 5 for Paul's market estimates). The company is currently shipping products to 55 stores in the U.S. and expects to ship to 750 stores by Fall of 2012. The average revenues-per-store-per-shipment is $1,200 and the company is currently doing two shipments per year. Paul expects this figure will increase to $3,000 by 2012 when he expects to ship five times per year and achieve around a 50% gross profit margin. See Exhibit 6 for details about Tenfold's financial projections.

Competitors. When asked to name competitors in their space, Paul noted the following:

Prairie Underground and Stewart & Brown would be the two that we focus on. Prairie Underground does use organic cotton, and so does Stewart & Brown. Stewart & Brown is a little higher on the price point than we are and Prairie Underground is probably pretty similar. I would say they are more similar to us than Stewart & Brown. In boutiques, it's really any fashion brand. For us, there is a fair amount of competition. We set ourselves apart, of course, through our story and the use of organic fabrics and natural dyes and the belief that people are going to care about that and place a value on that. Remember, we are also competing with everything else in the boutique, whether it is organic or not, and by nature of the target we're going after, we're not targeting organic boutiques. There aren't even a lot of them out there. We're targeting specialty boutiques that focus on fashion and that have a certain clientele that care about clothes and shopping, and we're positioning ourselves within that store as somebody to be set apart because of our values and transparency and what we're doing with the brand.

| Exhibit 5 | Paul's Estimate for U.S. Organic Apparel |

Organic Apparel (mil)	2007	% of total
Total Cotton	$912,800*	100%
Women's Apparel**	$483,784	53%
Men' Apparel	$264,712	29%
Children's Apparel	$164,304	18%
Distribution Channels Breakdown (mil)*		
Mass Merchandisers	30%	$145,135
Online Stores	22%	$106,432
Outdoor Apparel Stores	18%	$87,081
Department Stores	16%	$77,405
Specialty Boutiques	14%	$67,730
Women Total		483,784

*According to Packaged Facts (May 2008 report), global apparel figures were $450 billion in 2007. NPD group estimates U.S. apparel figures in 2007 to be $195 billion, which represents about 43.46% of global sales. U.S. sales are assumed to be about 43.46% of Global Cotton Apparel Sales. Packaged Facts estimates global cotton apparel sales were $2.1 billion in 2007.
**These category breakdowns are estimated using the figures from Exhibit 2.
*** Breakdown estimates for the sustainable apparel distribution are based on estimates provided by Packaged Facts.

Exhibit 6	Proposed Financial Plan

	2008	2009	2010	2011	2012
Revenues	$93,863	$648,469	$2,364,592	$4,200,000	$11,348,713
Cost of Goods Sold	$138,075	$515,000	$1,720,000	$2,630,941	$6,800,000
Gross Profit	**$(44,212)**	**$133,469**	**$644,592**	**$1,569,059**	**$4,548,713**
Marketing & Promotion					
Branding/Advertizing	$6,000	$6,000	$6,000	$12,000	$12,000
PR Campaign	$16,000	$6,000	$18,000	$18,000	$18,000
Marketing Materials	$4,000	$3,000	$3,000	$3,000	$3,000
Website Administration	$3,375	$6,938	$19,239	$63,672	$132,066
Total Marketing & Promotion	**$29,375**	**$21,938**	**$46,239**	**$96,672**	**$165,066**
Salaries and Wages					
Salary	$84,800	$39,450	$272,974	$282,000	$282,000
Commission	$6,615	$48,840	$139,995	$437,400	$672,624
Benefits/Taxes	$-	$-	$27,297	$28,200	$28,200
Total Salaries and Wages	**$91,415**	**$88,290**	**$440,266**	**$747,600**	**$982,824**
Sales, General & Administrative Expense					
Trade Shows/Marketing	$36,500	$44,500	$54,000	$54,000	$54,000
Samples	$44,500	$56,000	$76,000	$76,000	$76,000
Meals and Entertainment	$6,000	$12,000	$18,000	$18,000	$18,000
Travel and Lodging	$18,500	$30,000	$42,000	$42,000	$42,000
Rent	$-	$-	$-	$18,000	$18,000
Auto Expenses	$3,000	$3,000	$9,000	$9,000	$9,000
Dues/Subscriptions/Professional Fees	$6,000	$6,000	$6,000	$6,000	$6,000
Merchant/Bank Fees	$2,816	$14,954	$9,743	$34,603	$75,639
Telephone/Fax/Internet	$3,600	$3,600	$5,400	$5,400	$5,400
Office Supplies	$2,400	$900	$900	$900	$900
$720 $720 $720	$720	$720			
Total Sales Expense	**$124,036**	**$171,674**	**$221,763**	**$264,623**	**$305,659**
Total Expenses	**$244,826**	**$281,902**	**$708,268**	**$1,108,895**	**$1,453,549**
Interest Expense	$16,711	$38,811	$208,418	$308,449	$136,184
Net Income Before Taxes	**$(322,149)**	**$(187,244)**	**$(272,094)**	**$1,213,597**	**$2,958,980**

Source: The Company

Establishing the Brand. Paul intends to use a range of tactics to raise awareness among trade channel partners and consumers about chemical dyes and the benefits of organically dyed apparel. Trade shows and marketing materials will target channel partners, while customer touch points include online sales and advertising, as well as in-store clothing tags and materials. The focus will be on environmental responsibility through the use of his chemical-free organic brand. A public relations program will build awareness about chemical dyes and the company's organic brand:

> Using my experience from Jones Soda, I plan to employ various guerilla-style marketing tactics to increase the visibility and awareness of our brand. I am reviewing such ideas as product placement on reality fashion TV shows, or sponsorship of projects at leading fashion design schools. I am also planning to employ an influencer strategy by approaching noted celebrities that have taken on speaking out for environmental causes.

The company has taken some steps toward implementing the brand strategy. To connect with retail buyers, Paul and Amy will attend trade shows that target specialty boutiques and department stores. The initial focus will be on such Northwest shows as the Seattle Trend Show, and then expand to shows in the Southwest and East. They will also consider shows like Magic Marketplace, D&A and other industry-specific shows. While it may cost more to exhibit at Magic Marketplace and other similar shows, they strongly believe that a presence there is important to gain exposure among key audiences and sell the product.

Working with a Seattle-based graphic design and branding consultant, Paul designed the company's logos, website and brand identity. He and his associates have created marketing pieces for use at trade shows and sales calls. These materials provide information about the company, its unique dyeing process, benefits the company's brand offers, as well as images and details for each seasonal line. So far they have spent about $10,000 on such materials.

To foster a dialogue among boutiques and end customers about the use of chemical dyes and the benefits of choosing a garment that is organic throughout the production cycle, the company has retained On the Horizons Communications, a California-based public relations firm that has worked on industry and LOHAS[11] consumer publications, in print and Internet media. Its services cost about $1,500 per month. As a result,

Tenfold and its branded apparel have been mentioned in over ten trade and consumer publications and websites including Treehugger.com, MR Magazine, Seattle Business Monthly, and Textile Intelligence Magazine.

Pursuing Retail Sales. In 2008, the company began online retail operations; their site www.truly-organic.com is designed to showcase and sell products directly to consumers (see Exhibit 7). Says Paul, "Our online store enables us to have national retail coverage and the higher margins that accompany retail sales." Tenfold's wholesale margins are between 45 to 55%, which, according to Paul, are typical for the industry. The company is now employing search engine optimization (SEO) strategies and pay-per-click (PPC) advertising to drive traffic to the company's website and increase web sales.

Paul is also contemplating opening approximately 1,500 square feet of retail space in the third quarter of 2009. Notes Amy,

> We consider owning and operating retail space a key element in our ability to create and control the environment in which our consumers experience our products. It will also allow us to (1) interact with our customers directly so that we can educate them about our unique natural dye process and the benefits of our products, and (2) increase the velocity of the feedback cycle, giving us the ability to test new products and refine our designs to better suit the market. We intend to open one store in Q3 2009, a second store in Q1 2011, and three more in 2012. All of this will of course depend on the success of our first store and what we learn from it.

Exhibit 8 presents Paul's estimates for per-store start-up costs, monthly operating costs, and revenues per square foot. He estimates gross retail margins will be 75% of revenues.

Private-Label Strategy

The second prong of Tenfold's strategy was private label manufacturing. Tenfold's private-label strategy targets those companies interested in incorporating greater sustainability into their business practices. As Paul explains:

> We know that designers for companies such as Abercrombie & Fitch have created natural dye palettes for their brand, only to realize that they didn't have the ability to produce them. With our

relationships with our partner, we have the ability to assist domestic businesses in creating and manufacturing custom items using our naturally dyed organic fabrics. We have already completed a project for Aveda and are currently developing products for other manufacturers and retailers.[12]

| Exhibit 7 | Website selling "Truly Organic" Apparel |

Exhibit 8	Revenues Projections for Retail Stores 2009–2012

	2009	2010	2011	2012
Number of Stores (@1500 sq ft per store)	1	1	2	5
Total square feet of space	1,500	1,500	3,000	7,500
Revenues per square feet/year	$300	$400	$500	$600
Store Revenues	$112,500	$600,000	$1,500,000	$4,500,000
Cost of operations @ $25,000/month	$75,000	$315,000	$661,500	$1,732,500
Startup costs per store	$150,000	$0	$150,000	$750,000
Net Retail Store Revenues	$112,500	$285,000	$688,500	$2,017,500

*Estimates are starting the store in the 3rd quarter of 2009.

Paul concedes that pursuing this strategy requires considerable time and attention, and tends to be more transaction-based. However, such an approach requires little investment in working capital.

Target Customers. Tenfold targets department stores, parks and resorts, and companies attempting to improve their positioning with the "sustainable" apparel market. Notes Amy:

We are targeting companies that have set goals to try to improve their footprint, improve their sustainability profile and have picked up on the fact that their consumers care about that. And we know that, based on either marketing materials that express their preference or their inclusion of different suppliers that have those sustainability offerings, or because they have actually told us, hey, this is what we are trying to reach. They include retail stores like Nordstrom, who have their own private label brands; they include actual manufacturers like Patagonia; and they also include catalog. There is quite a bit of movement in the catalog industry as well.

Adds Paul,

Then you've got parks and resorts—we're talking to Disney Parks and Resorts, Warner Brothers, and those kinds of things. We have a targeted list of all the people that we think are looking at this space. They all see the same numbers that we see. We have a list, we're calling them, and we're making

contact. We send them a package where we tell our story and give them a sample of what we can do, and then we follow up.

In discussing Tenfold's marketing strategy to reach private-label manufacturing Amy observes, "It's not the kind of situation where trade advertising, or other tactics that often cost a lot of money, are really valuable. The most important thing is getting your stuff in front of them."

For private label apparel and custom-textile products, Tenfold will act as a sales agent, capturing 20% margins on any given transaction. Leveraging their exclusive relationship with Aura, Tenfold will coordinate the development, sampling and delivery process specific to an individual customer's needs.

Tenfold is already working on a few private label projects for apparel companies and a project for a retailer of sustainable home textiles. Some of these contacted the company through its website or through its listing with several sustainable fabric sourcing directories.

Progress

Since Paul's arrival the focus has been on writing a business plan, preparing to pitch the plan to potential investors, and getting the Truly Organic apparel into stores. So far, Tenfold Organic has progressed through several milestones set by Paul who completed the business plan in March 2008. He has assembled a management team of experienced marketing professionals, hired an agency to brand the company and a PR agency to promote it, and launched a website to sell the apparel. He is now in the process of assembling an experienced advisory team.

During the same period, Tenfold completed manufacturing its Spring/Summer 2008 line, which shipped to retailers and consumers in March 2008. They completed samples of the Fall/Winter 2008 line and were in the process of pre-selling the line to retailers. The design of the Spring/Summer 2009 line was completed, fabric ordered, and samples received by July 2008. As of April 2008, 55 retailers had placed purchase orders, with sales of $30,000 achieved.

On the private label front, the company recently completed 85,000 units of a custom drawstring bag for a new cosmetic brush for Aveda. This product is expected to be an ongoing item, with the bag standard packaging. Paul is also expecting orders from a retailer of organic home textiles.

To gather feedback before presenting their plan to professional investors, Paul and Amy presented the company's evolving business plan at two different forums. Out of 60 teams, Tenfold Organics became one of the four finalists to present at the University of Washington Business Plan Competition in May 2008, and Paul's team was one of four finalists (out of 16) at the 2008 Executive MBA Business Plan Challenge in June. They now felt ready to seek funding from professional investors.

THE CHALLENGES OF MOVING FORWARD

Between June and November 2008, Paul pitched Tenfold's business plan to a variety of Seattle investment groups including the Alliance of Angels, the Keiretsu Group, and the Zino Society. Paul sought a bridge round investment of $1 million, in the form of a convertible note. The funding was primarily designated for working capital, and for building the "Truly Organic" brand. A future round, in the range of $3-4 million, would be sought in around the third quarter of 2009 to accelerate market introduction and brand expansion.

Feedback from Investors

Paul and Amy's presentations garnered an enthusiastic reception. However, as of November 2008, no funding had been obtained. Some investors questioned Tenfold's relationship with Aura and whether this relationship was likely to last despite the longterm contract signed by the parties. Others were skeptical about Paul's two-pronged approach of building the brand while pursuing a private label strategy, believing that the former would require a large capital outlay and a significant amount of time to accomplish effectively. Some went so far as suggesting that Tenfold abandon its efforts to create branded apparel and focus solely on the private-label route.

Although Paul listened politely, he and his team were not yet ready to abandon Tenfold's goal of building its retail brand while pursuing private-label manufacturing. Paul explained,

> To us, branded products and private label are complementary, since each offsets the other's risk and reward. Branded products provide a wholesale margin of 50% and provide us the opportunity to create brand equity and establish a strong and leading presence in the market space. Because it is an inventory business, it requires more capital and comes with inventory risk. Private-label margins are somewhat lower, at 20%, but it is a transactional business and as such doesn't require the same cash outlays for inventory, or carry inventory risk. We see private label contracts as paid R&D—the experience from the contracts helps improve our branded products. Our strategy is to utilize private-label sales to generate positive cash flow, reach economies of scale quickly, and advance us along the learning curve while helping to fund and support our efforts to build the Truly Organic brand.

In the meantime, a global financial crisis and the resulting financial market meltdown in the U.S. and other countries was making it hard for small ventures to raise capital. In November 2008, Wally left the company due to lack of sales. In response to the new economic climate, Paul has revised his ask from $1 million to $500,000, in the form of equity and not a convertible loan.

Paul and Amy were invited to present at the Alliance of Angel's January 2009 meeting. Since this was the second presentation to the group, Paul felt they had a good shot at raising the capital, despite the poor economic climate. First, however, he had to decide whether to modify his presentation given the new economic reality. Since many of the investors had been skeptical about Tenfold's strategy, the issue was sure to be raised again. Was it time to revise the strategy and modify his business plan? Or, given market realities and poor economic conditions, would it be wiser to postpone or even abandon the idea of retail stores?

NOTES

1. Packaged Facts, International Market for Sustainable Apparel, May 2008. The same report notes, "There are many legal and regulatory statutes around the world that apply to textiles and clothing, and sustainable apparel must obviously meet all requirements and conditions for the country of production, and all import and export laws."

2. In the United States the organic label for agricultural products is regulated through the U.S. Department of Agriculture (USDA). The European Union has its own set of standards, as do Canada, Japan, and many other countries. In order to export a product to another country and sell it there, the product must meet that country's standards. However, there are some reciprocal agreements in place between countries to facilitate ease of trade.

3. Packaged Facts, May 2008.

4. Organic Exchange, Organic Cotton Market Report, 2007.

5. Packaged Facts, May 2008, p. 75.

6. These numbers are based on Organic Exchange market estimates. Alternatively, one could use Packaged Facts' global estimates for organic cotton apparel ($2.1 billion). It is worth noting again that the market for cotton organics is growing rapidly, and these figures are only estimates of the overall potential market.

7. Packaged Facts, May 2008.

8. The term "organic" is potentially confusing when applied to dye. Most dyes are "organic" in the chemical sense of being carbon-based compounds (while most pigments are inorganic compounds), which is not the same meaning "organic" has in the environmental arena. For practical purposes, we will use the term "natural dye."

9. Until World War I, Germany was the world leader in the production of synthetic dyes. The indigo dye molecule, for example, was first synthesized in 1870 and became commercially available in Germany after 1897. The demand for better and brighter synthetic dyes was an important factor in the development of the chemical manufacturing industry, which in turn led to the development of the pharmaceutical industry.

10. The Hartman Group, Inc., Sustainability from a Consumer Perspective, January 2007. Results are representative of the U.S. population.

11. LOHAS stands for Lifestyles Of Health And Sustainability. See, for example, www.lohas.com.

12. Aveda, Blaine, Minnesota based company started in 1978, manufacturers and sells profession plant?based hair care, skin care, makeup and lifestyle products. The company operates its own stores and also sells its products through 7,000 professional hair salons and spas in 24 countries worldwide (as of May 2009).

Case 6

The Air Express Industry: 40 Years of Expansion

Charles W. L. Hill,
The University of Washington

INTRODUCTION

The small package express delivery industry is that segment of the broader postal and cargo industries that specializes in rapid (normally 1–3 days) delivery of small packages (small packages are defined as those weighing less than 150 lbs or having less than 165 inches in combined length and girth). The modern express delivery industry in the United States began with Fred Smith's vision for Federal Express Company, which started operations in 1973. Federal Express transformed the structure of the existing air cargo industry and paved the way for rapid growth in the overnight package segment of that industry. A further impetus to the industry's development was the 1977 deregulation of the U.S. air cargo industry. This deregulation allowed Federal Express (and its emerging competitors) to buy large jets for the first time. The story of the industry during the 1980s was one of rapid growth and new entry. Between 1982 and 1989, small package express cargo shipments by air in the United States grew at an annual average rate of 31%. In contrast, shipments of air freight and air mail grew at an annual rate of only 2.7%.[1] This rapid growth attracted new entrants such as United Parcel Service (UPS) and Airborne Freight (which operated under the name Airborne Express). The entry of UPS triggered severe price cutting, which ultimately drove some of the weaker competitors out of the market and touched off a wave of consolidation in the industry.

By the mid 1990s, the industry structure had stabilized with four organizations —Federal Express, UPS, Airborne Express, and the United States Postal Service — accounting for the vast majority U.S. express shipments

via air. During the first half of the 1990s, the small package express industry continued to grow at a healthy rate, with shipments expanding by slightly more than 16% per annum.[2] Despite this growth, the industry was hit by repeated rounds of price cutting as the three big private firms battled to capture major accounts. In addition to price cutting, the big three also competed vigorously on the basis of technology, service offerings, and the global reach of their operations. By the late 1990s and early 2000s the intensity of price competition in the industry had moderated, with a degree of pricing discipline being maintained, despite the fact that the growth rate for the industry slowed down. Between 1995 and 2000, the industry grew at 9.8% per year. In 2001 the volume of express parcels shipped by air fell by 5.9%, partly due to an economic slowdown, and partly due to the aftereffects of the September 11 terrorist attack on the United States.[3] Growth picked up again in 2002. Estimates suggest that the global market for small package express delivery should continue to grow by a little over 6% per annum between 2005 and 2025. Most of that growth, however, is forecasted to take place outside of the now mature North American market. Within the United States, the annual growth rate is predicted to match the growth in United States GDP.[4]

In North America, the biggest change to take place in the 2000s was the 2003 entry of DHL with the acquisition of Airborne Express for $1 billion. DHL is itself owned by Deutsche Post World Net, formally the German post office, which since privatization has been rapidly transforming itself into a global express mail and logistics operation. Prior to 2003, DHL lacked a strong presence in the all-important United States market. The acquisition of Airborne gave DHL a foothold in the United States. DHL subsequently spent $1.5 billion trying to upgrade Airborne's delivery network in a quest for market share. Despite heavy investments, DHL failed to gain traction and after 5 years of losses, in 2009 it exited the United States market. With the exit of DHL, the United States market looks increasingly like a duopoly. In 2012, FedEx held onto 53% of the $15 billion Overnight Express market, UPS accounted for 42% and the U.S. Postal Service (USPS) held 5% (although the USPS actually contracted out its express deliveries to FedEx). UPS dominated the $34 billion ground market for small packages in 2012, with a 60% share, followed by FedEx with 24% and the USPS with 16%.[5]

THE INDUSTRY BEFORE FEDEX

In 1973, roughly 1.5 billion tons of freight were shipped in the United States. Most of this freight was carried by surface transport, with air freight accounting for less than 2% of the total.[6] While shipment by air freight was often quicker than shipment by surface freight, the high cost of air freight had kept down demand. The typical users of air freight at this time were suppliers of time-sensitive, high-priced goods, such as computer parts and medical instruments, which were needed at dispersed locations but which were too expensive for their customers to hold as inventory.

The main cargo carriers in 1973 were major passenger airlines, which operated several all-cargo planes and carried additional cargo in the holds of their passenger planes, along with a handful of all-cargo airlines such as Flying Tiger. From 1973 onward, the passenger airlines moved steadily away from all-cargo planes and began to concentrate cargo freight in passenger planes. This change was a response to increases in fuel costs, which made the operation of many older cargo jets uneconomical.

With regard to distribution of cargo to and from airports, in 1973 about 20% of all air freight was delivered to airports by the shipper and/or picked up by the consignee. The bulk of the remaining 80% was accounted for by three major intermediaries: (1) Air Cargo Incorporated, (2) freight forwarders, and (3) the U.S. Postal Service. Air Cargo Incorporated was a trucking service, wholly owned by 26 airlines, which performed pickup and delivery service for the airlines' direct customers. Freight forwarders were trucking carriers who consolidated cargo going to

the airlines. They purchased cargo space from the airlines and retailed this space in small amounts. They dealt primarily with small customers, providing pickup and delivery services in most cities, either in their own trucks or through contract agents. The U.S. Postal Service used air service for transportation of long-distance letter mail and air parcel post.[7]

THE FEDERAL EXPRESS CONCEPT

Founded by Fred Smith, Jr., Federal Express was incorporated in 1971 and began operations in 1973. At that time, a significant proportion of small-package air freight flew on commercial passenger flights. Smith believed that there were major differences between packages and passengers, and he was convinced that the two had to be treated differently. Most passengers moved between major cities and wanted the convenience of daytime flights. Cargo shippers preferred nighttime service to coincide with late-afternoon pickups and next-day delivery. Because small-package air freight was subservient to the requirements of passengers' flight schedules, it was often difficult for the major airlines to achieve next-day delivery of air freight.

Smith's aim was to build a system that could achieve next-day delivery of small-package air freight (less than 70 pounds). He set up Federal Express with his $8 million family inheritance and $90 million in venture capital (the company's name was changed to FedEx in 1998). Federal Express established a hub-and-spoke route system, the first airline to do so. The hub of the system was Memphis, chosen for its good weather conditions, central location, and the fact that it was Smith's hometown. The spokes were regular routes between Memphis and shipping facilities at public airports in the cities serviced by Federal Express. Every weeknight, aircraft would leave their home cities with a load of packages and fly down the spokes to Memphis (often with one or two stops on the way). At Memphis, all packages were unloaded, sorted by destination, and reloaded. The aircraft then returned back to their home cities in the early hours of the morning. Packages were ferried to and from airports by Federal Express couriers driving the company's vans and working to a tight schedule. Thus, from door to door, the package was in Federal Express's hands. This system guaranteed that a package picked up from a customer in New York at 5 p.m. would reach its final destination in Los Angeles (or any other major city) by noon the following day. It enabled Federal Express to realize economies in sorting and to utilize its air cargo capacity efficiently. Federal Express also pioneered the use of standard packaging with an upper weight limit of 70 pounds and a maximum length plus girth of 108 inches. This standard helped Federal Express to gain further efficiencies from mechanized sorting at its Memphis hub. Later entrants into the industry copied Federal Express's package standards and hub-and-spoke operating system.

To accomplish overnight delivery, Federal Express had to operate its own planes. Restrictive regulations enforced by the Civil Aeronautics Board (CAB), however, prohibited the company from buying large jet aircraft. To get around this restriction, Federal Express bought a fleet of twin-engine executive jets, which it converted to minifreighters. These planes had a cargo capacity of 6,200 pounds, which enabled Federal Express to get a license as an air taxi operator.

After 1973, Federal Express quickly built up volume. By 1976, it had an average daily volume of 19,000 packages, a fleet of 32 aircraft, 500 delivery vans, and 2,000 employees, and it had initiated service in 75 cities. After 3 years of posting losses, the company turned in a profit of $3.7 million on revenues of $75 million.[8] However, volume had grown so much that Federal Express desperately needed to use larger planes to maintain operating efficiencies. As a result, Smith's voice was added to those calling for Congress to deregulate the airline industry and allow greater competition.

DEREGULATION AND ITS AFTERMATH

In November 1977, Congress relaxed regulations controlling competition in the air cargo industry, 1 year before passenger services were deregulated. This involved a drastic loosening of standards for entry into the industry. The old CAB authority of naming the carriers that could operate on the various routes was changed to the relatively simple authority of deciding which among candidate carriers was fit, willing, and able to operate an all-cargo route. In addition, CAB controls over pricing were significantly reduced. The immediate effect was an increase in rates for shipments, particularly minimum- and high-weight categories, suggesting that prices had been held artificially low by regulation. As a result, the average yield (revenue per ton mile) on domestic airfreight increased 10.6% in 1978 and 11.3% in 1979.[9]

Freed from the constraints of regulation, Federal Express immediately began to purchase larger jets and quickly established itself as a major carrier of small-package air freight. Despite the increase in yields, however, new entry into the air cargo industry was limited, at least initially. This was mainly due to the high capital requirements involved in establishing an all-cargo carrier. Indeed, by the end of 1978, there were only four major all-cargo carriers serving the domestic market: Airlift International, Federal Express, Flying Tiger, and Seaboard World Airlines. While all of these all-cargo carriers had increased their route structure following deregulation, only Federal Express specialized in next-day delivery for small packages. Demand for a next-day delivery service continued to boom. Industry estimates suggest that the small-package priority market had grown to about 82 million pieces in 1979, up from 43 million in 1974.[10]

At the same time, in response to increasing competition from the all-cargo carriers, the passenger airlines continued their retreat from the all-cargo business (originally begun in 1973 as a response to high fuel prices). Between 1973 and 1978, there was a 45% decline in the mileage of all-cargo flights by the airlines. This decrease was followed by a 14% decline between 1978 and 1979. Instead of all-cargo flights, the airlines concentrated their attentions on carrying cargo in passenger flights. This practice hurt the freight forwarders badly. The freight forwarders had long relied on the all-cargo flights of major airlines to achieve next-day delivery. Now the freight forwarders were being squeezed out of this segment by a lack of available lift at the time needed to ensure next-day delivery.

This problem led to one of the major post-deregulation developments in the industry: the acquisition and operation by freight forwarders of their own fleets of aircraft. Between 1979 and 1981, five of the six largest freight forwarders became involved in this activity. The two largest were Emery Air Freight and Airborne Express. Emery operated a fleet of 66 aircraft at the end of 1979, the majority of which were leased from other carriers. In mid 1980, this fleet was providing service to approximately 129 cities, carrying both large-volume shipments and small-package express.

Airborne Express acquired its own fleet of aircraft in April 1980 with the purchase of Midwest Charter Express, an Ohio-based all-cargo airline. In 1981, Airborne opened a new hub in Ohio, which became the center of its small-package express operation. This enabled Airborne to provide next-day delivery for small packages to 125 cities in the United States.[11] Other freight forwarders that moved into the overnight mail market included Purolator Courier and Gelco, both of which offered overnight delivery by air on a limited geographic scale.

INDUSTRY EVOLUTION, 1980–1986

New Products and Industry Growth

In 1981, Federal Express expanded its role in the overnight market with the introduction of an overnight letter service, with a limit of 2 ounces. This guaranteed overnight delivery service was set up in direct competition with the U.S. Postal Service's Priority Mail. The demand for such a service was illustrated by its expansion to about 17,000 letters per day within its first 3 months of operation.

More generally, the focus of the air express industry was changing from being predominantly a conduit for goods to being a distributor of information—particularly company documents, letters, contracts, drawings, and the like. As a result of the growth in demand for information distribution, new product offerings such as the overnight letter, and Federal Express's own marketing efforts, the air express industry enjoyed high growth during the early 1980s, averaging more than 30% per year.[12] Indeed, many observers attribute most of the growth in the overnight delivery business at this time to Federal Express's marketing efforts. According to one industry participant, "Federal Express pulled off one of the greatest marketing scams in the industry by making people believe they absolutely, positively, had to have something right away."[13]

Increasing Price Competition

Despite rapid growth in demand, competitive intensity in the industry increased sharply in 1982 following the entry of UPS into the overnight-delivery market. UPS was already by far the largest private package transporter in the United States, with an enormous ground-oriented distribution network and revenues in excess of $4 billion per year. In addition, for a long time, UPS had offered a second-day air service for priority packages, primarily by using the planes of all-cargo and passenger airlines. In 1982, UPS acquired a fleet of 24 used Boeing 727-100s and added four DC-8 freighters from Flying Tiger. These purchases allowed UPS to introduce next-day air service in September 1982—at roughly half the price Federal Express was charging at the time.[14]

Federal Express countered almost immediately by announcing that it would institute 10:30 a.m. priority overnight delivery (at a cost to the company of $18 million). None of the other carriers followed suit, however, reasoning that most of their customers are usually busy or in meetings during the morning hours, so delivery before noon was not really that important. Instead, by March 1983, most of the major carriers in the market (including Federal Express) were offering their high-volume customers contract rates that matched the UPS price structure. Then three new services introduced by Purolator, Emery, and Gelco Courier pushed prices even lower. A competitive free-for-all followed, with constant price changes and volume discounts being offered by all industry participants. These developments hit the profit margins of the express carriers. Between 1983 and 1984, Federal Express saw its average revenue per package fall nearly 14%, while Emery saw a 15% decline in its yield on small shipments.[15]

Beginning around this time, customers began to group together and negotiate for lower prices. For example, Xerox set up accounts with Purolator and Emery that covered not only Xerox's express packages but also those of 50 other companies, including Mayflower Corp., the moving company, and the Chicago Board of Trade. By negotiating as a group, these companies could achieve prices as much as 60% lower than those they could get on their own.[16]

The main beneficiary of the price war was UPS, which by 1985 had gained the number 2 spot in the industry, with 15% of the market. Federal Express, meanwhile, had seen its market share slip to 37% from about 45% 2 years earlier. The other four major players in the industry at this time were Emery Air Freight (14% of market share), Purolator (10% of market share), Airborne Express (8% of market share), and the U.S. Postal Service (8% of market share).[17] The survival of all four of these carriers in the air express business was in question by 1986. Emery, Purolator, and the U.S. Postal Service were all reporting losses on their air express business, while Airborne had seen its profits slump 66% in the first quarter of 1986 and now had razor-thin margins.

INDUSTRY EVOLUTION, 1987–1996

Industry Consolidation

A slowdown in the growth rate of the air express business due to increasing geographic saturation and inroads made by electronic transmission (primarily fax machines) stimulated further price discounting in 1987 and early 1988. Predictably, this discounting created problems for the weakest companies in the industry. The first to go was Purolator Courier, which had lost $65 million during 1985 and 1986. Purolator's problems stemmed from a failure to install an adequate computer system. The company was unable to track shipments, a crucial asset in this industry, and some of Purolator's best corporate customers were billed 120 days late.[18] In 1987, Purolator agreed to be acquired by Emery. Emery was unable to effect a satisfactory integration of Purolator, and it sustained large losses in 1988 and early 1989.

Consolidated Freightways was a major trucking company and parent of CF Air Freight, the third largest heavy shipment specialist in the United States. In April 1989, Consolidated Freightways acquired Emery for $478 million. However, its shipment specialist, CF Air Freight, soon found itself struggling to cope with Emery's problems. In its first 11 months with CF, Emery lost $100 million. One of the main problems was Emery's billing and tracking system, described as a "rat's nest" of conflicting tariff schedules, which caused overbilling of customers and made tracking packages en route a major chore. In addition, CF enraged corporate customers by trying to add a "fuel surcharge" of 4 to 7% to prices in early 1989. Competitors held the line on prices and picked up business from CF/Emery.[19]

As a result of the decline of the CF/Emery/Purolator combination, the other firms in the industry were able to pick up market share. By 1994, industry estimates suggested that Federal Express accounted for 35% of domestic air freight and air express industry revenues; UPS had 26%; Airborne Express was third with 9%; and Emery and the U.S. Postal Service each held onto 4% of the market. The remainder of the market was split among numerous small cargo carriers and several combination carriers, such as Evergreen International and Atlas Air. (Combination carriers specialize mostly in heavy freight but do carry some express mail.)[20]

The other major acquisition in the industry during this time was the purchase of Flying Tiger by Federal Express for $880 million in December 1988. Although Flying Tiger had some air express operations in the United States, its primary strength was as a heavy cargo carrier with a global route structure. The acquisition was part of Federal Express's goal of becoming a major player in the international air express market. However, the acquisition had its problems. Many of Flying Tiger's biggest customers, including UPS and Airborne Express, were Federal Express's competitors in the domestic market. These companies had long paid Tiger to carry packages to those countries where they had no landing rights. It seemed unlikely that these companies would continue to give international business to their biggest domestic competitor. Additional problems arose in the process of trying to integrate the two operations. These problems included the scheduling of aircraft and pilots, the servicing of Tiger's fleet, and the merging of Federal's nonunionized pilots with Tiger's unionized pilots.[21]

During the late 1980s and early 1990s, there were also hints of further consolidations. TNT Ltd., a large Australian-based air cargo operation with a global network, made an unsuccessful attempt to acquire Airborne Express in 1986. TNT's bid was frustrated by opposition from Airborne and by the difficulties inherent in getting around U.S. law, which currently limits foreign firms from having more than a 25% stake in U.S. airlines. In addition, DHL Airways, the U.S. subsidiary of DHL International, was reportedly attempting to enlarge its presence in the United States and was on the lookout for an acquisition.[22]

Pricing Trends

In October 1988, UPS offered new discounts to high-volume customers in domestic markets. For the first time since 1983, competitors declined to match the cuts. Then in January 1989, UPS announced a price increase of 5% for next-day air service, its first price increase in nearly 6 years. Federal Express, Airborne, and Consolidated Freightways all followed suit with moderate increases. Additional rate increases of 5.9% on next-day air letters were announced by UPS in February 1990. Federal Express followed suit in April, and Airborne also implemented selective price hikes on non contract business of 5%, or 50 cents, per package on packages up to 20 pounds.

Just as prices were stabilizing, however, the 1990–1991 recession came along. For the first time in the history of the U.S. air express industry, there was a decline in year-on-year shipments, with express freight falling from 4,455 million ton miles in 1989 to 4,403 million ton miles in 1990. This decline triggered off another round of competitive price cuts, and yields plummeted. Although demand rebounded strongly, repeated attempts to raise prices in 1992, 1993, and 1994 simply did not stick.[23]

Much of the price cutting was focused on large corporate accounts, which by this time accounted for 75% by volume of express mail shipments. For example, as a result of deep price discounting in 1994, UPS was able to lure home shopping programmer QVC and computer mail-order company Gateway 2000 away from Federal Express. At about the same time, however, Federal Express used discounting to capture retailer Williams-Sonoma away from UPS.[24] This prolonged period of price discounting depressed profit margins and contributed to losses at all three major carriers during the early 1990s. Bolstered by a strong economy, prices finally began to stabilize during late 1995, when price increases announced by UPS were followed by similar announcements at Federal Express and Airborne.[25]

Product Trends

Second-Day Delivery   Having seen a slowdown in the growth rate of the next-day document delivery business during the early 1990s, the major operators in the air express business began to look for new product opportunities to sustain their growth and margins. One trend was a move into the second-day delivery market, or deferred services, as it is called in the industry. The move toward second-day delivery was started by Airborne Express in 1991, and it was soon imitated by its major competitors. Second-day delivery commands a substantially lower price point than next-day delivery. In 1994, Federal Express made an average of $9.23 on second-day deliveries, compared to $16.37 on priority overnight service. The express mail operators see deferred services as a way to utilize excess capacity at the margin, thereby boosting revenues and profits. Since many second-day packages can be shipped on the ground, the cost of second-day delivery can more than compensate for the lower price.

In some ways, however, the service has been almost too successful. During the mid 1990s, the growth rate for deferred services was significantly higher than for priority overnight mail because many corporations came to the realization that they could live with a second-day service. At Airborne Express, for example, second-day delivery accounted for 42% of total volume in 1996, up from 37% in 1995.[26]

Premium Services   Another development was a move toward a premium service. In 1994, UPS introduced its Early AM service, which guaranteed delivery of packages and letters by 8:30 a.m. in selected cities. UPS tailored Early AM toward a range of businesses that needed documents or materials before the start of the business day, including hospitals, who are expected to use the service to ship critical drugs and medical devices; architects, who need to have their blueprints sent to a construction site; and salespeople. Although demand for the service is predicted to be light, the premium price makes for high profit margins. In 1994, UPS's price for a letter delivered at 10:30 a.m. was $10.75, while it charged $40 for an equivalent Early AM delivery. UPS believes that it can provide the service at little extra cost because most of its planes arrive in their destination cities by 7:30 a.m. Federal Express and Airborne initially declined to follow UPS's lead.[27]

Logistics Services   Another development of some note was the move by all major operators into third-party logistics services. Since the latter half of the 1980s, more and more companies have been relying on air express operations as part of their just-in-time inventory control systems. As a result, the content of packages carried by air express operators has been moving away from letters and documents and toward high-value, low-weight products. By 1994, less than 20% of Federal Express's revenues came from documents.[28] To take advantage of this trend, all of the major operators have been moving into logistics services that are designed to assist business customers in their warehousing, distribution, and assembly operations. The emphasis of this business is on helping their customers reduce the time involved in their production cycles and gain distribution efficiencies.

In the late 1980s, Federal Express set up a Business Logistics Services (BLS) division. The new division evolved from Federal Express's Parts Bank. The Parts Bank stores critical inventory for clients, most of whom are based in the high-tech electronics and medical industries. On request, Federal Express ships this inventory to its client's customers. The service saves clients from having to invest in their own distribution systems.

It also allows their clients to achieve economies of scale by making large production runs and then storing the inventory at the Parts Bank.

The BLS division has expanded this service to include some assembly operations and customs brokerage and to assist in achieving just-in-time manufacturing. Thus, for example, one U.S. computer company relies on BLS to deliver electronic subassemblies from the Far East as a key part of its just-in-time system. Federal Express brings the products to the United States on its aircraft, clears them through customs with the help of a broker, and manages truck transportation to the customer's dock.

UPS moved into the logistics business in 1993 when it established UPS Worldwide Logistics, which it positioned as a third-party provider of global supply chain management solutions, including transportation management, warehouse operations, inventory management, documentation for import and export, network optimization, and reverse logistics. UPS's logistics business is based at its Louisville, Kentucky, hub. In 1995, the company announced that it would invest $75 million to expand the scope of this facility, bringing total employment in the facility to 2,200 by the end of 1998.[29]

Airborne Express also made a significant push into this business. Several of Airborne's corporate accounts utilize a warehousing service called Stock Exchange. As with Federal Express's Parts Bank, clients warehouse critical inventory at Airborne's hub in Wilmington, Ohio, and then ship those items on request to their customers. In addition, Airborne set up a commerce park on 1,000 acres around its Wilmington hub. The park was geared toward companies that wanted to outsource logistics to Airborne and could gain special advantages by locating at the company's hub. Not the least of these advantages is the ability to make shipping decisions as late as 2 a.m. Eastern time.

Information Systems

Since the late 1980s, the major U.S. air express carriers have devoted more and more attention to competing on the basis of information technology. The ability to track a package as it moves through an operator's delivery network has always been an important aspect of competition in an industry where reliability is so highly valued. Thus, all the major players in the industry have invested heavily in bar-code technology, scanners, and computerized tracking systems. UPS, Federal Express, and Airborne have also all invested in Internet-based technology that allows customers to schedule pickups, print shipping labels, and track deliveries online.

Globalization

Perhaps the most important development for the long-run future of the industry has been the increasing globalization of the air freight industry. The combination of a healthy U.S. economy, strong and expanding East Asian economies, and the move toward closer economic integration in Western Europe all offer opportunities for growth in the international air cargo business. The increasing globalization of companies in a whole range of industries from electronics to autos, and from fast food to clothing, is beginning to dictate that the air express operators follow suit.

Global manufacturers want to keep inventories at a minimum and deliver just in time as a way of keeping down costs and fine-tuning production, which requires speedy supply routes. Thus, some electronics companies will manufacture key components in one location, ship them by air to another for final assembly, and then deliver them by air to a third location for sale. This setup is particularly convenient for industries producing small high-value items (for example, electronics, medical equipment, and computer software) that can be economically transported by air and for whom just-in-time inventory systems are crucial for keeping down costs. It is also true in the fashion industry, where timing is crucial. For example, the clothing chain The Limited manufactures clothes in Hong Kong and then ships them by air to the United States to keep from missing out on fashion trends.[30] In addition, an increasing number of wholesalers are beginning to turn to international air express as a way of meeting delivery deadlines.

The emergence of integrated global corporations is also increasing the demand for the global shipment of contracts, confidential papers, computer printouts, and other documents that are too confidential for Internet transmission or that require real signatures. Major U.S. corporations are increasingly demanding the same kind of service that they receive from air express operators within the United States for their far-flung global operations.

As a consequence of these trends, rapid growth is predicted in the global arena. According to forecasts, the market for international air express is expected to grow at approximately 18% annually from 1996 to 2016.[31]

Faced with an increasingly mature market at home, the race is on among the major air cargo operators to build global air and ground transportation networks that will enable them to deliver goods and documents between any two points on the globe within 48 hours.

The company with the most extensive international operations by the mid 1990s was DHL. In 1995, DHL enjoyed a 44% share of the worldwide market for international air express services (see Exhibit 1).[32] Started in California in 1969 and now based in Brussels, DHL is smaller than many of its rivals, but it has managed to capture as much as an 80% share in some markets, such as documents leaving Japan, by concentrating solely on international air express. The strength of DHL was enhanced in mid 1992 when Lufthansa, Japan Airlines, and the Japanese trading company Nisho Iwai announced that they intended to invest as much as $500 million for a 57.5% stake in DHL. Although Lufthansa and Japan Airlines are primarily known for their passenger flights, they are also among the top five air freight haulers in the world, both because they carry cargo in the holds of their passenger flights and because they each have a fleet of all-cargo aircraft.[33]

TNT Ltd., a $6 billion Australian conglomerate, is another big player in the international air express market, with courier services from 184 countries as well as package express and mail services. In 1995, its share of the international air express market was 12%, down from 18% in 1990.[34]

Among U.S. carriers, Federal Express was first in the race to build a global air express network. Between 1984 and 1989, Federal Express purchased 17 other companies worldwide in an attempt to build its global distribution capabilities, culminating in the $880 million purchase of Flying Tiger. The main asset of Flying Tiger was not so much its aircraft, but its landing rights overseas. The Flying Tiger acquisition gave Federal Express service to 103 countries, a combined fleet of 328 aircraft, and revenues of $5.2 billion in fiscal year 1989.[35]

However, Federal Express has had to suffer through years of losses in its international operations. Start-up costs were heavy, due in part to the enormous capital investments required to build an integrated air and ground network worldwide. Between 1985 and 1992, Federal Express spent $2.5 billion to build an international presence. Faced also with heavy competition, Federal Express found it difficult to generate the international volume required to fly its planes above the break-even point on many international routes. Because the demand for outbound service from the United States is greater than the demand for inbound service, planes that left New York full often returned half empty.

Trade barriers have also proved very damaging to the bottom line. Customs regulations require a great deal of expensive and time-consuming labor, such as checking paperwork and rating package contents for duties. These regulations obviously inhibit the ability of international air cargo carriers to effect express delivery. Federal Express has been particularly irritated by Japanese requirements that each inbound envelope be opened and searched for pornography, a practice that seems designed to slow down the company's growth rate in the Japanese market.

Federal Express has also found it extremely difficult to get landing rights in many markets. For example, it took 3 years to get permission from Japan to make four flights per week from Memphis to Tokyo, a key link in the overseas system. Then in 1988, just 3 days before the service was due to begin, the Japanese notified Federal Express that no packages weighing more than 70 pounds could pass through Tokyo. To make matters worse, until 1995 Japan limited Federal Express's ability to fly on from Tokyo and Osaka to other locations in Asia. The Japanese claimed, with some justification, that due to government regulations, the U.S. air traffic market is difficult for foreign carriers to enter, so they see no urgency to help Federal Express build a market presence in Japan and elsewhere in Asia.[36]

After heavy financial losses, Federal Express abruptly shifted its international strategy in 1992, selling off its expensive European ground network to local

Exhibit 1	International Air Express Market Shares, 1995

Company	Market Share
DHL International	44%
Federal Express	21%
UPS	12%
TNT	12%
Others	11%

Source: Standard & Poor's, "Aerospace and Air Transport," Industry Surveys, February 1996.

carriers to concentrate on intercontinental deliveries. Under the strategy, Federal Express relies on a network of local partners to deliver its packages. Also, Federal Express entered into an alliance with TNT to share space on Federal Express's daily trans-Atlantic flights. Under the agreement, TNT flies packages from its hub in Cologne, Germany, to Britain, where they are loaded onto Federal Express's daily New York flight.[37]

UPS has also built up an international presence. In 1988, UPS bought eight smaller European air freight companies and Hong Kong's Asian Courier Service, and it announced air service and ground delivery in 175 countries and territories. However, it has not been all smooth sailing for UPS either. UPS had been using Flying Tiger for its Pacific shipments. The acquisition of Flying Tiger by Federal Express left UPS in the difficult situation of shipping its parcels on a competitor's plane. UPS was concerned that its shipments would be pushed to the back of the aircraft. Since there were few alternative carriers, UPS pushed for authority to run an all-cargo route to Tokyo, but approval was slow in coming. "Beyond rights," to carry cargo from Tokyo to further destinations (such as Singapore and Hong Kong), were also difficult to gain.

In March 1996, UPS sidestepped years of frustrations associated with building an Asian hub in Tokyo by announcing that it would invest $400 million in a Taiwan hub, which would henceforth be the central node in its Asian network. The decision to invest in an Asian hub followed closely on the heels of a 1995 decision by UPS to invest $1.1 billion to build a ground network in Europe. In September 1996, UPS went one step further toward building an international air express service when it announced that it would start a pan-European next-day delivery service for small packages. UPS hoped that these moves would push the international operations of the carrier into the black after 8 years of losses.[38]

INDUSTRY EVOLUTION, 1997–2012

Pricing Trends

The industry continued to grow at a solid rate through 2000, which helped to establish a stable pricing environment. In 2001, things took a turn for the worse. Recessionary conditions in the United States triggered a 7.6% decline in the number of domestic packages shipped by air. Even though the economy started to rebound in 2002, growth remained sluggish by historic comparison, averaging only 4% per annum.[39] Despite this, pricing discipline remained solid. Unlike the recession in 1990–1991, there was no price war in 2001–2002. Indeed, in early 2002, UPS pushed through a 3.5% increase in prices, which was quickly followed by the other carriers. The carriers were able to continue to raise prices at a fairly steady rate through until 2013. From 2007–2013, published rate increases averaged 4–5% per annum, although after negotiations the rate increases with large customers were more like 1–3% per annum.[40] FedEx and UPS were also successful in tacking on a fuel surcharge to the cost of packages to make up for sharply higher fuel costs.[41] During the 2002–2006 the average revenue per package at both UPS and FedEx increased as more customers opted for expedited shipments, and as both carriers shipped a high proportion of heavier packages.[42] The global financial crisis of 2008–2009 and the recession that it ushered in did lead to a slump in volume, a shift to deferred shipping, and more pricing pressures. At FedEx for example, the average revenue per overnight package fell from $18.42 in 2008 to $16.04 in 2010. However, volume and pricing trends improved in 2011 and 2012 along with the economy, and revenue per package at FedEx rose to $18.08 by the fourth quarter of 2010.[43]

Continuing Growth of Logistics

During 1997–2012 all players continued to build their logistics services. During the 2000s UPS was much more aggressive in this area than FedEx. By 2012, UPS's logistics business had revenues of $9.2 billion. UPS was reportedly stealing share from FedEx in this area. FedEx reportedly decided to stay more focused on the small package delivery business (although it continues to have a logistics business). Most analysts expected logistics services to continue to be a growth area. Outside of the North American market, DHL emerged as the world's largest provider of logistics services, particularly following its 2006 acquisition of Britain's Exel, a large global logistics business.

Despite the push of DHL and UPS into the global logistics business, the market remains very fragmented. According to one estimate, DHL, now the world's largest logistics company, has a 5.5% share of the global market in contract logistics, UPS has a 3% share and TNT has a 2.2% share.[44] The total global market for contract logistics was estimated to be worth over $200 billion in 2005. In 2006, TNT sold its logistics business to Apollo Management LP for $1.88 billion so that it could focus more on its small package delivery business.

Expanding Ground Network

In the late 1990s and early 2000s all the main carriers supplementing their air networks with extensive ground networks and ground hubs to ship packages overnight. With more customers moving from overnight mail to deferred services, such as second-day delivery, this shift in emphasis has become a necessity. Demand for deferred services help up reasonably well during 2001, even as demand for overnight packages slumped. Prices for deferred and ground services are considerably lower than are prices for air services, but so are the costs.

UPS has been the most aggressive in building ground delivery capabilities (of course, it already had extensive ground capabilities before its move into the air). In 1999, UPS decided to integrate overnight delivery into its huge ground transportation network. The company spent about $700 million to strengthen its ground delivery network by setting up regional ground hubs. By doing so, it found it could ship packages overnight on the ground within a 500-mile radius. Because ground shipments are cheaper than air shipments, the result was a significant cost savings for UPS. The company also deferred delivery of about 123 aircraft that were on order, reasoning that they would not be needed as quickly because more of UPS's overnight business was moved to the ground.[45]

FedEx entered the ground transportation market in 1998 with its acquisition of Caliber Systems for $500 million. This was followed by further acquisitions in 2001 and 2006 of significant U.S. trucking companies, including the 2006 acquisition of Watkins Motor Lines, a provider of long haul trucking services in the U.S. with sales of around $1 billion. Watkins was re-branded as FedEx National LTL. By 2002, FedEX was able to provide ground service to all U.S. homes, giving it a similar capability to UPS.

In addition, FedEx struck a deal in 2001 with the U.S. Postal Service (USPS), under which FedEx agreed to provide airport-to-airport transportation for 250,000 pounds of USPS Express Mail packages nightly and about 3 million pounds of USPS Priority Mail packages. The Priority Mail was to be moved on FedEx planes that normally sit idle during the day. The deal was reportedly worth $7 billion in additional revenues to FedEx over the 7-year term of the agreement. In addition, FedEx reaped cost savings from the better utilization of its lift capacity.[46] As of 2010, FedEx and the USPS still cooperated with each other.

Bundling

Another industry wide trend has been a move toward selling various product offerings—including air delivery, ground package offerings, and logistics services—to business customers as a bundle. The basic idea behind bundling is to offer complementary products at a bundled price that is less than would have been the case if each item had been purchased separately. Yet again, UPS has been the most aggressive in offering bundled services to corporate clients. UPS is clearly aiming to set itself up as a one-stop shop offering a broad array of transportation solutions to customers. FedEx has also made moves in this area. Airborne Express started to bundle its product offerings in mid 2001.[47]

Retail Presence

In 2001 UPS purchased Mail Boxes Etc. for $185 million. Mail Boxes Etc. had 4,300 franchisees, most in the United States, who operated small retail packaging, printing, and copying stores. At the time, Mail Boxes Etc was shipping some 40 million packages a year, around 12 million of which were via UPS. UPS stated that it would continue to allow the Mail Boxes stores to ship packages for other carriers. In 2003, the stores were re-branded as the UPS Store. While some franchisees objected to this move, the vast majority ultimately switched to the new brand.[48] In addition to the franchise stores, UPS has also begun to open wholly owned UPS stores, not just in the United States, but also internationally, and by 2006 had 5,600 outlets. In addition to The UPS Store, UPS put UPS Centers in office supplies stores, such as Office Depot, and by 2006 it had some 2,200 of these.

In 2004, FedEx followed UPS by purchasing Kinko's for $2.4 billion. Kinko's, which had 1,200 retail locations, 90% in the United States, focused on providing photo copying, printing and other office services to individuals and small businesses. FedEx has plans to increase the network of Kinko's stores to 4,000. In addition to providing printing, photocopying, and package services, FedEx is also experimenting using Kinko's stores as mini warehouses to store high value goods, such as medical equipment, for its supply chain management division.[49]

The Entry and Exit of DHL

In the late 1990s, DHL was acquired by Deutsche Post. Deutsche Post also spent approximately $5 billion to acquire several companies in the logistics business between 1997 and 1999. In November 2000, Deutsche Post went private with an initial public offering that raised $5.5 billion, and announced its intention to build an integrated global delivery and logistics network. Many believed it was only a matter of time before the company entered the United States. Thus, few were surprised when in 2003 DHL acquired Airborne. Under the terms of their agreement, Airborne Express sold its truck delivery system to DHL for $1.05 billion. Airborne's fleet of planes were spun off into an independent company called ABX Air, owned by Airborne's shareholders, and which continues to serve DHL Worldwide Express under a long term contract. This arrangement overcame the U.S. law that prohibits foreign control of more than 25% of a domestic airline. In the meantime DHL spun its own fleet of U.S. based planes into a U.S.-owned company called Astar, to also escape the charge that its U.S. airline was foreign owned. Between 2003 and 2005 DHL reportedly invested some $1.2 billion to upgrade the capabilities of assets acquired from Airborne.[50]

The DHL acquisition created three major competitors in both the U.S. and global delivery markets. By the fall of 2003, DHL had launched an ad campaign aimed at UPS and FedEx customers promoting the service and cost advantages that they would benefit from because of its merger with Airborne. DHL targeted specific Zip Code areas in its advertising promoting its claim to be the Number One in international markets, something important to many companies given the increasing importance of global commerce. In its ads, DHL reported that "current Airborne customers will be connected to DHL's extensive international delivery system in more than 200 countries."[51]

DHL's stated goal was to become a powerhouse in the U.S. delivery market. While its share of the U.S. small package express market remained small after the acquisition at around 10%, many thought that DHL would benefit from ownership by Deutsche Post, and from its own extensive ex-U.S. operations. When it first acquired Airborne, Deutsche Post stated that the U.S. operation would be profitable by the end of 2006.

However, the company ran into "integration problems" and suffered from reports of poor customer services and missed delivery deadlines. In 2006, DHL management stated that they now did not see the North American unit turning profitable until 2009. DHL lost some $500 million in the U.S. in 2006.[52] In 2007 they lost close to $1 billion. With corporate customers leaving for rivals, and market share sliding, in late 2008, DHL announced that it would exit the U.S. market. DHL shut down its air and ground hubs, laid off 9,600 employees, and took a charge against earnings of some $3.9 billion. In explaining the exit decision, DHL management stated that the underestimated just how tough it would be to gain share against FedEx and UPS.[53]

Continued Globalization

Between 1997 and 2012 UPS and FedEx continued to build out their global infrastructure. By 2012 UPS delivered to more than 200 countries. Much of the within country delivery is handled by local enterprises. The company has five main hubs. In addition to its main U.S. hub in Louisville, Kentucky, it has hubs in Cologne (for Europe), Shanghai (for Asia), Miami (serving Latin American traffic), and Shenzhen China (again, Asia). In 2004 UPS acquired Menio World Wide Forwarding, a global freight forwarder, to boost its global logistics business. In the same year, it also acquired complete ownership of its Japanese delivery operation (which was formally a joint venture with Yamato Transport Company). In 2005, UPS acquired operators of local ground networks in the UK and Poland, and it is pushing into mainland China, which it sees as a major growth opportunity.

Like UPS, FedEx serves more than 200 countries around the world, although also like UPS, most of the local ground delivery is in the hands of local partners. FedEx has recently been focusing upon building a presence in both China and India. The company recently developed a new Asian Pacific hub in Guangzhou China. This is FedEx's fifth international hub. The others are in Paris (handling intra-European express), the Philippines (handling intra-Asian express), Alaska (handles packages flowing between Asia, North America, and Europe) and Miami (for Latin America). In 2006, FedEx signaled its commitment to the Chinese market by buying out its joint venture partner, Tianjin Datian W. Group, for $400 million. The acquisition gave FedEx control of 90 parcel handling facilities and a 3,000 strong work force in China.[54]

While UPS and FedEx dominate the U.S. market for small package express delivery services, internationally DHL remains the largest carrier. DHL reportedly captured 37% of the European international express market in 2010, followed by UPS with 23%, TNT with 16% and FexEx with 10%. In the Asia Pacific region the figures were 34% for DHL, 21% for FedEx and 10% for UPS. In 2012 UPS made a $6.7 billion takeover bid for TNT, which would have significantly strengthened its position in Europe. However, the European Commission signaled that it would block the takeover due to its adverse impact on competition within the European Union, and UPS abandoned the proposed acquisition.

The U.S. and Global Markets in 2012

With DHL out of the picture in the United States, FedEx and UPS tightened their hold on the market. The USPS held onto a small share of the overnight express market and a somewhat bigger share of the ground market (see Exhibit 2). Despite challenging economic conditions, UPS and FedEx were both able to push through list rate increases of around 4–5% during the late 2000s, although after negotiations with large corporations, those increases were often reduced to 2–3%. They were also able to add fuel surcharges to prices, which helped given the high price of oil in the late 2000s.

Domestic volume continued to expand at a moderate pace, and tended to match the growth in U.S. GDP. Most of the domestic volume growth was in the ground network. International volume growth was correlated to the growth in international trade, and was generally higher than domestic growth. The volume of international trade had slumped in 2009, be rebounded in 2010–2012. While the volume of document shipments was declining due to electronic transmission, the slack was being picked up by increased shipment of goods purchased online, and growth of low weight high value inventory, such as electronic components. The globalization of supply chains and move towards just in time inventory was helping both companies.[55]

By 2012 UPS was shipping some 15 million packages a day through its global network, while FedEx was moving between 6 and 7 million. Peak volumes were hitting 26 million for UPS and 17 million for FedEx.

Both FedEx and UPS were solidly profitable in 2012. Profit margins in the industry were leveraged to volume; higher volume meant significant margin expansion. The USPS, however, was deep in the red. Traditional mail delivery was now a declining business as ever more mail was sent electronically. Some believed that the privatization of the USPS was inevitable.

Despite its exit from the U.S. market, DHL still was the largest operator globally in 2012 with $71 billion in revenues, and $3 billion in net income, followed by UPS and FedEx. TNT was in fourth place with $10 billion in revenues.

This case is intended to be used as a basis for class discussion rather than as an illustration of either effective or ineffective handling of the situation. Reprinted by permission of Charles W. L. Hill.

Exhibit 2	U.S. Market Share (%), 2012		
	Overnight Express	Deferred Air	Ground
FedEx	53%	47%	24%
UPS	42%	53%	60%
USPS	5%	0%	16%
Market Size	$15 billion	$6 billion	$38 billion

Source: W.J.Greene et al, "Airfreight and Surface Transport: Parcel Industry Primer 2.0", *Morgan Stanley*, March 11th, 2013.

NOTES

1. Standard & Poor's, "Aerospace and Air Transport," Industry Surveys, February 1996.
2. Ibid.
3. Standard & Poor's, Airlines, Industry Surveys, March 2002.
4. John Kartsonas, "United Parcel Service", *Citigroup Global Capital Markets*, November 13, 2006. W.J.Greene et al., "Airfreight and Surface Transport: Parcel Industry Primer", *Morgan Stanley*, May 25th, 2011.
5. W.J.Greene et al, "Airfreight and Surface Transport: Parcel Industry Primer 2.0", *Morgan Stanley*, May 11th, 2013.
6. Christopher H. Lovelock, "Federal Express (B)," Harvard Business School Case No. 579–040, 1978.
7. Standard & Poor's, "Aerospace and Air Transport," Industry Surveys, January 1981.
8. Lovelock, "Federal Express (B)."
9. Standard & Poor's, "Aerospace and Air Transport," Industry Surveys, January 1981.
10. Ibid.

11. Ibid.

12. Standard & Poor's, "Aerospace and Air Transport," Industry Surveys, January 1984.

13. Carol Hall, "High Fliers," Marketing and Media Decisions, August 1986, p. 138.

14. Standard & Poor's, "Aerospace and Air Transport," Industry Surveys, January 1984.

15. Standard & Poor's, "Aerospace and Air Transport," Industry Surveys, December 1984.

16. Brian Dumaine, "Turbulence Hits the Air Couriers," Fortune, July 21, 1986, pp. 101–106.

17. Ibid.

18. Chuck Hawkins, "Purolator: Still No Overnight Success," BusinessWeek, June 16, 1986, pp. 76–78.

19. Joan O'C. Hamilton, "Emery Is One Heavy Load for Consolidated Freightways," BusinessWeek, March 26, 1990, pp. 62–64.

20. Standard & Poor's "Aerospace and Air Transport," Industry Surveys, February 1996.

21. "Hold That Tiger: FedEx Is Now World Heavyweight," Purchasing, September 14, 1989, pp. 41–42.

22. Standard & Poor's, "Aerospace and Air Transport," Industry Surveys, April 1988.

23. Standard & Poor's, "Aerospace and Air Transport," Industry Surveys, February 1996.

24. David Greising, "Watch Out for Flying Packages," BusinessWeek, November 1994, p. 40.

25. Staff reporter, "UPS to Raise Its Rates for Packages," Wall Street Journal, January 9, 1995, p. C22.

26. Marilyn Royce, "Airborne Freight," Value Line Investment Survey, September 20, 1996.

27. Robert Frank, "UPS Planning Earlier Delivery," Wall Street Journal, September 29, 1994, p. A4.

28. Frank, "Federal Express Grapples with Changes in U.S. Market."

29. Company press releases (http://www.ups.com/news/).

30. Joan M. Feldman, "The Coming of Age of International Air Freight," Air Transport World, June 1989, pp. 31–33.

31. Standard & Poor's, "Aerospace and Air Transport," Industry Surveys, February 1996.

32. Ibid.

33. Peter Greiff, "Lufthansa, JAL, and a Trading Firm Acquire a Majority Stake in DHL," Wall Street Journal, August 24, 1992, p. A5.

34. Standard & Poor's, "Aerospace and Air Transport," Industry Surveys, February 1996.

35. "Hold That Tiger: FedEx Is Now a World Heavyweight."

36. Douglas Blackmon, "FedEx Swings from Confidence Abroad to a Tightrope," Wall Street Journal, March 15, 1996, p. B4.

37. Daniel Pearl, "Federal Express Plans to Trim Assets in Europe," Wall Street Journal, March 17, 1992, p. A3.

38. Company press releases (http://www.ups.com/news/).

39. C. Haddad and M. Arndt, "Saying No Thanks to Overnight Air," Business Week, April 1, 2002, p. 74.

40. W. J. Greene et al., "Airfreight and Surface Transport: Parcel Industry Primer 2.0", Morgan Stanley, May 11th, 2013.

41. Salomon Smith Barney Research, Wrap It Up—Bundling and the Air Express Sector, May 3, 2002. John Kartsonas, "United Parcel Service", Citigroup Global Capital Markets, November 13, 2006. W.J.Greene et al., "Airfreight and Surface Transport: Parcel Industry Primer 2.0", Morgan Stanley, May 11th, 2013.

42. John Kartsonas, "FedEx Corp", Citigroup Global Capital Markets, November 13, 2006.

43. W. J. Greene and A. Longson, "FedEx Corporation" Morgan Stanley Research, June 22nd, 2011.

44. Data from Deutsche Post World Net, 2005 Annual Report.

45. C. Haddad and M. Arndt, "Saying No Thanks to Overnight Air," Business Week, April 1, 2002, p. 74.

46. E. Walsh, "Package Deal," Logistics, February 2001, pp. 19–20.

47. Salomon Smith Barney Research, Wrap It Up—Bundling and the Air Express Sector, May 3, 2002.

48. R. Gibson, "Package Deal: UPS's purchase of Mail Boxes Etc. looked great on paper", Wall Street Journal, May 8, 2006, page R13.

49. Andrew Ward, "Kinko's plans to push the envelope further", Financial Times, August 7, 2006, page 22.

50. J. D. Schultz, "DHL crashes the party", Logistics, August 2005, page 59–63.

51. P. Needham, "Coming to America," Journal of Commerce, April 22, 2002, p. 12.

52. B. Barnard, "Logistics spurs Deutsche Post", Journal of Commerce, November 8, 2006, page 1.

53. A. Roth and M. Esterl, "DHL beats a retreat from the U.S.", Wall Street Journal, November 11th, 2008, page B1.

54. A. Ward, "A dogfight for courier service dominance", Financial Times, February 15, 2006, page 10.

55. W. J. Greene et al, "Airfreight and Surface Transport: Parcel Industry Primer", Morgan Stanley, May 25th, 2011.

Case 7

Airborne Express: The Underdog

Charles W.L. Hill, School of Business
University of Washington,
Seattle

This case was made possible by the generous assistance of Airborne Express. The information given in this case was provided by Airborne Express. Unless otherwise indicated, Airborne Express and Securities and Exchange Commission's 10–K filings are the sources of all information contained within this case. The case is based on an earlier case, which was prepared with the assistance of Daniel Bodnar, Laurie Martinelli, Brian McMullen, Lisa Mutty, and Stephen Schmidt. The case is intended as a basis for classroom discussion rather than as an illustration of either effective or ineffective handling of an administrative situation.

INTRODUCTION

Airborne Inc., which operated under the name Airborne Express, was an air-express transportation company, providing express and second-day delivery of small packages (less than 70 pounds) and documents throughout the United States and to and from many foreign countries. The company owned and operates an airline and a fleet of ground-transportation vehicles to provide complete door-to-door service. It was also an airfreight forwarder, moving shipments of any size on a worldwide basis. In 2003 Airborne Express held third place in the U.S. air express industry, with 9% of the market for small package deliveries. Its main domestic competitors were Federal Express, which had 26% of the market; United Parcel Service (UPS), which had 53% of the market. There were several smaller players in the market at the time, including DHL Airways, Consolidated Freightways (CF), and the U.S. Postal Service, each of which

This case was prepared by Charles W. L. Hill, University of Washington. Used by permission. Copyright © 2011 by Charles W. L. Hill.

held under 5% of the market share.[1] DHL however, had a huge presence outside of North America and was in fact the largest small package delivery company in the world. In 2003, after years of struggling to survive in the fiercely competitive small package express delivery industry, Airborne was acquired by DHL, which was itself owned by Deutsche Post, the large German postal, express package, and logistics company.

The evolution of the air express industry and the current state of competition in the industry were discussed in a companion case to this one, "The Evolution of the Air Express Industry, 1973–2010." The current case focuses on the operating structure, competitive strategy, organizational structure, and cultures of Airborne Express from its inception until it was acquired by DHL in 2003. It also deals with the aftermath of the DHL acquisition.

HISTORY OF AIRBORNE EXPRESS

Airborne Express was originally known as Pacific Air Freight when it was founded in Seattle at the close of World War II by Holt W. Webster, a former Army Air Corps officer. (See Table 1 for a listing of major milestones in the history of Airborne Express.) The company was merged with Airborne Freight Corporation of California in 1968, taking the name of the California company but retaining management direction by the former officers of Pacific Air Freight. Airborne was initially an exclusive airfreight forwarder. Freight forwarders such as Airborne arrange for the transportation of air cargo between any two destinations. They purchase cargo space from the airlines and retail this in small amounts.

Table 1   Major Milestones at Airborne Express[4]

1946: Airborne Flower Traffic Association of California is founded to fly fresh flowers from Hawaii to the mainland.

1968: Airborne of California and Pacific Air Freight of Seattle merge to form Airborne Freight Corporation. Headquarters are in Seattle, Washington.

1979–81: Airborne Express is born. After purchasing Midwest Air Charter, Airborne buys Clinton County Air Force Base in Wilmington, Ohio, becoming the only carrier to own and operate an airport. The package sort center opens, creating the "hub" for the hub-and-spoke system.

1984–86: Airborne is first carrier to establish a privately operated Foreign Trade Zone in an air industrial park.

1987: Airborne opens the Airborne Stock Exchange, a third-party inventory management and distribution service. In the same year, service begins to and from more than 8,000 Canadian locations.

1988: Airborne becomes the first air express carrier to provide same-day delivery, through its purchase of Sky Courier.

1990: The International Cargo Forum and Exposition names Airborne the carrier with the most outstanding integrated cargo system over the previous 2 years.

1991: A trio of accolades: Airborne is the first transportation company to receive Volvo-Flyg Motors' Excellent Performance Award. Computerworld ranks us the "most effective user of information systems in the U.S. transportation industry." In addition, we receive the "Spread the Word!" Electronic Data Interchange (EDI) award for having the largest number of EDI users worldwide in the air express and freight forwarding industry.

1992: Airborne introduces Flight-ReadySM - the first prepaid Express Letters and Packs.

1993: Airborne introduces Airborne Logistics Services (ALS), a new subsidiary providing outsourced warehousing and distribution services. IBM consolidates its international shipping operation with Airborne.

1994: Airborne opens its Ocean Service Division, becoming the first express carrier to introduce ocean shipping services. Airborne Logistics Services (ALS) establishes the first new film distribution program for the movie industry in 50 years. We also become the first company to provide on-line communication to Vietnam.

1995: Airborne Alliance Group, a consortium of transportation, logistics, third-party customer service operations and high-tech companies providing value-added services, is formed. Airborne opens a second runway at its hub, which is now the United States' largest privately owned airport. We also expand our fleet, acquiring Boeing 767–200 aircraft.

1996: Airborne Express celebrates 50 years of providing value-added distribution solutions to business.

1997: Airborne Express has its best year ever, with net earnings increasing three-and-a-half-fold over the previous year. Airborne's stock triples, leading to a two-for-one stock split in February, 1998.

1998: Airborne posts record profits and enters the Fortune 500. The first of 30 Boeing 767s is introduced to our fleet. The Business Consumer Guide rates Airborne as the Best Air Express Carrier for the 4th consecutive year.

1999: Airborne@home, a unique alliance with the United States Postal Service, is introduced. It enables e-tailers, catalog companies and similar businesses to ship quickly and economically to the residential marketplace. Optical Village is created. Part of Airborne Logistics Services, this new division brings together some of the biggest competitors in the optical industry to share many costs and a single location for their assembly, storage, inventory, logistics, and delivery options.

2000: Airborne announces several changes in senior management, including a new President and Chief Operating Officer, Carl Donaway. Several new business initiatives are announced, most notably a ground service scheduled to begin April 1, 2001. Airborne also wins the Brand Keys Customer Loyalty Award, edging out our competition for the second consecutive year.

2001: Airborne launches Ground Delivery Service and 10:30 a.m. Service, giving Airborne a comprehensive, full-service industry competitive capability. Airborne.com launches its Small Business Center, as well as a variety of enhancements to help all business customers speed and simplify the shipping process. We also release the Corporate Exchange shipping application, simplifying desktop shipping for customers while giving them greater control. Advanced tracking features are added to airborne.com and Airborne eCourier is released, enabling customers to send confidential, signed documents electronically.

2003: Airborne's ground operations acquired by DHL for $1.1 billion.

Source: http://www.airborne.com/Company/History.asp?nav=AboutAirborne/CompanyInfo/History

They deal primarily with small customers, providing pickup and delivery services in most cities, either in their own trucks or through contract agents.

Following the 1977 deregulation of the airline industry, Airborne entered the air express industry by leasing the airplanes and pilots of Midwest Charter, a small airline operating out of its own airport in Wilmington, Ohio. However, Airborne quickly became dissatisfied with the limited amount of control they were able to exercise over Midwest, which made it very difficult to achieve the kind of tight coordination and control of logistics that was necessary to become a successful air express operator. Instead of continuing to lease Midwest's planes and facility, in 1980 Airborne decided to buy "the entire bucket of slop; company, planes, pilots, airport and all."

Among other things, the Midwest acquisition put Airborne in the position of being the only industry participant to own an airport. Airborne immediately began the job of developing a hub-and-spoke system capable of supporting a nationwide distribution system. An efficient sorting facility was established at the Wilmington hub. Airborne upgraded Midwest's fleet of prop and propjet aircraft, building a modern fleet of DC-8s, DC-9s, and YS-11 aircraft. These planes left major cities every evening, flying down the spokes carrying letters and packages to the central sort facility in Wilmington, Ohio. There the letters and packages were unloaded, sorted according to their final destination, and then reloaded and flown to their final destination for delivery before noon the next day.

During the late 1970s and early 1980s, dramatic growth in the industry attracted many competitors. As a consequence, despite a high-growth rate price competition became intense, forcing a number of companies to the sidelines by the late 1980s. Between 1984 and 1990 average revenues per domestic shipment at Airborne fell from around $30 to under $15 (in 2003 they were just under $9).

Airborne was able to survive this period by pursuing a number of strategies that increased productivity and drove costs down to the lowest levels in the industry. Airborne's operating costs per shipment fell from $28 in 1984 to around $14 by 1990, and to $9.79 by 2001. As a consequence, by the late 1980s Airborne had pulled away from a pack of struggling competitors to become one of the top-three companies in the industry, a position it still held when acquired by DHL in 2003.

AIR EXPRESS OPERATIONS

The Domestic Delivery Network

As of 2002, its last full year as an independent enterprise, Airborne Express had 305 ground stations within the United States. The stations were the ends of the spokes in Airborne's hub-and-spoke system and the distribution of stations allows Airborne to reach all major population centers in the country. In each station there were about 50 to 55 or so drivers plus staff. About 80% of Airborne's 115,300 full-time and 7,200 part-time employees were found at this level. The stations were the basic units in Airborne's delivery organization. Their primary task was to ferry packages between clients and the local air terminal. Airborne utilized approximately 14,900 radio-dispatch delivery vans and trucks to transport packages, of which 6,000 were owned by the company. Independent contractors under contract with the company provided the balance of the company's pickup and delivery services.

Airborne's drivers made their last round of major clients at 5 p.m. The drivers either collected packages directly from clients or from one of the company's 15,300 plus drop boxes. The drop boxes were placed at strategic locations, such as in the lobbies of major commercial buildings. To give clients a little more time, in most major cities there were also a few central drop boxes that are not emptied until 6 p.m. If a client needed still more time, so long as the package could be delivered to the airport by 7 p.m. it would make the evening flight.

When a driver picked up a package, he or she read a bar code that is attached to the package with a hand-held scanner. This information was fed directly into Airborne's proprietary FOCUS (Freight, Online Control and Update System) computer system. The FOCUS system, which had global coverage, records shipment status at key points in the life cycle of a shipment. Thus, a customer could call Airborne on a 24-hour basis to find out where in Airborne's system their package is. FOCUS also allowed a customer direct access to shipment information through the Internet. All a customer needed to do is access Airborne's Web site and key the code number assigned to a package, and the FOCUS system would tell the customer where in Airborne's system the package was.

When a driver completed a pickup route, she or he took the load to Airborne's loading docks at the local airport. (Airborne served all 99 major metropolitan airports in the United States.) There the packages were loaded into C-containers (discussed later in this case study). C-containers were then towed by hand or by tractor to a waiting aircraft, where they were loaded onto a conveyor belt and in turn pass through the passenger door of the aircraft. Before long the aircraft was loaded and took off. It would either fly directly to the company's hub at Wilmington, or make one or two stops along the way to pick up more packages.

Sometime between midnight and 2 a.m., most of the aircraft would have landed at Wilmington. An old strategic air command base, Wilmington's location places it within a 600-mile radius (an overnight drive or 1 hour flying time) of 60% of the U.S. population. Wilmington has the advantage of a good-weather record. In all the years that Airborne operated at Wilmington, air operations were "fogged out" on only a handful of days. In 1995 Airborne opened a second runway at Wilmington. Developed at a cost of $60 million, the second runway made Wilmington the largest privately owned airport in the country. The runway expansion was part of a $120 million upgrade of the Wilmington sort facility.

After arrival at Wilmington the plane taxed down the runway and parked alongside a group of aircraft that were already disgorging their load of C-containers. Within minutes the C-containers were unloaded from the plane down a conveyor belt and towed to the sort facility by a tractor. The sort facility had the capacity to handle 1.2 million packages per night. At the end of 2001 the facility handled an average of 1 million packages a night. The bar codes on the packages were read, and then the packages were directed through a labyrinth of conveyor belts and sorted according to final destination. The sorting was partly done by hand and partly automated. At the end of this process, packages were grouped together by final destination and loaded into a C-container. An aircraft bound for the final destination was then loaded with C-containers, and by 5 a.m. most aircraft had taken off.

Upon arrival at the final destination, the plane was unloaded and the packages sorted according to their delivery points within the surrounding area. Airborne couriers then took the packages on the final leg of their journey. Packages had a 75% probability of being delivered to clients by 10:30 a.m., and a 98% probability of being delivered by noon.

Regional Trucking Hubs

Although about 71% of packages were transported by air and passed through Wilmington, Airborne also established 10 regional trucking hubs that deal with the remaining 29% of the company's domestic volume. These hubs sorted shipments that originate and had a destination within approximately a 300-mile radius. The first one opened was in Allentown, Pennsylvania, centrally located on the East Coast. This hub handled packages transported between points within the Washington, D.C., to Boston area. Instead of transporting packages by air, packages to be transported within this area were sorted by the drivers at pickup and delivered from the driver's home station by scheduled truck runs to the Allentown hub. There they were sorted according to destination and taken to the appropriate station on another scheduled truck run for final delivery.

One advantage of ground-based transportation through trucking hubs is that operating costs are much lower than for air transportation. The average cost of a package transported by air is more than five times greater than the cost of a package transported on the ground. However, this cost differential is transparent to the customer, who assumes that all packages are flown. Thus, Airborne could charge the same price for ground-transported packages as for air-transported packages, but the former yielded a much higher return. The trucking hubs also had the advantage of taking some of the load of the Wilmington sorting facility, which was operating at about 90% capacity by 2003.

International Operations

In addition to its domestic express operations, Airborne was also an international company providing service to more than 200 countries worldwide. International operations accounted for about 11% of total revenues in 2002. Airborne offered two international products: freight products and express products. Freight products were commercial-sized, larger-unit shipments. This service provides door-to-airport service. Goods were picked up domestically from the customer and then shipped to the destination airport. A consignee or an agent of the consignee got the paperwork and cleared the shipment through customs. Express packages are small packages, documents, and letters. This was a door-to-door service, and all shipments were cleared through customs by Airborne. Most of Airborne's international revenues come from freight products.

Airborne did not fly any of its own aircraft overseas. Rather, it contracted for space on all-cargo airlines or in the cargo holds of passenger airlines. Airborne owned facilities overseas in Japan, Taiwan, Hong Kong, Singapore, Australia, New Zealand, and London. These functioned in a manner similar to Airborne's domestic stations. (That is, they had their own trucks and drivers and were hooked into the FOCUS tracking system.) The majority of foreign distribution, however, was carried out by foreign agents. Foreign agents were large, local, well-established surface delivery companies. Airborne entered into a number of exclusive strategic alliances with large foreign agents. It had alliances in Japan, Thailand, Malaysia, and South Africa. The rationale for entering strategic alliances, along with Airborne's approach to global expansion, is discussed in greater detail later in this case.

Another aspect of Airborne's international operations was been the creation at its Wilmington hub of the only privately certified Foreign Trade Zone (FTZ) in the United States. While in an FTZ, merchandise is tax free and no customs duty is paid on it until it leaves. Thus, a foreign-based company could store critical inventory in the FTZ and have Airborne deliver it just-in-time to U.S. customers. This allowed the foreign company to hold inventory in the United States without having to pay customs duty on it until the need arose.

Aircraft Purchase and Maintenance

As of 2002, Airborne Express owned a fleet of 118 aircraft, including 24 DC-8s, 74 DC-9s, and 20 Boeing 767s. In addition, approximately 70 smaller aircraft were chartered nightly to connect smaller cities with company aircraft that then operate to and from the Wilmington hub. To keep down capital expenditures, Airborne preferred to purchase used planes. Airborne converted the planes to suit its specifications at a maintenance facility based at its Wilmington hub. Once it got a plane, Airborne typically gutted the interior and installed state-of-the-art electronics and avionics equipment. The company's philosophy was to get all of the upgrades that it could into an aircraft. Although this can cost a lot up front, there is a payback in terms of increased aircraft reliability and a reduction in service downtime. Airborne also standardized cockpits as much as possible. This made it easier for crews to switch from one aircraft to another if the need arose. According to the company, in the early 1990s the total purchase and modification of a secondhand DC-9 cost about $10 million, compared

with an equivalent new plane cost of $40 million. An additional factor reducing operating costs was that Airborne's DC-9 aircraft only require a two-person cockpit crew, as opposed to the three-person crews required in most Federal Express and UPS aircraft at the time.

After conversion, Airborne strove to keep aircraft maintenance costs down by carrying out virtually all of its own fleet repairs. (It was the only all-cargo carrier to do so.) The Wilmington maintenance facility could handle everything except major engine repairs and had the capability to machine critical aircraft parts if needed. The company saw this in-house facility as a major source of cost savings. It estimated that maintenance labor costs were 50–60% below the costs of having the same work performed outside.

In December 1995, Airborne announced a deal to purchase 12 used Boeing 767–200 aircraft between the years 1997 and 2000, and it announced plans to purchase a further 10 to 15 used 767–200s between the years 2000 and 2004. These were the first wide-bodied aircraft in Airborne's fleet. The cost of introducing the first 12 aircraft was about $290 million, and the additional aircraft would cost a further $360 million. The shift to wide-bodied aircraft was promoted by an internal study, which concluded that with growing volume, wide-bodied aircraft would lead to greater operating efficiencies.

During 2001, Airborne was using about 66.6% of its lift capacity on a typical business day. This compares with 76.7% capacity utilization in 1997, and 70% utilization in 2000. In late 2001, Airborne reduced its total lift capacity by some 100,000 pounds to about 4 million pounds a day. It did this to try and reduce excess capacity of certain routes and better match supply with demand conditions.

C-Containers

C-containers are uniquely shaped 60-cubic-foot containers, developed by Airborne Express in 1985 at a cost of $3.5 million. They are designed to fit through the passenger doors of DC-8 and DC-9 aircraft. They replaced the much larger A-containers widely used in the air cargo business. At six times the size of a C-container, A-containers can only be loaded through specially built cargo doors and require specialized loading equipment. The loading equipment required for C-containers is a modified belt loader, similar to that used for loading baggage onto a plane, and about 80% less expensive than the equipment needed to load A-containers. The use of

C-containers meant that Airborne did not have to bear the $1 million per plane cost required to install cargo doors that would take A-containers. The C-containers are shaped to allow maximum utilization of the planes' interior loading space. Fifty of the containers fit into a converted DC-9, and about 83 fit into a DC-8-62. Moreover, a C-container filled with packages can be moved by a single person, making them easy to load and unload. Airborne Express took out a patent on the design of the C-containers.

Information Systems

Airborne utilized three information systems to help it boost productivity and improve customer service. The first of these systems was the LIBRA II system. LIBRA II equipment, which included a metering device and PC computer software, was installed in the mailroom of clients. With minimum data entry, the metering device weighed the package, calculated the shipping charges, generated the shipping labels, and provided a daily shipping report. By 2002, the system was in use at approximately 9,900 domestic customer locations. The use of LIBRA II not only benefited customers but also lowered Airborne's operating costs since LIBRA II shipment data were transferred into Airborne's FOCUS shipment tracking system automatically, thereby avoiding duplicate data entry.

FOCUS was the second of Airborne's three main information systems. As discussed earlier, the FOCUS system was a worldwide tracking system. The bar codes on each package were read at various points (for example, at pickup, at sorting in Wilmington, at arrival, and so forth) using hand-held scanners, and this information was fed into Airborne's computer system. Using FOCUS, Airborne could track the progress of a shipment through its national and international logistics system. The major benefit was in terms of customer service. Through an Internet link, Airborne's customers could track their own shipment through Airborne's system on a 24 hour basis.

For its highest-volume corporate customers, Airborne developed Customer Linkage, an electronic data interchange (EDI) program and the third information system. The EDI system was designed to eliminate the flow of paperwork between Airborne and its major clients. The EDI system allowed customers to create shipping documentation at the same time they were entering orders for their goods. At the end of each day, shipping activities were transmitted electronically to Airborne's FOCUS system, where they are captured for shipment tracking and billing. Customer Linkage benefited the customer by eliminating repetitive data entry and paperwork. It also lowered the company's operating costs by eliminating manual data entry. (In essence, both LIBRA II and Customer Linkage pushed off a lot of the data-entry work into the hands of customers.) The EDI system also included electronic invoicing and payment remittance processing. Airborne also offered its customers a program known as Quicklink, which significantly reduced the programming time required by customers to take advantage of linkage benefits.

STRATEGY

Market Positioning

In the early 1980s Airborne Express tried hard to compete head-to-head with Federal Express. This included an attempt to establish broad market coverage, including both frequent and infrequent users. Frequent users are those that generate more than $20,000 of business per month, or more than 1,000 shipments per month. Infrequent users generate less than $20,000 per month, or less than 1,000 shipments per month.

To build broad market coverage, Airborne followed Federal Express's lead of funding a television advertising campaign designed to build consumer awareness. However, by the mid 1980s Airborne decided that this was an expensive way of building market share. The advertising campaign bought recognition but little penetration. One of the principal problems was that it was expensive to serve infrequent users. Infrequent users demanded the same level of service as frequent users, but Airborne would typically only get one shipment per pickup with an infrequent user, compared with 10 or more shipments per pickup with a frequent user, so far more pickups were required to generate the same volume of business. Given the extremely competitive nature of the industry at this time, such an inefficient utilization of capacity was of great concern to Airborne.

Consequently, in the mid 1980s Airborne decided to become a niche player in the industry and focused on serving the needs of high-volume corporate accounts. The company slashed its advertising expenditure, pulling the plug on its TV ad campaign, and invested more resources in building a direct sales force, which grew to be 460 strong. By focusing upon high-volume corporate accounts, Airborne was able to establish scheduled pickup routes and use its ground capacity more efficiently. This enabled the company to achieve significant reductions in its unit cost structure. Partly due to this factor, Airborne executives reckoned that their cost structure was as much as $3 per shipment less than that of FedEx. Another estimate suggested that Airborne's strategy reduced labor costs by 20% per unit for pickup, and 10% for delivery.

Of course, there was a downside to this strategy. High-volume corporate customers have a great deal more bargaining power than infrequent users, so they can and do demand substantial discounts. For example, in March 1987 Airborne achieved a major coup when it won an exclusive 3-year contract to handle all of IBM's express packages weighing less than 150 pounds. However, to win the IBM account, Airborne had to offer rates up to 84% below Federal Express's list prices! Nevertheless, the strategy does seem to have worked. As of 1995 approximately 80% of Airborne's revenues came from corporate accounts, most of them secured through competitive bidding. The concentrated volume that this business represents helped Airborne to drive down costs.

Delivery Time, Reliability, and Flexibility

A further feature of Airborne's strategy was the decision not to try to compete with Federal Express on delivery time. Federal Express and UPS have long guaranteed delivery by 10:30 a.m. Airborne guaranteed delivery by midday, although it offered a 10:30 guarantee to some very large corporate customers. Guaranteeing delivery by 10:30 a.m. would mean stretching Airborne's already tight scheduling system to the limit. To meet its 10:30 a.m. deadline, FedEx has to operate with a deadline for previous days' pickups of 6:30 p.m. Airborne could afford to be a little more flexible and can arrange pickups at 6:00 p.m. if that suited a corporate client's particular needs. Later pickups clearly benefit the shipper, who is, after all, the paying party.

In addition, Airborne executives felt that a guaranteed 10:30 a.m. delivery was unnecessary. They argued that the extra hour and a half does not make a great deal of difference to most clients, and they are willing to accept the extra time in exchange for lower prices. In addition, Airborne stressed the reliability of its delivery schedules. As one executive put it, "a package delivered consistently at 11:15 a.m. is as good as delivery at 10:30 a.m." This reliability was enhanced by Airborne's ability to provide shipment tracking through its FOCUS system.

Deferred Services

With a slowdown in the growth rate of the express mail market toward the end of the 1980s, in 1990 Airborne decided to enter the deferred-delivery business with its Select Delivery Service (SDS) product. The SDS service provides for next-afternoon or second-day delivery. Packages weighing 5 pounds or less are generally delivered on a next-afternoon basis, with packages of more than 5 pounds being delivered on a second-day basis. SDS shipment comprised approximately 42% of total domestic shipments in 1995. They were priced lower than overnight express products, reflecting the less time-sensitive nature of these deliveries. The company utilized any spare capacity on its express flights to carry SDS shipments. In addition, Airborne used other carriers, such as passenger carriers with spare cargo capacity in the bellies of their planes, to carry less urgent SDS shipments.

Early in 1996 Airborne began to phase in two new services to replace its SDS service. Next Afternoon Service was available for shipments weighing 5 pounds or less, and Second Day Service was offered for shipments of all weights. By 2001, deferred shipments accounted for 46% of total domestic shipments.

Ground Delivery Service

In April 2001, Airborne launched a Ground delivery Service (GDS) in response to similar offerings from FedEx and UPS. Airborne came to the conclusion that it was very important to offer this service in order to retain parity with its principle competitors, and to be able to offer bundled services to its principle customers (that is, to offer them air, ground, and logistics services for a single bundled price). Airborne also felt that they could add the service with a relatively minor initial investment, $30 million, since it leveraged of existing assets, including trucks, tracking systems, and regional ground hubs and sorting facilities.

The new service was initially been introduced on a limited basis, and targeted at large corporate customers. GDS was priced less than deferred services, reflecting the less time sensitive nature of the GDS offering. GDS accounted for 1.5% of domestic shipments in 2001, and 4% in the fourth quarter of 2001.

Logistics Services

Although small-package express mail remained Airborne's main business, through its Advanced Logistics Services Corp. (ALS) subsidiary the company increasingly promoted a range of third-party logistics services. These services provided customers with the ability to maintain inventories in a 1-million-square-foot "stock exchange" facility located at Airborne's Wilmington hub or at 60 smaller "stock exchange" facilities located around the country. The inventory could be managed either by the company or by the customer's personnel. Inventory stored at Wilmington could be delivered utilizing either Airborne's airline system or, if required, commercial airlines on a next-flight-out basis. ALS's central print computer program allowed information on inventories to be sent electronically to customers' computers located at Wilmington, where Airborne's personnel monitored printed output and shiped inventories according to customers' instructions.

For example, consider the case of Data Products Corp., a producer of computer printers. Data Products takes advantage of low labor costs to carry out significant assembly operations in Hong Kong. Many of the primary component parts for its printers, however, such as microprocessors, are manufactured in the United States and have to be shipped to Hong Kong. The finished product is then shipped back to the United States for sale. In setting up a global manufacturing system, Data Products had a decision to make either consolidate the parts from its hundreds of suppliers in-house and then arrange for shipment to Hong Kong, or contract out to someone who could handle the whole logistics process. Data Products decided to contract out, and they picked Airborne Express to consolidate the component parts and arrange for shipments.

Airborne controlled the consolidation and movement of component parts from the component part suppliers through to the Hong Kong assembly operation in such a way as to minimize inventory-holding costs. The key feature of Airborne's service was that all of Data Products' materials were collected at Airborne's facility at Los Angeles International Airport. Data Products' Hong Kong assembly plants could then tell Airborne what parts to ship by air as and when they are needed. Airborne was thus able to provide inventory control for Data Products. In addition, by scheduling deliveries so that year-round traffic between Los Angeles and Hong Kong could be guaranteed, Airborne was able to negotiate a better air rate from Japan Air Lines (JAL) for the transportation of component parts.

International Strategy

One of the major strategic challenges that Airborne faced (along with the other express mail carriers) was how best to establish an international service that is comparable to their domestic service. Many of Airborne's major corporate clients were becoming ever more global in their own strategic orientation. As this occurred, they were increasingly demanding a compatible express mail service. In addition, the rise of companies with globally dispersed manufacturing operations that relied upon just-in-time delivery systems to keep inventory holding costs down created a demand for a global air express services that could transport critical inventory between operations located in different areas of the globe (consider the example of Data Products discussed earlier in this case study).

The initial response of FedEx and UPS to this challenge was to undertake massive capital investments to establish international airlift capability and international ground operations based upon the U.S. model. Their rationale was that a wholly owned global delivery network was necessary to establish the tight control, coordination, and scheduling required for a successful air express operation. In the 1990s, however, FedEx pulled out of its European ground operations, while continuing to fly its own aircraft overseas.

Airborne decided upon a quite different strategy. In part born of financial necessity (Airborne lacks the capital necessary to imitate FedEx and UPS), Airborne decided to pursue what they refered to as a *variable cost strategy*. This involved two main elements: (1) the utilization of international airlift on existing air cargo operators and passenger aircraft to get their packages overseas, and (2) entry into strategic alliances with foreign companies that already had established ground delivery networks. In these two ways, Airborne hoped to be able to establish global coverage without having to undertake the kind of capital investments that Federal Express and UPS have borne.

Airborne executives defend their decision to continue to purchase space on international flights rather than fly their own aircraft overseas by making a number of points. First, they pointed out that Airborne's international business was 70% outbound and 30% inbound. If Airborne were to fly its own aircraft overseas, this would mean flying them back half-empty. Second, on many routes Airborne simply didn't have the volume necessary to justify flying its own planes. Third, national air carriers were giving Airborne good prices. If Airborne began to fly directly overseas, the company would be seen as a competitor and might no longer be given price breaks. Fourth, getting international airlift space was not a problem. While space can be limited in the third and fourth quarters of the year, Airborne was such a big customer that it usually had few problems getting lift.

On the other hand, the long-term viability of this strategy was questionable given the rapid evolution in the international air express business. Flying Tiger was once one of Airborne's major providers of international lift. However, following the purchase of Flying Tiger by FedEx, Airborne has reduced its business with Flying Tiger. Airborne worried that its packages will be "pushed to the back of the plane" whenever Flying Tiger had problems of capacity overload.

With regard to strategic alliances, Airborne had joint venture operations is Japan, Thailand, Malaysia, and South Africa. The alliance with Mitsui was announced in December 1989. Mitsui is one of the world's leading trading companies. Together with Tonami Transportation Co., Mitsui owns Panther Express, one of the top-five express carriers in Japan and a company with a substantial ground network. The deal called for the establishment of a joint venture between Airborne, Mitsui, and Tonami. To be known as Airborne Express Japan, the joint venture combined Airborne's existing Japanese operations with Panther Express. Airborne handled all of the shipments to and from Japan. The joint venture was 40% owned by Airborne, 40% by Mitsui, and 20% by Tonami. The agreement specified that board decisions had to be made by consensus between the three partners. A majority of two could not outvote the third. In addition, the deal called for Mitsui to invest $40 million in Airborne Express through the purchase of a new issue of nonvoting 6.9% cumulative convertible preferred stock and a commitment to Airborne from Mitsui of up to $100 million for aircraft financing. There is no doubt that Airborne executives saw the Mitsui deal as a major coup, both financially and in terms of market penetration into the Japanese market. The primary advantage claimed by Airborne executives for expanding via strategic alliances is that the company got an established ground-based delivery net-work overseas without having to make capital investments.

Organization

In 2001, Carl Donaway became CEO, replacing the long time top management team of Robert Cline, the CEO, and Robert Brazier, the president and COO, both of whom had been with the company since the early 1960s. Prior to becoming CEO, Donaway was responsible the airline operations, included managing the Wilmington hub, the package sorting facility, and all aircraft and flight maintenance operations. The philosophy at Airborne was to keep the organizational structure as flat as possible, to shorten lines of communication and allow for a free flow of ideas within the managerial hierarchy. The top managers generally felt that they were open to ideas suggested by lower-level managers. At the same time, the decision-making process was fairly centralized. The view was that interdependence between functions made centralized decision making necessary. To quote one executive, "Coordination is the essence of this business. We need centralized decision making in order to achieve this."

Control at Airborne Express was geared toward boosting productivity, lowering costs, and maintaining a reliable high-quality service. This was achieved through a combination of budgetary controls, pay-for-performance incentive systems, and a corporate culture that continually stressed key values.

For example, consider the procedure used to control stations (which contained about 80% of all employees). Station operations were reviewed on a quarterly basis using a budgetary process. Control and evaluation of station effectiveness stressed four categories. The first was service, measured by the time between pickup and delivery. The goal was to achieve 95 to 97% of all deliveries before noon. The second category was productivity, measured by total shipments per employee hour. The third category was controllable cost, and the fourth station profitability. Goals for each of these categories were determined each quarter in a bottom-up procedure that involved station managers in the goal-setting process. These goals are then linked to an incentive pay system whereby station managers can earn up to 10% of their quarterly salary just by meeting their goals with no maximum on the upside if they go over the goals.

The direct sales force also had an incentive pay system. The target pay structure for the sales organization was 70% base pay and a 30% commission. There was, however, no cap on the commissions for salespeople. So in theory, there was no limit to what a salesperson could earn. There were also contests that are designed to boost performance. For example, there was a so-called Top Gun competition for the sales force, in which the top salesperson for each quarter won a $20,000 prize.

Incentive pay systems apart, however, Airborne is not known as a high payer. The company's approach is not to be the compensation leader. Rather, the company tries to set its salary structure to position it in the middle of the labor market. Thus, according to a senior human resource executive, "We target our pay philosophy (total package—compensation plus benefits) to be right at the 50th percentile plus or minus 5%."

A degree of self-control was also achieved by trying to establish a corporate culture that focused employees' attention upon the key values required to maintain a competitive edge in the air express industry. The values continually stressed by top managers at Airborne, and communicated throughout the organization by the company's newspaper and a quarterly video, emphasized serving customers' needs, maintaining quality, doing it right the first time around, and excellent service. There was also a companywide emphasis on productivity and cost control. One executive, when describing the company's attitude to expenditures, said, "We challenge everything . . . . We're the toughest sons of bitches on the block." Another noted that "among managers I feel that there is a universal agreement on the need to control costs. This is a very tough business, and our people are aware of that. Airborne has an underdog mentality—a desire to be a survivor."

The DHL Acquisition and its Aftermath

By 2002 Airborne Express faced a number of key strategic opportunities and threats. These included (1) the rapid globalization of the air express industry, (2) the development of logistics services based on rapid air transportation, (3) the growth potential for deferred services and ground based delivery services, (4) lower margins associated with the new GDS offering, (5) the superior scale and scope of its two main competitors, FedEx and UPS, (6) an economic slowdown in the United States, and (7) persistently high fuel costs (oil prices rose from $18 a barrel in mid 1995 to $25 a barrel in 2002). The company's financial performance, which had always been volatile, was poor during 2001, when the company lost $12 million on revenues of $3.2 billion. In 2002, Airborne earned $58 million on revenues of $3.3 billion, even though average revenue per shipment declined to $8.46 from $8.79 a year earlier. Management attributed the improved performance to strong employee productivity, which improved 9.4% over the prior year. In their guidance for 2003, management stated that they would be able to further improve operating performance – then

in March 2003 DHL made its takeover bid for the company. Under the terms of the deal, which was finalized in 2003, DHL acquired the ground assets of Airborne Express, while the airline continued as an independent entity.

In the late 1990s DHL had been acquired by Deutsche Post, the German postal service. Deutsche Post had been privatized some years earlier. Deutsche Post spent approximately $5 billion to acquire several companies in the logistics business between 1997 and 1999. In November 2000, Deutsche Post went private with an initial public offering that raised $5.5 billion, and announced its intention to build an integrated global delivery and logistics network.

DHL's goal with the Airborne acquisition was to expand its presence in the United States, where it had long been a marginal player. In 2004–2005 DHL spent some $1.5 billion upgrading Airborne's network to handle higher volumes. The company also embarked upon an aggressive media advertising campaign, presenting itself as a viable alternative to FedEx and UPS. In doing this, DHL seemed to be departing from Airborne's highly focused niche strategy.

The results were disappointing. The company reportedly ran into significant "integration problems" and suffered from reports of poor customer services and missed delivery deadlines. In 2006, DHL management stated that they now did not see the North American unit turning profitable until 2009. DHL lost some $500 million in the U.S. in 2006.[2] In 2007 they lost close to $1 billion. With corporate customers leaving for rivals, and market share sliding, in November 2008, DHL announced that it would exit the U.S. market. DHL shut down its air and ground hubs, laid off 9,600 employees, and took a charge against earnings of some $3.9 billion. In explaining the exit decision, DHL management stated that the underestimated just how tough it would be to gain share against FedEx and UPS.[3]

NOTES

1. Standard & Poors Industry Survey, Airlines, March, 2002.
2. B. Barnard, "Logistics spurs Deutsche Post", *Journal of Commerce*, November 8, 2006, page 1.
3. A. Roth and M. Esterl, "DHL beats a retreat from the U.S.", *Wall Street Journal*, November 11th, 2008, page B1.

Case 8

Harley-Davidson's Focus Strategy

Syeda Masseeha Qumer and Debapratim Purkayastha

"Through our strategy to deliver results through Focus, which we rolled out in late 2009, we've been restructuring the business and focusing our investments in ways that will strengthen the Harley-Davidson brand, lower our cost structure, foster continuous improvement, and promote growth in the U.S. as well as globally. And while we feel good about all that we've achieved, we know it's crucial for us to stay fully on the throttle here."[i]

– Keith E. Wandell, President & CEO of Harley-Davidson Inc. in 2011.

In the fourth quarter ended December 31, 2011, US-based iconic motorcycle maker Harley-Davidson Inc. (Harley) posted a profit of US$105.7 million as against a net loss of US$46.8 million in the corresponding quarter of the previous year. For the full year 2011, income from continuing operations more than doubled to US$548.1 million and retail sales increased by 5.9% worldwide. Shipments rose 11% to 233,117 bikes. Commenting on the company's performance, Keith E. Wandell (Wandell), President and CEO of Harley, said, "Our improved performance in 2011 is the result of the tremendous efforts of all of our employees, dealers, and suppliers. Harley-Davidson is all about fulfilling dreams through remarkable motorcycles and extraordinary customer experiences. In 2011, we made strong progress at transforming our business to be more agile and effective than ever at exceeding customer expectations. The changes underway across the organization will enable Harley-Davidson to be world class and customer led like never before, with shorter product development lead times, flexible manufacturing, and an unmatched premium retail experience."[ii]

Founded in 1903, Harley was the world's leading manufacturer of heavyweight motorcycles. The company's bikes were sold through authorized dealers in more than 70 countries. Besides motorcycles, the company also offered a line of motorcycle parts & accessories[1] and general merchandise.[2] Over the years, Harley had established an image of raw power which became its unique selling proposition. The brand adopted a focused differentiation strategy wherein it targeted specific products at niche segments in the market. The Harley brand had achieved a cult status among its loyal customers as it characterized adventure, tradition, and power.

In 2008, the global economic recession and an aging customer base had significantly dented Harley's sales. In October 2009, the company launched a long-term business strategy called "Delivering Results through Focus" to get through the recession and expand the strength of the Harley-Davidson brand. The objective of this strategy was to enhance productivity and profitability through continuous improvement in manufacturing, product development, and business operations. As part of the strategy, Harley transformed its operations to make them more flexible and customer led. It focused on shortening product development lead times, implemented flexible manufacturing, expanded globally, and offered a premium retail experience to its customers. According to the company, the strategy had helped turn things around as evident from the fact that sales of its motorcycles and related products grew in 2011.

Despite delivering strong results in 2011, experts said the company needed to address its existing challenges if it wanted to retain its dominance in the heavyweight motorcycle industry. As the motorcycle market in the US was demographically dependent, a major problem for the company was its aging customer base. A majority of its customers who were from the baby boomers[3] generation were aging. Moreover, the company found it tough to attract young riders who preferred sports bikes and dual-purpose motorcycles to the heavyweight models. However, Harley was confident about attracting new customers and generating strong retail sales. According to John Olin, Chief Financial Officer and Senior Vice President of Harley, "We have made great strides toward transforming to a best-in-class manufacturing and product development, and have sharpened our focus on continuous improvement across the organization. We'll continue to prudently manage through any challenges the future might bring, and we are excited about the long term. We remain focused on executing against our strategies to complete the transfer–to complete the transformation of our organization and grow our business while delivering strong margins, strong returns, and value to our shareholders."[iii]

BACKGROUND NOTE

Harley was established in 1903 by William Harley and Arthur Davidson (Arthur) who built the first Harley motorcycle, a racer bike, in a small wooden shed in Milwaukee. Later, Arthur's brother, Walter Davidson (Walter), joined the business. In 1906, the company built a new factory in Milwaukee and also launched its first product catalog. In 1907, William A. Davidson, brother of Arthur and Walter, joined the company. The Harley-Davidson Motor Company was incorporated on September 17,1907. The popularity of Harley bikes rose after Walter rode a Harley motorcycle to victory in a 1908 race.[4] In 1909, Harley developed its first V-twin powered motorcycle.[5] The V-twin engine gave Harley motorcycles an aggressive appearance of raw power. Harley bikes had a characteristic design and were known for heavy customization that gave rise to the chopper style of motorcycle. By 1910, Harley had sold 3,200 motorcycles and its dealer network had grown to over 200 in the US. The company introduced its popular 'Bar & Shield' logo in 1910. To promote its bikes, Harley published advertisements in American expert magazines like *Bicycling World,*

Motorcycle Illustrated, Motorcyclist, and *The Western Bicyclist.* The company's advertisements, which featured leather clad riders and police officers on Harley motorcycles, gave the Harley a tough image. The company also launched an in-house magazine *Enthusiast* which published articles about the company's new motorcycle models and accessories.

By the end of 1920, Harley had become the largest motorcycle manufacturer in the world, supported by over 2,000 dealers in 67 countries. Harley motorcycles were used extensively by the US military during the First and Second World Wars.[6] The company supplied 90,000 motorcycles during the Second World War which earned it the coveted Army-Navy E[7] award for excellence in war time production for three consecutive years. After the Second World War, Harley shifted its focus to recreational bikes as it faced competition from foreign imports, mostly from Europe. To compete with the smaller, sportier motorcycles imported from Great Britain, Harley introduced the K-model with an integrated engine & transmission in 1952. By 1953, Harley was the sole American manufacturer of heavyweight motorcycles as its only competitor, the Indian Motorcycle Company, went out of business. It launched the XL Sportster,[8] a lightweight sports model, in 1957. The following year, Harley launched the Duo-Glide, the first motorbike with rear hydraulic suspensions and brakes.

During the late 1950s, Japanese motorcycle manufacturers entered the US market beginning with Honda Motor Co., Ltd[9] (Honda). Other companies like Yamaha Corporation,[10] Suzuki Motor Corporation,[11] and Kawasaki Motors Corp[12] soon followed. They marketed smaller and more fuel-efficient motorcycles that required little maintenance. Customers were enamored by the technical advances offered by the Japanese motorcycle manufacturers. During the late 1960s, the demand for Japanese motorcycles grew rapidly and they accounted for more than 85% of the motorcycle sales in the US.[iv] Harley, on the other hand, did little to offset the rise of Japanese competitors.

In the 1970s, under new owners American Machine and Foundry Company[13] (AMF), Harley's advertising strategy changed and the brand focused on the non-traditional market dominated by the Japanese motorcycle manufacturers. The change in the advertising approach alienated Harley's traditional customers.[14] During the 1970s, Japanese manufacturers continued to flood the US market with technologically sophisticated, low-priced motorcycles. Harley was now faced with a situation in which it was losing ridership to the

Japanese in the traditional biker segment and not attracting enough customers in nontraditional segments. Between 1973 and 1983, the company's market share plummeted from 77.5% to 23.3%. In 1980, AMF put Harley up for sale due to poor profitability.

In 1981, a group of senior Harley executives with support from the then CEO Vaughn Beals (Beals) reacquired the company from AMF. The new management orchestrated a remarkable turnaround of the company by adopting Japanese production methods. They formulated a new approach called productivity triad which focused on employee involvement,[15] use of JIT inventory practices,[16] and statistical operator control[17] (SOC). Harley based its marketing strategy on the idea of selling not just bikes, but a lifestyle. This idea led to the emergence of the Harley Owners Group (HOG) in 1983. The group aimed to strengthen relationships between customers, dealers, and employees of the company by sponsoring rallies and riding events. In 1986, Clyde Fessler (Fessler), the then Vice-president of business development at Harley, introduced a range of Harley MotorClothes which included shirts, jeans, kids wear, and fashion accessories for women. The company also began to license its popular bar & shield logo for various product categories including T-shirts, vehicle accessories, jewelry, leather goods, toys, and other products.

In 1986, Harley launched an initial public offering (IPO), and by the end of 1986, the company was able to regain a 25% share in the US motorcycle market. Two years later, in 1988, Richard Teerlink (Teerlink) was appointed as the CEO and chairman of the company. After rescuing the company from the verge of bankruptcy, Teerlink created a new organizational structure for Harley in 1992. Instead of the conventional hierarchical structure, the company adopted a circle-based organization structure to foster teamwork among the employees and do away with the command-and-control leadership style of management. Harley's organization chart comprised three overlapping circles — a Create Demand Circle (sales and marketing), a Produce Products Circle (engineering and manufacturing), a Support Circle (legal, financial, human resources, and communications issues). At the center where the three circles intersected, a Leadership and Strategy Council existed comprising members nominated from these circles (Refer to Exhibit I for the Circle Organization).

Between 1988 and 1995, the annual shipments of Harley motorcycles more than doubled. In 1993, to build

| Exhibit I | Harley-Davidson Circle Organization |

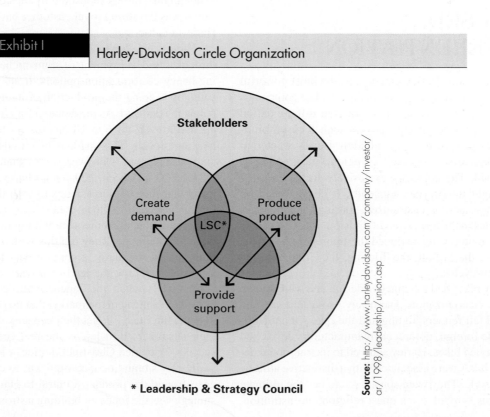

* **Leadership & Strategy Council**

Source: http://www.harleydavidson.com/company/investor/ar/1998/leadership/union.asp

sport motorcycles, Harley acquired a minority interest in the Buell Motorcycle company,[18] a manufacturer of performance motorcycles. Five years later, Harley purchased the remaining 49% of Buell. This gave the Harley management control of the company. In 1997, Teerlink was replaced by Jeffrey Bleustein as the company's CEO. In 1999, Harley launched the Custom Vehicle Operations (CVO) program to offer factory customized motorcycles to its customers. The company had also increased its production capacity significantly and it expected sales to reach 400,000 by 2007.[v] Harley's annual revenues grew from US$1.5 billion in 1996 to US$5 billion in 2004. Over the same period, net income increased from US$143 million to US$890 million. In 2002, the company introduced the VRSCA V-Rod, the first motorcycle in the company's history with a liquid cooled engine. In April 2005, James L. Ziemer (Ziemer) was appointed president and CEO of Harley. In 2007 Harley dealers sold 337,774 new Harley-Davidson motorcycle worldwide compared to 343,981 in 2006. In July 11, 2008, to expand the company's presence in Europe, Harley acquired the Italian motorcycle maker, the MV Agusta Group,[19] for US$109 million.

FOCUSED DIFFERENTIATION

Over the decades, Harley emerged as the most powerful and focused motorcycle brand in the US. The company's business strategy was based on focused differentiation wherein it targeted specific groups with focused products. Through focused differentiation, Harley wanted to gain a competitive edge and be unique in its industry, experts said. The company exclusively focused on the heavyweight motorcycle segment.[20] It concentrated on mini niches such as customized, touring, and standard motorcycles in the heavyweight division. The company's family of motorcycles included the Sportster, the Dyna, the VRSC, the Softail, the Touring, the Trike, and the CVO motorcycles.

Harley bikes had a distinctive design and were known for heavy customization. The heavy use of chrome and the styled tail fenders highlighted the bike's unique image. While foreign motorcycle manufacturers developed modern styled bikes, Harley adhered to its traditional design. The bikes were associated with a distinctive attitude and a lifestyle. They were considered to be "the ultimate biker status symbol . . . a quasi religion, an institution,

a way of life."[vi] According to industry experts, Harley motorcycles were not just products but symbols of American free-spiritedness as they demonstrated power, persuasion, and presence.

Despite the Japanese trying to beat Harley on their own playing field, the Milwaukee-based company retained its leadership position in the US motorcycle market by creating a lifestyle around its bikes and offering matchless riding experience. According to Bluestein "It is one thing to copy the products but quite another to create the lifestyle and total experience of a Harley — from the bike itself to the clothes and rallies and cachet. We've found that providing the total experience is key, and that is not quite as easy to copy."[vii] Harley's customers, popularly referred to as "enthusiasts", came from all walks of life and included police and military officers and celebrities. All of them contributed to building the image of the company. The company's core customer base comprised men over the age of 35. Noncore customers included young adults (aged between 18 and 34), women, and ethnically diverse adults. Harley instilled a strong sense of loyalty among its customers. The customers were so devoted to the brand that many of them tattooed the logo of the company on their bodies and traveled long distances to attend bike rallies sponsored by the company. Experts said it was the strong loyal customer base that had made Harley a cult brand.

Harley developed a strategy of value over price through the development of mini niches and by offering heavy customization options. It attempted to create value by keeping the production of its motorcycles well below the demand. As the demand for Harleys rose, buyers had to wait for 6 to 18 months for the delivery of a new motorcycle. This sparked an attitude of 'must-have' among customers who were more than willing to pay US$15,000 to US$30,000 for a Harley. "Since Harley knew that they couldn't compete with the prices of the foreign competitors, they made their brand such a high commodity that customers are willing to pay almost any price to obtain one. They did this with a combination of high quality standards, a commitment to tradition, and a refusal to follow the lead of foreign competitors. By "turning left when the Japanese turned right" Harley carved out a niche in the market that no other motorcycle manufacturer can fill; yet their capacity to turn left when their customers turn left is the real secret of Harley's success,"[viii] opined Christine Mattice, a journalist.

Harley's branding paradigm was to create an experience around the product. Central to Harley's marketing strategy was the focus on building a strong bond with the customer, maintaining a close relationship, and providing them with an engaging and interactive brand experience. According to experts, the sponsorship of HOG was one of the most creative and innovative strategies that helped convert the company's product into an experience. Considered to be the industry's largest company-sponsored motorcycle enthusiast organization, the group sponsored motorcycle events, including rallies and riding events, for Harley enthusiasts at local, regional, national, and international levels. The rallies featured live music, food booths, games, prizes, and vendor stalls. During the rallies, potential customers were given demonstration rides and they could even register their bikes and buy merchandise. Harley employees and senior executives also took part in the rallies. Analysts said that such events only strengthened the community and gave Harley owners a sense of belonging.

Harley identified the women's market as its fastest growing segment. To appeal to female riders, it produced models with lower frames and saddles and soft clutches. A group called "The Ladies of Harley" was created to generate interest among young women motorcyclists. To attract women customers, Harley dealers organized "garage parties" wherein women riders could learn the fundamentals of motorcycling, know which models of Harley suited them, and about various customization options. These parties which were hosted by Harley dealers provided an opportunity for female riders to bond with one another. The company also encouraged nontraditional riders to take up motorcycling through its Rider's Edge program started in 2000. The Rider's Edge program, initiated through Harley dealers, taught basic and advanced motorcycling skills and knowledge to new riders. The program also taught inexperienced female riders the techniques of handling and driving a heavy motorcycle. According to experts, Harley was selling a lifestyle by focusing on a niche segment that emphasized freedom.

TROUBLED RIDE

In 2008, Harley reported a decline in the demand for its motorcycles due to the global economic downturn. The recession affected the growth of the company as people were reluctant to spend money on luxury items. There were few takers for Harleys, which had a price tag of up to US$20,000 for a fully-rigged cruiser.[ix] In 2008, the company's revenue decreased by 2.3% to US$5.59 billion compared to the previous year. Sales were down by more than 7% and net income fell 29.9% to US$ 654.7 million.[x]

Analysts said that Harley had earlier survived economic downturns as it had attempted to create value by keeping the production of its motorcycles well below demand. However, down the line to compete with Japanese manufacturers it had increased production capacity, thereby becoming vulnerable to a cyclical economy.

Besides the downturn, another major challenge confronting the company was its aging customer base. Reports indicated that over 60% of Harley motorcycle riders were baby boomers aged between 35 and 54. The average age of Harley riders had been consistently increasing by about six months since the early 1990s. The median age of a Harley rider, which had been 35 years in 1987, reached 47 in 2005. To make matters worse for the company, analysts predicted that the number of potential US customers reaching the age of 47 had begun to drop, and would continue to drop at the rate of one million per year by 2019.[xi] Experts said that as baby boomers reached their prime riding age, they were less likely to ride a motorcycle due to physical constraints. Moreover, it was tough for the company to sell to young riders who preferred sport bikes and dual-purpose motorcycles to cruiser and touring bikes. The company's market share was slowly shrinking as Japanese competitors were luring customers by building sport bikes.[xii]

Besides an aging customer base, the company also faced competition from premium US motorcycle manufacturers such as Victory Motorcycles[21] and Big Dog Motorcycles LLC[22] which commanded a 41% premium over Harley bikes. According to Richard D'Aveni, professor of strategic management at the Tuck School of Business,[23] "The new rivals capitalized on the desire for a new image, a 'new American bike' in contrast with Harley's traditional Hells Angels open-highway leather-jacket-and-shades *Easy Rider* image. Victory and Big Dog's highly customized products were trumping Harley-Davidson's rebel image by changing motorcycle riding from an act of machismo into one of individualism and self-expression."[xiii]

Plagued by a difficult economic environment, an aging rider base, and increasing competition, Harley's sales dropped significantly. The company reported decreased revenue and net income for the third quarter of 2009 compared to the corresponding period of the previous year. Revenue from motorcycle sales declined 22.1% to US$803.3 million from US$1.03 billion a year ago. Net income for the third quarter was US$26.5 million, compared to US$166.5 million in the third quarter of 2008. Worldwide, the retail sales of new Harley motorcycles declined 21.3% in the third quarter. The company shipped 54,236 motorcycles, down 27.4% from the third quarter of 2008.

Through nine months, Harley reported revenue of US$3.57 billion, down 17.1% from the same period in the previous year[xiv]. "In the worst economic downturn in decades, 2009 was a year that required Harley-Davidson to respond with tough, courageous decisions. We had two key priorities. First, we executed on our strategy to manage the business effectively in the near term and address the immediate challenges. But we needed to do more than simply persevere. We needed to establish a bold, clear strategic direction that would maximize our opportunities going forward and restore the Company as a strong business that could consistently grow over the long haul. We set that direction, and the word that best describes our new strategy is "focus"[xv] said Wandell.

'DELIVERING RESULTS THROUGH FOCUS'

In October 2009, Wandell announced a long-term business strategy called "Delivering Results through Focus" to manage through the economic downturn and to enhance productivity and profitability. The key element of this strategy was to drive growth by focusing on the power of the Harley-Davidson brand and improve manufacturing, development, and business operations for sustained long-term growth.

Harley's go forward business strategy focused on new product development, global expansion, demographic outreach, and commitment to core customers. The basic pillars of this strategy were — growth, continuous improvement, leadership development, and sustainability (Refer to Exhibit II for the four basic pillars of Harley-Davidson's business strategy). The objective of this multi-generational and multi-cultural strategy was to increase sales to core customers and expand the company's strength as one of the most customer-centered brands in the world. According to Wandell, "As we execute on our strategy, we do not promise easy solutions. Consumers will likely continue to be cautious in an economic environment that remains challenging. However, we believe our strategy and the performance measures we have laid out are based on an appropriate and prudent approach to the market. Delivering on our plans will take discipline, determination, and intense focus, but we are confident we can achieve our goals through our strategy."[xvi]

As part of the strategy, the company restructured its manufacturing operations, divested itself of assets, cut costs, transformed product development, decreased motorcycle production, closed manufacturing plants, and laid off employees. To address immediate challenges in 2009, Harley reduced motorcycle shipments to dealers by nearly 27% compared to 2008.

Exhibit II	Strategic Pillars of Harley-Davidson's Focus Strategy

Growth – Consumers are increasingly influenced in purchase decisions by what companies are doing to support sustainable business practices, including reducing GHG emissions. We recognize that sustainability goes beyond the motorcycle to an integrated approach by the Company to society and the environment.

Continuous Improvement – Continuous improvement focuses on organizational engagement and process improvement transformation with the goal of delivering improved levels of business performance for quality, cost, and time to market. Our efforts to reduce energy use and make our facilities more energy efficient not only reduce GHG emissions, but also support this initiative, making sustainability an integral part of Continuous Improvement.

Leadership Development – Bold and decisive leadership is required to create company strategies and value through sustainable business practices, including reduction of GHG emissions. At Harley-Davidson, we are uniting the organization around a strategic plan that is resourced and evolving in step with the expectations of current and future owners and customers.

Sustainability – For Harley-Davidson, Sustainability means maintaining our business success forever, so that future generations can enjoy the Harley-Davidson riding experience. The Sustainability focus for Harley-Davidson will be to reduce waste, water and energy and related GHG emissions.

Adapted from Harley-Davidson 2009 Annual Report

DISCONTINUING BUELL, DIVESTING MV AGUSTA

In order to fully focus on the Harley brand, the company discontinued the Buell line of sport bikes and divested itself of MV Agusta. Commenting on the company's decision, Wandell said, "Buell and MV Agusta are great companies, with proud brands, high-quality exciting products, and passionate enthusiasm for the motorcycle business. Buell has introduced many innovative advancements in motorcycle design and technology over the years and MV Agusta is known in Europe for its premium, high-performance sport motorcycles. However, our strategy to focus on the Harley-Davidson brand reflects the fact that we believe our investments in that brand are a better utilization of overall company resources."[xvii]

Buell shipped just 13,119 motorcycles in 2008, compared with the 303,479 shipped by Harley. It accounted for 2.2% of Harley's revenues for that year.[xviii] It was reported that the Buell brand had lost US$18 million in 2008 and US$27 million by October 2009, including the US$14.2 million impairment charge.[xix] The discontinuation of the Buell line of motorcycles led to the elimination of 180 jobs and cost the company US$125 million in one-time expenses. However, the company decided to sell the remaining inventory of Buell motorcycles through authorized dealers and warranty coverage.

The discontinuation of the Buell line of motorcycles took many industry observers by surprise as the Buell bikes had won several design accolades and awards, numerous races, and championships over the years. They opined that the Buell bikes with their state-of-the-art liquid cooled engine technology, affordability, and easy maintenance competed strongly with the Japanese sports bikes. They felt it was a strategic oversight on the part of Harley's management to discontinue a product line which had the potential to attract young riders, one of the biggest challenges for the company.

In August 2010, Harley sold MV Agusta back to its founder Claudio Castiglioni and his wholly-owned holding company, MV Agusta Motor Holding, S.r.l. for an undisclosed sum. MV Agusta, one of the most iconic sportsbike brands in Europe, was rescued from the brink of bankruptcy by Harley. Despite the economic recession, MV Agusta sales increased by more than 50% during the first three months of 2010, compared to the same period in 2009. Analysts said despite the Italian motorcycle maker's satisfactory performance, Harley decided to divest itself of it. In the third quarter ended October 2009, Harley recorded a goodwill impairment charge of $18.9 million related to MV Agusta. According to Basem Wasef, an automotive journalist, "Blame the economy, bad timing, or simply bad luck, but Buell and MV Agusta are unfortunate victims of the financial hardship being suffered by Harley-Davidson. With two less sportbike brands to concern itself with, it seems Harley's efforts will eventually rest entirely on their own ailing, 106-year-old brand."[xx] On the other hand, the company's management said that they no longer wanted to spend money on brands that were not profitable.

TRANSFORMING PRODUCT DEVELOPMENT

As part of the focus strategy, Harley transformed its product development process to focus on the needs of riders, deliver relevant products in each global market, improve speed to market, and grow its customer base. The company changed its approach to product development by being leaner, faster, and smarter. As part of the product development process, Harley not only planned to strengthen its leadership in the heavyweight motorcycle segments, but also to develop modern bikes to attract customers in new demographic segments. "Our motorcycles and the experiences they provide have always been at the heart of our market leadership. Nothing will contribute more to our ability to grow and expand our reach still farther than bringing new generations of products to market. It is one of my highest priorities as CEO, and in 2010, we began the heavy lifting to fundamentally transform our entire approach to product development. Whether in the ongoing evolution of our iconic V-Twin motor-cycles, the development of alternate approaches to new motorcycles for the global market, or the deployment of advanced technologies, we are intent on further asserting our leadership as a global force on two-wheels,"[xxi] said Wandell.

The product development transformation focused on key areas such as reducing the time taken to bring new products to market through lean product development techniques, developing products that appealed across generations and cultures, and increasing production capacity by using best-in-class planning systems. It involved standardizing processes, scheduling projects logically, and reducing waste.

As the company wanted to be customer-led in its approach to products it gathered ideas from customers related to functionality, design, styling, and marketing of new bikes. To deliver matchless customer experiences, Harley launched the H-D1 factory customization option for its new Sportster 1200 Custom bike. Using tins option, customers could design a Sportster 1200 online, order it through a dealer, and get it built it at the factory. They could customize their bike in more than 2,600 ways by selecting different wheels, seats, handlebars, paint, foot control locations, etc. Moreover, the company's Dark Custom bikes like the Iron 883 and the 48 with their rebellious look were attracting young riders. Commenting on the company's customer-led product development approach, Matt Levatich (Levatich) President and COO of Harley, said, "We're lucky enough to be in the business of manufacturing dreams. And now, we have much better insight into those dreams and much better processes to tie that in to manufacturing. So they'll see more relevant innovation, better inventory availability, more customization of motorcycles — likethe factory custom concept in H-D1 — and more "wow" in styling and features, because we're listening in product development and responding in our manufacturing. Consumers today want what they want, how they want it, when they want it. "Customer-led" is about making the right products — more-focused products — more responsively."[xxii]

RESTRUCTURING MANUFACTURING OPERATIONS

As part of the company's strategy to focus on continuous improvement, save costs, and respond to the needs of its markets and riders, Harley embarked on a major consolidation and restructuring of its manufacturing operations which it expected to complete by 2012. The restructuring was expected to improve product quality and productivity, reduce administrative costs, and eliminate excess capacity. Experts said the restructuring of the manufacturing plants would build in greater flexibility and efficiency in product development by eliminating unnecessary processes and delivering the right product at the right time to the customer. Commenting on the company's decision to restructure its manufacturing processes, Levatich said, "So we needed to swallow

hard and step away from a manufacturing approach that worked for us when demand outpaced supply, but wasn't very flexible. With our historical manufacturing model, we were producing motorcycles in the fall that probably wouldn't have been sold until the spring. And that forced us to make three bets on the future: how many bikes to produce; which models to produce; and where those motorcycles were going to be sold at retail as we shipped them to our dealers. We expect our new production system to alleviate these issues."[xxiii]

Restructuring activities included streamlining the company's manufacturing operations, consolidating and redesigning the manufacturing facilities, implementing new flexible labor agreements at all its manufacturing locations in the US, and retraining the workforce. The company's manufacturing facilities were redesigned to produce multiple product families on the same assembly line every day for greater efficiency and flexibility. For instance, Harley's manufacturing plant in Kansas City build V-Rod and Sportster motorcycles on the same assembly line. "We need to be able to make any product on any line on any day. So we're structuring our manufacturing to be a lot more flexible. Some of the obvious benefits of commonality are cost savings and efficiency — there's simpler management of spare parts, for example, as well as standardized trainingof maintenance people, engineers, and technicians across the factories so that, as we move people and share knowledge across the factories, they see the same process they did in the other factory,"[xxiv] said Karl Eberle (Karl), Senior Vice President of Manufacturing at Harley. The company implemented common standards across its manufacturing facilities through groups called Best Practice Circles which comprised hourly and salaried employees from multiple locations and outside suppliers who shared specialized knowledge around a common process. The company had many best-practice circles in areas like safety, fabrication, and machining.

The first location that was restructured was the company's assembly plant at York, Pennsylvania. The York operation plant was consolidated into one building i.e. from a 1.5 million-square-foot factory to a 650,000 square feet plant. It focused on the core areas of motorcycle assembly, metal fabrication, and paint while other tasks were outsourced. The workforce at the plant was reduced from 1,950 to about 1,000 hourly employees. The production of all models that the facility produced was consolidated onto a single production line to reduce complexity. The redesigning of the plant, to be completed by the end of 2012, was expected to generate about US$100 million in annual operating savings. The company also planned to implement a new enterprise resource planning (ERP) system at the York plant in 2012 which would improve its supply chain and facilitate flexible production. "The new system will give us the flexibility to produce motorcycles closer to customer demand. Today, we do not have that capability. We know that change is never easy, and there is no doubt that we have asked everyone in our company to make a lot of changes in a short amount of time. But we are transforming the company not just to be sustainable, but to take advantage of the opportunities that we believe exist for the Harley-Davidson brand both in the United States and in the global marketplace,"[xxv] said Wandell.

In 2009, restructuring of manufacturing facilities reportedly led to a reduction of about 2,700 to 2,900 hourly production positions and 720 primarily salaried positions within the motorcycles division of Harley and around 100 salaried positions in the financial services segment. In December 2011, Harley shut down operations at New Castalloy, its Australian subsidiary and producer of cast motorcycle wheels and wheel hubs, and instead planned to source those components through other suppliers. With this decision, the company's workforce would be reduced by 200 employees by mid-2013.

It was reported that in 2011, the company had realized cumulative savings of US$217 million from restructuring activities initiated in October 2009.[xxvi] In the preceding year, the total savings were between US$135 million and US$155 million. Upon completion of all announced restructuring activities, Harley expected annual ongoing savings of US$315 million to US$335 million, beginning in 2014. It was reported that all the restructuring activities that began on October 2009 would incur one-time overall costs of US$500 million to US$520 million through 2013, including US$50 million to US$60 million in 2012.[xxvii] Experts said that when the revamped production system was fully implemented, Harley would have a best-in-class lean operating structure across all its operations. According to Levitich, "In the last 18 months, we've moved on a lot of fronts. There's transformation in our plants, culture, and workforce. The opportunity is bigger than any one plant, too. Being customer-led in manufacturing is leading us toward a common build process, with standard sequences and standard equipment wherever you go across our factories. It's unprecedented for us."[xxviii]

EXPANDING GLOBAL FOOTPRINT

As part of its long-term business strategy, Harley decided to expand its global presence and reach new demographics in the international markets as slow economic growth had curbed the demand for high-end motorcycles in the US. In 2010, Harley's international retail sales accounted for more than 35% of total sales, up from about 25% in 2006. In Europe, Harley earned the number two spot in the heavyweight market in 2010. The company planned to enhance its presence in Latin American regions, Europe, Japan, China, India, and other emerging markets by strengthening its operations and regional teams in these regions. Analysts felt that there was a significant opportunity for Harley to increase its sales in these markets which were witnessing rapid growth in disposable incomes and increase in demand for luxury and foreign brands.

Harley also planned to strengthen its worldwide dealer network and offer systems that would improve communication with retail customers, provide a premium retail experience, and strengthen dealer profitability. In 2010, Harley established dealer points in 13 developing markets including India, Russia, Mexico, Turkey, Jordan, China, and Ecuador. It planned to add around 150 dealer points through 2014. The company also opened regional headquarters offices in Singapore for the Asia Pacific region and in Miami for the Latin America region. By 2014, the company expected international retail unit sales to exceed 40% of total retail unit sales. The company planned to grow its brand globally by applying its customer-led principles of local insight and personal relevance through rallies and comradeship of HOG chapters in more than 70 countries.

ADOPTING A CUSTOMER LED MARKETING APPROACH

Historically, Harley marketed its products by promoting the experience of motorcycling to core customers. However, as demographic changes over the years were affecting sales, Harley planned to step up its efforts to appeal to a broader range of customers in the US and other emerging markets. In late 2010, Harley decided to adopt a multi generational and multi cultural marketing strategy in order to increase sales to noncore customers such as young adults (25-34-year-old men), women, and ethnically diverse adults. The company changed its marketing approach from a "one size fits all" agency-based marketing approach to a consumer-led model. It decided to implement a crowdsourcing approach toward its advertising wherein the company could draw on the ideas of Harley fans around the world to guide the direction of marketing for the brand. "We've always listened to our customers," said Mark-Hans Richer, chief marketing officer for the Milwaukee-based motorcycle manufacturer. "It only makes sense for us to tap into their passion, as well as the ideas they openly share with us to bolster our brand, rather than keeping our creativity bottled in the creative department of an agency of record."[xxix]

Using the concept of crowdsourcing, Harley developed a new agency support structure and called it the 'Creativity Model'. The Model began with Harley fans offering their ideas based on an advertising brief provided by the company. The best ideas were then developed and the creator rewarded. In this model, there was no lead agency or 'agency of record' as in a traditional model.

The company also worked closely with outside experts in media, digital marketing, public relations, and product placement to expand its marketing impact. According to analysts, Harley was one of the first major global companies to use the technique of crowdsourcing for its creative marketing development.

OTHER INITIATIVES

Besides growth and continuous improvement, sustainability was one of the four strategic pillars of the company's business strategy. Harley focused on reducing the environmental impact of its operations including efforts to reduce waste, increase recycling, and reduce water use, its carbon footprint, and energy consumption. Recycling operations across all the company facilities included paper, cardboard, metal, plastics, and packaging. The total amount of recycled materials increased from around 12,500 tons in 2004 to 13,342 tons in 2009. The company's greenhouse gas emissions dropped 40% from 2004 to 2010. "For Harley-Davidson sustainability means thinking differently to preserve and renew our brand for long-term success. We are passionate about future generations of riders sharing the Harley-Davidson experience that we enjoy. With that in mind, we

continue to focus on reducing energy use and associated greenhouse gas emissions in our plants, while building a broader sustainability framework into our strategic thinking,"[xxx] said Wandell.

As part of its leadership development strategy, Harley built an organizational structure that was team focused, with each team leader followed by a supervisor. Based on the principle of the inverted work triangle, the set up allowed any product in any line to be completed in record time. Accountability, focus on customers, creativity, and innovation were part of the company's leadership development process. In 2009, the company announced some organizational leadership changes to achieve operational excellence and drive growth.

In 2010, Harley made steady progress. The company reported a broad improvement in income from continuing operations. For the full year, income from continuing operations was US$259.7 million compared to US$70.6 million in 2009.[xxxi] However, revenue from the sales of Harley motorcycles decreased to US$3.14 billion in 2010, a decline of 1.2% from 2009 (Refer to Exhibit III for selected financial data of Harley-Davidson; Exhibit IV for the company's 2010 revenue distribution; and Exhibit V for year wise Harley-Davidson Motorcycles & Related Products Revenues). In 2010, the share price recovered to US$1.11 per share from US$0.30 per share in 2009. As of November 2010, Harley commanded about a 65% share of the Motorcycle, Bike & Parts Manufacturing industry in the US.[xxxii] (Refer to Exhibit VI market share of Harley-Davidson and Exhibit VII for 651+CC Motorcycle Registrations: Harley-Davidson Vs. Industry.) The company's financial-services arm — Harley-Davidson Financial Services (HDFS) — also turned profitable as credit quality improved. "In 2010, we expanded our international footprint, saw improvement in our motorcycle segment results driven by the restructuring of our operations and returned HDFS to solid profitability. A strong, financially sound Harley-Davidson is key to our ability to invest in the business and grow. While there is still hard work ahead and we remain cautious in our outlook, I am confident that we are positioning Harley-Davidson to succeed and deliver value for all our stakeholders into the future,"[xxxiii] Wandell said.

THE ROAD AHEAD

For the fourth quarter ended December 2011, Harley posted a profit of US$105.7 million, compared to a loss of US$42.1 million in the corresponding period of

Source: http://finapps.forbes.com/finapps/jsp/finance/comp-info/IncomeStatement.jsp?tkr=HOG

Exhibit III

Harley Davidson – Selected Financial Data

(Amount in thousands of US dollars)

Period Ending	2011	2010	2009	2008
Operating Revenue (Revenue/Sales)	5,311,713	4,859,336	4,781,909	5,594,307
Total Revenues	**5,311,713**	**4,859,336**	**4,781,909**	**5,594,307**
Cost of Sales	2,836,395	2,387,212	2,654,590	3,421,207
Cost of Sales with Depreciation	3,106,288	2,749,224	2,900,934	3,663,488
Gross Margin	2,475,318	2,472,124	2,127,319	2,173,100
Gross Operating Profit	2,475,318	2,472,124	2,127,319	2,173,100
Selling, Gen. & Administrative Expenses	1,077,974	1,113,489	1,148,590	984,560
Operating Income	**829,967**	**560,631**	**196,086**	**1,029,024**
Total Net Income	**599,114**	**146,545**	**(55,116)**	**654,718**
Normalized Income	616,070	423,177	323,306	654,718
Net Income Available for Common	548,078	259,669	70,641	654,718
Income Statement - Year-to-Date				
Revenues Year-to-Date	5,311,713	4,859,336	4,781,909	5,594,307
Income Year-to-Date from Total Ops.	599,114	146,545	(55,116)	654,718

*Data not available

Exhibit IV

Harley-Davidson 2010 Revenue Distribution (in million)

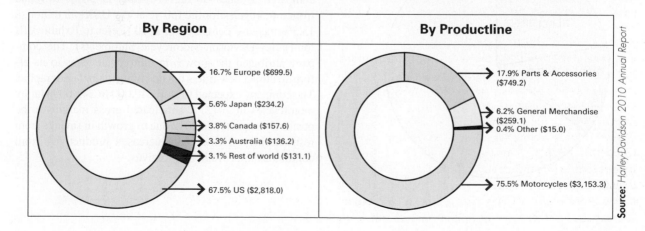

By Region

- 16.7% Europe ($699.5)
- 5.6% Japan ($234.2)
- 3.8% Canada ($157.6)
- 3.3% Australia ($136.2)
- 3.1% Rest of world ($131.1)
- 67.5% US ($2,818.0)

By Productline

- 17.9% Parts & Accessories ($749.2)
- 6.2% General Merchandise ($259.1)
- 0.4% Other ($15.0)
- 75.5% Motorcycles ($3,153.3)

Source: Harley-Davidson 2010 Annual Report

Exhibit V — Harley-Davidson Motorcycles & Related Products Revenues (Year Wise)

In millions of US Dollars

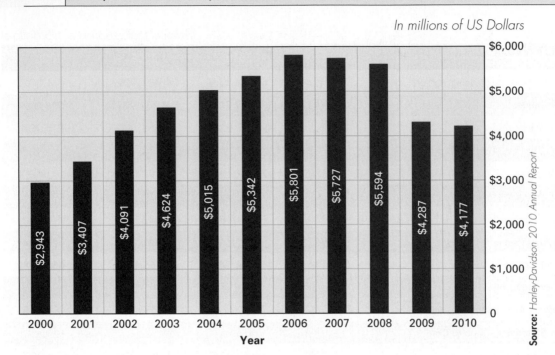

Year	Revenue
2000	$2,943
2001	$3,407
2002	$4,091
2003	$4,624
2004	$5,015
2005	$5,342
2006	$5,801
2007	$5,727
2008	$5,594
2009	$4,287
2010	$4,177

Source: Harley-Davidson 2010 Annual Report

Exhibit VI — Market Share of Harley-Davidson (in the US)

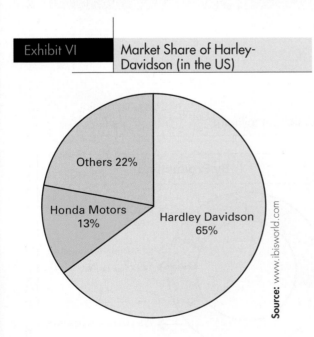

Others 22%

Honda Motors 13%

Hardley Davidson 65%

Source: www.ibisworld.com

2010[xxxiv]. Revenue from motorcycles during the quarter was US$791.9 million, up by 13.5% compared to the year-ago period. Globally, dealers sold 40,359 new Harley motorcycles in the fourth quarter of 2011, a 10.9% increase compared to the 36,390 motorcycles sold in the year ago period. For the full year, worldwide retail sales of new Harley motorcycles increased 5.9% to 235.188 units, compared to sales of 222,110 units in 2010. Revenue from motorcycles for the full year was US$3.55 billion, a 13.3% increase compared to 2010 (Refer to Exhibit VIII for Harley-Davidson-Motorcycle Shipments). The company attributed the growth in motorcycle sales to its efforts to attract new riders outside of its main demographic. The company expected to ship 240,000 to 245,000 Harley motorcycles in 2012. It anticipated gross margins to be positively impacted in 2012 due to growth in savings from restructuring activities and increased productivity from continuous improvement initiatives.

Exhibit VII	651+CC Motorcycle Registrations: Harley-Davidson Vs. Industry

(In '000)	Harley-Davidson	Rest	Total	Market Share (%)
US				
2000	155.9	185.0	340.9	45.7
2001	177.4	216.9	394.3	45.0
2002	209.9	232.3	442.2	47.5
2003	228.4	233.8	462.2	49.4
2004	244.5	250.4	494.9	49.4
2005	252.9	265.2	518.1	48.8
2006	267.7	275.2	542.9	49.3
2007	251.3	265.3	516.6	48.7
2008	218.3	262.0	480.3	45.4
2009	162.0	142.3	304.3	53.2
2010	142.7	117.0	259.7	54.9
Europe				
2000	23.2	299.5	322.7	7.2
2001	22.8	298.5	321.3	7.1
2002	23.5	309.8	333.3	7.1
2003	26.3	297.6	323.9	8.1
2004	25.9	310.8	336.7	7.7
2005	29.7	303.5	333.2	8.9
2006	34.3	327.0	361.3	9.5
2007	38.7	349.2	387.9	10.0
2008	41.1	348.6	389.7	10.6
2009	37.7	275.9	313.6	12.0
2010	38.3	263.0	301.3	12.7

Adapted from Harley-Davidson 2010 Annual Report

Exhibit VIII	Harley-Davidson - Motorcycle Shipments

(In Units)

	2011	2010	2009	2008	2007	2006	2005
Sporster	49,656	41,409	47,269	60,684	72,036	64,557	70,215
Custom	91,459	87,158	91,650	140,908	144,507	161,195	148,609
Touring	92,002	81,927	84,104	101,887	114,076	123,444	110,193
Total	**233,117**	**210,494**	**223,023**	**303,479**	**330,619**	**349,196**	**329,017**
Domestic	152,180	131,636	144,464	206,309	241,539	273,212	266,507
International	80,937	78,858	78,559	97,170	89,080	75,984	62,510
Total	**233,117**	**210,494**	**223,023**	**303,479**	**330,619**	**349,196**	**329,017**
BUELL	–	2,614	9,572	13,119	11,513	12,460	11,166

Source: http://inventer.harley-davidson.com/shipment Annual-1.pdf

As demographic changes were affecting sales, Harley planned to step up its efforts to appeal to a broader range of customers in the US and other emerging markets. Some experts opined that it was becoming increasingly important for Harley to address shifting demographics as its primary market was expected to grow to 122.7 million people in 2010 and to approximately 124.2 million people in 2020. They felt that the biggest challenge for the iconic company would be to increase sales by attracting young riders without alienating its traditional customer base. However, Wandell was positive that that the company's long-term business strategy would successfully leverage the unique strengths of the Harley-Davidson brand and ensure long-term profitability. "Our vision is clearly set on the future as we continue the transformative work that's underway, and we continue efforts to restore margins and profitability and to continue to meet the challenges of the ever-changing marketplace. By transforming our approach to product development, manufacturing, and the retail experience, we believe we will continue to exceed customers' expectations globally to create growth opportunities and sustain our business for all of our stakeholders,"[xxxv] said Wandell.

NOTES

i. "Harley-Davidson's CEO Discusses Q4 2010 Results - Earnings Call Transcript," http://seekingalpha.com, January 25, 2011.

ii. "Restructuring Helps Harley Profits Soar," www.biztimes.com, January 24, 2012.

iii. "Harley-Davidson's CEO Discusses Q4 2011 Results – Earnings Call Transcript," http://seekingalpha.com, January 24, 2012.

iv. Robert D. Buzzell and Dev Purkayastha, "Note on the Motorcycle Industry—1975," http://hbr.org, June 1, 1978.

v. Alex Taylor III, "Harley-Davidson's Aging Biker Problem," http://money.cnn.com, September 17, 2010.

vi. Robert M. Grant, Kent E, "Cases in Contemporary Strategy Analysis," Blackwell Publishing Ltd, 2003.

vii. Christine Mattice, "Harley Davidson: Defeating the Japanese and Riding Off into the Sunset," http://voices.yahoo.com, May 5, 2008.

viii. Ibid.

ix. Alex Taylor III, "Harley-Davidson's Aging Biker Problem," http://money.cnn.com, September 17, 2010.

x. Harley-Davidson 2008 Annual Report.

xi. "Demographic Headwinds Hitting Harley-Davidson," http://seekingalpha.com, July 17, 2009.

xii. Susanna Hamner, "Harley, You're Not Getting Any Younger," www.nytimes.com, March 21, 2009.

xiii. Richard D'Aveni, "How Harley Fell into the Commoditization Trap," www.forbes.com, March 17, 2010.

xiv. "Harley-Davidson Announces 3rd Quarter Results, Unveils Long-Term Business Strategy," http://investor.harley-davidson.com, October 15, 2009.

xv. Harley-Davidson 2009 Annual Report

xvi. Harley-Davidson 2008 Annual Report

xvii. "Harley-Davidson Announces 3rd Quarter Results, Unveils Long-Term Business Strategy," www.harley-davidson.com, October 15, 2009.

xviii. Hurley-Davidson 2008 Annual Report.

xix. David Schuyler, "Harley-Davidson to End Buell line, Cut 180 Jobs," www.bizjournals.com, October 15, 2009.

xx. Basem Wasef, "Industry Shock: Harley-Davidson to Discontinue Buell, Divest MV Agusta," http://motorcycles.about.com, October 15, 2009.

xxi. Harley-Davidson 2010 Annual Report

xxii. Harley-Davidson 2009 Annual Report

xxiii. Harley-Davidson 2010 Annual Report

xxiv. Ibid.

xxv. Rick Barrett, "Harley-Davidson is changing to Adapt Here and Globally," www.jsonline.com, April 30, 2011.

xxvi. Rick Barrett, "Harley-Davidson Says it Could Avoid Layoffs This Spring," http://m.jsonline.com, January 24, 2012.

xxvii. "Restructuring Helps Harley Profits Soar," www.biztimes.com, January 24, 2012.

xxviii. Harley-Davidson 2010 Annual Report

xxix. Rick Barrett, "Harley-Davidson Seeking Ideas Through 'Crowd Sourcing'," http://m.jsonline.com, November 18, 2010.

xxx. Harley-Davidson Sustainability Strategy Report 2010.

xxxi. "Harley-Davidson Reports Broad Improvement in Full-Year Results from Continuing Operations For 2010," http://investor.harley-davidson.com, January 25, 2011.

xxxii. Justin Molavi, "Motorcycle, Bike & Parts Manufacturing in the US," www.chopperexchange.com, November 2010.

xxxiii. "Harley-Davidson Reports Broad Improvement in Full-Year Results from Continuing Operations For 2010," http://investor.harley-davidson.com, January 25, 2011.

xxxiv. "Harley-Davidson Earnings, Retail Motorcycle Sales Show Continued Strength," www.harley-davidson.com, January 2, 2012.

xxxv. "Harley-Davidson's CEO Discusses Q4 2011 Results – Earnings Call Transcript," http://seekingalpha.com, January 24, 2012.

NOTES

1. Parts and Accessories (P&A) comprise replacement pails (Genuine Motor Parts) and mechanical and cosmetic accessories (Genuine Motor Accessories).

2. General Merchandise products include MotorClothes apparel and accessories.

3. In the US, the term Baby Boomer is used to describe a generation of individuals born between 1946 and 1964.

4. In 1908, Walter Davidson won the 7th Annual Federation of American Motorcyclists Endurance and Reliability Contest with a perfect score of 1,000 points.

5. The V-twin engine derived its name from its cylinders which were set opposite each other at a 45 degree angle. The V-twin powered motorcycle was the fastest motorcycle during those times and could travel at a speed of 60 miles per hour.

6. The First World War took place between 1914 and 1918 while the Second World War was fought between 1939 and 1945.

7. The Army-Navy "E" Award, also known as the Army-Navy Production Award, was an honor presented to a company during the Second World War for excellence in production of war equipment.

8. The Sportster with a 55 cubic inch overhead valve engine became known as one of the first Superbikes. It was a sleeker, less expensive alternative to the company's touring bikes.

9. Headquartered in Tokyo, Japan, Honda Motor Co., Ltd is one of the largest motorcycle manufacturers in the world. For the year ended March 31, 2011, the company's revenues were US$ 107.82 billion.

10. Yamaha Corporation is a global conglomerate based in Japan which manufactures a wide range of products such as electronics, motorcycles, and power sports equipment.

11. Headquratered in Hamamatsu, Japan, Suzuki Motor Corporation is a Japanese multinational corporation that specializes in manufacturing automobiles, a full range of motorcycles, all-terrain vehicles (ATVs), outboard marine engines, and a variety of small internal combustion engines. For the year ended 2010, the company's revenues were US$30.452 billion.

12. Kawasaki Motors Corp designs and manufactures motorcycles, sportbikes, cruisers, utility vehicles, and watercraft. It is headquartered in Irvine, California.

13. Founded in 1900, AMF initially manufactured automated machines for the tobacco industry. It started manufacturing a broad range of sporting equipment during the 1960s and 1970s. It was one of the largest recreational equipment companies in the US. It acquired Harley in 1969.

14. Harley's traditional bikers were those customers who maintained and customized their own bikes. Nontraditional bikers included recent converts to Harleys who earlier rode the smaller Japanese bikes.

15. First line workers were encouraged to contribute to the decision-making process. Workers were required to participate in the newly formed quality circles that were responsible for improving motorcycle quality.

16. A materials-as-needed (MAN) program based on Honda's JIT inventory control practices was implemented to

release cash by reducing WIP inventory. The company felt that by lowering the inventory levels, quality problems would become more apparent.

17. SOC taught employees how to detect and correct quality problems developed during the production process.

18. Buell Motorcycle Company was an American motorcycle manufacturer which basically manufactured sport bikes. It was founded in 1983 by Erik Buell.

19. The MV Agusta Group was an Italian motorcycle maker which manufactured premium, high-performance sport motorcycles under the MV Agusta brand and lightweight sport motorcycles under the Cagiva brand.

20. The company's heavyweight motorcycles segment comprised Standard, Touring, Custom, and Performance bikes. Standard motorcycles had no extra features, Touring products were meant for long distance travel, Custom bikes offered the customer the options to add on different parts and accessories, and Performance motorcycles had engines tuned for high speed travel.

21. In 1998 Polaris Industries Inc, a US-based manufacturer of snowmobiles, ATV, and electric vehicles started manufacturing large displacement cruiser motorcycles under the brand name Victory. Victory designs and manufactures motorcycles featuring sleek designs and American V-Twin muscle.

22. Started in 1994, Big Dog Motorcycles LLC is a leading manufacturer of custom American V-twin motorcycles.

23. The Tuck School of Business, a part of the Dartmouth College (a private Ivy League university in New Hampshire, US), is one of the leading business schools in the world.

Case 9

Auto-Graphics Corp and the Library Automation Industry

O. O. Sawyerr and Abraham Stanley

INTRODUCTION

Paul Cope, the president of Auto-Graphics (A-G), saw the rapid changes in technology occurring in his industry as new frontiers to be explored and conquered by A-G. A-G served public, academic, and consortia libraries, a segment of the library-automation industry. The industry was composed of firms that provided the computer architecture used by various types of libraries to service their patrons. A-G's products enabled library patrons to log into a library's catalog, search for information, check out materials, access various databases, and perform sundry other functions. The advent of the Internet and the emergence and dominance of companies such as Google and Amazon meant that A-G's primary customers, libraries, were being forced to reinvent themselves. With a new generation of patrons accustomed to Google-like searches and to obtaining all their information online, libraries could no longer survive doing business as usual.

Paul Cope envisioned a future in which virtual libraries maintained millions of items in their eHoldings. Patrons no longer needed to visit a brick-and-mortar building to obtain information. They searched for information from the cloud where the entire library's eHoldings were held as well as other authoritative resources.[i] Patrons downloaded eBooks, eReference materials, music, videos, digital collections, classroom assignments, and schedules for social activities, whatever they needed. They received e-alerts for new materials based on their interests. From where Paul Cope sat, these were truly exciting times. Libraries would no longer be places just to obtain information or borrow books. They would become community centers, gathering places for all ages with coffee shops, play areas for kids, movie theaters, family nights, local cultural events, and various activities that would bring in the community. Libraries would leverage their expertise to become centers for specialized knowledge and local information. This new frontier was not just a farfetched dream. It was becoming a reality.

Paul Cope was excited and extremely optimistic about the future possibilities of the library-automation industry. However, for A-G to be a critical part of the renaissance of libraries, he had to resolve the challenges facing the firm.

He explained A-G's situation in 2012 as follows:

> A major challenge facing A-G is how to grow in a mature market that is confronted with shrinking budgets. The library market is very mature. It is not going to grow. You are not seeing more libraries being built in the U.S. and the demand for library services is not growing. In the 1970s, when everyone converted to online electronic catalogs, there was a lot of growth in this industry. However, now everybody is electronic. So what we are really doing is taking business from one company to another; business is just moving back and forth.[1]

To Paul Cope, the maturing of A-G's primary market was an opportunity for A-G to identify a new strategic direction that would result in greater growth and profitability. Exactly how to do this weighed heavily on his mind over the past 18 months.

THE LIBRARY-AUTOMATION INDUSTRY

The library-automation industry focused on libraries as clients. The American Library Association (ALA) estimated there were 122,566 libraries in the U.S.: 99,180 school libraries (K-12), 9,214 public libraries, 8,906 special libraries, 3,827 academic libraries, 1,150 government libraries, and 289 Armed Forces libraries.[2] Comparable data for Canada were not readily available; however, there were an estimated 1,987 libraries in Canada with about 637 public libraries, 32 research libraries, and 51 correctional-facilities libraries.[3] Table 1 shows the estimated industry revenue and revenue-growth rate from 2004 to 2011 for North America (U.S. and Canadian markets).[4] The average annual growth rate during this period was 5.29%, which was a reflection of the economic conditions in North America and across the globe. By mid-2008, the U.S. and Canadian economies entered the deepest and longest economic downturn since the U.S. great depression of the 1930s. U.S. GDP growth contracted from 2.1% in 2007 to *minus* 2.4% in 2009,[5] after which the U.S. economy began a slow but uncertain recovery with real GDP growth of 3.0% in 2010 and 1.7% in 2011.[6] The Canadian economy contracted from a 2.7% growth in 2007 to a *minus* 2.4% in 2009. In 2010, the Canadian economy grew by 3.1% and in 2011 by 2.2%.[7] The economic recession of 2008–2009 and the subsequent uncertain recovery had significant negative impacts across a wide range of industries, including the library-automation industry. Industry sales began to pick up in 2009 with continued growth through 2011, a reflection of increased economic activity in North America.

Who Are the Customers?

The library-automation industry served three customer segments: *public and academic libraries* (both individual and combined into consortia), *K-12 school libraries* (both individual and district-centralized), and *special libraries* (including corporate and enterprise customers). As displayed in Figure 1, the *K-12 school libraries* segment dominated the industry with an 89% share of total installed products, followed by the *public and academic libraries* segment at 10% and the *special libraries* segment at 1.4%.[8]

Each market segment had a different automation need to which industry competitors had to be attuned in order to succeed in developing competitive products. For this reason, there were distinct products and competitors in each segment. Firms tended to specialize in meeting the needs of libraries in particular segments (see Tables 2 and 3 for a list of the firms that served the public- and academic-library segments in which A-G currently competed; Table 4 for the list of firms that served the K-12 segment; and Table 5 for the list of firms that served the special-libraries segment).

Public libraries require automated tools primarily to access their collections and reduce administrative

| Table 1 | North American Library-Automation Industry Sales and Sales Growth Rates 2004–2011 |

	2004	2005	2006	2007	2008	2009	2010	2011
Total Sales* (million $)	505	535	570	570	570	630	715	750
Sales Growth Rate (%)	1.0	5.9	6.5	0.0	0.0	10.5	13.5	4.9

Sources: Adapted from: Breeding, M. (April 1, 2007). Automation System Marketplace 2007: An Industry Redefined. *The Library Journal*. Retrieved on August 3, 2008, from www.libraryjournal.com/article/CA6429251.html; (April 1, 2009) Pressing onward in an uncertain economy, many industry players are adding staff and expanding development. *The Library Journal*. Retrieved on February 25, 2010, from http://www.libraryjournal.com/article/CA6645868.html?q=library+automation+industry; (April 1, 2010). Automation Marketplace 2010: New Models, Core Systems. *The Library Journal*. Retrieved on April 26, 2010, from http://www.libraryjournal.com/article/CA6723662.html?q=library+automation+industry; Breeding, M. (April 1, 2011). Automation Marketplace 2011: The New Frontier. *The Library Journal*. Retrieved on October 7, 2011, from http://www.libraryjournal.com/lj/home/889533-264/automation_marketplace_2011_the_new.html.csp; Breeding, M. (April 1, 2012). Automation Marketplace 2012: Agents of Change. Retrieved on June 15, 2012, from http://www.thedigitalshift.com/2012/03/ils/automation-marketplace-2012-agents-of-change/

*Represents total revenues of all companies that participate in the North American Library-Automation Industry

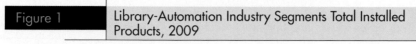

Figure 1 — Library-Automation Industry Segments Total Installed Products, 2009

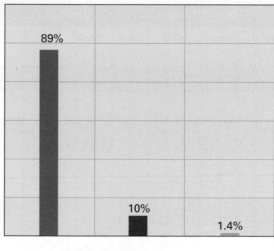

■ K-12 School Libraries
■ Public, Academic Libraries
■ Special Libraries

Source: *Developed from data in Breeding, M. (April 1, 2010). Automation Marketplace 2010: New Models, Core Systems.* The Library Journal. Retrieved on April 26, 2010, from http://www.libraryjournal.com/article/CA6723662.html?q=library+automation+industry

workloads, which helps them to use precious budget dollars efficiently. They had a higher rate of Software as a Service (SaaS) usage since most were moderately sized institutions that benefited from leveraging the vendor's technical infrastructure. High-volume public libraries also saw Radio Frequency Identification (RFID) technology as a way to improve efficiency, especially through automated sorting systems, patron self-check, and inventory control. With the pressure to be ever more efficient, libraries needed to generate automated reports to accurately report on library activity, which could positively impact staffing and funding. A-G was among the companies capitalizing on delivering full-featured automation products to otherwise underserved small public libraries.[9]

Academic libraries needed automated tools to manage and provide access to their extensive electronic collections. Electronic Resource Management (ERM) systems were becoming mainstream in these institutions because they helped to automate internal processes such as selection, licensing, and procurement of electronic content. One ongoing issue was that their patrons, a generation accustomed to Google-like search engines and

the latest and greatest technologies, had high expectations for a library's ease of use and breadth of content. Academic libraries hoped to live up to their patrons' expectations through improving interfaces and providing portals to institutional courseware and e-learning, using link resolvers that allowed users to link and navigate among licensed e-resources, and providing federated-search[ii] products to eliminate the laborious task of searching e-database collections individually.[10]

Libraries at K-12 schools had automated cataloging needs beyond a typical library. Schools needed to manage inventories of textbooks and other resources and support-assessment activities. Within this category, demand for a transition to more centralized systems was fueling a hot market for legacy migrations. Within the K-12 segment, a new giant had emerged—Follett, which had an estimated 70% market share, was ten times the size of its nearest competitor, and consolidated a large number of school products under one roof via acquisition of its competitors.[11]

The automation needs of the special-library (corporate) category were difficult to assess because companies

Table 2 Three-Year Sales Trends and Summary for the PAC Segment[a]

Company	System Name	New Customers			Total Sales			US Sales	2010 Non-US Sales	Total Installed
		2008	2009	2010	2008	2009	2010			
Auto-Graphics	AGent VERSO	23	16	85	24	18	86			394
Biblionix	Apollo	49	55	87	49	55	87	87		192
ByWater Solutions	Koha		7	40		1	155	154	1	167
Equinox Software	Evergreen		6	15	6	18	15			354
Equinox Software	Koha						11			12
Ex Libris	Aleph	23	38	30	26	47	39	1	38	2291
Ex Libris	Voyager	5	1	1	5	2	5	4	1	1251
Infovision Software	Evolve			5			73	81	0	81
Innovative Interfaces	Millenium	61	34	37	64	45	39	33	18	1412
Online Computer Library Center (OCLC)	Amlib Library Management Systems		5			5	12	39	1	
Polaris Library Systems	Polaris Integrated System	51	33	40	56	33	42			374
LibLime (PTFS)	Koha	40		42	40		63	35	28	800
SirsiDynix	Symphony	38		47	135		126	71	55	2255
SirsiDynix	Horizon	0		0	0		20	20		1406
The Library Corporation	Library Solutions	32	30	43	32	30	43	42	1	749
The Library Corporation	Carl X/Carl Solution	0	0	0	0	0	3			20
Visionary Technology in Library Solutions (VTLS)	Virtua	26	18	21	39	18	22	2	20	21

Source: Breeding, M. (April 1, 2011). Automation marketplace 2011: The new frontier. *The Library Journal*. Retrieved on April 7, 2012, from http://www.libraryjournal.com/lj/home/889533-264/automation_marketplace_2011_the_new.html.csp

[a]Blank spaces indicate that no data was provided, or companies gave only aggregate figures.

Table 3 — Competitors in the PAC Market Segment of the Library-Automation Industry in 2010

Name	Year Founded	Number of Libraries Served	Geographic Coverage
Auto-Graphics, Pomona CA	1950	434	National[a]
Biblionix, Austin TX	2003	313	National
ByWater Solutions, Santa Barbara CA	2009	449	National
Equinox, Norcross GA	2007	995	National
Ex Libris, Jerusalem, Israel	1986	2,976	International
Infovision Software, San Diego CA	2009	57	National
Innovative Interfaces Inc., Emeryville CA	1978	4,437	International
LibLime (PTFS), Bethesda MD	2005	454	International
Online Computer Library Center (OCLC), Dublin OH	1967	626	International
Polaris Library Systems, Syracuse NY	1930[b]	1,908	National
SirsiDynix, Provo UT	2005[c]	9,866	International
The Library Corporation (TLC), Inwood WV	1974	1,746	International
VTLS, Blacksburg VA	1974	414	International

Source: Library Technology Guides, Company Directory, Retrieved on April 7, 2012, from http://www.librarytechnology.org/?SID=20120407191802978

[a]Except for a small sales office in Ontario, Canada.
[b]Gaylord Information Systems, founded in 1930, was renamed Polaris Library Systems in 2005.
[c]Merger of Sirsi Corporation, founded in 1979, and Dynix Corporation, founded in 1983.

Table 4 — Three-Year Sales Trend of the Automation Systems for Schools and School Districts[a]

Company	System Name	New Customers			TOTAL SALES			2009		
		2007	2008	2009	2007	2008	2009	US Sales	Non-US Sales	TOTAL INSTALLED
Book Systems, Inc.	Atriuum	139	149	225	159	179	225	225	0	704
Book Systems, Inc.	Concourse	175	125	119	214	125	136	128	8	9,700
COMPanion Corp.	Alexandria	980			980	914	230			11,786
Follett Software Company	Circulation Plus and Catalog Plus	149	96		174					18,472
Follett Software Company	Destiny Library Manager for Districts	606	1,707	373	639		373			36,959

continues

Company	System Name	New Customers			TOTAL SALES			2009	
Follett Software Company	Destiny Library Manager for Schools	368	326	275	721	780			3,036
Follett Software Company	InfoCentre	35	15	8	43	9			3,267
Follett Software Company	Sagebrush Athena	30	0	1	35	1			2,750
Follett Software Company	Winnebago Spectrum	25	5		27			4	3,888
LibraryWorld, Inc.	LibraryWorld		550		550	483			1,717
Mandarin Library Automation	Mandarin Oasis (and Hosted)		114	36	114	36			313
Mandarin Library Automation	Mandarin M3	490	174	143	640	174	143		3,117
Media Flex	OPALS		216		216				627
Softlink America Inc.	Oliver	76	126		610	358			

Source: Breeding, M. (April 1, 2010). Automation Marketplace 2010: New Models, Core Systems. *The Library Journal.* Retrieved on April 26, 2010, from http://www.libraryjournal.com/article/CA6723662.html?q=library+automation+industry

[a]Blank spaces indicate that no data was provided, or companies gave only aggregate figures.

Table 5	Four-year Market Sales Trends and Summary for the Automation Systems for Special Libraries, 2007–2010[a]

Company	System Name	New Customers				Total Sales				2010		
		2007	2008	2009	2010	2007	2008	2009	2010	US Sales	Non-US Sales	Total Installed
CyberTools	Cybertools Libraries		30	32	31		30	32	31	31		326
EOS International	EOS.Web			48	97			186	97			1,097
Inmagic	DB/Text for Libraries		179				179					
Keystone Systems	KLAS	4	6	4		4	6	4		0		108

Source: Breeding, M. 2011. Automation marketplace 2011: The new frontier. Retrieved on April 7, 2012, from http://www.libraryjournal.com/lj/home/889533-264/automation_marketplace_2011_the_new.html.csp

[a]Blank spaces indicate that no data was provided, or companies gave only aggregate figures.

were reluctant to disclose information and their corporate customers often demanded nondisclosure.[12] The types of automation and product needs were also shifting further away from traditional library-automation models into the realm of knowledge management. Most special libraries relied heavily on e-content ranging from sensitive internal documents and external subscription-based materials to reports and research materials.

A trend across all segments was a fundamental shift from individual libraries/schools and PC-based systems to consortia and centralized, district-wide, web-based systems. These new consortia and resource-sharing environments helped increase efficiency and compensated for reduced budgets by providing technological developments that lowered automation costs and gave access to a larger collection of materials. Consortia were starting to merge together as well, creating "mega" consortia.[13]

Are Libraries Going the Way of the Dinosaur?

Were libraries going through a renaissance or were they going the way of the dinosaur? Most people believed that libraries would continue to exist, albeit in fewer numbers and doing the same things in very different ways. Technological advances forced libraries to reinvent themselves in order to remain relevant. The changes that libraries were making were not self-initiated, but rather were imposed by external forces—a new generation of technology-savvy users with very high expectations. Patrons no longer needed fact-based information because they could "google" it. However, Google searches were shallow or nonauthoritative searches. Patrons did not have to think too deeply about what they were looking for. In contrast, academic research required more complicated searches. Patrons needed help with developing search strategies, identifying the best database, generating search terms, determining how to search a particular subject term, interpreting search results, etc. According to one academic librarian:[14]

> In the future, libraries will take on more of an archival role of maintaining whatever remaining print media there are. They may work with digital archives such as the Civil War collection. There will be libraries, but there will be fewer librarians that won't need to help people as much while the technology becomes easier to use. Someone still has to play the role that we play. What we do has not changed that much—the core of what we do

is thinking about organizing information and accessing information. There will be a need for a librarian-type person to work with researchers to do the more sophisticated searching. We are doing more via email and chat.

> Defining our role in the world of Amazon and Google is a challenge. Decision-makers wonder why they have to spend more money on libraries. We are working a lot harder to promote what we have. Working with the website to make it easier to ask questions and find what patrons need.

Paul Cope felt that while librarians were demanding change, they were simultaneously resisting change. For example, one of the features of A-G's product suite enabled patrons to develop a list of books they had read and the authors they would like to read. Librarians were adamantly opposed to this feature because they did not want to deal with the legal ramifications of a third party demanding a list of books a patron had read. So, most librarians turned the function off. Or the example of book reviews from patrons, a common feature; but librarians were concerned about what was said by a user, when in fact these features were common place on the web today. Abuse occurs yes, but that abuse was self-correcting with the help of other users. According to Paul Cope, the challenge many firms in the industry faced was not so much the need to keep up with rapid advancements in technology by building new technology and infrastructure into their products, but having to deal with customers who were mostly an older generation of librarians who tended to forget *their* customers were younger more Internet-aware users. Further that the competitor for the user was not TV but e-Stores (Amazon or Barnes and Noble) where users could fill their needs by instantly downloading the materials or items they needed.

CURRENT PRODUCTS OFFERED TO LIBRARIES AND NEW PRODUCT TRENDS

The firms in the industry currently offered two basic software systems to all library segments. One was the Integrated Library System (ILS) that inventoried libraries' book collections; the other was the Inter-Library Loan

System (ILL) that allowed libraries to share their holdings through a borrowing-and-exchange program. The greatest opportunity for new ILS sales came in the form of legacy migration.[15] A legacy system referred to a system that an institution had been using for a period of time. Usually it contained outdated hardware and operating systems. The process of legacy migration meant updating the outdated hardware with a new system. In 2007, legacy migrations represented 63% of all ILS sales for the whole industry.[16] Libraries tended to defer replacing their legacy systems for as long as possible with the effect that these systems often remained in use many years past the point when new development ended. This was often caused by uncertainty regarding companies and technology trends. It was common for libraries to maintain a legacy ILS as long as possible but provide a new-generation interface to modernize its look for patrons.[17] In 2010, these new interfaces, the emergence of new technologies, and the global economic recession all worked in tandem to further the declining trend of complete ILS migrations.[18]

The decline in new ILS investments created a burgeoning market for interfaces such as discovery tools. These new products represented a growing portion of library-automation-industry sales.[19] According to one industry report:

> The challenge for academic libraries, caught in a seismic shift from print to electronic resources, is to offer an experience that has the simplicity of Google—which users expect—while searching the library's rich digital and print collections—which users need . . . Discovery tools are modeled on the Google-style approach of building and then searching a unified index of available resources, instead of searching each database individually. While Google's general index focuses on publicly available web content, these new discovery tools provide unified indexes of licensed scholarly publications combined with locally held content (like the catalog).[20]

A major product trend in the industry was enterprise-level solutions. While these solutions did not focus on the current ILS or ILL products, they aimed at providing frameworks to support a library's entire operations under one system. Instead of having a library subscribe to or purchase multiple systems including ILS, ILL, accounting, and purchasing systems, these products would enable libraries to run their entire enterprise using one system. These systems included Ex Libris's Alma,

currently in beta testing; OCLC's Web-scale Management Services (WMS) in the marketing and deployment cycle; and Kuali OLE (Open Library Environment), a research project supported through a major grant from the Andrew W. Mellon Foundation. These products were charting new territory and challenged existing products through precluding the need for multiple systems.[21]

Contracts—Securing Them and Counting Them

Firms in this industry obtained over 90% of their business through responding to requests for proposals (RFPs) submitted by libraries.[22] In an RFP, a library specified in detail its library-automation needs and invited vendors to submit proposals through a bidding process. The responding firms prepared proposals detailing how their products met the library's specifications and price. Libraries would then select the products that most closely met their needs at the lowest price.

A scorecard of a company's progress and activity was often measured by the number of contracts sold and the total number of installed products that a company had. While "counting contracts" was an important general measure, all contracts were not created equal and varied widely in value, number of libraries under a single contract (as in the case of consortia), collection sizes, and complexity of automation. For example, smaller library systems averaged $72,000 per contract, while large research libraries and consortia averaged over $300,000 per contract.[23]

Changing Business Model—SaaS[iii] or Licensing?

The advent of the Internet had resulted in a fundamental change in the business model of firms in the industry. The industry was moving away from licensing to some form of hosted service including SaaS and cloud-based services. The traditional business model involved libraries making large up-front investments in licensing fees for proprietary software and modest payments for maintenance over the life of the contract, usually five to seven years. In SaaS or cloud-based services, a library hosted its system and data on servers provided by the vendor and paid annual subscription fees in lieu of the licensing fees. Customers accessed the software and products through the Internet. This provided cost savings associated with administration and with installing and maintaining hardware and software. SaaS also freed up valuable IT or technical staff to support other projects.[24] This new model could result in significant cost reductions for libraries as it eliminated the need for local servers and the technical personnel to maintain them. The companies providing the hosting also experienced significant cost reductions due to very low unit costs, which further declined as the number of SaaS accounts increased.[25] The trend in 2011 was for companies to provide their new products as SaaS and to provide vendor-hosting options for their legacy products. To keep up with this trend, A-G and its competitors were making significant investments to increase their hosting capacity.[26]

Open-Source or Proprietary ILS— Which Will Libraries Choose?

Libraries were increasingly interested in more open-source products. The open-source movement allowed customers to own the product's source code, which could then be modified and customized to fit their specific needs. Revenues with this new business model were mostly from hosting, services, and custom development. Combined revenues of the firms supporting open source represented just over 1% of industry revenues.[27] In 2010, open source represented about 8% of total installed products.[28]

Three companies dominated in providing open-source ILS in 2011: LibLime (a division of Progressive Technologies Federal Systems, Inc. (PTFS)), ByWater Solutions, and Equinox (see Table 2). Public and academic libraries dominated those that had made official announcements to adopt open-source ILS at 57% for public libraries and 7% for academic libraries.[29]

Despite the seeming popularity of open source, Paul Cope had concerns:

> Open source appeals to the library mentality of sharing. Everything should be free. Open source said, "Here, just install it and run it yourself," and the libraries said, "OK, we'll give it a try." The libraries then found that it was more difficult than they had thought. They then realized the software is missing functions or features. This issue was addressed by the open-source "community" who said we will write that function, but no one is looking at the cost or time involved. For some libraries the operating system environment is perfect as it is today but others did not do their due diligence. They are enamored with the idea that they could get the source code, so they

would always be able to run the system. This idea was to address their concern related to the fact that the licensed software they had purchased was going to be "retired" and they had no more upgrade paths or if the upgrade existed it was expensive. Thus they became the "owner" of the code and they could find any hosting provider or they could always run it themselves.

Since 1972 A-G has taken the SaaS approach in its contracts by offering every customer every next version with no upgrade or migration fee. Further our contracts say, "If Auto-Graphics should fail, go out of business, or not offer you the next version of our software, while you have our software and are paying for it, we will give you the source code." So we have always had transparency. We are going to help you (the customer) keep running the software if we go out of business as our last will and testament.[30]

Although open sourcing currently represented a very small portion of the library-automation business, it had the potential to disrupt the industry's traditional business model of licensing if it became a permanent shift. Its impact could already be felt with the trend of proprietary-system providers giving customers the ability to customize their products, create new functionalities, collaborate, and share code and ideas.[31]

COMPETITION

A-G competed within the *public and academic libraries* segment of the industry. The number of total installed products determined market share in 2010 (see Table 2). The industry was concentrated as the top two companies, SirsiDynix and Ex Libris, commanded over 60% of the market share (see Figure 2). A-G was a small player with a little over 3% market share. The industry had begun to experience a rebound as indicated in Table 2. It experienced a 150% growth in new customers and an over 200% increase in total sales between 2009 and 2010 (see Figures 3 and 4 for 2010 sales figures for public and academic libraries). This was a sign that the industry might be seeing an end to the recession. A-G's competitors in the segment were Bilionix, ByWater Solutions, Equinox Software, Ex Libris, Infovision Software, LibLime (PTFS), Online Computer Library Center (OCLC), Polaris Library Systems, SirsiDynix, The Library Corporation (TLC), and Visionary Technology

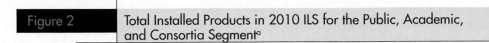

Figure 2 | Total Installed Products in 2010 ILS for the Public, Academic, and Consortia Segment[a]

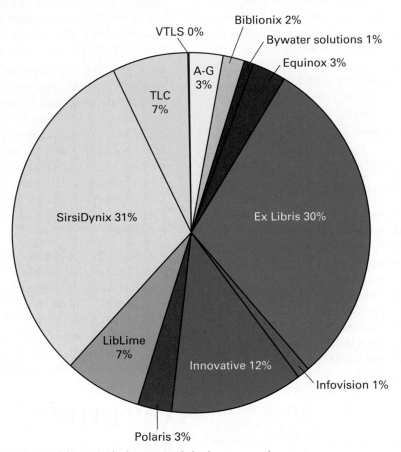

[a]Firms that are missing did not provide data or provided only aggregate data.

Source: Developed from data in Breeding, M. (April 1, 2011). Automation Marketplace 2011: The New Frontier. *The Library Journal.* Retrieved on October 7, 2011, from http://www.libraryjournal.com/lj/home/889533-264/automation_marketplace_2011_the_new.html.csp

in Library Solutions (VTLS).[32] See Table 3 for some basic facts about each competitor. A-G competed with the same firms in Canada; however, industry-share data was not broken down by U.S. and Canadian sales. A-G was private, as was the case with the majority of the competitors in this industry.

Biblionix

Biblionix was founded in 2003 by Alexander Charbonnet and was family owned. Its niche was small- and medium-sized public libraries which it served through SaaS. It introduced the Apollo ILS suite in 2008 and had since grown to a total customer base of 192. Twenty-four of its 87 new sales in 2010 were the product of a grant-funded project for the Central Texas and Alamo Area Library systems. The company experienced success in converting libraries in its niche market operating outdated or unsupported systems or those automating for the first time.[33]

ByWater Solutions

ByWater Solutions was founded in 2009 by Brendan A. Gallagher and Nathan A. Curulla as an official Koha Support Company.[34] ByWater was a small firm that specialized in support services for the open-source Koha ILS. ByWater won contracts from libraries that implemented

Figure 3	U.S. Public Library Sales 2010 (by number of contracts)ᵃ

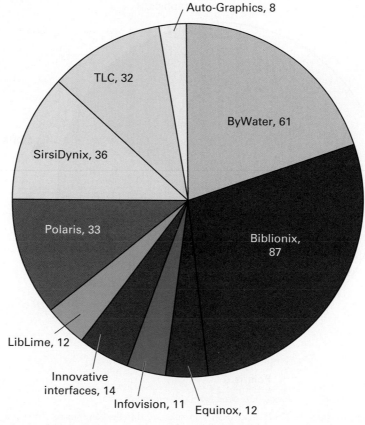

ᵃFirms that are missing did not provide data or provided only aggregate data.

Source: Breeding, M. (April 1, 2011). Automation Marketplace 2011: The New Frontier. *The Library Journal.* Retrieved on October 7, 2011, from http://www.libraryjournal.com/lj/home/889533-264/automation_marketplace_2011_the_new.html.csp

Koha on their own or from other support firms and from a wide range of those moving from a proprietary ILS to open-source systems. ByWater competed with LibLime in providing support for the Koha ILS in the U.S. ByWater developed software for Koha ILS as well as partnered with BibLibre, a French Koha Support Company.[35]

Equinox Software

Equinox was founded by the software team that developed Evergreen ILS at the Georgia Public Library Service for the Georgia Library PINES program. The firm specialized in services for open-source-library software with a focus on Evergreen ILS. In 2010 Equinox expanded its focus to include Koha ILS. Most of the development work on

Evergreen was conducted by Equinox; however, others such as PTFS also began providing development and service work for the ILS.

Ex Libris Group

Ex Libris was the second largest firm in the industry segment with a 30% market share. It focused on serving academic and research libraries as well as consortia in 78 international markets. The company's main ILS suite of products included Voyager and Aleph. These products were installed by over 50% of the Association of Research Libraries' members.[36] In 2010 Ex Libris was developing a new product branded Alma. The product aimed at providing libraries with a single system that

Figure 4	U.S. Academic Library Sales 2010 (by number of contracts)[a]

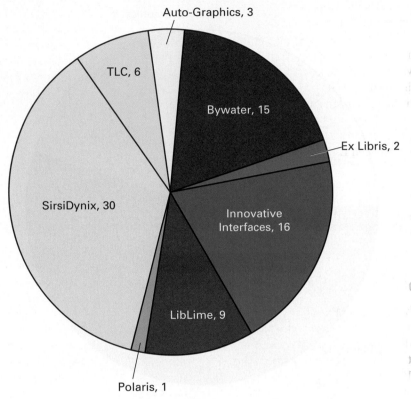

Auto-Graphics, 3

TLC, 6

Bywater, 15

Ex Libris, 2

SirsiDynix, 30

Innovative Interfaces, 16

LibLime, 9

Polaris, 1

[a]Firms that are missing did not provide data or provided only aggregate data.

Source: Breeding, M. (April 1, 2011). Automation Marketplace 2011: The New Frontier. *The Library Journal.* Retrieved on October 7, 2011, from http://www.libraryjournal.com/lj/home/889533-264/automation_marketplace_2011_the_new.html.csp

allowed them to manage all of their resources. This would negate the need for multiple systems such as ILS and ILL systems. It was planned to be offered via SaaS deployed on cloud-computing infrastructure. Alma was slated for general release in 2012.[37]

Infovision Software

Infovision was a very small player in the industry with less than 1% market share. It distributed the Australian-developed Amlib ILS in the U.S. Amlib was acquired in September 2008 by OCLC. Infovision ceased its association with Amlib after the acquisition and in 2009 began the development of Evolve, its own fully

web-based ILS, launched in 2010. Infovision's 81 installed products were mostly in public libraries, all in the U.S.

Innovative Interfaces, Inc.

Innovative Interfaces, Inc. (III, or Triple-I as it was known in the industry) was a leading contender in the academic and research libraries market segment. It also served additional libraries such as public, consortia, and digital libraries. It was a private firm founded by current Chairman Jerry Kline in 1978. It had installations in more than 52 countries and about 35% of its 2010 sales were derived from non-U.S. libraries.[38]

LibLime (PTFS)

LibLime was founded in 2005 to provide open-source software solutions to libraries. In March 2010, PTFS acquired LibLime. PTFS was a once relatively obscure firm in the industry because it supported libraries predominantly in the government and the military. It catapulted into the major leagues of library-system providers with the acquisition of LibLime.[39] PTFS was headquartered in Bethesda, MD.

LibLime was the leading firm in the open-source segment of the industry. Domestically, the Koha Support business was split primarily between ByWater Solutions and LibLime. The introduction of LLEK in 2009 had strained relations between LibLime and the broader Koha Support community, who felt that the company took advantage of a cooperatively developed resource without the reciprocity of contributing back the features it developed.[40] Despite this, LibLime had continued strong growth as open source continued to resonate with librarians.

Online Computer Library Center

OCLC was by far the largest and most global of all the firms that competed in the library-automation industry. It was founded as the Ohio College Library Center in 1967 and changed its name to Online Computer Library Center (OCLC) in 1981.[41] It had over 1,200 employees and total revenue of $228 million in 2010. However, only $17.3 million of revenue (7.6%) was derived from the library-automation industry, making it a mid-sized firm in the industry. OCLC entered the industry primarily through acquisitions of library-automation companies and through its own development of new products. OCLC differed from other firms in the industry because it was a non-profit membership-directed organization. It operated by having its members contractually bound to share intellectual content as well as resources.[42] Cooperative members had access to OCLC's library-automation systems and resources. In 2010, OCLC entered the marketing and deployment cycle of its new WMS system. The WMS system, like Ex Libris' Alma, aimed at providing enterprise-level solutions to libraries and obviating the need to purchase multiple systems such as ILL, ILS, etc.[43]

Polaris Library Systems

Polaris was A-G's closest competitor in terms of overall products and platforms as well as size.[44] It hoped to grow its business by providing products to midsized colleges. On January 15, 2010, Polaris announced an ownership change through a management buyout.[45] Its management team, under the leadership of CEO and President Bill Schickling, acquired the company from Croydon Company, which had owned it from its inception in 1997. Polaris was now owned through a holding company called PLS Solutions.[46] In 2009, Polaris created a new unit charged with maintaining high levels of customer satisfaction. Polaris had consistently maintained one of the highest ratios in the industry of customer-support staff to customer sites.[47]

SirsiDynix

Sirsi Corporation was founded in 1979 and Dynix Corporation in 1983. In June 2005, in the largest business acquisition in the industry's history, Sirsi, the smaller of the two, bought out Dynix and became SirsiDynix, making it the largest competitor in the segment with 31% of total installed product.[48] In 2009, while SirsiDynix signed a significant number of new clients for its Symphony ILS, it suffered a net loss of customers because of the defection of many libraries to competitors.[49] The company experienced a decline of over 56% in revenues between 2007 and 2008, after a 70% increase between 2006 and 2007.[50] This was attributed to the problems of integrating the two companies after the merger. SirsiDynix pulled the support for Dynix's products after the merger. Many customers were unhappy with having to pay more to upgrade to Sirsi's products. This created opportunities for smaller players in the industry, such as A-G, to grab additional market share.[51]

The Library Corporation

TLC, a family-owned and -operated company, was founded in 1974 to provide MARCFICHE to libraries. Its 2009 revenues were in the $30–$35 million range.[52] The company had an especially good year in 2010 in the K–12-school arena with eight sales of Library. Solution to school districts, including Jefferson County School District in Colorado, totaling 140 libraries serving 85,000 students.[53]

Visionary Technology in Library Solutions

Vinod Chachra at the Newman Library of Virginia Tech founded VLTS in 1974. In 1985, it separated from Virginia Tech as a for-profit company and ten years later it bought out Virginia Tech's interest in the company.[54] In 2009, VTLS won a contract for the Hong Kong Public Libraries, one of the largest public-library systems in the world. In 2010, it won a major contract with the Library of Congress to support procurement of materials using a customized version of VTLS's virtual-acquisitions module.[55]

THE COMPANY

Paul R. Cope had spent his entire career at A-G. A-G was founded by his grandfather Ira C. Cope in 1950 in Alhambra, CA. His father Robert S. Cope took the company public in 1969. Paul Cope became president of A-G in 2005. Robert Cope was chairman of A-G's Board of Directors. Besides Paul Cope and his father, two additional board members were Tom Dudley, a retired professor from Pepperdine University, and Larry Hubert, a professor at Pepperdine University. The board provided broad oversight and set strategic direction for the firm. A-G was headquartered in Pomona, CA.

A-G had evolved as technologies had evolved. When Robert Cope took the company public in 1969, it converted card catalogs into electronic catalogs for libraries. At that time, A-G also began building databases for libraries. It continued to reinvent itself as library technologies went from paper to microfilm and microfiche systems, then to online systems, CD-ROM cataloging, and finally to Internet web-based catalogs. As desktop publishing and Microsoft Word came along in the 1990s, A-G left the typesetting and publishing businesses almost completely.

In 1997, A-G acquired ISM Library Information Services Unit in Toronto, renamed it A-G Canada and maintained a small support and sales staff in its Toronto office. In 1998, A-G completely reengineered A-G Canada's major products by adding more than 32 million bibliographic and authority records to A-G Canada's extensive resource holdings and creating MARCit and TRACEit.[56]

A-G focused on library-automation systems and served more than 5,000 customers throughout North America.[57] According to Paul Cope:

> Times are changing of course, so things are different. That is the amazing thing. We used to say that we reinvented the company every ten years, and then we realized the cycle was five years, now it's every couple of years that we have to look at everything. The strategic plans had to be

rewritten every five years; now I'm down to every 18 months. Last time I wrote one (strategic plan) I was in the middle of the edit and update process, and it was already outdated.[58]

Table 6 depicts A-G's evolution over time.[59]

Paul attributed A-G's innovativeness to the flexibility and initiative of its management and employees. A-G had 32 employees in 2010 in the areas of development (7), support (7), sales (6), administration (3) and other areas (9).[60] A-G's management was especially proud of its ability to retain loyal, hard-working, and adaptable employees. Before Paul Cope was appointed President in 2005, he was the Chief Technology Officer and handled technology and new product development and product enhancements. When he became President, he hired three product managers to take care of the day-to-day technology part of the business so he could concentrate on running the company. One product manager was in charge of interfaces; the second was in charge of the ILL and statewide systems; and the third was in charge of the ILS. These three individuals were responsible for staying abreast of technology trends and of future product development. A-G hoped to attract the same caliber of employees as well as continue to hire people with experience in the library-automation industry.

Marketing for A-G typically happened at three national trade shows. Almost every state also had a library trade show and A-G attended those where it had a big statewide system in place to show its presence. It also relied on webinars, which were quite popular with clients. A-G also produced regular press releases and utilized email blasts. Press releases focused on informing clients and the public of new products or product enhancements. A-G utilized email blasts for the same purpose and reached a wider audience with these. A-G also utilized case studies to outline the benefits and/or features of a particular product and often included customer profiles and testimonials about how they were using the product.

Finance for A-G involved internal financing of new product development. In addition, it had a $1.0 million credit line at its bank. Paul described the product development and budget process at A-G as follows:

> In early September, Sales gives me a "preliminary forecast" for the next year. They are giving me a forecast of what they think they will be selling for the next year and in what areas. I take that detail and plug it into a budget based on the

current expectations of costs and then I am able to split the money into what I will spend on maintenance, support, or new projects. They can be enhancements to existing systems. Like last year we re-wrote our "book acquisition module" from scratch to really improve the workflow. This year we are improving the Inter-Library Loan function. We will see a more uniform, interstate loaning of books and materials. So those are development projects on existing products. So then what we do is sit down and set aside money that will go to the new products. The new product could be what we are calling "AGent Illuminar," which is our new user interface. We had made the decision last year that it was important to not just come up with a new webpage that looked the same. We wanted to go with the next step. We wanted to be different. So we went with Adobe and we have gone to a brand new Adobe Flex, which is a whole new technology and it provides a whole new user experience and it's great and customers love it.

In May 2004, A-G deregistered stock with the Security and Exchange Commission, thus allowing it to not deal with the new Sarbanes-Oxley laws with its added costs and reporting requirements. The company continued to do all of the standard reporting and audit it did in the past.[61]

A Wide Array of Products

A-G specialized in products for both large-scale resource-sharing projects and traditional library automation for public libraries both at the state level and for small libraries.[62] Its range of products rivaled its largest competitor, SirsiDynix. The main product suite and platform that A-G sold was called AGent. The AGent platform's primary core products were AGent VERSO™, AGent Iluminar™, AGent Resource Sharing™, and AGent Search™, but others included: iLib2Go (iPhone mobile application), MARCit, Digital Collections, TRACEit, Telephone Attendant, Content Management System (CMS), and Batch Services.[63] AGent Iluminar was A-G's product in the discovery tools category. A-G had remained innovative as could be seen from the evolution of its timeline displayed in Table 6 and the description of its products displayed in Table 7.

A-G's products could be customized and applied to institutions of any size. Any of these core products had over 16 modules and options that could be integrated into it, allowing A-G to fully customize any system. Core products and modules could further be customized through integrating partnership services and third-party products. The ability to customize products could be instrumental in cases where there were gaps in standards or when operating standards were not available. Modules and strategic partnerships also provided A-G with additional sources of revenue.

All of A-G's products ran off a standard browser, and products were delivered via three options:

1. SaaS—a library hosted its system and data on A-G's servers and paid annual subscription fees in lieu of licensing fees. Upgrades were free and immediately available to all subscribers through A-G's secure and backed-up servers. The library signed a five-year contract. This was A-G's primary business model in 2011.
2. Hosted license—a library made an initial capital investment in a license and then was supported via SaaS. Payment was a hybrid model, with libraries paying a licensing fee upfront and then paying the hosting and support and maintenance fees.
3. Licensing—a library made up-front investments in licensing fees for proprietary software and modest payments for maintenance over the life of the contract, usually five to seven years. It was suitable for large institutions with the budgets and IT staff to support A-G's products. Pricing was based on certain predetermined criteria, such as volume (how many records or items the system supported), activity, and number of users or staff the system supported. A-G moved away from the licensing model to the SaaS model in 2008. A-G offered AGent VERSO primarily through SaaS arrangements involving complete hosting and management.

Challenges in Moving Forward

Paul Cope was excited about the future of the library-automation industry and the tremendous possibilities created by new advances in technology. For the past 18 months, Paul Cope and his executive team considered how to adapt to the new realities of the library-automation industry and grow the company. A-G experienced a 4% average decline in total net sales between 2007 and 2011 and a 217% average decline in net income during the same time period (see Exhibits 1 and 2 for five

Table 6   A-G's evolution through different products

1950	1970	1986	1995	1999	2001	2002	2005	2006	2008	2009	2011
• Company founded	• First printed database library catalog	• Delivered CD-ROM based Public Access Library catalogs	• Released IOL (Impact On-Line). First internet based ILL (Inter-Library Loan) and cataloging system	• Released IOL2 (Impact On-Line 2) next generation ILL system	• Released AGent product line for virtual and hybrid ILL applications	• Released AGent portal to over 6,000 libraries	• Released AGent Verso - next generation ILS (Integrated Library System)	• Released AGent Search Web Service	• Introduced lib2Home, a preference tracking system, alerts, and other features that can be used as the basis for a program for home delivery of library materials	• Completed the initial development of AGent Illuminar, a new platform based on the Adobe Flex technology framework.	• Developed a new mobile application, iLib2Go; • Completed development of Circulation Interlibrary Loan Link (CILL), an NCIP-compliant utility that connects the circulation functions of an integrated library system (ILS) with an external interlibrary loan (ILL).

Sources: Adapted from A-G's website, data retrieved on October 7, 2011, from http://www4.autographics.com/company/history.htm; Breeding, M. (April 1, 2010). Automation Marketplace 2010: New Models, Core Systems. Library Journal. Retrieved on April 26, 2010, from http://www.libraryjournal.com/article/CA6723662.html?q=library+automation+industry; (April 1, 2011). Automation Marketplace 2011: The New Frontier. Library Journal. Retrieved on October 7, 2011, from http://www.libraryjournal.com/lj/home/889533-264/automation_marketplace_2011_the_new.html.csp; (April 1, 2012). Automation Market 2012: Agents of Change. Library Journal. Retrieved on August 25, 2012, from http://www.thedigitalshift.com/2012/03/ils/automation-marketplace-2012-agents-of-change/

Table 7	Auto-Graphics's Product Line

Product Name	Function
AGent VERSO	ILS that featured Google-like searches and provided libraries with a way to manage and track their inventory and resources by automating circulation activities like checking-in, checking-out, and transferring items; placing item-reserve requests and notifications; recovering fines, fees, and lost items; and administration and reporting activities. It was offered primarily through SaaS arrangements.
AGent Resource Sharing	Interlibrary Loan (ILL) system that allowed partner libraries to share resources and borrow from each other via a single interface regardless of the library's size or the ILS system used.
AGent Iluminar	A next-generation patron-user interface for AGent VERSO, which gave patrons more flexibility by allowing them to modify their own user experience through "My Lists" and "My Account" customization options.
AGent Search	A powerful federated search that quickly and intelligently searched resources and avoided information overload by ensuring that search results were not duplicated.
AGent MARCit	Provided a single point of access for public libraries to share over 20 million quality bibliographic records that ranged from individual library machine-readable (MARC) records to the Library of Congress database (MARC was a bibliographic-data format used for library cataloging).
AGent Digital Collections	Created, catalogued, and displayed digital content that was once limited only to internal library viewing.
AGent TRACEit	Extended resource sharing beyond traditional ILL boundaries and provided an efficient way to locate hard-to-find material.
AGent Telephone Attendant	Allowed libraries to provide automated services via telephone. Library hours, special-event information, renewing books, reviewing balances, and overdue items could all be done 24/7 at the patron's convenience.
AGent Enterprise	Provided modified versions of AGent Search and AGent Digital Collections and adapted them to corporations in various industries, using the newest data standard as its basic data structure – Extensible Mark-up Language (XML).
iLib2Go	An iPhone application which was a preference-tracking system with alerts and other features that could be used as the basis for a program for home delivery of library materials.

Sources: Cope, P. (May 26, 2009). Personal Interview; Auto-Graphics, Inc. The Company. Retrieved on October 27, 2009, from http://www4.auto-graphics.com/company/company.htm; Breeding, M. (April 1, 2007). Automation System Marketplace 2007: An Industry Redefined. *The Library Journal*. Retrieved on August 3, 2008, from www.libraryjournal.com/article/CA6429251.html; (April 1, 2009) Pressing onward in an uncertain economy, many industry players are adding staff and expanding development. *The Library Journal*. Retrieved on February 25, 2010, from http://www.libraryjournal.com/article/CA6645868.html?q=library+automation+industry; (April 1, 2010).

years of A-G's income statements and balance sheets). A-G performed better financially in 2011 as compared with 2010 with a 1% increase in total net sales as compared with a 10% decline between 2009 and 2010 and a 110% decline in net income as compared with a 696% decline between 2009 and 2010. A-G needed to find additional sources of long-term revenues and profits.

The library market was becoming an increasing challenge. A-G's customers experienced constantly changing and often shrinking budgets. To get new business, A-G bid on RFPs submitted by libraries listing their requirements and needs. However, libraries often had inflexible budgets and limited dollars to work with, and would often ask A-G to lower its bid if it was more than they could afford. This

Exhibit 1	Auto-Graphics, Inc. Consolidated Statements of Income

For the years ended December 31, 2007 through 2011 (in $)

	2007	2008	2009	2010	2011
Net Sales	5,617,675	5,576,737	5,300,038	4,752,383	4,815,155
Costs and expenses					
Cost of sales	1,429,727	1,253,499	1,305,711	1,362,644	1,265,776
Research and development	634,928	460,579	475769	445,150	491,536
Sales, marketing and customer service	2,398,651	2,521,221	2,362,128	2,540,393	1,920,699
General and administrative	900,599	1,100,082	1,054,495	1,014,378	1,048,540
Total costs and expenses	5,363,905	5,335,381	5,198,103	5,362,565	4,726,551
Income (loss) from operations	253,770	241,356	101,935	−610,182	88,604
Other income (expense):					
Foreign currency adjustment				−61,524	3,980
Other expense (income), net	−30,045	−16,306	−3,910	444	11,287
Interest expense, net					
Income before income taxes	283,815	257,662	105,845	−671,262	103,871
Income tax expense (benefit)	12,000	11,000	−9,295	15,000	34,000
Net income	271,815	246,662	115,140	−686,262	69,871
Earnings per share					
Basic income per share	0.05	0.06	0.03	(0.16)	0.02
Weighted average shares outstanding	4,327,377	4,778,277	4,273,210	4,272,860	4,272,610

Source: A-G.

could be a sticky situation. A-G risked losing the bid to a competitor if it did not acquiesce. However, lowering its price risked upsetting current customers that had bought the same product at a higher price. As a result, if A-G lowered the bid, it had to be clear how to remove some of the services so that other customers would not feel cheated.

The reliance of A-G's customers on state budgets and private grants sometimes made the library-automation industry very difficult to compete in

profitably. In an extreme case, when the Texas legislature found in mid-August that it was around $5 billion over budget it terminated A-G's previous account without warning. A-G's account was closed and funding ceased two weeks later. In most cases though, A-G had the opportunity to work with a library's reduced budget by scaling back services.[64]

Paul Cope would like to find more profitable growth alternatives within the library-automation industry. One

Exhibit 2	Auto-Graphics, Inc. Consolidated Balance Sheets

As of December 31, 2007 through 2011 (in $)

ASSETS	2007	2008	2009	2010	2011
Current assets:					
Cash and cash equivalents	803,949	1,026,571	1,014,158	823,815	610,536
Accounts receivable, less allowance for doubtful accounts	458,530	355,529	164,828	170,686	322,382
Deferred income taxes – current	54,000	68,000	154,000	145,000	175,000
Other current assets	76,934	139,144	199,353	224,515	228
Total current assets Software, net	1,393,413	1,589,244	1,532,339	1,364,016	1,335,563
	2,039,318	2,026,682	2,384,536	2,389,338	2,316,554
Equipment, furniture and leasehold improvements, net Other assets	240,287 22,522	270,155	225,706	285,568	333,417
Total assets	3,695,540	3,886,081	4,142,581	4,038,922	3,985,534
LIABILITIES & STOCKHOLDERS' EQUITY **Current liabilities**					
Line of credit				60,000	
Current maturities on long-term debt					11,945
Accounts payable	55,821	57,403	44,272	68,807	114,019
Deferred revenue	897,111	882,549	944,999	1,299,435	1,126,263
Accrued payroll and related liabilities	240,118	207,657	197,149	309,306	152,169
Other accrued liabilities Current portion of long-term debt	105,800	131,997	113,240	87,748	207,439
Total current liabilities	1,298,850	1,279,606	1,299,660	1,825,296	1,611,835
Long-term debt					46,783
Deferred income taxes	62,000	76,000	154,000	145	171,000
Total liabilities	1,360,850	1,355,606	1,453,660	1,970,296	1,829,618
Stockholders' equity		3,251,038	3,256,038	3,260,481	
Accumulated deficit	−867,395	−620,733	−505,593	−1,191,855	−1,121,984
Accumulated other comprehensive income (loss)	−42,841	−99,830	−61,524		8,778
Total stockholders' equity	2,334,690	2,530,475	2,668,921	2,068,626	2,155,916
Total liabilities and stockholders' equity	3,695,540	3,886,081	4,142,581	4,038,922	3,985,534

Source: A-G.

of the options available to A-G was further penetration into the California market. Although home to its headquarters, A-G had only three or four customers in California. The total number of libraries in California (not including school libraries) had remained flat since 1992 at 1,000 libraries. California public libraries (not including branches) in 2006 were estimated at 181, academic libraries at 121, special libraries at 117 and county law libraries at 58.[65] According to the California Department of Education, 97% of the 9,324 California public schools had an area designated as the library with significant variations in programs, staffing, and collections.[66] With California's ballooning budget deficit, libraries were living with what they had, because they had already invested large sums in licenses with other companies. However, Paul Cope felt that A-G's SaaS-subscription model could benefit over 60% of California libraries by providing the same level of service at a lower price than the libraries' current on-going support and maintenance fees with their original license companies. Although libraries were slow to change, liked what they had, and were loyal to original vendors,[67] fiscal conditions were forcing libraries to favor SaaS because it produced savings on local infrastructure and personnel and greater participation in larger-scale shared-automation systems such as consortia or statewide systems.[68] A-G could target California libraries that still had licenses and were considering moving to the SaaS model deployed on cloud-based architecture.

A related opportunity was legacy migrations. Several ILS systems were being phased out mostly due to acquisitions.[69] The libraries that were currently using these systems provided A-G with the opportunity for ILS sales. According to an industry report, a modest number of libraries were still using DynixClassic, which had been phased out by SirsiDynix. Several of these libraries were beginning to consider replacements. While SirsiDynix would like for them to switch to its flagship ILS Symphony, several of these libraries were up for grabs to the firms that could provide them the most cost efficient and effective solutions. Other ILSs that were in play were existing products of firms that were no longer in the industry such as Athena, Winnebago Spectrum, InfoCentre, and Circulation Plus. SirsiDynix's Horizon and Ex Libris's Voyager were currently receiving support from the two firms, but not as the flagship products. In 2010 Ex Libris's Voyager had 1,251 installed products while SirsiDynix's Horizon had 1,406 as compared with the total installed for A-G of 394 (see Table 2). Libraries with these systems were sales opportunities for A-G. Some of the smaller firms had begun to take advantage

of these opportunities. For example, 25 of the 33 contracts gained by Polaris in 2009 were migrations from one of SirsiDynix's products.[70] Significant numbers of Biblionix's 87 new sites in 2010 came from legacy migrations in the public-library segment.[71] A-G could target California libraries facing legacy migrations from any of these ILSs with subscriptions to AGent Verso using the SaaS model.

On a different front, Paul Cope showed interest in developing the enterprise market by creating products for special libraries such as law, medical, corporate, and enterprise libraries. Primarily four firms competed in this segment in 2010 as displayed in Table 6. CyberTools and EOS International served government, corporate, medical, law, and military libraries. Keystone Systems served the highly specialized niche of libraries that focused on clients with visual disabilities.[72] Inmagic provided social-knowledge networks for enterprise clients.[73] The total number of installed products for the segment in 2010 was about 14% of the total installed products for the public, academic and consortia (PAC) segment (see Table 2). Special libraries constituted 7% of the total number of libraries in the U.S. Growth in the segment paralleled that in the library-automation industry in general. Paul Cope believed firms that could find a special niche and serve it efficiently could be successful.[74]

In early 2007, A-G began to pursue this segment by creating products for the financial-services market, with the hopes of penetrating brokerage houses and banking institutions like Merrill Lynch, Fidelity Investments, Citibank, and Chase that were in need of federated-search products. A-G had originally planned on releasing products in the fall of 2007. However, because the housing and credit-crunch crises created gigantic losses and destroyed well-known companies in the financial services sector, money dried up immediately for buying new systems. However, with the improving economic environment, financial-services firms might be a niche in the special-libraries segment worth pursuing because there was a latent need, and very few competitors were currently targeting this niche. IBISWorld projected revenue growth for the financial-services industry to average about 3%; profit growth to average about 2.5%; and the number of establishments to grow at over 2.4% between 2012 and 2017.[75]

Non-U.S. sales of the library-automation industry declined from 237 units in 2008 to 138 in 2009; the 42% decline was a reflection of the global economic recession. In 2010 non-U.S. sales increased by 18% to 163 and by 68% to 274 in 2011.[76] Non-U.S. sales were expected to continue to grow and the international arena was expected to continue to provide opportunities for growth for U.S. companies. While library automation had reached maturity in the developed world, growth opportunities abounded in many emerging and developing markets. An example was VTLS's 2009 contract for the Hong Kong Public Libraries, one of the largest public library systems in the world. A-G currently had a small presence in the international market through its subsidiary, A-G Canada.

A-G Canada's office was currently small and focused primarily on selling MARCit to clients. Machine-Readable Cataloging Record (MARC) records contained bibliographic records of the type that were formerly placed on card catalogs such as author, date of publication, publisher, etc. MARC records allowed libraries to digitize their card catalogs by providing an industry standard of tags for each of the various components of a bibliographic record.[77]

In identifying growth opportunities, A-G also considered expanding its presence in Canada. It currently served 79 libraries in Canada and generated about 5% of its revenues from Canada. A-G could identify possible new markets for MARCit or expand its use among Canadian libraries where it was currently not being used as much such as in public libraries. MARCit Canadian clients were primarily special and academic libraries which made up 64% and 18% respectively of the number of libraries that A-G served in Canada. Although public libraries constituted only 14% of the libraries A-G served in Canada, they produced almost 30% of MARCit revenues in Canada.[78]

A-G could bundle MARCit with its portfolio of products in the U.S. market to attract and retain existing Canadian clients. It could leverage its relationships with current MARCit clients in the public, academic and special-library segments in Canada to push its ILS and supporting products through into the Canadian market. A-G had hesitated pursuing this option because of the expense of providing product capabilities in both French and English. Most competitive products in Canada utilized Unicode, which enabled them to accommodate multiple languages. Unicode capabilities were limited in A-G's current product suite. While it had responded to this need by creating patches that provided the capability for a French-speaking individual to search for information, the actual records themselves were still in English. A-G would have to incorporate French language capabilities into its suite of products if it wanted to successfully penetrate the Canadian market.

An advantage of A-G selling a full-suite of products in Canada was that MARCit would be part of a larger suite of solutions for the Canadian clients and A-G would be able to grow in the Canadian market. However, the Canadian market was very small compared to the U.S. and libraries in Canada were experiencing similar declines in funding as U.S. libraries.[79] However, library usage in Canada was up 45% in 2011 over the past decade, from 16.6 to 24.1 transactions on average per capita.[80] Also, as displayed in Table 1, the North American market was beginning to see an upsurge in demand. Making the necessary investment to incorporate Unicode into its AGent suite of products could give A-G the opportunity to ride the wave of growth in the international market as it would give A-G the ability to incorporate multiple language capabilities into its products.

Also, A-G had not pursued the sale of MARCit to its U.S. clients as aggressively as it had sales to its Canadian clients. The entrance of new bibliographic utilities such as Innovative Interfaces Inc.'s SkyRiver and Liblime's ≠biblios.net (both of which entered the market in 2009) might be the perfect opportunity to push MARCit. A-G could bundle MARCit as part of its AGent suite of products to its U.S. clients. A-G could also form partnerships with other firms that did not have their own bibliographic utility to bundle MARCit with partner ILSs. This would increase MARCit's market penetration in the U.S. as well as offer a value-added product to U.S. clients. This might give A-G an advantage in the U.S. market as there were only four bibliographic utilities in the industry (the three already mentioned and OCLC's WorldCat) and very few competitors had their own bibliographic utility that they could bundle with their ILSs. MARCit was highly competitive in terms of hit rates (quality and efficiency of searches) vis-à-vis competing products in the market.

All current indications in the library-automation industry pointed to incumbents gearing up for new product development that would result in improving their long-term competitive positions. According to one industry source, personnel grew by 15% in 2010 over the 2008 figure. Growth in development personnel was in preparation for the development of innovative products and new functionalities in current products. So, it made sense for A-G to revisit creating products for other markets, such as the financial services sector, or for the international markets such as Canada. A-G had consistently invested an average of 10% per annum of its revenues in R&D over the past seven years. Paul Cope and his executives had to decide where to invest future R&D investments: developing new products for the enterprise markets or developing multilanguage capabilities in its suite of products to expand in Canada and possibly into other international arenas.

CONCLUSION

Paul Cope knew that A-G's innovativeness and ability to change with the market for over 60 years were the foundation for its staying power and success. Advances in technology had provided A-G the opportunity to develop new products and new platforms to service current and future customers. Paul Cope was excited by the infinite possibilities of the new technologies. His job now was to figure out how to grow and strategically plan the next round of A-G's adaptation and evolution. He hoped that doing this would position A-G to compete strongly for another 60 years in the marketplace.

NOTES

1. Cope, P. (May 26, 2009). Personal Interview.
2. Numberof.net. Number of Libraries in the U.S. Retrieved on June 13, 2012, from http://www.numberof.net/number-of-libraries-in-the-us/
3. CARL 2009–2010 Statistics/Statistiques. (2012). Retrieved on June 13, 2012, from carl-abrc.ca/uploads/pdfs/stats/2010_CARL-Publication.pdt; Wiki Answers. How many libraries are in Canada. Retrieved on June 13, 2012, from http://wiki.answers.com/Q/How_many_libraries_are_in_Canada
4. Breeding, M. (April 1, 2007). Automation System Marketplace 2007: An Industry Redefined. *The Library Journal,*. Retrieved on August 3, 2008, from www.libraryjournal.com/article/CA6429251.html; (April 1, 2009) Pressing onward in an uncertain economy, many industry players are adding staff and expanding development. *The Library Journal.* Retrieved on February 25, 2010, from http://www.libraryjournal.com/article/CA6645868.html?q=library+automation+industry; (April 1, 2010). Automation Marketplace 2010: New Models, Core Systems. *The Library Journal.* Retrieved on April 26, 2010, from http://www.libraryjournal.com/article/CA6723662.html?q=library+automation+industry
5. CIA. (2010). The World Fact Book. Retrieved on July 21, 2010, from https://www.cia.gov/library/publications/the-world-factbook/geos/us.html
6. Bureau of Economic Statistics. (2012). Gross Domestic Product. Retrieved on June 15, 2012, from http://www.bea.gov/national/index.htm#gdp
7. Indexmundi. (2012). GDP Real Growth Rate – Canada. Retrieved on June 15, 2012, from http://www.indexmundi.com/g/g.aspx?c=ca&v=66
8. Breeding, M. (April 1, 2010).
9. Breeding, M. (April 1, 2009).
10. Breeding, M. (2004).
11. Breeding, M. (April 1, 2010).
12. Breeding, M. (April 1, 2005). Automation System Marketplace 2005: Gradual Evolution. *The Library Journal.* Retrieved on August 3, 2008, from www.libraryjournal.com/article/CA512267.html
13. Breeding, M. (2004).
14. Morgan, Ann. Personal Interview, December 2, 2011.
15. Ibid.
16. Breeding, M. (April 1, 2007).
17. Breeding, M. (April 1, 2009).
18. Breeding, M. (April 1, 2011). Automation Marketplace 2011: The New Frontier. *The Library Journal.* Retrieved on October 7, 2011, from http://www.libraryjournal.com/lj/home/889533-264/automation_marketplace_2011_the_new.html.csp
19. Breeding, M. (April 1, 2011).
20. Luther, J. and Kelly, M.C. (2011). The next generation of discovery. Retrieved on October 14, 2011, from http://www.libraryjournal.com/lj/home/889250-264/the_next_generation_of_discovery.html.csp
21. Breeding, M. (April 1, 2011).
22. Cope, P. (May 26, 2009).
23. Breeding, M. (2004).
24. Breeding, M. (April 1, 2009).
25. Ibid.
26. Breeding, M. (2011).
27. Breeding, M. (April 1, 2010).
28. Breeding, M. (April 1, 2011).
29. Breeding, M. (April 1, 2010).
30. Cope, P. (May 26, 2009).
31. Breeding, M. (April 1, 2011).
32. Ibid.
33. Ibid.
34. Library Technology Guides. ByWater company profile. Retrieved May 21, 2012, from http://www.librarytechnology.org/bywater.pl
35. Breeding, M. (April 2011).
36. Ex Libris Official Website. Retrieved on October 7, 2011, from http://www.Ex Librisgroup.com/category/Our Vision
37. Breeding, M. (April 1, 2011).
38. Ibid.
39. Hellman, E. (January 21, 2010). PTFS to Acquire LibLime and Move to Library Systems Premier League. Retrieved on July 27, 2010, from http://go-to-hellman.blogspot.com/2010/01/ptfs-to-acquire-LibLime-and-move-to.html
40. Breeding, M. (April 1, 2010).
41. Library Technology Guides. OCLC Company profile. Retrieved May 21, 2012, from http://www.librarytechnology.org/oclc.pl
42. OCLC Official Website. Retrieved May 21, 2012, from http://www.oclc.org/us/en/membership/benefits/default.htm
43. Breeding, M. (April 1, 2011).
44. Ibid.

45. Breeding, M. Management Buyout at Polaris. Retrieved November 4, 2011, from http://www.librarytechnology.org/ltg-displaytext.pl?RC=14779

46. Library Technology Guides. Polaris Library Systems Company Profile. Retrieved on November 4, 2011, from http://www.librarytechnology.org/polaris.pl

47. Breeding, M. (April 1, 2010).

48. SirsiDynix's Official Website. Retrieved on July 22, 2010, from http://www.sirsidynix.com; Breeding, M. (April 1, 2011).

49. Breeding, M. (April 1, 2009).

50. Breeding, M. (April 1, 2010).

51. Cope, P. (May 26, 2009).

52. Breeding, M. (April 1, 2010).

53. TLC's Official Website,

54. Library Technology Guides. VTLS company profile. Retrieved May 21, 2012, from http://www.librarytechnology.org/vtls.pl

55. Breeding, M. (April 2011).

56. A-G Company History. Internal company document.

57. Ibid.

58. Cope, P. (May 26, 2009).

59. Ibid.

60. Breeding, M. (April 2011).

61. Cope, P. (August 19, 2008).

62. Breeding, M. (April 1, 2010).

63. Auto-Graphics' Official Website.

64. Breeding, M. (2009).

65. Department of Finance. Number of California Libraries, 1990 to 2006. Retrieved on June 13, 2012, from www.dof.ca.gov/html/fs_data/sta-abs/documents/f5.pdf

66. Jeffus, B. (March 23, 2012). Statistics about California School Libraries. Retrieved June 13, 2012, from http://www.cde.ca.gov/ci/cr/lb/schoollibrstats08.asp

67. Ibid.

68. Breeding, M. (April 1, 2011).

69. Breeding, M. (April 1, 2010)

70. Ibid.

71. Breeding, M. (April 1, 2011)

72. Ibid.

73. Inmagic. About us. Retrieved on June 14, 2012, from http://www.inmagic.com/about-inmagic

74. Breeding, M. (April 1, 2011)

75. IBIS World Industry Reports. Retrieved on June 17, 2012, from http://0-clients.ibisworld.com.opac.library.csupomona.edu/industryus/industryoutlook.aspx?indid=1308

76. Breeding, M. (April 1, 2012). Automation Marketplace 2012: The Complete Survey Data. *The Library Journal*. Retrieved on June 17, 2012, from http://www.the-digitalshift.com/2012/03/ils/automation-marketplace-2012-the-complete-survey-data/; Breeding, M (April 1, 2010); Breeding, M. (April 1, 2009).

77. Library of Congress. Understanding MARC. Retrieved on October 10, 2011, from http://www.loc.gov/marc/umb/um01to06.html

78. Internal company documents.

79. Thompson, J. (September 12, 2011). City Manager recommends Toronto Public Library budget cuts and branch closures. Retrieved on June 13, 2012, from http://ourpubliclibrary.to/media-releases/city-manager-recommends-toronto-public-library-budget-cuts-and-branch-closures/; Cuts to N.S. librarians match trend seen in Ontario. (April 15, 2012). *The Canadian National Press*. Retrieved on June 13, 2012 from http://www.cbc.ca/news/canada/toronto/story/2012/04/15/ontario-group-decries-librarian-cuts.html

80. *The Canadian Press*. (November 27, 2011). Canadian Libraries thriving in ebook era. Retrieved on June 14, 2012, from http://m.ctv.ca/topstories/20111127/canadian-library-use-rising-in-ebook-era-111127.html

NOTES

i. Cloud computing enabled users to access applications and files stored on remote servers over the Internet using a web browser or a mobile device. It provided organizations "a way to increase capacity or add capabilities on the fly without investing in new infrastructure, training new personnel, or licensing new software. [It] encompasses any subscription-based or pay-per-use service that, in real time over the Internet, extends IT's existing capabilities" (Knorr, E. and Gruman, G. What Cloud Computing Really Means. Retrieved on May 14, 2012, from http://www.infoworld.com/d/cloud-computing/what-cloud-computing-really-means-031?page=0,1). It included many components including software as a service (SaaS).

ii. "Federated search was an information-retrieval technology that allowed the simultaneous search of multiple searchable resources. A user made a single query request that was distributed to the search engines participating in the federation. The federated search then aggregated the results that were received from the search engines for presentation to the user." Retrieved on May 14, 2012, from http://en.wikipedia.org/wiki/Federated_search.

iii. SaaS was a type of cloud computing that delivered "a single application through the browser to thousands of customers using a multitenant architecture. On the customer side, it meant no upfront investment in servers or software licensing; on the provider side, with just one application to maintain, costs were low compared to conventional hosting." Knorr, E. and Gruman, G. What Cloud Computing Really Means. Retrieved on May 14, 2012, from http://www.infoworld.com/d/cloud-computing/what-cloud-computing-really-means-031?page=0,1

Case 10

Nucor in 2013

Beverly B. Tyler,
Poole College of Management,
North Carolina State University

Frank C. Barnes,
Belk College of Business,
University of North Carolina-Charlotte

INTRODUCTION

What a time to be going out into the business world! Young Dan DiMicco faced a similar situation in 2000 when he took the reins of Nucor from the legendary Ken Iverson. Who could follow Ken's success in building a new kind of innovative steel company? "I think most executives, given a chance to run a steel company, would not have picked September 2000 as the time to start. The U.S. economy was entering into a 3-year slump, the worst economic period since the early 1980s. Dozens of steel companies were forced either into bankruptcy, reorganization or out of business altogether." But this is the hand Dan was dealt.

In January 2013, Dan was smiling as he turned over the leadership to a new chairman, John Ferriola. Nucor was better than ever. He happily reported Nucor's "total return to stockholders from the cyclical bottom of our share price on September 25, 2000 through the end of 2012 was 720%, compared with 187.7% for the S&P Steel Group Index and 25.4% for the S&P 500." Over all the challenges, he, or as he would say "his team," had prevailed; and he had the wealth to enjoy a long retirement, like his many employees would in time.

But how did he do it? This is not Apple or Facebook, but an American steel company in an industry the U.S. had given up on. How can a company or person face a messy, challenging situation and still achieve success?

In 1966 when Iverson began, the U.S. was liquidating its historic manufacturing businesses, like steel. Iverson took over a failing company, fought the trend and found a successful strategy; they became a model for the

second millennium. They faced many challenges over the years, adapted and prevailed.

In the spring of 2013, the U.S. had endured 4 years of recession and continued slow worldwide growth was expected. Like it or not, Nucor was now an international company and competition was intense. Imports were flooding the U.S. and domestic capacity utilization was down to 75%, depressing prices and profits. With so much production in emerging nations, the competition for the major raw material, scrap steel, was threatening long-term viability. And where many foreign competitors were supported by their governments, U.S. companies faced harassment, increased rules and regulations.

The challenges facing the company in 2013 had never been greater, but Dan said, "At Nucor, we view recessions differently; they are the pause that allows us to prepare ourselves to grow even stronger during the next economic expansion." Is their optimism justified, can they do it again?

BACKGROUND

Nucor Steel did not begin as a steel company but miraculously emerged from two corporate failures. First was Nuclear Consultants, a company formed after WW2 to ride the wave of growth coming in "nuclear" technology. When this didn't happen, Nuclear Corp. of America diversified to participate in the "conglomerate" trend popular at the time. Nuclear acquired various "high-tech" businesses, such as radiation sensors, semiconductors, rare earths, and air-conditioning equipment. However, the company still lost money and a fourth reorganization in 1966 put 40-year-old Ken Iverson in charge. The building of what we know as Nucor today began.

Ken Iverson had joined the Navy after high school in 1943 and had been transferred from officer training school to Cornell's Aeronautical Engineering Program. On graduation he selected Mechanical Engineering/Metallurgy for a Master's degree to avoid the long drafting apprenticeship in Aeronautical Engineering. His college work with an electron microscope earned him a job with International Harvester. After five years in their lab, his boss, and mentor, prodded him to expand his vision by going with a smaller company.

Over the next 10 years, Iverson worked for four small metals companies, gaining technical knowledge and increasing his exposure to other business functions. He enjoyed working with the presidents of these small companies and admired their ability to achieve outstanding results. Nuclear Corp., after failing to buy the company Iverson worked for, hired him as a consultant to find them another metals business to buy. In 1962, the firm bought a small joist plant in South Carolina that Iverson found, on the condition that he run it.

Over the next four years Iverson built up the Vulcraft division as Nuclear Corporation struggled. The president, David Thomas, was described as a great promoter and salesman but a weak manager. A partner with Bear Stearns actually made a personal loan to the company to keep it going. In 1965, when the company was on the edge of bankruptcy, Iverson, who headed the only successful division, was named president and moved the company's headquarters to Charlotte, North Carolina. He immediately began getting rid of the esoteric, but unprofitable, unrelated, high tech divisions and concentrated on the steel joist business he found successful. They built more joist plants and in 1968 began building their first steel mill in South Carolina to "make steel cheaper than they were buying from importers." By 1984 Nucor had six joist plants and four steel mills, using the new "mini-mill" technology.

The original owner of Vulcraft, Sanborn Chase was known at Vulcraft as "a scientific genius." He had been a man of great compassion, who understood the atmosphere necessary for people to self-motivate. Chase, an engineer by training, invented a number of things in diverse fields. He also established the incentive programs for which Nucor later became known. With only one plant, he was still able to operate with a "decentralized" manner. Before his death in 1960, while still in his 40s, the company was studying the building of a steel mill

using newly developed mini-mill technology. His widow ran the company until it was sold to Nucor in 1962.

Dave Aycock met Ken Iverson when Nuclear purchased Vulcraft and they worked together closely for the next year and a half. Located in Phoenix at the corporate headquarters, he was responsible to Iverson for all the joist operations and was given the task of planning and building a new joist plant in Texas. In late 1963 he was transferred to Norfolk, where he lived for the next 13 years and managed a number of Nucor's joist plants. Then in 1977 he was named the manager of the Darlington, South Carolina steel plant. In 1984, Aycock became Nucor's President and Chief Operating Officer, while Iverson became Chairman and Chief Executive Officer.

Aycock had this to say about Iverson: "Ken was a very good leader, with an entrepreneurial spirit. He is easy to work with and has the courage to do things, to take lots of risks. Many things didn't work, but some worked very well." There is the old saying "failure to take risk is failure." This saying epitomizes a cultural value personified by the company's founder and reinforced by Iverson during his time at the helm. Nucor was very innovative in steel and joists. Their plant was years ahead in wire rod welding at Norfolk. In the late '60s they had one of the first computer inventory management systems and design/engineering programs. They were very sophisticated in purchasing, sales, and managing and they beat their competition often by the speed of their design efforts.

By 1984 the bankrupt conglomerate became a leading U.S. steel company. It was a fairytale story. Tom Peters used Nucor's management style as an example of "Excellence," while the barons of old steel ruled over creeping ghettos. NBC featured Nucor on television and *New Yorker* magazine serialized a book about how a relatively small American steel company built a team, which led the whole world into a new era of steelmaking. As the NBC program asked: "If Japan Can, Why Can't We?" Nucor had! Iverson was rich, owning $10 million in stock, but with a salary that rarely reached $1 million, compared to some U.S. executive's $50 or $100 million. The 40-year-old manager of the South Carolina Vulcraft plant had become a millionaire. Stockholders chuckled and non-unionized hourly workers, who had never seen a layoff in the 20 years, earned more than the unionized workers of old steel and more than 85% of the people in the states where they worked. Many employees were financially quite secure.

Nucor owed much of its success to its benchmark organizational style and the empowered division managers.

There were two basic lines of business, the first being the six steel joist plants which made the steel frames seen in many buildings. The second line included four steel mills that utilized the innovative mini-mill technology to supply the joist plants at first and later outside customers. In 1984 Nucor was still only the seventh-largest steel company in America but they had established the organization design, management philosophy, and incentive system, which lead to their continued success.

NUCOR'S FORMULA FOR SUCCESS 1964–1999

In the early 1990s, Nucor's 22 divisions, one for every plant, had a general manager, who was also a vice president of the corporation. The divisions were of three basic types: joist plants, steel mills, and miscellaneous plants. The corporate staff consisted of less than 25 people. In the beginning Iverson had chosen Charlotte "as the new home base for what he had envisioned as a small cadre of executives who would guide a decentralized operation with liberal authority delegated to managers in the field," according to South magazine. The divisions did their own manufacturing, selling, accounting, engineering, and personnel management and there were only four levels from top to bottom (see Figure 1 for structure in 1991).

Iverson gave his views on keeping a lean organization:

Each division is a profit center and the division manager has control over the day-to-day decisions that make that particular division profitable

Figure 1 Nucor Organization Chart

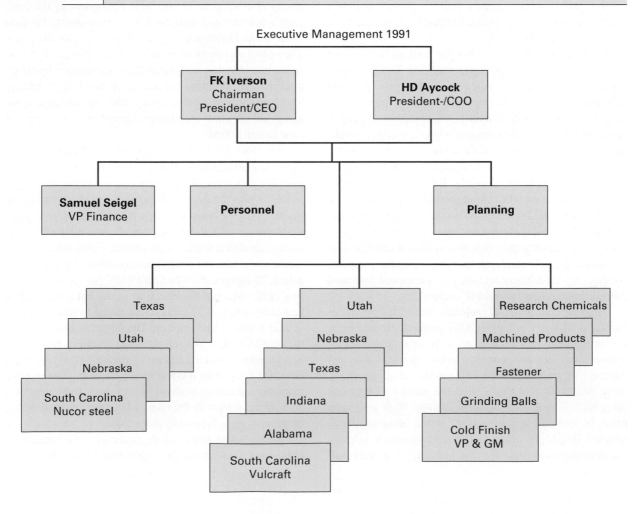

or not profitable. We expect the division to provide contribution, which is earnings before corporate expenses. And we expect a division to earn 25% return on total assets employed, before corporate expenses, taxes, interest or profit sharing. And we have a saying in the company if a manager doesn't provide that for a number of years, we are either going to get rid of the division or get rid of the general manager, and it's generally the division manager.

Nucor strengthened its position by developing strong alliances with outside parties. It did no internal research and development. Instead, they monitored other's work worldwide and attracted investors who brought them new technical applications at the earliest possible dates. Though Nucor was known for constructing new facilities at the lowest possible costs; their engineering and construction team consists of only three individuals. They did not attempt to specify exact equipment parameters, but asked the equipment supplier to provide this information and then held the manufacturer accountable. They had alliances with selected construction companies around the country who knew the kind of work Nucor wanted. Nucor bought 95% of its scrap steel from an independent broker who followed the market and made recommendations regarding scrap purchases. They did not have a corporate advertising department, corporate public relations department, or a corporate legal or environmental department. They had long-term relationships with outsiders to provide these services.

The steel industry had established a pattern of absorbing the cost of shipments so, regardless of the distance from the mill, all users paid the same delivered price. Nucor broke with this tradition and stopped equalizing freight. It offered all customers the same sales terms, price plus actual shipping costs. Nucor also gave no volume discounts, feeling that with modern computer systems there was no justification. Customers located next to the plant guaranteed themselves the lowest possible costs for steel purchases. Two tube manufacturers, two steel service centers, and a cold rolling facility had located adjacent to the Arkansas plant. These facilities accounted for 60% of the shipments from the mill. The plants were linked electronically to each other's production schedules allowing them to function in a just-in-time inventory mode. All new mills were built on large enough tracks of land to accommodate collaborating businesses.

Iverson didn't feel greater centralization would be good for Nucor. Hamilton Lott, a Vulcraft plant manager, commented in 1997, "We're truly autonomous; we can duplicate efforts made in other parts of Nucor. We might develop the same computer program six times. But the advantages of local autonomy make it worth it." Joe Rutkowski, manager at Darlington steel, agreed. "We're not constrained; headquarters doesn't restrict what I spend. I just have to make my profit contribution at the end of year."

South Magazine observed that Iverson had established a characteristic organizational style described as "stripped down" and "no nonsense." "Jack Benny would like this company," observed Roland Underhill, an analyst with Crowell, Weedon and Co. of Los Angeles, "so would Peter Drucker." Underhill pointed out that Nucor's thriftiness doesn't end with its "Spartan" office staff or modest offices. "There are no corporate perquisites," he recited. "No company planes, No country club memberships. No company cars."

Fortune noted, "Iverson takes the subway when he is in New York, a Wall Street analyst reports in a voice that suggests both admiration and amazement." The general managers reflected this style in the operation of their individual divisions. Their offices were more like plant offices or the offices of private companies built around manufacturing rather than for public appeal. They were simple, routine, and businesslike.

DIVISION MANAGERS

The corporate personnel manager described management relations as informal, trusting, and not "bureaucratic." He felt there was a minimum of paperwork, that a phone call was more common than memos and that no confirming memo was thought to be necessary.

A Vulcraft manager commented: "We have what I would call a very friendly spirit of competition from one plant to the next. And of course all of the vice presidents and general managers share the same bonus systems so we are in this together as a team even though we operate our divisions individually."

The divisions managed their activities with a minimum of contact with the corporate staff. Each day disbursements were reported to corporate office. Payments flowed into regional lock boxes. On a weekly basis, joist divisions reported total quotes, sales cancellations, backlog, and production. Steel mills reported tons rolled, outside shipments, orders, cancellations, and backlog. Each month the divisions completed a two page (11" × 17") "Operations

Analysis" which was sent to all the managers. Its three main purposes were (1) financial consolidation, (2) sharing information among the divisions, and (3) corporate management examination. The summarized information and the performance statistics for all the divisions were then returned to the managers.

The general managers met three times a year. In late October, they presented preliminary budgets and capital requests. In late February they met to finalize budgets and treat miscellaneous matters. Then, at a meeting in May, they handled personnel matters, such as wage increases and changes of policies or benefits. The general managers as a group considered the raises for the department heads, the next lower level of management for all the plants.

VULCRAFT—THE JOIST DIVISIONS

One of Nucor's major businesses was the manufacture and sale of open web steel joists and joist girders at Vulcraft divisions located in Florence, South Carolina; Norfolk, Nebraska; Ft. Payne, Alabama; Grapeland, Texas; St. Joe, Indiana; Brigham City, Utah, and Chemung, New York. Open web joists, in contrast to solid joists, were made of steel angle iron separated by round bars or smaller angle iron. These joists cost less, were of greater strength for many applications, and were used primarily as the roof support systems in larger buildings, such as warehouses and shopping malls.

The joist industry was characterized by high competition among many manufacturers for many small customers. With an estimated 40% of the market, Nucor was the largest supplier in the U.S. It utilized national advertising campaigns and prepared competitive bids on 80% to 90% of the buildings using joists. Competition was based on price and delivery performance. Nucor had developed computer programs to prepare designs for customers and to compute bids based on current prices and labor standards. In addition, each Vulcraft plant maintained its own Engineering Department to help customers with design problems or specifications. The Florence manager commented, "Here on the East Coast we have six or seven major competitors; of course none of them are as large as we are." He added, "It has been said to us by some of our competitors that in this particular industry we have the finest selling organization in the country."

Nucor aggressively sought to be the lowest cost producer in the industry. Materials and freight were two important elements of cost. Nucor maintained its own fleet of almost 150 trucks to ensure on time delivery to all of the states, although most business was regional due to transportation costs. Plants were located in rural areas near the markets they served. Nucor's move into steel production was a move to lower the cost of steel used by the joist business.

STEEL DIVISIONS

Nucor moved into the steel business in 1968 to provide raw material for the Vulcraft plants. Iverson said, "We got into the steel business because we wanted to build a mill that could make steel as cheaply as we were buying it from foreign importers or from offshore mills." Thus, they entered the industry using the new mini-mill technology after they took a task force of four people around the world to investigate new technological advancements. A case writer from Harvard recounted the development of the steel divisions:

> By 1967 about 60% of each Vulcraft sales dollar was spent on materials, primarily steel. Thus, the goal of keeping costs low made it imperative to obtain steel economically. In addition, in 1967 Vulcraft bought about 60% of its steel from foreign sources. As the Vulcraft Division grew, Nucor became concerned about its ability to obtain an adequate economical supply of steel and in 1968 began construction of its first steel mill in Darlington, South Carolina. By 1972 the Florence, South Carolina, joist plant was purchasing over 90% of its steel from this mill. The Fort Payne, Alabama plant bought about 50% of its steel from Florence. Since the mill had excess capacity, Nucor began to market its steel products to outside customers. In 1972, 75% of the shipments of Nucor steel were to Vulcraft and 25% were to other customers.

Between 1973 and 1981 they constructed three more bar mills and their accompanying rolling mills. Iverson explained in 1984:

> In constructing these mills we have experimented with new processes and new manufacturing techniques. We serve as our own general contractor and design and build much of our own equipment. In one or more of our mills we have built our own continuous casting unit, reheat furnaces, cooling beds and in Utah even our own mill stands. All of these to date have cost under $125 per ton of

annual capacity compared with projected costs for large integrated mills of $1,200–1,500 per ton of annual capacity, ten times our cost. Our mills have high productivity. We currently use <4 man hours to produce a ton of steel. Our total employment costs are less than $60 per ton compared with the average employment costs of the seven largest U. S. steel companies of close to $130 per ton. Our total labor costs are less than 20% of our sales price.

In 1987 Nucor was the first steel company in the world to begin to build a mini-mill to manufacture steel sheet, the raw material for the auto industry and other major manufacturers. This project opened up another 50% of the total steel market. The first plant in Crawfordsville, Indiana was successful and three additional sheet mills were constructed between 1989 and 1990. Through the years these steel plants were significantly modernized and expanded until the total capacity was 3 million tons per year at a capital cost of <$170 per ton by 1999. Nucor's total steel production capacity was 5.9 million tons per year at a cost of 300 dollars per ton of annual capacity. The eight mills, four bar mills and four sheet mills, sold 80% of their output to outside customers and the balance to other Nucor divisions.

A steel mill's work is divided into two phases: preparation of steel of the proper "chemistry" and the forming of the steel into the desired products. The typical mini mill utilized scrap steel, such as junk auto parts, instead of the iron ore, which would be used in larger, integrated steel mills. The typical bar mini mill had an annual capacity of 200–600 thousand tons, compared with the 7 million tons of Bethlehem Steel's integrated plant at Sparrow's Point, Maryland.

In the bar mills a charging bucket fed loads of scrap steel into electric arc furnaces. The melted load, called a heat, was poured into a ladle to be carried by overhead crane to the casting machine. In the casting machine the liquid steel was extruded as a continuous red hot solid bar of steel and cut into lengths weighing some 900 pounds called "billets." In the typical plant the billet, about four inches in cross section and about 20 feet long, was held temporarily in a pit where it cooled to normal temperatures. Periodically billets were carried to the rolling mill and placed in a reheat oven to bring them up to 2000°F at which temperance they would be malleable. In the rolling mill, presses and dies progressively converted the billet into the desired round bars, angles, channels, flats, and other products. After cutting to standard lengths, they were moved to the warehouse.

MANAGEMENT PHILOSOPHY

Aycock, while still the Darlington manager, stated,

"The key to making a profit when selling a product with no aesthetic value, or a product that you really can't differentiate from your competitors, is cost. I don't look at us as a fantastic marketing organization, even though I think we are pretty good; but we don't try to overcome unreasonable costs by mass marketing. We maintain low costs by keeping the employee force at the level it should be, not doing things that aren't necessary to achieve our goals, and allowing people to function on their own and by judging them on their results.

To keep a cooperative and productive workforce you need, number one, to be completely honest about everything; number two, to allow each employee as much as possible to make decisions about that employee's work, to find easier and more productive ways to perform duties; and number three, to be as fair as possible to all employees. Most of the changes we make in work procedures and in equipment come from the employees. They really know the problems of their jobs better than anyone else.

To communicate with my employees, I try to spend time in the plant and at intervals have meetings with the employees. Usually if they have a question they just visit me. Recently a small group visited me in my office to discuss our vacation policy. They had some suggestions and, after listening to them, I had to agree that the ideas were good."

In discussing his philosophy for dealing with the workforce, the Florence manager stated,

I believe very strongly in the incentive system we have. We are a non union shop and we all feel that the way to stay so is to take care of our people and show them we care. I think that's easily done because of our fewer layers of management… I spend a good part of my time in the plant, maybe an hour or so a day. If a man wants to know anything, for example an insurance question, I'm there and they walk right up to me and ask me questions, which I'll answer the best I know how.

We don't lay our people off and we make a point of telling our people this. In the slowdown of 1994, we scheduled our line for four days, but the men were allowed to come in the fifth day for maintenance work at base pay. The men in the plant on an average running bonus might make $17 to $19 an hour. If their base pay is half that, on Friday they would only get $8–$9 an hour. Surprisingly, many of the men did not want to come in on Friday. They felt comfortable with just working four days a week. They are happy to have that extra day off. About 20% of the people took the 5th day at base rate, but still no one had been laid off, in an industry with a strong business cycle.

In an earlier business cycle the executive committee decided in view of economic conditions that a pay freeze was necessary. The employees normally received an increase in their base pay the first of June. The decision was made at that time to freeze wages. The officers of the company, as a show of good faith, accepted a 5% pay cut. In addition to announcing this to the workers with a stuffer in their pay envelopes, meetings were held. Each production line, or incentive group of workers, met in the plant conference room with all supervision—foreman, plant production manager, and division manager. The economic crisis, the company was facing, was explained to the employees by the production manager and all of their questions were answered.

THE PERSONNEL POLICIES

The foremost characteristic of Nucor's personnel system was its incentive plan. Another major personnel policy was providing job security. Also all employees at Nucor received the same fringe benefits. There was only one group insurance plan. Holidays and vacations did not differ by job. Every child of every Nucor employee received up to $1,200 a year for four years if they chose to go on to higher education, including technical schools. The company had no executive dining rooms or restrooms, no fishing lodges, company cars, or reserved parking places.

Jim Coblin, Nucor's vice president of Human Resources at the time, described Nucor's systems for HR Magazine in a 1994 article, "No – frills HR at Nucor: a lean, bottom-line approach at this steel company empowers employees." Coblin, as benefits administrator, received part-time help from one of the corporate secretaries in the corporate office. The plants typically used someone from their finance department to handle compensation issues, although two plants had personnel generalists. Nucor plants did not have job descriptions, finding they caused more problems than they solved, given the flexible workforce and nonunion status of Nucor employees. Surprisingly, Coblin found performance appraisal a waste of time. If an employee was not performing well, the problem would be dealt with directly. The key, he believed, was not to put a maximum on what employee could earn and pay them directly for productivity. Iverson firmly believed that the bonus should be direct and involve no discretion on part of a manager.

Employees were kept informed about the company. Charts showing the division's results in return-on-assets and bonus payoff were posted in prominent places in the plant. The personnel manager commented that as he traveled around to all the plants, he found everyone in the company could tell him the level of profits in their division. The general managers held dinners at least once but usually twice a year with each of their employees. The dinners were held with 50 or 60 employees at a time, resulting in as many as 20 dinners per year. After introductory remarks the floor was open for discussion of any work related problems. There was a new employee orientation program and an employee handbook that contained personnel policies and rules. The corporate office sends all news releases to each division where they were posted on bulletin boards. Each employee in the company also received a copy of the Annual Report. For the last several years the cover of the Annual Report had contained the names of all Nucor employees.

Absenteeism and tardiness were not a problem at Nucor. Each employee had four days of absences before pay was reduced. In addition to these, missing work was allowed for jury duty, military leave, or the death of close relatives. After this, a day's absence cost them bonus pay for that week and lateness of more than a half-hour meant the loss of bonus for that day.

Safety was a concern of Nucor's critics. With ten fatalities in the 1980s, Nucor was committed to doing better. Safety administrators had appointed in each plant and safety had improved in the 1990s. The company also had a formal grievance procedure, although the Darlington manager couldn't recall the last grievance he had processed.

The average hourly worker's pay was over twice the average earnings paid by other manufacturing companies in the states where Nucor's plants were located. In many rural communities where Nucor had located, they provide better wages than most other manufacturers. The new plant in Hertford County illustrated this point as reported in a June 21, 1998 article in *The Charlotte Observer*, entitled "Hope on the horizon: in Hertford County, poverty reigns and jobs are scarce." Here the author wrote, "In North Carolina's forgotten northeastern corner, where poverty rates run more than twice the state average, Nucor's $300 million steel mill is a dream realized." The plant on the banks of the Chowan River in North Carolina's banks coastal district would have their employees earning a rumored $60,000 a year, three times the local average manufacturing wage upon completion. Nucor had recently begun developing its plant sites with the expectation of other companies co-locating to save shipping costs. Four companies have announced plans to locate close to Nucor's property, adding another 100 to 200 jobs. People couldn't believe such wages, but calls to the plant's chief financial officer got "we don't like to promise too much, but $60,000 might be a little low." The average wage for these jobs at Darlington was $70,000. The Plant's CFO added that Nucor didn't try to set pay "a buck over Wal-Mart" but went for the best workers. The article noted that steel work is hot and often dangerous, and that turnover at the plant may be high as people adjust to this and Nucor's hard-driving team system. He added, "Slackers don't last." The State of North Carolina had given $155 million in tax credits over 25 years. The local preacher said "In 15 years, Baron (a local child) will be making $75,000 a year at Nucor, not in jail. I have a place now I can hold in front of him and say 'Look, right here. This is for you.'"

In the early 2009 crisis, Nucor's unique policies with its employees were evident. Performance in 2008 had been good and $40 million in bonuses were still distributed, with an extra bonus on top because of the extraordinary year. The company paid $270 million in March in 2008 profit sharing. Gail Bruce, the new Vice-President of Human Resources, explained how Nucor had avoided the layoffs other plants experienced. First there was a history of open communications and a system designed to deal with the nature of the industry. Over the years there had been financial training for the workers explaining the cyclical nature of the industry. And if plants were idled, pay went automatically to a base pay which was about half the usual total income with bonuses. No one

was laid off and the well-paid workers could adapt, just like the company. He marveled, "The spirit in the operations is extraordinary." The cooperation extended to other solutions. Business Week reported "Work that used to be done by contractors, such as making special parts, mowing the lawns, and even cleaning the bathrooms, is now handled by Nucor staff. The bathrooms, managers say, was an employee suggestion." Business Week reported that DiMicco and other managers had received hundreds of cards and e-mails thanking them for caring about workers and their families.

THE INCENTIVE SYSTEM

There were four incentive programs at Nucor, one each for (1) production workers, (2) department heads, (3) staff people, such as accountants, secretaries, or engineers, and (4) senior management, which included the division managers (VP/General Managers of each division). All of these programs were based on group performance.

Within the production program, groups ranged in size from 25 to 30 people and had definable and measurable operations. The company believed that a program should be simple and that bonuses should be paid promptly. "We don't have any discretionary bonuses—zero. It is all based on performance. Now we don't want anyone to sit in judgment, because it never is fair ...," said Iverson. The personnel manager stated, "Their bonus is based on roughly 90% of historical time it takes to make a particular joist. If during a week they make joists at 60% less than the standard time, they receive a 60% bonus." The bonus was paid with the regular pay the following week. The complete pay check amount, including overtime, was multiplied by the bonus factor. A bonus was not paid when equipment was not operating: "We have the philosophy that when equipment is not operating everybody suffers and the bonus for downtime is zero." The foremen are also part of the group and received the same bonus as the employees they supervised.

The second incentive program was for department heads in the various divisions. The incentive pay here was based on division contribution, defined as the division earnings (net revenue) before corporate expenses and profit sharing are determined. Bonuses were reported to run between 0 and 90 % (averaging over 50%) of a person's base salary. The base salaries at this level were set at 75% of industry norms.

There was a third plan for people who were not production workers, department managers, or senior managers. Their bonuses were based on either the division return on assets or the corporate return on assets, depending on their unit. Bonuses were typically 30% or more of a person's base salary for corporate positions.

The fourth program was for the senior officers. This group had no employment contracts, pension or retirement plans, or other perquisites. Their base salaries were set at about 75% of what an individual doing similar work in other companies would receive. Once return on equity reached 9% (slightly below the average for manufacturing firms) 5% of net earnings before taxes went into a pool, which was divided among the officers based on their salaries. "Now if return on equity for the company reaches, say 20%, which it has, then we can wind up with as much as 190% of our base salaries and 115% on top of that in stock. We get both," the Personnel Director said half the bonus was paid in cash and half was deferred. Individual bonuses ranged from zero to several hundred percent, averaging 75% to 150%.

However, the opposite was true as well. In 1982 the return was 8% and the executives received no bonus. Iverson's pay in 1981 was approximately $300,000 but dropped the next year to $110,000. "I think that ranked by total compensation I was the lowest paid CEO in the Fortune 500. I was kind of proud of that, too." In his 1997 book, *Plain Talk: Lessons From a Business Maverick*, Iverson said, "Can management expect employees to be loyal if we lay them all off at every dip of the economy, while we go on padding our own pockets." Even so by 1986, Iverson's stock was worth over $10 million dollars and the former Vulcraft manager was a millionaire.

In lieu of a retirement plan, the company had a profit sharing plan with a deferred trust. Each year 10% of pretax earnings was put into profit sharing for all people below officer level. Twenty percent of this was set aside to be paid to employees in the following March as a cash bonus and the remainder was put into trust for each employee on the basis of percent of their earnings as a percent of total wages paid within the corporation. The employee was vested after the first year. Employees received a quarterly statement of their balance in profit sharing.

The company had an Employer Monthly Stock Investment Plan to which Nucor added 10% to the amount the employee contributed on the purchase of any Nucor stock and paid the commission. After each five years of service with the company, the employee received a service award consisting of five shares of Nucor stock. Moreover, if profits were good, extraordinary bonus payments would be made to the employees. For example, in December 1998 each employee received a $800 payment.

According to Iverson,

I think the first obligation of the company is to the stockholder and to its employees. I find in this country too many cases where employees are underpaid and corporate management is making huge social donations for self fulfillment. We regularly give donations, but we have a very interesting corporate policy. First, we give donations where our employees are. Second, we give donations that will benefit our employees, such as to the YMCA. It is a difficult area and it requires a lot of thought. There is certainly a strong social responsibility for a company, but it cannot be at the expense of the employees or the stockholders.

Having welcomed a parade of visitors over the years, Iverson had become concerned with the pattern apparent at other companies' steel plants: "They only do one or two of the things we do. It's not just incentives or the scholarship program; its all those things put together that results in a unified philosophy for the company."

BUILDING ON THEIR SUCCESS

Throughout the 1980s and 1990s Nucor continued to be a prime mover in steel as well as the industries vertically related to steel. For example in a seemingly risky move in 1986 Nucor began construction of a $25 million plant in Indiana to manufacture steel fasteners. Imports had grown to 90% of this market as U.S. companies failed to compete. Iverson said "We're going to bring that business back; we can make bolts as cheaply as foreign producers." A second plant, in 1995, gave Nucor 20% of the U.S. market for steel fasteners. Nucor also acquired a steel bearings manufacturer in 1986, which Iverson called "a good fit with our business, our policies and our people."

Also in 1986 Iverson announced plans for a revolutionary plant at Crawfordsville, Indiana, that would be the first mini-mill in the world to manufacture flat-rolled or sheet steel, the last bastion of the integrated manufacturers. This market alone was twice the size of the existing market for mini-mill products. It would be a quarter of a billion dollar gamble on a new technology. Nucor had spent millions trying to develop the process when it heard of some promising developments at a German company. In the spring of 1986, Aycock flew to

Germany to see the pilot machine at SMS Schloemann-Siemag AG. In December the Germans came to Charlotte for the first of what they thought would be many meetings to hammer out a deal with Nucor. Iverson shocked them when he announced Nucor was ready to proceed to build the first plant of its kind.

The gamble on the new plant paid off and Busse, the general manager of the plant, became a key man within Nucor. The new mill began operations in August of 1989 and reached 15% of capacity by the end of the year. In June of 1990 it had its first profitable month and Nucor announced the construction of a second plant in Arkansas. In 1994 the two existing sheet mills were expanded and a new $500 million 1.8 million ton sheet mill in South Carolina was announced, to begin operation in early 1997.

In 1987 in what the *New York Times* called their "most ambitious project yet," Nucor began a joint venture with Yamato Kogyo, Ltd. to make structural steel products in a mill on the Mississippi River in direct challenge to the Big Three integrated steel companies. He put John Correnti in charge of the operation. Correnti built and then became the general manager of Nucor-Yamato when it started up in 1988. In 1991 he surprised many people by deciding to double Nucor-Yamato's capacity by 1994. It became Nucor's largest division and the largest wide flange producer in the U.S. By 1995, Bethlehem Steel was the only other wide flange producer of structural steel products left and had plans to leave the business.

Nucor started up its first facility to produce metal buildings in 1987. A second metal buildings facility began operations in late 1996 in South Carolina and a new steel deck facility, in Alabama, was announced for 1997. At the end of 1997 the Arkansas sheet mill was undergoing a $120 million expansion to include a galvanizing facility.

The supply and cost of scrap steel to feed the mini-mills was an important future concern to Iverson. So at the first of 1993 Nucor announced the construction of plant in Trinidad to supply its mills with iron carbide pellets. The innovative plant would cost 60 million dollars and take a year and a half to complete. While other mini-mills were cutting deals to buy and sell abroad, Nucor was planning to ship iron from Brazil and process it in Trinidad.

In 1995 Nucor became involved in its first international joint venture to produce steel, an ambitious project with Brazil's Companhia Siderurgica National to build a $700 million steel mill in the state of Ceara.

Nucor set records for sales and net earnings in 1997. In the spring of 1998, as Iverson approached his 73rd birthday, he was commenting, "people ask me when I'm going to retire. I tell them our mandatory retirement age is 95, but I may change that when I get there." It surprised the world when, in October 1998, Ken Iverson left the board. He retired as Chairman at the end the year. Although sales for 1998 decreased 1% and net earnings were down 10%, the management made a number of long-term investments and closed draining investments. Start-up began at the new South Carolina steam mill and at the Arkansas sheet mill expansion. The plans for a North Carolina steel plate mill in Hertford were announced. This would bring Nucor's total steel production capacity to 12 million tons per year. Moreover, the plant in Trinidad, which had proven much more expensive than was originally expected, was deemed unsuccessful and closed. Finally, directors approved the repurchase of up to five million shares of Nucor stock.

Still, the downward trends at Nucor continued. Sales and earnings were down 3% and 7% respectively for 1999. However, these trends did not seem to affect the company's investments. Expansion was underway in the steel mills and a third building systems facility was under construction in Texas. Nucor was actively searching for a site for a joist plant in the Northeast. A letter of intent was signed with Australian and Japanese companies to form a joint venture to commercialize the strip casting technology. To understand the challenges facing Nucor, industry, technology and environmental trends in the 1980s and 1990s had to be considered.

EVOLUTION OF THE U.S. STEEL INDUSTRY

The early 1980's had been the worst years in decades for the steel industry. Data from the American Iron and Steel Institute showed shipments falling from 100-million tons in 1979 to the mid-80 levels in 1980 and 1981. A slackening in the economy, particularly in auto sales, led the decline. In 1986, when industry capacity was at 130-million tons, the outlook was for a continued decline in per-capita consumption and movement toward capacity in the 90–100-millionton range. The Chairman of Armco saw "millions of tons chasing a market that's not there: excess capacity that must be eliminated."

The large, integrated steel firms, such as U.S. Steel and Armco, which made up the major part of the industry, were the hardest hit. *The Wall Street Journal* stated, "The decline has resulted from such problems as high labor and energy costs in mining and processing iron ore, a lack of profits and capital to modernize plants, and conservative management that has hesitated to take risks." These companies produced a wide range of steels, primarily from ore processed in blast furnaces. They had found it difficult to compete with imports, usually from Japan, and had given market share to imports. They sought the protection of import quotas.

Imported steel accounted for 20% of the U.S. steel consumption, up from 12% in the early 1970s. The U.S. share of world production of raw steel declined from 19 to 14% over the period. *Iron Age* stated that exports, as a percent of shipments in 1985, were 34% for Nippon, 26% for British Steel, 30% for Krupp, 49% for USINOR of France, and less than 1% for every American producer on the list. The consensus of steel experts was that imports would average 23% of the market in the last half of the 1980s.

By the mid 1980s the integrated mills were moving fast to get back into the game: they were restructuring, cutting capacity, dropping unprofitable lines, focusing products, and trying to become responsive to the market. The industry made a pronounced move toward segmentation. Integrated producers focused on mostly flat-rolled and structural grades, reorganized steel companies focused on a limited range of products, mini-mills dominated the bar and light structural product areas, and specialty steel firms sought niches. There was an accelerated shutdown of older plants, elimination of products by some firms, and the installation of new product line with new technologies by others.

The American Iron and Steel Institute reported steel production in 1988 of 99.3 million tons, up from 89.2 in '87, and the highest in seven years. As a result of modernization programs, 60.9% of production was from continuous casters. Exports for steel increased and imports fell. Some steel experts believed the U.S. was now cost competitive with the Japan. However, 1989 proved to be a year of "waiting for the other shoe to drop," according to *Metal Center News*. U.S. steel production was hampered by a new recession, the expiration of the voluntary import restraints, and labor negotiations in several companies. Declines in car production and consumer goods hit flat-rolled hard. AUJ Consultants told MCN, "The U.S. steel market has peaked. Steel consumption is tending down. By 1990, we expect total domestic demand to dip under 90 million tons."

The economic slowdown of the early 1990's did lead to a decline in the demand for steel through early 1993, but by 1995 America was in its best steel market in 20 years and many companies were building new flat-roll mini-mills. A *Business Week* article at the time described it as "the race of the Nucor look-alikes." Six years after Nucor pioneered the low-cost German technology in Crawfordsville, Indiana, the competition was finally gearing up to compete. Ten new projects were expected to add 20 million tons per year of the flat-rolled steel, raising U.S. capacity by as much as 40% by 1998. These mills opened in 1997 just as the industry was expected to move into a cyclical slump. It was no surprise that worldwide competition increased and companies that had previously focused on their home markets began a race to become global powerhouses. The foreign push was new for U.S. firms who had focused on defending their home markets. U.S. mini-mills focused their international expansion primarily in Asia and South America. In the 1990's integrated mills market share fell to around 40%, while mini-mills share rose to 23%, reconstructed mills increased their share from 11% to 28%, and specialized mills increased their share from 1% to 6%.

In late 1997 and again in 1998 the decline in demand prompted Nucor and other U.S. companies to slash prices in order to compete with the unprecedented surge of imports. By the last quarter of 1998 these imports had led to the filing of unfair trade complaints with U.S. trade regulators, causing steel prices in the spot market to drop sharply in August and September before they stabilized. A press release by the U.S. Secretary of Commerce, William Daley, stated "I will not stand by and allow U.S. workers, communities and companies to bear the brunt of other nations' problematic policies and practices. We are the most open economy of the world. But we are not the world's dumpster."

The Commerce Department concluded in March 1999 that six countries had illegally dumped stainless steel in the U.S. at prices below production costs or home market prices. The Commerce Department found that Canada, South Korea, and Taiwan were guilty only of dumping, while Belgium, Italy, and South Africa also gave producers unfair subsidies that effectively lowered prices. However, on June 23, 1999, *The Wall Street Journal* reported that the Senate decisively shut off an attempt to restrict U.S. imports of steel despite industry complaints that a flood of cheap imports were driving them out of business. Advisors of President Clinton were reported to have said the President would likely veto the bill if it passed. Administrative officials opposed the bill because it would violate international trade law and leave the U.S. open to retaliation.

As the 90s ended, Nucor was the second-largest steel producer in the U.S., behind USX. The company's market capitalization was about two times that of the next smaller competitor. Even in a tight industry, someone can win. Nucor was in the best position because the industry was very fragmented and there are many marginal competitors.

MANAGEMENT EVOLUTION

Only five, not six, members of the Board were in attendance during the Board of Directors meeting in the fall of 1998, due to the death of Jim Cunningham. Near its end, Aycock read a motion, drafted by Siegel, that Ken Iverson be removed as Chairman. It was seconded by Hlavacek and passed. It was announced in October that Iverson would be a chairman emeritus and a director, but after disagreements Iverson left the company completely. It was agreed Iverson would receive five hundred thousand dollars a year for five years. Aycock left retirement to become Chairman.

The details of Iverson's leaving did not become known until June of 1999 when John Correnti resigned after disagreements with the Board and Aycock took his place. All of this was a complete surprise to investors and brought the stock price down 10%. Siegel commented "the board felt Correnti was not the right person to lead Nucor into the 21st century." Aycock assured everyone he would be happy to move back into retirement as soon as replacements could be found.

Aycock moved to increase the corporate office staff by adding a level of Executive Vice President's over four areas of business and adding two specialist jobs in strategic planning and steel technology. When Siegel retired, Aycock promoted Terry Lisenby to CFO and Treasurer, and hired a Director of IT to report to Lisenby (see Figure 2 for the organization chart in 2000).

Jim Coblin, Vice President of Human Resources, believed the additions to management were necessary, "It's not bad to get a little more like other companies." He noted that the various divisions did their business cards and plant signs differently; some did not even want a

| Figure 2 | Nucor Organization Chart |

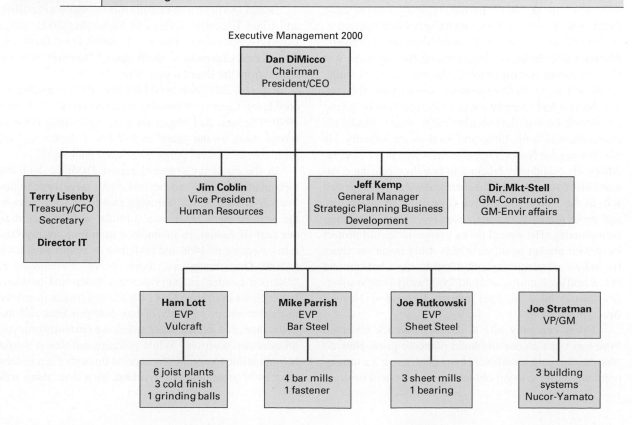

Executive Management 2000

Dan DiMicco
Chairman
President/CEO

Terry Lisenby
Treasury/CFO
Secretary

Director IT

Jim Coblin
Vice President
Human Resources

Jeff Kemp
General Manager
Strategic Planning Business
Development

Dir.Mkt-Stell
GM-Construction
GM-Envir affairs

Ham Lott
EVP
Vulcraft

Mike Parrish
EVP
Bar Steel

Joe Rutkowski
EVP
Sheet Steel

Joe Stratman
VP/GM

6 joist plants
3 cold finish
1 grinding balls

4 bar mills
1 fastener

3 sheet mills
1 bearing

3 building
systems
Nucor-Yamato

Nucor sign. Sometimes six different Nucor salesmen would call on the same customer. "There is no manager of human resources in the plants, so at least we needed to give additional training to the person who does most of that work at the plant," he stated. With these new additions there would be a director of information technology and two important committees, one for environmental issues and the second for audit.

He believed the old span of control of 20 might have worked well when there was less competition. Aycock considered it "ridiculous." "It was not possible to properly manage, to know what was going own. The top managers have totally lost contact with the company." Coblin was optimistic the use of Executive Vice Presidents would improve management. The three meetings of the general managers had slowly increased from about 1½ days to about 2½ days and become more focused. The new EVP positions would bring a perspective above the level of the individual plants. Instead of 15 individual detailed presentations, each general manager would give a short, five-minute briefing and then there would be an in-depth presentation on the Group, with team participation. After some training by Lisenby, the divisions had recently done a pretty good job with a SWOT analysis. Coblin thought these changes would make Nucor a stronger global player.

To Jeff Kemp, the new General Manager of Strategic Planning and Business Development, the big issue was how to sustain earnings growth. In the U.S. steel industry there were too many marginal competitors. The U.S. government had recently added to the problem by giving almost a billion dollars to nine mills, which simply allowed them to limp along and weaken the industry. He was looking for Nucor's opportunities within the steel industry. He asked why Nucor had bought a bearing company. His experience in the chemical industry suggested a need for Nucor to establish a position of superiority and grow globally, driving industry competition rather than reacting. He argued that a company should protect its overall market position, which could mean sacrifices for individual plants. Aycock liked Kemp's background in law and accounting, and had specifically sought someone from outside the steel industry to head up Nucor's strategic planning.

"Every company hits a plateau," Aycock observed "you can't just go out and build plants to grow. How do you step up to the next level? I wouldn't say it's a turning point but we have to get our strategic vision and strategic plans." He stated, "we are beginning Nucor's first ever strategic planning sessions, it was not necessary before."

Aycock believed Nucor needed to be quick to recognize developing technology in all production areas. He noted the joint venture to develop a new "strip caster," which would cast the current flat-rolled material in a more finished form. The impact could be "explosive," allowing Nucor to build smaller plants closer to markets. This would be particularly helpful on the West Coast. Nucor would own the U.S. and Brazilian rights, their partners the rest. He was also looking forward to the next generation of steel mills and wanted to own the rights, this time. He praised Iverson's skill at seeing technology and committing to it.

He was very interested in acquisitions, but "they must fit strategically." A bar mill in the upper central Midwest and a flat-rolled plant in the Northeast would be good. A significant opportunity existed in preengineered buildings. Aycock intended to concentrate on steel for the next five to six years, achieving an average growth rate of 15% per year. In about seven years he would like to see Nucor ready to move into other areas. He said Nucor had already "picked the low hanging grapes" and must be careful in its next moves.

Daniel DiMicco assumed the role of Nucor's President and Chief Executive Officer in September 2000, when David Avcock stepped down as planned. Peter Browning was elected Chairman of the Board of Directors. Aycock retired from the Board a year later.

Sales for 2000 increased 14% over 1999 to reach a record level. Earnings were also at record levels, 27% over 1999. The year had begun on a strong footing but had turned weak by the years' end. While Nucor remained profitable other steel companies faced bankruptcy.

In the company's annual report DiMicco laid out their plans for 2000 and beyond: "Our targets are to deliver an average annual earnings growth of 10–15% over the next 10 years, to deliver a return well in excess of our cost of capital, to maintain a minimum average return on equity of 14% and to deliver to return on sales a 8–10%. Our strategy will focus on Nucor becoming a, "'Market Leader' in every product group and business in which we compete. This calls for significant increases in market share for many of our core products and the maintenance of market share where we currently enjoyed a leadership position." While pointing out that it would be impossible to obtain this success through the previous strategy of greenfield construction, he added "there will now be a heavy focus on growth through acquisitions. We will also continue growing through the commercialization of new disruptive and leapfrog technologies."

THE EVOLUTION OF STEEL IN THE TWENTY-FIRST CENTURY

By October 2001, more than 20 steel companies in the U.S., including Bethlehem Steel Corp. and LTV Corp., the nations' third and fourth largest steel U.S. steel producers, respectively, had filed for bankruptcy protection. Over a dozen producers were operating under Chapter 11 bankruptcy-law protection, which allows them to maintain market share by selling steel cheaper than non-Chapter 11 steel makers. On October 20, 2001 *The Economist* noted that of the 14 steel companies followed by Standard & Poor, only Nucor was indisputably healthy. In the fall of 2001 25% of domestic steel companies were in bankruptcy proceedings, although the U.S. was the largest importer of steel in the world. Experts believed that close to half of the U.S. steel industry might be forced to close before conditions improved.

In 2001 the world steel industry found itself in the middle of one of its most unprofitable and volatile periods ever, in part due to a glut of steel that had sent prices to 20-year lows. While domestic steel producers were mired in red ink, many foreign steel-makers desperately needed to continue to sell in the relatively open U.S. market to stay profitable. The industry was hovering around 75% capacity utilization, a level too low to be profitable for many companies. New mega-steel makers could out-muscle U.S. competitors, which were less efficient, smaller and financially weaker than their competitors in Asia and Europe. At this time the largest U.S. steel maker, USX-U.S. Steel Group, was only the 11th largest producer in the world. Furthermore, while in 1990 mini-mills accounted for 36% of the domestic steel market, by 2000 the more efficient mini-mill had seized 50% of the market and the resulting competition had driven prices lower for integrated steel as well as mini-mills.

The year 2001 turned out to be one of the worst years ever for steel. There was 9/11, a recession, and a surge of imports. DiMicco broke with Nucor's traditional opposition to government intervention to make a major push for protective tariffs. He stated, "The need to enforce trade rules is similar to the need to enforce any other law. If two merchants have stores side by side, but one sells stolen merchandise at a vast discount, we know that it's

time for the police to step in." In March 2002 President Bush, after an investigation and recommendation by the ITC, imposed anti-dumping tariffs under section 201 of the Trade Act of 1974. This restricted some imports of steel and placed quotas of up to 30% on others. The move was opposed by many, including steel users. Columnist George Will in his editorial on March 10, 2002 criticized Bush for abandoning free-trade and pointed out that protection would hamper the necessary actions to restructure the steel industry in America by reducing excess capacity. The European Union immediately threatened reprisals and appealed to the WTO. In December China imposed its own 3-year program of import duties.

During 2003 prices of steel rose in the U.S. and Asia as global demand outpaced supply. China, with its booming economy, drove the market. An article in *Wall Street Journal*, October 15, quoted Guy Dolle, chief executives of Arcelor SA of Luxembourg, the world's largest steel maker in terms of steel product shipped, as saying "China is the wild card in the balance between supply and demand." World prices did not soar dangerously because the steel industry continued to be plagued by overcapacity. Yet steel-hungry China and other fast-growing nations added to their steel capacity. By February 2004, a growing coalition of U.S. steel producers and consumers were considering whether to petition to limit soaring exports of scrap steel from the U.S., the world's largest producer of steel scrap. One result was that the International Steel Group (ISG) replaced Nucor as the most profitable U.S. steel producer. ISG was created when investor Wilbur Ross acquired the failing traditional steel producers in America, including LTV, Bethlehem, and Weirton. These mills used iron ore rather than scrap steel.

Global competition continued. According to the *Wall Street Journal*, Posco steelworks in Pohang, South Korea enjoyed the highest profits in the global steel industry as of 2004. Moreover, *Business Week* reported that the company had developed a new technology called Finex, which turned coal and iron ore into iron without coking and sintering and was expected to cut production costs by nearly a fifth and harmful emissions by 90%. They had also expanded their 80 Korean plants by investing in 14 Chinese joint ventures. By December 2004 demand in China had slowed and it had become a net steel exporter, sparking concerns of global oversupply.

Global consolidation also continued. In October 2004 London's Mittal family announced that they would merge their Ispat International NV with LNM Group and ISG, to create the world's largest steel maker, with estimated annual revenue of $31.5 billion and output of 57 million tons. This would open a new chapter for the industry's consolidation, which had been mostly regional. Although the world's steel industry remains largely fragmented with the world's top 10 steelmakers supplying less than 30% of global production, Mittal Steel would have about 40% of the U.S. market in flat-rolled steel. Moreover Mittal, which had a history of using its scale to buy lower-cost raw materials and import modern management techniques into previously inefficient state-run mills, was buying ISG, a U.S. company which already owned the lowest-cost, highest profit mills in the U.S.

Globally steel mergers and acquisitions boomed during 2006–2008. For example, Arcelor SA took over Canadian steelmaker Dofasco Inc. for $4.85 billion in March 2006, followed by their merger in June with Mittal Steel Co. NV to create the world's largest steel company. In January 2007 Russian steelmaker Evraz SA acquired Oregon Steel Mills, a Portland based producer of specialty steel, for $2.3 billion and in March, Indian-based Tata Steel Ltd. completed its acquisition of UK-based Corus Group Plc for $12.4 billion. SSAB Svenskt Stal AB of Sweden completed its acquisition of IPSCO Inc. of Lisle, Illinois, for $7.7 billion in July 2007 and in October Steel Dynamics completed the acquisition of privately held OmniSource Corp., a scrap processor and trading company. In May 2008 OAO Severstal, a Russian-based steel company acquired ArcelorMittal's Sparrow Point steel plant in Maryland and in June they outbid Essar Steel Holdings Ltd., an India-based steel company for Esmark Inc. Also in June 2008 Tangsham Iron & Steel Group merged with Handan Iron & Steel Group; the new company called Hebei Iron & Steel Group Co. surpassed Baosteel Group Co. as China's largest steel producer. Despite all the transactions in 2006, 2007, and 2008, the industry remained fragmented, both domestically and internationally and more mergers were expected.

Future merger activity was expected to differ slightly as steel companies attempted to become more vertically integrated. Examples were integration forward with Esmark's service center's combination with Wheeling-Pittsburgh's steel production and integration backward into scrap with the takeover of OmniSource by Steel Dynamics in 2007 and Nucor's acquisition of David J. Joseph Co. in 2008. These represented a trend toward becoming less dependent on outside vendors. This

was due to the rising cost of scrap, which jumped from $185/tons in January 2006 to $635/ton in June 2008, and the highly concentrated nature of iron ore sources.

U.S. steelmakers saw a major transition in 2008. In the first quarter the combination of higher volume and increased prices led to a sizable gain in profits. At the end of July major U.S. steel makers' results were still supported by months of steel-price increases, which eased the burden of rising raw materials prices, as demand from emerging markets kept global steel supplies tight. However, in September 2008 steelmakers in the U.S. experienced a sharp pullback from buyers who were concerned with the credit crisis and a slowdown in automobile and construction markets. This caused inventories to rise and prices on some key products to drop 10%. The *Wall Street Journal* reported on November 17 that "Metals prices fell 35% in just four weeks last month-the steepest decline ever recorded, according to Barclays Capital." They also reported that big steel makers world-wide were cutting production as much as 35% and that U.S. Steel Corp. planned to lay off 2% of its work force. Chinese demand also slowed. This was a swift reversal in an industry that saw its profits increase 20-fold in five years. The pricing volatility was intensified by the global financial crisis as many hedge funds, pension funds, and other investors desperate to raise cash rapidly sold their commodities holdings. Still, the article said that ultimately the industry's problems were rooted in weakened demand, particularly in China, rather than the financial crisis.

In 2009, the producer price index for steel products in the U.S. fell 25.1%. This was due to the decrease in demand for steel resulting from the global financial crisis. Key markets (construction, industrial equipment, and durable consumer products) were hurt by the recession and fixed investment was hampered by tight credit conditions. Demand for certain steel products was propped up some by large public stimulus money for infrastructure. U.S. steel mills responded by cutting production 36.4% between 2008 and 2009. The domestic price of steel had exhibited high volatility because of exposure to world steel prices and exchange rate fluctuations.

As 2010 began, a recovery was expected and U.S. steel prices rose as demand for steel increased. Companies ramped up production but prices fell again in July when demand did not materialize. Despite predictions that world steel prices would remain weak for the rest of 2010. According to The World Steel Association 115 million metric tons (mmt) of crude steel was produced by 66 countries in July 2010, up 9.6% from

July 2009. Production was up 2.2% in China, 20.4% in Japan, 11.5% in Russia, and 32.9% in the U.S. However, the crude steel capacity utilization ratio of the 66 countries in July 2010 declined 5.3% in June 2010, but was 2.7% higher than in July 2009.

NUCOR STEEL IN THE TWENTY-FIRST CENTURY

Years 2000 to 2010 were some of the industry's rockiest times and yet Nucor had almost doubled its size (see Appendix A, B, and C), primarily through acquisitions, and even during the dark says of 2009 did not lay off any of its employees.

While many steel companies floundered, Nucor was able to take advantage of the weakened conditions. In March 2001, Nucor made its first acquisition in 10 years, purchasing a mini-mill in New York from Sumitomo Corp. Nucor had hired about five people to help plan for future acquisitions. DiMicco commented "it's taken us three years before our team has felt this is the right thing to do and get started making acquisitions." In the challenged industry, he argued it would be cheaper to buy than build plants. They purchased the assets of Auburn Steel, which gave them a merchant bar presence in the Northeast and helped the new Vulcraft facility in New York. They acquired ITEC Steel, a leader in the emerging load bearing light gauge steel framing market and saw an opportunity to aggressively broaden its market. Nucor increased its sheet capacity by roughly one third when it acquired the assets of Trico Steel Co. in Alabama for $120 million. In early 2002, they acquired the assets of Birmingham Steel Corp. The $650 million purchase of four mini-mills was the largest acquisition in Nucor's history. However, 2002 also proved to be a difficult year for Nucor. While they increased their steelmaking capacity by more than 25%, revenue increased 11%, and earnings improved 43% over weak 2001, their other financial goals were not met.

This did not stop Nucor from continuing their expansion through acquisitions to increase their market share and capacity in steel, and by actively working on new production processes that would provide them with technological advantages. They acquired the U.S. and Brazilian rights to the promising Castrip process for strip casting, the process of directly casting thin sheet steel. After development work on the process in Indiana they began full-time production in May 2002 and produced 7000 tons in the last 10 months of 2002.

Moreover, in April Nucor entered into a joint venture with a Brazilian mining company, CVRD, the world's largest producer of iron-ore pellets, to jointly develop low-cost iron-based products. Success with this effort would give them the ability to make steel by combining iron ore and coke rather than using scrap steel which was becoming less available.

When 2003 ended Nucor struck a positive note by reminding their investors that they had been profitable every single quarter since beginning operations in 1966. But while Nucor set records for both steel production and steel shipments, net earnings declined 61%. While the steel industry struggled, Nucor increased its market share and held on to profitability. They worked on expanding their business with the automotive industry, continued their joint venture in Brazil to produce pig iron, and pursued a joint venture with the Japanese and Chinese to make iron without the usual raw materials.

In 2004 and 2005 Nucor continued its aggressive geographic expansion and introduction of new products. For example, Nuconsteel ("Nucon"), a wholly owned subsidiary of Nucor which specialized in load bearing light gauge steel framing systems for commercial and residential construction markets, introduced two new low-cost automated fabrication systems for residential construction. And in March 2005, Nucor formed a joint venture with Lennar Corporation, named Nextframe, LP to provide comprehensive light gauge steel framing for residential construction. Nucor's 25% joint venture with the Rio Tinto Group, Mitsubishi Corporation and Chinese steel maker Shougang Corporation for a HIsmelt commercial plant in Kwinana, Western Australia started up in 2005. In 2004 Nucor acquired assets of an idled direct-reduced iron (DRI) plant in Louisiana and moved them to Trinidad. By December 2006 construction was completed and by 2008 Nu-Iron Unlimited produced 1,400,000 metric tons of DRI from Brazilian iron ore for the U.S.

By 2005, Nucor had 16 steel facilities producing three times as much as in 1999. The number of bar mills had grown to nine mills with capacity of 6,000,000 tons by the addition of Birmingham's four mills with 2,000,000 tons and Auburn's 400,000 tons. The sheet mills grew to four and increased capacity one-third with the acquisition of Trico. Nucor–Yamato's structural steel capacity was increased by half a million tons from the South Carolina plant. A new million ton plate mill, their second, had opened in North Carolina in 2000. Ninety-three percent of production was sold to outside customers.

By 2006 DiMicco had made many acquisitions while still managing to instill Nucor's unique culture in the new facilities. A *Business Week* article in May 2006 stated Nucor's culture and compensation system had changed very little since the 1990s. Michael Arndt reported that "Nucor gave out more than $220 million in profit sharing and bonuses to the rank and file in 2005. The average Nucor steelworker took home nearly $79,000 last year. Add to that a $2,000 one-time bonus to mark the company's record earnings and almost $18,000, on average, in profit sharing." He also noted that executive pay was still geared toward team building as "The bonus of a plant manager, a department manager's boss, depends on the entire corporation's return on equity. So there's no glory in winning at your plant if the others are failing."

In March of 2007, Nucor acquired Harris Steel Group Inc. of Canada for $1.06 billion in cash, adding 770,000 tons of rebar fabrication capacity and over 350,000 tons of capacity in other downstream steel products. This acquisition showed that Nucor saw growth opportunities in finishing steel products for its customers and in distribution rather than additional steelmaking capacity. While many large steel companies were buying other primary steelmakers around the world, Nucor was focusing its investments largely in North America's manufacturing infrastructure such as reinforced steel bars, platform grating and wire mesh for construction products ranging from bridges to airports and stadiums which according to Dan DiMicco "significantly advances Nucor's downstream growth initiatives." Through the acquisition of Harris, Nucor also acquired a 75% interest in Novosteel S. A., a Swiss-based steel trading company which matched buyers and sellers of steel products on a global basis and offered its customers logistics support, material handling, quality certifications, and schedule management. The Harris team was operating as a growth platform within Nucor and had completed several acquisitions. Nucor made several other acquisitions and some internal organic growth, increased Nucor's cold finish and drawn products' capacity by over 75% from 490,000 tons in 2006 to 860,000 tons at the end of 2007.

Harris kept its name, as a Nucor subsidiary, and was led by the previous Chairman and CEO John Harris. However, the Harris board consisted of Harris and three Nucor representatives. This was the first time Nucor had broken from its non-union tradition, as about half of Harris's 3,000 employees belonged to a mix of iron-workers, auto-workers, and steel workers unions. As Timna Tanners, a steel analyst in New York said, "It's definitely a stretch for Nucor, culturally, since they have managed to keep its other operations non-union by offering higher salaries and production incentives. But there are not many non-union options left in North America when it comes to acquisitions and expansion."

Nucor continued to invest in other downstream and upstream businesses (see Figure 3 for the organization chart in 2009). In the third quarter of 2007 they completed the acquisition of Magnatrax Corporation, a leading provider of custom-engineering metal buildings, for $275.2 million in cash. The Magnatrax acquisition, when combined with their existing Building Systems divisions and a newly constructed Buildings Systems division in Brigham City Utah, made Nucor the second largest metal building producer in the U.S., more than doubling their annual capacity to 480,000 tons of pre-engineered metal buildings.

In 2007, Nucor's seven Vulcraft facilities supplied more than 40% of total domestic buildings using steel joists and joist girders. In both 2006 and 2007 99% of its steel requirements were obtained from Nucor bar mills. Nucor nine steel deck plants supplied almost 30% of total domestic sales in decking, six of these plants were constructed by Nucor adjacent to Vulcraft joist facilities and three were acquired in November 2006 as a wholly owned subsidiary called Verco Decking. These decking plants obtained 99% of their steel requirements from Nucor sheet plants in 2006 but only 76% in 2007.

In March 2008, Nucor completed the acquisition of the David J. Joseph Company, the largest broker of ferrous and nonferrous scrap in the U.S. and one of the nation's largest processors of ferrous scrap for $1.44 billion. The company had been a supplier of scrap to Nucor since 1969. DJJ operated over 30 scrap processing facilities. This acquisition expanded Nucor's scrap-processing capabilities to four million short tons from 500,000 and provided them additional steelmaking raw materials through their brokerage operations, and rail services and logistics through its private fleet of some 2,000 scrap-related railcars. This allowed them to capture further margins in the steelmaking supply chain and to more closely control their raw-materials inputs. In May, they announced a plan to raise $3 billion for expansions and acquisitions, two-thirds to come from selling 25 million new shares. Nucor stopped making acquisitions in 2008 following their acquisition of 50% interest in a steel operation in Italy, due to the economic reversal that took place globally.

In 2009 Nucor's sales were down 53% and earnings per share dropped 116%. Steel production decreased 32%.

Figure 3   Nucor Organization Chart

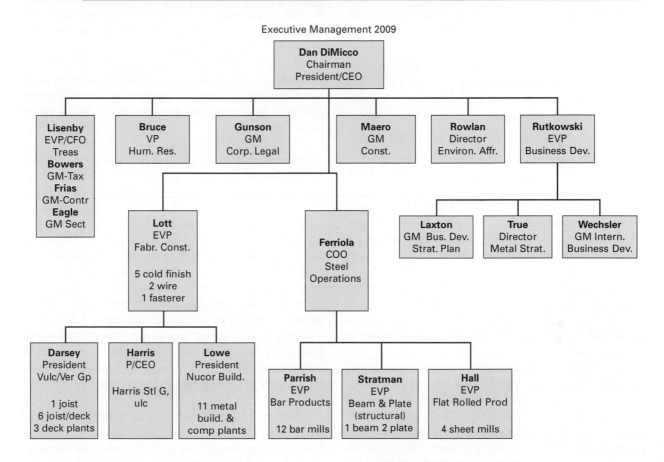

Executive Management 2009

Dan DiMicco
Chairman
President/CEO

Lisenby
EVP/CFO
Treas
Bowers
GM-Tax
Frias
GM-Contr
Eagle
GM Sect

Bruce
VP
Hum. Res.

Gunson
GM
Corp. Legal

Maero
GM
Const.

Rowlan
Director
Environ. Affr.

Rutkowski
EVP
Business Dev.

Lott
EVP
Fabr. Const.

5 cold finish
2 wire
1 fasterer

Ferriola
COO
Steel
Operations

Laxton
GM Bus. Dev.
Strat. Plan

True
Director
Metal Strat.

Wechsler
GM Intern.
Business Dev.

Darsey
President
Vulc/Ver Gp

1 joist
6 joist/deck
3 deck plants

Harris
P/CEO

Harris Stl G,
ulc

Lowe
President
Nucor Build.

11 metal
build. &
comp plants

Parrish
EVP
Bar Products

12 bar mills

Stratman
EVP
Beam & Plate
(structural)

1 beam 2 plate

Hall
EVP
Flat Rolled Prod

4 sheet mills

Vulcraft's production was down 46%. Nucor cut capital expenditures by 62%. Net earnings per share fell from a record $5.98 in 2008 to a low of $.94 in 2009. In addition to the collapse of sales, the company was hurt by commodity contracts based on the pre-recession prices. In their annual report they said that "2009 was one of the most tumultuous and difficult periods in Nucor's history."

As 2010 began, they expressed concern with the government response, noting that Nucor, and others, received no help from the "stimulus" money. They were concerned about recent legislative and regulatory proposals related to climate change and new interpretations of existing laws. They worried these might create new financial risks and competitive disadvantages for U.S. companies by increasing energy costs as well as the costs

of compliance, capital investment, and operation. They noted the challenges at their Louisiana iron-making plant where they were trying to develop alternatives to scrap steel but had been delayed by extended permitting processes and proposed climate change legislation.

UNCERTAINTY INTO THE TWENTY SECOND CENTURY

Although the global economic crisis resulted in a dramatic reduction in demand for steel, sending industry revenue plummeting 50.1% in 2009, it rebounded in 2010 and 2011 as prices recovered when demand for the industry's major markets bounced back. However, because near-term economic growth in Europe and the

U.S. remained uncertain, steel prices dropped again in 2012 hurting revenue. As the economy began to show sustained signs of improvement in 2013, steel prices were set to climb again.

In 2013 four major competitors had 54.3% of the U.S. market, down from 59.4% in 2010:

	2010	2013
AcelorMittal (Luxembourg based) with 18 plants	20.5%	19.7%
Nucor (U.S.) with 22 plants	19.9%	17.1%
United States Steel Corporation (U.S.) with 5 plants	13.0%	12.4%
AK Steel Holding Corporation (U.S.)	6.0%	5.1%

Increased international competition will characterize the next five years for the U.S. Steel industry. Frequent merger and acquisition activity is expected to reduce the number of enterprises operating in the U.S., but not as rapidly as it has over the past five years. Over the next five years to 2018, increases in steel prices are expected to drive revenue growth at a projected average annual rate of 3.5% to $142.3 billion. However, this growth is minimal compared to the iron and steel industries in competing nations.

The industry is increasingly globalized by the growing number of foreign-owned operations and the expanding U.S. presence in operations overseas. Acquisitions of foreign operations is attractive to U.S. producers because of the lower costs associated with operating steel production facilities in certain countries. This trend, flat domestic demand and frequent mergers, has reduced the number of domestic firms. During the five years leading to 2013, the number of firms has decreased at an average rate of 5.1%, to 435, largely due to the declines during the recession when more than 100 companies exited the industry. During this same period large profitable companies acquired their struggling competitors.

Conditions will likely remain challenging for many higher-cost steel manufacturers, such as operators of blast furnaces that contend with high variable costs due to labor and raw materials and their need for large-scale production to contain average costs. On the other hand, operators of electric arc furnaces and minimills have facilities that are generally less labor intensive and more flexible. Their share of industry production is 62% and expected to increase slightly throughout the next five years. This increasing dominance of electric arc furnaces, which require fewer workers, will continue to cut into industry employment. Larger firms that can leverage their iron and coal supply connections, either through contracts or vertical integration, are likely to enjoy higher profits.

By 2018, IBISWorld projects that the industry's average profit margin will reach 8.6% of revenue, slightly higher than the estimated 8.5% in 2013. Merger and acquisition activity is expected to continue as +a means to improve profitability, with the number of firms projected to fall at an annualized rate of 3.8% to 358 by 2018.

These small U.S. steel gains will pale in comparison to steel production growth in emerging economies, especially China and India. China already leads the world in steel production and its dominance is expected to grow. Over the next five years, import values are expected to grow at an average annual rate of 3.3%, while export values increase at an average annual rate of 4.5%. Eventually the growth in steel imports are expected to outpace growth in steel exports, as foreign producers with a cost advantage increasingly meet steel demand in the U.S.

As Dan DiMicco handed over the leadership of Nucor in 2013, he said, "When I became CEO, it was hard to hear what I had to say over the forces of all the skeptics. Nucor's best days were behind us, they said. Other companies were adopting the Nucor way and eliminating our edge." But he didn't buy that; he had succeeded.

He expected the same in the years ahead: "To achieve our goal, we said we would build on Nucor's strengths: product diversity, market leadership positions, a low and variable cost structure, financial strength, technological innovation, and, most importantly our unique Nucor culture." Still, it remains to be seen if this U.S. company will continue to prosper.

Case 11

Intel Corporation: 1968–2013

Charles W.L. Hill

School of Business, University of Washington
Seattle, WA 981095, June 2013

INTRODUCTION

In 2012 Intel was the leading manufacturer of microprocessors for personal computers in the world, a position that it had held onto for more than two decades. Over 80% of all personal computers sold in 2012 used Intel microprocessors. The company reported revenues of $53 billion and net profits of $11 billion. Meanwhile, Intel's only viable competitor, AMD, which in the early 2000s had been gaining share from Intel, lost $1.2 billion on sales of $5.4 billion.

Despite its historic dominance, the future looked uncertain for Intel. The rise of mobile devices had led to a strong substitution effect, with sales of PCs falling as consumers switched to smart phones and tablets for many of their computing needs. In the first quarter of 2013, global PC sales fell 14% on a year over year basis according to the research firm IDC. This was the worst yearly decline since IDC started tracking PC sales in 1994, and the fifth quarter in a row that PC sales had fallen. At the same time, sales of smart phones and tablets were booming. IDC predicted that sales of tablets would grow almost 60% in 2013, and that tablet shipments would exceed those of portable PCs.[1]

The crux of the problem for Intel is that most tablets and smart phones used microprocessors that are based on technology licensed from ARM Holdings PLC, a British company whose chip designs are valued for their low power consumption, which extends battery life. While Intel has a line of chips aimed at mobile devices—the Atom chips—microprocessors incorporating ARM's technology were found on 95% of smart phones in 2012 and over 30% of all mobile computing devices, a category that includes tablets and PC notebooks.[2] Moreover, in 2012 Microsoft issued a version of its Windows 8 operating system that ran on ARM chips, rather than Intel chips, creating a potential threat to Intel's core PC business.

THE FOUNDATION OF INTEL

Two executives from Fairchild Semiconductor, Robert Noyce and Gordon Moore, founded Intel in 1968. Fairchild Semiconductor was one of the leading semiconductor companies in the world and a key enterprise in an area south of San Francisco that would come to be known as Silicon Valley. Noyce and Moore were no ordinary executives. They had been among the eight founders of Fairchild Semiconductor. Noyce was general manager at the company, while Moore was head of R&D. Three years previously, Moore had articulated what came to be known as *Moore's Law*. IIe had observed that since 1958, due to process improvements the industry had doubled the number of transistors that could be put on a chip every year (in 1975 he altered this to doubling every two years).

Fairchild Semiconductor had been established in 1957 with funding from Sherman Fairchild, who had backed the founders on the understanding that Fairchild Semiconductor would be a subsidiary of his Fairchild Camera and Instrument Corporation on New York. By 1968 Noyce and Moore were chaffing at the bit under management practices imposed from New York, and both decided it was time to strike out on their own. Such were the reputations of Noyce and Moore that they were able to raise $2.3 million to fund the new venture "in an afternoon on the basis of a couple of sheets of paper containing one of the sketchiest business plans ever financed".[3]

When business reporters got wind of the new venture, they asked Noyce and Moore what they were intending to do, only to be greeted by vague replies. The two executives, however, knew exactly what they were going to do—manufacture silicon memory chips—they just didn't want potential competitors to know that. At the time, sales of mainframe computers were expanding. While these machines used integrated circuits to perform logic calculations, programs and data were stored on magnetic devices. Although inexpensive to produce, it was relatively slow to access information on a magnetic device. Noyce and Moore knew that if they could build a silicon based integrated circuit that could function as a memory device, they could speed up computers, making them more powerful, which would expand their applications and allow them to shrink in size.

These memory chips were knows as *dynamic random access memories* (DRAMs). While much of the theoretical work required to design an integrated circuit that could function as a memory device had already been done, manufacturing DRAMs cost efficiently had so far proved impossible. At the same time, some key research on manufacturing was being done at Fairchild. This research included a technique known as *metal oxide on silicon*, or MOS. Noyce and Moore wanted to mass-produce DRAMs, and after looking at other possible alternatives, they concluded that commercializing the MOS research was the way to do it. This prompted some cynics to note that Intel was established to steal the MOS process from Fairchild.

ANDY GROVE

To help them, Noyce and Moore hired a number of researchers away from Fairchild, including, most notably, a young Hungarian Jewish émigré called Andy Grove. At Fairchild, Grove had reported directly to Moore. At Intel he became the director of operations with responsibility for getting products designed on time and built on cost. Through the force of his own personality, Grove would transmute this position into control over just about everything Intel did, making him effectively the equal of Noyce and Moore, long before he was elevated to the CEO position in 1987.

Grove was an interesting character. Born in 1936, he went into hiding when the Germans invaded Hungary during World War II and managed to escape the Holocaust.

After WWII, the tyranny of the Germans was replaced by the tyranny of the Soviets as Hungary became a satellite state of the Soviet Union. In 1956, after the failure of an uprising against the Soviet puppet government, Grove escaped across the border to Austria, and made his way to the United States. He put himself through college in New York by waiting on tables, and then went to UC Berkley for graduate work, where he received a Ph.D. in chemical engineering in 1963. His next stop was Fairchild, where he worked until Moore recruited him away in 1968.

Over the next three decades, Grove would stamp his personality and management style on Intel. Regarded by many as one of the most effective managers of the late twentieth century, Grove was a very demanding and according to some, autocratic leader who set high expectations for everyone, including himself. He was detail orientated, pushed hard to measure everything, and was constantly looking for ways to drive down costs and speed up development processes. He was known for a confrontational "in your face" management style, and would frequently intimidate employees, shouting at those who failed to meet his expectations. Grove himself, who seemed to enjoy a good fight, characterized this behavior as "constructive confrontation". He would push people to their limits to get things done. As he once noted, "there is a growth rate at which everybody fails, and the whole situation results in chaos. I feel it is my most important function. . . . to identify the maximum growth rate at which this wholesale failure begins".[4]

Grove demanded discipline, insisting for example, that everybody be at their desks at 8 a.m., even if they had worked long into the night. He instituted a "late list", requiring that people who arrived after 8 a.m. sign in. If people arrived late for meetings, he would not let them attend. Every year he sent around a memo to employees reminding them that Christmas Eve was not a holiday, and that they were expected to work a full day. Known as the "Scrooge memo", many would be returned with nasty comments scrawled over them. *May you eat yellow snow*, said one. A very neat man, if people's desks were messy, Grove would publically criticize them. According to one observer, "Andy Grove had an approach to discipline and control that made you wonder how much he had been unwittingly influenced by the totalitarian regime he had been so keen to escape".[5]

Grove controlled managers through a regular budgeting process that required them to make detailed revenue and cost projections. He also insisted that all managers establish medium term objectives, and a set of key results by which success or failure would be measured.

He instituted regular one-on-one meetings where performance was reviewed against objectives, holding managers accountable for shortfalls. He also required monthly management reviews where managers from different parts of the company would meet to hear a presentation of its current strengths, weaknesses, opportunities and threats. The goal was to get managers to step back and look at the bigger picture, and to encourage them to help each other solve problems.

Grove would also practice management by walking around, inspecting facilities and offices, demanding that they be clean, something that earned him the nickname "Mr. Clean". He pushed the human resource department to institute a standard system of ranking and rating that had four performance categories; "superior", "exceeds expectations", "meets expectations", or "does not meet expectations". People were compared against others of their rank. Pay raises and later, stock option awards were based on these rankings.

Despite his autocratic style, Grove was grudgingly admired within the company. He was a brilliant problem solver, a man with tremendous control of facts and details, someone who was determined to master the challenging technical projects that Intel was working on. Moreover, while he drove everyone hard, he drove himself harder still, thereby earning the respect of many employees.

THE MEMORY CHIP COMPANY

Making a DRAM using MOS methods proved to be extremely challenging. One major problem—small partials of dust would contaminate the circuits during manufacturing, making them useless. So Intel had to develop "clean rooms" for keeping dust out of the process. Another was how to etch circuit lines on silicon wafers, without having the etched lines fracture and break as the wafer was heated and cooled repeatedly during the manufacturing process. The solution to this problem, identified by Moore, was to "dope" the metal oxide with impurities, making it less brittle. Intel subsequently went to some lengths to keep this aspect of the manufacturing process secret from competitors for as long as possible.

Intel, of course, was not alone in the race to develop a commercial process for manufacturing DRAMs. Among the potential competitors was another semiconductor company started in 1969 by Jerry Sanders, a former marketing director at Fairchild. Sanders started his company with the help several other Fairchild employees who had not been recruited by Intel. Called Advanced Micro devices, or AMD, the company found it tough to raise capital until it received an investment from non other than Robert Noyce, who saw something he liked in the flamboyant Sanders.

Driven by constant pressure from Andy Grove, whose "in your face" management style was bearing fruit, albeit at some human cost, by October 1970 Intel succeeded in producing a DRAM chip, named the 1103, in relatively high yields (which implied that relatively few chips had to be discarded). The 1103 could store 1,024 bits of information (zeros or ones), which was 4 times as much as the highest capacity semiconductor memory device currently available. Since the fixed costs required to establish a manufacturing facility were very high, the key to making money on the 1103 was high yields and high volume. If Intel could achieve both, unit costs would fall enabling Intel to make a lot of profit at low price points. In turn, low prices implied that DRAMs would start to gain wide adoption among computer manufacturers.

The 1103 put Intel firmly on the map. The chip soon became the memory technology of choice for computer makers, and by the end of 1971, 14 out of the world's 18 leading mainframe computer makers were using the 1103. However, Intel did not have the market entirely to itself. Computer makers did not want to become dependent upon a single source of supply for critical components. To avoid this, most computer makers mandated that components had to be at least duel sourced, and for Intel, this meant that if it wanted business, it had to license its technology to other companies. Intel first licensed the rights to produce the 1103 to a Canadian firm, MIL, in exchange for an upfront payment and per unit royalty fee. Before long, MIL was competing against Intel in the market for the 1103, but MIL made a critical mistake in their manufacturing processes, and it wasn't long before a stream of former MIL customers were knocking on Intel's door.

Along the way, Intel received an inquiry from two disgruntled engineers at Honeywell, asking if Intel was interested in building memory systems. The idea was to mount thousands of 1103 chips on a circuit board that could then be plugged into a mainframe computer to increase its memory capability. Impressed by the idea, Intel promptly hired the two engineers and set up a division to do this. Before long, the new division was selling circuit boards to customers running IBM mainframes. This was something of a coup: IBM would not even consider buying the 1103, and had started making its own memory chips. Now Intel had access to a formerly closed market that accounted for 70% of all memory sales.

Around the same time, an accidental discovery at Intel led to a second product line—erasable programmable read only memory (EPROM). Read only memory chips (ROM) were finding wide applications in computing. ROM had desired data, a program for example, permanently burnt into its circuits. ROM was used to store programs, such as a machine operating system, or part of that system. The troubling thing about ROM is that if an engineer made a mistake in programming the chip, he would have to burn another chip, which was a painstaking and time consuming process. While exploring the reason for failure of 1103 chips in the manufacturing process, Dov Froham, another ex Fairchild researcher at Intel, found that the cause was that some of the "gates" inside the chips had become disconnected; they were floating. Froham realized that this flaw in the 1103 had a potential use; it might enable an engineer to design a ROM chip that could be programmed with ease in a few minutes. Moreover, he found that the data on such chips could be erased and rewritten by shinning an ultra violet light on it and the EPROM was born.

Engineers loved the EPROM chip, and once Intel solved the manufacturing problem and started to produce EMROM chips in large quantities, demand surged. Better still, for two years Intel had a virtual monopoly on the product. While other companies tried to produce similar chips, they were unable to solve the manufacturing problems, enabling Intel to charge a relatively high price for a product whose cost was falling every day with advances in cumulative volume.

THE BIRTH OF THE MICROPROCESSOR

By 1971 Intel had already created two revolutionary innovations in the semiconductor industry, the DRAM and the EPROM chips. A third, the microprocessor, was also created that year. The microprocessor was born out of an inquiry from a Japanese company. The company asked Intel if it could build a set of eight logic chips to perform arithmetic functions in a calculator it was planning to produce. Intel took on the project. Ted Hoff, one of the

inventors of the DRAM, wondered if it might not make more sense to build a miniaturized general purpose computer, which could then be programmed to do the arithmetic for the company's calculator.

The project was given to Federico Faggin, an Italian engineer who made some of the basic breakthroughs on MOS technology while working at Fairchild. Although the Japanese company subsequently decided not to build the calculator, Intel pushed ahead with the project. Faggin, who worked 12 to 14 hour days for weeks on end, produced several prototypes in short order. (A source of irritation for Faggin was that despite the long hours, his boss, following Grove's lead, constantly complained that Faggin was late for work!)

Due to Faggin's efforts, by November 1971 Intel had its third product, the 4004 microprocessor. In an article in Electronic News that accompanied its introduction, and which described the 4004 as a computer on a chip, Gordon Moore heralded the 4004 as "one of the most revolutionary products in the history of mankind". No one paid much attention. People in the computer industry viewed the 4004 as a fascinating novelty. Although small and cheap, it could only process 4 bits on information at a time, which made it slow and thus unsuitable for use in the computers of the time. The 4004 was followed by the 8008 microprocessor, which could process eight bits of information at a time. Although faster, it too was a product in search of a market. In an attempt to speed adoption, Intel started to sell development tools that made it easier and faster for outside engineers to develop and test programs for new microprocessors. Slowly the microprocessor began to make inroads into the computer industry, primarily in peripherals such as printers and tape drives.

THE PERSONAL COMPUTER REVOLUTION

By the mid 1970s and embryonic new industry was appearing, the personal computer industry. A company called MITS based in Albuquerque, New Mexico produced the first true personal computer. The MITS Altair used an Intel 8080 microprocessor, which was priced at $360. The first program offered for sale with the Altair was a version of the BASIC programming language, written by Bill Gates and Paul Allen, and designed to run on the 8080. The two had moved to Albuquerque to be near to MITS, and they had established a company of their own, Microsoft. The Altair was sold primarily to hobbyists who wanted to write computer code at home (for which Microsoft Basic came in handy).

In short order, a number of companies sprung up making personal computers. The most successful of the early companies was Apple Computer, which introduced its revolutionary Apple II in 1977. By this time, a number of other companies were also producing microprocessors, including Motorola, whose processor Apple used in the Apple II. The Apple II was a big commercial success, in no small part because it was easy to use for, and because one of the most successful early programs, a spreadsheet called VisiCalc, was written to run on the Apple II.

The commercial success of the Apple II got the world's largest computer company, IBM, to take the nascent personal computer seriously. IBM started to develop its own personal computer in 1979 in a top-secret project. To speed the product to market, IBM took a monumental strategic decision—it decided to use "off the shelf components" to build the PC rather than develop everything itself, which had been the norm at IBM. Originally the company planned to use a microprocessor from Motorola and an operating system called CP/M from a company called Digital Research. However, Motorola was late developing its product, and Digital Research's CEO, Gary Kildall, proved to be difficult to work with. Casting around for alternatives, IBM contacted Intel, offering to purchase it's latest microprocessor, the 8088, which was a derivative of Intel's 8086 chip. However, IBM did not tell Intel what the microprocessor was to be used for (originally Intel was told that it was to go in a printer). As part of the deal, IBM insisted on alternative sources for the 8088. Reluctantly Intel allowed AMD and a number of other companies to produce the 8088 under license. A 1982 cross licensing agreement with AMD, which gave AMD the right to produce the 8088 chip, would come to haunt Intel for years to come.

For the operating system of its first PC, IBM decided to use MS-DOS, a Microsoft operating system. Originally developed by Seattle Computer, and called Q-DOS (which stood for quick and dirty operating system), Q-DOS was purchased by Microsoft for $50,000 when Bill Gates heard that IBM was looking for an operating system. Gates renamed the product, and quickly turned around and licensed MS-DOS to IBM. In what was to be a stroke of genius that had enormous implications for the future of all parties involved, Gates, sensing that IBM executives were desperate to get their hands on an operating system in order to get the IBM PC to market on time, negotiated a nonexclusive license with IBM.

Executives at Intel, who by now had realized that IBM was developing a personal computer, were profoundly unimpressed with the choice of MS-DOS and Microsoft. After a visit to Microsoft, one Intel executive noted: "These people are flakes. They're not original, they don't really understand what they are doing, their ambitions are very low, and it's not really clear that they have succeeded even at that."[6] For its part, Microsoft had to produce a version of MS-DOS that would run on the Intel microprocessor. From now on, like it or not, Microsoft and Intel would be joined at the hip.

Introduced in 1981, the IBM PC was an instant success. To stoke sales, IBM offered a number of applications for the IBM PC that were sold separately, including a version of VisiCalc, a word processor called EasyWriter, and well-known series of business programs from Peachtree Software. Over the next two years, IBM would sell more than 500,000 PCs, seizing market leadership from Apple. IBM had what Apple lacked, an ability to sell into corporate America.

As sales of the IBM PC mounted, two things happened. First, independent software developers started to write program to run on the IBM PC. These included two applications that drove adoptions of the IBM PC: word processing programs (Word Perfect) and a spread sheet (Lotus 1-2-3). Second, the success of IBM gave birth to clone manufacturers who made "IBM compatible" PCs that also utilized an Intel microprocessor and Microsoft's MS-DOS operating system. The first and most successful of the clone makers was Compaq, which in 1983 introduced its first personal computer, a 28-pound "portable" PC. In its first year, Compaq booked $111 million in sales, which at the time was a record for first year sales of a company. Before long, a profusion of IBM clone makers entered the market, including Tandy, Zenith, Leading Edge, and Dell Computer. This entry led to market share fragmentation in the PC industry.

By 1982, Intel had a replacement chip ready for the IBM PC, the 80286 microprocessor. The 80286 was desperately needed since the 8088 was painfully slow running some of the newer applications. IBM introduced a new PC, the AT, to use the 80286 chip, and priced it at a premium. Demand was so strong that IBM put the AT on allocation, which opened the door to clone makers, particularly Compaq. By now, 70% of the microprocessors sold to PC manufacturers were made by Intel, with AMD accounting for a significant portion of the remainder. For the 80286, Intel had cut the number of licenses down to 4. It also ran an intensive marketing and sales campaign, called Checkmate, which was successful in getting many Original Equipment Manufacturers (OEMs) to use Intel's version of the 80286 in their machines.

THE DRAM DEBACLE

In 1984 Intel booked revenues of $1.6 and made almost $200 million net profit, up from $134 million in revenues and $20 million in net profit a decade earlier. The growth had been dramatic. However, Intel's share of the DRAM market had been sliding for years. New entrants, particularly from Japan, had been grabbing ever more DRAM sales. They had done this by undertaking large scale investment to build efficient fabrication facilities (fabs) and paying meticulous attention to quality and costs, doing everything possible to drive up yields. One source suggested that while peak yields and U.S. DRAM plants, such as Intel's, were around 50%, in Japan they were closer to 80%. This translated into a huge cost advantage for the Japanese producers.

The American manufacturers, Intel included, had made the crucial mistake of underestimating the Japanese threat. Demands from computer companies for second sources had helped to facilitate diffusion of the underlying product technology and commoditized DRAMs. In such a market, advantage went to the most efficient, and this was the Japanese. Moreover, Japanese companies seized the lead in developing more powerful DRAM chips. While Intel had created the market for DRAMs, and dominated the market for 1K chips, in each subsequent generation it fell further and further behind. By 1983 when fifth generation 256K DRAMs started to appear, Intel was a year behind in the development cycle and as a consequence, was at a distinct cost disadvantage when it introduced its product.

Somehow, despite Grove's aggressive leadership, Intel's share had fallen to only 1% of the total DRAM market. To regain market share, management understood that Intel would have to build a new fabrication facility, at a cost of $600 million, and throw company R&D resources behind an effort to bring a next generation 1 megabyte DRAM chip to the market. To make matters worse, the DRAM market was in a big slump, bought on by overcapacity as a result of aggressive investments by Asian producers, and Intel was losing money in the DRAM business.

Faced with this bleak prospect, Intel's senior management had to decide whether to continue to compete in the DRAM business, the market they had created, or to focus resources on the more profitable microprocessor market. It was not an easy decision. Irrespective of the economics, there was enormous emotional attachment within the company to the DRAM business. Many at Intel wanted to build a 1 M DRAM. There were also valid arguments for staying in the DRAM business. Some thought that DRAMs were the technology driver in semiconductor manufacturing, and without the knowledge gained from making DRAMs, Intel's microprocessor business would suffer. In addition, there was the argument that customers would prefer to buy from a company that offered a full product range, and if it exited the DRAM business Intel would not be able to do that.

As Andy Grove describes it, a crucial point arrived when he and Gordon Moore were discussing what Intel's strategy should be. Grove asked Moore, "If we got kicked out, and the board bought in a new CEO, what would he do?" Moore's reply, "he would get us out of memories". Grove then said, "why don't we just walk out of the door, and come back and do it ourselves." It was one thing to make the decision, another to implement it. Grove removed the head of the DRAM division, recognizing that he was not the man to wield the ax, and replaced him with another manager, who promptly "went native" and started to argue for going ahead with the 1 megabyte DRAM chip. He too was replaced, and a year after the decision was made, Intel finally exited the DRAM business.

THE MICROPROCESSOR BUSINESS

In 1987 Gordon Moore stepped down as CEO of Intel, passing the torch on to Andy Grove, although Moore remained as Chairman. Grove, who held the CEO position through until 1998, and was then chairman until 2005, had no intention of letting Intel's dominance in microprocessors go the same way as its DRAM business.

Chip Design

By now, it was well understood at Intel that the market had an unquenchable thirst for more powerful microprocessors. Software was advancing rapidly, with new applications becoming available all the time. Running these applications quickly required more computing power, and users were willing to pay a premium for this. Intel knew that consumers would only be too happy to replace their old PCs with better, faster machines. It thus became critical to develop and introduce newer microprocessors. At the same time, the market demanded backward compatibility. The new machines had to run older software, and this implied that each new generation of chip should be able to run older programs. This requirement implied that too a degree, Intel was locked into the microprocessor architecture that had started with the 8086 (from which the 8088 was derived), and continued with the 80286. The next microprocessor in what was now known as the x86 architecture was the 80386, or i386 for short.

First introduced in October 1985, i386 was a 32-bit microprocessor that was much faster than the i286. Intel had been trying for over a year to get IBM to introduce a machine based on the i386, but IBM seemed to be dragging its feet. The problem for IBM was that an i386 PC would be very close in power to minicomputers that IBM was making a lot of money on. Fearing that i386 machines would cannibalize its product line, IBM seemed to want to keep the i386 of the market as long as possible. At the same time, Apple computer had introduced a new machine, the first Macintosh, which used a Motorola microprocessor. The Apple Mac was the first computer with a graphical user interface and a mouse. As it started to gain market share, Grove feared that the market might switch to the Apple standard, making it more critical than ever to get i386 based machines on the market.

Intel had an ally in Compaq Computer. In 1986, Compaq took advantage of IBM's sloth to be the first to introduce a PC built around the i386. Compaq seized the lead from IBM, other computer makers quickly followed, and from then on, IBM started to lose influence and share in the PC business. As the high margin i386 chip gained traction, Intel's sales exploded, hitting $2.9 billion in 1988, while profits surged to $450 million.

Over the next two decades Intel continued to drive the industry forward with regular advances in its x86 architecture. These included the i486 (introduced in 1989), the first Pentium chip (1993), The Pentium Pro (1995), various derivatives of the Pentium Pro architecture, and more recently, its 64-bit Core 2 Duo and Quad processor line, first introduced in 2006. The latest Intel processors have pushed the limits of performance by building two or four processors into a chip. Intel prices new chips at a premium then drops prices as manufacturing yields improve. It is not unusual to see prices drop by 30–50% in one year.

By continually increasing the performance of its chips, Intel was able to vanquish several potential competitors, including a series of fast chips from AMD in the early 2000s, and several chips based on an architecture known as reduce instruction set computing, or RISC, that during the 1990s seemed to threaten Intel's market dominance. One notable RISC chip arose out of an attempt by Apple, Motorola and IBM to seize momentum away from Intel with a RISC processor called the PowerPC. However, few companies outside of Apple adopted the processor. The limited volume meant high costs, which were further compounded by manufacturing problems at Motorola, and the PowerPC never gained wide acceptance. In 2006, Apple effectively killed the PowerPC when it announced that it would henceforth use Intel microprocessors in its machines.

Following Moore's law, successive generations of Intel chips have used ever-smaller micron geometries to cram ever more transistors on a chip. Intel's 8088 chip, introduced in 1979, had 29,000 transistors, the i486 chip, introduced in 1989, had 1.2 million transistors, and by 2012, its most powerful PC chips contained 1.48 billion transistors. By 2012 Intel was working with such small sub micro geometries that more than 100 million transistors could fit onto the head of a pin! Compared to its original 4004 chip introduced in 2012, the chips Intel was producing in 2012 ran 4,000 times as fast and each transistor used 5,000 times less energy, while the price per transistor had dropped by a factor of 50,000. Driving forward chip design and production requires very heavy R&D spending. By 2012, Intel was spending over $10 billion a year on R&D, or 19% of sales. This was split between spending on chip design, and spending on improving manufacturing processes.

Manufacturing Processes

Designing and manufacturing these devices requires constantly pushing against the limits of physics and technology. Microprocessors are built in layers on a silicon wafer through various processes using chemicals, gas and light. It is an extremely demanding process involving more than 300 steps and, on modern chips, 20 layers are connected with micro circuitry to form a complex three-dimensional structure. Intel is pushing the frontiers of sub micron geometry. The company is currently is producing transistors that measure just 22 nanometers, whereas most other semiconductor manufacturers are still making 45 nm or 32 nm chips (a nanometer is *one billionth* of a meter). Intel newest factory in Arizona, designed to come on line in 2014, will push this frontier still further making chips that have just 14 nm geometry. To carve features this small on a silicon chip, Intel uses a technique known as extreme ultra violet lithography. This is a way of printing circuit patterns onto silicon chips that goes beyond lasers and lenses, and utilizes xenon gas and microscopic reflectors. If it sounds incredibly complex and esoteric, this is because it is at the leading edge of what is scientifically possible. Indeed, each new generation of Intel chips relies upon pushing processes beyond what was attainable just a few years earlier.

So complex is the manufacturing process, that the high tech fabrication plants, or *foundries*, required to make microprocessors cost up to $5 billion each. By 2012 Intel had 16 of these plants around the world. Too equip its plants, Intel works very closely with equipment vendors. Due to its scale, Intel enjoys considerable leverage over equipment suppliers. In some cases, Intel will design a new machine itself, and then have equipment vendors manufacture it. In others, Intel works closely with the vendors on the design of a piece of equipment. As a result, Intel itself holds hundreds of patents relating to the processes for manufacturing semiconductors. Whenever equipment is developed specifically for Intel's requirements, vendors are generally prohibited from selling that equipment to other companies, such as AMD, for a given period.

When installing new equipment, the goal is to gain manufacturing efficiencies through increased yields, or other process improvements. For example, in the 2000s Intel switched from using 200 mm to 300 mm wafers in its manufacturing processes. The larger wafers allowed Intel to put more microprocessors on each, increasing throughput and significantly lowering costs. Intel is currently working to develop the commercialization of 450 mm wafers and is forecasting that it will start to make microprocessors on 450mm wafers by 2016/2017. If it can achieve this, it will be the first in the world to do so. This may give Intel an advantage in manufacturing efficiencies that will be very hard for other chipmakers to match.

To boost yields, raising the percentage of processors that come of the line operating perfectly, Intel uses sophisticated statistical process control procedures. Since even a microscopic piece of dust can contaminate a chip, the specifications that Intel works to are extremely demanding and tight. Over time, Intel has turned yield improvement into a precise science. With each succeeding generation of microprocessor geometry, the company seems able to achieve a steeper learning curve. By constantly pushing out the envelop with regard to manufacturing technology, product design, and yields, Intel has reportedly been able to reduce its unit manufacturing costs for a processor by as much as 25–30% a year.

Typically, Intel will refine new manufacturing processes in one factory, perfecting yields and reducing costs, and then transfer those processes to other facilities. To do this, it relies upon a methodology known as "Copy Exactly!" Under this methodology, engineers spend up to four years perfecting a new manufacturing technique in one of Intel's development factories in Hillsboro Oregon. Once they are satisfied with the results, they work to meticulously import every last detail to other factories around the world. Engineers strive to duplicate even the subtlest of manufacturing variables, from the color of a worker's gloves to the type of fluorescent lights in the building. Employees from around the world spend more than a year at the development factory, learning their small piece of the new recipe so they can bring it back to their home factory. The idea is to capture the infinite number of intangibles that have allowed a process to succeed in plants that have already brought it online. According to one Intel manager: "It's not just there's a specification or a recipe or a program you put into a machine. It also is what the human being does and how they interact with the machine."[7]

The extremes to which Intel engineers go to control the precise conditions in its dozen or so factories has become legendary. A few years ago Intel engineers were trying to figure out why one plant in Arizona wasn't hitting the benchmarks achieved at another in Oregon, where the processes were first developed. Then it hit them: Arizona's desert air was so much drier than the air in Portland, and the engineers in Arizona were skipping several steps taken in Oregon to dehumidify. Intel scientists theorized that the dehumidifying, besides removing water, also eliminated impurities such as ammonia. So engineers began adding water vapor to the air in the Arizona foundry, essentially making Portland air, and then subjected it to the same dehumidifiers used in Oregon. It worked! According to one engineer, this "shows the level of things you've got to worry about when you try to make something as complex as the chips we make."[8]

Intellectual Property

From the i386 chip onwards, Grove was determined to ensure that Intel was the only supplier in the world of its architecture. AMD, however, believed that under the terms of the 1982 technology sharing agreement between the two companies, it had rights to Intel's designs. Intel simply refused to hand over technical specifications for the i386 to AMD, sparking off a lengthy court battle between the two that persisted until 1995. In the end, the two chipmakers agreed to drop all pending lawsuits against each other, settled existing lawsuits, and signed a cross-licensing agreement. Irrespective of the final settlement, AMD had spent $40 million a year on legal fees alone. Senior management attention had been diverted by the ongoing legal battle. AMD had been slow to develop its own version of the i386, waiting instead to get specifications from Intel, which Intel only shared after ordered to in a 1990 ruling.

Intel Inside

For years, Intel had viewed its customers as original equipment manufacturers, focusing its marketing efforts on engineers within those companies. But the nature of the end market was changing. By the early 1990s increasingly sophisticated customers were making their own purchasing decisions, often in computer superstores, or buying direct from companies like Dell and Gateway. Consumers now had influence on the process, and could exercise choice over not just the machine, but also the components that went into it, including the microprocessor.

In 1991, Intel started to market directly to consumers with its *Intel Inside* campaign, effectively telling them that a computer with an Intel chip inside would guarantee advanced technology and compatibility with prior software. Supported by slick advertisements, the campaign was a stunning success. Within a year, Intel was listed as the third most valuable brand name on the planet. In 1993 Grove was able to claim that the number of consumers who preferred a PC with an Intel microprocessor had risen from 60 to 80%. By 1994, some 1,200 computer companies had signed on to the campaign, adhering "Intel Inside" logos on their machines, or including the logo on their product ads.

Complicating matters, one aspect of the long running legal battle between Intel and AMD was a trademark dispute. Intel had claimed that "386" referred to its trademark, and competitors like AMD could not use it. However, in 1991 a court had ruled that the name "386" was so widely used that it had become generic. The ruling infuriated Grove, who believed that clone makers would now be able to piggyback on Intel's marketing campaigns for the 386 and 486. He then made the suggestion that the next chip, which was to have been known as the i586, be given another name that could be trademarked, and the Pentium was born.

Forward Vertical Integration and Customers

Intel vertically integrated forward into the production of PCs in the mid 1980s, selling "boxes" without a screen, keyboard, or brand logo to well known computer companies who put there own brand on them and resold them. The move led to complaints from several of Intel's customers, who felt that Intel was indirectly competing against them in the end market and lowering barriers to entry into the PC industry. After push back, in the early 1990s Intel exited this business. However, the company continued to make motherboards, which are large printed circuit boards that hold the microprocessors, other critical chips, slots for connecting memory and graphics cards, and so on.

Intel's move into motherboards assured more rapid diffusion of each new generation of chips by making it much easier for PC companies to incorporate those chips into their machines. The move infuriated PCs manufacturers such as Compaq and IBM who generally made their own motherboards. Compaq had been able to gain a competitive advantage by bring PCs containing the latest generation Intel chips to market early. Compaq responded by trying to reduce their dependence on Intel. They used for chips from AMD and initially refused to participate in the Intel inside branding scheme. However, by the mid 1990s Intel's position was so strong that this had only marginal impact on the company.

Intel continued to make motherboards through the 2000s, even though profit margins were lower than on sales of stand-alone microprocessors. By 2007 some 24% of Intel's revenues came from the sale of motherboards. At this point, large branded OEMs with a global reach (HP, Dell, Lenovo, Acer, Toshiba and Apple), accounted for about 50–53% of global PC sales, with the remainder being captured by a long tail of smaller local brands. As of 2012, some 18% of Intel's total sales (stand alone chips and motherboards) went to Hewlett

Packard. Dell Computer accounted for another 14% and Lenovo for 11%.

The Microsoft Connection

Throughout the 1980s and much of the 1990s, the relationship between Intel and Microsoft, was an uneasy one. When Microsoft introduced Windows 3.0 in 1990, its first operating system with a graphical user interface, it boosted demand for new PCs to run graphics heavy programs. The same happened when Windows 95 was introduced five years later. In both cases, Intel was a beneficiary of the resulting upgrade cycle. Intel clearly needed Microsoft, but that did not mean that they respected the company. Intel was frustrated that Microsoft did not seem particularly interested in optimizing their software to run on Intel's chips. Microsoft's engineers seemed more concerned with adding features to their products, than in streamlining code so that it took advantage of the full capabilities of Intel's microprocessors.

Microsoft, one the other hand, was interested in making its Windows operating system as ubiquitous as possible, and that logically implied making a version of Windows that would run on other microprocessors, such as the new generation of RISC chips. During the 1990s Microsoft was eyeing users of powerful computer workstations, many of which used RISC chips. This was a potential nightmare for Intel, and it became all to real when Microsoft announced the development of Windows NT, a high end version of Windows that would run on both Intel and RISC microprocessors, including the PowerPC. What stopped the nightmare from occurring was the development of the Pentium Pro, which was so fast and efficient that it effectively eclipsed rivals who used RISC architecture.

Reflecting these underlying tensions, relationships between Andy Grove and Microsoft's Bill Gates were often rocky, and there were reports of meetings dissolving into shouting matches. This started to change in the mid 1990s. It may have been that after the failure of the RISC challenge to Intel, the two companies, and their respective leaders recognized their interdependence and decided that cooperation was better than conflict. Beginning in 1996, quarterly meetings were held between Grove and Gates, aimed at coordinating strategy and resolving differences.

In 2012 new cracks began to appear in the symbiotic relationship between Microsoft and Intel when Microsoft introduced a version of its Windows 8 operating system that would run on ARM processors. For Microsoft, this was a logical move given its strategy of having Windows 8 run on all devices, including tablets and smartphones where the low power consumption offered by ARM processors was highly valued. Microsoft reportedly made the decision to produce an ARM version of Windows 8 because Intel's atom processor consumed too much power to make it a compelling choice in tablets. The move opened the door for PC manufacturers to start building machines that ran on none Intel chips.

THE BARRETT ERA

In 1998 Craig Barrett succeeded Andy Grove as CEO. A former Stanford engineering professor who had become chief operating officer of Intel in 1993, Barrett's tenure as CEO was market by an aggressive push into new markets. By the 1990s the Internet was starting to take center place in computing, and Barrett saw opportunities in extending Intel's reach into chips to drive computer networking gear and wireless handsets. Moreover, Barrett was concerned that without product diversification, Intel would not be able to maintain its growth rate given the maturation of the PC market in many developed nations. In his first three years as CEO Intel spent some $12 billion on acquisitions and internal new ventures designed to strength the company's position in these emerging areas.

Barrett's push into these areas failed to yield any quick returns. By 2004 Intel only had 6% of the market for chips used in networking gear, and 7% of the market for processing chips within wireless phones. Part of the problem; Intel ran into stiff competition from embedded competitors. In the market for wireless phone chips, for example, Intel was competing against the likes of Texas Instruments and Qualcomm, both of whom had a strong market and technological position.

Moreover, Barrett's tenure was marred by some embarrassing product delays, capacity constraints that drove some customers to AMD, and product recalls. To make matters worse, in the early 2000s AMD seized the lead in chip design for the first time, and for two years AMD could boast that it was technological leader in the industry until Intel recaptured the lead with newer chips. Complicating matters, the PC industry went through a sharp contraction in 2001 that led to slumping sales and profits for Intel. While the industry recovered in 2002, growth rates since 2002 have been lower than in the 1990.

Some observers have blamed the problems of the Barrett era on management issues at Intel. The company, they say, had become too large, too bureaucratic, and was no longer the egalitarian entity of its early years. The "constructive confrontation" of the Grove years, which had kept managers on their toes, had been replaced by an autocratic culture dominated by people who got promoted for managing upwards. A management vacuum following Grove's departure led to a lack of accountability and control. To quote one critic: "In the Grove era, each leader who spearheaded an unsuccessful attempt left the company after the project failed. However, throughout the Barrett era each figure head has remained at Intel after the project failed".[9]

PAUL OTELLINI'S PLATFORM STRATEGY

In 2005 Barrett became chairman. Paul Otellini replaced him as CEO. Another long time Intel employee, Otellini was the first Intel CEO to not have an engineering background (Otellini was an MBA with a career in finance and marketing). As head of company wide sales and marketing, Otellini gained prominence at Intel during the late 1990s by pushing the company to adopt a more aggressive approach to market segmentation. By the late 1990s prices for low end PCs were falling to under $1,000, and in this commodity market OEMs were casting around for cheaper microprocessor and motherboard options. Ontellini came up with the idea of reserving the Pentium brand for higher end chips, and creating a new brand, *Celeron*, for lower performance chips aimed at low cost PCs.

In the early 2000s, Otellini pushed for the creation of the Centrino chip platform for lap top computers. While Intel engineers were focused on designing faster more powerful processors, Otellini argued that lap top users cared more about heat generation, battery life, and wireless capabilities. The Centrino platform was designed for them. It combined an Intel microprocessor with a WiFi chip (for wireless networking), and associated software. Personal computer manufacturers were initially skeptical about the value of the Centrino platform. For a while they continued to buy an Intel microprocessor while purchasing WiFi chips from other companies. But when performance tests showed that the Centrino platform worked well, most manufacturers shifted to purchasing this platform for their laptops and Centrino quickly became a recognizable brand.

Introduced in 2003, the Centrino was a huge hit, and helped to pull Intel out of its sales slump. Indeed, by the late 2000s Intel was dominating the market for lap top chips with its chipset offerings. Upon succeeding Barrett, Otellini called for the Centrino strategy to be applied to other areas of the computer industry. He wanted Intel to design separate "platforms" for corporate computers, home computers and lap top computers. Each platform was to combine several chips, and focus on providing utility to a specific customer set. The platform for corporate computers was to package a microprocessor with chips and software that enhance the security of computers, keeping them virus free, and allow for the remote management and servicing of computers (which could bring large cost savings to corporations). The platform for home computers was to combine a microprocessor with chips and software for a wireless base station (for home networking), chips for showing digital movies, and chips for three dimensional graphics processing (for computer games).

The goal was to enable Intel to capture more of the value going into every computer sold and that should increase the company's profitability and profit growth. To implement this plan, Otellini announced a sweeping reorganization of Intel, creating separate market focused divisions for mobile computing (lap tops), corporate computing, home computing, and health care computing (which Intel regarded as a promising growth market with its own unique set of customer requirements). Each division has its own engineering, software and marketing personnel, and is charged with developing a platform for its target market.

To further the strategy of capturing more value going into every computer sold, Intel moved into the graphics chip business, integrating graphics capabilities into its chipsets. Although Intel gained some share at the low end, ATI and Nvidia currently dominate the high-end graphics chip business. The most important and demanding applications for graphics chips are computer games. In 2006, AMD purchased ATI for $5.4 billion, signaling its intention to bundle both microprocessors and graphics chips together.

In mid 2008 Intel introduced a new line of low power consumption chips called Atom that were aimed at mobile internet devices (MIDs)—which was then defined as devices between a smart phone and a conventional laptop and included net-books (very small laptops meant primarily for web surfing). At the time the Atom chip was introduced, Apple had yet to revolutionized the computer market with the introduction of the iPad, although the iPhone had been introduced a year earlier. Unfortunately for Intel, smart phone and tablet makers, including Apple, quickly gravitated to low power consumptions chips based upon technology pioneered by the British company ARM Holdings Plc. The main advantage of ARM technology was that it generated far more computing power per watt than alternative designs, which implied extended battery life, a key requirement from consumers. ARM does not manufacture chips itself. Rather, it licenses its technology to other companies, including Apple, Samsung, NVIDIA and Qualcomm, who incorporated it in their chip designs. They then get the chips made by contract manufacturers. By 2012, ARM chips had become the de facto standard for mobile devices such as smart phones and tablets, leaving Intel at the fringe of the market.

INTEL IN 2013

Paul Otellini retired in May 2013. His legacy was a mixed one. On the positive side, he had helped Intel to reassert itself against a resurgent AMD and cemented the company's dominance in the PC market. The company's revenues grew from $39 billion to $54 billion, earnings per share increased from $1.40 to $2.39, and Otellini left Intel with a commanding market share lead in its core business. Moreover, its manufacturing capabilities remained unmatched in the industry. On the other hand, Intel had largely missed the move towards mobile computing, despite the introduction of the Atom chip, and the company was struggling to gain share against ARM chips.

More worrying still, PC sales were now in decline as demand switched towards tablets. That being said, no one expects the PC to disappear. Indeed, there is a belief that sooner or later the need to replace aging PC inventory will lead to a robust replacement cycle. There was some hope that the introduction of Windows 8 in 2012 might stimulate replacement demand, but many consumers were put off by the new tile based interface Microsoft utilized on Windows 8, and replacement demand remains muted for the time being.

That being said, there is a silver lining in the rapid switch towards mobile computing: Increasingly, these devices are using high-speed wireless links to store data on "the cloud" and access applications that resided on "the cloud". At the heart of the cloud are very large server farms containing hundreds of thousands of PC servers that are networked together. Most of these servers, as it happens, are based on PC architecture and run on Intel microprocessors. Thus the growth of mobile devices that are connected to the Internet through the cloud could result in more server farms and more demand for Intel microprocessors going forward. Nevertheless, for the time being Intel is clearly fighting headwinds in its microprocessor business.

Otellini's successor as CEO is Brian Krzanich, the former COO. A long time Intel employee, Krzanich made his mark in the company as head of the manufacturing organization. His elevation to the CEO position probably speaks volumes about the importance Intel attaches to the manufacturing aspect of its business. A key task for Krzanich is to make sure that the company remains relevant in the post PC era.

Intel is not sitting back and letting ARM chips dominate the mobile device market. It is introducing a new generation of its Atom chips that appear to be far more competitive with ARM chips, and deliver similar performance per watt. These are 22 nm chips and will be manufactured using the latest technology. If the new generation of Atom chips are competitive, it is possible that Microsoft will again focus just on writing Windows to run on Intel architecture, since producing two versions of Windows is a costly exercise. This could provide upside for Intel, particularly if Windows 8 and its successors gain traction in the tablet and smart phone markets— although to date that has yet to happen. Even if the Atom chip is successful, however, the economic impact for Intel might well be muted by the lower average selling price of chips for mobile devices, as opposed to PCs.

Another aspect of Intel's current strategy is to defend the laptop market from encroachment by ARM chips. In 2013 Intel introduced its Haswell chips that can run PC software but have longer battery life. Reportedly, laptops running on Haswell chips have a battery life of up to 10 hours, which represents a 50% improvement over prior generation chips and comparable with the battery life for a tablet.

Although Krzanich seems to be following the script laid out by Otellini, it is clear that he faces significant challenges going forward. The task for Intel is to remain relevant in the post PC era, to hold the rise of ARM chips in check, to continue to dominate its base, to revitalize, if possible, its long-term symbiotic relationship with Microsoft (a company that is itself facing significant challenges), and to gain meaningful traction in the rapidly growing mobile device market where Intel so far has been little more than a bystander.

REFERENCES

1. Anonymous, "Intel's Right Hand Turn", *The Economist*, May 14th, 2005, page 67.
2. Anonymous, "The empire strikes back", *The Economist*, December 2nd, 2006, page 69.
3. Anonymous, "Battlechips", The Economist, June 7th, 2008, pp 75–76.
4. B. Colman and L. Shrine, *Losing Faith*, Colman and Shrine, 2006.
5. R.P. Colwell, *The Pentium Chronicles*, John Wiley, New Jersey, 2006.
6. C. Edwards, "Getting Intel back on the Inside Track," *Business Week*, November 29th, 2004, page 39.
7. C. Edwards, "Shaking up Intel's Insides*", Business Week*, January 31st, 2005, page 35.
8. P. Frieberger and M. Swaine, *Fire in the Valley*, McGraw Hill, New York, 2000.
9. A. Hesseldahl, "AMD vs Intel: The challengers new plan", *Business Week Online*, July 11th, 2008, page 1.
10. A. Hesseldahl, "AMD wins another round against Intel", Business Week Online, June 9th, 2008, page 12.
11. Intel Corporation, Form 10K 2007.
12. T. Jackson, *Inside Intel*, Penguin Books, New York, 1997.
13. Lashinsky, "Is this the right man for Intel?", *Fortune*, April 18th, 2005, pp 110–120.
14. R. Parloff, "Intel's worse nightmare", *Fortune*, August 21st, 2006, pp 60–70.
15. B. Snyder Bulik, "Intel's New Strategy Demands a New Partner", *Advertising Age*, March 14th, 2005, pp 4–5.
16. Intel Corp. 10K Statement, 2012
17. Intel Corp: Assessing Intel's Atom Tablet Opportunity, *Morgan Stanley*, May 15th, 2013.
18. Vivek Arya, "Haswell: Mobility of a tablet, power of a PC", *Bank of America Merrill Lynch*, May 30th, 2013.
19. Anonymous, "Chip of the old Block: Intel v ARM", *The Economist*, May 2nd, 2013.

NOTES

1. T. Samson, "IDC: PC shipments worst than predicted, tablet shipments get better to exceed PC shipments by 2015", *InfoWorld*, May 28th, 2013.
2. D. Traviosm, "ARM Holdings and Qualcomm: The Winners in Mobile", *Forbes*, February 28th, 2013.
3. Tim Jackson, **Inside Intel**, Penguin Books, New York, 1997, page 18.
4. R.S. Redlow, "The Education of Andy Grove", **Fortune**, December 12th, 2005, page 116.
5. Tim Jackson, **Inside Intel**, Penguin Books, New York, 1997, page 33.
6. Tim Jackson, **Inside Intel**, Penguin Books, New York, 1997, page 206.
7. Anonymous, "When Intel says 'Copy Exactly', it means it", *Chinadaily.com*, May 30th, 2006.
8. Anonymous, "When Intel says 'Copy Exactly', it means it", *Chinadaily.com*, May 30th, 2006.
9. B. Coleman and L. Shrine, Losing Faith: How the Grove Survivors led the Decline of Intel's Corporate Culture (Logan and Shrine, 2006), page 117.

Case 12

Getting an Inside Look: Given Imaging's Camera Pill[1]

Melissa A. Schilling

Founded in 1998, Given Imaging is an Israeli medical device company that developed the "camera pill"—a tiny capsule shaped electronic device that, after being swallowed by a patient, sends visual images of the inside of the patient's gastrointestinal tract to a video pack worn around the patient's waist. These images can then be evaluated to diagnose numerous small intestine problems that had been hitherto very difficult to locate and diagnose.

Though Given's product offered numerous advantages in terms of both effectiveness and patient comfort, it be somewhat difficult to get doctors to adopt the product: many doctors and hospitals already had the equipment and training required for traditional endoscopy techniques, and were also risk averse about trying new methods. Analysts wondered if Given would be able to overcome physicians' reluctance and switching costs. Further complicating things, new competitors had emerged: Japanese camera companies were developing their own camera pills, some with intriguing special features Given's system did not possess. The race was on—how fast would the market emerge, and who would end up as leader?

THE HISTORY OF THE CAMERA PILL

Gavriel Iddan was an electro-optical engineer at Israel's Rafael Armament Development Authority, the Israeli authority for development of weapons and military technology. One of Iddan's projects was to develop the "eye" of a guided missile, which leads the missile to its target. In 1981, Iddan traveled to Boston on sabbatical to work for a company that produced X-ray tubes and ultrasonic probes. While there, he befriended a gastroenterologist (a physician who focuses on digestive diseases) named Eitan Scapa. During long conversations in which each would discuss their respective fields, Scapa taught Iddan about the technologies used to view the interior lining of the digestive system. Scapa pointed out that the existing technologies had a number of significant limitations, particularly with respect to viewing the small intestine.[2] The small intestine is the locale of a number of serious disorders. In the U.S. alone, approximately 19 million people suffer from disorders in the small intestine (including bleeding, Crohn's disease, celiac disease, chronic diarrhea, irritable bowel syndrome, and small bowel cancer).[3] Furthermore, the nature of the small intestine makes it a difficult place to diagnose and treat such disorders. The small intestine (or "small bowel") is about five to six meters long in a typical person and is full of twists and turns (see Figure 1 below). X-rays do not enable the physician to view the lining of the intestine, and endoscopes (small cameras attached to long, thin, flexible poles) can only reach the first third of the small intestine and can be quite uncomfortable for the patient. The remaining option, surgery, is very invasive and can be impractical if the physician does not know which part of the small intestine is affected. Scapa thus urged Iddan to try to come up with a better way to view the small intestine, but at that time Iddan had no idea how to do it.

Ten years later, Iddan visited the US again, and his old friend Scapa again inquired whether there was a technological solution that would provide a better solution for viewing the small intestine. By this time, very small *charge-coupled devices* (CCD) image sensors had been developed in the quest to build small video cameras.

Figure 1 — The Gastrointestinal Tract

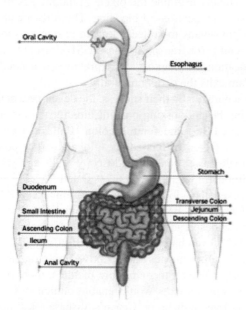

Figure 1 — **The Gastrointestinal Tract**

Iddan wondered if perhaps it would be possible to create a very small missile-like device that could travel through the intestine without a lifeline leading to the outside of the body. Like the missiles Iddan developed at Rafael, this device would have a camera "eye." If designed well, the body's natural peristaltic action would propel the camera through the length of the intestine.

When Iddan returned to Israel he began working on a way to have a very small CCD camera introduced into the digestive system, and transmit images wirelessly to a receiver outside of the body. Initially unsure whether images could be transmitted through the body wall, he conducted a very rudimentary experiment with a store-bought chicken: he placed a transmitting antenna inside the chicken and a receiving antenna outside the chicken. The results indicated that it was possible to transmit a clear video image. Encouraged by this, he set about overcoming the battery life problem: the small CCD sensors consumed so much energy that their batteries were often depleted within ten minutes. Fortunately, advancements in semiconductors promised to replace CCD imagers with a new generation of *complementary metal oxide semiconductors* (CMOS) that would consume a fraction of the power of CCD imagers. Iddan began developing

a prototype based on CMOS technology, and applied for an initial patent on the device in 1994. In 1995, he presented his product idea to Gavriel Meron, the CEO of Applitect Ltd., a company that made small endoscopic cameras. Meron thought the project was a fascinating idea, and founded Given Imaging (**GI** for gastrointestinal, **V** for video, and **EN** for endoscopy) to develop and market the technology.[4]

Unbeknownst to Iddan or Meron, another team of scientists in the UK was also working on a method for wireless endoscopy. This team included a physician named C. Paul Swain, a bioengineer named Tim Mills, and a doctoral student named Feng Gong. Swain, Mills and Gong were exploring using commercially available miniature video cameras and processors. They scouted out miniature camera technology at "spy shops" in London that supplied small video cameras and transmitters to private detectives and other users.[5] By 1994 they were developing crude devices to see if they could transmit moving images from within the gut using microwave frequencies. By 1996 they had succeeded in their first live animal trial. They surgically inserted their prototype device into a pig's stomach, and demonstrated that they could see the pylorus valve of the stomach open and close. Their next hurdle was to develop a device that could be swallowed instead of surgically inserted.

In the Fall of 1997, Gavriel Meron met Dr. Swain at a conference in Birmingham England, and the teams concluded that their progress would be much faster if they joined forces. Swain's team had superior expertise in anatomy and the imaging needs of diagnosing small intestine disorders while Iddan's CMOS-based sensors enabled the production of a smaller device with lower power requirements. The teams thus had complementary knowledge that each knew would be crucial to producing a successful capsule endoscope.

In 1999, the team got permission from the ethics committee at the Royal London Hospital to conduct their first human trial. Dr. Swain would be the patient, and Dr. Scapa (whose initial urgings had motivated Iddan to develop the wireless endoscope) would be the surgeon who would oversee the procedure. In October of 1999, in Scapa's clinic near Tel Aviv, Israel, Dr. Swain swallowed the 11 X 33 mm (0.43 inches X 1.3 inches) capsule. The first images were of poor quality due to the team's inexperience at holding the receiving antenna in an optimal position. The team was not sure how far the capsule had traveled so they used a radiograph to find the position of the capsule. The radiograph revealed that the device had reached Swain's colon, and thus had successfully traversed the entire length of the small intestine. The team was thrilled at this victory, and urged Swain to swallow another capsule, which he did the next morning. Now that the team was more practiced at optimizing the receiving antennae, and they achieved much better quality images. Swain remarked that he "enjoyed watching the lovely sea view" of his lower intestine. Though the first capsule had only transmitted for approximately two hours before its battery life was depleted, the second capsule transmitted for more than six hours, and the team knew they had obtained quality images of a substantial length of small intestine.[6]

Over the next few months the team conducted several animal and human trials, and by April of 2000 they had used the device to find a small intestinal bleeding source in three patients with "obscure recurrent gastrointestinal bleeding" (a difficult problem to diagnose and treat). An article on the device was published that year in Nature (a prestigious scientific journal), with a header reading "The discomfort of internal endoscopy may soon be a thing of the past."[7] By August of 2001 the device had received FDA clearance, and by October of 2001 Given Imaging had gone public, raising $60 million in its initial public offering.

Given Imaging marketed its device as a system that included its proprietary "RAPID" software, wearable video recording packs, and the swallowable capsules (called "PillCams") (see Figure 2). After swallowing the $450 PillCam, the patient goes about their day while the PillCam broadcasts images to a video recording pack the patient wears around their waist. When the patient returns the pack to the physician, the physician uploads the images and can both view them directly, and utilize Given's computer software that employs algorithms that automatically examine the pixels in the images to identify possible locations of bleeding. The software also enabled physicians to collect the data at remote sites and then send it (or transport it on a USB device) to a central location for diagnostic interpretation if needed. The PillCam exits the patient naturally.

Encouraged by their success, the developers at Given Imaging began working on PillCams for the esophagus (PillCam ESO) and for the colon (PillCam COLON). Whereas Given estimated the global market potential for small bowel capsule endoscopy (PillCam SB) was $1 billion (of which it had penetrated 15% by 2012), it believed the global market opportunity for PillCam COLON could be a multi-billion dollar opportunity due to widespread routine screening for colon cancer. By 2013, Given had also developed PillCam SB3, which offered sharper images and adaptive frame rate technology that enables it to snap more pictures, more quickly. These improvements would enable clinicians to better spot lesions indicating Crohn's disease—lesions that would go undetected by traditional endoscopic methods.[8] Crohn's disease is an auto-immune disorder in which the digestive tract attacks itself, leading to pain, diarrhea, and vomiting. More than one million people have been diagnosed worldwide, and many more cases were thought to be undiagnosed.

| Figure 2 | The PillCam |

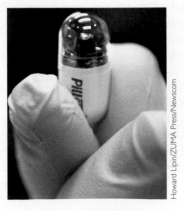

Howard Lipin/ZUMA Press/Newscom

COMPETITION IN THE ENDOSCOPY MARKET

Until 2005, Given enjoyed the benefits of offering a medical technology with tremendous advantages over the alternatives and having no competitors. However, in 2005, Japanese optics giant Olympus introduced its own camera pill—the "Endo Capsule." Given also faced competition from companies that produced traditional technologies for detecting gastrointestinal disorders (traditional endoscopy and radiological imaging).

In 2013, just four companies, Fujifilm Holdings, Olympus, Hoya, and Karl Storz, accounted for 77% of revenue in the traditional endoscope market, with Olympus alone accounting for roughly 50% and the others having nearly equal shares. Narrowing the market down to gastrointestinal endoscopes accentuated Olympus's lead: of this market it held roughly 73%, followed by Hoya at 17% and FujiFilm at 10%. The capsule endoscopy market (camera pills) was even more concentrated, with Olympus and Given Imaging accounting for nearly 100% of the market, but in this segment of the market Olympus was the underdog—Given Imaging controlled nearly 90% of the market.

Olympus

Olympus was founded in 1919 in Japan. Though known by most people as a camera maker, Olympus has a well-established history in medical devices, having developed and marketed medical microscopes, ultrasound equipment and endoscopes. In 1949, a Tokyo doctor asked Olympus to develop a camera that could photograph the inside of a patient's stomach. By 1950, Olympus had developed a prototype of an endoscope, too primitive for clinical use, but with clear potential for further development. Over the next several decades, Olympus was very active in the development of endoscopes, eventually introducing a wide range of endoscopic devices intended for diagnosis and endosurgery and achieving a leading global position.[9] It had legions of salespeople with well-developed relationships with gastroenterologists.

In 2005, Olympus announced its own capsule endoscopy system, "Endo Capsule." The device was launched into the European market in 2006 and into the U.S. market in 2007. Olympus's Endo Capsule offered higher resolution imaging than the PillCam, and real-time viewing, but the latter was seen as both an advantage and a disadvantage. On the one hand, immediacy can be important in some diagnostic situations; on the other hand, taking advantage of real-time viewing meant sitting with a gastroenterologist for the 8–12 hours it took the camera to traverse the patient's GI tract. Though Olympus was estimated to have only a 10% share of the global capsule endoscopy market, its size ($10.3 billion in revenues in 2012 compared to Given's $180.5 million) meant it had far greater resources to deploy.

Fujifilm Holdings

Also founded in Japan in 1919, Fujifilm was an early entrant into film production. By the 1930s, it was producing 35 mm photographic film, 16 mm motion picture film, and X-ray film, and by the 1960s it had offices in Brazil, U.S. and Japan. By the 1980s, the company was aggressively developing medical diagnostic equipment, and artificial "eyes" for robots, in addition to copiers, printers, and film. In 1999, Fuji developed the Sapientia, a digital endoscope system, followed by other endoscope products. In 2007, Fujinon, a division of Fujifilm, signed a strategic R&D agreement with Given Imaging permitting Fujinon to distribute Given's PillCam in various countries, including China. Then in October, 2012, Fujinon entered talks to acquire Given Imaging for $750 million. Given Imaging purportedly needed the cash, but ultimately announced that it would not sell (and Fujinon agreed to continue distributing Given's PillCam).

Hoya

Hoya was founded in Japan in 1941, and makes electro-optical components for high technology products, including medical devices. It acquired the Pentax camera company in 2007 primarily for its medical technologies (Pentax had extensive expertise and production in endoscopes, intraocular lenses, surgical loupes, and biocompatible ceramics), and sold off the other parts of the business to Taiwan Instrument Co., Ltd. and Ricoh Co., Ltd. Its endoscopes are still sold under the Pentax brand name. It also operates the Eyecity chain of contact lens stores in Japan. The company is also well known for making photomasks and photomask blanks for the IT industry.

MANUFACTURING

Given manufactured the PillCam capsules in Yoqneam, Israel. The process included a number of steps in which components were assembled into sub-assemblies, then into the final product, and then inspected, tested, and packaged. Most of the processes were fully- or semi-automated with machines that enabled high-volume manufacturing. A few products, such as sensor arrays and computer workstations (for customers that purchased Given's software preloaded on a workstation), were purchased from external vendors and tested and customized at Given's facilities. While many of its inputs could be obtained from multiple suppliers, Given relied on sole suppliers for some of its inputs, such as its imaging sensor and transmitter for the PillCam capsules.

MARKETING

Given's products were sold primarily to hospitals and gastroenterology offices. Though Given spent very little on advertising, the company benefited by significant free press due to the nature of its intriguing product. Articles compared the product to the movie, "The Fantastic Voyage," and on one occasion in 2005, Katie Couric shared footage of her gastrointestinal system with viewers on the *Today Show*.[10] Similarly, in July, 2012, BBC reporter Michael Mosley spent the entire day having live pictures of his gastrointestinal system transmitted to a public screen as an exhibit at the Science Museum in London.[11]

In 2013, Given was planning its first ever direct-to-consumer marketing campaign. The center of the campaign is a website that attempts to explain Crohn's disease and the PillCam in a user-friendly way. Jonathan Huber, Given's Vice President of Global Marketing noted that one of the obstacles to getting customers to adopt the product for use in identifying and managing Crohn's disease is that most people are unaware such a product exists. Many physicians already had training and equipment for traditional endoscopy methods rather than capsule endoscopy, and Physician's were unlikely to volunteer information about the PillCam to patients if they did not already use the system. The PillCam, however, was significantly more comfortable than traditional endoscopy methods; Huber was confident that if patients knew about the PillCam alternative, they would bring it up with their doctor.

Given also employed a force of 100 sales people to call on gastrointestinal physicians, and offered free training programs and webinars for doctors and staff to teach them how to read the PillCam video output. In 2012, Given held more than 55 "physician events" to promote its products. Given also focused on generating more clinical evidence of the effectiveness of the PillCam in diagnosing and monitoring Crohn's disease.

DISTRIBUTION

Given operated its own direct sales and marketing organizations in the U.S., Germany, France, Australia, Brazil, Canada, Japan, Hong Kong and Israel. It also used third-party distributors or independent sales representatives to sell in other countries (75 countries in total). Typically such distributors would be granted the exclusive right to sell Given's products in a particular country or region so long as they met minimum sales targets. Given would then be very reliant on that distributor for marketing the product in that region and ensuring that regulatory and reimbursement approvals were met. In 2012, 77% of Given's sales came from its direct sales locations, and 23% came from locations in which it relied on third-party distributors.

A VIEW TO THE FUTURE...

By the end of 2012, Given had sold more than 1.9 million capsules (mostly PillCam SB capsules), in over 75 countries, and had more than 5,500 active customers. Sales had grown to $181 million worldwide, with profits of $14 million (see Figure 3). Though it had expanded its product portfolio to other capsule endoscopy applications, and had acquired some complementary gastrointestinal pH measurement products, the bulk of its revenues (65%) still came from its original PillCam SB. Its PillCam COLON product, which it believed to have even bigger potential for the future, had received regulatory approval in Europe, Canada and Latin American, but not yet in Japan or U.S. Furthermore, even in the markets in which it had received regulatory approval, it was still not typically eligible for insurance reimbursement. This fact, combined with the reluctance of physicians to start using a new method for colon exams, had drastically slowed adoption. The future thus held both great promise and great uncertainty. On the one hand, Given's current markets for its PillCam SB were maturing, and competition was becoming more intense. Some of the competitors also had vastly more resources than Given possessed. On the other hand, if physicians would begin to use PillCam SB for monitoring Crohn's disease, and to use PillCam COLON for routine colon exams, Given had the potential for exponential growth.

Figure 3

Given Imaging's Revenues and Net Income, in $US million, 2003 to 2012

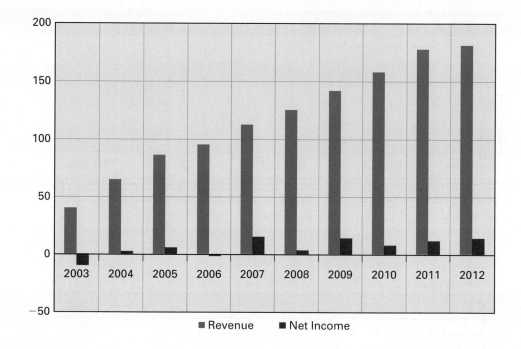

Exhibit 1

Given Imaging's Income Statement Data, in $US thousand, 2008–2012

	2012	2011	2010	2009	2008
Revenues	180,501	177,955	157,809	141,763	125,108
Cost of revenues	(42,971)	(41,466)	(37,629)	(33,145)	(33,001)
Gross profit	**137,530**	**136,489**	**120,180**	**108,618**	**92,107**
Operating expenses:					
Research and development, gross	(25,627)	(26,129)	(21,695)	(17,842)	(15,126)
In-process research and development acquired in a business combination	—	—	—	—	(4,700)
Government grants	1,439	1,113	1,477	1,109	1,530
Research and development, net	(24,188)	(25,016)	(20,218)	(16,733)	(18,296)

(continued)

Exhibit 1

Given Imaging's Income Statement Data, in $US thousand, 2008–2012 (continued)

	2012	2011	2010	2009	2008
Sales and marketing	(76,272)	(75,014)	(67,114)	(61,428)	(60,902)
General and administrative	(22,746)	(23,078)	(25,138)	(18,919)	(19,320)
Termination of marketing agreement	—	—	—	—	5,443
Other, net	(455)	(397)	(759)	(1,220)	(867)
Total operating expenses	**(123,661)**	**(123,505)**	**(113,229)**	**(98,300)**	**(93,942)**
Operating profit (loss)	13,869	12,984	6,951	10,318	(1,835)
Financial income, net	847	1,343	2,599	1,584	4,004
Profit before taxes on income	14,716	14,327	9,550	11,902	2,169
Income tax benefit (expense)	(459)	(2,158)	(1,362)	1,542	(250)
Net profit	**14,257**	**12,169**	**8,188**	**13,444**	**1,919**

Source: Given Imaging, 20-F filing, 2013

Exhibit 2

Given Imaging's Balance Sheet Data, in $US thousand, 2008–2012

	2012	2011	2010	2009	2008
Cash and cash equivalents	35,442	24,285	34,619	46,458	31,697
Short term investments	58,446	64,762	51,973	31,736	28,509
Working capital	122,282	116,613	105,339	100,586	85,154
Long term marketable securities	30,188	16,003	3,873	16,956	30,063
Total assets	274,314	248,265	222,200	185,720	177,915
Long-term liabilities	14,552	13,202	13,266	5,886	5,084
Total liabilities	51,366	50,340	49,412	33,114	31,751
Retained earnings (Accumulated deficit) [1]	1,621	(12,729)	(24,707)	(33,185)	(31,721)
Total shareholders' equity	222,948	197,634	172,688	151,928	144,171

[1]In March 2009 Given paid a dividend of approximately $15.8 million.
Source: Given Imaging, 20-F filing, 2013

NOTES

1. This case was developed through a combination of publicly available materials and documents provided by Given Imaging. The author is grateful for the valuable assistance of Sharon Koninsky of Given Imaging.

2. Iddan, G.J. & Swain, C.P. 2004. History and development of capsule endoscopy. *Gastrointestinal Endoscopy Clinics of North America*, 14:1–9.

3. Given Imaging Prospectus, 2004.

4. Anonymous, 2000. Given Imaging, *Wall Street Transcript - Bear, Stearns & Co. 15th Annual Healthcare Special* - September: 203–2006.

5. Iddan, G.J. & Swain, C.P. 2004. History and development of capsule endoscopy. *Gastrointestinal Endoscopy Clinics of North America*, 14: 1–9.

6. Iddan, G.J. & Swain, C.P. 2004. History and development of capsule endoscopy. *Gastrointestinal Endoscopy Clinics of North America*, 14:1–9.

7. Iddan, G., Meron, G., Glukhovsky, A., Swain P. 2000. Wireless capsule endoscopy. *Nature*, 405:417.

8. Arnold, M. 2013. A view to a pill. *Medical Marketing & Media*, June 1: 27–30.

9. www.olympus.com

10. Arnold, M. 2013. A view to a pill. *Medical Marketing & Media*, June 1: 27–30.

11. Mosley, M. 2012. The second brain in our stomachs. *BBC*, July 12.

Case 13

Skullcandy

Melissa A. Schilling

Marc Stamas/Getty Images

Founded in 2003 by Rick Alden, Skullcandy grew from a simple idea to a company with products distributed in approximately 80 countries and generating just under $300 million in revenues annually. The company's core products, headphones with an extreme sport aesthetic, were sold in both specialty shops (e.g., skateboard, surf, and snowboard shops) and mass market channels such as Target, Best Buy, college bookstores, and more, and its iconic skull logo was recognizable by its core youth market worldwide. Rather than the simplistic and streamlined ear buds that dominated the headphone category throughout the 1990s, many of Skullcandy's designs had large ear cups with integrated amplifiers, akin to those worn by disc jockeys. As Alden notes, one of their first set of headphones, the Skullcrushers, provided sound that "rattles your head and bleeds through your eyes. It's a damage-your-hearing kind of bass."[i] The headphones also came in bold colors and patterns (see Exhibit 1). Skullcandy had reinvented the headphone category from

a commodity-like product to one that was highly differentiated and branded, with distinct designs that became as much about fashion and identity as functionality. As a result, Skullcandy headphones commanded much higher prices, and greater brand loyalty than typical headphones.

After the company's 2011 initial public offering, however, Skullcandy's founder Rick Alden left the company to pursue other entrepreneurial ventures (starting, among other projects, the company Stance, which makes high performance sports socks with unique designs). This worried the young company's new stockholders. Furthermore, competitors began to eagerly imitate the Skullcandy strategy by developing large ear cup headphones with bolder aesthetics, and higher prices. Analysts began to wonder just how far Skullcandy could go.

CREATING AN ACTION SPORTS BRAND

In 2001, veteran snowboarder Rick Alden was riding up a ski lift and listening to music on an MP3 player when he heard his phone ringing, muffled in the pocket of his ski jacket. He fumbled around with his gloved hands, trying to get to the phone before it stopped ringing, worrying that he would drop either his gloves or his phone into the snow 30 feet below. At that moment he thought "why not have headphones that connect to both a cell phone and an MP3 player?"[ii] In January of 2002 he had his first prototype of a device called the "Link" built by a Chinese manufacturer. The device could plug into a cell phone and an MP3 player at the same time, and had a control switch on the cord with a microphone, a button that could switch between the phone and the MP3 player, and a volume control. The device was a hit. By January

Exhibit 1 | Skullcandy Headphone Product Range

Style	In Ear	On Ear	Over Ear
Product			
Price Range	$10–80 MSRP	$20–100 MSRP	$60–300 MSRP
Models	Jib Ink'd 2 Riot Chops Smokin' Buds Titan 50/50 Fix Heavy Medal	Icon 3 Uprock Lowrider Cassette Navigator	Hesh Agent Skullcrusher Crusher Aviator Mix Master

Source: Skullcandy 10-K, 2013. © Lipowski Milan/Shutterstock.com; Metal Hammer Magazine/ Contributor/Future/Getty Images; © Igor Lateci/Shutterstock.com

of 2003 he had taken out two mortgages on his home to launch his company, Skullcandy in Park City, Utah.[iii]

Alden had an extensive background in the snowboarding industry, having previously founded National Snowboard Incorporated (one of the first companies to promote snowboarding) and having developed and marketed his own line of snowboard bindings. His father, Paul Alden, had played many roles in the industry, including serving as the president of the North American Snowboard Association which helped open up ski resorts to snowboarders. His brother, David Alden, had been a professional snowboarder for Burton, and a sales representative for several snowboard lines. Thus when Alden began creating an image and brand for the headphones, it only made sense to create a brand that would have the kind of dynamic edginess that would attract snowboarders and skateboarders. Alden could also use his deep connections in the snowboarding and skateboarding worlds to line up endorsements by pro-riders and distribution by skate and snowboard shops. As Alden notes, "I'd walk into snowboarding and skateboarding shops that I'd sold bindings to or that I'd known for 15 years, and say, "Hey, man, I think you ought to sell headphones." Soon he was developing headphones that were integrated into Giro ski and snowboard helmets, and MP3-equipped backpacks and watches. The graphic imagery of the brand—which draws from hip-hop culture and features a prominent skull, helped to turned a once placid product category into an exciting and important fashion accessory for action sports enthusiasts.

The company grew quickly. By 2005, the company broke $1 million in sales, and in the following year sold almost $10 million worth of headphones and accessories. In 2007, Alden pitched Skullcandy's products to Best Buy, Target and Circuit City, never dreaming that all three would say "yes" and place orders for their U.S. stores. Suddenly the challenge was not selling, but production—could the company deliver that much product on time? Alden's team went to China and quickly figured out a way to increase the tooling cavities used to produce the headphones so that they could get more units out of each production run. Remarkably, they were able to deliver to all three chains by their deadlines.[iv] By the end of the year, Skullcandy had achieved $35 million in revenue, greatly exceeding even the stretch targets the company was shooting for. In 2008, almost 10 million people purchased Skullcandy headphones for total sales of $86.5 million, and by 2009 it had already broken $100 million in sales. In the same year, Alden was named *Entrepreneur* magazine's "Entrepreneur of the Year."

COMPETITION

Though Skullcandy had pioneered the market for action-sports headphones sold through specialty sports channels, in the mass market channels it faced competition from existing large consumer electronics brands that produced more traditional headphones (e.g., Sony, Sennheiser, Bose) and new entrants that entered directly in response to Skullcandy's success (e.g., Beats by Dr. Dre). The former category had the advantage of greater financial and distribution resources, and greater economies of scale. The latter had benefited mostly by observing Skullcandy's strategies to fine-tune their own market entry. For example, whereas Alden had not originally thought people would be willing to pay hundreds of dollars for headphones, managers at Beats by Dr. Dre had correctly surmised that if people are willing to pay hundreds of dollars for designer sunglasses, they might be willing to do so also with headphones. Alden conceded, "We have to give them a lot of credit for figuring out that one."[v] In addition, some sports brands (e.g., Nike and Adidas) had begun offering headphones bearing their brands.

The functionality and style trends in headphones were relatively easy to quickly imitate. The key source of advantage, then, was to create brand loyalty among consumers and distributors. Alden noted that though he had initially patented some of the individual headphone models or technologies, given the time lag between patent application and patent granting, and the expense involved in using patent attorneys, patenting didn't make much sense in his industry—he preferred to just beat his competitors to market with great products.[vi]

SKULLCANDY DISTRIBUTION

Alden was careful in his approach to selling to the mass market, vigilantly distinguishing between products that were sold to the core channel versus to big box retailers.[vii] Even though the core market only accounted for 10% of sales, they were disproportionately important to the reputation of the brand. Alden's philosophy was that "Conservative guys buy core products, but core guys will never buy conservative. In other words, we've got to be edgy and keep our original consumer happy, because without him, we'll lose people like me—old guys who want to buy cool young products too."[viii] To achieve this, Skullcandy restricted the sales of some of its products with the highest performance or edgiest designs to only specialty action-sports retailers such as dedicated skateboard, snowboard, or surf shops, while releasing the rest of the product lineup to broader channels. This helped to ensure that snowboarders and skaters who had bought the latest products at their local board shop were unlikely to see other types of customers with the same headphones, preserving some of the exclusivity of the brand.

MARKETING AT SKULLCANDY

Skullcandy's marketing relied primarily on in-store advertising, trade shows, and sponsoring highly visible sports events, action sports athletes, and music celebrities. Typical sponsorship contracts had a one to three-year term, required sponsored individuals to maintain a visible and exclusive association with Skullcandy headphones, and granted Skullcandy the right to use their names and likenesses in its other marketing. These Skullcandy "ambassadors" also received cash payments for wearing Skullcandy products during public appearances, in magazine photo shoots, or on the podium after a sports victory. The company also made extensive use of social media such as Twitter, Instagram, Facebook, and YouTube to promote its products.

NEW PRODUCT DEVELOPMENT AT SKULLCANDY

To develop a new headphone line, Skullcandy put together teams that included knowledgeable end users, industrial designers, and "creatives." For example, in 2009, the company began to develop a headphone line that would target the hip hop music aficionado market by partnering with key music industry veterans such as Calvin "Snoop Dogg" Broadus and Michael "Mix Master Mike" Schwartz of the Beastie Boys. The collaboration with Snoop Dogg resulted in the "Skullcrusher"—a headphone with extreme bass amplification perfect for listening to rap music.

The collaboration with Mix Master Mike was intended to produce the "ultimate DJ headphone" that would target disk jockeys/turntablists.

To develop the new product, a design team was assembled that included Mix Master Mike (who would lend insight into the key factors that would make the "ideal" DJ headphone, as well as lending his own personal design inspirations), Skullcandy's Director of Industrial Design, Pete Kelly (who would translate the desired features into engineering specifications), an external industrial design company that could quickly transform the team's ideas into photo-realistic renderings, Product Manager Josh Poulsen (who would manage the project milestones and communicate directly to the factory in China where the product would be manufactured), and team members with backgrounds in graphic arts or fine arts who would explore the potential color palettes, materials and form factors to use.

The small size and informal atmosphere at Skullcandy ensured close contact between the team members, and between the team and other Skullcandy personnel. For example, the Director of Industrial Design and the Art Director shared an office, and all of the graphic designers worked in a common bullpen.[ix] The team would schedule face-to-face meetings with Mix Master Mike and the external industrial design company, and Josh Poulsen would travel to China to have similar face-to-face meetings with the manufacturer.

In the first phase, the team met to analyze what functionality would be key to making a compelling product. For the DJ headphones, the team identified the following key factors that would help to significantly improve headphone design[x]:

- Tough, replaceable and/or washable ear pads made of antimicrobial materials (ear pads were prone to getting soiled or torn),
- Headphones that could be worn by "righty" or "lefty" DJs (DJs typically have a preference for leaning on one side while they work, and this side determines the optimal cable location),
- Sound quality that was not too clear, not too bass, and not too muddy (DJs typically were not looking for the clear quality of studio sound)
- Coiled cord or straight cord options (many DJs preferred coiled cords whereas mass market consumers typically preferred straight cords)

Above all, the team had the mandate given by Alden to create "headphones that don't look like headphones."

The product's aesthetic design was heavily influenced by Mix Master Mike. As noted by Dan Levine, "When you attach yourself to someone iconic, you try to figure out what inspires their form sensibilities. For example, Mike likes transformers, Japanese robots, Lamborghinis, furniture by B&B Italia . . . we use these design elements to build inspiration boards."[xi] The team initially met for three straight days in Mix Master Mike's studio. Then, after the team had created 6 to 12 initial sketches, they worked to narrow the list down to three of the best, and then fine-tuned those until they had one best sketch. The external industrial design firm created photorealistic renderings that precisely portrayed what the end product was to look like. At this point marketing people could be brought into the team to begin developing a marketing strategy around the product. The marketing team used "sneak peaks" of renderings and nonfunctioning prototypes to gain initial sales contracts.

The next phase was an iterative process of commercialization and design refinement. According to Levine, "That's when it feels like you're swimming in glue because it never happens fast enough. The design phase is exciting. Once you have that design you get impatient for it to come to market, but you can only work as fast as manufacturing capabilities dictate, and building technical products takes time."[xii] First, CAD files would be brought to China where a manufacturer would use a stereolithography apparatus (SLA) to create prototypes of each part of the headphone in a wax resin. As described by Alden, "you can't see the lasers—the part just rises up out of this primordial ooze. Then you can sand it down, paint it, screw it to your other parts. This part will end up costing $300 compared to the 30 cents the part will eventually cost when its mass produced using injection molding, but it's worth creating these SLA parts to make sure they're accurate."[xiii] SLA versions of the products were also often taken to the trade shows to solicit customer feedback and generate orders. Every week or two, the Product Manager would need to talk to the Chinese factory about building or modifying SLA parts, until eventually a 100% complete SLA product was achieved. At that point, it was time to begin "tooling" (the process of building molds that would be used to mass produce the product). This phase took four to six weeks to complete and was expensive. Several samples would be produced while final modifications were made, and then once a perfect sample was obtained, the tools would be hardened and mass production would begin. As Alden described, "after you've got everything in place—after you've made the first one, then it's just like making doughnuts."[xiv]

All of the steps of the project were scheduled using a Gantt chart (a type of chart commonly used to depict project elements and their deadlines). Project deadlines were determined by working backward from a target market release date and the time required to manufacture the product in China.[xv] In general, the firm sought to release new products in September (before the big Christmas sales season), which required having the tooling complete in July.

Team Roles and Management

Josh Poulsen, the Product Manager, was responsible for coordinating all of the team members and making sure all of the deadlines were met. Every major design decision was passed up to Dan Levine for approval, and when the design was ready for "tooling" (being handed off to manufacturing), it had to be approved by Rick Alden, as this phase entailed large irreversible investments. Most of the people at Skullcandy were involved with many projects simultaneously. As Levine emphasized, "This is a lean organization. At Nike you can work on a single or a few projects; when you have a brand that's small and growing fast, you work on a tremendous number of projects, and you also hire outside talent for some tasks."[xvi] According to Rick Alden, "We used to try to manage everything in-house, but we just don't have enough bodies. We've discovered that the fastest way to expand our development capacity is to use outside developers for portions of the work. We'll develop the initial idea, and then bring it to one of our trusted industrial design firms to do the renderings, for example."[xvii]

According to Alden, the biggest challenge associated with new product development is managing three different development cycles simultaneously. "You have your new stuff that you're coming out with that you haven't shown anyone yet—that's the really exciting stuff that everyone focuses on. Then you have the products you have just shown at the last show but that aren't done yet—maybe the manufacturing process isn't approved or the packaging isn't finished. You're taking orders but you haven't yet finished the development. Finally, you have all of the products you've been selling already but that require little improvements (e.g., altering how something is soldered, improving a cord, changing the packaging). We have so little bandwidth in product development that the big challenge has been managing all of these cycles. We just showed a product in January of this year [2009]

that we still haven't delivered and its now May. We were just too excited to show it. But that's risky. If you don't deliver on time to a retailer, they get really angry and they won't keep your product on the shelf."[xviii]

EMPLOYEE REVIEWS AND REWARDS

Team members did not receive financial rewards from individual projects. Instead, their performance was rewarded through recognition at monthly "Skullcouncil" meetings, and through quarterly "one touch" reviews. For the quarterly reviews, each employee would prepare a one-page "brag sheet" about what they had accomplished in the previous quarter, what they intended accomplish in the next quarter, and what their strengths and weaknesses were. These reviews would be used to provide feedback to the employee, and to determine the annual bonus. 75% of the annual bonus was based on the individual's performance, and 25% was based on overall company performance. According to Rick Alden, "In the early days, we did things very differently than we do now. Everyone received bonuses based on overall performance—there were so few of us that we all had a direct attachment to the bottom line. Now with a bigger staff, we have to rely more on individual metrics, and we have to provide quarterly feedback so that the amount of the annual bonus doesn't come as a surprise."[xix] The company also relied on some less conventional incentives. Each year the board of directors would set an overarching stretch target for revenues, and if the company surpassed it, Alden took the whole company on a trip. In 2006, he took everyone heli-boarding (an extreme sport where snowboarders are brought to the top of a snow-covered peak by helicopter). When the company achieved nearly triple its 2007 sales goal (earning $35 million instead of the targeted $13 million), Alden took the entire staff and their families to Costa Rica to go surfing.[xx]

The Future at Skullcandy

Alden had always been, first and foremost, an entrepreneur. Chafing under the direction of others, Alden had early in his life concluded that he was "completely unemployable," and set about creating his own economic opportunities. As an archetypal serial entrepreneur, he was happier creating new companies than managing established companies. In 2009, as the IPO process was unfolding, he noted to Jeremy Andrus (who had been with the company since 2005 and served as COO since 2008), "there are other entrepreneurial enterprises I'd like to focus on. I don't think I'll be sitting in public CEO seat for the next five years—it's time to do something different."[xxi] Thus one month after the IPO filing in January of 2009, Rick Alden startled the investment community by resigning as the CEO of Skullcandy (though he remained on the board of directors). Jeremy Andrus replaced Alden's position at the helm of Skullcandy, as Alden left to go work closely with his newest startup, Stance socks.

In the years that followed, management at Skullcandy sought to expand both its product portfolio and global reach. Though Skullcandy generated the vast majority of its revenues from headphones, the company also offered branded apparel, smartphone cases, and docking stations. Skullcandy also began to sell headphones designed specifically for videogaming (and acquired gaming handset manufacturer Astro Gaming for $10 million in early 2011).

The company also began to expand more aggressively internationally. Though prior to 2011 the company had only worked with third-party distributors to sell product into international markets, Andrus believed that such distributors were not invested in stewarding the brand. He thus used some of the capital raised through

the IPO to buy Skullcandy's European distributor (Kungsbacka 57 AB, who held an exclusive distribution license to sell Skullcandy products in Europe), and began making investments in brand, marketing and infrastructure to accelerate growth in Europe. Skullcandy also began marketing directly to Mexico, Japan and China, and began sponsoring international athletes, musicians, and artists. By 2013, Skullcandy products could be found in roughly 80 countries, and was earning 30% of its sales in markets outside of the U.S.

Though the Skullcandy name was becoming more and more well-known and its products were available in an ever wider range of outlets, investors still had some concerns. Though revenues had continued to increase, so had competition, and Skullcandy's net margin had decreased from 18% and 17% in 2007 and 2008 respectively, to 8% and 9% in 2011 and 2012 respectively (see Exhibit 2). Alden's departure had given investors concern in 2011, and the 2013 announcement that Andrus would also be departing (Alden returned as Interim CEO while a new leader was sought) had intensified those concerns. As a result, the stock price of the company had fallen from its IPO price of $20 per share to $5.73 per share in June of 2013 (see Exhibit 3). The young and fast-growing company was making the transition to adulthood, and it was anyone's guess what that adulthood look like. Would it continue to grow and diversify, leveraging the brand

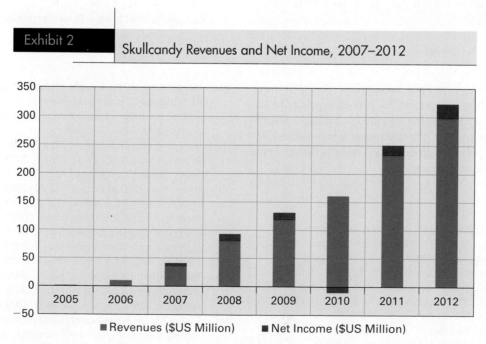

Exhibit 2 Skullcandy Revenues and Net Income, 2007–2012

Source: Skullcandy 10-K, 2013.

| Exhibit 3 | Skullcandy Stock Price and Trading Volume, August 2011–June 2013 |

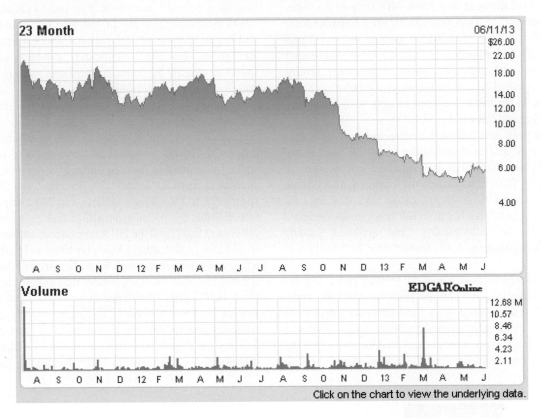

Source: Nasdaq.com

profitably to more product categories? Would it stay focused and lean, deepening its presence primarily in action-sports headphones? Or would it stumble, enabling competitors to displace it in the market it had pioneered? The next few years would be pivotal ones as the answers to these questions emerged.

NOTES

i. Alden, R. 2008. How I did it. *Inc.* September.
ii. Osmond, A. 2007. Rick Alden: Founder & CEO Skullcandy. *Launch,* March/April.
iii. Interview with Rick Alden, May 5, 2009.
iv. Alden, R. 2008. How I did it. *Inc.* September.
v. Alden, R. 2012. Speech given at New York University Executive Education seminar, "Breakthrough Strategic Thinking," October.
vi. Interview with Rick Alden, February 2012.

vii. Anonymous. 2008. Caught on tape: Rick Alden, CEO of Skullcandy. *Transworld Business*, October 24th.
viii. Alden, R. 2008. How I did it. *Inc.'s Small Business Success Newsletter*, September.
ix. Interview with Dan Levine, May 2, 2009.
x. Interview with Dan Levine, May 2, 2009.
xi. Interview with Dan Levine, May 2, 2009.
xii. Interview with Dan Levine, May 2, 2009.
xiii. Interview with Rick Alden, May 5, 2009.
xiv. Interview with Rick Alden, May 5, 2009.
xv. Interview with Dan Levine, May 2, 2009.
xvi. Interview with Dan Levine, May 2, 2009.
xvii. Interview with Rick Alden, May 5, 2009.
xviii. Interview with Rick Alden, May 5, 2009.
xix. Interview with Rick Alden, May 5, 2009.
xx. Interview with Rick Alden, May 5, 2009.
xxi. Lewis, M. 2011. Skullcandy CEO Jeremy Andrus breaks the silent period. *Transworld Business,* August 29th.

Case 14

Tesla Motors

Melissa A. Schilling

In 2013, Tesla Motors was a 4500-person company on track to set history. It had created two cars that most people agreed were remarkable. It had posted its first quarterly profit in 2013, and had repaid its government loans ahead of the major auto conglomerates. Most importantly, it looked like it might *survive*. Perhaps even thrive. This was astonishing as there had been no other successful auto manufacturing start up in the U.S. since the 1920s.

The road leading up to Tesla's position in 2013 had not always been smooth, and there were many doubts that still lingered. Tesla had benefited from the enthusiasm of the "eco-wealthy"—a rather narrow portion of the market. How would Tesla fare when it was in direct competition with General Motors, Ford, and Nissan for the mass market? Would it be able to turn a sustainable profit on its automaking operations? Furthermore, some questioned whether Tesla's goals to sell to the mass market even made sense. In the niche market, it had a privileged position with customers that were relatively price-insensitive and were seeking a stylish, high performance car that made an environmental statement. To compete for the mass market, the car would have to provide good value for the money (involving trade-offs that might conflict with Chairman Elon Musk's ideals), and the obstacles to charging would have to be overcome.

HISTORY OF TESLA

In the year 2003, an engineer named Martin Eberhard was looking for his next big project. A tall, slim man with a mop of gray hair, Eberhard was a serial entrepreneur who had launched a number of start-ups, including a company called NuvoMedia, which he sold to Gemstar

in a $187 million deal. Eberhard was also looking for a sports car that would be environmentally friendly—he had concerns about global warming and U.S. dependence on the Middle East for oil. When he didn't find the car of his dreams on the market he began contemplating building one himself, even though he had zero experience in the auto industry. Eberhard noticed that many of the driveways that had a Toyota Prius hybrid electric vehicle (or "dork mobile" as he called it) also had expensive sports cars in them—making Eberhard speculate that there could be a market for a high performance environmentally friendly car. As explained by Eberhard, "It was clear that people weren't buying a Prius to save money on gas—gas was selling close to inflation-adjusted all-time lows. They were buying them to make a statement about the environment."[i]

Eberhard began to consider a range of alternative fuel options for his car: hydrogen fuel cells, natural gas, diesel. However he soon concluded the highest efficiency and performance would come from a pure electric vehicle. Luckily for Eberhard, Al Cocconi (founder of AC Propulsion and one of the original engineers for GM's ill-fated EV-1) had concluded the same thing, and had produced a car called the tzero. The tzero could go from zero to 60 miles per hour in 4.1 seconds, but it was powered with extremely heavy lead-acid batteries, limiting its range to about 60 miles between charges. Eberhard approached Cocconi with the idea of using the lighter lithium ion batteries, which offered six times more energy per pound. Cocconi was eager to try out the idea (he had, in fact, been experimenting with lithium ion batteries himself), and the resulting lithium ion based tzero accelerated to 60 miles per hour in 3.6 seconds, and could travel more than 300 miles. Eberhard licensed the electric-drive-train technology from AC Propulsion, and founded his company, Tesla Motors (named after Nikola Tesla, a late 19th century and early 20th century inventor who developed, among other things, the AC electrical systems used in the U.S. today).[ii]

Meanwhile, there was another entrepreneur—one with much deeper pockets—also interested in developing electric vehicles based on the tzero: Elon Musk. In 2002, Elon Musk was a 31-year-old South African living in California, who had founded a company that ultimately became PayPal. After selling PayPal to eBay in 2002 for $1.5 billion, he started a company called SpaceX with the ambitious goal of developing cheap, consumer space travel. (SpaceX's Dragon spacecraft ultimately made history in May of 2012 by becoming the first commercial vehicle to launch and dock at the International Space Station.[iii]) Musk was also the chairman of a high profile clean tech venture in Northern California called Solar City. Musk's glamorous and assertive style, and his astonishing record of high-tech entrepreneurship, made him one of the inspirations for the Tony Stark character in Jon Favreau's Iron Man movies.

Like Eberhard, Musk thought electric cars were the key to the U.S. achieving energy independence, and he approached Cocconi about buying the tzero. Tom Gage, who was then AC Propulsion's CEO, suggested that Musk collaborate with Eberhard. After a two hour meeting in February of 2004, Musk agreed to fund Eberhard's plan with $6.3 million. He would be the company's chairman and Eberhard would serve as CEO.

The first Tesla prototype, named the Roadster, was based on the $45,000 Lotus Elise, a fast and light sports car that seemed perfect for the creation of Eberhard and Musk's grand idea (see Figure 1a). The car would have 400 volts of electric potential, liquid-cooled lithium ion batteries, and a series of silicon transistors that would give the car acceleration so powerful the driver would be pressed back against their seat.[iv] It would be about as fast as a Porsche 911 Turbo, would not create a single emission, and would get about 220 miles on a single charge from the kind of outlet you would use to power a washing machine.[v]

While the men at first worked well together, personality clashes soon began to emerge. Both were technically savvy and vigorously addressed problems within the company. As described by Laurie Yoler, Eberhard was "just brilliant, and he has this tenacity that is unbelievable . . . He is the guy you want around in those early days when you have naysayers all around." However, Eberhard could also be abrasive and critical. Musk, in turn, was not content to just financially back the company—he

Figure 1a   Tesla Roadster

began to get intimately involved in decisions about the car's design and the operation of the company. Soon Musk and Eberhard were at odds over decisions such as the body panels (Eberhard preferred to stick with the fiberglass panels used in the original Elise; Musk wanted to use the lighter, stronger—and more expensive—carbon fiber), marketing (Eberhard had approved the hiring of PR professionals to build publicity for the car before its launch; Musk fired them, believing his own involvement and the car itself would generate enough publicity), and even the chassis (Eberhard wanted to reap the cost savings of sticking with the Elise's original crash-tested, off-the-rack chassis; Musk wanted to lower the doorsills by two inches to make the car easier to enter and exit). Musk also wanted to redesign the headlights and door latches, and replace the Elise's seats with more comfortable—and expensive—custom seats.[vi]

In each case, Musk's preference prevailed. As Musk insisted, "you can't sell a $100,000 car that looks like crap," and Musk's views were hard to ignore given that he was putting more and more of his personal wealth into the company. By 2007 he had put in $55 million of his own money into the company, and had also raised money from his other wealthy entrepreneur friends (that included eBay's second employee, Jeff Skoll, and Google founders Sergey Brin and Larry Page).

Musk's insistence on the best materials and parts, however, combined with Eberhard's inexperience as the manager of a major firm, resulted in delays and runaway costs. At a staff meeting in June 2007, Tom Colson, head of manufacturing, revealed a cost analysis suggesting that the average cost of the cars would be over $100,000 for the first 50, and would decline only slightly with increased volume. Eberhard could not answer the financial questions of the venture capitalists on Tesla's board, and their confidence in him was eroded even further by his defense of "In any other company it's the CFO that provides those numbers . . . I'm an engineer, not a finance guy." In August of 2007, the board removed him as CEO and demoted him to president of technology. Then in October of 2007, Musk arranged for Eberhard to be ousted from the company entirely. Furious, Eberhard started a blog detailing what he called the "Stealth Bloodbath" going on at Tesla, and he would later sue Musk for libel, slander, and breach of contract.[vii]

Meanwhile, Eberhard's temporary replacement was Michael Marks, former CEO of Flextronics. Marks immediately created a priority list that identified items with potential to delay the car. He mothballed any plans for side projects and focused the entire business on streamlining costs and getting the Roadster out. Despite his efforts, the Roadster missed its deadline for beginning production at the Lotus facility, triggering a penalty built into the manufacturing contract Eberhard had signed with Lotus: a $4 million fee.

By the beginning of 2008 morale was at an all-time low. In March, however, production began on the Roadster, and by July of 2008, most of the production problems had been forgotten as the first seven Roadsters (the "Founder's Series") hit the road. Enthusiasm for the cars was astonishing—the cars boasted an all-star list of celebrities with reservations to buy a car, and everywhere the Roadster drove, people (albeit mostly men) stopped to stare.[viii]

Musk's ambitions did not stop at a niche high-end car, however. He wanted to build a major U.S. auto company—a feat that had not been successfully accomplished since the 1920s. To do so, he knew he needed to introduce a less expensive car that could attract a higher volume of sales, if not quite the mass market. In June of 2008, Tesla announced the Model S—a high performance all-electric sedan that would sell for a price ranging from $57,400 to $77,400, and compete against cars like the BMW 5-series (see Figure 1b). The car would have an all-aluminum body, and a range of up to 300 miles per charge.[ix] The Model S cost $500 million to develop,[x] however offsetting that cost was a $465 million loan Tesla received from the U.S. government to build the car, as part of the U.S. government's initiative to promote the development of technologies that would help the U.S. to achieve energy independence.

Figure 1b   Tesla Model S

Mark Von Holden/WireImage/Getty Images

By May of 2012 Tesla reported that it already had 10,000 reservations for customers hoping to buy the Model S, and Musk confidently claimed the company would soon be producing—and selling—20,000 Model S cars a year. Musk also noted that after ramping up production, he expected to see "at least 10,000 units a year from demand in Europe and at least 5,000 in Asia."[xi] The production of the Model S went more smoothly than that of the Roadster, and by June of 2012 the first Model S cars were rolling off the factory floor. The very first went to Jeff Skoll, eBay's first president, and a major investor in Tesla. On the day of the launch, Skoll talked with Musk about whether it was harder to build a rocket or a car (referring to Musk's SpaceX company): "We decided it was a car. There isn't a lot of competition in space."[xii]

To build the car, Tesla bought a recently closed automobile factory in Fremont California that had been used for the New United Motor Manufacturing Inc. (NUMMI) venture between Toyota and General Motors. The factory, which was far bigger than Tesla's immediate needs, would give the company room to grow. Furthermore, though the plant and the land it was on had been appraised at around $1 billion before NUMMI was shut down, Tesla was able to snap up the idled factory for $42 million.[xiii] Tesla also used the factory to produce battery packs for Toyota's RAV4, and a charger for a subcompact Daimler AG electric vehicle. These projects would supplement Tesla's income while also helping it to build scale and learning curve efficiencies in its technologies. Musk also had plans to produce a sport utility vehicle, the Model X, which would cost $250 million to develop and would go into production in late 2013.

OBSTACLES TO THE ADOPTION OF ELECTRIC VEHICLES

There were a number of obstacles slowing the adoption of electric vehicles. The first was the price: Electric vehicles were, typically, significantly more expensive than comparable internal combustion models. Complicating matters still further, most consumers had a very difficult time estimating how much their cost of ownership for an electric car would be: How much would they pay to charge at home? How much would they pay to charge away from home? What would the maintenance and repairs of an electric vehicle cost? How long would the battery and/or car last? Would it have resale value? To lessen these concerns, Elon Musk set out to make the cost of owning a Tesla as certain as possible. First, he created a "Supercharger" network that Model S owners could use for free, for the life of the car. As noted by Musk, "The clearest way to convey the message that electric cars are actually better than gasoline cars is to say charging is free."[xiv] The hitch was that a user had to be within range of one of the Supercharger stations. Second, Musk announced an unprecedented price protection guarantee that permitted a Model S owner to trade in their car for a designated residual value anytime within the first three years of the cars life. Musk also announced plans to offer free repairs, and a free replacement car while a customer's car was being repaired. Needless to say, analysts were scratching their heads at the potential costs of these promises.

The second major obstacle to the adoption of electric vehicles was their limited range and associated "range anxiety" (people's concerns about driving in places where they were not sure they would be able to charge their cars). These concerns were not so much of an issue for the Tesla cars due to their exceptionally long range. The other "mass market" electric vehicles faced tougher hurdles. For example, though a Nissan Leaf could be charged at an ordinary 110 household outlet, a full charge by this method could take eight hours. Level 2 charging with a 220-volt outlet could shorten that time to four hours, but this was still completely impractical for recharging during a trip. DC Fast Chargers and Tesla's "Superchargers" promised to fully charge a vehicle in 30 minutes or less. While this is still significantly longer than the typical 6-minute gasoline fill-up, it meant that charging could be feasible if it were colocated with other services that drivers might appreciate, such as restaurants or coffee shops. There were, however, only six Tesla Supercharging stations in the world at the beginning of 2013.[xv] DC Fast Chargers and Tesla's Supercharging stations were expensive to purchase and install—up to $250,000 depending on the location—and they needed to be close to heavy-duty electricity transformers.

COMPETITION IN THE ELECTRIC VEHICLE MARKET

Hybrid electric vehicles (HEV, such as the Toyota Prius) made their appearance in the U.S. auto market in 2000. These vehicles were readily adopted by consumers because they require no change in typical consumer usage habits—they are filled with gasoline and will automatically switch between electric miles and gasoline miles. Most such HEVs, however, have extremely limited electric range. For many, ten miles of electric driving before switching over to gas is the norm. This limits their ability to reduce carbon emissions or to influence energy usage. All-electric vehicles (also called Plug-in Electric vehicles, known alternatively as AEV or PEV) get all of their energy from electricity. They are thus considered true zero-emission vehicles. Plug-in Hybrid Electric vehicles (PHEV) such as the Chevy Volt plugged in to charge, but could also use gas.

A number of automakers were introducing electric vehicles by 2013—in large part due to California's CARB standards that mandated that for automobiles to be sold in California, a certain portion of an automaker's fleet had to be emission free. As a result, some automakers were willing to produce all-electric vehicles at a loss in order to be able to also sell more lucrative internal combustion models. (It was these California's zero-emissions mandates that had spurred a flurry of introductions of electric vehicles in the early 1990s. The subsequent downscaling of California's zero-emission mandate in the late 1990s led GM, Toyota, Honda, and Ford to shut down their loss-making EV programs, including most notoriously, GM's EV-1s, which were literally torn from their owners and crushed, as shown in the film "Who Killed the Electric Car?") Other automakers opted to buy zero-emission credits from those companies that sold more than their required proportion of zero-emission vehicles. Tesla was one such automaker who had surplus credits (since it produced no internal combustion vehicles), and as a result Tesla earned roughly $68 million selling its ZEV credits in the first quarter of 2013.

Several companies had attempted to enter the all-electric vehicle market, but run out of cash and ceased operations. These included Fisker, Coda, Azure Dynamics, Bright Automotive, and others. The more serious competition was coming from established automakers who had deeper pockets to withstand the losses of building the electric vehicle market. Among these, there were a few competing cars that had sold significant (though still small) numbers of cars into the market. The Nissan Leaf, for example, retailed for about $35,000, and had a range of about 90-100 miles per charge. It had sold 25,000 units in the U.S. and 50,000 worldwide by June of 2013. The Chevy Volt was a plug-in hybrid that could travel about 40 all-electric miles per charge, and an additional 340 miles on gasoline (making it a good solution for individuals that primarily made short commutes, but also wanted to be able to drive the car long distances without "range anxiety"). It also retailed for about $35,000, and had sold over 20,000 units in the U.S. by June of 2013 (see Figure 2).

Figure 2   U.S. Electric Vehicle Sales

Company	June 2013	June 2012	% Change	YTD 2013	YTD 2012	% Change
Ford	**7736**	**1354**	**471.34**	**46197**	**8992**	**413.76**
Ford C-Max Hybrid	2889	0	–	17858	0	–
Ford C-Max Energi PHEV	455	0	–	2482	0	–
Ford Escape Hybrid	0	17	–	0	1281	–
Ford Focus Electric	177	89	98.88	900	97	827.84
Ford Fusion Hybrid	3057	797	283.56	20283	4988	306.64
Ford Fusion Energi PHEV	390	0	–	1584	0	–
Lincoln MKZ Hybrid	768	451	70.29	3090	2626	17.67
GM	**2831**	**1927**	**46.91**	**10660**	**10020**	**6.39**
Chevy Volt	2698	1760	53.30	9855	8817	11.77
Other hybrids	133	167	−20.36	805	1203	−33.06
Honda	**1758**	**1566**	**12.26**	**9302**	**10712**	**−13.16**
Honda Civic Hybrid	568	548	3.65	3141	4118	−23.73
Honda CR-Z	393	409	−3.91	2415	2404	0.46
Honda Insight	384	494	−22.27	2362	4041	−41.55
Honda Fit EV	208	0	–	291	0	–
Honda Accord PHEV	42	0	–	200	0	–
Acura ILX Hybrid	163	115	41.74	893	149	499.33
Mitsubishi						
Mitsubishi i	39	33	18.18	882	333	164.86

Company	June 2013	June 2012	% Change	YTD 2013	YTD 2012	% Change
Nissan						
Nissan Leaf	2225	535	315.89	9839	3148	212.55
Porsche	**66**	**67**	**-1.49**	**372**	**909**	**-59.08**
Porsche Cayenne S Hybrid	62	42	47.62	294	669	-56.05
Porsche Panamera Hybrid	4	25	-84.00	78	240	-67.50
Toyota	**30663**	**25776**	**18.96**	**176506**	**169113**	**4.37**
Toyota Prius Liftback	14066	11514	22.16	76809	83205	-7.69
Toyota Prius C	3442	3657	-5.88	20575	16251	26.61
Toyota Prius V	2987	3284	-9.04	18616	22851	-18.53
Toyota Prius PHEV	584	695	-15.97	4214	4347	-3.06
Toyota Camry Hybrid	3878	3459	12.11	23834	23538	1.26
Toyota Highlander Hybrid	550	496	10.89	2960	3051	-2.98
Toyota Avalon Hybrid	1394	0	–	8348	0	–
Toyota RAV4 EV	44	0	–	408	0	–
Lexus Hybrids	3718	2671	39.20	20742	15870	30.70
Volkswagen						
Volkswagen Jetta Hybrid	438	0	–	2219	0	–
Total 100% Electrics	**2693**	**657**	**309.89**	**12320**	**3578**	**244.33**
Total PHEVs	**4169**	**2455**	**69.82**	**18335**	**13164**	**39.28**
Total Conv. Hybrids	**38894**	**28146**	**38.19**	**225322**	**186485**	**20.83**
TOTAL	**45756**	**31258**	**46.38**	**255977**	**203227**	**25.96**

Source: EVObsession, June Electric Vehicle Sales, Published July 4, 2013 at http://evobsession.com/electric-vehicles-sales-update-june-2013-sales/june-electric-vehicle-sales/

TESLA'S STRATEGIES

Automated Manufacturing

In 2013, all of Tesla's manufacturing was performed at its Fremont plant. Its manufacturing process was highly automated, with extensive use of eight-to ten-foot-tall red robots, reminiscent of Iron Man. Each robot had a single multi-jointed arm. While typical auto factory robots perform only one function, Tesla's robots perform up to four tasks: welding, riveting, bonding, and installing a component. Eight robots might work on a single car at each station of the assembling line in a choreographed pattern like ballet. The robots produce up to 83 cars a day, and can be reprogrammed to produce the Model X on the same assembly line.[xvi]

Distribution

Musk saw the franchise-dealership arrangements that U.S. car companies use to sell cars as an expensive, margin-killing model. He chose instead to own and operate Tesla dealerships himself (a controversial move that has provoked the ire of dealership networks). Furthermore, Tesla dealerships are more like "stores" in upscale shopping malls (in 2013 the company had 35 stores across the U.S., Europe, and Asia). Salespeople answer customer questions without using high-pressure sales tactics. The company also sells direct to consumers on the internet.

Marketing

Tesla spends no money on advertising, nor does it have any plans to hire advertising agencies or run ads in the future. Its in-house marketing team had only seven staff people, and an internal team runs the website. Nissan, by contrast, spent $25 million advertising the Leaf in 2012. According to Alexis Georgeson, Tesla spokesperson, "Right now, the stores are our advertising. We're very confident we can sell 20,000-plus cars a year without paid advertising . . . It may be something we'll do years down the road. But it's certainly not something we feel is crucial for sales right now."[xvii]

LOOKING TO THE FUTURE . . .

In the first quarter of 2013, Tesla announced its first quarterly profit. The company had taken in $562 million in revenues, and reported an $11.2 million profit. Then more good news came: the Model S had earned Consumer Reports' highest rating, and had outsold similarly priced BMW and Mercedes models in the first quarter.[xviii] In May of 2013, the company raised $1 billion by issuing new shares, and then surprised investors by announcing that it had paid back its government loan. After repaying the loan, Tesla had about $679 million in cash. Musk had announced confidently that he felt it was his obligation to pay back taxpayer money as soon as possible, and that the company had sufficient funds now to develop its next generation of automobiles without the loan, and without issuing further shares.[xix]

Tesla's success was surprising and inspiring. The company had survived its infancy, appeared to be solvent, and was meeting its sales objectives even though serious obstacles remained for electric vehicles. It was also competing against companies with far greater scale. As noted by O'Dell, a senior editor at auto information sites Edmunds.com, on Tesla's success, "A lot of people have been very, very skeptical . . . when you want to be an automaker, you are competing with multibillion-dollar conglomerates . . . It's entrepreneurism on steroids . . . They had a huge learning curve but they've powered through it." Theo O'Neill, an analyst at Wunderlich Securities adds that "It's going to prove everybody in Detroit wrong . . . They all say what Tesla is doing isn't possible."[xx]

However, some investment analysts were more skeptical. The 2013 profits had included a one-time $10.7 million DOE stock warrant profit, and $68 million in ZEV credit sales.[xxi] The warrant revenues would not be repeated, and nobody knew what the yearly demand for ZEV credits would be and whether such revenues were sustainable. Competition from the major automakers was also increasing steadily. Furthermore, what was the true market size for electric vehicles, and what portion of that market would pay the higher price of a Tesla? On top of this, Tesla's stock had risen meteorically and many investors were concerned that Tesla's stock price was an overinflated bubble (see Figure 3). In June of 2013 Tesla's market capitalization was $11 billion—more than Fiat's and roughly a quarter of General Motors. While Tesla's success surely warranted praise and enthusiasm, it was difficult for many people to reconcile such a large market capitalization with Tesla's sales. Furthermore, if the stock was overvalued and began to drop precipitously, it could undermine people's faith in the company. In short, Tesla was not out of the woods yet.

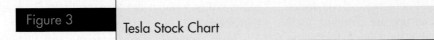

Figure 3 — Tesla Stock Chart

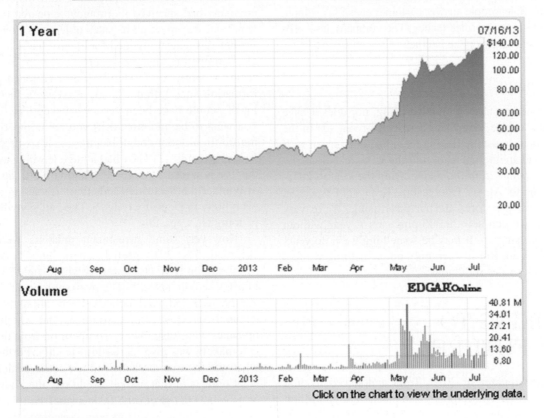

Source: Nasdaq.com

Exhibit 1 — Tesla Financials, in Thousand US$

	March 2013	2012	2011	2010
Revenues				
Automotive sales	555,203	385,699	148,568	97,078
Development services	6,589	27,557	55,674	19,666
Total revenues	561,792	413,256	204,242	116,744
Cost of revenues				
Automotive sales	461,818	371,658	115,482	79,982
Development services	3,654	11,531	27,165	6,031
Total cost of revenues (1)	465,472	383,189	142,647	86,013
Gross profit	96,320	30,067	61,595	30,731

(continued)

	March 2013	2012	2011	2010
Operating expenses				
Research and development (1)	54,859	273,978	208,981	92,996
Selling, general and administrative (1)	47,045	150,372	104,102	84,573
Total operating expenses	101,904	424,350	313,083	177,569
Income/Loss from operations	**−5,584**	**−394,283**	**−251,488**	**−146,833**
Interest income	10	288	255	258
Interest expense	−118	−254	−43	−992
Other income (expense), net (2)	17,091	−1,828	−2,646	−6,583
Income (loss) before income taxes	11,399	−396,077	−253,922	−154,155
Provision for (benefit from) income taxes	151	136	489	173
Net income (loss)	**11,248**	**−396,213**	**−254,411**	**−154,328**
Net income (loss) per common share, basic (3)	0.1	(3.69)	(2.53)	(3.04)

NOTES

i. Copeland, M.V. 2008. Tesla's wild ride. *Fortune*, Vol. 158, issue 2, pg. 82–94.

ii. Copeland, M.V. 2008. Tesla's wild ride. *Fortune*, Vol. 158, issue 2, pg. 82–94.

iii. Boudreau. J. 2012. In a Silicon Valley milestone, Tesla Motors begins delivering Model S electric cars. *Oakland Tribune*, June 24: Breaking News Section.

iv. Copeland, M.V. 2008. Tesla's wild ride. *Fortune*, Vol. 158, issue 2, pg. 82–94.

v. Williams, A. 2009. Taking a Tesla for a status check in New York. *New York Times*, July 19, ST.7.

vi. Copeland, M.V. 2008. Tesla's wild ride. *Fortune*, Vol. 158, issue 2, pg. 82–94.

vii. Garthwaite, J. 2011. Tesla sues "Top Gear," *New York Times*, April 3, AU.2.

viii. Williams, A. 2009. Taking a Tesla for a status check in New York. *New York Times*, July 19, ST.7.

ix. Ramsey, M. 2011. Tesla sets 300-mile range for second electric car. *Wall Street Journal (Online)*, March 7: n/a.

x. Aggregated from Tesla's first quarter 2013 10Q and 2012 10K.

xi. Sweet, C. 2013. Tesla posts its first quarterly profit. *Wall Street Journal (Online)*, May 9: n/a.

xii. Boudreau. J. 2012. In a Silicon Valley milestone, Tesla Motors begins delivering Model S electric cars. *Oakland Tribune*, June 24: Breaking News Section.

xiii. Anonymous. 2010. Idle Fremont plant gears up for Tesla. *Wall Street Journal (Online)*, October 20: n/a.

xiv. Woody, T. 2012. Billionaire car wars. *Forbes*, December 10: pg. 90–98.

xv. Woody, T. 2012. Billionaire car wars. *Forbes*, December 10: pg. 90–98.

xvi. Markoff, J. 2012. Skilled work, without the worker. *New York Times*, August 19:A.1.

xvii. McCarthy, M. 2013. Tesla generates small sales, huge buzz without paid ads. *Advertising Age*, June 10:pg. 9.

xviii. Levi, M. 2013. How Tesla pulled ahead of the electric-car pack. *Wall Street Journal*, June 21:A.11.

xix. White, J.B. 2013. Corporate News: Electric car startup Tesla repays U.S. loan. *Wall Street Journal*, May 23:B.3.

xx. Boudreau. J. 2012. In a Silicon Valley milestone, Tesla Motors begins delivering Model S electric cars. *Oakland Tribune*, June 24: Breaking News Section.

xxi. Tesla 10-Q, May 2013.

Case 15

Charles Schwab

Charles Hill

INTRODUCTION

In 1971, Charles Schwab, who was 32 at the time, set up his own stock brokerage concern, First Commander. Later he would change the name to Charles Schwab & Company, Inc. In 1975, when the Securities and Exchange Commission abolished mandatory fixed commissions on stock trades, Schwab moved rapidly into the discount brokerage business, offering rates that were as much as 60% below those offered by full commission brokers. Over the next 25 years, the company experienced strong growth, fueled by a customer centric focus, savvy investments in information technology, and a number of product innovations, including a bold move into online trading in 1996.

By 2000, the company was widely regarded as one of the great success stories of the era. Revenues had grown to $7.1 billion and net income to $803 million, up from $1.1 billion and $124 million respectively in 1993. Online trading had grown to account for 84% of all stock trades made through Schwab, up from nothing in 1995. The company's stock price had appreciated by more than that of Microsoft over the prior ten years. In 1999, the market value of Schwab eclipsed that of Merrill Lynch, the country's largest full service broker, despite Schwab's revenues being more than 60% lower.

The 2000s proved to be a more difficult environment for the company. Between March 2000 and mid 2003 share prices in the U.S. tumbled, with the technology heavy NASDAQ index losing 80% of its value from peak to trough. The volume of online trading at Schwab slumped from an average of 204,000 trades a day in 2000 to 112,000 trades a day in 2002. In 2003 Schwab's revenues and net income fell sharply and the stock price tumbled from a high of $51.70 a share in 1999 to a

low of $6.30 in early 2003. During this period Schwab expanded through acquisition into the asset management business for high net worth clients with the acquisition on U.S. Trust, a move that potentially put it in competition with independent investment advisors, many of who used Schwab accounts for their clients. Schwab also entered the investment banking business with the purchase of Soundview Technology Bank.

In July 2004 founder and chairman Charles Schwab, who had relinquished the CEO role to David Pottruck in 1998, fired Pottruck and returned as CEO. Before stepping down in 2008 he refocused the company back on its discount brokering roots, selling off Soundview and U.S. Trust. At the same time, he pushed for an expansion of Schwab's retail banking business, allowing individual investors to hold investment accounts and traditional bank accounts at Schwab. Schwab remains chairman of the company.

In 2007–2009 a serious crisis gripped the financial services industry. Some major financial institutions went bankrupt, including Lehman Brothers and Washington Mutual. The widely watched Dow Industrial Average Index plunged from over 14,000 in October of 2007 to 6,600 in March 2007. Widespread financial collapse was only averted when the Government stepped in to support the sector with a $700 billion loan to troubled companies. Almost alone amongst major financial service firms, Schwab was able to navigate through the crisis with relative ease, remaining solidly profitable and having no need to place a call on Government funds. By 2010–2013 the company was once again on a growth path, fueled by

School of Business, University of Washington, Seattle, WA 98105, June 2013.

expanded offerings including the establishment of a market place for Exchange Traded Funds (EFTs). Schwab's asset base expanded at around 6% per annum during this period. The major strategic question going forward was how to continue to grow profitably in what remained a challenging environment for financial service firms.

THE SECURITIES BROKERAGE INDUSTRY[1]

A security refers to financial instruments, such as a stocks, bonds, commodity contracts, stock option contracts, and foreign exchange contracts. The securities brokerage industry is concerned with the issuance and trading of financial securities, as well as a number of related activities. A broker's clients may be individuals, corporations, or government bodies. Brokers undertake one or more of the following functions; assist corporations to raise capital by offering stocks and bonds, help governments raise capital through bond issues, give advice to businesses on their foreign currency needs, assist corporations with mergers and acquisitions, help individuals plan their financial future and trade financial securities, provide detailed investment research to individuals and institutions so that they can make more informed investment decisions.

Industry Background

In 2011 there were 4,456 broker-dealers registered in the United States, down from 9,515 in 1987. The industry is concentrated with some 200 firms that are members of the New York Stock Exchange (NYSE) accounting for 87% of the assets of all broker-dealers, and 80% of the capital. The 10 largest NYSE firms accounted for almost 57.9% of the gross revenue in the industry in 2011, up from 48% in 1998. The consolidation of the industry has been driven in part by deregulation, which is discussed in more detail below.

Broker-dealers make their money in a number of ways. They earn **commissions** (or fees) for executing a customer's order to buy or sell a given security (stocks, bonds, option contracts, etc). They earn **trading income**, which is the realized and unrealized gains and losses on securities held and traded by the brokerage firm. They earn money from **underwriting fees**, which are the fees charged to corporate and government clients for managing an issue of stocks or bonds on their behalf. They earn

asset management fees, which represent income from the sale of mutual fund securities, from account supervision fees, or from investment advisory or administrative service fees. They earn **margin interest**, which is the interest that customers pay to the brokerage when they borrow against the value of their securities to finance purchases. They earn **other securities related revenue** comes from private placement fees (i.e. fees from private equity deals) subscription fees for research services, charges for advisory work on proposed mergers and acquisitions, fees for options done away from an exchange and so on. Finally, many brokerages earn **non-securities revenue** from other financial services, such as credit card operations or mortgage services.

Exhibit 1 illustrates the breakdown between the various income sources for brokers in 2004, 2007 and 2011. Of particular note is the surge in "other securities revenue" in 2007. This reflects the boom in private equity deals, derivatives contracts, and associated fees that were *not* executed through an exchange, and therefore were unregulated. The high volume of derivatives, in particular, was a major factor in the 2008 turmoil in global financial markets, since many of the derivatives were tied to mortgage-backed securities, the value of which collapsed during 2008.

Industry Groups

Brokerage firms can be segmented into five groups. First, there **are national full line firms**, which are the largest full service brokers with extensive branch systems. They provide virtually every financial service and product that a brokerage can offer to both households (retail customers) and institutions (corporations, governments, and other nonprofit organizations such as universities). Examples of such firms include Merrill Lynch, Morgan Stanley Smith Barney, and A.G. Edwards. Most of these firms are headquartered in New York. For retail customers, national full line firms provide access to a personal financial consultant, traditional brokerage services, securities research reports, asset management services, financial planning advice, and a range of other services such as margin loans, mortgage loans, and credit cards. For institutional clients, these firms will also arrange and underwrite the issuance of financial securities, manage their financial assets, provide advice on mergers and acquisitions, and provide more detailed research reports than those normally provided to retail customers, often for a fee.

| Exhibit 1 | Brokers' Line of Business, as a Percentage of Revenues, 2004, 2007 and 2011 |

Item	2004 (%)	2007 (%)	2011 (%)
Commissions	16.5	8.2	17.4
Trading Gain	10.9	−2.9	1.0
Investment Gain	1.04	0.9	0.0
Underwriting	10.5	6.6	12.4
Margin Interest	3.9	8.3	3.3
Asset Management Fees	8.8	6.1	17.4
Commodities	0.6	0.2	1.7
Other Securities Revenue	37.2	60.4	32.7
Other Revenue	6.8	10	13.8

Source: SIFMA

Large investment banks are a second group. This group includes Goldman Sachs. These banks have a limited branch network and focus primarily on institutional clients, although they also may have a retail business focused on high net worth individuals (typically individuals with more than $1 million to invest). In 2008 Lehman Brothers went bankrupt, a casualty of bad bets on mortgage backed securities, while the large bank, JP Morgan, acquired Bear Stearns, leaving Goldman Sachs as the sole stand alone representative in this class.

A third group are **regional brokers**, which are full service brokerage operations with a branch network in certain regions of the country. Regional brokers typically focus on retail customers, although some have an institutional presence.

Fourth, there are a number of **New York City Based** brokers, who conduct a broad array of financial services, including brokerage, investment banking, traditional money management, and so on.

Finally, there are the **discounters**, who are primarily involved in the discount brokerage business and focus on executing orders to buy and sell stocks for retail customers. Commissions are their main source of business revenue. They charge lower commissions than full service brokers, but do not offer the same infrastructure such as personal financial consultants and detailed research reports. The discounters provide trading and execution services at deep discounts online via the Web. Many discounters, such as Ameritrade and E*Trade, do not maintain branch offices. Schwab, which was one of the first discounters, and remains the largest, has a network of brick and mortar offices, as well as a leading online presence.

Earnings Trends

Industry revenues and earnings are volatile, being driven by variations in the volume of trading activity (and commissions), underwriting, and merger and acquisition activity. All of these tend to be highly correlated with changes in the value of interest rates and the stock market. In general, when interest rates fall, the cost of borrowing declines so corporations and governments tend to issue more securities, which increases underwriting income. Also, low interest rates tend to stimulate economic growth, which leads to higher corporate profits, and thus higher stock values. When interest rates decline, individuals typically move some of their money out of low interest bearing cash accounts or low yielding bonds, and into stocks, in an attempt to earn higher returns. This drives up trading volume and hence commissions. Low interest rates, by reducing the cost of borrowing, can also increase merger and acquisition activity. Moreover, in a rising stock market, corporations often use their stock as currency with which to make acquisitions of other companies. This drives up drives up merger and acquisition activity, and the fees brokerages earn from such activity.

The 1990s was characterized by one of the strongest stock market advances in history. This boom was driven by a favorable economic environment, including falling interest rates, new information technology, productivity gains in American industry, and steady economic expansion, all of which translated into growing corporate profits and rising stock prices.

Also feeding the stock market's advance during the 1990s were favorable demographic trends. During the 1990s American baby boomers started to save for retirement, pumping significant assets into equity funds. In 1989 some 32.5% of U.S. households owned equities. By 1999 the figure had risen to 50.1% (see Exhibit 2). In 1975, some 45% of the liquid financial assets of American households were in financial securities, including stocks, bonds, mutual funds, and money market funds. By 2011 this figure had increased to 72.6%. The total value of household liquid financial assets increased from $1.7 trillion to $25.6 trillion over the same period.

Adding fuel to the fire, by the late 1990s stock market mania had taken hold. Stock prices rose to speculative highs rarely seen before as "irrationally exuberant" retail investors who seemed to believe that stock prices could only go up made increasingly risky and speculative "investments" in richly valued equities.[2] The market peaked in late 2000 as the extent of overvaluation became apparent. It fell significantly over the next two years as the economy struggled with a recession. This was followed by a recovery in both the economy and the stock market, with the S&P 500 returning to its old highs by October of 2007. However, as the global credit crunch unfolded in 2008, the market crashed, falling precipitously in the second half of 2008 to return to levels not seen since the mid 1990s. Although the market has since recovered, US households still have less of their liquid financial assets in stocks and mutual funds than at the peak of the 1990s boom (see Exhibit 2).

The long stock market boom drove an expansion of industry revenues, which for brokerages that were

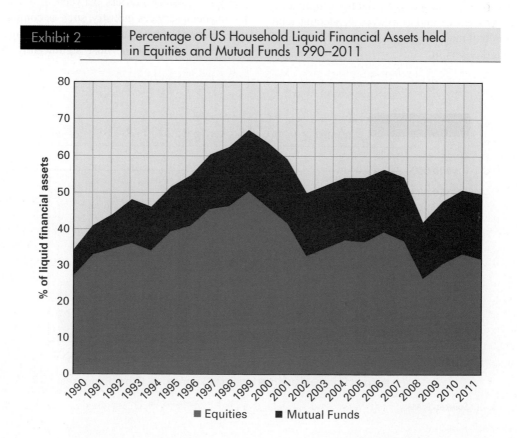

| Exhibit 2 | Percentage of US Household Liquid Financial Assets held in Equities and Mutual Funds 1990–2011 |

members of the NYSE, grew from $54 billion in 1990 to $245 billion in 2000. As the bubble burst and the stock market slumped in 2001 and 2002, and brokerage revenues plummeted to $144 billion in 2003, forcing brokerages to cut expenses. By 2007 revenues had recovered again and were a record $352 billion. In 2008 the financial crisis hit and industry revenues contracted $178 billion. In that year the industry lost $42.6 billion. As of 2011 they remained depressed at $147 billion, while industry profits were $7.7 billion.

The expense structure of the brokerage industry is dominated by two big items: interest expenses and compensation expenses (see Exhibit 3). Together these account for about three quarters of industry expenses. Interest expenses reflect the interest rate paid on cash deposits at brokerages, and rise or fall with the size of deposits and interest rates. As such, they are generally not regarded as a controllable expense (since the interest rate is ultimately set by the U.S. Federal Reserve and market forces). Compensation expenses reflect both employee headcount and bonuses. For some brokerage firms, particularly those dealing with institutional clients, bonuses can be enormous, with multi million dollar bonuses being awarded to productive employees. Compensation expenses and employee headcount tend to grow during bull markets, only to be rapidly curtailed once a bear market sets in.

As shown in Exhibit 4, which graphs the return on equity in the brokerage industry between 1990 and 2011. The profitability of the industry is volatile, and depends critically upon the overall level of stock market activity. Profits were high during the boom years of the 1990s. The bursting of the stock market bubble in 2000–2001 bought a period of low profitability, and although profitability improved after 2002, it did not return to the levels of the 1990s. The financial crisis and stock market crash of 2007–2009 clearly impacted profitability for the industry.

Deregulation

The industry has been progressively deregulated since May 1st, 1975, when a fixed commission structure on securities trades was dismantled. This development allowed for the emergence of discount brokers such as Charles Schwab. Until the mid 1980s, however, the financial services industry was highly segmented due to a 1933 Act of Congress know as the Glass-Steagall Act. This Act, which was passed in the wake of wide spread bank failures following the stock market crash of 1929, erected regulatory barriers between different sectors of the financial services industry, such as commercial banking, insurance, saving and loans, and investment services (including brokerages). Most significantly, Section 20

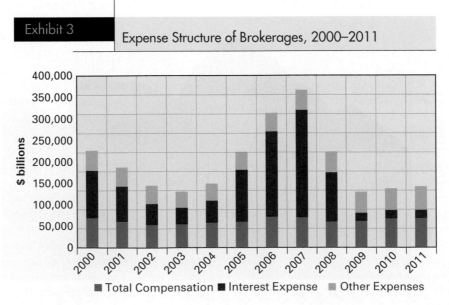

Exhibit 3 — Expense Structure of Brokerages, 2000–2011

■ Total Compensation ■ Interest Expense ■ Other Expenses

Source: SIFMA

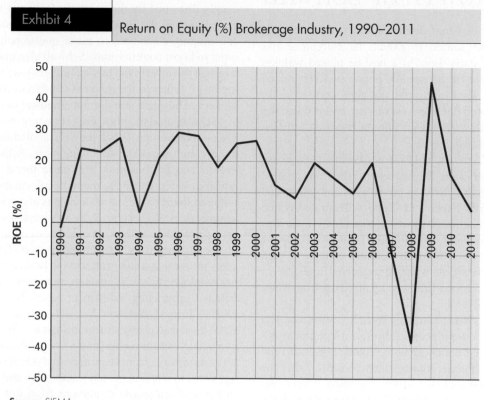

| Exhibit 4 | Return on Equity (%) Brokerage Industry, 1990–2011 |

Source: SIFMA

of the Act erected a wall between commercial banking and investment services, barring commercial banks from investing in shares of stocks, limiting them to buying and selling securities as an agent, prohibiting them from underwriting and dealing in securities, and from being affiliated with any organization that did so.

In 1987, Section 20 was relaxed to allow banks to earn up to 5% of their revenue from securities underwriting. The limit was raised to 10% in 1989 and 25% in 1996. In 1999, the Gramm-Leach-Bliley (GLB) Act was past, which finalized the repeal of the Glass-Steagall Act. By removing the walls between commercial banks, broker-dealers, and insurance companies, many predicted that the GLB Act would lead to massive industry consolidation, with commercial banks purchasing brokers and insurance companies. The rational was that such diversified financial services firms would become one stop financial supermarkets, cross-selling products to their expanded client base. For example, a financial supermarket might sell insurance to brokerage customers, or brokerage services to commercial bank customers. The leader in this process

was Citigroup, which was formed in 1998 by a merger between Citicorp, a commercial bank, and Traveler's, and insurance company. Since Traveler's had already acquired Salmon Smith Barney, a major brokerage firm, the new Citigroup seemed to signal a new wave of consolidation in the industry. The passage of the GLB Act allowed Citigroup to start cross selling products.

However, industry reports suggest that cross selling is easier in theory than practice, in part because customers were not ready for the development.[3] In an apparent admission that this was the case, in 2002 Citigroup announced that it would spin off Traveler's Insurance as a separate company. At the same time, the fact remains that the GLB Act has made it easier for commercial banks to get into the brokerage business, and there have been several acquisition to this effect. Most notably, in 2008 Bank of America purchased Merrill Lynch, and JP Morgan Chase purchased Bear Stearns. Both of the acquired enterprises were suffering from serious financial troubles due to their exposure to mortgage backed securities.

THE GROWTH OF SCHWAB

The son of an assistant district attorney in California, Charles Schwab started to exhibit an entrepreneurial streak from an early age. As a boy he picked walnuts and bagged them for $5 per 100 pound sack. He raised chicken in his backyard, sold the eggs door to door, killed and plucked the fryers for market, and peddled the manure as fertilizer. Schwab called it "my first fully integrated businesses".[4]

As a child, Schwab had to struggle with a sever case of dyslexia, a disorder that makes it difficult to process written information. To keep up with his classes, he had to resort to Cliffs Notes and Classics Illustrated comic books. Schwab believes, however, that his dyslexia was ultimately a motivator, spurring him on to overcome the disability and excel. Schwab excelled enough to gain admission to Stanford, where he received a degree in economics, which was followed by an MBA from Stanford Business School.

Fresh out of Stanford in the 1960s, Schwab embarked upon his first entrepreneurial effort, an investment advisory newsletter, which grew to include a mutual fund with $20 million under management. However, after the stock market fell sharply in 1969, the State of Texas ordered Schwab to stop accepting investments through the mail from its citizens because the fund was not registered to do business in the State. Schwab went to court and lost. Ultimately, he had to close his business, leaving him with $100,000 in debt and a marriage that had collapsed under the emotional strain.

The Early Days

Schwab soon bounced back. Capitalized by $100,000 that he borrowed from his uncle Bill, who had a successful industrial company of his own called Commander Corp, in 1971 Schwab started a new company, First Commander. Based in San Francisco, a world away from Wall Street, First Commander was a conventional brokerage that charged clients fixed commissions for securities trades. The name was changed to Charles Schwab the following year.

In 1974, at the suggestion of a friend, Schwab joined a pilot test of discount brokerage being conducted by the Securities and Exchange Commission. The discount brokerage idea instantly appealed to Schwab. He personally hated selling, particularly cold calling; the constant calling on actual or prospective customers to encourage them to make a stock trade. Moreover, Schwab was deeply disturbed by the conflict of interest that seemed everywhere in the brokerage world, with stock brokers encouraging customers to make questionable trades in order to boost commissions. Schwab also questioned the worth of the investment advice brokers gave clients, feeling that it reflected the inherent conflict of interest in the brokerage business and did not empower customers.

Schwab used the pilot test to fine tune his model for a discount brokerage. When the SEC abolished mandatory fixed commission the following year, Schwab quickly moved into the business. His basic thrust was to empower investors by giving them the information and tools required to make their own decisions about securities investments, while keeping Schwab's costs low so that this service could be offered at a deep discount to the commissions charged by full service brokers. Driving down costs meant that unlike full service brokers, Schwab did not employee financial analysts and researchers who developed proprietary investment research for the firm's clients. Instead, Schwab focused on providing clients with third party investment research. These "reports" evolved to include a company's financial history, a smatter of comments from securities analysts at other brokerage firms that had appeared in the news and a tabulation of buy and sell recommendations from full commission brokerage houses. The reports were sold to Schwab's customers at cost (in 1992 this was $9.50 for each report plus $4.75 for each additional report).[5]

A founding principle of the company was a desire to be the most useful and ethical provider of financial services. Underpinning this move was Schwab's own belief in the inherent conflict of interest between brokers at full service firms and their clients. The desire to avoid a conflict of interest caused Schwab to rethink the traditional commission based pay structure. As an alternative to commission based pay, Schwab paid all of its employees, including its brokers, a salary plus a bonus that was tied to attracting and satisfying customers and achieving productivity and efficiency targets. Commissions were taken out of the compensation equation.

The chief promoter of Schwab's approach to business, and marker of the Schwab brand, was none other than Charles Schwab himself. In 1977, Schwab started to use pictures of Charles Schwab in its advertisements, a practice it still follows today.

The customer centric focus of the company led Schwab to think of ways to make the company accessible to customers. In 1975, Schwab became the first discount broker to open a branch office and to offer access 24 hours a day seven days a week. Interestingly, however, the decision to open a branch was not something that Charles Schwab initially embraced. He wanted to keep costs low and thought it would be better if everything could be managed by way of a telephone. However, Charles Schwab was forced to ask his Uncle Bill for more capital to get his nascent discount brokerage off the ground. Uncle Bill agreed to invest $300,000 in the company, but on one condition, he insisted that Schwab open a branch office in Sacramento and employee Uncle Bill's son in law as manager![6] Reluctantly Charles Schwab agreed to Uncle Bill's demand for a show of nepotism, hoping that the branch would not be too much of a drain on the company's business.

What happened next was a surprise; there was an immediate and dramatic increase in activity at Schwab, most of it from Sacramento. Customer inquiries, the number of trades per day, and the number of new accounts, all spiked upwards. Yet there was also a puzzle here, for the increase was not linked to an increase in foot traffic in the branch. Intrigued, Schwab opened several more branches over the next year, and each time noticed the same pattern. For example, when Schwab opened its first branch in Denver it had 300 customers. It added another 1,700 new accounts in the months following the opening of the branch, and yet there was a big spike up in foot traffic at the Denver branch.

What Schwab began to realize is that the branches served a powerful psychological purpose—they gave customers a sense of security that Schwab was a real company. Customers were reassured by seeing a branch with people in it. In practice, many clients would rarely visit a branch. They would open an account, and execute trades over the telephone (or later, via the Internet). But the branch helped them to make that first commitment. Far from being a drain, Schwab realized that the branches were a marketing tool. People wanted to be "perceptually close to their money", and the branches satisfied that deep psychological need. From 1 branch in 1975, Schwab grew to have 52 branches in 1982, 175 by 1992, and 430 in 2002. The next few years bought retrenchment however, and Schwab's branch fell to around 300 by 2008.

By the mid 1980s, customers could access Schwab in person at a branch during office hours, by phone day or night, by a telephone voice recognition quote and trading service known as TeleBroker, and by an innovative proprietary online network. To encourage customers to use TeleBroker or its online trading network, Schwab reduced commissions on transactions executed this way by 10%, but it saved much more than that because doing business via computers was cheaper. By 1995, Telebroker was handling 80 million calls and 10 million trades a year, 75% of Schwab's annual volume. To service this system, in the mid 1980s Schwab invested $20 million in four regional customer call centers, routing all calls to them rather than branches. Today these call centers have 4,000 employees.

Schwab was the first to establish a PC based online trading system in 1986, with the introduction of its Equalizer service. The system had 15,000 customers in 1987, and 30,000 by the end of 1988. The online system, which required a PC with a modem, allowed investors to check current stock prices, place orders, and check their portfolios. In addition, an "offline" program for PCs enabled investors to do fundamental and technical analysis on securities. To encourage customers to start using the system, there was no additional charge for using the online system after a $99 sign up fee. In contrast, other discount brokers with PC based online systems, such as Quick and Riley's (which had a service known as "Quick Way"), or Fidelity's (whose service was called "Fidelity Express") charged users between 10 cents and 44 cents a minute for online access depending on the time of day.[7]

Schwab's pioneering move into online trading was in many ways just an evolution of the company's early utilization of technology. In 1979, Schwab spent $2 million, an amount equivalent to the company's entire net worth at the time, to purchase a used IBM System 360 computer, plus software, that was leftover from CBS's 1976 election coverage. At the time, brokerages generated and had to process massive amounts of paper to execute buy and sell orders. The computer gave Schwab a capability that no other brokerage had at the time; take a buy or sell order that came in over the phone, edit it on a computer screen, and then submit the order for processing without generating paper. Not only did the software provide for instant execution of orders, it also offered what were then sophisticated quality controls, checking a customer's account to see if funds were available before executing a transaction. As a result of this system Schwab's costs plummet as it took paper out of the system. Moreover, the cancel and rebill rate—a measure of the accuracy of trade executions—dropped from an average of 4 to 0.1%.[8] Schwab soon found it could handle twice the transaction volume of other brokers, at less cost, and with much greater accuracy. With two years, every other broker in the nation had developed similar systems, but Schwab's early investment had given it an edge and underpinned the company's belief in the value of technology to reduce costs and empower customers.

By 1982, the technology at Schwab was well ahead of that used by most full service brokers. It was this commitment to technology that allowed Schwab to offer a product that was similar in conception to Merrill Lynch's revolutionary Cash Management Account, which was introduced in 1980. The CMA account automatically sweeps idle cash into money market funds and allows customers to draw on their money by check or credit card. Schwab's system, know as the Schwab One Account, was introduced in 1982. It went beyond Merrill's in that it allowed brokers to execute orders instantly through Schwab's computer link to the exchange floor.

In 1984 Schwab moved into the mutual fund business, not by offering its own mutual funds, but by launching a mutual fund marketplace, which allowed customers to invest in some 140 no-load mutual funds (a "no-load" fund has no sales commission). By 1990, the number of funds in the market place was 400 and the total assets involved exceeded $2 billion. For the mutual fund companies, the mutual fund marketplace offered distribution to Schwab's growing customer base. For its part, Schwab kept a small portion of the revenue stream that flowed to the fund companies from Schwab clients.

In 1986, Schwab made a gutsy move to eliminate the fees for managing Individual Retirement Accounts (IRAs). IRAs allow customers to deposit money in an account where it accumulates tax free until withdrawal at retirement. The legislation establishing IRAs had been passed by Congress in 1982. At the time, estimates suggest that IRA accounts could attract as much as $50 billion in assets within ten years. In actual fact, the figure turned out to be $725 billion!

Initially Schwab followed industry practiced and collected a small fee for each IRA. By 1986 the fees amounted to $9 million a year, not a trivial amount for Schwab in those days. After looking at the issue, Charles Schwab himself made the call to scrap the fee, commenting that "It's a nuisance, and we'll get it back."[9] He was right; Schwab's No-Annual Fee IRA immediately exceeded the company's most optimistic projections.

Despite technological and product innovations, by 1983 Schwab was scrapped for capital to fund expansion. To raise funds, he sold the company to Bank of America for $55 million in stock and a seat on the bank's board of directors. The marriage did not last long.

By 1987 the bank was reeling under loan losses, and the entrepreneurially minded Schwab was frustrated by banking regulations that inhibited his desire to introduce new products. Using a mix of loans, his own money, and contributions from other managers, friends and family, Schwab led a management buyout of the company for $324 million in cash and securities.

Six months later on September 22, 1987 Schwab went public with an IPO that raised some $440 million, enabling the company to pay down debt and leaving it with capital to fund an aggressive expansion. At the time, Schwab had 1.6 million customers, revenues of $308 million, and a pre tax profit margin of 21%. Schwab announced plans to increase its branch network by 30% to around 120 offices over the next year. Then on Monday, October 19, 1987, the United States stock market crashed, dropping over 22%, the biggest one day decline in history.

October 1987–1995

After a strong run up over the year, on Friday, October 16th the stock market dropped 4.6%. During the weekend, nervous investors jammed the call centers and branch offices, not just at Schwab, but at many other brokerages, as they tried to place sell orders. At Schwab, 99% of the orders taken over the weekend for Monday morning were sell orders. As the market opened on Monday morning, it went into free fall. At Schwab, the computers were overwhelmed by 8am. The toll free number to the call centers was also totally overwhelmed. All the customers got when they called were busy signals. When the dust had settled, Schwab announced that it had lost $22 million in the fourth quarter of 1987, $15 million of which came from a single customer who had been unable to met margin calls.

The loss which amounted to 13% of the company's capital, effectively wiped out the company's profit for the year. Moreover, the inability of customers to execute trades during the crash damaged Schwab's hard earned reputation for customer service. Schwab responded by posting a two page ad in the Wall Street Journal on October 28th, 1987. On one page there was a message from Charles Schwab thanking customers for their patience, on the other an ad thanking employees for their dedication.

In the aftermath of the October 1987 crash, trading volume fell by 15% as customers, spooked by the volatility of the market, sat on cash balances. The slowdown prompted Schwab to cut back on its expansion plans. Ironically, however, Schwab added a significant number of new accounts in the aftermath of the crash as people looked for cheaper ways to invest.[10]

Beset by weak trading volume through the next 18 months, and reluctant to layoff employees, Schwab sought ways to boost activity. One strategy started out as a compliance issue within Schwab. A compliance officer in the company noticed a disturbing pattern; a number of people had given other people limited power of attorney over their accounts. This in itself was not unusual—for example, the middle aged children of an elderly individual might have power of attorney over their account—but what the Schwab officer noticed was that some individuals had power of attorney over dozens, if not hundreds of accounts.

Further investigation turned up the reason—Schwab had been serving an entirely unknown set of customers, independent financial advisors who were managing the financial assets of their clients using Schwab accounts. In early 1989 there were some 500 financial advisors who managed assets totaling $1.5 billion at Schwab, about 8% of all assets at Schwab.

The advisors were attracted to Schwab for a number of reasons, including cost and the company's commitment not to give advice—which was the business of the advisors. When Charles Schwab heard about this he immediately saw an opportunity. Financial advisors, he reasoned, represented a powerful way to acquire customers. In 1989, the company rolled out a program to aggressively court this group. Schwab hired a marketing team and told them to focus explicitly on financial planners, set apart a dedicated trading desk for them, and gave discounts of as much as 15% on commissions to financial planners with significant assets under management at Schwab accounts. Schwab also established a Financial Advisors Service, which provided its clients with a list of financial planners who were willing to work solely for a fee, and had no incentive to push the products of a particular client. At the same time, the company stated that it wasn't endorsing the planners' advice, which would run contrary to the company's commitment to offer no advice. Within a year, financial advisors had some $3 billion of client's assets under management at Schwab.

Schwab also continued to expand its branch network during this period, at a time while many brokerages, still stunned by the October 1987 debacle, were retrenching. Between 1987 and 1989 Schwab's branch network increased by just five, from 106 to 111, but in 1990 it opened up an additional 29 branches and another 28 in 1991.

By 1990s Schwab's positioning in the industry had become clear. Although a discounter, Schwab was by no means the lowest price discount broker in the country. Its average commission structure was similar to that of Fidelity, the Boston Based mutual fund company that had moved into the discount brokerage business, and Quick & Reilly, a major national competitor (see Exhibit 5). While significantly below that of full service brokers, the fee structure was also above that of deep discount brokers. Schwab differentiated itself from the deep discount brokers, however, by its branch network, technology, and the information (not advice) that it gave to investors.

In 1992 Schwab rolled out another strategy aimed at acquiring assets—OneSource, the first mutual fund "supermarket". OneSource was created to take advantage of America's growing appetite for mutual funds. By the early 1990s there were more mutual funds than individual equities. On some days Fidelity, the largest mutual fund company, accounted for 10% of the trading volume on the New York Stock Exchange. As American baby boomers aged, they seemed to have an insatiable appetite for mutual funds. But the process of buying and selling mutual finds had never been easy. As Charles Schwab explained in 1996:

"In the days before the supermarkets, to buy a mutual fund you had to write or call the fund distributor. On Day Six, you'd get a prospectus. On Day Seven or Eight you call up and they say you've got to put your money in. If

Exhibit 5	Commission Structure in 1990

Type of Broker	Average Commission Price on 20 trades averaging $8,975 each.
Deep Discount Brokers	$54
Average Discounters	$73
Banks	$88
Schwab, Fidelity and Quick & Reilly	$92
Full Service Brokers	$206

Source: E.C.Gottschalk, "Schwab forges ahead as other brokers hesitate", **Wall Street Journal**, May 11th, 1990, page C1.

you're lucky, by Day Ten you've bought it. . . . It was even more cumbersome when you redeemed. You had to send a notarized redemption form."[11]

One Source took the hassle out of owning funds. With a single visit to a branch office, telephone call, or PC based computer transaction, a Schwab client could buy and sell mutual funds. Schwab imposed no fee at all on investors for the service. Rather, in return for shelf space in Schwab's distribution channel and access to the more than 2 million accounts at Schwab, Schwab charged the fund companies a fee amounting to 0.35% of the assets under management. By inserting itself between the fund managers and customers, Schwab changed the balance of power in the mutual fund industry. When Schwab sold a fund through One Source, it passed along the assets to the fund managers, but not the customers' names. Many fund managers did not like this, because it limited their ability to build a direct relationship with customers, but they had little choice if they wanted access to Schwab's customer base.

One Source quickly propelled Schwab to the number three position in direct mutual fund distribution, behind the fund companies Fidelity and Vanguard. By 1997, Schwab customers could choose from nearly 1,400 funds offered by 200 different fund families and Schwab customers had nearly $56 billion in assets invested through One Source.

1996–2000: eSchwab

In 1994, as access to the World Wide Web began to diffuse rapidly throughout America, a two year old startup run by Bill Porter, a physicist and inventor, launched its first dedicated web site for online trading. The company's name was E*Trade. E*Trade announced a flat $14.95 commission on stock trades, significantly below Schwab's average commission which at the time of $65. It was clear from the outset that E*Trade and other online brokers, such as Ameritrade, offered a direct threat to Schwab. Not only were their commission rates considerably below those of Schwab, but the ease, speed, and flexibility of trading stocks over the Web suddenly made Schwab's proprietary online trading software, Street Smart seemed limited. (Street Smart was the Windows based successor to Schwab's DOS based Equalizer program). To compound matters, talented people started to leave Schwab for E*Trade and its brethren, which they saw as the wave of the future.

At the time, deep within Schwab, William Pearson, a young software specialist who had worked on the development of Street Smart, quickly saw the transformational power of the Web and believed that it would make proprietary systems like Street Smart obsolete. Pearson believed that Schwab needed to develop its own Web based software, and quickly. Try as he might, though, Pearson could not get the attention of his supervisor. He tried a number of other executives, but found support hard to come by. Eventually he approached Anne Hennegar, a former Schwab manager that he knew who now worked as a consultant to the company. Hennegar suggest that Pearson meet with Tom Seip, an Executive Vice President at Schwab who was know for his ability to think outside of the box. Hennegar approached Seip on Pearson's behalf, and Seip responded positively, asking her to set up a meeting. Hennegar and Pearson turned up expecting to meet just Seip, but to their surprise in walked Charles Schwab, his Chief Operating Officer, David Pottruck, and the Vice Presidents in charge of strategic planning and the electronic brokerage arena.

As the group watched Pearson's demo of how a web based system would look and work, they became increasingly excited. It was clear to those in the room that a Web based system based on real time information, personalization, customization, and interactivity all advanced Schwab's commitment to empowering customers. By the end of the meeting, Pearson had received a green light to start work on the project.

It soon transpired that several other groups within Schwab had been working on projects that were similar to Pearson's. These were all pulled together under the control of Dawn Lepore, Schwab's chief information officer, who headed up the effort to develop the Web based service that would ultimately become eSchwab. Meanwhile, significant strategic issues were now beginning to preoccupy Charles Schwab and David Pottruck. They realized that Schwab's established brokerage and a Web based brokerage business were based on very different revenue and cost models. The Web based business would probably cannibalize business from Schwab's established brokerage operations, and that might lead people in Schwab to slow down or even derail the Web based initiative. As Pottruck later put it:

"The new enterprise was going to use a different model for making money than our traditional business, and we didn't want the comparisons to form the basis for a measurement of success or failure. For example, eSchwab's per trade revenue would be less than half that of the mainstream of the company, and that could be seen as a drain on resources rather than a response to what customer would be using in the future".[12]

Pottruck and Schwab understood that unless eSchwab was placed in its own organization, isolated and protected from the established business, it might never get off the ground. They also knew that if they did not cannibalize their own business with eSchwab, someone would do it for them. Thus they decided to set up a separate organization to develop eSchwab. The unit was headed up by Beth Sawi, a highly regarded marketing manager at Schwab who had very good relations with other managers in the company. Sawi set up the development center in a unit physically separated from other Schwab facilities.

eSchwab was launched in May 1996, but without the normal publicity that accompanied most new products at Schwab. Schwab abandoned its sliding scale commission for a flat rate commission of $39 (which was quickly dropped to $29.95) for any stock trade up to 1,000 shares. Within two weeks 25,000 people had opened eSchwab accounts. By the end of 1997 the figure would sore to 1.2 million, bringing in assets of about $81 billion, or ten times the assets of E*Trade.

Schwab initially kept the two businesses segmented. Schwab's traditional customers were still paying an average of $65 a trade while eSchwab customers were paying $29.95. While Schwab's traditional customers could make toll free calls to Schwab brokers, eSchwab clients could not. Moreover, Schwab's regular customers couldn't access eSchwab at all. The segmentation soon gave rise to problems. Schwab's branch employees were placed in the uncomfortable position of telling customers that they couldn't set up eSchwab accounts. Some eSchwab customers started to set up traditional Schwab accounts with small sums of money so that they could access Schwab's brokers and Schwab's information services, while continuing to trade via eSchwab. Clearly the segmentation was not sustainable.

Schwab began to analyze the situation. The company's leaders realized that the cleanest way to deal with the problem would be to give every Schwab customer online access, adopt a commission of $29.95 on trading across all channels, and maintain existing levels of customer service at the branch level, and on the phone. However, internal estimates suggested that the cut in commission rates would reduce revenues by $125 million, which would hit Schwab's stock. The problem was compounded by two factors; first, employees owned 40% of Schwab's stock, so they would be hurt by any fall in stock price, and second, employees were worried that going to the web would result in a decline in business at the branch level, and hence a loss of jobs there.

An internal debate ranged within the company for much of 1997, a year when Schwab's revenues surged 24% to $2.3 billion. The online trading business grew by more than 90% during the year, with online trades accounting for 37% of all Schwab trades during 1997, and the trend was up throughout the year.

Looking at these figures, Pottruck, the COO, knew that Schwab had to bite the bullet and give all Schwab customers access to eSchwab (Pottruck was now running the day to day operations of Schwab, leaving Charles Schwab to focus on his corporate marketing and PR role). His first task was to enroll the support of the company's largest shareholder, Charles Schwab. With 52 million shares, Charles Schwab would take the biggest hit from any share price decline. According to a Fortune article, the conversation between Schwab and Pottruck went something like this:[13]

Pottruck: "We don't know exactly what will happen. The budget is shaky. We'll be winging it."
Schwab: "We can always adjust our costs".
Pottruck: "Yes, but we don't have to do this now. The whole year could be lousy. And the stock!"
Schwab: "This isn't that hard a decision, because we really have no choice. It's just a question of when, and it will be harder later".

Having got the agreement of Schwab's founder, Pottruck formed a task force to look at how best to implement the decision. The plan that emerged was to merge all of the company's electronic services into Schwab.com, which would then coordinate Schwab's online and off line business. The base commission rate would be $29.95 whatever channel was used to make a trade—online, branch, or the telephone. The role of the branches would change, and they would start to focus more on customer support. This required a change in incentive systems. Branch employees had been paid bonuses on the basis of the assets they accrued to their branches, nut now they would be paid bonuses on assets they came in via the branch, or the Web. They would be rewarded for directing clients to the web.

Schwab implemented the change of strategy on January 15, 1998. Revenues dropped 3% in the first quarter as the average commission declined from $63 to $57. Earnings also came in short of expectations by some $6 million. The company's stock had lost 20% of its value by August 1998. However, over much of 1998 new money poured into Schwab. Total accounts surged, with Schwab gaining a million new customers in 1998, a 20% increase, while assets grew by 32%. As the year progressed, trading volume grew, doubling by year end. By the third quarter Schwab's revenues and earnings were surging past analysts' expectations. The company ultimately achieved record revenues and earnings in 1998. Net income ended up 29% over the prior year, despite falling commission rates, aided by surging trading volume and the lower cost of executing trades over the Web. By the end of the year, 61% of all trades at Schwab were made over the Web. After its summer lows, the stock price recovered, ending the year up 130%, pushing Schwab's market capitalization past that of Merrill Lynch.[14]

2000–2004: After the Boom

In 1998 Charles Schwab appointed his long time number two, David Pottruck, co-CEO. The appointment signaled the beginning of a leadership transition, with Schwab easing himself out of day today operations. Soon Pottruck had to deal with some major issues. The end of the long stock market boom of the 1990s hit Schwab hard. The average number of trades made per day through Schwab fell from 300 million to 190 million between 2000 and 2002. Reflecting this, revenues slumped from $7.1 billion to $4.14 billion and net income from $803 million to $109 million. To cope with the decline, Schwab was forced to cut back on its employee headcount, which fell from a peak of nearly 26,000 employees in 2000 to just over 16,000 in late 2003.

Schwab's strategic reaction to the sea change in market conditions was already taking form as the market implosion began. In January 2000, Schwab acquired U.S. Trust for $2.7 billion. U.S. Trust was a 149-year-old investment advisement business that manages money for high net worth individuals whose invested assets exceed $2 million. When acquired, U.S. Trust had 7,000 customers and assets of $84 billion, compared to 6.4 million customers and assets of $725 billion at Schwab.[15]

According to Pottruck, widely regarded as the architect of the acquisition, Schwab made the acquisition because it discovered that high net worth individuals were starting to defect from Schwab for money managers like U.S. Trust. The main reason; as Schwab's clients got older and richer they started to need institutions that specialized in services that Schwab didn't offer—including personal trusts, estate planning, tax services, and private banking. With baby boomers starting to enter middle to late middle age, and their average net worth projected to rise, Schwab decided that it needed to get into this business or lose high net worth clients.

The decision though, started to bring Schwab into conflict with the network of 6,000 or so independent financial advisors that the company has long fostered through the Schwab Advisers Network, and who funneled customers and assets into Schwab accounts. Some advisors felt that Schwab was starting to move in on their turf, and they were not too happy about it.

In May 2002, Schwab made another move in this direction when it announced that it would launch a new service targeted at clients with more than $500,000 in assets. Know as Schwab Private Client, and developed with the help of U.S. Trust employees, for a fee of 0.6% of assets Private Client customers can meet face to face with a financial consultant to work out an investment plan and return to the same consultant for further advice. Schwab stressed that the consultant would not tell clients what to buy and sell—that is still left to the client. Nor will clients get the legal, tax and estate planning advice offered by U.S. trust and independent financial advisors. Rather, they get a financial plan and consultation regarding industry and market conditions.[16]

To add power to this strategy, Schwab also announced that it would start a new stock rating system. The stock rating system is not the result of the work of financial analysts. Rather, it is the product of a computer model, developed at Schwab, that analyzes more than 3,000 stocks on 24 basic measures, such as free cash flow, sales growth, insider trades, and so on, and then assigns grades. The top 10% get an A, the next 20% a B, the middle 40% a C, the next 20% a D, and the lowest 10% an F. Schwab claims that the new system is "a systematic approach with nothing but objectivity, not influenced by corporate relationships, investment banking, or any of the above".[17]

Critics of this strategy were quick to point out that many of Schwab's branch employees lacked the qualifications and expertise to give financial advice. At the time the service was announced, Schwab had some 150 qualified financial advisers in place, and planned to have 300 by early 2003. These elite employees required a higher salary than the traditional Schwab branch employees, who in many respects were little more than order takers and providers of prepackaged information.

The Schwab Private Client service also caused further grumbling among the private financial advisors affiliated with Schwab. In 2002 there were 5,900 of these. In total their clients amounted to $222 billion of Schwab's $765 billion in client assets. Several stated that they would no longer keep clients' money at Schwab. However, Schwab stated that it would use the Private Client Service as a device for referring people who wanted more sophisticated advice than Schwab could offer to its network of registered financial advisers, and particularly an inner circle of 330 advisers who have an average of $500 million in assets under management and 17 years of experience.[18] According to one member of this group, "Schwab is not a threat to us. Most people realize the hand holding it takes to do that kind of work and Schwab wants us to do it. There's just more money behind the Schwab Advisors Network. The dead wood is gone, and firm's like ours stand to benefit from even more additional leads".[19]

In 2003 Charles Schwab finally stepped down as co-CEO, leaving Pottruck in charge of the business (Charles Schwab stayed on as chairman). In late 2003, Pottruck announced that Schwab would acquire Soundview Technology Group for $321 million. Soundview was a boutique investment bank with a research arm that covered a couple of hundred companies and offered this research to institutional investors, such as mutual fund managers. Pottruck justified the acquisition by arguing that it would have taken Schwab years to build similar investment research capabilities internally. His plan was the have Soundview's research bundles for Schwab's retail investors.

2004–2008: The Return of Charles Schwab

The Soundview acquisition proved to be Pottruck's undoing. It soon became apparent that the acquisition has a huge mistake. There was little value to be had for Schwab's retail business from Soundview. Moreover, the move had raised Schwab's operating costs. By mid 2004, Pottruck was trying to sell Soundview. The board, which was disturbed at Pottruck's vacillating strategic leadership, expressed their concerns to Charles Schwab. On July 15th, 2004, Pottruck was fired, and the 66-year-old Charles Schwab returned as CEO.

Charles Schwab moved quickly to refocus the company. Soundview was sold to the investment bank UBS for $265 million. Schwab reduced the workforce by another 2,400 employees, closed underperforming branches, and removed $600 million in annual cost. This allowed him to reduce commissions on stock trades by 45%, and take market share from other discount brokers such as Ameritrade and E*Trade.

Going forward, Charles Schwab reemphasized the tradition mission of Schwab—to empower investors and provide them with ethical financial services. He also reemphasized the importance of the relationships that Schwab had with independent investment advisors. He

noted: "Trading has become commoditized. The future is really about competing for client relationships".[20] One major new focus of Charles Schwab was the company's retail banking business. This had been established in 2002, but it had been a low priority for Pottruck. Now Schwab wanted to make the company a single source for banking, brokerage, and credit card services—one that would give Schwab's customers something of value: a personal relationship they could trust. The goal was to lessen Schwab's dependence on trading income, and give it a more reliable earnings stream and a deeper relationship with clients.

In mid 2007 Schwab's reorientation back to its traditional mission reached a logic conclusion when U.S. Trust was sold to Bank of America for $3.3 billion. Unlike in the past, however, Schwab was no longer earning the bulk of its money from trading commissions. As a percentage of net revenues, trading revenues (mostly commissions on stock trades) was down from 36% in 2002 to 17% in 2007. By 2007, asset management fees accounted for 47% of Schwab's net revenue, up from 41% in 2002, while net interest revenue (difference between earned interest on assets such as loans and interest paid on deposits) was 33%, up from 19% in 2002.[21] Schwab's overall performance had also improved markedly. Net income in 2007 was $1.12 billion, up from a low of $396 million in 2003.

The Great Financial Crisis and its Aftermath: 2008–2012

The great financial crisis that hit the financial services industry in 2008–2009 had its roots in a bubble in housing prices in the United States. Financial service firms had been bundling thousands of home mortgages together into bonds, and selling them to investors worldwide. The purchasers of those bonds thought that they were buying a solid financial asset with a guaranteed payout—but it turned out that the quality of many of the bonds was much lower than indicated by bond rating agencies such as Standard & Poor's. Put differently, there was an unexpectedly high rate of default on home mortgages in the United States.

At the top of the housing bubble, many people were paying more than they could afford to for homes. Banks were only to happy to lend them this money because they assumed, incorrectly as it turned out, that if the borrower faced default, the home could be sold for a profit and the balance on the mortgage paid off. The flaw in this reasoning was the assumption that the underlying asset—the house—could be sold and that home pricing would continue to advance. There had been massive overbuilding in the U.S. By 2007 home prices were falling as it became apparent that there was too much excess inventory in the system. The net result; many supposedly high quality mortgage backed bonds turned out to be nothing more than junk and prices for these bonds fell precipitously. Institutions holding these bonds had to write down their value, and their balance sheets started to deteriorate rapidly. As this occurred, other financial institutions became increasingly reluctant to lend money to those institutions seen as being overexposed to the housing market. Suddenly the banking system was facing a major credit crunch.

As the crisis unfolded, several major financial institutions went bankrupt, including Lehman Brothers (a major player in the market for mortgage backed securities) and Washington Mutual (one of the nation's largest mortgage originators). AIG, a major insurance company which had built a big business in the 2000s selling default insurance to the holders of mortgage backed securities, faced massive potential claims and had to be rescued from bankruptcy by the U.S, Government. The Government took an 80% stake in AIG in return for providing loans worth $182 billion. The U.S. Government also created a $700 billion fund—the Troubled Asset Relief Program—that banks could draw upon the shore up their balance sheets and meet short-term obligations. While these actions managed to arrest what was the most serious crisis to hit the global financial system since the Great Depression of 1929, they could not stave off a sever and prolonged recession and a major decline of the market value of most financial institutions.

Almost alone among major financial institutions, Schwab sailed through the financial crisis with relative ease. The firm had steered well clear of the feeding frenzy in the U.S. housing and mortgage markets. Schwab did not originated mortgages and nor did it hold mortgage backed securities on its balance sheet. Schwab had no need to draw on Government funds to shore up its balance sheet. The company remained profitable, and although revenues and earnings did fall from 2007 though to 2009, the balance sheet remained strong.

By 2010, Schwab was once more on a growth path, although extremely low interest rates in the United States and elsewhere limited its ability to earn money from the spread between what it paid to depositors, and the amount it could earn by investing depositors money on the short-term money markets. Some 40% of Schwab's revenues are tied to interest rates, and so long as interest rates remain very low, Schwab's ability to earn profit here is limited. On the other hand, earnings could expand significantly if rates return to pre crisis levels.

Charles Schwab himself stepped down as CEO on July 22nd, 2008, passing the reins of leadership to Walter Bettinger, although Schwab continues to be involved in major strategic decisions as an active chairman. Under Bettinger the company has charted a conservative course. The main goal has been to grow the net asset base of the firm by attracting more clients. The stellar performance of Schwab though the financial crisis, and its continuing strong brand, has certainly helped in this regard. From 2008 to 2012 Schwab has been able to generate 5 to 8% annual growth in its asset base. To keep doing so going forward, the company has launched couple of other initiatives.

First, in 2011 it announced a plan to start expanding its physical retail presence. Schwab's branches had declined in number from 400 in 2003 to around 300 by 2011 as more and more customers transacted online with the company. Despite this decline, Schwab has come to the conclusion that a physical retail presence remains a powerful means of gathering in new accounts and holding onto existing accounts. Rather than open more storefronts itself, however, which entails significant costs, the company has opted for a different strategy; it has decided to open additional retail branches using independents operators in what amounts to a franchise system. The goal is to ultimately triple the branch network to around 1,000. Detractors worry that Schwab risks diluting its powerful brand if the independent operators do not offer the same level of service that people have become accustomed to at traditional Schwab branches. For its part, Schwab executives have stated that it is their intention that a client walking into an independently owned Schwab branch will not know the difference, and would get the same service and products as at company owned branches.[22]

Second, Schwab has made a big push into the exchange traded fund business (EFTs). EFTs are passively managed index funds, such as an S&P 500 index fund. EFTs have grown into a $1.4 trillion dollar industry since the first EFT was introduced just 20 years ago. EFTs are attractive because they trade like stocks on a regulated exchange while providing diversity within a single investment product. Since EFTs are passively managed, expense ratios are typically lower than those for actively managed mutual funds. Schwab started to offer EFTs in the 2000s, and in 2013 it announced the launch of Schwab EFT OneSource trading platform. Modeled on Schwab's successful mutual fund market place, this provides access to 105 EFTs and offers $0 online trade commissions. Schwab will make money from charging fund distribution fees, the same way as it does with mutual funds.

NOTES

1. Material for this section is drawn from *Securities Industry and Financial Markets Association Fact Book 2012,* SIFMA, New York, 2012.
2. Robert E. Shiller. *Irrational Exuberance,* Princeton University Press, Princeton, NJ, 2002.
3. Anthony O'Donnell, "New thinking on convergence", *Wall Street & Technology*, May 2002, pages 16–18.
4. Terence P. Pare, "How Schwab wins investors", *Fortune*, June 1, 1992, pages 52–59.
5. Terence P. Pare, "How Schwab wins investors", *Fortune*, June 1st, 1992, pages 52–59.
6. John Kador, *Charles Schwab: How One Company Beat Wall Street and Reinvented the Brokerage Industry*, John Wiley & Sons, New York, 2002.
7. Earl C. Gottschalk, "Computerized Investment Systems Thrive as People Seek Control over Portfolios", *Wall Street Journal*, September 27, 1988, page 1.
8. John Kador, *Charles Schwab: How One Company Beat Wall Street and Reinvented the Brokerage Industry*, John Wiley & Sons, New York, 2002.
9. John Kador, *Charles Schwab: How One Company Beat Wall Street and Reinvented the Brokerage Industry*, John Wiley & Sons, New York, 2002, page 73.
10. G.C. Hill. "Schwab to Curb Expansion, Tighten Belt Because of Post Crash trading Decline", *Wall Street Journal*, December 7, 1987, page 1.
11. John Kador, *Charles Schwab: How One Company Beat Wall Street and Reinvented the Brokerage Industry*, John Wiley & Sons, New York, 2002, page 185.
12. John Kador, *Charles Schwab: How One Company Beat Wall Street and Reinvented the Brokerage Industry*, John Wiley & Sons, New York, 2002, page 217.
13. Erick Schonfeld, "Schwab puts it all online", *Fortune*, December 7, 1998, pages 94–99.
14. Anonymous, "Schwab's e-Gambit", *Business Week*, January 11, 1999, page 61.
15. Amy Kover. "Schwab makes a grand play for the rich", *Fortune*, February 7th, 2000, page 32.
16. Louise Lee and Emily Thornton, "Schwab v Wall Street", *Business Week*, June 3, 2002, page 64–70.
17. Quoted in Louise Lee and Emily Thornton, "Schwab v Wall Street", *Business Week*, June 3, 2002, page 64–70.
18. Erin E. Arvedlund, "Schwab trades up", *Barron's*, May 27, 2002, pages 19–20.
19. Erin E. Arvedlund, "Schwab trades up", *Barron's*, May 27, 2002, page 20.
20. B. Morris, "Charles Schwab's Big Challenge", *Fortune*, May 30, 2005, pp 88–98.
21. Charles Schwab, 2007 10K form.
22. E. MacBride, "Why Schwab is embracing a franchise like strategy to fast forward branch growth", *Forbes*, February 14, 2011.

Case 16

Toyota In 2013: Lean Production and the Rise of the World's Largest Automobile Manufacturer

Charles W. L. Hill

INTRODUCTION

The growth of Toyota has been one of the great success stories of Japanese industry during the last half century. In 1947, the company was a little-known domestic manufacturer producing around 100,000 vehicles a year. In 2012 Toyota sold 9.4 million light vehicles globally, making it the largest automobile manufacturer in the world ahead of Volkswagen with 9.1 million units sold and GM with 7.7 million units.

For all of its success, however, the last few years had been challenging for Toyota. As a consequence of the global financial crisis, demand for vehicles fell sharply in 2008 and 2009, pushing most of the world's major automobile companies into the red. GM, one of Toyota's main global rivals, had to file for Chapter 11 bankruptcy protection in 2009. However, the GM that emerged from Chapter 11 2 years later was a leaner and more viable competitor to Toyota. At the same time, the South Korean company, Hyundai-Kia, emerged from the financial crisis in a strong position as the 4th largest automobile manufacturer in the world and the most profitable. Volkswagen too, has strengthening its position and closing in on Toyota in terms of sales volume.

Not only did Toyota face stronger global rivals than hitherto, its own position was damaged when a series of product recalls, mostly in the United States, tarnished its brand and corporate image. The most infamous of these was the "sticky accelerator pedal" issue that allegedly led to sudden uncontrolled vehicle acceleration and in some cases serious accidents. Toyota recalled some 9 million vehicles to in 2009–2010, the largest product recall in industry history, and temporarily suspended some sales while it tried to identify and solve the issue. An investigation by

the U.S. National Highway Transport & Safety Agency found no electronic fault with Toyota's "drive-by-wire" throttle system, which was initially blamed for the issue, and instead attributed the problem to mechanical causes (including pedals caught under floor mats), and "driver error." Irrespective of the failure to identify a clear cause, in 2012 Toyota agreed to pay $1.1 billion to settle a class action lawsuit related to the issue. More importantly perhaps, Toyota's legendary reputation for product quality had taken a major knock. The question for Toyota's management now, was how could they reestablished the company as the undisputed leader in quality, and how could they fend of stronger competitors in a rapidly globalizing marketplace?

THE ORIGINS OF TOYOTA

The original idea behind the founding of the Toyota Motor Company came from the fertile mind of Toyoda Sakichi.[1] The son of a carpenter, Sakichi was an entrepreneur and inventor whose primary interest lay in the textile industry, but he had been intrigued by automobiles since a visit to the United States in 1910. Sakichi's principal achievement was the invention of an automatic loom that held out the promise of being able to lower the costs of weaving high-quality cloth. In 1926 Sakichi set up Toyoda Automatic Loom to manufacture this product. In 1930 Sakichi sold the patent rights to a British textile concern, Platt Brothers, for about 1 million yen,

Foster School of Business, University of Washington, Seattle, WA 98185, May 2013.

a considerable sum in those days. Sakichi urged his son, Toyoda Kiichiro, to use this money to study the possibility of manufacturing automobiles in Japan. A mechanical engineer with a degree from the University of Tokyo, in 1930 Kiichiro became managing director of loom production at Toyoda Automatic Loom.

Kiichiro was at first reluctant to invest in automobile production. The Japanese market was at that time dominated by Ford and General Motors, both of which imported knock-down car kits from the United States and assembled them in Japan. Given this, the board of Toyoda Automatic Loom, including Kiichiro's brother-in-law and the company's president, Kodama Risaburo, opposed the investment on the grounds that it was too risky. Kiichiro probably would not have pursued the issue further had not his father made a deathbed request in 1930 that Kiichiro explore the possibilities of automobile production. Kiichiro had to push, but in 1933 he was able to get permission to set up an automobile department within Toyoda Automatic Loom.

Kiichiro's belief was that he would be able to figure out how to manufacture automobiles by taking apart U.S.-made vehicles and examining them piece by piece. He also felt that it should be possible to adapt U.S. mass-production technology to manufacture cost efficiently at lower volumes. His confidence was based in large part upon the already considerable engineering skills and capabilities at his disposal through Toyoda Automatic Loom. Many of the precision engineering and manufacturing skills needed in automobile production were similar to the skills required to manufacture looms.

Kiichiro produced his first 20 vehicles in 1935, and in 1936 the automobile department produced 1,142 vehicles—910 trucks, 100 cars, and 132 buses. At this time, however, the production system was essentially craft-based rather than a modern assembly line. Despite some progress, the struggle might still have been uphill had not fate intervened in the form of the Japanese military. Japan had invaded Manchuria in 1931 and quickly found American-made trucks useful for moving men and equipment. As a result, the military felt that it was strategically important for Japan to have its own automobile industry. The result was the passage of an automobile manufacturing law in 1936 which required companies producing more than 3,000 vehicles per year in Japan to get a license from the government. Moreover, to get a license over 50% of the stock had to be owned by Japanese investors. The law also placed a duty on imported cars, including the knock-down kits that Ford and GM brought into Japan. As a direct result of this legislation, both GM and Ford exited from the Japanese market in 1939.

Once the Japanese government passed this law, Kodama Risaburo decided that the automobile venture could be profitable and switched from opposing to proactively supporting Kiichiro (in fact, Risaburo's wife, who was Kiichiro's elder sister, had been urging him to take this step for some time). The first priority was to attract the funds necessary to build a mass-production facility. In 1937 Risaburo and Kiichiro decided to incorporate the automobile department as a separate company in order to attract outside investors—which they were successful in doing. Kiichiro Toyoda was appointed president of the new company. The company was named the Toyota Motor Company. (The founding family's name, "Toyoda," means "abundant rice field" in Japanese. The new name had no meaning in Japanese.)

Upon incorporation, Risaburo and Kiichiro's vision was that Toyota should expand its passenger car production as quickly as possible. However, once again fate intervened in the form of the Japanese military. Toyota had barely begun passenger car production when war broke out; in 1939 the Japanese government, on advice from the military, prohibited passenger car production and demanded that the company specialize in the production of military trucks.

THE EVOLUTION OF THE TOYOTA PRODUCTION SYSTEM

After the end of World War II, Kiichiro was determined that Toyota should reestablish itself as a manufacturer of automobiles.[2] Toyota, however, faced a number of problems in doing this:

1. The Japanese domestic market was too small to support efficient-scale mass-production facilities such as those common in America by that time.
2. The Japanese economy was starved of capital, which made it difficult to raise funds to finance new investments.
3. New labor laws introduced by the American occupiers increased the bargaining power of labor and made it difficult for companies to lay off workers.
4. North America and Western Europe were full of large auto manufacturers eager to establish operations in Japan.

In response to the last point, in 1950 the new Japanese government prohibited direct foreign investment in the automobile industry and imposed high tariffs on the importation of foreign cars. This protection, however, did little to solve the other problems facing the company at this time.

Limitations of Mass Production

At this juncture a remarkable mechanical engineer entered the scene: Ohno Taiichi. More than anyone else, it was Ohno who was to work out a response to the above problems. Ohno had joined Toyoda Spinning and Weaving in 1932 as a production engineer in cotton thread manufacture and entered Toyota when the former company was absorbed into the latter in 1943. Ohno worked in auto production for 2 years, was promoted and managed auto assembly and machine shops between 1945 and 1953, and in 1954 was appointed a company director.

When Ohno Taiichi joined Toyota the mass-production methods pioneered by Ford had become the accepted method of manufacturing automobiles. The basic philosophy behind mass production was to produce a limited product line in massive quantities to gain maximum economies of scale. The economies came from spreading the fixed costs involved in setting up the specialized equipment required to stamp body parts and manufacture components over as large a production run as possible. Since setting up much of the equipment could take a full day or more, the economies involved in long production runs were reckoned to be considerable. Thus, for example, Ford would stamp 500,000 right-hand door panels in a single production run and then store the parts in warehouses until they were needed in the assembly plant, rather than stamp just those door panels that were needed immediately and then change the settings and stamp out left-hand door panels, or other body parts.

A second feature of mass production was that each assembly worker should perform only a single task, rather than a variety of tasks. The idea here was that as the worker became completely familiar with a single task, he could perform it much faster, thereby increasing labor productivity. Assembly line workers were overseen by a foreman who did not perform any assembly tasks himself, but instead ensured that the workers followed orders. In addition, a number of specialists were employed to perform nonassembly operations such as tool repair, die changes, quality inspection, and general "housecleaning."

After working in Toyota for 5 years and visiting Ford's U.S. plants, Ohno became convinced that the basic mass-production philosophy was flawed. He saw five problems with the mass-production system:

1. Long production runs created massive inventories that had to be stored in large warehouses. This was expensive both because of the cost of warehousing and because inventories tied up capital in unproductive uses.
2. If the initial machine settings were wrong, long production runs resulted in the production of a large number of defects.
3. The sheer monotony of assigning assembly line workers to a single task generated defects, since workers became lax about quality control. In addition, since assembly line workers were not responsible for quality control, they had little incentive to minimize defects.
4. The extreme division of labor resulted in the employment of specialists such as foremen, quality inspectors, and tooling specialists, whose jobs logically could be performed by assembly line workers.
5. The mass-production system was unable to accommodate consumer preferences for product diversity.

In addition to these flaws, Ohno knew that the small domestic market in Japan and the lack of capital for investing in mass-production facilities made the American model unsuitable for Toyota.

Reducing Setup Times

Given these flaws and the constraints that Toyota faced, Ohno decided to take a fresh look at the techniques used for automobile production. His first goal was to try to make it economical to manufacture autobody parts in small batches. To do this, he needed to reduce the time it took to set up the machines for stamping out body parts. Ohno and his engineers began to experiment with a number of techniques to speed up the time it took to change the dies in stamping equipment. This included using rollers to move dies in and out of position along with a number of simple mechanized adjustment mechanisms to fine-tune the settings. These techniques were relatively simple to master, so Ohno directed production workers to perform the die changes themselves. This in itself reduced the need for specialists and eliminated the idle time that workers previously had enjoyed while waiting for the dies to be changed.

Through a process of trial and error, Ohno succeeded in reducing the time required to change dies on stamping equipment from a full day to 15 minutes by 1962, and to as little as 3 minutes by 1971. By comparison, even in the early 1980s many American and European plants required anywhere between 2 and 6 hours to change dies on stamping equipment. As a consequence, American and European plants found it economical to manufacture in lots equivalent to 10 to 30 days' supply and to reset equipment only every other day. In contrast, since Toyota could change the dies on stamping equipment in a matter of minutes, it manufactured in lots equivalent to just one day's supply, while resetting equipment three times per day.

Not only did these innovations make small production runs economical, but they also had the added benefit of reducing inventories and improving product quality. Making small batches eliminated the need to hold large inventories, thereby reducing warehousing costs and freeing up scarce capital for investment elsewhere. Small production runs and the lack of inventory also meant that defective parts were produced only in small numbers and entered the assembly process almost immediately. This had the added effect of making those in the stamping shops far more concerned about quality. In addition, once it became economical to manufacture small batches of components, much greater variety could be included into the final product at little or no cost penalty.

Organization of the Workplace

One of Ohno's first innovations was to group the work force into teams. Each team was given a set of assembly tasks to perform, and team members were trained to perform each task that the team was responsible for. Each team had a leader who was himself an assembly line worker. In addition to coordinating the team, the team leader was expected to perform basic assembly line tasks and to fill in for any absent worker. The teams were given the job of housecleaning, minor tool repair, and quality inspection (along with the training required to perform these tasks). Time was also set aside for team members to discuss ways to improve the production process (the practice now referred to as "quality circles").

The immediate effect of this approach was to reduce the need for specialists in the workplace and to create a more flexible work force in which individual assembly line workers were not treated simply as human machines. All of this resulted in increased worker productivity.

None of this would have been possible, however, had it not been for an agreement reached between management and labor after a 1950 strike. The strike was brought on by management's attempt to cut the work force by 25% (in response to a recession in Japan). After lengthy negotiations, Toyota and the union worked out a compromise. The work force was cut by 25% as originally proposed, but the remaining employees were given two guarantees, one for lifetime employment and the other for pay graded by seniority and tied to company profitability through bonus payments. In exchange for these guarantees, the employees agreed to be flexible in work assignments. In turn, this allowed for the introduction of the team concept.

Improving Quality

One of the standard practices in the mass-production automobile assembly plants was to fix any errors that occurred during assembly in a rework area at the end of the assembly line. Errors routinely occurred in most assembly plants either because bad parts were installed or because good parts were installed incorrectly. The belief was that stopping an assembly line to fix such errors would cause enormous bottlenecks in the production system. Thus it was thought to be more efficient to correct errors at the end of the line.

Ohno viewed this system as wasteful for three reasons: (1) since workers understood that any errors would be fixed at the end of the line, they had little incentive to correct errors themselves; (2) once a defective part had been embedded in a complex vehicle, an enormous amount of rework might be required to fix it; and (3) since defective parts were often not discovered until the end of the line when the finished cars were tested, a large number of cars containing the same defect may have been built before the problem was found.

In an attempt to get away from this practice, Ohno decided to look for ways to reduce the amount of rework at the end of the line. His approach involved two elements. First, he placed a cord above every workstation and instructed workers to stop the assembly line if a problem emerged that could not be fixed. It then became the responsibility of the whole team to come over and work on the problem. Second, team members were taught to trace every defect back to its ultimate cause and then to ensure that the problem was fixed so that it would not reoccur.

Initially, this system produced enormous disruption. The production line was stopping all the time and workers became discouraged. However, as team members began to gain experience in identifying problems and tracing them back to their root cause, the number of errors began to drop dramatically and stops in the line became much rarer, so that today in most Toyota plants the line virtually never stops.

Developing the Kanban System

Once reduced setup times had made small production runs economical, Ohno began to look for ways to coordinate the flow of production within the Toyota manufacturing system so that the amount of inventory in the system could be reduced to a minimum. Toyota produced about 25% of its major components in-house (the rest were contracted out to independent suppliers). Ohno's initial goal was to arrange for components and/or subassemblies manufactured in-house to be delivered to the assembly floor only when they were needed, and not before (this goal was later extended to include independent suppliers).

To achieve this, in 1953 Ohno began experimenting with what came to be known as the kanban system. Under the kanban system, component parts are delivered to the assembly line in containers. As each container is emptied, it is sent back to the previous step in the manufacturing process. This then becomes the signal to make more parts. The system minimizes work in progress by increasing inventory turnover. The elimination of buffer inventories also means that defective components show up immediately in the next process. This speeds up the processes of tracing defects back to their source and facilitates correction of the problem before too many defects are made. Moreover, the elimination of buffer stocks, by removing all safety nets, makes it imperative that problems be solved before they become serious enough to jam up the production process, thereby creating a strong incentive for workers to ensure that errors are corrected as quickly as possible. In addition, by decentralizing responsibility for coordinating the manufacturing process to lower-level employees, the kanban system does away with the need for extensive centralized management to coordinate the flow of parts between the various stages of production.

After perfecting the kanban system in one of Toyota's machine shops, Ohno had a chance to apply the system broadly in 1960 when he was made general manager of the Motomachi assembly plant. Ohno already had converted the machining, body stamping, and body shops to the kanban system, but since many parts came from shops that had yet to adopt the system, or from outside suppliers, the impact on inventories was initially minimal. However, by 1962 he had extended the kanban to forging and casting, and between 1962 and 1965 he began to bring independent suppliers into the system.

Organizing Suppliers

Assembly of components into a final vehicle accounts for only about 15% of the total manufacturing process in automobile manufacture. The remaining 85% of the process involves manufacturing more than 10,000 individual parts and assembling them into about 100 major components, such as engines, suspension systems, transaxles, and so on. Coordinating this process so that everything comes together at the right time has always been a problem for auto manufacturers. Historically, the response at Ford and GM to this problem was massive vertical integration. The belief was that control over the supply chain would allow management to coordinate the flow of component parts into the final assembly plant. In addition, American firms held the view that vertical integration made them more efficient by reducing their dependence on other firms for materials and components and by limiting their vulnerability to opportunistic overcharging.

As a consequence of this philosophy, even as late as the mid-1990s General Motors made 68% of its own components in-house, while Ford made 50% (in the late 1990s both GM and Ford de-integrated, spinning out much of their in-house supply operations as independent enterprises). When they didn't vertically integrated, U.S. auto companies historically tried to reduce the procurement costs that remain through competitive bidding—asking a number of companies to submit contracts and giving orders to suppliers offering the lowest price.

Under the leadership of Kiichiro Toyoda during the 1930s and 1940s, Toyota followed the American model and pursued extensive vertical integration into the manufacture of component parts. In fact, Toyota had little choice in this matter, since only a handful of Japanese companies were able to make the necessary components. However, the low volume of production during this period meant that the scale of integration was relatively small. In the 1950s, however, the volume of auto production began to increase dramatically. This presented Toyota with a dilemma: should the company increase its capacity to manufacture components in-house in line with the growth in production of autos, or should the company contract out?

In contrast to American practice, the company decided that while it should increase in-house capacity for essential subassemblies and bodies, it would do better to contract out for most components. Four reasons seem to bolster this decision:

1. Toyota wanted to avoid the capital expenditures required to expand capacity to manufacture a wide variety of components.
2. Toyota wanted to reduce risk by maintaining a low factory capacity in case factory sales slumped.
3. Toyota wanted to take advantage of the lower wage scales in smaller firms.
4. Toyota managers realized that in-house manufacturing offered few benefits if it was possible to find stable, high-quality, and low-cost external sources of component supply.

At the same time, Toyota managers felt that the American practice of inviting competitive bids from suppliers was self-defeating. While competitive bidding might achieve the lowest short-run costs, the practice of playing suppliers off against each other did not guarantee stable supplies, high quality, or cooperation beyond existing contracts to solve design or engineering problems. Ohno and other Toyota managers believed that real efficiencies could be achieved if the company entered into long-term relationships with major suppliers. This would allow them to introduce the kanban system, thereby further reducing inventory holding costs and realizing the same kind of quality benefits that Toyota was already beginning to encounter with its in-house supply operations. In addition, Ohno wanted to bring suppliers into the design process since he believed that suppliers might be able to suggest ways of improving the design of component parts based upon their own manufacturing experience.

As it evolved during the 1950s and 1960s, Toyota's strategy toward its suppliers had several elements. The company spun off some of its own in-house supply operations into quasi-independent entities in which it took a minority stake, typically holding between 20% and 40% of the stock. It then recruited a number of independent companies with a view to establishing a long-term relationship with them for the supply of critical components. Sometimes, but not always, Toyota took a minority stake in these companies as well. All of these companies were designated as "first-tier suppliers." First-tier suppliers were responsible for working with Toyota as an integral part of the new product development team. Each first tier was responsible for the formation of a "second tier" of suppliers under its direction. Companies in the second tier were given the job of fabricating individual parts. Both first- and second-tier suppliers were formed into supplier associations.

By 1986 Toyota had three regional supply organizations in Japan with 62, 135, and 25 first-tier suppliers. A major function of the supplier associations was to share information regarding new manufacturing, design, or materials management techniques among themselves. Concepts such as statistical process control, total quality control, and computer-aided design were rapidly diffused among suppliers by this means.

Toyota also worked closely with its suppliers, providing them with management expertise, engineering expertise, and sometimes capital to finance new investments. A critical feature of this relationship was the incentives that Toyota established to encourage its suppliers to focus on realizing continuous process improvements. The basic contract for a component would be for 4–5 years, with the price being agreed in advance. If by joint efforts the supplier and Toyota succeeded in reducing the costs of manufacturing the components, then the additional profit would be shared between the two. If the supplier by its own efforts came up with an innovation that reduced costs, the supplier would keep the additional profit that the innovation generated for the lifetime of the contract.

As a consequence of this strategy, Toyota outsourced more production than almost any other major auto manufacturer. By the late 1980s Toyota was responsible for only about 27% of the value going into a finished automobile, with the remainder coming from outside suppliers. In contrast, at the time General Motors was responsible for about 70% of the value going into a finished automobile. Other consequences included long-term improvements in productivity and quality among Toyota's suppliers that were comparable to the improvements achieved by Toyota itself. In particular, the extension of the kanban system to include suppliers, by eliminating buffer inventory stocks, in essence forced suppliers to focus more explicitly on the quality of their product.

Consequences

The consequences of Toyota's production system included a surge in labor productivity and a decline in the number of defects per car. Exhibit 1 compares the number of vehicles produced per worker at General Motors, Ford, Nissan, and Toyota between 1965 and 1983.

Exhibit 1	Vehicles Produced per Worker (adjusted for vertical integration), 1965–1983

Year	General Motors	Ford	Nissan	Toyota
1965	5.0	4.4	4.3	8.0
1970	3.7	4.3	8.8	13.4
1975	4.4	4.0	9.0	15.1
1979	4.5	4.2	11.1	18.4
1980	4.1	3.7	12.2	17.8
1983	4.8	4.7	11.0	15.0

Source: M. A. Cusumano, The Japanese Automotive Industry (Cambridge, Mass.: Harvard University Press, 1989), Table 48, p. 197.

Exhibit 2	General Motors's Framingham Plant versus Toyota's Takaoka Plant, 1987

	GM Framingham	Toyota Takaoke
Assembly Hours per Car	31	16
Assembly defects per 100 Cars	135	45
Inventory of Parts	2 weeks	2 hours

Source: J. P. Womack, D. T. Jones, and D. Roos, The Machines That Changed the World (New York: Macmillan, 1990), Figure 4.2, p. 83.

These figures are adjusted for the degree of vertical integration pursued by each company. As can be seen, in 1960 productivity at Toyota already outstripped that of Ford, General Motors, and its main Japanese competitor, Nissan. As Toyota refined its production system over the next 18 years, productivity doubled. In comparison, productivity essentially stood still at General Motors and Ford during the same period.

Exhibit 2 provides another way to assess the superiority of Toyota's production system. Here the performance of Toyota's Takaoka plant is compared with that of General Motors's Framingham plant in 1987. As can be seen, the Toyota plant was more productive, produced far fewer defects per 100 cars, and kept far less inventory on hand.

A further aspect of Toyota's production system is that the short setup times made it economical to manufacture a much wider range of models than is feasible at a traditional mass-production assembly plant. In essence, Toyota soon found that it could supply much greater product variety than its competitors with little in the way of a cost penalty. In 1990 Toyota was offering consumers around the world roughly as many products as General Motors (about 150), even though Toyota was still only half GM's size. Moreover, it could do this at a lower cost than GM.

Distribution and Customer Relations

Toyota's approach to its distributors and customers as it evolved during the 1950s and 1960s was in many ways just as radical as its approach toward suppliers. In 1950 Toyota formed a subsidiary, Toyota Motor Sales, to handle distribution and sales. The new subsidiary was headed by Kaymiya Shotaro from its inception until 1975. Kaymiya's philosophy was that dealers should be treated as "equal partners" in the Toyota family. To back this up, he had Toyota Motor Sales provide a wide range of sales training and service training for dealership personnel.

Kaymiya then used the dealers to build long-term ties with Toyota's customers. The ultimate aim was to bring customers into the Toyota design and production process. To this end, through its dealers, Toyota Motor Sales assembled a huge database on customer preferences. Much of these data came from monthly or semiannual surveys conducted by dealers. These asked Toyota customers their preferences for styling, model types, colors, prices, and other features. Toyota also used these surveys to estimate the potential demand for new models. This information was then fed directly into the design process.

Kaymiya began this process in 1952 when the company was redesigning its Toyopet model. The Toyopet was primarily used by urban taxi drivers. Toyota Motor Sales surveyed taxi drivers to try to find out what type of vehicle they preferred. They wanted something reliable, inexpensive, and with good city fuel mileage—which Toyota engineers then set about designing. In 1956 Kaymiya formalized this process when he created a unified department for planning and market research whose function was to coordinate the marketing strategies developed by researchers at Toyota Motor Sales with product planning by Toyota's design engineers. From this time, on marketing information played a critical role in the design of Toyota's cars and in the company's strategy. In particular, it was the research department at Toyota Motor Sales that provided the initial stimulus for Toyota to start exporting during the late 1960s after predicting, correctly, that growth in domestic sales would slow down considerably during the 1970s.

Expanding Internationally

Large-scale overseas expansion did not become feasible at Toyota until the late 1960s for one principal reason: despite the rapid improvement in productivity, Japanese cars were still not competitive.[3] In 1957, for example, the Toyota Corona sold in Japan for the equivalent of $1,694. At the same time the Volkswagen Beetle sold for $1,111 in West Germany, while Britain's Austin company was selling its basic model for the equivalent of $1,389 in Britain. Foreign companies were effectively kept out of the Japanese market, however, by a 40% value-added tax and shipping costs.

Despite these disadvantages, Toyota tried to enter the United States market in the late 1950s. The company set up a U.S. subsidiary in California in October 1957 and began to sell cars in early 1958, hoping to capture the American small car market (which at that time was poorly served by the U.S. automobile companies). The result was a disaster. Toyota's cars performed poorly in road tests on U.S. highways. The basic problem was that the engines of Toyota's cars were too small for prolonged high-speed driving and tended to overheat and burn oil, while poorly designed chassis resulted in excessive vibration. Sales were slow and in 1964 Toyota closed down its U.S. subsidiary and withdrew from the market.

The company was determined to learn from its U.S. experience and quickly redesigned several of its models based on feedback from American consumer surveys and U.S. road tests. As a result, by 1967 the picture had changed considerably. The quality of Toyota's cars was now sufficient to make an impact in the U.S. market, while production costs and retail prices had continued to fall and were now comparable with international competitors in the small car market.

In the late 1960s Toyota reentered the U.S. market. Although sales were initially slow, they increased

steadily. Then the OPEC-engineered fourfold increase in oil prices that followed the 1973 Israeli/Arab conflict gave Toyota an unexpected boost. U.S. consumers began to turn to small fuel-efficient cars in droves, and Toyota was one of the main beneficiaries. Driven primarily by a surge in U.S. demand, worldwide exports of Toyota cars increased from 157,882 units in 1967 to 856,352 units by 1974 and 1,800,923 units by 1984. Put another way, in 1967 exports accounted for 19% of Toyota's total output. By 1984 they accounted for 52.5%.

Success brought its own problems. By the early 1980s political pressures and talk of local content regulations in the United States and Europe were forcing an initially reluctant Toyota to rethink its exporting strategy. Toyota already had agreed to "voluntary" import quotas with the United States in 1981. The consequence for Toyota was stagnant export growth between 1981 and 1984. Against this background, in the early 1980s Toyota began to think seriously about setting up manufacturing operations overseas.

Transplant Operations

Toyota's first overseas operation was a 50/50 joint venture with General Motors established in February 1983 under the name New United Motor Manufacturing, Inc. (NUMMI). NUMMI, which is based in Fremont, California, began producing Chevrolet Nova cars for GM in December 1984.[4] The maximum capacity of the Fremont plant is about 250,000 cars per year.

For Toyota, the joint venture provided a chance to find out whether it could build quality cars in the United States using American workers and American suppliers. It also provided Toyota with experience dealing with an American union (the United Auto Workers Union) and with a means of circumventing "voluntary" import restrictions. For General Motors, the venture provided an opportunity to observe in full detail the Japanese approach to manufacturing. While General Motors's role was marketing and distributing the plant's output, Toyota designed the product and designed, equipped, and operated the plant. At the venture's start, 34 executives were loaned to NUMMI by Toyota and 16 by General Motors. The chief executive and chief operating officer were both Toyota personnel.

By the fall of 1986 the NUMMI plant was running at full capacity and the early indications were that the NUMMI plant was achieving productivity and quality levels close to those achieved at Toyota's major Takaoka plant in Japan. For example, in 1987 it took the NUMMI plant 19 assembly hours to build a car, compared to 16 hours at Takaoka, while the number of defects per 100 cars was the same at NUMMI as at Takaoka—45.[5]

Encouraged by its success at NUMMI, in December 1985 Toyota announced that it would build an automobile manufacturing plant in Georgetown, Kentucky. The plant, which came on stream in May 1988, officially had the capacity to produce 200,000 Toyota Camrys a year. Such was the success of this plant, however, that by early 1990 it was producing the equivalent of 220,000 cars per year. This success was followed by an announcement in December 1990 that Toyota would build a second plant in Georgetown with a capacity to produce a further 200,000 vehicles per year.[6]

By 2012, Toyota had 14 vehicle assembly plants in North America, 10 of them in the United States, which collectively produced 7 out of every 10 Toyota cars sold in the region. In addition, the company had six other plants producing a range of components, including engines and transmissions. The company also has two R&D and design centers in the United States, its only such facilities outside of Japan. By 2012, Toyota's cumulative investment in the United States exceeded $19.5 billion. In April 2013, Toyota announced that it would move production of one of its luxury Lexus vehicles from Japan to the United States, marking the first time that the company had produced a luxury vehicle outside of Japan. At the same time, Toyota announced that it would invest another $2.5 billion to expand U.S. production capacity.[7]

In addition to its North American transplant operations Toyota moved to set up production in Europe in anticipation of the 1992 lowering of trade barriers among the 12 members of the European Economic Community. In 1989 the company announced that it would build a plant in England with the capacity to manufacture 200,000 cars per year by 1997. It opened a second plant in France in 2001, and by 2008, Toyota had four assembly plants in Europe with a total production capacity of 800,000 vehicles.

The company also expanded China during the first decade of the twentieth century. In China, it had three assembly plants by 2008 that were capable of producing over 440,000 vehicles a year. In the rest of South East Asia Toyota had another 10 plants that could produce almost one million vehicles. There were also significant assembly plants in South Africa, Australia, and South America.

Despite Toyota's apparent commitment to expand global assembly operations, it was not all smooth sailing. One problem was building an overseas supplier network comparable to Toyota's Japanese network. For example, in a 1990 meeting of Toyota's North American supplier's association, Toyota executives informed their North American suppliers that the defect ratio for parts produced by 75 North American and European suppliers was 100 times greater than the defect ratio for parts supplied by 147 Japanese suppliers—1,000 defects per million parts versus 10 defects per million among Toyota's Japanese suppliers. Moreover, Toyota executives pointed out that parts manufactured by North American and European suppliers tend to be significantly more expensive than comparable parts manufactured in Japan.

Because of these problems, Toyota had to import many parts from Japan for its U.S. assembly operations. However, for political reasons Toyota was being pushed to increase the local content of cars assembled in North America. By the mid-2000s, the local content of cars produced in North America was over 70%. To improve the efficiency of its U.S.-based suppliers, Toyota embarked upon an aggressive supplier education process. In 1992, it established the Toyota Supplier Support Center to teach its suppliers the basics of the Toyota production system. By the mid-2000s over 100 supplier companies had been through the center. Many have reportedly seen double- and triple-digit productivity growth as a result, as well as dramatic reductions in inventory levels.[8]

Product Strategy

Toyota's initial production was aimed at the small car/basic transportation end of the automobile market. This was true both in Japan and of its export sales to North America and Europe. During the 1980s, however, Toyota progressively moved up market and abandoned much of the lower end of the market to new entrants such as the South Koreans. Thus, the company's Camry and Corolla models, which initially were positioned toward the bottom of the market, have been constantly upgraded and now are aimed at the middle-income segments of the market. This upgrading reflects two factors: (1) the rising level of incomes in Japan and the commensurate increase in the ability of Japanese consumers to purchase mid-range and luxury cars and (2) a desire to hold onto its U.S. consumers, many of whom initially purchased inexpensive Toyotas in their early twenties and who have since traded up to more expensive models.

The upgrading of Toyota's models reached a logical conclusion in September 1989 when the company's Lexus division began marketing luxury cars to compete with Jaguars, BMWs, and the like. Although the Lexus brand initially got off to a slow start—in large part due to an economic recession—by 2001 Toyota was selling over 200,000 Lexus models a year in the United States, making it the best-selling luxury brand in the country.

In the mid-1990s Toyota's U.S. research suggested that the company was losing younger buyers to hipper brands like Volkswagen. The result was a brand designed specially for the United States market, the Scion. Established with its own dealer network, the Scion has been a hit for Toyota.

TOYOTA IN 2000–2012

The first 8 years of the 21st century were ones of solid growth for Toyota. In 2004 it overtook Ford to become the second largest car company in the world. The company surpassed General Motors in 2008, and seemed on track to meet its goal of capturing 15% of the global automobile market by 2010. Toyota was now a truly international company. Its overseas operations had grown from 11 production facilities in nine countries in 1980 to 48 production facilities in 26 countries around the world.[9] In the important United States market, the world's largest, Toyota held an 18.4% share of passenger car sales in mid-2008, up from 11% in 2000. Ford's share was 15.4% while GM held onto a 19.3% share.[10]

The company was very profitable. In the financial year ending March 2008 it earned $17.5 billion net profits on sales of $183 billion. Both General Motors and Ford lost money that year.

According to data from J.D. Power, Toyota was the quality leader in the United States market in 2008. For cars that had been on the market for over 3 years, Toyota's Lexus brand led the pack for the 14th consecutive year with 120 problems per 100 vehicles, compared to an industry average of 206 problems per 100 vehicles. The Toyota brand had 159 problems per 100 vehicles, compared to 177 for Honda, 204 for Ford, 226 for GMC, 229 for Chrysler, and 253 for Volkswagen. Toyota also had a strong record in the industry when measured by problems reported in the first 90 days after a sale—99 problems per 100 cars for the Lexus brand and 104 for the Toyota brand versus an industry average of 118 problems per 100 cars.[11]

J.D. Power also found that Toyota led the market in Japan. A survey found that for vehicles purchased in 2002, Toyota had 89 problems per 100 vehicles compared to an industry average of 104. Honda was next with 91 problems per 100 vehicles, followed by Nissan with 108 problems per 100 vehicles.[12]

On the productivity front, Toyota's lead seemed to have narrowed. While it was clearly the productivity leader in the United States in 2003, where it took an average of 30.1 hours to make a car, compared to 35.2 hours at General Motors and 38.6 hours at Ford, by 2007 Toyota was taking 30.37 to build a car, compared to 32.29 at GM and 33.88 at Ford (see Exhibit 3).[13] On the other hand, according to J.D. Power, Toyota has the three most efficient assembly plants in the world, all of which are located in Japan.[14]

Higher quality and greater productivity helped Toyota to make far more money per car than its large rivals. In 2007, Toyota made a pretax profit of $922 per vehicle in the United States, compared with losses of $729 and $1,467 at GM and Ford respectively. These losses also reflect the fact that Ford and GM still pay more for health care, pensions, and sales incentives than Toyota. Also, Ford and GM support more dealers relative to their market share than Toyota.[15]

Toyota's ability to stay on top of productivity and quality rankings can be attributed to a company wide obsession with continuing to improve the efficiency and effectiveness of its manufacturing operations. The latest round of these was initiated in 2000 by Toyota President,

Exhibit 3	Total Manufacturing Productivity in the U.S. Automobile Industry (Total Labor Hours per Unit)	
Company	**2003**	**2007**
Ford	38.6	33.88
Chrysler	37.42	30.37
General Motors	35.2	32.39
Nissan	32.94	32.96
Honda	32.36	31.33
Toyota	30.01	30.37

Note: Includes assembly, stamping, engine, and transmission plants.
Source: *Oliver Wyman's Harbour Report*, Oliver Wyman, June 2008.

Fujio Cho. Cho, who worked for a while under Toyota's legendary engineer, Taichi Ohno, introduced an initiative known as "Construction of Cost Competitiveness for the 21st Century," or CCC21. The initiative has as a goal slashing component part costs by 30% on all new models. Attaining this goal necessitated Toyota working closely with suppliers—something it has long done.

By the mid-2000s Toyota was close to attaining its CCC21 goal. In implementing CCC21, no detail has been too small. For example, Toyota took a close look at the grip handles mounted above the doors inside most cars. By working closely with suppliers, they managed to reduce the number of parts in these handles from 34 to 5, which cut procurement costs by 40% and reduced the time need for installation from 12 seconds to 3 seconds.[16]

More generally, Toyota continues to refine its lean production system. For example, in die making, by 2004 Toyota had reduced the lead time to engineer and manufacture die sets for large body panels to 1.7 months, down from 3 months in 2002. By reducing lead time, Toyota reduces the startup costs associated with producing a new model, and the development time.[17]

In welding, Toyota has developed and installed a simplified assembly process known as the "Global Body Line" or GBL. First developed in a low volume Vietnamese assembly plant in 1996, and introduced into its first Japanese plant in 1998, by 2004 the GBL was operating in some 20 of the company's 50 assembly plants and was found in all plants by 2007. The GBL system replaced Toyota's Flexible Body Line assembly philosophy that has been in place since 1985. The GBL system is based upon a series of programmable robotic wielding tools. Under the old FBL system each car required three pallets to hold body parts in place during the wielding process; each gripping either a major body side assembly or the roof assembly. The GBL system replaces these three pallets with a single pallet that holds all three major body panels in place from the inside as wielding proceeds.[18]

According to Toyota, the GLB system has the following consequences:

- 30% reduction in the time a vehicle spends in the body shop.
- 70% reduction in the time required to complete a major body change.
- 50% cut in the cost to add or switch models.
- 50% reduction in the investment to set up a line for a new model.
- 50% reduction in assembly line footprint.

The floor space freed up by the GLB allows two assembly lines to be placed in the space traditionally required for one, effectively doubling plant capacity. Moreover, using GLB technology as many as eight different models can be produced on a single assembly line. To achieve this, Toyota has pushed for consistency in design across model ranges, particularly with regard to the "hard points" that are grasped by the single master pallet.

Meanwhile, Toyota has also been accelerating the process of moving towards fewer vehicle platforms, the goal being to build a wide range of models on a limited range of platforms that use many of the same component parts or modules. The company is reportedly working towards a goal of having just 10 platforms, down from over 20 in 2000.[19]

While Toyota is undoubtedly making progress refining its manufacturing efficiency, the fact remains that the productivity and quality gap between Toyota and its global competitors has narrowed. General Motors and Ford have both made significant strides in improving their quality and productivity in recent years. Moreover, in the American market at least, Toyota has suffered from the perception that its product offerings lack design flair and are not always as well attuned to consumer tastes as they might be. Here too, however, there are signs that Toyota is improving matters interestingly enough, by listening more to its American designers and engineers.

A pivotal event in the changing relationship between Toyota and its American designers occurred in the late 1990s. Japanese managers had resisted their U.S. colleagues' idea that the company should produce a V8 pickup truck for the American market. To change their minds, the U.S. executives took flew their Japanese counterparts over from Japan and took them to a Dallas Cowboys football game—with a pit stop in the Texas Stadium parking lot. There the Japanese saw row upon row of full-size pickups. Finally, it dawned on them that Americans see the pickup as more than a commercial vehicle, considering it primary transportation. The result of this was Toyota's best-selling V8 pickup truck, the Toyota Tundra.[20]

American designers also pushed Toyota to redesign the Prius, its hybrid car first introduced in Japan 1997. The Americans wanted a futuristic design change so that people would notice the technology. The result, the new Prius, has become a surprise hit with Toyota hitting cumulative global sales of over one million vehicles in mid-2008. By 2010 Toyota was making more than one million hybrids a year.[21]

Toyota's Americanization runs deeper than just product design issues. On the sales front, the company now sells more cars and trucks in North American than it does in Japan, and 70% to 80% of Toyota's global profits come from North America. On the personnel front, President Cho himself made his reputation by opening Toyota's first U.S. production plant in Georgetown Kentucky in 1988. Another senior executive, Yoshi Inaba, spent 8 years in the U.S. and has an MBA from Northwestern University. Americans are also starting to make their way into Toyota's top ranks.[22]

Another concern of Toyota has been the aging of its customer base. According to J.D. Power, the average Toyota customer is 44 years old, compared with 38 for Volkswagen and 41 for Honda. Concerned that it was loosing its cache with the younger generation, some 60 million of whom will reach driving age over the next few years, Toyota introduced a new car brand, the Scion, into America in June 2004. Scion cars are targeted at young entry-level buyers and can be purchased over the web in addition to through traditional Toyota dealers. Toyota's initial sales goals for the brand were 100,000 cars in 2005, but in October 2004 it raised that target to 170,000. The average buyer in the months following launch was 31 years old.[23]

THE 2008–2009 CRISIS AND ITS AFTERMATH

Starting in mid-2008, sales in the global automobile industry collapsed at unprecedented rates, falling by around 40%. The sales collapse was a direct consequence of the global financial crisis that started in the American mortgage market, and then spilled over into other sectors. A combination of tight credit and uncertainty about the future caused consumers to buy far fewer new cars. For an industry with high fixed costs, a sales decline of this level was catastrophic.

Toyota was caught flat-footed by the decline. Toyota had been adding to its production capacity in the United States, its largest market, and pushing into the full sized pick up truck segment, when the storm hit. It had also been adding significant capacity elsewhere, a move that seemed sensible only 12 months earlier given that the company had been struggling to keep up with demand for its vehicles. Indeed, between 2001 and 2007 Toyota added about 500,000 cars worth of production capacity per year, a pace that now seems to be aggressive.[24]

By April 2009 Toyota's sales in the U.S. were down 42% compared to the same month a year earlier. Moreover, there were sales declines in all other major national markets as well, including China, where Toyota sales fell by 17% in the first quarter of 2009, even though that market was one of the few that continued to grow. Toyota's problems in China reflected a slow response to increasing demand outside of China's big cities for small affordable cars. Toyota exports from Japan were also hit hard by a rise in the value of the Japanese Yen against the dollar and euro during 2008 and early 2009.

In the United States, Toyota responded to the recession by placing the planned addition of a new production plant in Mississippi on hold, and idling a production line in Texas. In Japan, production was cut by as much as 40% in some factories. These actions created a huge problem for Toyota, which adheres to a policy of lifetime employment, and has not made any significant workforce reductions since the 1950s. Toyota's initial response was to send underutilized employees to training sessions, and to have them work on identifying ideas for cost savings. However, the company did start to lay off temporary workers and many questioned whether Toyota would be able to stick to its commitment of lifetime employment, particularly if the recession drags on.

Toyota also launched an "Emergency Profit Improvement Committee," whose job was to find $1.4 billion in savings in 2009. These cost savings came upon some $3.3 billion in cost reductions attained during the preceding few years. In typical Toyota style, no action seems too small. Employees have been encouraged to take the stairs rather than use elevators to save electricity. The heat in factories has been turned down. Teams of workers are looking for any way to shave costs out of a production system that is already the world's most efficient.[25]

To try and boost sales in the United States, Toyota introduced 0% financing in late 2008, but sales continued to falter. Ironically, one of Toyota's best-selling cars in the United States during much of 2007 and 2008, the fuel-efficient Prius, which carries a relative high price sticker, also saw steep sales declines in early 2009 as gasoline prices fell, and consumers who did purchase switched to low priced small cars from Kia and even Ford.

Meanwhile, Toyota was also going through a changing of senior management ranks. In June 2009, Akio Toyoda, grandson of the company's founder, succeeded outgoing CEO Katsuaki Watanabe. With an MBS from

Babson College in the U.S., and time working in both New York and London, Toyoda is without question the most cosmopolitan CEO to take the helm at Toyota. He did so at a particularly challenging time for the company. His major challenge was to weather the storm and return the company to its growth path.

By 2012 it looked as if he had succeeded in doing that. Toyota had regained the mantel of the world's largest automobile company. Its reputation for quality, which had been badly tarnished by the sudden acceleration problems in the United States, was again riding high. Accordingly to J.D. Power's annual Vehicle Dependency Study, after slipping in 2009 and 2010, Toyota brands regained the top spot in 2011 and 2012. That being said, Toyota faced invigorated competitors who were fast closing in on the company. Most notably, Hyundai-Kia of South Korea had grown its output from just 2.4 million units in 2000 to 7.1 million in 2012, making it the 4th largest automobile maker in the world. Hyundai was now more profitable than Toyota, and produced more vehicles per employee, suggesting that Toyota might be losing its crown as the most productive automobile company in the world. In addition, Volkswagen was investing aggressively in capacity, particularly in China, now the world's largest national automobile market, and was well position to challenge Toyota for global market share leadership. Rounding out the top four global automobile makers was General Motors, which had emerged from bankruptcy a smaller but stronger company. Indeed, on global measures of labor productivity, GM now surpassed Toyota. Moreover, GM was well positioned in the large and rapidly growing Chinese market, where Toyota had struggled due to anti-Japanese sentiment. The future thus presented numerous challenges for Toyota.[26]

END NOTES

1. This section is based primarily on the account given in M. A. Cusumano, *The Japanese Automobile Industry*, (Cambridge, Mass: Harvard University Press, 1989).

2. The material in this section is drawn from three main sources: M. A. Cusumano, *The Japanese Automobile Industry*; Ohno Taiichi, *Toyota Production System* (Cambridge, Mass.: Productivity Press, 1990; Japanese Edition, 1978); J. P. Womack, D. T. Jones, and D. Roos, *The Machine That Changed the World* (New York: Macmillan, 1990).

3. The material in this section is based on M. A. Cusumano, The Japanese Automobile Industry.

4. Niland Powell, "U.S.-Japanese Joint Venture: New United Motor Manufacturing, Inc.," *Planning Review*, January–February 1989, pp. 40–45.

5. From J. P. Womack, D. T. Jones, and D. Roos, *The Machine That Changed the World*.

6. J. B. Treece, "Just What Detroit Needs: 200,000 More Toyotas a Year," *Business Week*, December 10, 1990, p. 29.

7. P. Eisensteon, "Toyota investing over $500 million to launch US Lexus production," *NBC News*, April 19, 2013.

8. P. Strozniak, "Toyota Alters the Face of Production," *Industry Week*, August 13, 2001, pp. 46–48.

9. Anonymous, "The Car Company out in Front," *The Economist*, January 29, 2005, pp 65–67.

10. R. Newman, "How Toyota could become the US sales champ," *US News and World Reports*, June 9, 2008.

11. J.D. Power Press Release, August 7 2008, "Lexus Ranks Highest in Vehicle Dependability for 14th Consecutive Year." J.D. Power press Release, June 4, 2008, "Overall Initial Quality Improves Considerably."

12. J.D. Power Press Release, "Toyota Ranks Highest in Japans First Long Term Vehicle Dependability Study," September 2, 2004.

13. *Oliver Wyman's Harbour Report*, Oliver Wyman, June 2008.

14. *Oliver Wyman's Harbour Report*, Oliver Wyman, June 2008.

15. *Oliver Wyman's Harbour Report*, Oliver Wyman, June 2008.

16. B. Bremner and C. Dawson, "Can Anything stop Toyota," *Business Week*, November 17, 2003, pp 114–117.

17. M. Hara, "Moving Target," *Automotive Industries*, June 2004, pp. 26–29.

18. B. Visnic, "Toyota Adopts New Flexible Assembly Process," Wards Auto World, November 2002, pp. 30–31. M. Bursa, "A Review of Flexible Automotive Manufacturing," *Just Auto*, May 2004, p. 15.

19. M. Hara, "Moving Target," *Automotive Industries*, June 2004, pp. 26–29.

20. C. Dawson and L. Armstrong, "The Americanization of Toyota," *Business Week*, April 15, 2002, pp. 52–54.

21. Chuck Squatriglia, "Prius sales top 1 million," *Autopia*, May 15, 2008.

22. A. Taylor, "The Americanization of *Toyota*," Fortune, December 8, 2004, p. 165.

23. N. Shirouzu, "Scion Plays Hip-Hop Impresario to Impress Young Drivers," *Wall Street Journal*, October 5, 2004, p. B1.

24. Y. Takahashi, "Toyota record $7.74 billion quarterly loss," *Wall Street Journal*, May 11, 2009, p. 3.

25. I. Rowly, "Toyota's cost cutting drive," *Business Week*, January 1, 2009, p. 15.

26. Stuart Pearson et al, "Global Autos: A Clash of Titans," *Morgan Stanley Blue Paper*, January 22, 2013.

Case 17

Costco Wholesale Corporation

Ankur Anand*

Charles WL Hill

A man who looks like Wilford Brimley (an American actor) walks into a Costco warehouse store in the Seattle suburb of Issaquah, Washington, on a bright Columbus Day morning, easily blending into the throngs of shoppers picking up Kellogg's Cornflakes, toilet paper, and cashmere sweaters. But as soon as Costco CEO Jim Sinegal crosses the threshold of this vast, 150,000-square-foot theater of retail, it's abundantly clear that he's not just a spectator—he's the executive producer, director, and critic. "Jim's in the building!" crackles over the walkie-talkie of warehouse manager Louie Silveira. In the apparel section, Silveira's infectious grin morphs into a look of slight panic.[1]

A sudden hop in his step, Silveira, who can log 15 miles a day walking the aisles, scurries over to Sinegal. Unsmiling, hands in his pockets, a coffee stain on his $12.99 Costco shirt, Sinegal turns out to be a no-nonsense connoisseur of detail. He greets his manager with a barrage of questions: "What's new today?"

"We just moved this $800 espresso machine to an endcap," Silveira responds, meaning he moved it out from the middle of the aisle to a more prominent location at the end.

"How are in-stocks?"

"We're good there."

"What did we do in produce last week?"

"$220,000."

Wielding a barcode scanner like a six-shooter, Silveira answers each query to Sinegal's satisfaction, but evidently that's not often the case.

INTRODUCTION

Costco Wholesale Corporation is a membership-only warehouse club that provides a wide selection of merchandise. As of July 2012, it is the second largest retailer in the United States, the seventh largest retailer in the world and the largest membership warehouse club chain in the United States.[2]

Costco operates membership warehouses based on the concept that offering its members low prices on a limited selection of nationally branded and private-label products in a wide range of merchandise categories will produce high sales volumes and rapid inventory turnover. This turnover, when combined with the operating efficiencies achieved by volume purchasing, efficient distribution and reduced handling of merchandise in no-frills, self-service warehouse facilities, enables Costco to operate profitably at significantly lower gross margins than traditional wholesalers, mass merchandisers, supermarkets, and supercenters.[3]

Costco's typical warehouse averages approximately 143,000 square feet; newer units tend to be slightly larger. Floor plans are designed for economy and efficiency in the use of selling space, the handling of merchandise, and the control of inventory. Because shoppers are attracted principally by the quality of merchandise and the availability of low prices, Costco's warehouses do not have elaborate facilities. By strictly controlling the entrances and exits of its warehouses and using a membership format, Costco has limited inventory losses (shrinkage) to less than two-tenths of 1% of net sales in the last several fiscal years—well below those of typical discount retail operations.

Costco's warehouses generally operate on a 7-day, 69-hour week, open weekdays between 10:00 a.m. and 8:30 p.m., with earlier weekend closing hours. Gasoline

*This case was written by Ankur Anand under the direction of Charles W.L. Hill. Please send requests for permission to Charles Hill. (itzankur@gmail.com)

(chill@u.washington.edu), Foster School of Business, University of Washington, Seattle, WA 98195.

operations generally have extended hours. Because the hours of operation are shorter than those of traditional retailers, discount retailers and supermarkets, and due to other efficiencies inherent in a warehouse-type operation, labor costs are lower relative to the volume of sales. Merchandise is generally stored on racks above the sales floor and displayed on pallets containing large quantities, thereby reducing labor required for handling and stocking.

Costco's strategy is to provide its members with a broad range of high-quality merchandise at prices consistently lower than they can obtain elsewhere. Costco seeks to limit specific items in each product line to fast-selling models, sizes, and colors. Therefore, Costco carries an average of approximately 3,600 to 4,000 active stock keeping units (SKUs) per warehouse in its core warehouse business, as opposed to 45,000 to 140,000 SKUs or more at discount retailers, supermarkets, and supercenters. Many consumable products are offered for sale in case, carton, or multiple-pack quantities only.[4]

In keeping with its policy of member satisfaction, Costco generally accepts returns of merchandise. On certain electronic items, they generally have a 90-day return policy and provide, free of charge, technical support services, as well as an extended warranty.[5]

THE COMPANY HISTORY[6]

Costco Wholesale Corporation and its subsidiaries (Costco or the Company) began operations in 1983 in Seattle, Washington. In October 1993, Costco merged with The Price Company, which had pioneered the membership warehouse concept. In January 1997, after the spin-off of most of its nonwarehouse assets to Price Enterprises, Inc., the Company changed its name to Costco Companies, Inc. On August 30, 1999, the Company reincorporated from Delaware to Washington and changed its name to Costco Wholesale Corporation, which trades on the NASDAQ Global Select Market under the symbol "COST".

As of December 2012, the Company operated a chain of 622 warehouses in 41 states and Puerto Rico, nine Canadian provinces (85 locations), Mexico (32 locations), the United Kingdom (23 locations), Japan (13 locations),

Positioning

The wholesale club store format is positioned as having a lower shopping frequency and less range than a conventional supermarket

Major supermarket-type retail store formats by positioning model

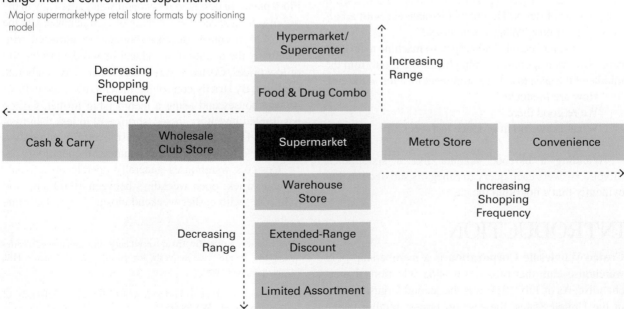

Costco Timeline

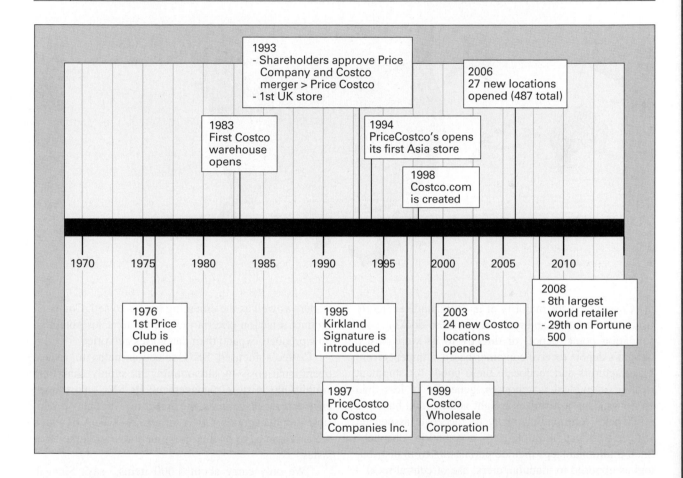

1993
- Shareholders approve Price Company and Costco merger > Price Costco
- 1st UK store

2006
27 new locations opened (487 total)

1983
First Costco warehouse opens

1994
PriceCostco's opens its first Asia store

1998
Costco.com is created

1970 1975 1980 1985 1990 1995 2000 2005 2010

1976
1st Price Club is opened

1995
Kirkland Signature is introduced

2003
24 new Costco locations opened

2008
- 8th largest world retailer
- 29th on Fortune 500

1997
PriceCostco to Costco Companies Inc.

1999
Costco Wholesale Corporation

Korea (nine locations), Taiwan (nine locations, through a 55%-owned subsidiary) and Australia (three locations). The Company also operates Costco online, electronic commerce web sites, at www.costco.com (U.S.), www.costco.ca (Canada), and www.costco.co.uk (United Kingdom).

COSTCO'S STRATEGY

Price

"We always look to see how much of a gulf we can create between ourselves and the competition," Sinegal says. "So that the competitors eventually say, '#*** 'em, these guys are crazy. We'll compete somewhere else.'"[7]

To illustrate, Sinegal recounts a story about denim. "Some years ago we were selling a hot brand of jeans for $29.99. They were $50 in a department store. We got a great deal on them and could have sold them for a higher price, but we went down to $29.99. Why? We knew it would create a riot."[8]

But it is the customer, more than the competition that keeps Mr. Sinegal's attention. "We're very good merchants, and we offer value," he said. "The traditional retailer will say: 'I'm selling this for $10. I wonder whether I can get $10.50 or $11.' We say: 'We're selling it for $9. How do we get it down to $8?' We understand that our members don't come and shop with us because of the fancy window displays or the Santa Claus or the piano player. They come and shop with us because we offer great values."[9]

622 Locations as of December 31, 2012

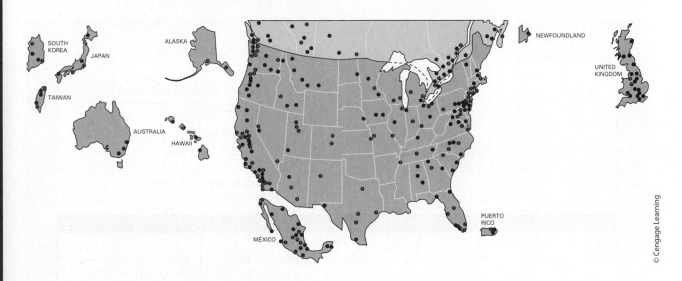

© Cengage Learning

Costco buys the majority of its merchandise directly from manufacturers and routes it to a cross-docking consolidation point (depot) or directly to its warehouses. Costco's depots receive container-based shipments from manufacturers and reallocate these goods for shipment to their individual warehouses, generally in less than 24 hours. This maximizes freight volume and handling efficiencies, eliminating many of the costs associated with traditional multiple-step distribution channels. Such traditional steps include purchasing from distributors as opposed to manufacturers, use of central receiving, storing and distributing warehouses, and storage of merchandise in locations off the sales floor.

Because of its high sales volume and rapid inventory turnover, Costco generally sells inventory before it is required to pay many of its merchandise vendors and thus take advantage of early payment discounts when available. Thanks to the rapid turnover, an increasingly greater percentage of inventory gets financed through payment terms provided by suppliers rather than by Costco's working capital.[10]

Scarcity

A key tenet of Costco's business strategy is to limit the number of different items on its shelves. The Company evaluates SKUs individually and selects both category leaders as well as the emerging brands to sell. Company product selection criteria include value, sales potential, how products expand their categories and price.

Costco's focused SKU selection helps to reduce operational costs by streamlining its supply chain and simplifying in-store management. Its SKU-constrained environment also limits the freedom available to consumer product goods (CPG) companies—many of which are accustomed to owning prominent real estate in-store aisles.

"We only carry about 4,000 items," says Sinegal, "compared with 40,000 in a typical supermarket and 150,000 in a Wal-Mart supercenter. Of that 4,000, about 3,000 can be found on the floor all the time. The other 1,000 are the treasure-hunt stuff that's always changing. It's the type of item a customer knows they'd better buy because it will not be there next time, like Waterford crystal. We try to get that sense of urgency in our customers."

The limited-variety approach isn't for everyone, though. Sinegal explains: "We carry a 360-count bottle of Advil for $18.49," he says. "Lots of customers don't want to buy 360. If you had ten customers come in to buy Advil, how many are not going to buy any because you just have one size? Maybe one or two. We refer to that as the intelligent loss of sales: We are prepared to give up that one customer. But if we had four or five sizes of

Advil, as grocery stores do, it would make our business more difficult to manage. Our business can only succeed if we are efficient. You can't go on selling at these margins if you are not."

The more efficient the product sourcing, the more latitude Sinegal can give his sto re managers in how they lay out those big bottles of Advil. "There are certain merchandise displays that all warehouses do," he says. "TVs are always in the front, for example".

Private-Label Power

Kirkland Signature is Costco's store brand, otherwise known in the retail industry as an "own-brand," "house brand" or "private label." It is found at Costco's website, Costco warehouses and on Amazon.com.

When Costco introduced Kirkland Signature as its house brand in 1995, the idea was to face private-label competition at many major retailers including Wal-Mart's Great Value, Target's Archer Farms and CVS's branded product line. Costco's strong private-label offering, Kirkland Signature, competes with brands in an ever-expanding range of categories.

Many private-label brands provide consumers with economical options for their shopping lists, and Kirkland Signature is typically 10 to 20% lower than its branded counterparts. That said, Kirkland Signature also competes directly with many national CPG firms on quality. This focus on value has evolved to position Kirkland Signature products as slightly more expensive in many categories as comparable national brands—including canned tuna, salsa, and pet snacks.[11]

Positioning Kirkland Signature as a premium-priced brand—but not the most expensive option—gives Costco the opportunity to brand itself as a quality product with a slight value (price) advantage over its CPG competitors.

Marketing

Costco generally limits marketing and promotional activities to new warehouse openings, occasional direct mail to prospective new members, and regular direct marketing programs (such as The Costco Connection, a magazine that Costco publishes for our members, coupon mailers, weekly email blasts from costco.com, and handouts)to existing members promoting selected merchandise. These practices result in lower marketing expenses as compared to typical retailers.[12]

Membership Model

Since Costco offers steep discounts on its merchandise, it attempts to make up for it via a membership fee. The retailer charges an annual membership fee of $55 for business and business add-on membership, and $110 for executive membership.

A warehouse club's true value lies in its ability to attract bulk buyers. Thus, despite low margins, a warehouse club can generate significant amount of dollar profits due to rapid inventory turnover. Such a value proposition is lucrative to customers who tend to buy large amounts of merchandise, and thus despite paying a membership fee save money due to discounts. Costco offers a variety of merchandise categories such as groceries, hardlines and softlines, and ancillary services such as gas station, pharmacy, food court etc. Groceries account for more than half of Costco's revenues.[13]

Executive members, who account for about one-third of Costco's total members, and two-third of its sales, are the most valuable customers for the retailer. These members pay around $110 annually, as opposed to $55 paid by the other members. For the higher fee, executive members are given 2% redeemable reward against their annual purchases (maximum limit of $750). The percentage of executive members enrollment increased from 33% in fiscal 2009 to 38% at the end of fiscal 2012. An increase in executive members will provide strong support to Costco's future growth. The fact that these members pay a higher membership fee implies that they tend to buy a lot more in order to take advantage of their 2% annual rewards.

Readmore:http://www.nasdaq.com/article/how-does-costco-make-money-cm205766#ixzz2UuPbWqpU

COSTCO.COM

Costco went online in November 1998 (three years after Amazon). Currently, Costco.com ranks 17th[14] among online retailers. Amazon ranks first and Wal-Mart fourth (Staples is second and Apple is third)[15]—and both are growing faster than Costco. Costco.com sells about $2 billion worth of goods.[16]

Costco sells online only in the United States and Canada for now, but hopes to expand to other countries in the coming year.[17]

Costco offers distinct products in its stores and e-commerce site to keep its customers interested. About

80 to 90% of its products offered online do not overlap with the store inventory. This allows the retailer to operate two distinct channels without having to worry about self-cannibalization.[18] Also, shipping is included in most purchases and features "white-glove delivery," which means the item (if needed) is assembled in the room of your choice and the service covers disposal of the packaging.

However, nonmembers are required to pay a 5% fee to buy from Costco online. That means an expensive enough purchase could make the $55 standard membership fee worth the investment.

"A lot of other chain retailers, including Wal-Mart, are doing things sooner, better and quicker, including going international. Wal-Mart has included Sam's Club (a Costco competitor) in its aggressive plans for overseas online sales, including China, and Wal-Mart is buying social-media space to get hold of the always-connected buyer."[19]

Mark Brohan, director of research for International Journal of Electronic Commerce.

"We don't advertise and we don't pay for search. We're moving to a new platform that will be structured in a way to be picked up by search engines."[20]

Ginnie Roeglin, senior vice president of Costco's e-commerce and publishing operations.

According to Roeglin, Costco is exploring social media options and is planning to expand to other countries very soon.

COSTCO EMPLOYEE RELATIONS[21]

"When employees are happy, they are your very best ambassadors."

-Jim Sinegal, CEO, Costco.

Costco enjoys a reputation for having the best benefits in retail, a sector where labor costs account for about 80% of a typical company's total expenses. Costco Wholesale Corp. often is held up as a retailer that does it right, pays well and offers generous benefits.

Costco pays starting employees at least $10 an hour, and with regular raises a full-time hourly worker can make $40,000 annually within 3.5 years. Cashiers are paid $10.50 to $17.50 an hour.

Costco also pays 92% of its employees' health-insurance premiums, much higher than the 80% average at large U.S. companies. Wal-Mart pays two-thirds of health-benefit costs for its workers. Costco's health plan offers a broader range of care than Wal-Mart's does, and part-time Costco workers qualify for coverage in six months, compared with two years for Wal-Mart part-timers.

"From day one, we've run the company with the philosophy that if we pay better than average, provide a salary people can live on, have a positive environment and good benefits, we'll be able to hire better people, they'll stay longer and be more efficient," says Richard Galanti, Costco's chief financial officer.

Costco has several advantages over Wal-Mart that help it extend such unusually generous pay and benefits. Costco has a more-upscale reputation than Sam's Club, helping it attract shoppers with higher incomes. The average Costco store rings up $115 million in annual sales, almost double the Sam's Club average. And Costco, which charges $55 to $110 for yearly memberships, doesn't spend any money on advertising.

Costco says its higher pay boosts loyalty: Its employee turnover rate is 24% a year. Wal-Mart's overall employee turnover rate is 50%, about in line with the retail-industry average. Wal-Mart doesn't break out turnover rates at Sam's Club. High turnover creates a significant added expense for retailers because new workers those have to be trained and are not as efficient.[22]

Probably one of the biggest differences between Costco and other discounters is that the chain pays relatively high wages for retail. Luxury department stores can pay higher base wages or high commissions because they can maintain big markups, but Costco's shoppers are more price sensitive. The big advantages for Costco here are shrinkage, turnover, and public relations, but these factors don't seem like enough to convince most discounters to pay higher wages.

Costco's wages may have helped boost another financial metric, net income per employee. Costco's earning is more than twice as much profit per employee as Wal-Mart. (Table below[23])

"Wall Street grumbles that Costco cares more about its customers and employees than its shareholders; it pays workers an average of $17 an hour and covers 90% of health-insurance costs for both full-timers and part-timers. Yet revenues have grown by 70% in the past five years, and its stock has doubled."

-Jim Sinegal, CEO, Costco.

In 2008, *Ethisphere* named Sinegal one of the 100 Most Influential People in Business Ethics (ranked at #37).[24]

	WAL-MART	COSTCO
1. Net income per employee	$7,039	$17,174
2. Employees covered by company health insurance	48%	82%
3. Insurance-enrollment waiting periods (for part-time workers)	2 years	6 months
4. % Employees covered for health insurance	66%	92%
5. Annual worker turnover rate	50%	24%

"Senegal is known as a leader who is fair to his employees, and Costco has been reaping the benefits for some time. It doesn't appear that he'll change his ways in 2008 amidst the financial crisis. In fact, he's also ramping up Costco's sustainability initiatives such as investing in solar power and, according to one interview, changing the shape of cashew containers in order to let them stack more efficiently and take trucks off the road."[25]

Ethisphere's analysis concluded that the emphasis on employees at Costco is the key to the Company's success and ability to consistently provide a better shopping experience for its members. It also said that Jim Sinegal is the perfect example of how the tone at the top sets the tone for the entire company.

While talking about Costco's employee-first philosophy, Mr. Jim Sinegal said that,

"Because it's part of the DNA of our company. It's the culture. . . . It's not altruistic. This is good business, hiring good people and paying them good wages and providing good jobs for them and opportunities for a career. If you accept the premise that we pay the highest wages in our industry [hourly workers average more than $20 an hour, including bonuses] and have the richest health care and benefit plan in our industry and the lowest price on merchandise and run the lowest-cost operation, then it must follow we're getting better productivity."[26]

-Jim Sinegal, CEO, Costco.

Many executives once believed that you can't keep prices low if a company pays high wages and benefits. Costco is proof that this isn't always the case. Costco executives understand the impact and importance that good employees can have in an organization. Perks such as high wages, benefits and opportunity for growth allow Costco to attract a large pool of high-quality candidates who are committed to their jobs. A Workforce article, "Welcome to the Club", reported that:

In addition to offering some of the best wages and benefits in the retail industry, Costco rewards employees with bonuses and other incentives. It promotes from within, encourages workers to make suggestions and to air grievances and gives managers autonomy to experiment with their departments or stores to boost sales or shave expenses as they see fit.

Much of the emphasis on culture and values at Costco is attributed to the personal interests of Sinegal, its CEO. In an interview when asked for his opinion on the rising gas prices, Sinegal responded that:

"Even employees who work at Costco—who make the type of wages that we pay—are being hit at the gas pump. We're working very hard to schedule people from the same part of town so they can drive together. We're encouraging van pools. We're even testing 10-hour days, something we've never done in the past. If we can schedule some employees for four 10-hour days, that's one day they don't have to drive to work. They've got a 20% savings in their gas right there."

His response to the question shouldn't be surprising, but it is surprising to find a CEO who actually takes these types of external factors into consideration when planning for their business. Costco's executives focus on putting their employees first, which has lead to low employee turnover rates. In the long run, this increased rate of retention has allowed Costco to save on labor costs while continuing to provide employees with significant wages and benefit packages. When employees feel important and that there is value in the work that they do, it makes it harder to leave their current position and seek out new work.

Front-line employees are the ones who interact with your company's customers each day and are ultimately the ones who communicate the values and culture of your brand to the public. When employees are not passionate about their work or their brand, their attitudes have the ability to influence the customer's shopping experience. Sinegal started out his retail career as a bagger[27], working through the ranks to VP Merchandising and Operations at FedMart- eventually cofounding Costco in 1983. Since he has worked in a variety of retail positions throughout his career, Sinegal understands the motivators and impact that every position has on the overall success of Costco.

In one of their articles about Costco, Tech Crunch[28] discussed the factors of success at Costco, stating that:

"The company's per-employee sales are considerably higher than those of key rivals such as Target and Wal-Mart; customer service at the stores is phenomenal and fast; and Costco continues to expand, both in number of warehouses and in products and services for business and consumer customers."[29]

The Costco story teaches us all a few lessons that can be applied to our own workplaces: think of the long-term impact of your actions, reduce employee turnover and, at all times, let your employees know they matter.

COSTCO VS. WALMART 2012	COSTCO	WALMART
Average Hourly Wage	$17.00	$12.54
Annual Health Costs per Worker	$7,127	$4,750
Covered by health plan	82%	49%
Annual Retirement costs per worker	$1,330	$996
Employee turnover	12%	37%
Labor and overhead	9.60%	19.50%
Sales per square foot	$986	$425
Net profits per employee	$946	$656
Yearly operating income growth	16.10%	−0.04%
Chairman Salary (incl. bonus)	$548,400	$1,264,775
Stock Price as of 11/28/2012	101.8	70.43

*CEO-Chairman is S. Robson Walton@33% ownership

BIG BOX, BIG BUCKS[30]

Costco sells more efficiently than its low-margin peers. It even outdoes plusher names like Nordstrom, and holds its own against higher-markup "category killers" like Best Buy.

COMPANY	SALES PER SQUARE FOOT, ANNUAL
Target	$307
Nordstrom	$369
Home Depot	$377
Wal-Mart*	$438
BJ's	$445
Sam's Club*	$552
Costco	$918
Best Buy	$941

Source: Company data; UBS, 2009
*Estimate

COMPETITION

Warehouse clubs compete with each other on factors such as price, merchandise quality and selection, location, and member service. Warehouse clubs also compete with a wide range of other types of retailers, including retail discounters such as Wal-Mart and Dollar General, supermarkets, general merchandise chains, specialty chains, gasoline stations, and most recently Internet retailers (which now represents one of the biggest threats). Wal-Mart, the world's largest retailer, competes directly with Costco not just via its Sam's Club subsidiary but also through its Wal-Mart stores, which sell many of the same SKUs at attractively low prices. Target and Kohl's have also emerged as significant retail competitors in certain merchandise categories. Low-cost, single category retailers, including Lowe's, Home Depot, Office Depot, Staples, Best Buy, Circuit City, PetSmart, and Barnes & Noble, also compete with Costco and have significant market shares in their respective product categories.

There have been three main players in the wholesale club industry—Costco Wholesale, Sam's Club (612 membership warehouse clubs in the U.S., Brazil, China and Mexico), and BJ's Wholesale Club (190 locations in 15 states). At the end of 2010, there were just over 1,200 warehouse locations across the United States and Canada; most every major metropolitan area had one, if not several, warehouse clubs. Costco held a nearly 55% share of warehouse club sales across the United States and Canada, with Sam's Club (a division of Wal-Mart) holding roughly 36% share and BJ's Wholesale Club and several small warehouse club competitors making up the remaining 9% share.

The wholesale club and warehouse retail segment is estimated to be $140 billion[31] in annual revenue, and it is growing about 20% faster than retailing as a whole.[32,33]

Below are brief profiles of Costco's two primary competitors in North America: Sam's Club and BJ's Wholesale Club.

Sam's Club

Wal-Mart opened the first Sam's Club in 1984. In the beginning, many Sam's Club locations were located adjacent to Wal-Mart Supercenters. The concept of the Sam's Club format was to sell merchandise at very low profit margins (lower than Wal-Mart stores), resulting in low prices to members.

Sam's Club warehouses range from 70,000 to 190,000 square feet, with a typical size of about 132,000 square feet. Similar to Costco, all Sam's Club warehouses feature concrete floors, sparse décor, with goods displayed on pallets, simple wooden shelves, or racks. Sam's Club stocks branded merchandise, including hard goods, some soft goods, institutional-size grocery items, and selected private-label items sold under the Member's Mark, Bakers & Chefs, and Sam's Club brands.

Most Sam's Club locations also carry software, electronics, jewelry, sporting goods, toys, tires, batteries, stationery and books. The majority of clubs have fresh-foods departments that include bakery, meat, produce, floral products, and a Sam's Café. Members can also shop online at www.samsclub.com. Like Costco, Sam's Club stocks about 4,000 SKUs, most of which are standard items and a small fraction of which are special, limited time offerings. However, these limited time offerings tend to be of lesser quality and carry a lower price tag than those at Costco.

The annual fee for "Sam's saving" members is $45 for the primary membership card, with an additional houeholdcard available at no additional cost.[34]

A "Sam's Plus" membership costs $100 with an additional household card available at no additional cost. Businesses with a plus membership can have up to 16 add-ons for $45 each.[35]

Regular hours of operation for Sam's Club are Monday through Friday 10:00 a.m. to 8:30 p.m., Saturday 9:30 a.m. to 8:30 p.m., and Sunday 10:00 a.m. to 6:00 p.m.

Approximately two-thirds of the merchandise at Sam's Club is shipped from the division's own distribution facilities and, in the case of perishable items, from some of Wal-Mart grocery distribution centers. The balance is shipped by suppliers direct to Sam's Club locations.

Like Costco, Sam's Club distribution centers employ cross-docking techniques whereby incoming shipments are transferred immediately to outgoing trailers destined for Sam's Club locations; shipments typically spend less than 24 hours at a cross-docking facility and in some instances are there for only an hour. The Sam's Club distribution center network consisted of seven company-owned-and-operated distribution facilities, 13 third-party-owned-and-operated facilities, and two third-party-owned-and-operated import distribution centers.

A combination of company-owned trucks and vehicles from independent trucking companies are used to transport merchandise from distribution centers to club locations.[36]

BJ's Wholesale Club

BJ's Wholesale Club, Inc., commonly referred to simply as BJ's, is a membership-only warehouse club chain operating on the United States. Headquartered in Westborough, MA, BJ's Wholesale Club, Inc. (www.bjs.com), is a leading operator of membership warehouse clubs in the Eastern United States. The Company currently operates over 190 Clubs in 15 states from Maine to Florida and employs more than 24,000 Team Members. BJ's is traded on the New York Stock Exchange under the symbol "BJ."[37]

On September 30, 2011, BJ's Wholesale Club was acquired by Beacon Holding Inc., an affiliate of Leonard Green & Partners, L.P., and funds advised by CVC Capital Partners.[38]

Merchandise in BJ's is generally displayed on pallets containing large quantities of each item, thereby reducing labor required for handling, stocking, and restocking. Backup merchandise is generally stored in steel racks above the sales floor. Similar to Costco and Sam's, BJ's sells high-quality, branded merchandise at prices that are significantly lower than the prices found at supermarkets, discount retail chains, and specialty retail stores such as Best Buy[39]. Its merchandise lineup of about 7,500 items includes consumer electronics, prerecorded media, small appliances, tires, jewelry, health and beauty aids, household products, computer software, books, greeting cards, apparel, furniture, toys, seasonal items, frozen foods, fresh meat and dairy products, beverages, dry grocery items, fresh produce, flowers, canned goods, and household products.

Paid membership is an essential part of the warehouse club concept. In addition to providing a source of revenue it helps offer low prices and reinforces customer loyalty. BJ's offers two types of memberships: Inner Circle® memberships and business memberships. Most Inner Circle members are likely to be homeowners whose incomes are above the average for the Company's catchment area.

Inner Circle® memberships usually cost $50 per year for a primary member and includes one free supplemental membership. Members in the same household may purchase additional supplemental memberships for $25 each. A primary business membership also costs $50 per year and includes one free supplemental membership. Additional supplemental business memberships cost $25 each. These fees were increased on January 3, 2011. Prior to that date, primary Inner Circle and business memberships cost $45 per year and supplemental memberships cost $20 each.

APPENDIX

Costco Financials[41]

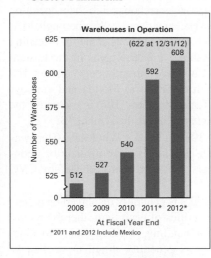

Warehouses in Operation

(622 at 12/31/12)

Year	Number
2008	512
2009	527
2010	540
2011*	592
2012*	608

At Fiscal Year End
*2011 and 2012 Include Mexico

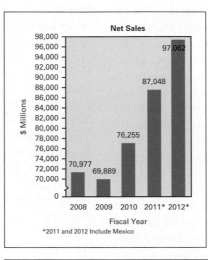

Net Sales ($ Millions)

Year	Sales
2008	70,977
2009	69,889
2010	76,255
2011*	87,048
2012*	97,062

Fiscal Year
*2011 and 2012 Include Mexico

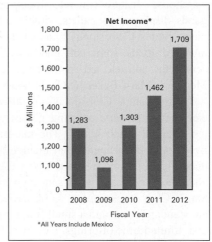

Net Income* ($ Millions)

Year	Income
2008	1,283
2009	1,096
2010	1,303
2011	1,462
2012	1,709

Fiscal Year
*All Years Include Mexico

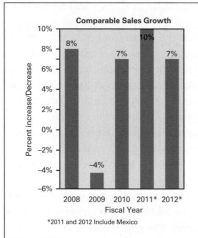

Comparable Sales Growth

Year	Percent increase/Decrease
2008	8%
2009	−4%
2010	7%
2011*	10%
2012*	7%

Fiscal Year
*2011 and 2012 Include Mexico

Membership

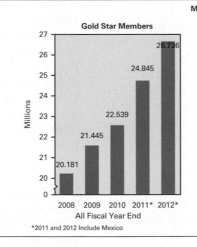

Gold Star Members (Millions)

Year	Members
2008	20.181
2009	21.445
2010	22.539
2011*	24.845
2012*	26.736

All Fiscal Year End
*2011 and 2012 Include Mexico

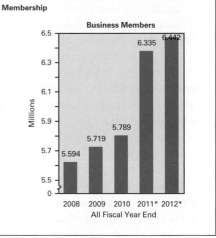

Business Members (Millions)

Year	Members
2008	5.594
2009	5.719
2010	5.789
2011*	6.335
2012*	6.442

All Fiscal Year End

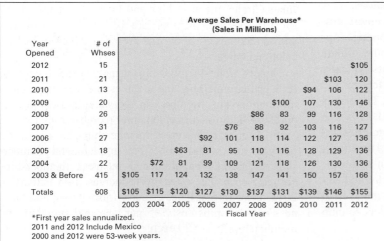

Average Sales Per Warehouse*
(Sales in Millions)

Year Opened	# of Whses	2003	2004	2005	2006	2007	2008	2009	2010	2011	2012
2012	15										$105
2011	21									$103	120
2010	13								$94	106	122
2009	20							$100	107	130	146
2008	26						$86	83	99	116	128
2007	31					$76	88	92	103	116	127
2006	27				$92	101	118	114	122	127	136
2005	18			$63	81	95	110	116	128	129	136
2004	22		$72	81	99	109	121	118	126	130	136
2003 & Before	415	$105	117	124	132	138	147	141	150	157	166
Totals	608	$105	$115	$120	$127	$130	$137	$131	$139	$146	$155

Fiscal Year

*First year sales annualized.
2011 and 2012 Include Mexico
2000 and 2012 were 53-week years.

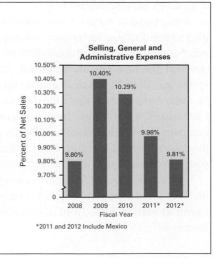

Selling, General and Administrative Expenses (Percent of Net Sales)

Year	Percent
2008	9.80%
2009	10.40%
2010	10.29%
2011*	9.98%
2012*	9.81%

Fiscal Year
*2011 and 2012 Include Mexico

Like Costco and Sam's, BJ's Rewards Membership® program, is geared to high frequency, high volume members, offering a 2% rebate, capped at $500 per year, on most in-club purchases. The annual fee for a BJ's Rewards Membership is $100. At the end of 2010, Rewards Members accounted for approximately 7.8% of BJ's primary members and approximately 17% of BJ's merchandise sales during the year.

BJ's top management believed that several factors set BJ's Wholesale operations apart from those of Costco and Sam's Club:

- Offering a wide range of choice—7,500 items versus 4,000 items at Costco and Sam's Club:
- Focusing on the individual consumer via merchandising strategies that emphasized a customer-friendly shopping experience
- Clustering club locations to achieve the benefit of name recognition and maximize the efficiencies of management support, distribution, and marketing activities
- Supplementing the warehouse format with aisle markers, express checkout lanes, self-checkout lanes and low-cost video-based sales aids to make shopping more efficient for members
- Offering longer working hours than competitors
- Offering smaller package sizes for many items
- Accepting manufacturers' coupons
- Accepting more credit card payment options[40]

CONCLUSION

Looking forward, the issue facing Costco is how to maintain its historically high performance? As the Company has become larger, several markets have neared saturation and maintaining historic growth rates has become more challenging. Moreover, Costco faces a potentially strong challenge from online retailers, most notably Amazon, which offers a vast array of goods at low prices. Moreover, as Amazon builds out its distribution system it will soon be able to offer next day delivery to most locations within the United States. Will this be enough to draw customers away from Costco and end the Company's impressive rise to dominance in deep discounting retailing?

NOTES

1. http://money.cnn.com/magazines/fortune/fortune_archive/2006/10/30/8391725/
2. http://en.wikipedia.org/wiki/Costco
3. COSTCO Annual report FY 2011
4. http://www.coriolisresearch.com/pdfs/coriolis_understanding_Costco.pdf
5. COSTCO Annual report FY 2011
6. http://phx.corporate-ir.net/phoenix.zhtml?c=83830&p=irol-reportsannual
7. http://money.cnn.com/magazines/fortune/fortune_archive/2006/10/30/8391725/
8. http://money.cnn.com/magazines/fortune/fortune_archive/2006/10/30/8391725/
9. http://www.nytimes.com/2005/07/17/business/yourmoney/17costco.html?pagewanted=all&_r=0
10. COSTCO Annual report FY 2011
11. http://www.lek.com/sites/default/files/lek-why_costco_and_other_warehouse_club_retailers_matter.pdf
12. COSTCO Annual report FY 2011
13. http://www.nasdaq.com/article/how-does-costco-make-money-cm205766#ixzz2UuPFCPCq
14. http://seattletimes.com/html/businesstechnology/2018150010_costco06.html
15. http://netonomy.net/2013/01/30/top-5-largest-online-retailers-who-companies-how-did-they-make-it/
16. http://seattletimes.com/html/businesstechnology/2018150010_costco06.html
17. http://www.cisco.com/web/about/ac79/docs/retail/Costco-com_UK.pdf
18. http://www.forbes.com/sites/greatspeculations/2013/05/29/costco-earnings-swelling-membership-will-fuel-its-sales-growth/
19. http://o.seattletimes.nwsource.com/html/businesstechnology/2018150010_costco06.html
20. http://seattletimes.com/html/businesstechnology/2018150010_costco06.html
21. http://www.businessweek.com/stories/2004-05-30/online-extra-at-costco-good-jobs-and-good-wages
    http://www.seattlepi.com/business/article/Costco-s-love-of-labor-Employees-well-being-key-1140722.php
    http://beta.fool.com/enovinson/2012/07/26/several-ways-costco-differs-other-discounters/7886/
22. http://www.priceviewer.com/costco/costco_employment.htm
23. http://reclaimdemocracy.org/costco_employee_benefits_walmart/
24. http://ethisphere.com/100-most-influential-people-in-business-ethics-2008/#37
25. http://ethisphere.com/100-most-influential-people-in-business-ethics-2008/#37
26. http://www.tlnt.com/2011/12/19/generous-benefits-costco-ceo-says-they-are-just-good-business/
27. http://en.wikipedia.org/wiki/James_Sinegal
28. TechCrunch is a web publication that offers technology news and analysis, as well as profiles of startup companies, products, and websites. It was founded by Michael Arrington in 2005, and was first published on June 11, 2005.

29. http://techcrunch.com/2010/03/20/integrating-ethics-into-the-core-of-your-startups-why-and-how/

30. http://money.cnn.com/magazines/fortune/fortune_archive/2006/10/30/8391725/

31. https://www.deloitte.com/assets/Dcom-UnitedStates/Local%20Assets/Documents/ConsumerProducts/us_cp_Club%20Strategy_011813.pdf

32. http://www.lek.com/sites/default/files/lek-why_costco_and_other_warehouse_club_retailers_matter.pdf

33. https://www.deloitte.com/assets/Dcom-UnitedStates/Local%20Assets/Documents/ConsumerProducts/us_cp_Club%20Strategy_011813.pdf

34. https://m.samsclub.com/membership/join

35. https://m.samsclub.com/membership/join

36. http://www.walmartstores.com/sites/annualreport/2011/financials/2011_Five_Year_Summary.pdf

37. BJ's 2011 Annual Report (LINK)

38. http://www.bjs.com/company-background.content.about_background.A.about

39. BJ's 2011 Annual Report (LINK)

40. BJ's 2011 Annual Report (LINK)

41. Costco 2012 Annual report

Case 18

IKEA in 2013: Furniture Retailer to the World

Charles W.L. Hill

INTRODUCTION

IKEA is one of the world's most successful global retailers. By 2012 IKEA had 320 home furnishing superstores stores in 40 countries and was visited by some 776 million shoppers. IKEA's low-priced, elegantly designed merchandise, displayed in large warehouse stores, generated sales of €27.5 billion in 2012, up from €4.4 billion in 1994, and €4.2 billion in net profit. Although the privately held company refuses to publish detailed financial data, its net profit margins were rumored to be around 10%, high for a retailer. The founder, Ingvar Kamprad, now in his 80s but still an active "advisor" to the company, is rumored to be one of the world's richest men.

COMPANY BACKGROUND

IKEA was established by Ingvar Kamprad in Sweden in 1943 when he was 17 years old. The fledgling company sold fish, Christmas magazines and seeds from his family farm. It wasn't his first business—that had been selling matches which the enterprising Kamprad had purchased wholesale in 100 box lots (with help from his Grandmother who financed the enterprise) and then resold individually at a higher mark-up. The name IKEA was an acronym, I and K being his initials, while E stood for Elmtaryd, the name of the family farm, and A stood for Agunnaryd, the name of the village in Southern Sweden where the farm was located. Before long Kamprad had added ballpoint pens to his list and was selling his products via mail order. His warehouse was a shed on the family farm. The customer fulfillment system utilized the local milk truck, which picked up goods daily and took them to the train station.

In 1948 Kamprad added furniture to his product line and in 1949 he published his first catalog, distributed then as now, for free. In 1953 Kamprad found himself struggling with another problem, the milk tuck had changed its route and he could no longer use it to take goods to the train station. Kamprad's solution was to buy an idle factory in nearby Almhult and convert it into his warehouse. With business now growing rapidly, Kamprad hired a 22 year old designer, Gillis Lundgren. Lundgren originally helped Kamprad to do photo shoots for the early IKEA catalogs, but over time he started to design more and more furniture for IKEA, eventually designing as many as 400 pieces, including many best sellers.

IKEA's goal as it emerged over time was to provide stylish functional designs with minimalist lines that could be manufactured cost efficiently under contract by suppliers and priced low enough to allow most people to afford them. Kamprad's theory was that "good furniture could be priced so that the man with that flat wallet would make a place for it in his spending and could afford it".[1] Kamprad was struck by the fact that furniture in Sweden was expensive at the time, something that he attributed to a fragmented industry dominated by small retailers. Furniture was also often considered a family heirloom, passed down across the generations. He wanted to change this: to make it possible for people of modest means to buy their own furniture. Ultimately, this led to the concept of what IKEA calls "democratic design"—a design that, according to Kamprad, "was not just good, but also from the start adapted to machine production and thus cheap to assemble".[2] Gillis

School of Business, University of Washington, Seattle, WA 98105

Lundgren was instrumental in the implementation of this concept. Time and time again he would find ways to alter the design of furniture to save on manufacturing costs.

Gillis Lundgren also stumbled on what was to become a key feature of IKEA furniture: self-assembly. Trying to efficiently pack and ship a long-legged table, he hit upon the idea of taking the legs off and mailing them packed flat under the tabletop. Kamprad quickly noticed is that flat packed furniture reduced transport and warehouse costs, and also reduced damage (IKEA had been having a lot of problems with furniture damaged during the shipping process). Moreover, customers seemed willing to take on the task of assembly in return for lower prices. By 1956, self-assembly was integral to the IKEA concept.

In 1957 IKEA started to exhibit and sell its products at home furnishing fairs in Sweden. By cutting retailers out of the equation and using the self-assembly concept, Kamprad could undercut the prices of established retail outlets, much to their chagrin. Established retailers responded by prohibiting IKEA from taking orders at the annual furniture trade in Stockholm. Established outlets claimed that IKEA was imitating their designs. This was to no avail however, so the retailers went further, pressuring furniture manufacturers not to sell to IKEA. This had two unintended consequences. First, without access to the designs of many manufacturers, IKEA was forced to design more of its products in house. Second, Kamprad looked for a manufacturer who would produce the IKEA designed furniture. Ultimately he found one in Poland.

To his delight, Kamprad discovered that furniture manufactured in Poland was as much as 50% cheaper that furniture made in Sweden, allowing him to cut prices even further. Kamprad also found that doing business with the Poles required the consumption of considerable amounts of vodka to celebrate business transactions, and for the next 40 years his drinking was legendary. Alcohol consumption apart, the relationship that IKEA established with the Poles was to become the archetype for future relationships with suppliers. According to one of the Polish managers, there were three advantages of doing business with IKEA: "One concerned the decision making; it was always one man's decision, and you could rely upon what had been decided. We were given long-term contracts, and were able to plan in peace and quite. . . . A third advantage was that IKEA introduced new technology. One revolution for instance, was a way of treating the surface of wood. They also mastered the ability to recognize cost savings that could trim the price."[3] By the early 1960s, Polish made goods were to be found on over half of the pages of the IKEA catalog.

By 1958, an expanded facility at the Almhult location became the first IKEA store. The original idea behind the store was to have a location where customers could come and see IKEA furniture set up. It was a supplement to IKEA's main mail order business; but it very quickly became an important sales point in its own right. The store soon started to sell car roof racks so that customers could leave with flat packed furniture loaded on top. Noticing that a trip to an IKEA store was something of an outing for many shoppers (Almhult was not a major population center, and people often drove in from long distances), Kamprad experimented with adding a restaurant to the Almhult store so that customers could relax and refresh themselves while shopping. The restaurant was a hit and it became an integral feature of all IKEA stores.

The response of IKEA's competitors to its success was to argue that IKEA products were of low quality. In 1964, just after 800,000 IKEA catalogs had been mailed to Swedish homes, the widely read Swedish magazine *Allt i Hemmet* (Everything for the Home) published a comparison of IKEA furniture to that sold in traditional Swedish retailers. The furniture was tested for quality in a Swedish design laboratory. The magazine's analysis, detailed in a 16-page spread, was that not only was IKEA's quality as good if not better than that from other Swedish furniture manufacturers, the prices were much lower. For example, the magazine concluded that a chair bought at IKEA for 33 kroner ($4) was better than a virtually identical one bought in a more expensive store for 168 kroner ($21). The magazine also showed how a living room furnished with IKEA products was as much as 65% less expensive than one furnished with equivalent products from four other stores. This publicity made IKEA acceptable in middle-class households, and sales began to take off.

In 1965, IKEA opened its first store in Stockholm, Sweden's capital. By now, IKEA was generating the equivalent of €25 million and had already opened a store in neighboring Norway. The Stockholm store, its third, was the largest furniture store in Europe and had an innovative circular design that was modeled on the famous Guggenhiem Art Museum in New York. The location of the store was to set the pattern at IKEA for decades. The store was situated on the outskirts of the city, rather than downtown, and there was ample space for parking and good access roads. The new store generated a large amount of traffic, so much so that employees could not keep up with customer orders, and long lines formed at the checkouts and merchandise pick up areas. To try and reduce the lines, IKEA experimented with a self-service pick up solution, allowing shoppers to enter the warehouse, load flat packed furniture onto trolleys, and then take them through the checkout. It was so successful that this soon became the norm in all stores.

INTERNATIONAL EXPANSION

By 1973 IKEA was the largest furniture retailer in Scandinavia with 9 stores. The company enjoyed a market share of 15% in Sweden. Kamprad, however, felt that growth opportunities were limited. Starting with a single store in Switzerland over the next 15 years the company expanded rapidly in Western Europe. IKEA meet with considerable success, particularly in West Germany where it had 15 stores by the late1980s. As in Scandinavia, Western European furniture markets were largely fragmented and served by high cost retailers located in expensive downtown stores and selling relatively expensive furniture that was not always immediately available for delivery. IKEA's elegant functional designs with their clean lines, low prices and immediate availability were a breath of fresh air, as was the self-service store format. The company was meet with almost universal success even though, as one former manager put it: "We made every mistake in the book, but money nevertheless poured in. We lived frugally, drinking now and again, yes perhaps too much, but we were on our feet bright and cheery when the doors were open for the first customers, competing in good Ikean spirit for the cheapest solutions".[4]

The man in charge of the European expansion was Jan Aulino, Kamprad's former assistant, who was just 34 years old when the expansion started. Aulino surrounded himself with a young team. Aulino recalled that the expansion was so fast paced that the stores were rarely ready when IKEA moved in. Moreover, it was hard to get capital out of Sweden due to capital controls, so the trick was to make a quick profit and get a positive cash flow going as soon as possible. In the haste to expand, Aulino and his team did not always pay attention to detail, and he reportedly clashed with Kamprad on several occasions and considered himself fired at least four times, although he never was. Eventually the European business was reorganized and tighter controls were introduced.

IKEA was slow to expand in the UK, however, where the locally grown company Habitat had built a business that was similar in many respects to IKEA, offering stylish furniture and at a relatively low price. IKEA also entered North America, opening up seven stores in Canada between 1976 and 1982. Emboldened by this success, in 1985 the company entered the United States. It proved to be a challenge of an entirely different nature.

On the face of it, America looked to be fertile territory for IKEA. As in Western Europe, furniture retailing was a very fragmented business in the United States. At the low end of the market were the general discount retailers, such as Wal*Mart, Costco, and Office Depot, who sold a limited product line of basic furniture, often at a very low price. This furniture was very functional, lacked the design elegance associated with IKEA, and was generally of a fairly low quality. Then there were higher end retailers, such as Ethan Allen, who offered high-quality, well-designed, and high-priced furniture. They sold this furniture in full service stores staffed by knowledgeable sales people. High-end retailers would often sell ancillary services as well, such as interior design. Typically these retailers would offer home delivery service, including set up in the home, either for free or for a small additional charge. Since it was expensive to keep large inventories of high-end furniture, much of what was on display in stores was not readily available, and the client would often have to wait a few weeks before it was delivered.

IKEA opened its first U.S. store in 1985 in Philadelphia. The company had decided to locate on the coasts. Surveys of American consumers suggested that IKEA buyers were more likely to be people who had travelled abroad, who considered themselves risk takers, and who liked fine food and wine. These people were concentrated on the coasts. As one manager put it, "there are more Buicks driven in the middle than on the coasts".[5]

Although IKEA initially garnered favorable reviews, and enough sales to persuade it to start opening additional stores, by the early 1990s it was clear that things were not going well in America. The company found that its European-style offerings didn't always resonate with American consumers. Beds were measured in centimeters, not the king, queen, and twin sizes with which Americans are familiar. American sheets didn't fit on IKEA beds. Sofas weren't big enough, wardrobe drawers were not deep enough, glasses were too small, curtains too short, and kitchens didn't fit U.S. size appliances. In a story often repeated at IKEA, managers noted that customers were buying glass vases and using them to drink out of, rather than the small glasses for sale at IKEA. The glasses were apparently too small for Americans who like to add liberal quantities of ice to their drinks. To make matters worse, IKEA was sourcing many of the goods from overseas and they were priced in Swedish Kroner, which was strengthening against the U.S. dollar. This drove up the price of goods in IKEA's American stores. Moreover, some of the stores were poorly located, and the stores were not large enough to offer the full IKEA experience familiar to Europeans.

Turning around its American operations required IKEA to take some decisive actions. Many products had to be redesigned to fit with American needs. Newer and larger store locations were chosen. To bring prices down, goods were sourced from lower cost locations and priced in dollars. IKEA also started to source some products from factories in the United States to reduce both transport costs and dependency on the value of the dollar. At the same time, IKEA was noticing a change in American culture. American's were becoming more concerned with design, and more open to the idea of disposable furniture. It used to be said that American's changed their spouses about as often as they changed their dinning room table, about 1.5 times in a life time, but something was shifting in American culture. Younger people were more open to risks and more willing to experiment, and there was a thirst for design elegance and quality. Starbucks was tapping into this, as was Apple Computer, and so did IKEA. According to one manager at IKEA, "ten or 15 years ago, travelling in the United States, you couldn't eat well. You couldn't get good coffee. Now you can get good bread in the supermarket, and people think that is normal. I like that very much. That is more important to good life than the availability of expensive wines. That is what IKEA is about".[6]

To tap into America's shifting culture, IKEA reemphasized design, and it started promoting itself with a series of quirky hip advertisements aimed at a younger demographic; young married couples, college students, and twenty to thirty something singles. One IKEA commercial, called "Unboring", made fun of the reluctance of Americans to part with their furniture. One famous ad featured a discard lamp, forlorn and forsaken in some rainy American city. A man turns to the camera sympathetically. "Many of you feel bad for this lamp," he says in thick Swedish accent, "That is because you are crazy". Hip people, the commercial implied, bought furniture at IKEA. Hip people didn't hang onto their furniture either, after a while they discarded it and replaced it with something else from IKEA.

The shift in tactics worked. IKEA's revenues doubled in a 4-year period to $1.27 billion in 2001, up from $600 million in 1997. By 2012 the United States was IKEA's largest market after Germany, with 44 stores accounting for 14% of the global total revenues.

Having learnt vital lessons about competing in foreign countries outside of continental Western Europe, IKEA continued to expand internationally in the 1990s and 2000s. It first entered the UK in 1987 and by 2012 had 18 stores in the country. IKEA also acquired Britain's Habitat in the early 1990s, and continued to run it under the Habitat brand name. In 1998, IKEA entered China, where it had 14 stores by 2012, followed by Russia in 2000 (14 stores by 2012), and in 2006 Japan, a country where it had failed miserably 30 years earlier (by 2012 IKEA had 6 stores in Japan). In total, by 2012 there were 320 IKEA stores in 40 countries and territories. The company's plans call for continued global expansion, opening 20 to 25 stores per year, funded by an investment of around €20billion.

IKEA's latest target market is India, where it has plans to invest €1.5 billion and ultimately open 25 stores. In late 2012 India's foreign investment board approved IKEA's plans to open stores in the country. However, the approval came with strings attached. The board denied IKEA to offer products in areas that the government thinks are politically sensitive, and where it wants to protect local retailers. These include food and beverage outlets, which are a standard feature of its stores around the world, and 18 of the 30 product categories it had initially applied for. Those 18 categories include gift items, fabrics, books, toys, and consumer electronics. It remains to be seen how IKEA will adapt to these retractions.[7]

As with the United States, some local customization has been the order of the day. In China, for example, the store layout reflects the layout of many Chinese apartments, and since many Chinese apartments have balconies, IKEA's Chinese stores include a balcony section. IKEA also has had to adapt its locations in China, where car ownership is still not widespread. In the West, IKEA stores are generally located in suburban areas and have lots of parking space. In China, stores are located near public transportation, and IKEA offers delivery services so that Chinese customers can get their purchases home. IKEA has also adopted a deep price discounting model in China, pricing some items as much as 70% below their price in IKEA stores outside of China. To make this work, IKEA has sourced a large percentage of its products sold in China from local suppliers.

On thing that IKEA has refused to adapt to, however, are business practices that clash with its values. The company prides itself on its "clean" image and is willing to halt investment in order to protect that. In the mid 2000s it put investment in Russia on hold as a protest against endemic corruption. It subsequently fired two senior executives in the country for allegedly turning a bribe to a subcontractor to secure electricity supply for its St Petersburg outlets.[8]

Senior executives at IKEA have been know to complain that they could expand the business faster, were it not for administrative "red tape" in many countries that slows down the rate of expansion. According to the current CEO, Mikael Ohlsson, the amount of time it takes to open a store has roughly doubled to 5 or 6 years since the 1990s. Ohlsson singled out German local authorities as having planning restrictions designed to protect local city center shops that are detrimental to IKEA's expansion plans. Ohlsson argues that such regulations are holding back investment by IKEA, and thus job creation, across the European Union.[9]

THE IKEA CONCEPT AND BUSINESS MODEL

IKEA's target market is the young upwardly mobile global middle class who are looking for low-priced but attractively designed furniture and household items. This group is targeted with somewhat wacky offbeat advertisements that help to drive traffic into the stores. The stores themselves are large warehouses festooned in the blue and yellow colors of the Swedish flag that offer 8,000 to 10,000 items, from kitchen cabinets to candlesticks. There is plenty of parking outside, and the stores are located with good access to major roads.

The interior of the stores is configured almost as a maze that requires customers to pass through each department to get to the checkout. The goal is simple; to get customers to make more impulse purchases as they wander through the IKEA wonderland. Customers who enter the store planning to buy a $40 coffee table can end up spending $500 on everything from storage units to kitchenware. The flow of departments is constructed with an eye to boosting sales. For example, when IKEA managers noticed that men would get bored while their wives stopped in the home textile department, they added a tool section just outside the textile department, and sales of tools skyrocketed. At the end of the maze,

just before the checkout, is the warehouse where customers can pick up their flat packed furniture. IKEA stores also have restaurants (located in the middle of the store) and child-care facilities (located at the entrance for easy drop off) so that shoppers stay as long as possible.

Products are designed to reflect the clean Swedish lines that have become IKEA's trademark. IKEA has a product strategy council, which is a group of senior managers who establish priorities for IKEA's product lineup. Once a priority is established, product developers survey the competition, and then set a price point that is 30 to 50% below that of rivals. As IKEA's web site states, "we design the price tag first, then the product". Once the price tag is set, designers work with a network of suppliers to drive down the cost of producing the unit. The goal is to identify the appropriate suppliers and least costly materials, a trial and error process that can take as long as three years. In 2008 IKEA had 1380 suppliers in 54 countries. The top sourcing countries were China (21% of supplies), Poland (17%), Italy (8%), Sweden (6%), and Germany (6%).

IKEA devotes considerable attention to finding the right supplier for each item. Consider the company's best-selling Klippan love seat. Designed in 1980, the Klippan, with its clean lines, bright colors, simple legs, and compact size, has sold over 1.5 million units by 2010. IKEA originally manufactured the product in Sweden but soon transferred production to lower-cost suppliers in Poland. As demand for the Klippan grew, IKEA then decided that it made more sense to work with suppliers in each of the company's big markets to avoid the costs associated with shipping the product all over the world. In 2010 there were five suppliers of the frames in Europe, plus three in the United States and two in China. To reduce the cost of the cotton slipcovers, IKEA concentrated production in four core suppliers in China and Europe. The resulting efficiencies from these global sourcing decisions enabled IKEA to reduce the price of the Klippan by some 40% between 1999 and 2005.

Although IKEA contracts out manufacturing for most of its products, since the early 1990s a certain proportion of goods have been made internally (today around 90% of all products are sources from independent suppliers, with 10% being produced internally). The integration into manufacturing was born out of the collapse of communist governments in Eastern Europe after the fall of the Berlin Wall in 1989. By 1991 IKEA was sourcing some 25% of its goods from Eastern European manufacturers. It had invested considerable energy in building long-term relationships with these suppliers, and had often helped them to develop and purchase new technology so that they could make IKEA products at a lower cost. As communism collapsed and new bosses came in to the factories, many did not feel bound by the relationships with IKEA. They effectively tore up contracts, tried to raise prices, and under invested in new technology.

With its supply base at risk, IKEA purchased a Swedish manufacturer, Swedwood. IKEA then used Swedwood as the vehicle to buy and run furniture manufacturers across Eastern Europe, with the largest investments being made in Poland. IKEA invested heavily in its Swedwood plants, equipping them with the most modern technology. Beyond the obvious benefits of given IKEA a low cost source of supply, Swedwood has also enabled IKEA to acquire knowledge about manufacturing processes that are useful both in product design and in relationships with other suppliers, giving IKEA the ability to help suppliers adopt new technology and drive down their costs.

For illustration, consider IKEA's relationship with suppliers in Vietnam. IKEA has expanded its supply base here to help support its growing Asian presence. IKEA was attracted to Vietnam by the combination of low cost labor and inexpensive raw materials. IKEA drives a tough bargain with its suppliers, many of whom say that they make thinner margins on their sales to IKEA than they do to other foreign buyers. IKEA demands high quality at a low price. But there is an upside; IKEA offers the prospect of forging a long-term, high volume business relationship. Moreover, IKEA regularly advises its Vietnamese suppliers on how to seek out the best and cheapest raw materials, how to set up and expand factories, what equipment to purchase, and how to boost productivity through technology investments and management process.

ORGANIZATION AND MANAGEMENT

In many ways IKEA's organization and management practices reflect the personal philosophy of its founder. A 2004 article in Fortune describes Kamprad, then one of the world's richest men, as an informal and frugal man who "insists on flying coach, takes the subway to work, drives a ten year old Volvo, and avoids suits of any kind. It has long been rumored in Sweden that when his self-discipline fails and he drinks an overpriced Coke out of a hotel mini bar, he will go down to a grocery store to buy a replacement".[10] Kamprad's thriftiness is attributed

to his upbringing in Smaland, a traditionally poor region of Sweden. Kamprad's frugality is now part of IKEA's DNA. Managers are forbidden to fly first class and expected to share hotel rooms.

Under Kamprad, IKEA became mission driven. He had a cause, and those who worked with him adopted it too. It was to make life better for the masses, to democratize furniture. Kamprad's management style was informal, nonhierarchical, and team based. Titles and privileges are taboo at IKEA. There are no special perks for senior managers. Pay is not particularly high, and people generally work there because they like the atmosphere. Suits and ties have always been absent, from the head office to the loading docks. The culture is egalitarian. Offices are open plan, furnished with IKEA furniture, and private offices are rare. Everyone is called a "coworker", and first names are used throughout. IKEA regularly stages anti bureaucracy weeks during which executives work on the store floor or tend to registers. In a Business Week article then CEO, Andres Dahlvig, described how he spent sometime earlier in the year unloading trucks and selling beds and mattresses.[11] Creativity is highly valued, and the company is replete with stories of individuals taking the initiative; from Gillis Lundgren's pioneering of the self assemble concept to the store manager in the Stockhom store who let customers go into the warehouse to pick up their own furniture. To solidify this culture, IKEA had a preference for hiring younger people who had not worked for other enterprises, and then promoting from within. IKEA has historically tended to shy away from hiring the highly educated status oriented elite because they often adapted poorly to the company.

Kamprad seems to have viewed his team as extended family. Back in 1957 he bankrolled a weeklong trip to Spain for all 80 employees and their families as reward for hard work. The early team of employees all lived near each other. They worked together, played together, drank together, and talked about IKEA around the clock. When asked by an academic researcher what was the fundamental key to good leadership, Kamprad replied "love". Recollecting the early days, he noted that "when we were working as a small family in Aluhult, we were as if in love. Nothing whatsoever to do with eroticism. We just liked each other so damn much."[12] Another manager noted that "we who wanted to join IKEA did so because the company suits our way of life. To escape thinking about status, grandeur and smart clothes."[13]

As IKEA grew, the question of taking the company public arose. While there were obvious advantages associated with doing so, including access to capital, Kamprad decided against it. His belief was that the stock market would impose short-term pressures on IKEA that would not be good for the company. The constant demands to produce profits, regardless of the business cycle, would in Kamprad's view, make it more difficult for IKEA to take bold decisions. At the same time, as early as 1970 Kamprad stared to worry about what would happen if he died. He decided that he did not want his sons to inherit the business. His worry was that they would either sell the company, or they might squabble over control of the company, and thus destroy it. All three of his sons, it should be noted, went to work at IKEA as managers.

The solution to this dilemma created one of the most unusual corporate structures in the world. In 1982 Kamprad transferred his interest in IKEA to a Dutch based charitable foundation, Stichting Ingka Foundation. This is a tax exempt, non-profit making legal entity that in turn owns Ingka Holding, a private Dutch firm that is the legal owner of IKEA. A five-person committee chaired by Kamprad and which includes his wife runs the foundation. In addition, the IKEA trademark and concept was transferred to IKEA Systems, another private Dutch company, whose parent company, Inter-IKEA, is based in Luxembourg. The Luxembourg company is in turn owned by an identically named company in the Netherlands Antilles, whose beneficial owners remain hidden from public view, but they are almost certainly the Kamprad family. Inter-IKEA earns its money from a franchise agreement it has with each IKEA store. The largest franchisee is none other than Ingka Holdings. IKEA states that franchisees pay 3% of sales to Inter-IKEA.

Thus, Kamprad has effectively moved ownership of IKEA out of Sweden, although the company's identity and headquarters remains there, and established a mechanism for transferring funds to himself and his family from the franchising of the IKEA concept. Kamprad himself moved to Switzerland in the 1980s to escape Sweden's high taxes, and he has lived there ever since.

In 1986, Kamprad gave up day-to-day control of IKEA to Andres Moberg, a 36 year old Swede who had dropped out of college to join IKEA's mail order department. Despite relinquishing management control, Kamprad continued to exert influence over the company as an advisor to senior management and an ambassador for IKEA, a role he was still pursuing with vigor in 2012, despite being in his mid 80s.

LOOKING FORWARD

In its half century, IKEA had established an enviable position for itself. It had become one of the most successful retail establishments in the world. It had expanded into numerous foreign markets, learning from its failures and building on its successes. It had bought affordable, well-designed, functional furniture to the masses, helping them to, in Kamprad's words, achieve a better everyday life. IKEA's goal is to continue to grow opening 25 stores by 2020. Achieving that growth would mean continued expansion into non-western markets, including most notably China and India. Could the company continue to do so? Was its competitive advantage secure?

Exhibit 1	IKEA by the numbers in 2012
IKEA Stores	238 in 40 countries
IKEA Sales	€27.5 billion
IKEA Suppliers	1,380 in 54 countries[14]
The IKEA Range	9,500 products
IKEA Coworkers	154,000 in 40 countries

Source: Company website

Exhibit 2		Sales and Suppliers	
Top Five Sales Countries		**Top Five Supplying Countries**	
Germany	15%	China	21%
USA	12%	Poland	17%
France	10%	Italy	8%
US	7%	Sweden	6%
Sweden	6%	Germany	6%

Source: Company Website

Case Discussion Questions

1. By the early 1970s IKEA had established itself as the largest furniture retailer in Sweden. What was the source of tits competitive advantage at that time?
2. Why do you think IKEA's expansion into Europe went so well? Why did the company subsequently stumble in North America? What lessons did IKEA learn from this experience? How is the company now applying these lessons?
3. How would you characterize IKEA's strategy prior to its missteps in North America? How would you characterize its strategy today?
4. What is IKEA's strategy towards its suppliers? How important is this strategy to IKEA's success?
5. What is the source of IKEA's success today? Can you see any weaknesses in the company? What might it do to correct these?

SOURCES

1. Anonymous, "Furnishing the World", *The Economist*, November 19, 1995, pp. 79–80.
2. Anonymous. "Flat pack accounting", *The Economist*, May 13, 2006, pp. 69–70.
3. K. Capell, A. Sains, C. Lindblad, and A.T. Palmer, "IKEA," *BusinessWeek*, November 14, 2005, pp. 96–101.
4. K. Capell et al., "What a Sweetheart of a Love Seat," *BusinessWeek*, November 14, 2005, p. 101.
5. C. Daniels, "Create IKEA, Make Billions, Take Bus," *Fortune*, May 3, 2004, p. 44.
6. J. Flynn and L. Bongiorno, "IKEA's new game plan", *BusinessWeek*, October 6, 1997, pp. 99–102.
7. R. Heller, "Folk Fortune", *Forbes*, September 4, 2000, page 67.
8. IKEA Documents at www.ikea.com

9. J. Leland, "How the disposable sofa conquered America", *New York Times Magazine*, October 5, 2005, page 40–50.
10. P.M. Miller, "IKEA with Chinese Characteristics," *Chinese Business Review*, July–August 2004, pp. 36–69.
11. B. Torekull, *Leading by Design: The IKEA Story*, Harper Collins, New York, 1998.
12. Anonymous, "The Secret of IKEA's success", *The Economist*, February 24, 2011.

NOTES

1. Quoted in R. Heller, "Folk Fortune", *Forbes*, September 4, 2000, page 67.
2. B. Torekull, *Leading by Design: The IKEA Story*, Harper Collins, New York, 1998, page 53.
3. B. Torekull, *Leading by Design: The IKEA Story*, Harper Collins, New York, 1998, pages 61–62.
4. B. Torekull, *Leading by Design: The IKEA Story*, Harper Collins, New York, 1998, page 109.
5. J. Leland, "How the disposable sofa conquered America", *New York Times Magazine*, October 5, 2005, page 45.
6. J. Leland, "How the disposable sofa conquered America", *New York Times Magazine*, October 5, 2005, page 45.
7. Manu Kaushik, "Conditions Apply", *Business Today*, December 23, 2010.
8. Anonymous, "The secrete of IKEA's success", *The Economist*, February 24, 2011.
9. Richard Milne, "Red tape frustrates IKEA's plans for growth", *Financial Times*, January 25, 2013.
10. C.Daniels and A. Edstrom, "Create IKEA, make billions, take a bus", *Fortune*, May 3, 2006, page 44.
11. K. Capell et al, "Ikea", *Business Week*, November 14, 2005, pp. 96–106.
12. B. Torekull, *Leading by Design: The IKEA Story*, Harper Collins, New York, 1998, page 82.
13. B. Torekull, *Leading by Design: The IKEA Story*, Harper Collins, New York, 1998, page 83.
14. The supplier figures are for 2008. IKEA has not published detailed data on suppliers in recent years.

Case 19

Starbucks, 2013

Melissa A. Schilling
New York University

In 2013, Starbucks was the undisputed world leader in specialty coffee retail, with over $13 billion in annual revenues (see Exhibit 1). Starbucks had nearly 200,000 employees, and over 17,000 Starbucks-branded cafes in forty countries (about 9,000 of those were owned and operated by Starbucks itself while the remaining 8,000 were operated by licensees and franchisees). In addition, Starbucks owned the Seattle's Best Coffee, Torrefazione Italia, Teavana's Heaven of Tea brands, and more.[i]

The company had grown remarkably fast over its short life, and was still exceptionally profitable with a 17.6% return on assets in 2012 (compared to 6.8% at Peet's Coffee and Tea, 10.9% at Green Mountain Coffee, 16% at McDonald's, and 3.4% at Dunkin Donuts). However, its growth had not always been smooth—in fact, Starbucks had shuttered about 900 stores during 2008 and 2009. As its domestic market appeared to be approaching saturation, Starbucks began to focus on growing its international locations, and diversifying into other product lines where its now iconic brand could create value.

THE HISTORY OF STARBUCKS

In 1971, three Seattle entrepreneurs, Jerry Baldwin, Zev Siegl, and Gordon Bowher, started selling whole-bean coffee in Seattle's Pike Place Market. They named their store Starbucks, after the first mate in *Moby Dick*. By 1982, the business had grown to a bustling business of five stores, a small roasting facility, and a wholesale business selling coffee to local restaurants. At the same time, Howard Schultz had been working as VP of U.S. operations for Hammarplast, a Swedish housewares company in New York, marketing coffee makers to a number of retailers, including Starbucks. Through selling to Starbucks, Schultz was introduced to the three founders who recruited him to bring marketing savvy to the loosely run company. Schultz, 29 years old and recently married, was eager to leave New York, so he moved to Seattle and joined Starbucks as manager of retail sales and marketing.

One year later, Schultz visited Italy for the first time on a buying trip. As he strolled through the piazzas of Milan one evening, he was inspired by a vision. Coffee is an integral part of the romantic culture in Italy; Italians start their day at an espresso bar, and return with their friends later. There were 200,000 coffee bars in Italy, and 1,500 in Milan alone. Schultz believed that given the chance, Americans would pay good money for a premium cup of coffee and a stylish, romantic place to enjoy it. Enthusiastic about his idea, Schultz rushed back to tell the Starbucks owners of his plan for a national chain of Starbucks cafes stylized on the Italian coffee bar. The owners, however, were less enthusiastic, and said that they did not want to be in the restaurant business. Undaunted, Schultz wrote a business plan, videotaped dozens of Italian coffee bars and began to look for investors. By April 1986 he had opened his first coffee bar, Il Giornale (named after the Italian newspaper), where he served Starbucks coffee. Following Il Giornale's immediate success, Schultz opened a second coffee bar in Seattle, and then a third in Vancouver. In 1987, the owners of Starbucks finally agreed to sell to Schultz for $4 million. The Il Giornale coffee bars took on the name of Starbucks, and a star was born.

Convinced that Starbucks would one day be in every neighborhood in America, Schultz was intent on growing the company slowly with a very solid foundation. He hired top executives away from corporations such as PepsiCo, and was determined that future profits would be well worth early losses. At first, the company's losses almost doubled, to $1.2 million from fiscal 1989 to 1990 as overhead and operating expenses ballooned with the expansion.[ii] Starbucks lost money for three years running, and the stress was hard on Schultz, but he stuck to his conviction not to "sacrifice long-term integrity and values for short-term profit."[iii] In 1991 sales shot up 84%, and the company broke into the black. Everywhere Starbucks opened, people flocked to pay upwards of $2.00 and more for a cup of coffee. Enthusiastic analysts began to predict that Starbucks would top $1 billion by the year 2000, but Schultz preferred to play the company's early successes down, asserting that it is better to "underpromise and over-deliver." The analysts, it turned out, had *underestimated* Starbucks' success—by the year 2000 it was taking in over $2 billion in revenues. In the twenty years between 1993 and 2013, Starbucks averaged an annual revenue growth rate of 28% a year.

COMPETITION IN THE SPECIALTY COFFEE SEGMENT

In the US in 2012, specialty coffee accounted for 37% of all coffee cups consumed, and for nearly 50% of all coffee revenue. Though the US was the single largest buyer of un-roasted coffee in the world in 2012, emerging markets were exhibiting strong growth, and many experts anticipated that Brazil would surpass the United States in coffee consumption sometime between 2014 and 2016.

Worldwide, independent coffee shops still make up the majority of coffee-house locations, though prominent chains have emerged in many regions. Starbucks has long held a leading position in its home market, selling over 50% of the specialty coffee purchased in cafes in the US over the last several decades, and easily dominating local specialty coffee competitors such as Caribou Coffee or Peet's Coffee & Tea. However, in recent years Both Dunkin' Donuts and McDonald's began targeting Starbucks' growing customer base with coffee offerings based on high quality Arabica brews at a lower cost than Starbucks' beverages. With a very large number of existing stores (see Exhibit 1), both competitors posed big threats if they were effective in

wooing customers away from Starbucks. Furthermore, Starbucks faces other more entrenched competition in many of its international markets (see Exhibit 2 for a breakdown of market share by regional areas).

Caribou Coffee

Founded in 1992, Caribou Coffee operates 410 coffee houses in about 20 states, and has an additional 170 franchised outlets, including many in international markets (particularly in the Middle East and South Korea). Its 2011 sales were $326.5 million. Its stores are designed to look like mountain lodges and sell only specialty coffee, baked goods, and coffee brewing supplies. However, like Starbucks, the company also sells roasted coffee to grocery stores and has a licensing agreement to make single-serve k-cups for home brewing using Keurig machines.

McDonald's

Founded in 1948 in San Bernardino, California, McDonald's grew to become the world's largest quick-service restaurant. Boasting almost 34,500 restaurants in 119 countries and $27.6 billion in sales (see Exhibit 1), McDonald's is probably the best known restaurant in the world. Though its menu is most famous for hamburgers and fries, in the last two decades McDonald's has developed healthier food items in response to social pressure mounted against burger chains. In 1993, a McDonald's licensee, Ann Brown, created the McCafé—a coffeehouse style outlet that would offer high-end coffee beverages similar to Starbucks. In response to its early success, McDonald's also introduced a line of special coffee drinks called McCafé into its other restaurants.

Dunkin' Donuts

Originally founded as the Open Kettle Doughnut shop in Quincy, Massachusetts in 1948, its founder, William Rosenburg changed its name to Dunkin' Donuts in 1950 began franchising the shops five years later. The popular franchise became famous for its wide variety of donuts, and expanded to become the world's leading donut chain with 10,000 outlets in about 30 countries, and earned $658.2 million in sales in 2012 (see Exhibit 1). Though it had long offered coffee, the company did not begin offering espresso drinks until 2003. The Dunkin Brands group also owns the Baskin-Robbins ice cream and Togo sandwiches chains.

Exhibit 1	Selected Data for Starbucks, McDonald's, and Dunkin Donuts, 2012			
	Starbucks	**McDonald's**	**Dunkin**	**Industry Median**
Stores	17,651	34,500	10,000	
Annual Sales	$13.30B	$27.57B	$658.18M	
Employees	160,000	440,000	1,104	
Market Cap	$38.00B	$88.45B	$3.52B	
Gross Profit Margin	56.54%	39.24%	78.09%	37.62%
Pre-Tax Profit Margin	15.44%	29.31%	24.61%	14.90%
Net Profit Margin	10.49%	19.82%	16.46%	10.43%
Return on Equity	28.85%	36.82%	19.83%	32.26%
Return on Assets	17.57%	15.98%	3.36%	11.70%
Return on Invested Cap	25.60%	18.33%	2.67%	16.47%
Days Sales Outstanding	12.02	17.94	19.28	11.28
Inventory Turnover	5.36	140.47	–	24.38
Asset Turnover	1.67	0.81	0.2	1.12
Current Ratio	1.9	1.45	1.19	1.15
Quick Ratio	1.14	1.09	0.86	14.16
Leverage Ratio	1.61	2.31	9.28	2.73
Total Debt/Equity	0.11	0.89	5.36	0.97
Interest Coverage	69.72	16.64	3.19	10.45

REDEFINING "A CUP OF JOE"

Starbucks' coffee quality begins with bean procurement. Whereas historically Americans had drunk a commodity-like coffee composed of Arabica beans mixed with less-expensive Robusta filler beans, Starbucks coffee is strictly specialty varietals of Arabica beans, and the company goes to great lengths to ensure that only the highest quality beans are used. Starbucks' bean procurement standards are demanding and the company conducts exacting experiments in order to get the proper balance of flavor, body and acidity. Brews are subjected to "cupping"—a process similar to wine tasting that involves inhaling the steam ("the strike" and "breaking the crust"), tasting the coffee, and spitting it out ("aspirating" and "expectorating")—to evaluate the aroma and taste.

From the company's inception, it has worked on developing relationships with the countries from which it buys coffee beans. Prior to Starbucks' rise, Americans were notorious for buying poor quality coffee beans—most of the premium coffee beans were bought by Europeans and Japanese. In 1992, however, Starbucks set a new precedent by outbidding European buyers for the exclusive Narino Supremo bean crop. This Columbian coffee bean crop is very small and grows only in the high regions of the Cordillera mountain range. For years, the Narino beans were guarded zealously by Western Europeans who prized its colorful and complex flavor. It was usually used for upgrading blends. Starbucks was determined to make them available for the first time as

Exhibit 2 Specialty Coffee Market Shares by Region[1]

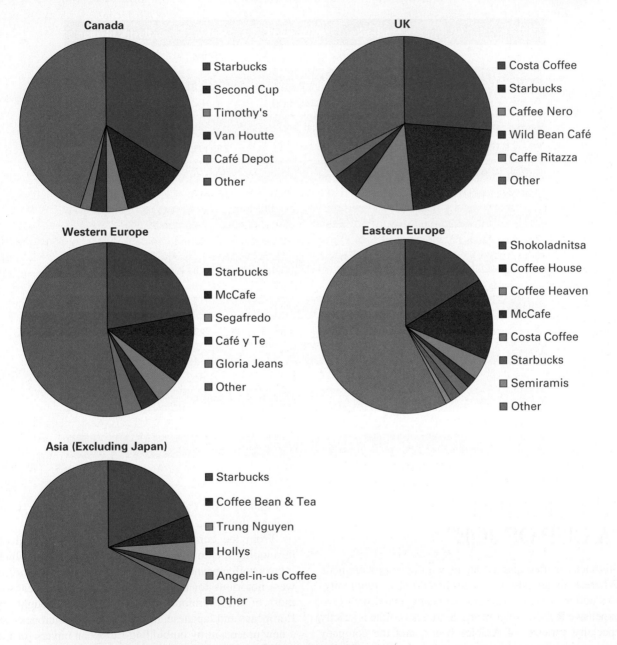

Canada
- Starbucks
- Second Cup
- Timothy's
- Van Houtte
- Café Depot
- Other

UK
- Costa Coffee
- Starbucks
- Caffee Nero
- Wild Bean Café
- Caffe Ritazza
- Other

Western Europe
- Starbucks
- McCafe
- Segafredo
- Café y Te
- Gloria Jeans
- Other

Eastern Europe
- Shokoladnitsa
- Coffee House
- Coffee Heaven
- McCafe
- Costa Coffee
- Starbucks
- Semiramis
- Other

Asia (Excluding Japan)
- Starbucks
- Coffee Bean & Tea
- Trung Nguyen
- Hollys
- Angel-in-us Coffee
- Other

[1]Data from 2008 Bernstein Research Report, "Starbucks: Getting its Buzz Back."

a pure varietal. This required breaking Western Europe's monopoly over the beans by convincing the Columbian growers that it intended to use "the best beans for a higher purpose." Starbucks collaborated with a mill in the tiny town of Pasto, located on the side of the Volcano Galero.

There they set up a special operation to single out the particular Narino Supremo bean, and Starbucks guaranteed to purchase the entire yield. This enabled Starbucks to be the exclusive purveyor of Narino Supremo, purportedly one of the best coffees in the world.

Procurement is not the only area where extreme care differentiates Starbucks' product: roasting is close to an art form at Starbucks. Unlike most specialty coffee retailers, Starbucks roasts its own beans in its private roasting facilities in California, Nevada, Pennsylvania, South Carolina, Washington, and the Netherlands. Roasters are promoted from within the company and trained for over a year, and it is considered quite an honor to be chosen. The coffee is roasted in a powerful gas oven for 12 to 15 minutes while roasters use their sight, smell and hearing to judge when beans are perfectly done. The color of the beans is even tested in an Agtron blood-cell analyzer, with the whole batch being discarded if the sample is not deemed perfect.

Despite the attention to quality, Starbucks' effort at bringing a premium coffee and Italian-style beverage experience to the American market could have been lost on consumers had it not invested in consumer education. Starbucks spends far less on advertising than most chain restaurants (in 2012, for example, Starbucks spend $182.4 million on advertising—just 1.3% of sales, compared to McDonalds' $787.5 million, or 3% of its sales).[iv] Instead, it invests in securing highly visible locations, innovating in its menu, and building an iconic, ubiquitous brand. Starbucks' logo has evolved from an original 16th century Norse woodcut of a visibly topless mermaid, to a version in which her flowing hair afforded more modesty (which was crucial for entry into countries with strong cultural taboos around nudity), to the current version which omits the nameplate, permitting Starbucks to symbolize a broader product range than just coffee (see Figure 1 below).

Starbucks also seeks to develop a close connection with customers. Starbucks employees are encouraged to help customers make decisions about beans, grind, and coffee/espresso machines and instruct customers on home brewing. The objective is to create a long-term relationship with customers.

In order to create American coffee enthusiasts with the dedication of their Italian counterparts, Starbucks needed to provide a seductive atmosphere in which to imbibe. The stores are sleek, yet comfortable. Coffee preparers are referred to as "baristas," Italian for bartender, and *biscotti* is available in glass jars on the counter. The stores are well lighted, feature plenty of burnished wood and brass, and sophisticated artwork hangs on the walls. Jazz or opera music plays softly in the background. According to Schultz, "We're not just selling a cup of coffee, we are providing an experience."

Many of the stores offer light lunch fare including sandwiches and salads, and an assortment of pastries, bottled waters and juices. Starbucks also launched a line of packaged and prepared teas in 1995 in response to growing demand for tea houses and packaged tea. Tea is a highly profitable beverage for restaurants to sell, costing only 2 cents to 4 cents a cup to produce.

PAMPERING EMPLOYEES

Schultz believes that happy employees are the key to competitiveness and growth. He states, "We can't achieve our strategic objectives without a work force of people who are immersed in the same commitment as management. Our only sustainable advantage is the quality of our work force. We're building a national retail company by creating pride in—and stake in—the outcome of our labor."[v] Starbucks has accomplished this through

---

Figure 1   Evolution of the Starbucks Logo

| 1971–1987 | 1992–2011 | 2011–Present |

Courtesy of Starbucks

an empowering corporate culture, exceptional employee benefits and employee stock ownership programs. While Starbucks enforces almost fanatical standards about coffee quality and service, the culture at Starbucks towards employees is laid back and supportive. Employees are empowered to make decisions without constant referral to management, and are encouraged to think of themselves as partners in the business. Starbucks wants employees to use their best judgment in making decisions and will stand behind them. This is reinforced through generous compensation and benefits packages.

Starbucks offers its benefits package to both part-time and full-time employees. The package includes medical, dental, vision and short-term disability insurance, as well as paid vacation, paid holidays, mental health/chemical dependency benefits, an employee assistance program, a 401 (k) savings plan and a stock option plan. They also offer career counseling and product discounts. The decision to offer benefits even to part-time employees garnered the firm a great deal of attention in the press. It was difficult to get insurers to sign Starbucks up since they did not understand why Starbucks would want to cover part-timers. However, while many companies scrimp on these essentials, Schultz believes that without these benefits, people do not feel financially or spiritually tied to their jobs. The stock options and the complete benefits package increase employee loyalty and encourage attentive service to the customer. Bradley Honeycutt (director of compensation and benefits) also points out that "part-timers are on the front line with our customers. If we treat them right, we feel they will treat (the customers) well."[vi]

Employee turnover is also discouraged by Starbucks' stock option plan (known as the Bean Stock Plan). Implemented in August of 1991, the plan made Starbucks the first company to offer stock options unilaterally to all employees, including part-time workers. After one year, employees may join a 401 (k) plan. There is a vesting period of five years; it starts one year after the option is granted, then vests the employee at 20% every year. In addition, every employee receives a new stock option award each year, and a new vesting period begins. This plan required the then privately-held Starbucks to get an exemption from the Security Exchange Commission, since any company with more than 500 shareholders has to report its financial performance publicly—a costly process that reveals valuable information to competitors.

The option plan did not go uncontested by the venture capitalists and shareholders on the board. Craig Foley, a director and managing partner of Chancellor Capital Management Inc. (and the largest shareholder before the public offering) says, "Increasing the shareholders substantially dilutes our interest. We take that very seriously." Inthe end they were won over by a study conducted by Orin Smith that revealed the positive relationship between employee ownership and productivity rates, and a scenario analysis of how many employees would be vested. Foley conceded that the company's culture was a major component of its profitability. "The grants are tied to overachieving. If you just come to work and do your job, that isn't as attractive as if you beat the numbers."

Training programs are extensive at Starbucks. Each employee takes at least 24 hours worth of classes. Classes cover everything from coffee history, to a 7-hour workshop called Brewing the Perfect Cup at Home. Starbucks employees even undergo rigorous training about how to respond to cranky customers through the "Latte Method" of responding to unpleasant situations: "We Listen to the customer, Acknowledge their complaint, Take action by solving the problem, Thank them, and then Explain why the problem occurred."[vii] Store managers (who have gone through facilitation workshops and are certified by the company as trainers) teach the classes. The classes emphasize the empowering culture at Starbucks, and teach the employees to make decisions that will enhance customer satisfaction without requiring manager authorization. For example, if a customer comes into the store complaining about a how their beans were ground, the employee is authorized to replace them on the spot. While most restaurants use on-the-job training, Starbucks holds bar classes where employees practice taking orders and preparing beverages in a company training room. This allows employees to hone their skills in a low-stress environment, and also protects Starbucks' quality image by only allowing experienced baristas to serve customers.

Schultz is also known for his sensitivity to the well-being of employees. Once when an employee had come to tell Schultz that he had AIDS, Schultz reassured him that he could work as long as he wanted to, and when he left, Starbucks would continue to cover his insurance. After the employee left the room, Schultz sat down and wept. Schultz attributes his concern for his employees to his memories of his father. According to Schultz his father "struggled a great deal and never made more than $20,000 a year, and his work was never valued, emotionally or physically, by his employer . . . This was an injustice . . . I want our employees to know we value them."

In 1995 Starbucks demonstrated that its concern for employee welfare extended beyond the U.S. borders. After a human-rights group leafleted the stores complaining that Guatemalan coffee pickers received less than $3 a day, Starbucks became the first agricultural commodity importer to implement a code for minimal working conditions and pay for foreign subcontractors. The company's guidelines called for overseas suppliers to pay wages and benefits that "address the basic needs of workers and their families" and to only allow child labor when it does not interrupt required education. This move set a precedent for other importers of agricultural commodities, and earned the company high praise from global human-rights activists.

In 2000, Schulz transitioned to being the chairman and chief global strategist, but continued to stay very actively involved in the company's operations and taking a strong stance on ethical business. Working in combination with Conservation International, Starbucks introduced new ethical coffee-sourcing guidelines in 2001, and began actively promoting its Coffee and Farmer Equity (CAFE) Practices that provide measurable standards for such factors as economic transparency, fair and humane working conditions, and water and energy conservation.

GROWTH, DIVERSIFICATION, AND INTERNATIONAL EXPANSION

In Starbucks' early years, Schultz had professed a strict slow-growth policy. While other coffee houses or espresso bars were being franchised, Starbucks owned all of its stores outright with the exception of key locations where the only way in was through a license agreement (e.g., airports, stadiums). Hundreds of willing investors would call every day, but Schultz turned them all down, arguing that it was important to the company's integrity to keep all stores company owned. Furthermore, in each market that Starbucks entered, imitators would rapidly emerge. Thus rather than creating outposts in all the potential markets as soon as possible, Starbucks went into a market and completely dominated it before setting its sights further abroad. Despite this, the company was consistently one of the fastest growing companies in the US (see Figure 2). Over time, Starbucks loosened its licensing policy, and began accelerating the rate at which it permitted licensed stores. Licensing was particularly

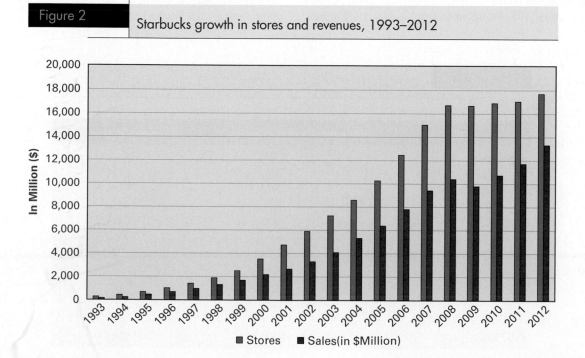

Figure 2 — Starbucks growth in stores and revenues, 1993–2012

■ Stores ■ Sales(in $Million)

important for many international markets in which having a foreign partner reduced both the difficulty and risk of entry (see Exhibit 2).

The combination of the high quality products and service, well-managed branding, and a reputation for social responsibility made the company attractive to both consumers and investors. By 2007, the company had over 15,000 stores. However, a combination of competition, the recession, and Starbucks' own saturation of many markets began to spell trouble for the company. Sales declined for the first time ever in 2009. From 2007 to 2010, many Wall Street analysts were whispering that the company's best days were behind it.[viii] Feeling that the company was in crisis, Schultz decided to return to the role of chief executive officer in 2008, noting "This has been my life's work, as opposed to a job. I didn't come back to save the company—I hate that description—I came back to rekindle the emotion that build it." Though Schultz was advised to lower prices and cut benefits to employees, he opted instead to invest in a two-year transformation of Starbucks that he called "the company's holistic restoration."[ix] Though some stores had to be closed (Starbucks closed about 900 company-operated stores in 2008–2009), he focused most of his effort on reinvigorating what he saw as the heart of the company—its commitment to exceptional service and quality. He invested in developing new product lines and line extensions, and he even closed all of the US stores for three hours on the evening of February 26th, 2010 to retrain about 135,000 in-store employees. His gambles paid off, and the company began to again climb to new sales and profitability highs.

In addition to expanding its menu selection to include more food products and drink options, Starbucks has begun diversifying in other ways. It now offers a range of cafe formats (including expanding the number of drive-through service locations), and in 2009, Starbucks introduced single-serve coffee packets targeted at the home brewing, office, and hotel coffee markets. The single-serve packs are designed to be brewed in Green Mountain Coffee's Keurig brewers, and are distributed by Green Mountain. In 2012, Starbucks acquired Bay Bread and its La Boulange bakery brand, marking its entry into the French-style bakery market. It also acquired Evolution Fresh, a fruit and vegetable juice beverage company.

By 2013, Starbucks had also expanded well beyond its US origins. The company's international presence had expanded from a single store opened in Japan in 1996, to a well-diversified presence around the world by 2013 (see Exhibit 3). Recognizing that the US market was maturing, Schultz acknowledged that most of the future growth would come from emerging markets. In 2013, Schultz was focusing most of his attention on Brazil, China, India, and Vietnam.

Perhaps more importantly, Schultz no longer thinks of Starbucks as just a coffee company. As Schultz explains, the next great challenge is to deepen the company's involvement in health and wellness. "I think despite the growth and development and the size of the company, we're still in the early days of what Starbucks might become."[x]

| Exhibit 3 | Starbucks Stores Open as of 2012 by Geographical Area |

	Company-Operated Stores	Licensed Stores
Americas:		
US	6866	4262
Canada	878	303
Chile	41	
Brazil	53	
Puerto Rico	19	
Mexico		356
Other		125
Total Americas	**7857**	**5046**

(continued)

	Company-Operated Stores	Licensed Stores
Europe/Middle East/Africa		
UK	593	168
Germany	157	
France	67	
Switzerland	50	
Austria	12	
Netherlands	3	
Turkey		171
United Arab Emirates		99
Spain		78
Kuwait		65
Saudi Arabia		64
Russia		60
Greece		42
Other		240
Total EMEA	**882**	**987**
China/Asia Pacific		
China	408	292
Thailand	155	
Singapore	80	
Australia	23	
Japan		965
South Korea		467
Taiwan		271
Philippines		201
Malaysia		134
Indonesia		133
Hong Kong		131
New Zealand		34
Total China/Asia Pacific	**666**	**2628**
Totals Across Regions	**9405**	**8661**

NOTES

i.   Data compiled from Starbucks SEC filings 1996–2013; and Hoovers, March 2013. Interviews also conducted with Susan Mecklenberg, Director of Environmental Affairs at Starbucks, and Troy Alstead, Director of International Planning and Finance at Starbucks.

ii. Rothman, M. 1993. Into the black. *Inc.*, January.

iii. Abramovitch, I. 1993. Miracles of Marketing: How to reinvent your product. *Success Magazine*, April.

iv. Morrison, M. 2011. Starbucks: Forging a moment of connection. *Advertising Age*, 82(40):30; and Morrison, M. 2011. Bang for its Starbucks: Hits No. 3 despite limited spend. *Advertising Age*, 82(18):1–100.

v.   Rothman, M. 1993. Into the black. *Inc.*, January.

vi. Roberts, S. 1995. Working part time pays off at Starbucks Coffee. *Business Insurance*, March 27.

vii. Duhigg, C. 2012. *The Power of Habit: Why we do what we do in life and in business*. New York: Random House.

viii. Gertner, J. 2012. The World's 50 Most Innovative Companies: Starbucks—For infusing a steady stream of new ideas to revive its business. *Fast Company*, 163:112–149.

ix. Ostdick, JH. 2012. Rekindling the heart & soul of Starbucks. *Success Magazine*.

x.   Gertner, J. 2012. The World's 50 Most Innovative Companies: Starbucks—For infusing a steady stream of new ideas to revive its business. *Fast Company*, 163:112–149.

Case 20

Apple Inc., 1976–2013

Charles W.L. Hill

INTRODUCTION

Back in 1997 Apple Computer was in deep trouble. The company that had pioneered the personal computer market with its easy to use Apple II in 1978, and had introduced the first graphical user interface with the Macintosh in 1984, was bleeding red ink. Apple's worldwide market share, which had been fluctuating between 7 and 9% since 1984, had sunk to 4%. Sales were declining. Apple was on track to lose $378 million on revenues of $7 billion, and that on top of a $740 million loss in 1996. In July 1997, the cofounder of the company, Steve Jobs, who had left Apple back in 1985 after being stripped of any operating responsibility, returned as CEO. At an investor conference, Michael Dell, CEO of Dell Inc., then the world's largest and most successful PC manufacturer, was asked what Jobs should do as head of Apple. Dell quipped "I'd shut it down and give the money back to shareholders."[1]

By early 2013 the situation could not look more different. Apple was the world's most valuable company with a market capitalization of over $450 billion. The stock price, which had traded as low as $6 a share in 2003, had run as high as $705 a share in 2012. Revenues in the financial year ending September 2012 were $157 billion and net income was $41.7 billion. The company had generated $41.5 billion of free cash flow in 2012, and was sitting on over $120 billion in cash on its balance sheet. Meanwhile Dell Inc., with a market capitalization roughly 5% of Apple's, was struggling to remain relevant in the rapidly changing computer industry.

Driving the transformation had been a string of game changing innovations that included the introduction of Apple's iPod music player in 2001, music downloads from the iTunes store in 2003, the iPhone in 2007, and the iPad in 2010. Throughout this period, Apple had continued improve and refine its line of desktop and lap top computers, producing stylish models that set the standard for the industry in design elegance and ease of use. The MacBook Air, an ultra lightweight notebook computer introduced in 2008, had become a benchmark against which all other notebooks were compared. Apple had also vertically integrated forward in to the retail business, opening its first Apple store in 2001. By late 2012 the company had 390 Apple stores worldwide. The stores were themselves a phenomenon. In the U.S., the average store generated sales per square foot of $6,050 in 2012, a retail industry record and twice that of second place Tiffany and Co, which had sales per square foot of $3,017.[2] To emphasize the broadening product portfolio of the company, Apple had dropped "computer" from its name.

Once considered a perennial also ran, Apple was now on top of the world. It's successful iPhone and iPad lines had made the company a driving force behind an industry wide shift towards mobile computing and cloud services. It's iCloud cloud storage and synchronization service, introduced in October 2011, already had more than 250 million users by January 2013.[3]

However, the future was less clear. In 2011 the driving force of the company's transformation, founder and CEO Steve Jobs, died of cancer. Observers wondered if the company could maintain its innovative momentum without the creative genius of Jobs at the helm. Competitors were also snapping at Apple's heals. Smart phones using Google's Android operating system were outselling Apple's iPhone by 4 to 1 world wide in 2012 (although Apple was reportedly captured 72% of all

School of Business, University of Washington, Seattle, 98195, February 2013, Copyright Charles W.L. Hill © 2008, 2013

profits from smart phone sales in 2012). In the tablet market, while the iPad captured 53.8% of the global market in 2013, devices running the Android operating system had 42.7%.[4] In April 2012, Google offered its own cloud storage and synchronization service, Google Drive, in an attempt to create an ecosystem that rivaled Apple's. There were also signs that Microsoft was starting to wake up from a decade of slumber and missed opportunities to compete head to head with Apple. In late 2012 Microsoft introduced its Windows 8 operating system. Windows 8, which has touch screen capabilities, can be configured to run on any computing device, from desktop and laptop to tablet and smart phone. Microsoft also offers a cloud storage and synchronization service, SkyDrive, raising the possibility that the company can become a third player in the emerging mobile computing/cloud services format war.

APPLE 1976–1997

The Early Years

Apple's genesis is the stuff of computer industry ledged.[5] On April Fools Day, 1976, two young electronics enthusiasts, Steve Jobs and Steve Wozniak, started a company to sell a primitive personal computer that Wozniak's had designed. Steve Jobs was just twenty, Wozniak, or Woz as he was commonly called, was 5 years older. They had known each other for several years, having been introduced by a mutual friend who realized that they shared an interest in consumer electronics. Woz had designed the computer just for the fun of it. That's what people did in 1976. The idea that somebody would actually want to purchase his machine had not occurred to Woz, but it did to Jobs. Jobs persuaded a reluctant Woz to form a company and sell the machine. The location of the company was Steve Jobs's garage. Jobs suggested they call the company Apple and their first machine the Apple I. They sold around 200 of them at $666 each. The price point was picked as something of a prank.

The Apple I had several limitations—no case, keyboard, or power supply being obvious ones. It also required several hours of laborious assembly by hand. By the late 1976 Woz was working on a replacement to the Apple I, the Apple II.[6] In October 1976, with the Apple II under development, Jobs and Woz were introduced to Mike Markkula. Only 34, Markkula was already a retired millionaire having made a small fortune at Fairchild and Intel. Markkula had no plans to get back into business anytime soon, but a visit to Jobs's garage changed all that. He committed to investing $92,000 for one-third of the company, and promised that his ultimate investment would be $250,000. Stunned, Jobs and Woz agreed to let him join as a partner. It was a fateful decision. The combination of Woz's technical skills, Jobs's entrepreneurial zeal and vision, and Markkula's business savvy and connections, was a powerful one. Markkula told Jobs and Woz that neither of them had the experience to run a company, and persuaded them to hire a president, Michael Scott, who had worked for Markkula at Fairchild.

The Apple II was introduced in 1977 at a price of $1,200. The first version was an integrated computer with a Motorola microprocessor and included a keyboard, power supply, monitor, and the BASIC programming software. It was Steve Jobs who pushed Woz to design an integrated machine—he wanted something that was easy to use and not just a toy for geeks. Jobs also insisted that the Apple II looked good. It had an attractive case and no visible screws or bolts. This differentiated it from most personal computers at the time, which looked as if they had been assembled by hobbyists at home (as many had).

In 1978, Apple started to sell a version of the Apple II that incorporated something new—a disk drive. The disk drive enabled third party developers to write software programs for the Apple II that could be loaded via floppy disks. Soon programs started to appear, among them EasyWriter, a basic word processing program, and VisiCalc, a spreadsheet. VisiCalc was an instant hit, and pulled in a new customer set, business types who could use VisiCalc for financial planning and accounting. Since VisiCalc was only available for the Apple II, it helped to drive demand for the machine.

By the end of 1980, Apple had sold over 100,000 Apple II's, making the company the leader in the embryonic personal computer industry. The company had successfully executed an IPO, was generating over $200 million in annual sales, and was profitable. With the Apple II series selling well, particularly in the education market, Apple introduced its next product, the Apple III, in the fall of 1980. It was a failure. The computer was filled with bugs and crash constantly. The Apple III had been rushed to market. Apple reintroduced a reengineered Apple III in 1981, but it continued to be outsold by Apple II. Indeed, successive versions of the Apple II family, each an improvement on the proceeding version, continued to be produced by the company until 1993. In total, over 2 million Apple II computers were sold. The series became a standard in American classrooms where it was valued for its intuitive ease of use. Moreover, the Apple II was the mainstay of the company until the late 1980s, when an improved version of the Macintosh started to garner significant sales.

The IBM PC and its Aftermath

Apple's success galvanized the world's largest computer company, IBM, to speed up development of its entry into the personal computer market. IBM had a huge and very profitable mainframe computer business, but it had failed to develop a personal computer, despite two attempts. To get to market quickly with its third PC project, IBM broke with its established practice of using its own proprietary technology to build the PC. Instead, IBM adopted an "open architecture," purchasing the components required to make the IBM PC from other manufacturers. These components included a 16 bit microprocessor from Intel, and an operating system, MS-DOS, which was licensed from a small Washington State company, Microsoft.

Microsoft had been in the industry from its inception, writing a version of the BASIC software programming language for the MITS Atari in 1977, the first PC ever produced. IBM's desire to license BASIC brought them to Redmond to talk with the company's CEO, Bill Gates. Gates, still in his early 20s, persuaded IBM to adopt a 16-bit processor (originally IBM had been considering a less powerful 8 bit processor). He was also instrumental is pushing IBM to adopt an open architecture, arguing that IBM would benefit from the software and peripherals that other companies could then make.

Initially IBM was intent on licensing the CP/M operating system, produced by Digital Research, for the IBM PC. However, the current version of CP/M was designed to work on an 8 bit processor, and Gates had persuaded IBM that it needed a 16 bit processor. In a series of quick moves, Gates purchased a 16 bit operating system from a local company, Seattle Computer, for $50,000. Gates then hired the designer of the operating system, Tim Paterson, renamed the system MS-DOS, and offered to license it to IBM. In what turned out to be a masterstroke, Gates persuaded IBM to accept a nonexclusive license for MS-DOS (which IBM called PC-DOS).

To stoke sales, IBM offered a number of applications for the IBM PC that were sold separately, including a version of VisiCalc, a word processor called EasyWriter, and well-known series of business programs from Peachtree Software.

Introduced in 1981, the IBM PC was an instant success. Over the next 2 years, IBM would sell more than 500,000 PCs, seizing market leadership from Apple. IBM had what Apple lacked, an ability to sell into corporate America. As sales of the IBM PC mounted, two things happened. First, independent software developers started to write program to run on the IBM PC. These included two applications that drove adoptions of the IBM PC; word processing programs (Word Perfect) and a spread sheet (Lotus 1-2-3). Second, the success of IBM gave birth to clone manufacturers who made "IBM compatible" PCs that also utilized an Intel microprocessor and Microsoft's MS-DOS operating system. The clone makers included Compaq, Tandy, Zenith, Leading Edge, and Dell.

The Birth of the Macintosh

By 1980 two other important projects were underway at Apple: Lisa and the Macintosh. Lisa was originally conceived as a high-end business machine, and the Macintosh as a low-end portable machine.

The development of both the Lisa, and ultimately the Macintosh, were influenced by two visits Steve Jobs paid to Xerox's fabled Palo Alta Research Center (PARC) in November and December 1979. Funded out of Xerox's successful copier business, PARC had been set up to do advanced research on office technology. Engineers at PARC had developed a number of technologies that were later to become central to personal computers, including a graphical user interface (GUI), software programs that were made tangible through on screen icons, a computer mouse that let a user click on and drag on screen objects, and a laser printer. Jobs was astounded by what he saw at PARC, and decided on the spot that these innovations had to be incorporated into Apple's machines.

Jobs initially pushed the Lisa team to implement PARC's innovations, but he was reportedly driving people on the project nuts with his demands, so President Mike Scott pulled him of the project. Jobs reacted by essentially hijacking the Macintosh project, and transforming it into a skunk works that would put his vision into effect. By one account:

He hounded the people on the Macintosh project to do their best work. He sang their praises, bullied them unmercifully, and told them they weren't making a computer, they were making history. He promoted the Mac passionately, making people believe that he was talking about much more than a piece of office equipment.[7]

It was during this period that Bud Tribble, a software engineer on the Mac project, quipped that Steve Jobs could create a "reality distortion field." Jobs insisted that the Mac would ship by early 1982. Tribble knew that the schedule was unattainable, and when asked why he didn't point this out to Jobs, he replied: "Steve insists that we're shipping in early 1982, and won't accept answers to the contrary. The best way to describe the situation is a term from Star Trek. Steve has a reality distortion field. . . . In his presence, reality is malleable. He can convince anyone of practically anything. It wears off when he's not around, but it makes it hard to have realistic schedules."[8]

Andy Hertzfeld, another engineer on the Macintosh project, thought Tribble was exaggerating. . . . "until I observed Steve in action over the next few weeks. The reality distortion field was a confounding mélange of a charismatic rhetorical style, an indomitable will, and an eagerness to bend any fact to fit the purpose at hand. If one line of argument failed to persuade, he would deftly switch to another. Sometimes, he would throw you off balance by suddenly adopting your position as his own, without acknowledging that he ever thought differently.[9]

Back at Apple things were changing too. Mike Scott had left the company after clashes with other executives, including Markkula, who had become chairman. Steve Jobs persuaded John Sculley to join Apple as CEO. Sculley was the former executive vice president of marketing at Pepsi, where he had become famous for launching the Pepsi Challenge. Jobs had reportedly asked Sculley *Do you want to sell sugar water for the rest of your life, or do you want to change the world?* Sculley opted for changing the world. A Wharton MBA, Sculley had been hired for his marketing savvy, not his technical skills.

While the Lisa project suffered several delays, Jobs pushed the Macintosh team to finish the project and beat the Lisa team to market with a better product. Introduced in 1984, the Macintosh captured attention for its stylish design, and utilization of a GUI, icons, and a mouse, all of which made the machine easy to use and were not found on any other personal computer at the time. Jobs, ever the perfectionist, again insisted that not a single screw should be visible on the case. He reportedly fired a designer who presented a mockup that had a screw that could be seen by lifting a handle.

Early sales were strong; then they faltered. For all its appeal, the Macintosh lacked some important features—it had no hard disk drive, only one floppy drive, and insufficient computer memory. Moreover, there were few applications available to run on the machine, and the Mac proved to be a more difficult machine to develop applications for than the IBM PC and its clones. Jobs, however, seemed oblivious to the problems, and continued to talk about outsized sales projections, even when it was obvious to all around him that they were unattainable.

In early 1985, Apple posted its first loss. Aware that drastic action was necessary, but could not be taken while Jobs was running the Macintosh division, Sculley got backing from the board of directors to strip Jobs of his management role and oversight of the Macintosh division. In late 1985 an embittered Jobs resign from Apple, sold all of his stock, and left to start another computer company, aptly named NeXT.

Sculley's Apple

With Jobs gone, Sculley shut down the Lisa line, which had done poorly in the market due to a very high price point of $10,000, and pushed developers to fix the problems with the Macintosh. In January 1986 a new version of the Macintosh, the Mac Plus, was introduced. This machine fixed the shortcomings of the original Mac, and sales started to grow again.

What helped was Apple's domination of the desktop publishing market. Several events came together to make this happen. Researchers from Xerox PARC formed a company, Adobe, to develop and commercialize the PostScript page description language. Postscript enabled the visual display and printing of high quality page layouts loaded with graphics (e.g. colored charts, line drawings and photos). Apple licensed PostScript and used it as the output for its Apple LaserWriter printer, which was introduced in 1985. Shortly afterwards, a Seattle company, Aldus, introduced a program called Page Maker for the Mac. Page Maker used Adobe's Post Script page description language for output. Although Aldus introduced a version of Page Maker for MS-DOS in 1986, Apple already had a lead, and with the Macs GUI interface appealing to graphic artists, Apple's tightened its hold on the desk top publishing segment. Apple's position in desk top publishing was further strengthened by the release Adobe Illustrator in 1987 (a freehand drawing program), and Adobe Photoshop in 1990.

The period between 1986 and 1991 were in many ways the golden years for Apple. Since it made both hardware and software, Apple was able to control all aspects of its computers, offering a complete desktop solution that allowed customers to "plug and play." With the Apple II series still selling well in the education market, and the Mac dominating desktop publishing, Apple was able to charge a premium price for its products. Gross margins on the Mac line got as high as 55%. In 1990 Apple sales reached $5.6 billion. Its global market share, which had fallen rapidly as the IBM compatible PC market had grown, stabilized at 8%, the company had a strong balance sheet and was the most profitable personal computer manufacturer in the world.

During this period executives at Apple actively debated the merits of licensing the Mac operating system to other computer manufacturers, allowing them to make Mac clones. Sculley was in favor of this move. So was Microsoft's Bill Gates, who wrote two memos to Sculley laying out the argument for licensing the Mac OS. Gates argued that the closed architecture of the Macintosh prevented independent investment in the standard by third parties, and put Apple at a disadvantage versus the IBM PC standard. However, some senior executives at Apple were against the licensing strategy, arguing that once Apple licensed its intellectual property, it would be difficult to protect it. In one version of events, senior executives debated the decision at a meeting, and took a vote on whether to license. Given the controversial nature of the decision, it was decided that the vote in favor had to be unanimous. It wasn't—a single executive voted against the licensing decision, and it was never pursued.[10] In another version of events, Jean-Louis Gassee, head of R&D at Apple, vigorously opposed Sculley's plans to clone, and Sculley backed down.[11] Gassee was deeply distrustful of Microsoft, and Bill Gates, and believed that Gates's probably had an ulterior motive given how the company benefited from the IBM standard.

Ironically, in 1985 Apple had licensed its "visual displays" to Microsoft. Reportedly Gates had strongarmed Sculley, threatening that Microsoft would stop developing crucial applications for the Mac unless Apple granted Microsoft the license. At the time, Microsoft had launched development of its own GUI. Called Windows, it mimicked the look and feel of the Mac operating system, and Microsoft didn't want to be stopped by a lawsuit from Apple. Several years later, when Apple did file a lawsuit against Microsoft, arguing that Windows 3.1 imitated the "look and feel" of the Mac, Microsoft was able to point to the 1985 license agreement to defend its right to develop Windows—a position which the judge in the case agreed with.

Apple in Decline: 1990–1997

By the early 1990s, the prices of IBM compatible PCs were declining rapidly. So long as Apple was the only company to sell machines that utilized a GUI, its differential appeal gave it an advantage over MS-DOS based PCs with their clunky text based interfaces, and the premium price could be justified. However, in 1990 Microsoft introduced Windows 3.1, its own GUI that sat on top of MS-DOS, and Apple's differential appeal began to erode. Moreover, the dramatic growth of the PC market had turned Apple into a niche player. Faced with the choice of writing software to work with an MS-DOS/Windows operating system and an Intel microprocessor, now the dominant standard found on 90% of all personal computers, or the Mac OS and a Motorola processor, developers logically opted for the dominant standard (desk top publishing remained an exception to this rule). Reflecting on this logic, Dan Eilers, then vice president of strategic planning at Apple, reportedly stated "The company was on a glide path to history"[12].

Sculley too, thought that the company was in trouble. Apple seemed boxed into its niche. Apple had a high cost structure. It spent significantly more on R&D as a percentage of sales than its rivals (in 1990 Apple spent 8% of sales on R&D, Compaq around 4%). Its microprocessor supplier, Motorola, lacked the scale of Intel, which translated into higher costs for Apple. Moreover, Apple's small market share made it difficult to recoup the spiraling cost of developing a new operating system, which by 1990 amounted to at least $500 million.

Sculley's game plan to deal with these problems involved a number of steps.[13] First, he appointed himself chief technology officer in addition to CEO—a move that raised some eyebrows given Sculley's marketing background. Second, he committed the company to bring out a low cost version of the Macintosh to compete with IBM clones. The result was the Mac Classic, introduced in October 1990 and priced at $999. He also cut prices for the Mac's and Apple II's by 30%. The reward was a 60% increase in sales volume, but lower gross margins. So third, he cut costs. The workforce at Apple was reduced by 10%, the salaries of top managers (including Sculley's) were cut by as much as 15%, and Apple shifted much of its manufacturing to subcontractors (for example, the PowerBook was built in Japan—a first for Apple). Fourth, he called for the company to maintain its technological lead by bringing out hit products every 6 to 12 months. The results include the first Apple portable, the PowerBook notebook, which was shipped in late 1991 and garnered very favorable reviews, and the Apple Newton hand held computer, which bombed. Fifth, Apple entered into an alliance with IBM, which realized that it had lost its hold on the PC market to companies like Intel, Microsoft, and Dell.

Toyota Pebble Recall

The IBM alliance had several elements. One was the decision to adopt IBM's Power PC microprocessor architecture, which IBM would also use in its own offerings. A second was the establishment of two joint ventures—Taligent, which had the goal of creating a new operating system, and Kaleida to develop multimedia applications. A third was a project to help IBM and Apple machines work better together.

While Sculley's game plan helped to boost the top line, the bottom line shrunk in 1993 due to a combination of low gross margins and continuing high costs. In 1994 Sculley left Apple. Michael Spindler, a German engineer who had gained prominence as head of Apple Europe, replaced him.

Spindler finally took the step that had been long debated in the company—he decided to license the Mac OS to a handful of companies, allowing them to make Mac clones. The Mac OS would be licensed for $40 a copy. It was too little too late—the industry was now waiting for the introduction of Microsoft's Windows 95. When it came, it was clear that Apple was in serious trouble. Windows 95 was a big improvement over Windows 3.1, and it closed the gap between Windows and the Mac. While many commentators criticized Apple for not licensing the Mac OS in the 1980s, when it still had a big lead over Microsoft, ironically Bill Gates disagreed. In a 1996 interview with Fortune, Gates noted that:

> As Apple has declined, the basic criticism seems to be that Apple's strategy of doing a unique hardware/software combination was doomed to fail. I disagree. Like all strategies, this one fails if you execute poorly. But the strategy can work, if Apple picks its markets and renews the innovation in the Macintosh.[14]

Spindler responded to Windows 95 by committing Apple to develop a next generation operating system for the Macintosh—something that raised questions about the Taligent alliance with IBM. At the end of 1995, IBM and Apple parted ways, ending Taligent, which after $500 million in investments had produced little.

By then, Spindler had other issues on his mind. The latter half of 1995 proved to be a disaster for Apple. The company seemed unable to predict demand for its products. It overestimated demand for its low-end Macintosh Performa computers, and was left with excess inventory, while underestimating demand for its high-end machines. To compound matters, its new PowerBooks had to be recalled after batteries started to catch fire, and a price war in Japan cut margins in one of its best markets. As a consequence, gross margins slumped and Apple lost $68 million in 1995. Spindler responded by announcing 1,300 layoffs. He suggested that up to 4,000 might ultimately go—some 23% of the workforce.[15] That was his last significant act. Gilbert Amelio replaced him in February.

Amelio, joined Apple from National Semiconductor where he had gained a reputation for his turnaround skills. He lasted just seventeen months. He followed through on Spindler's plans to cut headcount and stated that Apple would return to its differentiation strategy. His hope was that the new Mac operating system would help, but work on that was in total disarray. He took the decision to scrap the project after an investment of over $500 million. Instead, Apple purchased NeXT, the computer company founded by none other than Steve Jobs after he left Apple, for $425 million. The NeXT machines had received strong reviews, but had gained no market traction due to a lack of supporting applications. Amelio felt that the NeXT OS, a UNIX based operating system, could be adapted to run on the Mac. He also hired Steve Jobs as a consultant, but Jobs was rarely seen at Apple—he was too busy running Pixar, his computer animation company that was riding a wave of success after a huge hit with the animated movie, Toy Story.[16]

Amelio's moves did nothing to stop the slide in Apple's fortunes. By mid 1997, market share had slumped to 3%, from 9% when Amelio took the helm. The company booked a loss of $742 million in 1996 and was on track to lose another $400 million in 1997. It was too much for the board. In July 1997 he was fired. With market share falling, third party developers and distributors were rethinking their commitments to Apple. Without them, the company would be dead.

THE SECOND COMING OF STEVE JOBS

Following Amelio's departure, Steve Jobs was appointed interim CEO. In April 1998, he took the position on a permanent basis, while staying on at Pixar as CEO. Jobs moved quickly to fix the bleeding. His first act was to visit Bill Gates and strike a deal with Microsoft. Microsoft agreed to invest $150 million in Apple and to continue producing Office for the Mac through until at least 2002. Then he ended the licensing deals with the clone makers, spending over $100 million to acquire the assets of the leading Mac clone maker, Power Computing, including its license. Jobs killed slow selling products, most notably the Apple Newton handheld computer, and reduced the number of product lines from 60 to just 4. He also pushed the company into online distribution, imitating Dell Computer's direct selling model. While these fixes brought the company time, and a favorable reaction from the stock market, they were not enough to generate growth.

New Computer Offerings

Almost immediately Jobs started to think about a new product that would embody the spirit of Apple. What emerged in May 1998 was the iMac. The differentiator for the iMac was not its software, or its power, or its monitor—it was the design of the machine itself. A self contained unit that combined the monitor and central processing unit in translucent teal and with curved lines, the iMac was a bold departure in a world dominated by putty colored PC boxes (see Exhibit 1).

To develop the iMac, Jobs elevated a team of designers headed by Jonathan Ive, giving them an unprecedented say in the development project. Ive's team worked closely with engineers, manufacturers, and marketers, and most importantly, with Jobs himself. To understand how to make a plastic shell look exciting rather than cheap, the designers visited a candy factory to study the finer points of making jellybeans. They spent months working with Asian partners designing sophisticated process capable of producing millions of iMacs a year. The designers also pushed for the internal electronics to be redesigned, to make sure that they looked good through the thick shell. Apple may have spent as much as $65 a machine on the casing, compared with perhaps $20 for the average PC.[17]

Priced at $1,299, iMac sales were strong with orders placed for 100,000 units even before the machine was available. Moreover, one-third of iMac purchases were by were first time buyers according to Apple's own research.[18] The iMac line was continually updated, with faster processors, more memory, and bigger hard drives being added. The product was also soon available in many different colors. In 1999, Apple followed up the iMac with introduction of the iBook portable. Aimed at consumers and students, the iBook had the same design theme as the iMac and was priced aggressively at $1,599.

Sales of the iMac and iBook helped push Apple back into profitability. In 1999, the company earned $420 million on sales of $6.1 billion. In 2000, it made $611 million on sales of almost $8 billion.

To keep sales growing, Apple continued to invest in development of a new operating system, based on the technology acquired from NeXT. After 3 years work by nearly 1,000 software engineers, and a cost of around $1 billion, the first version of Apple's new operating systems was introduced in 2001. Known as OS X, it garnered rave reviews from analysts who saw the UNIX based program as offering superior stability and faster speed than the old Mac OS. OS X also had an enhanced ability to run multiple programs at once, to support multiple users, connected easily to other devices such as digital camcorders, and was easier for developers to write applications for. In typical Apple fashion, OS X

| Exhibit 1 | The iMac and iBook |

it also sported a well-designed and intuitively appealing interface. Since 2001, new versions of OS X have been introduced every 12 to 18 months. The most recent version, OS X Mountain Lion, was introduced in 2012 and sold for $19.99.

To get the installed base of Mac users to upgrade to OS X, who at the time numbered 25 million, Apple had to offer applications. The deal with Microsoft ensured that its popular Office program would be available for the OS X. Steve Jobs had assumed that the vote of confidence by Microsoft would encourage other third part developers to write programs for OS X, but it didn't always happen. Most significantly, in 1998 Adobe refused to develop a Mac version of their consumer video-editing program, which was already available for Windows PCs.

Shocked, Jobs directed Apple to start working on its own applications. The first fruits of this effort were two video-editing programs, Final Cut Pro for professionals, and iMovie for consumers. Next was iLife, a bundle of multimedia programs now preinstalled on every Mac, which includes iMovie, iPhoto, Garage Band, and the

| Exhibit 2 | iMac G5 Introduced in 2004 |

Finnbarr Webster/Alamy

iTunes digital jukebox. Apple also developed its own web browser, Safari.

Meanwhile, Apple continued to update its computer lines with eye-catching offerings. In 2001 Apple introduced its Titanium PowerBook G4 notebooks. Cased in Titanium, these ultra-light and fast notebooks featured a clean postindustrial look that marked a distinct shift from the whimsical look of the iMac and iBook. As with the iMac, Jonathan Ive's design team took the lead in the products development. A core team of designers set up a design studio in a San Francisco warehouse, far away from Apple's main campus. They worked for 6 weeks on the basic design then headed to Asia to negotiate for widescreen flat panel displays and to work with toolmakers.[19]

The Titanium notebooks were followed by a redesigned desktop line that appealed to the company's graphic design customers, including the offering of elegantly designed very wide screen cinema displays. In 2004, Ive's design team came out with yet another elegant offering, the iMac G5 computer which PC Magazine described as a "simple stunning all in one design (see Exhibit 2)."[20] This was followed in 2008 with the release of yet another strong design, the ultra thin MacBook Air that weighed just 3 pounds and was only 0.76 of an inch thick at its widest point.

For all of Apple's undisputed design excellence, and the loyalty of its core user base, during the early 2000s Apple's global market share remained anemic, trailing far behind industry leaders Dell, Hewlett Packard, and IBM/Lenovo. Weak demand, combined with its low market share, translated into another loss for Apple in 2001, leading some to question the permanence of Steve Jobs's turnaround. However, while Apple's share in its core U.S. market fell to under 3% in 2004, it started to pick up again in 2005, rising to 8.5% by 2008. Driving growth during 2005–2008 was the surging popularity of Apple's iPod music player and in 2007, iPhone. These two products had raised Apple's profile among younger consumers and was having a spill over effect on Mac sales.[21]

Intel Inside, Windows on the Desktop

Since the company's inception, Apple had had not used Intel microprocessors, which had become the industry standard for microprocessors following the introduction of the IBM PC in 1981. In June 2005, Apple announced that it would start to do so. Driving the transition was growing frustration with the performance of the PowerPC chip line made by IBM that Apple had been using for over a decade. The PowerPC had failed to keep up with the Intel chips, which were both faster and had lower power consumption—something that was very important in the portable computer market, where Apple had a respectable market share.

The transition to an Intel architecture created significant risks for Apple. Old applications and OS X had to be rewritten to run on Intel processors. By the spring of 2006 Apple had produced Intel compatible versions of OS X and its own applications, but many other applications had not been rewritten for Intel chips. To make transition easier, Apple provided a free software program, known as Rosetta, which enabled users to run older applications on Intel based Macs. Moreover, Apple went a step further by issuing a utility program, known as Boot Camp, which enabled Mac owners to run Windows XP on their machines.

Reviews of Apple's Intel based machines were favorable, with many reviewers noting the speed improvement over the older PowerPC Macs.[22] In late 2006 Apple reported that its transition to Intel based architecture was complete, some 6 months ahead of schedule. The move may have helped Apple to close the price differential that had long existed between Windows based PCs and Apple's offerings. According to one analysis, by September 2006 Apple's products were selling at a *discount* to comparable product offerings from Dell and Hewlett Packard.[23]

Moving into Retail

In 2001 Apple made another important strategic shift—the company opened its first retail store. In an industry that had long relied upon third party retailers, or direct sales as in the case of Dell, this shift seemed risky. One concern was that Apple might encounter a backlash from Apple's long-standing retail partners. Another was that Apple would never be able to generate the sales volume required to justify expensive retail space; the product line seemed too thin. However, Apple clearly felt that it was hurt by a lack of retail presence. Many computer retailers didn't carry Apple machines, and some of those that did often buried Mac displays deep in the store.

From the start, Apple's stores exhibited the same stylish design that characterized its products with clean lines, attractive displays, and a postindustrial feel. Steve Jobs himself was intimately involved in the design

process. Indeed, he is one of the named inventors on a patent Apple secured for the design of the signature glass staircase found in many stores, and he was apparently personally involved in the design of a glass cube atop a store on New York's 5th Avenue that opened in 2006. In an interview, Jobs noted that "we spent a lot of time designing the store, and it deserves to be built perfectly."[24]

Customers and analysts were immediately impressed by the product fluency that the employees in Apple stores exhibited. One hallmark of Apple stores seems to be the personal attention paid to customer by smiling sales staff, an approach that is remonstrant of upscale retailers like Nordstrom. They also liked the highlight of many stores, a "genius bar" where technical experts helped customers fix problems with their Apple products. The wide-open interior space, however, did nothing to allay the fears of critics that Apple's product portfolio was just too narrow to generate the traffic required to support premium space.

The critics couldn't have been more wrong. Spurred on by booming sales of the iPod, and then the iPhone and iPad Apple's stores have done exceptionally well. By late 2012 Apple had some 390 stores in upscale locations. Sales per square foot are extraordinary, averaging $6,050 per U.S. store in 2012, making Apple the envy of other retailers.[25]

iPod and iTunes

In the late 1990s and early 2000s the music industry was grappling with the implications of two new technologies. The first was the development of inexpensive portable MP3 players that could store and play digital music files such as Diamond Media's Rio, which was introduced in 1997 and could hold 2 hours of music. The second was the rise of peer-to-peer computer networks such as Napster, Kazaa, Grokster and Morpheus that enabled individuals to efficiently swap digital files over the Internet. By the early 2000s, millions of individuals were downloading music files over the Internet without the permission of the copyright holders, the music publishing companies. For the music industry, this development was devastating. After years of steady growth, global sales of music peaked in 1999 at $38.5 billion, falling to $32 billion in 2003. Despite the fall in sales, the International Federation of the Phonographic Industry (IFPI) claimed that demand for music was higher than ever, but that the decline in sales reflected the fact that "the commercial value of music is being widely devalued by mass copying and piracy."[26]

The music industry had tried to counter piracy over the Internet by taking legal action to shut down the peer-to-peer networks, such as Napster, and filing law suits against individuals who made large numbers of music files available over the Internet. Its success had been limited, in part because peer-to-peer networks offered tremendous utility to consumers. They were fast, immediate, and enabled consumers to unbundled albums, downloading just the tracks they wanted while ignoring junk filler tracks. And of course, they were free. The music industry was desperate for a legal alternative to illegal downloading.

Then along came the iPod and iTunes. These products were born out of an oversight—in the late 1990s when consumers were staring to burn their favorite CDs, Macs did not have a CD burner, or software to manage their digital music collections. Realizing the mistake, CEO Steven Jobs ordered Apple's software developers to create the iTunes program to help Mac users manage their growing digital music collections. The first iTunes program led to the concept of the iPod. If people were going to maintain the bulk of their music collection on a computer, they needed a portable MP3 player to take music with them. While there were such devices on the market already, they could only hold a few dozen songs each.

To run the iPod Apple licensed software from PortalPlayer. Apple also learnt that Toshiba was building a tiny 1.8 inch hard drive that could hold over 1,000 songs. Apple quickly cut a deal with Toshiba, giving it exclusive rights to the drive for 18 months. Meanwhile, Apple's focused on designing the user interface, the exterior styling, and the synchronization software to make it work with the Mac. As with so many product offerings unveiled since Jobs returned to the helm, the design team led by Jonathan Ive played a pivotal role in giving birth to the iPod. Ive's team worked in secrecy in San Francisco. The members, all paid extremely well by industry standards, worked together in a large open studio with little personal space. The team was able to figure out how to put a layer of clear plastic over the white and black core of an iPod, giving it tremendous depth of texture. The finish was superior to other MP3 players, with no visible screws or obvious joins between parts. The serial number of the iPod was not on a sticker, as with most products, it was elegantly etched onto the back of the device. This attention to detail and design elegance, although not with cost implications, was to turn the iPod into a fashion accessory.[27]

The iPod was unveiled in October 2001 to mixed reviews. The price of $399 was significantly above that of competing devices, and since the iPod only worked with Apple computers it seemed destined to be a niche product. However, initial sales were strong. It turned out that consumers were willing to pay a premium price for the iPod's huge storage capacity. Moreover, Jobs made the call to develop a version of the iPod that would be compatible with Windows. After it was introduced in mid 2002, sales took off.

By this times Jobs was dealing with a bigger strategic issue—how to persuade the music companies to make their music available for legal downloads. Jobs meet with executives from the major labels. He persuaded them that it was in their best interest to support a legal music download business as an alternative to wide spread illegal downloading. People would pay to download music over the Internet, he argued. Although all of the labels were setting up their own online businesses, Jobs felt that since they were limited to selling music owned by the parent companies, demand would be limited too. What was needed was a reputable independent online music retailer, and Apple fit the bill. If it was going to work, however, all of the labels needed to get on board. Under Jobs scheme, iTunes files would be downloaded for $0.99 each. The only portable digital player that the files could only be stored and played on was an iPod. Jobs's argument was that this closed world made it easier to protect copyrighted material from unauthorized distribution.

Jobs also meet with 20 of the worlds top recording artists, including U2's Bono, Sheryl Crow, and Mick Jagger. His pitch to them—digital distribution is going to happen, and the best way to protect your interests is to support a legal online music distribution business. Wooed by Jobs, these powerful stakeholders encouraged the music recording companies to take Apple's proposal seriously.[28]

By early 2003 Jobs had all of the major labels onboard. Apple launched the online iTunes store in April 2003. Within days it was clear that Apple had a major hit on its hands. A million songs were sold in the first week. By the end of 2004 customers were downloading over 4 million songs per week, which represented a run rate of more than 200 million a year. The reach of iTunes has expanded enormously since then. By the end of 2012 the iTunes store had a song catalog of 20 million, and Apple was seeing 15,000 downloads a minute. In February 2013, Apple announced that 25 billion songs had been downloaded from iTunes.[29] Early on Steve Jobs stated that Apple was not making much money from iTunes downloads, probably only $0.10 a song, but it was making good margins of sales of the iPod—and sales of the iPod ballooned after the launch of the iTunes online store.

Success such as this attracts competitors. RealNetworks, Wal*Mart, Yahoo, Napster, Microsoft, Google and Amazon all set up legal downloading services to compete with iTunes. However, iTunes has continued to outsell its rivals by a wide margin. In mid 2012, downloads from iTunes accounted for 64% of the entire U.S. digital music market and 29% of all music sold in the U.S. (including both digital and physical formats).[30] Coming in a distant second was Amazon MP3, which had a 16% share of the digital market. Microsoft's Zune Music Pass and Google's Google Play each had less than a 5% share of the market. Helping Apple to maintain share is the fact that iTunes comes preinstalled on all Apple devices, and through iCloud, a subscriber's iTunes music library is synchronized across all devices that run iTunes, including Windows devices.

The iPhone and App Store

In June 2007 Apple introduced the iPhone. The iPhone was a smart phone that was also able to browse the web, take pictures and function as an iPod digital music player. Designed by the team led by Jonny Ive, the iPhone was differentiated from established smart phone offerings by revolutionary touch screen that replaced the traditional mechanical keypad and allowed users to quickly and easily switch between functions. As was typical for Apple products, it was elegantly designed and made extensive use of expensive materials including a body of brushed aluminum and a screen made of tough "gorilla glass" from Corning. Up to this point, most phones had used plastic bodies and all had plastic screens. Steve Jobs reportedly hated the ascetic of plastic, and complained that plastic screens were too easily scratched. He insisted on a glass screen, which had previously been rejected because it broke or cracked too easily. Designers at Apple had heard about a very strong form of glass Corning had developed, but which was not in manufacture. Jobs reportedly flew out to Corning, visited with the CEO, and personally persuaded him to put the material into mass production.[31]

The iPhone used a version of Apple's OS X operating system and the company's Safari web browser. Apple struck a deal with AT&T, under which it was to be the exclusive provider of wireless service for the iPhone. Under the deal, AT&T would share a percentage of its service fees from iPhone users with Apple (the percentage was rumored to be 30%, but neither company would confirm this).

Priced between $599 and $499 depending on the model, the iPhone was positioned at the high end of the smart phone market. Some were skeptical that the device would be able to gain share from established smart phones such as Research in Motion with its Blackberry, and offerings from Palm, Motorola and Nokia, all of which had gained a following among business users.

Steve Jobs announced that the goal was to try and grab 1% of the total global market for wireless phones in the first full year that the iPhone was on the market. With a total market in excess of 1 billion units, most of which were not smart phones, this suggested a goal of selling 10 million iPhones in fiscal 2008 (which ended September 2008).

There was some disappointment that the iPhone would use AT&T's slower data network, rather than the faster 3G network that was more suited to web browsing. There was also disappointment that the iPhone did not contain a GPS location finding function.

Despite the high price and perceived limitations, early demand for the iPhone was strong with long lines forming outside Apple stores on the day the device was released. Although some consumers experienced activation problems, most were happy with their purchase. The device got rave reviews for its design elegance, ease of use, and compelling touch screen interface. Apple sold over 250,000 iPhones in the first 2 days the device was on the market and it soon became clear that the company had another hit on its hands.

In June 2008, Apple introduced a second version of its iPhone, the iPhone 3G. Designed to run on a faster 3G networks, the new phone also incorporated GPS functionality. AT&T was again the exclusive service provider in the United States. However, Apple shifted the business model. Instead of giving a share of service fees to Apple, AT&T agreed to pay a subsidy to Apple for each iPhone sold. The subsidy allowed Apple to drop the price for the iPhone to as low as $199 for an entry level model. Yet again long lines formed outside Apple stores and in the first 3 days the iPhone 3G was on the market over 1 million units were sold. By the end of fiscal 2008, Apple had sold 11.63 million iPhones (see Exhibit 3).

One feature of the iPhone 3G that started to garner a lot of attention was the rapid growth in third party applications. In July 2008 Apple opened an online store for applications that were written to run on the iPhone. Known as the App Store, consumers could download applications through their iTunes account. Some of these apps are free, while others are sold, typically for a few dollars. In the first month the phone was on the market, more than 60 million applications were downloaded.

Apple keeps 30% of the proceeds from application sales, letting program creators retain the other 70%. Among the top sellers were game applications.[32]

By the end of 2012, Apple had over 700,00 applications available for download on the App Store. Apple generated $4.9 billion in revenue from App Store downloads in 2012 and in total some 40 billion applications had been downloaded by early 2013. According to Apple, this has resulted in net payments of around $7 billion to third party developers since the App Store went live in 2008. Of the ten top paid apps of all time, eight were games. The top ten free apps include Facebook, Pandora Radio, Skype, and Google Search.[33]

The iPhone 3G was followed by the iPhone 4 and iPhone 5, each of which included more powerful features and functionality. In 2011 Apple ended its exclusive relationship with AT&T when Verizon, the largest U.S. wireless service provider, started to offer the iPhone.

Expanded service coverage in the United States, plus surging overseas sales, helped propel sales of the iPhone, which reached 125.04 million units in 2012. Apple made $80.5 billion in revenues from iPhone sales in 2012, making it by far the biggest revenue generator in Apple's portfolio of products. By comparison, the venerable line of Mac computers generated revenues of $23.2 billion in 2012.

Competition in the Smart Phone Market

When the iPhone was introduced in 2007, it redefined what a smart phone had to look like and do. Before the iPhone, smart phones had physical keyboards and relatively small screens. Moreover, the dominant smart phones players, such as Blackberry, sold their phones to business users. From the outset, Apple focused on the consumer and gave them a device that was a phone, computing tool, and fashion accessory rolled into one.

In 2007, 122 million smartphones were sold worldwide. The largest vendor at the time was Nokia with 63.5% of the market. The Nokia phones used the Symbian operating system. While Symbian had many of the features also found on the iPhone, including web browsing, a music player, and a camera, it lacked the design elegance of the iPhone, the connection with iTunes, and a rapidly expanding network of 3rd party application developers. The other major players in 2007 were Blackberry (with 9.6% of the market), and Microsoft Windows Mobile (which was used on phones from various manufactures, and had 12% of the market).

By late 2008 phones powered by Google's Android operating systems started to reach the market. Like Apple's iOS smart phone operating system, Android was designed for touchscreen mobile devices. However, whereas Apple designed and sold a physical phone that ran on iOS, Google adopted a very different approach— it licensed Android for free to smart phone manufacturers. Android is an *open source* operating system, which allows the code to be freely modified and distributed by device manufacturers and wireless carriers. This led to rapid adoption of Android by handset manufacturers who were caught flat-footed by the sudden success of the iPhone and needed a competitive offering of their own.

Exhibit 3	World Wide iPhone Unit Sales

Year	World Wide iPhone Unit Sales (millions)
2007	1.46
2008	11.63
2009	20.73
2010	39.93
2011	72.3
2012	125.04

Source: Apple annual 10K Reports

Exhibit 4	Global Smart Phone Market Share (%), Q4 2012

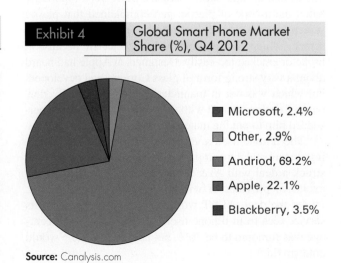

- Microsoft, 2.4%
- Other, 2.9%
- Andriod, 69.2%
- Apple, 22.1%
- Blackberry, 3.5%

Source: Canalysis.com

To further drive adoption of Android, Google established its own applications store in 2008. Known as Google Play, by late 2012 the store had some 700,000 apps available for download to Android devices, about the same number as at the Apple app store. However, reports suggest that Google earned only about one-quarter of Apple's revenues from app downloads in 2012, or some $1.25 billion. This suggests that Apple's customers are more valuable to third party application developers.

The Android operating system started to diffuse very rapidly. By 2010 Android overtook Apple iOS to become the most widely used smartphone platform in the world. In the fourth quarter of 2012, 69.2% of the 216 million smart phones sold worldwide ran on Android. Apple had a 22.1% share, followed by Blackberry with 3.5% and Microsoft with 2.4% (see Exhibit 4). However, Apple continued to capture the bulk of the profits in the industry. In the last quarter of 2012 Apple earned 72% of all profits from smart phone sales worldwide. Samsung, which used Android on its phones, picked up the rest of the profits. No other device manufacturer made money on handset sales.[34]

Driven by the widespread appeal of Android and the iPhone, smartphone sales grew rapidly from 122 million in 2007 to 712 million in 2012. In total, 1.7 billion mobile phones were sold worldwide in 2012, with smart phone sales account for around 42% of the global total.[35] Smart phone sales are forecasted to continue expanding, and are expected to hit 1 billion in 2013 out of total mobile phone sales of 1.9 million according to estimates from Gartner.[36]

Faced with devastating market share losses, in 2011 Nokia decided to drop the Symbian operating system in favor of a new smart phone operating system from Microsoft. For its part, Microsoft redesigned its smart phone operating system from the ground up. In 2012 it introduced its Windows 8 operating system. Sporting a radically designed interface based on "tiles," Windows 8 utilizes a touchscreen capability and can be used on any digital device from smart phone to tablet and personal computer. Microsoft has also established an App Store. By late 2012, Microsoft had 125,000 apps available at its store, less than 20% of those available from Apple and Google's app stores.

Microsoft Windows 8 phones began appearing at the end of 2012. So far market share gains have been slow, despite positive reviews. Some research analysts, however, expect Microsoft to gain traction. They point out that over 90% of the worlds PCs still use Windows, and that having the same operating system on your phone and your computer is a major advantage. Microsoft can also leverage a wide array of other assets to gain share, including its SkyDrive cloud computing service, Xbox live, and well-known applications such as Office. As a result, the research group Gartner estimates that Microsoft's OS will be found on around one-quarter of all smart phones shipped in 2016.[37] Gartner sees Android losing share, while Apple holds onto its share.

The iPad

In 2010 Apple introduced its iPad, a revolutionary tablet computer with a touch screen keyboard, and WiFi and 3G wireless service support. Named after a device used in the Star Trek TV series, the iPad was powered by the same iOS operating system found on the iPhone, had similar functionality, and could run the same applications. The iPad had the design elegance that was now the hallmark of all Apple's products and utilized the same expensive materials as the iPhone, including an aluminum case and Gorilla glass. The iPad was powerful enough to download and watch full-length movies on at high resolution, and light enough to slip into a bag.

In many ways, the iPad finally fulfilled Steve Jobs's vision for what a computer should be. According to a speech given by Apple cofounder Steve Wozniak in 2011, the iPad was in Jobs's mind from the beginning. Back in 1983, Jobs's had stated that. . . .

> *What we want to do is have an incredibly great computer in a book that you can carry around with you and learn how to use in 20 minutes. . . . we really want to do it with a radio link in it so you don't have to hook up to anything and you're in communication with all of these larger databases and other computers.*[38]

In 1983, this was not technically possible, but by the 2000s technology had advanced to the point where it was feasible. Some early table computers, including an offering from Microsoft in 2002, used a stylus as an input device. But Jobs's dismissed any tablet that used a stylus as "a failure." From the start, he wanted a tablet to be created from scratch using a glass touch screen. Work on that idea reportedly happened before the idea of an Apple smartphone. In his words:

> *I had this idea about having a glass display, a multitouch display you could type on with your fingers. I asked our people about it. And six months later, they came back with this amazing display. And I gave it to one of our really brilliant UI guys. He got scrolling working and*

some other things, and I thought, 'my God, we can build a phone with this!' So we put the tablet aside, and we went to work on the iPhone.[39]

Introduced in April 2010, the iPad was an immediate success. 300,000 iPads were sold on the first day of availability. Sales passed a million units in less than a month. Between April 2010 and December 2012 Apple sold a total of 98 million iPads. By early 2013, Apple was selling a 4th generation iPad that included a high-resolution retina display.

As with the iPhone, Apple's success led to rapid imitation. Most rivals introduced tablets using Google's Android operating system. The most successful of these was the Galaxy tablet introduced by Samsung 5 months after the launch of the iPad. In the fourth quarter of 2012, Samsung captured 15% of the global market, while Apple's share dropped to 44%, down from 52% a year earlier. Other notable competitors included Amazon.com, which captured 12% of shipments with its Kindle Fire tablet. Microsoft too, entered the fray in late 2012 with its Surface tablet that utilized the Windows 8 operating system. The Surface represented a distinct break for Microsoft, since it manufactured the product itself. While early sales of the Surface were disappointing, a more powerful version introduced in February 2013 was starting to garner considerable interest.[40]

iCloud

In October 2011 Apple launched its iCloud cloud storage, computing, and synchronization service. The service allows customers to store data such as music, movies, books, documents and applications on remote servers. iCloud automatically synchronizes such data across all of a subscriber's Apple devices. While iCloud is not a totally new offering (Apple has had some form of cloud based service since 2000) it is the most comprehensive offering yet. iCloud had more than 20 million users within one week of launch. By the end of 2012, there were 250 million subscribers on the service. Although basic iCloud services are free, Apple is charging a small annual subscription for music storage and synchronization services.

STRATEGIC ISSUES

In early 2013 Apple found itself in an interesting position. In many ways the company was at the top of its game (see Exhibit 5). For over a decade it had set the agenda in the computer industry with a stream of market changing innovations including the iPod, iPhone, and iPad. It had established a thriving ecosystem that encapsulated all of its devices, cloud services, iTunes, and the growing number of applications available through the App Store. After a decade of spectacular revenue and earnings growth, Apple was the most valuable company in the world measured by market capitalization.

On the other hand, the company had lost its visionary, its driving force, and one of the world's great entrepreneurial geniuses. Dead at 56, Steve Jobs had left a creative vacuum that would be hard to fill. Could the company continue to innovate in the post Jobs world? The new CEO, Tim Cook, had been COO under Jobs and was widely admired as a brilliant operations manager, but could he keep Apple's creative juices flowing? Johnny Ive still ran Apple's design operation, and his group still took the lead on product development efforts, but without Job to inspire and push them, and to give them a vision, could Ive's team continue to maintain their high standards?

Moreover, rivals were not sitting back. Google had established an ecosystem similar to Apple's. Its Android operating system was found on many of the world's most successful smart phones and tablets. Its Google Drive cloud service did all that iCloud did, and arguably more. Google's own app store offered just as many applications as Apple's. And with the advent of the Chrome book in 2012, a cheap laptop running on Google's Chrome operating system, Google was pushing into the desktop and laptop business as well.

Microsoft too, was finally putting together a coherent strategy after disappointing for years. The combination of Windows 8 on phones, tablets, lap tops, and the desktop, together with its SkyDrive cloud service and Windows app store, held out the promise of a third ecosystem to rival those of Apple and Google. Microsoft's presence in the smart phone and tablet space was still tiny, but with Windows sitting on 90% of the world's

1.5 billion PCs, it would be foolish to write the company off.

For his part, Tim Cook had to figure out how to keep these rivals at bay? Moreover, he had to match investors' expectations for continued growth at Apple—not an easy thing when you are already the world's largest computer company.

| Exhibit 5 | Net Sales by Operating Segment and Net Sales and Unit Sales by Product, 2012 (Dollars in Millions and Units in Thousands). |

	2012	Change over 2011
Net Sales by Operating Segment:		
Americas net sales	$57,512	50%
Europe net sales	$36,323	31%
Japan net sales	$10,571	94%
Asia-Pacific net sales	$33,274	47%
Retail net sales	$18,828	33%
Total net sales	$156,508	45%
Net Sales by Product:		
Desktops	$6,040	–6%
Portables	$17,181	12%
Total Mac net sales	$23,221	7%
ipod	$5,615	–25%
Other music related products and services	$8,534	35%
iPhone and related products and services	$80,477	71%
iPad and related products and services	$32,424	59%
Peripherals and other hardware	$2,778	19%
Software, service and other sales (h)	$3,459	17%
Total net sales	$156,508	45%
Unit Sales by Product:		
Desktops (a)	4,656	0%
Portables (b)	13,502	12%
Total Mac unit sales	18,158	9%
iPod unit sales	35,165	–17%
iPhone units sold	125,046	73%
iPad units sold	58,310	80%

Source: Apple 2012 10K Form

NOTES

1. Quoted in Pete Burrows, "Steve Jobs" Magic Kingdom," *Business Week*, February 6, 2006, page 62–68.

2. Seth Fiegerman, "Apple has Twice the Sales per Square Foot of Any Other U.S. Retailer," Mashable, November 12, 2012 (http://mashable.com/2012/11/13/apple-stores-top-sales-per-square-foot/)

3. Anthony Ha, "Apple's iCloud was Grown to 250 million Users," techcrunch, January 23, 2013 (http://techcrunch.com/2013/01/23/apple-icloud-250m/).

4. Dan Graziano, "Android is nipping at Apple's Heels in the Tablet Market," BGR, December 5, 2012 (http://bgr.com/2012/12/05/tablet-market-share-2012/).

5. Much of this section is drawn from P. Freiberger and M. Swaine, *Fire in the Valley*, New York: McGraw-Hill, 2000

6. For a detailed history of the development of the Apple II see Steve Weyhrich, *Apple II History*, http://apple2history.org/history/ah01.html

7. P. Freiberger and M. Swaine, *Fire in the Valley*, New York: McGraw-Hill, 2000, page 357.

8. Andy Hertzfeld, "Reality Distortion Field," http://www.folklore.org/ProjectView.py?project=Macintosh

9. Andy Hertzfeld, "Reality Distortion Field," http://www.folklore.org/ProjectView.py?project=Macintosh

10. This version of events was told to the author by a senior executive who was present in the room at the time.

11. Jim Carlton, "Playing catch up – Apple finally gives in an attempts cloning," *Wall Street Journal*, October 17, 1994, page A1.

12. D.B. Yoffie, "Apple Computer 1992," Harvard Business School Case, 792–081

13. Andrew Kupfer, "Apple's Plan to Survive and Grow," *Fortune*, May 4, 1992, pp. 68–71. B.R. Schlender, "Yet Another Strategy for Apple," *Fortune*, October 22, 1990. pp. 81–85.

14. B. Schlender, "Paradise lost: Apple's quest for life after death," *Fortune*, February 1996, pp. 64–72.

15. Jim Carlton, Apple's losses to stretch into 2nd period," *Wall Street Journal*, January 18, 1996, page B7.

16. Peter Burrows, "Dangerous limbo," *Business Week*, July 21, 1997, page 32.

17. Peter Burrows, The man behind Apple's design magic," *Business Week*, September 2005, pp. 27–34.

18. A. Reinhardt, "Can Steve Jobs keep his mojo working," *Business Week*, August 2, 1999, page 32.

19. Peter Burrows, The man behind Apple's design magic," *Business Week*, September 2005, pp. 27–34.

20. Apple iMac G5 Review, *PC Magazine*, on line at http://www.pcmag.com/article2/0,1759,1648796,00.asp

21. *Standard & Poor's Industry Surveys*, Computers: Hardware, "Global Demand for PCs accelerates," December 8, 2005. Mark Veverka, *Wall Street Journal*, "Barron's

22. insight: Apple's Horizon Brightens," July 23, 2006, page A4.

23. Peter Lewis, "Apple's New Core," *Fortune*, March 29, 2006, pp. 182–184.

24. Citigroup Global Markets, "Apple Computer: New products position Apple well for Holidays," September 13, 2006.

25. N. Wingfield, "How Apple's store strategy beat the odds," *Wall Street Journal*, May 17, 2006, page B1.

26. Seth Fiegerman, "Apple has Twice the Sales per Square Foot of Any Other U.S. Retailer," Mashable, November 12, 2012 (http://mashable.com/2012/11/13/apple-stores-top-sales-per-square-foot/)

27. IFPI News release. Global music sales down 5% in 2001. www.ifpi.org

28. Peter Burrows, The man behind Apple's design magic," *Business Week*, September 2005, pp. 27–34.

29. N. Wingfield and E. Smith. "U2's Gig: Help Apple sell IPods," *Wall Street Journal*, October 20, 2004, page D5. Apple Computer Press Release, "iTunes Music Store Downloads top 150 Million Songs," October 14, 2004.

30. Hayley Tsukayama, "Apple Announces 25 billion iTunes downloads," *The Washington Post*, February 6, 2013.

31. Hisham Dahud, "iTunes Dominates Music Sales, While Pandora's Footprint Soars," Hyperbot.com, September 19, 2012 (http://www.hypebot.com/hypebot/2012/09/itunes-dominates-music-sales-while-pandoras-footprint-soars-study.html)

32. Doug Aamoth, "A Story about Steve Jobs, Steel Balls and Gorilla Glass," *Time*, January 11, 2013

33. N. Wingfield, "iphone softwear sales take off," *Wall Street Journal*, August 11, 2008, page B1.

34. Matt Hamblen, "Apple wins top score for App Store," *Computerworld*, January 2, 2013.

35. Adrian Diaconescu, "Canalys: Android Rules Global Smartphone Market with 69% share," Android Authority, February 8, 2013 (http://www.androidauthority.com/canalys-android-ios-smartphone-market-share-q4-2012-154743/).

36. Data are from IDC. "Strong demand for smartphones and heated vendor competition at the end of 2012," IDC Press Release, January 24, 2013.

37. Charlie Osborne, "Cell phone sales dip globally, Gartner says," *CNET*, February 13, 2013.

38. Louis Columbus, "2013 Roundup of Smartphone and Tablet Forecasts and Market Estimates," Forbes, January 17, 2013.

39. Panzarino, Matthew (2012–10–02). "Rare full recording of 1983 Steve Jobs speech reveals Apple had been working on iPad for 27 years." *The Next Web*. Retrieved October 2, 2012.

40. John Paczkowski, "Apple CEO Steve Jobs live at D8," All Things D, June 1, 2010 (http://allthingsd.com/20100601/steve-jobs-session/)

41. D. Kucera, "Samsung Doubles Tablet PC Market Share Amid Apple Lead," *Bloomberg*, January 31, 2013.

Case 21

High Noon at Universal Pipe: Sell Out or Risk Everything?

Arieh A. Ullmann, Binghamton University (SUNY)

It was mid-November 2004, and as Dave Butler, CEO of Universal Pipe, Inc. (UPI), packed his overnight bag for the flight early the next morning, he was thinking about the upcoming decisive meeting with the Japanese majority owners of UPI in their mid-town Manhattan office. The continued existence of the company was at stake. The fate of UPI, one of the larger U.S. PVC-pipe manufacturers, and its employees depended on him.

Rumors were already circulating that bankruptcy was imminent and that a private equity firm would buy the company and hold a fire sale of its assets in order to pay the former owners and make a handsome profit. Butler felt that this would be unfair to suppliers and employees whose interests would be sacrificed in such a process. He figured that companies involved in the pipe industry might be interested in buying the company as a going concern as well, although, given UPI's checkered past and difficult financial situation, this possibility faced significant obstacles. If this option were pursued, serious questions remained: What price could be negotiated? How quickly could a sale to a new owner other than the private equity firm be executed? Would not the impact on workers be just as detrimental as the bankruptcy/private equity option? Finally, Butler considered the idea of raising the capital to buy the company himself. This would be a major challenge since he had limited personal resources and, should the company fail, his personal assets would be at risk.

While it seemed certain that the current owners were determined to sell the firm, the ultimate outcome depended on Butler's ability to persuade potential buyers and/or capital providers that an option other than selling UPI to private equity would be more advantageous for them. If Butler was able to convince the Japanese owners that another option would better serve their interests, disaster for suppliers and workers could be averted.

AT A CROSSROADS

Three years after 9/11, business was still slow. Demand was sluggish and prices for pipe stayed low. Worse yet, UPI's Japanese owners wanted to get out. They had purchased the company in 1996 with bold expansion plans in mind, which did not materialize. The planned diversification into vinyl siding never happened. The 1999 acquisition of a rival plant in Jonestown, Georgia, had turned out to be a disaster. Since 2001, UPI had reported losses year after year (see Exhibit 6). Butler was blunt in his assessment:

The Japanese parent company was getting fed up with us. The Japanese didn't like us Americans very much anyway. We were the only manufacturing operation they had. They did not understand manufacturing and they especially did not understand manufacturing inventory. They were a trading company. They were the 39th largest corporation in the world and were used to owning inventory for 5 minutes. We were a tiny speck in their portfolio. The only inventory they had on their balance sheet was ours—and they rounded it to millions of dollars!

There were other reasons for the disinterest of the Japanese owners. A few months earlier, on April 1, 2004, a new, billion-dollar company had been formed under the name of Sojitz that combined two of UPI's owners, Nissho Iwai and its American subsidiary and

Copyright © 2011 by the *Case Research Journal* and by Arieh A. Ullmann. An earlier version of this case received the Silver Award at the 2009 NACRA Conference in Santa Cruz, California.

another firm called Nichimen, into a giant with eight business divisions. Within this entity, UPI was practically nonexistent. The merger and its ramifications relegated a business of the size of UPI even more to the sidelines.

Explained Butler:

Eventually our Japanese owners stopped believing that we would ever be able to turn a profit, and in 2003 they decided that the only way out was to sell us. They didn't understand manufacturing, they didn't understand inventory and they certainly didn't understand what our management was doing and there were some people in the U.S. that we reported to that went back to Tokyo and just said: "Give it up!" That turned out to be fairly good for us because by 2003 we were turning the company around. But they didn't believe it. They changed management. In April [2003] they made me CEO and then they said: "We are going to sell the company."

THE NORTH AMERICAN PVC-PIPE MANUFACTURING INDUSTRY

Pipes have been around for a very long time; clay pipes that were used by the ancient Romans have been found in archeological excavations. A wide array of industries used pipes, such as agriculture, oil and gas, construction, and machinery. Pipes came in a variety of materials, such as clay, concrete, metal (lead, copper, iron, steel), rubber, and thermoplastic polymers (which includes PVC) derived from oil and natural gas. Given their widespread applications, pipes could vary dramatically in diameter, ranging from less than an inch to several feet.

PVC Resin and Suppliers

Polyvinyl chloride (PVC), the main material used in UPI's products, was accidentally discovered in the nineteenth century. In 1925, the B.F. Goodrich Company invented a method to plasticize PVC. The first PVC pipes were manufactured in Germany in 1934. The invention of the extruder in the 1940s provided the complimentary

product to establish PVC's usefulness for pipes. Extrusion converted beads of resin and additives under heat and pressure into a liquid analogous to squeezing toothpaste from a tube. The liquid could be shaped into the desired hollow form and then cooled, which caused it to harden. Given its chemical composition and production process, PVC belonged to the family of thermoplastic polymers. PVC made its debut in the U.S. in 1952 and quickly gained popularity. Since then, numerous new applications for PVC have been created in industries ranging from oil extraction to packaged food.

PVC offered significant advantages compared to other materials.[1] It was light, yet extremely durable. It did not rust, rot, or suffer bacterial contamination because PVC pipe had a very smooth surface. Materials flowing through were less likely to get stuck and provide a substrate for bacterial contamination. PVC was malleable and could be bent. It was easy to saw and drill with standard tools and could be glued. It absorbed shocks instead of cracking, which expanded the range of applications even further. Overall, compared to other materials, PVC pipe was cheaper by length of pipe. For these reasons, pipes made from PVC were ideal for the construction industry, for water systems, underground wiring, and sewer lines. Rising prices of copper, the raw material traditionally used for many types of pipes, also stimulated the use of PVC as the raw material of choice. PVC was not without disadvantages, notably with regard to its environmental impact when it caught fire. But this was less of an issue for PVC used in pipes.

The suppliers of PVC resin could be split into two groups. One was comprised of large multinational oil, gas, or chemical corporations, like Chevron Phillips Chemical Company, Dow Plastics, or Saudi Basic Industries Corporation, that were vertically integrated into resin production since PVC resin was based on ethylene, a chemical derived from oil cracking. The second group of suppliers consisted of smaller specialists that customized PVC resins and purchased basic raw materials from the first group.

PVC Pipe

By the early 2000s, PVC was one of the world's most widely used thermoplastic polymers. It consumed about a third of the global chloride output and about 5% of the global oil and gas supply.[2] As of 2002, 40% of the global PVC resin output was used for pipes and fittings.[3] In construction, the market consisted of three applications:

1. Buried water (fresh, sewer),
2. Above ground water (plumbing), and
3. Electrical conduit/telecommunication (insulation).

In the U.S. and Canada, PVC was the dominant material used for drinking water distribution and waste water mains. In fresh water distribution, PVC pipes accounted for about two-third of the market, in sanitary sewer they accounted for 75%, and in wire and cable they accounted for about 60%.

The market could be segmented by users into industrial and municipal uses. The latter comprised drinking water distribution, sanitary sewer mains, storm sewer, and drainage, which were the markets UPI served. Drinking water distribution as well as other uses required pipes to be pressure resistant, whereas sewer systems used so-called gravity pipes that were not designed to transport pressurized materials. As of 2004, PVC claimed a dominant share in the municipal segment. Statistics showed that PVC's share declined in the potable water and sewer segments with increasing pipe diameter primarily for technical reasons.

Exhibit 1	Municipal Pipe Material Usage in the U.S. and Canada (2004)

Rows denote percentage use by application.

	PVC	HDPE*	Ductile Iron**	Corrugated Steel	Concrete	Other
Potable Water	78	2	18	0	2	0
Sanitary Sewer	81	6	9	0	2	2
Storm Sewer	24	46	0	10	18	2
Drainage	0	86	0	11	3	0
Municipal Total	48	34	8	5	4	1

*HDPE: High Density Polyethylene designed for specific uses such as laundry detergent bottles, milk jugs, natural gas, and water pipes.
**Type of cast iron that is not brittle, but flexible and elastic.
Source: Rahman 2007.

The U.S. drinking water infrastructure was huge. It comprised 54,000 systems serving almost 90% of the U.S. population with 2 million miles of water distribution and transmission pipe. The sanitary sewer infrastructure consisted of 60,000 systems with 2.5 million miles of sewer mains and service lines.

Between 1975 and 2002, North American demand for PVC pipe and fittings grew from .5 million metric tons to 3.1 million,[4] and more recently, during the 5 to 7 years prior to 2002, at about 2.3% annually. Demand was sensitive to the economy in that it depended on construction (housing, roads), industrial activity, and the need to replace an aging infrastructure. Demand varied regionally as a function of population growth, which, in turn, was affected by migration patterns.

Aside from the economy, pipe resin prices, like those of other commodities, were susceptible to many other factors and changed monthly. The weather was key in that

hurricanes could shut down production capacity of resin or of feedstock like oil or chlorides causing a sudden spike in prices. The addition of a new plant that could add 1 billion pounds per year would exert a downward pressure on prices, whereas terrorist attacks such as 9/11, a war in an oil producing region like Iraq, or political turmoil somewhere in key locations caused price spikes. At times, producers would try to hike prices but not every increase would stick, i.e., be followed by rival producers.

PVC-Pipe Manufacturers

Until the late 1970s, the number of U.S. players in the PVC-pipe industry expanded rapidly. Later, mergers and acquisitions consolidated the industry fueled by rivals that pursued acquisitive growth as a way to boost market power and share in search of profits. In the 1990s, foreign corporations started acquiring U.S. pipe producers.

In terms of plant capacity, a survey of North American injection molders indicated that while plant capacity varied considerably, the bulk was medium sized, that is, ranged between 250,000 and 600,000 tons. Plants consisted of multiple extrusion lines. The difference between a large and a small plant was the number of lines on the factory floor connected to raw material silos on the input side and finished good warehouses on the other end. With regard to geographic spread, plants were scattered across the country and not colocated with the resin producers that had their capacity primarily along the Gulf.

Pipe manufacturers complied with product standards that established minimum performance criteria such as inside/outside diameter, wall thickness, weight, elasticity, strength, and response to temperature changes. These standards were developed consensually within the industry through the Plastic Pipe and Fittings Association. Standards were crucial because they served as the basis for code requirements issued by states, counties, or cities and as proof of compliance assessed by third parties such as Underwriters Laboratories.

Because pipes were standardized, the possibilities to differentiate on features were limited. Buyers tended to be very price sensitive since pipes and their function were a necessity but added little to the final product beyond "doing their job." Municipalities tended to go with the lowest bidder, and the construction companies that used the pipes were subject to penalties if they could not complete a project on time and at cost. Therefore, for pipe users, low price and on-time delivery were crucial.

Changing needs and regulatory requirements, such as protecting the environment or reducing fresh water leakage, stimulated product innovation in a variety of directions, in particular with regard to ease of assembly, lower installation costs (e.g., replacing trenches for underground pipe installation with holes through which pipe was pushed or pulled), or better joints given that these were the weak link in a pipeline.

Exhibit 2	Sample Market Prices for Pipe PVC

Date	Price (cents/pound)
February 2002	19–20
May 2002	23–24
December 2003	29–30

Source: PlasticsTechnology, various issues.

Exhibit 3	North American Pipe Market Share (2003)

Top ten combined market share	38%
Remaining 228 firms	62%

Source: Plastic News.

Exhibit 4	Distribution of Plant Capacity (1000)

Smaller than 100 tons	23%
100–349 tons	41%
350–749 tons	24%
750–1,199 tons	8%
1,200–1,999	2%
2,000 tons and larger	2%

Source: Plastic News.

Exhibit 5	Geographical Distribution of Pipe Manufacturing Plants

Top Locations	Total Plants
California	39
Ohio	38
Illinois	30
Texas	27
Michigan	25
Georgia	24
Pennsylvania	21
Ontario	19
New Jersey	17
Indiana	15
Missouri	15
North Carolina	15
U.S.	428
Canada	37
Mexico	9

Source: Plastic News.

Pipe manufacturing was scale sensitive to some extent. Labor, shipping, and energy were the major cost items in manufacturing, representing roughly 75% of total cost. Depending on location, labor represented between 44 and 51% of operating cost, energy between 7 and 12%, and shipping from 14 to 18%.

In the early 2000s, the global plastic pipe industry comprised 400–500 companies,[5] and for the U.S. and Canada the trade journal *PlasticNews* listed about 200 firms engaged as pipe, profile, and tubing producers. The 2002 survey of the U.S. Census Bureau listed 441 establishments in NAICS 326122 (plastics, pipe, and pipe fitting manufacturing) with a total value of shipments close to $5.5 billion and 21,570 employees. The players in this industry varied in a number of ways:

- Vertical Scope: Some pipe manufacturers were subsidiaries of resin or chemicalproduct manufacturers. For example, Performance Pipe was a division of Chevron Phillips Chemical Company LP, one of the largest producers of polyethylene piping products in North America; North American Pipe was a subsidiary of Westlake Chemical and grew outwards via acquisitions from its original base in Georgia, Kentucky, and Mississippi.
- Horizontal Scope: Some rivals were exclusively or primarily operating in the pipe business, like UPI, whereas for others pipes were but one product line in a broad array of building materials. An example of the latter was CertainTeed, a subsidiary of SaintGobain, a French multinational involved in glass and construction products.
- Geographic Scope: The largest players owned many plants spread across North America (e.g., North American Pipe Corporation), others owned a few plants concentrated regionally (e.g., UPI), and the smallest operated out of one plant with limited geographical scope.

UNIVERSAL PIPE, INC.

UPI was founded in 1974 under the name Mirapipe as a 50:50 joint venture between Culver Stevens, Sr., a Shreveport, Louisiana, businessman, and a Japanese partner. The company was located in Mattydale, near Syracuse in upstate New York. Before 1974, Miraculous Technical Products, a manufacturer of wire products, occupied the site.

To form the joint venture, the Japanese partner created a Japanese company named Shintech. Two years later, in 1976, Shintech became a wholly owned subsidiary of ShinEtsu, originally a Japanese fertilizer manufacturer that sought to expand globally with this, its second foreign acquisition. In 1984, in the aftermath of an investigation by the New York State Department of Environmental Conservation, the New York site was named a Superfund site and placed on the National Priorities List due to high levels of contamination with volatile organic constituents going back to the first owner's use of toxic solvents for cleaning wires. This meant that any construction on the site or change of its use or ownership required U.S. Environmental Protection Agency (EPA) approval.

Mirapipe grew, changed hands several times, and went through bankruptcy along the way. In 1996, now renamed UPI, it was sold again. The new owners were three Japanese companies: Nissho Iwai American Corp., a New York based trading company with an 80% share; the Japanese conglomerate Nissho Iwai Corp. (NIC), which was the parent of Nissho Iwai American Corp.; and the Japanese chemical maker Kaneka Corp., with a 10% share each. In Japan, NIC was known as a major vinyl extruder that operated seven plants. Kaneka manufactured various plastics products and owned two small PVC additives plants in the U.S. but was not directly involved in the pipe or PVC resin business. At the time, UPI operated two plants, the main one in upstate New York with eighteen extrusion lines, and the other in Knoxville, Tennessee, that had 11 extrusion lines. The new owners retained the president, J. Randy Tagg, as well as all agents and sales representatives. They announced ambitious plans to grow via acquisitions in the pipe industry and by broadening the product line. The new market was to be housing siding, one of NIC's main markets in Japan. After the acquisition had been completed, UPI reported to Nissho Iwai American Corp., the trading subsidiary, located in New York City. No direct link to NIC or Kaneka, the two minority owners, was established.

Vinyl siding production also used PVC (in a different formulation) as the main raw material and relied on a process called coextrusion that combined two layers of material in a continuous process. In the U.S., vinyl siding came in many qualities with regard to thickness, durability, color, and appearance. The Vinyl Siding Institute, the industry's trade association, maintained a product certification program to independently certify product quality in terms of weatherability, windload, and impact resistance. Given the many different climates in the U.S., the range of houses that could be clad in vinyl siding, and the varying preferences of builders and home-owners, the market offered a broad variety of products. Prices varied as well, so much so that a website featured a vinyl siding cost calculator that gave various price ranges, one of which was labeled "Outrageously Over-priced Competitor's Vinyl Siding Cost Selling Range."[6] Only one company, Saint-Gobain's CertainTeed Co., was engaged in both PVC-pipe and vinylsiding manufacturing. It was the only pipe producer that had made the investments in the extra equipment needed for siding and had developed the distribution system and sales force required to sell it.

Butler became UPI's CFO and second–in–command in 1996 after the company had changed ownership. For 1995, the company reported sales of $65.8 million and was ranked twenty-ninth among the North American pipe producers. Butler had broad industry experience. "I've been in manufacturing all my life and have worked for twenty businesses in twenty different industries," he explained, not without pride. After working in the factory on the shop floor his first management job was foreman. Upon graduating with a bachelor's degree he worked in accounting, and then, after he got his MBA, in a variety of companies and positions climbing through the ranks. In 1996, when Butler joined UPI, he had prior experience as CFO and COO. His diverse back-ground came in handy when he started in his new job because, even though he was the CFO, he "was helping in manufacturing."

At that time, the company's performance was subpar in many respects. Manufacturing efficiency was average at best. It was a command-and-control shop and little was done to train and motivate the labor force or to elicit their ideas for continuous improvement. Butler set out to change this.

UPI sold exclusively through wholesale distributors. Some of them were large with nationwide coverage, while others were regional. UPI's sales territory cov-ered the entire northeastern U.S., some areas west of the Mississippi, and southeastern Canada. It employed three in-house sales managers and about 40 indirect sales rep-resentatives spread over the sales territory. UPI offered price breaks depending on volume, order size, and order frequency, a practice that reflected the industry norm. The company produced PVC pipes ranging from 1.5" to 24" in diameter for the three major applications—underground (water and sewer), above ground (plumb-ing), and electrical conduit. On average, the company received 40 orders a day and each order comprised about five items. These orders were sold through sales reps in different territories who serviced the distributors. Com-petition varied from region to region, which meant that prices differed from one customer to the next and by ter-ritory. Managing such a set-up required substantial at-tention to detail and was fairly complex. One of the few ways pipe manufacturers could differentiate themselves from their rivals was the manner in which they handled customer complaints. Providing good, reliable service and being understanding and helpful even when a com-plaint was not the pipe manufacturer's fault could earn the trust and loyalty of a customer.

MARKET SHARE FIRST

Butler was critical of the mode of competition in the in-dustry and of UPI's strategy, which he believed inflicted pain on all pipe producers:

> When the industry was formed there were a lot of very wealthy people who had high goals set for their businesses based on a system of who was king of the mountain, who had the most sales. . . . So if their volume started to drop off they would cut their prices in order to maintain a certain volume.

This strategy of emphasizing sales above profits was compounded by the ups and downs of resin prices. Explained Butler:

> Resin is a commodity with a certain supply and demand. How do you determine what your [product] price is going to be? If a resin sup-plier raises their price to us by one cent in one month and we do 250 million pounds of pipe a year that basically cost us another $2.5 million a year. And so the tiny fractions of money that we deal with mean that we have to count every fraction of a penny. So a one-penny increase to us is significant. There were times when suppli-ers announced two-cent increases every month for 6 months in a row. . . . One of the unique difficulties in our market is that we have to take the resin and turn it into pipe, and that's a 60 to 90 day process. So the contracts to buy resin would be for a month at a time. We buy resin in January. In February we received that resin and started to make it into pipe. In February/March

we would put that pipe into our inventory and in April we'd sell that pipe out of our inventory. So resin that was priced to us in January actually goes out to the customer in April because we have a 30-day supply in our inventory. So, from the point of purchase to sales you're looking at a 90–120 day period before we can convert resin purchases into sales, which means that a two-cent increase of the price of resin in January converts to 3 months of increased costs before we start to get the revenue back. In terms of mode of payment, everyone is on 30 to 60 day terms. We buy resin on terms of ship date from the Gulf Coast and then deliver at a certain date to our customer, which creates this time lag, which is actually closer to 75–105 days. So if there are 4 consecutive months of cost increases, to us the costs are piling up fairly significantly before our revenues come back and that becomes difficult.

He continued:

So what happens then is that our competitors are going out trying to discount pipe sales at a time when costs are going up in an effort to increase volume quicker. They find themselves easy money. We don't want to do that. So our customers come back to us because nobody can pass these price increases on quickly enough and we end up going back to the resin people and tell them that we're just not going to buy anymore. Our customers won't take the price increases so they stop buying, we stop buying, and the resin people stop selling. So, instead of having six two-cent increases for a total of 12 cents, all of a sudden they're [the pipe manufacturers] backed up to selling for 4 cents less than they were at the beginning [to get rid of their inventory]. It's like bouncing one of these super balls against the floor and when it hits the ceiling it comes back faster than when it went up and the resin makers lose more than they gain.

On September 1, 1999, UPI acquired a plant from North American Pipe Corporation in Jonestown, Georgia. When corporate management disclosed the plan to add capacity via acquisition, UPI's management was concerned, but their objections and request to be included in the on-site visit were ignored. North American Pipe ranked sixth among North American pipe extruders with 1998 sales of $320 million. The Jonestown plant had 75 employees, eight extrusion lines, and a capacity of 100 million pounds. UPI's 1999 annual capacity was 240 million pounds before the acquisition. The purchase was part of UPI's long-term growth strategy of expanding the service territory that Sojitz's management had formulated. With its three plants, UPI now covered the Eastern Seaboard. The Jonestown plant enabled the company to better serve its nearby customers by cutting delivery time and shipping costs. The plant would be overhauled from top to bottom. Storage silos and additional extruder lines would be added to handle the increased production.

Butler reminisced:

We were running fairly well [at the time after I joined the company] except that we had a couple of years we were doing really well, in 1999 and 2000. And then our company's parent, corporate management, decided that the best thing for us was to get bigger. So we bought another business in the South and this turned out to be not a good acquisition. It was too much volume and it was difficult to operate. That company produced a lot of scrap; they had poor factory management. We were trying to raise the skill level of management. But we had excess capacity. We had about 240 million pounds of sales before and after the purchase. We had excess capacity, more cost and they were inefficient in the other location.

The acquisition strategy imploded in early 2002, a few months after 9/11. UPI had signed a contract that promised delivery of 40 million pounds of pipe at very low prices. UPI's management figured it would work out and yield a profit thanks to better capacity utilization. They assumed that the new facility could produce 20 million pounds per month and payment would be received within 4 months. Instead, only two or three of the eight extruder lines could be used and it took more than a year to fulfill the contract, which resulted in a great loss. In July 2003, the Jonestown plant was idled; some distribution operations were kept at the location for a little while longer before they were stopped as well. In the midst of all these problems, the original plan to diversify into vinyl siding was shelved. UPI's management never heard about it again. "I assume the Japanese dropped their plan to make siding when they discovered how diverse that business would be," said Butler.

A NEW STRATEGY—FOR NAUGHT?

In the aftermath of the Jonestown debacle, Butler realized that pursuing market share was a prescription for disaster. Profitability needed to come first, even at the expense of sales. This ran counter to industry practice. Butler recalled a large merger that had occurred in the early 2000s that would have granted the new entity some pricing power, which it could have used to raise prices.

> *But after the acquisition they had all this volume that wasn't selling fast enough, so they were emphasizing volume again. They had an opportunity to control the price in the market; they were so big. But instead of using price they used volume again because that had been their target from the beginning.*

Butler and his lieutenants embarked on what he labeled a "scientific" analysis. UPI had about 3,000 customers. Butler and his team succeeded in breaking down profitability by SKU to determine which products were lucrative and which were not, and by sales rep to learn who was profitable and who was not. Finally, profits were segmented by territory, because each region differed in the level of competition, which affected pricing. Since transportation costs were an important factor—shipping pipes essentially means shipping a lot of air since pipes are hollow—distance mattered. Butler explained:

> *When we looked at freight that was a key. We found out for instance that it'll cost an extra nickel a pound to go across the Mississippi [i.e., to more distant customers] and therefore we brought our territory back in to the east of the Mississippi only. At the time we had some fairly large customers west of the Mississippi. And we realized that we couldn't sell to them anymore and make a profit even though selling to them meant a higher volume.*

Further problems needed to be addressed. In the fourth quarter of 2001, UPI was hemorrhaging cash. Management approached two of UPI's five resin suppliers and told them that UPI would no longer buy from them because their prices were higher by fractions of a cent. These suppliers were subsidiaries of multibillion-dollar companies. The move backfired because the two large suppliers decided to stop selling to UPI, which increased the leverage of the other three suppliers, and they began charging UPI higher prices. To make matters worse, UPI was having difficulties paying its suppliers on a timely basis. "So we owed them an awful lot of money and instead of paying them we went to argue with them that they were taking advantage of us and we shouldn't have to pay them so much money and they didn't really like that," admitted Butler. The difficulties on the supply end impacted deliveries and so customers were unhappy as well.

In March 2003, Butler became CEO when Tagg retired after 10 years at the helm. Little did he know that a year later he was given a difficult order—making himself and everyone else in the company obsolete!

The first task Butler set himself was making amends. He spent months on the road and visited suppliers and customers repeating time and again the same message—that new management was in place, that UPI would honor all contracts, and that he as the new CEO was apologizing for what had happened in the past.

> *When I took over I went back to the vendor with whom we had haggled the year before and said: "We're going to pay you. Whatever we owe you, we're going to pay you. It will take some time. Will you work with us?" And they agreed to work with us. We paid them back everything and they were really pleased with it. They had a very diligent, hard-nosed Japanese gentleman who ran that business.*

Ultimately Butler was able to convince suppliers and customers that he was serious with his creed "to do the right thing—period—whatever that is."

Butler also achieved his second objective: he managed to convince suppliers of the detrimental effects of sudden large price hikes. They understood that it was better for all to have multiple one-cent price increases spread over several months rather than a one-time six-cent jump.

By summer 2003, UPI had closed the Jonestown plant and moved some of the equipment to New York and Tennessee to enhance the two plants' efficiency and boost capacity. The in-depth market analysis that Butler had earlier put together with his team helped to make the decisions to become profitable again. Now they had the data needed to target training, to revamp processes, and to invest in plant and equipment. Earlier, in a break with UPI's long-standing organizational culture, Butler went to the work force and asked for their ideas and support.

He promised to share the benefits of their contributions with them. Now, productivity improvements accelerated. Yet, UPI's owners showed little interest in these initiatives; their attention was fixated on the bottom line, which continued to show a loss.

In fall 2004, Butler learned of corporate management's plan. Butler was convinced that a sale to private equity would mean the end of UPI. Private equity would extract any value possible from the company to pay for the purchase and make a profit. Before long, every one of the people with whom he had worked for the last 8 years and for whom he felt responsible would be fired. The managers would find new jobs, but the fate of many workers was dire given the weak economy in upstate New York, which had experienced an exodus of manufacturing jobs for some time. Butler also knew that UPI's suppliers who were owed millions would suffer, since bankruptcy would allow the new owners to walk out on some of the existing obligations (see Exhibit 7). To him, given the likely consequences for the employees and the suppliers, a leveraged buyout combined with bankruptcy was an immoral proposition.

An alternative would have to be found quickly; the Japanese owners were resolved to dispose of UPI by the end of the year—in less than two months. What were his options? Butler learned from a few discreet phone calls that a direct competitor and two suppliers might be interested in acquiring the company. But at what price and how quickly?

Would not such an acquisition be just as detrimental for the workers? A leveraged buyout and the invariable post-merger streamlining would cause layoffs like the ones UPI had implemented at the Jonestown plant albeit for different reasons.

Since an acquisition also entailed negative consequences, he wondered whether he could buy the company. In recent months, UPI had been performing better. Sooner or later demand would pick up, he told himself. Housing sales and total construction forecasts looked good and mortgage rates were holding steady. Could he do a better job than the companies that had signaled an interest in UPI? Could he secure UPI's profitability on a long-term basis, and thereby keep the employees on UPI's payroll? Assuming that he could gain control of UPI, what should be the strategy going forward? The current one seemed to be working. Could he convince suppliers and customers to keep doing business with UPI given its checkered recent past and the rumor mill overheating?

How could he come up with the requisite funds to buy UPI? He did not have the kind of money required. He had learned from his bosses that the private equity buyer proposed to pay in the neighborhood of $3 million, which was about twice the amount that he might be able to raise. The "private equity sharks," as he labeled them, would not pay upfront, but in installments over 3 years as they proceeded to extract profits from the operations and turn the acquired assets into cash. He was aware that the Sojitz executives were uncomfortable with private equity's 3-year installment plan. But they seemed inclined to accept it because they wanted to offload UPI quickly. Maybe he could make up for a lower offer by paying upfront instead? Would corporate management, given that they were Japanese, be amenable to the argument that their plan would be heavily criticized locally once it became public and possibly embarrass them? Would banks be willing to lend him the money?

Also, such an acquisition was complex, involving many steps. The site was a Superfund site, a plot that the EPA had designated as a high–pollution site requiring a costly cleanup. A change in ownership could not go forward without involving the EPA. Federal agencies were not known for the speed with which they handled transactions. A multitude of appraisals and legal documents would be required that could not be completed without all sorts of lawyers. It was doubtful that these steps could be executed as fast as his superiors demanded, given that they wanted to get out before the end of the year.

Furthermore, he had never been an entrepreneur; this would be a new experience for him. And this at an age when many of his peers were thinking about retirement! If he were to acquire UPI, should he invite his managers and workers to become shareholders as well? No, he decided, he did not want this. He strongly believed in sharing success with all the employees since he knew that their contributions were essential. But he equally strongly felt that their savings should not be put at risk.

As if this uncertainty was not enough, the bank UPI had worked with was less than forthcoming when he laid out his options. It withheld the last $1.5 million of UPI's credit line and would not budge even when Butler presented the most recent quarterly statements showing that the strategy was working. The bank's managers were worried since the market was very competitive and demand was still languishing. UPI's liquidity was very tight; the company had $22 million in debt and the bank's decision closed access to a critical cash reserve in case of an emergency (see Exhibit 6).

Exhibit 6   Financial Statements

Income Statement	1999	2000	2001	2002	2003	2004 Q1	2004 Q2
Sales volume (1,000 lbs.)	239,785	241,221	239,502	230,783	206,734	55,093	54,203
Production volume (1,000 lbs.)	251,772	256,855	244,799	222,458	212,531	45,656	55,752
PVC sale price (avg.)	0.3960	0.5300	0.3800	0.3950	0.4400	0.4433	0.5156
Sale price (std. dev.)	0.057	0.063	0.0025	0.057	0.020	0.014	0.018
PVC resin cost (avg.)	0.2380	0.3535	0.2540	0.2660	0.3170	0.3107	0.3509
PVC resin cost (std. dev.)	0.053	0.024	0.046	0.056	0.021	0.005	0.010
Gross Sales ($000)	95,978	129,713	91,030	90,533	92,522	24,772	28,276
Less Returns & Allowances ($000)	90	846	354	427	466	59	73
Less Customer Discounts ($000)	1,719	2,346	1,637	1,659	1,746	361	511
Net Sales ($000)	94,169	126,521	89,039	88,447	90,310	24,352	27,692
Manufacturing ($000)	73,004	101,076	84,077	77,355	83,984	22,037	22,194
Freight In/Out	5,813	6,269	6,566	6,200	5,911	1,647	1,765
Shipping	1,138	1,431	1,206	1,320	1,338	335	327
Total Manufacturing	79,955	108,776	91,849	84,875	91,233	24,019	24,286
Gross Profit	14,214	17,745	(2,810)	3,572	(923)	333	3,406
General and Administrative	3,257	3,725	3,224	3,482	3,502	882	756
Selling Cost	4,129	5,334	3,497	3,887	3,143	672	722
Total Selling, G & A	7,386	9,059	6,721	7,369	6,645	1,554	1,478
Manufacturing Income	6,828	8,686	(9,531)	(3,797)	(7,568)	(1,221)	1,928
Other Op. Income (Expense)	11	43	–	181	–	–	–
Net Income From Operations	6,839	8,729	(9,531)	(3,616)	(7,568)	(1,221)	1,928
Interest Expense—Term Loans	1,504	1,914	1,834	1,408	1,645	450	527
Interest (Income) Expense	(313)	(428)	(174)	(29)	–	(66)	(62)
Amortization—Other	223	–	1,500	–	3,476	–	9
Net Other (Income) Expense	1,414	1,486	3,160	1,379	5,121	384	474
Net Income Before Incentive	5,425	7,243	(12,691)	(4,995)	(12,689)	(1,605)	1,454

Income Statement	1999	2000	2001	2002	2003	2004 Q1	2004 Q2
Incentive Pay	542	754	–	–	–	–	–
Net Income Before Tax	4,883	6,489	(12,691)	(4,995)	(12,689)	(1,605)	1,454
Income tax	2,032	2,740	(5,315)	(1,934)	(4,139)	(664)	554
Net Income (Loss)	**2,851**	**3,749**	**(7,376)**	**(3,061)**	**(8,550)**	**(941)**	**900**

Balance Sheet ($000)	1999	2000	2001	2002	2003
Assets					
Cash	9,367	5,244	15	443	957
Accounts Receivable—total	16,179	10,901	10,539	8,084	8,064
Inventories—total	14,350	24,023	18,486	25,741	17,378
Prepaid Expenses	97	209	289	336	282
Total Current Assets	39,993	40,377	29,329	34,604	26,681
Fixed Assets	28,755	33,935	36,430	43,163	33,441
Less Depreciation	(4,164)	(6,184)	(8,196)	(10,613)	(8,388)
Fixed Assets—net	24,591	27,751	28,234	32,550	25,053
Other Assets	59	226	2,371	4,483	188
Total Assets	64,643	68,354	59,934	71,637	51,922
Liabilities					
Short Term Debt	676	739	10,743	27,438	14,441
Accounts Payable—total	18,213	17,713	9,872	19,374	33,258
Accrued Liabilities—total	3,587	3,710	2,419	2,088	2,340
Total Current Liabilities	22,476	22,162	23,034	48,900	35,598
Long-Term Debt—net	26,597	26,372	21,769	10,550	23,372
Deferred Income Tax	1,842	2,341	–	–	–
Liabilities—total	50,915	50,875	44,830	59,450	58,970
Common Stock	10,000	10,000	15,000	15,000	15,000
Retained Earnings	3,728	7,479	104	(2,813)	(22,046)
Shareholders' Equity	13,728	17,479	15,104	12,187	(7,046)
Total Liabilities & Equity	64,643	68,354	59,934	71,637	51,924

Source: Company records.

The issue that kept bothering him the most was allowing the company to enter into bankruptcy coupled with a reorganization and private equity as owners. How could he let this happen, he wondered, since throughout his life he had tried "to do the right thing—period—whatever that is?"

Exhibit 7	Private Equity Buyouts

The purchase of a company by a privately owned company is called a private equity acquisition. The most common form is a leveraged buyout in which the purchasing company takes control by using the acquired company's assets as collateral to raise the capital for the acquisition. Often, the target company is ailing and new management is put in place to improve the company's performance, a process that may involve selling off parts of the company, liquidating assets, and putting new incentives in place to enhance productivity.

A large scale study by Lerner and Gurung (2008) of more than 20,000 private equity transactions over a 27-year-period in multiple countries showed that, overall, leveraged buyouts in their many forms had positive effects: Firms that underwent buyouts tended to become more innovative. Employment initially declined in the wake of buyouts, but in the post-buyout phase grew at levels comparable to similar firms.

Private equity buyouts have gained a bad reputation due to the massive restructuring and associated reductions of the workforce that often accompanies such an acquisition. Investors tend to be most concerned with the purchase price and the debt that will be realized in conjunction with the acquisition. This often compels the private equity firm to make the purchased firm file for bankruptcy. Bankruptcy allows the new owners to relieve some of the financial pressure. Essentially, by filing for bankruptcy, the firm can reduce the inherited debt owed to creditors and suppliers or even eliminate it.

In a small percentage of private equity buyouts, the private equity firms have shown no interest in fixing the acquired company. Instead, a company is bought only to be sold for a higher profit as quickly as possible, a practice called a quick flip. The acquirer chooses to disband the firm and sell off the assets piece–by–piece in order to maximize profits. In such a situation, all employees of the acquired firm will be out of work, with a related impact on the local economy.

U.S. law distinguishes between two types of corporate bankruptcies. A Chapter 7 bankruptcy entails liquidation of the business. A trustee is appointed by the courts who collects and sells all nonexempt assets of the debtor and distributes the proceeds to the creditors and the business ceases to exist. Creditors are grouped into secured creditors that get paid off first because their loan is based on the value of a specific asset (e.g., bank loans) followed by the unsecured creditors, which are divided into unsecured priority creditors and general unsecured creditors (e.g., bondholders)

A Chapter 11 bankruptcy provides the company in difficulty with an opportunity to reorganize itself and re-emerge on a more solid foundation. It involves developing a reorganization (turnaround) plan that has to be approved by the creditors. Just like Chapter 7, the reorganization bankruptcy also requires the appointment of a trustee and the involvement of the courts. Sometimes a Chapter 11 bankruptcy is followed by a Chapter 7 liquidation.

A third option is an out–of–court settlement to which all creditors have to agree. A contract is drawn up between the company and its creditors that specifies at what rate each creditor will be paid off. This contract is part of a retrenchment/turnaround plan.

Sources: Lerner, J., and A. Gurung. 2008. The global economic impact of private equity report. World Economic Forum.Pearce II, J. A., and S. A. DiLullo. 1998. When a strategic plan includes bankruptcy. *Business Horizons.* September–October, 67–73.

NOTES

1. "How the PVC Pipe Has Changed the World." *Article Base* (May 20, 2008). Acessed May 28, 2009, at http://www.articlesbase.com/home–improvement–articles/howthe–pvc–pipe–has–changed–the–world–420237.html

2. Shah Rahman, "PVC Pipe and Pipe Fittings: Underground Solutions for Water and Sewer Systems in North America." Paper presented at the 2nd Brazilian PVC Congress, Sao Paulo, Brazil (June 19–20, 2007). Accessed June 6, 2009, at http://www.institutodopvc.org/congresso2/Shah-Rahman.pdf.

3. Ibid.

4. Ibid.

5. "World Plastic Pipe Market," *Freedonia* (November 2008). Accessed May 27, 2009, at http://www.reportlinker.com/p099485/World-Plastic-Pipe-Market.html.

6. "Vinyl Siding Cost Analysis Sheet," *Siding4U.com.* Accessed April 21, 2010, at http://www.siding4u.com/vinyl-siding-cost-analysis.php.

Case 22

Principled Entrepreneurship and Shared Leadership: The Case of TEOCO (The Employee Owned Company)*

Prof. Thomas Calo, Prof. Olivier Roche, Prof. Frank Shipper
Perdue School of Business Salisbury University Salisbury

INTRODUCTION

Fairfax, October 6, 2009. Atul Jain, founder of TEOCO, a provider of specialized software for the telecommunications industry, had been meeting all day to finalize a partnership agreement with TA Associates, a private equity firm. For Atul, the pace of activities had been relentless on this special day.[1] By all accounts, the last 12 hours had been hectic but the closing of the transaction was a success. The event had started with back-to-back meetings between TEOCO's senior management and their new partner's representatives and had culminated with the usual press conference to mark the occasion. The senior management teams of both organizations announced to the business community that TA Associates [TA] had made a minority equity investment of $60 million in TEOCO. It was indeed a memorable day, the culmination of intense and uneven negotiations between two organizations that did not have much in common except for deep industry knowledge and a shared interest in seeing TEOCO succeed.

This new partnership marked the end of a marathon, but Atul did not feel the excitement that usually comes with crossing the finish line. It was late and he was tired. Back in the quiet of his office, he reviewed, once again, the draft of the press release relating the day's event. As he read the various statements captured from the meetings, he still had the uneasy feeling that comes with making life-changing decisions when one does not have all the required information. There were so many unknowns. Partnering with the right investor, like many

other entrepreneurial endeavors, was not a decision made in a vacuum. It was all about good timing, cold analysis, gut feeling and luck; the latter was last but by no means least. Despite all the uncertainty, Atul felt that this was a worthy endeavor.

Atul had come a long way since his humble beginnings in India and a lot was at stake, not only for him but also for the 300 employees of the company. The TEOCO enterprise had been a successful business endeavor and at the same time a very personal journey. What had begun as a result of frustration with his old job in Silicon Valley 15 years ago had become one of the fastest growing businesses in the telecom software industry; and the fast pace of the company's development had not gone unnoticed. For quite some time now, TEOCO had been on the "radar screen" of investors looking for high-growth opportunities. However, Atul had never cultivated a relationship with potential external investors; he had remained congruous with his long-held business beliefs that an alliance with external financiers was rarely in the best interest of a company and its employees.

> Atul [CEO & Chairman]: "I am often asked why we didn't approach an investor for money or seek venture capital. I have two answers to this question. My first answer is: that's not our way of

*The authors would like to thank the employee owners of TEOCO who graciously shared their knowledge, experiences and perspectives about the company. Their viewpoints were invaluable in ensuring that this case provides a true representation of the culture and practices of the company.

doing business. I believe that every entrepreneur must aspire to be debt-free and profitable from the very first day. My second answer is: nobody would have given me the money even if I had asked! I also had a fear – that external investment might impact the culture and values that I wanted TEOCO to promote and cherish. I wanted to steer the TEOCO ship along a very different course. My dream was to set up an enterprise based on a model of shared success. TEOCO's success wouldn't just be my success; it would be our success. TEOCO wouldn't just have one owner; it would be owned by each of its employees – who would therefore be called employee owners."

But several months earlier, events had taken an unexpected turn; unsolicited financiers approached TEOCO once again, this time offering to invest a substantial amount of capital. Still, Atul was reluctant to engage in negotiations with a party that, as far as he knew, did not share TEOCO's values.

Atul: "[In the early days]we took a conscious decision not to accept venture capital. I have always had a healthy disdain for venture capital because it numbs the entrepreneur's competitive edge and enfeebles him. I still remember TEOCO's early battles with [competitors] Vibrant and Broadmargin and how difficult it was for us to compete with all that extra money flowing into the rival's coffers. But we took the hard road – and survived. . . . What, then, went wrong with Broadmargin or Vibrant? If I have to over-simplify, I'd say that both were done in by venture capital. VC is an impatient master; it forces you to always go for the home run, and always push hard on the gas. With certain kinds of businesses this works; indeed, it might be the only way. Think of Google: their business space is so vast that only continuous and unbridled growth can sustain the venture. But TEOCO's space is very different; there is no exponential growth here that everyone can go chasing . . . I would guess that the size of the telecom Cost Management business is no larger than $100 million per year; so to survive you have to be patient and play your cards carefully. This isn't the place to be if you are in a tearing hurry to grow. . . . While this strategy of focusing on niche markets significantly limits our market potential, it does keep the sharks away. The big companies *are not bothered by niche products for telecom carriers; they don't want to swim in small ponds."*

Atul's comment reflected the situation a few years ago; TA's recent partnership offer was made in a new context. In this rapidly changing industry, there are constantly new directions in technology and the landscape continually shifts. The industry, consolidating quickly, required that in order to remain a viable player, TEOCO would have to change gears—sooner rather than later.

Until now, the primary focus of the company had been on the North American telecom carriers. However, with the anticipated consolidation of the telecom industry in North America, TEOCO needed to focus on international expansion. In addition, to leverage TEOCO's deep expertise in cost, revenue and routing, the company would soon need to fish "outside the pond" and enter the global business support system/operations support system (BSS/OSS) market. Here, TEOCO could find itself in competition with much larger players and it would be valuable to have a strong financial partner.

Indeed, the company had reached an important threshold in its organizational development. But if TEOCO was at a crossroads, so was its founder. Atul was in his late forties and he was not getting any younger. In this industry Atul had known many entrepreneurs who, like himself, had rapidly grown their businesses only to find out that "you are only as good as your last call." For a few of these entrepreneurs, one or two poor decisions had triggered a descent that had been as swift as their earlier ascent and they ended up with very little to show for their efforts. These were the intangibles. During rare moments of quiet reflection, Atul realized that his "risk return profile" had changed imperceptibly over time. Having all his eggs in the same basket and going for all or nothing had been fun in his mid-thirties when everything was possible, but it would be much less so in his early fifties when starting from scratch would be a very unappealing scenario for Atul and his family. Furthermore, he felt an obligation to create liquidity for the employees who had supported him on this 15-year journey and had their own dreams and goals. At the end of the day, any business has only three exit options: it could get listed, be sold or go bankrupt! And the latter option is not particularly appealing.

It was in this context and mindset that he had agreed to listen to what TA Associates had to offer. Founded in 1968, TA had become one of the largest private equity firms in the country. The company was managing more than $16 billion in capital by 2009 and it had an extensive knowledge of the industry. Atul was impressed by TA's approach, its willingness to take a minority position, and Kevin Landry, Chairman and the "spirit" of TA. This private equity firm not only managed capital; it also had impressive network of relationships. In addition, TA executives had been adamant that Atul remain in charge, and he was keen on continuing as the controlling shareholder. The fund would appoint two board members [see Appendix 1] but TEOCO's current management team would still lead the company as they had in the past.

Reviewing the details, Atul could not spot any flaws in the logic of the transaction. It was neither a marriage of love nor a "shotgun wedding," just a pragmatic alliance between two companies with complementary skills and resources at a time when such alliance was valuable to both parties: TA looking for a good investment and TEOCO shareholders looking for partial liquidity. As Atul reread the press release and a few of his quotes, he reflected that he meant every word.

> Atul: "We are pleased to welcome TA as our first institutional investor. As a company that has avoided external capital for 15 years, we are delighted to find a partner that will strengthen TEOCO without changing the culture of our organization. We see this as the beginning of a new phase in TEOCO's history where we look to add even greater value to communications service providers worldwide."

This was definitely a new era and there would be no turning back. For better or for worse, this partnership had to work. Atul made minor corrections to the wording of the document and authorized its release.

COMPANY BACKGROUND AND ACTIVITIES

TEOCO's predecessor, Strategic Technology Group (STG), was founded as an S corporation in 1994. The company's initial focus was to provide high quality consultancy for IT projects. STG's first clients included Mobil, Siemens, Cable & Wireless, SRA, TRW and Freddie Mac. The company started operations in April 1995 and 3 years later, in March 1998, the company name was changed to TEOCO (The Employee-Owned Company). At the same time, TEOCO made the strategic decision to

shift its business from consultancy to product development and to focus on the telecommunications industry. This was achieved through the acquisition of a fledgling software product that processed invoices of telecom payables. BillTrak Pro would ultimately become TEOCO's best-selling network cost management software.

Subsequently, the company grew rapidly. As the number of employees exceeded 75, the maximum numbers of shareholders an S corporation can have, the company changed its status to a C corporation to enable a broad-based employee ownership. Over the years preceding the burst of the "Dot.com" bubble, TEOCO not only expanded its client base for its basic products but also invested substantial amounts of capital in three startups. These entities were: *netgenShopper.com* for online auctions; *Eventrix,* an event planning portal; and *AppreciateYou.com* to support employee retention. These internet startups functioned as separate entities, each at their own location, with their own business goals and core values, managed by different entrepreneurs/managers; at the same time, they each relied on TEOCO's cash flow for their development.

Ultimately, none of these ventures emerged as viable businesses and this left TEOCO in a difficult financial situation. As a result, TEOCO registered its first year of losses in 2000.

> Atul: "This failure was devastating, but also a humbling experience. I learned the hard way that no entrepreneur can survive inside a technology incubator. We had to pay a price for all these transgressions . . . Our revenues were still impressive, but the money in the bank was dwindling rapidly . . . We were truly caught in deep and dangerous waters. I have often wondered what went wrong. It wasn't as if we made one big mistake. . . . I guess we just took our eyes off the ball. Somewhere along the way, we lost our focus; we tried to do too many things at the same time and ended up getting nothing right. We had to quickly get back to our knitting. The question was: how?"

Under Atul's leadership, TEOCO made the judicious decision to refocus its activities on its core industry expertise and its largest clients. To achieve this, the organization solidified its position in the telecom sector by improving its services and developing new products. In 2004, research and development efforts resulted in the patented XTrak technology which today represents the core of the company's invoice automation solution.

In addition, TEOCO was able to migrate from software licensing to the far more lucrative software-as-a-service model. Instead of a fixed licensing fee, the company charged a recurring monthly fee based on the volume of data processed for each client. As the recurring revenue model took hold, it became much easier to grow revenues from year to year and improve company's profitability.

In 2006, TEOCO acquired Vibrant Solutions, bringing in cost management and business intelligence assets with its 24 employees. Ultimately this resulted in the important development of TEOCO's SONAR solution for cost, revenue and customer analytics. Finally, in 2008, Vero systems was acquired, adding routing management and its 36 employees to the repertoire of communication service provider solutions.

This stream of acquisitions and internal development left TEOCO with a staff of about 300 employees and a portfolio of three major activities: cost management, least cost routing and revenue assurance.

Cost Management

Cost management solutions include invoice automation and payable processing. Powered by XTrak, TEOCO's invoice automation solution processes over 1,000,000 invoices annually. This facilitates the audit and analysis of billions of dollars in current billings due to each telecom company. While the usual scanning of paper bills relies on optical character recognition technologies that routinely require hands-on intervention to correct misrepresented characters on complex invoices, the XTrak technology mines the original formats which produced the paper to create files for loading into cost management solutions. By eliminating the tedious, costly and error-prone task of manual invoice data entry, telecom companies increase productivity and reduce costs by increasing the number of disputes filed and resolved and by reducing late-payment charges. In addition, TEOCO also processes "payables" on behalf of clients by managing the full lifecycle of invoice payment, including account coding, management review, and payment reconciliation. TEOCO's employees audit client invoices, comparing rates, inventory and usage with other source data to identify and recover additional savings. Finally, the company manages disputed claims on behalf of its clients from creation through resolution. TEOCO has the technical capability to capture all correspondence between parties and can review and track every claim to resolution.

With regard to cost management, it is worth noting that the Sarbanes-Oxley Act of 2002 requires every listed company to implement a reliable reporting system. TEOCO's services support this compliance by improving the details and timeliness of the reports generated by/for telecom companies. TEOCO's rapid development in this area coincided with a market need that was augmented by the legal requirements imposed by the Act.

Least Cost Routing

TEOCO's routing solutions help telecom companies determine the optimal route between two customers with regard to cost, quality of service and margin targets. Capable of supporting multiple services and various networks, the company is able to monitor CDRs (Call Detail Records) in near real time to identify bottlenecks, reroute traffic and improve the quality of services for greater satisfaction of its clients' customers.

Revenue Assurance

Communications service providers can lose 5 to 15% of gross revenue due to revenue leakage. TEOCO's SONAR solution is an industry first in supporting switch-to-bill reconciliation. TEOCO combines its specialized industry expertise with high-capacity data warehouse appliances to create a unified CDR and makes a high volume of current and historical CDR data available on a single platform for in-depth analysis. This helps telecom companies uncover billing discrepancies, detect fraudulent behavior, reveal usage patterns, understand customer profitability, conduct margin analysis, and determine the financial viability of reciprocal compensation agreements.

INDUSTRY LANDSCAPE: CONTINUOUS CHANGE

Competitors

TEOCO operates in a fragmented and highly competitive industry. Appendix 2 lists its competitors in each of the three major business segments. TEOCO operates mostly in North America; therefore, the main competitors in the cost management segment are Razorsight, Connectiv and Subex. These same companies compete for revenue assurance, as well as others such as cVidya and Wedo. Finally, in the least cost routing segment, TEOCO faces a different set of competitors: Pulse Networks, Global Convergence Solutions and Telarix.

> Brian [Marketing & Communications Department]: "So [from the customer's point of view] what we bring to the table is just end-to-end solutions that reach all of these different categories. While we still compete with certain people, it's on a specific product; not across the board."

Indeed, with the possible exception of Subex, none of the above competitors operate in the same three business segments as TEOCO; and Subex does not provide a domestic least cost routing in North America. Since TEOCO derives 50% of its revenue from cost management and 25% from revenue assurance, Razorsight and Subex could be considered TEOCO's main business competitors. Faye summarizes TEOCO's current market position.

> Faye [General Manager/Account Management]: "...In North America, we dominate the cost management space. We've got a decent lock on least cost routing, which is a very operational and technical function that bridges between network and finance."

One of the ways TEOCO differs from most of its VC backed competitors is its focus on internal cost management. This manifests itself in two different ways. The management begins the year by making a conservative revenue plan for the year. The company then manages its expenses to be a fixed percentage of the projected revenues. Investments in Sales, Marketing, and R&D are adjusted throughout the year to ensure that expenses stay within the pre defined limits. The second way cost management manifests itself is how the cost of each individual transaction is closely managed and monitored whether it be purchasing hardware, leasing office space, renewing supplier contracts, recruiting new employees, or planning business travel.

One of the consequences of this strong discipline of cost management is that TEOCO is consistently profitable, something most of its competitors struggle to accomplish. This enables the company to focus its energy on clients and innovation.

Clients

TEOCO operates in an industry where clients are known and clearly identifiable. One of the key reasons clients buy from TEOCO is because its solutions have a strong ROI (Return on Investment). In other words, TEOCO's products quickly pay for themselves and then begin to generate profits for the companies that subscribe to them.

> Faye: "The telecommunication space is who we sell to exclusively, and within that space, we have a relatively known and discreet customer list or target list, if you will. We don't sell cookies. Not everybody's going to buy what we're selling . . . I know who those customers are and I can identify groups within that addressable market that fall into natural tiers. So either because of their size or because of the market that they cater to, themselves, whether they're wireless or wire line or whether they're cable companies, I can identify who they are and then try to focus products and services that I think will best meet their needs."

There are four telecom companies that drive about 65% of TEOCO's domestic revenue: Verizon, Sprint, AT&T and Qwest; these are the "platinum" accounts. For obvious reasons, they get a lot of attention from both the engineering and product delivery standpoints. Thirty-five other companies, including Cricket, Global Crossing, Metro PCS, Level 3, and Bell Canada, account for the remaining balance of revenues.

TEOCO, like most of its competitors, is client-centered. Smooth customer interactions are not only critical to increase sales and garner new relationships but also to develop new products. Over the years, most of the ideas for new products or improvements to existing products have come out of discussions with customers.

> Hillary [Marketing & Communications Department]: "Our number one avenue for receiving customer feedback is our TEOCO summit, our annual user meeting . . . where customers are able to talk one-on-one with not only TEOCO representatives but also with other customers to learn what they are doing . . . and then circling back with TEOCO."

Initially, TEOCO used its generic products, either developed in-house or brought in via acquisitions, to start relationships with new clients. More recently, however, the company has innovated solutions driven by specific clients. These, in turn, are adjusted to suit the needs of other clients. Dave describes this "evolutionary loop."

> Dave [Software Architect]: "With our first product [BillTrak Pro], we sold it to a number of different carriers resulting in a broad footprint of wireline and wireless carriers. Then we had

account managers engage with our customers, and it's through conversations with our existing customers, generally, that the ideas for the next set of products come out . . . More recently, I'd say that most of our products are customer-driven, so what will happen is we'll have someone in the company that will identify a need at a specific customer. Then, we'll enter into some kind of partnership with them, whether we'll develop the application specifically to their needs and then work to resell that and make it useful to other customers as well."

GROWTH STRATEGIES

TEOCO's Product Strategy: "Spidering" through Clients' Organizations

Since the number of clients is limited, two other ways to grow the business are cultivated. A company like TEOCO can either "productize" its current services or acquire a competitor with a different client base and cross-sell its products.

Faye: ". . .But for the products we're selling, if we have two new sales a year, that's significant . . . maybe you could squeak out a third in a good year. So the majority of the sales growth really comes from existing accounts . . . most of the growth though is coming from those large platinum accounts. Those are the ones that have money to spend and where we're driving products, driving solutions, trying to help them tell us or help them identify where they have needs. The other way to grow the business is to acquire companies that have a different business and then cross-sell services. For instance, with the Vero acquisition, we added another 'vertical' line of business [least cost routing . . . And then Vero had a relatively separate client base . . . so we were able to cross-sell products into each other's companies' portfolio of clients [i.e., TEOCO's clients buying least cost routing services and Vero's clients buying cost management products]."

Faye joined the company in March 2010, a few months after the TA's investment in TEOCO with a charter to grow TEOCO's revenues with its smaller customers.

With Faye in position, the company became more market-driven and far more aggressive in cross-selling its services and products among the three main lines of business. As well, it adopted a more cohesive approach to expand the client base, including leveraging its reputation for excellence and for having the technical ability to solve problems across various business segments.

Faye : "We're 'spidering' through [our clients'] organizations. With each additional organization that we enter into, the stickier we become. Our software products run the gamut from mission critical to nice-to-have. And the more mission criticals and nice-to-haves we get, the stickier we are in that organization, in all the organizations. . . . [For instance] . . . I'm not going outside AT&T, but I have – instead of two customers at AT&T, I now have ten. And they're distinctly different sales each time."

TEOCO's Acquisition Strategy

For the first 10 years of TEOCO's existence, Atul had built the business based on the premise that growth had to be organic and financed through internal cash flow. To some extent, his views on acquisition were consistent with his opinions about external financing from VCs and private funds. For Atul, acquisition and growth financed by external funds represented a risky development strategy that could dilute a company's culture.

However, as noted earlier, internal growth through innovation had been slow and limited in scope. Cross-selling products between vertical lines of business coming from acquired companies with a different client base offered far more potential for the organization's growth. Therefore, it was just a matter of time before TEOCO would decide to "experiment" with acquisitions:

Atul: "When we started building TEOCO, I was very focused on organic growth. I felt that acquisitions tend to dilute culture and values. But then we happened to acquire a company called Vibrant Solutions (in 2006) and that acquisition went so phenomenally well, it gave us a lot of encouragement. The people were great, the product was solid and the client relationships were very valuable. They integrated well into our company and into our culture. We felt it made TEOCO a much stronger company. We had just broadened from cost management into revenue management before we acquired Vibrant, but I don't believe we would have been as successful in delivering on that without the expertise of the people that came from that acquisition."[2]

The subsequent acquisition of Vero in 2008 brought TEOCO closer to the network and strengthened its position in the market place, particularly with the larger customers. This reinforced TEOCO's belief that acquisition of carefully selected targets should be a key component of its overall growth strategy.

Atul: "So at the end of that I said to myself maybe my narrow-minded thinking about acquisition diluting the culture was wrong, that in fact, if you do it right, you have an opportunity to strengthen the culture."[3]

From these two positive experiences, Atul established guidelines for the kinds of companies to target when scanning the market for future acquisitions. TEOCO would look for companies that:

Had people with deep industry expertise;
Offered solutions/products that the marketplace valued;
Had a solid customer base that had been established over time;
Offered potential synergies with current products/services offered by TEOCO;
Had not been able to develop their full potential due to poor management;
Had a manageable size to facilitate their integration into TEOCO's current businesses.

Atul: "One thing you will see in the companies we acquire is that before the acquisition those companies were not running that smoothly. If they were, perhaps they wouldn't be up for sale or be affordable. We tend to acquire companies that present a challenge but also an opportunity for us to improve the business and make it much stronger and more valuable."[4]

What enabled TEOCO to successfully integrate Vibrant and Vero into its business? TEOCO brought to the table: (1) a solid core business that generated a positive and stable cash flow; (2) a well-established strength in cost management (not only for its clients but also for itself); and (3) a disciplined approach to the management of human resources. Indeed, TEOCO is conservatively managed and Atul is recognized by employees for his

ability to select and retain the best while optimizing the use of the organization's human resources. TEOCO core strengths, when applied to the business of Vibrant and Vero, resulted in a bigger and better company.

TTI Acquisition Rationale: Going Global and Getting "Closer to the Network"

In December 2009, TEOCO began to consider the acquisition of the company that would become in 2010 its biggest acquisition ever—TTI Telecom. TTI was an Israel-based global supplier of service assurance solutions to communications service providers. The company had 300 employees and was listed on NASDAQ (TTIL). Through this acquisition, TEOCO would gain access to wide array of intellectual property including a Mediation Platform, Fault Management and Performance Management Systems, and valuable expertise in 4G and data-centric networks. Service assurance is important in a data environment because it reduces jitter and packet loss during the delivery of high value data transfer. To some extent, TEOCO's existing portfolio of services and products would expand on TTI's well-recognized expertise in the next generation network (i.e., 4G). In addition, TTI had an international client base that offered the potential to cross-sell TEOCO's existing product lines. On August 2010, TEOCO completed the acquisition, thus taking a big step in a new direction which, as of this writing, has yet to show conclusive results, but is considered a positive move.

Atul (at the time of the TTI acquisition): "Our last acquisition was Vero Systems (in October, 2008) and that brought us one step closer to the network. We were doing least cost routing and in that world you are trying to help determine how to terminate calls in the most cost-effective manner. The Vero solution got us working with network players and got us into the switches. It became clear that the closer we got to the network, the better business value we could create. So we started looking for companies that have intellectual property and an international client base that would bring us even closer to the network. TTI [Telecom] really fit that bill for us. TEOCO has traditionally been focused on North America so we thought acquiring a company with an international client base was of value *to us. Their solutions in fault management, performance management and service management all bring us closer to network and assuring Quality of Service. We are good at handling large volumes of data and deriving intelligence out of that data. And we convert that intelligence into business value. A lot of people can derive intelligence from data but they aren't able to create actionable intelligence that creates bottom line value. We think we will be able to improve the economics of the data TTI collects for our customers. It may be a little into the future, but we believe this acquisition positions us to get to that future."*[5]

TTI Acquisition Challenges

From a technical and marketing point of view, the acquisition of TTI represented a very logical move that would allow TEOCO to expand its business while remaining focused on telecom carriers. It fit many of the acquisition criteria that Atul had laid out (see prior section), but it also represented a substantial departure from previous acquisitions in three critical aspects: its size, its location and culture, and the means of its acquisition.

1. The Size of the Target Company. In terms of revenues, TTI was four to five times larger than the last acquisition made by TEOCO and this purchase effectively doubled the size of the organization. On that point, Atul was the first to recognize that TEOCO was entering uncharted territories.

Atul: "All the other acquisitions were small. We bought a company with 24 employees, we bought a company with 36 employees, and this time we bought a company with 300 plus employees. So, this is going to present a completely different challenge and I don't know what that is going to be because I haven't dealt with it. So, it's yet to come."

From the outset, and unlike prior acquisitions, TTI remained an entity that was managed separately. Therefore, one of the key issues to be addressed in the short to medium term would be the degree of integration between the two companies.

2. The Location and Culture of the Target Company. TEOCO had essentially been operating in the US, whereas TTI was located in Israel and was far more international in its operations. This created tremendous opportunities for marketing synergies and for cross-selling products to a different client base.

Faye: "So I see leveraging a lot of the existing sales and marketing resources in Israel. I mean they have a strong presence in Israel, but they're really European. EMEA is big. But also CIS, they do a lot in Russia. . . . MTS is one of their customers, which is just a huge, huge Russian company. Internationally, it's a brand new client base into which we can cross-sell the least cost routing and probably not the cost management products because they don't translate outside of North America as well. But certainly the least cost routing products. Taking their products into the North American base is definitively something we can do. And as far as clients' crossover versus new, they have about ten North American customers, only four of whom are existing customers of ours."

At the same time, however, it also exposed TEOCO's business to a pool of larger competitors that competed on a global basis. TTI was "swimming in a different pond" in which blue chip companies with well-recognized brands and deep pockets were aggressively marketing their services.

Faye: "We participate in a handful of shows, and again, that's expanding quite a bit this year because of the international presence and customer base . . . it's further complicated, though, by this acquisition of TTI because . . . they are a very sales and marketing-centric company, and it's going to be interesting to see how the cultures meld. . . . I see a lot of Advil for me between now and then. We're going to have to get there. Traditionally, TTI has gone to a lot of shows and they like to build brand new booths and spend hundreds of thousands of dollars for each of these shows on their presence there, and [at TEOCO] we don't do that."

Indeed, TEOCO's management was cost conscious and not prepared to invest heavily in shows and other marketing activities where Return on Investment (ROI) is difficult to measure. It was not evident how the two cultures would merge. TTI management might argue that substantial resources would be needed to compete in their market segment while TEOCO's management would probably take the position that overspending on marketing and poor cash-flow management were the reasons for TTI's financial problems prior to its acquisition.

3. The Means of Acquisition. One cannot understand the acquisition of TTI without first understanding how the alliance with TA changed the company's and CEO's ways of doing business, as well as their risk/return profile. To some extent TA gave TEOCO's management both the means and the incentives to take more risks. TA's involvement provided TEOCO with the credentials to approach financial institutions and increase the company's financial leverage to acquire a large target. It is one thing when a US$50 million company approaches a bank to finance the acquisition of another company of equivalent size. It is quite another when a US$16 billion equity firm with a substantial stake in the acquirer approves the transaction at the board level. Following TA's equity participation, no one ever asked TEOCO if they had the means to acquire TTI and complete the transaction. The legitimacy provided by TA's participation was essential for the financing of the acquisition of a listed company where time is of the essence.

> Avi Goldstein [CFO]: ". . . Before TA came on board, taking debt was something that was not on the table. And when TA came on board and they asked us, 'Are you willing to take debt to finance acquisitions?' and we said, 'Yes' . . . And maybe without TA we wouldn't go after TTI because of the debt, not so much because of the size of TTI."

While providing the means to be more aggressive in TEOCO's growth strategy, the partnership with TA also reduced Atul's aversion to risk. It was the TA "push-and-pull" strategy (i.e., providing the financial means while reducing the acceptable risk threshold) that allowed this transaction to materialize.

> Atul: "I haven't fully understood how the TA transaction has changed us. I think, over time, I will understand how it has changed us. All I can tell you is that I feel a degree of financial independence and I personally feel that it is more important for me to focus on making a greater difference for the world. I don't know that I could have supported this acquisition if I hadn't gotten liquidity because this acquisition had a much higher risk profile."

COMPANY CULTURE AND PHILOSOPHY

The background and evolution of TEOCO provide the context for exploring the unique way in which the organization functions, which in turn explains the basis for its success. Three different lenses provide the focus for this understanding: shared leadership; a culture of employee ownership; and human resources as a strategic function. These three characteristics have combined to contribute to TEOCO's success, as well as its competitive advantage.

Shared Leadership

The shared leadership team is comprised of three leaders of the organization with distinctly different, but complementary, skills and responsibilities. These leaders are Atul Jain (Chairman and CEO), Philip M. Giuntini (Vice Chairman and President) and John Devolites (Vice President and General Manager). [See Appendix 3]

Atul is the central figure in the story of TEOCO. By understanding Atul's background, philosophy of life, vision and style, the organization and its unique culture create a cohesive portrait.

Atul was born in India in the early 60's. He has an older sister and an older brother. His father was a mid-level civil servant in India, now retired. Both of his parents live with him and his family, which is customary in Indian culture. Atul is married and has three children. His intellect and abilities were identified at an early age. When he was a teenager, he was invited to attend the prestigious Indian Statistical Institute, known as one of the best schools in India for the study of statistics, which required that the young Atul move away from home to live in another part of the country.

Atul was raised in the Indian religion of Jainism, an important aspect of his background that shaped his view of people and organizations. While he does not wear his religion "on his sleeve," it is evident that his religious beliefs and upbringing have had a significant impact on his leadership style and the culture he has shaped within TEOCO. Atul does not go to temple and does not even pray, so in that sense he does not consider himself to be a religious person. On the other hand, he expressed that he has internalized the culture and religion and that it manifests in his thinking about business. Jainism is an ancient but minority religion in India,[6] yet its influence far exceeds its size, as Jains represent some of the wealthiest Indians. Among its core beliefs are a philosophy of nonviolence towards all living things, vegetarianism, a strong belief in self-help and self-support, and a continual striving towards the liberation of the soul. These tenets can be seen in Atul as he believes that everyone is an "independent soul," and that consequently he "can't make you do anything that you don't want to do." What stands out is that this type of thinking is very uncharacteristic for a leader.

> Atul: "As a CEO of the company, I understand that I have no control over anybody. I can't get anybody to do anything . . . so I don't spend my time trying to control people . . . what I try to do is to conduct myself in a manner that may encourage people to work in a certain way. I can try to create an environment that is encouraging; an environment in which people wish to excel."

When he came to the United States it was not to be an entrepreneur but to study for a doctorate degree in Probability and Statistics. He describes himself as an "accidental entrepreneur." A disillusioning experience working for a Silicon Valley firm led him to reconsider his options. When commitments regarding future assignments and compensation were not honored, and he felt disrespected by the company's CFO, he became motivated to take the risk to establish his own company to prove that "you don't have to be an *&%$# in order to succeed in business". At the same time, this experience impressed upon him the importance of treating his future colleagues with fairness and respect.

Atul's personal leadership style, which is reflected by the organization, overall, is quite atypical, especially for an entrepreneur. Atul openly admits his shortcomings. While manifesting many of the traits of an entrepreneur, he sets himself apart by claiming that one of his greatest strengths is that he knows what he does not know. In fact, he even says "I know that I don't know how to run a business." In conjunction with his perceived shortcomings, he also believed that you create joy at work by sharing the decision making with others in the organization. The end result was his desire to establish a structure of shared leadership within TEOCO. He demonstrated this by establishing a "Steering Committee" of the senior employees within one year of the existence of the company, much prior to his association with Philip and John.

While there has been much discussion in the management literature on the potential value of shared leadership, few organizations have attempted it, and even fewer have utilized it successfully. In many respects, the notion of shared leadership is quite contrary to traditional beliefs about leadership in US organizations, which have strongly followed the military model of command and control. Atul's personal background and beliefs, coupled with a unique confluence of circumstances, have made shared leadership a major factor contributing to the success of TEOCO.

To understand why shared leadership at TEOCO was both possible and successful requires an understanding of the unique combination of personalities, leadership strengths and styles, along with the career and life circumstances—not only of Atul, the founder and CEO, but also the other two members of the leadership team; Philip, President; and John, General Manager.

Philip was a very successful, retired executive. Atul read an article in the *Washington Post* in September, 1998, that profiled Philip's retirement from American Management Systems (AMS) after 28 years. He contacted Philip, established a relationship with him, and eventually persuaded him to become a member of TEOCO's Board of Advisors. Within a year, Philip agreed to come out of retirement to serve as the Vice Chairman and President.

John followed a path similar to Philip's. He served as President of Professional Services for Telecordia. His earlier career experiences included executive positions at PriceWaterhouseCoopers, American Management Systems (AMS), and Booz Allen Hamilton. He became a member of the board in 2000, and in February 2004 he joined the company as a senior executive. In January 2005, he assumed the role of General Manager of its Telecom Business unit.

Personalities In contrast with these two veteran executives, Atul was an entrepreneur with little or no experience in running a sizable business. However, he was a leader with a vision, strong intellect and a passion to build a successful company. In explaining why shared leadership works at TEOCO when it has not worked at many other organizations, Atul says that "I recognize that Philip and John are far more seasoned business professionals than me. . . . I go to them for guidance and advice and I will rarely do things that they do not agree with." That said, Atul acknowledged that there are many challenges to shared leadership.

Atul: "The single biggest thing it requires on my part is to give up a ton of decision-making authority, and most people in a CEO chair are not willing to do that. I have to be subservient to John and Philip, and I'm happy to bePersonalitiesI feel that it is not in my personality to be authoritative . . . being forced to conduct myself in an authoritative manner is offensive to my soul."

John underlined the importance of personality in ensuring the success of shared leadership. While working at consulting firms, he had studied this concept and he commented, "I will tell you that when you look at the situation, it comes back to the individuals and the egos that they have. And if they have large egos, this would not work." When first asked about describing shared leadership at TEOCO, he responded by suggesting, "How about shared fate?"

Complementary Management Skills. The skill sets of these leaders are very complementary, and together form a powerful combination for organizational success. This was described separately, and consistently, by each of them. Atul excels at cost management and judging people.

Atul: "I really see my role as primarily focusing on culture and values and candidly I own all the decisions related to the ownership structure and internal management. However, I don't build anything and I don't sell anything."

Referring to Atul's strengths in cost management and people management, as opposed to direct customer interface, John noted that Atul rarely has customer interface, as Atul entrusts this responsibility to him. John's own skills and interests are focused on creativity and client relations. He sees his job as assembling people around clients and projects, and keeping customers happy. Finally, Philip is the one who makes it all happen. He is skilled at running a business that will endure, and has the organizational skills to free up Atul and John to do what they do best. As Philip describes, "We are all strong in a different place. Collectively, when we are together, we basically combine our strengths and eliminate our weaknesses . . . we do not compete with each other in our strong areas, and I think that is the key to it." John adds, "We would not be as successful if one of the other two of us weren't here." Atul shares the same view but from a different angle.

Atul: "I understand that I have certain strengths, and I tend to focus on playing to those strengths, and I have an understanding of what I'm not. . . . I think incompetence can be valuable, if you know it. If you recognize that you don't know what to do, you're forced to ask others and the resulting collaborative environment has a power of its own."

Career and Life Circumstances. While personality and skills are important factors, it appears as well that life circumstances were a necessary precondition to the effectiveness of the collaborative model at TEOCO. In their own way, each of these leaders acknowledged that at a different time and place, shared leadership would not necessarily have been a model they would have liked or one with which they would have been successful. As John described, "I think you have to be at a point in your life where you're pretty comfortable with who you are." All three of these men, as a result of their career circumstances, have done well in their professional life. All of them have "builder" personalities; they derive a great deal of satisfaction from growing a business. For these leaders, the journey of growing TEOCO into a successful enterprise is as important as the end result.

Culture of Employee Ownership

Atul has shaped the culture of TEOCO and ensures that it is continuously reinforced. This culture is founded upon the core values of the company. As he expresses it, "I define success as 'living up to your values.'" Those values are rooted in a business philosophy he calls "principled entrepreneurship," which he defines as "a business where you have a set of values and you commit to living up to those values while trying to create business success." He further specifies, "They have to be a clear set of articulated values." In describing his success, he says that "what motivates me is to make as big a difference as I can for as many people as I can. And I was never in it solely for the money."

TEOCO has a clearly articulated set of core values [see Appendix 4] and a very distinct culture. Atul explains that the former were established even before he knew what the words "core values" meant. The initial slogan for the company was: "We'll take care of our employees, they'll take care of our clients, and that will take care of the business." He says that the actual articulation of and focus on "core values" began after he read a 1999 *Inc. Magazine* article based on the book *Built To Last: Successful Habits of Visionary Companies,*[7] which caused him to ask, "*Who* are we?" rather than focusing primarily on "*What* do we want to be?"

A hallmark of TEOCO is the ownership culture that is embedded in the company. As an employee-owned company, Atul wants all employees to buy and own TEOCO stock. Yet consistent with his overall philosophy of life, he does not believe he can make anybody buy the stock; he can only give them information and the opportunity to make that decision. He strongly believes that the environment created by employee ownership leads to better organizational performance and stronger employee commitment.

> Atul: "I believe in the model of shared success. And I believe that if you share your success with the people that actually influence it and create it, then you create [something] extremely powerful. So, I'm fond of saying that TEOCO is a difficult company to beat – not because we are so good, but because it's tough beating a bunch of employee owners that feel so passionately about what they do."

He and the leadership team continuously seek to create and reinforce an "ownership culture" and have employees take an active part in ownership. Carrie (Director of Human Resources) has worked for TEOCO for 7 years; previously she had worked for other organizations with stock programs that create an ownership stake in the company.

> Carrie: "I would say that TEOCO is the first company I've worked for where it is as big of a deal. And we make it such a large component of the culture and we spend a ton of time from an HR perspective making sure people understand all the different elements of ownership, why we feel it's important to us, what different programs and mechanisms are out there to provide ownership and allow them to have an ownership stake in the company."

Hillary is an employee who has worked for TEOCO for 5 years in various professional positions, but has not worked at any other companies. She said she realized how much she appreciates the overall work environment at TEOCO when she compared her circumstances with friends. To describe the differences that may exist in working for an employee-owned company as opposed to a traditional company, she said, "I think the employees here at TEOCO have a lot more knowledge about what's going on."

Dave, one of the earliest and longest-serving employees, when asked what employee ownership meant to him, said "I've got a stake in the game. My kid's college education is riding on this whole thing. There are no two ways about it. . . . I think a lot of the people in the company think that way."

Additionally, John, General Manager, explains further,

> ". . . It's keeping people motivated. It's keeping them focused. I think employee ownership helps us with some of those things. . . . [It's] a very powerful ally when you're in a market that's got a lot of competition in it."

In addition to the organization's core values and corporate culture, the sense of ownership is reinforced through three distinct types of mechanisms: (1) Employees' involvement in the decision-making process; (2) Bonus and Stock Ownership; and (3) A Philosophy of Total Compensation.

Employee Involvement in the Decision-Making Process

The secret to making it work, according to Atul, is that "you have to create a culture of sharing in the decision-making process." The core values of TEOCO are manifested in the degree of employee involvement within the organization, as well as in the many significant ways employees contribute.

"All-Hands Meeting" At 11:00 a.m. on the first Thursday of every month, an "all-hands meeting" is held for all employees. This is a standing meeting, never moved or cancelled for any reason—one for US-based employees and one for employees in India. For those US-based employees who are geographically dispersed from corporate headquarters, a video feed goes out and an audio feed comes back so that questions can be posed from off-site locations. Each meeting lasts from 60 to 90 minutes and concludes with a pizza lunch.

These meetings have a structured format so that employees know what to expect. First, new employees are introduced; next, employee service anniversaries are acknowledged and celebrated (five, ten and 15 years' service awards are presented); and then there is a monthly drawing for the TeoStar Award. The second half of the meeting more formally introduces its principal objective: leadership providing a business update, as well as any news of particular interest to employees.

Once per quarter the meeting is devoted to detailed financial updates. This is described as an "open book" presentation; there is a review of the balance sheet and client revenues, an update from each line of business, and a discussion of new business prospects. Avi, CFO, elaborated that it is "not only one page of the P & L and one page of the balance sheet; it's pretty extensive." Based on his prior experiences as a CFO, he said this is "like having a shareholder's meeting every quarter." Further, he specified that the company practices "open book management" and that the employees can see the books at any time.

The February meeting each year is devoted to a presentation on the year-end financials, and employees are informed what percent of their target bonus they will receive. As of 2011, all employees with 3+ years of service have received more than 100% of their target bonus for the last several years. Miscellaneous presentations are also made on topics of relevance, such as an update on the internal stock market.

Every meeting concludes with an open segment called "benefits and concerns." First, employees are encouraged to discuss any benefits received or positive experiences that have happened in the company. Mutual support and a form of company "cheerleading" is adopted. This is followed by a unique opportunity for any employee to raise any issue of concern. No question is considered out of bounds, and senior management is expected to respond openly and fully. The only ground rule is that every question must be phrased in the format of "I wish I knew. . . ." For example, "I wish I knew why our financials were not as good this quarter," or "I wish I knew why we do not have a benefit such as. . . ." Atul said that this protocol ensures that concerns are presented in an impersonal and nonoffensive manner; rather than being a challenge, each question focuses on looking for an explanation. He said that this approach has been "a game changer," "has really changed the tone of the meetings," and reflects the way in which owners would treat each other.

The A-Team In addition to the opportunity to raise issues at the "all-hands meeting," a standing group of employee representatives meets each month. TEOCO's Advisory Team, simply called the A-Team, serves as an interface between the employee-owners and the leadership team. The team is comprised of 12 people: eight full-time members and four alternates. Any employee can bring any issue to the A-Team, and the A-Team can bring any issue they choose to the leadership of the company. Similarly, the leadership can bring any issue to the A-Team. This is considered a mechanism to involve employees in the governance of the business; its chief function is to provide a voice to the employee-owners. The membership rotates each year, and outgoing members choose the incoming team. By design it is not intended to be composed of management, and the majority of the members are lower-level employees. As well, it intentionally includes a cross section of members: single, married, from all geographic areas and from different levels within the organization.

Bonus and Stock Ownership

All employees receive an annual cash bonus. The program seems to function more like a traditional profit sharing plan, as it is not individual performance-related. The bonus pool equals 15% of pretax and pre-bonus profit of the company for the calendar year. The plan is designed to be entirely transparent. Each employee has a target bonus of 8% of base salary. The eligibility for the bonus percentage increases as the employee rises to different organizational levels, as follows:

20–40% - Executive Leadership
20% - Vice President;
16% - Senior Principal;
12% - Principal;
8% - all other employees.

Titles have no meaning at TEOCO in the traditional sense of their relationship to a level of job responsibility. Rather, titles are determined on the basis of the employee's value to the company. There is a vice president, for example, who does not manage anyone.

In addition to bonuses, employees can purchase stock or receive stock options. At the initial founding of TEOCO in 1994, the only ownership vehicle was for employees to purchase stock outright. At the beginning of the company, Atul offered employees a specific number of shares to purchase, and he claims that every employee took full advantage of this opportunity. However, by 1999–2000, the value of the stock had risen to a level that Atul explains made it difficult for employees to purchase outright, so traditional stock options were awarded, instead of requiring employees to fully purchase the shares at the time of the grant. While acknowledging that options are necessary, Atul strongly believes that "option holders are not the same as shareholders," because he believes that the mere granting of options does not create ownership.

With regard to purchasing stock, it should be noted that employees have the option of taking their annual bonus in stock up to a maximum of 60%. The remaining 40% is intended for use in paying taxes.

The stock plan also provides for repurchase rights. If an employee terminates, the company has the right to repurchase the stock, with two exceptions. If an employee worked for the company for at least 5 years and owned the stock for a minimum of 3 years or if an employee worked for the company for 10 years and owned the stock for at least a year, they may retain the stock, with the rationale that since they contributed many years of service to the success of the company, they should be able to continue to benefit. However, for others the stock is typically repurchased by the company.

Starting in January, 2007, the company decided to replace its 401K match with an ESOP. When the ESOP was implemented, it was both a bold and controversial decision. Atul came to the reluctant conclusion that if he wanted to create a broad-based ownership, an ESOP was needed as an involuntary mechanism. This was a difficult decision for him as it risked making existing employees unhappy, but he finally realized that it "was the only method to create broad-based ownership [because] educating and cajoling and encouraging was never going to work broadly enough."

His struggle with the ESOP was further complicated by the fact that Philip and John were not initially supportive. Their resistance delayed implementation for a year or two. This issue put the shared leadership model to a test; still, he said that even though he is the CEO, "there are times I know the right answer and they just don't see it, and I accept their decision." Only when these two had fully embraced it was the ESOP adopted. In the end, ESOP became very successful. While some employees were initially unhappy, they eventually saw how the TEOCO stock has outperformed the market since its inception in 2007.

Despite his belief in the need for the ESOP, Atul maintains that it does not create "ownership culture" in the same way that voluntarily investing one's own money to buy shares does. However, he wanted to achieve a broad-based ownership which, in his opinion, would not have been possible otherwise. From his perspective, ownership means wealth and the real benefit would be realized if the company was sold or went public. A successful and attractive company, especially one in the high tech field, can expect to sell at a high multiple of the price-to-earnings ratio, which would result in an impressive return for employees, rewarding them for their exemplary performance and company loyalty.

A Philosophy of Total Compensation

Atul's philosophy of compensation is that base salaries should be in the range of 0–10% below the going market rate. He believes that employees can accept this as a trade-off for a supportive and respectful work environment, a sizable bonus, along with the benefits of employee ownership. He even prefers it when a new employee takes a modest pay cut to join TEOCO, because he believes it is "a very resounding affirmation that they believe in our company and in our core values."

> Atul: "We work our hardest if we are happier, if we enjoy our work and if we feel that we belong. That's why TEOCO has chosen to be an employee owned company; you don't work for an employer here, you work for yourself."

Since every TEOCO employee owns some company stock and receives an annual bonus and generous benefits, he feels that they are not underpaid. This full range of benefits seems to be highly valued and appreciated by employees. Hillary, for example, said that these make it difficult for her to consider leaving to work at another company. In comparing TEOCO's benefits with those her friends receive at other organizations, she is especially appreciative; 3 weeks instead of two weeks of vacation, the casual work environment and the flexible schedule were all cited.

Finally, TEOCO never misses an opportunity to recognize employees' commitment to the company, as well as their performance, by distributing awards. These awards reinforce the core values of the company: excellence, dedication and team work. It should be noted that these are peer-to-peer awards in which fellow employees are recognized for actions that exemplify one of the core values. [See Appendix 5 for an exhaustive list of TEOCO benefits and awards.]

Human Resources as a Strategic Function

In addition to shared leadership and employee ownership programs, the third component of TEOCO's competitive advantage is the way the senior executive team emphasizes the importance of managing TEOCO's main asset: its human resources. In many organizations, Human Resources is seen as a necessary cost of doing business; the HR function typically operates at a functional level or, at best in far fewer companies, at the executive level.[8] At TEOCO, however, Atul has elevated HR to the strategic level. While there is a dedicated human resources director, Atul effectively serves as the organization's Chief Human Resources Officer.

For most organizations, the human resources policies and practices are transactional in nature. At TEOCO, the HR function has become the principal means of cultural transmission and reinforcement. In addition, Atul devotes strategic focus on HR because of his belief in the potential of an empowered work force. To some extent, part of the company's overall strategy is working from the "bottom up." The company relies on the abilities of its employees to understand what the market needs and develop new products. An example of how the empowered workforce functions at TEOCO was related by Dave [Software Architect]:

> We are not structured in a way that we have a team for incubating products . . . it's through conversations with our existing customers, generally, that the ideas for the next set of products come out.

Meanwhile, it is the shared leadership model that provides the opportunity for Atul to be so strongly and strategically focused on HR while depending on John, Faye and others to bring in the revenues. In an organization whose principal assets and competitive advantage are its human and intellectual capital, Atul and the shared leadership team have recognized the strategic importance of HR to its success.

The culture at TEOCO revolves singularly around the principle of employee ownership; it is embedded in the language, the policies and practices, the daily activities and even the rituals at TEOCO. There is a formal HR policy manual which is kept continuously current. While the manual is comprehensive in its scope, it is somewhat limited in specific details. Atul's stated philosophy of a policy manual is that "less is more," and the existing manual is larger than he would prefer. His rationale for not wanting to embed detailed procedures into the policy manual is that he prefers to have as few rules as possible. He believes that every employee will always want to do what is in the best interest of the company, and to reinforce the culture at TEOCO he believes that doing the right thing might at times require violating a policy.

TEOCO's articulated core values, and the resulting organizational culture, are evident in the working environment as well as in the HR policies and practices. The overall environment could be described as one of collegiality and mutual respect. Atul's background and beliefs support his desire for peace at the office, wanting employees to respect one another and not wanting employees to feel insecure about their jobs. Hillary validated this perception when she said "I think the environment is one of my favorite things about TEOCO." She claims that Atul comes by her office every week, and she thinks it is the same for many other employees as well. She described that "he walks around" and is very interactive. Brian independently said that "I get high-fives from Atul probably four days a week." He noted that many new employees, especially those who come from larger organizations, often comment on how surprised they are that the CEO recognizes them, let alone that they see him come down to their floor. Further, Brian mentioned that interpersonal relationships are very important at TEOCO. For many employees some of their best friends work there, and "that's a really big benefit that isn't on any paperwork or on any contract."

The socialization process at TEOCO begins at new employee orientation and is continuously reinforced through the HR policies and practices. Carrie (Director of HR) believes that the principal mission of HR is to help shape employee perceptions, especially as it relates to employee ownership, and to impress upon every employee the core value of "driving for progress through ownership."

The HR policies and practices, themselves, demonstrate their critical importance through the resulting work environment. Taken together, the culture of employee ownership, combined with the strategic focus on HR, serve to recruit, motivate and retain the TEOCO workforce.

The importance of human assets to the company's success is highlighted by the active involvement of its CEO and chairman in the hiring process. He interviews every applicant before a hiring decision is made. As he says, "Nobody gets hired without meeting me, and nobody gets hired without getting my nod." The two areas in which he exercises tight-fisted control are hiring and cost management. He believes he has developed unique expertise to know "who to hire and what to look for." His focus is not only on technical competence, but on "cultural fit" as well. In many ways Atul could be described as the keeper of the culture. He gets so deeply involved in the hiring process that he says he is sometimes asked if he doesn't have anything better to do, and he responds by saying that there is nothing more important because the hiring process is so vital to the company's continued success.

TA, TTI AND THE FUTURE OF TEOCO

How will the story of TEOCO unfold with the investment by TA and the acquisition of TTI? From a purely business perspective, these decisions were justifiably necessary and defensible. However, each of the three distinctive characteristics of TEOCO's model of success, the shared leadership model, the culture of employee ownership and the resulting HR policies and practices, are being challenged in this post-acquisition environment.

Impact on Shared Leadership

The scope of the combined enterprise presents challenges that may strain the shared leadership model. TA's investment already added two influential directors to TEOCO's board. While directors usually have a "nose in, hands out" approach to management, the representatives of investment funds appointed to a company's board tend to be far more proactive in their "dialogues" with the senior team managing their investment. The subsequent acquisition of TTI added a fourth executive, Eitan Naor, into the leadership mix and in the last 2 years, Avi (TEOCO's CFO) has also become a key member of the Executive Leadership Team. Considering the distance between TEOCO and TTI, as well as their respective nearly equal sizes, it remains to be seen how the strengths and weaknesses of each leader will play out in the management of this new entity. For instance, Atul's well-recognized skills in hiring and motivating employees on a daily basis may not prove as beneficial or essential for TTI.

Impact on the Culture of Employee Ownership

Avi claims that the cultures have nothing in common. Yet the senior management team seems adamant that the culture of TEOCO has not and will not change. Faye says, "I don't think there's been significant change." Still, she acknowledged the inevitability that an aggregated culture will arise in which each organization impacts the other. But she adds, "I can see [Atul] sitting in that chair right now saying, 'It's not going to happen.'"

These statements are not surprising, as it is nearly universal that in this situation company executives proclaim that their acquisition will not change the corporate culture. Yet some degree of change is inevitable, and change has already occurred. These events will inevitably impact business activities and decision-making. The TTI acquisition and the investment of TA enhance the likelihood that within the next 3 years TEOCO may be acquired by a larger corporation, go public or require some other fundamental organizational realignment. Before agreeing to the TA investment, Atul says that he went to the employees for their consent. He believes the employees were comfortable with the transaction or he would not have done it; he says that the employees are aware of its positive impact as well as the potential outcome.

Atul is determined to continue on the same path as before these major events. He points out that a condition of TA's investment in TEOCO was that he retain the role of CEO because he is so essential to the culture of the company. The bank, as a condition of the loan for the purchase of TTI, had the same requirement. Meanwhile, Atul is intent on TA receiving a good return on their investment in TEOCO.

> Atul: "But I will no longer do that with a sense of obligation; I will do that with a sense of joy. You know, if you do something out of joy, you do it differently than when you do it out of a sense of obligation."

An immediate impact is that these two events place a strain on employee ownership. The ownership mix shifted significantly with the TA investment. Prior to this equity transaction, Atul controlled 75% of the shares, while employees owned 25% from all combined sources. Post-TA, the employee share was halved as they were offered approximately 60% liquidity on their previous ownership.. Given Atul's ownership, and his intention to maintain a controlling interest in the company, coupled with TA's sizable equity stake, an issue that arises is whether there is any meaningful future opportunity to expand employee ownership. This is further compounded by the near doubling of the total number of employees.

An interesting paradox, according to Atul, is that despite the lower total employee ownership, there is a perception that the TA liquidity has strengthened the culture of ownership. He said that he "predicted that post-TA our payroll deductions [to purchase stock] would go down. It has increased . . . because [the employees] see a success story," even though the stock purchase price has since increased. Atul attributes this pattern to the fact that employees witnessed other employees making significant sums of money from the TA transaction. He claims that now they truly understand and value ownership. As he says, "Once you've made money out of ownership, it changes you forever. And until you do, you don't believe it." Atul felt a very deep sense of gratitude to his long-term employees for their loyalty and sacrifice in creating value for TEOCO. The TA transaction allowed him to fulfill his commitment that one day they would get a return on their investment of time and money into TEOCO.

While these events will inevitably bring about changes in the way the company is managed, John believes that these will not dilute the culture. The TA investment "allowed TEOCO to preserve something that I think is pretty important to the way we operate, which is having employee ownership in the business, and that employees have a piece of it." A firm believer in employee ownership, he has "worked at the world's largest employee-owned company, for Telecordia, which was owned by SAIC." He claims that TEOCO is heavily modeled after SAIC in terms of employee ownership as a mechanism.

> John: "If you're just paying people to show up to work and they get an annual bonus – those are two factors. But if you introduced the third factor of employee ownership –why wouldn't you treat that as a means to motivate the employees beyond just simply giving them a salary and giving them a bonus? . . . And that's what Dr. Beyster [the founder of SAIC] figured out before anybody else figured it out."

These perceptions by senior management were validated by Carrie, HR Manager. When asked about the relatively small percentage of total stock owned by employees, she claims that the perception of employee ownership continues to be important, and that all employees still have opportunity to build additional equity. She cited, for example, that every new employee is granted a certain amount of ownership rights; they determine how much stock they want to purchase either through payroll deduction or the internal stock market. Brian validated this further when he said that once employees realize the benefits of being invested in the company, it changes their perspective. Like Atul, he underlined that this reality became clear for many employees when they witnessed others cashing out a portion of their equity with the TA investment. As he said, "Once that clicks in, it builds on it."

It remains to be determined if the employees of TTI will become owners, and whether they will embrace the culture of ownership. It is also uncertain how TEOCO's employee perceptions may change in terms of the growing price of ownership and the potential diminished opportunity for share availability.

Impact on Human Resources as a Strategic Function

The TTI acquisition will strain Atul's role as the organization's chief human resources officer and as someone who has been intimately and deeply involved in all HR-related decisions of the company. Dave describes Atul's current role in HR activities.

> Dave: "Atul is very, very, very engaged at the staffing and who's working on what and the hiring process. Its personnel stuff. Personnel and costs are the two things he focuses on . . . it blows my mind the level of detail and recollection he has on individual people and what's going on in the company."

As the company continues to grow, and as the complexity of issues expands, it will become increasingly difficult to maintain this level of involvement in details. A further challenge will be the issue of the standardization and consistency of application of HR-related policies and practices. Atul has a strong aversion to formal policies, preferring instead to have maximum flexibility and discretion in deciding HR issues.

> Atul: "Life is all about making decisions and the reason management exists is to use judgment. Too many people want to make too many rules and they don't want to use judgment and I feel that if judgment doesn't exist then management doesn't have a job."

Given the increasingly litigious and regulated work environment for organizations, such a philosophy can create challenges for HR. When asked about Atul's philosophy of a policy manual where "less is more," HR Director Carrie admitted that there are some policies "that do cause me a little heartburn just because it's a little tough to administer without having something solid." One example she cited is that the sick leave policy is administered on an honor system. The only way to monitor abuse, she says, is indirectly by the impact such abuse may have on employee performance. As the company gets larger, she believes it would be easier if there were specific guidelines to turn to in a dilemma, to be able to say, "Here's the policy." Yet despite the lack of specifications, she claims there appears to be a high degree of consistency in the administration of HR policies.

Whether HR will continue to be viewed as a strategic function and receive the executive focus that it has had will be tested as well in the new corporate environment.

Impact on TEOCO's Core Competencies

While Atul believes that corporate culture and philosophy have played "key roles in our success", he says "that without its distinctive core competencies the company could not have been successful." Whether the core competencies that TEOCO has built can carry over in the post acquisition environment is an unanswered question. That TTI is similar in size to TEOCO and that they are geographically separated are two factors that will pose challenges in transferring specialized expertise from the acquiring company to the acquired company and vice versa. Also, given that the two companies had different cultures at the time of acquisition, additional work will have to be done to ensure successful transference of core competencies.

CONCLUSION

The challenge for any organization with a strong culture and a loyal workforce is to sustain them and adapt them in the face of organizational change. Over a very short period of time, TEOCO has changed its capital structure and expanded its business. How and to what extent TEOCO manages these changes will determine whether it maintains its competitive advantage and, finally, what will be its overall fate.

APPENDIX 1: Board of Directors

In addition to John Devolites, Philip M. Giuntini and Atul Jain, TEOCO's board is composed of a majority of outside board members with deep telecom industry expertise:

Gabriel Battista, Former Chairman, Talk America

Gabe Battista formerly served as Chairman of the Board of Directors of Talk America, where he previously served as CEO. Prior to joining Talk America in January of 1999, Mr. Battista served as CEO of Network Solutions, Inc. Before joining Network Solutions, Mr. Battista served as CEO, President and COO of Cable & Wireless, Inc. He also held management positions at US Sprint, GTE Telenet and The General Electric Company. He serves as a director of Capitol College, and Systems & Computer Technology Corporation (SCTC).

Brian J. Conway, Managing Director, TA Associates

Mr. Conway heads TA Associates' Boston office Technology Group, focusing on recapitalizations, buyouts and minority growth investments of technology-based growth companies. He is also a member of TA Associates' Executive Committee. Prior to joining TA Associates, Mr. Conway worked with Merrill Lynch in Mergers and Acquisitions and Corporate Finance. He serves on the Board of Directors for Epic Advertising, IntraLinks, and Numara Software.

Hythem T. El-Nazer, Senior Vice President, TA Associates

Mr. El-Nazer's focus at TA Associates is on recapitalizations, management-led buyouts, and growth capital investments in telecommunications, media and other technology-based services companies. Prior to joining TA Associates, Mr. El-Nazer worked with McKinsey & Company and Donaldson, Lufkin & Jenrette—Investment Banking. He serves on the Board of Directors for eSecLending, Radialpoint, and is Board Observer at Orascom Telecom Holding S.A.E. and Weather Investments S.p.A.

Robert J. Korzeniewski, Former Executive Vice President, VeriSign

As VeriSign's Executive Vice President, Corporate Development and Strategy, Mr. Robert Korzeniewski is responsible for providing a consistent strategy and focus for investments and merger-and-acquisition activity. Mr. Korzeniewski served from 1996-2000 as CFO of Network Solutions, Inc., which was acquired by VeriSign in June 2000. Mr. Korzeniewski came to Network Solutions from SAIC, where from 1987 to 1996, he held a variety of senior financial positions.

Source: *TEOCO's website*

APPENDIX 2: Industry Landscape / Major Competitors

(1) Least Cost Routing

Vendors	Regions				OVERALL	Market Segments	
	NA	CALA	EMEA	APAC		Mobile	PSTN
Ascade	P	—	NP	NP	NP	NP	NP
Connective-Sol	NP	—	—	—	P	NP	P
GCS	NP	—	—	—	NP	NP	NP
OrcaWave	NP	—	P	—	P	P	NP
Prime Carrier	P	—	P	P	P	P	P
Pulse Networks	NP	—	—	—	NP	NP	NP
Subex	—	NP	—	—	—	—	—
Telarix	ML	P	ML	—	ML	ML	ML

(2) Revenue Assurance

VENDORS	Regions				OVERALL	Market Segments	
	NA	CALA	EMEA	APAC		MOBILE	PSTN
Connectiva	P	P	NP	NP	NP	NP	NP
Connectiv	NP	—	—	—	P	NP	P
Cvidya	NP	—	—	NP	—	—	NP
Razorsight	P	—	—	—	P	P	P
Subex	NP	P	ML	ML	ML	ML	ML
Qosmos	P	—	P	P	P	P	P
Wedo	NP	—	ML	NP	ML	ML	ML

(3) Cost Management

VENDORS	Regions				OVERALL	Market Segments	
	NA	CALA	EMEA	APAC		MOBILE	PSTN
Connectiv	P	—	—	—	P	P	P
Martin Dawes	—	—	NP	—	P	NP	P
Razorsight	ML	—	—	—	NP	NP	NP
Subex	P	NP	ML	ML	ML	ML	ML

Note: NA = North America; CALA = Central America & Latin America; EMEA = Europe, Middle East and Africa; APAC = Asia & Pacific. PSTN = Public Switched Telephone Network; P = has a presence in the market; NP = has a notable presence in the Market; ML = is a market leader
Source: TEOCO Marketing Department

APPENDIX 3: TEOCO/TTI Leadership

Atul Jain, Chairman and CEO

Atul Jain founded TEOCO Corporation in 1994. Prior to starting TEOCO Corporation, Mr. Jain was with a Silicon Valley firm called TIBCO for 7 years. At TIBCO, Mr. Jain's focus was to work with Fortune 500 clients to design and build state-of-the-art software solutions leveraging the company's trademark TIB platform.

Philip M. Giuntini, Vice Chairman and President

Philip M. Giuntini joined TEOCO in February 2000 as Vice Chairman and President. Prior to joining TEOCO, Mr. Giuntini was President and on the Board of Directors of AMS, a $1B international business and information technology consulting firm headquartered in Fairfax, Virginia.

John Devolites, Vice President and General Manager

John Devolites is currently the Vice President and General Manager at TEOCO focusing on solutions for the communications service provider industry. Previously, Mr. Devolites served as President of Professional Services for Telcordia. His other work experiences include executive positions at PricewaterhouseCoopers, E-Commerce Industries, Andersen, American Management Systems (AMS), Alexander Proudfoot PLC, and Booz Allen Hamilton.

Avi Goldstein, Chief Financial Officer (CFO)

Avi Goldstein joined TEOCO in October 2008 and was nominated TEOCO's CFO on April 2009. Prior to joining TEOCO, Mr. Goldstein co-founded several startup companies as well provided consulting services in the Telecom arena with a strong focus on Mergers and Acquisitions. Prior to that Mr. Goldstein served as an Executive Vice President and CFO of ECtel Ltd. (NASDAQ: ECTX) from its establishment until 2005. Mr. Goldstein led ECtel to a successful IPO as well as private placements and M&A activities.

Eitan Naor, General Manager and CEO of TTI

Eitan Naor joined TEOCO in August 2010 and brings more than 25 years of leadership and experience in the global telecom and service assurance markets. Prior to joining TEOCO, Mr. Naor served as President and CEO of Magic Software (NASDAQ:MGIC), where he led a significant restructure of the business and regained focus in its worldwide network of partners, resulting in a significant increase in sales and a return to profitability in less than one year. Mr. Naor also had great success in his other professional roles, including President and CEO of ECTEL (NASDQ:ECTX, Division President at AMDOCS, and Vice President with ORACLE Israel.

Source: *TEOCO's website*

APPENDIX 4: TEOCO's Core Values & Value Proposition

At TEOCO, The Employee-Owned Company, we are driven by our core values. These values are our guiding principles in all business initiatives:

Alignment with Employees, Clients and Community We act in the best interest of our employees, clients and community, consistently seeking partnership and mutual benefit.

Integrity, Honesty and Respect We value our reputation and conduct our business with integrity, honesty and respect for each individual.

Acting with Courage We demonstrate a willingness to take risks, while conducting our business in a responsible manner.

Drive for Progress through Ownership We are committed to a relentless pursuit of excellence, never being satisfied with the status quo. We are a team whose sum is greater than its parts and devoted to constant innovation.

TEOCO sets standards of excellence that others strive to emulate in our areas of focus—cost management, routing, and revenue management. TEOCO's value proposition is as follows:

Innovation TEOCO's committed emphasis on one industry allows us unparalleled customer focus. We commit a significant share—up to 30%—of our annual revenues to research and development to address your precise needs.

Stability TEOCO is the only firm in our industry segment that is financially sound, debt free, and employee owned. You can rest assured that we are responsive to your needs and will be there tomorrow.

Integrity At TEOCO, acting with integrity is one of our essential core values. We focus intensely on developing mutually beneficial, trust-based relationships with customers and communicating honestly in every situation.

Deep Industry Expertise Our team includes experienced professionals, many of whom have substantial telecommunications experience and/or have worked directly in service provider cost management organizations.

Source: *TEOCO's website*

APPENDIX 5: TEOCO's Benefits and Awards

Flexible Schedule

Flexible working hours occur on an informal basis and vary from job to job and department to department. While there is no formal HR policy on flexible working hours or working from home, this approach is consistent with its performance-driven culture in that what ultimately matters is employee performance. Even though employees may be permitted flexibility with schedules and working from home, employees are expected to be available nights, weekends and even vacations when there are pressing deadlines or problems to trouble shoot.

Snacks and Beverages

Company-provided snacks, coffee and other beverages are made available throughout the day for all employees.

"Splash Vacation"

After completing 5 years of service (and on every subsequent fifth-year anniversary) employees are provided with an extra week of paid vacation. They are also provided with a reimbursement of up to $2,000 for expenses incurred (transportation, lodging, etc.) in taking a vacation for themselves and their family to any place of their choosing.

ACE Award

ACE stands for Attitude, Commitment and Excellence. This is TEOCO's version of an "Employee of the Year" award, and is given annually to the employee who best exemplifies these three qualities. The winner, who receives stock and a cash award, is chosen by a committee which is comprised of previous winners of the ACE Award.

MVP Award

The Most Versatile Player Award, similar in concept to the ACE Award, is given annually to an employee who may not rise to that level of excellence, but who contributes to the organization in multiple ways. The winner receives stock and a cash award. Like the ACE Award, the winner is chosen without any management involvement, and the selection committee is comprised of previous winners of the award.

TEOCO Star Award

This is a peer-to-peer award in which employees recognize fellow employees for doing something that exemplifies one of the core values. This award would be TEOCO's version of a "spot bonus," with the exception that it is peer-to-peer rather than given by a supervisor. For example, one employee being helpful to another on a project might garner them a recommendation for the award. At the monthly "all-hands meeting," there is a drawing amongst all those nominated that month, and the winner receives a $150 Amex gift card as well as official acknowledgement.

One-Year Service Award

All new employees, on their first anniversary of employment, are given a plant, a balloon and a card signed by other employees to acknowledge their first anniversary.

Notes:

1. All employees are referred to in this case by their first name including the CEO because that is standard practice at TEOCO.
2. http://www.billingworld.com/articles/2010/09/teoco-ceo-reversal-on-acquisitions-complete.aspx
3. Ibid.
4. http://www.billingworld.com/articles/2010/09/teoco-ceo-reversal-on-acquisitions-complete.aspx
5. http://www.billingworld.com/articles/2010/09/teoco-ceo-reversal-on-acquisitions-complete.aspx

6. Jainism is the least populous of the Indian religions; comprising approximately 0.5% of the population (Hindus represent approximately 80%, Muslims approximately 12% and Christians approximately 3%).

7. James C. Collins and Jerry I. Porras. New York: Harper Collins Publishers, 1994.

8. As Peter Drucker said, "All organizations now say routinely, 'people are our greatest asset.' Yet few practice what they preach, let alone believe it." *"The New Society of Organizations," Harvard Business Review,* Sept/Oct, 1992.

Case 23

3M—The First 110 Years

Charles W.L. Hill

School of Business
University of Washington
Seattle, WA 98105
June 2013

Established in 1902, by 2012 3M was one of the largest technology driven enterprises in the United States with annual sales of almost $30 billion, two-third of which were outside the United States. The company was solidly profitable, earning $6.5 billion in net income in 2012 and generating a return on invested capital (ROIC) of 19.5%. Throughout its history 3M's researchers had driven much of the company's growth. In 2012 the company sold over 50,000 products, including Post-it Notes, Flex Circuits, various kinds of Scotch tape, abrasives, specialty chemicals, Thinsulate insulation products, Nexcare bandage, optical films, fiber optic connectors, drug delivery systems and much more. Around 7,350 of the company's 80,000 employees were technical employees. 3M's annual R&D budget exceeded $1.6 billion. The company had garnered over 8,000 patents since 1990. 3M was organized into 35 different business units grouped together into six main areas; consumer and office products; display and graphics; electronics and telecommunications; health care; industrial and transportation; safety, security, and protection services (see Exhibit 1 for details).

The company's 100-year anniversary in 2002 was a time for celebration, but also one for strategic reflection. During the prior decade, 3M had grown profits and sales by between 6–7% per annum, a respectable figure but one that lagged behind the growth rates achieved by some other technology based enterprises and diversified industrial enterprises like General Electric. In 2001, 3M took a step away from its past when the company hired the first outsider to become CEO, James McNerney Jr. McNerney, who joined 3M after heading up GE's fast growing medical equipment business (and losing out in the race to replace legendary GE CEO, Jack Welch) was quick to signal that he wanted 3M to accelerate its growth rate. McNerney set an ambitious target for 3M—to grow sales by 11% per annum and profits by 12% per annum. Many wondered if McNerney could achieve this without damaging the innovation engine that had propelled 3M to its current stature. In the event, the question remained unanswered, as McNerney left to run the Boeing Company in 2005. His successor, however, George Buckley, another outsider, seemed committed to continuing on the course McNerney had set for the company.

THE HISTORY OF 3M: BUILDING INNOVATIVE CAPABILITIES

The story 3M goes back to 1902 when five Minnesota business men established the Minnesota Mining and Manufacturing company to mine a mineral that they thought was corundum, which is ideal for making sandpaper. The mineral, however, turned out to be low grade anorthosite, nowhere near as suitable for making sandpaper, and the company nearly failed. To try and salvage the business, 3M turned to making the sandpaper itself using materials purchased from another source.

In 1907, 3M hired a 20-year-old business student, William McKnight, as assistant bookkeeper. This turned out to be a pivotal move in the history of the company. The hardworking McKnight soon made his mark. By 1929 he was CEO of the company and in 1949 he became chairman of 3M's board of directors, a position that he held through until 1966.

From Sandpaper to Post it Notes

It was McKnight, then 3M's president, who hired the company's first scientist, Richard Carlton, in 1921. Around the same time, McKnight's interest had been peaked by an odd request from a Philadelphian printer by the name of Francis Okie for samples of every sandpaper grit size that 3M made. McKnight dispatched 3M's East Coast sales manager to find out what Okie was up to. The sales manager discovered that Okie had invented a new kind of sandpaper that he had patented. It was waterproof sandpaper that could be used with water or oil to reduce dust and decrease the friction that marred auto finishes. In addition, the lack of dust reduced the poisoning associated with inhaling the dust of paint that had a high lead content. Okie had a problem though; he had no financial backers to commercialize the sandpaper. 3M quickly stepped into the breach, purchasing the rights to Okie's Wetodry waterproof sandpaper, and hiring the young printer to come and join Richard Carlton in 3M's lab. Wet and Dry sandpaper went on to revolutionize the sandpaper industry, and was the driver of significant growth at 3M.

Another key player in the company's history, Richard Drew, also joined 3M in 1921. Hired straight out of the University of Minnesota, Drew would round out the trio of scientists, Carlton, Okie and Drew, who under McKnight's leadership would do much to shape 3M's innovative organization.

McKnight charged the newly hired Drew with developing a stronger adhesive to better bind the grit for sand paper to paper backing. While experimenting with adhesives, Drew accidentally developed a weak adhesive that had an interest quality—if placed on the back of a strip of paper and stuck to a surface, the strip of paper could be pealed off the surface it was adhered to without leaving any adhesive residue on that surface. This discovery gave Drew an epiphany. He had been visiting autobody paint shops to see how 3M's wet and dry sand paper was used, and he noticed that there was a problem with paint running. His epiphany was to cover the back of a strip of paper with his weak adhesive, and use it as "masking tape" to cover parts of the auto body that were not to be painted. An excited Drew took his idea to McKnight, and explained how masking tape might create an entirely new business for 3M. McKnight reminded Drew that he had been hired to fix a specific problem, and pointedly suggested that he concentrate on doing just that.

Chastised, Dew went back to his lab, but he could not get the idea out of his mind, so he continued to work on it at night, long after everyone else had gone home. Drew succeeded in perfecting the masking tape product, and then went to visit several autobody shops to show them his innovation. He quickly received several commitments for orders. Drew then went to see McKnight again. He told him that he had continued to work on the masking tape idea on his own time, had perfected the product, and got several customers interested in purchasing it. This time it was McKnight's turn to be chastised. Realizing that he had almost killed a good business idea, McKnight reversed his original position, and gave Drew the go ahead to pursue the idea.[1]

Introduced into the market in 1925, Drew's invention of masking tape represented the first significant product diversification at 3M. Company legend has it that this incident was also the genesis for 3M's famous 15% rule. Reflecting on Drew's work, both McKnight and Carlton both agreed that technical people could disagree with management, and should be allowed to go and do some experimentation on their own. The company then established a norm that technical people could spend up to 15% of their own workweek on projects that might benefit the consumer, without having to justify the project to their manager.

Drew himself was not finished. In the late 1920s he was working with cellophane, a product that had been invented by Du Pont, when lightening struck for a second time. Why, Drew wondered, couldn't cellophane be coated with an adhesive and used as a sealing tape? The result was Scotch Cellophane Tape. The first batch was delivered to a customer in September 1930, and Scotch tape went on to become one of 3M's best selling products. Years later, Drew noted that "Would there have been any masking or cellophane tape if it hadn't been for earlier 3M research on adhesive binders for 3M™ Wetordry™ Abrasive Paper? Probably not!"[2]

Over the years, other scientists followed Drew's footsteps at 3M, creating a wide range of innovative products by leveraging existing technology and applying it to new areas. Two famous examples illustrate how many of these innovations occurred—the invention of Scotch Guard, and the development of the ubiquitous "Post it Notes".

The genesis of Scotch Guard was in 1953 when a 3M scientist named Patsy Sherman was working on a new kind of rubber for jet aircraft fuel lines. Some of the latex mixture splashed onto a pair of canvas tennis shoes.

Over time, the spot stayed clean while the rest of the canvas soiled. Sherman enlisted the help of fellow chemist Sam Smith. Together they began to investigate polymers, and it didn't take long for them to realize that they were onto something. They discovered an oil and water repellant substance, based on the fluorocarbon fluid used in air conditioners, with enormous potential for protecting fabrics from stains. It took several years before the team perfected a means to apply the treatment using water as the carrier, thereby making it economically feasible for use as a finish in textile plants.

Three years after the accidental spill, the first rain and stain repellent for use on wool was announced. Experience and time revealed that one product could not, however, effectively protect all fabrics, so 3M continued working, producing a wide range of Scotch Guard products that could be used to protect all kinds of fabrics.[3]

The story of Post it Notes began with Spencer Silver, a senior scientist studying adhesives.[4] In 1968 Silver had developed an adhesive with properties like no other; it was a pressure sensitive adhesive that would adhere to a surface, but was weak enough to easily peel off the surface and leave no residue. Silver spent several years shopping his adhesive around 3M, to no avail. It was a classic case of a technology is search of a product. Then one day in 1973, Art Fry, a new product development research who had attended one of Silver's seminars, was singing in his church choir. He was frustrated that his bookmarks kept falling out of his hymn book, when he had a "Eureka" moment. Fry realized that Silver's adhesive could be used to make a wonderfully reliable bookmark.

Fry went to work next day, and using 15% time, started to develop the bookmark. When he started using sample to write notes to his boss, Fry suddenly realized that he had stumbled on a much bigger potential use for the product. Before the product could be commercialized, however, Fry had to solve a host of technical and manufacturing problems. With the support of his boss, Fry persisted and after 18 months the product development effort moved from 15% time to a formal development effort funded 3M's own seed capital.

The first Post it Notes were test marketed in 1977 in four major cities, but customers were lukewarm at best. This did not gel with the experience within 3M, where people in Fry's division were using samples all the time to write messages to each other. Further research revealed that the test marketing effort, which focused on ads and brochures, didn't resonate well with consumers, who didn't seem to value Post it Notes until they had the actual product in their hands. In 1978, 3M tried again, this time descending on Boise Idaho, and handing

out samples. Follow up research revealed that 90% of consumers who tried the product said they would buy it. Armed with this knowledge, 3M rolled out the national launch of Post it Notes in 1980. The product subsequently went on to become a best seller.

Institutionalizing Innovation

Early on McKnight set an ambitious target for 3M—a 10% annual increase in sales and 25% profit target. He also indicated how he thought that should be achieved with a commitment to plow 5% of sales back into R&D every year. The question though, was how to ensure that 3M would continue to produce new products?

The answer was not apparent all at once, but rather evolved over the years from experience. A prime example was the 15% rule, which came out of McKnight's experience with Drew. In addition to the 15% rule and the continued commitment to push money back into R&D, a number of other mechanisms evolved at 3M to spur innovation.

Initially research took place in the business units that made and sold products, but by the 1930s 3M had already diversified into several different fields, thanks in large part to the efforts of Drew and others. McKnight and Carlton realized that there was a need for a central research function. In 1937 they established a central research laboratory which was charged with supplementing the work of product divisions and undertaking long run basic research. From the outset, the researchers at the lab were multidisciplinary, with people from different scientific disciplines often working next to each other on research benches.

As the company continued to grow, it became clear that there was a need for some mechanism to knit together the company's increasingly diverse business operations. This led to the establishment of the 3M Technical Forum in 1951. The goal of Technical Forum was to foster idea sharing, discussion and problem solving between technical employees located in different divisions and the central research laboratory. The Technical Forum sponsored "problem solving sessions" at which businesses would present their most recent technical nightmares in the hope that somebody might be able to suggest a solution—and that often was the case. The forum also established an annual event in which each division put up a booth to show off its latest technologies. Chapters were also created to focus on specific disciplines, such as polymer chemistry or coating processes.

During the 1970s the Technical Forum cloned itself, establishing forums in Australia and England. By 2001 the forum had grown to 9,500 members in 8 U.S.

locations and 19 other countries, becoming an international network of researchers who could share ideas, solve problems, and leverage technology.

According to Marlyee Paulson, who coordinated the Technical Forum from 1979 to 1992, the great virtue of the Technical Forum is to cross pollinate ideas. To quote:

3M has lots of polymer chemists. They may be in tape; they may be medical or several other divisions. The forum pulls them across 3M to share what they know. It's a simple but amazingly effective way to bring like mind together.[5]

In 1999, 3M created another unit within the company, 3M Innovative Properties (3M, IPC) to leverage technical know-how. 3M IPC is explicitly charged with protecting and leveraging 3M's intellectual property around the world. At 3M there has been a long tradition that while divisions "own" their products, the company has a whole "owns" the underlying technology, or intellectual property. One task of 3M IPC is to find ways in which 3M technology can be applied across business units to produce unique marketable products. Historically, the company has been remarkably successful at leveraging company technology to produce new product ideas (see Exhibit 1 for some examples).

Another key to institutionalizing innovation at 3M has been the principle of "patient money". The basic idea is that producing revolutionary new products requires substantial long-term investments, and often repeated failure, before a major payoff occurs. The principle can be traced back to 3M's early days. It took the company 12 years before its initial sandpaper business started to show a profit, a fact that drove home the importance of taking the long view. Throughout the company's history,

Exhibit 1	Examples of Leveraging Technology at 3M[6]

Richard Miller, a corporate scientist in 3M Pharmaceuticals, began experimental development of an antiherpes medicinal cream in 1982. After several years of development, his research team found that the interferon-based materials they were working with could be applied to any skin-based virus. The innovative chemistry they were working with was applied topically and was more effective than other compounds on the market. They found that the cream was particularly effective to interfering with the growth mechanism of genital warts. Competitive materials on the market at the time were caustic and tended to be painful. Miller's team obtained FDA approval for its Aldara (imiquimod) line of topical patient-applied creams in 1997.

Miller then applied the same Aldara-based chemical mechanism to basal cell carcinomas and found that, here too, it was particularly effective to restricting the growth of the skin cancer. "The patient benefit is quite remarkable," says Miller. New results in efficacy have been presented for treating skin cancers. His team recently completed phase III clinical testing and expects to apply later this year for FDA approval for this disease preventative. This material is already FDA-approved for use in the treatment of genital warts. Doctors are free to choose to use it to treat those patients with skin cancers.

Andrew Ouderkirk is a corporate scientist in 3M's Film & Light Management Technology Center. 3M has been working in light management materials applied to polymer-based films since the 1930s, according to Ouderkirk. Every decade since then 3M has introduced some unique thin film structure for a specific customer application from high-performance safety reflectors for street signs to polarized lighting products. And every decade, Ws technology base has become more specialized and more sophisticated. Their technology has now reached the point where they can produce multiple-layer interference films to 100-nm thicknesses each and hold the tolerances on each layer to within +/− 3 nm. "Our laminated films are now starting to compete with vacuum-coated films in some applications," says Ouderkirk.

Rick Weiss is technical director of 3M's Microreplication Technology Center, one of 3M's 12 core technology centers. The basic microreplication technology was discovered in the early 1960s when 3M researchers were developing the fresnel lenses for overhead projectors. 3M scientists have expanded upon this technology to a wide variety of applications including optical reflectors for solar collectors, and adhesive coatings with air bleed ribs that allow large area films to be applied without having the characteristic "bubbles" appear. Weiss is currently working on development of dimensionally precise barrier ribs that can be applied to separate the individual "gas" cells on the new high resolution large screen commercial plasma displays. Other applications include fluid management where capillary action can be used in biological testing systems to split a drop of blood into a large number of parts.

similar examples can be found. Scotchlite reflective sheeting, now widely used on road signs, didn't show much profit for 10 years. The same was true of fluro-chemicals and duplicating products. Patient money doesn't mean substantial funding for long periods of time, however. Rather, it might imply that a small group of five researchers is supported for 10 years while they work on a technology.

More generally, if a researcher creates a new technology or idea, they can begin working on it using 15% time. If the idea shows promise, they may request seed capital from their business unit managers to develop it further. If that funding is denied, which can occur, they are free to take the idea to any other 3M business unit. Unlike the case in many other companies, requests for seed capital do not require that researchers draft detailed business plans that are reviewed by top management. That comes later in the process. As one former senior technology manager has noted. . . .

> In the early stages of a new product or technology, it shouldn't be overly managed. If we start asking for business plans too early and insist on tight financial evaluations, we'll kill an idea or surely slow it down[7].

Explaining the patient money philosophy, Ron Baukol, a former executive vice president of 3M's international operations, and a manager who started as a researcher, has noted that. . . .

> You just know that some things are going to be worth working on, and that requires technological patience. . . . you don't put too much money into the investigation, but you keep one to five people working on it for twenty years if you have to. You do that because you know that, once you have cracked the code, it's going to be big.[8]

An internal review of 3M's innovation process in the early 1980s concluded that despite the liberal process for funding new product ideas, some promising ideas did not receive funding from business units, or the central research budget. This led to the establishment in 1985 of Genesis Grants, which provide up to $100,000 in seed capital to fund projects that do not get funded through 3M's regular channels. About a dozen of these grants are given every year. One of the recipients of these grants, a project that focused on creating a multilayered reflective film, has subsequently produced a break though reflective technology that may have applications in a wide range of businesses, from better reflective strips on road signs to computer displays and the reflective linings in light fixtures. Company estimates in 2002 suggest that the commercialization of this technology might ultimately generate $1 billion in sales for 3M.

Underlying the patient money philosophy is recognition that innovation is a very risky business. 3M has long acknowledged that failure is an accepted and essential part of the new product development process. As former 3M CEO Lew Lehr once noted:

> We estimate that 60% of our formal new product development programs never make it. When this happens, the important thing is to not punish the people involved.[9]

In an effort to reduce the probability of failure, in the 1960s 3M started to establish a process for auditing the product development efforts ongoing in the company's business units. The idea has been to provide a peer review, or technical audit, of major development projects taking place in the company. A typical technical audit team is composed of 10 to 15 business and technical people, including technical directors and senior scientists from other divisions. The audit team looks at the strengths and weaknesses of a development program, and its probability of success, both from a technical standpoint and a business standpoint. The team then makes nonbinding recommendations, but they are normally taken very seriously by the managers of a project. For example, if an audit team concludes that a project has enormous potential, but is terribly under funded, managers of the unit would often increase the funding level. Of course, the converse can also happen, and in many instances, the audit team can provide useful feedback and technical ideas that can help a development team to improve their projects chance of success.

By the 1990s, the continuing growth of 3M had produced a company that was simultaneously pursuing a vast array of new product ideas. This was a natural outcome of 3M's decentralized and bottom up approach to innovation, but it was problematic in one crucial respect, the company's R&D resources were being spread too thinly over a wide range of opportunities, resulting in potentially major projects being under funded. To try and channel R&D resources into projects that had blockbuster potential, in 1994 3M introduced what was known as the Pacing Plus Program.

The program asked business to select a small number of programs that would receive priority funding, but 3M's senior executives made the final decision on which programs were to be selected for the Pacing Plus Program. An earlier attempt to do this in 1990 had met with limited success because each sector in 3M submitted as many as 200 programs. The Pacing Plus Program narrowed the list down to 25 key programs that by 1996 were receiving some 20% of 3M's entire R&D funds (by the early 200s the number of projects funded under the Pacing Plus Program had grown to 60). The focus was on "leapfrog technologies", revolutionary ideas that might change the basis of competition and led to entirely new technology platforms that might in typical 3M fashion, spawn an entire range of new products.

To further foster a culture of entrepreneurial innovation and risk taking, over the years 3M established a number of reward and recognition programs to honor employees who make significant contributions to the company. These include the Carton Society award, which honors employees for outstanding career scientific achievements and the Circle of Technical Excellence and Innovation Award, which recognizes people who have made exceptional contributions to 3M's technical capabilities.

Another key component of 3M's innovative culture has been an emphasis on duel career tracks. Right for its early days, many of the key players in 3M's history, people like Richard Drew, chose to stay in research, turning down opportunities to go into the management side of the business. Over the years, this became formalized in a dual career path. Today, technical employees can choose to follow a technical career path or a management career path, with equal advancement opportunities. The idea is to let researchers develop their technical professional interests, without being penalized financially for not going into management.

Although 3M's innovative culture emphasizes the role of technical employees in producing innovations, the company also has a strong tradition of emphasizing that new product ideas often come from watching customers at work. Richard Drew's original idea for masking tape, for example, came from watching workers uses 3M wet and dry sandpaper in auto body shops. As with much else at 3M, the tone was set by McKnight who insisted that salespeople needed to "get behind the smokestacks" of 3M customers, going onto the factory floor, talking to workers and finding out what their problems were. Over the years this theme has become ingrained in 3M's culture, with salespeople often requesting time to watch customer work, and then brining their insights about customer problems back into their organization.

By the mid 1990s, McKnight's notion of getting behind the smokestacks had evolved into the idea that 3M could learn a tremendous amount from what were termed "lead users", who were customers working in very demanding conditions. Over the years, 3M had observed that in many cases, customer themselves can be innovators, developing new products to solve problems that they face in their work setting. This was most likely to occur for customers working in very demanding conditions. To take advantage of this process, 3M has instituted a lead user process in the company in which cross functional teams from a business unit go and observe how customers work in demanding situations.

For example, 3M has a $100 million business selling surgical drapes, which are drapes backed with adhesives that are used to cover parts of a body during surgery and help prevent infection. As an aid to new product development, 3M's surgical drapes business formed a cross functional team that went to observe surgeons at work in very demanding situations—including on the battlefield, hospitals in developing nations, and in vets offices. The result was a new set of product ideas, including low cost surgical drapes that were affordable in developing nations, and devices for coating a patient's skin and surgical instruments with antimicrobial substances that would reduce the chance of infection during surgery.[10]

Driving the entire innovation machine at 3M has been a series of stretch goals set by top managers. The goals date back to 3M's early days and McKnight's ambitious growth targets. In 1977, the company established "Challenge 81", which called for 25% of sales to come from products that had been on the market for less than 5 years by 1981. By the 1990s, the goal had been raised to the requirement that 30% of sales should come from products that had been on the market less than four years.

The flip side of these goals were that over the years, many products and businesses that had been 3M staples were phased out. More than 20 of the businesses that were 3M mainstays in 1980, for example, had been phased out by 2000. Analysts estimate that sales from mature products at 3M generally fall by 3 to 4% per annum. The company has a long history of inventing businesses, leading the market for long periods of time, and then shutting those businesses down, or selling them off, when they can no longer meet 3M's own demanding growth targets. Notable examples include the duplicating business, a business 3M invented with Thermo-Fax copiers (which were ultimately made obsolete my Xerox's patented technology) and the video and audio magnetic tape business. The former division was sold off in 1985, and the later in 1995. In both cases the company exited these areas because they had become low growth commodity businesses which could not generate the kind of top line growth that 3M was looking for.

Still, 3M was by no means invulnerable in the realm of innovation and on occasion squandered huge opportunities. A case in point was the document copying business. 3M invented this business in 1951 when it introduced the world's first commercially successful Thermo-Fax copier (which used specially coated 3M paper to copy original typed documents). 3M dominated the world copier business until 1970, when Xerox overtook the company with its revolutionary xerographic technology that used plane paper to make copies. 3M saw Xerox coming, but rather than try and develop their own plane paper copier, the company invested funds in trying to improve its (increasingly obsolete) copying technology. It wasn't until 1975 that 3M introduced its own plane paper copier, and by then it was too late. Ironically, 3M turned down the chance to acquire Xerox's technology 20 years earlier, when the company's founders had approached 3M.

Building the Organization

McKnight, a strong believer in decentralization, organized the company into product divisions in 1948 making 3M one of the early adopters of this organizational form. Each division was set up as an individual profit center that had the power, autonomy and resources to run independently. At the same time, certain functions remained centralized, including significant R&D, human resources, and finance.

McKnight wanted to keep the divisions small enough that people had a chance to be entrepreneurial, and focused on the customer. A key philosophy of McKnight's was "divide and grow". Put simply, when a division became too big, some of its embryonic businesses were spun of into a new division. Not only did this new division then typically attain higher growth rates, but the original division had to find new drivers of growth to make up for the contribution of the businesses that had gained independence. This drove the search for further innovations.

At 3M the process of organic diversification by splitting divisions became known as "renewal". The examples of renewal within 3M are legion. A copying machine project for Thermo-Fax copiers grew to become the Office Products Division. When Magnetic Recording Materials was spun off from the Electrical Products division, it grew to become its own division, and then in turn spawned a spate of divisions.

However, this organic process was not without its downside. By the early 1990s some of 3M's key customers were frustrated that they had to do businesses with a large number of different 3M divisions. In some cases, there could be representatives from 10 to 20 3M divisions calling on the same customer. To cope with this problem, in 1992 3M started to assign key account representatives to sell 3M products directly to major customers. These representatives typically worked across divisional lines. Implementing the strategy required many of 3M's general managers to give up some of their autonomy and power, but the solution seemed to work well, particularly for 3M's consumer and office divisions.

Underpinning the organization that McKnight put in place was his own management philosophy. As explaining in a 1948 document, his basic management philosophy consisted of the following values:[11]

As our business grows, it becomes increasingly necessary to delegate responsibility and to encourage men and women to exercise their initiative. This requires considerable tolerance. Those men and women to whom we delegate authority and responsibility, if they are good people, are going to want to do their jobs in their own way.

Mistakes will be made. But if a person is essentially right, the mistakes he or she makes are not as serious in the long run as the mistakes management will make if it undertakes to tell those in authority exactly how they must do their jobs.

Management that is destructively critical when mistakes are made kills initiative. And it's essential that we have many people with initiative if we are to continue to grow.

At just 3% per annum, employee turnover rate at 3M has long been among the lowest in corporate America, a fact that is often attributed to the tolerant, empowering and family like corporate culture that McKnight helped to establish. Reinforcing this culture has been a progressive approach towards employee compensation and retention. In the depths of the Great Depression, 3M was able to avoid laying off employees while many others did because the company's innovation engine was able to keep building new businesses even through the worst of times.

In many ways, 3M was ahead of its time in management philosophy and human resource practices. The company introduced its first profit sharing plan in 1916, and McKnight instituted a pension plan in 1930 and an employee stock purchase plan in 1950. McKnight himself was convinced that people would be much more likely to be loyal in a company if they had a stake in it. 3M also developed a policy of promoting from within, and of giving its employees a plethora of career opportunities within the company.

Going International

The first steps abroad occurred in the 1920s. There were some limited sales of wet and dry sandpaper in Europe during the early 1920s. These increased after 1929 when 3M joined the Durex Corporation, a joint venture for international abrasive product sales in which 3M was involved along with eight other United States companies. In 1950, however, the Department of Justice alleged that the Durex Corporation was a mechanism for achieving collusion among U.S. abrasive manufactured, and a judge ordered that the corporation be broken up. After the Durex Corporation was dissolved in 1951, 3M was left with a sandpaper factory in Britain, a small plant in France, a sales office in Germany, and a tape factory in Brazil. International sales at this point amounted to no more than 5% of 3M's total revenues.

Although 3M opposed the dissolution of the Durex Corporation, in retrospect it turned out to be one of the most important events in the company's history, for it forced the corporation to build its own international operations. By 2010, international sales amounted to 63% of total revenues.

In 1952 Clarence Sampair was put in charge of 3M's international operations and charged with getting them off the ground. He was given considerable strategic and operational independence. Sampair and his successor, Maynard Patterson, worked hard to protect the international operations from getting caught up in the red tape of a major corporation. For example, Patterson recounts how….

> I asked Em Monteiro to start a small company in Columbia. I told him to pick a key person he wanted to take with him. "Go start a company", I said," and no one from St Paul is going to visit you unless you ask for them. We'll stay out of your way, and if someone sticks his nose in your business you call me".[12]

The international businesses were grouped into an International Division that Sampair headed. From the get go the company insisted that foreign ventures pay their own way. In addition, 3M's international companies were expected to pay a 5 to 10% royalty to the corporate head office. Starved of working capital, 3M's International Division relied heavily on local borrowing to fund local operations, a fact that forced those operations to quickly pay their own way.

The international growth at 3M typically occurred in stages. The company would start by exporting to a country and working through sales subsidiaries. In that way, it began to understand the country, the local marketplace, and the local business environment. Next 3M established warehouses in each nation, and stocked those with goods paid for in local currency. The next phase involved converting products to the sizes and packaging forms that the local market conditions, customs and culture dictated. 3M would ship jumbo rolls of products from the United States, which were then broken up and repackaged for each country. The next stage was designing and building plants, buying machinery and getting them up and running. Over the years, R&D functions were often added, and by the 1980s considerable R&D was being done outside of the United States.

Both Sampair and Patterson set an innovative, entrepreneurial framework that according to the company, still guides 3M's International Operations today. The philosophy can be reduced to several key and simple commitments: (1) Get in early (within the company, the strategy is known as FIDO—"First in Defeats Others"), (2) Hire talented and motivated local people, (3) Become a good corporate citizen of the country, (4) Grow with the local economy, (5) American products are not one size fit all around the world; tailor products to fit local needs, and (6) Enforce patents in local countries.

As 3M stepped into the international market vacuum, foreign sales surged from less than 5% in 1951 to 42% by 1979. By the end of the 1970s 3M was beginning to understand how important it was to integrate the international operations more closely with the U.S. operations, and to build innovative capabilities overseas. It expanded the company's international R&D presence (there are now more than 2,200 technical employees outside the U.S.), built closer ties between the U.S. and foreign research organizations, and started to transfer more managerial and technical employees between businesses in different countries.

In 1978 the company started the Pathfinder Program to encourage new product and new business initiatives born outside the United States. By 1983, products developed under the initiative were generating sales of over $150 million a year. 3M Brazil invented a low cost, hot melt adhesive from local raw materials, 3M Germany teamed up with Sumitomo 3M of Japan (a joint venture with Sumitomo) to develop electronic connectors with new features for the worldwide electronics industry, 3M Philippines developed a Scotch-Brite cleaning pad shaped like a foot after learning that Filipinos polished floors with their feet, and so on. On the back of such developments, in 1992 international operations exceeded 50% for the first time in the company's history.

By the 1990s 3M started to shift away from a country-by-country management structure to more regional management. Drivers behind this development included the fall of trade barriers, the rise of trading blocks such as the European Union and North American Free Trade Agreement (NAFTA), and the need to drive down costs in the face of intense global competition. The first European Business Center (EBC) was created in 1991 to manage 3M's chemical business across Europe. The EBC was charged with product development, manufacturing, sales and marketing for Europe, but also with paying attention to local country requirements. Other EBCs soon followed, such as EBCs for Disposable Products and Pharmaceuticals.

As the millennium ended, 3M was transforming the company into a transnational organization characterized by an integrated network of businesses that spanned the globe. The goal was to get the right mix of global scale to deal with competitive pressures, while at the same time maintaining 3M's traditional focus on local market differences and decentralized R&D capabilities.

THE NEW ERA

The DeSimone Years

In 1991, Desi DeSimone became CEO of 3M. A long time 3M employee, the Canadian born DeSimone was the epitome of a 21st century manager—he had made his name by building 3M's Brazilian business and spoke five languages fluently. Unlike most prior 3M CEOs, DeSimone came from the manufacturing side of the business, rather than the technical aide. He soon received praise for managing 3M through the recession of the early 1990s. By the late 1990s, however, his leadership had come under fire from both inside and outside the company.

In 1998 and 1999 the company missed its earnings targets, and the stock price fell as disappointed investors sold. Sales were flat, profit margins fell and earnings slumped by 50%. The stock had underperformed the widely tracked S&P 500 stock index for most of the 1980s and 1990s.

One cause of the earnings slump in the late 1990s was 3M's sluggish response to the 1997 Asian crisis. During the Asian crisis the value of several Asian currencies fell by as much as 80% against the U.S. dollar in a matter of months. 3M generated a quarter of its sales from Asia, but it was slow to cut costs there in the face of slumping demand following the collapse of currency values. At the same time, a flood of cheap Asian products cut into 3M's market share in the United States and Europe as lower currency values made Asian products much cheaper.

Another problem was that for all of its vaunted innovative capabilities, 3M had not produced a new blockbuster product since Post it Notes. Most of the new products produced during the 1990s were just improvements over existing products, not truly new products.

DeSimone was also blamed for not pushing 3M hard enough earlier in the decade to reduce costs. An example was the company's supply chain excellence program. Back in 1995, 3M's inventory was turning over just 3.5 times a year, subpar for manufacturing. An internal study suggested that every half point increase in inventory turnover could reduce 3M's working capital needs by $700 million, and boost its ROIC. But by 1998 3M had made no progress on this front.[13]

By 1998 there was also evidence of internal concerns. Anonymous letters from 3M employees were sent to the board of directors, claiming that DeSimone was not committed to research as he should have been. Some letters complained that DeSimone was not funding important projects for future growth, others that he had not moved boldly enough to cut costs, and still others that the company's duel career track was not being implemented well, and that technical people were underpaid. Critics argued that he was a slow and cautious decision maker in a time that required decisive strategic decisions. For example, in August 1998 DeSimone announced a restructuring plan that included a commitment to cut 4,500 jobs, but reports suggest that other senior managers wanted 10,000 job cuts, and DeSimone had watered down the proposals.[14]

Despite the criticism, 3M's board, which included four previous 3M CEOs among its members, stood behind DeSimone until he retired in 2001. However, the board began a search for a new top executive in February 2000 and signaled that it was looking for an outsider. In December 2000 the company announced that it had found the person they wanted, Jim McNerney, a 51 year old General Electric veteran who ran GE's medical equipment businesses, and before that GE's Asian operations. McNerney was one of the front runners in the race to succeed Jack Welsh as CEO of General Electric, but lost out to Jeffrey Immelt. One week after that announcement, 3M hired him.

McNerney's Plan for 3M

In his first public statement days after being appointed, McNerney said that his focus would be on getting to know 3M's people and culture and its diverse lines of business:

I think getting to know some of those businesses and bringing some of GE here to overlay on top of 3M's strong culture of innovation will be particularly important.[15]

It soon became apparent that McNerney's game plan was exactly that: to bring the GE play book to 3M and use it to try and boost 3M's results, while simultaneously not destroying the innovative culture that had produced the company's portfolio of 50,000 products.

The first move came in April 2001 when 3M announced that the company would cut 5,000 jobs, or about 7% of the workforce, in a restructuring effort that would zero in on struggling businesses. To cover severance and other costs of restructuring, 3M announced that it would take a $600 million charge against earnings. The job cuts were expected to save $500 million a year. In another effort to save costs, the company streamlined its purchasing processes, for example, by reducing the number of packaging suppliers on a global basis from 50 to 5, saving another $100 million a year in the process.

Next, McNerney introduced the Six-Sigma process, a rigorous statistically based quality control process that was one of the drivers of process improvement and cost savings at General Electric. At heart, Six-Sigma is a management philosophy, accompanied by a set of tools, that is rooted in identifying and prioritizing customers and their needs, reducing variation in all business processes, and selecting and grading all projects based on their impact on financial results. Six-Sigma breaks every task (process) in an organization down into increments to be measured against a perfect model.

McNerney called for Six-Sigma to be rolled out across 3M's global operations. He also introduced a 3M like performance evaluation system at 3M under which managers were asked to rank every single employee who reported to them.

In addition to boosting performance from existing business, McNerney quickly signaled that he wanted to play a more active role in allocating resources between new business opportunities. At any given time, 3M has around 1,500 products in the development pipeline. McNerney stated that was too many, and he indicated that wanted to funnel more cash to the most promising ideas, those with a potential market of $100 million a year or more, while cutting funding to weaker looking development projects.

In the same vein, he signaled that he wanted to play a more active role in resource allocation than had traditionally been the case for a 3M CEO, using cash from mature businesses to fund growth opportunities elsewhere. He scrapped the requirement that each division get 30% of its sales from products introduced in the past four years, noting that:

To make that number, some managers were resorting to some rather dubious innovations, such as pink Post it Notes. It became a game, what could you do to get a new SKU?[16]

Some long time 3M watchers, however, worried that by changing resource allocation practices McNerney might harm 3M's innovative culture. If the company's history proves anything, they say, it's that it is hard to tell which of today's tiny products will become tomorrow's home runs. No one predicted that Scotch Guard or Post it Notes would earn millions. They began as little experiments that evolved without planning into big hits. McNerney's innovations all sound fine in theory, they say, but there is a risk that he will transform 3M into "3E" and lose what is valuable in 3M in the process.

In general though, securities analysts greeted McNerney's moves favorably. One noted that "McNerney is all about speed", and that there will be "no more Tower of Babel-everyone speaks-one language". This "one company" vision was meant to replace the program under which 3M systematically spun off successful new products into new business centers. The problem with this approach, according to the analyst, was that there was no leveraging of best practices across businesses.[17]

McNerney also signaled that he would reform 3M's regional management structure, replacing it with a global business unit structure that will be defined by either products or markets.

At a meeting for investment analysts, held on September 30 2003, McNerney summarized a number of achievements.[18] At the time, the indications seemed to suggest that McNerney was helping to revitalize 3M. Profitability, measured by ROIC, had risen from 19.4% in 2001 and was projected to hit 25.5% in 2003. 3M's stock price had risen from $42 just before McNerney was hired to $73 in October 2003.

Like his former boss, Jack Welsh at GE, McNerney seemed to place significant value on internal executive education programs as a way of shifting to a performance oriented culture. McNerney noted that some 20,000 employees had been through six-sigma training by the third quarter of 2003. Almost 400 higher level managers had been through an Advanced Leadership Development Program set up by McNerney, and offered by 3M's own internal executive education institute. Some 40% of participants had been promoted on graduating. All of the company's top managers had graduated from an Executive Leadership Program offered by 3M.

McNerney also emphasized the value of five initiatives that he put in place at 3M; indirect cost control, global sourcing, e-productivity, Six-Sigma, and the 3M Acceleration Program. With regard to indirect cost control, some $800 million had been taken out of 3M's cost structure since 2001, primarily by reducing employee numbers, introducing more efficient processes that boost productivity, benchmarking operations internally and leveraging best practices. According to McNerney, internal benchmarking highlighted another $200 to $400 million in potential cost savings over the next few years.

On global sourcing, McNerney noted that more than $500 million had been saved since 2000 by consolidating purchasing, reducing the number of suppliers, switching to lower cost suppliers in developing nations, and introducing duel sourcing policies to keep price increases under control.

The e-productivity program at 3M embraced the entire organization, and all functions. It involves the digitalization of a wide range of processes, from customer ordering and payment, through supply chain management and inventory control, to managing employee process. The central goal is to boost productivity by using information technology to more effectively manage information within the company, and between the company and its customers and suppliers. McNerney cited some $100 million in annual cost savings from this process.

The six-sigma program overlays the entire organization, and focuses on improving processes to boost cash flow, lower costs (through productivity enhancements), and boost growth rates. By late 2003, there were some 7,000 six-sigma projects in process at 3M. By using working capital more efficiently, six-sigma programs had helped to generate some $800 million in cash, with the total expected to rise to $1.5 billion in by the end of 2004. 3M has applied the six-sigma process to the company's R&D process, enabling researcher to engage customer information in the initial stages of a design discussion, which according to Jay Inlenfeld, the VP of R&D, six-sigma tools:

Allow us to be more closely connected to the market and give us a much higher probability of success in our new product designs.[19]

Finally, the 3M Acceleration Program is aimed at boost the growth rate from new products through better resource allocation, particularly by shifting resources from slower growing to faster growing markets. As McNerney noted:

3M has always had extremely strong competitive positions, but not in markets that are growing fast enough. The issue has been to shift emphasize into markets that are growing faster.[20]

Part of this program is a tool termed 2X/3X, 2X is an objective for two times the number of new products that were introduced in the past, and 3X is a business objective for three times as many winning products as there were in the past (see Exhibit 2). 2X focuses on generating more "major" product initiatives, and 3X on improving the commercialization of those initiatives. The process illustrated in Exhibit 3 is 3M's "stage gate" process, where each gate represents a major decision point in the development of a new product, from idea generation to post launch.

Other initiates aimed at boosting 3M's organization growth rate through innovation include Six-Sigma process, leadership development programs, and technology leadership (see Exhibit 3). The purpose of these initiatives was to help implement the 2X/3X strategy.

As a further step in the Acceleration Program, 3M decided to centralize its corporate R&D effort. Prior to the arrival of McNerney, there were 12 technology centers

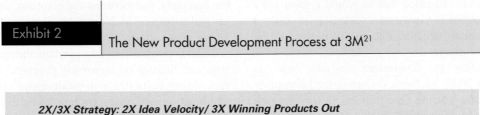

Exhibit 2   The New Product Development Process at 3M[21]

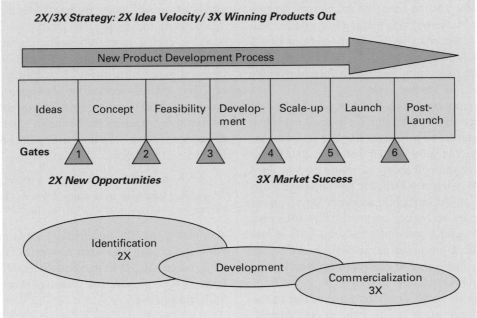

staffed by 900 scientists that focused on core technology development. The company is replacing these with one central research lab, staffed by 500 scientists, some 120 of whom will be located outside the United States. The remaining 400 scientists will be relocated to R&D centers in the business units. The goal of this new corporate research lab is to focus on developing new technology that might fill high growth "white spaces", which are areas where the company currently has no presence, but where the long-term market potential is great. An example is research on fuel cells, which is currently a big research project within 3M.

Responding to critics' charges that changes such as these might impact on 3M's innovative culture, VP of R&D Inlenfeld noted that:

We are not going to change the basic culture of innovation at 3M. There is a lot of culture in 3M, but we are going to introduce more systematic, more productive tools that allow our researchers to be more successful.[23]

For example, Inlenfeld repeatedly emphasized that the company remains committed to basic 3M principles, such as the 15% rule and leveraging technology across businesses.

By late 2003 McNerney noted that some 600 new product ideas were underdevelopment and that collectively, they were expected to reach the market and generate some $5 billion in new revenues between 2003 and 2006, up from $3.5 billion 18 months earlier. Some $1 billion of these gains were expected to come in 2003.

George Buckley Takes Over

In mid 2005 McNerney announced that he would leave 3M to become CEO and Chairman of Boeing, a company on whose board he had served for some time. He was replaced in late 2005 by another outsider, George Buckley, the highly regarded CEO of Brunswick Industries. Buckley, a Brit with a PhD. in electrical engineering, describes himself as a scientist at heart. Over the

Exhibit 3	R&D's Role in Organic Growth[22]

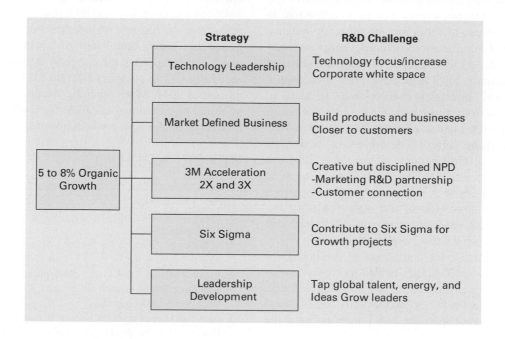

next year in several presentations Buckley outlined his strategy for 3M, and it soon became apparent that he was sticking to the general course laid out by McNerney, albeit with some important corrections.[24]

Buckley did not see 3M as an enterprise that needed radical change. He saw 3M as a company with impressive internal strengths, but one that had been too cautious about pursuing growth opportunities.[25] Buckley's overall strategic vision for 3M was that the company must solve customer needs through the provision of innovative and differentiated products that increase the efficiency and competitiveness of customers. Consistent with long-term 3M strategy, he saw this as being achieved by taking 3M's multiple technology platforms, and applying them to different market opportunities.

Controlling costs and boosting productivity through Six-Sigma continued to be a major thrust under Buckley. This was hardly a surprise, since Buckley had pushed Six-Sigma at Brunswick. By late 2006 some 55,000 3M employees had been trained in Six-Sigma methodology, 20,000 projects had been completed, and some 15,000 were under way. 3M was also adding techniques gleaned

from Toyota's lean production methodology to its six-sigma tool kit. As a result of Six-Sigma and other cost control methods, between 2001 and 2005 productivity measured by sales per employee increased from $234 to $311, and some $750 million were taken out of overhead costs.

However, Buckley departed from McNerney's playbook in one significant way, he removed Six-Sigma from the labs. The feeling of many at 3M was that Six-Sigma rules choked those working on innovation. As one 3M researcher noted, "It's really tough to schedule innovation".[26] When McNerney left 3M in 2005, the percentage of sales from new products introduced in the last 5 years had fallen to 21%, down from the company's long-term goal of 30%. By 2010, after 5 years of Buckley's leadership, the percentage was back up to 30%. According to many in the company, Buckley has been a champion of researchers at 3M, devoting much of his personal time to empowering researchers, and urging them to restore the luster of 3M.

Buckley stressed the need for 3M to more aggressively pursue growth opportunities. He wanted the company to use its differentiate brands and technology to continue to develop core businesses and extend those core business into adjacent areas. In addition, like McNerney, Buckley wanted the company to focus R&D resources on emerging business opportunities, and he too seemed to be prepared to play a more proactive role in this process. Areas of focus include filtration systems, track and trace information technology, energy and mineral extraction, and food safety. 3M made a number of acquisitions since 2005 to achieve scale and acquire technology and other assets in these areas. In addition, it increased its own investment in technologies related to these growth opportunities, particularly nanotechnology.

Buckley made selective divestures of businesses not seen as core. Most notably, in November 2006 3M reached an agreement to sell its pharmaceutical business for $2.1 billion. 3M took this step after deciding that a combination of slow growth, and high regulatory and technological risk, made the sector an unattractive one that would dampen the company's growth rate.

Finally, Buckley was committed to continuing internationalization at 3M. 3M doubled its capital investment in the fast growing markets of China, India, Brazil, Russia, and Poland between 2005 and 2010. All of these markets are seen as expanding 2 to 3 times as fast as the United States.

Judged by the company's financial results, the McNerney and Buckley eras did seem to be improving 3M's financial performance. The first decade of the 21st century was a difficult one, marked by sluggish growth in the United States, and in 2008–2009, a steep recession triggered by a global financial crisis. 3M weathered this storm better than most, bouncing out of the recession in 2010 with strong revenue and income growth, helped in large part by its new products and exposure to fast growing international markets. For the decade, revenues expanded from $16 billion in 2001 to $26.66 billion in 2010, earnings per share expanded from $1.79 to $5.63, while ROIC increased from the mid teens in the 1990s to the mid 20s form most of the decade.

Inge Thulin: Back to the Future

In early 2012 Georg Buckley retired after a successful tenure during which he had skillfully navigated 3M through the great financial crisis of 2008–2009. The company's COO, Inge Thulin replaced him. Thulin was originally from Sweden and first joined 3M in 1979. Fluent in five languages, Thulin has worked for 3M in Europe, the Middle East, Canada and Hong Kong. Within the company he is seen as one of the chief architects of 3Ms successful international business, which he oversaw as executive vice president for international operations. He is also seen as an insider who knows 3M's culture intimately, and who places a high value on innovation. In his first shareholder meeting, he reaffirmed this, stating that "innovation is the center of our plan", and committing the company to increasing R&D spending to 6% of company sales by 2017, up from 5.4% of sales in 2012. More generally, Thulin has stated that he would be continuing to follow the road map laid out by George Buckley, with whom he worked closely.

REFERENCES

1. J.C. Collins and J.I. Porras. *Built to Last*, Harper Business, New York, 1994.
2. Michelle Conlin. "Too much doodle?" *Forbes*, October 19, 1998, page 54–56.
3. M.Dickson. "Back to the Future", *Financial Times*, 1994, May 30, page 7.
4. Joseph Hallinan. "3M's next chief plans to fortify results with discipline he learned at GE unit", *Wall Street Journal*, December 6, 2000, page B17.
5. Eric Von Hippel et al, "Creating Breakthroughs at 3M", *Harvard Business Review*, September–October 1999.
6. Rick Mullin. "Analysts rate 3M's new culture", *Chemical Week*", September 26, 2001, pages 39–40.
7. 3M. *A Century of Innovation*, the 3M Story. 3M, 2002. Available at http://www.3m.com/about3m/century/index.jhtml
8. 3M Investor Meeting, September 30, 2003, archived at http://www.corporate-ir.net/ireye/ir_site.zhtml?ticker=MMM&script=2100
9. Tim Studt. 3M – where innovation rules, *R&D Magazine*, April 2003, Vol 45, pages 20–24.
10. De'Ann Weimer, "3M: The heat is on the boss", *Business Week*, March 15, 1999, page 82–83.
11. Jerry Useem. "(Tape) + (Light bulb) = ?", *Fortune*, August 12, 2002, pages 127–131.
12. M. Gunther, M. Adamo, and B. Feldman, "3M's innovation revival", *Fortune*, September 27, 2010, pp. 73–76.

NOTES

1. Sources: M.Dickson. "Back to the Future", *Financial Times*, 1994, May 30, page 7. http://www.3m.com/profile/looking/mcknight.jhtml.
2. http://www.3m.com/about3M/pioneers/drew2.jhtml
3. Source:http://www.3m.com/about3M/innovation/scotchgard50/index.jhtml

4. 3M. A Century of Innovation, the 3M Story. 3M, 2002. Available at http://www.3m.com/about3m/century/index.jhtml

5. 3M. A Century of Innovation, the 3M Story. 3M, 2002, page 33. Available at http://www.3m.com/about3m/century/index.jhtml

6. Tim Studt. 3M – where innovation rules, *R&D Magazine*, April 2003, Vol 45, pages 20–24.

7. 3M. A Century of Innovation, the 3M Story. 3M, 2002, page 78. Available at http://www.3m.com/about3m/century/index.jhtml

8. 3M. A Century of Innovation, the 3M Story. 3M, 2002, page 78. Available at http://www.3m.com/about3m/century/index.jhtml

9. 3M. A Century of Innovation, the 3M Story. 3M, 2002, page 42. Available at http://www.3m.com/about3m/century/index.jhtml

10. Eric Von Hippel et al., "Creating Breakthroughs at 3M", Harvard Business Review, September–October 1999.

11. From 3M web site at http://www.3m.com/about3M/history/mcknight.jhtml

12. 3M. A Century of Innovation, the 3M Story. 3M, 2002, page 143–144. Available at http://www.3m.com/about3m/century/index.jhtml

13. Michelle Conlin. "Too much doodle?" *Forbes*, October 19, 1998, page 54–56.

14. De'Ann Weimer, "3M: The heat is on the boss", *Business Week*, March 15, 1999, page 82–83.

15. Joseph Hallinan. "3M's next chief plans to fortify results with discipline he learned at GE unit", *Wall Street Journal*, December 6, 2000, page B17.

16. Jerry Useem. "(Tape) + (Light bulb) = ?", *Fortune*, August 12, 2002, pages 127–131.

17. Rick Mullin. "Analysts rate 3M's new culture", *Chemical Week*", September 26, 2001, pages 39–40.

18. 3M Investor Meeting, September 30, 2003, archived at http://www.corporate-ir.net/ireye/ir_site.zhtml?ticker=MMM&script=2100

19. Tim Studt, "3M—Where innovation rules", R&D Magazine, April 2003, page 22.

20. 3M Investor Meeting, September 30, 2003, archived at http://www.corporate-ir.net/ireye/ir_site.zhtml?ticker=MMM&script=2100

21. Adapted from presentation by Jay Inlenfeld, 3M Investor Meeting, September 30, 2003, archived at http://www.corporate-ir.net/ireye/ir_site.zhtml?ticker=MMM&script=2100

22. Adapted from presentation by Jay Inlenfeld, 3M Investor Meeting, September 30, 2003, archived at http://www.corporate-ir.net/ireye/ir_site.zhtml?ticker=MMM&script=2100

23. Tim Studt, "3M—Where innovation rules", R&D Magazine, April 2003, page 21.

24. Material here drawn from George Buckley' presentation to Prudential's investor conference on "Inside our Best ideas", September 28, 2006. This and other relevant presentations are archived at http://investor.3m.com/ireye/ir_site.zhtml?ticker=MMM&script=1200

25. Jeffery Sprague, "MMM: Searching for Growth with new CEO leading", *Citigroup Global Markets*, May 2, 2006.

26. M. Gunther, M. Adamo, and B. Feldman, "3M's innovation revival", *Fortune*, September 27, 2010, pp. 74.

Case 24

The Tata Group, 2013

Melissa A. Schilling & Nora Scott

The Tata Group is India's largest industrial conglomerate. Throughout its 145-year history the growth of the company has advanced in parallel with the Indian economy, increasing both the scope of businesses in which it participates, and its scale in those businesses. By 2013 the company had sales of over $100 billion a year, and operated more than 90 companies in sectors as diverse as automobiles, steel, tea, hotels, telecommunications, chemicals, and more. More remarkable still was that despite its immense size and diversification, the company had maintained a return on assets of 7% or more throughout most of its history, in contrast to the conventional wisdom that giant conglomerates typically underperform more specialized companies.

The Tata Group is managed by the holding company, Tata Sons. The original Tata family owns about 3% of Tata Sons, and a large portion of the rest of the equity of the group is held by charitable trusts that were created by the family. Since its inception in 1868, the Tata Group has had only six chairmen, two for negligible amounts of time. Tata's expansion into the massive holding company that it is today was shaped by both the evolution of the economic and political climate of India, as well as the vision of the four major chairmen who steered the Group. To understand Tata's evolution and performance, it is necessary to understand both the business context of India, and the mission of its founding family.

THE HISTORY OF THE HOUSE OF TATA

Jamsetji Nusserwanji Tata founded the his company as a textile trading company in 1868. Then in 1869, he expanded into textile manufacturing through the purchase of a bankrupt mill, which he later sold for a profit after improving its efficiency. His professed goals for the company that would later be known as House of Tata were to help industrialize India. His plan was to set up an iron and steel company that would supply the expanding railroads, a hydro-electric power plant, a luxury hotel and a world-class learning and research institution[i]. Only one of those goals was fulfilled within his lifetime, the Taj Mahal Hotel in Bombay was opened (1903), at the time the only hotel in India to have electricity.

After Jamsetji Tata's death (1904) he was succeeded by his eldest son, Dorabji Tata. Dorabji Tata actualized his father's remaining goals and opened India's first private steel company in 1907 (one hundred years later it would be the country's largest private-sector steel company), the Indian Institute of Science in 1909, and the hydro-electric power plant in 1911.[ii] Dorabji Tata further diversified Tata Group's interests when he created the New India Assurance Company in 1919, which was the largest general insurance company in India. These became the cash pillars of Tata Group and allowed the company to reinvest in new projects without having to borrow capital from lending institutions.

In 1932, J.R.D. Tata (the son of Dorabji's cousin) took the help of the Tata group. Under J.R.D. Tata, the Tata Group continued to be at the forefront of India's development, opening India's first airline in 1932, Tata Chemicals in 1939, Tata Engineering & Locomotive in 1945. Tata Engineering & Locomotive had been founded to make steam locomotives, but after collaborating with Diamler-Benz in 1954 to enter truck production, the Tata Gropu began producing began producing commercial vehicles in earnest. In 1968, Tata founded India's first software firm 1968. In total, under J.R.D. Tata's control, the Tata portfolio expanded from 14 businesses to 95 businesses that they had either started or in which Tata held a controlling interest. If one includes subsidiary and associate companies, Tat was involved in over 300 businesses. Also under his chairmanship the assets of the Tata Group rose from US $100 million to over US $5 billion.

Many of the sectors the Tata Group entered were new for India at the time of its entry. Whereas in the US or Western Europe entrepreneurs could access investor funds or debt to found new ventures or scale-up businesses, India did not have strong capital markets. Weak investing norms and infrastructure, poor enforcement of contracts, and corruption meant that capital came at too high of a price or was not available at all. Tata's subsidization of new businesses from the high income generating, mature businesses thus allowed the Tata Group to expand in ways that independent companies could not. By internally funding new ventures this giant conglomerate was able to create large infrastructure projects without having to issue bonds or borrow from banks.

In 1991, Ratan Tata (great-grandson of Jamsetji Tata) took over as chairman from J.R.D. Tata. He had studied architecture at Cornell before returning to India to work shoveling limestone at Tata Steel.[iii] While the economic setting in India led J.R.D. Tata to create an insular system of companies that were able to cross fund each other without having to seek external capital, when Ratan Tata assumed the position as chairman in the early 90s, India's government had begun to relax its regulation of both domestic industry and the licensing regime that protected Indian industry from foreign investment. The loosening of restrictions gave Indian businesses more autonomy, but also exposed them to more foreign competition. Indian regulations mandated that foreign firms could enter India only by collaborating with a domestic company. The Tata Group's prominence and reputation for high ethical standards made many of their group companies popular partners. As a result, Tata companies created alliances with AT&T, Cummings Engine, IBM, Honeywell, Mercedes-Benz and Silicon Graphics as well as others during the 1990s. Tata's involvement with these companies enhanced its global exposure and strengthened its ability to expand into foreign markets.

Ratan Tata sought to increase the competitiveness of Tata's operating companies by cutting costs as well as employee ranks. One example of this approach is Tata Steel (the world's sixth largest producer after the $12.1 billion acquisition of UK-based Corus in 2007). Tata Steel has increased output per worker eightfold in just over a decade. Tata Steel cut costs to improve the production of blast furnaces by continually adjusting them to burn at maximum efficiency based on the incoming coal blends.[iv] This example of improved industrial efficiency is paralleled in Tata Power's decision to lower its capital expenditures by identifying inexpensive designs for large-scale projects. For example, when planning a new 4,000 mega-watt facility Tata engineers used cheaper welded tubes instead of seamless ones in feed-water heaters, and redesigned the layout of the turbine generator station. By making these types of adjustments Tata Power was able to save more than $100 million in capital expenditures while preserving the base capacity of the plant and still meeting India's standards for safety. Cutting employee ranks at Tata Steel served to reduce the number of management layers, from 13 to 5, thus increasing employee accountability. These organizational changes improved the competitiveness and the quality of products and services.

Under Ratan's stewardship, Tata engaged in a series of international acquisitions, including the Corus steel deal, the purchase of UK teabag maker Tetley, iconic automakers Land Rover and Jaguar (which were purchased from Ford), and Singapore's National Steel. By 2008, it was earning a majority of its profit from outside of India. Though the Tata Group had been founded with a mission to serve India through economic and industrial development, it was now being transformed into a truly global company. The acquisition of the two luxury brand vehicles (Jaguar and Land Rover)particularly increased international awareness of the Tata Group, while simultaneously giving Tata Motors access to new technology and markets. At his 2012 retirement Ratan Tata was replaced as Chairman by Cyrus Mistry, the first non-Indian to head the Tata Group, and only the second without the surname Tata.

THE INDIAN BUSINESS CONTEXT

When Jamsetji Tata originally founded his company, India was under British rule. India's independence did not come until the Tata Group had been around for 79 years, in 1947. Since its independence, India's government has developed into a federation system with a parliament. Post Independence India still adhered to socialist policies with economic policies that leaned toward protectionism and state monitoring of industrialization, import substitution and state intervention. High tariffs and the need for an import license worked to prevent foreign goods from reaching India's market. Firms were required to obtain a license in order to invest or develop their product.[v] These economic government policies are what caused J.R.D.Tata to structure the Tata Group in such an insular fashion. Following an economic crisis, in which the Indian government was close to default, the Liberalization Act in 1991 opened India's economy to trade and investment, broke the state monopolies, and eased the licensing requirements. The effect of the liberalization act enabled foreign direct investment to increase dramatically, both inward and outward (see Figure 1). Unshackling Indian businesses from the cumbersome regulation allowed new businesses to more rapidly form, and productivity to accelerate. As shown in Figure 2, while the population in India shows linear

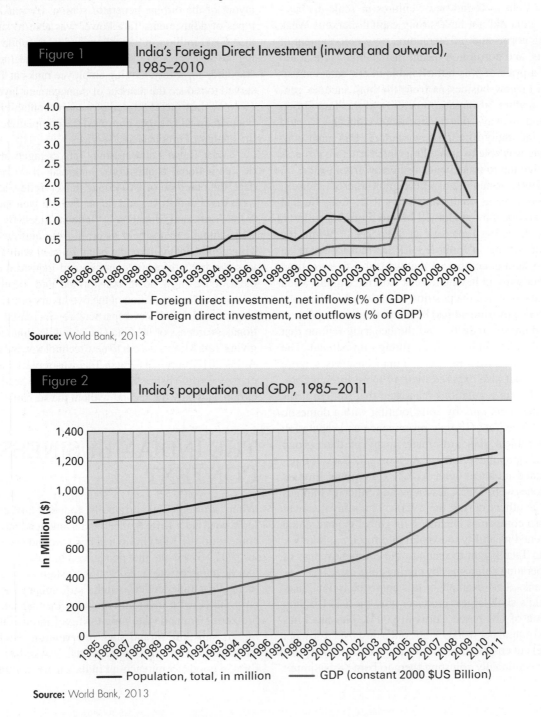

Figure 1 India's Foreign Direct Investment (inward and outward), 1985–2010

— Foreign direct investment, net inflows (% of GDP)
— Foreign direct investment, net outflows (% of GDP)

Source: World Bank, 2013

Figure 2 India's population and GDP, 1985–2011

— Population, total, in million   — GDP (constant 2000 $US Billion)

Source: World Bank, 2013

growth, the gross domestic product (GDP) began to increase exponentially. By 2011, India's economy was worth $1.85 trillion, making it the world's tenth largest by nominal GDP and the third largest by purchasing power parity.[vi]

TATA INDUSTRIES IN 2013

Before his 2012 retirement, Ratan Tata began an initiative to streamline and consolidate the Tata Group. Ratan Tata felt that the myriad of companies tied only by the Tata name needed to be realigned, with a stronger and more unified focus. He divested some operating companies while consolidating the others into seven categories: consumer products; energy; engineering; information systems and communications; services; chemicals; and materials (see Figure 3). Every Tata company has its own board of directors and shareholders to which it is accountable. The largest Tata companies are Tata Steel, Tata Motors, Tata Consultancy Services, Tata Power, Tata Chemicals, Tata Global Beverages, Tata Teleservices, Titan, Tata Communications, and Indian Hotels.

Consumer Products

This sector made up 4% of Tata Group's sales in 2011–12. From high-end designer furniture to bottled water, the various companies have an array of products priced to appeal to those of varied income. One company offers fine-bone china (selling to Wedgewood, Royal Doulton. . .) and also sells industrial china to institutional customers. Titan Industries and Tata Global Beverages (the largest tea company in the world) are part of this group.

Energy

The Energy sector represented 6% of sales for 2011–12. Tata Power, now 102 years old and the parent company of all the others in the energy division, has a presence in all the segments of the power sector from power generation, such as thermal, hydro, solar, wind, geothermal and waste gas, to the transmission, distribution and trading of power. Its areas of focus are power generation, green energy, transmission and distribution, fuel assets, shipping and logistics, trading and power project related services. Tata Power has interests in Australia, South Africa, Nepal and Bhutan, fuel assets and geothermal projects in Indonesia as well as logistics operations in Singapore.

Engineering

Engineering made up 39% of Tata Group's sales for 2011–12, making it Tata's largest sector. The various business in this sector offer consulting services, precision tool design and manufacturing, automation, construction, and temperature engineering (essential in a country where temperatures can reach 104 in the summer months). Tata Motors is one of the businesses within the Engineering sector. It was established (as Tata Engineering and

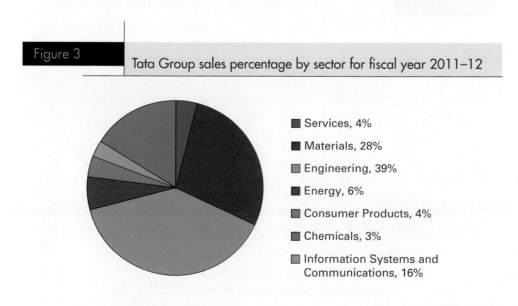

Figure 3 Tata Group sales percentage by sector for fiscal year 2011–12

- Services, 4%
- Materials, 28%
- Engineering, 39%
- Energy, 6%
- Consumer Products, 4%
- Chemicals, 3%
- Information Systems and Communications, 16%

Locomotive Company, or TELCO) in 1945, and is South Asia's largest auto manufacturer, and produces passenger cars, commercial vehicles, vans, and coaches. Jaguar and Land Rover are also part of this group.

Information Systems and Communications

This was the Tata Group's third-largest sector in 2011–12, bringing in 16% of the sales for Tata Group. The range of businesses clustered in this division offer services such as industrial automation, telecommunications, software and information systems. Notably, India has seen massive growth in the penetration of communication technologies such as mobile cellular subscriptions and internet use in the last decade (see Figure 4). Tata's information technologies consulting company, Tata Consultancy Services was the largest source of revenue for the group in 2012 (see Exhibit 1 for a breakdown of Tata's sales and profits by its major businesses). Tata Consultancy Services also employees over 250,000 consultants.

Services

The Service section comprises Tata's interests in the hospitality sector, insurance, realty and financial services primarily. This sector made up 4% of the Tata Group's sales for 2011–12. Indian Hotels, Taj Air, Tata Capital, Tata AIG General Insurance, among others, are part of this group.

Chemicals

Chemicals was the smallest of Tata's sectors, only comprising 3% of the company's sales. The Tata Group is one of the largest producers of soda ash (sodium carbonate) in the world. With a plethora of uses soda ash can be used as a water softener, a food additive, and a stabilizer in glass production. The businesses in this sector also have interests in fertilizers and pharmaceuticals.

Materials

This sector is accounts for 28% of the Tata Group's sales for 2011–12. Tata Steel has investments in Corus (UK, renamed Tata Steel Europe), Mellennium Steel (renamed Tata Steel Thailand), and NatSeel Holdings (in Singapore). It operates in over 20 countries, has a commercial presence in over 50, and has the capacity to produce over 30 million tons of crude steel every year, making it one of the largest steel producers in the world.

THE NANO PROJECT

On a rainy day in 2002, Ratan Tata, Chairman of India's Tata Group, was driving to the airport in Bangalore. In front of him was a typical sight: an entire family on a two-wheel scooter. The father drove the scooter with a young child standing in front of him, and his wife held

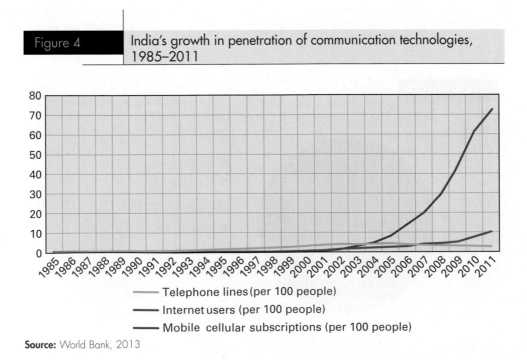

Figure 4 India's growth in penetration of communication technologies, 1985–2011

—— Telephone lines (per 100 people)

—— Internet users (per 100 people)

—— Mobile cellular subscriptions (per 100 people)

Source: World Bank, 2013

Exhibit 1	2012 Sales figures for select Tata Group companies

2012	Sales	Net Profit/Loss	Return on Sales
CMC	952.96	143.33	15%
Indian Hotels Company	1,808.73	145.35	8%
Tata Global Beverage	2,035.29	302.68	15%
Tata Consultancy	38,858.54	10,975.98	28%
Tata Elxsi	514.46	33.95	7%
Tata Investment	202.10	161.59	80%
Mount Everest Mineral Water	18.34	−1.64	−9%
Tata Teleservices (Maharashtra)	2,470.25	−517.55	−21%
Tayo Rolls	138.04	−53.12	−38%
Nelco	139.11	1.09	1%
Tata Metaliks	1,132.92	−90.60	−8%
Tinplate Company of India	627.03	16.55	3%
Rallis India	1,178.05	101.39	9%
Tata Motors	54,217.22	1,242.23	2%
Titan Industries	8,838.38	600.16	7%
Tata Chemicals	7,987.28	586.60	7%
Tata Power	8,569.08	1,169.73	14%
Trent	869.88	47.27	5%
Tata Coffee	506.73	78.85	16%
Tata Sponge Iron	633.71	75.68	12%
TRF, Ltd.	800.70	15.58	2%
Tata Communications	4,091.77	171.34	4%
Tata Steel	33,838.51	6,696.42	20%
Voltas	5,169.76	151.87	3%

a small baby in back. Suddenly the scooter skidded and overturned, sending the family tumbling. Tata and his driver narrowly escaped running over the poor family.[vii] At that moment, Ratan Tata conceived of a dream that would take five years and the help of a global network of 800 suppliers to realize: a car that was affordable by the masses of India. In a seemingly off-handed comment Tata mentioned to a reporter that the car would be priced at around Rs. 1 Lakh (approximately $2200). Despite extreme difficulties in meeting this price point, and increases in both parts and commodity prices during its development, Tata upheld what he viewed as a promise to the Indian public: to produce a Rs. Lakh car.

Developing the Nano

Ratan Tata decided to stay personally involved in the Nano project, and also put Ravi Kant, the Vice Chairman of Tata Motors, in charge of the project to ensure that the project had senior support. At the time Tata began developing the Nano, the least expensive car in the world was the Chinese QQ3, priced at $5,000. It quickly became clear that trying to make a Rs. 1 Lakh car by benchmarking against existing cars and trying to make them less expensive was not going to be successful, so Tata and Kant decided to instead benchmark many of the systems in the car against two-wheel scooters.

Many things that were taken for granted about producing a car had to be challenged. For example, rather than an engine with at least three cylinders, the Nano would be designed with two cylinders, which would both reduce the cost and weight of the car. The car would not have electric windows or locks, anti-lock brakes, or air bags. Its tires would have innertubes, its seats would have a simple three-position recline, and there would be only one windshield wiper and one rear-view mirror for the entire car.

Meeting many of the design challenges of the car was incredibly difficult, but many of Tata's suppliers looked at the project as an exciting challenge. Rather than being given a design dictated by Tata, they were given weight and cost objectives and given free reign to try to find a way to meet them. Many suppliers came up with startlingly unique ways of lowering the cost of the car, such as a hollow steering column and a single fuel injection valve for both of the engines cylinders. Power steering was unnecessary due to the low weight of the car. Radios were not included with the base model of the car, but could be purchased as an optional accessory.

Every thing about car design had to be reconceptualized to realize the Nano, from the car's frame, to it's major power systems, to even its trim. As summarized by Girish Wagh, head of the Tata team, "The entire system was being re-invented. Innovation at the aggregate level trickled down to system, then to sub-systems, then to parts. We went through a tremendous amount of iteration in the design process. The entire engine was redesigned thrice, the entire body was redesigned twice, and the floor plan of the car redesigned around ten times, the wiper system designed more than 11 times."[viii]

The Launch

The Nano was officially launched in March of 2009, at its intended price of Rs. 1 Lakh, and meeting all of the Indian government's safety and emissions standards. It weighed 1,320 pounds, and was rated at 50 miles to the gallon.[ix] Ratan Tata, who is exceptionally tall, even sat in the car (to demonstrate that the Nano had ample interior space despite its small size), and remarked, "We made a promise to the world and we kept it."

Demand for the Nano was very strong, but the car was not without its early struggles. First, plans to manufacture the car in West Bengal met with resistance by farmers, forcing a costly move of both Tata's manufacturing and many suppliers.[x] Then several Nanos caught fire, leading to extremely bad publicity for the car. Tata reinforced the exhaust systems of the car to avoid such problems in the future, but it would take some time for the car's reputation to recover.

The Future of Nano

Ratan Tata envisions a new market niche worldwide for the Nano, especially in developing countries where motorcycles and scooters dominate the rural travel options. Ratan Tata became involved in South Africa after noticing the enormous disparity of wealth and meeting Thabo Mbeki (before he became president). In a 2005 interview Ratan Tata described the process of entering other countries, "I said we [the Tata Group] really wanted to do something in South Africa to give to the country rather than take away from it." Tata Group set up schools to train people in trades, Ratan Tata then joined Mbeki's investment council. Tata said, "Eventually, this led to our launching our cars and trucks in South Africa, where we became quite successful, and then we were awarded a second network operator's contract for telecommunications in all of South Africa."[xi]

The Nano is set to arrive in the United States in three years[xii], but Tata has yet to announce how it will distribute the Nano, as it doesn't have preset distribution channels in place. In a 2005 interview Ratan Tata addressed this problem when he spoke of the ability to create "small satellite units, with very low breakeven points, where some of the cars could be assembled, sold, and serviced." [xiii] This approach would replace the dealer and the dealer's margin, keeping the cost low for the consumer. For the US market Tata is planning on creating a more "potent" vehicle with a bigger engine, a wider stance and more substantial crash protection.

THE FUTURE FOR TATA GROUP

As Tata Group navigates its new global role it must strike a balance between economic growth and investment in its country of origin. When Jamsetji Tata founded the company his goals of growing India's economy in conjunction with his company were complemented by his desire to give back to the Indian people. This was his professed goal in creating a world-class learning facility, the Indian Institute of Science. The Nano was emblematic of these goals – it aligned perfectly with Tata's mission to serve the bottom of the financial pyramid in India. Many of the company's other businesses, however, faced pressures of a more global nature. Did Tata's mission-based management make sense for a company that earned the majority of its profits abroad? Furthermore, analysts questioned whether Tata's large and diversified holding group would continue to make sense in an increasingly modern India. India's capital markets were becoming more robust, lessening the value to be gained through cross-subsidization of businesses. Furthermore, since many of Tata's businesses could now easily access global capital markets,

any constraints remaining in India's capital markets were becoming less relevant. Would Tata ultimately be split apart? What were the advantages and costs of keeping so many businesses united under a single family name, and under the watchful eye of Tata Sons? On a more tactical level, what should be Tata's plans for the Nano? Did it viable chance of succeeding in the international markets that Ratan had imagined? How could the learning that the company had reaped in its development be harnessed for future advantage?

NOTES

i. Sivakumar, N. 2007. The Business Ethics of Jamsetji Nusserwanji Tata—A Forerunner in Promoting Stakeholder Welfare. *Journal of Business Ethics*, (2008) 83:353–361.

ii. Hoovers, April 1, 2013.

iii. Raynal, W. 2012. The smartest guy in the room. *Automotive News,* 00051551, Vol. 87. Issue 6546.

iv. Dhwan, Rajat, Swaroop, Gautam, Zainulbhai, Adil. 2012. How Tata Group is raising its game. *McKinsey Quarterly*, 00475394, Issue 2.

v. India: the economy, BBC. 3, December, 1998.

vi. World Bank.

vii. Freiburg, K, Freiburg, J. & Dunston, D. 2011. *Nanovation: How a little car can teach the world to think big and act bold.* Nashville, TN: Thomas Nelson.

viii. Palepu, K., Anand, B. & Tahilyani, R. 2011. Tata Nano—The People's Car. *Harvard Business School Case*, 9-710-420: page 8.

ix. Taylor, A. 2011. Tata takes on the world: Building an auto empire in India. *Fortune*, 163(6):86–92.

x. Taylor, A. 2011. Tata takes on the world: Building an auto empire in India. *Fortune*, 163(6):86–92.

xi. Pandit, Ranjit. 2005. What's next for the Tata Group: An interview with its chairman. *The McKinsey Quarterly,* No. 4.

xii. Kurylko, Diana. 2012. Tata will redo Nano for the U.S. *Automotive News,* 00051551. Vol. 87. Issue 6538.

xiii. Pandit, Ranjit. 2005. What's next for the Tata Group: An interview with its chairman. *The McKinsey Quarterly,* No. 4.

Case 25

Genzyme's Focus on Orphan Drugs

Melissa Schilling[i]

In 2012, Genzyme, a subsidiary of Sanofi, was one of the world's leading biotech companies. With approximately $1.8 billion in annual revenues, it had 12,000 employees in locations around the world. Genzyme's products and services were focused on rare, inherited disorders, kidney disease, cancer, transplant and immune diseases, and multiple sclerosis. The company was consistently recognized as a leader across many dimensions of its operations. It had been named to numerous national "best places to work" lists, and the journal *Science* had regularly named Genzyme a "Top Employer" in its annual survey of scientists.[ii] The company had also won numerous awards for practicing environmental sustainability and ethical responsibility. In 2007, Genzyme received the National Medal of Technology, the highest honor awarded by the President of the United States for technological innovation.

Genzyme's focus on rare diseases had made it very unique in its early history. However, by 2012, many more competitors were beginning to explore the "orphan drug" opportunity ("orphan drugs" are drugs that receive special government protection to target rare diseases). Many large pharmaceutical companies were falling off a "patent cliff"—the patents of large numbers of blockbuster drugs were expiring, leaving the companies scrambling to refill their drug pipelines. As a result of this, and the fact that orphan drugs could be sold for extremely high prices and received special protection and incentives, "big pharma" companies were now actively pursuing orphan drugs, making the drug market for rare diseases a more hotly contested one.

HUMBLE BEGINNINGS

Genzyme was founded in Boston in 1981 by a small group of scientists who were researching genetically inherited enzyme diseases. People with these rare disorders (e.g., Gaucher disease, Fabry disease, MPS-1) lack key enzymes that regulate the body's metabolism, causing sugar, fats, or proteins to build up in the body and resulting in constant pain and early death. In 1983, the scientists were working out of the 15th floor of an old building in Boston's seedy "Combat Zone," when they were joined by Henri Termeer, who took the role of president and eventually chief executive officer of the company. Termeer had left a well-paying executive vice president position at Baxter to join the 2-year-old start-up, and many people thought he was crazy to do so.[iii] However, Termeer thought Genzyme was well positioned to pursue a novel strategy in the drug industry: target the small markets for rare diseases.

Focusing on rare diseases was close to heresy in the pharmaceutical industry. Developing a drug takes 10 to 14 years and costs an average of $1.9 billion to perform the research, run the clinical trials, get FDA approval, and bring a drug to market.[iv] Pharmaceutical companies thus focused on potential "blockbuster" drugs that would serve a market that numbered in the millions. A drug was considered a "blockbuster" if it earned revenues of $1 billion or more, and achieving this level required many thousands of patients, with chronic diseases such as hypertension, diabetes, or high cholesterol. Genzyme, however, challenged the notion that a firm needed a blockbuster drug to succeed. Genzyme would focus on drugs that were needed by only a few thousand patients with severe, life-threatening diseases.[v] Though there would be few patients for these drugs, there would also be few competitors. Furthermore, the small number of patients and the severity of the diseases would make insurance companies less likely to actively resist reimbursement. Both of these factors suggested that drugs for rare diseases might support higher margins than typical drugs. Additionally, whereas pharmaceutical companies typically needed large sales forces and considerable marketing budgets to promote their drugs, a company focusing on drugs for rare diseases could have a much smaller, more targeted sales approach. There were only a small number of physicians specializing in rare diseases so Genzyme could go directly to those doctors rather than funding a large sales force and expensive ad campaigns. Finally, therapies with significant clinical value in smaller populations required much smaller clinical trials (though it was more difficult to find the study candidates).

THE ORPHAN DRUG ACT

Genzyme's timing was auspicious. In 1983, the Food and Drug Administration established the Orphan Drug Act to induce development of drugs for rare diseases. The act provides significant tax breaks on research costs and 7 years of market exclusivity to any company putting an orphan drug on the market. This market exclusivity amounted to significantly more protection from rivalry than a typical patent. When a firm secures a patent on a drug, that patent only prevents another firm from marketing the same drug; it does not prevent another firm from marketing a drug that achieves the same or similar action through other means. Thus when a firm introduced a patented drug that met an important medical need, the race was on by competitors to introduce a different (hopefully improved) version of the drug that could also be patented and compete with the original drug. Drugs for orphan diseases would be shielded from such competition for 7 years, hopefully permitting them to recoup their development costs and earn a rate of return that would make the venture attractive.

To qualify for orphan drug status, a disease had to afflict less than 200,000 people worldwide. Big pharma remained uninterested because of the small market sizes and high risks of developing therapies for them. Even most biotech firms failed to see the opportunity in the act that might suit their rapidly evolving technologies. Genzyme's eventual success, however, would ultimately attract their attention to this small but lucrative market.

THE FIRST BIG SUCCESS

Genzyme's first commercial product was Ceredase—a replacement protein designed to treat fewer than 10,000 people afflicted with a deadly, rare genetic disorder called Gaucher's disease. Children born with this disease rarely live past their 10th birthday, and adults who develop this fatal disease suffer from chronic, liver, kidney, heart, and spleen damage. Clinical trials for Ceredase began in 1984, and in March of 1985 the U.S. Food and Drug Administration designated Ceredase an orphan drug. Genzyme was first allowed to make Ceredase available to patients outside of the United States in 1990, and was approved by the FDA to market Ceredase in the United States in 1991.

Creating a therapy to treat a patient with Gaucher's disease required extracting proteins from human tissue, and the most productive source of these proteins was found in human placentas. The expense and difficulty of this provided a substantial barrier to competitive entrants. Not many experts believed Genzyme could be commercially successful with this product. As Termeer noted, "The FDA thought we were out of our minds." In an interview, Termeer explained, "The hurdles to raise more finance for the trials were formidable. Not least was the fact that human placentas were the source of the enzyme and to provide a year's dose for just one patient, more than 22,000 placentas were needed. To overcome this, Genzyme built a plant in France to take unwanted placental tissue which would have otherwise been burnt and extracted the enzyme. At one point 35% of all placentas from the United States were passing through the French plant. Ceredase was the only drug made from placentas that the U.K. government allowed to be used in Britain."[vi] By 1991, Genzyme was collecting a million placentas a year, and knew it could not produce enough of the enzyme to treat all the patients who needed it. Fortunately, by 1993, Genzyme had developed a recombinant form of the enzyme, Cerezyme, which obviated the need for human tissue and made efficient production possible. In the meantime, Genzyme had also begun work on gene therapies and had begun investigating potential treatments for another rare enzyme disorder, Fabry disease.

REMAINING INDEPENDENT

Genzyme also broke with industry norms in its decision to *not* work with large pharmaceutical companies. Whereas most biotech companies licensed their technologies to large pharmaceutical firms to tap the larger company's greater capital resources, manufacturing capabilities and marketing and distribution assets, Termeer felt strongly that the company should remain independent, stating, "If we worked with a very large corporation, we would lose our strategic direction and be dependent . . . we've tried to stay as self-sufficient as we possibly can."[vii] Performing its own testing, manufacturing, and sales meant incurring much greater risks, but it also meant that the company would keep all of the profits its drugs earned. To generate revenues to fund the research, Termeer entered into a number of side ventures including a chemical supplies business, a genetic counseling business, and a diagnostic testing business. He also took the company public in 1986, raising $27 million. Termeer's gamble paid off: Patients taking Cerezyme paid an average of $170,000 a year for their medication, and with about 4,500 patients committed to taking the drug for life, this amounted to more than $800 million in annual revenue from Cerezyme alone.[viii]

THE COMPETITION IN BIOTECH

The global biotechnology industry included about 7,000 companies in 2012, with total revenues of about $140 billion.[ix] Just over half of that ($80 billion) came from the United States, though other major biotech regions included Canada, Australia, and Europe.[x] Over half of the U.S. biotech revenues, however, came from just six firms: Amgen ($17.3 billion), Gilead Sciences ($9.7 billion), Biogen Idec ($5.5 billion), Celgene ($5.5 billion), Genentech ($2.4 billion), and Genzyme ($1.8 billion). Genentech was the oldest, formed in 1976; Amgen and Genzyme were established in the early 1980s. Many competitors were small, emerging companies with less than 500 employees. In fact, more than 50% of biotech companies had fewer than 50 employees.[xi]

Most biotech start-ups followed a similar path of evolution. The firms would start out as a research and development firm, with employees coming from university science labs or big pharma. If the start-up survived the lean years and had prospects for producing a commercially viable therapy, the young firm would seek alliances with large pharma firms for late-stage development, manufacturing, and marketing. For example, both Genentech and Gilead formed relationships with Roche, and Amgen formed a relationship with Abbott Laboratories. If a firm's drugs achieved commercial success, it could negotiate higher royalties and attract capital investment.

Genzyme differed from all its peers and from later biotech companies by being profitable early on (Genzyme posted a profit of just over $20 million in 1991, losses in 1992 and 1993, and a profit of over $16 million in 1994), and until only recently, remaining independent of partners. "We wanted a diversified company that could use technology to make a difference for people with serious diseases, and to get profitable so we can continue to develop new medicines," Termeer said.[xii] In the late 2000s, most analysts believed that no other developer was likely to pursue Genzyme's strategic path, even with the benefits offered under the Orphan Drug Act. While both Amgen and Genentech had produced orphan drugs, it had not been their strategic focus.

THE GROWING COMPETITION IN ORPHAN DRUGS

It is estimated that there are between 5,000 and 8,000 known rare diseases in the world. In the decade leading up to 1983, only 10 orphan drugs entered the market, according to the FDA. However, from passage of the act until the end of 2012, 415 orphan drugs were approved by the FDA (see Figure 1). The European Union passed similar legislation protecting "orphan medicinal products," granting them market exclusivity for 10 years after approval. Japan, Singapore, and Australia also began offering subsidies and other incentives to develop drugs for rare diseases. As of 2010, roughly 200 orphan diseases had become treatable.[xiii]

Genzyme had proven that a business could be built around small disease populations and demonstrated its ability to profitably serve markets that seemed financially unjustified. Even large pharmaceutical companies, who were struggling by 2012 due to the "patent cliff", began to pay more attention to the orphan drug opportunity.

| Figure 1 | Cumulative Number of U.S. FDA Orphan Drug Approvals, 1983–2012 |

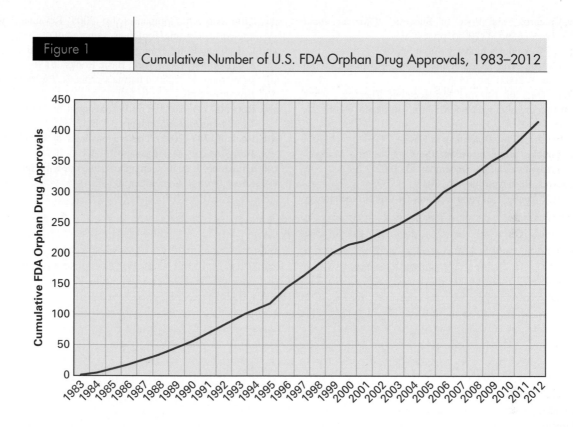

While this was good news for sufferers of rare diseases, it meant significantly more competition for Genzyme. Companies such as Pfizer, Isis Pharmaceutical, NPS Pharmaceuticals, GlaxoSmithKline, and Shire were all beginning to target orphan drugs. As noted by Francois Nader, chief executive of NPS Pharmaceuticals, shifts is science and economics had made the orphan drug market more viable. Researchers could identify ahead of time "the patients that would benefit from a particular drug, rather than using the shotgun approach we used in the past."[xiv] Ironically, despite the small numbers of patients served, high prices enabled almost one-third of orphan drugs to achieve $1 billion in sales[xv]—making them the new blockbusters.

INDEPENDENCE NO MORE

Growing competition wasn't the only challenge Genzyme was facing. A series of manufacturing problems created shortages that impaired its sales of Cerezyme and Fabrazyme in 2009 and 2010. To make matters worse,

plant contamination problems caught the FDA's attention in 2010, resulting in fines and sending the stock into a tumble, making the company vulnerable to a takeover. Pharmaceutical company Sanofi began making overtures that, while initially friendly, also included signals that the company was considering a hostile takeover of Genzyme. Genzyme rebuffed the initial offers, saying that they undervalued the company,[xvi] but after months of negotiation Genzyme was acquired by Sanofi for $20.1 billion, ending its 30-year run as an independent biotechnology drug maker. Henri Termeer resigned, and Sanofi CEO Christopher Viehbacher took over. The company retained its name and its facilities in Cambridge, Massachusetts, becoming Sanofi's new headquarters for rare diseases.

NOTES

i. Adapted from a NYU Teaching Case by Jane Cullen and Melissa A. Schilling.

ii. Company Web site: http://www.genzyme.com/corp/structure/awards_genz.

iii. S. Calabro, "The Price of Success," *Pharmaceutical Executive* 26, no. 3 (2006), pp. 64–80.

iv. Standard & Poor's Industry Surveys, 2013.

v. N. Watson, "This Dutchman Is Flying," *Fortune* (Europe) 148, no. 1 (2003), pp. 55–57.

vi. "Ten Years of Enzyme Replacement Therapy," www .gaucher.org.uk/tenyearsapr03.htm, retrieved April 21, 2006.

vii. N. Watson, "This Dutchman Is Flying."

viii. D. Shook, "Biotechs Adopt the Orphan-Drug Market," *BusinessWeek Online*, December 13, 2002.

ix. Hoovers, Retrieved June 25, 2013

x. Ernst Y Young's Beyond Borders Global Biotechnology Report, 2012.

xi. "Top Biotech Companies by 2005 Revenue," www .bioworld.com/img/TopDrugs_sample.pdf.

xii. C. Robbins-Roth, *From Alchemy to IPO: The Business of Biotechnology* (New York: Basic Books, 2000), p. 44.

xiii. Armstrong, W. 2010. Pharma's orphans. *Pharmaceutical Executive*, May.

xiv. Rockoff, J.D. 2013. The big business of orphan drugs. *Wall Street Journal,* January 31, B.1.

xv. Rockoff, J.D. 2013. The big business of orphan drugs. *Wall Street Journal,* January 31, B.1.

xvi. Jannarone, J. 2010. Genzyme's time out with Sanofi. *Wall Street Journal,* September 28th, C.10.

Case 26

Usha Martin: Competitive Advantage Through Vertical Integration

Nitin Pangarkar (National University of Singapore), Mohit Agarwal (Indian Institute of Technology, Kharagpur) and Natasha Pangarkar (Williams College).

In June 2012, Usha Martin, a prominent Indian engineering conglomerate, faced key decisions about maintaining its past performance. The company, which was founded for making steel wire ropes, had undertaken end-to-end vertical integration by making massive investments in steel making, captive power plants and even coal mines which had afforded it significant advantages in terms of consistent product quality and stable supply while shielding it from fluctuations in input prices. The broader economic environment was changing, however, and it could have a significant impact on the continued feasibility of Usha Martin's strategy. Specifically, economic growth in India, which accounted for more than 70% of Usha Martin's sales in most years, had slowed down significantly. In this slow growth environment, Usha Martin's extensive vertical integration, especially the large recent investments made in steel making, coal mines and power generation, could prove to be problematic. The export markets of the company were also slowing, further adding to the challenge of utilizing the extensive capacity.

HISTORY

Usha Martin was founded in 1961 by two brothers, Mr Basant K (or BK) Jhawar and Mr Brij K Jhawar. The Scottish company Martin-Black partnered the Jhawars by providing resources such as technology and capital and hence the name—Usha Martin. The foundation stone for the company's first factory—a 100,000 sq ft facility which could produce 3,600 tonnes of wire ropes—was laid on 15th August 1961 in Ranchi, then a modest-sized town in northern India. Wire ropes were an attractive product for the startup company because they could be used in a wide variety of applications such as oil exploration (rigs), elevators, cranes, fishing, construction, mining and general engineering sectors. Bihar, the Indian state of which Ranchi was a part, was extremely rich in minerals such as coal and iron ore and this factor probably played a significant role in the location of the plant which took eight months to complete. Soon after startup the company faced an acute water shortage because the nearby river was running dry but the company was able to overcome this challenge with the cooperation of the local community. Despite the initial difficulties, in the plant's first full year of operations (1963), the company earned its maiden profits and also paid out its maiden dividend. The company also successfully adapted the technology shared by Martin Black to suit the Indian conditions including a redesigned rod-patenting furnace which could use kerosene. Having successfully commenced production, expansion was the next challenge and the company embarked on expanding its output from 3,600 tonnes to 7,200 tonnes. However, all was not smooth sailing and in 1965 the India-Pakistan war broke out which derailed the Indian economy and pressurized demand and sales. In what was to become the norm, the founders saw the adverse environmental development as an opportunity rather than a threat. The company managed to not only boost its production but with the domestic market stagnating, it ventured into international markets.

By 2012, the Usha Martin Group had become one of India's biggest industrial conglomerates, not only present in the domestic market but also in several international markets (see Exhibit 1 for a timeline of the

C-347

Exhibit 1	Timeline of Usha Martin's development

Date	Event description	Category of Strategic initiative or accomplishment
1960	Usha Martin Industries (UMIL) begins construction of a wire rope plant with 3,600 tonnes per annum capacity	Start up plant construction
1962	Production commences at the plant	
1965	Collaboration with CCL Systems of UK to form Usha Ismal to manufacture rope accessories and splicing equipment	Product extension/diversification
1972	Forms Usha Alloys and Steels (UASL) to manufacture steel billets	Product extension/diversification
1975	Sets up a machinery division at Bangalore for manufacture of wire drawing and allied products in collaboration Marshall Richards Barcro, UK	Product extension/diversification
1979	UASL sets up a wire rod rolling mill at Jamshedpur to supply wire rods for its wire rope plant	Backward integration
1980	Usha Siam Steel Industries formed in Thailand as a joint venture for manufacture of wire, wire ropes and auto cables	Internationalization
1986	Usha Beltron (UBL) incorporated as a joint venture between Usha Martin Industries and Bihar State Electronics Development Corporation, AEG Kabel, Germany (now Kabelrhydt and a member of the Alcatel group) and DEG, Germany to manufacture jelly filled telephone cables (JFTC).	Product extension
1991	Successfully completes thencontract to supply the parallel wire stay cables for the Second Hooghly Bridge at Kolkata and establishes the company's capability for manufacturing sophisticated special cables.	Completion of a key contract
1988	UASL merged into UMIL	Rationalization of internal portfolio
1990	Usha Ismal merged with UMIL	Rationalization of internal portfolio
1995	UMIL sets up a mini blast furnace at Jamshedpur to reduce cost and improve productivity.	Vertical integration
1996	UMIL sets up a wire rod mill at Jamshedpur to produce higher weight coils for better productivity	Product extension
1998	UMIL merged with UBL	Rationalization of internal portfolio
2000	IT division within the parent company demerged and named Usha Martin Infotech (UMITL).	Rationalization of internal portfolio
	UM Cable established as a wholly owned subsidiary to set up a greenfield plant	Product extension
	Commissioned a 25 MW thermal power plant at Jamshedpur for captive consumption.	Vertical integration
	Acquired majority stake in Usha Siam Steel Industries, Bangkok because of financial troubles of the joint venture partner	Restructuring of an international JV
	Acquired an 80% stake in Brunton Shaw, UK, from Carclo Group	Internationalization

(continued)

Date	Event description	Category of Strategic initiative or accomplishment
2001	Usha Matin Singapore (Pty.) to set up as a distribution facility at Singapore for wire ropes.	Internationalization
	In order to increase the capacity the company sets up second unit in at Jamshedpur	Capacity expansion
2003	Divested its rolling mill division at Agra with an intention to focus on core business.	Product and facility rationalization
	Company name changed to Usha Martin	Name change
	Joint venture with Gustav Wolf of West Germany to form Brunton Wolf Wire Ropes FZCO located in Dubai.	Internationalization
	Obtains a prestigious order from Otis Elevators for supplying cables on a world-wide basis	
	Successfully creates new facilities by modifying the cable plant to manufacture value added products such as bright bars, special wires and conveyor cords.	Key customer account
2004	Starts its DRI and WHRB power plant at its steel division in Jamshdedpur	Vertical integration
2005	Signed an MOU with Joh. Pengg for manufacturing of the speciality oil tempered spring steel wire.	Product extension
	Acquired JCTL's steel division.	Backward integration through acquisition
	incorporates Brunton Shaw America Inc as a new subsidiary of the company.	
2007	Acquired Netherlands based De Ruiter Staalkabel B.V. engaged in business of distribution and rigging.	Forward integration
	Starts wire rope plant in Houston, US.	New facility
	Buys a 76% stake in UK outsourcing services provider Converso Contact Centres for an undisclosed fee	Unrelated diversification
2010	Raises Rs 4681.5 million Qalified Investor Placement	Capital raising

Sources: Profile-Usha Martin, 23 April 2012, ACE Equity - Indian Company Profiles, Accord Fintech For the information about the Converso acquisition, Personnel Today, 9/18/2007

company's development and Exhibit 2 for the sales achieved by the company by 2011). Its range of products and services was diverse and included the manufacture and distribution of special steels, alloys, cables and wires; telecoms cables; industrial ropeways; cable car assemblages and hydraulic systems. The company was also involved in the implementation of major engineering infrastructure projects and a few rapidly growing and technologically intensive services such as outsourcing services for the telecoms industry (see Exhibit 3 for a breakdown of the revenues contributed by the different product groups in 2011).[1]

STRATEGY

Usha Martin had adopted a simple strategy to compete in wire ropes, its first product. *Business Today*, an India based business publication summarized its strategy thus:

(Usha Martin's) (S)trategy is simple: make high-end products in specialized steel and wire ropes, and cash in on the low-cost advantage of India.[2] The simple strategy had, however, evolved over time. There were six cornerstones to its strategy: seeking continuous cost reductions through several strategies; acquiring external knowledge to supplement its internal capabilities; proactively spending resources on Corporate Social Responsibility; building close relations with the local governments; continuously enhancing its product range often through moving into adjacent product areas and exercising control over the key inputs to its plants to insulate it from volatility of quality, availability and prices.

Seeking continuously improved operations and lower costs

Usha Martin continuously sought to improve its cost position. Vertical integration, discussed under a separate

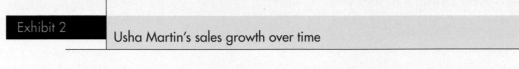

Exhibit 2 — Usha Martin's sales growth over time

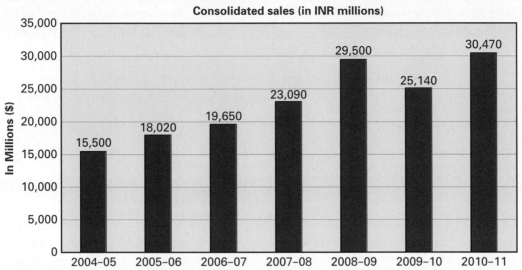

Consolidated sales (in INR millions)

Source: Annual Report (2010–11) Exchange rates as at 31st Dec of each year were (INR/ US$): 2011 (53.88), 2010 (45.34); 2009 (46.3); 2008 (49.72); 2007 (39.43); 2006 (44.12); 2005 (45.20); 2004 (43.73);

Exhibit 3 — Usha Martin's revenue breakdown across different product divisions

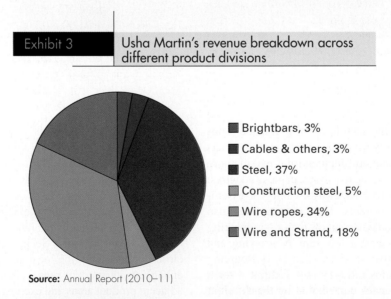

- Brightbars, 3%
- Cables & others, 3%
- Steel, 37%
- Construction steel, 5%
- Wire ropes, 34%
- Wire and Strand, 18%

Source: Annual Report (2010–11)

heading, was an important aspect of this strategy. While seeking cost reductions, Usha Martin ensured, however, that the product quality was not sacrificed. In fact, it believed that high quality was the most effective differentiator. To this end, it also ensured that it deployed the latest technology and capital equipment available in the market—Italian drawing machines at its Ranchi plant which were preferred over the products of a sister company being one such example. Specific examples of its cost reduction strategy included the following:

- TPM, or Total Productive Maintenance, deployed within its plants was a key element of this cost reduction strategy. TPM which involves a zero loss concept at its core—zero breakdowns, zero accidents, and zero defects, allowed achievement of high levels of productivity through total and complete participation of all people inside the organization and developing self-managing abilities. After initial trials in a few plants Usha Martin had introduced TPM in all of its plants enabling it to become more resilient through the twin benefits of reduced production costs and increased competitiveness.

- Usha Martin had also implemented ERP systems for managing and enhancing business processes. On July 1, 2011, it also began its TQM (Total Quality Management) initiative, through which it would seek to continuously improve the quality of products and processes.

- Its cost consciousness extended to international operations as well. To save energy costs, for instance, Usha Siam (Thailand) was using natural gas.

- The company also sought to increase volume through capacity additions and technological upgrading, which, in turn, saved costs through economies of scale. Though its steel making plant had started with a modest installed capacity mostly to supply steel to its wire ropes plants, Usha Martin had undertaken an aggressive capital expenditure program to increase the plant's capacity manifold. In 2011, for instance, the company had undertaken many new additions to its plant which were aimed at decreasing overheads, optimizing utilization of the available capacity and achieving complete end-to-end integration. These new initiatives had followed on the heels of upgrades, in 2009–10 which had boosted the production of steel from from 280,000 tonnes to 500,000 tonnes. This increased steel production had not only served the needs of the sister wire-producing units but had also served the growing market of specialty steel market.

Acquiring external knowledge and expertise

Right from inception when it tapped into the technological expertise of Martin Black, its UK collaborator, Usha Martin had been open to 'importing' knowledge and expertise from external sources.

- Usha Martin worked with experts and top universities including IIT Kharagpur, a world-renowned technology institute, to design better products.

- With an aim to make its plants zero accident zones and create a safe working environment, Usha Martin

also conducted external audits at all of its facilities to "take stock of existing safety measures and address any lacunae"[3]

- The company also sought out joint ventures with other companies to fill gaps in its expertise and enter new product segments. In 2006–07, for instance, the company entered into three joint ventures: with Joh Pengg AG of Australia to form Pengg Usha Martin Wires Pvt. Ltd. For manufacturing oil tempered and other specialty wires in Ranchi; with CCL group of UK to form CCL Usha Martin Stressing Systems Ltd. for post tensioning in civil works; and with the Emta Group to form Dove Airlines to offer charter air services

Corporate Social Responsibility

Right from its inception, Usha Martin had taken its Corporate Social Responsibility seriously by going well beyond the legal requirement. The company chose to partner with the community in developmental activities which would be scalable and sustainable. The successful efforts of the company in the social sector resulted in the company being awarded the TERI Corporate Award for Environmental Excellence and Corporate Social Responsibility for 2004–05.

As early as 1971 when it was still a small company, it used a bottom up approach and came up with KGVK—Krishi Gram Vikas Kendra (which translates to Centre for the Development of Villagers and Villages). KGVK worked on an extrapolated model of TPM which Usha Martin called TVM—Total Village Management—a unique process to create real difference in the lives of the rural poor through sustainable and inclusive rural transformation (see Exhibit 4 for a schematic). The broad sweep of areas covered by TVM included Natural Resource Management, Education, Health and Sanitation, Livelihood, Women's Empowerment, Renewable Energy and Capacity Building. By 2010–11, KGVK spanned 23 villages and specific initiatives included getting water to the villages through installation and repair of wells, organizing health camps, livelihood programs, capacity building programs like training of teachers and offering education facilities through KGVK schools, among others. To achieve widespread adoption and dissemination of TVM activities, the company had formed TVM Gurukul which was a formal campus and included a primary school, a rural BPO, an auxiliary nursing cum midwifery school, demonstration farms, dairy entrepreneurship models and residential hostels. The results of

Exhibit 4   A schematic for Total Village Management

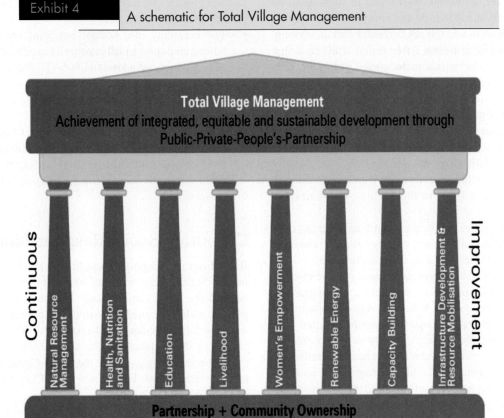

Source: Usha Martin Annual Report (2010–11)

these CSR efforts were quite impressive. Between April 2009 and March 2011, the KGVK program had: improved access to healthcare for 30,000 people, improved access to drinking water for 72,100 people, and created sustainable income through self-employment or new job opportunities for 10,158 people.[4] Co-operation of local villagers was a key advantage derived by the company through KGVK. This cooperation enabled Usha Martin to set up its projects quickly—e.g., it was able to start up its mines in record times for the Indian context.

The company also paid close attention to environmental issues. Its wire ropes and specialty products division had reduced pollution by converting from oil to LPG and eliminating emission of un-burnt fuels in the atmosphere.[5] Its steel and specialty products divisions enjoyed certification under the ISO 14001 Environment Management Systems from DNV of UK.[6]

In 2001, the company had also started an Academy (Usha Martin Academy) which would provide trained manpower to meet the needs of its home country. The degree courses offered by the Academy spanned two areas (Management and Computing) and were intended to provide a balanced mix of theoretical knowledge and practical training with industry professional as mentors. The Academy was started in collaboration with the Indian Institute of Technology (Madras) and funded by the Usha Martin group.

Cooperation with government agencies

Cooperation with various government agencies was another cornerstone of Usha Martin's strategy. The first such cooperation happened in 1971 when India and Pakistan went to war over Bangladesh (which used to be East Pakistan) breaking away from Pakistan to become a separate country. The defense department of the Indian government needed special ropes for the INS Vikrant, its aircraft carrier, for which the government approached Usha Martin. The company completed the task in record time, which earned it praise and goodwill from the government.

The firm's next notable project was the second Hooghly Bridge (an arm of the Ganges river) in Kolkata (Calcutta at that time). Kolkata had the first Hooghly Bridge, which was considered to be a civil engineering marvel in India at the time, and needed another bridge across Hooghly to handle the heavy traffic. Usha Martin manufactured the cables to support the bridge, the work for which commenced in 1979, under extremely tight deadlines, thus enhancing its reputation and also strengthening its relationships with the government.

Since 2002, World Bank's International Finance Corporation (IFC) had supported the company in improving its existing technology and infrastructure. The financing from the agency had been especially useful for establishment of captive Coal Preparation Plant (for power generation) and Direct Reduced Iron plants (for steel-making) and thus achieving end-to-end integration. In 2003, IFC owned a stake of 14% in the company and had invested as much as US$21 million.[7]

Probably in recognition of its past contributions to important government projects and also its social contributions, in 2008, the government of Jharkhand gave Usha Martin a lease to mine iron ore deposits, the only steel company to be granted a lease in the last twenty five years.[8]

Exhibit 5	Usha Martin's Integrated Business Model

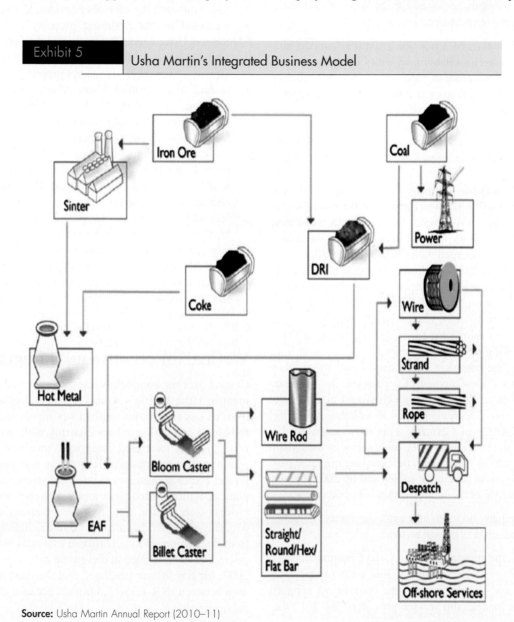

Source: Usha Martin Annual Report (2010–11)

Product extension

Throughout its history Usha Martin had sought and exploited opportunities to extend its product range. This had included many 'backward' movements in its value chain (e.g., in making raw materials or intermediate products), a few 'forward' movements in the value chain (e.g., into products with greater value added or in implementation of projects which utilized its key product of wire ropes) as well extension into related products (e.g., into niche or sector-specific applications such as telecom cables) and sometimes even into products unrelated to its core business (see Exhibit 5 for a schematic of the company's end-to-end integration).

- In 1965, it formed a new joint venture named Usha Ismal Limited in collaboration with CCL Systems Ltd, UK for manufacture of rope accessories and splicing equipment at its factory at Ranchi. The new company was merged with the parent company in 1990.
- In a forward integration move, Usha Breco, a joint venture with Breco (UK), was formed in 1969 to design, manufacture, erect and commission ropeways in India.
- In 1975, another company "Usha Alloys & Steels Limited" (or UASL) was formed for the manufacture of steel billets at Adityapur, Jamshedpur (at a distance of 106 km from the original Ranchi plant). This company was also merged with the parent in 1988.
- In 1975, it set up its Machinery Division at Bangalore for manufacture of wire drawing and allied products in collaboration Marshall Richards Barcro Ltd. UK.
- In 1979, in order to obtain steady supply of wire rods for its wire rope plant, UASL set up a Wire Rod Rolling Mill at Jamshedpur.
- In 1986, the company joined hands with Bihar State Electronics Development Corporation, to promote Usha Beltron Ltd. (UBL) which would manufacture Jelly Filled Telephone Cables in collaboration with AEG KABEL of Germany. This move came on the heels of the opening up of the cable sector by the Indian government in 1985. Later, the company migrated part of its output to fibre optic cables and by 2001 it commanded 15% of the Indian market for optic cables.[9]

The company had also undertaken a number of unrelated product diversification moves.

- In 1994, the company formed Usha Communications Technology (later renamed UshaComm) to provide billing and customer care and operational support systems for telecom service providers. By 2012 the company was able to claim a number of accomplishments including a network of offices in foreign countries such as UK, S Africa and the USA, prestigious ISO and industry-specific certifications and patronage (sometimes repeat business) from global clients such as Vodafone.[10]
- In 1995 it partnered with Telekom Malaysia and other international investors to form Usha Martin Telekom Ltd., a GSM cellular network operator in Kolkata. The venture was sold to the Hong-Kong based Hutchison Wampoha in July 2000.[11]
- In 2007, the company acquired a 75% stake in UK based outsourcing services provider, Converso.
- Attracted by the booming property sector, it had formed Usha Breco Realty Limited to construct affordable housing. By 2010, the new subsidiary had already commenced its second project in Mumbai.[12]
- It had also formed Usha Martin Education & Solutions Limited (UMESL). In 2009, UMESL had forayed into providing standardized end-to-end solutions and school management services to enable the creation of a national network of high quality English medium K-12 schools with a focus on smaller towns and cities in India. The company had tied up with Pearson to help the schools access content such as books, worksheets and assessment tools. UMESL also aimed to offer schools Pearson's cutting edge ERP software solutions for schools.[13] In 2010, UMESL also launched Usha Martin people search which would offer innovative recruitment solutions to the industry while simultaneously offering placement services to the students of Usha Martin Academy.[14]

Vertical (or end-to-end) integration

Control over the complete value chain formed a key element of Usha Martin's strategy, which also set it apart from its key rivals who sourced key inputs such as wire rods from external suppliers. Starting with making wire ropes, it had backward integrated into making steel, which was the raw material for making wire ropes. It had further backward integrated into coal mining and power plant operation which were inputs into the steel making process (see Exhibit 5). From the company's perspective, this end-to-end control over value chain shielded it from fluctuations in availability of inputs as well as their prices and thus enabled achievement of stable profits. In 2007, Mr BK Jhawar predicted that the company would save between INR 1.3 to 1.5 billion because of its vertical integration.[15]

One instance of the constraint posed by availability of inputs happened in 2004–05 when the company faced bottlenecks in production due to poor availability of inputs like iron ore and coal and was also seeing fluctuating profits due to the volatility in prices of steel. Following this, the company proactively commissioned a steel plant and also secured rights to coal mining with production commencing in 2005–06. Interestingly, all of the key activities such as wire making, steel making, coal mining and power plant operation were located in geographic proximity (100 kilometers) to each other. The company also rapidly scaled up its steel-making capacity and started supplying almost half of its specialty steel to external customers in automobile and engineering industries.

Mr BK Jhawar, USha Martin's Chairman identified total control over the quality of wire rods as another important benefit of its vertical integration strategy. The benefits of its integrated business were well summarized in its 2010–11 annual report. "Cost competitiveness has been the driving force behind the integrated business model followed by the company. The benefits are all the more visible in current regime of high commodity prices. Ongoing projects . . . will further strengthen company's cost competitiveness. Captive mines provide not only a cost advantage but also a better quality due to control on inputs and more importantly, consistent production free of uncertainties in supply of raw materials."

Evolution of strategy

While following its three-pronged strategy of capacity expansion, product extension and end-to-end integration, the company also exploited opportunities as they became available—specifically it pursued acquisitions (rather than its usual modes of organic growth or joint ventures) to bolster its competitive position, enter new products or extend its geographic footprint, or a combination of the above. In 2004, the company executed a MOU with the north India based JCT Ltd. for acquisition of the company's steel business—which would bring into its control the company's facilities for manufacturing steel wire and wire rope products in North India. In 2006–07, the company took over a steel rolling plant in Agra which it slotted into its Construction Steel Division. It had also undertaken other acquisition such as those of EMMC, Brunton Shaw and Converso, which were discussed under the heading 'Product Extension'.

INTERNATIONALIZATION

Usha Martin's first international foray was its joint venture in Yugoslavia for production of steel wire ropes and strands—Unis Usha Tvornica Celicne Uzabi Visegrad. After the disintegration of Yugoslavia in 1991, Usha Marin walked away from the joint venture but was invited back to manage the joint venture by the Bosnian government in 2003.[16]

In 1980, Usha Martin registered a joint venture company in Thailand, called Usha Siam, in which it held a 49% stake. Usha Siam manufactured rope wires and wire ropes, the core products of the company, which were used in various applications in different industries. Usha Siam also served as the company's manufacturing hub outside India. Commercial production commenced in 1982 with an. initial capacity of the plant at 10,000 tonnes per year, which had increased to 39,000 tonnes by 2011. The plant was the largest integrated plant in Thailand and 40% of Usha Siam's products were exported to USA and Europe.

The Asian financial crisis had a major negative impact on several Asian economies, especially in east Asia. The crisis began from Thailand with the collapse of the Thai Baht. This development affected Usha Siam significantly because its partner faced financial troubles. Adopting a long term perspective, Usha Martin acquired the partner's stake and made it a wholly owned subsidiary.

In 1988, Usha Martin began penetration of the UK market with a representative office in Scotland. Within 2–3 years, Usha Martin products had been successfully adapted and introduced in several European countries such as the UK, Germany, Italy and Holland. In 1994, a wholly owned wholesale distribution company, Usha Martin International Limited (UMIL) was started. With a warehousing facility in UK the company was expected to help its parent deepen the penetration of its products. Wire rope manufactured in India and Thailand was imported and sold via the distribution company. Subsequently, Usha Martin recognized a need to expand business and identified opportunities to add value to its portfolio by entering oil services and rigging operations. To this end, in 1997, the group acquired EMMC, an emerging company in the wire rope application for the oil and gas sector in the North Sea.

The next opportunity identified by the firm was the acquisition of Brunton Shaw, a specialist rope manufacturer based in UK in October 2000. Brunton Shaw was the

2nd largest wire ropes manufacturer in the UK with an annual capacity of 6,000 tonnes. More importantly, Brunton Shaw operated in a niche branded segment offering rope for mining, cranes, elevators and nylon-coated wires and its revenue realization per tonne of wire rope was almost twice that of Usha Martin (US$3000 per tonne versus US$1600 per tonne).[17] The additional capabilities complemented Usha Martin's portfolio and enhanced its manufacturing capabilities to allow production of niche products for the European market. After the acquisition, Usha Martin further enhanced Brunton Shaw's capabilities and competitiveness by consolidating rigging facilities, expanding the fishing rope business, growing the crane rope market share and cutting fixed costs. It also undertook additional capital investments. Both these initiatives strengthened the company's ability to serve customers in markets such as Canada.[18]

In 2001, Usha Martin set up a company in Singapore, Usha Martin Singapore Pte. Ltd., to fulfill its orders in the South East Asian region and simultaneously grow its market share. Because of its proximity to the two key manufacturing hubs of India and Thailand, the Singapore operations enjoyed a status as the regional distribution center in Southeast Asia and the Pacific. In fact, Usha Martin's subsidiary in Australia—Usha Martin Australia Pte Ltd.—was fully funded by the Singapore operation—and by 2011 the subsidiary had achieved sales of US$10 million and also earned positive profits. The Singapore company also oversaw the conversion of representative offices in Vietnam and Indonesia into subsidiaries and oversees the company's business in New Zealand, Australia, Indonesia, Vietnam, Malaysia, Myanmar, Korea and China.

By 2003, UMIL had recognized the potential of the Middle East and Africa markets and set up a joint venture company (60% stake by Usha Martin) in Dubai to manufacture wire ropes in collaboration with Gustav Wolf of Germany–Brunton Shaw Middle East FZE which specialized in manufacturing of wire ropes. With a production capacity of 6000 tonnes per annum, the company was expected to serve as a manufacturing base and supply markets outside Asia. The company was later renamed to Brunton Wolf Wire Rope Company FZCo (BWWR)

Also, in 2005–06, the company hatched plans of setting up a wire manufacturing facility in USA under Brunton Shaw Americas Inc., a new subsidiary. Brunton Shaw Americas Inc was to be a production and manufacturing center while Usha Martin Americas Inc was the distribution center of the company in America.

With an aim to exploit the huge demand created by the infrastructure boom in China, the company set up offices in China in 2007 and planned to sell special quality wire ropes for elevators, mining and the construction sector through its factory in Bangkok (which served the rest of the Asian markets) and warehouses in Singapore. The company did not make greater resource commitments to China however. As stated by one of its senior managers (Dr Bhattacharya): "It is fine to jump into the bandwagon headed to China, but my interest is greater in Europe, which offers the high-end market."[19] In another publication, Mr BK Jhawar, the company's Chairman at the time said: "China is a complex market. I understand there are over 500 factories in China making some 400,000 tonnes of wire and rope. Though by far the world's biggest producer of rope, Chinese capacity remains highly fragmented. It is also a very complex market. I can't tell you at this stage whether Usha Martin should be building a factory in China or have a marketing alliance with a local company."[20]

In 2007, Usha Martin acquired a Dutch company called De Reuiter Staalkabel B.V. Netherlands which focused on high tech non rotational ropes for off shore applications (oil and gas sector). Subsequently, the newly acquired operation was made into a subsidiary of Usha Martin International Ltd.

Exhibit 6 shows the international organization of Usha Martin and Exhibits 7 and 8 show the performance of Usha Martin's internationalization efforts.

PERFORMANCE

Usha Martin's performance was impressive with regard to varied performance metrics. Exhibit 2 shows the sales growth attained by the company between 2004–05 and 2010–11. Profits before tax had grown from 133.5 million for the year ended March 2003 to 1384 million for the year ended March 2007 and further to 1453 million for the year ended March 2011 (see Exhibit 9). The sales and profit growth had been attained by successfully operating several manufacturing plants, captive iron ore and coal mines and a vast network of distribution centers and marketing offices which supported an ever growing and diverse customer base. For the 2010–2011 year, it exported approximately 16.26% of its total sales, which represented a decline from 25.39% previous year.[21] The company's success in international markets was even greater for specific product lines. It exported 60% of its wire rope output, for instance.[22] In addition to these

Exhibit 6 — Usha Martin's International Organization

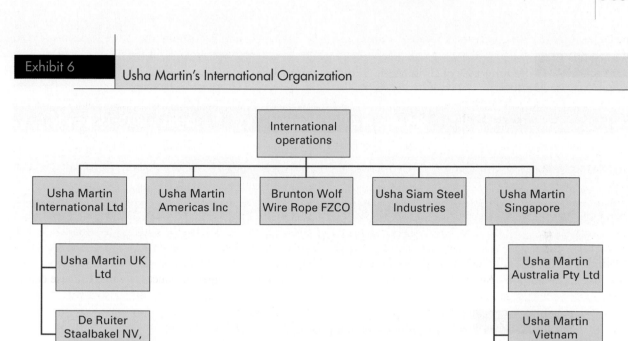

Source: Usha Martin Annual Report (2010–11)

Exhibit 7 — Usha Martin's revenue breakdown across key geographic regions

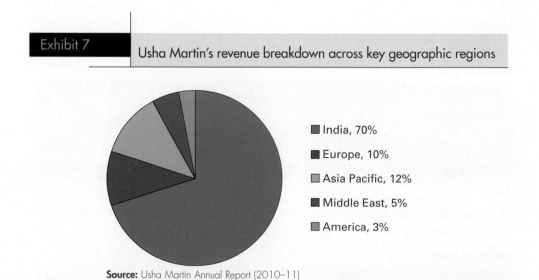

- India, 70%
- Europe, 10%
- Asia Pacific, 12%
- Middle East, 5%
- America, 3%

Source: Usha Martin Annual Report (2010–11)

metrics, the company had earned accolades from its partners (such as financiers), analysts and customers alike.

- Mr SB Nair, Deputy Managing Director and Group Executive of India's largest bank, the State Bank of India, said: "Usha Martin is one of our best clients. . . . We share certain characteristics of believing in long term relationships and a tempered outlook. . . . For a decade we have supported all of their ventures, domestic and international—and we see huge potential

Exhibit 8

Performance of Usha Martin's foreign operations

	Revenues in 2010–11 (growth)	Profits in 2010–11 (growth)
Usha Martin International Limited	GBP 41.0 million (–17.01%)	GBP 2.6 million (–18.75%)
Usha Martin Americas Inc	US$15.2 million (–21.25%)	US$1.1 million (–8.34%)
Brunton Wolf Wire Rope FZCO	US$18.8 million (+12.5%)	US$1.5 million (–6.67%)
Usha Siam Steel Industries	Thai Baht 1628 million (+9.04%)	Thai Baht 86 million (+21.12%)
Usha Marin Singapore	US$30 million (–10%)	US$1.7 million (–52.78%)

Source: Usha Martin Annual Report (2010–11)

Exhibit 9

Income Statement (all figures in INR millions)

	2010–11	2009–10	2006–07
INCOME			
Net (of excise duty) sales turnover (revenues) and including other income	30671	25399	19816
PROFIT BEFORE TAXATION	2041	2400	1829
Provision for taxation	458	470	441
Profit after tax	1400	1715	1379
BALANCE SHEET			
Liabilities			
Shareholder's funds	15570	14997	7210
Loan funds (including deferred tax liability)	18240	10092	8928
Total liabilities	**33811**	**25089**	**16138**
Assets			
Fixed assets (net of depreciation)	27475	22491	9000
Capital work in progress	3824	6084	1971
Total fixed assets	**31,300**	**28575**	**10971**
Investments	1869	1869	1601
Current assets	16500	11343	8411
Current Liabilities	15858	16699	4875
Net current assets	**642**	**-5356**	**3536**

Note: All figures in INR millions. Exchange rates as at 31st Dec of each year were (INR/ US$): 2011 (53.88), 2010 (45.34); 2009 (46.3); 2008 (49.72); 2007 (39.43); 2006 (44.12).

Source: Usha Martin Annual Report (2010–11)

for the future. . . . Brand and Quality are two of Usha Martin's biggest strengths and this definitely gives them an advantage.[23]

- In 2009, while complimenting the company on its past strategy and performance, one analyst made the following comment: "For Usha Martin, the path to sustainable growth was long; the management constantly tried out innovative business practices. With initiative to diversify the customer base by venturing into the international markets, moving up the value chain and fully integrating its business process to maximize stakeholder value."[24]

- Mr Nimish Deshpande, Director of Engineering at Schindler India, a subsidiary of one of the largest manufacturers of elevators of escalators in the world (Schindler AG), said: Our association dates to more than a decade in the field of elevator ropes. It has been an extremely rewarding partnership and we have had no complaints on either quality or supply.[25]

- In 2009–10, Usha Martin's wire ropes and specialty division received an award for Excellence in Consistent TPM commitment from the Japan Institute for Plant Maintenance.[26]

The company's competitive and past performance had also enabled it to raise substantial capital in global markets. For instance, in 2005–06, the company had successfully raised US$5 million through the issue of Global Depository Receipts listed on the Luxembourg stock exchange. In 2010, the company had raised INR 4.68 billion through placement to qualified investors. It had also received funding from the IFC.

THE ROAD AHEAD

Though its strategy of aggressive capital investments, end-to-end integration and proactive product extension had helped Usha Martin achieve significant competitive advantage and strong financial performance in the past, the future outlook remained far less certain. Analysts expected weak economic performance through most major economies around the world, mature as well as emerging, and this weakness would significantly affect the demand for Usha Martin's products. A demand slowdown would be particularly problematic because of Usha Martin's end-to-end integration, which significantly increased its fixed costs. In fact, despite a 20% growth in consolidated sales, consolidated profits for the year ended March 2011 were lower than March 2010. Clearly, more challenging

times lay ahead and the company needed to think about possible adaptations to its past strategy.

NOTES

1. The bridge builder. By: Warwick, Martyn, Euronet, 13676792, Jul 2001, Issue 13
2. Usha Martin: A high wire act, Business Today, December 2, 2007
3. Annual Report 2010–11, Managing Director's Statement, Page 10
4. 2010–11 Annual Report
5. 2010–11 Annual Report
6. (2010–11 Annual Report).
7. Jhawars to take over Bosnian plant, The Economic Times, 29th Sep 2003, http://articles.economictimes.indiatimes.com/2003–09–29/news/27565184_1_wire-rope-jhawars-plant
8. Preparing for take-off *Kunal Bose*. Metal Bulletin Monthly. London: Feb 2008. , Iss. 445; pg. 16, 3 pgs
9. The bridge builder. By: Warwick, Martyn, Euronet, 13676792, Jul2001, Issue 13
10. http://www.ushacomm.com/corporate.html#Milestones
11. http://prashantjhawar.com/Person_PersonalProfile.asp
12. Usha Breco announces housing project NBM & CW. New Delhi: Dec 23, 2010.
13. Usha Martin Education & Solutions forays into School Management. Accord Fintech. Mumbai: Dec 17, 2009
14. Usha Martin Education flies high on launching Usha Martin People Search Accord Fintech. Mumbai: Aug 20, 2010
15. Usha Martin: A high wire act, Business Today, December 2, 2007.
16. Bosnia woos back Usha Martin, The Economic Times, Oct 2, 2003, http://articles.economictimes.indiatimes.com/2003-10-02/news/27548851-1-wire-rope-prashant-jhawarusha- martin-group
17. Usha Martin plans to buy European distribution company, wee.livemint.com, Sanchita Das, , 18 May 2007
18. Indian wire finds global markets *Kunal Bose*. Metal Bulletin Monthly. London: Apr 2006. , Iss. 424; pg. 23, 3 pgs
19. Usha Martin plans to buy European distribution co Sanchita Das,www.livemint.com, 8 May 2007
20. Indian wire finds global markets, *Kunal Bose*. Metal Bulletin Monthly. London: Apr 2006. , Iss. 424; pg. 23, 3 pgs
21. Calculated based on data provided on page 52 of the 2010–11 Annual Report
22. Profile-Usha Martin, 23 April 2012, ACE Equity - Indian Company Profiles, Accord Fintech.
23. SB Nair, Dy Managing Director and Group Executive, State Bank of India
24. Profile: Usha Martin Infotech, ACE Quity: Indian Company Profiles by Accord Fintech. 3rd August 2009
25. 2010–2011 Annual Report
26. 2010–2011 Annual Report

Case 27

Disaster in Bangladesh: The Collapse of the Rana Plaza Building

Charles WL Hill

On the morning of Wednesday April 24, 2013, an eight storey industrial and commercial building in Bangladesh collapsed, killing over 1,100 people, most of them workers in one of the five garment factories that occupied six floors of the building. This was not the first high profile accident in the Bangladesh garment industry. The prior November, a factory fire had killed 112 garment workers. Just days after the building collapse, a fire in another garment factory killed eight people. The spat of accidents led to calls for Western clothing retailers to do more to improve working conditions and safety in Bangladesh and other poor nations from which they source production. Some interest groups went further, arguing that Western companies should refuse to source production from countries where working conditions were so bad. One high profile Western company, Walt Disney, had already made this decision. In March 2013, Disney removed Bangladesh from the list of countries where it authorized partners to produce clothing and other merchandise for Disney. Politicians in Bangladesh responded to the Disney announcement with dismay. They argued that the economy of Bangladesh was very dependent upon the garment industry, and that "the whole nation should not be made to suffer" because of these accidents.

THE GARMENT INDUSTRY IN BANGLADESH

Bangladesh, one of the world's poorest countries, has long depended heavily upon exports of textile products to generate income, employment, and economic growth. Most of these exports are low-cost finished garments sold to a wide range of retailers in the West, such as Wal-Mart, The Gap, H&M, and Zara. For decades, Bangladesh was able to take advantage of a quota system for textile exports that gave it, and other poor countries, preferential access to rich markets such as the United States and the European Union. On January 1, 2005, that system was scrapped in favor of one that was based on free trade principles. From 2005 on, exporters in Bangladesh would have to compete for business against producers from other nations such as China and Indonesia. Many analysts foresaw the quick collapse of Bangladesh's textile industry. They predicted a sharp jump in unemployment, a decline in the country's balance of payments accounts, and a negative impact on economic growth.

The collapse didn't happen. Bangladesh's exports of textiles continued to grow, even as the rest of the world plunged into an economic crisis in 2008. Bangladesh's exports of garments rose to around $20 billion in 2012, up from $8.9 billion in 2006, making it the largest export industry in the country and a primary driver of economic growth. By 2012 the textile industry in Bangladesh comprised of some 5,000 factories whish were the source of employment for 3 million people, 85% of whom were women with few alternative employment opportunities.

As a deep economic recession took hold in developed nations during 2008–2009, big importers such as Wal-Mart increased their purchases of low-cost garments from Bangladesh to better serve their customers, who were looking for low prices. Li & Fung, a Hong Kong company that handles sourcing and apparel manufacturing, stated its production in Bangladesh jumped 25% in 2009, while production in China, its biggest supplier, slid 5%.

Bangladesh's advantage is based on a number of factors. First, labor costs are low, in part due to low hourly

Foster School of Business, University of Washington

wage rates and in part due to investments by textile manufacturers in productivity-boosting technology during the past decade. The minimum wage rate in Bangladesh is currently $38 a month, compared to a minimum wage in China of $138 a month. Wage rates in the textile industry are about $50 to $60 a month, less than a fifth of the going rate in China. Textile workers may have to work 12-hour shifts and can work 7 days a week during busy periods. While the pay rate is dismally low by Western standards, in a country where the gross national income per capita is only $850 a year the pay is better than that available in many other unskilled and low skilled occupations.

Second, there are few regulations in Bangladesh, and as one foreign buyer says, "there are no rules whatsoever that cannot be bent". The lack of effective regulations keeps costs down. Another source of advantage for Bangladesh is that it has an established network of supporting industries that supply inputs to its garment manufacturers. Some three-quarters of all inputs are made locally. This saves garment manufacturers transport and storage costs, import duties, and the long lead times that come with the imported woven fabrics used to make shirts and trousers.

Bangladesh also has the advantage of not being China. Many importers in the West have grown cautious about becoming too dependent upon China for imports of specific goods for fear that if there was disruption, economic or other, their supply chains would be decimated unless they had an alternative source of supply. Thus, Bangladesh has benefited from the trend by Western importers to diversify their supply sources. Although China remains the world's largest exporter of garments, Bangladesh is now second. Moreover, Chinese wage rates are now rising fast, suggesting the trend to shift textile production away from China may continue.

Bangladesh, however, does have some negatives; most notable are the constant disruptions in electricity because the government has underinvested in power generation and distribution infrastructure. Roads and ports are also inferior to those found in China.

The demand for garments from low-cost sources such as Bangladesh has been driven by intense competition among Western clothing retailers. U.S. consumers, for example, have become accustomed to spending relatively little on clothing. In 2012 US consumers devoted just 3% of their annual spending to clothing and footwear, compared to around 7% in 1970. One reason Americans now spend so little on clothing is that real prices have fallen

significantly over the last two decades Since 1990, clothing prices in the US have risen by just 10% in nominal terms, compared to an 82% jump in nominal food prices during the same period. Adjusted for price inflation, clothing prices have fallen. The sluggish U.S. economy and stagnant wage growth have increased pressure on clothing retailers by capping consumers' disposable income. At the same time, the desire to shop for fashionable new outfits remains strong. The result has been strong price competition among retail apparel chains.

FACTORY COLLAPSE

The building that collapsed on April 24 was an eight storey complex called the Rana Plaza after its owner, Sohel Rana, a local politician and member of the ruling political party. The builders of the Rana Plaza only had approval for the construction of a five-storey structure, but in Bangladesh rules can be bent, so the builders added three extra floors. Five garment factories occupied six floors in the building. At the time of the collapse, it is estimated that they were making clothes for some 30 Western apparel brands.

In retrospect, the building collapse should not have been a total surprise. Parts of the complex had been built on a pond filled with sand, making for an unstable foundation. The entire building vibrated whenever its diesel generator was working. The day before the collapse, visible cracks had appeared in the building, promoting some workers to run out. Both the local police and the Bangladesh Garment Manufacturers and Exporters Association warned Sohel Rana that the building was unsafe. Rana disagreed, and the complex stayed open for business. Two inspectors were in the building when it collapsed. Both died. Some survivors stated that their employees had pressured them to turn up for work as usual on Wednesday. After the collapse Sohel Rana fled. He was found and arrested four days later on the border with India and charged with criminal negligence.

The death toll from the factory collapse was initially pegged at 250, but over the following days and weeks it kept increasing. By mid May it was clear that over 1,100 people had died in the collapsed building, making it the second worst industrial disaster in the history of South Asia after the infamous Bhopal disaster in 1984. The Bangladesh government stated that it would pay $250 in compensation to each family that lost a member in the building collapse.

AFTERMATH

The building collapse prompted some soul searching on the part of Western retailers who sourced production from Bangladesh. Critics were quick to point out that desires to drive prices down may have contributed to the situation in Bangladesh. Factory owners might bid low to get business from Western companies. While these factories themselves might meet the standards required by Western companies, such as they are, it is common-place for them to outsource production to a shadow economy of subcontractors where regulations are rou-tinely ignored and workers are paid less than the legal minimum wage. Indeed, this is how they make a profit. That being said, all of the factories operating in the Rana Plaza seem to have been among the country's 1,500 or so regular exporters.

Some Western companies had already taken steps to improve working conditions in Bangladesh prior to the collapse of the Rana Plaza building. In October 2012, The Gap announced a $22 million fire and building safety plan with its suppliers in Bangladesh, without identify-ing which factories it was using there or how many facto-ries would be improved under the plan. In early April, in response to the factory fire the prior November that had killed 112, Wal-Mart pledged $1.8 million to train 2,000 Bangladesh factory managers about fire safety. Critics noted that these commitments represented a drop in the bucket. Some non-governmental organizations estimated that it would cost some $3 billion to make the needed fire safety and building improvements to ensure that Bangladesh's 5,000 garment factories were safe.

Three weeks after the building collapse several of the world's largest apparel retailers—including the retailer H&M, Inditex, the owner of the Zara chain, Benetton, Marks & Spencer, and Tesco—agreed to sign a legally binding agreement designed to improve safety conditions in Bangladesh's garment factories. Under the five-year agreement, the signatories agreed not to hire manufac-turers whose factories fail to meet safety standards and committed to help pay for necessary repairs and renova-tions. Signatories will form a governing board to over-see safety inspections of up to 5,000 factories over two years, with results being made public. The governing board will include three representatives from retailers, three labor representatives, and a chairman chosen by the UN International Labor Organization. Participation will

cost each company a maximum of $2.5 million each over the 5-year period of the agreement.

Several major U.S. retailers, including Wal-Mart, Gap, Sears, and JC Penny, did not initially sign the pact. Gap Inc. stated that it would not sign the pact because the language makes it legally binding in the U.S., and if they failed to comply they could be sued in U.S. courts. Instead Gap Inc. put forward an amendment calling for retailers to be publically expelled from the group if they fail to comply with arbitration. Wal-Mart too, cited the legally binding language as a reason for not signing the pact. Instead Wal-Mart said that it would hire an outside auditor to inspect 279 Bangladesh factories and publish results on its web site by June 1 2013. When fire or building issues are found, Wal-Mart said that it would require factory owners to make necessary renovations or risk being removed from its list of authorized sup-pliers. Wal-Mart stated that it would not pay for factory renovations, but expected the cost of improvements to be reflected in the costs of goods they purchased. Wal-Mart will also set up an independent call center for garment workers to report unsafe working conditions. For its part, the government of Bangladesh stated that it would raise the minimum wage for garment workers in the country and tighten building and fire regulations.

CASE DISCUSSION QUESTIONS

1. From an economic perspective, was the shift to a free trade regime in the textile industry good for Bangladesh?
2. Economically who benefits when retailers in Europe and the United States source textiles from low-wage countries such as Bangladesh? Who might lose? Do the gains outweigh the losses?
3. What the causes of the weak safety record of the Bangladesh garment industry? Do Western com-panies that import garments from Bangladesh bear any responsibility for what happened at the Rana Plaza and other workplace accidents?
4. Do you think the legally binding agreement signed by H&M, Zara, Tesco and others will make a dif-ference? Does it go far enough? What else might be done?

5. What do you think about Walt Disney's decision not to purchase merchandise from Bangladesh? Is this an appropriate way of dealing with the problem?

6. What do you think of Wal-Mart's approach to this problem? Is the company doing enough? What else could it do?

SOURCES

- S. Banjo, "Promises in Bangladesh", *Wall Street Journal*, May 14, 2013.
- S. Banjo, "Wal-Mart Crafts own Bangladesh Safety Plan", *Wall Street Journal*, May 15, 2013.
- K. Bradsher, "Jobs Vanish as Exports Fall in Asia," *The New York Times,* January 22, 2009, p. B1
- "Knitting Pretty," *The Economist,* July 18, 2008, p. 54.
- "The new collapsing building", *The Economist*, April 25, 2013.
- "Rags in the ruins", *The Economist*, May 4, 2013.
- K. Bradsher, "Competition Means Learning to Offer More Than Just Low Wages," *The New York Times,* December 14, 2004, p. C1.
- V. Bajaj, "As Labor Costs Rise in China, Textile Jobs Shift Elsewhere," *The New York Times,* July 17, 2010, pp. 1, 3.
- S. Greenhouse, "Bangladesh fears exodus of apparel firms", *New York Times*, May 2, 2013.
- S. Greenhouse, "Major retailers join Bangladesh safety plan", *New York Times*, May 13, 2013.
- A. Zimmerman and N. Shah, "American tastes fuel boom in Bangladesh", *Wall Street Journal*, May 13, 2013.

Case 28

Frog's Leap Winery in 2011—The Sustainability Agenda [Case and Video]

Armand Gilinsky, Jr., Sonoma State University

There's an old saying in the wine industry that goes, "In order to make a small fortune you need to start out with a *large* one." Unfortunately, I'd never heard of that "rule" before I started out. I came here to the Napa Valley 27 years ago with $40 in my pocket, sold my motorcycle for $5,000 to start a winery, and now I owe $22 million to the bank. And I still haven't been able to buy back my motorcycle, because the current loan covenants with the bank do not permit me to ride, so I'm not sure that I am a success story, really. –John Williams, founder & CEO, Frog's Leap Winery.[1]

From the autumn of 1999 to late spring 2011, most Napa Valley premium wineries were embracing modernity—launching websites, using viral marketing, developing wine clubs, and shifting distribution channels from on-premises accounts to direct sales. John Williams, the co–founder, owner, and CEO/winemaker of Frog's Leap Winery in Rutherford, California, had followed suit by making modest investments in these marketing programs. Williams nevertheless remained skeptical that these changes would dictate his winery's future. In May 2011, Williams reflected upon his heritage as the son of upstate New York dairy farmers and his 35 years' working in the wine industry, since graduation from Cornell University. Williams not only displayed his normally irreverent humor, but also acknowledged that he had quietly developed the industry's most sophisticated environmental management system.[2] Environmental management systems (EMS) had risen in importance for wine businesses, as they confronted survival threats from the natural world, such as rising energy prices, water scarcity, mounting concerns about chemical exposure, and climate change.[3] Yet Williams wondered aloud:

"How could Frog's Leap, which has grabbed the 'low–hanging fruit' of environmental management, become even more sustainable?" See Exhibit 1 for a timeline of events in Frog's Leap's evolution.

NAPA VALLEY AND THE PREMIUM WINE INDUSTRY

Napa Valley was a prominent American Viticultural Area (AVA) in California's North Coast wine-producing region, which encompassed Lake, Napa, Mendocino, and Sonoma counties. [See "Glossary of Common Wine Industry Terminology" at the end of this case.] Since 1999, the number of premium wineries in the North Coast had grown from 329 to 1,250.[4] Of that number, nearly 92% could be classified as small or 'boutique' wineries, that is, those producing fewer than 50,000 cases per year. The number of boutique wineries increased dramatically during the 12–year period, from 249 to 1,133. By contrast, midsized wineries (those producing between 50,000 to 499,999 cases per year) and large wineries (those producing more than 499,999 cases per year) grew more modestly in number during the same period, from 80 to 117.

After the height of the global economic downturn in 2008–2009, during the following year the premium wine industry witnessed a small but significant rebound in growth. Mid-priced and high-priced wines led that growth. See Table 1 for data comprising the U.S. premium wine industry's percent sales growth, margins, and pretax profits

Exhibit 1	Evolution of Frog's Leap Winery

Year	Major events
1884	Welcoming building built as the Adamson Winery
1972	As undergraduate at Cornell, John Williams obtains internship at Taylor Wine company, falls in love with wine as a result
1975	While touring Napa Valley with a friend, John meets Larry Turley at Larry's newly bought farmstead; returns in summer to begin graduate work in enology at UC Davis; starts working part-time at Stag's leap Wine cellars (under Warren Winiarski); makes (and consumes) with Turley the first unofficial Frog's leap vintage, a fizzy chardonnay
1980	John returns to Napa Valley to become head winemaker at Spring mountain, marries Julie Johnson; first Frog's leap vintage, a cabernet Sauvignon, is (somewhat unofficially) crushed
1981	John Williams forms Frog's leap Winery in Napa with Larry Turley; winery is bonded; winery makes its first Sauvignon Blanc and Zinfandel
1984	Julie Williams becomes Frog's leap's first employee
1985	John leaves Spring Mountain to work full time at Frog's leap
1989	Frog's leap certifies its first organic vineyard
1992	First Frog's leap merlot (1990) is released
1993	Larry and John agree to create separate wineries; John and Julie buy Frog's leap from Larry and begin to look for new home for winery; Larry starts Turley Wine cellars on original Frog's leap site (the Frog Farm)
1994—1995	John and Julie purchase defunct Adamson Winery from Freemark abbey and re-start Frog's leap at the "red Barn" ranch in Rutherford
1999	First appearance of winery's Rutherford label (1996 vintage); underground barrel chai (barrel hall) next to the red Barn completed; John and Julie are divorced; Julie starts her own winery, Tres Sabores
2002	At urging of John, Rutherford dust Society begins Napa River Restoration project; debut of winery's Syrah and La Grenouille Rouganté, a dry rosé
2005	Photovoltaic system goes live after installation of 1,020 panels at the red Barn vineyard; original green mailbox at winery entrance is removed and road signage to winery added
2006	Frog's leap completes ten–year plan for winery and opens new LEED certified hospitality and administrative offices; red Barn rebuilt
2009	Frog's leap creates wine club, "Fellowship of the Frog" and begins developing "wine by the glass program" by packaging wines for delivery to restaurants in half kegs

Sources: Casewriters' research; Beer, J. (2007), *Organically Sublime, Sustainably Ridiculous: The First Quarter Century of Frog's Leap*, Kennett Square, Pa: Union Street Press.

from 2002–2010. See Table 2 showing volume and value changes for various price points of wines during 2010.

CONSUMER SEGMENTS FOR PREMIUM WINES

The U.S. surpassed both France and Italy in 2008 as the world's largest consumer of wine by dollar value. In 2010,

U.S. wine consumption in terms of volume reached an all-time peak of 2.54 gallons per resident over 21. In that same year, 25- to 44-year-olds emerged as the largest segment of wine consumers, supplanting the 'Baby-Boom' generation that had led much of the industry's growth during the prior 30 years. See Table 3 for 2010 data on consumer demographics of the U.S. wine industry.

Trends in consumer health awareness also had a considerable impact on U.S. wine consumption. The 'Baby-Boomers' increasingly desired to stave off aging and

Table 1

U.S. Premium Wine Industry—Key Financial Data, 2002—2010

	12/31/02	12/31/03	12/31/04	12/31/05	12/31/06	12/31/07	12/31/08	12/31/09	12/31/10
Sales Growth (yr. on yr.)	5.2%	17.6%	25.5%	19.4%	21.2%	22.3%	2.0%	−3.8%	10.8%
Gross Margin	51.5%	50.2%	51.5%	52.8%	54.5%	57.1%	55.3%	52.4%	53.7%
Pretax Profit	3.2%	6.3%	7.6%	12.6%	11.3%	16.3%	9.5%	2.2%	6.7%

Source: Silicon Valley Bank, 2011–12 *State of the Wine Industry*, April 2011, p. 11.

Table 2

U.S. Premium Wine industry—Price Segment data, 12/31/09—12/31/10

Last 52 wks Volume	Price segment	Value % change		Value % change	
		Last 52 wks	Last26 wks	Last 52 wks	Last 26 wks
100.0%	Total table wine	+4.5%	+4.8	+3.2%	+3.5
8.4	$0—$2.99	−1.3	−2.5	−2.4	−2.6
29.3	$3—$5.99	+4.4	+4.2	+4.8	+4.9
20.2	$6—$8.99	−3.4	−3.3	−1.0	−0.9
20.8	$9—$11.99	+10.0	+10.5	+12.4	+12.5
10.0	$12—$14.99	+7.8	+8.1	+10.3	+10.2
6.2	$15—$19.99	+7.0	+9.4	+7.7	+10.3
5.0	>$20	+11.4	+11.8	+9.2	+11.0

Note: shaded areas indicate double–digit growth.
Source: The Nielsen Companies, in Silicon Valley Bank, 2011–12 *State of the Wine Industry*, April 2011, p. 4.

infirmity by incorporating better nutrition and wellness into their lives. The postulated positive health aspects of drinking red wine in moderation contributed to increasing wine sales across all age groups.

So-called "green" consumers comprised an emerging demographic segment called LOHAS (Lifestyles of Health and Sustainability). This segment sought a better world for themselves and their children. LOHAS consumers were savvy, sophisticated, ecologically and economically aware and believed that society had reached a watershed moment in history because of increasing public scrutiny of corporations' environmental and ethical practices.[5] The LOHAS consumer focused on health and fitness, the environment, personal development,

Table 3	U.S. Wine Industry—2010 Consumer Demographics Data		
	Unemployment Rate	**% of population**	**% of wine drinking population**
Race/Ethnicity			
White	8.5%	68.9%	78.5%
Hispanic	13.0%	13.4%	8.9%
African–American	15.8%	10.8%	7.3%
Age			
21–24	15.3%	7.4%	4.0%
25–34	10.1%	18.7%	13.6%
35–44	7.8%	19.6%	16.3%
45–54	7.5%	20.6%	22.0%
55+	6.9%	33.7%	44.1%
Education			
High school diploma	15.3%	19.2%	10.2%
Some college	10.6%	28.4%	20.2%
College grad	4.9%	24.3%	39.9%

Source: The Nielsen Companies, in Silicon Valley Bank, 2011–12 *State of the Wine Industry*, April 2011, p. 13.

sustainable living and social justice. The segment was estimated at about 38 million people, or 17% of the U.S. adult population, with spending power of $209 billion annually.[6] Among all ages of consumers, younger consumers, aged 14–24, were reported to be most concerned about issues such as climate change and environmental protection, and were the major drivers of growth in the LOHAS segment. See Table 4 for demographic data on "green" consumers vs. all consumers.

Yet considerable confusion remained among wine consumers of all ages regarding organic wine vs. wine made from organically grown grapes. Organic wine was fermented and aged without sulfites, regardless of how the grapes were grown. Wine made from organically grown grapes might or might not have sulfites added to preserve shelf life. The two products were considerably different in origin, composition, and potential shelf lives.[7] Furthermore, wines labeled as organic or biodynamic were typically placed in a separate section away from other mainstream brands in supermarkets and specialist shops. Nevertheless, U.S. sales of certified organic wine and those made with organic grapes reached $80 million in 2006, and rose to nearly $130 million in 2008, an increase of 28% over 2004, according to the Organic Trade Association.[8]

SUSTAINING THE CALIFORNIA WINE INDUSTRY

After a period of unprecedented and sustained growth from 2002–2007, wine producers sought an edge to differentiate their brands and also to reduce costs during

| Table 4 | The Green Consumer |

	All consumers	"Green" consumers
Average age	44	40
Gender		
Female	51%	54%
Male	49%	46%
Ethnicity		
Caucasian/other	75%	62%
Hispanic	13%	21%
African–American	11%	16%
College educated	25%	31%
Median household income	$58,700	$65,700

Source: Brooks, S. (2009). The green consumer, *Restaurant Business*, September, pp. 20–21.

the 2008–2009 industry downturn. Many wineries faced financial difficulties due to market saturation. Almost all 6,785 wineries across the U.S. (of which 3,306 were in California) faced downward pressure on prices and margins. Some industry observers opined that wine producers faced a newly "hyper-competitive" trading environment: the rate of new brand introductions slowed in 2009 and 2010, in a period when wholesalers and distributors of wine were struggling to sell off a backlog of wine inventory and thus less receptive to taking on new wines to sell.[9]

Barbara Banke was co-proprietor of Jackson Family Wines in Santa Rosa, California (Sonoma County), a wine business known for its Kendall-Jackson, Hartford Family, Matanzas Creek, and Cardinale brands. Banke listed sustainability as one of the greatest challenges the wine industry faced in 2011:

We've had a reduction in the workforce last year, and we focused on controlling our costs and not investing so much capital. We have a constant battle to get the recognition we deserve with all the work we've done on sustainability. The industry is very green—and yet that's something that's not widely known. The California wine industry should work on enhancing its reputation for sustainability.[10]

To many in the wine industry, sustainability was defined as the 'triple bottom line,' meaning that producers needed to measure the impacts of their activities upon 'people, planet, and profit,' that is, creating social, environmental, and economic value. That the wine industry was greening was borne out by a report issued by the California Sustainable Winegrowing Alliance in 2009.[11] Some 1,237 California vineyard and 329 winery owners voluntarily participated in the Sustainable Winegrowing Program (SWP), despite widespread perceptions that sustainable farming practices increased the cost of production and lowered crop yields. Information about the SWP is shown in Exhibit 2. According to the Napa Valley Vintners Association, Napa Valley boasted 404 premium wineries, of which 60 were classified as "Green" or "Sustainable" in some fashion. See Exhibit 3 for more information on the 60 "Green" wineries in Napa in 2011.

Frog's Leap had hosted a Sustainable Wine Growers conference each year since 2006. The purpose of these conferences was to share information and best practices. Attendance had grown from ten to over 250 California wineries (out of 329 members of the California Sustainable Winegrowing Alliance) in just five years. At the 2010 conference, Ted Hall, owner of Long Meadow

| Exhibit 2 | About the California Sustainable Winegrowing Program |

Wine institute and the California Association of Wine Growers (CAWG) partnered to design and launch the Sustainable Winegrowing Program (SWP) in 2002. The California Sustainable Winegrowing Alliance (CSWA) was incorporated a year later to continue implementing this program.

Mission

The long-term mission for the SWP includes:

- Establishing voluntary high standards of sustainable practices to be followed and maintained by the entire California wine community;
- Enhancing grower-to-grower and vintner-to-vintner education on the importance of sustainable practices and how self-governance improves the economic viability and future of the wine community; and
- Demonstrating how working closely with neighbors, communities, and other stakeholders to maintain an open dialogue addresses concerns, enhances mutual respect, and accelerates positive results.

Vision

The vision of the SWP is the sustainability of the California wine community for future generations. In the context of winegrowing, the program defines sustainability as wine grape growing and winemaking practices that are sensitive to the environment (Environmentally Sound), responsive to the needs and interest of society at-large (Socially Equitable), and economically feasible to implement and maintain (Economically Feasible). The combination of these three principles is often referred to as the three E's of sustainability. These important principles are translated into information and education about specific practices that are documented in the program's comprehensive code workbook and are conveyed during the program's targeted education events that are aimed to encourage the adoption of improvements over time.

SWP Voluntary Participation data (as of July, 2009)

Vineyard Data Comparison	2004	2009	
Number of Distinct Vineyard Organizations	813	1,237	
Total Vineyard Acres Farmed by 1,237 Organziations	223,971	358,121	(68.1% of 526,000 total statewide acres)
Number of Vineyard Acres Accessed by the 1,237 Organziations	137,859	241,325	(45.9% of 526,000 total statewide acres)
Number of Vineyard Organzations that Submitted Assessment Results	614	868	(70.2% of 1,237 total organizations)
Total Vineyard Acres from 868 Organzations Assessed and Submitted	124,576	206,899	(39.3% of 526,000 total statewide acres)

Winery Data Comparison	2004	2009	
Number of distinct Winery organizations	128	329	
Total Winery Cases Produced by 329 Organizations	145.6M	150M	(62.5% of 240 million total statewide cases)
Number of Winery Cases Assessed by 329 Organizations	126.6M	141.5M	(59% of 240 million total statewide cases)
Number of Winery Organizations that Submitted Assessment Results	86	173	(52.6% of 329 total organizations)
Total Winery Cases from 173 Organizations Assessed and Submitted	96.8M	134.6M	(56.1% of 240 million total statewide cases)

Sources: California Wine community, Sustainability report 2009, pp. 6–7; Brodt, S. & Thrupp, A. (2009, July), "Understanding Adoption and Impacts of Sustainable Practices in California Vineyards," California Sustainable Winegrowing alliance, pp. 5–8, www.sustainablewinegrowing.org.

Exhibit 3   "Green" Wineries in Napa Valley as of 2011

Winery name	Annual case production (est.)	Certified Napa Green Land (1)	Certified Napa Green Winery (2)	Sustainable practices (3)
1 Araujo Estate Wines	5,000–49,999	X	X	X
2 Artesa	50,000–499,999	X		X
3 Beaulieu Vineyard	500,000+	X		X
4 Beringer Vineyards	500,000+	X	X	X
5 Boeschen Vineyards	<1,000		X	X
6 Bouchaine Vineyards	5,000–49,999	X		X
7 CADE Winery	5,000–49,999		X	X
8 Cain Vineyard & Winery	5,000–49,999	X		X
9 Cakebread Cellars	50,000–499,999	X	X	X
10 Chateau Boswell Winery	1,000–4,999	X	X	X
11 Chateau Montelena	5,000–49,999		X	X
12 Clark–Claudon Vineyards	1,000–4,999	X		X
13 Clos Du Val	50,000–499,999	X	X	X
14 Clos Pegase	5,000–49,999	X		X
15 CONSTANT	1,000–4,999		X	X
16 Cuvaison Estate Wines	50,000–499,999	X	X	X
17 Duckhorn Vineyards	50,000–499,999	X		X
18 Etude	5,000–49,999	X	X	X
19 Franciscan Estate	50,000–499,999	X	X	
20 Frog's Leap	50,000–499,999	X	X	X
21 Gargiulo Vineyards	1,000–4,999	X		
22 HALL	5,000–49,999	X		X
23 HdV Wines–Hyde de Villaine	1,000–4,999	X		X
24 Heitz Wine Cellars	5,000–49,999	X		X
25 Hess Collection Winery, The	500,000+	X	X	X
26 Honig Vineyard & Winery	5,000–49,999	X		X
27 Jericho Canyon Vineyard	1,000–4,999	X	X	X
28 Joseph Phelps Vineyards	50,000–499,999	X		X
29 Judd's Hill	1,000–4,999		X	X
30 Krupp Brothers	5,000–49,999	X		X
31 Ladera Vineyards	5,000–49,999	X		X
32 Larkmead Vineyards	5,000–49,999		X	X
33 Long Meadow Ranch Winery	5,000–49,999	X		X
34 Markham Vineyards	50,000–499,999	X		
35 Merryvale Vineyards	50,000–499,999	X	X	X

(continued)

Winery name	Annual case production (est.)	Certified Napa Green Land (1)	Certified Napa Green Winery (2)	Sustainable practices (3)
36 Mumm Napa	50,000–499,999		X	X
37 Opus One	5,000–49,999	X	X	X
38 Ovid Napa Valley	<1,000		X	X
39 Parry Cellars	5,000–49,999	X		X
40 Peju	<1,000	X		X
41 Quintessa	5,000–49,999	X		X
42 Robert Craig Winery	5,000–49,999		X	X
43 Robert Mondavi Winery	50,000–499,999	X		X
44 Saintsbury	50,000–499,999	X		X
45 Salvestrin	1,000–4,999	X		X
46 Schramsberg Vineyards	50,000–499,999	X	X	
47 Silver Oak Cellars	5,000–49,999	X		
48 Silverado Vineyards	50,000–499,999	X		X
49 Spottswoode Estate Vineyard & Winery	1,000–4,999	X	X	X
50 St. Supéry Estate	50,000–499,999	X		X
51 Stag's Leap Wine Cellars (4)	50,000–499,999	X	X	X
52 Stags' Leap Winery (5)	50,000–499,999	X		
53 Sterling Vineyards	50,000–499,999	X	X	X
54 Stony Hill Vineyard	5,000–49,999	X		X
55 Trefethen Family Vineyards	50,000–499,999	X	X	X
56 Trinchero Napa Valley	500,000+	X		X
57 V. Sattui Winery	50,000–499,999	X		X
58 Volker Eisele Family Estate	50,000–499,999	X		
59 White Rock Vineyards	1,000–4,999	X		X
60 William Hill Estate Winery	50,000–499,999	X		X

Notes:

1. The **Certified Napa Green Land** program was a third party certified, voluntary program for Napa vintners and grape growers. The program sought to restore, protect and enhance the regional watershed and included restoration of wildlife habitat, healthy riparian environments, and sustainable agricultural practices. As of 2011, approximately 45,000 acres were enrolled in this program and more than 19,000 acres were certified.

2. Founded in 2007, the **Certified Napa Green Winery** designation was developed by the Napa Valley Vintners association in coordination with the County's Department of Environmental Management (DEM), and was based on the Association of Bay Area Government's (ABAG) Green Business Program. ABAG's winery-specific checklist included: water conservation, energy conservation, pollution prevention, and solid waste reduction.

3. The Napa Valley Vintners association defined **Sustainable practices** as environmentally sound, economically viable, and socially responsible winegrowing methods. Examples of sustainable practices that pertained to resource conservation and/or effective vineyard management included:

   - Cover crops
   - Reduced tillage
   - Reduced-risk pesticides

Winery name	Annual case production (est.)	Certified Napa Green Land (1)	Certified Napa Green Winery (2)	Sustainable practices (3)

- Use only organic inputs
- Erosion control measures
- Hedgerows/habitat management
- Installing bird boxes
- Integrated Pest management (monitoring of pests & beneficial plants, reduced-risk materials, leaf-pulling)
- Energy conservation
- Weather station
- Renewable energy (solar, biofuels)
- Creek and river restoration

4. Founder Warren Winiarski sold Stag's leap Winery in 2007 to a joint venture between chateau Ste. Michelle (Washington state) and Marchesi Antinori (Italy). Notably, Stag's leap's cabernet Sauvignon won a gold medal in the famous Paris wine tasting in 1978, an event that suddenly put Napa on the map as a global wine producer. Warren Winiarski was John Williams' first employer in the Napa wine industry.

5. Often misspelled and confused with Stag's leap Winery, Stags' leap was purchased by Beringer Wine Estates in 1999, and is currently owned by Treasury Wine Estates, a recent spinoff of Foster's Group (Australia).

Sources: Napa Valley Vintners Association Green Wineries Program, http://www.napavintners.com/wineries/napa_green_wineries. asp, accessed May 23, 2011, company websites, *Wines and Vines*.

Ranch, an organic Napa vineyard located in the Mayacamas Mountains above the valley, said:

> There is only one reason we farm organically, and that's because it results in higher quality and lower costs. Organic growing could double the life of a vineyard, perhaps to 40 years. That should be considered in calculating its costs. The fundamental objective of organic farming is to create a healthy plant. We're trying to create a plant that is balanced and appropriate for its site, slope and conditions. A healthy plant can produce fantastic flavors at full physiological ripeness without practices like water stress and long hang–time that can weaken the plant. You have to take a systems approach to organic growing. You can't just substitute organic pesticides or fertilizers for conventional chemicals. As much as we like to believe when we tell the rest of the world about the value of the Napa Valley appellation, not every piece of [Napa vineyard] property is suitable for growing quality grapes [organically] at a reasonable cost.[12]

A 2011 survey of 98 U.S. wine producers found that wineries appeared highly aware of sustainability issues and recognized the importance of caring for the environment.[13] Notably, about one third of the respondents had increased investment in EMS during the recent recession. However, although many reportedly had adopted some sustainable practices such as organic and biodynamic cultivation, energy efficient production, and dry farming, the *perceived* benefits of going beyond those practices to the adoption of a formal EMS program remained unclear. There was a perception of a cost advantage benefit to a formal EMS program, but not necessarily a differentiation benefit, with the possible exception of an increased ability to enter new market segments.

FROG'S LEAP IN 2011

Frog's Leap commenced production with 653 cases of Sauvignon Blanc in 1981. By 2010 the winery produced 62,000 cases of predominantly red wines. Varietal brands included white wines made from Sauvignon Blanc ($18 retail) and Chardonnay grapes ($26), and red wines from Zinfandel ($27), Merlot ($34), two wines made from Cabernet Sauvignon ($42 and $70), and Petite Sirah ($35). Frog's Leap also sold the amusingly named Frogenbeerenauslese ($25), a 100% Riesling, and La Grenouille Rougante ($14), a rosé blend made from Gamay and a touch of Riesling. In addition, the winery produced its own olive oil and honey.[14]

Staff headcount at Frog's Leap grew 100% over 12 years, from 25 to 50 personnel. Most of the new hires were fieldworkers. Other employees included those in its tasting room, such as Shannon Oren, Tasting Room Assistant. In 2011, three managers reported to John Williams. Paula Moschetti, after five years' service as enologist for the firm, was promoted to Assistant Winemaker. Jonah Beer, former director of sales for Stag's Leap Wine Cellars, was hired as Director of Sales, Marketing and Public Relations in August 2003, and soon after became the winery's first General Manager. Upon the retirement of Gary Gates, Frog's Leap's longtime financial consultant, the firm hired Doug DeMerritt as its Chief Financial Officer. DeMerritt had served in a similar capacity at another Napa winery, Duckhorn Vineyards, from 2002 until that company's acquisition by a private equity firm in August 2007.

From 1999 to 2010, Frog's Leap purchased 100 acres of vineyards in the surrounding Rutherford area in Napa Valley, effectively doubling its acreage under production in an area where land for vineyards was valuable and seldom available for purchase. Wine case production grew comparatively more modestly, from 59,000 cases to 62,000 cases. Williams commented,

> The true growth of Frog's Leap over the last ten years has been the acquisition and planting of vineyards which has reduced our income, increased our debt and added significantly to our operating costs in the short term BUT has guaranteed a high quality source of grapes for the future—a future which seems to be heading in the direction of grape supply shortage and rising prices.

Company net sales grew from $7 million in 1999 to $12 million in 2010. Frog Leap's portfolio of premium wines was sold primarily via what was called the "Three-tier distribution" chain in the alcoholic beverages industry. Resellers included wine specialists and selected supermarkets (off-premises accounts) or restaurants and hotels (on-premises accounts). Approximately 80% of 2010 company net sales in the U.S. were to resellers. Exports, primarily to Japan, accounted for about 7 to 8% of company net sales. The remainder was sold to consumers from Frog's Leap's tasting room and hospitality center, opened in 2006, and its "Fellowship of the Frog" wine club, created in 2009. Direct sales to consumers, where permitted by state laws regarding the sale of alcohol, had become increasingly important to wineries during the 2008–2010 recession to reduce backlogged inventories of wine. Direct sales to consumers also generated higher gross profit margins for wineries than sales to resellers, as wineries could charge consumers full retail prices (or provide a slight discount for wine club members), whereas wines to resellers

typically sold at 50% off the retail price, in order to provide markup incentives for moving products along the chain.

Although Frog's Leap's reputation in the wine industry had begun with a 1982 review by Terry Robards in the *New York Times* ("Frog's Leap: A Prince of A Wine"), Williams subsequently paid little attention to ratings of his wines by popular wine critics. While many winemakers and winery owners depended on high ratings by wine critics to drive consumer demand, Williams commented on the fact that only two of his wines had ever been reviewed:

> . . . we built our brand on Frog's Leap and fun. We started developing a loyal following that reduced our reliance on establishing our brand through traditional channels. I've made wine for 27 years, and I think [that] only two of our wines have ever been reviewed by Robert Parker [editor of *Wine Advocate*]. That's just fine with me. I don't have to worry about reviews that fail to recognize the brilliance of our wines, because our customers will go out and buy the wine because they love it no matter what other people say. The love of our brand evolved out of our approach, and it has allowed me to be freer as a winemaker, and more edgy in my winemaking.[15]

A PHILOSOPHY OF SUSTAINABILITY

Frog's Leap adhered to pre-1970s Napa Valley winemaking traditions, such as dry farming. Dry farming involved growing grape vines without using drip irrigation systems. Growing grapes without drip irrigation resulted in minimal water use and a more European style and wine flavor profile, with far lower alcohol content and fruitiness than the wines that had been produced by other Napa Valley wineries since 1970.

Other EMS practices adopted by Frog's Leap over the years included organic and biodynamic growing techniques. According to Williams, both techniques primarily involved building soil health through the use of cover crops and compost. Healthy, living soils produced healthy, living plants that naturally resisted disease. Natural-based soil fertility worked to regulate the vigor of the grapevine and naturally conferred its health and balance to the fruit, and thus to the fermenting wine, thereby avoiding many of the problems he would otherwise have had to confront in the wine cellar at a later stage of the production process.

Creating its own source of compost was another money saver for Frog's Leap. Field workers gathered the major byproducts of winemaking (like stems and pomace, or grape skins), added in all the coffee grounds, garden waste, and vegetable or fruit scraps from the kitchen, covered the pile, and let it turn into compost. Temperature readings indicated when and how often the compost pile needed to be turned. Frog's Leap saved money by not paying someone to haul the waste away, which was in keeping with the tenets of sustainable farming.

Why did Frog's Leap convert its grape production to organic and biodynamic and develop an EMS? According to Paula Moschetti, Assistant Winemaker,

> It's what we believe. We know that it not only produces better quality wine, but it just makes sense for the quality of life for the employees; it makes sense for giving back to society; it makes sense for the environment. Like everybody says, 'Respect where the grapes are grown.' We try to optimize that, but also to not take wine too seriously. We want to make great, world-class wine, but with a sense of humor, a tongue-in-cheek attitude. And I think people really respond to that.[16]

Meanwhile, Frog's Leap moved towards energy self-sufficiency via investments in geothermal and solar power. Williams would not disclose the cost of the geothermal system, but it was known to be one of the relatively few such systems in California. Cost of the solar power system, installed in February 2005, was $1.2 million, offset by a $600,000 cash rebate from the local power utility company. That system generated sufficient electricity to power 150 homes, and any excess power generated was sold back to the public utility. Jonah Beer, General Manager, described some of the cost advantages provided by Frog's Leap's energy systems:

> There is virtually no cost to operate the geothermal heating and cooling system . . . and the cost payback is only about six years. It comes with a 30-year warranty for the pumps, and the wells have a lifetime warranty. The exchanger itself is 70% more efficient at its job because it only has to do one thing. Plus, our pumps use the electricity from our own solar power. The savings from solar is very obvious; what's amazing is that everyone *isn't* doing it. While the up-front cost estimate was $1.2 million, Pacific Gas & Electric

(PG&E) gave [us] a $600,000 cash rebate up front, and [our] bank gave [us] a loan on the rest. As far as payback goes, we're actually paying less on the loan per month than we were paying on our electric bill. We're cash flow positive, and we'll be paid back in seven years. The system has a 25-year warranty. So we get 18 years of free electricity. Even if you don't care about green at all, it's kind of silly not to do it. [Our] system produces 450,000 KW-hours of electricity, which will save CO2 emissions equal to not driving four million miles.[17]

In 2006 Frog's Leap opened the industry's first LEED certified wine tasting and office facility, primarily from recycled building materials. LEED was an acronym for Leadership in Energy and Environmental Design. Buildings attained LEED certification from the U.S. Green Business Council. Lower operation costs were typically associated with a LEED building: approximately 30 to 40% less energy use and 40% less water. Application for LEED certification of an existing property could cost upwards of $10,000, depending upon the size of the building, the number of rooms, and the level of certification sought.[18]

Frog's Leap provided full-time, year-round employment and benefits for winery personnel, who were mostly immigrant laborers. According to Williams:

> The Mexican workforce has been wonderful for us, and we try to return that favor. The workers don't have to be laid off after pruning in January until tying canes in May, or from leafing until harvest. In between, our workers can prune trees, turn compost, bottle Sauvignon Blanc, harvest broccoli, rack and wash barrels, thin pears and apples, bottle Merlot, etc. They work full time— and get paid, three-week vacations, 401(k) plans, and health benefits. We also have fewer safety issues, because they're well-trained and experienced. They're an engaged and highly motivated workforce. Are there higher overall labor costs? How can you really measure your labor costs? The workers get stable wages, they don't have to worry about housing and healthcare and where their kids go to school. They're a community of workers. There are fewer problems with documentation, better health, less crime and use of the community's safety net.[19]

While other winery operators remained dubious about the cost/benefit tradeoff of investing in EMS and providing full-time employment to immigrant workers, Frog's Leap remained mostly profitable during the 2009–2010 recession.[20] To generate incremental cash flows, Frog's Leap augmented its sales via conventional distribution channels by an innovative "wine-by-the glass" program using kegs (instead of bottles) of wine, and by initiating direct-to-consumer programs, including a tasting room, and "Fellowship of the Frog" wine club. See Exhibit 4 for the disguised income statements provided by Frog's Leap for fiscal years 2000–2001 and 2009–2010. See Exhibit 5 for the disguised balance sheets for fiscal years 2000–2001 and 2009–2010. Williams commented:

> Over the long term, we have seen that our methods are viable. This is not just an experiment. We are a thriving business with above average margins and below average operating expenses. Our cost here for making a bottle of wine is equal to or less than the industry average.[21]

For purposes of comparison, see Exhibit 6 for 2000–01 and 2009–10 financial ratios compiled by Silicon Valley Bank, based on actual data from several anonymous wineries similar in size to Frog's Leap.

A reporter for the *San Francisco Chronicle* opined, "Frog's Leap could be the poster child for a new generation of Napa wineries: beautifully appointed, genteel, terroir oriented and dedicated to a green agenda."[22]

OPEN OTHER END

Early in Frog's Leap's history, John Williams had managed to persuade the U.S. Alcohol Tobacco Tax and Trade Bureau (known in the industry as the TTB) that has to approve all bottle labeling that it was not frivolous to mark the bottom of his wine bottles with a sage precaution: "Open Other End". The word "Ribbit" was printed on the cork of every bottle of Frog' Leap wine.

Humorous presentations aside, Williams remained serious about sustaining growth of his business while remaining at the same level of production output. "How can we continue to grow sales and profits while remaining a small winery production-wise? I know that some business people are trained to think outside of the box, but first I want to know *where* the box is and what is *in*

Exhibit 4	Frog's leap Winery Statements of income, 2000—2001 and 2009—2010

All dollar amounts are in $000	FYI 2000	% of Sales	FY 2001	% of Sales	FY 2009	% of Sales	FY 2010	% of Sales
Cases Sold	61,000		54,000		53,000		62,000	
Sales	$9,638	100%	$9,180	100%	$10,017	100%	$12,152	100%
Costs of Goods Sold	**4,514**	**46.8%**	**4,050**	**44.1%**	**4,346**	**43.4%**	**4,960**	**40.8%**
Gross Profit	5,124	53.2%	5,130	55.9%	5,671	56.6%	7,192	59.2%
Operating Expenses:								
Sales & Marketing	1,580	16.4%	1,615	17.6%	2,853	28.5%	3,337	27.5%
General & administrative	**1,200**	**12.5%**	**1,300**	**14.2%**	**1,678**	**16.8%**	**1,483**	**12.2%**
Total Operating Expenses	**2,780**	**28.8%**	**2,915**	**31.8%**	**4,531**	**45.2%**	**4,820**	**39.7%**
Operating Income	2,344	24.3%	2,215	24.1%	1,140	11.4%	2,372	19.5%
Interest Expense	**450**	**4.7%**	**875**	**9.5%**	**1,420**	**14.2%**	**1,420**	**11.7%**
Earnings bef. Tax	$1,894	19.7%	$1,340	14.6%	$(280)	−2.8%	$952	7.8%
Depreciation & amortization	675	7.0%	900	9.8%	1,250	12.5%	1,100	9.1%

Source: Frog's leap Winery. Some data have been disguised by the company, but the relationships are accurate.

Exhibit 5	Frog's leap Winery Balance Sheets, 2000–2001 and 2009–2010 (FYE 12/31)

All amounts are in $000	FYI 2000	% of Total Assets	FY 2001	% of Total Assets	FY 2009	% of Total Assets	FY 2010	% of Total Assets
ASSETS								
Current Assets								
Cash	$130	0.7%	$80	0.4%	$10	0.0%	$20	0.1%
Accounts Receivable	400	2.1%	550	2.6%	1,650	4.1%	1,950	5.0%
Inventory	6,500	33.5%	7,560	35.5%	12,010	30.1%	11,550	29.5%
Prepaid and other Expenses	**125**	**0.6%**	**250**	**1.2%**	**320**	**0.8%**	**325**	**0.8%**
Total Current Assets	7,155	36.9%	8,440	39.6%	13,990	35.0%	13,845	35.4%
Property, Plant and Equipment	15,250	78.6%	16,150	75.8%	36,750	92.1%	37,100	94.9%
Less: Accumulated Depreciation & Amort.	**3.150**	**16.2%**	**3,450**	**16.2%**	**10,925**	**27.4%**	**11,950**	**30.6%**
Net Property, Plant and Equipment	12,100	62.4%	12,700	59.6%	25,825	64.7%	25,150	64.3%
Other Assets	**150**	**0.8%**	**175**	**0.8%**	**100**	**0.3%**	**110**	**0.3%**
Total Assets	$19,405	100.0%	$21,315	100.0%	$39,915	100.0%	$39,105	100.0%
LIABILITIES & CAPITAL								
Current Liabilities								
Notes Payable	$3,150	16.2%	$4,370	20.5%	$2,425	6.1%	$2,425	6.2%
Accounts Payable and Accruals	2,610	13.5%	1,470	6.9%	2,325	5.8%	2,150	5.5%
Current Portion of LTD	**540**	**2.8%**	**960**	**4.5%**	**890**	**2.2%**	**950**	**2.4%**
Total Current Liabilities	6,300	32.5%	6,800	31.9%	5,665	14.2%	5,525	14.1%
Long-term Debt	5,030	25.9%	7,040	33.0%	20,400	51.1%	19,500	49.9%
Total Libilities	11,330	58.4%	13,840	64.9%	26,065	65.3%	25,025	64.0%
Shareholder Equity	8,075	41.6%	7,475	35.1%	13,850	34.7%	14,080	36.0%
Total Liabilities and Equity	$19,405	100.0%	$21,315	100.0%	$39,915	100.0%	$39,105	100.0%

Source: Frog's leap Winery. Some data have been disguised by the company, but the relationships are accurate.

the box before I think about what's outside," he quipped in May 2011.

One option for sustaining Frog's Leap's growth was to pursue other EMS projects. Williams maintained that Frog's Leap still had a long way to go to become a truly sustainable winery:

We're not 100% there. We're not even close. But we've done a lot of interesting things, and a lot of the big projects are behind us. Now we're into some of the more fun and challenging ideas that will help us take our philosophy further: Healthier field workers; healthier, longer living

Exhibit 6	Financial ratios for Similar-Sized Wineries, 2000–2001 and 2009–2010

	FYI 2000	FY 2001	FY 2009	FY 2010
Growth Rate, Cased Goods Revenue		−14.1%		+2.9%
Current Ratio (x)	2.11x	1.76x	1.91x	2.29x
Quick Ratio (x)	0.49x	0.30x	0.22x	0.08x
Working Capital ($000)	$4,203	$3,941	$6,063	$8,518
Cased Goods Revenues/Net Working Capital (x)	1.67x	1.53x	1.84x	1.35x
Account Receivable Days (365)	95.3	91.1	39.8	14.8
Inventory Days	575	805	1,118	1,533
Tangible Net Worth (TNW, $000)	$4,499	$4,361	$12,863	$13,597
Total Liabilities to TNW (x)	0.9x	1.3x	1.6x	1.7x
Senior Liabilities/TNW + Subordinate debt (x)	0.9x	1.3x	1.4x	1.4x
Gross Profit Margin (%)	45.70%	45.30%	67.20%	70.00%
Sales & Marketing Expenses/Sales (% of sales)	9.50%	12.20%	10.90%	9.80%
Net Margin (Return on Sales, %)	14.70%	5.70%	9.10%	9.70%
EBITDA ($000)	$1,528	$799	$3,964	$4,269
EBITDA, Less Distributions or Dividends ($000)	$218	$325	$3,502	$4,062
Debt Service Coverage (x)	6.4x	3.9x	2.0x	2.4x
Total Interest/Total Senior Debt (%)	7.50%	4.90%	6.80%	6.00%
Conventional ROE (%)	22.70%	7.80%	7.90%	8.20%
Operating Return on Assets (%)	11.90%	3.50%	3.00%	3.10%

Source: Casewriter's research, based on data provided by Silicon Valley Bank that were compiled from anonymous wineries similar in size to Frog's leap. For more highly aggregated financial data, see: Jordan, D.J., Aguilar, d., & Gilinsky, A. (2010), "Benchmarking Northern California Wineries," *Wine Business Monthly*, October, 60–67.

vineyards; enriched soil fertility; less erosion; lessened environmental contamination; greater trust with our consumers; and even considerably higher wine quality, converting farm equipment to biodiesel and reducing employee car use by commuting. Start-ups are going to be more expensive. There's no getting around it. However, if you take the long view of it, once you get past 10 years, the costs are less, and you've got a vineyard that will outlast everyone else's.[23]

Over time, it has developed that every decision at Frog's Leap is weighed at least in some measure by its social and ecological costs and benefits. We believe that these are the kinds of questions

all businesses will have to ask and answer if we wish [to have] a sustainable future. . . .[24]

Williams felt that pursuing any new sustainability projects in the near-to-medium term would have highly uncertain associated costs and benefits. Building out the direct-to-consumer sales channels (tasting room and wine club) was another option under consideration, but might come at the expense of taking attention away from distributors. A longer-term question about sustainability was also nagging at him: Frog's Leap's debt load. Williams and his former wife, Julie (who now owned another winery, Trés Sabores), had three sons who would presumably take over the business someday:

Right now my kids think my legacy is $22 million of debt (laughs). You know I don't really think about my legacy too often. I'm happy about growing grapes and making wine and having fun doing it. But I believe our winery has changed the dialogue about the healthy growing of grapes, conservation of soil and natural resources. I hope to be remembered for that.[25]

Williams' eldest son was working for another winery, his middle child was starting business school in Fall 2011, and his youngest was preparing to start law school. Now entering his mid-50s, Williams wondered aloud how to "position the business to be successful for the next 10 to 20 years, after which time the transition to that next generation would *inevitably* begin."

Glossary of Common Wine Industry Terminology

American Viticultural Area (AVA)—A designated "viticultural area" (e.g. Napa Valley, Sonoma, Central Coast) that must produce 85% of the grapes processed for bottling and sale. For a specified vineyard name, a particular vineyard must grow 95% of the grapes and all grapes used must be from the AVA.

Appellation—Similar to an AVA, the term appellation is used by other wine producing nations to demarcate a legally defined and specific region where wine grapes are grown. A wine claiming to be sourced from a named boundary (e.g. Côtes du Rhône in France, Chianti in Italy, or Rioja in Spain) must be comprised of at least 75% of the grapes grown within that boundary.

Biodynamics—Biodynamics, a growing agricultural movement both in the U.S. and internationally, is based on a series of lectures given in the 1920s by Austrian philosopher Rudolf Steiner. The movement views the vineyard (or farm) as an ecological whole—not just the vines, but also the soil, insects and other local flora and fauna. Like organic farmers, biodynamic growers are interested in naturally healthy plants, and in enriching their soil without artificial fertilizers or pesticides. Where biodynamics differs from classic organics, however, is in the belief that agriculture can be aligned to the spiritual forces of the cosmos. This may mean harvesting grapes when the moon is passing in front of a certain constellation, or sometimes by creating a homeopathic mixture that, when sprayed on the vines, will—in theory—help the grapes ripen and improve their flavors.

Brand—The name of the product. This can be a made-up name, the name of the actual producer, a virtual winery, or it could be a restaurant or grocery store chain that contracts with a winery for a "special label" purchase.

Chai—A barrel *chai* is a wine shed, or other **storage** place above ground, used for storing **casks**, common in Bordeaux. Usually different types of wine are kept in separate sheds. The New World counterpart to the chai may be called the barrel hall. In Bordeaux, the person in charge of vinification and aging of all wine made at an estate, or the chais of a **négociant**, is titled a *Maître de Chai*.

Dry farming—For most of the history of agriculture, grape growers dry-farmed their lands, and they still do in many wineries in Europe. Then, in the 1970s, drip irrigation conquered the world. A farming practice as old as agriculture itself fell to the wayside as wells were drilled, streams tapped, and pipes and hoses were run through thousands of acres of vineyards and orchards. By no coincidence, water supplies have now entered an era of decline in California, where land is subsiding in many regions as the aquifers below are emptied. Above ground, many small streams have drained into the earth; they may still flow—just underground. Dry-farmed wines, many sources say, are better, as grapevines, working under stressed conditions, produce smaller grapes than watered vines. The result is a greater quantity of tannin-rich skins and seeds to volume of juice, which can render denser, richer wines. For a dry farmer, the challenge is to lock the winter and spring rainfall in the soil for the duration of the dry season.

Economy wine—Regardless of where they are produced, table wines that retail for less than $3.00 per 750ml bottle are deemed to be in the generic, economy, or "jug" wine category.

Organic grapes—Organically grown grapes follow a broad definition of organic farming issued by the U.S. Department of Agriculture: "Organic farming is a production system which avoids or largely excludes the use of synthetically compounded fertilizers, pesticides, growth regulators, and livestock feed additives. To the maximum extent feasible, organic farming systems rely on crop rotations, crop residues, animal manures, legumes, green manures, off farm organic wastes and aspects of biological pest control to maintain soil productivity and tilth, to supply plant nutrients and to control insects, weeds and other pests. The concept of soil as a 'living system' is central to this definition." Wines made from organically grown grapes must be referred to as "wines made from organic grapes" (or organically grown grapes), as they are allowed to contain up to 100 ppm of added sulfites.

Organic wine—Organic wine is defined by the U.S. Department of Agriculture as "a wine made from organically grown grapes *and* without any added sulfites."

Premium wine—Wines selling for more than $3.00 per bottle are considered to be in the premium wine category. Most bottled wines in the premium category show a vintage date on their labels, that is, the product is made with at least 95% of grapes harvested, crushed and fermented in the calendar year shown on the label and also uses grapes from an appellation of origin (i.e. Napa Valley, Central Coast, Willamette Valley). Several market segments within the premium category are based on retail price points, typically double the wholesale value of a bottle or case of wine. *Impact Databank, Review & Forecast of the Wine Industry*, classifies wines "Sub–Premium" as those that retail for $3.00 to $6.00 per bottle; the "Premium" category retail for $7.00 to $9.99; the "Super–Premium" category retail for $10.00 to $13.99 per bottle, while the "Deluxe" segment are wines commanding a retail price above $14.00. Motto Kryla Fisher, a Napa Valley wine consulting firm, further refines the "Deluxe" segment into sub–segments: "Ultra Premium" wines, priced from $14.00 to $29.99, and "Luxury" wines, that retail in excess of $30.00 per bottle.

Three–tier distribution—A myriad of state laws and regulations restricting the sale of alcoholic beverages generally require wineries to use a "three-tier" distribution system (winery to distributor to retailer to consumer). However, distributor consolidation (through termination or acquisition) increased substantially since the May 16, 2005 *Granholm v. Heald* U.S. Supreme Court decision, prohibiting discrimination between in-state products and products from out–of–state, and that subsequently served to increase liberalization of shipping wine across some state lines, direct from producers to consumers.

Varietal—A type of grape (i.e., Merlot, Cabernet Sauvignon, Zinfandel, Chardonnay, etc.). To declare a "varietal" on the label, at least 75% of the wine must consist of that variety of grape. Some wineries use almost 100% of the same varietal. Some blend a principal varietal (the one named on the label) with wines made from other varieties of the same color for better flavor balance. Others blend in "filler" varieties, which usually go unlisted, to get the most out of their supply of then-popular varieties, which are the ones touted on the label. If the label mentions a varietal, it will always be in conjunction with an appellation to inform consumers of the source of the varietal grape.

Vintage—The year in which the harvest of the wine grapes occurs. By law, grapes grown in a declared vintage year (harvest year) must account for 95% of the wine if the label declares a vintage year.

Source: Casewriters' research; Modern Distribution Management (MDM).

NOTES

1. Originally quoted in Rainsford, P. (1999) "Frog's Leap Winery" (video case presented to the North American Case Research Association conference in Santa Rosa, California). Williams updated this quotation during interviews at Frog's Leap Winery in May and September 2011; Jonah Beer, Doug DeMerritt, and Shannon Oren also agreed to be interviewed on camera for the video case.

2. Intardonato, J. (2007, June 15) "Frog's Leap pursues their green vision," *Wine Business Monthly online*, http://www.winebusiness.com/wbm/?go=getArticle& dataId=48589, accessed April 10, 2011.

3. Hertsgaard, M. (2010) "Grapes of wrath," *Mother Jones*, July/August, pp. 37–39.

4. Wines and Vines (1999, 2004, 2009) *Wines and Vines Annual Directory*, San Francisco, CA.

5. Ekberg, P. (2006) "The keyword is LOHAS," *Japan Spotlight*, Japan Economic Foundation (JEF), March 1, 146.

6. As cited by Brooks, S. (2009) "The green consumer," *Restaurant Business*, September, pp. 20–21.

7. Delmas, M.A. and Grant, L.E. (2008, Mar.) "Eco-labeling strategies: The ecopremium puzzle in the wine industry," *AAWE working paper* no. 13; Guthey, G.T. and Whiteman, G. (2009) "Social and ecological transitions: Winemaking in California," *E:CO*, Vol. 11, No. 3, pp. 37–48.

8. Delmas, M.A. and Grant, L.E., op. cit.

9. Penn, C. (2011, Feb. 15) "Review of the industry: Outlook and trends," *Wine Business Monthly*, p. 70.

10. Ibid.

11. Brodt, S. & Thrupp, A. (2009, July) "Understanding adoption and impacts of sustainable practices in California vineyards," California Sustainable Winegrowing Alliance, www.sustainable winegrowing.org, accessed April 12, 2011.

12. Franson, P. (2010) "Organic grapegrowing for less," *Wines & Vines*, July 28, http://www.winesandvines.com/template.cfm?section=news&content=76728, accessed April 10, 2011.

13. Atkin, T., Gilinsky, A., & Newton, S.K. (2011) "Sustainability in the wine industry: Altering the competitive landscape?" Paper presented to the 6th Academy of Wine Business Research conference, June 9–11, Bordeaux, FR.

14. Saekel, K. (2009, May 13) "Napa Frog's Leap comes with a bit of whimsy," *San Francisco Chronicle*, http://www.seattlepi.com/default/article/Napa-winery-Frog-s-Leap-comes-with-a-bit-of-whimsy-1303945.php, accessed April 10, 2011.

15. As quoted in Cutler, L. (2008, Feb. 15) "Industry round-table: Humor in the wine trade," *Wine Business Monthly online*, http://www.winebusiness.com/wbm/?go=getArticle&dataId=54456, accessed April 10, 2011.

16. Brenner, D. (2006) "Paula Moschetti," *Women of the Vine*, Hoboken, NJ: John Wiley & Sons, p. 168.

17. Intardonato, J., op. cit.

18. For more on LEED certified buildings in Northern California, see: http://www.mlandman.com/gbuildinginfo/leedbuildings.shtml (updated every 8 weeks, accessed 5/25/2011).

19. Franson, P. (2010) "Winegrowers cash in on other crops," *Wines & Vines*, May 25, http://www.winesandvines.com/template.cfm?section=news&content=74538&htitle= Winegrowers%20Cash%20in%20on%20Other%20Crops, accessed April 10, 2011.

20. Hertsgaard, op. cit.; Guthey, G.T. and Whiteman, G. op. cit.

21. Intardonato, J., op. cit.

22. Saekel, K., op. cit.

23. As quoted by Saekel, K., op. cit.

24. As quoted by Daniel, L. (2011, November 1) "Grapegrower interview: John Williams: winegrowing from the roots up," http://www.allbusiness.com/agriculture-forestry/agriculture-animal-farming/16738095-1.html#ixzz1kPJtKSHF, accessed January 26, 2012.

25. Walters, C. (2010, May 3) "How organic and biodynamic viticulture will change the way you think: An interview with Frog's Leap Owner and Winemaker John Williams," *Indigo Wine Blog*, http://indigowinepress.com/2010/05/how-organic-and-biodynamic-viticulture-will-change-the-way-you-think-an-interview-with-frogs-leap-owner-and-winemaker-john-williams/, accessed January 29, 2011.

Glossary

absolute cost advantage A cost advantage that is enjoyed by incumbents in an industry and that new entrants cannot expect to match.

absorptive capacity The ability of an enterprise to identify, value, assimilate, and use new knowledge.

acquisition When a company uses its capital resources to purchase another company.

adaptive culture A culture that is innovative and encourages and rewards middle- and lower-level managers for taking the initiative to achieve organizational goals.

anticompetitive behavior A range of actions aimed at harming actual or potential competitors, most often by using monopoly power, and thereby enhancing the long-run prospects of the firm.

availability error A bias that arises from our predisposition to estimate the probability of an outcome based on how easy the outcome is to imagine.

barriers to imitation Factors that make it difficult for a competitor to copy a company's distinctive competencies.

behavior control Control achieved through the establishment of a comprehensive system of rules and procedures that specify the appropriate behavior of divisions, functions, and people.

brand loyalty Preference of consumers for the products of established companies.

broad differentiation strategy When a company differentiates its product in some way, such as by recognizing different segments or offering different products to each segment.

broad low-cost strategy When a company lowers costs so that it can lower prices and still make a profit.

bureaucratic costs The costs associated with solving the transaction difficulties between business units and corporate headquarters as a company obtains the benefits from transferring, sharing, and leveraging competencies.

business ethics Accepted principles of right or wrong governing the conduct of businesspeople.

business model The conception of how strategies should work together as a whole to enable the company to achieve competitive advantage.

business unit A self-contained division that provides a product or service for a particular market.

business-level strategy The business's overall competitive theme, the way it positions itself in the marketplace to gain a competitive advantage, and the different positioning strategies that can be used in different industry settings.

capabilities A company's skills at coordinating its resources and putting them to productive use.

chaining A strategy designed to obtain the advantages of cost leadership by establishing a network of linked merchandising outlets interconnected by information technology that functions as one large company.

code of ethics Formal statement of the ethical priorities to which a business adheres.

cognitive biases Systematic errors in human decision making that arise from the way people process information.

commonality Some kind of skill or competency that when shared by two or more business units allows them to operate more effectively and create more value for customers.

competitive advantage The achieved advantage over rivals when a company's profitability is greater than the average profitability of firms in its industry.

control system Provides managers with incentives for employees as well as feedback on how the company performs.

corporate headquarters staff The team of top executives, as well as their support staff, who are responsible for overseeing a company's long-term multibusiness model and providing guidance to increase the value created by the company's self-contained divisions.

corruption Can arise in a business context when managers pay bribes to gain access to lucrative business contracts.

credible commitment A believable promise or pledge to support the development of a long-term relationship between companies.

cross-selling When a company takes advantage of or "leverages" its established relationship with customers by way of acquiring additional product lines or categories that it can sell to customers. In this way, a company increases differentiation because it can provide a "total solution" and satisfy all of a customer's specific needs.

customer defection Rate percentage of a company's customers who defect every year to competitors.

customer response time Time that it takes for a good to be delivered or a service to be performed.

devil's advocacy A technique in which one member of a decision-making team identifies all the considerations that might make a proposal unacceptable.

dialectic inquiry The generation of a plan (a thesis) and a counterplan (an antithesis) that reflect plausible but conflicting courses of action.

diseconomies of scale Unit cost increases associated with a large scale of output.

distinctive competencies Firm-specific strengths that allow a company to differentiate its products and/or achieve substantially lower costs to achieve a competitive advantage.

diversification The process of entering new industries, distinct from a company's core or original industry, to make new kinds of products for customers in new markets.

diversified company A company that makes and sells products in two or more different or distinct industries.

divestment strategy When a company decides to exit an industry by selling off its business assets to another company.

dominant design Common set of features or design characteristics.

economies of scale Reductions in unit costs attributed to a larger output.

economies of scope The synergies that arise when one or more of a diversified company's business units are able to lower costs or increase differentiation because they can more effectively pool, share, and utilize expensive resources or capabilities.

employee productivity The output produced per employee.

environmental degradation Occurs when a company's actions directly or indirectly result in pollution or other forms of environmental harm.

escalating commitment A cognitive bias that occurs when decision makers, having already committed significant resources to a project, commit even more resources after receiving feedback that the project is failing.

ethical dilemmas Situations where there is no agreement over exactly what the accepted principles of right and wrong are, or where none of the available alternatives seems ethically acceptable.

ethics Accepted principles of right or wrong that govern the conduct of a person, the members of a profession, or the actions of an organization.

experience curve The systematic lowering of the cost structure, and consequent unit cost reductions, that have been observed to occur over the life of a product.

external stakeholders All other individuals and groups that have some claim on the company.

first mover A firm that pioneers a particular product category or feature by being first to offer it to market.

first-mover disadvantages Competitive disadvantages associated with being first.

fixed costs Costs that must be incurred to produce a product regardless of the level of output.

flexible production technology A range of technologies designed to reduce setup times for complex equipment, increase the use of individual machines through better scheduling, and improve quality control at all stages of the manufacturing process.

focus differentiation strategy When a company targets a certain segment or niche, and customizes its offering to the needs of that particular segment through the addition of features and functions.

focus low-cost strategy When a company targets a certain segment or niche, and tries to be the low-cost player in that niche.

focus strategy When a company decides to serve a limited number of segments, or just one segment.

format wars Battles to control the source of differentiation, and thus the value that such differentiation can create for the customer.

fragmented industry An industry composed of a large number of small- and medium-sized companies.

franchising A strategy in which the franchisor grants to its franchisees the right to use the franchisor's name, reputation, and business model in return for a franchise fee and often a percentage of the profits.

functional managers Managers responsible for supervising a particular function, that is, a task, activity, or operation, such as accounting, marketing, research and development (R&D), information technology, or logistics.

functional structure Grouping of employees on the basis of their common expertise and experience or because they use the same resources.

functional-level strategies Strategy aimed at improving the effectiveness of a company's operations and its ability to attain superior efficiency, quality, innovation, and customer responsiveness.

general managers Managers who bear responsibility for the overall performance of the company or for one of its major self-contained subunits or divisions.

general organizational competencies Competencies that result from the skills of a company's top managers that help every business unit within a company perform at a higher level than it could if it operated as a separate or independent company.

generic business-level strategy A strategy that gives a company a specific form of competitive position and advantage vis-à-vis its rivals that results in above-average profitability.

geographic structure A way of grouping employees into different geographic regions to best satisfy the needs of customers within different regions of a state or country.

global matrix structure A structure in which horizontal differentiation proceeds along two dimensions: product division and geographic area.

global standardization strategy A business model based on pursuing a low-cost strategy on a global scale.

global strategic alliances Cooperative agreements between companies from different countries that are actual or potential competitors.

greenmail A source of gaining wealth by corporate raiders who benefit by pushing companies to either change their corporate strategy to one that will benefit stockholders, or by charging a premium for these stocks when the company wants to buy them back.

harvest strategy When a company reduces to a minimum the assets it employs in a business to reduce its cost structure and extract or "milk" maximum profits from its investment.

hierarchy of authority The clear and unambiguous chain of command that defines each manager's relative authority from the CEO down through top, middle, to first-line managers.

holdup When a company is taken advantage of by another company it does business with after it has made an investment in expensive specialized assets to better meet the needs of the other company.

horizontal integration The process of acquiring or merging with industry competitors to achieve the competitive advantages that arise from a large size and scope of operations.

hostage taking A means of exchanging valuable resources to guarantee that each partner to an agreement will keep its side of the bargain.

illusion of control A cognitive bias rooted in the tendency to overestimate one's ability to control events.

industry A group of companies offering products or services that are close substitutes for each other.

information asymmetry A situation where an agent has more information about resources he or she is managing than the principal has.

information distortion The manipulation of facts supplied to corporate managers to hide declining divisional performance.

information manipulation When managers use their control over corporate data to distort or hide information in order to enhance their own financial situation or the competitive position of the firm.

inside directors Senior employees of the company, such as the CEO.

intangible resources Nonphysical entities such as brand names, company reputation, experiential knowledge, and intellectual property, including patents, copyrights, and trademarks.

integrating mechanisms Ways to increase communication and coordination among functions and divisions.

integrating roles Managers who work in full-time positions established specifically to improve communication between divisions.

internal capital market A corporate-level strategy whereby the firm's headquarters assesses the performance of business units and allocates money across them. Cash generated by units that are profitable but have poor investment opportunities within their business is used to cross-subsidize businesses that need cash and have strong promise for long-run profitability.

internal new venturing The process of transferring resources to and creating a new business unit or division in a new industry to innovate new kinds of products.

internal stakeholders Stockholders and employees, including executive officers, other managers, and board members.

international division A division created by companies that expand abroad and group all of their international activities into one division; often characterizes single businesses and diversified companies that use the multidivisional organizational form.

intrapreneurs Managers who pioneer and lead new-venture projects or divisions and act as inside or internal entrepreneurs.

just-in-time (JIT) inventory system System of economizing on inventory holding costs by scheduling components to arrive just in time to enter the production process or as stock is depleted.

killer applications Applications or uses of a new technology or product that are so compelling that customers adopt them in droves, killing the competing formats.

leadership strategy When a company develops strategies to become the dominant player in a declining industry.

learning effects Cost savings that come from learning by doing.

leveraging competencies The process of taking a distinctive competency developed by a business unit in one industry and using it to create a new business unit in a different industry.

limit price strategy Charging a price that is lower than that required to maximize profits in the short run, but is above the cost structure of potential entrants.

localization strategy A strategy focused on increasing profitability by customizing the company's goods or services so that the goods provide a favorable match to tastes and preferences in different national markets.

location economies The economic benefits that arise from performing a value creation activity in an optimal location.

management by objectives A system in which employees are encouraged to help set their own goals so that managers manage by exception, intervening only when they sense something is not going right.

market development When a company searches for new market segments for a company's existing products to increase sales.

market segmentation The way a company decides to group customers based on important differences in their needs to gain a competitive advantage.

market structure A way of grouping employees into separate customer groups so that each group can focus on satisfying the needs of a particular customer group in the most effective way.

marketing strategy The position that a company takes with regard to pricing, promotion, advertising, product design, and distribution.

mass customization The use of flexible manufacturing technology to reconcile two goals that were once thought to be incompatible: low cost, and differentiation through product customization.

mass market One in which large numbers of customers enter the market.

matrix structure A way of grouping employees in two ways simultaneously—by function and by product or project—to maximize the rate at which different kinds of products can be developed.

merger An agreement between two companies to pool their resources and operations and join together to better compete in a business or industry.

mission The purpose of the company, or a statement of what the company strives to do.

multidivisional company A company that competes in several different businesses and has created a separate self-contained division to manage each.

multidivisional structure A complex organizational design that allows a company to grow and diversify while also reducing coordination and control problems because it uses self-contained divisions and has a separate corporate headquarters staff.

multinational company A company that does business in two or more national markets.

network effects The network of complementary products as a primary determinant of the demand for an industry's product.

new-venture division A separate and independent division established to give its managers the autonomy to develop a new product.

niche strategy When a company focuses on pockets of demand that are declining more slowly than the industry as a whole to maintain profitability.

non-price competition The use of product differentiation strategies to deter potential entrants and manage rivalry within an industry.

on-the-job consumption A term used by economists to describe the behavior of senior management's use of company funds to acquire perks (such as lavish offices, jets, etc.) that will enhance their status, instead of investing it to increase stockholder returns.

operating budget A blueprint that states how managers intend to use organizational resources to most efficiently achieve organizational goals.

opportunism Seeking one's own self-interest, often through the use of guile.

opportunistic exploitation Unethical behavior sometimes used by managers to unilaterally rewrite the terms of a contract with suppliers, buyers, or complement providers in a way that is more favorable to the firm.

opportunities Elements and conditions in a company's environment that allow it to formulate and implement strategies that enable it to become more profitable.

organizational culture The specific collection of values, norms, beliefs, and attitudes that are shared by people and groups in an organization and that control the way they interact with each other and with stakeholders outside the organization.

organizational design skills The ability of the managers of a company to create a structure, culture, and control systems that motivate and coordinate employees to perform at a high level.

organizational design The process of deciding how a company should create, use, and combine organizational structure, control systems, and culture to pursue a business model successfully.

organizational slack The unproductive use of functional resources by divisional managers that can go undetected unless corporate managers monitor their activities.

organizational structure The means through which a company assigns employees to specific tasks and roles and specifies how these tasks and roles are to be linked together to increase efficiency, quality, innovation, and responsiveness to customers.

output control The control system managers use to establish appropriate performance goals for each division, department, and employee and then measure actual performance relative to these goals.

outside directors Directors who are not full-time employees of the company, needed to provide objectivity to the monitoring and evaluation of processes.

outside view Identification of past successful or failed strategic initiatives to determine whether those initiatives will work for project at hand.

parallel sourcing policy A policy in which a company enters into long-term contracts with at least two suppliers for the same component to prevent any problems of opportunism.

personal control The way one manager shapes and influences the behavior of another in a face-to-face interaction in the pursuit of a company's goals.

personal ethics Generally accepted principles of right and wrong governing the conduct of individuals.

positioning strategy The specific set of options a company adopts for a product based upon four main dimensions of marketing: price, distribution, promotion and advertising, and product features.

potential competitors Companies that are currently not competing in the industry but have the potential to do so.

price leadership When one company assumes the responsibility for determining the pricing strategy that maximizes industry profitability.

price signaling The process by which companies increase or decrease product prices to convey their intentions to other companies and influence the price of an industry's products.

primary activities Activities related to the design, creation, and delivery of the product, its marketing, and its support and after-sales service.

principle of the minimum chain of command The principle that a company should design its hierarchy with the fewest levels of authority necessary to use organizational resources effectively.

prior hypothesis bias A cognitive bias that occurs when decision makers who have strong prior beliefs tend to make decisions on the basis of these beliefs, even when presented with evidence that their beliefs are wrong.

process innovation Development of a new process for producing products and delivering them to customers.

product bundling Offering customers the opportunity to purchase a range of products at a single combined price; this increases the value of a company's product line because customers often obtain a price discount when purchasing a set of products at one time, and customers become used to dealing with only one company and its representatives.

product development The creation of new or improved products to replace existing products.

product innovation Development of products that are new to the world or have superior attributes to existing products.

product proliferation strategy The strategy of "filling the niches," or catering to the needs of customers in all market segments to deter entry by competitors.

product structure A way of grouping employees into separate product groups or units so that each product group can focus on the best ways to increase the effectiveness of the product.

product-team structure A way of grouping employees by product or project line but employees focus on the development of only one particular type of product.

profit center When each self-contained division is treated as a separate financial unit and financial controls are used to establish performance goals for each division and measure profitability.

profit growth The increase in net profit over time.

profitability The return a company makes on the capital invested in the enterprise.

public domain Government- or association-set standards of knowledge or technology that any company can freely incorporate into its product.

quasi integration The use of long-term relationships, or investment into some of the activities normally performed by suppliers or buyers, in place of full ownership of operations that are backward or forward in the supply chain.

razor and blade strategy Pricing the product low in order to stimulate demand, and pricing complements high.

reasoning by analogy Use of simple analogies to make sense out of complex problems.

reengineering The process of redesigning business processes to achieve dramatic improvements in performance, such as cost, quality, service, and speed.

related diversification A corporate-level strategy that is based on the goal of establishing a business unit in a new industry that is related to a company's existing business units by some form of commonality or linkage between their value-chain functions.

representativeness A bias rooted in the tendency to generalize from a small sample or even a single vivid anecdote.

resources Assets of a company.

restructuring The process by which a company streamlines its hierarchy of authority and reduces the number of levels in its hierarchy to a minimum to lower operating costs.

restructuring The process of reorganizing and divesting business units and exiting industries to refocus upon a company's core business and rebuild its distinctive competencies.

risk capital Capital that cannot be recovered if a company fails and goes bankrupt.

risk capital Equity capital for which there is no guarantee that stockholders will ever recoup their investment or earn a decent return.

scenario planning Formulating plans that are based upon "what-if" scenarios about the future.

sector A group of closely related industries.

segmentation strategy When a company decides to serve many segments, or even the entire market, producing different offerings for different segments.

self-contained division An independent business unit or division that contains all the value-chain functions it needs to pursue its business model successfully.

self-dealing Managers using company funds for their own personal consumption, as done by Enron, for example, in previous years.

self-managing teams Teams where members coordinate their own activities and make their own hiring, training, work, and reward decisions.

shareholder value Returns that shareholders earn from purchasing shares in a company.

span of control The number of subordinates reporting directly to a particular manager.

stakeholders Individuals or groups with an interest, claim, or stake in the company—in what it does and in how well it performs.

standardization strategy When a company decides to ignore different segments, and produce a standardized product for the average consumer.

standardization The degree to which a company specifies how decisions are to be made so that employees' behavior becomes measurable and predictable.

stock options The right to purchase company stock at a predetermined price at some point in the future, usually within 10 years of the grant date.

strategic alliances Long-term agreements between two or more companies to jointly develop new products or processes that benefit all companies that are a part of the agreement.

strategic commitments Investments that signal an incumbent's long-term commitment to a market, or a segment of that market.

strategic control systems The mechanism that allows managers to monitor and evaluate whether their business model is working as intended and how it could be improved.

strategic leadership Creating competitive advantage through effective management of the strategy-making process.

strategic outsourcing The decision to allow one or more of a company's value-chain activities to be performed by independent, specialist companies that focus all their skills and knowledge on just one kind of activity to increase performance.

strategy A set of related actions that managers take to increase their company's performance.

strategy formulation Selecting strategies based on analysis of an organization's external and internal environment.

strategy implementation Putting strategies into action.

substandard working conditions Arise when managers underinvest in working conditions, or pay employees below-market rates, in order to reduce their production costs.

supply chain management The task of managing the flow of inputs and components from suppliers into the company's production processes to minimize inventory holding and maximize inventory turnover.

support activities Activities of the value chain that provide inputs that allow the primary activities to take place.

sustained competitive advantage A company's strategies enable it to maintain above-average profitability for a number of years.

switching costs Costs that consumers must bear to switch from the products offered by one established company to the products offered by a new entrant.

SWOT analysis The comparison of strengths, weaknesses, opportunities, and threats.

takeover constraint The risk of being acquired by another company.

tangible resources Physical entities, such as land, buildings, equipment, inventory, and money.

tapered integration When a firm uses a mix of vertical integration and market transactions for a given input. For example, a firm might operate limited semiconductor manufacturing itself, while also buying semiconductor chips on the market. Doing so helps to prevent supplier holdup (because the firm can credibly commit to not buying from external suppliers) and increases its ability to judge the quality and cost of purchased supplies.

team Formation of a group that represents each division or department facing a common problem, with the goal of finding a solution to the problem.

technical standards A set of technical specifications that producers adhere to when making the product, or a component of it.

technological paradigm shift Shifts in new technologies that revolutionize the structure of the industry, dramatically alter the nature of competition, and require companies to adopt new strategies in order to survive.

threats Elements in the external environment that could endanger the integrity and profitability of the company's business.

total quality management increasing product reliability so that it consistently performs as it was designed to and rarely breaks down.

transfer pricing The price that one division of a company charges another division for its products, which are the inputs the other division requires to manufacture its own products. The problem of establishing the fair or "competitive" price of a resource or skill developed in one division that is to be transferred and sold to another division.

transferring competencies The process of taking a distinctive competency developed by a business unit in one industry and implanting it in a business unit operating in another industry.

transnational strategy A business model that simultaneously achieves low costs, differentiates the product offering across geographic markets, and fosters a flow of skills between different subsidiaries in the company's global network of operations.

turnaround strategy When managers of a diversified company identify inefficient and poorly managed companies in other industries and then acquire and restructure them to improve their performance—and thus the profitability of the total corporation.

two-boss employees Employees who report both to a project boss and a functional boss.

unrelated diversification A corporate-level strategy based on a multibusiness model that uses general organizational competencies to increase the performance of all the company's business units.

value chain The idea that a company is a chain of activities that transforms inputs into outputs that customers value.

value innovation When innovations push out the efficiency frontier in an industry, allowing for greater value to be offered through superior differentiation at a lower cost than was previously thought possible.

values A statement of how employees should conduct themselves and their business to help achieve the company mission.

vertical disintegration When a company decides to exit industries either forward or backward in the industry value chain to its core industry to increase profitability.

vertical integration When a company expands its operations either backward into an industry that produces inputs for the company's products (backward vertical integration) or forward into an industry that uses, distributes, or sells the company's products (forward vertical integration).

virtual corporation When companies pursued extensive strategic outsourcing to the extent that they only perform the central value creation functions that lead to competitive advantage.

vision The articulation of a company's desired achievements or future state.

worldwide area structure A structure in which the world is divided into geographic areas; an area may be a country or a group of countries, and each area operates as a self-contained and largely autonomous entity with its own set of value creation activities, with headquarters retaining authority for the overall strategic direction of the firm and financial control; favored by companies with a low degree of diversification and a domestic structure based on functions that are pursuing a localization strategy.

worldwide product divisional structure A structure in which each division is a self-contained, largely autonomous entity with full responsibility for its own value creation activities, with headquarters retaining responsibility for the overall strategic development and financial control of the firm; adopted by firms that are reasonably diversified and originally had domestic structures based on product divisions.

Index